AUSTRALIAN
REAL PROPERTY LAW

CANADA AND U.S.A.

The Carswell Company Ltd
Agincourt, Ontario

HONG KONG

Bloomsbury Books Ltd

NEW ZEALAND

University Bookshop (Auckland) Ltd
The University Bookshop, Christchurch
Bell's Techbooks Ltd, Wellington

UNITED KINGDOM

Sweet & Maxwell Ltd
London

Australian
Real Property
Law

ADRIAN J. BRADBROOK

M.A. (Cantab.), LL.M. (Osgoode Hall), Ph.D. LL.D. (Melbourne)
*Barrister and Solicitor of the Supreme Courts of
Nova Scotia and Victoria,
Professor of Law, University of Adelaide*

SUSAN V. MacCALLUM

LL.M. (Melbourne)
*Barrister and Solicitor of the Supreme Court of Victoria,
Senior Lecturer in Law, University of Melbourne*

ANTHONY P. MOORE

J.D. (Chicago), LL.M. (Melbourne)
Associate Professor of Law, University of Adelaide

THE LAW BOOK COMPANY LIMITED

1991

Published in Sydney by

The Law Book Company Limited
    44-50 Waterloo Road, North Ryde, N.S.W.
    490 Bourke Street, Melbourne, Victoria
    40 Queen Street, Brisbane, Queensland
    81 St George's Terrace, Perth, W.A.

First edition 1991
    second impression 1991

National Library of Australia
Cataloguing-in-Publication entry

Bradbrook, Adrian J. (Adrian John).
    Australian real property law.

    Includes bibliographical references and index.
    ISBN 0 455 20992 8.
    ISBN 0 455 20993 6 (pbk).

    1. Real Property—Australia.I. MacCallum, Susan V.
    II. Moore, Anthony P. III. Title

346.94043

Designed and edited by Lynne Smith
Typeset in Baskerville, 10½ on 11 point, by Mercier Typesetters Pty Ltd,
    Granville, N.S.W.
    Printed by Robert Burton Printers Pty Limited, Sefton, N.S.W.

Preface

The dominant purpose of this text is to provide a succinct but comprehensive account of Australian real property law. Over the past 15 years there have been numerous textbooks published in Australia on a wide variety of mainstream legal subjects. The stage has now been reached where Australian textbooks have largely supplanted the traditional reliance placed by legal practitioners and law students on English textbooks. One area where this has not yet occurred is real property law, where extensive use is still made of textbooks such as Megarry and Wade, *The Law of Real Property*, and Cheshire and Burn, *The Modern Law of Real Property*. These texts have always had to be used with caution because of some basic differences between real property law in the two countries. Ever increasing differences enhance the need for a purely Australian book on real property law.

The book represents a comprehensive discussion of the current state of Australian law on all the major features of the law of real property. This discussion has been organised under fairly traditional categories to facilitate access to the mass of material. We have, however, at an early stage set out the principles of the Torrens system and have endeavoured to ensure that the principles of this system have been applied in all subsequent topics. Furthermore, we have drawn attention to the social role and development of real property law in Australia. We have dealt with a number of emerging areas such as retirement villages and retail tenancies. In our treatment of each of the topics we have endeavoured to ensure that the book is equally important and relevant to legal practitioners working in the area of property law and to law students enrolled in property law courses at the various university law schools around the country.

There are two restrictions on the scope of this book. First, we have not included matters relating to real property law that are commonly discussed in textbooks on other areas of law. The prime illustration of this is family property, which forms a significant part of modern Australian family law textbooks. Another illustration is mining law, in respect of which separate Australian textbooks have been prepared. Secondly, we have not discussed Australian Capital Territory and Northern Territory legislation. We have excluded this legislation on pragmatic grounds. The small size of the potential readership did not in our view justify the additional fragmentation of the text to deal with the further differences of the law in the Territories.

The problems of fragmentation for a text on Australian real property law flow from the differences between the statutes of the States and Territories. Whilst most readers will be concerned solely with the law of one particular State, the text is often endeavouring to make statements of general application. Nonetheless we have endeavoured to draw attention to all significant differences between the various statutes and to set out comprehensive statutory references. We have adopted a shorthand reference to the major statutes so that reference is, for example, simply made to the Torrens system statutes. The list of abbreviated statutes is set out after the Table of Statutes. We have also referred to the major texts simply by way of the names of the authors. The list of abbreviated books is set out after the list of abbreviated statutes.

We agonised at some length as to whether to include a discussion of the legal principles regarding general law land. We decided eventually to do so for the sake of completeness. Although the vast majority of land in Australia is now under the Torrens system, there are still significant tracts of land in the eastern States which remain under the old general law system.

Responsibility for the preparation of the manuscript has been shared equally between the three authors. The only exception to this is paragraphs 1.39-1.52 relating to Aboriginal land rights. This was written by Mr Richard Johnstone, Lecturer in Law at the University of Melbourne Law School. We gratefully acknowledge his important contribution.

In relation to Australian materials, the book represents the law as it stands on 1 May 1990. In relation to overseas materials, the discussion is based on the publications reaching the University of Adelaide and the University of Melbourne law libraries by the same date.

For invaluable research assistance we wish to thank Susan Gunter and Mary Heath of the University of Adelaide Law School; Joan Wright, Kathryn Forrest and Philip Crutchfield of the University of Melbourne Law School; and Andrea Burke, a Melbourne librarian. Many others have provided information and comment; in particular we wish to thank Don MacCallum, a Melbourne practitioner. Steven Thomas, of the University of Adelaide Law School has prepared the very comprehensive and detailed index. We are deeply indebted to him. Finally, we wish to express our gratitude to the secretarial staff of the Adelaide and Melbourne Law Schools (particularly Helen Doungas of Melbourne and Linda Lambie and Judy Smith of Adelaide), who cheerfully and competently typed numerous drafts of each chapter.

ADRIAN BRADBROOK
ANTHONY MOORE
SUSAN MacCALLUM

October 1990

Table of Contents

Table of Cases

Table of Statutes

Queensland

South Australia

Australian Capital Territory

Northern Territory

New Zealand

Abbreviated Statutes

Torrens system statutes

N.S.W.:   Real Property Act 1900
Vic.:   Transfer of Land Act 1958
Qld: Real Property Act 1861
S.A.:   Real Property Act 1886
W.A.:   Transfer of Land Act 1893
Tas.:   Land Titles Act 1980

Property law statutes

N.S.W.:   Conveyancing Act 1919
Vic.:   Property Law Act 1958
Qld: Property Law Act 1974
S.A.:   Law of Property Act 1936
W.A.:   Property Law Act 1969
Tas.:   Conveyancing and Law of Property Act 1884

Residential tenancies statutes

N.S.W.:   Residential Tenancies Act 1987
Vic.:   Residential Tenancies Act 1980
Qld: Residential Tenancies Act 1975
S.A.:   Residential Tenancies Act 1978
W.A.:   Residential Tenancies Act 1987
Tas.:   —

Settled land legislation

N.S.W.:   Conveyancing and Law of Property Act 1898
Vic.:   Settled Land Act 1958
Qld: —
S.A.:   Settled Estates Act 1880
W.A.:   —
Tas.:   Settled Land Act 1884

Trustee statutes

N.S.W.:   Trustee Act 1925
Vic.:   Trustee Act 1958
Qld: Trusts Act 1973
S.A.:   Trustee Act 1936
W.A.:   Trustees Act 1962
Tas.:   Trustee Act 1898

Strata title statutes

N.S.W.:   Strata Titles Act 1973
Vic.:   Subdivision Act 1988; Subdivision (Body Corporate)
             Regulations
Qld: Building Units and Group Titles Act 1980
S.A.:   Strata Titles Act 1988
W.A.:   Strata Titles Act 1966
Tas.:   Conveyancing and Law of Property Act 1884

Retirement village legislation

N.S.W.:   Retirement Villages Act 1989
Vic.:   Retirement Villages Act 1987
Qld: Retirement Villages Act 1988
S.A.:   Retirement Villages Act 1987
W.A.:   —
Tas.:   —

Limitation statutes

N.S.W.:   Limitation Act 1969
Vic.:   Limitation of Actions Act 1958
Qld: Limitation of Actions Act 1974
S.A.:   Limitation of Actions Act 1936
W.A.:   Limitation Act 1935
Tas.:   Limitation Act 1974

Select Bibliography

Bradbrook and Croft	Bradbrook and Croft, *Commercial Tenancy Law in Australia*, Butterworths, Sydney, 1990.
Bradbrook, MacCallum and Moore	Bradbrook, MacCallum and Moore, *Residential Tenancy Law and Practice—Victoria and South Australia*, The Law Book Co. Ltd, Sydney, 1983.
Bradbrook and Neave	Bradbrook and Neave, *Easements and Restrictive Covenants in Australia*, Butterworths, Sydney, 1981.
Butt	Butt, *Land Law*, 2nd ed., The Law Book Co. Ltd, Sydney, 1988.
Cheshire and Burn	*Cheshire and Burn's Modern Law of Real Property* 13th ed. by Burn, Butterworths, London, 1982.
Cheshire and Fifoot	*Cheshire and Fifoot's Law of Contract*, 5th Aust. ed. by Starke, Seddon and Ellinghaus, Butterworths, Sydney, 1988.
Gale	*Gale on Easements*, 15th ed. by Maurice, Sweet & Maxwell, London, 1986.
Ford and Lee	Ford and Lee, *Principles of the Law of Trusts* ,2nd ed., The Law Book Co. Ltd, Sydney, 1990.
Gray and Symes	Gray and Symes, *Real Property and Real People*, Butterworths, London, 1981.
Hardingham, Neave and Ford	Hardingham, Neave and Ford, *Wills and Intestacy in Australia and New Zealand*, 2nd ed., The Law Book Co. Ltd, Sydney, 1989.
Meagher, Gummow and Lehane	Meagher, Gummow and Lehane, *Equity Doctrines and Remedies*, 2nd ed., Butterworths, Sydney, 1984.
Megarry and Wade	Megarry and Wade, *The Law of Real Property*, 5th ed., Stevens, London, 1984.
Preston and Newsom	*Preston and Newsom's Restrictive Covenants Affecting Freehold Land*, 7th ed., Sweet & Maxwell, London, 1982.
Redfern and Cassidy	Redfern and Cassidy, *Australian Tenancy Practice and Precedents*, Butterworths, Sydney, 1987 (looseleaf).
Robinson	Robinson, *Transfer of Land in Victoria*, The Law Book Co. Ltd, Sydney, 1979.
Sackville and Neave	*Sackville and Neave's Property Law—Cases and Materials*, 4th ed. by Neave, Rossiter and Stone, Butterworths, Sydney, 1988.
Sappideen and Butt	*The Perpetuities Act 1984*, The Law Book Co. Ltd, Sydney, 1986.
Snell	*Snell's Principles of Equity*, 28th ed. by Baker and Langan, Sweet & Maxwell, London, 1982.
Spry	Spry, *Principles of Equitable Remedies*, 3rd ed., The Law Book Co. Ltd, Sydney, 1984.

Sykes	Sykes, *The Law of Securities*, 4th ed., The Law Book Co. Ltd, Sydney, 1986.
Teh and Dwyer	Teh and Dwyer, *Introduction to Property Law*, Butterworths, Sydney, 1988.
Voumard	Voumard, *The Sale of Land in Victoria*, 4th ed. by Wikrama, The Law Book Co. Ltd, Sydney, 1986.
Whalan	Whalan, *The Torrens System in Australia*, The Law Book Co. Ltd, Sydney, 1982.
Woodman	Woodman, *The Law of Real Property in New South Wales, Vol. 1*, The Law Book Co. Ltd, Sydney, 1980.

1

Nature and Development of Real Property Law

I. DEVELOPMENT OF REAL PROPERTY LAW IN AUSTRALIA

[1.01] Real property law has had an important part in law school curricula in Australia throughout the history of legal education in this country.[1] Similarly real property transactions have formed a significant aspect of legal practice. This text is however the first attempt to provide a comprehensive text on Australian real property law. Aspects of real property law have been dealt with: there are several important texts on the Torrens system[2] and on the sale of land;[3] other texts have covered topics ranging from strata titles[4] to easements and covenants[5] to Crown lands;[6] real property law generally in New South Wales has been analysed.[7] Unlike areas such as torts and contract, real property law has an extensive statutory base and those statutes differ markedly from State to State. Practitioners and law teachers therefore acquire familiarity with the laws of their State but are inhibited by the strangeness of at least the appearance of the laws of other States. One of the aims of this text is to enable more ready interstate comparisons.

[1.02] Upon settlement of the various Australian States in the early 19th century British statute and common law was received and applied. Of most immediate impact was the feudal doctrine that all land is owned by

1. A general history of South Australian legal education is provided in Castles, Ligertwood and Kelly (eds), *Law on North Terrace* (1984).
2. These texts include Hogg, *The Australian Torrens System* (1905); Kerr, *The Principles of the Australian Lands Titles (Torrens) System* (1927); Baalman, *The Torrens System in New South Wales* (1951); Ruoff, *An Englishman Looks at The Torrens System* (1957); Francis, *The Law and Practice Relating to Torrens Title in Australasia* (Vol 1-1972, Vol. 2-1973); Whalan.
3. These texts include Voumard; Robinson; Butt, *The Standard Contract for the Sale of Land in New South Wales* (1985); Duncan and Weld, *The Standard Land Contract in Queensland* (2nd ed., 1984).
4. Bugden, *Strata Title Management in New South Wales* (5th ed., 1988); Collins and Robinson, *Strata Title Units in New South Wales* (2nd ed., 1982); Ilken, *Strata Title Management and the Law* (1989); Moses and Tzannes, *Strata Titles* (1978).
5. Bradbrook and Neave.
6. Lang, *Crown Land in New South Wales* (1973); Fry, *Freehold and Leasehold Tenancies of Queensland* (1946); Brierley and Irish, *The Crown Lands Acts of New South Wales* (3rd ed., 1914).
7. Butt; Hargreaves and Helmore, *Introduction to the Principles of Land Law* (1963).

the Crown and that private rights depend upon a grant from the Crown. But there was a mass of law relating to proprietary rights in land. Much of the conceptual framework was well established: the doctrines of tenure and estates, the role of equity in the protection of trusts, the nature of mortgages as a result of redemption and foreclosure, and the concept of incorporeal hereditaments such as profits à prendre and easements. Case law in the 19th century was to mark out the implied covenants of a lease, define the characteristics of an easement, create restrictive covenants as new proprietary interests, and to specify equitable intervention in response to common law formality rules. The contribution of Australian courts to this legal growth was insignificant.

[1.03]   The feudal system was irrelevant to the system of land grants in Australia. Consequently tenure principles were uncomplicated and all grants were by way of free socage tenure. However the spread of land development led to the first Australian real property law innovations. Official efforts were made to constrain the early settlement to an area surrounding Sydney. Nonetheless actual development spread well beyond the official limits giving rise to the class of pastoralists known as the squatters. Subsequently some security of title was sought for this illegal landholding and the early colonial legislature was sympathetic to the squatters' claims. A system of Crown grants of leasehold interests[8] evolved. There were many different forms of leasehold tenure and special rules applicable to the various forms. These tenures were peculiar to the conditions of the colonies. In recent times the various tenures have been simplified but much of rural Australia remains subject to Crown leasehold arrangements.

The squatters gained some security of tenure through the system of leasehold grants. But they also needed access to money. Mid 19th century banking practice was averse to accepting land as a security.[9] Bank charters and banking regulations forbade loans on the security of a mortgage over land.[10] Moreover the squatters' title was not permanent. From 1843 legislation was introduced to allow for security to be granted over stock and crops through stock mortgages, wool liens and fruit or crop liens. These arrangements conferred interests in crops yet to be harvested and wool yet to be shorn. The legislation sought to prop up a shaky security and paid particular attention to the problems of possible invalidity on the subsequent bankruptcy of the squatter.[11]

[1.04]   Subsequent to the initial settlement a policy of land sales at substantial prices was adopted largely from the theories of Edward Gibbon Wakefield.[12] Land speculation led to fraudulent dealings which exploited the cumbersome English process of land transfer. Consequently the Torrens system was introduced to simplify the process and make land

---

8. On Crown grants of leasehold interests, see below **[19.03]**.
9. Holden, *Securities for Bankers' Advances* (2nd ed., 1957), p. 15.
10. Davidson and Wells, "The Land, The Law and The State: Colonial Australia 1788-1900" (1982) 2 *Law in Context* 89 at 109.
11. Sykes, p. 499.
12. The Wakefield theories are outlined below **[19.07]**.

titles more certain.[13] Land speculation had encouraged acquisition and dealing in land by absentee landholders without regard for the development of the land. As the transactions were little more than paper exchanges the opportunities for bogus chains of title and even bogus land areas were considerable. The Torrens system provided a register which described the land and designated the owners of interests in that land. Dealings in the land were effected by entries upon the register. The Torrens system was first introduced in South Australia in 1858 and quickly followed in the other Australian States and subsequently in many overseas jurisdictions. However the system has not become universal because land alienated prior to the system's coming into force was not automatically brought under the system. Much land in Victoria and New South Wales in particular remains outside the system. Only in Queensland and South Australia is the process of bringing all land within the system practically complete.

Whilst the Torrens system was principally about the method of obtaining title and thus built upon the common law statement of estates and interests in land it did effect some change to these interests. The greatest change was with respect to the nature of mortgages. Whereas under the common law the credit provider or mortgagee became the owner and the borrower or mortgagor had an equitable right to get back the land on payment of debt, interest and costs, under the Torrens system the mortgagor remained the legal owner and the mortgagee held a statutory charge over the land. As well as changes to the nature of interests, primacy of the register affected informal interests. Whilst interests not on the register were not denied recognition their enforceability against third parties became much more vulnerable because only fraud and not notice actual or constructive would affect a subsequent registered proprietor.

Alongside the Torrens system, all States had statutes dealing with property matters in general. In most cases these statutes dealt with personal as well as real property. In all jurisdictions in some instances the statutes are intended to apply to Torrens system land but in many instances provisions overlap in a confusing way. The content of the property statutes has in most cases been derivative from British statutes though the extent to which statutes were copied varies from time to time and State to State. Moreover even in the earliest times there were sparks of originality such as a desire to simplify common conveyancing documents.[14]

[1.05] In Britain in the second half of the 19th century land law was to be significantly affected by the freeing of land for development through the settled land legislation and by the reforms of the court structure by the *Judicature Act* of 1873. Settlements were a device for the spreading of land title throughout family generations and thus a denial to the current holder of any absolute title. The settled land legislation empowered that holder

---

13. Torrens, *The South Australian System of Conveyancing by Registration of Titles* (1859), p. 8.
14. The preamble to the South Australian *Law of Property Act* 1838 refers to this goal.

to deal with the land and transferred rights of family members to the proceeds of any disposition. The existence of separate interests at common law and equity was a peculiar feature of the British system: the different interests were protected by different courts. The *Judicature Act* meant there was but one court hierarchy although it still administered separate legal and equitable principles with little attempt until very recently at fusion of principles. In Australia, formal settlements had not been common so the settled land legislation was not needed to free land in the same way as in Britain but there were many common situations where the legislation did facilitate dealings. Consequently all States adopted some parts of the legislation. The separate system of courts had been inherited and again the *Judicature Act* was copied in all States but in New South Wales not until 1970.

[1.06]   The Commonwealth of Australia came into being on 1 January 1901—its existence in formal legal terms deriving from the British *Commonwealth of Australia Constitution Act* 1900. The Constitution provides for the executive government of the Commonwealth and by s. 61 the executive power is vested in the Queen and exercisable by the Governor-General as the Queen's representative. The executive power includes the power to acquire land. The Commonwealth may also gain land by the surrender of territory by a State—any surrender must be approved by the Parliament of the State and accepted by the Commonwealth.[15]

Compulsory acquisition of property by the Commonwealth may be authorised by laws of the Commonwealth parliament. Under s. 51(xxxi) of the Constitution the Commonwealth may make laws for the acquisition of property on just terms from any State or person for any purpose for which the Commonwealth has power to make laws. Whilst this section is an enabling provision and makes it clear that the Commonwealth may acquire property from the States the section places significant limits on the exercise of power. Any acquisition must be on just terms and for a purpose which is a subject of Commonwealth legislative power. Just terms involve reasonable compensation—a concept which is the subject of much judicial consideration.[16] The protection from compulsory acquisition without reasonable compensation is not applied by the Constitution to acquisitions by the States. The States confer power by legislation upon State instrumentalities to acquire property compulsorily and that legislation provides for compensation. However, there is no constitutional base to attack the compensation thus provided as being in any particular instance unjust, or to attack any restriction on land use by planning legislation, for example, as a taking for which no compensation is paid.

Property of the Commonwealth and the States is protected from taxes by each other. Under s. 114 of the Constitution a State shall not impose any tax on property of any kind belonging to the Commonwealth and the Commonwealth shall not impose any tax on property of any kind

---

15. Constitution: s. 111.
16. The leading cases include *Grace Bros Pty Ltd v. Commonwealth* (1946) 72 C.L.R. 269 and *Bank of New South Wales v. Commonwealth* (1948) 76 C.L.R. 1.

belonging to a State. A limited interpretation has been given to this protection in that a customs duty has been held to be not a tax on property but a tax on the act of importation.[17]

The Commonwealth is given exclusive legislative power by s. 52(1) of the Constitution with respect to all places acquired by the Commonwealth for public purposes. The exclusive nature of this power means that State laws cannot apply to such places.[18] To overcome an absence of civil and criminal laws in such places the *Commonwealth Places (Application of Laws) Act* 1970 (Cth) adopts for them the laws in force from time to time in the States in which the places are situated.

The statement of legislative powers in the Constitution says little about land. Of its nature land was regarded as local and thus an appropriate subject for State laws. The structure of the Constitution is such that State laws apply in the absence of any exclusive Commonwealth power and in the absence of any inconsistent Commonwealth law on a subject on which the Commonwealth has a non-exclusive power (the effect of ss 108 and 109 of the Constitution). The non-exclusive legislative powers of the Commonwealth are extensive in relation to intangible property: currency, coinage and legal tender (s. 51(xii)); bills of exchange and promissory notes (s. 51(xvi)); and copyright, patents and trademarks (s. 51(xviii)). In relation to land some of the Commonwealth non-exclusive powers enable laws that may affect land transactions (interstate trade and commerce—s. 51(i); bankruptcy and insolvency—s. 51(xvii); and trading or financial corporations—s. 51(xx)). The bankruptcy power was not significantly used by the Commonwealth until the *Bankruptcy Act* 1924 and the trade and commerce and corporations powers were not significantly used to make laws with respect to commercial transactions in interstate trade or by corporations until the *Trade Practices Act* 1974.

[1.07] One legislative reform of the turn of the century affecting land was the enactment by all States of fences legislation: see below **[14.27]**. This legislation establishes a procedure for the sharing of fencing costs. A landowner proposing to erect a boundary fence serves notice on the neighbour setting out details of the proposal. Counter-proposals may be made. Disputes may be determined by local courts. The legislation establishes a general liability between neighbours to share fencing costs and provides a relatively simple and inexpensive means of enforcing the liability and resolving disputes. The legislation appears to have been unique at the time to Australasia perhaps drawing on practices of local courts. To some extent the law is reflecting the Australian concern for a detached dwelling on a defined quarter acre.

[1.08] The relationship between allotments was also affected by that aspect of British property law involving the ability to acquire easements through long use as a result of the doctrines of prescription and lost

---

17. *Attorney-General (N.S.W.) v. Collectors of Customs (N.S.W.)* (1908) 5 C.L.R. 818; cf. *Essendon Corporation v. Criterion Theatres Ltd* (1947) 74 C.L.R. 1; *Queensland v. Commonwealth* (1987) 69 A.L.R. 207.
18. *Worthing v. Rowell and Muston Pty Ltd* (1970) 123 C.L.R. 89; *R. v. Phillips* (1970) 125 C.L.R. 93.

modern grant. The applicability of these doctrines produced a rare judicial outburst of colonial independence. In *Sheehy v. Edwards, Dunlop & Co.*[19] Manning J. stated:

> "Can one say that a [prescriptive right to light] is reasonably applicable . . .? When people were looking forward to the future of this country, to large cities and towns being established, when the streets and roads were first laid out in spots still then uncultivated, was it reasonable that a man, by acquiring a plot of ground and building as they did in those days a small shanty . . . should be able after 20 years' enjoyment to prevent his neighbour building so as to interfere with the light entering into that one window? If that were so, a man by buying alternate allotments through . . . Sydney would have had it in his power to block completely the erection of any buildings of a more substantial size."

This view was not to prevail at least in courts. In *Delohery v. Permanent Trustee Company (N.S.W.)*[20] the High Court ruled that rights of light could be acquired through the doctrine of lost modern grant. However, the legislatures acted and in the case of Western Australia in 1902 even before the High Court decision. Between 1902 and 1911 all Australian States enacted legislation to prevent the coming into existence of any right to the access or use of light by reason of the enjoyment of such access to use for any period. In all States except South Australia the legislation extends to air as well as light: see below **[16.31]**. The legislation has no international basis but rather reflects acceptance of sentiments similar to those voiced by Manning J.

[1.09]   Concern over boundary disputes also led some States from the 1920s to enact encroachments legislation.[21] A landowner is enabled to apply for a determination that a building or structure encroaches onto her or his land. If an encroachment exists an order may be made for its removal. But, most significantly, the court is given a discretion to amend the boundary to allow for the encroachment on the condition of payment of compensation for the land thus gained.

[1.10]   The interaction of urban development, economic circumstances and the necessities of war caused the more significant legislative actions with respect to land from the early part of the century to the 1950s. This interaction is reflected in controls on land use and subdivision, housing standards and arrangements between landlords and tenants. The general trends flowed from concerns after the First World War for a more pleasant urban environment, after the depression to eliminate slums and curb exploitation by speculators and landlords, during the Second World War to regulate extensively in the national interest, and after the Second World War to set a framework for orderly reconstruction.

---

19. (1897) 13 W.N. (N.S.W.) 166 at 168.
20. (1904) 1 C.L.R. 283.
21. The legislation in its current form is analysed below **[14.25]**.

After faltering initial steps in the 1920s, land-use planning was a central concern of reconstruction after the Second World War.[22] More effort was probably directed to the preparation of elaborate schemes for the dominant and ever-sprawling capital cities than the implementation of sensible and workable controls but the landholder's freedom to develop as he or she pleased was controlled. Public housing authorities were set up after the depression to tackle the physical manifestations of unsatisfactory living conditions and in particular the disadvantage faced by children growing up in such conditions.[23] The establishment of these authorities may be viewed as simply adding another, albeit public, landowner but the authorities did have extensive powers of compulsory land acquisition (which caused much dislocation), and powers to order works by private landowners to eliminate substandard housing conditions. Moreover because efforts were directed to governmental housing construction little attention was given to private landlord and tenant relationships and at a policy level to more subtle economic measures to alleviate substandard housing conditions. Private landlord and tenant relationships[24] were controlled during the First and Second World Wars on the basis of housing shortages caused by emergency conditions. Security of tenure and rental controls were imposed.[25] These controls were taken over by the States after the war and somewhat haphazardly lingered on thereafter.

An emphasis upon home ownership and the growth of the major metropolitan areas led by the 1960s to a need for alternatives to the suburban quarter acre allotment. Whilst high-rise accommodation tended to be rented public housing, the combination of land ownership and more compact housing tested the ingenuity of Australian property lawyers. The most common technique adopted was the formation of a company to own the allotment and the grant of shares in that company to persons seeking to acquire residences within that allotment. Those shares carried with them rights of occupation but the company was the legal beneficial owner of the land and the individuals' shares conferred rights against the company. Ultimately legislation was introduced in all jurisdictions for the system of strata titles which kept the company structure and company ownership of common property but gave the individuals a registered title to their residences: see below [13.03].

[1.11] The reformist period of the 1970s produced little by way of change in property law. In the longer term the general regulation of commercial practice by the *Commonwealth Trade Practices Act* 1974 has probably more significance even for land dealings than other reforms. The 1976 amendments to the *Trade Practices Act* introduced specific proscriptions against misleading statements on the sale of land. However, remedies in land transactions have come from the general prohibition of

---

22. Hutchings and Bunker (eds), *With Conscious Purpose: A History of Town Planning in South Australia* (1986).
23. Bradbrook, MacCallum and Moore, pp. 27-36.
24. See Bradbrook; "The Evolution of Australian Landlord and Tenant Law" in Ellinghaus, Bradbrook and Duggan, *The Emergence of Australian Law* (1989) pp. 114-118.
25. See Bellhouse, "National Security (Landlord and Tenant) Regulations" (1947) 20 A.L.J. 470.

misleading or deceptive conduct and the remedies of damages and contractual avoidance for those injured by breach.[26] In the late 1980s these provisions were copied in State laws and the general prohibitions extended to unconscionable conduct.[27] Credit transactions underlying land mortgages are particularly susceptible to unconscionability attack.

One traditional property area—that of perpetuities—was tackled during this period. The complexity of the common law rules against perpetuities had long been exploited to the suffering of law students and the embarrassment of legal practitioners. Reform was not a uniquely Australian movement and has had a theoretical rather than practical bent with little regard for the needs of legal simplification. Again the Australian States went in their own separate directions in legislative changes through the 1970s and 1980s: see below [8.01].

[1.12] Throughout this period Queensland has been regarded as politically the most conservative of the States. However, that State did achieve a fundamental restatement of general property law in the *Property Law Act* 1974. Whilst the passing of the statute can probably be attributed to its technical nature and lack of radical change it does achieve a modern coherent and cohesive statement of the law. The Act adopts the English position that all future interests are equitable rather than legal. It adopts a preference for tenancy in common over joint tenancy and establishes third party rights under contracts and conveyances. It sets out rights and obligations of landlord and tenant and mortgagee and mortgagor including the imposition of a duty of care on sale by a mortgagee.

[1.13] One social reform in the land law area given attention by the national Poverty Commission Inquiries of 1974 was that of residential landlord and tenant law.[28] Reform was urged on the general basis of the imbalance caused by reliance on freedom of contract, the procedural difficulties of the local court system and the inappropriateness of rules based on a feudal agricultural society to the 20th century urban situation. Again Queensland led the way with minor reforms[29] but a comprehensive restatement of the law came first in South Australia with the *Residential Tenancies Act* 1978. Similar comprehensive statements of the law now exist in all States except Tasmania: see below [11.02]. Further reforms in the landlord and tenant area have been designed to address the problems of the small shopkeeper in particular: see below [11.11].

The different needs caused by compact housing forms have resulted in particular problems for the aged who have been encouraged into specialist accommodation through such factors as the existence of a more compatible community and the availability of nursing care. Regulation in this area has come from retirement villages legislation: see below [13.32].

Planning laws have sought to preserve natural and artificial features of the environment. Restrictions upon owners of heritage buildings have

26. Moore and Tarr, "Consumer Protection" in Baxt and Kewley, *Annual Survey of Law* (Law Book Co. Ltd, 1987), pp. 176-180.
27. Ibid., pp. 181-182, 185-186.
28. Sackville, *Law and Poverty in Australia* (1975), Chap. 3.
29. *Residential Tenancies Act* 1975 (Qld).

become onerous.[30] Resort to property techniques rather than regulation has been evidenced in the development of land management agreements between landowners and government agencies.[31] These agreements extend beyond the negative covenants between neighbouring owners enforced by equity to impose positive obligations for land management and are registered as encumbrances on title.

[1.14] Whilst the adoption of the Torrens system has been the most significant feature of the Australian land law even that step has not been achieved by uniform legislation amongst the States. South Australia was the first State to adopt the system in 1858 but perhaps because of that position it undertook substantial revisions of its statute between 1858 and 1886. The Queensland statute remains closest to the original legislation but New South Wales and Western Australia have only tinkered with their legislation. The Victorian Act has undergone substantial changes and rewriting and Tasmania passed on an entirely rewritten *Land Titles Act* 1980. This Act is perhaps most noteworthy for its restatement of the indefeasibility principle. In all jurisdictions adaptation to technology has provoked interest in amendment.

A plea for uniformity of the Torrens system system was made by Hogg in 1927[32] and repeated by Professor Whalan in 1982.[33] Professor Whalan added his concern for land data banks. Concerns probably reflect whatever is otherwise the focus of authors' attention. Whereas Professor Whalan was describing the registration system the current authors are describing real property law in Australia. They must therefore not only cope with a lack of uniformity of Torrens system statutes but a lack of universality of the Torrens system. There are registration procedures outside the Torrens system which affect such land but generally land outside the system is governed by a mix of common law and general property law statutes. Again those property law statutes vary markedly from State to State. Equally distressingly their relationship with the Torrens system statutes varies and can be most obscure. The general property law statutes may have been seen as having only a limited life once the Torrens system was introduced but there is a pressing need today to examine which of the principles can meaningfully apply to the Torrens system land.

The Torrens system statutes adopt common principles as to indefeasibility of title and agree in the restructuring of the form of a mortgage. But even with respect to title there may be differences as to the effect of forgery and the protection of volunteers. There are differences as to the prima facie form of co-ownership and as to the recognition of claims based on adverse possession and the recognition of implied easements and of restrictive covenants. The point at which to divide between informal and formal leases and the extent or protection for informal leases is not

---

30. Jensen, "Conversion of Historic Buildings, Redevelopment and Town Planning: A Problem of Environmental Design" (1984) 1 E. & P.L.J. 212.
31. Fowler, "Vegetation Clearance Controls in South Australia—A Change of Course" (1986) 3 E. & P.L.J. 49.
32. In the preface to Kerr, op. cit.
33. Whalan, p. viii.

agreed upon and, if anything, is made more obscure by recent legislation. The differences between the property law statutes reflect more the extent to which common law technicalities have been overcome by statute. Thus it is still possible that a distinction must be drawn between covenants in esse and those in posse when the enforceability of covenants in a lease between successors in title is considered. These differences reflect the assiduity of Stage legislatures in copying British statutory reforms. It is difficult to believe that a conscious preference was exercised in favour of the settled land legislation of 1877 over that of 1882. Whilst South Australia has been the leader in social reforms (residential tenancies, retirement villages) it has been most neglectful of technical property reforms.

The differences between the States with respect to the content of Torrens system and general property law statutes might be ascribed to the greater independence from one another both politically and geographically of the then Australian colonies of the 19th century. Related statutes such as those concerning settled land and limitation of actions might be similarly explained. But the States continue to frame statutes about real property matters with a diversity which can only be described as perverse. Thus the boundary between unit property and common property is placed differently in the strata titles legislation[34] and the definition of a retirement village[35] is different in each statute on the topic. The differences in no way appear to reflect peculiar circumstances in the various States. Legal resources are wastefully consumed on analysis of differing wordings. Differences in land-use planning laws are so great that it has been almost impossible for planning lawyers to get together nationally to discuss common problems.[36]

[1.15] If the state of Australian real property law is a cause for concern then much blame must be attributed to academic neglect and the shortcomings of Australian legal education. Two great works on the Torrens system in the early part of the century (by Hogg[37] and Kerr[38]) seem to have had no connection with the universities. Two significant writers who published well-known books, Baalman[39] and Voumard,[40] were practitioners with conveyancing specialisations in Sydney and Melbourne respectively. After the Second World War a study of land law principles[41] was written by Dr Helmore of the University of Sydney on the law of New South Wales alone, a constant feature of works on land law eminating from Sydney.

As late as the time of the Vietnam war the property law course at the University of Melbourne did not acknowledge the existence of the Torrens

34. On strata boundaries, see below [13.23].
35. On the retirement village definition, see below [13.36].
36. Ryan, "Metropolitan Planning in Australia: The Instruments of Planning— Regulation" (1988) 5 E. & P.L.J. 147.
37. Hogg, op. cit.
38. Kerr, op. cit. Dr Kerr was an Adelaide practitioner; he received his doctorate for work on public law: see Castles, Ligertwood and Kelly, op. cit., p. 27.
39. Baalman, op. cit.
40. Voumard.
41. Hargreaves and Helmore, op. cit.

system. No record was kept by the University of Adelaide of the essays commissioned to mark the centenary of the Torrens system. Indeed many University property law courses up to the 1970s reflected a view that the remainder and perpetuity rules provided a good mental exercise even if settlements were uncommon in Australia. The University of Queensland did have a local focus as can be seen in Fry's published notes and Professor Harrison's[42] casebook. A considerable change in legal education came with the publication of Sackville and Neave's *Property Law Cases and Materials* in 1971. Not only did the work concentrate on the Torrens system and socially relevant problems in Australia at that time but it examined what was special about property rights.[43] Professor Sackville also chaired the Law and Poverty section of the Poverty Commission Inquiry and again academic investigation can be seen to lead to property law reform (residential tenancies) whereas earlier reforms (such as fencing and strata title laws) reflected practical concerns and initiatives.

II.   SIGNIFICANCE OF AUSTRALIAN REAL PROPERTY LAW

[1.16]   A guide to the mass of Australian statutes and cases could claim for that fact alone to be a useful reference. But the authors believe that that mass goes well beyond a superficial accretion to English law as received and as developed subsequently in England. The historical sketch has attempted to show that divergences have occurred on a number of fundamental issues.

[1.17]   A different approach is taken by the authors of *Understanding Land Law* who claim in their preface "The existing law of real property is feudal: its fundamental principles were laid down in a period and society far removed from the present."[44] Consequently the authors set out those rules and terminology so that they could be understood by the modern reader. In view of the fact that Sydney is the place of publication, that modern reader is intended to be an Australian reader. The necessary inference is that an understanding of English feudal land law will provide an Australian reader in the 1990s with a basis for knowledge of Australian land law.

[1.18]   The most obvious objection to this proposition is that most land in Australia is held under the Torrens system and that system is unique to the country. If substantial amounts of land in Victoria and New South Wales in particular have remained outside the system, a duality of knowledge has been necessary. Moreover, the significance of the system is increased because yet again in recent years governments have shown an interest in the conversion of all land to the Torrens system. This interest

---

42. A biographical note at the time of Professor Harrison's professorial appointment appears at 21 A.L.J. 437.
43. Conceptually it owes much to Jackson, *Principles of Property Law* (1970).
44. Oxley-Oxland and Stein, *Understanding Land Law* (1985), Chap. V.

has been sparked by the introduction of computer-based title records and the linking of title records with satellite-picture-based information systems of land use.[45]

The unfriendly onlooker can dismiss the Torrens system as one concerned with the transfer of interests in land rather than one concerned with the nature of interests in land. The system can then be said to be relevant to conveyancing rather than land law. It is true that the Torrens system builds from the range of interests in land at common law. However it is fundamental to the Torrens system that title stems from the fact of registration. Thus any interest can only exist in so far as the system allows it to exist. Consequently the enforceability in Australia of restrictive covenants has not flowed as readily as in England because of the difficulties of bringing those interests (which postdated the Torrens system) within the registration process.

Not only does the existence of interests within the Torrens system depend on the system's willingness to allow them to be registered or otherwise protected but the system has wrought vast changes to the nature of interests. It is customary to equate registered with legal interests and unregistered with equitable interests. In general, registered interests are enforceable against the whole world, but that quality derives from the absolute and indefeasible status conferred by the Torrens system legislation and is subject to its qualifications—principal of which is the ease of being displaced as the registered proprietor. Furthermore although unregistered interests like equitable interests are vulnerable, they are far more vulnerable than equitable interests because of the exemption of registered proprietors from the doctrine of notice. The protection of unregistered interests and priority between such interests also depends largely upon the caveat system.

The Torrens system has retained fee simple and life estates and in some instances fee tail estates. But traditional settlements have been virtually unknown. The doctrine of tenure has little meaning for those who hold an estate but has been applied to deny recognition to interests not based on a Crown grant. Mortgages have been substantially reshaped under the Torrens system. Leases and easements have retained their common law characteristics. The system has however considerably restricted the recognition of the creation of interests through the fact of possession.

[1.19] Beyond the Torrens system, Australian real property law has had to adapt to the demands of Australian geography and society. Adaptation has occurred through statutes and common law development. The historical development of this adaptation has already been outlined. The impact of these developments will be appreciated in the succeeding substantive Chapters. After the process of securing title through registration under the Torrens system, attention turns to dealings between parties. Much of the law of formalities and fair dealings between parties has been reshaped by Australian courts through such doctrines as estoppel and unconscionability. Many landlord and tenant relationships are now

45. Lang, "Computerised Land Title and Land Information" (1984) 10 Mon. U.L.R. 196.

governed not by the rules relevant to a rural feudal society but by statutory codes. New arrangements have been authorised by statute to allow multiple rights of ownership of land and buildings through strata titles, time-sharing and retirement villages. Several statutory enactments have been made to deal with boundary disputes. Some of the law of easements and covenants has been shaped in this century to cope with intensive urban relationships though Australian innovation has been less pronounced. Significant statutory regulation has however affected the rights of mortgagees and mortgagors. Finally consideration is given to the variety of forms of tenure through Crown leases and licences applicable to much rural land; these forms have been a distinctive Australian development.

III. SOCIAL PURPOSE OF REAL PROPERTY LAW

[1.20] The historical survey of real property law developments in Australia is based on an initial assumption that land will be subject to private ownership. That assumption has not been seriously questioned during the period of European occupation. The acceptance of the principle of tenure has meant that there is a relationship between the individual and the State in relation to all land but this relationship has been largely theoretical and for a long time private freehold owners have been free from any obligations to the State arising from the tenurial relationship. The system of leasehold tenure has been used where it has been desired to impose obligations towards the State. The only other consideration of financial burdens on land owners has arisen in the context of the basis of land rates and taxes imposed on land owners in favour of local and State governments. Some experimentation has occurred through the levying of rates on the unimproved value of land on the theory that landowners are thereby encouraged to seek an economic return from the land.[46]

Private land ownership has been supported by traditional economic analysis on the basis that it not only encourages maximum utilisation of the land but that it also ensures consideration of the future condition of the land. The rational landowner will not exploit the land to the point where current returns are outweighed by future loss of productivity. This assertion does rest on an assumed capacity properly to discount future income. Nonetheless the position of the private owner is contrasted with public enjoyment of physical resources. Each individual with access to public facilities is encouraged to overexploit because that individual will derive the total benefit from overexploitation but the burdens will be shared by everyone with rights of access.[47] It is therefore suggested that the success of the agrarian revolution is tied to enclosure and the removal

---

46. Hagman, "The Single Tax and Land-Use Planning: Henry George Updated" (1963) 12 U.C.L.A.L.R. 762; *Osborne v. Commonwealth* (1911) 12 C.L.R. 321; Stein, *Urban Legal Problems* (1974), pp. 49-59
47. Hardin, "The Tragedy of the Commons" (1968) 162 *Science* 1243; Posner, *Economic Analysis of Law* (2nd ed., 1977), Chap. 3.

of rights of commons. In current affairs, pollution is blamed on public access to air and water. The polluter reaps the profit of the polluting activity but the burdens are transferred to society as a whole.

The economic basis for private land ownership leads to the conclusion that the initial allocation of land should be to the person who is likely to make the most efficient use of that land.[48] This conclusion lends support for the selling of Crown land by public auction (a process which has occurred in the Australian Capital Territory) and the related and highly publicised process of tendering for new radio and television broadcasting licenses. These processes are supported on the basis that the most efficient user is able to outbid others. But whatever the initial allocation a more efficient user will be in a position to buy the land.

The intitial allocation is relatively unimportant in terms of ensuring the ultimate most efficient use of the land if land can be readily transferred. If the initial owner's use of the land is the most efficient use of that land, the value placed on the land by that person will be higher than that of rival bidders. Conversely if someone else's use is more efficient that person will offer the current owner sufficient for the land that the current owner will agree to sell. Transaction costs are the major impediment to this movement. They may result not merely from the land transfer process but for example from an excessive fragmentation of initial allocations. Urban redevelopment faces the problem of dealing with a number of holders of small allotments; this difficulty is then used to justify government intervention through compulsory acquisition. At the same time initial allocation is not totally irrelevant to the transfer process and may affect the ability to bid. At an extreme, if land is the sole resource and all land is allocated to one person, others have nothing with which to bid.

[1.21] Traditional English real property law centred on obstacles to the acquisition of land for its most efficient use. The strict settlement gave the current landholder only a limited interest in the land and guaranteed the right of future generations. The purpose of the settlement was to prevent the alienation of land away from the families by which it was held. The retention of personal power was sought even at the price of a less efficient use of land. On the other hand efforts were made to pierce the settlement and allow the transfer of the land. How successful settlements were in preserving the position of the landed families is unclear; what is commonly accepted is that at the start of the First World War much of the land in England was owned by a small group of persons.[49]

One of the key issues affected by real property law in Australia was the control of rural land. The legal theory that all land was owned by the Crown and that title depended on Crown grant was used to exclude aborigines from much of the land they had held from ancient times. Conversely legal recognition was given to the claims of squatters who seised land beyond the official limits of settlement. Again control of rural land was affected by the rights of free selection. The success of legal

---

48. Posner, op. cit., pp. 31-33.
49. Langbein, *The Twentieth Century Revolution in Family Wealth Transmission* (University of Chicago Occasional papers No. 25).

resistance to the selectors—legal resistence involving manipulation of processes established by statute—ensured the wealth and power of the squatters.

The Australian system of landholding has been pre-eminently a capitalist enterprise.[50] Land was granted on conditions as to its development. The insecurity of the squatters' title emphasised that the value of the land lay in the capacity to exploit it. Pastoral development where, for example, fencing was a key to increased returns involved heavy reliance on borrowings so that efficient use was necessary to pay back the financiers. The Torrens system meant that land could be readily transferred or mortgaged. Land thus became (in Professor Whalan's words) a commodity.

Australian real property history may be seen as a triumph for efficiency of land use over attempts to provide greater equity through the distribution of land rights. Attempts to provide for small landholders have generally failed: from Governor Macquarie's attempts to create a peasant farming class to free selection to soldier settlements to reward those who served in the world wars. These small holders were generally unable to compete with the large pastoralists.

[1.22] If the battle for control of rural land was vital to the acquisition of wealth and power, the rights of the landholders have been long established and current signs of rebellion seem very dim. A study of real property law might then seem today to be irrelevant to an understanding of the holding of wealth in society.[51] The study seems to be confined to an analysis of the processes for the transfer of land.[52] If that characterisation is true then the central role of real property courses should properly be challenged.

A criticism that a study of real property law is confined to relatively unimportant land transfer processes vastly underestimates the scope of that law. Many significant relationships are regulated by real property law and the balance struck by the law does greatly affect wealth and power. Probably the relations between landlord and tenant and mortgagee and mortgagor are the most significant contests affecting land. Rights for strata unit holders and retirement village residents have enhanced the position of these persons. Real property law also has many gender aspects: the rights of married women to own land are now assumed but often the interests of a female partner stem from informal arrangements and real property law has emphasised formality.

Moreover the economic significance of the processes of transfer[53] has already been stated. The Torrens system has been important in allowing the cheap alienation of land with certainty as to the title obtained as a

---

50. Davidson and Wells, "The Land, The Law and The State: Colonial Australia 1788-1890" (1982) 2 *Law in Context* 89.
51. Mossman, "Toward 'New Property' and 'New Scholarship': An Assessment of Canadian Property Scholarship" (1985) 23 Osgoode Hall L.J. 633.
52. Ackerman, *Economic Foundations of Property Law* (1975), Chap. IX.
53. Johnstone, "Land Transfers: Process and Processors" (1988) 22 Val U.L.R. 493.

result of a land transfer. Similarly the system has facilitated the use of land as a security through the Torrens system mortgage. The greatest impediment to the cheapness of land transfers has come from the impositions of State governments who have seen the opportunity for revenue through stamp duties. Moreover government authorities have been reluctant to allow the paramountcy of the register to defeat any of their claims by way of charges over the land for unpaid rates and taxes. Much recent effort in the development of real property law has been to provide protection for purchasers from these claims by government authorities.

[1.23] Whilst fears about the value of the study of real property law may be allayed, it should be acknowledged that its relative importance has been diminished by the lesser significance of land as a source of wealth and power. Attention has turned to the processes of manufacture carried out by organisations and the issues of the control of corporate organisations, their access to finance and their dealings with the workforce. Moreover in a technological society value comes more from ideas rather than from the exertion of physical labour. Intangible rights which protect those ideas, such as trademarks and patents, assume greater significance. The creation and protection of these rights requires greater sophistication than regulation of dealings in land or goods. These tasks impose demands and provide opportunities for lawyers. And because the capacity for ideas is most unevenly distributed amongst members of society, the significance of property in intangibles as a wealth-creator has implications for relative equality within society.

Not only have corporations law and intellectual and industrial law assumed greater significance than real property law, the scope for development of these areas of law is less restricted. The need for certainty in real property law because of the ordering of affairs on the basis of that law is most pronounced. Thus the courts have established a range of interests in land and new situations have been dealt with by way of application of the definitions of these interests. The Torrens system has further restricted the creative scope of the courts. By and large a registration system defines the things which can be registered and limits the range of things which can be recognised to those which can be registered.

The scope for creativity is greater in disputes relating to the exploitation of land rather than those dependent on the definition of interests in land and the processes for their transfer. Real property law does affect relations between landholders through the law of easements and covenants and that of strata unit holders. But the extent to which one landholder can interfere with another landholder is largely the province of the law of nuisance and in Australia (as in England) this branch of the law is regarded as part of the law of torts. Similarly the statutory land use planning and environmental laws have been treated separately from real property law. It is significant as an indication of their importance and scope for creativity that many of the illustrations of the application of economic analysis to land law concern nuisance cases. The authors of the current text accept the established practices as to the treatment of these areas of law with some misgivings and suggest that those practices produce a fragmented analysis of the rights of exploitation of land.

[1.24] Real property law is not confined to the issue of the nature of interests in land and as has been already emphasised much development has occurred in defining the relationships between holders of different interests and the processes by which transfers occur. But even new interests have been recognised by the courts and by the legislatures. As will be explained more fully in the substantive analysis, the constructive trust has been developed by the courts to protect investments of both money and labour against what has been described as unconscionable appropriation (see below [6.35]) and the legislatures have acted with surprising speed to protect residents of retirement villages: see below [13.32].

In terms of values to which the courts and legislatures have responded in real property matters, that of reaping without sowing has a special place. The idea that the fruits of a person's labour belong to that person has long been regarded as an almost natural principle.[54] It has clear utility connotations in that a person is encouraged to labour if that person retains the results of the effort. In its application the idea relates not just to the products of physical exertion but to those of financial exertion. At the same time the retirement village example indicates that protection is most readily afforded to those who already have some degree of power.

Even in the current society the distribution of real property does matter in terms of wealth and power. The Commission of Inquiry into Land Tenures observed that the relatively high level of home ownership (approximately 70 per cent of households) was the greatest factor in favour of equality of wealth in Australia.[55] Apart from the value of equality in terms of individual dignity, the spread of home ownership does assist social cohesion and stability. Persons become petty capitalists; they work and conform to maintain their mortgage commitments. The value placed upon this spread of real property interests has been most pronounced under the Commonwealth-State Housing Agreements under which government assistance was directed to assisting house purchasers rather than the less advantaged residential tenants.[56] Similarly strata titles can be seen as enabling ownership even of limited spaces.

IV. NATURE AND CLASSIFICATION OF PROPERTY RIGHTS

[1.25] Protection of residents of retirement villages by the creation of a new proprietary interest has been remarked upon as a rapid legislative intervention. That interest is designated as proprietary because residents have been protected from eviction not just as against a management authority with whom they contracted but against holders of security

---

54. See Teh and Dwyer, p. 4; Hamilton, "Property According to Locke" (1932) 41 Yale L.J. 864; Sackville and Neave, p. 31.
55. Commission of Inquiry into Land Tenures, *Final Report* (1976), pp. 12-13.
56. Bradbrook, MacCallum and Moore, p. 34.

interests over that land and subsequent purchasers of the land. The fact of the existence of the village is recorded on title and rights have flown on to residents of the village.

Whereas retirement village residents have been given statutory rights thus classified as proprietary, boarders and lodgers have been explicitly denied the protections given to occupants of residential premises. Some of the protections were regarded as inappropriate for boarders and lodgers but such persons have been totally denied status as holders of proprietary rights. A dependence on contractual rights is seen even as a denial of all rights, but only because the emphasis upon freedom of contract and the assumption that their landlords would frame contracts favourable to the landlords has been seen as producing few contractual rights of substance.

[1.26] Understanding the differences between retirement village residents and boarders and lodgers necessitates an analysis of what is special about property rights.[57] In its simplest form property is inherently involved with a thing. When I say "That is my pencil" I am referring to an object which is in my possession, is mine to do with as I please, is free from any obligations to other persons, and may be disposed of as I see fit. Ownership and possession are merged and there is but a single relationship with the object. The notion of property becomes more sophisticated and involved with power and politics as things serve purposes other than to provide for the enjoyment of their owner. The continued application of the idea that property and things co-exist leads to misconception as other purposes are introduced. Thus a landowner will protest at the restrictions on the owner's rights if the owner is told that land cannot be entered because a tenancy has been granted or cannot be developed because of planning controls. These instances illustrate that land at least cannot in today's society serve simply the interest of one person. Therefore the question of what is meant by ownership is posed and the existence of rights that relate to but do not fully encompass a thing is recognised.

Once the concept that something can be mine is divorced from the totality of the object, the focus turn to rights in that object. Private property can usefully be contrasted with the enjoyment of unappropriated natural resources. A public lake provides water to swim in or to drink. But I cannot claim any of that water from anyone else. Similarly property can be contrasted with contractual rights. A right of occupation could be a proprietary or contractual right: the essence lies in the range of persons against whom enforcement is possible. A right of occupation which is enforceable merely against a grantor is not a property right since if a third party interferes with the occupation the grantee has no complaint against that third party. Similarly my enjoyment of the public lake gives me no standing to complain of a polluter. The essence of the idea that something is mine is that I have rights to prevent interference by third parties. Thus in our legal system both landlords and tenants can claim that a house is theirs since they will be protected against third parties.

---

57. See generally Sackville and Neave, pp. 1-14.

The exclusion of others from something is a meaningful course of action only if others want that thing. If there are ready alternatives for the thing then others will not want it and exclusion is pointless. There is thus a sense in which property is a factor of scarcity. A limited supply of a thing causes competition for that thing. But scarcity can be created even though there is a sufficient supply of things to meet all demands for consumption of that thing. Patents created a scarcity of particular applications of knowledge. Things may be appropriated to an individual and thus excluded from others even though that individual has more of the things than the individual can consume. Control of the things can enable the individual to impose terms for the transfer or even mere use of the things. Property is thus a source of power over others. The exercise of that power in turn requires an enforcement mechanism. In Australia private property exists because it is protected by the legal system. The ability of that legal system to impose its decision to a large extent depends on the common acceptance of the system of government but also on the physical force which sustains that system.

The exclusion of others can be most readily understood in relation to material objects. Thus land and goods are the most obvious subjects of property. As already mentioned patents confer the right to exploit a particular idea. The reproduction of a particular combination of words is protected by copyright. Recent legislation has protected plant variety rights. Once property in the idea or statement or species is recognised, the owner may exclude others and is able to demand payment to dispose of the thing.

[1.27] In terms of this basic definition a retirement village resident has a proprietary interest because that interest can be enforced against third parties generally. These parties include purchasers and credit providers. On the other hand the existence of a proprietary interest does not necessarily mean that all third parties are subject to it. The dividing line is drawn between rights enforceable only against another party and those enforceable generally against others.

[1.28] Not all arrangements relating to land confer proprietary interests in relation to that land. As well as the freehold and leasehold estates the principal proprietary interests in land recognised by the common law are mortgages, rentcharges, profits à prendre, easements and restrictive covenants. To determine whether an arrangement confers a proprietary interest, the arrangement must be examined to see if it satisfies the definition of any one of the recognised proprietary interests. Because lawyers are often involved in the framing of arrangements relating to land rather than involved only subsequently when a dispute has arisen, arrangements may be given particular features so as to bring them within one of the definitions. Thus although the right to display advertising signs was held by the House of Lords in *King v. David Allen & Sons Billposting Ltd*[58] to confer only personal rights, a similar arrangement was extended to include exclusive possession of the outside walls and thus

---

58. [1916] 2 A.C. 54.

amount to a lease of that area and thereby confer a proprietary interest: *Claude Neon Ltd v. Melbourne & Metropolitan Board of Works.*[59]

[1.29] Whilst not all rights to be on land are proprietary rights, grants of proprietary interests do confer rights to be on land. Those without permission to be on land are trespassers. The great bulk of those who are on land with permission do not have a proprietary interest but some form of licence. Some licences are attached to proprietary interests so that the right to remove gravel (a profit à prendre) carries with it a right to cross the land to get to the gravel. These licences are described as licences coupled with an interest and take on the qualities of the proprietary interest to which they are attached. A bare licence is a gratuitous permission. Since our legal system does not enforce promises without consideration the permission can be withdrawn at any time: dinner guests can be asked to leave before the main course. The bare licensee must be given a reasonable time to get off the premises but thereafter becomes a trespasser and the legal system allows a degree of self-help through the use of physical force to remove a trespasser.[60]

[1.30] Many licences arise from commercial arrangements: permission to be on the land is granted pursuant to a contract. Contractors or employees performing work on the land, students at a fee-paying institution, paying spectators at the theatre or a sporting event, and boarders and lodgers are all contractual licensees. Does the fact that they do not have a proprietary interest mean that their licence may be revoked at any time? Obviously the licence must be subject to some limits which are not express but must be implied: theatre-goers may be asked to leave in the event of a fire or bomb threat, a student suspended for drug dealing, or a punter removed for illegal gambling. But these problems relate to the definition of the contract. The issue under discussion is the revocability of the licence in breach of contract.

Breach of contract gives rise to an action in damages. Normally in the contractual licence context this right is dismissed as an entitlement to a refund of the entrance fee. But substantial damages for breach of contract are not inconceivable. If I can prove that I had $1,000 committed to what turned out to be the 50 to one winner of the last race is my $50,000 loss too remote? If the anguish of upset travel plans is compensable[61] should not a football fan receive something for missing her or his team's first premiership in 25 years? If removal is taken as a sign of wrongdoing, are not damages available for the loss of reputation amongst those who have witnessed or learnt of the removal?

The right of the contractual licensee to stay put came before the High Court in *Cowell v. Rosehill Racecourse Co.*[62] In that case a spectator had been

---

59. (1969) 43 A.L.J.R. 69; Kitto and Windeyer JJ. dissented on the basis that since no arrangements were made with the so-called tenants on matters such as exterior cleaning the tenants did not genuinely have control and thus exclusive possession.
60. See Fleming, *The Law of Torts* (7th ed., 1987), pp. 78-79.
61. *Athens-MacDonald Travel Service Pty Ltd v. Kazis* [1970] S.A.S.R. 264; *Falko v. James McEwan & Co. Pty Ltd* [1977] V.R. 447; see also Cheshire and Fifoot, p. 663.
62. (1937) 56 C.L.R. 605. See also *Graham H. Roberts Pty Ltd v. Maurbeth Investment Pty Ltd* [1974] 1 N.S.W.L.R. 93.

asked to leave a race meeting and when he refused to do so he was forcibly evicted. He sued for damages for assault on the basis that the licence had not been validly revoked.

One issue which entered the analysis but which was properly irrelevant was that of formalities. Nineteenth century decisions on similar facts were claimed to rest on the absence of a deed granting the right to come onto the land and with the passing of the *Judicature Act*, rules of equity became relevant and they would relieve against the absence of a deed. But a deed is only needed and its absence only a matter of concern if one is involved with the grant of a proprietary interest. That issue was made clear by the High Court. It further rejected the view that the category of licences coupled with an interest extended beyond licences associated with the grant of proprietary interests to licences whereby the grantee had some contractual interest in being on the land.

Cowell's Case has nothing to do with proprietary interests or formalities connected with such interests. It concerns the effectiveness of an action (withdrawal of a licence) in breach of contract. At an extreme would be the approach of Oliver Wendell Holmes that a contractor has the choice of performing or paying damages for breach.[63] But Latham C.J. in one of the majority judgments in *Cowell* took the narrower ground that a contract to provide an entertainment was not one in respect of which equity would decree specific performance or whose breach equity would restrain by an injunction. Therefore the licence had been withdrawn and the only redress was a claim for damages for breach of contract. In dissent Evatt J. challenged this limited view of equitable intervention. It was, he stated, a broad and just principle of equity to restrain revocation of the licence in breach of contract. Evatt J. further reasoned that if equity would restrain the revocation, the position of the parties would be no different if the timing meant they were unable to seek equitable assistance until after the event.

Subsequent English decisions have lent support to the dissenting judgment.[64] It is clear that in some cases at least a revocation of a licence in breach of contract will be restrained and certainly equitable remedies will not be made available to assist the revocation. Some doubts on the decision in *Cowell* were cast by dicta in the High Court decision in *Forbes v. N.S.W. Trotting Club Ltd.*[65]

[1.31]   The analysis of licences to be on land is an orthodox application of the definition of proprietary rights as those enforceable against third parties generally. Thus the issue of sphere of enforceability is separated from that of remedies to enforce the right. This division should not however be overstated. One of the reasons why some rights are denied recognition as proprietary is that specific performance is inappropriate. The relationship between boarders or lodgers and their landlord is customarily one of close residential contact. Similarly residents of

---

63. The approach is discussed in Gilmore, *The Death of Contract* (1974).
64. *Winter Garden Theatre (London) Ltd v. Millenium Productions Ltd* [1948] A.C. 173; *Hounslow London B. C. v. Twickenham Garden Developments Ltd* [1971] Ch. 233.
65. (1979) 25 A.L.R. 1.

University Colleges have been excluded from residential tenancy legislation. Specific performance of whatever contractual rights these persons have would involve compelling them and the other parties to sustain a living relationship in what might be unpleasant circumstances.

[1.32] Normally something that can be excluded from others has value not only for its use by its owner but because of the ability to dispose of it.[66] However the right of alienation is not a universal aspect of a proprietary interest. Thus a right of personal residence has been classified as a proprietary interest as a conditional life estate—a person has an interest for the person's lifetime provided he or she lives on the property. However the right of alienation is normally associated with a proprietary interest and in relation to tenants the courts have reasoned that because they have proprietary interests they have interests which are prima facie assignable.[67]

[1.33] If specific enforceability is not confined to proprietary interests in relation to land, specific enforceability is normally assumed to be available to protect proprietary interests. However that protection is not assumed in relation to goods. Damages are asserted to be a sufficient remedy because goods can be replaced.[68] Obviously an exception for heirlooms and precious paintings and similar objects can be justified. But the general position in relation to goods means that the owner's right of exclusion does not enable her or him to retrieve the object itself. However a range of legal rights do attach to what would commonly be regarded as the owner's property. There are limited rights of self-defence to prevent taking by others; the criminal law and its enforcement processes operate to apprehend a taker and return the goods. Objects acquire for their owners personal significance so that the loss felt on a housebreaking is more than the economic setback.[69]

Similarly whilst the holder of contractual rights can directly enforce those rights only against other contracting parties, remedies may affect third parties. If the holder learns of a prospective attempt to induce the other party to breach the contract, injunctive relief may be available to prevent that action.[70] Similarly the tort of interference with contractual relations provides damages against third parties in some cases where those third parties have induced non-performance by a contracting party.[71]

[1.34] Like all definitions that of proprietary interests is a help to understanding but should not be utilised in a mechanistic fashion. Far more rigid were the classifications or subdivisions of property rights adopted by a common law. These classifications were often applied with significant consequences. Few of those consequences remain. The terms are still often used in legal documents including statutes and wills. The

---

66. This attribute is discussed in *Milirrpum v. Nabalco Pty Ltd* (1971) 17 F.L.R. 141 at 272 amongst a general discussion of the incidents of proprietary rights.
67. See the discussion of the tenant's rights below **[10.31]**.
68. Fleming, op. cit., pp. 66-68.
69. Reeve, *Property* (1986), p. 5.
70. Cheshire and Fifoot, p. 674.
71. Fleming, op. cit., pp. 651-659.

greatest problems arise where technical words are used without full appreciation of their precise meaning.

[1.35] The most basic division was that between real and personal property. This division lives on in common language, such as the term real estate agent, where real property is assimilated to land. However the division comes from the late Norman period and real property means that which can be recovered in kind—the thing (res) is recoverable. At the time the only things recoverable in kind were the freehold estates in land. Everything else was personal property. The freehold estates were those of indefinite duration (the fee simple, fee tail and life estates); those estates of definite duration were less than freehold and thus termed leasehold. It is an anomaly that an estate for a 1000 years is less than one for a lifetime. But for the process of classification, because the only forms of real property were the freehold estates, leasehold estates were personal property. The basis of the distinction was to disappear with the development of the action of ejectment whereby a leaseholder could be restored to possession. Nonetheless the division had been made and as a result personal property encompasses leasehold interests, interests in goods and intangible rights. Because of this scope personal property was divided between chattels real (leasehold interests) and chattels personal (other forms of personalty).

Legal consequences flowed from the division between real and personal property. Until the *Statute of Wills* 1540 real property could not be left by will but passed automatically to the heir (a concept giving preference to males over females and amongst males to the first-born over others). Even after that statute a difference flowed in the passing of real and personal property on the death of an owner without a will. Again real property passed to the heir whereas personalty passed to the next of kin (a concept giving priority according to the closeness of the relationship). In the 19th century statutes in all Australian jurisdictions providing for the administration of estates removed this residual vestige of male preference. The categories of real and personal property are still part of legal language. One consequential linguistic distinction is that to leave realty by will is to devise whereas to leave personalty by will is to bequeath.

[1.36] A less significant and less understood general distinction is that between corporeal and incorporeal hereditaments. The term hereditament refers to interests that pass to the heirs (basically freehold estates other than the life estate). The distinction between corporeal and incorporeal is a distinction between tangible and intangible. In the sense that property is a form of right all property is intangible. However the division depended upon whether the right involved possession and enjoyment or some more limited use of the land. Thus the estates are corporeal interests whereas rights of access (easements) are incorporeal.

V. SPECIAL FORMS OF LAND RIGHTS

1. Introduction

[1.37] This text is concerned generally with private property rights in land. The rights of the Crown and even local government in public land is beyond its consideration. The distinction between proprietary and contractual interests has already been explained. There are two general systems of property rights in land in Australia: one where the Crown has granted freehold rights in the land to a private person; the other where the Crown has granted a leasehold interest. The private rights that exist in such cases stem from general principles of statutory and common law. There are however three forms of private land rights which exist under separate regimes; first, rights to minerals subject to specific mining legislation; secondly, those of aborigines resulting from specific native land rights legislation; and thirdly, those of partners to a family relationship subject to the jurisdiction of the family court and related State courts.

2. Mining Rights

[1.38]   The extent to which rights to land include minerals in that land is discussed in Chapter 14. However, today the acquisition of rights to minerals stems from separate legislation which does vary from State to State. Every State has separate regimes for petroleum and minerals, though even the statutory definitions of petroleum and minerals vary. Despite the considerable differences between the States' legislation, each petroleum and minerals statute prescribes a similar framework for exploitation of the resource. This framework consists of the grant by the Crown in relation to petroleum or minerals of exploration licences or leases. These licences or leases permit works to be undertaken to ascertain the likely existence of petroleum or minerals. Actual mining is subject to the further grant of petroleum or minerals production leases or licences. The legislation also provides for the payment of royalties, the compensation of owners or occupiers of the surface land, a system of mine inspection and control, and various environmental safeguards.[72]

3. Aboriginal Land Rights

[1.39]   Prior to the establishment of the colony of New South Wales by Captain Phillip in 1788, the Australian continent was occupied solely by the Australian Aborigines.[73] Aboriginal society was, and still is, diverse and culturally sophisticated, emphasising the group and its cultural obligations ahead of the individual. This emphasis, of course, is a direct contrast to the individualism at the heart of contemporary non-Aboriginal society in Australia. Aboriginal law was, and is, an integral part of Aboriginal society, and covered cultural, spiritual, social and economic behaviour. The law has always had a crucial role in the manner in which

---

72. For a detailed discussion of this legislation, see Forbes and Lang, *Australian Mining and Petroleum Laws* (2nd ed., 1987).
73. The term "Aborigine" is used reluctantly, as it refers to the indigenous group of any country, and detracts from the named identity of the "Aboriginal people" in Australia. "Aborigines" in Australia in fact have their own general names for all "Aboriginal people", which differ in different regions of Australia—for example, the term "Koori" is used by the people in Victoria, Tasmania, New South Wales and Southern Queensland to refer to "Aborigines" in general, and "Nyungga" by the people in South Australia. "Aborigine" will be used in this book because it is a book for general use in Australia.

Aboriginal culture reflects the interaction between the people of the present, their ancestors, and the environment.

Central to Aboriginal culture, spirituality and sustenance is a complex and important relationship of the group with the land.[74] It is a spiritual, intellectual and economic relationship. The land is a source of food and shelter, the home of Aboriginal "totems",[75] and a future resting place for the spirits of individual Aborigines. Aborigines believe they have come from the land, that they are one with the land, and will return to the land when they die. To Aborigines, the land was created, with all its features, together with the law, the people, the culture, and other forms of life, by ancestral beings and every piece of land is marked with the passage of these ancestral beings. In their movement over the land, the ancestral beings determined the spirit centres for both humans and animals. The map of their travels—the "songs" for the particular country—are the property of the senior traditional owners of the land.

It is the duty of these owners to care for the land, and the duty is passed down through families. Caring for the land, or "growing up the country", involves making sure the country grows up, thrives and is in a suitable physical and spiritual conditions to be handed down to future generations of the group. Aborigines see themselves as the land's inherent and perpetual custodians. The individual is therefore part of a continuum of culture. He or she links the past, the present and the future of the land. This process has been repeated since the earliest generations, and it is through the strict observation of this process, the law, that the country has continued to flourish. The activities of the spirit ancestors are commemorated in the rich Aboriginal oral tradition, and in Aboriginal ritual and social life. Aboriginal communities accept a collective responsibility for their country, and live in the "tracks" of ancestral beings. For Aborigines land is the central and inseparable part of their being.

Knowledge of the land is central to Aboriginal self-identity and pivotal in the creation and fulfilment of obligations in Aboriginal society. Acquiring knowledge of the land is a lifelong task, and dispensing of it a lifelong obligation. This knowledge of the land involves an intimate understanding of the plants, animals and geographic formations on the

74. For descriptions of this relationship, see Dodson "Aborigines and the Criminal Justice System" (1987) 28 *Aboriginal Law Bulletin* 4; Butcher and Turnbull, "Aborigines, Europeans and the Environment" in Burgmann and Lee (eds), *A People's History of Australia since 1788, Vol. 1: A Most Valuable Acquisition* (McPhee Gribble/Penguin, Melbourne, 1988), p. 19; Christie, *Aborigines in Colonial Victoria 1835-1886* (Sydney University Press, 1979) pp. 22-23; Toyne and Vachon *Growing Up the Country: The Pitjantjatjara Struggle for Their Land* (McPhee Gribble/Penguin, Melbourne, 1984), pp. 5-8.

75. "Totemism" means that Aborigines see humans and the natural species as part of one social and ceremonial whole, so that there is no dichotomy between humans and the things of nature. In Aboriginal society, each person, clan, local descent group, and part of land was identified with a natural species or object. A person saw the totem as a guide and a helper, and in return would respect and refrain from injuring the totem. The totems linked the individual with the creation of society, and is a reminder of social and ceremonial obligations: see Christie, op. cit., pp. 21-22.

land, and of the near inexhaustible food and medicinal resources that the land can yield.[76] It means understanding the importance of geographic features as signs of the activities of ancestral beings, as links with the past and as deserving of respect and love.

This approach is in strong contrast with European systems of land law, where land is a commodity, to be bought and sold, to be commercially developed and exploited, to be a source of profit. The European concept of land ownership gives the owner exclusive rights to use the land without any obligation to look after it in the longer term. In contrast, Aborigines do not own the land. If anything, the land owns them, and they belong to the land. Land is not a source of material wealth as in European communities, but a source of comfort. Aborigines consider it important to die in one's own country, so that the spirits might be at home. "It is their identity with the land, achieved through knowledge and understanding, that distinguishes Aborigines from the Europeans, who treat the land as a passive resource rather than an active ally".[77]

[1.40] This integration of the spiritual, cultural and economic aspects of Aboriginal life, particularly the relationship with the land, left Aboriginal societies very vulnerable when their connection with the land was broken. From the establishment of white "settlement" in 1788, Aborigines were defined as British subjects and were entitled to the protection of British law. They did not, however, have any recognised title to land, and their culture was fundamentally misunderstood to the extent that they were regarded as "primitive, if not subhuman".[78] As the frontiers of settlement expanded, more and more Aboriginal land was taken, and Aborigines were likely to be treated violently if they resisted the takeover of their lands.[79]

As a consequence, during the following two centuries the relationship of most Aboriginal communities with their land was shattered. Many Aborigines tried to ignore the dispossession of their lands, but free-range hunting and gathering were no longer possible because of the new laws of trespass and property ownership.[80] Without their land, Aborigines' whole system of knowledge and economic life has been endangered, and they have been "cut off from the privileges of their birthright".[81] The dispossession of their land and culture has caused Aboriginal communities distress at being unable to perform their true responsibilities to the land and to their past and future generations.

76. See e.g., Christie, op. cit., pp. 14-15 and Toyne and Vachon op. cit., pp. 7-8.
77. Butcher and Turnbull, op. cit., p. 19.
78. Australian Law Reform Commission, *The Recognition of Aboriginal Customary Laws*, Report No. 31 (A.G.P.S., Canberra, 1986), para. 23.
79. See generally Reynolds, *The Other Side of the Frontier: Aboriginal Resistance to the European Invasion of Australia* (Penguin, 1982); Reynolds, *Frontier* (Allen and Unwin, 1987); and Rowley, *The Destruction of Aboriginal Society* (Penguin, 1972).
80. See Koori Miller, *A Will to Win. The Heroic Resistance and Triumph of Black Australia* (Angus & Robertson, 1985), pp. 51-54.
81. Eyre, *Journals of Expeditions into Central Australia* (London, 1840), Vol. 2, reproduced in Stone (ed.), *Aborigines in White Australia: A Documentary History of the Attitudes Affecting Official Policy and the Australian Aborigine 1697-1973* (Heinemann, 1974), p. 66.

[1.41] Concern about the reduction in size of the Aboriginal population and of their mistreatment led to the appointment in the 1830s of Protectors in New South Wales, South Australia and Western Australia to protect Aborigines from abuse and to provide remaining populations around the towns with some rations, blankets and medicine. This policy proved unsuccessful, and was replaced after the 1860s with more formal and extensive policies of "Protection". This involved isolating and segregating "full blood" Aborigines on reserves and restricting contact and interbreeding between them and outsiders. The purpose of the reserves, therefore, was not to restore the relationship between Aborigines and the land. Rather it was a means of isolating the Aboriginal population. The missions that were sometimes entrusted with the running of the reserves were sometimes unsympathetic to Aborigines continuing their traditional way of life. The policy also aimed to assimilate "half castes", especially their children who were often removed to "boarding houses" to be educated in European ways.[82]

From the 1950s the Commonwealth and all the State Governments adopted the policy of "assimilation", which involved the expectation that all Aborigines would be expected to attain the same manner of living as of other Australians and to live as members of a single Australian community, with the same rights and privileges and accepting the same customs and influenced by the same beliefs as other Australians.[83] This policy involved expenditure on health, housing, education and training programs, and an attempt to remove restrictive and discriminatory legislation, and the mechanisms of protection. Aborigines became entitled to vote at federal elections in 1962, and in the 1967 referendum the Commonwealth Parliament was given power to pass laws specifically for the benefit of the Aboriginal people.

During the late 1960s, there was an increased questioning of the general policy of assimilation. The policy took no account of the value or resilience of Aboriginal culture, and did not allow Aborigines to observe their own languages and traditions. There was a gradual movement away from "assimilation" towards a general recognition of the value of Aboriginal culture and the right of Aborigines to retain their languages and customs and to maintain their own distinctive communities. Early initiatives focused on increased funding and improved programs in health, education and employment, but there were also measures taken to increase funding for Aboriginal community projects. In 1972 a separate federal Department of Aboriginal Affairs was established.

Hand in hand with these developments was a gradual movement towards the assertion of rights, including land rights, for the Aboriginal people. Whilst the campaign for recognition of Aboriginal rights has never ceased since the time of European invasion and settlement, it received a renewed impetus in the late 1960s, and inevitably the focus was on land rights, on the basis of traditional association with the land, long occupancy, and economic need. In 1966 Gurindji stockmen went on strike in protest against conditions of employment with the Vestey beef cattle

---

82. Australian Law Reform Commission, op. cit., para. 25.
83. Ibid., para. 26, fn 26.

interests in the Northern Territory, and then the entire community walked off Wave Hill Station and moved to establish camp on a portion of their traditional land at Wattle Creek in what was clearly a claim for land rights.[84]

[1.42] Thereafter clans at Yirrkala on the Gove peninsula in the Northern Territory brought an action in the Northern Territory Supreme Court to assert their continuing ownership of their traditional lands and challenged the validity of mining leases granted over their land by the Commonwealth government. In *Milirrpum v. Nabalco Pty Ltd*[85] Blackburn J. held, inter alia, that (a) that the doctrine of communal native title (which would recognise at common law the rights under Aboriginal law or custom of Aboriginal communities to land) did not form, and had never formed, part of the law of any part of Australia, and that such a doctrine had no place in a settled colony (which New South Wales was held to be[86]) except under express statutory provisions; (b) that the Aboriginal clans in the Gove Peninsula had established a recognisable system of law; (c) that this system of law did not provide for any proprietary interest in the clans in any part of the land claimed; (d) in any event, in the circumstances of the case, the plaintiffs had not established that, on the balance of probabilities, their predecessors had, at the time of the acquisition of their territory by the Crown as part of the colony of New South Wales, the same links to the same areas of land as those claimed by the plaintiffs.

This decision has been strongly criticised by many writers, for its findings that New South Wales was a settled colony, that the doctrine of communal native title was never part of the Australian common law, and that the clans' law did not recognise proprietary interests.[87] One of the responses of the Aboriginal population to the decision, and to the McMahon government's refusal to contemplate any substantial recognition of land rights in the Northern Territory, was to establish an "Aboriginal Embassy" tent encampment on the lawns in front of Parliament House in Canberra. Its presence there over several months highlighted the land rights claim.[88] The Australian Labor Party at a federal level eventually decided to include an election pledge to move towards the recognition of Aboriginal land rights in the Northern Territory.

84. See "The Original Wave Hill Mob Letter" reproduced in (1986) 20 *Aboriginal Law Bulletin* 11, and Miller, op. cit., p. 194.
85. (1971) 17 F.L.R. 141; [1972-73] A.L.R. 65.
86. Following *Cooper v. Stuart* (1889) 14 A.C. 286 a Privy Council decision which had absolutely nothing to do with Aboriginal title.
87. See Reynolds, *The Law of the Land* (Penguin, Ringwood, 1987); Blumm and Malbon, "Aboriginal Title, the Common Law and Federalism: A Different Perspective" in Ellinghaus, Bradbrook, and Duggan, op. cit.; Hookey, "The Gove Land Rights Case: A Judicial Dispensation for the Taking of Aboriginal Lands in Australia?" (1972) 5 F.L.R. 85; Hocking, "Does Aboriginal Law Now Run in Australia" (1979) 10 F.L.R. 16; Bartlett, "Aboriginal Land Claims at Common Law" (1983) U.W.A.L.R. 16.
88. Nettheim, "Pcoples' and Populations—Indigenous Peoples and the Rights of Peoples" in Crawford (ed.), *The Rights of Peoples* (Clarendon Press, Oxford, 1988), p. 109.

[1.43]   Land Trusts were set up by legislation in South Australia,[89] New South Wales,[90] Victoria[91] and Western Australia[92] to administer the remaining Aboriginal Reserves in those States in the late 1960s and early 1970s. While these developments did not result in land rights regimes totally acceptable to Aborigines, they did in some cases "symbolise the principle of ownership of Aboriginal Reserves by those Aborigines who live on the reserves".[93] These trust arrangements proved to be unsatisfactory, largely because the policy, powers and practices of the trusts were seen to be subject to excessive ministerial control and because the trusts were too bureaucratic and removed.[94] Nevertheless in 1982 the Queensland government abolished the existing reserves, and transferred former reserve lands by "Deeds of Grant in Trust" to trustees appointed from the local community.[95] These arrangements continue today. Local councils have limited powers of mangement and control, and no powers over mining. There is no process for claims for additional lands. Legislation in 1985 enabled individual families in reserve communities to take out perpetual leases over their house blocks in town areas and any other area less than one hectare.[96] Individuals could also take out long-term leases over large areas for commercial purposes, subject to the approval of the elected community council. The grant of such a lease results, however, in loss of community title and control over the area leased.[97]

[1.44]   The first genuine land rights legislation was initiated by the national government. In 1973 the newly elected Whitlam Labor government commissioned Mr A. E. Woodward Q.C. (formerly Senior Counsel for the plaintiffs in the *Milirrpum* case) as Aboriginal Land Rights Commissioner to inquire into and report on the "appropriate means to recognise and establish the traditional rights and interests of Aborigines to and in relation to lands". In particular the Commissioner was to report on arrangments for vesting title to, and granting rights in, land in the Northern Territory already reserved for the use and benefit of Northern Territory Aborigines, and to inquire into the desirability of establishing appropriate procedures for the examination of claims to Aboriginal traditional rights and interests in land in the Northern Territory outside Aboriginal reserves.

89. *Aboriginal Land Trusts Act* 1966 (S.A.).
90. *Aborigines (Amendment) Act* 1973 (N.S.W.).
91. *Aboriginal Lands Act* 1970 (Vic.).
92. *Aboriginal Affairs Planning Authority Act* 1972 (W.A.).
93. Pepper, *You Are What You Make Yourself To Be: The Story of a Victorian Aboriginal Family 1842-1980* (Hyland House, Melbourne, 1980).
94. For a discussion and criticism of these Land Trust arrangements see Keon-Cohen and Morse "Indigenous Land Rights in Australia and Canada" in Hanks and Keon-Cohen (eds), *Aborigines and the Law* (Allen & Unwin, 1984), pp. 74, 83-85.
95. *Land Act (Aboriginal and Islander Land Grants) Amendment Act* 1982-84 (Qld). The Governor-in-Council can remove any trustee from office if of the opinion that it is in the public interest to do so. See also *Community Services (Aborigines) Act* 1984 (Qld) and *Community Services (Torres Strait) Act* 1984 (Qld).
96. *Aborigines and Torres Strait Islanders (Land Holding) Act* 1985 (Qld).
97. See Brennan, "Aboriginal Aspirations to Land: Unfinished History and an Ongoing National Responsibility" in Hocking (ed.), *International Law and Aboriginal Human Rights* (Law Book Co. Ltd, 1988), Chap. 8.

The Commissioner's two reports[98] contemplated that Aboriginal reserves and certain other defined areas were to be vested in an appropriate Aboriginal body in fee simple. Claims to "vacant Crown land", if not accepted by the government, were to be referred to an independent Aboriginal Land Commission for investigation and recommendation to the government. Title granted to Aborigines in land should be communal and inalienable (except for the transfer of land from one Aboriginal body to another) and vested in a trust, with the trustees being nominated by Land Councils. The Councils were also to provide administrative services and to give directions in certain matters. The formal title to Aboriginal land was to be held in an Aboriginal corporation known as a Land Trust which was to hold the land for the benefit of all those having traditional interests or rights over the land. The Land Councils were, inter alia, to represent Aborigines in negotiations with the government in relation to land rights, to protect the interests of traditional owners in all negotiations concerning the use of land, and to co-ordinate and make traditional claims to vacant Crown lands.

The government was to support an Aboriginal Land Fund to finance the acquisitions of pastoral leases or land within towns, where claims could be made on traditional grounds or for social or economic reasons. It was recommended that minerals and petroleum should remain the property of the Crown, but that Aborigines should have the right to prevent exploration on traditional lands. The power of veto was to be overridden only if the government formed the opinion that it was in the national interest to do so. Land Councils were to have the power to negotiate with prospective miners on behalf of the traditional owners.

[1.45] The Whitlam government introduced a bill containing most of these recommendations in October 1975, but it lapsed with the dissolution of Parliament the following month. The Coalition government passed a revised *Aboriginal Land Rights (Northern Territory) Act* (Cth) in 1976. The Act provided for the setting up by the Commonwealth government of at least two Land Councils, which were to have the functions enumerated in the Commissioner's Reports. The making of "traditional land claims" was to be based on the spiritual attachment of Aboriginal clans to an area of land over which they were entitled to forage by Aboriginal law. Only unalienated Crown land could be the subject of a land claim. In accordance with the Woodward Reports, which envisaged the traditional owners, not the Land Councils, would have power over the land, the Land Councils were only able to act with the consent of the local Aboriginal communities. In 1980, however, the Act was amended[99] to provide that if the Land Council agreed to mining, that agreement was valid even if the consent of the local Aboriginal communities had not been obtained.

Under the Act land claims are heard by an Aboriginal Land Commissioner, who is a judge of the Supreme Court of the Northern Territory. The Commissioner determines whether the Aboriginal

98. Aboriginal Land Rights Commission, *First Report* Parliamentary Paper No. 138 (1973); *Second Report* Parliamentary Paper No. 69 (1974).
99. *Aboriginal Land Rights (Northern Territory) Amendment Act* 1980 (Cth).

claimants have traditional links with the land being claimed. This inquiry involves visiting the land in question, witnessing ceremonies, obtaining evidence from the Aboriginal people as to their traditions, and receiving "expert" evidence from anthropologists. If the Commissioner decides in favour of the claimants, a recommendation is made to the Minister for the granting of an area of land to the traditional owners. Upon receiving this advice the Minister is required to transfer the land to a Land Trust.[100] Members of the Land Trust act at the direction of the local Land Council.[101] At the middle of 1989, a total of 258,000 square kilometres of former reserves and land held by missions had been granted to Aboriginal Land Trusts from the time of the commencement of the Act. In addition, following successful claims by traditional Aboriginal owners, 21 deeds of grant had been handed over to Aboriginal Land Trusts. These deeds covered areas totalling 193,075 square kilometres.[102]

[1.46] During the 1980s, a number of State governments enacted or initiated land rights legislation. These innovations can only be studied on a State by State basis in a roughly chronological order.

[1.47] South Australia passed the *Pitjantjatjara Land Rights Act* 1981 and the *Maralinga Tjarutja Land Rights Act* 1984. The *Pitjantjatjara Land Rights Act* transferred just under 100,000 square kilometres of land to the Pitjantjatjara people (about 10 per cent of the State's land area) and the *Maralinga Tjarutja Land Rights Act* involved a 50,000 square kilometre tract of land.[103] The statutes set up statutory Aboriginal corporations to be the holders of special title to traditional lands. All members of the relevant Aboriginal community are members of the corporate body. The body's principal functions are to administer the land vested in it; to ascertain the wishes and opinions of all traditional owners in relation to the management, use and control of the land; and to seek, where practicable, to give effect to those wishes or opinions. The body corporate has wide powers to permit or deny access to lands, and there can be no mining operations without the consent of the body corporate, although unreasonable refusal of consent may lead to arbitration. South Australia has not set up any open-ended claims procedure for vacant Crown lands, as in the Northern Territory, and has preferred to deal with each major land grant on a one off legislative basis.

[1.48] The New South Wales *Aboriginal Land Rights Act* 1983 makes provision for the transfer of former reserves or Trust lands to the ownership of local Aboriginal Land Councils and for claims by Land Councils of "claimable" Crown Land. The legislation allocates 7.5 per

100. For accounts of the land claims processes under the Act, see Bell, "In the Case of the Lawyers and the Anthropologists" (1986) 11 *Legal Service Bulletin* 202; and Neate, *Aboriginal Land Rights Law in the Northern Territory, Volume 1* (A.P.C.O.L., 1989).
101. For a criticism of the legal structures imposed by the Act for the setting up of Land Councils, see McGill, "Northern Territory Land Councils: European Systems Don't Meet Aboriginal Needs" (1980) 5 *Leg. Ser. Bull.* at 269.
102. Department of Aboriginal Affairs, *Annual Report 1988-89* (A.G.P.S.), p. 37.
103. The Maralinga peoples had been moved from these lands in the 1950s and 1960s for the convenience of British testing of nuclear weapons.

cent of Land Tax revenues for 15 years to a three tier system of Aboriginal Land Councils (State, Regional and Local) and enables the purchase of land on the open market.[104] "Claimable" Crown land excludes lands lawfully used or occupied and those lands which, in the opinion of the Minister, are needed or are likely to be needed for either an "essential public purpose" or for "residential land". As neither of these terms are defined in the Act, the Minister has a wide discretionary power to block claims.[105] An Aboriginal Land Council has a right of appeal to the New South Wales Land and Environment Court if dissatisfied with the Minister's exercise of discretion. By February 1990 8,552 claims had been made under the legislation, of which 582 had been granted (involving 34,240 hectares of freehold grants and 1,562 hectares of Western Lands leases) and 1,000 claims were still under investigation.[106] The Greiner government came to power in New South Wales in 1988 with a pledge to abolish land rights. Initial moves were blocked by the New South Wales Upper House and the Supreme Court.[107]

[1.49] Victoria does not have an open-ended land claims procedure and therefore follows South Australia in contrast to the Northern Territory and New South Wales. Land rights, in the form of freehold land, have been granted at Lake Condah (half a square kilometre) and Framlingham (11 square kilometres)[108] to Aboriginal corporations who have full power of management, control and enjoyment over the land. Eligibility for membership of the Aboriginal corporations is determined by the relevant Committee of Aboriginal elders. The elders are given extensive powers over the management of the corporation and the land. The provisions in the Act relating to mining are based on the *Pitjantjatjara Land Rights Act* 1981 (S.A.). The Victorian Act provides special protection for sacred or significant sites. It also establishes a procedure for balancing the interest of the miners and the Aboriginal owners. Mining rights created after the date of the Act may not be exercised without the permission of the relevant Aboriginal corporation. If permission is refused, or is granted on conditions to which the applicant objects, the applicant can ask the Minister to resolve the matter by conciliation, and, if need be, arbitration.

[1.50] In Western Australia, a proposed Aboriginal Land Bill 1985 (W.A.) which would have transferred the control and ownership of reserves to local councils and set up a claims procedure for vacant Crown Lands, was rejected by the Upper House. Consequently, the reserves remain under the control of the Aboriginal Affairs Planning Authority. In

---

104. Land rights were also vested in the Wreck Bay Aboriginal Community Council by the *Aboriginal Land Grant (Jervis Bay Territory) Act* which granted 403 hectares of land in the Jervis Bay Territory, geographically located on the south coast of New South Wales.

105. See Chalk, "New South Wales Land Rights . . . All Just an Act?" (1988) 32 *Aboriginal Law Bulletin* 4.

106. Figures supplied by the New South Wales Department of Lands.

107. Nettheim, "Developing Aboriginal Rights" (1989) 19 V.U.W.L.R. 403 at 409.

108. *Aboriginal Land (Lake Condah and Framlingham Forest) Act* 1987 (Cth) enacted by the Commonwealth Parliament at the request of the Victorian Government after the Victorian Legislative Council refused to pass the legislation.

1986-87 a joint Commonwealth-State program was established to provide Aboriginal communities with secure tenure for reserve land, excisions from other areas of land, and improved living conditions for communities through the adequate servicing of the land.[109]

[1.51] This account of State land rights legislation indicates the problems arising from leaving the issue of the grant of land rights in the hands of State governments. There has been no consistent land rights model adopted, and Aboriginal rights to land vary considerably from State to State. There has been only one attempt by the Federal government to use its constitutional power (inserted by the 1967 referendum to make "special laws")[110] to vest land rights in the Aboriginal people.

In 1985 the Federal government published a "Preferred National Aboriginal Land Rights Model"[111] which included a commitment to the principles that Aboriginal land would be held under inalienable freehold title, and sacred sites protected. A previous commitment to Aboriginal control of mining on Aboriginal land was watered down to a proposal that the relevant government (Commonwealth, State or Territory) have the power to determine mining applications in cases where miners and Aboriginal communities could not agree on the terms and conditions under which mining was to occur. The government would receive recommendations from a tribunal before making these decisions. It would also be up to the government to determine the proportion of royalties payable to Aborigines. An earlier commitment to the negotiation of compensation for lost land was abandoned. The "Preferred Model" was heavily constrained by the Federal government's concern to reduce the prospects of Federal-State conflict over land rights legislation, and was particularly accommodating to the views of the Western Australian State government. Early in 1986 the Federal government, in the face of a lack of community support, allowed the proposal to die.

[1.52] The granting of Aboriginal land rights is a crucial aspect of the recognition of Aboriginal rights and culture. In many senses, it is the most important single issue in the dispensation of justice for Australian Aborigines. The passage of the Northern Territory Act and the success of subsequent land claims, has, for example, been described as "the catalyst . . . for an unprecedented cultural revival" in that "some people have been able to go back and resume their legal responsibility for caring for the country".[112]

---

109. Department of Aboriginal Affairs, *Annual Report 1988-89* 34.

110. Section 51 (xxvi) now empowers the federal government to make laws with respect to "the people of any race for whom it is deemed necessary to make special laws".

111. See generally Brennan, "Aboriginal Aspirations to Land: Unfinished History and an Ongoing National Responsibility" in Hocking (ed.), op. cit., pp. 168-171.

112. Dodson, "Aborigines and the Criminal Justice System" (1987) 28 Aborig. Law Bull. 4.

4. Property Rights in Family Relationships

(a) Introduction

[1.53]   The *Family Law Act* 1975 (Cth) provides a separate regime for the distribution of property upon the breakdown of a marriage. In New South Wales and Victoria, there is legislation providing a separate regime for the distribution of property upon the breakdown of a de facto relationship. That is, in both these cases legislative intervention has ensured that property disputes between particular persons are not to be resolved according to the general legal and equitable principles of property law. The basic reason for the intervention is that the ordinary laws of property are ineffective to produce a just result in such situations. In the case of legal marriage and perhaps to a lesser extent in the de facto relationship, the relationship involves "a sharing of economic existence"[113] and an intention that it should last, if not for life, then at least for an indefinite time in the future. If the parties choose to arrange their affairs in such a way that one partner engages in financially productive work and the other does not, the latter should not be penalised by her or his lack of direct financial contribution to property. In most instances the ordinary principles of property law would so penalise such a partner: see below **[6.33]**.

(b) Married persons

[1.54]   The married women's property legislation introduced in England and in all Australian States[114] in the late 19th centry overturned the insidious system pursuant to which the rights of a woman to the use, management and control of her property were lost upon marriage.[115] At common law, upon marriage a husband and wife became one person. The 19th century legislation introduced a regime which ensured a system of separation of property. A husband and a wife could each hold their own property and were able to institute court proceedings to have any property dispute between them settled.

It was intended that the legislation provide an equality in law between men and women but the social context within which the relevant issues arose meant that the concept of separation of property very often did not result in an equal division of property upon separation of the parties to a marriage. Usually the wife involved herself in homemaking activities which did not result in the acquisition of funds with which to purchase her

---

113. Dickey, "The Moral Justification for Alteration of Property Interests under the *Family Law Act*" (1988) 11 U.N.S.W.L.J. 158 at 165.
114. The married women's property legislation now in force is as follows: *Married Persons (Property and Torts) Act* 1901 (N.S.W.); *Marriage Act* 1958 (Vic.); *Married Women's Property Act* 1890 (Qld); *Law of Property Act* 1936 (S.A.) ss 92-111; *Married Women's Property Act* 1892 (W.A.); *Married Women's Property Act* 1935 (Tas.). Although this legislation is in force, it is rarely used because of the provisions of the *Family Law Act* 1975 (Cth) discussed below.
115. For a detailed account of the position before the introduction of the married women's property legislation see Hardingham and Neave, *Australian Family Property Law* (Law Book Co. Ltd, 1984), Chap. 1.

own separate property. On the other hand, the financially productive partner, usually the husband, was in a position to build up assets as his own separate property. Also that partner usually had greater access to the supply of credit and indeed be favoured by the policies of credit providers. Although in recent years changing social patterns may have altered the traditional roles of husband and wife, it is still more likely that the wife will use a greater proportion of her time in financially non-productive homemaking and parenting than will the husband.

For a long period of time, it was assumed that the relevant provisions in the married women's property legislation only gave the court the power to declare existing property interests. During the 1950s and 1960s, however, the English Court of Appeal interpreted s. 17 of the *Married Women's Property Act* 1882 (Eng.) in a manner which effectively gave the courts the power to redistribute the existing property rights of husband and wife to achieve a fair result.[116] This approach was called "palm tree justice". The approach recognised the inherent practical inequality in the ability to acquire assets which existed between husband and wife and attempted to redress the balance by taking into account for example, the contributions of the wife as a homemaker and parent. The approach of the Court of Appeal was brought to an end by the House of Lords[117] and apart from one possible exception,[118] it was never accepted in Australia.[119]

[1.55] Although few would have advocated a return to the system where the husband and the wife were one person at law, most accepted the notion that marriage was a partnership which extended into the financial, economic arena. A husband and a wife who chose to arrange their affairs in such a way that the husband was the financially more productive partner did not thereby adhere to a law which would result in the husband being solely entitled to all assets acquired with his earnings. The concept of separation of property as enshrined in the married women's property legislation ensured, however, that this was the case. The need for change to the legislation was obvious. Apart from in Victoria,[120] however, the married women's property legislation remained as it was.

The need for change to State legislation diminished drastically because in 1959 the Commonwealth used its constitutional powers to legislate in the area of family law and produced a different system for property determination. The *Matrimonial Causes Act* 1959 (Cth) provided a number

---

116. See e.g. *Rimmer v. Rimmer* [1953] 1 Q.B. 63; *Cobb v. Cobb* [1955] 2 All E.R. 696; *Hine v. Hine* [1962] 3 All E.R. 345. See also *Bendall v. McWhirter* [1952] 2 Q.B. 466.
117. *Pettitt v. Pettitt* [1970] A.C. 777; *Gissing v. Gissing* [1972] A.C. 886.
118. *Wood v. Wood* [1956] V.L.R. 478.
119. *Wirth v. Wirth* (1956) 58 C.L.R. 228.
120. In Victoria, an attempt was made to give the court the power to redistribute property between husband and wife and to achieve a fair result and to provide for a presumed joint tenancy of the matrimonial home: see *Marriage Act* 1958 (Vic.), s. 161(3) and (4) inserted in 1962. The drafting of the legislation however ensured that the aims of the legislation were not fulfilled: see *Hogben v. Hogben* [1964] V R 468; *Haskin v. Haskin* [1964] V.R. 37. See generally Sackville, "The Emerging Australian Law of Matrimonial Property" (1970) 7 M.U.L.R. 353 at 366ff.

of grounds for divorce and gave the courts wide discretionary powers to redistribute the property of the parties to a marriage when the proceedings for property relief were ancillary to proceedings for principal relief. In order to reach a just and equitable result, a number of factors such as the means and needs of the parties were taken into account.

In 1975, the Commonwealth replaced the *Matrimonial Causes Act* 1959 (Cth) with the *Family Law Act* 1975 (Cth). In contrast to the *Matrimonial Causes Act* which provided a number of grounds for divorce, the *Family Law Act* 1975 provides only one ground for dissolution of marriage. The ground for dissolution is irreconcilable differences as evidenced by 12 months' separation. As in the earlier legislation, the court is given power to order an alteration of the property interests of husband and wife to achieve a just and equitable result. Section 79(1) of the *Family Law Act* 1975 provides:

> "In proceedings with respect to the property of the parties to a marriage or either of them, the court may make such order as it considers appropriate altering the interests of the parties in the property, including an order for a settlement of property in substitution for any interest in the property and including an order requiring either or both of the parties to make, for the benefit of either or both of the parties or a child of the marriage, such settlement or transfer of property as the court determines."

Pursuant to s. 79(4), the court must take into account a number of factors in considering what order to make. Pursuant to s. 79(4)(a) and (b), the court must take into account the financial and non-financial contributions made directly or indirectly to the acquisition, conservation or improvement of the property of the parties or either of them. Further, by s. 79(4)(c) the court is directed to take into account the contribution made by a party to the marriage to the welfare of the family including any contribution in the capacity as homemaker or parent. All of the factors referred to above comprise the retrospective or "contribution" element of a property order. The court is further directed to take into account a number of prospective or "maintenance" elements. The effect of a proposed order on the earning capacity of either party to the marriage, the age and state of health of the parties, the general means and needs of the parties, the duration of the marriage and the extent to which it has affected the respective earning capacities, and any child support under the *Child Support (Assessment) Act* 1989 (Cth) that a party provides for a child of the marriage are some of the factors to which the court must direct is attention. A party's future entitlement to superannuation is one specific factor which may be very important. After the matrimonial home, such an entitlement may be the greatest asset built up during the marriage and the fact that one party alone may benefit from it in the future must be taken into account in any property order. Various methods of taking such an entitlement into account have been used but it seems that in general, insufficient weight has been given to this matter.[121]

---

121. Australian Law Reform Commission, *Matrimonial Property*, Report No. 39 (1987).

[1.56] The task of balancing the respective contributions of the parties and of evaluating non-financial contributions has proved to be an immensely difficult one for the Family Court. As a means of attempting to provide some certainty, the Family Court developed a rule of thumb that at least in marriages of long standing duration and at least with respect to property with a matrimonial flavour, the contributions (whatever they comprised) of the parties should be viewed as being equal.[122] (The prospective element may of course have resulted in an order which did not effect an equal division.) In *Mallett v. Mallett*,[123] however, the High Court disapproved the guideline of the Family Court, taking the view that the legislation required the court to consider the factors listed in s. 79(4) in each case. It seems however that an assessment of contributions on an asset by asset approach is not required in every case: where more appropriate, the use of a "global" approach is permissible.[124]

[1.57] The matrimonial property regime in Australia, a judicial discretion regime permitting alteration of existing property interests, is based upon the notion that marriage comprises, inter alia, economic partnership and that due regard should be paid to varying contributions to that partnership. Where one party's contribution has been wholly non-financial that party is clearly in a better position under such a system than he or she would be under a pure separation of property system. The system of judicial discretion provides greater flexibility but has been criticised as also providing a system of great uncertainty. The Australian Law Reform Commission in its report on matrimonial property considered alternative schemes for the division of property between husband and wife on the breakdown of a marriage.[125] Although the Commission took the view that there was merit in schemes of community and deferred community of property under which parties are entitled to fixed shares computed by reference to a set formula, it opted for a retention of the judicial discretion system. Often the parties are not in a position of financial equality when the marriage breaks down. Curtailed employment opportunities and the care of children, for example, may mean that the future financial positions of the parties are quite disparate and incapable of being balanced by a fixed half share.

Despite favouring a judicial discretion regime the Commission recommended, however, that the exercise of this judicial discretion be circumscribed by much clearer and more precise guidelines. Most importantly, and in order to overcome the major problem of evaluation and comparison of differing contributions, the Commission suggested that there should be a rule of equal sharing of the value of the property of the marriage. These equal shares could then be varied to take account of specific special circumstances such as a possible future financial disparity

---

122. See e.g. *Wardman and Hudson* (1978) F.L.C. 90-466; *Rolfe and Rolfe* (1979) F.L.C. 90-629.
123. (1984) 52 A.L.R. 193.
124. *Norbis v. Norbis* (1986) 161 C.L.R. 513.
125. A.L.R.C., Report No. 39. This report is considered in Charlesworth, "Domestic Contributions to Matrimonial Property" (1989) A.J.F.L. 147.

if the disparity were wholly or partly attributable to a party's responsibility for the future care of children or to the income earning capacity of a party having been affected by the marriage. The recommendations of the Commission have not as yet been adopted and in view of the criticisms of its report it is perhaps unlikely that they will be. There have been adverse reactions to the concept of reducing judicial discretion[126] and to the primary recommendation that there should be an equal sharing of the value of the property of the marriage. Although it is not demonstrably the case, the party who has made the greater share of financial contributions sees her or himself as being placed in a worse position under the recommended regime.

(c) De facto relationships

[1.58] In addition to property disputes between parties to a legal marriage, property disputes may arise between parties involved in other types of family relationships. Property disputes may arise between parties in a de facto marriage, parties in a homosexual relationship and parties in other family relationships such as between parent and child. Apart from property disputes between partners to a de facto relationship arising in New South Wales or Victoria, these disputes are dealt with by an application of the ordinary legal and equitable principles of property law. Recent developments in the area of the constructive trust have increased the range of circumstances in which the person without legal title may claim an equitable interest. It remains the case, however, that the availability of a remedy is entirely dependent on the general rules of common law and equity. These principles are discussed in Chapter 6.

For a long time, the law disapproved the concept of heterosexual cohabitation outside marriage and refused to be involved in any process which could be viewed as encouraging such cohabitation. Thus, a contract between parties to a de facto relationship seeking to provide for their respective property rights was deemed contrary to public policy and thus unenforceable.[127] The large numbers of couples who chose, nevertheless, to live in a de facto relationship led to a change in community attitudes. This in turn led to changes in the common law's conception of matters considered to be contrary to public policy.[128] It seems clear that contracts for which the sole consideration is not the provision of meretricious sexual services and which provide for property division between the parties to a de facto relationship would now be enforceable.[129]

The acceptance of the de facto relationship in turn led to a consideration of whether the de facto relationship should be accorded further legal recognition.[130] Of particular interest in this context was the issue of

---

126. See e.g. the comment by Fowler, Chairman of the Family Law section of the Law Council of Australia: *The Age*, 24 September 1987.
127. See *Fender v. Mildmay* [1938] A.C. 1; *Zapletal v. Wright* [1957] Tas. S.R. 211.
128. See e.g. *Andrews v. Parker* [1973] Qd R. 93; *Seidler v. Schallhofer* [1982] 2 N.S.W.L.R. 80.
129. *Seidler v. Schallhofer* [1982] 2 N.S.W.L.R. 80.
130. New South Wales Law Reform Commission, *Summary of Issues Paper: De Facto Relationships* (1981).

whether a regime for the settlement of property disputes should be set up. Valid arguments favouring and rejecting the imposition of a statutory regime have been made.[131] Arguments in favour of statutory intervention held sway in both New South Wales and Victoria. Perhaps the most important factor in favour of intervention is that the lack of regulation provides the opportunity for one partner to exploit the other. In New South Wales, the *De Facto Relationships Act* 1984 contains property and maintenance powers and permits the parties to enter cohabitation and separation contracts relating to financial matters between them. By contrast in Victoria the *Property Law Amendment Act* 1987[132] provides only for a regime of division of property interests.[133] The provisions in the New South Wales legislation and the Victorian legislation governing property disputes between de facto couples are very similar. One important difference is that in Victoria the court may only make an order in respect of real property.

[1.59] In New South Wales and Victoria a de facto partner[134] who fulfils particular criteria may apply to the court for an adjustment of property interests.[135] The de facto relationship must not have ended before the introduction of the legislation[136] and the action must be commenced within two years of the termination of the relationship. A de facto partner may only seek an alteration of property interests in three circumstances. The first circumstance is where the relationship has been of a duration of two years or more. The second circumstance is where there is a child of the relationship. The third circumstance is where a serious injustice would result to a partner making the application and that partner has made substantial contributions which would not otherwise be adequately compensated or has the care and control of a child of the other de facto partner.[137]

In making a decision as to whether to alter the existing proprietary interests of the parties, the court must have regard to direct and indirect financial and non-financial contributions to the property of either of them and the contributions to the welfare of the family.[138] Thus, the types of

---

131. Ibid.
132. See *Property Law Act* 1958 (Vic.), ss 275-302.
133. The De Facto Relationships Bill (Vic.) included provisions relating to maintenance but did not pass through the Upper House.
134. *De Facto Relationships Act* 1984 (N.S.W.), s. 3(1) provides that de facto relationship "means the relationship between de facto partners, being the relationship of living or having lived together as husband and wife on a bona fide domestic basis although not married to each other". *Property Law Act* 1958 (Vic.), s. 275 states that de facto relationship "means the relationship between de facto partners of living or having lived together as if they were husband and wife although not married to each other".
135. *De Facto Relationships Act* 1984 (N.S.W.), s. 20; *Property Law Act* 1958 (Vic.), s. 279(1).
136. In New South Wales the Act commenced on 1 July 1985 and in Victoria the Act commenced on 1 June 1988.
137. *De Facto Relationships Act* 1984 (N.S.W.), s. 17; *Property Law Act* 1958 (Vic.), s. 281
138. *De Facto Relationships Act* 1984 (N.S.W.), s. 20; *Property Law Act* 1958 (Vic.), s. 285.

contribution which the court must take into account are the same as those which are taken into account under the *Family Law Act* 1975 (Cth).[139] The vital difference from the *Family Law Act* 1975 is that neither New South Wales nor the Victorian legislation makes any provision for a "prospective" or maintenance element in its property order. It has been argued that the omission of this element may lead to injustice particularly for the financially unproductive homemaker. "The financial consequences of role division can be the same whatever the legal status of the relationship."[140]

It is unclear whether the other States will follow the lead of New South Wales and Victoria and introduce legislation governing property disputes between de facto couples. The recent developments in the area of the constructive trust have lessened the immediate need for such legislation. Nevertheless, the precise ambit of the new style constructive trust, particularly in situations where one partner has adopted solely the homemaking role, has yet to be settled: see below **[6.33]**. The certainty of specific legislation requiring the court to take into account particular factors provides advantages in many situations in New South Wales and Victoria and would do so in the other States.

VI.   LAND RIGHTS AND LAND USE

[1.60]   In his text *Property: Illusions of Ownership*, John Clough builds his analysis around the story of the settlement of Bayocean on the American Pacific coast south of Portland, Oregon. The point of the story is that this settlement was destroyed by the ocean because of sand erosion caused by an inappropriate jetty siting. The story should not be strange to Australian readers and indeed at the time of writing the Henty Estate—a subdivision near the town of Portland Victoria—was being reclaimed by the sea.[141] Again works at one point on the coast had changed the balance of coastal forces and caused a rather rapid coastal erosion. At both Bayocean Oregon and the Henty Estate Victoria individuals had purchased from developers private allotments of land. Natural forces rendered those rights worthless.

Over the past 25 years environmental awareness has become part of Australia's social and political thinking. The great bulk of the Australian population clings to the rim of the island continent. The greatest environmental threat—the greenhouse effect—is likely to lead to a rise in sea levels because of the melting of the polar icecaps and could pose

139.   Some early decisions have suggested that Family Court decisions on interpretation of the "contribution" element may not be a reliable guide to construing s. 20 of the *De Facto Relationships Act* 1984 (N.S.W.): see e.g. *D. v. McA* (1986) 11 Fam. L.R. 214; *Wilcock v. Sain* (1986) 11 Fam. L.R. 302. This should not be the case. The wording of the provisions is very similar: see Finlay and Bailey-Harris, *Family Law in Australia* (4th ed., Butterworths, 1989), pp. 392. There has also been a suggestion that the homemaker contribution may be undervalued: see Finlay and Bailey-Harris, op. cit., pp. 392-393.

140.   Finlay and Bailey-Harris, op. cit.

141.   *The Age*, 16th January 1990.

serious problems for a coastal population. As well, climatic changes must be a concern for a nation so heavily dependent on primary production. More localised pollution problems pose more immediate problems: the great beaches around Sydney threaten to become sewerage wastelands; the sprawling cities are heavily dependent upon private motor cars and consequently prone to smog alerts; increasing salinity in the Murray River poses risks for Adelaide's water supply. Preservation of natural areas ranging from Kakadu and the tropical rain forests in the north to the Tasmanian wilderness have provoked bitter confrontation. Social problems arising from the segregation of many of the nation's poor into the western suburbs of Melbourne and Sydney also reflect on urban planning.

[1.61] The problems and the significance of the legal responses to them cannot be denied. However, they fall outside the subject matter of this text.[142] The text is about property rights which, as explained above, are claims to land as against other people. The use and development of land is then regulated by general laws, almost exclusively statutory. However, the property rights themselves can be so delineated as to provide restraints on land use. The tenure system has the potential to be so used but it has been only in Crown leases that conditions relating to land use have been imposed. Recently developed land management agreements do combine land use conditions into the definition of land rights by setting out those conditions as an encumbrance on the land.

Leasehold covenants, easements and restrictive covenants are recognised property interests which impinge upon land use and can be used as planning devices. They tend to provide more for local adjustments of neighbouring land use as they can be enforced only by landlords or neighbouring land-owners. Leasehold covenants allow the landlord of a shopping centre, for instance, to balance and integrate commercial activities. Easements allow for the supply of utilities and for access without public roads and are particularly useful for more compact housing. Restrictive covenants allow minimum standards to be set for neighbourhoods, though their name has been sullied by their use in the United States for racial segregation.[143]

The value of some property law principles to restrain development should not lead to any conclusion that the direction of the development of legal principle has been in favour of conservation. The requirement of a Crown grant has allowed almost total displacement of the Aboriginal communities. Conditions attached to Crown leases have been overwhelmingly designed to ensure the clearing and development of land. Whilst property settlements were uncommon in Australia, nonetheless holders of interests less than a fee simple were constrained by their limited powers of disposition and limits on use flowing from the law of waste. The settled land legislation sought to overcome these limits. The utility of easements and restrictive covenants for broad community planning was

142. Planning laws are discussed by Fogg, *Australian Town Planning Law* (1974) and Ryan, *Urban Development Law and Policy* (1987).
143. Such covenants were declared unconstitutional in *Shelley v. Kraemer* 334 U.S. 1 (1948).

severly curtailed by the rule that they could only be enforced by neighbouring landowners. Indeed most easements in Australia exist in favour of government utilities as a result of special statutory provisions.

[1.62] Whilst environmental awareness has increased in recent times, pollution problems in particular date from the industrial revolution. Even such advances as the elimination of coal-burning trains have been major environmental improvements. The protection of private rights of enjoyment of land was in the 19th century the province of the law of nuisance. Any unreasonable interference with the enjoyment of land was actionable at the suit of the owner of that land. What was reasonable depended on the nature of the neighbourhood so complaint could not be made about the shoe factories of Collingwood.[144]

[1.63] The more formal segregation of conflicting land uses has been one of the functions of planning laws. In their simplest form these laws aim to prevent glue factories in residential areas. At a more sophisticated level they seek to provide proper intercommunication, a balance of residential forms, and access to service, retail and commercial activities. Segregation has not met with universal acclaim as some critics claim that a mix of uses is preferable to suburban sterility. All Australian States now have elaborate planning systems, involving specialist planning authorities and local government. General planning standards and zoning charts have been established. Any development—normally defined to include any building or change of land use—requires permission from the relevant authority. One feature of Australian planning systems has been the right of appeal to independent judicial bodies. These bodies have produced an enormous outpouring of planning law principle, most often, unfortunately, on a State by State basis.

Segregation of land use is a crude and localised method of combatting environmental degradation. Planning laws can include standards for development to reduce that degradation. Major projects can be subject to detailed anlaysis and investigation to assess environmental impact. The preparation of environmental impact statements began as a technique to catch projects (particularly of government authorities) and dimensions not provided for by the planning process. However, the process of preparation of these statements had gradually been integrated into the planning process and different levels of detail required according to the magnitude of the project.[145]

[1.64] Environmental harm must come from activity on land or sea or in the air. But not all activity on land can be related to the development of the land by landowners. Activities such as the use of motor cars or of aerosols cannot usefully be regulated as part of controls upon land development. Thus pollution laws are necessary. However, land development and use is a significant polluting activity and is subject to a range of pollution laws in addition to planning controls.[146] These laws seek

144. Fleming, op. cit., pp. 387-388.
145. Fowler, "Legislative Bases for Environmental Impact Assessment" (1985) 2 E. & P.L.J. at 200.
146. Bates, *Environmental Law in Australia* (2nd ed., 1987), Chap. 10.

to restrain noxious discharges into seas, rivers and other waters or into the air, to control noise, and to enhance soil conservation. Typically in Australia a government agency has been established with responsibility for a particular problem. That agency is then empowered to set standards, issue permits and enforce compliance.

VII. ARRANGEMENT OF THE TEXT

[1.65] This introduction has already emphasised the fact that this text is about Australian land law and that for most land in Australia the key factor is that title is held under the Torrens system. Furthermore, as a property text, stress is placed upon competition between claimants to interests in land. Many interests arise from contracts and the nature of those interests cannot be adequately ascertained without reference to those contracts. Nonetheless this is not a text about contractual rights and obligations as between vendor and purchaser, landlord and tenant, mortgagee and mortgagor, or the Crown and holders of Crown leases. Detailed analysis of such contracts will be found in specialist texts. Whilst equitable interests in land and management powers and responsibilities for land as between trustees and beneficiaries are fully analysed, many aspects of the law of trusts again form a separate specialist area.

Already mention has been made of the link between proprietary rights and specific remedies (normally equitable in nature). However, as Evatt J. argued persuasively in *Cowell v. Rosehill Racecourse Co. Ltd*,[147] specific remedies are not confined to the protection of proprietary interests. Since that time such remedies have been significantly advanced for the protection of contractual rights both through the common law and the *Trade Practices Act*. However, contracts for the sale of land are ones where the courts are predisposed to grant specific performance on the basis that each parcel of land is unique.[148] Furthermore an owner of land will sometimes be seeking to eject someone unlawfully on the land and landlords seek eviction as a remedy against defaulting tenants. Orders with respect to the register of titles maintained under the Torrens system provide a means of giving effect to determinations about rights in land. This text will be concerned with remedies peculiarly associated with land rather than general principles of remedies whether at law or in equity.[149]

[1.66] The text commences with an examination of what is meant by ownership of land and the nature of the interests conferring ownership. The means of establishing ownership including the conferral of title by registration are then considered. Thereafter analysis of the operation of property principles will be primarily directed towards this system of registered title but allowance is made for the continued existence in

147. (1937) 56 C.L.R. 605.
148. *Pianta v. National Finance & Trustees Ltd* [1965] A.L.R. 737 at 738 and *Coulls v. Bagot's Executor & Trustee Co.* (1967) 119 C.L.R. 406 at 502-3.
149. Chapter 6 of Sackville and Neave tends to concentrate on discretionary aspects of equitable remedies but that work is concerned with property generally and not just property in land.

several States of much land outside the Torrens system. After examination of the nature of interests and means of establishing title attention is directed to the major forms of dealings or dispositions of land. Chapters 2 to 6 therefore can be described as concerned with title and transfers.

Property rights are commonly shared amongst several persons. This sharing can involve rights at different points of time such as rights for one person during that person's lifetime and for others after the person's death. Analysis of future interests and the rule against perpetuities covers this form of sharing. A simpler division is that between a number of concurrent owners. Division by the grant of rights of occupation is achieved by leases and the landlord and tenant relationship normally reflects a lack of any capital investment by the tenant. All divisions of the property in land create issues as to the responsibility for management. Special schemes for unit titles represent more sophisticated divisions and management responsibilities. Chapters 7 to 13 therefore have this common theme of the division of property rights.

Just as property rights in individual allotments may be divided and relationships between the holders of divided interests regulated, so relationships between neighbouring landholders give rise to matters for determination. Parcels of land have to be defined as to their extent both horizontally and vertically and as to the incidents within those physical dimensions. The title to land as defined by dealings and registration may come in conflict with actual control or possession and the law of adverse possession provides for adjustment of title to reflect sustained control (in some cases because of inaccurate boundaries). Total independence of one landowner from her or his neighbour may unduly impede the use of the land. Rights of access from one piece of land to another or shared drainage or communications systems may be achieved by easements and further optimum efficiency. Conversely land use may need protection from adverse impacts and neighbours may restrict that use through covenants. Chapters 14 to 17 are concerned with the definition and adjustment of rights between landowners.

Land is a stable, readily identified and valuable asset. As such it provides a useful security for the borrowing of money. Often the loan enables the purchase of the land itself. The lender can be confident of the availability of an asset to cover a debt in the case of default in performance of the primary personal obligation to repay the loan. The common form of security in land in Australian law is the mortgage and it is analysed in Chapter 18.

As will be seen, after a freehold grant of land by the Crown under tenurial theory, an interest in that land is still retained by the Crown. However, this interest is largely theoretical. In much of rural Australia the Crown has sought to retain a greater and more significant interest and has granted only leasehold rights. The nature of the interests created by these arrangements involves issues as to the applicability of many of the real property law principles. Crown leases are the subject of the concluding Chapter 19.

[1.67] Although this text considers principles relating to land subject to the Torrens system and those relating to land outside that system (general law land), in Queensland and South Australia the amount of land outside the Torrens system is insignificant. Therefore the analysis of principles applicable to general law land will be confined to New South Wales, Victoria, Western Australia and Tasmania. Moreover there are separate bodies of real property law in both the Northern Territory and the Australian Capital Territory and that law can be expected to develop in individual ways since both territories are self-governing. To an extent the real property law of the two territories is derived from and still similar to that of South Australia and New South Wales respectively with which the two territories were once associated. However, the law in these territories will be considered only in Chapter 19 because as will be explained in that Chapter both urban and rural land grants have commonly been of only leasehold tenure and general real property principles can be applied only in a qualified way. This approach has been adopted by the authors with some reluctance but the differences between six jurisdictions constantly threaten to fragment the text and destroy its cohesion. The evident frustration caused by these problems may be thought to colour the authors' plea for uniformity of the law in Australia but the frustration stems more from the lack of meaning behind the differences and the sense of individuality for individuality's sake.

2

Tenure, Estates and Trusts

I. THE DOCTRINE OF TENURE

[2.01]   The doctrine of tenure, and its influence upon modern land law, have been analysed in detail by many writers.[1] Although it is not intended to discuss the doctrine of tenure in detail here, some discussion of this historical area is necessary in order to understand clearly the law of real property and, more specifically, to gain some insight into the reasons why fragmentation of proprietary interests is so much an accepted part of the law. It is important to note that the doctrine of tenure itself is now of little more than historical significance: see below **[2.04]**.

[2.02]   Although much land was held in feudal tenure before the Norman Conquest, it was during the reign of William I that a feudalised regime became highly developed. After the Conquest, the King considered that he owned all of the land in England. He did not, however, seize the ownership of the land of the English landowners and share it out among his followers: rather he retained ownership and granted land to Englishmen who recognised him as King. The King did not transfer absolute ownership but set up complex feudal ties pursuant to which land was granted subject to the grantee performing and fulfilling certain duties and conditions (for example, rendering of services or payment of money). A person holding directly of the King was called the tenant-in-chief. In turn, the tenant-in-chief granted part of the land to another who, in return, promised to fulfil certain conditions. This process could be repeated many times with respect to the same piece of land. The process was called subinfeudination. The tenant-in-demesne was the person in actual possession of the land and the persons in the pyramid between the King and tenant-in-demesne were called mesne lords.[2] Feudal tenures were established throughout the Norman period and extended to all parts of the kingdom. A feudal pyramid emerged with the King at the top owning all of the land: many tenurial relationships could and did exist with respect to one piece of land. Tenure could be free tenure or non-free tenure. The forms of free tenure comprised spiritual tenure (frankalmoign) and lay tenure. Lay tenure took the form of tenure by knight service, tenure by serjeanty or socage tenure. Non-free tenure

---

1. See e.g. Cheshire and Burn, pp. 9-26; Megarry and Wade, pp. 12-37; Butt, Chs 3 and 4; Hargreaves and Helmore, *Introduction to the Principles of Land Law (New South Wales)* (Law Book Co. Ltd, Sydney, 1963), pp. 8-18 and pp. 30-36.
2. Seignories were the lords.

comprised villeinage which was later termed copyhold. Each of these forms of tenure involved various incidents and involved different rights and obligations.[3]

[2.03] The tenure system became increasingly complex and gradually many services became difficult to enforce. The first attempt to simplify the system and to prevent even more complex feudal ties developing was made in 1290. The *Statute of Quia Emptores*, passed in 1290, changed the law in two respects. First, a person was able to alienate the whole or part of land without the consent of the lord. Secondly, further subinfeudination was prohibited. Thus, for example, if A held the land from a lord X, and alienated part or all of the land to B, B stood in A's shoes: no new subtenancy between A and B could be created. A substitution only was permitted.[4] The statute did not apply to land that was not held in a fee simple estate. Further, it did not prevent subinfeudination where the holder of a fee simple estate granted a fee tail or a life estate and the statute did not bind the Crown. Nevertheless, the result of the *Statute of Quia Emptores* was that the number of tenure relationships existing with respect to the one piece of land lessened. The statute, together with the incident of escheat, which provided that the land "escheated" or was forfeited to the immediate lord if the tenant died without an heir, both led to a diminution in the number of persons involved in tenure relationships between the Crown and the tenant-in-demesne.

The simplification of tenures in each piece of land was aided further by the disappearance of many services associated with tenure. Labour services, such as the provision of agricultural labour, arising from socage tenure were gradually converted into fixed money rents. With the fall in the value of money, the fixed payment became an insignificant amount, barely worth the trouble of collecting and fell into oblivion. Mesne tenants had little reason to assert their rights and socage tenants gradually became tenants-in-chief.[5] This process was aided by the rule that a tenant is deemed to hold the land directly of the King if there is no evidence to the contrary. By contrast, tenure by knight service did not disappear as readily because of the incidents of wardship and marriage which could, in certain circumstances, give the mesne lord the control of the land. Nevertheless, the mesne lords were also subject to these incidents and the king, who was the only person in the position with everything to gain but nothing to lose, was eventually the only person interested in the maintenance of tenure by knight service. Gradually, many parts of the tenure system fell into disuse. It was not until 1660, however, that statutory intervention occurred. The *Statute of Tenures* 1660 abolished most of the incidents of tenure. It abolished the military tenures of knight

---

3. See Cheshire and Burn, pp. 16ff.
4. The *Statute of Quia Emptores* applies in Australia. In New South Wales, Victoria and Queensland, the statute has been repealed and re-enacted in a simpler form. N.S.W.: *Imperial Acts Application Act* 1969, s. 36; Vic.: *Imperial Acts Application Act* 1980, s. 5 and *Imperial Law Re-enactment Act* 1980, inserting s. 18A; Qld: *Property Law Act* 1974, s. 21.
5. This in turn was aided by the *Statute of Wills* 1540 which permitted the disposition of land by will and thus lessened the possibility of escheat.

service and grand serjeanty[6] by converting them into socage tenure. The incident of most value in socage tenure, aids, was abolished. The only incident of value in socage tenure which was retained was that of escheat. In view of the *Statute of Wills* 1540 permitting devise by will, this incident was in itself of less practical importance than it had been previously.[7]

[2.04] The doctrine of tenure is part of the law of Australia.[8] Its practical importance, however, is very limited: feudalism and feudal tenure as a means of landholding were never in existence in Australia. All land held in fee simple is held in socage tenure directly of the Crown.[9] In *Milirrpum v. Nabalco Pty Ltd and Commonwealth* Blackburn J. reiterated the proposition that the doctrine of tenure was part of the law of Australia and explained clearly its significance for Australia:[10]

> "[A]ll the Australian cases to which I was referred . . . affirm the principle, fundamental to the English law of real property, that the Crown is the source of title to all land; that no subject can own allodially, but only an estate or interest in it which he holds mediately or immediately of the Crown. On the foundation of New South Wales, therefore, and of South Australia, every square inch of territory in the colony became the property of the Crown. All titles, rights and interests whatever in land which existed thereafter in subjects of the Crown were the direct consequence of some grant from the Crown."

II. POSSESSION AND SEISIN

[2.05] The doctrine of tenure, as described above, militated against any concept of absolute ownership in land. The tenant in possession could not be regarded as having "ownership" as a failure to perform the requisite services resulted in the lord being able to recover the land. Neither could the lord be said to have absolute "ownership" as he had no right to possession of the land provided the services were performed by the tenant.

[2.06] In fact, English law has never recognised a concept of absolute ownership of land. The early real actions for the recovery of land demonstrated that English law, in analysing a person's interest in or

---

6. The honorary services relating to grand serjeanty were specifically retained. See Hargreaves and Helmore, op. cit., p. 36.
7. Note that frankalmoign and copyhold were retained at this stage. See Megarry and Wade, pp. 31-32.
8. See *Milirrpum v. Nabalco Pty Ltd and Commonwealth* (1971) 17 F.L.R. 141.
9. The land is held in socage tenure free of all its incidents apart from escheat. Where a tenant in fee simple dies intestate and without any next of kin, the land "escheats" to the Crown, the only feudal overlord in Australia. In most States, this now occurs pursuant to the statutory principle of bona vacantia (based on the common law principle of escheat): see below **[6.02]**.
    It is interesting to note that one incident of socage tenure, a rental payment, was used in the early days of settlement in the nature of a quit rent reserved to the Crown. See Hargreaves and Helmore, op cit., p. 36. See generally Chapter 19.
10. (1971) 17 F.L.R. 141 at 245.

relationship to land, concentrated upon the right to seisin or possession rather than a right to absolute ownership. As Chesire has commented, "it may be said without undue exaggeration that so far as land is concerned there is in England no law of ownership, but only a law of possession."[11] In disputes concerning land the question to be decided as between the plaintiff and the defendant was which party had the better right to seisin. The courts were unconcerned as to whether the plaintiff or the defendant had a right enforceable against the whole world. The concept of relativity of title rather than absolute ownership was firmly established in English land law from very early times and has remained one of the cornerstones of Anglo-Australian real property law. The emphasis on possession in English law is to be contrasted with the position in Roman law. In Roman law, the doctrine of dominium meant that a person had either absolute and complete ownership of land or nothing at all. A person who enjoyed possession had some personal remedies for interference with his right, but was not considered to have any proprietary interest in or "ownership" of the land.

The ancient remedy for recovery of land, the writ of right, concentrated upon whether the plaintiff or the defendant had the earlier, and therefore, the better right to seisin. The fact that the plaintiff was unable to prove a title good against the whole world was irrelevant. The procedure relating to this old writ was complex and lengthy. In order to decide disputes concerning rights to land, simpler remedies, the possessory assizes, were introduced by the common law.[12] These protected recent invasions of possession. The possessory assizes considered only the question as to whether the plaintiff had been wrongfully disseised by the defendant. Even an "owner" of land who was disseised and failed to regain possession quickly (four days), lost seisin to the disseisor and the disseisor could use the possessory assizes to protect his seisin even against the owner. The "owner" having lost seisin was no longer entitled to use the possessory assizes. The writ of right, where the question was who had the earlier, and therefore the better right to seisin, could still be used by the "owner" but, as stated above, its use involved a complex and lengthy procedure.

Eventually, the writs of entry replaced the possessory assizes. They gave some further and simpler protection to the "owner" and covered the instances where the disseisin was not of very recent origin. Although the disseisor gained seisin, he was subject to a right of entry by the person disseised. The person disseised could thus attempt to regain possession of the land (he had a right of entry), and in doing so was not subject to any action by the disseisor for doing so. The right of entry, however, was not a right which the common law considered an alienable one.[13] In contrast, seisin which remained in the disseisor, was a fully alienable right.

11. Cheshire and Burn, p. 27.
12. For a concise description of the various remedies, see Sackville and Neave, pp. 101-102.
13. Pursuant to statute, the right of entry is now alienable. General Law Statutes: N.S.W.: s. 50(1); Vic.: s. 19(1)(b); Qld: s. 31(2), S.A.: s. 10(b); Tas.: s. 80(1); quaere W.A. See, however, s. 50(2) of the *Conveyancing Act* 1919 (N.S.W.) which limits the alienability of a right of entry by providing that the conveyance of such

[2.07]   The above analysis demonstrates that it was seisin which was protected by the courts. How then is this term defined? In early times, it appears that no distinction was drawn between seisin and possession. With respect to real property, the law developed in such a manner that a real and important distinction between the two evolved. Seisin means the possession of land by a person holding a *freehold* estate in land. Only a person seised of a freehold estate in land was able to use the old real actions for the recovery of land. In this Chapter, the doctrine of estates will be analysed. In outline, it will be seen that estates in land fall into two distinct categories—freehold estates and estates less than freehold (leasehold estates). A person holding a leasehold estate was regarded as being in possession of the land the subject to the lease, but was not "seised" of the land. A leasehold interest was viewed as a personal transaction between the lessor and the lessee and gave the lessee a chattel interest or personal property only. The old actions for the recovery of land—the real actions, the possessory assizes and the writs of entry— could only be used to protect seisin. Thus, a lessee, who was dispossessed of the land, had no right to recover possession of the land. During the term of the lease, seisin remained in the lessor. This unsatisfactory situation, whereby a lessee had no right to recover land of which he or she was dispossessed, was remedied by the development of the action of ejectment. The action of ejectment permitted the lessee to recover the land. Because the action of ejectment provided a simpler means of recovering land than did the old actions, freeholders wished to use it too and, by the use of a fiction which the courts accepted,[14] began to do so. In time, the action in ejectment largely replaced the older actions as a means of recovering land for freeholders. The modern actions for the recovery of land are based on the action of ejectment and concentrate upon relative rights to possession of land.[15]

The separate terms "seisin" and "possession" are still used by the courts and writers alike but it is clear that the use of the action of ejectment as a general action for the recovery of land and the subsequent abolition of the old real actions have rendered the distinction of little practical importance. As Sackville and Neave state:[16] "the authorities tend to support the straightforward view that possession of land, like possession of goods, creates an interest in the possessor enforceable against the whole world, except someone with a superior right to possession."

---

13. *Continued*
    a right is only effective against the person in possession, if the person conveying, or any person through whom he claims, has been in possession of the land within 12 months of the date of the conveyance. See Baalman, "The Mystery of Pretensed Titles" (1957) 31 A.L.J. 450 where it is argued that s. 50(2) should be repealed. See also Maitland, "The Mystery of Seisin" (1886) 2 L.Q.R. 481 and Note (1969) 43 A.L.J. 301. See also *Morgan v. 15 Bannerman St Pty Ltd* [1971] 1 N.S.W.L.R. 601.
14. The nature of this fiction is described in Megarry and Wade, pp. 1156-1157.
15. See e.g. *Supreme Court Act* 1970 (N.S.W.), s. 79.
16. Sackville and Neave, p. 101.

[2.08] A number of cases demonstrate the importance of possession in Anglo-Australian land law and illustrate the generally accepted view that there is no concept of absolute ownership. In a dispute concerning land, the courts approach the matter by considering whether the plaintiff or the defendant has a relatively better right to the land. Possession does give rise to an interest in the land and a plaintiff who is dispossessed of land by the defendant will succeed in recovering the land unless the defendant can prove a superior right to possession. The defendant may prove such a superior right by showing he or she has the documentary title or that he or she has a prior and thereby superior right to possession. Because of the statutory principle of limitation of actions discussed in Chapter 15, it must be remembered that a person who has such a superior right does not retain the right indefinitely. After a set period of time, the person's right to bring an action to recover the land is lost.

[2.09] In *Asher v. Whitlock*[17] Williamson took possession of two pieces of land in 1842 and 1850 respectively. Documentary title to the land was held by L. Williamson died in 1860 and in his will he devised the pieces of land he had enclosed to his widow for life or until her remarriage and then to his daughter. Williamson's widow and his daughter remained in possession of the land. In 1861 the widow married Whitlock who also came to reside on the land. In February 1863, the daughter died. The plaintiff in the action, Asher, was the daughter's heir. In March 1863, the widow died. Asher brought an action in ejectment against Whitlock.

The court held in favour of the plaintiff. Cockburn C.J. stated the clear proposition that if Whitlock had dispossessed Williamson, Williamson would have had a right to recover the land from Whitlock. Williamson's prior, and therefore better, possessory interest would have given him a better right to the land than Whitlock. "[P]ossession is good against all the world except the person who can shew a good title."[18] The court held that the possessory interest is clearly a devisable one and thus Asher, who was the heir of the daughter, stood on the shoes of her predecessors-in-title (Williamson and his daughter) and could rely upon the prior possessory right in the action in ejectment against Whitlock. The only way in which Whitlock could have succeeded is if he had maintained possession in his own right for the period of time (then 20 years) necessary to bar the right of action of the holder of the prior possessory interest.

Although Cockburn C.J. and Mellor J. reached the same decision, it is interesting to note the differences in terminology used in their respective judgments. Cockburn C.J. discarded the distinction between seisin and possession and stated simply that possession itself gives rise to an interest which is enforceable against all but the true owner. In contrast, Mellor J. retained the distinction in holding that possession is "prima facie evidence of seisin in fee" and thereby implying that the plaintiff's proprietary interest was based on seisin, rather than simply possession. Although the judgment of Mellor J. is strictly more correct than that of Cockburn

17. (1865) L.R. 1 Q.B. 1.
18. (1865) L.R. 1 Q.B. 1 at 5 per Cockburn C.J.

C.J.,[19] there seems little reason for continuing to use terminology which is effectively outdated.

[2.10]   Although the issue was not raised directly in *Asher v. Whitlock*, the case is often cited as authority for the proposition that the defendant in an action to recover land cannot raise successfully the plea of jus tertii. The plea of jus tertii is effectively a plea that if a third party to the proceedings has a better right to the land than either the plaintiff or the defendant, the plaintiff cannot succeed even if he or she has a better possessory interest than the defendant. With respect to the land enclosed by Williamson in 1850, L retained the best right to the land. The limitation period was 20 years and thus in 1865, the limitation period had not expired. It appears that the plea was not raised by the defendant in *Asher v. Whitlock*. Thus, although by inference the court rejected its use, the court was not required directly to consider the issue.[20] The Privy Council in *Perry v. Clissold*[21] rejected the use of the plea of jus tertii and although there are some judgments in the High Court decision of *Allen v. Roughley*[22] which imply that the plea may be raised, on balance the law appears to be that such a plea cannot be raised successfully.

[2.11]   The fact situation in *Allen v. Roughley* was complex and the following is a version sufficient for an understanding of its relevance to this area of the law. Cusbert took possession of the land in dispute in 1880 and remained there until his death in 1895. He did not hold the documentary title. By his will, Cusbert devised the land to his son, William, for life and the remainder in fee simple to his other children. The defendant, Allen, who was a son-in-law of Cusbert took possession of the land in 1898 and remained there. William lived on the land with Allen and his wife from 1898-1900. From 1900-1915 he resided in New Zealand and on his return he lived in a hut on part of the land and, for some periods of time, with Allen in the homestead until his death in 1942. In 1950, an action to recover the land from Allen was commenced. It was effectively an action by the remaindermen pursuant to Cusbert's will (that is, his other children). They claimed that their possessory interest deriving from Cusbert was prior in time to any such interest claimed by Allen and that even if Allen had taken adverse possession, he had not barred their right to bring an action as their right only arose in 1942 upon the death of William, the life tenant. When the matter reached the High Court Allen had accepted that he was unable to defeat the plaintiff's claim by relying upon the fact that he had extinguished all other claims to the land through adverse possession. He claimed, however, that the plaintiffs could only defeat his interest if they could prove title to the land and that they could only do this by showing a good documentary title or a possessory title which was proved to be the best interest in the land by 20 years' (the

---

19. See Hargreaves, "Terminology and Title in Ejectment" (1940) 56 L.Q.R. 376 at 381-386 and Sackville and Neave, p. 113.
20. Cf. *Doe d. Carter v. Barnard* (1849) 13 Q.B. 945; 116 E.R. 1524 where the plea of jus tertii was raised successfully.
21. [1907] A.C. 73.
22. (1955) 94 C.L.R. 98; [1955] A.L.R. 1017. See below **[2.12]**.

limitation period) uninterrupted possession. His argument was based on the views of Holdsworth.[23]

The High Court rejected the defendant's argument and held, as had the court in *Asher v. Whitlock*, that possession for less than the statutory period gives rise to an interest in land which is sufficient to maintain an action in ejectment against a dispossessor.[24] The court drew attention to the fact that a person who takes possession of land and then abandons it, has no right of action to recover land as against a person who subsequently takes possession. Thus, it may be that a plaintiff in ejectment is required to prove a prior possessory interest and to prove that the possessory interest has not been abandoned.

[2.12] The decision of the High Court demonstrates clear approval of the theory of relativity of title. By inference it would be thought that such an approval would involve the unacceptability of the plea of jus tertii. If the task of the court is to determine whether the plaintiff or the defendant has the relatively better title, the implication must be that the proof of a better title than either the plaintiff or the defendant in a third party, would be irrelevant to the dispute at hand. This conclusion is not, however, wholly clear in some of the judgments of the High Court. Fullagar J. indorsed, in a stronger fashion than the other justices, that possession gives rise to an interest in the land which is enforceable against all possessors but a person with a superior interest, and unless the possession is abandoned, any subsequent possessor cannot hold a superior interest. The whole tenor of his judgment militates against the availability of the plea of jus tertii. Dixon C.J. and Taylor and Williams JJ. viewed possession as being prima facie evidence of title. It is possible to argue on this analysis that the plaintiff's claim is based on prima facie proof of title and a defendant who could prove that title is in fact in a person other than the plaintiff (the plea of jus tertii) would succeed. However, the better view is that the justices would have rejected the use of the plea of jus tertii. When referring to possession as being prima facie evidence of title, it seems the Dixon C.J., in particular, was referring to possession as prima facie evidence of a possessory title, rather than prima facie evidence of an absolute title. Their Honours clearly supported the concept of relativity of title, a concept which involves an acceptance that a dispute concerning land must be decided according to whether the plaintiff or the defendant has the better right to the land. It is a little more difficult to conclude that Kitto J. would have rejected the plea of jus tertii. Kitto J. viewed possession as being prima facie evidence of a fee simple estate, of absolute ownership. Arguably, proof that the best title was in a third person would, on the analysis of Kitto J., have destroyed the plaintiff's case. Subsequent decisions have taken the view that jus tertii is not a good defence[25] and

23. Holdsworth, *A History of English Law* (2nd ed., Vol. 7, 1937), pp. 62-65.
24. Cf. the judgment of Williams J. who took a different view of the facts: see (1955) 94 C.L.R. 98 at 118. On his Honour's analysis, the periods of possession by Cusbert and William, the life tenant, taken together comprised a 20 year period. Quaere whether in view of the judge's findings of fact, such a view was possible.
25. See e.g. *Spark v. Whale Three Minute Car Wash (Cremorne Junction) Pty Ltd* (1970) 92 W.N. (N.S.W.) 1087; *Mulcahy v. Curramore* [1974] 2 N.S.W.L.R. 464; *Newington v. Windeyer* [1986] 3 N.S.W.L.R. 555.

although doubt remains in view of some of the judgments in the High Court in *Allen v. Roughley*, it is suggested on balance that the plea cannot be raised successfully.

III.   THE DOCTRINE OF ESTATES

[2.13]   The doctrine of tenure demonstrated that several persons could hold interests in the one piece of land. The doctrine thereby laid the groundwork for the division of interests in land in ways other than pursuant to the tenurial relationship. From early times, it was recognised that the permanent nature of land lent itself readily to the concept of the creation of successive interests in land. The idea was that it should be possible for a person to have an interest in the land giving a present right to possession, whilst other persons would have interests which would give them rights to possession in the future. Although the holder of a future interest had no present right to possession, the interest was still a present and full one in the sense that the interest was capable of alienation. In order to give effect to this concept of fragmentation of a proprietary interest on the basis of time, English law developed the notion of the ''estate'' (the doctrine of estates). The estate was separate from the land. By viewing the estate as a thing separate from the land, it was simpler to accept, for instance, the notion of the alienation of a future right to possession of the land.[26]

The estate gives its holder a right to seisin or possession and the nature of the estate determines the extent and duration of the right to seisin or possession. For example, if A is the holder of a life estate in Blackacre, her right to seisin is limited to the duration of her life. Estates are classified into estates of freehold and estates less than freehold. The second category comprises what is more commonly termed the leasehold estate. Estates of freehold are created where the length of the duration of the estate is uncertain. Estates of less than freehold are created when the duration of the estate is certain or capable of being rendered certain.

[2.14]   When the concept of the estate was first developed, it was only estates of freehold, the fee simple, the fee tail and the life estate, which were recognised as estates in land. Leases were seen as comprising a simple, personal transaction between the landlord and the tenant. Whilst the tenant was entitled to possession of the land, seisin and therefore the right to use the real actions to recover possession of the land, remained with the landlord. A tenant who was dispossessed of the land could not use the old real actions to recover possession of the land: the only remedy was to sue the landlord for a breach of contract. As explained above **[2.07]**, in the 15th century the action of ejectment was developed and gave the dispossessed tenant the right to recover the land. Consequently, it was recognised that the lease gave its holder proprietary rights in the land, rather than simply personal rights pursuant to contract and the estate less than freehold, the leasehold estate, became established.

26.   See Sackville and Neave, p. 148 and Hargreaves and Helmore, op. cit., pp. 40ff.

1. Estates of Freehold

[2.15]   The three estates of freehold are the fee simple, the fee tail and the life estate.

(a) Fee simple

[2.16]   The fee simple is the largest estate in duration. It is the closest estate to absolute ownership. As Megarry and Wade state: "its proprietor is commonly called the owner of the land."[27] It is only the doctrine of tenure which theoretically means the Crown is the owner of all land, that still prevents the holder of an estate in fee simple from being regarded as an absolute owner.

[2.17]   At first, the fee simple estate was not such an enduring, absolute estate as it is now. The word "fee" denoted that the estate was an inheritable one and the word "simple" meant that the estate could pass to heirs generally and was not, like the fee tail, limited to a particular class of heirs. In early times, the heir was viewed as having a current clear interest in the land and the holder of the fee simple estate could not alienate the estate to another without the consent of the heir. The estate was considered to be one of inheritance in a strict sense and was enforced as such. By 1200, the situation had changed and the holder of a fee simple estate was able to alienate the estate, inter vivos. Nevertheless, the fee simple estate continued only for as long as the original holder or the heirs survived.[28] Even if the holder had conveyed the estate to another person before her or his death, the estate failed if the holder died without leaving heirs. Gradually the fee simple estate became a more enduring interest. By early in the 14th century, it was clear that if the holder of a fee simple estate alienated the estate and subsequently died without heirs, the fee simple estate would continue in the new holder as long as the new holder had heirs. The right of the holder of a fee simple estate to dispose of the estate by will and so defeat the claim of the heir, was longer in coming. The "use" effectively made it possible to dispose of land in this way (discussed below **[2.51]-[2.69]**), and in 1540, the *Statute of Wills* enabled direct testamentary dispositions of fee simple estates. In modern law, the fee simple estate continues whether or not there are heirs. The holder may dispose of the estate during her or his lifetime or by testamentary devise. If the holder dies intestate, the estate passes to her or his next of kin.[29] Where a person dies intestate and without next of kin, the Crown takes the property.[30]

---

27. Megarry and Wade, p. 13.

28. "Heirs" included blood relations and their heirs. For a detailed account of the meaning of term "heir" see Megarry and Wade, pp. 540ff.

29. This is according to statutory formulae: see below **[6.02]**.

30. At common law, the fee simple passed or escheated to the feudal overlord in certain circumstances: one instance where this occurred was if the holder of a fee simple estate died intestate and without next of kin. For the relevant statutory provisions, see below **[6.02]**.

(b) Fee tail

[2.18] The fee tail is an estate of inheritance, but unlike the fee simple, inheritance is limited to a particular person and her or his specified lineal descendants. As explained above, the fee simple estate as originally formulated and enforced could pass to collateral relations (for example, a brother) or ascendants if there were no direct descendants. The idea of the fee tail estate was to keep the estate within a particular branch of the family: the estate would revert to the grantor when the grantee and the specified descendants were dead.

The grant could be restricted further than to the lineal descendants and could be formulated so as to descend only to a specified class of lineal descendants. For example, the grant could specify that only female or male descendants were to take ("to A and the female heirs of his body" or "to A and the male heirs of his body"). Such grants together with the ordinary fee tail described above, "to A and the heirs of his body", have been termed "general tail".[31] Alternatively, the grant could be restricted to heirs descended from a particular spouse ("to A and the heirs of his body begotten of his wife, Z"). This type of grant may be classified as a "special tail".

[2.19] The common law interpreted these grants as the grants of fee simple estates subject to the condition that heirs of the specified class existed. Once a descendant of the specified class was born, the common law deemed the condition to be fulfilled and the grantee was then deemed to be in the same position as the holder of a fee simple. Thus, the holder had the power to alienate to another and so defeat the intention of the grantor and the possible interests of persons falling within the specified class of descendants. The power to alienate in the grantee was so clearly against the intention of the grantor that the law was altered by the statute, *De Donis Conditionalibus* 1285. This statute created the freehold estate of the fee tail. Pursuant to the statute, it was provided that conditional grants of the type described were to be interpreted as the grantor intended. Thus, even if the grantee purported to alienate, the estate descended to the specified line of descendants upon the death of the grantee. When the grantee and all the issue were dead, the estate reverted to the grantor. Effectively, the holder of a fee tail estate could only alienate an interest lasting for her or his lifetime. It follows then that the holder of a fee simple estate who created a fee tail from the fee simple, retained an interest in the land: the whole of the estate had not been given away. In such circumstances, the holder of the fee simple held a reversion or a vested remainder in another person may have been created.

[2.20] The fee tail estate effectively prevented alienation of the land. The specified descendants were not bound by an alienation by the tenant in tail. More specifically, the rights of the issue could not be affected by partial forms of alienations, such as rentcharges and leases. The effective management of land became very difficult for the holder of the fee tail estate. Statutory change to remedy the situation was not possible as the

---

31. See Megarry and Wade, p. 55.

large landowners still favoured the fee tail estate as a means of keeping the property in the family, tying descendants to the property and preserving it from forfeiture.

Various fictitious procedures evolved as a means of converting the fee tail estate into a fee simple estate. In order to effect such a conversion successfully, it was necessary to bar the rights of the specified line of descendants and the rights of any persons, reversioners or remaindermen, who would take in the event of the failure of heirs. The two devices which were used successfully were the common recovery and the fine. They involved the use of an established action at law and relied upon the binding nature of a court judgment. The ways in which these devices operated have been explained fully elsewhere. In view of the fact that fees tail can no longer be created in most Australian States, they will not be discussed in detail here.[32]

It is sufficient to state that if the device of the common recovery was used properly, the fee tail estate was converted into a fee simple estate. The collusive action of the fine, being ineffective to bar the interests of persons holding estates in remainder or reversion, resulted in the creation of a base fee, an estate similar to a determinable fee simple. The result was that the estate continued only for as long as the entail would have continued had it not been barred. The fine, as a device to end an estate in tail, was therefore not as effective as the common recovery. Nevertheless, because its scope and use were not as limited as the common recovery, the fine was a popular means of barring an entail. The procedures for the use of the common recovery were simplified with the introduction of the *Fines and Recoveries Act* 1833 (Eng.).

[2.21] The estate of fee tail was rarely used in Australia. Different social and economic conditions existed in Australia and there was little interest by landowners in keeping land within the family, or a particular branch of it, by use of the fee tail estate: see below **[12.04]**.[33] Recoveries and fines were not used in New South Wales. However, the *Registration of Deeds Act* 1825 (N.S.W.), s. 8 provided that a deed acknowledged in a particular manner would have the same effect as the suffering of a recovery or the levy of a fine.[34]

[2.22] In four States, New South Wales, Victoria, Queensland and Western Australia, fees tail can no longer be created at all.[35] In these States, any attempt to create a fee tail estate results in the creation of a fee simple estate. In New South Wales, Queensland and Western Australia, it was provided further that all existing fee tail estates were converted into fee simple estates. These statutory provisions were reiterated by the repeal in New South Wales, Victoria and Queensland

---

32. See Megarry and Wade, pp. 78-85 and Butt, pp. 101-104.
33. Cf. Sackville and Neave, pp. 624-628.
34. See Hargreaves and Helmore, op. cit., p. 70, Sackville and Neave, p. 146 and Butt, p. 104
35. General Law Statutes: N.S.W.: s. 19 (from 1 July 1920) and s. 19A (from January 1971); Vic.: s. 249 (from 1 January 1886); Qld: s. 22 (from 1 December 1975); W.A.: s. 23 (from 1 August 1969).

of the *De Donis Conditionalibus* statute.[36] In Victoria, ss 250-266 of the *Property Law Act* 1958 (Vic.) provide detailed rules for the barring of the entail with respect to fee tail estates which came into existence before 1 January 1886. It is thought that few, if any, estates tail exist in Victoria.[37]

In Tasmania, it has not been possible to create an estate tail over Torrens land since 8 December 1886.[38] Limitations coming into effect after that date which purport to create a fee tail estate, create instead a fee simple estate. As in Victoria, it is thought that few, if any, fee tail estates exist. There are provisions for the barring of the entail.[39] In South Australia, the fee tail estate continues to exist and, it seems, may still be created over Torrens land and any general law land which still exists: see below **[4.05]**. The *Estates Tail Act* 1881 (S.A.), which substantially adopted the English *Fines and Recoveries Act* 1833, provides the means by which the holder of an estate tail can bar the entail.

[2.23]   The holder of a fee tail estate enjoys the same rights of enjoyment apart from the right of alienation as are held by the holder of a fee simple estate. As stated above, there are various types of entail (for example, tail male, special tail) and the entail may be determinable or conditional in the same way as the other freehold estates.

(c) Life estate

[2.24]   The life estate, although an estate of freehold, is not an estate of inheritance as it clearly ends on the death of the tenant. The life estate may take one of two forms. First, it may be granted for the life of the grantee. Thus, a grant "to A for life" creates a life estate in A.[40] Secondly, a life estate may be granted for the life of a person other than the grantee, an estate pur autre vie. A grant "to A for the life of B" creates an interest in A which lasts, not for the length of his lifetime, but for the length of B's life. The cestui que vie, B in this example, is the person whose lifetime fixes the duration of the estate. An estate pur autre vie often arises, not by way of a direct grant, but by the holder of a life estate conveying her or his interest to another. For example, if B holds a

36. N.S.W.: *Imperial Acts Application Act* 1969, s. 8; Vic.: *Imperial Acts Application Act* 1980, s. 5; Qld: *Property Law Act* 1974, s. 3, Sched. 6.
37. Whalan, p. 99. Note that the provisions in ss 250-266 differ in a number of respects from the *Estates Tail Act* 1881 (S.A.) adopting the *Fines and Recoveries Act* 1833 (Eng.). E.g., a disposition by will of the tenant in tail subject to certain criteria, may bar the entail in Victoria but not in South Australia or Tasmania: s. 251. In Victoria where a parent and child are granted successive life estates and the grandchild an estate tail in remainder, the parent and child may bar the entail as if the entail had been given to the child: s. 250. This is not possible under the South Australian or the Tasmanian legislation.
38. See now *Land Titles Act* 1980 (Tas.), ss 113-116.
39. *Estates Tail Act* 1853 (Tas.). This Act sets out a scheme for converting the fee tail to a fee simple absolute. The scheme is similar to the provisions in the *Property Law Act* 1958 (Vic.) but still bears more of the trappings of the old actions of levying a fine or suffering a common recovery. See above, fn. 37.
40. Other forms of life estate, dower and curtesy, arose by operation of law. They can no longer exist. See Butt, pp. 107-110 for a description of these forms of life estate.

life estate and conveys his interest to A, A holds a life estate pur autre vie (for the life of B).

[2.25] Problems arose with respect to the estate pur autre vie if the holder of the estate predeceased the cestui que vie. As the estate was not one of inheritance, the holder of an estate pur autre vie could not devise the interest in her or his will and nor would it devolve to her or his next of kin upon an intestacy. The doctrine of occupancy was invented by the common law to solve the problem. If the holder of the estate pur autre vie held the land pursuant to a grant which was worded, as in the example above, "to A for the life of B", the first person to enter the land after A's death was entitled to the estate pur autre vie. He was so entitled as "general occupant" for the remainder of B's life with no liability for A's debts. If, however, the grant of the estate pur autre vie specifically mentioned A's heirs, for example, "to A and his heirs for the life of B", A's heir was entitled to the land as "special occupant" for the remainder of the life of the cestui que vie's life. The heir did not take by way of inheritance but simply because the word "heirs" was mentioned in the grant. As he did not take by descent, neither was the land held by the special occupant subjected to the debts of A.

The doctrine of occupancy is no longer part of the law. Statutory provisions now ensure that the holder of an estate pur autre vie may leave the interest by will. If the holder dies intestate, the interest forms part of the intestate's estate and devolves according to set statutory formulae: see below **[6.02]**.

[2.26] In order to ensure the land was retained and maintained in a proper manner for those who would succeed to the land upon the death of the life tenant, a number of restrictions regarding use and enjoyment were placed on the life tenant. The law of waste, in particular, restricted the life tenant's use of the land. The law of waste and statutory provisions regarding the rights and duties of life tenants are discussed in Chapter 12.

2. Leasehold Estates

[2.27] As stated above, leasehold estates may be distinguished from freehold estates by the fact that their duration must be certain or capable of being rendered certain. The various types of leasehold estates are considered below. A detailed analysis of the substantive and formal criteria necessary for the creation of these estates and of the law, both common law and statutory, governing the landlord and tenant relationship is undertaken in Chapters 10 and 11.

(a) Lease for a fixed term of years

[2.28] A lease for a fixed term of years is, in fact, a lease for any fixed period of time which comes to an end automatically at the expiration of the period.[41] The rule is that the maximum period of duration must be

---

41. See Chapter 11 for statutory exceptions to this rule.

certain and the fact that a lease may come to an end before that, does not invalidate it. For example, a lease, "to A for five years as long as she continues to live on the premises" is a valid lease for a fixed term of years.

(b) Periodic tenancies

[2.29] A periodic tenancy continues from period to period until it is determined by proper notice. Periodic tenancies may be created by reference to any period of time. The most common forms of periodic tenancy are the yearly, the monthly and the weekly. The notice required to terminate the tenancy depends upon the type of periodic tenancy. For example, a yearly tenancy is terminated by six months' notice.

Periodic tenancies appear, then, to have an uncertain maximum duration. However, they have been treated as complying with the rules as to certainty of maximum duration as the tenancy is regarded as being one for a definite term of the relevant period (for example, one year, one month, one week). If the tenancy is not determined at the end of the relevant period, it is considered to continue for another term.[42]

(c) Tenancy at will

[2.30] A tenancy at will is created when a tenant occupies the land as a tenant on the basis that either party may terminate the tenancy at any time. There is no agreement as to duration, and usually, no agreement as to payment of rent. The tenancy at will arises in a variety of situations. The simplest example is where a person, with the permission of the landlord, takes possession of a property rent free and for an indefinite period.

Such a tenancy may also arise where at the expiration of a lease, the tenant holds over with the landlord's consent and pays no rent. Of course, if the tenant subsequently pays rent on a periodic basis and the rent is accepted by the landlord, the tenancy at will is converted into a periodic tenancy. Although it has been argued that the tenancy at will should not be classified as a leasehold estate because the maximum duration is uncertain, it is generally accepted that the landlord and tenant relationship exists between the parties.

The tenancy at will determines automatically if the tenant purports to alienate her or his interest or if he or she dies.[43]

(d) Tenancy at sufferance

[2.31] The tenancy at sufferance arises when the tenant holds over at the expiration of a lease without the consent of the landlord. The landlord

---

42. *Commonwealth Life (Amalgamated) Assurance Ltd v. Anderson* (1945) 46 S.R. (N.S.W.) 47 at 50-51; *Mitchell v. Weiriks; Ex parte Weiriks* [1975] Qd R. 100.

43. See Megarry and Wade, p. 654. The tenancy also terminates if the landlord assigns her or his interest or dies but the tenant cannot be ejected unless he or she knows of the event terminating the tenancy. *Doe d. Davies v. Thomas* (1851) 6 Exch. 854 at 857; 155 E.R. 792. The tenancy at will is discussed further: see below **[10.12]**.

may bring an action for recovery of possession against the tenant, but he or she cannot sue for damages for trespass as the original entry was lawful.

The tenancy at sufferance is not strictly a leasehold estate as there is no agreement or tenure between the parties. Nevertheless, it often arises where such a relationship has formerly existed between the parties and some remedies normally applicable to the landlord-tenant relationship, such as a claim by the landlord for "use and occupation", are available where the tenancy is one at sufferance.[44] It seems that the designation of a "tenancy" for this situation may have originally occurred in order to prevent the occupation being viewed as "adverse possession" which could in time bar the landlord's title. The old rules of adverse possession have changed and a tenant at sufferance is now considered an adverse possessor from the commencement of the "tenancy". As Megarry and Wade state: "[t]he old rules as to adverse possession have long disappeared, and this 'tenancy' might be permitted to go with them."[45]

3. Words of Limitation

[2.32] The characteristics and nature of each type of freehold estate have been set out above. In order to create each of the estates, however, a particular form of words, "words of limitation", had to be used. An incorrect formulation in a grant resulted in the grantor's intention not being effected. The words of limitation mark out the type of estate which is to be taken. On the other hand, words of purchase set out the person who is to take the estate.

Before setting out the correct words for each grant, three important points must be noted. First, the courts treated grants inter vivos and dispositions by will very differently. If the grant was made inter vivos, the common law adopted a very strict approach and required the exact and proper words of limitation in order to effect the grant intended. If the gift was made by will, the courts adopted a far more lenient approach. Provided the testator's intention (as to the type of estate he or she intended to create) was clear, the intention was effected despite any incorrect use of the words of limitation. Secondly, statutory provisions in all Australian States, except South Australia, have gradually modified the position. Strict adherence to the "correct" words of limitation is no longer required. Nevertheless, a knowledge and understanding of the words of limitation remain important as the statutory modifications apply only to grants made after the date of the relevant statutory provision. Thirdly, the use of correct words of limitation has never been necessary where the land falls under the Torrens system of land registration and it is a legal interest which is to be created or conveyed: see below, Chapter 5. The statutory provisions relating to the creation and passing of interests in Torrens land set out particular forms which must be used for the transfer, mortgage and passing of other types of interest in the land. Further, unlike the position

---

44. *Bayley v. Bradley* (1848) 5 C.B. 396 at 406; 136 E.R. 932; *Leigh v. Dickeson* (1884) 15 Q.B.D. 60. There cannot be any claim for rent as such as there is no relationship of landlord and tenant.
45. Megarry and Wade, p. 43.

with respect to general law land, it is the registration of the particular form or document which passes the interest in the land rather than the document itself: see below, Chapter 5.

(a) Word of limitation for a fee simple estate

(i) Dispositions inter vivos

[2.33] The correct formulation to create a fee simple estate at common law required the use of the words "heirs" after the grantee's name. Thus, a grant in fee simple to A was effected by the phrase, "to A and his heirs". The words "and his heirs" were the words of limitation. They marked out the quantity of the estate—a fee simple estate. They were not words of purchase, and therefore, did not give A's heirs any interest in the land. A's heir had an expectation of succeeding to the estate if A died without having disposed of the estate but the heir acquired no estate by virtue of the grant. An incorrect use of the words of limitation resulted in the grantee obtaining a life estate only. Thus, for example, a grant "to A in fee simple" meant that A obtained a life estate only and that there would be a reversion in the grantor.[46] As a corporation cannot die or have heirs, a grant of land to a corporation without the use of the words "and his heirs" effected a conveyance of the fee simple estate.[47] In Australia the correct use of the words of limitation was, and remains in relation to grants made before statutory modifications, necessary to create the fee simple estate.[48]

As stated above, the common law position has been modified by statute. In New South Wales, Victoria, Queensland, Western Australia and Tasmania a disposition without the correct words of limitation now passes the fee simple estate unless there is a contrary intention. Therefore, dispositions such as "to A", "to A in fee simple", "to A forever", and "to A in fee" pass the fee simple estate.[49]

46. See Megarry and Wade, pp. 50-51 for further examples and special rules.
47. *Re Woking U.D.C. (Basingstoke Canal) Act 1911* [1914] 1 Ch. 300 at 312. See Megarry and Wade, pp. 51-52 for the position regarding corporations sole.
48. *Sexton v. Horton* (1926) 38 C.L.R. 240. It should be noted that the relevant interests created in *Sexton v. Horton* were equitable, rather than legal, in nature. A discussion of legal and equitable interests in land is found in Chapter 6. Nevertheless, the rules concerning the creation of freehold legal estates were applied. Where technical conveyancing terms are used in the grant, as was the case in *Sexton v. Horton*, the correct and strict words of limitation must be used for the creation or passing of an equitable fee simple. See also *Perpetual Trustee Co. Ltd v. Griffin* [1963] N.S.W.R. 465 which followed *Sexton v. Horton*. Cf. the view of Baalman, "Sacred Cow of the Common Law" (1965) 39 A.L.J. 197 and the decision of the Privy Council in *Adeyinka Qyeckan v. Musendiku Adele* [1957] 1 W.L.R. 876.
49. General Law Statutes: N.S.W.: s. 47(1) and (2) after 1 July 1920; Vic.: s. 60(6), from 31 January 1905 to 31 December 1918—the words "to A in fee" and "to A in fee simple" in addition to the correct words of limitation "to A and his heirs" passed a fee simple estate. S. 60(1), after 31 December 1918 the fee simple passed without the use of correct words of limitation unless there was a contrary intention — "to A", "to A forever"; Qld: s. 29(1) after 4 December 1952; W.A.: s. 37(1) and (2), after 1 August 1969; Tas.: s. 61(2), after 18 September 1874.

Further as noted above, fee tail estates can no longer be created in New South Wales, Victoria, Queensland and Western Australia and words of limitation which would formerly have created a fee tail estate, or in some cases, which show an intention to create a fee tail, result in the creation of a fee simple estate.[50]

In South Australia, there has been no statutory modification and the correct words of limitation, "to A and his heirs" must be used to dispose of the fee simple estate.

(ii) Dispositions by will

[2.34] From 1540 when devises of land were recognised as being lawful and effective,[51] the courts took a more lenient approach where a disposition was by will. The courts did not insist on the use of the magical words "and his heirs" in order for a fee simple estate to pass. Nevertheless, the will had to evince an intention to pass the fee simple estate and the devisee had to prove that the will demonstrated such an intention. A devise "to A in fee simple" or "to A forever" demonstrated such an intention but a devise "to A" was insufficient, without further evidence, to prove an intention to pass the fee simple. Statutory provisions in all Australian States now provide that a disposition without the correct words of limitation passes the fee simple estate unless a contrary intention is shown.[52] The onus of proof has been effectively reversed.

---

50. General Law Statutes: N.S.W.: s. 19(1) and s. 47(1), after 1 July 1920; Vic.: s. 249 — a limitation which would have created a fee tail e.g. "to A and the heirs of his body" created a fee simple estate from 1 January 1886; s. 60(6) — a limitation which showed an intention to create a fee tail e.g. "to A in tail male" "to A in tail" created a fee simple estate from 31 January 1905. Quaere a limitation "to A in fee tail"; Qld: s. 22 after 1 December 1975; W.A.: s. 23(1) after 1 August 1969. In Queensland and Western Australia, it appears that where there is a clear intention to create a fee tail but words are used which would not have been sufficient to create a fee tail (e.g. "to A in tail") the common law remains applicable and a life estate by default would result. Neither of the relevant provisions (ss 22 and 29 in Queensland and s. 23(1) and s. 37 in Western Australia) appear to apply. See Note (1953) 26 A.L.J. 648.

51. *Statute of Wills* 1540.

52. The current legislation is given: in many instances it derives from earlier legislation. N.S.W.: *Wills, Probate and Administration Act* 1898, s. 24 after 1 January 1840; Vic.: *Wills Act* 1958, s. 26 after 1851 when Victoria became a separate colony; Qld: *Succession Act* 1981, s. 28 after 1 January 1840 (see *Succession Act* 1867, s. 74); S.A.: *Wills Act* 1936, s. 31; W.A.: *Wills Act* 1970, s. 27(e) after 4 July 1839; Tas.: *Wills Act* 1840, Sched., cl. 28 after 1 April 1841. See *In the Will of Hoare* [1908] V.L.R. 369; *Re Ridgeway* (1900) 26 V.L.R. 254; *Campbell v. Glasgow* (1919) 27 C.L.R. 31; *Pead v. Pead* (1912) 5 C.L.R. 510. These statutory provisions are all very similar to s. 28 of the *Wills Act* 1837 (Eng.). In *Nichols v. Hawkes* (1853) 10 Hare. 342; 68 E.R. 958 it was held that s. 28 did not apply to the creation of new interests in a will: in this case, the correct words of limitation had to be used. Thus, for example, if 'T' has a fee simple absolute in Blackacre and devises to X a rentcharge (without use of the correct words of limitation) X would take a rentcharge for life only subject to a contrary intention.

(b) Words of limitation for a fee tail estate

(i) Dispositions inter vivos

[2.35] In order to create a fee tail estate the word "heirs" had to be used as for the fee simple estate and had to be followed by words which confined the estate to the lineal descendants of the grantee. These words were termed "words of procreation". The most common form of words to create the fee tail were "to A and the heirs of his body". However, any words of procreation which indicated an intention to limit the estate to lineal descendants of the grantor, sufficed. Other examples of words of procreation included "from him proceeding" and "of his flesh". As stated above, the entail could be defined further by limiting it to a particular class of lineal descendants. For example, the descendants could be limited to female or male descendants ("to A and the female heirs of her body" or "to A and the male heirs of his body") or to the descendants of a specified wife ("to A and the heirs of his body begotten of his wife, Z"). The words following the name of the grantee were considered words of limitation and not words of purchase and therefore did not give any estate to the heirs of A, but merely a "spec successionsis".

Up until the various times when statutory provisions in New South Wales, Victoria, Queensland and Western Australia made it impossible to create new fee tail estates,[53] the correct words of limitation and of procreation as described above had to be complied with in order to create a fee tail estate. Dispositions such as "to A in tail", "to A in fee tail", "to A in tail female" were ineffective to create a fee tail estate and instead created by default, a life estate in the grantee. In South Australia, the common law requirements remain in force and the correct words of limitation must be used to create a fee tail estate (for example, "to A and the heirs of his body"). In Tasmania, where it remains possible to create a fee tail estate over general law land, strict adherence to the correct words of limitation has been unnecessary since 1884.[54] Dispositions "to A in tail", "to A in tail female" and "to A in tail male" are effective to create fee tail estates.

(ii) Dispositions by will

[2.36] As in the case of the fee simple, the courts adopted a more lenient approach when construing dispositions in wills and did not insist upon strict compliance with the correct words of limitation. Clear words which evinced an intention to create a fee tail estate sufficed. Thus, expressions such as "to A in fee tail", to "A and his issue", "to A and his seed", "to A and his heirs male" created a fee tail estate if found in a will. In those jurisdictions, New South Wales, Victoria, Queensland and Western Australia, where it is no longer possible to create fees tail, limitations in wills which would formerly have created fee tail estates, create fee simple estates. In South Australia and Tasmania, the fee tail estate is created if there are clear words in the will showing an intention to create a fee tail estate.

---

53. See above, fn. 50.
54. *Conveyancing and Law of Property Act* 1884 (Tas.), s. 65, after 1 January 1884.

(c) Words of limitation for a life estate

(i) Dispositions inter vivos

[2.37] A life estate was created if the grantor evinced an intention to create a life estate, such as in a grant "to A for life". A life estate was also created by default when the grantor intended to create a fee simple estate or a fee tail estate but failed to use the correct words of limitation. The statutory changes in New South Wales, Victoria, Queensland and Western Australia described above, permitting the creation of fee simple estates in the absence of the use of the correct words of limitation, have indirectly resulted in a situation where a grantor must now use clear words to create a life estate (for example, "to A for life"). The creation of a life estate by default in A would now be rare in these jurisdictions.[55] In Tasmania, however, there is one area where a life estate, created by default, may still arise. As stated above, it is still possible in Tasmania to create a fee tail over general law land but it appears that only particular forms of words will suffice. These are the strict common law form of words, "to A and the heirs of his body" or like terminology and the expressions "to A in tail", "to A in tail female" and "to A in tail male".[56] If the grantor uses a form of words insufficient to create a fee tail estate, for example "to A in fee tail" it is suggested that A obtains a life estate only. In South Australia, where there have been no statutory modifications, the life estate may arise pursuant to a direct grant, or by default, where the grantor intends to create a fee simple estate or a fee tail estate but fails to use the correct words of limitation.

(ii) Dispositions by will

[2.38] A specific devise of the life estate, for example, "to A for life" passes the life estate. Life estates created by default were less common where the disposition was in a will. As the courts did not insist upon the use of the correct words of limitation to create a fee simple estate and a fee tail estate, a life estate passed only if the testator failed to show a clear intention to pass the fee simple or the fee tail. The statutory reversal of the onus of proof described above, now means that a life estate is only created in a disposition in a will if there is a clear intention to create a life estate.

(d) Equitable interests under the Torrens system

[2.39] It has been stated above that the rules demanding strict compliance with the correct words of limitation have never been applied to the creation or passing of legal interests in land falling under the Torrens system of land registration: see above [2.32]. Statutory provisions set out particular forms and documents which must be used for this purpose. As under the general law land system, however, equitable

---

55. It is important to note that the changes in some jurisdictions occurred gradually and the life estate by default did not disappear at any particular point in time. Further, in Queensland and Western Australia dispositions which would have been ineffective to create fees tail, e.g. "to A in tail" may not take effect as fees simple, but rather take effect as life estates by default.

56. *Conveyancing and Law of Property Act* 1884 (Tas.), s. 65, after 1 January 1884.

interests may exist in land falling under the Torrens system and the question has arisen as to whether the strict requirement of correct words of limitation applies to documents creating or passing such equitable interests. Conflicting approaches to this problem have been taken by Australian courts. In *Re Austin's Settlement; Strachan v. Austin*,[57] Dean J. held that the principle expressed in *Sexton v. Horton* applied to equitable interests under the Torrens system. His Honour rejected the argument that because the legal estate under the Torrens system could be transferred without words of inheritance, the equitable estate could be transferred in the same way because equity follows the law.[58] Dean J. referred to the fact that the Torrens statutes do not make express provision for the transfer of equitable interests and stated that: "[I]t would, therefore, . . . be impossible for equity to follow the law in such a case and accordingly the freedom given in relation to the transfer of the legal fee simple cannot be extended to transfers of an equitable fee simple which remains in the same position as before."[59] In contrast, Roper J. in *Carroll v. Chew*[60] stated that: "[T]he transferor of the legal estate having being freed from the purely technical requirements as to the use of words of limitation it appears to me that the creator of equitable estates should have the same freedom."[61] One of the aims of the Torrens system is to ensure that interests may be alienated in a simple and certain manner. At least where the grantor of an equitable interest accurately describes the equitable estate to be transferred, for example, "to A for an equitable estate in fee simple", it is suggested that a non-compliance with strict words of limitation should not invalidate the grant.[62] Nevertheless, the matter remains unclear.

(e) The rule in Shelley's case

[2.40] The rule in *Shelley's Case*[63] was a notorious one and provided many difficulties for conveyancers: see below [7.09]. It applied strictly to grants inter vivos and dispositions by will. The rule provided that a grant "to A for life, remainder to his heirs" or "to A for life, remainder to the heirs of his body" created immediately a fee simple in A in the first example and a fee tail in A in the second example. This was despite the clear intention of the grantor that A was to obtain a life estate only and the remainder in fee simple or fee tail was to be vested in his heirs. The heirs acquired no interest as the words used which purported to give them

---

57. [1960] V.R. 532.
58. [1960] V.R. 532 at 534.
59. [1960] V.R. 532 at 534. See also *Re Bennett (decd)* [1951] Q.S.R. 202.
60. (1946) 47 S.R. (N.S.W.) 229.
61. (1946) 47 S.R. (N.S.W.) 229 at 232.
62. This suggestion was made in Note (1952) 25 A.L.J. 683 at 684. It is noted, however, that the author of the note did not consider that the facts of *Carroll v. Chew* should have resulted in the grantee obtaining an equitable fee simple. The actual words used were, in his view, insufficiently accurate to describe an equitable fee simple ("upon trust for A if and when she shall attain the age of 21 years").
63. (1581) 1 Co. Rep. 93b; 76 E.R. 206.

a grant were construed as words of limitation.[64] For various reasons[65] the rule survived and clearly outlasted any usefulness it ever had.

In New South Wales, Victoria, Queensland and Western Australia the rule has now been abolished.[66]

4. Determinable and Conditional Interests

[2.41] Each of the estates could be further limited by the imposition in the grant or disposition of factors designed to limit the duration of the estate in particular circumstances. These limits were permitted by placing a determinable limitation on the grant or by inserting a condition subsequent to the grant. The difference between a determinable limitation and conditional limitation is not easy to define precisely, but very different consequences result from a finding that grant is determinable or conditional.

(a) Determinable interests

[2.42] A determinable interest is one which terminates on the occurrence or non-occurrence of a specified event. In the case of a determinable fee simple, the specified event must not be one which is bound to happen in the future as it is an essential characteristic of the fee simple that it may last forever. "The (determinable) limitation marks the bounds or compass of the estate, and the time of its continuance."[67] It sets out the type of estate and marks its extent by setting out the time for which it will last. As Megarry and Wade state: "the determining event in a determinable fee itself sets the limit for the estate first granted."[68] Where the grantor creates a determinable fee simple, he or she has a possibility of reverter as there is a possibility that the estate will revert to the grantor. If the determining event does occur, the fee simple reverts to the grantor or to her or his estate if the grantor is dead. It was not possible at common law to create a fee simple after a determinable fee simple (or a determinable fee tail): see below **[7.04]**. Thus, a limitation "to A and his heirs until A ceases to reside in Malvern and then to B and his heirs" was ineffective to give B any interest in the land even when the terminating factor had occurred.[69] Statutory provisions have now ensured, however, that the possibility of reverter is an alienable right both inter vivos and by testamentary disposition.[70]

---

64. Even if the grant were "to A for life, remainder to B for life and then remainder to A's heirs", the rule applied so that A obtained a life estate in possession and a fee simple remainder to follow the life estate of B.
65. See **[7.09]** and Sackville and Neave, p. 159.
66. General Law Statutes: N.S.W.: s. 17, after 1 July 1920; Vic.: s. 130 after 18 December 1929; Qld: s. 28 after 1 December 1975; W.A.: s. 27 after 1 August 1969. In South Australia and Tasmania, it appears that the rule continues to exist: see below **[7.18]**.
67. See *Zapletal v. Wright* [1957] Tas S.R. 211 at 218 per Crisp J. quoting from *Preston on Estates*, Vol. 1, p. 49.
68. Megarry and Wade, p. 69.
69. If a grantor wishes to make such a grant effectively, the limitation must be in the form of an equitable future interest. See below Chapter 7 for a discussion of the legal contingent remainder rules and equity's role in the area of future interests.
70. See above, fn. 13 and below, fn. 102. See below **[7.17]**.

A grantor may create a determinable life interest. In this case, it is possible for the grantor to follow the determinable life interest with a gift over to another person if the determining event occurs. A grant "to A for life, or until he becomes bankrupt and then to B and his heirs" would be an effective one.[71] A leasehold estate for a term of years may also be the subject of a determinable limitation. An example is: "to A for three years or until he ceases his law studies at the University of Melbourne."

Once the determining event can no longer occur, the grant becomes an absolute one. Sometimes, the determining limitation may be a void one.[72] If it is, the grant fails entirely for there is then no proper limitation of the estate. The terminating limitation marks the extent of the estate, and if it is declared void the grant fails altogether for to sever the determining factor from the grant and treat it as an absolute grant would be to change completely the nature of the estate intended, an estate intended to last only until the occurrence or non-occurrence of a particular event.

Although reference must always be made to the basic principle described above, the use of words in a grant such as "while", "as long as", "until" and "during" tend to suggest a determinable interest rather than a conditional interest.

(b) Conditional interests

[2.43] A conditional interest comprises the grant of an estate, for example, a fee simple, which has some condition subsequent attached to it pursuant to which the grantee's fee simple may be cut short. For example, a grant "to A and his heirs on condition that A does not marry B" gives A a fee simple estate which may be lost if he marries B. The conditional subsequent "has its operation in defeating the estate before it attains the boundary or has completed the space of time described by the limitation".[73] It is an extra clause added to a limitation of a complete estate, for example, a fee simple estate.[74] A passage from Chesire sums up succinctly the difference between the determinable interest and the conditional interest. "[I]f the terminating event is an integral and necessary part of the formula from which the size of the interest is to be ascertained, the result is the creation of the determinable interest; but if the terminating event is external to the limitation, if it is a divided clause from the grant, the interest granted is an interest upon a condition."[75]

If the event set out in the condition subsequent occurs, the grantor or her or his estate has a right of re-entry. It is not until the grantor or her or his successor exercises this right of re-entry, however (by gaining possession through a court order or by physically taking possession), that the interest of the grantee terminates. This is to be compared to the

---

71. A common form of determinable life interest takes the form of a protective trust.
72. See below [2.44]-[2.47] for a discussion of this matter. Note that limitations in determinable interests are less likely to be declared void than conditions subsequent in conditional interests.
73. See *Zapletal v. Wright* [1957] Tas. S.R. 211 at 218 per Crisp J. quoting from *Preston on Estates*, Vol. 1, p. 49.
74. See Megarry and Wade, p. 69.
75. Cheshire and Burn, p. 347.

situation where the event set out in the determining limitation occurs. In this case, as shown above, the estate automatically reverts to the grantor.

The use of words such as "on condition that", "provided that", "but if" tend to suggest the creation of a conditional interest.

As in the case of the determinable fee simple, it was not possible to create a fee simple to come into operation after a conditional fee simple. Neither was it possible for the grantor to alienate the right of re-entry. However, statutory provisions now ensure that the grantor can dispose of the right of re-entry.[76] In contrast to the position relating to determinable interests, at common law it was not possible to create a remainder to come into effect after a life estate defeasible by a condition subsequent. A grant "To A for life on condition that if she marries then to B and his heirs" failed to give B any interest upon the marriage of A. Such a disposition conflicted with several rules, one of which was a legal contingent remainder rule that prohibited a remainder from cutting short a prior particular estate.[77] A disposition in the form of the example could now be effected by placing the dispositions in trusts and creating a future equitable interest in B. As will be seen later, future equitable interests are not bound by the stringent common law rules which governed the creation of legal future interests: see below [2.57] and [7.11].

An estate granted subject to a condition subsequent must be distinguished from an interest which is granted subject to a condition precedent. The condition precedent relates to a condition which marks the time for the beginning of an estate: for example, a grant "to A and his heirs when A reaches 21 years" contains a condition precedent to the estate coming into being. This type of interest is dealt with later: see below [2.49]-[2.50] and [7.06].

(c) Void conditions

[2.44] Several types of conditions subsequent are void when attached to the grant of an interest. If the condition is held to be void, the condition is severed and the grant becomes absolute. Conditions which are contrary to public policy, conditions which are uncertain and conditions which are repugnant to the interest granted, are void.[78]

If the void limitation appears in a determinable limitation the whole grant fails and there is a reversion to the grantor. The determinable limitation sets the bounds of the estate and to sever such a limitation would be to treat the grant as absolute and would change the nature of the estate granted. Very different results ensue then depending upon whether the limitation is considered to take the form of a conditional or determinable one. In some instances, limitations which are void when appearing as a conditional limitation are valid when used in a determinable limitation.[79] For instance, determinable limitations providing that a gift is to last "until marriage", "until the bankruptcy of

---

76. See above, fn. 13 and below, fn. 102.
77. See generally, Cheshire and Burn, p. 349.
78. Ibid., pp. 349ff.
79. E.g. restraints on alienation: see below [2.46].

the grantee" or "until the grantee purports to alienate" will be valid as the limitations set the absolute bounds of the estate. Nevertheless, even a determinable limitation which is to operate on the occurrence of a stated event, and which is against public policy, would fail.

(i) Conditions contrary to public policy

[2.45] Any condition which is illegal, immoral or otherwise conflicts with the interest of the community is contrary to public policy, and therefore, void. Examples of such conditions are many and varied. Conditions in restraint of marriage are often encountered and with respect to realty,[80] it may be said that a condition in partial restraint of marriage is good. For example, a condition prohibiting marriage with a Scotsman or a Papist is valid.[81] However, a total prohibition on marriage is void unless the object of the condition is to provide for the grantee whilst unmarried rather than simply to restrain marriage.[82] Further, such a condition is good if the condition is to prevent a second or subsequent marriage.[83]

A condition which encourages the separation or divorce of a married couple is void as being contrary to public policy.[84] It has also been held that a condition which encourages extra-marital cohabitation is void.[85] The classes of acts which are said to be against the policy of the law are capable of change in the light of changing social conditions and it is arguable that a condition encouraging extra-marital cohabitation would no longer be considered a void one.[86]

A condition which is designed to separate a parent from her or his child is void.[87] A condition forbidding a change of religion, at least in an adult grantee, is valid.[88]

(ii) Conditions repugnant to the interest granted

[2.46] A condition which purports to place a substantial restraint on alienation by the grantee is void as "the power of alienation is necessarily and inseparably incidental to ownership".[89] Thus, conditions prohibiting

---

80. See Cheshire and Burn, p. 352 for the stricter law pertaining to conditions in restraint of marriage where the property involved is personalty.
81. *Perrin v. Lyon* (1808) 9 East. 170; 103 E.R. 538; *Duggan v. Kelly* (1848) 10 Ir. Eq. Rep. 473.
82. *Jones v. Jones* (1876) 1 Q.B.D. 279.
83. *Newton v. Marsden* (1862) 2 J. & H. 356; 70 E.R. 1094; *Allan v. Jackson* (1875) 1 Ch. D. 399. Note also that there can be no general restraint on a tenant in tail as such a restraint would be repugnant to the interest.
84. *Re Moore* (1888) 39 Ch. D. 116; *Re Johnson's Will Trusts* [1967] Ch. 387; [1967] 1 All E.R. 152. Cf. *Re Lovell* [1920] 1 Ch. 122 where the parties are already separated.
85. *Zapletal v. Wright* [1957] Tas S.R. 211.
86. See *Andrews v. Parker* [1973] Qd R. 93; *Seidler v. Schallhofer* [1982] 2 N.S.W.L.R. 80. See also the legislation governing property disputes between de facto couples in New South Wales (*De Facto Relationships Act* 1984) and Victoria (*Property Law (Amendment) Act* 1987). Such legislation gives recognition to the de facto status and is indicative of a change in prevailing attitudes to the status.
87. *Re Sandbrook* [1912] 2 Ch. 471; *Re Piper* [1946] 2 All F.R. 503.
88. *Blathwayt v. Lord Cawley* [1976] A.C. 397; [1975] 3 All E.R. 625.
89. Cheshire and Burn, p. 349.

alienation during a person's life[90] or alienation by mortgage[91] or will[92] are void. Further illustrations of void conditions are conditions prohibiting the alienation of the property for a certain period or to anyone other than a named person.[93] Nevertheless, some conditions in partial or limited restraint of alienation have been held to be valid. Two cases which are commonly contrasted are *Re Macleay*[94] and *Re Rosher*.[95] In *Re Macleay*, a devise to X "on condition that he never sells it outside the family" was held to be valid as being only a limited restraint on alienation. In *Re Rosher*, there was a devise to the testator's son in fee simple, with a proviso that if the son, his heirs or devisees wished to sell the property in the lifetime of the testator's wife, she should have the option to purchase the property for £3,000 (which was considerably less than its value). Pearson J. held that this restraint on alienation was void even though it was only partial in its scope and limited in time. As these cases illustrate, it is difficult to reconcile the existing authorities, and there appears to be no firm principle which can be applied to determine with certainty whether a particular partial restraint is valid or void.

In the same way as conditions restraining alienation are void as being repugnant to the concept of ownership, so too have conditions attempting to exclude the bankruptcy laws been held to be void.[96] The operation of the bankruptcy laws may be seen as an alienation of ownership, albeit an involuntary one.

It is important to note, however, that in the case of life interests subject to a limitation that the grantee must not alienate or may only hold the interest until he or she becomes bankrupt, the limitation is more likely to be considered valid. The courts treat the limitation as a determinable one rather than a conditional one if at all possible. This makes an important difference as the courts interpret conditions subsequent more strictly than determinable limitations and are likely to hold them to be void. A condition subsequent gives rise to a right of forfeiture and the courts insist upon the circumstances in which forfeiture will occur being clear and precise. More specifically, in the context of limitations regarding alienation and bankruptcy, a determinable limitation is not repugnant to the interest granted in the same way as is a condition subsequent. For example, a grant "to A for life until he becomes bankrupt" (a determinable life estate) sets the bounds of the estate granted: the estate is only intended to last until A's bankruptcy and the occurrence of the determining event does not cut short a larger interest or take away any incidents of the estate granted. Such a grant is valid. In contrast, a grant "to A for life on condition that on his bankruptcy he forfeits the interest" purports to grant A an absolute life estate and then to take away one of

90. *Re Rosher* (1884) 26 Ch. D. 801; *Corbett v. Corbett* (1888) 14 P.D. 7.
91. *Ware v. Cann* (1830) 10 B. & C. 433; 109 E.R. 511.
92. *Re Dunstan* [1918] 2 Ch. 304.
93. *Attwater v. Attwater* (1853) 18 Beav. 330; 52 E.R. 131; *Re Cockerill* [1929] 2 Ch. 131. See further illustrations in Megarry and Wade, p. 72.
94. (1875) L.R. 20 Eq. 106.
95. (1884) 26 Ch. D. 801.
96. *Re Machu* (1882) 21 Ch. D. 838.

its incidents, liability for debts. The condition is void and is severed from the grant.[97]

(iii) Uncertain conditions

[2.47]   In view of the fact that a condition subsequent gives rise to a right of forfeiture and possible defeat of an absolute and vested estate, the courts have insisted upon the condition being clear and precise in wording and in operation. If it is uncertain, the condition will be declared void and severed from the main grant. For example, conditions requiring the grantee "to be a member" of the Church of England,[98] restraining marriage with a person "not of Jewish parentage and of the Jewish faith",[99] and requiring the grantee "to reside in Canada", [100] have been declared void as being insufficiently certain.[101]

5. Remainders and Reversions

[2.48]   The doctrine of estates recognised and indorsed the concept of the creation of successive interests in land, and thereby recognised the fact that future interests in land could exist: see below Chapter 7 for a detailed discussion of future interests. At first, the common law recognised two types of future interests: the estate in remainder and the estate in reversion. An estate in possession gives a present right to possession of the land. The future interest, whether it be a remainder or a reversion, is one which gives a right to possession of the land in the future. The reversion comprises the residue of the grantor's estate when he or she has granted a lesser portion of the interest to another person. For example, if X, the fee simple owner, grants a life estate to A, X has a reversion, a present right to future enjoyment and possession of the property upon A's death. During his life, A has an estate in possession, a life estate. A remainder is the grant of a future interest to a person who was not previously entitled to the land. For example, if X grants his fee simple estate to A for life and then to B and his heirs, A has a life estate in possession and B has a fee simple in remainder. B, or his estate if he is dead, will be entitled to possession of the property upon A's death. As in the example given with respect to the reversion, B's interest is a present right to future enjoyment. His interest is a future one only in the sense that the right to possession of the property will arise in the future: his right is vested in interest immediately and exists as an estate during A's life. B has an interest in the land which he can alienate inter vivos or dispose of by will.

[2.49]   Future interests may be vested or contingent. Vested interests may be "vested in interest" or "vested in possession". If an interest is "vested in possession", as are the life estates of A in the examples above, the interest is clearly not a future one: a present right to possession of the land is given. If the interest is one which is "vested in interest", but not

---

97. See Cheshire and Burn, p. 351 and Megarry and Wade, p. 1178. See generally Chapter 8.
98. *Re Tegg* [1936] 2 All E.R. 878.
99. *Clayton v. Ramsden* [1943] A.C. 320; [1943] 1 All E.R. 116; *Re Krawitz Will Trusts* [1959] 1 W.L.R. 1192; [1959] 3 All E.R. 793.
100. *Sifton v. Sifton* [1938] A.C. 656; [1938] 3 All E.R. 425.
101. For further examples, see Cheshire and Burn, pp. 355-356.

in possession, as are the reversion and the remainder in the examples above, the interest is termed a future one as the right to possession will arise in the future. Nevertheless, as explained above, the interest is a currently existing one in the property even though the right to possession is postponed. The contingent interest is quite different and in theory, is not an estate in land at all. It gives no right at all to the recipient until the occurrence of some particular future event. Thus if, X grants land to A for life, remainder to B in fee simple if B has attained the age of 21 years at A's death, B has a contingent remainder. B has only the possibility of an estate. The right is neither vested in possession nor in interest and B (or his estate) would not gain any estate if, at A's death, B was not 21 years or more. Effectively, there is a condition precedent to B's right becoming a vested interest. (In these circumstances, the estate reverts to the grantor, X, or his estate.) At common law, B the holder of a contingent remainder had no right to assign the expectancy. Statute has now made assignment possible.[102] If B attained the age of 21 years before A's death, B's contingent remainder is converted into a vested remainder.

A future interest is said to be vested, rather than contingent, if two criteria are met. First, the identity of the person who is to take must be clear. Secondly, there must not be any condition precedent to the interest taking effect in possession other than the regular and natural termination of the prior particular estate. Usually it is a simple task to determine if a remainder is vested or contingent. Sometimes, however, the wording in the grant is unclear. In these circumstances, the courts lean in favour of holding the remainder to be vested.

[2.50] The common law evolved very strict rules for the creation of future interests. Most of these rules concerned contingent remainders. These rules are discussed in Chapter 7. Because of these rules, contingent remainders were very precarious interests. Although techniques evolved to prevent their destruction and although statutory intervention rendered them less precarious, they remained uncertain in various ways: see Chapter 7. In the meantime, a vital development in English land law had taken place: the fragmentation of estates between legal and beneficial ownership. Inter alia, this development made the creation and durability of future interests simpler and more certain. It has led to a situation where legal contingent remainders, with all their uncertainties, are rarely used today. For the most part, future interests are now created in equity, rather than at law.

IV.   THE DEVELOPMENT OF THE USE AND THE TRUST: THE CREATION OF THE EQUITABLE INTEREST

[2.51] From as early as the Middle Ages, it was becoming clear that the doctrine of tenure and the doctrine of estates alone could not forever

---

102. *Deed*—General Law Statutes: N.S.W.: s. 50(1); Vic.: s. 19(1)(a); Qld: s. 31; S.A.: s. 10(a) (wills too); Tas.: s. 80(1); quaere W.A. *Wills*—N.S.W.: *Wills Probate and Administration Act* 1898, s. 5; Vic.: *Wills Act* 1958, s. 5, Qld. *Succession Act* 1981, s. 7(2)(b); S.A.: *Wills Act* 1936, s. 4; W.A.: *Wills Act* 1970, s. 6; Tas.: *Wills Act* 1840, s. 1.

provide the sole basis of land law in England. The social and economic conditions were changing and the many fetters on the enjoyment of a freehold estate at common law gradually became less appropriate to prevailing conditions and were a source of resentment to freeholders. In order to understand the development of the modern-day trust, it is necessary to consider some of the stringent conditions placed on the freeholder which led the freeholder to consider alternative ways of dealing with her or his interest.

1. Disadvantages of the Common Law

(a) Rules relating to conveyancing

[2.52] To ensure that there was no doubt as to who held the freehold estate in land, the common law insisted that every conveyance of a freehold estate be public and formal. The effective enforcement of feudal dues depended upon the lord who had the right to collect the dues knowing exactly who was seised of the land. Thus, every conveyance of a freehold estate had to be "effected by an open and public delivery of seisin, either upon or within view of the land conveyed".[103] Those residing within the area could then provide evidence of the identity of the current freeholder. This method of conveyance was called *feoffment by livery of seisin* (the important part was the delivery). This strict rule had the consequence that a freeholder, who for valid reasons wished to transact a conveyance that was not public to the world at large, was unable to do so.

(b) Inability to dispose of estate by will

[2.53] As stated above, the common law did not permit a freeholder to dispose of an estate by will. The estate automatically passed to the heir (eldest son or other heir) and any purported disposition by will to another person had no effect. Although the freeholder could alienate the interest during lifetime, this method did not aid the freeholder who wished to retain the estate up until death. Further, if the fee simple holder died without an heir, the land automatically escheated to the overlord.

(c) Feudal burdens

[2.54] The freeholder was subjected to many, heavy feudal dues. The most burdensome feudal dues were payable upon the death of the freeholder. For example, feudal dues named "relief" were payable to the overlord by the heir before the heir could succeed to the land. Further, in order to prevent the loss of feudal dues which resulted if land were conveyed to a body which never died, for example, a religious body, any lands conveyed to such a body were forfeited to the overlord.[104]

The fetters referred to above stimulated interest in finding other ways of dealing with land and it was outside the traditional bounds of the common law that the answer was found.

103. Cheshire and Burn, p. 40.
104. *Statutes of Mortmain* 1279 and 1290 (Eng.).

2. Origin and Development of the Use

[2.55]   From its inception, the Chancery was involved in administering the rules of the common law. It was the Chancery which issued writs enabling actions to be commenced at common law. From the beginning of the 14th century, the forms of writs which could be issued were clearly defined and set. More and more frequently, a person with a legitimate complaint could not find a writ which fitted the cause of action and therefore, could not obtain a remedy in the common law courts. Such a person could, however, petition the King directly in an attempt to obtain a remedy. Despite the creation of the common law courts in the 11th and 12th centuries, the King had retained a residual judicial power and it was to this power that a person turned when there was no remedy available at common law. Originally, the King's Council, of which the Chancellor was a member, heard those special petitions but by the end of the 14th century, the King and his council had delegated the task to the Chancellor. The Chancery Council (the Court of Chancery later) with the Chancellor presiding, heard the petitions. The judicial power of the Chancery was clearly recognised by the end of the 15th century and the rules administered by it became known as the rules of equity. In fact, the "rules" varied markedly at first and were apt to change from Chancellor to Chancellor. Gradually, the Chancery began using the common law system of binding precedent and by the end of the 17th century a set of rules in the true sense had developed. Thus, a system evolved whereby two sets of rules, the rules of common law and the rules of equity, existed side by side and were enforced in two different courts. It is important to note that the Chancellor did not have, or seek to have, jurisdiction over all inequities existing in the legal system. Rather, the Chancellor's jurisdiction was confined to situations where the common law could not act because, for example, there was no recognised writ the plaintiff could use for the type of damage he or she had suffered. Equity did not attempt to destroy the rules of common law but only to affect the way in which they operated.

[2.56]   In the area of land law, the Chancellor played a vital role. It was his enforcement of the "use" which gave rise to the distinction between legal and equitable interests in land. In order to avoid the fetters created by the common law, the freeholder began to employ the use.[105] It operated in the following way. The freeholder conveyed the land to a trusted person with the proviso that that person held the land, not for her or his own use and benefit, but for the use and enjoyment of the grantor. The person taking the legal estate pursuant to the conveyance was called the "feoffee to uses" (in modern terms the trustee) and the person entitled to the use of the land was called the cestui que use (in modern terms, the beneficiary). Thus, for example if B, the holder of a fee simple estate conveyed his interest "to A and his heirs to the use of B and his heirs", A was the feoffee to uses and B was the cestui que use.

[2.57]   The common law recognised A alone as having an interest in the land. At common law, A was seised of the land and if A refused to honour

---

105. See Cheshire and Burn, p. 43.

the agreement and permit B the use of the land, B had no remedy at common law. If the device proceeded as planned and the feoffee to uses permitted the cestui que use to use and enjoy the land, the advantages for the cestui que use, the former freeholder, were many. First, the freeholder effectively gained the power to dispose of the estate by will. During his lifetime, the freeholder, A, conveyed the land to B to the use of himself, A, for life and the remainder to such uses as set out in his will. Secondly, the conveyance of land to uses provided a means of evading heavy feudal burdens payable on the death of the freeholder. By conveying the land to two or more feoffees to joint uses, and preventing the number of feoffees from falling below two, these dues were avoided. Upon the death of one of the joint holders of an estate, the land vested in the surviving holder(s) by survivorship, not by inheritance and therefore feudal dues payable on death were inapplicable. The former freeholder, the cestui que use after the conveyance, possessed the land but no dues were payable on his death as he was not seised of the land. Thirdly, the conveyance to uses permitted a form of conveyancing not bound by the strict common law rules of conveyancing. Finally, it became possible to create future interests which were not bound by the strict legal remainder rules: see below [7.11].

[2.58]   The obvious disadvantage for the cestui que use was the inability to enforce the use against the feoffee in the common law courts. From the beginning of the 15th century, the Court of Chancery began to protect the cestui que use and enforce the use against the feoffee. The Chancery insisted that the feoffees exercise their legal rights in accordance with the use. Equity acted in personam specifically against the feoffee who refused to hold the land on behalf of the beneficiaries.[106] The use was enforced against the heirs or devisees of the feoffee as the Chancery took the view that the conscience of such persons was affected in the same way as the original feoffee. Eventually, a purchaser of the legal estate from the feoffee, who took with notice of the use, was also required by the Chancery to hold the land for the benefit of the cestui que use.[107] A situation was reached whereby the equitable rights of the cestui que use were enforceable against persons generally, except a purchaser of the legal estate for value without notice of the use. Thus, equitable rights, originally enforceable in personam against the feoffee, arguably became, or became akin to, rights in rem, that is, rights normally enforceable against third parties generally.[108] These equitable rights became a new type of proprietary interest, commonly called the equitable interest.

[2.59]   The Chancellor, by his enforcement of the use in the manner described effectively created a new form of interest in land, the equitable estate. As it was his own creation he could have permitted the creation of different types of equitable interests or estates unknown to the common law. For the most part, however, the Chancellor chose to accept and follow

---

106. See generally Cheshire and Burn, pp. 44-45.
107. See Chapter 3 for a discussion of the doctrine of notice.
108. There is still dispute as to whether equitable rights are properly termed rights in rem or rights in personam. See Spry, p. 36. Meagher, Gummow and Lehane, pp. 89-90; Jackson, *Principles of Property Law* (Law Book Co. Ltd, Sydney, 1967), pp. 83-85.

the common law as to the types of interests and estates which could be created. Thus, equity adopted the doctrine of estates so that it was possible, for example, to have an equitable fee simple, an equitable fee tail, an equitable life interest and an equitable leasehold interest.[109] Although equity adopted much of the common law without modification, there were a number of clear examples where equity modified the common law. For instance, in the area of future interests, the legal remainder rules were not in general adopted and thus equitable remainders were not as liable to destruction. Further, there was the capacity for equity to permit the creation of interests unattainable at common law and equity did, and continues to, use this capacity from time to time. The creation of remaiders, reversions and life interests in leasehold estates, the estate contract and the mortgagor's equity of redemption are examples of equity acting in this manner.[110] A more recent example is that of the restrictive covenant, an interest in land which can exist in equity alone.[111]

[2.60] Effectively a grant "to A and his heirs to the use of B and his heirs" gave A the legal estate and B the equitable estate. A's holding of the legal estate gave A no rights to the use and enjoyment of the land: it is often said that A had the bare legal estate. It was B, the beneficial owner, who was entitled to the use and enjoyment of the land and any profits arising from it.

3. The Statute of Uses

[2.61] The King, being at the top of the feudal pyramid, was the person who was bound to lose more than any other person from the reduction in the payment of feudal dues brought about by the introduction and enforcement of the use. At Henry VIII's instigation the *Statute of Uses* was passed in 1535 to vest the legal estate and seisin in the cestui que use. Upon the death of the cestui que use, feudal burdens would again be payable. Thus, in a conveyance "to A and his heirs to the use of B and his heirs", B took the legal fee simple and A obtained nothing at all. Effectively, the statute *executed* the use. Before the *Statute of Uses*, such a grant resulted in A obtaining the legal fee simple and B, the equitable fee simple.

The aim of the statute was to abolish uses. This aim was not fully realised as not all uses were executed by the statute and there were some instances where the feoffee was required by the Chancellor to perform the obligations set out in the grant. It was one of these instances which led to the general re-emergence of the equitable interest and the development of the modern day trust of land. The uses not executed by the statute included the following.

(a) Leaseholds

[2.62] The statute applied to execute a use only where one person was seised to the use of another person. If the grant were "to A for 20 years

---

109. A further example is that equity used the common law rules of descent.
110. See Chapters 6 and 18 for a detailed discussion of these interests.
111. *Tulk v. Moxhay* (1848) 2 Ph. 774; 41 E.R. 1143; see below Chapter 18.

to the use of B for 10 years", the Chancellor enforced the use in favour of B. A held a legal leasehold estate for 20 years and B held an equitable leasehold estate for ten years. The grantor, the landlord remained seised of the land throughout the term, A being entitled to possession only. That is, A was not seised of the land to the use of B, and therefore, the grant did not fall within the purview of the statute.

(b) Active uses

[2.63] The statute did not execute the use where the feoffee had active duties to perform. For example, if the feoffee were seised to collect rents and profits and hold and pay them to the use of the cestui que use the Chancellor continued to enforce the use: the feoffee held the legal interest and the cestui que use held the equitable interest.

(c) Seised to own use

[2.64] Where a person was seised to her or his own use, the statute did not execute the use. The feoffee held the legal fee simple pursuant to the common law.

(d) Use upon a use

[2.65] Before the *Statute of Uses*, it had been held that it was not possible to have a use upon a use. In a grant "to A and heirs to the use of B and heirs to the use of C and his heirs", A took the legal fee simple, B took the equitable fee simple and C took nothing. The use in favour of C was void as it was repugnant to the use in favour of B. Soon after the enactment of the *Statute of Uses*, it was held in *Tyrel's Case* that the statute did not execute the second use. Thus, in the example above, B took the legal fee simple and C took nothing. As there was no valid use in favour of C before 1535, there was nothing the statute could execute.

4. Re-emergence of the Equitable Interest

[2.66] The reason for the *Statute of Uses* had been to control the loss of revenue by the King. By 1660, feudal dues had become of little relevance (see generally above [2.03])[112] and the reason for the desire to destroy the equitable interest had disappeared. At about this time, the chancellor began to recognise again the equitable interest and he did so by enforcing the use upon a use as an equitable interest. In a grant, "to A and his heirs, to the use of B and his heirs to the use of C and his heirs", B took the legal fee simple (the *Statute of Uses* having executed the use) and C was viewed as holding the equitable interest. C's equitable interest was equivalent to the equitable interest created by one single use before the *Statute of Uses*. The distinction between the legal interest and the equitable interest had thus re-emerged. In order to avoid confusion, the terminology used to describe the second use was changed and a grant in which B was intended to take the legal fee simple and C the equitable fee simple was worded "to A and his heirs to the use of B and his heirs on

112. Military tenures had been abolished: *Statute of Tenures* 1660.

trust for C and his heirs''. Eventually, A's name was removed altogether and the words in a grant, "unto and to the use of B and his heirs on trust for C and his heirs'' were effective to give B the legal fee simple and C the equitable fee simple.[113] B, the feoffee to uses become known as the trustee and C, the cestui que use, became known as the cestui que trust or the beneficiary.

5. Statute of Wills 1540

[2.67]   One of the effects of the *Statute of Uses* was that feudal dues were again payable on the death of the cestui que use who after the statute held the legal estate. It was also thought that the statute resulted in the cestui que use, as the holder of a legal estate and subject to the common law rules, being unable to devise the interest. This part of the *Statute of Uses* was so vehemently criticised that in 1540 the *Statute of Wills* restored the power of the cestui qui use to devise land. Tenants of land under socage tenure were able to devise the whole of their lands. No feudal incidents of value were payable on this type of tenure. Tenants who held land by knight service could devise two-thirds of their land. Feudal dues were payable by the devisee if the devisee were also the heir. The *Statute of Tenures* in 1660 effectively changed all freehold tenure into socage tenure and it was from this time, that absolute power to dispose of land by will was obtained.[114]

6. Repeal of the Statute of Uses in New South Wales, Victoria and Queensland

[2.68]   In New South Wales,[115] Victoria[116] and Queensland,[117] the *Statute of Uses* has been repealed. Effectively the position in these States has returned to the pre 1535 period in England. Accordingly, to create a trust of land and ensure that A (the trustee) takes the legal fee simple and B (the beneficiary) takes the equitable fee simple, the disposition is worded simply "to A in fee simple on trust for B in fee simple".[118]

In South Australia, Western Australia and Tasmania, a grant whereby one person is to take the legal fee simple and hold it for the use and enjoyment of another who is to take the equitable fee simple (a trust of land) is still effected by the old terminology "unto and to the use of B on trust for C".

[2.69]   Finally, it is important to note that statutory provisions in all jurisdictions provide that in a will, the whole of the legal estate of the

---

113. See Cheshire and Burn, p. 55 for a detailed analysis of how this was achieved.
114. See Sackville and Neave, p. 207 on the question of whether the *Statute of Uses* executed uses in wills. *Baker v. White* (1875) L.R. 20 Eq. 166.
115. N.S.W.: *Imperial Acts Application Act* 1969, s. 8.
116. Vic.: *Imperial Acts Application Act* 1980, s. 5.
117. Qld: *Property Law Act* 1974, ss 3, 7, Sch. 6, Pt 1.
118. In the pre 1535 terminology the wording would have been "to A and his heirs, to the use of B and his heirs". See also *Property Law Act* 1958 (Vic.), s. 19A discussed in **[7.22]**.

testator vests in her or his executor upon the testator's death.[119] The devisee obtains the beneficial interest and can only acquire the legal estate when the executor conveys the land to her or him. After payment of all debts, the executor is under a duty to carry out the instructions of the testator, but it is not until the legal estate is formally conveyed to the devisee that he or she so obtains it.[120]

7. Equitable Remedies

[2.70]   The common law developed a limited range of remedies. These remedies included orders for damages, for the recovery of land and for a liquidated sum due as a debt. A plaintiff who demonstrated that the criteria for a particular cause of action existed, was automatically entitled as of right to the appropriate legal remedy.[121] In contrast, the equitable remedies were always discretionary. For instance, even where the plaintiff proves that a cause of action exists, equity may refuse to assist her or him if it would be unconscionable in the circumstances to grant a remedy. The use of this discretionary power is exercised according to settled principles which have developed over the years.[122] For example, a plaintiff who has acted dishonestly ("equity assists only those who come with clean hands"), delayed inordinately the bringing of the action ("he who seeks equity must do equity") or instituted a trivial claim, may be deprived of the benefit of an equitable remedy.

[2.71]   The main forms of equitable relief are specific performance and the injunction.[123] Specific performance is an order directing a person to carry out her or his obligation. Generally, the plaintiff must establish the existence of a contract enforceable at law.[124] Specific performance may then be granted in two instances. First, where the contract is executory, the plaintiff may seek specific performance in order to make the other party perform her or his side of the bargain.[125] Secondly, where the contract is executed the plaintiff may seek specific performance in order to enforce one or more particular obligations contained in the contract.[126]

---

119. N.S.W.: *Wills Probate and Administration Act* 1898, s. 44; Vic.: *Administration and Probate Act* 1958, s. 13; Qld: *Succession Act* 1981, s. 44; S.A.: *Administration and Probate Act* 1919, ss 45 and 46; W.A.: *Administration Act* 1903, s. 8; Tas.: *Administration and Probate Act* 1935, s. 4. After the grant of probate, the executor proceeds to distribute the estate.

120. *Re Beavis; Beavis v. Beavis* (1906) 7 S.R. (N.S.W.) 66; *In the Will of Malin* [1912] V.L.R. 259; *Barrett v. Barrett* (1918) 18 S.R. (N.S.W.) 637.

121. See generally Megarry and Wade, p. 115.

122. See generally Spry, passim and Sackville and Neave, p. 336.

123. There are other forms of equitable relief. E.g., equity may order the rectification of a document for fraud or mistake: *Smith v. Jones* [1954] 2 All E.R. 823; *Downie v. Lockwood* [1965] V.R. 257.

124. There are exceptions to this rule. See e.g. the equitable doctrine of part performance, discussed below [6.37]-[6.40].

125. See *Wolverhampton & Walsall Rly Co. v. London & North Western Rly Co.* (1873) L.R. 16 Eq. 433; *Turner v. Bladin* (1951) 82 C.L.R. 463.

126. It has been argued that, in a strict sense, specific performace is limited to the first situation. For a short discussion of this matter, see Sackville and Neave, p. 341.

Apart from refusing to grant the remedy where equity took the view that it would be unconscionable to do so, a decree of specific performance will also usually be refused if the decree would involve the court in constant supervision[127] or compel the performance of services or the maintenance of a personal relationship.[128]

The injunction is an order to restrain a person from doing a particular act (prohibitory) or to compel a person to do some act (mandatory). The mandatory injunction may issue against a person who has acted unlawfully (for example, the erection of a building in breach of a covenant) and require that person to put right the wrong (demolish the building erected unlawfully). Alternatively, the mandatory injunction may be issued to ensure the carrying out of a contractual obligation.[129] The courts issue mandatory injunctions sparingly.[130]

[2.72] Equity could not award the legal remedy of damages for breach of contract. It could make an order for specific performance that a money payment be made where no remedy lay at law. For example, where a trustee had dissipated the trust funds equity could order the trustee to pay the sum to the beneficiary. It was not until the *Chancery Amendment Act* 1858 (Eng.) that equity was given any power to award damages for breach of contract. The provisions of the *Chancery Amendment Act (Lord Cairns' Act)* have been adopted in the Australian States.[131] This statute only permitted equity to award such damages if an equitable remedy (specific performance or injunction) were available.[132] According to the strict view, equity only had the power to award damages if in its discretion it would have been prepared to grant specific performance or an injunction.[133] It has been argued that a less stringent view is to be preferred and that the court should be able to order equitable damages even where in its discretion, it may refuse to order an equitable remedy.[134] It has been argued that the terminology of the legislation allowing an application for equitable damages where the court "has jurisdiction to entertain an application" for specific performance or an injunction, permits this more lenient interpretation.[135]

---

127. *J. C. Williamson Ltd v. Lukey and Mulholland* (1931) 45 C.L.R. 282; [1931] A.L.R. 157. Cf. *Wolverhampton Corporation v. Emmons* [1901] 1 K.B. 515 (building contract).

128. See Meagher, Gummow and Lehane, p. 479; *Giles v. Morris* [1972] 1 All E.R. 960.

129. The relationship of this type of injunction with a decree for specific performance is unclear. See Sackville and Neave, p. 346.

130. There are further distinctions — e.g. the distinction between perpetual and interlocutory injunctions. See Meagher, Gummow and Lehane, pp. 562ff.; Sackville and Neave, p. 347.

131. N.S.W.: *Supreme Court Act* 1970, s. 68; Vic.: *Supreme Court Act* 1986, s. 38; S.A.: *Supreme Court Act* 1935, s. 30; W.A.: *Supreme Court Act* 1935, s. 25(10); Tas.: *Supreme Court Civil Procedure Act* 1932, s. 11(3); Qld: see *Conroy v. Lowndes* [1958] Qd R. 375.

132. *Lavery v. Pursell* (1888) 39 Ch. D. 508; *Johnson v. Agnew* [1980] A.C. 367 at 400.

133. *J. C. Williamson Ltd v. Lukey and Mulholland* (1931) 45 C.L.R. 282 at 294 per Starke J. See also Megarry and Wade, p. 116.

134. Jolowicz, "Damages in Equity — A Study of Lord Cairns' Act" (1975) 34 C.L.J. 224 at 246.

135. Sackville and Neave, p. 357.

[2.73] The equitable remedies were used in a number of situations. They were used to settle disputes concerning rights which were recognised only in equity, for example, trusts (exclusive jurdisdiction). They were also used, however, to enforce legal rights where equity offered more appropriate remedies than the legal remedy of damages (concurrent and auxiliary jurisdication). For example, the remedy of specific performance to enforce a contract for the sale of land has long been recognised as a more appropriate remedy than an award of damages.[136]

[2.74] Before the Judicature Acts, which ensured that the rules of law and equity could be enforced in the one court, judgments of the common law courts and the Court of Chancery could conflict. The Chancellor had the power to issue an injunction to prevent the execution of the common law judgment or to stay proceedings in the court in some instances. For example, where possible the Court of Chancery ensured that the trustee of land did not exercise her or his legal rights so as to deny the beneficiary the use and enjoyment of the land.

8. The Judicature Acts

[2.75] Before the *Judicature Act* 1873 (Eng.), separate courts administered the rules of law and equity. The courts of common law—the Queen's Bench, Exchequer and Common Pleas—heard actions based on common law claims and granted legal remedies. The Court of Chancery granted equitable relief. The disadvantages of such a system were all too obvious. For instance, a plaintiff seeking damages at law and an injunction was forced to commence proceedings in two separate courts.[137] There were numerous examples of duplication of proceedings concerning the same dispute. Although it was clear that the Court of Chancery would ensure that equitable rules prevailed over the rules of common law if there was a conflict, it was obvious that the legal system would be streamlined considerably by the introduction of a scheme whereby one court had jurisdiction with respect to both law and equity.

The *Judicature Act* 1873 (Eng.) abolished the separate courts and established one Supreme Court, comprising the High Court of Justice, the jurisdiction of first instance, and the Court of Appeal. The Supreme Court was invested with both legal and equitable jurisdication. The High Court of Justice was divided into a number of divisions, each division dealing with certain matters.[138] Thus, there was one court invested with legal and equitable jurisdiction which could grant both legal and equitable remedies. The already established principle that the rules of equity should prevail if there was a dispute between the rules of law and equity, was statutorily enacted.[139] The *Judicature Act* did not destroy the distinction

---

136. It is to be noted that in the grant of an injunction in the exclusive jurisdiction, the existence of a proprietary right in the plaintiff is not a criterion for the issue of the injunction — see Sackville and Neave, p. 348.
137. See Sackville and Neave, p. 56 for a brief description of attempts to alleviate the situation.
138. Each division, however, had the same jurisdiction.
139. *Judicature Act* 1879 (Eng.), s. 25.

between the rules of law and equity: rather, it simplified the procedure for enforcing these rules by providing that the one court had both legal and equitable jurisdication.[140] All Australian States now have legislation similar to the *Judicature Act* 1873 (Eng.). The rules of law and of equity were both part of the law of the colony of New South Wales taken from England.[141] Although they were administered by one court, the Supreme Court, two quite separate divisions of the Supreme Court administered the rules of law and equity. The procedures and proceedings of these divisions were quite different and separate. Matters which concerned legal or equitable rules could only be heard in the appropriate division. Thus, although there was theoretically only one court, effectively the system in New South Wales was the same as that which existed in England before the *Judicature Act* 1873.

Although some ad hoc changes were made to alleviate the situation,[142] it was not until 1970 in New South Wales that legislation similar to the English *Judicature Act*, was passed. The *Supreme Court Act* 1970 (N.S.W.) provides that the court must administer concurrently the rules of law and equity. By s. 5 of the *Law Reform (Law and Equity) Act* 1972 it is provided that where there is a conflict between the rules of law and equity, the rules of equity prevail.

In the other jurisdictions, the changes were made at much earlier dates.[143]

9. The Trust Today

[2.76] For a long period of time, the subject matter of a trust was invariably land. The concept of tying up the land for future generations was strongly advocated and adapted by the landed classes and for many years this was achieved by a type of trust called the strict settlement: see below [12.04]-[12.08]. In recent times, the trust has been used in many more diversified ways to achieve a range of varied objects. The subject matter of the modern trust is more likely to comprise shares in companies, than it is to comprise land.

Some examples of the situations in which the trust is used are given here.[144] First, the trust is still used where there is a desire to provide for successive interests in property. This may be done by will or inter vivos. If there is a desire to keep the contents of such a trust private, the trust would be set up during the settlor's lifetime because a will becomes a

---

140. Cf. however the views in *Joseph v. Lyons* (1884) 15 Q.B.D. 280 and *United Scientific Holdings Ltd v. Burnley B.C.* [1978] A.C. 904 at 924-5; [1977] 2 All E.R. 62 at 67-68 per Lord Diplock. See on this point generally, Sackville and Neave, pp. 359-361.
141. See Butt, p. 87.
142. Ibid., pp. 87-89.
143. A full account of these changes is to be found in Meagher, Gummow and Lehane, pp. 16-22.
144. See Parker and Mellows, *The Modern Law of Trusts* (5th ed., Sweet and Maxwell, London, 1983), pp. 1-4 and Heydon, Gummow and Austin, *Cases and Materials on Equity and Trusts* (Butterworths, Sydney, 1982), pp. 343-344 for further details.

document freely available to the public once probate has been granted. Secondly, trusts, and in particular discretionary trusts, have been used for the purpose of minimising income taxation. Although there are many ways in which such trusts can be used, typically the idea is to distribute the income of trust property amongst the objects of the trust in such a manner so as to reduce income taxation burdens. Changes to taxation laws in the past decade have resulted in this form of taxation avoidance being less useful in achieving its purpose. Thirdly, the trust has been used to enable unincorporated associations to hold property in a viable manner. Unincorporated associations are not separate legal entities and would have faced virtually insurmountable difficulties in holding property. The vehicle of the trust has been used to enable trustees to hold property on behalf of unincorporated associations. Fourthly, in many cases pension and superannuation schemes operate under a trust. The funds of the scheme, whether the scheme be contributory or non-contributory, are held by trustees. The employee is thereby assured that her or his employer cannot dispose of the funds. Fifthly, the trust is used to enable investment through unit trusts. Under these schemes, the trustees purchase shares in a large number of companies and then individual persons acquire ''units'' or shares in the overall trust fund. The trustees are often full-time professional managers of the trust. They receive the income and then pay the administrative costs, distribute wholly or partially to the unit holders and reinvest the remainder. From the point of view of the unit holder, the unit trust offers an opportunity to invest in many companies and thereby offset the risks. Other uses of the trust include the protective trust, the charitable trust and trusts under which debenture stock is issued by a company.[145]

Apart from the use of the express trust in these varied ways, trusts may arise by operation of law. The resulting and constructive trusts are examples of this form of trust. They are discussed in detail in Chapter 6. Trusts also arise in a variety of situations where persons have failed to follow the proper formalities for the creation or passing of a legal estate. These trusts are discussed in several places: see above **[2.59]** and below **[6.37]** and **[10.06]**.

145. Ibid.

3

Priorities Under the General Law

I. INTRODUCTION

[3.01] In general terms, a priorities dispute arises where two or more persons have inconsistent proprietary interests in the one piece of land. For example, if A, the owner of land enters into an equitable mortgage in favour of B and subsequently contracts to sell the property to C, both B and C have valid equitable interests in the property. The internal validity of each of these transactions is without defect: the inconsistency between the two interests arises as a result of A, the grantor, purporting to create a second interest which may be wholly or partially inconsistent with the first interest. As Sykes states: "Any invalidity attributable to one of the dispositions exists . . . by inconsistency with the other disposition or the result sought to be obtained by that other disposition."[1] It does not exist by reason of the internal invalidity of either of the dispositions.

[3.02] Disputes concerning rights to the one piece of land may arise, however, in a different way. If A purports to convey to B and it is subsequently revealed that there was some defect or invalidity in the transaction by which A claims to have originally acquired title from X, a dispute may arise between B and X. If the document under which A claims an interest is void because it involved, for example, a forgery or an agent acting beyond authority, A acquires no interest at all and the maxim nemo dat quod non habet[2] provides the answer to the dispute between B and X. A had no title and B, who can have no better title than A had, loses in a dispute with X. In the strict sense, the type of dispute described above is not a priorities dispute, for B really has no interest with which to compete with X.[3] Sometimes, however, a party in B's position may succeed in gaining "priority" over a party in X's position. If X has been fraudulent or negligent in some manner, she may be estopped from denying that B acquired an interest from A.[4] In a sense, B's title arises independently of the defect in A's title. Although this sort of dispute is not a priorities dispute in the narrow sense, it will be considered here.

---

1. Sykes, pp. 28-29.
2. No one gives who possesses not.
3. See Sykes, p. 31, where he draws a distinction between "independent" and "dependent" title, that is, the situations described above, and rejects any contention that there is no distinction between the two.
4. See below **[3.07]-[3.13]** and the discussion of the decision in *Walker v. Linom* [1907] 2 Ch. 104.

85

[3.03] A further important aspect affecting both types of disputes described above concerns the statutory concept of indefeasibility of title. In the area of real property, this concept is applicable to all land falling under the Torrens system of land registration. In outline, it results in the person who is registered as the holder of an estate taking an interest which is unaffected by any prior claims. Although the paramountcy concept is hedged by many and varied exceptions, the resolution of priorities problems in a system adopting the concept of indefeasibility is thus different, where at least the later interest is registered, from the resolution of such disputes in a system free of the concept of indefeasibility. For this reason, some types of priority disputes arising under the Torrens system will be dealt with separately. It is important to note, however, that with respect to some types of priority disputes arising under Torrens land, the basic principles governing their resolution are the same as the principles applicable to like priority disputes arising under general law land. Thus, the same principles are used to resolve a dispute between equitable interest holders, a dispute between the holders of a mere equity and a full equitable interest and, arguably, a dispute between the holders of a prior legal interest and a subsequent equitable interest. Differences in the operation of the two systems mean that different factors may influence the operation of the principle. This is particularly evident where the competition is between the holders of equitable interests and for this reason this type of dispute is dealt with both in this Chapter and in Chapter 5. With respect to the two other types of dispute mentioned above, both the position under the general law and the position under the Torrens system are dealt with in this Chapter: see below **[3.07]** and **[3.49]-[3.51]**.

[3.04] It is important to note at the outset that the resolution of a priority dispute in favour of one party does not automatically result in the absolute loss of the interest of the other party. The interest of the losing party may operate subject only to the interest of the other party. Of course, if the interests are wholly inconsistent, for instance as between the holders of two absolute interests, the interest of the losing party is lost. Further, if the dispute is between the holder of an absolute interest and the holder of an interest which is not absolute and the former wins the dispute, the interest of the latter in the land is eliminated. For example, the resolution of a dispute between the holders of a prior equitable mortgage and a subsequent legal fee simple in favour of the holder of the legal fee simple, results in the loss of the mortgagee's security interest in the property.[5] In contrast, a decision in the above example in favour of the holder of the equitable mortgage would result in the holder of the legal fee simple retaining the fee simple but subject to the mortgage.

[3.05] The solution to a priorities dispute is governed by the rules of common law and equity. The solution arrived at pursuant to these rules may, however, be affected by the system of registration of deeds contained

---

5. Note that the contract between the mortgagor and the mortgagee remains good.

in the general property law statutes[6] and by the legislative provisions concerning frauds on purchasers.[7] In this Chapter it is intended to analyse the legal and equitable principles pertaining to priority disputes. In general terms, the dispute is resolved by reference to the time of creation of the competing interests. The intervention of equity, however, has resulted in modifications to this general principle. Equity was far less rigid than the common law and was prepared to overrule the rule of priority in time in situations where a fairer result could be achieved by doing so. In fact, many of the principles governing priority disputes were formulated by the Court of Chancery.

II. LEGAL ESTATE AND LEGAL ESTATE

[3.06] A dispute between the holders of two legal estates is resolved by determining when the interests were created (which is generally the date of execution of the document pursuant to which the interest was created) and according priority to the interest which was created first in time. Thus, where A, the holder of a fee simple, grants a legal lease to B and subsequently conveys the legal fee simple to C, B's prior legal interest takes priority over the legal fee simple of C. In such a case of partial inconsistency, C takes the legal fee simple subject to the legal lease in B. If A had conveyed the legal fee simple to B and subsequently had purported to convey the legal fee simple to C, B's interest, being first in time, would prevail. The dispositions are totally inconsistent and the one in favour of C is a nullity. It may be argued that this example is simply an application of the maxim nemo dat quod non habet, and that it is not a case of conflicting interests. Whilst it is difficult to separate precisely the principle of nemo dat and a true priorities dispute,[8] the preliminary analysis above supports the view that this type of conflict is a priorities dispute. Each of the documents purporting to convey the fee simple to B and to C was an internally valid document and the decision to be made concerns priority between the two. Nevertheless, the answer to the dilemma is unclear. The distinction matters little for it is clear that the first in time prevails pursuant to either view. It is important to note however, that the principles discussed below pursuant to which a prior legal interest may lose priority to a subsequent equitable interest may also operate to overturn the natural priority in time enjoyed by the holder of the first legal interest.[9]

6. See generally Chapter 4. *Conveyancing Act* 1919 (N.S.W.), ss 184A-J; *Property Law Act* 1958 (Vic.), Pt 1; *Property Law Act* 1974 (Qld), ss 241-249; *Registration of Deeds Act* 1935 (S.A.); *Registration of Deeds Ordinance* 1856 (W.A.) now *Registration of Deeds Act* 1856; *Registration of Deeds Act* 1935 (Tas.).
7. General Law Statutes: N.S.W.: s. 37B; Vic.: ss 173-174; Qld: s. 229; S.A.: s. 87; W.A.: ss 90, 91; Tas.: s. 41. These provisions are infrequently used now. They are discussed briefly in Sykes, p. 416.
8. Discussed in Sackville and Neave, pp. 221-222.
9. See, however, *Northern Counties Fire Insurance Co. v. Whipp* (1884) 26 Ch. D. 482 (C.A.) and *Walker v. Linom* [1907] 2 Ch. 104 discussed below **[3.08]-[3.11]**.

III.   LEGAL ESTATE AND SUBSEQUENT EQUITABLE ESTATE

[3.07]   If this type of dispute is uncomplicated by any factor of fraud or negligence on the part of the legal interest holder, the prior legal estate prevails against the subsequent equitable estate. However, in some circumstances, the holder of the legal interest has been postponed because of blameworthy conduct or because of some estoppel.

Often the circumstances do not give rise to a priorities dispute in the strict sense. The dispute covers circumstances of the type described above [3.02]. Thus where the grantor, A, is a person with no valid title, a dispute may arise between X, the true holder of the legal fee simple and C, the purported grantee from A. As stated above, however, disputes of this nature will be discussed in this section.

[3.08]   In the case of *Northern Counties Fire Insurance Co. v. Whipp*,[10] the English Court of Appeal considered the circumstances in which postponement of the legal estate may occur. C was the manager of the plaintiff company. He gave a legal mortgage over his property to the plaintiff company. The title documents, including the mortgage, were handed to the plaintiff company and placed in the company safe. Subsequently, C, who had a key to the safe, removed the title documents except for the mortgage and gave them to the defendant as a security in return for a loan of money from the defendant to C. Pursuant to this transaction, the defendant gained an equitable mortgage.[11] C failed to make the requisite payments under the mortgage to the plaintiff and the plaintiff sought to foreclose the mortgage. Foreclosure results in the extinguishment of the mortgagor's equity of redemption and confers upon the mortgagee an unencumbered legal fee simple in the land: see below [18.40]-[18.43]. Whipp, the equitable mortgagee, defended the action and counter-claimed seeking a declaration that the plaintiff company's mortgage was fraudulent and void against her and that therefore its mortgage should be postponed to her later equitable mortgage.

Although on the facts of the instant case the Court of Appeal refused to accord priority to the subsequent equitable interest holder, it set out two instances where the holder of the prior legal estate may be postponed to the holder of the later equitable interest. First, where the holder of the legal estate has been a party to a fraud and the fraud has led to the creation of the equitable interest, the legal interest holder will lose priority. The following situation provides an example. A, the holder of the legal fee simple enters into a legal mortgage in favour of B and subsequently B and A collude to induce C to lend A money on the security of the property, inducing C to believe that there is no other outstanding mortgage over the property. B and A could achieve this result by B handing the title deeds (minus the mortgage) back to A and by A then using the title deeds as

---

10.   (1884) 26 Ch. D. 482.
11.   After the transaction between C and the plaintiff company, C retained an equitable interest in the land, the equity of redemption, and thus, there was no question of the nemo dat maxim applying.

security for the loan from C. On the facts of *Whipp's* case, the plaintiff company had not been a party to a scheme to defraud the defendant. The plaintiff company's extreme carelessness in its handling of the security documents did not amount to fraud: the plaintiff company had not combined with C to induce the defendant to lend her money.

[3.09]   Although the Court of Appeal held in *Whipp's* case that negligence in the custody of the title deeds was insufficient to postpone the interest of the holder of a prior legal interest, it seems that a negligent failure to get in the title deeds may suffice to postpone the holder of a prior legal interest.[12] Further, in order to lead to postponement it seems that the negligent failure to get in the title deeds must constitute "gross" negligence. Although the term "gross negligence" does not lend itself to simple definition,[13] it connotes more than mere carelessness.[14] "[S]ome special degree of want of prudence" must be demonstrated.[15]

In *Walker v. Linom*[16] that "special degree of want of prudence" was found and the legal interest holder was postponed. Walker was the holder of the legal fee simple. He conveyed the legal fee simple to trustees to be held on certain trusts. The relevant trusts were to Walker for life or until he attempted to alienate, then to his wife for life and thereafter upon other stated trusts. The solicitors who acted for both Walker and the trustees took possession of the title deeds but unbeknown to them or to the trustees, Walker retained the deed in the chain by which the land had originally been conveyed to him. At a later date, Walker, by using the deed, held himself out to be the legal owner of the property and procured a loan from X on the security of the deed. He also purported to execute a formal legal mortgage in favour of X. Subsequently, X sold to Linom. The dispute that came before the court was between the trustees, who held the legal estate, and Linom. Unlike the situation in *Whipp's* case, it seemed apparent that Linom had no subsisting legal or equitable interest in the land at all. Walker had no legal estate to give X and thus X could have no legal estate to give to Linom. Neither did Walker have any equitable estate out of which could be carved an interest in favour of X and Linom: his equitable life estate under the trust determined upon alienation. Nevertheless, the court treated the dispute as one between a prior legal interest and a subsequent equitable interest. Although it is not explicitly expressed, it appears that the court is suggesting that in such circumstances, the legal interest holder is estopped by her or his conduct from denying the existence of an equitable estate in the other claimant party.[17] It was held that the legal estate of the trustees must be postponed

---

12.   See e.g. *Clarke v. Palmer* (1882) 21 Ch. D. 124; *Walker v. Linom* [1907] 2 Ch. 104; see also Sykes, p. 397.
13.   See Sykes, p. 397.
14.   *Hudston v. Viney* [1921] 1 Ch. 98—gross negligence is something more than mere carelessness.
15.   Sykes, p. 397.
16.   [1907] 2 Ch. 104.
17.   See Sykes, p. 401. Cf. Megarry and Wade, p. 990 where it is suggested that the party in Linom's position is said to have had an equitable interest, not from any interest that the party in Walker's position had the power to create, but from an intervention of the court.

to the equitable estate in Linom. The trustees had been guilty of gross negligence in failing to get in all the title deeds in the chain of title.[18]

Despite the decision in *Walker v. Linom*, it appears that a failure to get in the title deeds will not always lead to postponement of the legal interest holder.[19] The criterion for postponement is gross negligence and in the unlikely event that a legal mortgagee, for example, can demonstrate that there was a good reason for the failure to get in the title deeds and thereby prove that he or she was not grossly negligent, postponement may not result. Sometimes, the holder of the legal interest may get in the title deeds but later permit them to leave her or his possession. If the title deeds are then used fraudulently to induce a third party to lend money, the legal mortgagee may lose priority to the third party. Unless these is some very good and plausible reason for parting with the title deeds, the conduct of the legal mortgagee in so parting with the deeds will be considered to be grossly negligent.[20]

[3.10]   Gross negligence which is not comprised either by a failure to get in the title deeds or possibly by parting with them will probably not lead to the postponement of the legal interest.[21] The cases do not support a general proposition that gross negligence per se by the holder of the legal interest will lead to postponement of the legal interest.[22]

[3.11]   The Court of Appeal in *Whipp's* case envisaged a second way in which the holder of the legal estate could be postponed to the holder of a later equitable interest. The court expressed the rule in the following way: "where the owner of the legal estate has constituted the mortgagor his agent with authority to raise money, and the estate thus created has by the fraud or misconduct of the agent been represented as being the first estate."[23] The rule is a poorly expressed one and arguably covers a wider variety of circumstances than a strict reading of it would suggest. For example, if the holder of the legal estate hands the indicia of title to an agent with authority to raise a limited amount of money using the title deeds as security for that amount and the agent borrows a larger sum than the authority permitted, the legal owner would be bound by the security so created. Similarly, a legal mortgagee is bound by a subsequent mortgage if he or she permits the mortgagor to use the title deeds to raise

---

18. No attention appears to have been given to the fact that, in turn, Linom must have relied upon one single document as evidence of title in Walker.
19. See *Hudston v. Viney* [1921] 1 Ch. 98. Note, however, that this case concerned a competition between a prior equitable interest and a subsequent legal interest.
20. Cf. *Saltoon v. Lake* [1978] 1 N.S.W.L.R. 52 and Meagher, Gummow and Lehane, pp. 238-239. This conduct may often be subsumed under the second category discussed below **[3.11]**. If the legal mortgagee holds on trust for beneficiaries, the beneficiaries may rely on their equitable title to defeat any subsequent interest holder. *Shropshire Union Rlys & Canal Co. v. R.* (1875) L.R. 7 H.L. 496. Cf. the situation where the legal interest holder/trustee fails to get in the title deeds. In this situation, the equitable interest of the beneficiaries falls with the trustee's title: see *Walker v. Linom* [1907] 2 Ch. 104.
21. See Meagher, Gummow and Lehane, p. 238; cf. Sykes, p. 397.
22. See e.g. *Northern Counties Fire Insurance Co. v. Whipp* (1884) 26 Ch. D. 482.
23. (1884) 26 Ch. D. 482 at 494.

a limited amount on the security of the property (the security created to take precedence over the first mortgage) and the mortgagor exceeds the authority and borrows a larger amount. The legal interest holder here is not postponed on the basis of any fraud but rather on an estoppel basis. By entrusting the agent/mortgagor with the indicia of title the mortgagee has held out to the world at large that the mortgagor has an unlimited authority to raise money on the security of the property. The legal interest holder is bound by her or his implied representation.[24]

On the facts in *Whipp's* case, the court had to decide if the plaintiff company had constituted C as its agent to raise money by permitting C to have possession of a key to the safe where the title documents were kept. The court was not prepared to conclude that C's possession of the key amounted to an implied authority to deal with the plaintiff company's security.

However, in the case of *Perry-Herrick v. Attwood*,[25] this second instance envisaged in *Whipp's* case did lead to the postponement of the holder of the prior legal interest. In this case, the legal mortgagees who were two sisters permitted the mortgagor to retain the title deeds so that he could give a first mortgage to another party, X, to secure a particular limited sum owed by the mortgagor to X. The deeds were deposited with X. At a later date the mortgagor regained possession of the title deeds from X, without X's concurrence, and mortgaged the estate to the plaintiffs in return for a loan of a much larger amount. The plaintiffs had no knowledge of the mortgage in favour of the sisters. The legal interest of the sisters was postponed to the equitable mortgage of the plaintiffs. The court held that the conduct of the sisters in handing over the title deeds to the mortgagor and permitting the mortgagor to raise a specific sum of money and create a security which was to take priority over their own security, had placed the mortgagor in a position to represent himself as an unencumbered owner of a legal fee simple estate. As against the plaintiffs who had advanced money on the faith of the mortgagor's possession of the deeds, the legal mortgagees could not complain that the mortgagor had raised a larger sum than had been agreed upon.

The principle also appeared to lead to the postponement of the holder of the legal interest in the case of *Brocklesby v. Temperance Permanent Building Society*.[26] The father, who was the holder of a legal fee simple estate, gave his son an authority to collect the title deeds to the property to raise a loan of £2,250 on the security of the deeds. The authority contained no reference to any limitation. The son procured a loan of £3,500 on the security of the property and the equitable mortgage thereby created in the lender was held to be enforceable against the legal interest of the father.

[3.12] Apart from the instances mentioned in *Whipp's* case and in *Walker v. Linom*, a legal owner may also be postponed to the holder of a

---

24. Cf. Mason and Deane JJ. in *Heid v. Reliance Finance Corporation Pty Ltd* (1983) 154 C.L.R. 326 at 340; 49 A.L.R. 229 at 238-239 where their Honours argue that the findng of a "representation" in these circumstances is artificial.
25. (1857) 2 De G. & J. 21; 44 E.R. 895.
26. [1895] A.C. 173.

subsequent equitable interest in circumstances where, pursuant to some document other than the title deeds, he or she effectively permits another party to hold out that the legal estate will vest in that other party. For example, a legal mortgagee may place in the hands of the mortgagor a document which implies that the mortgage has been paid off. In *Barry v. Heider*[27] the interest of the legal fee simple holder, Barry, was postponed to that of a subsequent equitable mortgagee. Barry executed a transfer of his land in favour of Schmidt. As the land transferred to Schmidt did not contain the whole of the land Barry owned, the Titles Office had to issue a new certificate of title. At the time the transfer from Barry to Schmidt was executed, the new title had not issued and therefore the transfer could not be registered immediately. Schmidt then obtained a loan from one Heider on the basis that the land contained in the transfer from Barry to Schmidt would provide security for the loan. He got Barry to sign an authority, addressed to the Registrar-General, requesting that the new certificate of title be delivered to Heider. The loan from Heider was obtained on the security of the transfer and the authority.

Subsequently, Barry alleged that he had a right to have the transfer to Schmidt set aside because of fraud. He claimed that he had offered to sell the land for £4,000, that his signature for £1,200 had been obtained by fraud, and that, in any event, he had not been paid any part of the purchase money. He sought an injunction restraining registration of the transfer to Schmidt. Further, Barry claimed that his registered title should not be subject to the mortgage to Heider.[28] The High Court upheld Barry's claim that the transfer to Schmidt had been obtained by the fraud of Schmidt, and cancelled it. However, the High Court held further that Barry's legal registered interest was subject to the equitable interest of Heider. The transfer and authority "operated as . . . representation(s), addressed to any person into whose hands (they) might lawfully come, that Schmidt has such an assignable interest", that is, that Schmidt had a full beneficial interest.[29]

[3.13] All of the situations in which the holder of a legal interest has had her or his interest postponed to a later equitable interest appear to be based on two principles.[30] The first principle is the estoppel theory: a person is estopped from denying certain facts which he or she has represented to exist by words or conduct and which have been relied upon by another. The second principle, named the "innocent person" theory by Isaacs J.,[31] concentrates upon some default on the part of the legal interest holder. The legal interest holder should lose priority where her or his fraudulent or, in certain instances, negligent acts, have induced an

---

27. (1914) 19 C.L.R. 197. Note that this case concerned Torrens land.
28. There was a further mortgage to one Gale but for the purposes of this discussion, the relevance and position of the Gale mortgage will not be analysed here.
29. Griffith C.J. and Barton J. appeared to take the view that either the transfer or the authority would have acted as a sufficient representation. Isaacs J. was of the opinion that the transfer comprised the representation. He specifically attached no importance to the authority.
30. See *Barry v. Heider* (1914) 19 C.L.R. 197 at 216-218 per Isaacs J. See also Sykes, pp. 399-401.
31. (1914) 19 C.L.R. 197 at 218.

"innocent person" to act to her or his detriment. In fact, it seems that resort must be had to both principles in order to bring in all the instances where a prior legal interest is postponed to a later equitable interest. In some cases, there may have been no direct representation by the legal interest holder, and yet, the holder may be postponed by fraudulent or negligent conduct. For example, a legal owner who fails to get in the title deeds makes no direct representation to the world as would be required by a strict estoppel theory about title to the property and yet, the owner's negligent conduct has permitted another to make a representation. The default is the important component and the legal interest holder is then estopped from denying the truth of the representation.

The principles upon which this priority rule is based appear also to be the principles upon which the priority rule governing conflicts between the holders of equitable interests is based: see below [3.47]. In both instances, the court must decide whether sufficient reason exists to displace the natural priority enjoyed by the earlier legal or equitable interest and thereby accord priority to the holder of a later created equitable interest. It is not surprising, therefore, that similar base principles have been used by the courts for deciding both types of priority dispute.

IV. EQUITABLE ESTATE AND SUBSEQUENT LEGAL ESTATE

[3.14] The development of the equitable interest in land by the Court of Chancery has been discussed in Chapter 2. As the common law courts did not recognise these equitable interests, it was the Court of Chancery which developed priority principles where there was a dispute between an equitable interest and a legal interest, or indeed, between two equitable interests. In general, the Court of Chancery took the view that it would not interfere with a legal interest unless the conscience of the legal interest holder was not clear. Thus, in the early days where there was a conveyance to uses, equity acted in personam against the feoffee to uses (the trustee) who refused to exercise her or his legal rights in accordance with the use. The Court of Chancery insisted that the rights be exercised in accordance with the use and that the trustee hold the land on behalf of the beneficiaries. In time, equity took the view that the conscience of a purchaser of the legal estate was not clear if the purchaser took with notice of a prior equitable interest and the equitable interest was thus enforced against the purchaser too. In so doing, the Court of Chancery developed the rule that has become known as the polar star of equity: a bona fide purchaser of the legal estate for value without notice of prior equitable interests takes free of prior equitable interests.[32] Thus, for instance, if A, the holder of the legal fee simple creates an equitable mortgage in B and then purports to convey the unencumbered legal fee simple to C, C is not bound by the mortgage in B provided C is a bona fide purchaser and has taken without notice of B's interest.

32. *Pilcher v. Rawlins* (1872) L.R. 7 Ch. 259.

[3.15] There is considerable doubt concerning the onus of proof in these disputes.[33] Although the preponderance of authority favours the view that the holder of the legal estate must prove that he or she purchased for value without notice,[34] there are decisions which support the view that the holder of the prior equity must prove that the legal interest holder had notice.[35] The matter remains unresolved.

1. Bona Fide Purchaser for Value

[3.16] The principle outlined makes it clear that the holder of the legal interest may only take free of prior equitable interests if a purchaser. A person who takes the legal interest by way of gift is a volunteer and is thus bound by existing equitable interests. The equitable maxim, equity will not assist a volunteer, gave rise to this part of the principle. A person who has given no value must take the land with all its burdens. A purchaser includes a grantee of any type of legal estate such as a fee simple, a mortgage or a lease.

[3.17] Further, the principle provides that the purchaser must be a "bona fide purchaser". That is, the purchaser must act in good faith. According to general principles then, a purchaser guilty of unconscionable conduct may not be able to take advantage of the principle. As Lord Wilberforce stated in *Midland Bank Trust Co. Ltd v. Green*[36] the bona fide requirement is "a separate test which may have to be passed even though absence of notice is proved". In practice, however, the bona fide criterion does not appear to operate separately but is subsumed under the part of the principle which requires a purchaser to take without notice.

[3.18] The legal interest holder must be a bona fide purchaser *for value*. The reason for the inclusion of the words "for value" is because the technical legal meaning of "purchaser" does not necessarily show that value has been given. In discussing estates in Chapter 2, a distinction was drawn between words of limitation in a grant, which define the nature of the estate granted, and words of purchase which designate the person who is the grantee. The person named as the grantee by the words of purchase is the "purchaser". A purchaser in this technical sense is simply a person who takes by way of grant, whether pursuant to a gift or sale. "For value" means consideration in money, money's worth or marriage. It does not mean full value.[37] Money's worth means services, shares, other land or any form of consideration in the contractual sense.[38] Marriage will only suffice as "value" with respect to a future marriage.[39] Consideration

---

33. See generally Meagher, Gummow and Lehane, p. 248.
34. See e.g. *Re Nisbet and Potts' Contract* [1905] 1 Ch. 391; *Wilkes v. Spooner* [1911] 2 K.B. 473; *Mills v. Renwick* (1901) 1 S.R. (N.S.W.) (Eq.) 173.
35. *Corser v. Cartwright* (1875) L.R. 7 H.L. 731. See generally Meagher, Gummow and Lehane, p. 249.
36. [1983] A.C. 513 at 528.
37. *Bassett v. Nosworthy* (1673) Rep. Finch 102; 23 E.R. 55.
38. E.g. satisfaction of an existing debt: *Thorndike v. Hunt* (1859) 3 De G. & J. 563; 44 E.R. 1386.
39. *Attorney-General v. Jacobs Smith* [1895] Q.B. 341.

stated to be for natural love and affection of a stated person or persons does not constitute "value" for this purpose.[40]

2. Taking a Legal Estate without Notice

[3.19]   Where a purchaser simultaneously provides the consideration and obtains the legal estate, and does so without notice of a prior equity, he or she is not bound by the prior equity. The position is more complex where the dates of the payment of consideration and of the taking of the legal estate are not the same. The general rule is that the purchaser must not have notice at the date he or she furnishes the consideration. If a purchaser has no notice at the time of payment of the consideration and this lack of notice continues until the date of the acquisition of the legal estate, the purchaser is clearly not bound by the prior equity.[41] The position of a purchaser who pays the purchase moneys, then receives notice of a prior equity and then takes the legal interest, may be different. It seems that a purchaser who pays the purchase moneys without notice of a prior equitable interest and acquires the legal estate at a later time and after acquiring notice is protected, provided the conveyance of the legal estate is not in breach of trust.[42]

[3.20]   The latter situation often arises where a person originally intends to take only an equitable estate but subsequently seeks to get in the legal estate upon discovering that a prior equitable interest exists, of which he or she had no notice at the time of taking the later equitable estate. The person gets in the legal estate pursuant to a separate transaction from the one under which he or she acquired the equitable estate. The aim is to acquire a title not subject to the prior equitable interest. This situation involves the doctrine of tabula in naufragio: see below [18.17]-[18.21]. In a situation such as that described, provided the conveyance of a legal estate does not constitute a breach of trust by the grantor, the person taking the legal estate acquires a title which is not subject to the prior equitable interest.[43] Without acquisition of the legal interest the rule of qui prior est tempore potior est jure[44] would usually have resulted in loss of priority to the earlier equitable estate.

The difficult question is as to when it will be considered that there has been a breach of trust. In *Mumford v. Stohwasser*,[45] a lessee granted an equitable sublease and subsequently, as security for a loan of money to him, granted an equitable mortgage by deposit of title deeds to the defendant. At the time of taking his equitable interest, the defendant had no notice of the earlier equitable interest. Upon discovering its existence

---

40. *Goodright v. Moses* (1774) 2 Wm. Bl. 1019; 96 E.R. 599.
41. See e.g. *Pilcher v. Rawlins* (1872) L.R. 7 Ch. 259. This is so even if the purchaser takes from a trustee selling in breach of trust.
42. *Bailey v. Barnes* [1894] 1 Ch. 25; *Saunders v. Dehew* (1692) 2 Vern. 271; 23 E.R. 775; *Mumford v. Stohwasser* (1874) L.R. 18 Eq. 556; *Taylor v. Russell* [1892] A.C. 244; *Blackwood v. London Chartered Bank* (1874) L.R. 5 P.C. 92. Cf. *Wigg v. Wigg* (1739) 1 Atk. 382; 26 E.R. 244.
43. See e.g. *Bailey v. Barnes* [1894] 1 Ch. 25.
44. He who is first in time has the strongest claim in law.
45. (1874) L.R. 18 Eq. 556.

the defendant, not wishing to be bound by the earlier interest, procured a legal mortgage in his favour from the lessee. It was held, however, that the defendant could not succeed on the basis of his acquisition of the legal estate: the lessee was said to be a trustee for the equitable sublessee and had acted in breach of trust: see below **[18.18]**. As has been suggested, the concept of a trustee is applied in a wide sense and it may be that where a legal interest holder creates an equitable interest, he or she will be considered a trustee for the equitable interest holder whilst he retains the legal interest.[46] It appears that the person getting in the legal estate where the conveyance involves a breach of trust by the grantor, will be defeated whether or not he or she knew the conveyance was in breach of trust. On the other hand, it seems that the grantor must know the grant was in breach of trust in order for the exception to apply.[47]

In order for the breach of trust to defeat the plea of the acquisition of the legal estate, the trust must not be in favour of some third party unconnected with the proceedings. It must be in favour of the person against whom the legal estate is set up. In *Taylor v. Russell*,[48] Walker, who held the legal estate as trustee for particular beneficiaries, entered into a legal mortgage. Apparently having forgotten about the mortgage, Walker subsequently purported to convey the legal fee simple free of encumbrances to T. T thereby acquired an equitable fee simple. T then created equitable mortgages, first in the plaintiff and secondly, in the defendant. Neither the plaintiff nor the defendant had knowledge of the original legal mortgage when taking their interests and the defendant was unaware of the plaintiff's interest at the time he took his mortgage. Upon discovering the existence of the plaintiff's interest, the defendant arranged for the legal mortgagees to reconvey the legal estate to Walker and then procured a conveyance of the legal estate from Walker to himself.

The plaintiff's action to establish the priority of his mortgage over that of the defendant was unsuccessful. The legal estate obtained by the defendant entitled him to priority over the first equitable mortgage. The plaintiff argued that Walker's actions constituted a breach of trust vis-a-vis the beneficiaries under the orginal trust. Whilst not deciding whether or not such a breach was present, the House of Lords affirming the decision of the Court of Appeal took the view that even if such a breach were proved, it was not a breach of trust which would aid the plaintiff's case. Fry L.J. in the Court of Appeal stated:[49]

> "a plaintiff cannot rely on some breach of trust towards third persons who assert no title to the estate and take no part in the litigation. The plaintiff, to deprive the defendant of the benefit of the legal estate, must rely on an equity of his own, not on that of a stranger."

[3.21]   Sometimes a person may intend to acquire the legal estate from the beginning as part of one transaction but for some reason acquires only

---

46. Sykes, p. 391.
47. *Mumford v. Stohwasser* (1874) L.R. 18 Eq. 556 at 563 per Jessel M.R. See also Sykes, pp. 391-392.
48. [1891] 1 Ch. 8 (C.A.); [1892] A.C. 244 (H.L.(E)).
49. [1891] 1 Ch. 8 at 28.

an equitable interest at the time of paying the purchase moneys. If the person gains notice of a prior equitable interest after taking an equitable interest but before acquiring the legal estate, a question arises as to whether the fact that the grantor acts in breach of a trust in conveying to her or him will destroy the protection afforded by acquisition of the legal estate in the same manner as protection is lost in the true tabula doctrine. Although the authorities do not appear to distinguish between the tabula situation and the continuous transaction, it has been argued that the legal interest holder may retain the protection if he or she did not know of the trust or any possible breach at the time of taking the equitable interest.[50] One form of "tacking" in relation to mortgages comes within the tabula in naufragio doctrine.[51]

[3.22]   In the situations described above, a person must take the legal estate before any protection against prior equitable interests is afforded. In one instance, however, a purchaser without notice may obtain priority over the holder of a prior equitable interest even before acquisition of the legal estate. This is the case where the subsequent purchaser who has taken an equitable interest has a superior right to call for the legal estate. This appears to be a special example or an extension of the tabula principle.[52] Such a superior right exists where it can be proved that the legal estate is held upon a trust for the second purchaser.[53] For example, if the subsequent purchaser arranges that the conveyance be made to a third party and not himself, on the basis that the third party is to hold on trust for him, and neither the purchaser nor the trustee had notice of a prior equitable interest, the interest of the subsequent purchaser prevails.[54] In these circumstances, the subsequent purchaser has a superior right to call for the legal estate. In short, a better right to call for the legal estate is equated with possession of the legal estate. The issue of the exact circumstances required in order for a superior right to call for the legal estate to exist has been discussed in a number of decisions.[55] It appears that there must be some positive act by the legal estate holder "operating in favour of the claimant". An express declaration of trust is a clear example. In a mortgage situation where the mortgagor creates two equitable interests, the holder of the subsequent equitable interest may be able to claim a superior right to the legal estate if, for example, the legal estate holder, the mortgagee, had lodged the title deeds with her or him or had joined in the conveyance of the equitable interest to her or him.[56]

It has been argued that this principle was only intended to operate where the dispute is between two equitable mortgagees—as it is (when

50. *Saunders v. Dehew* (1692) 2 Vern. 271; 23 E.R. 775; *Dodds v. Hills* (1865) 2 H. & M. 424; 71 E.R. 528—both discussed in Sykes, p. 392.
51. Tacking is discussed below **[18.17]-[18.21]**.
52. See Meagher, Gummow and Lehane, p. 242 and Sykes, p. 393.
53. *Stanhope v. Earl Verney* (1761) 2 Ed. 81 at 85; 28 E.R. 826 at 828 per Lord Henley L.C.
54. Ibid.
55. *Wilkes v. Bodington* (1707) 2 Vern. 599; 23 E.R. 991; *Taylor v. London & County Banking Co.* [1901] 2 Ch. 231; *Assaf v. Fuwa* [1955] A.C. 215.
56. Ibid.

confined in this way) an extension of the tabula in naufragio rule.[57] The extension to other types of competing equitable claims seems to provide an unnecessary and unacceptable exception to the bona fide purchaser rule.

3. Notice

[3.23]   As set out above the holder of a legal estate must take without notice of the prior equitable interest in order to take priority over it. Notice may be actual, constructive or imputed. These categories of notice were recognised by the common law and are now set out in statutory form in all States except Western Australia.[58] The statutory provisions were adopted from the *Conveyancing Act* 1882 (Eng.).[59] Section 199 of the *Property Law Act* 1958 (Vic.) for example, provides:

> "(1) A purchaser shall not be prejudicially affected by notice of any instrument, fact or thing unless—
>
> (a) it is within his own knowledge, or would have come to his knowledge if such inquiries and inspections had been made as ought reasonably to have been made by him; or
>
> (b) in the same transaction with respect to which a question of notice to the purchaser arises, it has come to the knowledge of his counsel, as such, or of his solicitor or other agent, as such, or would have come to the knowledge of his solicitor or other agent, as such, if such inquiries and inspections had been made as ought reasonably to have been made by the solicitor or other agent.
>
> (2) This section shall not exempt a purchaser from any liability under, or any obligation to perform or observe, any covenant condition, provision or restriction contained in any instrument under which his title is derived, mediately or immediately; and such liability or obligation may be enforced in the same manner and to the same extent as if this section had not been passed.
>
> (3) A purchaser shall not by reason of anything in this section be affected by notice in any case where he would not have been so affected if this section had not been passed.
>
> (4) This section shall apply to purchases made either before or after the commencement of this Act."

The statutory provisions do not alter the kinds of notice recognised by the common law. The case law on what constitutes each type of notice remains relevant. The statutory provisions simply ensure that no new form of notice can be created except by statute.

---

57. See Meagher, Gummow and Lehane, pp. 223, 242 where it is argued that even this extension of the tabula in naufragio principle is unacceptable.
58. General Law Statutes: N.S.W.: s. 164; Vic.: s. 199; Qld: s. 256; S.A.: s. 117; Tas.: s. 5.
59. The relevant English provision is now contained in s. 199 of the *Law of Property Act* 1925 (Eng.).

(a) Actual notice

[3.24] Actual notice means actual knowledge of the relevant facts. Although rumours of a fact do not amount to notice of the fact, clear and relevant information relating to the property—even if obtained from a third party to the transaction—cannot be ignored.[60] The dividing line between what will and will not constitute notice of a fact may sometimes be difficult to draw accurately. A person is not necessarily deemed to have actual knowledge of facts which he or she may have become aware of in transactions preceding the transaction in question.[61] Where the purchaser is a trustee who acts for more than one trust, he or she is not affected with notice of facts which were discovered by the trustee whilst administering another trust.[62]

(b) Constructive notice

[3.25] Constructive notice comprises notice of matters which would have come to the purchaser's attention if the purchaser had made all the usual and proper inquiries and inspections. Thus, a purchaser of a legal estate is only able to plead lack of constructive notice if he or she has made all the reasonable inquiries and has found nothing to indicate the presence of a prior, existing equitable interest. In general a purchaser should make such inquiries as a reasonable purchaser would make in like transactions.[63] This includes making further inquiries about a particular fact if a reasonable person with due regard to her or his interest would have done so.

[3.26] The deeds registration system sets up a scheme pursuant to which instruments creating or affecting interests in general law land may be registered.[64] It is reasonable to expect that a purchaser of an interest in general law land will search the deeds register to determine if there are any subsisting interests in the land of which he or she may otherwise have been unaware. Thus, it has been held that a purchaser is usually deemed to have constructive notice of any interest, the existence of which could have been discovered by a search of the deeds register.[65] In certain instances or transactions, however, a search of the deeds register is not considered necessary. For example, where a trustee conveys to beneficiaries who have become sui generis such a search is considered unnecessary.[66]

[3.27] There are provisions in some States which confine the number and the extent of searches which are required to be made. Generally these

60. Cf. *Williamson v. Bars* (1900) 21 N.S.W.L.R. (Eq.) 302 with *Lloyd v. Banks* (1868) 3 Ch. A. 488.
61. *Brennan v. Pitt Son and Badgery* (1898) 20 N.S.W.L.R. (Eq.) 179.
62. See e.g. *Trustee Act* 1958 (Vic.), s. 35. Similar provisions exist in all other States except Tasmania.
63. *Bailey v. Barnes* [1894] 1 Ch. 25.
64. See generally Chapter 4.
65. *Mills v. Renwick* (1901) 1 S.R. (Eq.) 173.
66. See generally Meagher, Gummow and Lehane, pp. 244-245. See *Re Ball* (1890) 2 Ir. 313; *Mills v. Renwick* (1901) 1 S.R. (Eq.) 173.

provisions affect persons who are purchasing from companies, executors or trustees for sale.[67]

[3.28] Constructive notice and its parameters have given rise to considerable dispute. Apart from the specific matters mentioned above, what are the usual and proper inquiries that a purchaser should make? Basically, a purchaser's duties fall into two main areas. First, the purchaser has a duty to inspect the land and secondly, the purchaser has particular duties relating to the title documents.[68]

(i) Duty to inspect the land

[3.29] In *Barnhart v. Greenshields*[69] it was held that possession of the land by a person other than the vendor is notice of the interest that the possessor has in the land. The following provides an example. A, the legal fee simple holder of Blackacre, enters into an agreement for a lease for four years in favour of B. B thereby acquires an equitable interest in the land.[70] B enters into possession pursuant to the agreement for lease. Subsequently, A sells the land to C and C becomes the holder of the legal fee simple. Even if C were unaware of the existence of B, C would be bound by B's prior equitable tenancy. Reasonable inquiries by C would reveal that B was in possession under a tenancy agreement. A purchaser is always said to have constructive notice of the interest of a tenant in possession and, in fact, of the interest of a person in possession who holds possession pursuant to an arrangement other than a tenancy. Thus, if a person holds an equitable interest pursuant to an agreement for a lease or a contract of sale and is in possession of the land, any person who subsequently takes a legal interest in the land will be deemed to have notice of the prior equitable interest.[71]

[3.30] Although occupation by a tenant is notice of the tenant's interest and other rights associated with the tenancy, it does not constitute notice of rights, such as an equity of rectification, which cannot be gleaned from the lease.[72] Neither is a purchaser under a duty to investigate to whom the tenant pays her or his rent. In *Hunt v. Luck*,[73] Hunt had an equitable right to have a conveyance of his land to Gilbert set aside because of Gilbert's fraud. Before Hunt took action, Gilbert executed a legal mortgage in favour of the defendants. Throughout the whole of this period the property had been tenanted and the rent was paid, through an estate agent, to Hunt. Although the defendants had no actual notice of Hunt's beneficial interest, it was argued that they had constructive notice. It was so argued on the basis that if the tenant had been asked about the final destination of his rent, his reply would have revealed that Hunt, as

---

67. A good summary of these statutory provisions can be found in Meagher, Gummow and Lehane, pp. 245-246.
68. These provisions are discussed in Meagher, Gummow and Lehane, pp. 244-245.
69. (1853) 9 Moo. P. C. 18; 14 E.R. 204.
70. (1882) 21 Ch. D. 9.
71. *Marsden v. Campbell* (1897) 18 N.S.W.L.R. (Eq.) 33; *Short v. Gill* (1892) 13 N.S.W.L.R. (Eq.) 155.
72. *Smith v. Jones* [1954] 1 W.L.R. 1089; [1954] 2 All E.R. 823. Cf. *Downie v. Lockwood* [1965] V.R. 257.
73. [1902] 1 Ch. 428.

recipient of the moneys, had some beneficial interest in the property. It was held that the principle of constructive notice should not be extended in such a manner. Although the purchaser has constructive notice of the interest of a person in possession, the purchaser does not have constructive notice of the interest of a person to whom the occupier is paying rent. The "reasonable inquiries" of the purchaser do not include ascertaining the final destination of rent.

[3.31] Generally then, possession of the land by a person other than the vendor provides notice of any equitable interest the possessor holds. The position is less clear where the vendor is in possession of the land but another person or persons are in possession with the vendor. In these circumstances, is the possession of the person without legal title, "notice" of any beneficial interest he or she holds? The early view taken in *Caunce v. Caunce*[74] was that the purchaser was not affected with notice of the interest of such a person unless the possession was clearly inconsistent with the title of the vendor. Thus, in *Caunce v. Caunce* where the husband and wife lived together on a property to which the husband held sole legal title, possession of the land by the vendor's wife was not deemed to constitute notice of the equitable interest she held in the property. As Stamp J. remarked:[75] "[neither would the bank have been fixed] . . . with notice of the equitable interest of any other person who might also be resident on the premises, e.g., the vendor's father, his Uncle Harry or his Aunt Matilda."

Subsequent English decisions have taken, however, a broader view of constructive notice in these circumstances.[76] Two of these cases, *Hodgson v. Marks*[77] and *Williams and Glyn's Bank Ltd v. Boland*[78] concerned land falling under the *Land Registration Act* 1925 (Eng.) and thus the bona fide purchaser rule and constructive notice per se were inapplicable. Rather, the question to be decided in those cases was whether the persons living with the legal title holder had an "overriding interest", as against the purchaser of the legal title. The interest of a person in "actual occupation" is protected as an "overriding interest" under the *Land Registration Act* 1925 (Eng.).[79] Nevertheless, the decisions have ramifications for the area of constructive notice. The type of occupation which gives rise to constructive notice of the rights of the occupier in unregistered land may arguably be equated with the type of occupation considered to be "actual occupation" and an overriding interest in registered land.[80] In fact, Russell L.J. in *Hodgson v. Marks* stated that he was "prepared to assume . . . that s. 70(1) (g) of the *Land Registration Act*

---

74. [1969] 1 W.L.R. 286; [1969] 1 All E.R. 722.
75. [1969] 1 W.L.R. 286 at 293; [1969] 1 All E.R. 722 at 728.
76. *Hodgson v. Marks* [1971] Ch. 892; *Williams and Glyn's Bank Ltd v. Boland* [1980] 3 W.L.R. 138; [1980] 2 All E.R. 408; *Kingsnorth Trust Ltd v. Tizard* [1986] 2 All E.R. 54.
77. [1971] Ch. 892.
78. [1980] 3 W.L.R. 138; [1980] 2 All E.R. 408.
79. S. 70(1)(g).
80. See McNicol, "Constructive Notice of a Spouse in Actual Occupation" (1981) 13 M.U.L.R. 226.

1925 is designed only to apply to a case in which the occupation is such, in point of fact, as would in the case of unregistered land affect a purchaser with constructive notice of the rights of the occupier."[81]

In both of these cases, the co-occupation of the person with an equitable title (a lodger and a wife, respectively) with the legal title holder was held to be "actual occupation" by the co-owner and thus an overriding interest enforceable against the subsequent holder of the legal title. In both decisions, disapproval with the statements of Stamp J. in *Caunce v. Caunce* was expressed.[82] Lord Wilberforce in the *Williams and Glyn's Bank Ltd* case rejected the notion that a wife's occupation was simply a "shadow" of her husband's occupation, and more specifically, rejected the dichotomy drawn between "consistent" and "inconsistent" occupation in the *Caunce* decision. As his Honour asked rhetorically,[83] "How can it be said that the presence of a wife in the house as occupier, is consistent or inconsistent with the husband's rights until one knows what rights she has? The only solution . . . is to read the paragraph for what it says. Occupation, *existing as a fact*, may protect rights if the person in occupation has rights."

In the third relevant English decision, *Kingsnorth Trust Ltd v. Tizard*[84] the land was unregistered and the issue of constructive notice was raised directly. The husband held the legal title. The marriage broke down and although the wife often slept at her sister's home, in most cases she returned to the matrimonial home daily to get ready for work and to look after the two children. When the husband was away, she slept at the home. The husband decided to take out a legal mortgage over the property. An agent of the mortgagee inspected the property for the mortgagee and reported that the property was occupied by the husband and his son and daughter. Subsequently, the mortgagee wished to enforce the charge and the wife claimed that she had an equitable interest which was enforceable against the subsequent legal interest of the mortgagee. She claimed that she was in occupation of the property and that this gave the mortgagee constructive notice of her interest. Judge Finlay Q.C. upheld the submission of the wife and in doing so, noted and relied upon the decisions in *Hodgson v. Marks* and *Williams and Glyn's Bank Ltd v. Boland* and their disapproval of the *Caunce* decision. His Honor took the view that a person could be in occupation even though such a person's presence on the property was not exclusive, continuous or uninterrupted. The fact that the wife was in the home on most days was sufficient to show that she had not ceased her "occupation". In the circumstances the agent of the mortgagee had not inquired or inspected with sufficient diligence: first, the occupation of the children should have alerted the mortgagee to the possibility of a spouse; secondly, the husband had originally described himself as spouse and admitted to being married but separated; and thirdly, the time of inspection was set up by the husband.

---

81. [1971] Ch. 892 at 931.
82. [1971] Ch. 892 at 934-935 per Russell L.J.; [1980] 2 All E.R. 408 at 505 per Lord Wilberforce.
83. [1980] 2 All E.R. 408 at 505-506. Emphasis added.
84. [1986] 2 All E.R. 54.

The decision in the *Kingsnorth* case is one of a single judge. Nevertheless, in conjunction with *Hodgson v. Marks* and the *Williams and Glyn's Bank* case, it suggests that purchasers (including mortgagees) of a legal title will have to take quite stringent precautions in order to avoid being subject to the rights of even intermittent occupiers who have prior equitable interests.[85] Even in a case such as *Kingsnorth*, where the legal title holder deliberately tries to conceal the occupation of a person with an equitable interest and is successful in doing so, a purchaser may be held to have constructive notice of the interest of the occupier if the particular circumstances suggest that the purchaser should have made further inquiries.

[3.32] The post-*Caunce* decisions demonstrate an awareness of and a willingness to change what had amounted to an indirect gender bias of the law in favour of males. In the greater proportion of cases where a man and a woman are living together in a property where the legal title is held by only one of them, the man will be the party holding the legal title: see above **[1.58]-[1.59]**. The person relying upon an equitable interest in the land and possession as a means of protecting that interest will be the woman. The woman's claim to an equitable estate may be based on such matters as direct and indirect contributions to the purchase price and may in some instances be difficult to prove: see below **[6.30]-[6.36]**. The protection given to the holder of an equitable estate, even where the holder is in possession with the holder of the legal title, ensures that there is some means of retention of the interest against a bona fide purchaser even where the legal title holder purports to deal with the property as the owner of an unencumbered property.[86]

(ii) Duty to inspect the title documents

[3.33] The other main duty that a purchaser must attend to is an investigation of the title documents. Where the law requires that the vendor produce a good chain of title to the land, a reasonable purchaser would search the documents in the chain. Thus a purchaser is said to have constructive notice of all the equitable interests which he or she would have discovered had a search been made of the vendor's chain of title. In the absence of statutory provisions restricting necessary searches, a prudent purchaser would need to search all documents in the vendor's chain of title going back to the original Crown grant.

[3.34] In all States except South Australia there are statutory provisions which attempt to limit the searches required of a purchaser.[87] In Victoria, for example, s. 44(1) of the *Property Law Act* 1958 (Vic.) provides that the vendor is only obliged to produce documents proving title for 30 years preceding the date of contract, providing the documents go back to a

---

85. See generally Sackville and Neave, p. 292.
86. See McNicol, op. cit. and cf. the possibly weaker position of the holder of such an equitable estate under the Torrens system: see below **[5.19]**.
87. General Law Statutes: N.S.W.: s. 53(1); Vic.: s. 44(1); Qld: s. 237(1); Tas.: s. 35(1); *Sale of Land Act* 1970 (W.A.), s. 22. Presumably the 60 year period insisted upon at common law in England is the relevant period for South Australia. Cf. position in England now *Law of Property Act* 1969 (Eng.), s. 23.

"good root of title". A good root of title has been described as "an instrument of disposition dealing with or proving on the face of it, ownership of the whole of the estate sold containing a description by which the land can be identified".[88] The most obvious example of a document showing a good root of title is a conveyance of the legal fee simple. Thus a purchaser only has a legal right to require production of documents in the chain going back 30 years providing the documents go back to a good root of title. A conveyance of the legal fee simple 28 years before the date of contract would not be considered to constitute compliance with s. 44(1): the vendor is required to produce a document showing a good root of title which was made at least 30 years before the contract. The vendor must also, of course, produce any other documents in the chain of title from that date.

In four States there are provisions such as s. 44(6) of the *Property Law Act* 1958 (Vic.) which complete the picture from the purchaser's point of view by providing that a purchaser is not deemed to have notice of any matter which if he or she had investigated title prior to the statutory period set out in s. 44(1), he or she might have had notice (unless the purchaser had actual notice). It has been suggested that the same result may ensue in South Australia as a result of the general notice section.[89]

[3.35] The following example demonstrates the way in which these statutory provisions operate to reduce the searches required of a purchaser and to limit the interests of which a purchaser is deemed to have constructive notice. Assume that there are six documents in the chain of title to Blackacre: document 1 is the Crown grant to X in 1860, document 2 is a conveyance of the legal fee simple from X to Y in 1920, document 3 evidences the creation of a restrictive covenant in favour of Z over Blackacre in 1922, document 4 is a conveyance of the legal fee simple interest from Y to P in 1940 and document 5 is a further conveyance of the legal fee simple from P to Q in 1945. In 1988, Q contracts to sell to R. Pursuant to s. 44(1), Q produces as evidence of title, the 1945 conveyance from P to himself. When the transaction is completed and R becomes the legal fee simple holder, pursuant to s. 44(6), R would not be deemed to have constructive notice of the equitable interest, the restrictive covenant, in Z. In the absence of statutory provisions such as those discussed above, R would have been held to have constructive notice of Z's interest.

[3.36] If a purchaser has actual or constructive notice of a particular document, he or she will only be held to have constructive notice of the contents of the document if the document is one which necessarily affects title.[90]

[3.37] It has been held that a purchaser has constructive notice of the contents of all the documents comprising the chain of title.[91] (In the case

---

88. Voumard, p. 333.
89. See Sackville and Neave, pp. 364-365 and *Law of Property Act* 1936 (S.A.), s. 117. Quaere the Western Australian position.
90. *Reeve v. Berridge* (1888) 20 Q.B.D. 523. See generally Sykes, p. 387.
91. *Carter v. Carter* (1857) 3 K. & J. 617; 69 E.R. 1256.

where it has been statutorily provided that the vendor only has to produce documents going back for a particular time the chain of title would for those purposes, necessarily only include the documents within that time.) Where a vendor deliberately removes deeds from a chain of title but prima facie the chain seems complete and satisfactory thus giving the purchaser no reason to suspect their existence and, no means of discovering their existence, this would appear to be unduly harsh for the vendor. In *Pilcher v. Rawlins*[92] it was held that constructive notice should not be extended so far and that in these circumstances, a purchaser is not deemed to have constructive notice of interests created by such deeds.

[3.38]   If the purchaser fails to investigate the title at all or investigates the title for a shorter period than the law requires, he or she has constructive notice of any interest which would have been discovered had the search been properly undertaken.[93] Thus for example, if the purchaser discovers that the vendor does not have possession of all or some of the title deeds and does not inquire as to who holds them and in what capacity, the purchaser has constructive notice of the interest of any person who is holding the title deeds.[94] However, if the purchaser inquires as to the whereabouts of the title deeds and receives a reasonable explanation, he or she will not be deemed to have constructive notice of the equitable interest of a person holding the deeds.[95] A vendor who claimed he was too busy at the time of the transaction but would produce the deeds later was said to have provided a "reasonable" explanation for non-production of the deeds.[96] It has been argued that this is an exceptional rule which derogates from the usual principle of notice requiring the vendor to make all usual and proper inquiries.[97]

(c) Imputed notice

[3.39]   Imputed notice is notice acquired or deemed to be acquired by an agent of the purchaser of the legal estate. If a purchaser employs an agent, such as a solicitor, any actual or constructive notice the agent receives is imputed to the purchaser.[98] In order for notice to be imputed to the purchaser, knowledge of the fact must be brought to the agent's attention in the course of the agency and not whilst the agent is pursuing her or his own independent activities.[99] However, the common law position is that in order for the notice to be imputed to the purchaser the knowledge need not have been acquired by the agent in the course of the particular transaction provided the knowledge is in the mind of the agent

---

92. (1872) 7 Ch. A. 259.
93. *Worthington v. Morgan* (1849) 16 Sim. 547; 60 E.R. 987; *Re Nisbet and Potts' Contract* [1905] 1 Ch. 391.
94. *Worthington v. Morgan* (1849) 16 Sim. 547; 60 E.R. 987.
95. *Hewitt v. Loosemore* (1851) 9 Hare. 449; 68 E.R. 586.
96. Ibid.
97   See Megarry and Wade, pp. 151, 991. The reason for this rule may lie in the principle discussed in *Oliver v. Hinton* [1899] 2 Ch. 264 and *Hudston v. Viney* [1921] 1 Ch. 98 discussed below **[3.41]**.
98. *Wyllie v. Pollen* (1863) 3 De G.J. & S. 596; 46 E.R. 767.
99. *R. v. Biggan; Ex parte Fry* [1955] V.L.R. 36.

whilst he or she is engaged in the transaction in question.[100] In New South Wales, Victoria, South Australia and Tasmania this principle has been overturned by specific statutory provisions. For example, s. 199(1) (b) of the *Property Law Act* 1958 (Vic.) provides that a purchaser is only affected with notice if the knowledge or deemed knowledge is obtained by the agent in the course of the same transaction with respect to which a question of notice arises.[101]

The knowledge of an agent is not imputed to the purchaser if the thing of which the agent had notice comes from the agent's own fraud.[102]

4. Other Principles

[3.40]   The discussion above demonstrates that in a competition between a prior equitable interest and a subsequent legal interest, the holder of the legal interest has priority over the holder of the equitable interest if he or she is a bona fide purchaser of the legal estate for value without notice of the equitable interest. There is, however, one instance where the purchaser of a legal estate who has notice of a prior equitable interest can take priority over the equitable interest.[103] A purchaser of the legal estate for value without notice of prior equitable interests can give a good clear title to a purchaser of the legal title from her or him even though the latter has notice of the equitable interest. The rationale for such a rule appears to have been to ensure that the first purchaser can sell the land. There are exceptions to the principle set out in *Wilkes v. Spooner*. First, a trustee who sells in breach of trust to a purchaser without notice, and then re-acquires the legal title, holds the property on the trust again; and secondly, a person who acquires a property by actual fraud cannot defeat the interest of the prior equitable interest holder by purchasing from a bona fide purchaser of the legal title without notice.

[3.41]   It has been suggested that there is another priority rule affecting a conflict between a prior equitable interest and a subsequent legal interest. In *Oliver v. Hinton*[104] the court took the view that the holder of a subsequent legal interest would lose priority to the holder of a prior equitable interest if the former were guilty of any fraud or gross negligence. It is suggested that in cases where fraud or gross negligence exists, the person holding the legal title would fail to gain priority anyway on the basis of the bona fide purchaser rule described above. For example, gross negligence in getting in and searching the title deeds would

---

100. *Brotherton v. Hatt* (1706) 2 Vern. 574; 23 E.R. 973; *Hargreaves v. Rothwell* (1836) 1 Keen. 154; 47 E.R. 21.
101. See General Law Statutes: N.S.W.: s. 164(1)(b); Qld: s. 256(1)(b); S.A.: s. 117(1)(b); Tas.: s. 5(1)(b). Cf. the position in Western Australia where there is no statutory provision to this effect. Imputed notice may not be as narrowly defined. See *Brotherton v. Hatt* (1706) 2 Vern. 574; 23 E.R. 973; *Gerrard v. O'Reilly* (1823) 3 Dr. & War. 414 at 431; 61 E.R. 97 at 104; *Hargreaves v. Rothwell* (1836) 1 Keen. 154; 48 E.R. 265; Sykes, p. 388.
102. *Schultz v. Corwill Properties Pty Ltd* (1969) 90 W.N. (Pt 1) (N.S.W.) 529 discussed below **[5.47]-[5.48]**. Cf. *Boursot v. Savage* (1866) L.R. 2 Eq. 134.
103. See *Kettlewell v. Watson* (1882) 21 Ch. D. 685 at 707; *Wilkes v. Spooner* [1911] 2 K.B. 473.
104. (1899) 2 Ch. 264.

constitute constructive notice of any prior equitable interests. Although there appears little if any scope for this separate priority rule the case of *Oliver v. Hinton* sets it out clearly as an alternative.

V. EQUITABLE ESTATE AND EQUITABLE ESTATE

[3.42]   As is the case in relation to legal interests, equitable interests take effect according to their dates of creation. However, equity has taken a broader view than the law when determining the nature and extent of priority conflicts. Where, for example, A enters into a contract to sell property to B and subsequently contracts to sell to C, equity does not apply strictly the maxim nemo dat quod non habet and hold that C has no equitable interest. Equity has been prepared to view both B and C as having equitable interests in the land arising from their respective contracts of sale and to decide which party has the better interest. It has sometimes been stated that the use of the maxim, qui prior est tempore potior est jure[105] provides the answer to a dispute between the holders of equitable interests. This, however, is only partly true. Equity prefers to search for the "better equity" and to use priority of time to decide the issue only if the interests are equal. In *Rice v. Rice*[106] Kindersley V.-C. stated the rule in the following terms: "As between persons having only equitable interests, if their equities are *in all other respects* equal, priority of time gives the better equity; or, qui prior est tempore potior est jure."[107]

[3.43]   Kindersley V.-C. in *Rice v. Rice* treated priority of time as the decisive factor only if the equities were equal. This approach has been followed in some decisions[108] but in other judgments, the order of the relevant matters for consideration appears to have been reversed.[109] For example, in *Heid v. Reliance Finance Corporation Pty Ltd*[110] Gibbs C.J., in the course of deciding a dispute between equitable interest holders, although quoting with approval the formulation of Kindersley V.-C. in *Rice v. Rice*, remarked:[111]

"In the present case, the interest of the appellant was first in time. The question therefore is whether his conduct . . . has the consequence that [the holder of the second equitable interest] has the better equity, and that the appellant's interest should be postponed."

It is doubted whether the order of consideration of these relevant matters is of practical importance in the resolution of individual cases. The important issue is to determine the means by which the courts have decided if "the equities are equal".

105. He who is first in time has the strongest claim in law.
106. (1853) 2 Drew. 73; 61 E.R. 646.
107. (1853) 2 Drew. 73 at 78; 61 E.R. 646 at 648.
108. See e.g. the judgment of Mason and Deane JJ. in *Heid v. Reliance Finance Corporation Pty Ltd* (1983) 154 C.L.R. 326 at 339; 49 A.L.R. 229 at 237.
109. *Abigail v. Lapin* [1934] A.C. 491; *J. & H. Just (Holdings) Pty Ltd v. Bank of New South Wales* (1971) 125 C.L.R. 546. *Heid v. Reliance Finance Corporation Pty Ltd* (1983) 154 C.L.R. 326 at 333; 49 A.L.R. 229 at 233 per Gibbs C.J.
110. (1983) 154 C.L.R. 326; 49 A.L.R. 229. Note that this case concerned Torrens land.
111. (1983) 154 C.L.R. 326 at 333; 49 A.L.R. 229 at 233.

[3.44]   In *Rice v. Rice*, Kindersley V.-C. took the view that in looking at the relative merits of the parties, the court must direct its inquiries to three matters: first, the nature and condition of the respective equitable interests; secondly, the circumstances and manner of acquisition; and thirdly, the whole conduct of the parties. The plaintiff conveyed the legal estate to X. He gave the title deeds to X and a receipt stating that he had received the purchase price. In fact, the purchase price had not been paid and thus the plaintiff had an equitable lien over the land. Subsequently, X created an equitable mortgage in the defendant by way of deposit of title deeds. The court found nothing in the differing nature of the interests to distinguish them. In considering the conduct of the parties, however, the court took the view that the plaintiff's conduct in handing the title deeds to X and in signing the receipt which stated that all purchase moneys had been paid, had armed the purchaser X with the power to deal with the estate as an absolute legal and equitable owner. The equitable mortgagee was blameless and entitled to assume in the circumstances that X was the unencumbered owner of the property. The fact that the defendant had possession of the title deeds was considered a factor in his favour but the court was careful to make it clear that the possession of title deeds does not in every case confer priority. A party may be in possession of the title deeds under such circumstances that no advantage is conferred.[112]

[3.45]   In subsequent decisions, the emphasis has been placed on the third criterion set out by Kindersley V.-C., that is the conduct of the parties. It appears that distinctions between different types of equitable interests, for example, an equitable fee simple and an equitable mortgage, are unlikely alone to provide a solution in any dispute and that the criterion concerning circumstances and manner of acquisition, whilst important, is usually dealt with under the more general criterion of "conduct of the parties".

Although theoretically the conduct of both parties is relevant in a practical sense concentration upon the conduct of the holder of the first equitable interest holder is inevitable. In the absence of any act or omission by the first equitable interest holder, he or she will win the dispute on the basis of priority of time. The conduct of the holder of the second equitable interest may be directly relevant if an act or omission on the part of the first holder is demonstrated: it may act as a counter-balance in "weighing" the relative merits of the equities when the court is required to answer the question as to whether there is any factor making it inequitable for the first equitable interest holder to rely on priority of time.

Despite the emphasis on the conduct of the holder of the first equity, Mason and Deane JJ. in the High Court decision of *Heid v. Reliance Finance Corporation Pty Ltd* reiterated the basic *Rice v. Rice* test and the need to determine if the "equities are equal" by comparing fully the interests of each party.

---

112. (1853) 2 Drew. 73 at 82; 61 E.R. 646 at 649.

[3.46] What conduct is considered "displacing" or "postponing" conduct? What is an act or omission which will lead to the holder of the first equitable interest being postponed to the holder of a subsequent equitable interest? The facts of *Rice v. Rice* provide an example of where the holder of the first equitable interest armed a third party "to go into the world under false colours". The acts of the holder enabled a third party to present himself as the unencumbered owner of the fee simple. A similar "arming" process may be said to arise where the conflict is between two equitable mortgagees and the first mortgagee is entitled under the agreement to get in the title deeds from the mortgagor but has failed to do so. By leaving the title deeds with the mortgagor, the first mortgagee has enabled the mortgagor to hold her or himself out as the holder of an unencumbered fee simple.[113] Similarly, a first equitable mortgagee who takes possession of the title deeds but returns them to the mortgagor and fails to press for their return may be postponed to a second equitable mortgagee who has taken all the reasonable precautions.[114] Fraud or gross negligence of types other than those described above on the part of a first equitable interest may lead to the postponement of the earlier interest in favour of the later one.[115]

Attention to usual conveyancing practices may be relevant to the issue of what is and what is not, "displacing" conduct. For example, the handing over of title deeds and a signed conveyance acknowledging payment to his independent solicitor by a vendor for the purpose of allowing the solicitor to complete the transaction and take the money from the purchaser on his behalf, is a common conveyancing practice. If the solicitor acted fraudulently and the consequence was a dispute between the vendor's equitable lien and a subsequent equitable interest, the vendor's conduct would not necessarily be considered "displacing", that is, conduct pursuant to which it was reasonably foreseeable that a second equity could be created.[116]

[3.47] There has been considerable dispute and uncertainty as to the underlying basis for the granting of priority to a later equitable interest holder. In a number of decisions, it has been suggested all such findings have their basis in the doctrine of estoppel: that is, the holder of the first equitable interest should be estopped from asserting the priority of her or his interest because her or his words or conduct have induced the holder of the second equity to act to her or his detriment.[117] Whilst many cases of postponement may be justified pursuant to the doctrine of estoppel, it

---

113. See e.g. *Farrand v. Yorkshire Banking Co.* (1888) 40 Ch. D. 182. Attention must be paid to common conveyancing practice here. A mortgagee who takes a first equitable mortgage should take possession of the title deeds to protect her or his security.
114. *Waldron v. Sloper* (1852) 1 Drew. 193; 61 E.R. 425.
115. *Taylor v. Russell* [1891] 1 Ch. D. 8.
116. Cf. the facts of *Heid v. Reliance Finance Corporation Pty Ltd* (1983) 154 C.L.R. 326; 49 A.L.R. 229. See generally below **[5.108]**.
117. See e.g. *Rimmer v. Webster* [1902] 2 Ch. 163; Gibbs C.J. in *Heid v. Reliance Finance Corporation Pty Ltd* (1983) 154 C.L.R. 326 at 335; 49 A.L.R. 229 at 234.

seems that not all can be.[118] An estoppel by representation requires a representation by words or conduct upon the faith of which the representee acted to her or his detriment. In many instances where the dispute arises because of the fraud of a third party, it is difficult to find a "representation" by the holder of the first equitable interest. The following fact situation provides an example. A, the holder of the fee simple creates an equitable mortgage in B who is entitled to take the title deeds but fails to do so. Subsequently, A fraudulently uses the title deeds to create an equitable mortgage in C who is induced to believe that this mortgage will be the first and only security over the land. The "representation" is made by A, the third party, and it is straining the interpretation of the term "representation" to conclude that the representation can be attributed to B. B did not give authority actual or implied for A to make such a representation. As Mason and Deane JJ. in *Heid's* case remarked: "While the conduct of the holder of the first equity may, in such a case, be blameworthy, the operative representation was neither made nor authorized by him."[119] Further, detriment means that there must be a material disadvantage and the mere alteration of position by entry into a contract is insufficient in itself to constitute detriment.[120]

Some commentators and judges have taken the view that a more generalised principle may be at the base of such decisions. This is the principle described above, and involves a general evaluation of which equity is the better one. Within such a principle the fraudulent or negligent conduct of the holder of the first equity becomes the central issue.

Mason and Deane JJ. in *Heid's* case took the view that "elements of both negligence and estoppel [are] found in the statements of general principle"[121] and adopted Sykes' broad test, which includes both notions in the test for deciding a priority conflict between equitable interests. Sykes suggests that the court approaches the matter by "inquiring whose is the better equity, bearing in mind the conduct of both parties, the question of any negligence on the part of the prior claimant, the effect of any represenation as possibly raising an estoppel and whether it can be said that the conduct of the first or prior owner has enabled such a representation to be made".[122]

Although the test as stated is a mix of the principles of estoppel and negligence, in other parts of the joint judgment it is submitted that the emphasis is on a comparison of the equities and thus, by definition, on the possibly negligent conduct of the holder of the first equity. Mason and Deane JJ. in the *Heid* case illustrate such an emphasis by using the language of negligence rather than estoppel.

118. *Cappel v. Winter* [1907] 2 Ch. 376; *Rice v. Rice* (1853) 2 Drew. 73; 61 E.R. 646; *Heid v. Reliance Finance Corporation Pty Ltd* (1983) 154 C.L.R. 326 at 340; 49 A.L.R. 222 at 238 per Mason and Deane JJ.
119. (1983) 154 C.L.R. 326 at 341; 49 A.L.R. 229 at 238-239.
120. *Jacobs v. Platt Nominees Pty Ltd* [1990] V.R. 146 at 153.
121. (1983) 154 C.L.R. 326 at 341-342; 49 A.L.R. 229 at 239.
122. Sykes, p. 403.

Under the broad principle enunciated by Mason and Deane JJ.in the *Heid* case, it is important to note that more is required than a simple causal connection between the conduct of the holder of the equity and the acquisition of the interest by the holder of the second equity. It appears that the court should concern itself only with particular types of conduct in the holder of the first equity: conduct pursuant to which it is reasonably foreseeable that a later equitable interest will be created and that the holder of the second equity will assume no first equity exists. The use of such terms as "reasonable foreseeability" and "breach of duty" in the joint judgment is the use of "negligence-based language" and is an indicator of the drift away from the pure estoppel rationale as the basis for the principle governing conflicts between the holders of equitable interests.[123] Much earlier in *I.A.C. (Finance) Pty Ltd v. Courtenay*,[124] similar language of "reasonable foreseeability" had been used.

In the recent Victorian decision of *Jacobs v. Platt Nominees Pty Ltd*,[125] the Full Court accepted the dichotomy of views expressed by the High Court in the *Heid* case and indicated its view that priority disputes may be settled according to either of these principles. In some cases, estoppel by representation may be the more appropriate principle and in others, the broad principle suggested by Mason and Deane JJ. may be more appropriate. A number of cases may be equally well decided under an "estoppel" or a "negligence" approach. In fact, in the *Jacobs* case the Full Court analysed each of the principles and attempted to apply each of them to the facts. As it was a case in which the failure to caveat was the only possible omission, the court took the view that the application of estoppel by representation was inapposite.

In essence, however, the matter is one of semantics. In cases where it is possible to say that A (the holder of the first equity), should not be postponed to B (the holder of the second equity), because it was not "reasonably foreseeable" that A's conduct would lead to the creation of a second equity, it would also be possible to find that A's conduct did not amount to a representation of an unencumbered estate, such that, she should be estopped from asserting the priority of her interest over B.

[3.48]   Where the holder of the first equitable interest is a beneficiary under a trust, the priority rules may vary. Where the trustee deals with the title deeds in a fraudulent or negligent manner and another equitable interest is created the beneficiary does not lose priority because of the conduct of the trustee.[126] That is, the beneficiary's equitable interest is not tainted with the reprehensible conduct of the trustee. The underlying reason for this principle is that a beneficiary, unless entitled to call for the legal estate, is not entitled to possession of the title deeds. It would be

---

123. (1983) 154 C.L.R. 326 at 342-343; 49 A.L.R. 229 at 240-242.
124. (1963) 110 C.L.R. 550; [1964] A.L.R. 971. Discussed below **[5.106]**.
125. *Jacobs v. Platt Nominees Pty Ltd* [1990] V.R. 146.
126. *Shropshire Union Rlys & Canal Co. v. R.* (1875) L.R. 7 H.L. 496.

unfair, therefore, to penalise a beneficiary not entitled to possession of the title deeds, for misuse of the deeds by the trustee.[127]

VI.   EQUITY AND SUBSEQUENT EQUITABLE ESTATE

1. The Nature of the Equity

[3.49]   Apart from legal interests and equitable interests, it appears to be accepted that there is a third somewhat ill-defined category of proprietary interests.[128] Interests falling within this category are called "equities". The term "an equity" or "a personal equity" is sometimes used to connote the right to bring an action to obtain equitable remedies against a defendant. Such a right is, however, a personal right only and incapable of assignment or of enforcement against a third party. In certain circumstances, the courts have been prepared to enforce some categories of these rights against third parties and where this has happened "the equity" has thereby assumed a proprietary character.[129]

Equities which have so assumed such a proprietary character are nevertheless "at the bottom of a hierarchy of proprietary interests consisting of legal interests, equitable interests and equities."[130] In other words the sphere of enforceability of the equity is less than that of either the legal interest or the equitable interest. Before stating the priority rule some of the possible proprietary interests existing as equities will be set out below.

[3.50]   One such equity which is clearly defined, is the equity of rectification. If a written lease, for instance, does not reflect the actual agreement between the parties to it, the right of the parties to have the document rectified is an equity.[131]

[3.51]   A further possible example of an equity which is proprietary in nature, is the right of a grantor to have a conveyance set aside because of the fraud of the grantee. In *Latec Investments Ltd v. Hotel Terrigal Pty Ltd*[132] the nature of this right was the subject of a detailed analysis by the

127. Cf. the position where the reprehensible conduct of the trustee concerns a failure to get in the title deeds: see *Walker v. Linom* [1907] 2 Ch. 104 discussed above [3.09]. In this case the beneficiary's interest falls in with that of the trustees and the beneficiary is in no better position than her trustees. This distinction has been criticised (see *Coleman v. London County & Western Bank Ltd* [1916] 2 Ch. 353 at 360-361 and Sykes, p. 496) but it appears to represent the correct legal position. Further cf. and see *Lloyd's Bank v. Bullock* [1896] 2 Ch. 192 for an example of a situation where the beneficiary may be postponed to a later equitable interest holder despite the basic rule in the *Shropshire* case. Cf. the *Lloyd's Bank* case with *Cappel v. Winter* [1907] 2 Ch. 376.

128. See e.g. Meagher, Gummow and Lehane, pp. 111-114; Sackville and Neave, pp. 298-311; Jackson, *Principles of Property Law* (Law Book Co. Ltd, Sydney, 1967), pp. 72-77.

129. Meagher, Gummow and Lehane, p. 111; Neave and Weinberg, "The Nature and Function of Equities" (1978-80) 6 U. Tas. L.R. 24 (Pt 1) and 115 (Pt 11).

130. Neave and Weinberg, op. cit. at 24.

131. *Smith v. Jones* [1954] 1 W.L.R. 1089; [1954] 2 All E.R. 823. Cf. *Downie v. Lockwood* [1965] V.R. 257.

132. (1965) 113 C.L.R. 265; [1966] A.L.R. 775.

High Court. Latec was the registered mortgagee of Torrens system land owned by Terrigal. When Terrigal fell into arrears with its repayments Latec exercised the mortgagee's power of sale and sold to Southern, a wholly owned subsidiary of Latec. The court was satisfied that Terrigal had a right to have the sale set aside because of the fraud of Latec and Southern. Latec had shown a lack of good faith by opting for a very high reserve, by arranging a very short advertising period for the auction and by selling subsequently to Southern at a price well below the reserve. Southern, Latec's subsidiary, was a party to this fraud. The problem was that before Terrigal had proceeded to have the sale set aside, Southern had created an equitable interest in M.L.C. Nominees. The conflict was one between the right of Terrigal and the equitable interest of M.L.C. Nominees.

Much of the reasoning in the decision concerned the nature of the interest of the right to have a transaction set aside because of fraud. Menzies J. noted that there were two different lines of authority in relation to this issue. The first line, illustrated in the case of *Stump v. Gaby*,[133] reflects the view that the right constitutes a full equitable interest in land. In *Stump v. Gaby* the issue was whether the right to have a sale set aside because of fraud was capable of being devised. In holding that it was, the court held the right to be an equitable interest. As Menzies J. remarked, the *Stump v. Gaby* analysis concentrates upon and assumes the result of the eventual avoidance or setting aside of the conveyance.[134] Once such a claim is upheld the purchaser holds the legal estate on trust for the defrauded vendor. (That is, the vendor holds a full equitable interest.) The second line of authority illustrated in *Phillips v. Phillips*[135] involved, as did the *Latec* case, a priority dispute between the holder of the right to have a transaction set aside and the holder of a subsequent full equitable interest. In the *Phillips* case attention was directed to the nature of the right before a court has made an order upon it. That is, before the party has gone to court to get the transaction set aside what is the nature of the right? What is the nature of the *right to sue* in these circumstances? It was held that the right is a mere equity at this stage and subject to defeat by the purchaser of a subsequent equitable interest for value without notice.

Menzies J. attempted to reconcile the two lines of authority by suggesting that there is room for the application of each principle in the appropriate circumstances. As the facts concerned a priorities dispute Menzies J. adopted the *Phillips* line of authority and held the right to be a mere equity. The approach of Menzies J. is not wholly satisfactory for a single dispute concerning aspects of both lines of authority could arise.

Kitto J. also held that Terrigal's right was a mere equity and that M.L.C. Nominees' subsequent equitable interest was not subject to it because M.L.C. Nominees was a bona fide purchaser of the equitable estate for value without notice. Kitto J. concluded that the right contained two separate parts. His Honour took the view that Terrigal's right to have

133. (1852) 2 De G.M. & G. 623, 42 E.R. 1015.
134. (1965) 113 C.L.R. 265 at 290; [1966] A.L.R. 775 at 790.
135. (1861) 4 De G.F. & J. 208; 45 E.R. 1164.

a transaction set aside because of fraud, that is the right to sue in these particular circumstances, is a mere equity. However, if there had been a court order setting aside the sale, Kitto J. took the view that Terrigal's right would then have ripened into a full equitable interest. The sale would not have been set aside literally: rather Southern, the registered proprietor, would have been required to hold title subject to the equitable right of Terrigal to regain the legal title upon repayment of the mortgage moneys. Terrigal would be seen as having an interest akin to the equity of redemption (a full equitable interest) under general law land.[136]

Taylor J. held the interest of Terrigal to be a full equitable interest. However, where the equitable interest was one which required the "assistance of a court of equity to remove an impediment to . . . title as a preliminary" to assertion of the interest, Taylor J. held that the holder of the equitable interest lost priority to a subsequently created equitable interest where the holder of the later interest was a bona fide purchaser of the equitable interest for value without notice.[137] The use of this priority rule in a dispute between equitable interests is peculiar. If the dispute is in reality one between equitable interests, it is suggested that the priority rule which should have been used is the principle of all other things being equal first in time prevails.[138] Nevertheless, Taylor J. reached the same result as Menzies and Kitto JJ.

In *Breskvar v. Wall*[139] the High Court, without undertaking a detailed review of the authorities, took the view that the right to have a sale set aside because of fraud was an equitable interest. Detailed analysis of the nature of the right was unnecessary in the circumstances because even when put at its highest as a full equitable interest, the right of the Breskvars was inferior to the right of the subsequent equitable interest holder. The priority rule applicable between equitable interests ensured that in view of the conduct of the Breskvars, the holders of the first equitable interest, their natural priority in time would be lost: see below **[5.26]** and **[5.107]**.

[3.52]   Where there has been no postponing conduct by a person who has a right to have a sale set aside because of fraud, the nature of such a person's right may be very important if a subsequent equitable interest has been created before the sale has been set aside. Although the High Court decision in *Breskvar v. Wall* is more recent than its decision in the *Latec* case, it is suggested that the majority view in the *Latec* case would prevail. The right asserted is one which involves going to court to seek equitable remedies. Whilst the result of such court action may result in the acquisition of a full equitable interest, it is submitted that the right to seek such a remedy is not in itself a full equitable interest from the time of the fraudulent conduct.

136. (1965) 113 C.L.R. 265 at 275; [1966] A.L.R. 775 at 778-779. See also *Re Pile's Caveat* [1981] Qd R. where the difference between on the one hand, an equity to set aside a sale because of fraud which may or may not eventually result in an acquisition of an equitable interest, and, on the other hand, an existing equitable interest, was emphasised.
137. (1965) 113 C.L.R. 265 at 286; [1966] A.L.R. 775 at 786.
138. *Rice v. Rice* (1853) 2 Drew. 73; 61 E.R. 646.
139. (1971) 126 C.L.R. 376; [1972] A.L.R. 205.

[3.53] The interest which the Court of Appeal recognised in the defendant in *Inwards v. Baker*[140] has been described as an equity of acquiescence.[141] In this case, the son expended money building a bungalow on his father's land, with his father's encouragement, in the expectation of being able to live on the land indefinitely. When the father died, the father's successor in title, Inwards, sought to eject the son. It was held that the facts gave rise to an equity in the son which in the circumstances should be satisfied by permitting the son to remain on the property indefinitely. The son's right would also have been enforceable against a purchaser with notice. Where the circumstances are such as to give rise to this equity, a court has a wide discretion as to the relief to be given to the person asserting the equity.[142] That is, the court, in its discretion, must decide how to "satisfy" the equity. Although there is no clear authority on point, it appears that a person who fits within the criteria for this type of equity and who becomes involved in a priority dispute with a third party before he or she has been to court to have the equity declared and "satisfied", may only rely upon having a mere equity in the priority dispute. This is so even if the court would have been prepared to satisfy the equity as against the original owner of the land who actually encouraged the expenditure, by ordering a transfer of the whole beneficial estate. The equity is a right to go to court to seek a remedy. It seems if the court sees fit to grant a remedy resulting in the grant of an interest such as a life estate or a fee simple, it would do so on the basis that such an interest arose as from the time of the court order.

[3.54] Often, the facts which give rise to the equity described above may also be analysed in terms of the constructive trust based on unconscionable conduct: see below **[6.30]-[6.36]**. The law in this area is in a state of flux. Before the landmark decision of the High Court in *Baumgartner v. Baumgartner*[143] the constructive trust appeared to operate as an institution in a recognised class of cases.[144] Although its imposition necessarily contained a remedial function at least indirectly, where the facts fell within the recognised class, a constructive trust was imposed irrespective of intention and gave rise to an equitable interest as from the time of the conduct giving rise to it. Examples of the traditional constructive trust include mutual wills and breach of fiduciary duty.[145] Thus pursuant to the orthodox view, the equitable interest "exists": the constructive trust is not a remedy with its existence being dependent upon the court's desire.

The decision in the *Baumgartner* case, however, demonstrates a willingness to confer a clearly remedial function on the constructive trust.

140. [1965] 2 Q.B. 29; [1965] 1 All E.R. 446. Discussed below **[6.42]-[6.47]**.
141. See Neave and Weinberg, op. cit. at 25. It may be, however, that the equity of acquiescence is a full equitable interest from the outset.
142. See e.g. *Pascoe v. Turner* [1979] 1 W.L.R. 431 where the person asserting the equity was awarded the full fee simple estate in the disputed land.
143. (1987) 164 C.L.R. 137; 76 A.L.R. 5. Discussed below **[6.34]**.
144. Cf. *Muschinski v. Dodds* (1985) 160 C.L.R. 583 at 613-615; 62 A.L.R. 429 at 450-451 per Deane J. where his Honour argues that the constructive trust is, in a broad sense, an institution and a remedy.
145. See e.g. Meagher, Gummow and Lehane, p. 145 on breach of fiduciary duty.

A constructive trust was imposed to prevent the unconscionable assertion of sole legal title. In both the *Baumgartner* case and another High Court case, *Muschinski v. Dodds*,[146] the remedial and highly discretionary nature of rights arising pursuant to the trust and the need to protect the position of third parties have been emphasised. Thus, for example, it was suggested by Deane J. that the enforceability of rights arising under a constructive trust may not be operative until the date the court so decrees they will be operative.[147]

The comments of Deane J. take up the debate concerning the function of the constructive trust.[148] The following suggestion must remain in the realm of speculation in view of this uncertain but developing area of the law. It is arguable that a person who seeks the exercise of the court's discretion in her or his favour on the basis that it would be unconscionable for the legal title holder to retain sole title, does not hold an equitable interest under a constructive trust in the period of time before the court has made its decision. Such a person may be viewed as holding an equity—a right to go to court to seek an equitable remedy. Although not absolutely clear, this equity would probably be more than a personal right. It would be a right akin to the right of a person to have a sale set aside because of fraud. If the legal title holder has created a further interest (whether legal or equitable) in a third party before the court has declared a constructive trust, a priority dispute could arise. The person seeking the imposition of the constructive trust on the basis of unconscionable conduct may have only an equity with which to enter the dispute.[149] It is important to note that in some cases the person seeking the imposition of the constructive trust will be in possession of the land and such possession will provide notice of the interest to the holder of a subsequent equitable or legal interest.[150]

2. The Priority Rule

[3.55]   If the conflict is held to be one between a prior equity and a subsequent equitable interest, the holder of the prior equity loses priority to a bona fide purchaser of the subsequent equitable interest who takes without notice of the equity.[151] In *Latec Investments Ltd v. Hotel Terrigal Pty Ltd* (in liq.),[152] discussed above, two of the three High Court judges held that M.L.C. Nominees, the bona fide purchaser of the equitable interest for value without notice of the prior equity in Terrigal, was not subject

---

146. (1985) 160 C.L.R. 583; 62 A.L.R. 429.
147. *Muschinski v. Dodds* (1985) 160 C.L.R. 583 at 615; 62 A.L.R. 429 at 451 per Deane J.
148. The debate is discussed by Goulding J. in *Chase-Manhattan Bank v. Israel-British Bank (London Ltd)* [1981] Ch. 105. In particular, his Honour considered the divergence between the English and American views of the constructive trust. In America, the constructive trust is viewed as a remedy.
149. Cf. the view of Goulding J. in *Chase-Manhattan Bank v. Israel-British Bank (London Ltd)* [1981] Ch. 105.
150. Cf. the situation under the Torrens system discussed below **[5.19]** and **[5.79]**.
151. *Smith v. Jones* [1954] 1 W.L.R. 1089; [1954] 2 All E.R. 823; *Latec Investments Ltd v. Hotel Terrigal Pty Ltd* (1965) 113 C.L.R. 265; [1966] A.L.R. 775.
152. (1965) 113 C.L.R. 265; [1966] A.L.R. 775.

to the interest of Terrigal. Although the matter was not specifically raised in the *Latec* case, presumably "notice" in this context includes actual, constructive and imputed notice.[153] Further, it is important to note that the land in dispute in the *Latec* case fell under the Torrens system of land registration. It is submitted that the priority principle expounded with respect to a competition between a prior equity and a subsequent equitable interest is equally applicable to general law land.

If a competition arose under general law land between the holders of a prior equity and a subsequent legal interest, it is suggested that the principle expressed in the *Latec* case is to be applied. If such a dispute arose under Torrens land, however, the *Latec* principle would be inapplicable in view of the statutory concept of indefeasibility of title: see below **[5.20]-[5.35]**.

---

153. For a full discussion of notice, see above **[3.24]-[3.39]**.

4

General Law Registration

I. HISTORY AND BACKGROUND TO THE INTRODUCTION OF THE DEEDS REGISTRATION SYSTEM

[4.01] The effectiveness of any system concerning the conveyance of and the dealing with interests in land depends largely upon the provision and promotion of security and certainty of title and the existence of a simple, speedy and inexpensive method for such dealings. The system of private conveyancing, unaffected by statutory modifications, failed to provide a simple system and it failed also to provide a secure, certain title for a purchaser.

Once the earliest form of conveyancing, the feoffment and livery of seisin, fell into disuse,[1] purchasers had to rely upon the written records of dealings relating to the land in order to satisfy themselves that the vendor in fact had the title proposed to be sold. Thus, a purchaser had to inspect all documents concerning dealings with the land in question in order to verify the vendor's title. Although in England the practice was to limit the length of the search to 60 years even before formal statutory limits were introduced,[2] in Australia the purchaser's task required an examination by the purchaser of all documents in the "chain of title" commencing with the Crown grant. It was, and is, a lengthy and time-consuming task and a task requiring particular skills in the searcher. Further, it was clear that even an exhaustive and thorough search did not provide the purchaser with an absolute certainty that the vendor had the title purportedly being sold. For example, if a deed creating a legal easement over the land had been removed whether deliberately or accidently from the chain of title, the purchaser may have been unaware of the interest affecting the land and yet subject to that interest. A prior legal interest is enforceable against a subsequently created legal interest. The purchaser would be so subject despite the fact that discovery of the interest was impossible from a search of the chain of title. Similarly, if the vendor acted fraudulently and conveyed the fee simple interest to a purchaser, but retained or retrieved from the first purchase the chain of title and then purported to convey to a second purchaser, the second

---

1. The feoffment and livery of seisin is described in Megarry and Wade, p. 47. This method of conveyance comprised a ceremony carried out on the land in the presence of witnesses whereby the grantor (the feoffor) passed over the grantee (the feoffee) a sod of earth and then left the feoffee in possession.
2. Voumard, p. 350 and Sackville and Neave, p. 363.

purchaser would usually take no interest at all, for on the principle of nemo dat quod non habet[3] the legal interest would have already passed to the first purchaser.[4] Alternatively, a document in the chain of title may be a void document, for example through forgery or non est factum and thus ineffective to pass any interest. In each of these instances described, the most careful, skilled and thorough of searches of the chain of title would fail to reveal the fact that the purchaser would not receive the exact interest promised.

Sometimes defects in the title may be very difficult, though not impossible, to detect from a search of the chain. For instance, a failure to use the correct words of limitation to create a fee simple estate may have resulted in a grantee in the chain receiving a life estate instead of the fee simple. The grantee would then only have a life estate to convey: see above [2.32]-[2.38]. Further, interests acquired by means other than document are not reflected in the chain of title.[5] Although some such interests may be discovered by a search of the land, not all can be.

Thus, the process of searching a chain of title was complex and lengthy and even a thorough investigation did not ensure that the vendor had the exact title he or she was purporting to sell. Legislative initiatives (see above [3.33]-[3.35]) in most States attempted to reduce the length and complexity of the searches required by the purchaser but these failed to fulfil their purpose. Although the relevant provisions fix the period of commencement of title and provided that a purchaser is not deemed to have notice of interests created before that date, a purchaser is nevertheless subject to any outstanding legal interests affecting the title, whenever they were created. Legal interests are enforceable against the whole world including any subsequently created legal interests. In order to avoid the possibility of receiving a title subject to such an interest, prudent purchasers search the whole chain of title (when it is available) back to the Crown grant.[6] The benefit of statutory provisions limiting the searches required is therefore lost.

[4.02]   In short, it was the purchaser's inability to discover and verify in a certain and simple manner the preceding dealings relating to the land which created the main problem. It was thought that a central, complete and publicly available register containing abstracts or memorials of all dealings relating to the land would simplify the searching procedure. Thus, the first legislative attempts towards alleviating the problem in the Australian jurisdictions involved the creation of a facility for the registration of deeds and other documents concerning dealings with interests in land. In New South Wales, the *Registration of Deeds Act* was

---

3. "No one gives who does not possess."
4. See e.g. *Pilcher v. Rawlins* (1872) 7 Ch. A. 259. In some circumstances, the second purchaser may be successful in acquiring an interest which has priority over the interest of the first purchaser: see *Northern Counties of England Fire Insurance Co. v. Whipp* (1884) 26 Ch. D. 482 and *Walker v. Linom* [1907] 2 Ch. 104 discussed above, [3.08]-[3.11].
5. E.g. interests arising through adverse possession and easements by long user.
6. See Voumard, p. 369.

passed and registration of deeds legislation was passed in all other States.[7]
The legislation in New South Wales, Victoria, Queensland and Tasmania
is similar. The South Australian and Western Australian provisions differ
from each other and both sets of provisions are substantially different from
the relevant provisions in the eastern States.[8]

[4.03] In none of the States does registration affect the validity of
documents purporting to convey or deal with interests in land. For
example, if A's solicitor forges A's name to a conveyance of the fee simple
of A's land in favour of B, no interest passes to B because the deed is void
as a result of the forgery. The fact that B registers the deed does not
enhance B's position.[9] Unlike the Torrens system of land registration,
discussed in Chapter 5, registration does not confer title. Therefore, it was
necessary to find a means of encouraging registration in order to ensure
as complete a register as possible. In most States the means adopted was
to confer priority on registered over unregistered and subsequently
registered instruments.[10]

[4.04] As is explained below, the deeds registration system failed to
provide an adequate solution to the problems which beset private
conveyancing and the Torrens system of land registration was introduced
into all States by 1875: see below **[5.01]-[5.02]**. In every State, all land
alienated from the Crown after the introduction of the Torrens system
falls under the operation of that system. Therefore, only land which was
alienated by the Crown before the introduction of the Torrens system
(and which has not been subsequently converted to Torrens system land)
is general law land. With some exceptions,[11] it is only instruments
affecting general law land which fall within the ambit of the deeds
registration system.

---

7. The current legislation is contained in the following Acts. N.S.W.: *Conveyancing
    Act* 1919, Pt 23; Vic.: *Property Law Act* 1958, Pt I; Qld: *Property Law Act* 1974,
    ss 241-249; S.A.: *Registration of Deeds Act* 1935; W.A.: *Registration of Deeds Act* 1856;
    Tas.: *Registration of Deeds Act* 1935.

8. See Sykes, p. 408, for a discussion of the possible historical bases for the differing
    legislative provisions.

9. See e.g. *Re Cooper* (1881) 20 Ch. D. 611.

10. Cf. the position in South Australia and Western Australia. See below **[4.09]** and
    Sykes, pp. 413-414.

11. Any document affecting Torrens land cannot be registered under the deeds
    registration system in Victoria (*Property Law Act* 1958, s. 4), South Australia
    (*Registration of Deeds Act* 1935, s. 9) and Tasmania (*Registration of Deeds Act* 1935,
    s. 3). In New South Wales, only those instruments which are registered under the
    Real Property Act are excluded from registration under the deeds registration
    system. See below **[4.07]**. It has been argued that this is the case in Queensland
    and Western Australia too: see Sykes, p. 409. Sykes argues that in addition to
    unregistrable instruments such as contracts of sale of Torrens land being
    registrable under the deeds registration system, so too might instruments in
    registrable form, prior to registration under the Torrens system, be capable of
    registration under the deeds registration system. If this were the case, priority
    disputes between holders of equitable interests might be affected. Cf., however,
    Saunder v. Twigg (1887) 13 V.L.R. 765 at 783-784.

[4.05]   The pool of general law land has lessened considerably over the years, more in some States than in others.[12] In New South Wales, Victoria and Tasmania considerable areas of land remain under the general law but in South Australia and Queensland, general law land has virtually disappeared:[13] see below **[5.135]**ff. In Western Australia small pockets of general law land remain. In view of the virtual elimination of general law land in South Australia and Queensland the following analysis is limited to a discussion of the operation of the deeds registration system in New South Wales, Victoria, Tasmania and Western Australia.

II. OPERATION OF THE DEEDS REGISTRATION SYSTEM

[4.06]   It is necessary to consider the types of interests which may be registered and the effect of registration.

1. Registrable Instruments

[4.07]   In general, any instrument which affects an interest in land is capable of registration. For example, in Victoria s. 6 of the *Property Law Act* 1958 provides that all deeds, conveyances and other instruments in writing relating to or affecting any lands, may be registered. Except in Tasmania, wills affecting real estate may be registered. Therefore, instruments such as a contract for the sale of land, an equitable mortgage in writing and an agreement to grant an easement are registrable instruments. Three States have specific provisions relating to leases. In Victoria, leases for less than three years cannot be registered,[14] in Tasmania leases for less than 14 years cannot be registered[15] and in Western Australia bona fide leases at a rack rent for a term exceeding 14 years cannot be registered.[16]

In Victoria and Tasmania documents affecting Torrens land cannot be registered at all.[17] In New South Wales, the exclusion is less widely based: only instruments which are registered or required to be registered under the Torrens system are excluded from registration under the deeds registration system. Thus, theoretically, a contract of sale giving rise to an equitable interest may be capable of registration and thus capable of affecting a priority dispute.[18] The position in New South Wales may also exist in Western Australia.[19] In Western Australia and Tasmania it is

---

12. See **[5.135]**-**[5.145]** for a discussion of the conversion schemes.
13. By the end of June 1990, it is expected that no general law land at all will remain in Queensland: conversation with G. Topfer of the Registrar's Office (9/3/90).
14. General Property Statutes: Vic., s. 6.
15. *Registration of Deeds Act* 1935 (Tas.), s. 3.
16. *Registration of Deeds Act* 1856 (W.A.), s. 3
17. See above fn. 11.
18. Ibid.
19. Ibid.

specifically provided that judgments are registrable instruments[20] and in New South Wales and Tasmania instruments affecting Crown lands appear to be registrable:[21] see generally Chapter 19.

2. Effect of Registration

[4.08] In New South Wales, Victoria and Tasmania, a registered instrument prevails over an unregistered or subsequently registered instrument provided the former is made and executed bona fide and for valuable consideration and registered in conformity with the relevant provisions of the Act.

The principle affects the priority principles described above. Therefore, for example, the holder of an equitable interest under a registered agreement for a lease would take priority over the holder of a subsequent unregistered, or later registered, conveyance of a legal fee simple. The prior registration of the agreement for the lease ensures priority for the equitable lessee: under the general law, the result of such a priority dispute depends upon whether the holder of the subsequent legal interest is a bona fide purchaser of the legal estate for value without notice.[22]

Indirectly, the priority rule affects the application of the principle of nemo dat quod non habet. For example if A, the owner of Blackacre conveys the legal fee simple to B and subsequently purports to convey the same estate to C and C registers a memorial of her conveyance first, C gains priority over B because of the registration. At common law, the interest of B would prevail. At common law, C would be viewed as having no interest at all as A had nothing to give at the time of the conveyance. As Stawell C.J. in *Andrews v. Taylor* remarked:[23]

"[T]he intention of the 'Registration Acts' is to give priority to the registered owner over the unregistered owner. In other words, in the case of two conveyances, either of which would be valid if the other was removed to give by virtue of the registration of one of them, priority to it over the unregistered conveyance."

It is important to reiterate, however, that registration does not cure the defect in an instrument which in inherently invalid. Neither does registration of such a document give priority over an unregistered or subsequently registered but inherently valid instrument. Thus a document which is void because of a forgery for instance, is of no greater effect because it is registered.

[4.09] The Western Australian provisions arguably accord greater importance and effect to registration or the lack of it than the registration provisions in New South Wales, Victoria and Tasmania. Priority is decided according to the date of registration and there is no proviso such as exists in the eastern States concerning bona fides or consideration. By

20. *Registration of Deeds Act* 1856 (W.A.), s. 2; *Registration of Deeds Act* 1935 (Tas.), ss 5, 9.
21. See *Blackwood v. London Chartered Bank* (1870) 9 S.C.R. (N.S.W.) (Eq.).
22. See *Pilcher v. Rawlins* (1872) 7 Ch. A. 259.
23. (1869) 6 W.W. & A'B. (L) 223 at 224.

s. 3 any unregistered instrument is invalid as against any subsequent bona fide purchaser for value of the same land. This appears to be the case whether or not the subsequent purchaser has registered her or his instrument of grant. It has been suggested that the net effect of these provisions is to ensure that registration is vital in the protection of interests in land under the general law.[24] First, where there is a dispute between two instruments, one or both of which are registered, the instrument registered or first registered is accorded priority whether or not the person so registering lacked bona fides[25] or was a volunteer. Secondly, in a dispute between two unregistered instruments, s. 3 appears to provide that the second instrument prevails provided the holder of the interest under the second instrument took bona fide and for value.[26] The discussion at [4.10] and [4.15] applies equally to Western Australia.

There are limitations to the operation of the priority principle.

(a) Unregistrable transactions

[4.10] Certain instruments and transactions affecting land cannot be registered. For example, as noted above in Victoria, leases in writing for less than three years cannot be registered. Further, there are many instances where interests in land may be created without any writing at all. In such cases, there is of course no instrument to register. For example, an oral agreement for the grant of an interest in land supported by sufficient acts of part performance gives rise to an equitable interest in the grantee. Other examples of the creation of interests in land without writing include an easement by long user (see below [16.31]-[16.33]) and an interest based on adverse possession: see below Chapter 15.

If an interest is acquired pursuant to an unregistrable instrument or without an instrument at all, it is not defeated by the registration of an inconsistent instrument.[27] The priority principle expressed in the provision such as s. 6 of the *Property Law Act* 1958 (Vic.) has no operation. In such circumstances, the priority principles discussed in Chapter 3 are applied to decide the dispute.

(b) Bona fide and for valuable consideration

[4.11] Reference has been made to the fact that in New South Wales, Victoria and Tasmania a registered instrument prevails over an unregistered instrument or a subsequently registered instrument if made and executed bona fide and for valuable consideration.

[4.12] A person who is actually fraudulent in procuring the execution of an instrument under which he or she is the grantee is clearly not "bona fide" and cannot benefit by the registration.[28] However, it seems that

24. Sykes, p. 414.
25. Sykes, p. 414 argues that the omission of the requirement of bona fides in the priority provision must be given full weight in view of the fact that it is used in the avoidance provision.
26. As to the interpretation of bona fide, see [4.12].
27. See *White v. Neaylon* (1886) 11 A.C. 171.
28. It is the fraud of the *grantee* which is the relevant consideration: see *Davidson v. O'Halloran* [1913] V.L.R. 367. See also New South Wales s. 12(2).

something less than fraud may also constitute a lack of the requisite bona fides. It is strongly arguable from the decision in *Sydney & Suburban Mutual Permanent Building & Land Investment Assoc. v. Lyons*[29] that a person who registers an instrument having actual or constructive notice of prior unregistered interests at the time of taking the interest, lacks the requisite bona fides. In this case one Lyons purchased eight lots of an estate at an auction. Contracts of sale between Lyons and the vendor were signed. Subsequently, the vendor gave a legal mortgage over the whole estate (including the eight lots) to the Sydney and Suburban Land Association. The Association knew at the time it advanced the mortgage moneys that unspecified parts of the estate had been sold. The Association registered a memorial of the mortgage. In the priority dispute which ensued between Lyons and the Association, the Association relied upon the registration of the instrument of mortgage. It was held that as the Association had notice of Lyons' equitable interest, it had not satisfied the bona fide criterion. The equitable interests of Lyons arising from the contracts of sale took priority.[30] Although the appellant probably had actual notice, the court implied that constructive notice would be sufficient to demonstrate a lack of bona fides in this context.[31]

[4.13]   The benefits of registration are conferred only upon a person who has given valuable consideration. Nevertheless, a volunteer should register the instrument pursuant to which he or she claims an interest. This is to ensure that any natural priority over later created and registered interests is not lost. For example, if A acquires a legal interest by way of gift and registers the deed pursuant to which the legal interest passed to her, A's interest may not be defeated merely by the subsequent acquisition and registration of another legal or equitable interest in the land. Arguably, the registration of A's interest may constitute notice of A's interest and thus ensure that any subsequent registration of an instrument cannot be bona fide on the view of bona fide taken in the *Lyons* case.[32] In a priority dispute where neither claimant can rely upon registration of an instrument as being made "bona fide and for valuable consideration", the normal priority rules would be used to resolve the dispute. If A has a legal interest prior in time, A's interest will prevail. On the other hand, a failure to register by A may result in the defeat of A's interest by the holder of a later registered interest.

[4.14]   As mentioned above, in Western Australia the priority principle does not require that the instrument registered be made and executed bona fide and for valuable consideration: see above **[4.09]**.

---

29. [1894] A.C. 260. See also *Scholes v. Blunt* (1917) 17 S.R. (N.S.W.) 36.
30. The court ordered specific performance of the contracts and ordered that the Association join in the execution of the required conveyances.
31. See also *Marsden v. Campbell* (1897) 18 L.R. (N.S.W.) (Eq.) 33; cf. *Agra Bank v. Berry* (1874) L.R. 7 H.L. 135. See *Le Neve v. Le Neve* (1747) Amb. 436; 27 E.R. 291. These decisions are discussed in Sykes, p. 411.
32. See generally Sykes, pp. 412-413.

(c) Inconsistent instruments

[4.15]   In some instances difficult questions may arise in determining whether or not there is an inconsistency between two instruments. It is only where there is such an inconsistency that the priority principle applies. Where the owner of land executes two separate instruments which are inconsistent with each other and one is registered, there is a clear case for the application of the priority principle.[33] If, however, the two instruments are executed by different parties (for example, by the holder of the fee simple and a person claiming through the holder of the fee simple such as a trustee in bankruptcy), an issue arises as to whether there are conflicting instruments. For example, suppose that A, the owner of the land, conveyed her interest to B and subsequently was declared bankrupt. If the trustee in bankruptcy of A's estate conveyed the same land to X and X registered the conveyance, a question arises as to whether the instruments operating in favour of B and X respectively are "conflicting instruments" so that registration of the conveyance to X gives X's interest priority. It has been argued that there can be no conflict between the instruments because the second deed would only be purporting to convey any "right, title or interest" remaining in the grantor after the execution of the first conveyance. It has been held, however, that this argument is not well-founded and that registration does confer the better title in these circumstances.[34] As the Chief Justice remarked in *Smith v. Deane*:[35] "The effect of registration is to vest the land again in the conveying party, in such a way as to feed the estate of the party who registers, and to give him priority over any previous unregistered purchaser."

Similarly, the question as to whether there are conflicting instruments so that the statutory provision is brought into play may arise where there is a conveyance of land by a specific description and a subsequent conveyance of land by a general description. If the land generally described in the second conveyance could include the land specifically described in the first conveyance, are the conveyances "conflicting instruments" so that registration of the second conveyance gives priority? Arguably, the instruments may be wholly consistent with each other if there is a simple finding that the land of general description in the second grant includes only land *to which the grantor is entitled at the time of the*

---

33. *Boyce v. Beckman* (1890) 11 L.R. (N.S.W.) (L) 139.
34. See e.g. *Warburton v. Loveland* (1832) 2 Dow. & Cl. 480 6 E.R. 806; 6 Bligh N.S.I. 5 E.R. 499; *Dorward v. Salter* (unreported Full Ct of Sup. Ct, Victoria, *Argus Newspaper* 8 December 1859) referred to in Voumard, p. 365; *Smith v. Deane* (1889) 10 L.R. (N.S.W.) (Eq.) 207; 6 W.N. (N.S.W.) 8. Cf. *Andrews v. Taylor* (1869) 6 W.W. & A'B. (L) 223. Some of these cases are discussed in Voumard, pp. 364-366.
35. *Smith v. Deane* (1889) 10 L.R. (N.S.W.) (Eq.) 207 at 208. Cf. the situation where there is a sale by a sheriff. Here the estate of the debtor does not vest in the sheriff but in the purchaser who takes any "right, title and interest" of the debtor on a sale by the sheriff. In this case registration by the purchaser of a conveyance would not confer priority over the interest of a person taking under a previous conveyance from the debtor—no conflicting instruments. See generally, Voumard, p. 365.

conveyance. Land which is the subject of the first grant would thereby be excluded. In *Boyce v. Beckman*,[36] however, the court was concerned to give as wide a scope as possible to the registration priority principle. Innes J. stated:[37]

> "Such words, then as 'lands to which I am entitled', when used by a vendor, must be held to mean 'such lands as I possess and am entitled to, whether included in any previous conveyance by me or not, if that conveyance remains unregistered,' and cannot be held to except lands previously conveyed by him, so long as that conveyance remains unregistered. To hold otherwise would, in our opinion, be to defeat the very object of the Act."

Although it is often stated that registration does not confer title under a deeds registration system, the examples above demonstrate that there are instances where registration has the effect of conferring title. It is important to note, however, that where a document is itself void, registration is ineffective to validate the documents and confer title.

36. (1890) 11 L.R. (N.S.W.) (L) 139.
37. (1890) 11 L.R. (N.S.W.) (L) 139 at 146.

5

The Torrens System

I. INTRODUCTION

1. Background

[5.01] The defects of the general law system of conveyancing have been described above: see above **[4.01]**. Although the systems of registration of deeds introduced in all jurisdictions ameliorated some of the difficulties encountered in the private conveyancing system, the basic and major problems associated with this system of conveyancing remained. The certainty and security of title were not, and could not, be assured under this system because of what Sir Robert Torrens described as "the dependent nature of titles".[1] A purchaser of land could only be assured of receiving the estate bargained for if each document in the chain of title relating to the land was an internally valid document and effectively conveyed the interest which was intended to be conveyed. Further, the doctrine of notice sometimes resulted in a purchaser being subject to interests in the land which were not evidenced in the chain of title and of which the purchaser may have been unaware in fact. As discussed above, the searches required were complicated, time-consuming and expensive and absolute accuracy could not be guaranteed.

[5.02] The impetus for a different method of conveying land was strong. As it needed to be, the system eventually adopted in all Australian jurisdictions was totally different in its conception, form and operation from that of private conveyancing. It was a system of title by registration and it became known as the Torrens system. The Torrens system of land registration is a system pursuant to which a central register is set up. The Register contains records and dealings relating to individual lots of land. Interests in land pass upon registration not upon the execution of any dealing document and the State guarantees the correctness of the Register.

It is important to note, however, that the doctrine of estates and the types of interests in land which can exist at common law have not been discarded under the Torrens system. Generally, the types of interests which can exist under the Torrens system are the same as those which can exist under the general law system. It is the means by which title passes in such interests which is wholly different under the Torrens system. The new system was named after Sir Robert Richard Torrens. There has been

---

1. Torrens, *The South Australian System of Conveyancing by Registration of Title* (1859), p. 8, quoted in Whalan, p. 14.

much debate surrounding the origins of the Torrens system and the exact nature of Sir Robert Torrens' contribution to the overall structure and the detailed provisions of the system. The researches of a number of authors demonstrate that the ideas and proposals put forward by Torrens were not totally new and original concepts.[2] Indeed, Torrens himself conceded this.

[5.03] The system appears to have been derived from a number of sources, including the Imperial Merchant Shipping Acts dealing with registration of title to ships, the system of registration of title to land in some Hanseatic towns and some suggestions made in the 1857 Report of English Royal Commissioners, a report which proposed the introduction of a system of registration of titles.[3] The issue of the relative importance of these sources and influences is probably incapable of authoritative resolution. Robinson, for example, has argued that the legislation enacted showed a strong and clear link with the Hanseatic system of land registration whilst others have argued that the system was derived from a number of sources.[4]

[5.04] Likewise, the issue of the input and importance of the role of Sir Robert Torrens has drawn widely varying views. In early times, it seems to have been accepted by some that Torrens conceived the idea for the system and worked out the structure and detail of the legislation, putting the scheme into effect with only a little assistance from the Merchant Shipping Acts.[5] This view of Torrens as the originator and author of a new system of registration of title has long since been discredited.[6] As explained above, it is clear that the ideas emanated from a number of different sources and it is also clear that several other individuals played important roles in the formulation of the system.[7] Robinson has argued that Dr Ulrich Hübbe, a German lawyer, is the person who should receive the greatest credit for the form and content of the legislation introducing the Torrens system.[8] Others prefer the view that credit is to be spread more evenly among a number of individuals including Torrens and Hübbe. Whatever the original contributions of Sir Robert Torrens to the structure and detail of the legislation, it is conceded by most authors that he was, in the words of Professor Whalan: "the most influential person in the introduction of registration of titles to land in Australasia."[9]

[5.05] Robert Richard Torrens emigrated to South Australia in 1840. From about 1852 he worked with enormous enthusiasm towards the introduction of a new system of land law. Although there was public support for a new system, the work of Torrens and his supporters was

2. See e.g. Hogg, *Australian Torrens System with Statutes* (1905), Chaps 1-4.
3. See generally Whalan, pp. 5-6. The relative importance of these sources is discussed by Robinson, pp. 1-25 and by Whalan, "The Origins of the Torrens System and its Introduction into New Zealand" in *The New Zealand Torrens System Centennial Essays* (1971), pp. 1-12.
4. Ibid.
5. See generally Sackville and Neave, p. 383.
6. See Hogg, op. cit., and Whalan, pp. 5-6.
7. See Whalan, pp. 4-6 and Whalan, op. cit., pp. 3-12.
8. Robinson, pp. 11-25.
9. Whalan, p. 5.

carried out against a barrage of eloquent opposition and criticism from the legal profession. The Torrens legislation in South Australia, the first Torrens legislation in Australian jurisdictions, went through a number of drafts before being enacted in 1858 as the *Real Property Act*.[10] Despite the care taken in the drafting there were many problems which required amendments to be made.[11] Further amendments were made in 1861 and in 1886 the *Real Property Act* was rewritten.[12] The introduction of the Torrens system of land registration in most other jurisdictions followed quickly[13] and by 1863, all jurisdictions except Western Australia had enacted Torrens legislation. In Western Australia, the Torrens statute came into operation in 1875.[14] From these respective dates, all land alienated by the Crown fell under the Torrens system of registration. The involvement of Torrens had not ended with the introduction of the legislation in South Australia. He continued to campaign for Torrens statutes in the other jurisdictions and provided practical help and support to the framers of the Torrens statutes in the other jurisdictions.[15]

[5.06] Although the Torrens statutes have retained the basic tenets of the system first introduced in the 1860s, many amendments have been made over the years to the original statutes. In New South Wales, the current Act is the *Real Property Act* 1900: important amendments have been made to this Act. In Victoria, the *Transfer of Land Act* 1958, as amended, is the present statute. There were major changes to the Victorian Torrens legislation in 1890, 1915, 1928 and 1954. In Queensland, the legislation is contained in the *Real Property Act* 1861 and the *Real Property Act* 1877 but there have been many significant amendments to these Acts. In South Australia, the *Real Property Act* 1886 as amended is the current legislation and in Western Australia the *Transfer of Land Act* 1893 as amended is the current legislation. In Tasmania, the Torrens legislation was amended and consolidated in the *Land Titles Act* 1980.

[5.07] Although the essence and the basic features of the Torrens system are contained within each of the Australian Torrens statutes, there are some quite significant differences which will be outlined in this Chapter. As Whalan has argued, this lack of uniformity, although not as vital as in areas such as company law or criminal law, may prevent an Australia wide land data bank.[16]

[5.08] Perhaps the most important reforms and amendments to the Torrens legislation which have occurred in the past decade concern the efforts in some jurisdictions to introduce a computerised automated title

---

10. Ibid.
11. These amendments were made in 1858.
12. See Whalan, pp. 7-8 for a discussion of various problems faced by the courts in interpreting the Torrens legislation.
13. In 1861 in Queensland (*Real Property Act*); in 1862 in Victoria and Tasmania (*Transfer of Land Act* and *Real Property Act* respectively) and in 1863 in New South Wales (*Real Property Act* 1862).
14. *Transfer of Land Act* 1874.
15. See Whalan, pp. 9-12.
16. Whalan, p. 12.

system and to speed up the process of conversion of general law land to
Torrens title land in those jurisdictions where general law land titles
remain.[17] In New South Wales, a system under which all manual Torrens
titles are to be converted to a computerised system of titles (known as
A.L.T.S.) was introduced by amendments to the *Real Property Act* 1900 in
1979.[18] The first conversions to computer titles were made in 1983[19] and
by early 1990, some two million titles had been computerised.[20] In
Queensland, the *Real Property Acts and Other Acts Amendment Act* 1986
provides for the computerisation of land titles in Queensland although
process of conversion of titles has yet to start.[21] In Victoria, the *Transfer
of Land (Computer Register) Act* was passed in 1989 but as of March 1990
had not been proclaimed. Although there has been computerisation of
some functions associated with title registration in other jurisdictions,[22]
computerisation of land titles has not occurred. There seems little doubt,
however, that computer land title registers will eventually replace the
manual or "paper" registers.[23] A further aim is to provide a system
whereby the computer registers of title can be integrated with other
information concerning the property in question where the additional
information is held by other Government agencies.[24] For instance,
information concerning local rates and taxes is held by local councils. This
aim will be more easily achieved in view of schemes such as Landata in
Victoria. Landata aims to provide "a centralised system of collecting and
providing land information held by Government"[25] and thus reduce the
number of individual and separate inquiries which need to be made by
purchasers.

The schemes introduced to accelerate the conversion of general law to
Torrens title are discussed below: see below **[5.135]-[5.145]**.

---

17. There are still areas of general law land in New South Wales, Victoria, Western
    Australia and Tasmania.
18. See generally Butt, p. 492.
19. Ibid.
20. Butt, p. 493 and Sackville and Neave, pp. 389-390 where a detailed account of
    the formal plan for conversion is set out.
21. Sackville and Neave, p. 390 and Preece, "The Real Property Acts and Other
    Acts Amendment Act" (1986) 16 Qld Law Soc. J. 103. Disussion with G. Topfer,
    Registrar's Office (Qld), 15 March 1990.
22. E.g. in Victoria unregistered dealings are computerised.
23. See Whalan, p. 80 where he comments on legislative changes which would need
    to be made in order for titles to be computerised. See the amendments made to
    the *Real Property Act* 1900 (N.S.W.) (e.g. s. 31B(3), (4), s. 3(1)(a)) discussed in
    Butt, pp. 493-494. See also Victorian Law Reform Commission (Vic. L.R.C.),
    The Torrens Register Book, Report No. 12 (November 1987), pp. 18-20 where the
    Commission discusses some of the problems of an automated Register. See the
    large number of legislative changes to the *Transfer of Land Act* 1958 (Vic.), made
    by the *Transfer of Land (Computer Register) Act* 1989 (Vic.) (not proclaimed as of
    May 1990). This legislation is outlined in fn. 29.
24. Vic. L.R.C., Report No. 12. See *Land (Transaction Information) Act* 1988 (Vic.)
    which makes provision to implement a computerised public inquiry service on
    property.
25. Vic. L.R.C., Report No. 12, p. 4. Landata was first established in Victoria in
    1982. See also Lang, "Computerized Land Title" (1983) 1 J.L.I.S. 230.

2. The Torrens System in Outline

[5.09] In all States, the Registrar[26] is directed to keep a Register[27] in which he or she keeps a record of all parcels of land falling under the Torrens system and of the persons holding interests in the parcels.[28] In Victoria,[29] South Australia and Western Australia the Registrar registers[30] all Crown grants and certificates of title[31] and any other instruments pertaining to the land which may be registered. Thus the Registrar sets out the type of estate and a description of the land for which the grant, certificate or folio has been issued and the name of the person in whose favour the grant is made and then notes any dealings, such as mortgages and leases which have been made with respect to the land. Crown grants and certificates of title pertain to a particular physical area or horizontal stratum of land. Each Crown grant or certificate of title constitutes a separate folium of the Register.[32] These folios are then placed

---

26. In Victoria, Queensland and Western Australia, the term is Registrar of Titles; in New South Wales and South Australia, the term is Registrar-General and in Tasmania, the term is Recorder of Titles. For ease of expression the term "Registrar" is generally used in this Chapter except where discussion is specifically concerned with one State: in such cases the strictly correct term, such as Registrar-General in New South Wales, is used.

27. In Victoria, South Australia and Western Australia, the Registrar keeps a "Register Book" and in New South Wales, Queensland and Tasmania, the Registrar keeps a "Register".

28. Torrens statutes: N.S.W.: s. 31B(1), (2); Vic.: s. 27; Qld: s. 32(1); S.A.: s. 47; W.A.: s. 48; Tas.: s. 33. Separate particular registers may also be set up: e.g. in South Australia and Western Australia a Register of Crown leases is kept. Torrens statutes: S.A.: s. 93; W.A.: s. 81A. See Chapter 19.

29. It is important to note that the position and terminology as described for Victoria do not include the amendments made to the *Transfer of Land Act* 1958 (Vic.), by the *Transfer of Land (Computer Register) Act* 1989 (Vic.). As of May 1990 this amending Act had not been proclaimed to come into operation. The following provides a brief summary of the effect of the Act. The *Transfer of Land (Computer Register) Act* 1989 (Vic.), is intended to facilitate the automation of the Land Titles Register. Thus it provides for the Registrar to keep the Register in or on any form or medium or combination of forms or mediums: s. 27(2). A medium includes a computer, microfilm or paper: s. 27(3). The Register comprises folios of the Register, each folio containing recordings permitted to be made and a distinctive identifying reference: s. 27(5) & (6). The Act contains detailed provisions as to the Register itself, recordings in the Register, the construction of references and the issue of certificates of title (a certificate of title is effectively a copy of the current recordings in the Register and occupies the same place in the system as the duplicate certificate of title). Although there are differences from the legislation which has enabled the computerisation of titles in New South Wales and Queensland, much of the terminology in the Victorian Act is similar. Thus, the Register (not the Register Book) comprises folios which may consist of various mediums and the certificate of title is not part of the Register but merely a copy of the existing recordings.

30. "Registers" in Victoria (s. 27); "files" in South Australia (s. 48); "registers by binding up" in Western Australia (s. 48).

31. A Crown grant is issued where the land is granted directly from the Crown and a certificate of title is issued where, for example, general law land is brought under the Torrens system. There is no difference in effect between the two: see Robinson, p. 135.

32. Torrens statutes: Vic.: s. 29(1); S.A.: s. 49; W.A.: s. 48.

in volumes. In Victoria, the registration of a Crown grant or certificate of titles takes place when it is signed or initialled by the Registrar. In South Australia and Western Australia, a grant or certificate of title is not registered until the folio and volume number has been marked on it.[33] All grants and certificates of title and folios are automatically issued in duplicate. The original is placed in the Register and the duplicate is handed to the registered proprietor.[34]

[5.10] In New South Wales, Queensland and Tasmania, the terminology used is different. In New South Wales, the Registrar-General is required to create a folio in the Register describing the land to which it relates and the estate or interest held in the land by the named proprietor or owner.[35] The Registrar-General is only required to issue a certificate of title which is effectively a copy of the folio if he or she is requested to do so by the registered proprietor or a registered mortgagee or chargee.[36] Because of the gradual computerisation of titles in New South Wales a folio may be a manual folio (that is, in traditional written form) or a computer folio.[37] In Queensland, the Registrar is required to maintain a register of every parcel of land and of all estates or interests which are required or permitted to be registered in each parcel of land. The Register may be maintained on paper, on microfilm, in or on such other medium as the Registrar considers appropriate or in such device for storing or processing information as the Registrar considers appropriate.[38] A certificate of title, which is an instrument evidencing the estate in fee simple or other estate or interest in land,[39] is effectively a copy of the relevant register and is issued to the person entitled thereto.[40] In Tasmania, the Recorder is directed to keep a Register which comprises folios and dealings.[41] Each folio is the record of title to a parcel of land[42] and a certificate of title is effectively the copy.[43] In these jurisdictions, land is subject to the Torrens statute and registered land when the Registrar creates a folio or, in Queensland, a register, relating to the specified land.[44] In order to so create a folio or a register inter alia the Registrar must allocate to the folio a distinctive reference or number.[45]

[5.11] Apart from the Registrar issuing a certificate of title or creating a folio for a fee simple estate, a certificate or folio may be issued for a life

33. Torrens statutes: Vic.: s. 29(2); S.A.: s. 50; W.A.: s. 52.
34. Torrens statutes: Vic.: s. 28; S.A.: s. 48; W.A.: s. 48. Cf. *Transfer of Land (Computer Register) Act* 1989 (Vic.), s. 7 (unproclaimed in May 1990).
35. Torrens statutes: N.S.W.: ss 31B, 32(1).
36. Torrens statutes: N.S.W.: s. 33. The certificate of title takes the place of the duplicate certificate of title and is used in the same way as the duplicate.
37. Torrens statutes: N.S.W.: s. 3(1)(a). See also *Transfer of Land (Computer Register) Act* 1989 (Vic.), which provides for similar terminology to that used in New South Wales.
38. Torrens statutes: Qld: s. 32(1), (4).
39. Torrens statutes: Qld: s. 3.
40. Torrens statutes: Qld: s. 33(3).
41. Torrens statutes: Tas: s. 33(4).
42. Torrens statutes: Tas: s. 33(5).
43. Torrens statutes: Tas: s. 33(8), (9).
44. Torrens statutes: N.S.W.: ss 31B, 32(1); Qld: s. 34(1); Tas.: s. 33(7).
45. Torrens statutes: N.S.W.: s. 32(1); Qld: s. 32(3); Tas.: s. 33(5)(b).

estate.[46] In some jurisdictions, long-term lessees of land which is not under the Torrens system may apply to have the leasehold estate registered under the system.[47] Further, in some jurisdictions, a lessee of Torrens land may apply for the issue of a separate certificate for the leasehold estate.[48] This may prove very useful where the lease itself is to be the subject of a number of dealings.[49] Separate certificates of title may be issued for tenants in common.[50]

[5.12] Once a Crown grant, certificate of title or folio has issued, the person named as the holder of the estate or interest—the registered proprietor—may deal with the estate or interest. The Torrens statutes set out the types of dealings which may be entered into by the registered proprietor. The relevant provisions in the Victorian statute provide an example and are similar to the provisions in the other States. Inter alia, the registered proprietor may transfer,[51] lease,[52] sublease[53] and mortgage[54] her or his interest in the land. Any such dealing must be effected by the use of the appropriate form as set out in the Torrens statutes[55] and it is only upon registration of the appropriate form or memorandum by the Registrar on the Crown grant, title or folio that title passes and the benefits of registration are obtained by the transferee. Thus, there are specific forms for each of the possible dealings, such as transfers, mortgages and leases, which may be registered.[56] Some interests although not registrable, may be noted or recorded on the Register. Thus, for example, restrictive covenants may be noted on the certificate of title of the burdened land in New South Wales, Victoria, Western Australia and Tasmania: see below [17.11]. Effectively, such notification ensures that a purchaser of the burdened land is bound by the restrictive covenant: see below [5.38]-[5.39] and [17.11]. Indefeasibility of title

46. See Whalan, pp. 85-86 for a discussion on the issues and difficulties arising when a life interest and a remainder exist.
47. Torrens statutes: N.S.W.: s. 14(2)(b) (a lease for a life or lives or a lease with 25 years to run); Vic.: s. 9(2) and W.A.: s. 39 (a lease for a life or lives or a lease with ten years to run). Except in Queensland and Tasmania, Crown leases fall under the operation of the Torrens system: see Chapter 19.
48. Torrens statutes: N.S.W.: s. 32(3); Qld: s. 34; W.A.: s. 39; Tas.: s. 33(6)(a), (8), s. 71.
49. See Whalan, p. 87.
50. Torrens statutes: N.S.W.: s. 100(2), (3); Vic.: s. 30(2); Qld: s. 40; S.A.: s. 74; W.A.: s. 60; Tas.: s. 33(6)(d). Quaere the position of joint tenants. It seems that separate certificates may only be issued in Tasmania: s. 33(6)(d), (8). A more detailed examination of the nature of interests pursuant to which grants or certificates may issue can be found in Whalan, p. 12.
51. Torrens statutes: Vic.: s. 45.
52. Torrens statutes: Vic.: s. 66 (for a term not less than three years).
53. Torrens statutes: Vic.: s. 71 (for a term not less than three years).
54. Torrens statutes: Vic.: s. 74.
55. Even in jurisdictions where permissive terminology is used, the use of the prescribed form has been held to be mandatory: see *Crowley v. Templeton* (1914) 17 C.L.R. 457 at 463 per Griffith C J.
56. As to registration of incorporeal hereditaments: see below [16.40], [16.44], [16.45]. It seems that profits à prendre may be registered: see *Ellison v. Vukicevic* (1986) 7 N.S.W.L.R. 104 at 119.

does not, however, attach to the interest so noted: see below **[5.20]-[5.35]** and **[17.11]**.

[5.13] Apart from instruments of dealing, a person may be entitled to obtain a registered interest pursuant to a transmission. The law in each State sets out particular events pursuant to which title may be acquired by transmission. Events which operate to pass title from a registered proprietor include the death or bankruptcy of the proprietor.[57] In some States where a person who is registered as a joint proprietor dies, the surviving joint proprietor may apply to the Registrar to be registered as proprietor and upon proof of the death, the Registrar so registers the survivor.[58]

[5.14] The Registrar's powers are set out in the provisions defining the particular duties and functions of the Registrar. Further, the Registrar has general powers including the power to call for documents[59] and to. require persons to appear before her or him.[60] Many powers of the Registrar are discretionary but the Registrar cannot refuse to register an instrument produced in proper form.[61] The statutes contain appeal provisions and decisions of the Registrar may be appealed.

[5.15] An issue arises as to the terminology to be used in relation to registered interests. Does the registered proprietor hold a "registered" interest or a "legal" interest? If a mortgage is registered, does the mortgagee hold under a "registered" mortgage or a "legal" mortgage? Although the legal and equitable interest distinction in the Torrens system was eschewed in the early days (see below **[5.78]**) the dichotomy is now clearly established and it seems to be accepted that "the statutory form of transfer . . . when registered . . . is effective to pass the legal title".[62] It is important to note, however, that the registered or legal interest under the Torrens system differs from the legal interest under the general law. Their respective spheres of enforceability are quite different. Although the term registered interest may be used more often, the terms "registered" and "legal" interest may generally be used interchangeably. It is arguable that they cannot *always* be so used because some interests may be "legal" in character although not registered. An example of such an interest may be the short-term tenancy. In Victoria, for example, only a lease for a term exceeding three years may be registered.[63] Despite the lack of

---

57. See generally, Torrens statutes: N.S.W.: s. 3(1)(a), Pt XI; Vic.: ss 4(1), 49, 51; Qld: ss 3, 86, 89 (note that s. 89 (death) requiring an application to the Supreme Court); *Real Property Act* 1877, ss 32-33; S.A.: ss 3, 175-187; W.A.: ss 4(1), 187, 203, 221, 234; Tas.: ss 3(1), 49, 98, 99, 100. For a detailed discussion of the operation of these provisions, see Whalan, Chap. 18.
58. Torrens statutes: Vic.: s. 50; S.A.: s. 188; W.A.: s. 227; Tas.: s. 100. Cf. New South Wales and Queensland: see below **[9.26]-[9.27]**.
59. Torrens statutes: N.S.W.: s. 12(1)(a); Vic.: ss 104, 105; Qld: s. 11(1); S.A.: s. 220; W.A.: s. 180; Tas.: s. 160(1).
60. Torrens statutes: N.S.W.: s. 12(1)(b); Vic.: ss 104(3), 116A; Qld: s. 11(2); S.A.: s. 220; W.A.: s. 180; Tas.: s. 160(2), (6).
61. *Perpetual Executors & Trustees Association of Australia v. Hosken* (1912) 14 C.L.R. 286.
62. *Abigail v. Lapin* [1934] A.C. 491 at 500.
63. Torrens statutes: Vic.: s. 66(1).

registration, a lease for three years or less may be, however, "legal" rather than "equitable" in nature. The contention is that if there is a means provided in the Torrens legislation by which an interest can be registered pursuant to a registrable instrument, the interest can only be, at best, an equitable interest if it is not registered. However, where there is no means of registering, such as the case of the short-term tenancy in Victoria, it is suggested that the interest is of the same type as it would have been under the general law.[64] Alternatively, the view may be taken that all unregistered interests, whether registrable or not, are equitable in character. In most instances, the nature of unregistrable interests would be equitable under the general law. In most cases, the nature of the interest (that is, whether it is legal or equitable) does not affect the outcome of any dispute. The interest of a tenant in possession in Victoria for example, is specifically protected whether it is termed a legal or equitable interest: see **[5.59]-[5.60]** and **[10.87]**.

[5.16] It is clear, then, that the starting point of the Torrens system of registration is to provide a record relating to each piece of land. "The unit of land [is] the basis of record."[65] If this is so, the unit of land must be accurately defined. Although precise definition is possible now, in the early days surveys were often inaccurate and this caused and still causes, some problems. Once a Crown grant, certificate of title or folio has been created with respect to any piece of land, the Registrar registers all dealings in the land if such dealings are presented in registrable form.[66] In relation to any one piece of land the Register is thereby intended to provide a record of the state of the title so that intending purchasers have only to search the one folio in order to determine the nature of any interests existing over the land and the identity of the holders of these interests. The concept is that a person who acquires land or an interest in it (bona fide and for consideration, and takes a registered interest), should be subject only to those interests he or she can discover from a search of the Register.

[5.17] In reality, the position is more complicated. First, various statutes which give rise to interests in land may override the relevant State Torrens legislation and thus permit the enforceability of interests not disclosed on the Register as against the registered proprietor: see below **[5.65]-[5.67]**. Secondly, all of the Torrens statutes provide, to a greater or lesser degree, for particular interests to prevail over the title of a registered interest holder: see below **[5.40]-[5.62]**. Although the discussion of these paramount exceptions below demonstrates that there

---

64. This conclusion is suggested by Sykes, p. 219. See *Josephson v. Mason* (1912) 12 S.R. (N.S.W.) 249; *Munro v. Stewart* (1924) 41 S.R. (N.S.W.) 203. The sphere of enforceability of a legal but not registered interest is presumably the same as the enforceability of a legal interest under the general law. It would not survive against a registered interest. Note, however, that in the case of the short term tenancy, the interest of the tenant is expressly protected: see below **[5.59]-[5.60]** and **[10.87]**.

65. Whalan, p. 18; cf. the system of private conveyancing discussed in Chaps 3 & 4.

66. The Registrar's discretion in registering dealings which contain errors is discussed in Whalan, pp. 147-148. This discretion varies from State to State.

is a need for such provisions, their presence inevitably means that the Register itself will not contain a record of all interests binding the registered proprietor. Thirdly, it is clear that interests in the land may exist outside the Register and although this factor does not directly interfere with the integrity of the Register, it can complicate the simple picture of a registered proprietor being subject only to prior registered interests. Various provisions of the Torrens statutes themselves, by providing for caveats to protect unregistered interests (see below [5.81]- [5.86]) and by referring to declarations of trust,[67] reveal that it was always envisaged that interests in the land, which might be termed unregistered or equitable interests,[68] could exist in Torrens land.[69] Such interests may arise, for example, through the previous registered proprietor having made a declaration of trust or entered into a specifically enforceable contract. The adequacy and correctness of the Register, at least from the point of view of providing a record of interests in the land which will bind any person subsequently taking a registered interest, is not threatened by the presence of unregistered interests in the same way as it is in the first two examples. This is because the bona fide purchaser who becomes a registered proprietor is not subject to any such equitable unregistered interests which would have bound the previous registered proprietor in personam: he or she takes subject only to interests on the Register.

Although their existence is probably inevitable, the very presence of interests existing off the Register necessarily means that the Register may not reflect all interests existing in the land. Further, although a purchaser with notice of a prior, unregistered interest is not bound by it once registered, difficult factual issues may arise when a court is asked to consider whether the "notice" actually amounted to "fraud" within the meaning of the Torrens statute. As will be discussed below, a registered proprietor who registers with fraud will effectively be subject to the prior unregistered interest: see below [5.40]-[5.49].

[5.18]   The caveat is designed to provide some protection for unregistered interests. The provision for lodgment of caveats was one of the clearest indicators that unregistered interests in land can exist. It is the caveat against dealings which is a means of providing some protection for the unregistered interest. The provisions relating to caveats are discussed below [5.40]-[5.49].

[5.19]   Of course, in order to protect an unregistered or equitable interest by caveat, the holder of the interest must be aware that he or she does hold such an interest. As will be discussed in Chapter 6, equitable interests may arise from a variety of informal transactions. Very often the holder of an equitable interest arising pursuant to an informal transaction

---

67. Subject to limited exceptions, the Registrar cannot make any entry of any notice of any type of trust. It is expressly provided, however, that trusts of Torrens land can be created. Torrens statutes: N.S.W.: s. 82(1), (2); Vic.: s. 37; Qld: ss 77, 78, 79; S.A.: s. 162; W.A.: s. 55; Tas.: s. 132.
68. See generally Chapter 6 for a discussion of the nature of these interests.
69. The High Court in *Barry v. Heider* (1914) 19 C.L.R. 197 removed any doubt as to the existence of unregistered or equitable interests in Torrens land.

may be unaware of the possibility that her or his actions have given rise to a proprietary interest in land. If so unaware, the recipient will fail to use the means available to protect the interest. That is, he or she will fail to lodge a caveat. In a system where the emphasis is on the registration and recording of interests, the holder of such an equitable interest is often in an invidious position. Not only might there be difficulty in establishing the existence of the interest but the lack of protection of the interest at a time when the holder was unaware of her or his rights may result in loss of the interest if a bona fide transferee becomes registered. Effectively, a person holding such an equitable interest may be in a worse position than if he or she held such an interest under the general law system. Although social patterns and the traditional roles of men and women have changed during the latter part of the 20th century, it is still the case that women rather than men are more likely to hold equitable interests arising out of informal transactions. The Torrens system with its emphasis on the recording of interests may thus be viewed as a form of gender bias.

II. INDEFEASIBILITY OF TITLE

1. Introduction and Statutory Provisions

[5.20] The term "indefeasibility of title" is one which is so well entrenched in the Torrens system language that any reader in the area would expect to find a clear and simple definition of it in each of the Torrens statutes. The reverse is the case. In fact, the word "indefeasible" is used in only two jurisdictions[70] and is specifically defined only in the Tasmanian statute. Instead, the concept of indefeasibility is to be gleaned from a composite of provisions in the statutes. These sets of provisions have been categorised by a number of authors as the "paramountcy", the "ejectment", the "notice" and the "protection" (or "protection of purchasers") provisions.[71]

[5.21] The "paramountcy" sections are the provisions which set out the most positive statement of indefeasibility. In all States except South Australia and Tasmania, the paramountcy section provides that notwithstanding the existence in any other person of any estate or interest which but for this Act may be held to have priority, the registered proprietor of any estate or interest in the land shall except in the case of fraud and subject to other various exceptions which differ from jurisdiction to jurisdiction hold the land, estate or interest subject only to the encumbrances, liens, estates or interests noted to the Register.[72] Although differently set out, the paramountcy provisions in South Australia and Tasmania have a similar effect. In South Australia, it is

---

70. Torrens statutes: S.A.: s. 69; Tas.: s. 40.
71. See e.g. Harrison, "Indefeasibility of Torrens Title" (1952) 2 U.Q.L.J. 206; Sykes, p. 446; and Whalan, pp. 293ff. Note that Harrison and Sykes also refer to the "priority" provision which sets out that instruments registered in respect of the same estate or interest are entitled to priority according to the date of registration and not according to the date of each instrument.
72. Torrens statutes: N.S.W.: s. 42; Vic.: s. 42; Qld: s. 44; W.A.: s. 68.

provided that the title of the registered proprietor is absolute and indefeasible, subject only to encumbrances, liens, estates or interests noted on the Register and other particular listed exceptions, one of which is fraud.[73] In all other cases the registered proprietor's title prevails over the estate or interest of any other person which but for the Act might have been held to have priority.[74] In Tasmania, it is provided that subject to the listed exceptions, the title of the registered proprietor is indefeasible.[75] Indefeasible is defined as "subject only to such estates and interests as are recorded on the folio of the Register or registered dealing evidencing title to the land". The title of the registered proprietor prevails notwithstanding the existence of any other estate or interest in any person which but for the Torrens statute might have been held to have priority.

Thus the basic theme of the Register accurately reflecting title is reinforced by the corollary that the person named as a registered interest holder does so hold the estate and, apart from stated exceptions, is not subject to the estate or interest of any other person which in the absence of the Torrens legislation, may have been held to be paramount. Common law principles relating to the relevance of validity of documents and priority rules are displaced. In several jurisdictions, the paramountcy sections are reinforced by the "ejectment" provisions which effectively provide that no person can maintain an action to recover the land against the registered proprietor except in particular named circumstances.[76]

[5.22]   As stated above, the paramountcy provisions are those which state the principle of indefeasibility of title most positively. The "notice" and the "protection" provisions set out in more detail and explain more fully the consequences of having a concept of indefeasibility of title. Arguably, these provisions do not expand the meaning of indefeasibility: it may have been possible to assume their content from the paramountcy provisions. For example, if the registered proprietor's title is subject only to estates or interests noted on the Register, the inevitable conclusion is that the registered proprietor is not subject to an unregistered interest even if he or she had notice of it.

The notice and protection provisions direct attention to the position of a person who intends to take a registered interest and is for this purpose dealing with the registered proprietor. Pursuant to the notice provisions, a transferee is not affected by actual or constructive notice of any unregistered interests and is not required to enquire into the circumstances under, or the consideration for which the transferor or any

---

73. Torrens statutes: S.A.: s. 69.
74. Torrens statutes: S.A.: s. 70.
75. Torrens statutes: Tas.: s. 40.
76. Torrens statutes: N.S.W.: s. 124; Qld: s. 123; W.A.: s. 199; Tas.: s. 149. It should be noted that the particular named circumstances in which ejectment can be maintained do not always coincide with the exceptions in the paramountcy provisions. As Whalan states "the 'ejectment provision' is thus more of a corollary to the 'paramountcy provision' than the converse of it": Whalan, p. 295.

previous proprietor was registered.[77] The relevant provisions have been interpreted so that protection against notice is provided only upon registration by the transferee.[78] The protection provisions have some differences in wording but have similar meanings.[79] They provide that nothing in the Act is to be interpreted so as to leave subject to an action for recovery of damages, or to an action for possession or ejectment or to deprivation of the estate in respect of which he or she is registered as proprietor, any purchaser or mortgagee bona fide for valuable consideration on the ground that her or his vendor or mortgagor may have been registered through fraud or error or may have derived through or from a person registered as proprietor through fraud or error.[80] This is the case whether the fraud or error consists of wrong description of the boundaries or the parcels of land or otherwise.[81]

As in the case of the notice provision, it may be argued that the protection provision is simply explanatory of the general principle expounded in the paramountcy provision. By providing that the registered proprietor, if not fraudulent, takes free of any other claims or interests not noted on the Register, the paramountcy provision is indirectly providing, for example, that any fraud by a previous registered proprietor cannot affect the validity of the current registered proprietor's title. The protection provisions specifically make it clear any such fraud or error one step away from the registered proprietor does not affect the registered proprietor's title.

[5.23] As Whalan has argued, the term "indefeasibility" as meaning incapable of being annulled, defeated or abrogated is an inappropriate term to describe the protection afforded to a Torrens title.[82] Indefeasibility of title under the Torrens system means that the title, if considered at a given time, cannot be defeated. It does not mean that the title is incapable of defeat at that time and any time in the future. A registered proprietor with an indefeasible title may lose that title if another person becomes the registered proprietor without fraud: indefeasibility attaches to the second proprietor, the person currently registered. A number of the cases discussed below are examples of such a scenario which is most often caused by the intervention of a fraudulent third party: see below **[5.25]-[5.32]**.

[5.24] Despite the inappropriateness of the term "indefeasibility" it is suggested that it is too embedded in the Torrens language for any change

---

77. Torrens statutes: N.S.W.: s. 43; Vic.: s. 43; Qld: s. 109; S.A.: ss 186, 187; W.A.: s. 134; Tas.: s. 41. The terminology of the Queensland provision is simpler than the wording of this provision in the other States. See Whalan, p. 295 and Robinson, p. 201ff. See also Sykes, pp. 447-448 where the differences in the provisions are discussed.
78. *Templeton v. The Leviathan Pty Ltd* (1921) 30 C.L.R. 34.
79. Torrens statutes: N.S.W.: s. 135; Vic.: s. 44(2); Qld: s. 126; S.A.: s. 207; W.A.: s. 202; Tas.: s. 42.
80. Victoria and Western Australia "purchaser"; South Australia "transferee", "encumbrancee" and "lessee". See Sykes, p. 448 for a discussion of the differences in the wording of the provisions.
81. Robinson, p. 209 comments on the inapt wording of the "protection" provision.
82. Whalan, p. 296.

to be made. The exact extent of protection given by indefeasibility has been the subject of much dispute and has been examined in numerous cases. It is examined below.

2. The Meaning and Extent of Indefeasibility

(a) The current position in outline

[5.25] The Torrens system sets up a regime pursuant to which title is acquired by registration. As described above, registration is a process separate from the process of transfer: see **[5.09]-[5.16]**. The process of transfer involves the parties to the transaction executing registrable documents: the process of registration involves the Registrar in actually registering the documents. Whilst for a time it was held that particular invalidities in the process of transfer could prevent title passing even after the completion of registration, it is now clear that if a document is registered, title passes to the registered transferee whatever the invalidity in the process of transfer.[83] If the registered transferee can prove that the invalidity in the process of transfer did not amount to fraud on her or his part and that he or she was not fraudulent in any other way, the title will be indefeasible. Where the invalidity in the process of transfer involves fraud on the part of the registered transferee, or there is otherwise fraud by that party, title still vests in the transferee but it is a defeasible title. A previous registered proprietor who has been defrauded is able to bring an action to recover the title.

[5.26] The High Court decision in *Breskvar v. Wall*[84] demonstrates clearly the dichotomy between the processes of transfer and registration, and highlights the fact that registration is the means by which title passes. The Breskvars were the registered proprietors of land. As security for a loan provided by Petrie they handed the duplicate certificate of title to Petrie and they also executed a transfer of the land. The name of the transferee was left out. Pursuant to the *Stamps Act* 1894 (Qld), a transfer executed in such a way was a void document. The intention of the parties was that the transfer should only be completed and registered if the Breskvars defaulted in repayment. Despite there having been no such default, the name of Petrie's grandson, Wall, was inserted into the transfer and Wall became the registered proprietor. Wall was a party to the fraud aimed at depriving the Breskvars of their land. Before the Breskvars had discovered the fraud, Wall had contracted to sell the land to Alban Pty Ltd and had executed a transfer.

It was argued on behalf of the Breskvars that they had retained title because registration of a void instrument (the transfer being void because

---

83. *Breskvar v. Wall* (1971) 126 C.L.R. 376; [1972] A.L.R. 205. Cf. *Chasfild Pty Ltd v. Taranto* (1990) V. Conv. R. 54-367. Note that registration of a discharge of an interest, for example, a discharge of mortgage, results in indefeasibility in the same way as the registration of, for example, the mortgage itself: see *Schultz v. Corwill Properties Pty Ltd* (1969) W.N. (Pt I) N.S.W. 59.
84. (1971) 126 C.L.R. 376; (1972) 46 A.L.J.R. 68.

of the *Stamps Act*) was ineffective to pass any interest or title to Wall.[85] All members of the High Court rejected this submission and took the view that an invalidity in the process of transfer did not have the effect of preventing the passing of title upon registration.[86] The fact that Wall had been fraudulent resulted in his title being defeasible but whilst remaining on the title, Wall was the registered proprietor and could create valid interests in third parties. The dispute between the two innocent parties, the Breskvars and Alban Pty Ltd was thus a dispute between holders of unregistered interests: the Breskvars having a right to sue to recover the land and have the Register rectified as against Wall and Alban Pty Ltd having an equitable interest under the contract of sale.[87] This dispute was resolved in favour of Alban Pty Ltd.[88]

(b) The deferred versus immediate indefeasibility debate

[5.27] The material above suggests that in the absence of fraud indefeasibility of title occurs immediately upon registration. Whilst this is accepted as the case now,[89] for many years the most elusive question in the debate about the nature of indefeasibility concerned the time at which indefeasibility attaches to the registered title and it is intended to trace this development here. The debate may be termed the "deferred" versus "immediate" indefeasibility clash. Does a registered proprietor gain indefeasibility of title immediately upon registration or is the indefeasibility deferred?

An example is the clearest means of demonstrating the distinction between these concepts and of illustrating why and how it can become important. Assume A, the registered proprietor of Blackacre leaves her duplicate certificate of title with her solicitor, S, for safekeeping and that S forges A's name to a transfer of the land in favour of B. Subsequently, the transfer is registered and B becomes the registered proprietor. A and B are both innocent parties. Does B, who is now the registered proprietor, have an indefeasible title or can A successfully maintain an action to recover "her" land? On the theory of immediate indefeasibility, B's title is indefeasible.[90] On the theory of deferred indefeasibility, B's title is not indefeasible: indefeasibility is "deferred" to one transaction away from the problem dealing.[91] Thus, if B subsequently transferred the land to C and C became the registered proprietor, C's title would be indefeasible and not subject to any attack by A.[92]

---

85. Reliance was placed on the decisions in *Gibbs v. Messer* [1891] A.C. 248 and *Clements v. Ellis* (1934) 51 C.L.R. 217 discussed below [5.28].
86. The High Court followed the reasoning of the Privy Council in *Frazer v. Walker* [1967] 1 A.C. 569.
87. *Barry v. Heider* (1914) 19 C.L.R. 197.
88. Discussed further below [5.31], [5.107] and [5.111].
89. Cf. *Chasfild Pty Ltd v. Taranto* (1990) V. Conv. R. 54-367.
90. The "paramountcy" provisions support this result.
91. The "protection" provisions support this result.
92. Ibid.

For many years, the Australian courts following the Privy Council decision in *Gibbs v. Messer*[93] adopted deferred indefeasibility as the test.[94] However, since the decision of the Privy Council in 1967 in *Frazer v. Walker*[95] the theory of immediate indefeasibility has been embraced.

[5.28] In *Gibbs v. Messer*, Mrs Messer, the registered proprietor of land, left her duplicate certificate of title with her solicitor, Cresswell. Cresswell forged Mrs Messer's name to a transfer of the land in favour of "Cameron", a non-existent person, and "Cameron" became the registered proprietor. Cresswell then prepared a mortgage from "Cameron" to the McIntyres, other clients of his, as security for a loan of money from the McIntyres to "Cameron". The mortgage in favour of the McIntyres was registered and Cresswell absconded with the money. Mrs Messer discovered what had happened and she brought an action to cancel the certificate of title and to have issued to her a new certificate of title in her name, subject to no encumbrance.[96] The Privy Council held in favour of Mrs Messer and ordered that her name be restored to the Register. The mortgage of the McIntyres was held not to constitute an encumbrance on her title.[97]

A number of possible reasons for the decision have been advanced. First, the decision may have stood for the proposition that a person registering any void instrument does not obtain an indefeasible title. This interpretation means that if a document is void for any reason on ordinary principles of law, it cannot be validated by registration. Forgery, lack of capacity, and non est factum in the making of a document all render the document null and void. The relevant Torrens legislation contained no specific exception to indefeasibility based on the voidness of a document through which registration was obtained: as explained above, the tenor of the statutes was that fraud *in the person* obtaining registration, was to prevent the acquisition of indefeasibility of title. The validity of this possible ratio with the Torrens legislation requires an acceptance that this vital part of the Torrens legislation cannot be read alone, but must be read in light of general principles relating to the voidness of documents.

Secondly, and more narrowly, it can be argued that the decision was based upon a holding that a person registering an instrument void, specifically because of forgery, cannot obtain an indefeasible title. This possible ratio was based upon that part of s. 43 of the Victorian Act, the notice provision, which requires that a person must deal with the registered proprietor on the faith of the Register in order to gain an indefeasible title. Where there is a forgery, the innocent person becoming

---

93. [1891] A.C. 248.
94. See e.g. *Clements v. Ellis* (1934) 51 C.L.R. 217 (cf. the dissenting judgments of Rich J. at 229 and Evatt J. at 260).
95. [1967] 1 A.C. 569. The issue of indefeasibility in light of *Frazer v. Walker* is discussed by Sackville, "The Torrens System—Some Thoughts on Indefeasibility and Priorities" (1973) 47 A.L.J. 526.
96. Alternatively if the mortgage were held to be valid, the plaintiff sought that she be at liberty to redeem the mortgage with moneys paid out of the Assurance Fund.
97. Thus the McIntyres lost their mortgage and had no claim against the Assurance Fund.

registered has not dealt with the registered proprietor, but a forger.[98] Finally, it has been said that the decision in *Gibbs v. Messer* was based on the registration of a non-existent person as registered proprietor.[99]

Whatever the reason for the decision, the Privy Council clearly accepted, however, that a bona fide purchaser from the McIntyres would have obtained an indefeasible title.[100] Indefeasibility was to be "deferred" to one step away from the void document. If, for example, Cresswell had perpetrated the fraud by transferring the fee simple to himself instead of "Cameron", the McIntyres' mortgage would then have been indefeasible. The document of mortgage from Cresswell to the McIntyres would have been an internally valid one and they would have been bona fide purchasers.[101]

[5.29] Some 15 years later the Privy Council in *Assets Co. Ltd v. Mere Roihi*[102] had the opportunity to look again at the nature and extent of indefeasibility of title. Although it is strongly arguable that the Privy Council favoured a theory of immediate indefeasibility, various factors resulted in its actual decision not reflecting this unambiguously.[103] In New Zealand, the view was taken that the *Assets* case did support immediate indefeasibility. For example, in *Boyd v. Mayor of Wellington*,[104] a proclamation vesting part of the plaintiff's land in the Wellington Corporation was registered. The plaintiff argued that the proclamation was void as it was ultra vires. It was held that even if the proclamation were void, registration of it conferred an indefeasible title on the Corporation. The majority relied upon *Assets Co. Ltd v. Mere Roihi.*[105] In Australia, the courts took a different course and followed a theory of deferred indefeasibility.[106] Compliance with the provision requiring that there had been a dealing with the registered proprietor was insisted upon and registration of a forged document did not confer indefeasibility. The acceptance of deferred indefeasibility continued until 1967 when the Privy Council decided the case of *Frazer v. Walker*. The Privy Council firmly indorsed the concept of immediate indefeasibility.

98. See *Clements v. Ellis* (1934) 51 C.L.R. 217 and the rather strained interpretations by Dixon J. at 236-237 and McTiernan J. at 272-275 of the phrase "dealing with the registered proprietor".
99. The Privy Council in *Frazer v. Walker* [1967] 1 A.C. 569 distinguished *Gibbs v. Messer* on this basis. Note, however, that Lord Watson in *Gibbs v. Messer* specifically denied that the decision was based on the non-existence of "Cameron".
100. The "protection" provisions, such as s. 44(2) of the Victorian Act would ensure this result.
101. Bona fide purchasers of the mortgage.
102. [1905] A.C. 176.
103. Two of the three appeals could clearly have been decided on the basis of deferred indefeasibility. See the discussion by Whalan, p. 300.
104. [1924] N.Z.L.R. 1174.
105. The New Zealand courts followed the decision in the *Boyd* case and accepted immediate indefeasibility. See e.g. *Pearson v. Aotea District Maori Land Board* [1945] N.Z.L.R. 542.
106. See e.g. *Clements v. Ellis* (1934) 51 C.L.R. 217.

[5.30] The facts in *Frazer v. Walker* were as follows. The Frazers were registered proprietors of the land in question and Mrs Frazer forged her husband's signature to a mortgage of the property in favour of Radomski. As she failed to meet the mortgage payments Radomski, the registered mortgagee, exercised his power of sale and sold to Walker who became the registered proprietor. When Walker attempted to obtain possession of the land, Mr Frazer claimed that the mortgage to Radomski was a nullity because of the forgery and asked for the entries on the Register of the mortgage to Radomski and that the interest of Walker be cancelled. It was strictly unnecessary for the Privy Council to consider the immediate and deferred indefeasibility clash. The essential dispute was between the Frazers and Walker. Walker was one transaction removed from the invalid document (the forged mortgage from the Frazers to Radomski) and thus, as a bona fide purchaser would have defeated the Frazers even on the concept of deferred indefeasibility.[107] The Privy Council took the opportunity, however, to express its views on the debate.

The court held in favour of the theory of immediate indefeasibility. It held that the title of Radomski, whilst on foot, was an indefeasible title from the time of registration. Radomski had taken without fraud on his part and the fact that the mortgage document was a void document at common law did not affect the indefeasibility of his title. The Privy Council relied upon its earlier decision in *Assets Co. Ltd v. Mere Roihi* and on the case of *Boyd v. Mayor of Wellington Corporation*. The decision in *Gibbs v. Messer* was not overruled but distinguished on the basis that it involved a fictitious person. The basis for distinguishing *Gibbs v. Messer* was flawed as it seems that the Privy Council's decision in the *Gibbs* case would have been the same even if "Cameron" had been a real person.

It is clear that the basis of the decision in *Gibbs v. Messer*, that is, support for deferred indefeasibility, is no longer good law. Nevertheless, the fact that the decision has not been overruled and the method by which it was distinguished in *Frazer v. Walker* leaves open the possibility that if a set of facts arose, identical to those in *Gibbs v. Messer*, the decision in *Gibbs v. Messer* may be applicable. Such a result would be inappropriate for it would be an unnecessary and an anomalous exception to immediate indefeasibility.[108]

[5.31] The Privy Council in *Frazer v. Walker* stated clearly that indefeasibility of title was subject to the exceptions of fraud and to any rights in personam. These exceptions are discussed below: see **[5.40]**-

---

107. This was the manner in which the case was decided by the New Zealand Court of Appeal: [1966] N.Z.L.R. 331.
108. See generally: Whalan, p. 308 and Brookfield, "The Land Transfer System Problems and Developments since Frazer v. Walker" [1975] N.Z.L.J. 473, discussed in Whalan, where a possible extension to the fictitious person category is discussed. See also *Wicklow Enterprises Pty Ltd v. Doysal Pty Ltd* (1986) 45 S.A.S.R. 247 where the plaintiff sought to rely on *Gibbs v. Messer*. The court held that the intention to defraud is an essential element of forgery and as there was no such intention on the facts, the principle of *Gibbs v. Messer* (whatever it might be) was inapplicable. For a discussion of this case see Moore, "Interpretation of the Real Property Act" (1988) 11 Adel. L.R. 405.

[5.49] and **[5.68]-[5.72]**. The principle of immediate indefeasibility was rapidly accepted and applied in several State Supreme Court decisions[109] and in 1971, the High Court in *Breskvar v. Wall*[110] accepted the applicability of the principle. As Barwick C.J. commented:[111]

"[A] registration which results from a void instrument is effective according to the terms of the registration. The affirmation by the Privy Council in *Frazer v. Walker* of the decision of the Supreme Court [sic.] of New Zealand in *Boyd v. Mayor of Wellington* now places that conclusion beyond question."

The *Breskvar* case is considered in more detail above and below.[112]

[5.32] Despite the general acceptance of the concept of immediate indefeasibility, it has recently been held that in certain circumstances immediate indefeasibility is inapplicable in Victoria. In *Chasfild Pty Ltd v. Taranto*[113] Gray J. held that the presence of s. 44(1), a provision unique to Victoria, effects such a result. The dispute in the case was between the registered proprietor and the registered mortgagee. The actions of fraudulent third parties had resulted in the forged mortgage being registered on the title: the registered proprietor and the registered mortgagee were both innocent parties. The registered proprietor knew nothing of the mortgage and when repayment of the principal sum was not made, the mortgagee sought an order for possession and the registered proprietor counter-claimed seeking rectification of the Register by removal of the plaintiff's registered mortgage.

Section 44(1) provides:

"Any certificate of title or entry alteration removal or cancellation in the Register Book procured or made by fraud shall be void as against any person defrauded or sought to be defrauded thereby and no party or privy to the fraud shall take any benefit therefrom."

Section 44(1) was inserted into the Victorian Torrens statute in 1954 at the same time as the ejectment provision was deleted, seemingly as being obsolete.[114] In fact, s. 44(1) was not a wholly new provision but rather a rewording of s. 104 in the 1928 Victorian Act.[115] Section 44(1) was

109. See *Mayer v. Coe* (1968) 88 W.N. (Pt 1) (N.S.W.) 549; *Ratcliffe v. Watters* (1969) 89 W.N. (Pt 1) (N.S.W.) 497; *Schultz v. Corwill Properties Pty Ltd* (1969) 90 W.N. (Pt 1) (N.S.W.) 529.
110. (1971) 126 C.L.R. 376; [1972] A.L.R. 205.
111. (1971) 126 C.L.R. 376 at 385-386; [1972] A.L.R. 205 at 209.
112. See above **[5.26]** and below **[5.107]** and **[5.111]**. See also *Tyre Marketers (Aust.) Ltd v. Martin Alstergren Pty Ltd* (1989) V. Conv. R. 54-335.
113. (1990) V. Conv. R. 54-367.
114. The ejectment provisions in the other States are discussed above **[5.21]**. Although the ejectment provisions reiterate the paramountcy provisions, it is submitted that they do not add in substance to the concept of indefeasibility. See Whalan, p. 294 who describes the ejectment provisions as "re-inforcing negative statements".
115. The provision orginally came into operation pursuant to s. 15 of the *Transfer of Land Act 1890 Amendment Act* 1914 *(No. 2)*. (It was enacted as s. 104 in the consolidated Act: The *Transfer of Land Act* 1915.) There appears to be no record of the reason for its insertion. It was originally inserted as part of a provision setting out criminal penalties and appears to have been directed to the civil position as between the fraudulent and defrauded parties.

intended to correct the obvious drafting error in s. 104(1)[116] to make it
clear that any entry procured or made by fraud was void *as against any
person defrauded*.

In the *Chasfild* case, Gray J. took the view that the term "fraud" in
s. 44(1) was to be accorded a wider meaning than "fraud" as used in s. 42
and that it was not limited to fraud in the person seeking to rely on a
registered interest. Gray J. stated:[117]

> "In my opinion the effect of the present Victorian provisions is that
> 'fraud' in s. 44(1) means fraud associated with the registration and
> that a proprietor who becomes registered in such circumstances, even
> if innocent of the fraud, may be divested at the suit of a defrauded
> previous proprietor until there is a sale to a bona fide purchaser who
> becomes registered. In this connection, fraud includes forgery."

Whilst it is the case that s. 44(1) is capable of the interpretation given
it in the *Chasfild* case, it is submitted that it was not intended to have the
far-reaching effect suggested. Its terms lend support to the view that
s. 44(1) is directed simply to the position as between the defrauded party
and the fraudulent party. The concluding words of s. 44(1) "and no party
or privy to the fraud shall take any benefit therefrom" reiterate this.[118]
These words also suggest that it is only the fraud of a registered proprietor
or her or his agent which is sufficient to impeach the title.[119] The
interpretation suggested here leaves little, if any scope, for an independent
operation for s. 44(1) as s. 42(1) standing alone would cover the content
of s. 44(1). Although in other areas this may support an interpretation
which gives some effect to s. 44(1) overlap between provisions in the
Torrens statutes is not uncommon and has been so recognised as a
consequence, albeit an unpalatable one, of the original drafting and
subsequent numerous amendments to the Torrens statutes.

In the *Chasfild* case, Gray J. in reaching the conclusion he did, placed
considerable reliance on the insertion of s. 44(1) into the 1954 Act. *Gibbs
v. Messer* and *Clements v. Ellis* were both cases which emanated from the
Victorian jurisdiction and were decided upon provisions which were
substantially the same as the provisions of the Torrens statutes considered
in *Frazer v. Walker* and *Breskvar v. Wall*. Barwick C.J. stated that *Clements
v. Ellis* had been wrongly decided and although *Gibbs v. Messer* has not
been overruled, its authority is, at best, extremely limited: see above
[5.30]. Gray J. accepted that only a change in the Victorian Torrens
legislation would enable him to reach a decision in favour of the
mortgagor.[120] It is suggested that the insertion s. 44(1) did not constitute
a change of substance to the Torrens statute but was a re-enactment of an
earlier provision (s. 104(1)) with the necessary changes to correct the

---

116. See *Votes and Proceedings*, Vol. 1, Legislative Assembly, Session 1954-1955,
     Vol. 1, 911 (evidence of A. Garran, Assistant Parliamentary Draftsman) quoted
     in the judgment of Gray J., in the *Chasfild* case (1990) V. Conv. R. 54-367 at
     64,584.
117. *Chasfild Pty Ltd v. Taranto* (1990) V. Conv. R. 54-367 at 64,584.
118. *Chasfild Pty Ltd v. Taranto* (1990) V. Conv. R. 54-367 at 64,585.
119. See Robinson, p. 208.
120. *Chasfild Pty Ltd v. Taranto* (1990) V. Conv. R. 54-367 at 64,584.

drafting error in s. 104. If this view is correct, immediate indefeasibility would remain applicable in Victoria. It is important to note that the decision in the *Chasfild* case has the potential to affect indefeasibility of title only within the parameters of s. 44(1). Thus, for example, if a dealing document is void as a result of circumstances not arising out of fraud, the registration would confer indefeasibility of title on the transferee.

(c) Indefeasibility and the protection of individual terms in registered documents

[5.33] A further issue relating to indefeasibility of title concerns the extent of the protection accorded to individual terms in registered documents. Does indefeasibility attach to all covenants in a registered document? In *Mercantile Credits Ltd v. Shell Co. of Australia Ltd* [121] the High Court took the view that the registration of an instrument does not necessarily "give priority or the quality of indefeasibility to every right which the instrument creates".[122] Only those covenants which are effectively part of the estate or interest in the land attract the quality of indefeasibility. Personal convenants which do not affect the estate or interest in the land are not "indefeasible" simply because they are contained within a registered document. In the *Mercantile Credits* case an option to renew, contained in the registered lease, was held to derive indefeasibility from the registration of the lease.[123] The option to renew was held to be a covenant touching and concerning the land and not personal in nature. In contrast an option to purchase contained in a registered lease may be viewed as a separate and independent covenant and not one concerning the tenancy or its terms. Thus it would not attract the quality of indefeasibility by virtue simply of being included in a registered lease.[124] It is important to note, however, that in New South Wales, Queensland and South Australia, it is provided specifically that an option to purchase may be included in a registered lease.[125] Where it is

121. (1976) 136 C.L.R. 326. Discussed at **[10.85]**.
122. (1976) 136 C.L.R. 326 at 342 per Gibbs J. Cf. protection given to covenants in an unregistered lease: see below **[10.87]**; *Davies v. Wickham Properties Pty Ltd* (1988) A.N.Z. Conv. R. 218; cf. *Downie v. Lockwood* [1965] V.R. 257 discussed below **[10.87]**. See Bradbrook, "The Scope of Protection for Leases under the Victorian Transfer of Land Act" (1988) 16 M.U.L.R. 837.
123. See also *Medical Benefits Fund of Australia Ltd v. Fisher* [1984] 1 Qd R. 606. Further, see *Re Eastdoro Pty Ltd* [1990] 1 Qd R. 424 where the lessee held under a registered lease for three years with options for renewal of two further leases of two years each. The issue arose as to whether the purchasers were bound by the second option to renew. At first instance, it was held that the purchasers were not bound by the second option as the lessee must still be holding under the registered lease containing the option to renew in order for indefeasibility to attach to the option. The first option was exercised but no new lease was executed and at the time the respondent purchased the land, the lessee held only under an equitable lease. On appeal, the Full Court reversed the decision and held in favour of the tenant on the basis that as the option was contained in the original registered lease, it gained protection. Protection is thus afforded even where the original registered lease containing the option has expired. See (1990) 4 Aust. Prop. Law Bull. 58.
124. (1976) 136 C.L.R. 326 at 346-347 per Gibbs J. Cf. Whalan, pp. 114-119.
125. Torrens statutes: N.S.W.: s. 53(3); Qld: s. 53; S.A.: s. 117.

so included, the option to purchase acquires indefeasibility in the same way as the lease itself.[126]

[5.34]   In some cases, an option to renew or an option to purchase (in those States where indefeasibility can attach to an option to purchase) may be illegal or void. An issue arises as to the effect of registration of the lease in these circumstances. Where the option in a registered lease is illegal, it seems that it does not gain the protection of indefeasibility by registration of the lease. In *Travinto Nominees Pty Ltd v. Vlattas*[127] it was held that such an option would be incapable of specific performance because of the illegality. On the other hand, where the option is void, registration would cure the defect in the same way as it would if the instrument of lease itself were void.[128]

(d)   Overview

[5.35]   In general, the acceptance by the courts of the theory of immediate indefeasibility was welcomed.[129] It involved a straightforward reading of the statutes, unimpeded as far as possible by general law principles. The central core of the Torrens system, title by registration, seemed to have been firmly established. Indefeasibility of title is not, however, as "indefeasible" as it may appear to be from decisions such as *Breskvar v. Wall*. The threat to indefeasibility of title may come in the future from all the possible exceptions to it. Some of the exceptions are extremely open-ended and in some instances, the courts have not been adverse to giving a wide, rather than a strict interpretation to them.[130]

III.   EXCEPTIONS TO INDEFEASIBILITY

[5.36]   The Torrens statutes specifically set out a number of exceptions to the indefeasibility of title. These will be considered under the heading of express exceptions. Apart from these express exceptions, a number of other exceptions to the indefeasibility of title exist and these will be considered under a heading of other exceptions.

[5.37]   The express exceptions vary markedly from State to State. In many instances, it is unlikely that clear reasons exist for these variations. In order to ensure the smooth passage of the Torrens statutes, a number of provisions were inserted in response to objections from various groups and it seems that this may account for the number of exceptions and for the variations which exist from State to State. This non-uniform and

---

126. See e.g. *Mercantile Credits Ltd v. Shell Co. of Australia Ltd* (1976) 136 C.L.R. 326 at 341.
127. (1973) 129 C.L.R. 1.
128. *Frazer v. Walker* [1967] 1 A.C. 569; *Breskvar v. Wall* (1971) 126 C.L.R. 376; [1972] A.L.R. 205.
129. See e.g. Sackville, "The Torrens System—Some Thoughts on Indefeasibility and Priorities" (1973) 47 A.L.J. 526 at 528-532. Cf. Taylor, "Scotching Frazer v. Walker" (1970) 44 A.L.J. 248.
130. See e.g. the judgment of Mason C.J. and Dawson J. in *Bahr v. Nicholay* (1988) 164 C.L.R. 604 at 610; 78 A.L.R. 1 at 3.

ad hoc treatment of the area of exceptions to indefeasibility has played a significant role in the interpretation of the Torrens system by the courts. In a number of instances the narrowness of an express exception or the lack of an express exception which should arguably have been included, or at least expressly addressed, has resulted in the courts interpreting an alternative exception in a strained manner. The courts have sometimes adopted the role of filling gaps or inadequacies in the legislation. Inevitably the balances adopted have varied from time to time and from jurisdiction to jurisdiction and have led to further uncertainty and lack of uniformity. A number of examples may be cited. In South Australia, the exception relating to tenancies is very narrow and tenants who fail to fall within the express exception have attempted to use another express exception, that of fraud, in order to gain protecton for their interests. Thus the courts have been required to interpret the fraud exception in order to determine if an inadequacy in the express exception can be corrected. In all States except South Australia, there is no express exception to indefeasibility where the dealing document is forged. Neither is there an express provision stating that a forged document, once registered, is effective to pass title. If the transferee were fraudulent, the fraud exception applies to make the transferee's registered title defeasible. If, however, the transferee were not involved in the forgery, a question arises as to the indefeasibility of her or his title. Effectively, the courts have been required to determine whether or not to fill a possible gap and create a further exception to indefeasibility of title. The attitude of the courts on this issue has varied over the years and is the basis of the deferred versus immediate indefeasibility clash. This debate is discussed above [5.27]-[5.32]. The changing perception of the courts on this issue has led to periods of considerable uncertainty.

A further area of uncertainty exists with respect to volunteers. The Torrens legislation does not contain a specific provision setting out the position of volunteers. Is a volunteer who becomes a registered proprietor intended to obtain an indefeasible title? Again the courts have been required to consider the issue and fill the gap: the law on this point still remains uncertain.

1. Express Exceptions

[5.38]   In all States, the title of the registered proprietor of an estate or interest is subject to all estates, interests, encumbrances or liens notified on the Register.[131] Any person intending to take an interest in Torrens land can check the Register to determine the state of title. It seems reasonable that such a person, on obtaining a registered interest, is subject to the interests and estates already noted on the Register.

[5.39]   The decision in *Bursill Enterprises Pty Ltd v. Berger Bros Trading Co. Pty Ltd*,[132] however, demonstrates that even this seemingly simple area of exception is not free from difficulty. A registered proprietor of land

131. Torrens statutes: N.S.W.: s. 42; Vic.: s. 42; Qld: s. 44; S.A.: s. 69; W.A.: s. 68; Tas.: s. 40.
132. (1971) 124 C.L.R. 73.

granted to a neighbouring registered proprietor, an extension of an existing right of way over his land and what was, in effect, a transfer of part of his land comprising a horizonal stratum of airspace ("together with all buildings on the road and the right to pull down the buildings and rebuild others at a height of not less than 12' from the ground over the road"). The certificate of title relating to the grantor's land had a notification that there was an encumbrance over the land referring to it as "right of way created by and more fully set out in Transfer No. 7922". A dispute arose between the successors-in-title to the original registered proprietors, Bursill being the successor of the grantor and Berger being the successor of the grantee. The question was whether the title of Bursill was subject to Berger's claimed right to a fee simple interest in the horizontal stratum of airspace. In turn, the answer to this dispute depended upon whether this interest had been "notified" on the Register. A person who becomes the registered proprietor takes subject to any interests noted on the Register. Thus, if the interest had been noted on the Register, Bursill would hold subject to it. The High Court held that the transfer of the airspace had been "noted" on the Register. Such a finding is predicated on an acceptance that, in order to protect itself, Bursill should have looked further than the folio relating to the land it was purchasing. Bursill should have searched the relevant document, namely Transfer No. 7922 to determine the nature and extent of the "right of way". As Windeyer J. remarked: "[A] prudent conveyancer acting for a purchaser of the land that is now Bursill's would have ascertained what it was that Transfer 7922 . . . effected . . . [S]urely no prudent person, seeing the reference to a right of way, would neglect to ascertain what exactly was the nature of the right of way."[133]

The majority of the High Court in the *Bursill* case thus took the view that if an interest is noted on the Register, even if it is noted under the wrong name, the registered proprietor is bound by it if by some further searching he or she could have discovered the exact nature of the interest.

A requirement necessitating such searches goes against one of the aims of the Torrens system that in order to keep searches simple, the Register should accurately reflect the state of the title. Nevertheless, the additional search that could have been undertaken by Bursill was not a particularly onerous or difficult one. It has been argued that what is more troubling is the notion that the intended and true import of an instrument prevails over the Registrar's notification of its import.[134]

(a) Fraud

[5.40] It is clear that the exception of fraud relates only to fraud by the current registered proprietor or her or his agent.[135] Fraud in transactions occurring before the transaction pursuant to which the registered

---

133. (1971) 124 C.L.R. 73 at 93. Cf. the judgment of Menzies J. at 84.
134. See Butt, pp. 520-521. See also *Mercantile Credits Ltd v. Shell Co. of Australia Ltd* (1976) 136 C.L.R. 326 discussed above **[5.33]**.
135. See e.g. *Assets Co. Ltd v. Mere Roihi* [1905] A.C. 176 at 210. As to the agency point see below **[5.47]-[5.49]**.

proprietor took her or his interest is of no importance and cannot affect the indefeasibility of the registered proprietor's title. Fraud by the current registered proprietor may be perpetrated against the prior registered proprietor or the holder of a prior unregistered interest.[136] Many of the reported decisions on the fraud exception have concerned fraud against a prior unregistered interest holder.[137]

[5.41] How then is "fraud" defined for the purpose of the Torrens legislation? The statutes do not contain positive definitions of fraud and to a large degree the interpretation of the term fraud has been left to the courts. The statutes provide some guidance in that they provide that knowledge of an unregistered interest or trust is not of itself to be imputed as fraud.[138] In itself such a provision suggests that a tight, narrow definition of fraud is intended and that concepts of constructive or equitable fraud are to be inapplicable. The courts have taken this view and excluded from the definition of fraud, any conduct which might be considered equitable fraud. In *Wicks v. Bennett*,[139] Knox C.J. and Rich J. stated that fraud as interpreted under the Torrens system was "something more than mere disregard of rights of which the person sought to be affected had notice. It imports something in the nature of 'personal dishonesty' or 'moral turpitude'."[140] In *Assets Co. Ltd v. Mere Roihi* the Privy Council stated that: "[Fraud means] actual fraud, that is, dishonesty of some sort, not what is called constructive or equitable fraud."[141]

[5.42] Although it is simple to state that on the one hand, fraud connotes dishonesty, and that, on the other hand, knowledge of a prior unregistered interest is not of itself fraud, the dividing line is much more difficult to draw in individual cases. In *Loke Yew v. Port Swettenham Rubber Co. Ltd*[142] the rubber company purchased a large area of land from the registered proprietor, Eusope. Although not registered as such, Loke Yew was the owner of part of this land and Eusope only agreed to sell the whole of the land to the rubber company when he was given an assurance by the company that it would not disturb Loke Yew's possession. Upon becoming the registered proprietor, the rubber company asserted that it was entitled to the whole of the land and Loke Yew sought relief. On the evidence, the court was satisfied that the rubber company had been fraudulent and it ordered the rubber company to execute a transfer of the

---

136. See, however, *Australian Guarantee Corporation Ltd v. De Jager* [1984] V.R. 483 where it was held that if the registered proprietor lodges a dealing which he or she knows has not complied with the necessary formalities (and the document would not have been accepted without them) the conduct of the registered proprietor may constitute fraud. This is so even if the fraud is really against the Registrar.
137. Whalan, p. 312.
138. See the "notice" provisions discussed above **[5.22]**.
139. (1921) 30 C.L.R. 80.
140. (1921) 30 C.L.R. 80 at 91.
141. [1905] A.C. 176 at 210.
142. [1913] A.C. 491.

land in dispute.[143] The court took the view that the rubber company had more than mere knowledge of Loke Yew's prior unregistered interest. The statement by Glass (the representative of the company), that the rights of Loke Yew would be protected, had been falsely and fraudulently made to induce Eusope to sign the transfer. In effect, the court was satisfied that there had been a deliberate plan to deprive Loke Yew of his land.

[5.43] The decision in *Loke Yew v. Port Swettenham Rubber Co. Ltd* is to be contrasted with decisions such as *R.M. Hosking Properties Pty Ltd v. Barnes*,[144] and *Friedman v. Barrett*,[145] where the person becoming the registered proprietor knew of an earlier unregistered interest and yet, in the absence of proof of a deliberate fraudulent scheme, was held to have an indefeasible title. In the *R.M. Hosking* case, the defendants held possession under a two year unregistered lease with an option to renew for a further two years. During the term of the lease, the lessor sold the land to the plaintiff who knew of the terms of the lease and agreed to accept title subject to the occupation of the defendants. Subsequently, the defendants sought to exercise the option to renew and the plaintiff gave notice to quit[146] stating that it was not bound by the terms of the unregistered lease. Unlike the situation in the *Loke Yew* case, there was no proven plan of dishonesty or fraud, no evidence that the lessor had been induced to sign the transfer by the plaintiff's statement. Although there was knowledge of the prior unregistered interest, this was not sufficient to constitute fraud. Further, it seems that the knowledge that the prior unregistered interest will be defeated by registration is insufficient per se to constitute fraud by the person becoming the registered proprietor.[147] Nor is it fraud to register an instrument expeditiously in the knowledge that such registration would defeat the claim of a person who is attempting to establish that claim in litigation.[148]

[5.44] Cases such as the *R.M. Hosking* case illustrate clearly the sharp contrast between the general law system and the Torrens system in the area of notice. Under the general law system, the holder of a subsequent legal interest is subject to all prior equitable interests of which he or she

---

143. Quaere whether the court could have simply ordered a rectification of the Register. See the discussion in Sackville and Neave, p. 424 and Harrison, *Cases on Land Law* (2nd ed., Law Book Co. Ltd, Sydney, 1965), pp. 613-614.
144. [1971] S.A.S.R. 100. See also *Oertel v. Hordern* (1902) 2 S.R. (N.S.W.) (Eq.) 37 and *Munro v. Stuart* (1924) 41 S.R. (N.S.W.) 203.
145. [1962] Qd R. 498. In Queensland, there is no provision in the "notice" section that knowledge of a trust does not constitute fraud. Thus the decision in the *Friedman* case supports strongly the notion of a strict definition of fraud. It has been argued that the in personam exception should have been applied in the *Friedman* case: see Robinson,"Friedman v. Barrett—Wrongly Decided" (1984) Qld Law Soc. J. 259.
146. Payment of rent from the defendant to the plaintiff had been made on a weekly basis. Thus the defendants were weekly tenants of the plaintiff but this tenancy was determinable by appropriate notice.
147. See also *Bahr v. Nicholay* (1988) 164 C.L.R. 604 at 653; 78 A.L.R. 1 at 35 per Brennan J. See also *Mills v. Stokman* (1967) 116 C.L.R. 61 at 78 per Kitto J.
148. *Waimiha Sawmilling Co. Ltd (in liq.) v. Waione Timber Co. Ltd* [1926] A.C. 101.

has notice: see above **[3.14]-[3.48]**. Under the Torrens system, notice per se does not render the holder of the legal (registered) interest subject to the interest of the holder of a prior equitable (unregistered) interest.

[5.45] Although notice of a prior unregistered interest does not constitute fraud, *knowledge* of a fraud by which a previous proprietor has been deprived of an interest may affect the title of the registered proprietor. In *Assets Co. Ltd v. Mere Roihi* the Privy Council defined fraud as follows:[149]

> "Fraud by persons from whom he claims does not affect him unless knowledge of it is brought home to him or his agents. The mere fact that he might have found out fraud if he had been more vigilant, and had made further inquiries which he omitted to make does not of itself prove fraud on his part. But if it be shown that his suspicions were aroused, and that he abstained from making inquiries for fear of learning the truth, the case is very different, and fraud may be properly ascribed to him."

The latter part of this judgment suggests a broader definition of fraud than does the analysis above. The varied judicial comments on the definition of fraud cannot all be reconciled satisfactorily. In Australia, however, the majority of the cases suggest a strict rather than broad definition of fraud and if there is doubt in a given instance, it is more likely that there will be finding of no fraud.[150]

[5.46] Another issue which has been considered again recently is whether the fraud must occur in the period of time leading up to the registration or whether fraud can be established by the actions of the registered proprietor after registration.[151] In the past the accepted view has been that it is only fraud prior to registration (that is circumstances leading to acquisition) which is sufficient to render the registered proprietor's title defeasible.[152] However, at least two judges in the High Court decision of *Bahr v. Nicholay*[153] suggested that fraud can occur after registration by the dishonest repudiation of a prior interest which the registered proprietor has agreed to recognise as a basis for acquiring title. In the *Bahr* case the Bahrs were the registered proprietors of the land in dispute and they agreed to sell to Nicholay. The contract of sale included an agreement by Nicholay to lease the property back to the Bahrs for three years and upon the expiration of the lease to enter into a contract to resell

---

149. [1905] A.C. 176 at 210. Expressly approved by the Supreme Court of Victoria in *Australian Guarantee Corporation v. De Jager* [1984] V.R. 483.

150. Cf. the broader manner in which the New Zealand courts have dealt with the issue of fraud. See e.g. *Efstratiou v. Glantschnig* [1972] N.Z.L.R. 594. See generally Whalan, "The Meaning of Fraud under the Torrens System" (1975) 6 N.Z.U.L.R. 207 and Butt, "Fraud in the Torrens System: A Comparative Analysis" (1977) 13 U.W.A.L.R. 354.

151. See *Bahr v. Nicholay* (1988) 164 C.L.R. 604; 78 A.L.R. 1.

152. Note that some of the relevant provisions may be interpreted in such a way that they seem to require specifically that the fraud be in the period prior to registration: see e.g. South Australian Act, s. 69I.

153. (1988) 164 C.L.R. 604 at 615; 78 A.L.R. 1 at 6-7 per Mason C.J. and Dawson J. Quaere the view of Brennan J. at 34-35 and 653-655.

the land to the Bahrs. Nicholay became the registered proprietor and then sold the property to the Thompsons. The Thompsons knew of the agreement between the Bahrs and Nicholay and, at Nicholay's insistence, the contract for sale from Nicholay to the Thompsons contained an express acknowledgment of it. After the Thompsons became registered, their actions made it clear that they acknowledged the rights of the Bahrs. For example, they wrote to the Bahrs acknowledging their (the Thompsons) obligation to sell and had made offers to do this. (These offers had lapsed.) Subsequently, however, the Thompsons sought to rely on their registered title to defeat the rights of the Bahrs. Thus, the evidence showed that the Thompsons had accepted the obligation and after registration had sought to extinguish it: any dishonest conduct occurred *after* registration.

In deciding whether the title of the Thompsons was indefeasible, the High Court considered whether either the fraud or the in personam exception was applicable. As to fraud, Mason C.J. and Dawson J. took the view that the fraud exception includes the fraudulent repudiation of a prior interest which the registered proprietor has acknowledged or agreed to recognise as a basis for obtaining title.[154] In the view of their Honours there had been no "definitive pronouncements that fraud is confined to fraud in the obtaining of a transfer or in securing registration".[155] Further, they stated that "there is no difference between the false undertaking which induced the execution of the transfer in *Loke Yew* and an undertaking honestly given which induces the execution of a transfer and is subsequently repudiated for the purpose of defeating the prior interest."[156] In contrast, Wilson and Toohey JJ. adopted the more accepted and conservative approach in holding that fraud under the Torrens legislation can only be constituted by dishonest conduct in the period leading up to registration. There was no proof of such dishonest conduct by the Thompsons.[157]

In the view of Wilson and Toohey JJ., fact situations such as the one in the *Bahr* case were more properly dealt with under the in personam exception. The in personam exception is discussed below: as will be shown there, all justices in the *Bahr* case took the view that the in personam exception was applicable and thus, in the end result, the Thompsons were subject to the rights of the Bahrs: see below [5.70]-[5.72].

The weight of authority[158] favours the view that it is only fraud in the period prior to registration which is capable of falling within the fraud exception and rendering the registered proprietor's title defeasible. One of the basic aims of the Torrens system is to confer an indefeasible title

---

154. (1988) 164 C.L.R. 604 at 615; 78 A.L.R. 1 at 6-7 per Mason C.J. and Dawson J.
155. (1988) 164 C.L.R. 604 at 615; 78 A.L.R. 1 at 6 per Mason C.J. and Dawson J.
156. (1988) 164 C.L.R. 604 at 615; 78 A.L.R. 1 at 7 per Mason C.J. and Dawson J.
157. The view of Brennan J. on this point is not absolutely clear. It appears that his Honour's reasons for decision are based on the in personam exception. The more likely interpretation is that he would not support the view of Mason C.J. and Dawson J. on this point. Cf. the Headnote (1988) 78 A.L.R. 1.
158. See e.g. *Loke Yew v. Port Swettenham Rubber Co. Ltd* [1913] A.C. 491; *Waimiha Sawmilling Co. Ltd (in liq.) v. Waione Timber Co. Ltd* [1926] A.C. 101.

on any person who purchases bona fide and enters the instrument of dealing on the Register. The satisfaction of this aim only requires that an inquiry be made into the bona fides of the registered proprietor up until the time of registration. In view of the fact that the in personam exception appears to cover the *Bahr* type fact situation, the extension to the fraud exception suggested by Mason C.J. and Dawson J. may be unnecessary.

Fraud by the agent

[5.47]   It is clear from the cases of *Assets Co. Ltd v. Mere Roihi* and *Schultz v. Corwill Properties Pty Ltd*[159] that the title of the registered proprietor may sometimes be impeached even though he or she has not been personally fraudulent or if her or his agent either has been fraudulent or has knowledge of a fraud. Both of the decisions referred to above show that it is necessary to look at two separate situations in order to determine if the title of the registered proprietor is rendered defeasible.

[5.48]   First, the situation where the fraud is actually committed by or "brought home to" the agent, must be considered. To determine if the fraud of the agent is the fraud of the principal (the registered proprietor), the ordinary agency principle of respondeat superior is applied. If the agent acted within the scope of her or his actual or apparent authority, then the fraud of the agent becomes the fraud of the principal. Further "an act of an agent within the scope of his actual or apparent authority does not cease to bind his principal merely because the agent was acting fraudulently and in furtherance of his own interests."[160] In *Schultz v. Corwill Properties Pty Ltd*, however, an application of the principle of respondeat superior resulted in the fraud of the agent not being held to be the fraud of the principal. In this case, a solicitor who acted for both parties in the dispute[161] was the fraudulent party. The execution of a mortgage from the registered proprietor to the registered mortgagee was a forgery, the solicitor having forged the registered proprietor's execution of it. Inter alia, the issue arose as to whether the fraud of the agent became the fraud of the registered mortgagee so as to make her registered mortgage defeasible. The court held that it did not, as it was not within the scope of the solicitor's actual or apparent authority to forge the registered proprietor's execution of the mortgage. "The forged execution of the mortgage was in furtherance of a felonious (activity). . . . It was an independent activity entirely in furtherance of his own interests."[162]

[5.49]   Secondly, where an agent has knowledge of a fraud in the transaction in issue, a question arises as to whether this knowledge is to be imputed to the principal. Clearly, if the registered proprietor knows personally that a fraud has been committed, whereby for example, a

159. (1969) 90 W.N. (Pt 1) (N.S.W.) 529.
160. *Bowstead on Agency* (15th ed., Sweet & Maxwell, London, 1985), p. 279.
161. In fact, the personal representative (the husband) of one of the parties was the plaintiff in the action as the aggrieved party, the wife, had died.
162. (1969) 90 W.N. (Pt 1) (N.S.W.) 529 at 540. In view of this decision, quaere when the fraud of the agent will be considered the fraud of the principal. The decision suggests that there must be some direction concerning the fraudulent activity from the principal to the agent.

previous registered proprietor has been deprived of all or part of her or
his interest, that knowledge is sufficient to impeach the title of the
registered proprietor.[163] Knowledge by the agent of a fraud, however,
only becomes the knowledge of the principal in the relevant sense if the
agent's knowledge can be imputed to the principal.[164] There is a
presumption that the agent has communicated to the principal any
information concerning the transaction of which he or she has express
knowledge.[165] However, if the matter concerns the agent's own fraud or
the agent's participation in a fraudulent scheme, the principal is able to
rebut the presumption of imputed notice for the agent is unlikely to have
communicated knowledge of a fraud where the agent her or himself has
been involved in the fraud. On the facts of the *Schultz* case, the solicitor's
knowledge that a fraud had been committed whereby the registered
proprietor had been deprived of part of its interest was not imputed to the
registered mortgagee because the agent himself had perpetrated the
fraud.[166]

(b) Forgery, insufficient power of attorney or disability

[5.50]   South Australia is the only State in which the Torrens statute
provides specifically that if a certificate of title or other instrument of title
is obtained by forgery or by means of an insufficient power of attorney or
from a person under some legal disability, the certificate of title or other
instrument is void.[167] The proviso sets out, however, "that a registered
proprietor who has taken bona fide for valuable consideration shall not be
affected by reason that a certificate or other instrument of title was
obtained by any person through whom he claims title from a person under
disability, or by any of the means aforesaid". The interpretation of the
proviso, in particular the last seven words, has given rise to some difficulty
and ambiguity. In *Wicklow Enterprises Pty Ltd v. Doysal Pty Ltd*[168]
O'Loughlin J. concluded that the provision should be read as if it were
expressed in the following terms:[169]

> "Provided that the title of a registered proprietor who has taken bona
> fide for valuable consideration shall not be affected by reason that a
> certificate of title was obtained
>
> (a) By any person through whom he claims title *from* a person under
>   some legal disability;

163. See *Assets Co. Ltd v. Mere Roihi* [1905] A.C. 176.
164. *Schultz v. Corwill Properties Pty Ltd* (1969) 90 W.N. (Pt 1) (N.S.W.) 529 at 583.
165. *Schultz v. Corwill Properties Pty Ltd* (1969) 90 W.N. (Pt 1) (N.S.W.) 529 at
      583-584.
166. In fact, in the *Schultz* case, there had also been a forged discharge of mortgage
      so the end result was a victory for the registered proprietor, not the registered
      mortgagee. See also *Ratcliffe v. Watters* (1969) 89 W.N. Pt 1 (N.S.W.) 497 and
      Australian Guarantee Corporation Ltd v. De Jager [1984] V.R. 483. In the latter case,
      it was suggested that knowledge of fraud may be imputed from agent to principal
      even where the agent does not have actual knowledge but has deliberately
      "closed his eyes" to the fraud.
167. Torrens statutes: S.A.: s. 69II.
168. (1986) 45 S.A.S.R. 247.
169. (1986) 45 S.A.S.R. 247 at 260.

or

(b) By any of the means aforesaid (namely by forgery or *by* means of an insufficient power of attorney).''

Thus, with respect to forgery, for example, the interpretation of O'Loughlin J. would result in a certificate of title obtained by forgery being void provided that a certificate of title obtained by forgery by a registered proprietor, who has taken bona fide for valuable consideration, being valid. Clearly, this interpretation leaves little scope for the operation of the forgery section. It does, however, result in immediate indefeasibility of title where the title is obtained by forgery or by means of an insufficient power of attorney. In view of the wide acceptance of immediate indefeasibility, it is not surprising that an interpretation which supports immediate over deferred indefeasibility was sought and supported.

Nevertheless, it has been stated that as s. 69II is an express proviso, the issue is not about the relative merits of deferred and immediate indefeasibility but is about the section's construction.[170] It has been argued that the more obvious interpretation, and the one supported by the historical data concerning the introduction of the provision, requires the ''deferred indefeasibility proviso'' to be applied to forgery and insufficient power of attorney in addition to disability.[171] Thus, the argument is that the correct construction of the proviso requires that it be read as if it were expressed:[172]

''Provided that the title of a registered proprietor who has taken bona fide for valuable consideration shall not be affected by reason that a certificate of title was obtained by any person through whom he claims title

(a) from a person under a disability

or (b) by forgery

or (c) by means of an insufficient power of attorney.''

The logic of this construction is clear. Nevertheless the decision and interpretation of O'Loughlin J. remains as a relevant authority in interpreting this provision.

(c) Prior certificate of title or folio

[5.51] The title of a registered proprietor is not indefeasible against the interest or estate of a registered proprietor claiming the same land under a prior grant, certificate of title or folio.[173] Thus, in the situation where two certificates of title (or folios or grants) are issued in respect of the same land, the interest of the registered proprietor under the prior one, prevails.[174]

---

170. Moore, op. cit. at 408.
171. Moore, op. cit. at 408-410.
172. Moore, op. cit. at 408.
173. Torrens statutes: N.S.W.: s. 42(a); Vic.: s. 42(1)(a); Qld: s. 44; S.A.: s. 69v; W.A.: s. 60; Tas.: s. 40(3)(b).
174. *Lloyd v. Mayfield* (1885) 7 A.L.T. 48; *Stevens v. Williams* (1886) 12 V.L.R. 152.

This may occur where the two certificates cover exactly the same area of land or where there is only a partial incompatibility.[175] It is clear that the registered proprietor under the second certificate cannot rely on the "protection" provision, such as s. 44(2) of the Victorian Act.[176] The fact that the registered proprietor under the second certificate is a bona fide purchaser for value is of no assistance in relation to this exception. In this instance the "paramountcy" provision giving protection to the registered proprietor under the first certificate has priority over the "protection" provision.[177] Further, the conflict arises as soon as the second title covering the same land is issued and is resolved whenever the dispute arises in favour of the certificate or folio first issued whether the dispute is between the original parties or their successors.[178]

(d) Erroneous description of land

[5.52] In all States, the registered proprietor's title is not indefeasible with respect to any portion of land which may have been included in the grant, certificate or folio by wrong description of parcels or boundaries.[179] Except in Queensland and Tasmania, the relevent statutory provisions provide that the exception is inapplicable where the registered proprietor is a bona fide purchaser for value or someone deriving from or through such a purchaser. Even in Queensland and Tasmania, the position is probably the same as in the other States despite the lack of the specific statutory provision.[180]

[5.53] The exception applies very specifically to cases of a "wrong description". Thus, for example, if an applicant describes incorrectly the land for which he or she intends to apply and the description of the land thereby includes land for which he or she did not intend to apply, the land incorrectly included falls within this exception.[181] The title to the land so included in the certificate because of the wrong description stays with the true owner.[182] If, on the other hand, the applicant describes correctly the land for which he or she intends to apply but the land or part of it is not actually the applicant's, any grant, certificate or folio issued including the land is not an instance of "wrong description". This is a complete lack of title but if the applicant becomes the registered proprietor without fraud, he or she will obtain an indefeasible title.[183]

---

175. A partial incompatibility will most often arise because of a mistake in survey.
176. *Registrar of Titles and Esperance Land Co.* (1899) 1 W.A.L.R. 118. See generally Whalan, p. 318.
177. Ibid.
178. Any other interpretation could lead to ridiculous results: see Whalan, p. 319. Robinson, p. 191 suggests that this proviso is subject to no other exception being applicable: see e.g. *National Trustees Co. v. Hassett* [1907] V.L.R. 404.
179. Torrens statutes: N.S.W.: s. 42(c); Vic.: s. 42(1)(b); Qld: s. 44; S.A.: s. 69III; W.A.: s. 68; Tas.: s. 40(3)(c).
180. See *Zachariah v. Morrow and Wilson* (1915) 34 N.Z.L.R. 892.
181. See generally Voumard, p. 429.
182. *Marsden v. McAlister* (1887) 8 N.S.W.L.R. (L) 300; *Ex parte Solling* (1893) 14 N.S.W.L.R. (L) 399.
183. *Hamilton v. Iredale* (1903) 3 S.R. (N.S.W.) 535. See Voumard, p. 429.

[5.54] In some cases there may be an overlap and conflict between this exception and the exception discussed above where the same land is included in two certificates, grants or folios. Although the prior certificate was included by wrong description, the subsequent certificate prevails. In other words, where both exceptions could apply, the exception relating to wrong description of the land is applicable and prevails.[184]

[5.55] In itself, however, the exception relating to wrong description of parcels or boundaries is more limited than that relating to two certificates pertaining to the same land. This is because the exception is inapplicable to a registered proprietor who purchased for value or who derived from or through such a purchaser and intentionally purchased the whole of the land described in the certificate.[185] Where a purchaser transferee relies upon the description of the land in the certificate and intends to purchase what is set out in that certificate, the exception is inapplicable.

[5.56] Difficulties may arise in certain circumstances. The following provides an example. The physical portion of land intended to be sold is a shop. The certificate of title for the land upon which the shop is built includes an additional area of land beside the shop, which area of land has been included by "wrong description". Negotiations for the sale of the shop from the vendor to the purchaser proceed upon the basis that the purchaser intends to purchase the area of land upon which the shop is built. When the purchaser becomes the registered proprietor, a dispute may ensue as to entitlement to the extra piece of land included in the certificate. In such a case, it seems that the proviso to the exception would not apply so as to give the purchaser an indefeasible title to the whole of the land described in the certificate.[186] This is because the purchaser was not a bona fide purchaser for value for all of the land included in the certificate of title. Rather, the intention was to buy the land on which the shop stood.

(e) Easements

[5.57] The Torrens statutes in all States provide that particular unregistered easements are an exception to the indefeasibility of the registered proprietor's title.[187] The scope of the exception varies from jurisdiction to jurisdiction. This exception is discussed in detail below **[16.40]**.

(f) Adverse possession

[5.58] As is the case in relation to easements, the adverse possession exception to the indefeasibility of the registered proprietor's titles, varies considerably from State to State. The exception is discussed in detail below **[15.82]-[15.86]**.[188]

---

184. *National Trustees Co. v. Hassett* [1907] V.L.R. 404.
185. *Pleasance v. Allen* (1889) 15 V.L.R. 601.
186. *Pleasance v. Allen* (1889) 15 V.L.R. 601. The facts of the example posited are based upon the fact situation in the *Pleasance* case.
187. Torrens statutes: N.S.W.: s. 42(b); Vic.: s. 42(2)(d); Qld: s. 44; S.A.: s. 69ɪᴠ; W.A.: s. 68; Tas.: s. 40(3)(c).
188. See also the exception in the South Australian Act in s. 69ᴠɪ discussed below **[15.85]**. Note also s. 46 of the Tasmanian Act.

(g) Tenancies

[5.59] In all States, some measure of protection is given to unregistered leases or tenancies.[189] The extent of the protection given varies markedly from the very wide protection given in Victoria to the situation in South Australia where only a tenant in actual possession under a tenancy for a term not exceeding one year is protected. The exception is discussed in detail below [10.87].

[5.60] Although it has been argued that the protection given to tenants in Victoria is too wide,[190] it is apparent that the exception in South Australia is too narrow. The fact is that many persons holding under a tenancy exceeding one year do not register their leases. Transaction costs of placing the document in registrable form and actual registration costs deter registration. Such a tenant cannot enforce the lease against a purchaser from the landlord even if the purchaser knows about the lease.[191] The new registered proprietor has an indefeasible title except in the case of fraud. The narrowness of the exception encourages, therefore, disputes about whether a registered proprietor's "notice" was actually more than notice and constituted "fraud".

The Western Australian exception, which gives protection to lessees where the term does not exceed five years, provides a balance between the interests of the tenant and the interests of a purchaser from the landlord. A lease exceeding five years represents a substantial investment on the part of the tenant and it seems reasonable in these circumstances to require that the lessee register the lease in order to gain protection.

(h) Rates and taxes

[5.61] In all States, there are specific Acts which impose rates, taxes, duties and charges against land and provided that these remain unpaid they override the title.[192]

In view of the overriding nature of the relevant statutes, a specific statutory exception to indefeasibility is strictly unnecessary. Nevertheless, in Victoria s. 42(2)(f) of the *Transfer of Land Act* 1958 provides that the title of the registered proprietor is subject to taxes and rates created under the *Land Tax Act* 1958, the *Local Government Act* 1958, the *Sewerage District Act* 1958 and the *Water Act* 1958.[193] In Tasmania, there is a specific exception

189. Torrens statutes: N.S.W.: s. 42(d); Vic.: s. 42(2)(e); Qld: *Real Property Act* 1877, ss 11, 18; S.A.: s. 69VIII; W.A.: s. 68; Tas.: s. 40(3)(d).
190. Cf. Vic. L.R.C., Report No. 12, p. 11 where it is suggested that the exception be retained in its current form. Additional costs would be incurred if leases had to be registered. The Commission however, took the view that an equity of rectification should not be protected under the exception: cf. *Downie v. Lockwood* [1965] V.R. 257.
191. *R.M. Hosking Properties Pty Ltd v. Barnes* [1971] S.A.S.R. 100.
192. See the discussion on overriding statutes: below [5.65]-[5.67]. See below [6.61]-[6.62] on the current required disclosures by the vendor when a contract of sale is entered into.
193. Discussed in Vic. L.R.C., Report No. 12, p. 12.

with respect to money charged on land under an Act[194] and in South Australia, there is an exception for unpaid succession duty.[195]

It has been suggested that if governments and local councils wish to bind the land with respect to unpaid rates for instance, they should be required to place a note on the title.[196] As soon as centralised land-information networks, such as Landata in Victoria, are fully operational and linked with the source of title, any purchaser will be able to discover all such information from one single inquiry.[197]

(i) Section 71 South Australian Act

[5.62] Unlike the other States, the South Australian Torrens statute contains a general saving provision setting out that the indefeasibility of the registered proprietor's title is subject to a number of matters.[198] It provides:

"71. Nothing in the two preceding sections contained shall be construed so as to affect any of the following rights or powers, that is to say—

(I) the power of the Sheriff to sell the land of a judgment debtor under writ of execution:

(II) the power of the Court to order the sale of land:

(III) the right of the Official Receiver or of any trustee to land transmitted on the bankruptcy or statutory assignment of the registered proprietor:

(IV) the rights of a person with whom the registered proprietor shall have made a contract for the sale of land or for any other dealing therewith:

(V) the rights of a *cestui que trust* where the registered proprietor is a trustee, whether the trust shall be express, implied, or constructive:

(VI) the right of promoters of an undertaking to vest land in themselves by deed-poll pursuant to the Compulsory Acquisition of Land Act, 1925, or any Act amending the same:

Provided that no unregistered estate, interest, power, right, contract, or trust shall prevail against the title of a registered proprietor taking *bona fide* for valuable consideration, or of any person *bona fide* claiming through or under him."

Even without the provision it seems that each of these matters is an exception to indefeasibility either under the overriding statute or the in personam exceptions discussed below. Thus, although not specifically

---

194. Torrens statutes: Tas.: s. 40(3)(g).
195. Torrens statutes: S.A.: s. 69ix.
196. See Whalan, p. 331.
197. See Vic. L.R.C., Report No. 12, p. 13.
198. See also Torrens statutes: S.A.: s. 69vii for a further outdated exception relating to a wife's separate property.

mentioned in the other statutes, it is submitted that the matters listed above in the South Australian statute do constitute exceptions to indefeasibility of title.[199]

2. Other Possible Exceptions to Indefeasibility of Title[200]

[5.63] Some exceptions to indefeasibility of title which arise outside the Torrens statutes themselves are necessary in order for transactions to proceed in an efficient manner. The range and extent of these exceptions has been criticised.[201] As Whalan commented in 1982:[202] "[t]his type of exogenous growth forms a serious and constantly increasing threat to the integrity of the Torrens system."

(a) Registered volunteers

[5.64] The Torrens statutes themselves do not specifically provide that a registered proprietor obtains an indefeasible title only if a bona fide purchaser for value. In other words, there is no specific provision denying indefeasibility of title to a registered proprietor who is a volunteer. The "paramountcy" provisions, such as s. 42 of the Victorian Act, provide simply that the registered proprietor, except in the case of fraud, holds the land subject only to those interests noted on the Register but absolutely free from all other encumbrances. There are, however, a number of provisions in the Torrens statutes which suggest that a registered volunteer is not intended to obtain an indefeasible title. For example, in the Victorian Act, provisions such as s. 43 ("notice" provision); s. 44(2) ("protection" provision); ss 52 and 110(3), all suggest that it is only a purchaser who should benefit by the protection offered in the Act.[203] In the Victorian decision of King v. Smail,[204] Adam J. held that a registered volunteer did not acquire an indefeasible title free from prior unregistered interests. In part, his Honour's decision relied upon the provisions mentioned above which support the notion that protection is intended only for the registered proprietor/purchaser.[205] King v. Smail was decided, however, at a time when deferred indefeasibility was the accepted theory. As has been stated above (see above [5.28]) the theory of deferred indefeasibility required a reading of the relevant statute which did not give clear prominence to the provisions such as s. 42 of the Victorian Act.[206] Since the decision in Frazer v. Walker, and the inherent acceptance there of the importance of the "paramountcy" provision, it has been argued

---

199. See Whalan, pp. 331-332. See also *Real Property Act* 1877 (Qld), s. 51.
200. Apart from the following exceptions there is a further issue as to whether the Crown is bound by the Torrens statutes. See Victorian Act s. 3(3). It is submitted that in many circumstances the Crown is bound but the authorities do conflict. For a clear discussion see Whalan, pp. 336-337.
201. Vic. L.R.C., Report No. 12, p. 3.
202. Whalan, p. 332.
203. See also *Gibbs v. Messer* [1891] A.C. 248; *Clements v. Ellis* (1934) 51 C.L.R. 217.
204. [1958] V.R. 273.
205. It is to be noted that a decision in favour of the registered volunteer would essentially have permitted the registered proprietor to succeed in a scheme to defraud her husband's creditors.
206. The "paramountcy" provisions.

that registered volunteers should now acquire an indefeasible title. This is because the vital "paramountcy" provisions do not specifically require that the registered proprietor be a volunteer. In fact, in 1988 in *Bogdanovic v. Koteff*[207] this line of reasoning was adopted by the New South Wales Court of Appeal in holding that a registered volunteer obtained an indefeasible title and was thereby not subject to a prior unregistered interest created by the previous registered proprietor.[208]

Despite the relative importance of the paramountcy provisions, these provisions cannot be considered in isolation and it still remains the case that a number of other provisions in the Torrens statutes imply that indefeasibility of title only attaches to the registered proprietor who is a purchaser. It is suggested that the framers of the Torrens legislation intended that only purchasers for value acquire indefeasibility and that there is no compelling reason existing now pursuant to which volunteers should obtain an indefeasible title.[209] It might be thought that the *King v. Smail* type of fact situation lends strong support to this argument that volunteers should not get an indefeasible title. In *King v. Smail*, the court was concerned to ensure that the registered volunteer could not simply by registration, defeat the interests of the creditors of her husband. However, a number of fact situations similar to *King v. Smail* would now be covered by the "claw-back" provisions in the bankruptcy legislation.[210]

(b) Overriding legislation

[5.65] It has been suggested that the overriding statute exception to indefeasibility of title "pose(s) perhaps the greatest single threat to public confidence in the Torrens system".[211] In all jurisdictions provisions of the Torrens statutes are capable of being overruled or effectively repealed by a later statute.[212] It is not necessary that the later statute specifically

207. (1988) 12 N.S.W.L.R. 472.
208. Leave to appeal to the High Court was refused as the substance had been removed from the dispute: the holder of an unregistered interest who was attempting to maintain a right to occupation against the volunteer registered proprietor had entered a nursing home and thus had no need to pursue her right to occupation.
209. See *Official Receiver v. Klau; Ex parte Stephenson Nominees Pty Ltd* (1987) 74 A.L.R. 67. If the principle that a volunteer does not acquire an indefeasible title had been argued in two recent cases, arguably fairer decisions would have resulted: see particularly *State Bank of New South Wales v. Berowra Waters Holdings Pty Ltd* (1986) 4 N.S.W.L.R. 398 and also *Medical Benefits Fund of Australia Ltd v. Fisher* [1984] Qd R. 606 both discussed in Teh and Dwyer, p. 100.
210. *Bankruptcy Act* 1966 (Cth), ss 115-116, 120-123.
211. Butt, p. 532. See also Whalan, pp. 338ff.
212. *South-Eastern Drainage Board (S.A.) v. Savings Bank of South Australia* (1939) 62 C.L.R. 603; *Miller v. Minister of Mines* [1963] A.C. 484 (P.C.). See also *Attorney-General (N.T.) v. Minister for Aboriginal Affairs* (1990) 90 A.L.R. 59 where it was found that there was a conflict between relevant provisions of the *Aboriginal Land Rights (Northern Territory) Act* 1976 (Cth) and the operation of the indefeasibility provisions in the *Real Property Act* 1886 (N.T.). In such a case the *Real Property Act*, a law of the Northern Territory, cannot confer an indefeasible title which would operate inconsistently with the *Land Rights Act*, a law of the Commonwealth, unless the Commonwealth legislation is stated to be subject to the provisions of the Northern Territory Act.

provides that earlier statutes or parts thereof are repealed: it is sufficient
that repeal is the ordinary and proper implication to be drawn from the
later statute.[213] The result of this exception is that rights and charges
relating to land which are created pursuant to a later statute may be
enforceable against the title of the registered proprietor even though the
registered proprietor did not know of them and in some instances had no
means of finding out about them.[214] In a minority of cases, the statute
may provide for the right created to be entered on the Register and may
further provide that the right is ineffective until so registered. This system
fits with the Torrens system ideal of the Register reflecting accurately the
state of the title. It is suggested that all legislative enactments which
purport to detract from the indefeasibility of the registered proprietor's
title be drafted in such a manner.

[5.66]   The reality is, however, that most statutes which create rights
and interests having the potential to interfere with the indefeasibility of
the registered proprietor's title, do not require the interest to be entered
on the Register, and in some cases, make no provision at all for such
rights to be so recorded. The case of *Pratten v. Warringah S.C.*[215] provides
an example. An unregistered interest of the council (a drainage reserve)
created pursuant to a provision of the *Local Government Act* took priority
over the title of the registered proprietor of the land. Before purchasing
Pratten had made inquiries of the Council asking if it claimed any interest
and he had made a thorough search of the title. The Council assured
Pratten that it claimed no interest in the land. After Pratten became the
registered proprietor, the Council asserted its rights claiming that it was
the owner of the land in dispute. The court held in favour of the Council
on the basis that the title of the registered proprietor is inherently subject
to rights created by overriding statutes. In this case, the *Local Government
Act* overrode the *Real Property Act*. The absolute indefeasibility of title
ordinarily flowing from registration does not help, where "the fee simple
has in effect been removed from the registration system".[216]

[5.67]   A registered proprietor who loses part or all of her or his interest
because of the operation of an overriding statute may not be able to claim
compensation from the Assurance Fund. In *Trieste Investments Pty Ltd v.*

---

213.   *Miller v. Minister of Mines* [1963] A.C. 484 (P.C.).
214.   *Pratten v. Warringah S.C.* [1969] 2 N.S.W.L.R. 161. This can be accomplished
       by the setting up of a separate registration system for particular rights (e.g.
       mining registers of mining leases, licences) or by allowing for the creation of
       interests which do not have to be on the Register.
215.   [1969] 2 N.S.W.L.R. 161.
216.   [1969] 2 N.S.W.L.R. 161 at 166. The fact that the Council did not apply for
       its interest to be placed on the Register when that became possible as a result
       of a statutory amendment did not amount to an estoppel against the Council.
       This was because there was no duty on the Council to do so. Further, letters
       written by the Council stating it had no interest in the land did not amount to
       an estoppel as the Council had no right to dispose of its interests in land without
       the consent of the Governor-in-Council. See also *Travinto Nominees Pty Ltd v.
       Vlattas* (1973) 29 C.L.R. 1 at 33-35.

Watson,[217] a person in a similar position to Pratten claimed damages from the Fund on the basis that the certificate of title contained an error, misdescription or omission: see below [5.127]. It was held that because there was no duty on the Registrar-General to note the resumption on the certificate of title, the certificate could not be said to contain an error or misdescription. Such a narrow reading was probably unnecessary. Ferguson J., in dissent, took the view that an order to pay compensation need not imply that the Registrar-General has neglected his duty but simply that the registered proprietor sustained loss by relying on the certificate.[218]

(c) Rights in personam

[5.68]   Although the extent and limits of the in personam exception has been the subject of some debate recently,[219] its nature is clear and has been clear from very soon after the commencement of the Torrens legislation. The exception, if indeed it is properly so called, acknowledges that the concept of indefeasibility of title enshrined in the Torrens legislation does not affect the personal obligations of the registered proprietor. A registered proprietor is subject to contracts he or she has entered into and also to trusts, whether express or implied, over the property. Thus, if a registered proprietor enters into a contract to sell the land the purchaser can seek specific performance of the contract if the registered proprietor refuses to complete. The registered proprietor cannot defend the action successfully by arguing that her or his title is indefeasible and thus not subject to rights or interests not noted on the Register: rights in personam are enforceable against the registered proprietor.[220] Similarly, if the registered proprietor is a trustee of the land for another person, that other person, the beneficiary, can enforce the trust against the registered proprietor.[221]

217. (1963) 64 S.R. (N.S.W.) 98.
218. Cf. *Parker v. Registrar-General* [1977] 1 N.S.W.L.R. 22 and see below [5.127].
219. See e.g. *Bahr v. Nicholay* (1988) 164 C.L.R. 604; 78 A.L.R. 1 discussed in Butt, "Fraud and Personal Equities under the Torrens System" (1988) 62 A.L.J. 1036.
220. Cf. *State Bank of New South Wales v. Berowra Waters Holdings Pty Ltd* (1986) 4 N.S.W.L.R. 398 and *Palais Parking Station Pty Ltd v. Shea* (1980) 20 S.A.S.R. 425. It is arguable that cases such as the *Palais* case and *Boyd v. Mayor of Wellington* [1924] N.Z.L.R. 1174 (see above [5.29]) should have given rise to a successful in personam claim against the registered proprietor. Where a transaction, such as a resumption of land pursuant to statute, has not been performed in accordance with the relevant statutory provisions, it seems that the previous proprietor should have a right in personam to have the land retransferred. Courts faced with this problem have tended to assume that such a result would detract from the concept of immediate indefeasibility of title and have been concerned to reinforce the notion that registration of a void instrument can confer an indefeasible title. It is suggested that the result posited does not concern the issue of indefeasibility of title: rather, it explains a situation where an exception to indefeasibility of title, the in personam exception, is applicable.
221. See the specific provisions in Torrens statutes: S.A.: s. 71; Qld: *Real Property Act* 1877, s. 51.

[5.69] The principle has been set out clearly in a number of cases over the years.[222] In 1967 the Privy Council in *Frazer v. Walker* whilst adopting the principle of immediate indefeasibility, stressed that: "this principle in no way denies the right of a plaintiff to bring against a registered proprietor a claim in personam, founded in law or in equity, for such relief as a court acting in personam may grant."[223] The personal obligations enforceable against the registered proprietor may arise pursuant to actions of the registered proprietor before or after he or she became registered.[224] They may give rise to rights in law or in equity and they may or may not give rise to interests which are proprietary in nature.

[5.70] The High Court decision in *Bahr v. Nicholay* makes clear that the in personam exception may also arise where the registered proprietor purchases the property having acknowledged the existence of a prior unregistered interest or right binding on the vendor and having agreed either expressly or by implication to take subject to that interest or right. The facts of the *Bahr* case are set out above: see above **[5.46]**. All of the High Court judges in the *Bahr* case found that the Thompsons were bound in personam to respect the interests of the Bahrs. However, different views emerged as to the precise nature of the in personam claim. Wilson and Toohey JJ. took the view that the Thompsons, by undertaking to respect the claim of the Bahrs, became constructive trustees for the Bahrs.[225] Further, and unexceptionally, in the view of their Honours, the indefeasibility provisions do not protect a registered proprietor from her or his own actions where those actions have given rise to a personal equity in another. In contrast, Mason C.J. and Dawson J. reviewed the evidence and found that the "matrix of circumstances" was sufficient to establish that there was an intention to create an express trust. The effect of the trust was that the Thompsons held their interest subject to the rights of the Bahrs created under the agreement pursuant to which the Bahrs had sold to Nicholay.[226]

[5.71] The decision in *Bahr v. Nicholay* highlights that in particular fact situations there may be a fine dividing line between the "fraud" exception and the "in personam" exception. In fact, the judgments of Mason C.J. and Dawson J. demonstrate that in some cases there is no dividing line between the two but an overlap where either or both exceptions may be applicable.

[5.72] The *Bahr* case probably does not widen the nature and extent of the in personam exception. It does, however, provide a thorough

---

222. See e.g. *Barry v. Heider* (1914) 19 C.L.R. 197.
223. [1967] 1 A.C. 569 at 585.
224. *Bahr v. Nicholay* (1988) 164 C.L.R. 604; 78 A.L.R. 1; *Logue v. Shoalhaven S.C.* [1979] 1 N.S.W.L.R. 537 at 543ff. per Mahoney J. See also *Silovi Pty Ltd v. Barbaro* (1988) 13 N.S.W.L.R. 466 where the reasoning of the High Court in the *Bahr* case was impliedly approved although not applied.
225. (1988) 164 C.L.R. 604 at 638; 78 A.L.R. 1 at 24 per Wilson and Toohey JJ. The conduct of the Thompsons gave rise to the constructive trust: see *Binions v. Evans* [1972] Ch. 359.
226. (1988) 164 C.L.R. 604 at 618; 78 A.L.R. 1 at 8-9 per Mason C.J. and Dawson J. Quaere the view of Brennan J.

exposition of the principles governing the exception.[227] Further, it demonstrates clearly that the in personam exception may be applicable in many cases where the plaintiff does not have quite enough proof to satisfy the strict definition of "fraud". If a registered proprietor has "notice" of a prior unregistered interest, such notice is insufficient per se to bind the title of the registered proprietor. If a registered proprietor has "notice" of a prior unregistered interest and implies that he or she will abide by that interest but after registration refuses to do so, such action may not constitute fraud but it may come within the in personam exception. Although the result in the *Bahr* case is unobjectionable, it is submitted that the in personam exception has the capacity to cause significant inroads into the concept of indefeasibility of title. As Whalan stated, "the trusteeship concept must be very carefully and sparingly used in the context of indefeasibility or it will undermine the system of registration of titles."[228]

(d) Registrar's power to correct the Register

[5.73] In all States, there are provisions in the Torrens statutes giving the Registrar powers to correct the Register.[229] The very existence of such powers raises the question as to whether the concept of indefeasibility of title is thereby impinged upon. In its purest form, indefeasibility connotes that the Register contains all information relating to the title and that any changes to entries on the Register derogate from the concept of indefeasibility of title. There will be circumstances, however, where the smooth running of the registration system requires the Registrar to have some powers of correction. For example, mistakes in entries on the Register by the Registrar's staff are bound to occur from time to time and a means of correction should be available.

[5.74] In all States except in Victoria, the Torrens statutes contain two sets of provisions relating to the Registrar's power to correct the Register.[230] First, in all States the Registrar may[231] correct errors in the Register and supply omitted entries, but the Registrar must ensure that in doing so the original entry is not erased or made illegible.[232] Corrections or entries made are to have the same effect as if the error or omission had not occurred but without prejudicing any rights acquired from an entry on the Register before the time of correcting the error or supplying the omitted entry.[233] Thus, whatever power the Registrar has

---

227. See also the judgment of Mahoney J. in *Logue v. Shoalhaven S.C.* [1979] 1 N.S.W.L.R. 537 at 543ff.
228. Whalan, p. 335.
229. Torrens statutes: N.S.W.: s. 12(1)(d); Vic.: s. 103(2); Qld: s. 11(4); S.A.: s. 220(4); W.A.: s. 188(ii); Tas.: s. 139.
230. There is overlap between the sets of provisions.
231. In Western Australia, the Registrar "shall" upon the direction of the Commissioner correct errors in the Register Book.
232. Torrens statutes: N.S.W.: s. 12(3); Vic.: s 103(2); Qld: s. 11(4); S.A.: s. 220(4); W.A.: s. 188(ii); Tas.: s. 139(2)(a).
233. Cf. S.A.: s. 220(4).

under this provision is limited to the period before a bona fide purchaser or mortgagee acquires a title having relied upon the Register as it was.[234]

Secondly, except in Victoria if the Registrar is satisfied that a certificate of title, entry, indorsement or instrument has been fraudulently or wrongfully obtained or that a certificate of title, duplicate, dealing or instrument has been fraudulently or wrongfully retained, the Registrar may summon or require delivery up to him of the relevant document for cancellation or correction.[235] Further, this procedure is applicable except in Victoria and Queensland if the Registrar is satisfied that any entry or indorsement has been made in error on a certificate of title, dealing or instrument.[236] These provisions provide considerable overlap with the first set of provisions described above.

[5.75]   In *Frazer v. Walker* the Privy Council considered the equivalent sets of provisions in the New Zealand Torrens legislation. The Privy Council took the view that the first provisions, and the only provisions relating to the Registrar's power to correct the Register in Victoria, were merely ''slip'' provisions and had no substantive importance. However, in the opinion of the Privy Council, the second set of provisions was significant and had the capacity to derogate from the principle of indefeasibility of title. It is submitted, however, that so far the provisions have not been used to create a further exception to indefeasibility of title and the courts have encouraged this position by suggesting that the power should only be used in very clear cases where no difficult issues of law or fact are involved.[237] Further, although it is not specifically provided in the second set of provisions, if a bona fide purchaser has taken an interest on the basis of the Register, any power of the Registrar to correct is lost.[238]

The second set of provisions does contain an inherent capacity for a further exception to indefeasibility to be created. In view of the Privy Council's comments in *Frazer v. Walker*, however, it is perhaps unlikely that Registrars will exercise the power in such a manner as to create a further exception. Thus, where a registered proprietor would have an immediately indefeasible title under the *Frazer v. Walker* principle but there is evidence to show that fraud (but not the fraud of the registered proprietor) was involved in procuring the registration, it is suggested that the Registrar, although having the power, is unlikely to use the power to correct. If the power were so used it would render nugatory the indefeasibility of the registered proprietor's title.[239]

---

234. See *James v. Registrar-General* (1967) S.R. (N.S.W.) 361. Cf. however s. 12(3) of the New South Wales Act discussed in Butt, p. 531.

234. See *James v. Registrar-General* (1967) S.R. (N.S.W.) 361. Cf. however s. 12(3) of the New South Wales Act discussed in Butt, p. 531.
235. Torrens statutes: N.S.W.: ss 136, 137; Qld: ss 130-135; S.A.: ss 60-63; W.A.: ss 76, 77; Tas.: ss 163, 164.
236. Torrens statutes: N.S.W.: s. 136; S.A.: s. 60; W.A.: s. 76; Tas.: s. 163.
237. See e.g. *Re Macarthy and Collins* (1901) 19 N.Z.L.R. 545; *State Bank of New South Wales v. Berowra Waters Holdings Pty Ltd* (1986) 4 N.S.W.L.R. 398.
238. *Frazer v. Walker* [1967] 1 A.C. 569; *James v. Registrar-General* (1967) 69 S.R. (N.S.W.) 361. Cf. s. 12(3) of New South Wales Act.
239. Cf. *District Land Registrar v. Thompson* [1922] N.Z.L.R. 627 referred to in Whalan, p. 371.

[5.76]   The Registrar's powers are discretionary (apart from in Western Australia) and the court will not interfere with the exercise of the Registrar's discretion.[240]

[5.77]   Apart from the specific provisions discussed above, the Registrar also has other various powers to correct the Register. These powers emanate from the express statutory exceptions to indefeasibility. The powers exist quite independently of the specific correction powers and can be used whether or not a bona fide purchaser for value has taken a registered interest.

IV.   EQUITABLE OR UNREGISTERED INTERESTS

1. General

[5.78]   There is a provision in each of the Torrens statutes which suggests that unregistered interests cannot exist under the Torrens system. Section 40(1) of the *Transfer of Land Act* 1958 (Vic.), for example, provides:[241]

"Subject to this Act no instrument until registered as in this Act provided shall be effectual to create vary extinguish or pass any estate or interest or encumbrance in on or over any land under the operation of this Act, but upon registration the estate or interest or encumbrance shall be created varied extinguished or pass in the manner and subject to the covenants and conditions specified in the instrument or by this Act prescribed or declared to be implied in instruments of a like nature."

However, as has already been mentioned (see above **[5.17]**) there are other provisions in the Torrens statutes which make clear that unregistered interests may exist. Over the years, there has been considerable debate as to the precise nature of these "interests". In early times, there was support for the notion that rights created before, or outside, the Register were simply contractual or personal rights and did not give rise to any proprietary interest in the land. This view has received coherent support more recently.[242] It places considerable reliance on the provisions referred to above, which state that no estate or interest in the land can pass until registration. The far more widely accepted view, however, is that these unregistered interests are to be regarded as equitable estates or interests in the land.[243] It seems that all transactions or sets of circumstances which would lead to the creation of equitable interests under the general law conveyancing system, will also lead to the creation of equitable or unregistered interests under the Torrens system. Thus, a specifically enforceable contract of sale gives rise to an equitable

240. *Ex parte Mutual Trust & Investment Society Ltd* (1885) 11 V.L.R. 166.
241. See Torrens statutes: N.S.W.: s. 41; Qld: s. 43; S.A.: s. 67; W.A.: s. 58; Tas.: s. 49(1).
242. Robinson, Chaps 5 & 6.
243. Sackville and Neave, p. 404 (although not fully agreeing with the result, accepting that the interests are so viewed); Whalan, p. 282. See *Barry v. Heider* (1914) 19 C.L.R. 197.

interest in the purchaser[244] and a properly executed trust relating to land gives rise to an equitable interest in the beneficiary. Similarly, implied trusts are applicable to Torrens land: see generally Chapter 6. Further, a person holding an unregistered but registrable instrument has an equitable interest.[245] A question arises as to how the s. 40(1) type provision can be reconciled with the now entrenched view that equitable interests may exist outside the Register. The judgment of Isaacs J. in *Barry v. Heider* provides the answer. Isaacs J. stated:[246]

> "The Torrens statutes do not touch the form of contracts. A proprietor may contract as he pleases, and his obligation to fulfil the contract will depend on ordinary principles and rules of law and equity. [The provision] in denying effect to an instrument until registration, does not touch whatever rights are behind it. Parties may have a right to have such an instrument executed and registered; and that right, according to accepted rules of equity, is an estate or interest in land."

Thus, one looks to the transaction behind the instrument to determine if an equitable interest has been created.[247] As a result of the development, sometimes the term "unregistered interest" is used and sometimes the term "equitable interest" is used by judges and authors. In this section the terms are used interchangeably.

[5.79] Although it may be generally accepted that equitable or unregistered interests can exist under the Torrens system, these interests are far more vulnerable under the Torrens system than they are if existing under the general law system. The doctrine of notice is inapplicable to Torrens land and subject to certain exceptions, a registered proprietor gains an indefeasible title. The vulnerability of an equitable interest in Torrens land is most aptly demonstrated by comparing the means of resolution of a dispute between a prior equitable interest and a subsequent legal, or in Torrens terminology, registered interest under both the general law system and the Torrens system. Under the general law system, the legal interest would only prevail over the equitable interest if the holder of the legal interest had purchased bona fide for value and without notice (actual, constructive or imputed) of the prior equitable interest. In contrast, under the Torrens system the registered interest would prevail over the unregistered interest unless fraud on the part of the holder of the registered interest could be proved. In short, the holder of the registered interest has an indefeasible title subject to the named exceptions which include fraud.

[5.80] Disputes may arise between holders of equitable or unregistered interests. Despite some criticism of the approach,[248] priority between

244. *Barry v. Heider* (1914) 19 C.L.R. 197.
245. According to Isaacs J. in *Barry v. Heider* (1914) 19 C.L.R. 197 at 216 the contract behind the instrument creates the equitable interest. Cf. the view of Griffith C.J. to the effect that the registrable instrument itself creates the interest at 208.
246. (1914) 19 C.L.R. 197 at 216.
247. Cf. the view of Griffith C.J.
248. Robinson, Chap. 5; Robinson, "Caveatable Interests—Their Nature and Priority" (1970) 44 A.L.J. 351.

unregistered interests is decided by applying the general priority rules governing conflicts between equitable interests under the general law: see above **[3.42]-[3.48]**. Although the principles to be applied are the same, an application of the principles to a dispute under the Torrens system necessarily involves a consideration of factors which are exclusive to the Torrens system. Thus, for example, the lodgment or non-lodgment of a caveat is a factor to be considered in any application of the general principles. Apart from this proviso, the principles and underlying bases for deciding disputes between the holders of equitable interests are equally applicable to Torrens land.

It is intended first to discuss the provisions relating to the caveat against dealings. The priority rules as applicable to Torrens land will then be analysed. Finally, various statutory provisions having the potential to affect priorities between unregistered interests, will be discussed.

2. Caveats

(a) General

[5.81]　Although it is registration which confers title and protection, the Torrens statutes permit some degree of protection for holders of unregistered interests. This protection is afforded through the use of the caveat. Perhaps the most used and probably the most litigated type of caveat, is the caveat lodged by a person who claims an estate or interest in the land and who wishes to prevent the registration of any dealing inconsistent with her or his interest. Detailed attention is directed to this type of caveat below. There are, however, many other situations where various provisions of the Torrens statutes permit the lodgment of caveats.[249] The range of caveats varies from State to State. For example, a person claiming an interest in the land in question may lodge a caveat against the bringing of land under the Torrens statutes[250] and against the grant of a title based on an adverse possession claim.[251] Further, in certain circumstances, the Registrar her or himself may lodge a caveat against dealings. Thus, the Registrar may enter a caveat on behalf of the Queen or a person under a disability for that person's protection restraining any dealing in any land.[252] Further, the Registrar may enter a caveat to prevent fraud or error or to prohibit any dealing with land in which the Registrar is of the view that there has been a misdescription of the land in the Register or any dealing document.[253] Except in Tasmania, a document creating a trust may be deposited with the Registrar but not registered.[254] In New South Wales, the Registrar must lodge a caveat

---

249. A detailed list is set out in Whalan, pp. 223-225.
250. Torrens statutes: N.S.W.: s. 74B; Vic.: s. 12; Qld: s. 23; S.A.: s. 39; W.A.: s. 30; Tas.: s. 14.
251. Torrens statutes: N.S.W.: s. 74F; Vic.: s. 61; Qld: *Real Property Acts Amendments Act* 1952, s. 56; S.A.: s. 80F; W.A.: s. 223A; Tas.: s. 118.
252. Torrens statutes: N.S.W.: s. 12(1)(f); Vic.: s. 106(a); Qld: s. 11(5); S.A.: s. 220(5); W.A.: 188(iii); Tas.: s. 160(3).
253. Ibid.
254. Torrens statutes: N.S.W.: s. 82(2); Vic.: s. 37; Qld: s. 78 ("must"); S.A.: s. 162; W.A.: s. 55.

prohibiting the registration of dealings not in compliance with the trust.[255] In the other States, except Queensland, the Registrar appears to have a power to lodge a caveat to protect the interests under the trust.[256]

(b) Caveat against dealings lodged by a person claiming an estate or interest in the land

[5.82] The holder of an unregistered interest is in a vulnerable and precarious position. The caveat against the registration of inconsistent dealings provides some protection. In outline, the caveat against registration of dealings operates in the following manner.

A person claiming an estate or interest in the land may lodge a caveat prohibiting the registration of all, or specifically named, dealings in the land which would affect the estate protected by the caveat.[257] A memorandum of the caveat is noted in the Register[258] and, except in Queensland, remains there until a dealing inconsistent with the caveator's claim is lodged for registration or proceedings are commenced under the relevant statutory provisions for the removal of the caveat.

When a dealing is lodged for registration, the caveator is given notice of this fact. The caveator has a set period in which to consent to registration or to take action to demonstrate the validity of her or his interest and thus show cause why the dealing should not be registered.[259] If the caveator takes no action, the caveat lapses and the dealing is registered. The lapsed caveat cannot be renewed. If the caveator does prove the interest, a priority dispute may ensue between the unregistered interests of the caveator and the person who has lodged the dealing. Such a dispute is resolved according to the various priority rules discussed below (see below **[5.97]-[5.112]**) and the presence of the caveat itself may be a factor in the resolution of the dispute.

The caveat aids both intending purchasers and caveators: a search of the title reveals to any intending purchaser that there is an existing interest over the land and the lodgment of a dealing for registration has the effect of alerting the caveator.

(i) Nature of caveatable interest

[5.83] It is well established law that caveats may only be lodged to protect interests in land.[260] Whether an estate or interest exists in land

---

255. Torrens statutes: N.S.W.: s. 82(3). See Whalan, p. 121 where it is argued that the N.S.W. provision derogates from the aim that trusts not be registered.
256. Torrens statutes: Vic.: s. 37; S.A.: s. 220(5) (power to lodge caveat to prevent fraud and improper dealing); W.A.: s. 55.
257. Torrens statutes: N.S.W.: s. 74F; Vic.: s. 89(1); Qld: s. 98; S.A.: s. 191; W.A.: s. 137; Tas.: s. 133.
258. Torrens statutes: N.S.W.: s. 74G "for the purpose only of acknowledging receipt of caveat" and "if satisfied that the caveat complies with the requirements made in respect of if"; Vic.: s. 89(2); S.A.: s. 191II; W.A.: s. 141; Tas.: s. 133(3). Cf. Queensland: no specific provision but recording made in practice.
259. Torrens statutes: N.S.W.: s. 74I (21 days); Vic.: s. 90(1), (2) (30 days); W.A.: s. 138 (14 days); Tas.: s. 136 (28 days). Cf. Queensland and South Australia: see below **[5.90]-[5.91]**.
260. See e.g. *Miller v. Minister of Mines* [1963] A.C. 484 (P.C.).

must be determined by the general principles discussed in Chapter 6. Although the emergence of new types of proprietary interest in land is not a common occurrence, new interests are defined and accepted by the courts[261] or the legislature from time to time and such developments are to be noted for the purpose of determining the existence or non-existence of a caveatable interest. It has sometimes been suggested that in order for a caveatable interest to exist, the estate or interest claimed must be one which, if established, "results in an entry being made on the Register".[262] In other words, the proposition is that the interest claimed must be capable of being placed on the Register. However, there is a preponderance of Australian authority which does not require that the interest be capable of being noted on the Register.[263]

A number of fact situations clearly give rise to caveatable interests. The claim of a beneficiary under a trust, the interest of an optionee under an option to purchase provided the terms and conditions are set out in the option, the rights under an agreement for a mortgage[264] or a lease or an easement, the interest of a purchaser of a registered interest under a contract for sale and a vendor's lien all give rise to caveatable interests. Each of the transactions gives rise to an equitable interest in the land. In contrast, merely contractual rights associated with land or interests in land, and not per se giving rise to proprietary rights in the land are not caveatable rights.[265] Thus, a licence to occupy land does not give rise to a caveatable interest.[266] Neither does a pre-emptive right, such as a right of first refusal to purchase, give rise to a right capable of supporting a caveat.[267] A spouse's claim under matrimonial property law for an interest in the other spouse's property is not per se a caveatable interest.[268] Generally, the cases support the notion that a purchaser under a conditional contract for sale does not have a caveatable interest until the condition is fulfilled.[269]

261. See e.g. *Tulk v. Moxhay* (1848) 2 Ph. 774; 41 E.R. 1143.
262. See Robinson, "The Nature of Cautionable Interests" (1971) 35 Conv. (N.S.) 21 at 24 relying upon statements of the Privy Council in *Miller v. Minister of Mines* [1963] A.C. 484.
263. See Whalan, p. 229. Cf. however, *Bacon v. O'Dea* (1989) 88 A.L.R. 486 at 496-497.
264. *Zafiropoulos v. Recchi* (1978) 18 S.A.S.R. 5.
265. See *Bacon v. O'Dea* (1989) 88 A.L.R. 486.
266. See e.g. *La Martina v. Penney* [1968] S.A.S.R. 411.
267. *Eudunda Farmers' Co-operative Society Ltd v. Mattiske* [1920] S.A.L.R. 309. A pre-emptive right may lead to an equitable interest capable of supporting a caveat. If the terms and conditions are such that it is possible to find an offer and an acceptance, an enforceable contract for the land may have been formed: see *Pata Nominees Pty Ltd v. Durnsford Pty Ltd* [1988] W.A.R. 365. See also Purich, "The Caveat: An Uncertain Instrument in an Exact System" (1982) 47 Saskatchewan L.R. 353.
268. *Re Pile's Caveat* [1981] Qd R. 81. Cf. *Ioppolo v. Ioppolo* (1978) 4 Fam. L.R. 124. See Butt, "Moot Point Caveat Caveator" (1980) 54 A.L.J. 166. See also *Sonenco (No. 77) Pty Ltd v. Silvia* (1990) 89 A.L.R. 437.
269. See e.g. *Re Dimbury's Pty Ltd Caveat* [1986] 2 Qd R. 348. See also *Batagol Nominees Pty Ltd v. Similar or Equal Approved Products Pty Ltd* [1989] Vic. Con. R. 54-342 where it was held that if the parties have agreed that the contract is not to be binding until the exchange of parts, the purchaser has no caveatable interest until such exchange. See also Note, "Caveats and Conditional Contracts" (1987) 61 A.L.J. 306. See generally, Chapter 6.

[5.84] A question arises as to whether a person may lodge a caveat against her or his own registered title. Such a course of action may be necessary if, for example, the duplicate certificate of title has been lost or stolen and there is a danger that a dealing affecting the registered proprietor's title may be lodged. In New South Wales, the legislation now specifically permits the registered proprietor to lodge a caveat in these circumstances.[270] Case law supports the view that the position in the other States is the same as in New South Wales despite the lack of specific statutory provision.[271] Although technically it could be argued that a registered proprietor may only lodge a caveat to protect a separate and distinct interest in the land,[272] an acceptance of the practice of permitting a registered proprietor to lodge a caveat provides an important protection for the registered proprietor whose duplicate certificate of title is stolen.

[5.85] It is to be noted that the relevant statutory provisions require only that the caveator "claims" an estate or interest in the land. It is not a requirement that the interest is "established". Further, it is not the duty of the Registrar to check the validity of the caveator's claimed interest.[273] It might be thought that the admixture of the above factors may lead to the lodgment of frivolous and vexatious caveats. A further provision, however, provides some protection against such caveats. In all States, any person who lodges a caveat without reasonable cause is liable to pay compensation to any person who suffers loss as a consequence of the caveat.[274] It seems that if a caveator who believes on reasonable grounds that he or she has an interest sufficient to support a caveat, he or she will not be held to have lodged the caveat "without reasonable cause".[275]

(ii) Describing the claimed interest

[5.86] The Torrens statutes in all jurisdictions provide that caveats must be lodged in a particular form and manner.[276] The nature and probably the quantum[277] of the estate or interest claimed, a description of the land over which the estate is claimed and the facts upon which the claim is based, must be set out in the caveat. Strict compliance is necessary and a caveat may be deemed defective for small, seemingly unimportant errors. In New South Wales, the provisions relating to caveats and to their formal requirements have recently been revised and

---

270. Torrens statutes: N.S.W.: s. 74F(2).
271. See e.g. *Barry v. Heider* (1914) 19 C.L.R. 197; *J. & H. Just (Holdings) Pty Ltd v. Bank of New South Wales* (1971) 125 C.L.R. 546; [1972] A.L.R. 323. Cf. *Sinclair v. Hope Investments Pty Ltd* (1983) A.N.Z. Conv. R. 184.
272. See Teh and Dwyer, p. 105 and Whalan, p. 232.
273. See specifically Torrens statutes: N.S.W.: s. 74Q.
274. Torrens statutes: N.S.W.: s. 74P; Vic.: s. 118; Qld: s. 103; S.A.: s. 191x; W.A.: s. 140; Tas.: s. 138.
275. Teh and Dwyer, p. 104. The onus of proof is on the plaintiff to show that the caveator acted without reasonable cause. See generally *Bedford Properties Pty Ltd v. Surgo Pty Ltd* [1981] 1 N.S.W.L.R. 106; *Hooke v. Holland* [1984] W.A.R. 16; *D.F.C. of T.C.W.A. v. Corwest Management Pty Ltd* [1978] W.A.R. 129.
276. Torrens statutes: N.S.W.: s. 74F(5); Vic.: s. 89(1); Qld: ss 98, 100; S.A.: s. 191I; W.A.: s. 137; Tas.: s. 133(1), (2).
277. Although this generally seems to be required, Whalan suggested that the statutory provisions do not justify this: Whalan, p. 233.

changed. Whilst the caveator must still use a particular form for caveating and must specify her or his interest in the land and verify this by a statutory declaration,[278] a failure to comply strictly with the formalities is to be disregarded by the courts.[279]

(iii) Effect of caveat

[5.87]   A caveat effectively operates as an injunction to the Registrar by restraining the Registrar from registering any dealing. The Registrar is prevented from registering any dealing prohibited by the caveat until the caveator has had an opportunity to establish her or his claim. Although it is not mandatory in all jurisdictions, the caveat is noted on the Register but not on the duplicate certificate of title. As it is noted on the Register, the caveat may have the effect of operating as notice to the world of the caveator's claimed interest but its primary purpose is as a direction to the Registrar. The Registrar gives notice to the registered proprietor that a caveat has been lodged.[280]

[5.88]   The Registrar is restrained from registering only those dealings which affect the estate or interest of the caveator. Thus, it may be argued that a caveat lodged by an equitable mortgagee should not prevent the registration of a transfer to a purchaser from the first registered mortgagee who has exercised her or his power of sale. The second equitable mortgage is carved from the registered proprietor's notional "equity of redemption" and has no priority over the registered mortgage. Arguably, a sale by the registered mortgagee does not affect the interest of the equitable mortgagee.[281] Nevertheless, in a Victorian decision[282] it was held that such a caveat by a second equitable mortgagee effectively prevented registration of a transfer from the registered mortgagee.[283] An amendment to the *Transfer of Land Act* now ensures that a caveat protecting a second unregistered mortgage does not prevent the registration of a transfer by the registered mortgagee who has exercised her or his power of sale.[284] In the other States, statutory provisions are in place which would prevent a caveat lodged by a second unregistered mortgagee having the effect of restraining the registration of a transfer.[285]

[5.89]   Apart from the exception referred to above, there are some other situations where the Registrar is empowered to register a dealing despite the existence of a caveat on the title. These exceptions vary in detail from

---

278.   Torrens statutes: N.S.W.: s. 74F(5).
279.   Note, however, the comments of Butt suggesting that the requirements under the New South Wales Act remain very detailed and are similar to the requirements developed by the courts: see Butt, p. 502.
280.   Torrens statutes: N.S.W.: s. 74F(6); Vic.: s. 89(3); Qld: s. 99; S.A.: s. 191II; W.A.: s. 138; Tas.: s. 133(3)(b). See *N.R.M.A. Insurance Ltd v. Martin* (1988) 84 A.C.T.R. 1.
281.   See MacCallum, "Dilemmas for Torrens System Mortgagees" (1981) 13 M.U.L.R. 248 at 250.
282.   *Forster v. Finance Corporation of Australia Ltd* [1980] V.R. 63.
283.   Discussed in MacCallum, op. cit.
284.   See now Torrens statutes: Vic.: s. 91(2A).
285.   Torrens statutes: N.S.W.: ss 74H(5)(g), 74H(1)(b); Qld: s. 101; S.A.: s. 136(2); Tas.: s. 137. Quaere W.A.: s. 141A.

State to State but generally concern matters such as registration of transmissions,[286] vesting orders, discharges of mortgages and transfers pursuant to writs.[287] Further, except in Queensland, any registrable dealing lodged for registration before the lodgment of a caveat is not affected by the caveat: registration of the dealing proceeds despite the caveat.[288] In Queensland, a caveat lodged after the lodgment of instrument for registration, prevents the registration of the registrable instrument.[289] Sometimes an instrument may be lodged for registration but may not be in registrable form. In these circumstances a question arises as to whether the subsequent lodgment of a caveat prevents registration of such an instrument. In New South Wales, the relevant provision states clearly that the instrument must be in registrable form for the registration to proceed despite the caveat.

There are some provisions which allow for "permissive" or "conditional" caveats. For example, in Victoria, South Australia and Western Australia the caveat may forbid the registration of any dealing unless it expressed to be subject to the claim of the caveator.[290] Where such a caveat is lodged, it is effective in preserving the claim of the caveator as against a purchaser who becomes the registered proprietor.[291]

[5.90] Thus, generally when a dealing is lodged for registration the Registrar cannot proceed to register it if there is a caveat on the title restraining the registration of the dealing. In all States except Queensland and South Australia, the Registrars must, however, notify the caveator that a dealing has been lodged for registration and the caveator then has a set time, varying from 14-30 days, to agree to the registration of the dealing or to commence proceedings to establish the right to maintain the caveat. Effectively, the caveator must, within the specified time period, obtain a court order extending the caveat until the rights of the competing parties are settled in a fully argued court action. At the first stage, the court does not decide the rights of the parties and will usually grant an extension of the caveat unless it is shown that the caveator has no possible

---

286. This varies from State to State. There is provision for the registration of transmissions based on particular facts where there is a caveat on title in N.S.W.: s. 74H(5); Vic.: ss 90(1)(a), 91(1); W.A.: s. 142 (very limited circumstances); Tas.: s. 137(3)(g). Whalan suggests that the practice of registering transmissions despite the existence of a caveat where there is no statutory provision enabling such registration may not be justified: see Whalan, p. 240.
287. See generally Torrens statutes: N.S.W.: s. 74H(5); Vic.: ss 90(1), 91(1), 90(2A), 90(2B); Qld: s. 101; S.A.: s. 136; Tas.: s. 137.
288. Torrens statutes: N.S.W.: s. 74H(4); Vic.: s. 91(2); S.A.: s. 191III; W.A.: s. 139(2); Tas.: s. 137(2)(a).
289. Torrens statutes: Qld: ss 98, 101.
290. Torrens statutes: Vic.: s. 90(1)(d); S.A.: s. 191; W.A.: s. 137. See also the "after notice" provisions forbidding registration until the caveator has been notified in the manner provided in the caveat—Torrens statutes: Vic.: ss 89(1), 90(1)(e); Qld: s. 98; W.A.: s. 137 and the "written consent" provisions— Torrens statutes: N.S.W.: s. 74H(5)(i); Vic.: s. 90(1)(b); Qld: s. 101; Tas.: s. 137(1).
291. *Coles K.M.A. Ltd v. Sword Nominees Pty Ltd* (1986) 44 S.A.S.R. 120.

interest in the land and that any further action by the caveator would be frivolous or vexatious.[292] The extension is granted only for a period of time sufficient to ensure that the fully argued case can be heard by a court.

[5.91] In Queensland, a caveat against dealings does not simply remain on the title until an instrument is lodged for registration. Rather, the caveator must take proceedings to establish her or his claim within three months of lodging the caveat. If such proceedings are not taken the caveat lapses.[293] In South Australia, the position is more open-ended. The registered proprietor may seek to have the caveat removed. The Registrar then gives the caveator 21 days in which to obtain a court order for extension of the caveat.[294] If no such order is obtained, the caveat lapses.

(iv) Methods by which a caveat may be removed from title

[5.92] In most States once a caveat against dealings has been removed or lapsed, the caveator cannot lodge another caveat based on the same facts against the title.[295] A caveator in this position wishing to prevent the registration of further dealings would need to go to court and seek an injunction.[296]

[5.93] **Withdrawal.** A caveator may withdraw the caveat at any time.[297]

[5.94] **Application for removal of caveat.** In all States, an application may be made to the court seeking removal of a caveat.[298] In Western Australia only the registered proprietor or any person claiming under any instrument signed by the registered proprietor can make such an application. In the other States, the provision is wider.[299] For example, in Victoria any person adversely affected by a caveat may make an

---

292. Torrens statutes: Vic.: s. 90(2) and W.A.: s. 138 which provide that the court grants the stay if the caveator provides an undertaking or security or lodges a sum set by the court sufficient to indemnify persons who may suffer loss as a result of the continuing presence of the caveat on the title. See *Dralter Pty Ltd v. Channel Land Co. Pty Ltd* (1988) V. Conv. R. 54-324—if the caveator is impecunious, an effective security cannot be given.

293. *Real Property Act* 1877 (Qld), s. 39.

294. Torrens statutes: S.A.: s. 191v, vi, vii. See *Galvasteel Pty Ltd v. Monterey Building Pty Ltd* [1974] 10 S.A.S.R. 176.

295. Torrens statutes: N.S.W.: s. 74o; Vic.: s. 91(4); Qld: *Real Property Act* 1877, s. 40; S.A.: s. 191xi; W.A.: s. 138. Quaere "withdrawn". Cf. Tasmanian Act where successive caveats are prohibited only with respect to caveats against applications: s. 14(4). See also s. 134 and note the comments of Whalan, p. 264.

296. This appears to be possible: see e.g. the comments in *Halaga Developments Pty Ltd v. Grime* (1986) 5 N.S.W.L.R. 740.

297. Torrens statutes: N.S.W.: s. 74m(1)(a); Vic.: s. 89(1); Qld: s. 102; S.A.: s. 191viii; W.A.: s. 137; Tas.: s. 133(5), (6).

298. In New South Wales the application is made for an order that the caveat be "withdrawn": s. 74ma.

299. Torrens statutes: N.S.W.: s. 74ma; Vic.: s. 90(3); Qld: *Real Property Act* 1877, s. 38; S.A.: s. 191iv; W.A.: s. 138; Tas.: s. 135. In *N.R.M.A. Insurance v. Martin* (1988) 84 A.C.T.R. 1 it was held that a registered mortgagee is a "registered proprietor" of an interest in the land and was thus entitled to make application to have a caveat removed.

application for its removal. The court may make such order as it thinks fit. The court will not order the removal of a caveat if the caveator establishes the right to maintain the caveat or if there is some doubt as to the caveator's right to maintain the caveat. In the latter case the caveat would remain on title at least until sufficient time has elapsed for the matter to have been fully litigated.[300] If it is clear that there were no proper grounds for lodging the caveat or that the caveatable interest has since been lost, the court will order the removal of the caveat. Further, in a case where a dealing is awaiting registration and an application for removal of caveat has been made, the court will order the removal of the caveat if the caveator clearly does not have an interest which is enforceable against the registered interest holder who has executed the registrable instrument. This may arise in the case where there is a registered mortgage followed by an equitable mortgage protected by a caveat. As Holland J. remarked in *Kerabee Park Pty Ltd v. Daley*:[301]

> "[A] caveator should have no right to prohibit registration of a dealing to which his alleged interest in the land would not entitle him to object, if he were to invoke the assistance of the court. A subsequent incumbrancer, registered or unregistered, has no right whatever to interfere in, or object to, a proper exercise by a mortgagee of the mortgagee's power of sale, and would have no ground on which to seek the intervention of the court, notwithstanding the fact that registration of the transfer to the purchaser would discharge or defeat all mortgage interests in the land whether registered or not."

Although there is some doubt, the better view is that the caveator carries the onus of proof. On an application for removal, the caveator must justify the maintenance of the caveat.[302]

[5.95]   Lapse of caveat. This is discussed under the effect of a caveat.

[5.96]   Removal by Registrar. The methods of removal of a caveat described above do not provide a simple method for a registered proprietor to get a caveat removed from her or his title. In cases where it is clear the caveator has no caveatable interest, it is important that the registered proprietor has an effective way of securing the removal of the caveat. In all States except Tasmania, such a method is provided for in the legislation. An application may be made to the Registrar seeking removal of the caveat.[303] The form and content of the application vary

---

300. *McMahon v. McMahon* [1979] V.R. 239. Sometimes the parties may agree for the substantive matter to be decided at the hearing of the application for removal of the caveat.
301. (1978) 2 N.S.W.L.R. 222 at 228. See also *Lewenberg v. Direct Acceptance Corporation Ltd* [1981] V.R. 344. Cf. *Zombolas v. L.R.G. Credit & Finance Pty Ltd* (1988) V. Conv. R. 54-302.
302. *Re Little; Ex parte Thorne's Bankstown Estate Ltd* (1929) 29 S.R. (N.S.W.) 401; *Lewenberg v. Direct Acceptance Corporation Ltd* [1981] V.R. 344; *Commonwealth Bank of Australia v. Schierholter* [1981] V.R. 292; *Smith v. Callegar* (1988) V. Conv. R. 54-300.
303. Torrens statutes: N.S.W.: s. 74J; Vic.: s. 89A; Qld: s. 102; S.A.: s. 191V; W.A.: s. 141A.

from State to State.[304] The Registrar gives notice to the caveator and if no response is received within a set time the caveat is removed.

3. Priority between Unregistered Interests[305]

[5.97] It has often been stated that equity applies the maxim "qui prior est tempore potior est jure" to decide priority disputes between holders of equitable interests. In reality, the position is more complex. As has been discussed earlier in deciding a dispute between equitable interests, the court searches for the better equitable interest by considering all the circumstances of the case including the conduct of the parties. In the language of *Rice v. Rice*,[306] if all other things are equal, the first in time is accorded priority. As has been discussed in Chapter 3 this suggests that the date of acquisition of the interest is used to determine the dispute only where the circumstances and conduct of the parties do not provide a means of according priority to one. In other decisions, the principle has been expressed in a way which suggests that priority is to be determined primarily by the dates of acquisition of interests and that first in time is only to lose priority if there is some conduct on the part of the first equitable interest holder which would merit postponement of the interest.[307]

Reference has been made earlier to the fact that it is unlikely this distinction in itself would result in different decisions on the same set of facts. Reference has also been made to recent cases which lend support to the view that in determining if all other things are equal the courts appear to be using two different, if overlapping principles in according priority between equitable interests.[308] The use of one or other of these principles in any given fact situation seems to depend upon the nature of the fact situation. The first, as evidenced in the judgments of Gibbs C.J. and Wilson J. in *Heid v. Reliance Finance Corporation Pty Ltd*,[309] is a use of the principle of estoppel by representation to decide such a priority dispute. The second approach is to use a broad principle which takes into account all the circumstances and the conduct of both parties to determine who has the better equity and comprises elements of both estoppel and negligence.

---

304. Ibid.
305. For principles relating to the resolution a dispute between (1) a prior registered interest and a subsequent unregistered interest, see *Barry v. Heider* (1914) 19 C.L.R. 197, discussed at [3.12] and generally [3.07]-[3.13]; (2) a prior unregistered interest and a subsequent registered interest, see above [5.36]-[5.77]; (3) a prior equity and a subsequent equitable interest, see *Latec Investments Ltd v. Hotel Terrigal Pty Ltd (in liq.)* (1965) 113 C.L.R. 265, discussed at [3.51] and [3.55].
306. (1853) 2 Drew. 73; 61 E.R. 646.
307. *Abigail v. Lapin* [1934] A.C. 491; *Heid v. Reliance Finance Corporation Pty Ltd* (1983) 154 C.L.R. 326 at 333; 49 A.L.R. 229 at 233 per Gibbs C.J.
308. See above [3.47]. For a discussion of these principles, see Nicholson, "Owning and Owing—In What Circumstances Will the Responsibility of Ownership Preclude the Assertion of the Rights of an Owner?" (1988) 16 M.U.L.R. 784.
309. (1983) 154 C.L.R. 326 at 333; 49 A.L.R. 229 at 233 per Gibbs C.J.; Wilson J. agreed with the judgment of Gibbs C.J.

Judgments in which this second broad approach has been used have
tended to the use of negligence-based language.[310]

The operation of the equitable rule and these underlying principles
have been discussed in Chapter 3. It is intended here to analyse factors
arising under the Torrens system which affect the way in which these
principles are applied. Most important of these factors is the caveat.

(a) The impact of the caveat and other relevant Torrens factors

[5.98] The relevance of the caveat in disputes between holders of
unregistered interests has been considered in many cases. However, its
relative importance in priority disputes has varied markedly over the
years and although the most recent interpretations tend to downplay its
importance, a clear and unequivocal view has yet to emerge. Perhaps such
a situation is inevitable in view of the widely varying fact situations in
which disputes between holders of equitable interests may arise.

[5.99] The Law Reform Commission of Victoria has suggested that
irrespective of the fact situation, caveats should be used as a determinative
factor in priorities disputes.[311] Such an approach would possibly provide
more certainty in the settlement of priority disputes. It would, however,
give the caveat a role and importance in the operation of the Torrens
system which was probably not intended and it may have unexpected
consequences. The equitable interest of a person who holds pursuant to
an informal arrangement would become even more precarious than it is
at present. The holder of such an interest may be unaware that he or she
holds an interest and thus would be clearly unaware of the need to lodge
a caveat.

(i) The nature of disputes

[5.100] Some knowledge of the more usual of the fact situations
involving competitions between equitable interests is important in giving
a basis and substance to the ensuing discussion of the relevant principles
and authorities.

[5.101] Disputes may very often arise between holders of unregistered
mortgages. An unregistered mortgagee who takes possession of the
duplicate certificate of title may be confident of claiming priority over the
interest of any subsequently created unregistered mortgage.[312] The

---

310. (1983) 154 C.L.R. 326 at 342-343; 49 A.L.R. 229 at 239-240 per Mason and
      Deane JJ.
311. Vic. L.R.C., *Priorities*, Report No. 22 (April 1989), pp. 10-12.
312. *J. & H. Just (Holdings) Pty Ltd v. Bank of New South Wales* (1971) 125 C.L.R. 546;
      [1972] A.L.R. 323. The certificate of title in New South Wales, Queensland and
      Tasmania is the equivalent of the duplicate certificate of title. See Vic. L.R.C.,
      Sale of Land, Report No. 20 (June 1989) p. 27 where it is argued that duplicate
      certificates of title should be removed from the system. The Commission argues
      that there is no need for duplicate certificates of title except to facilitate
      unregistered mortgages which are secured by the deposit of the duplicate. The
      Commission had suggested elsewhere that all holders of equitable interests,
      including equitable mortgagees, should protect their interests by caveat: see Vic.
      L.R.C. Report No. 22, p. 12.

possession of the duplicate certificate of title protects the first mortgagee as against a subsequent mortgagee even where the former has not lodged a caveat. This is because reasonable conduct on the part of the subsequent mortgagee requires that party to inform her or himself as to the physical whereabouts of the duplicate certificate of title in order to ensure that it has not been deposited as a security for another loan. The position may be different if the dispute is between the holders of second and third unregistered mortgages. If the first mortgagee has possession of the duplicate certificate of title, the second mortgagee may need to use an alternative means, such as the lodgment of a caveat, to protect her or his interest.[313] Similarly if the dispute is between an equitable mortgage and subsequent equitable interest created under a contract of sale, the possession of the duplicate certificate of title by the mortgagee may not provide such a complete protection.[314] In these circumstances the lodgment of a caveat by the mortgagee may ensure priority.

[5.102] A priority dispute between unregistered interest holders which tends to become very common in times of rapidly increasing prices is that between purchasers of the same land. A vendor who enters into a contract of sale may discover some weeks later that he or she could obtain a much higher price and may proceed to "forget about" the first contract and enter into a contract of sale in favour of another purchaser. Although in some cases protection for the deposit moneys of these purchasers is provided by legislation requiring the vendor's agent to place the deposit in a trust account,[314a] the issue as to which purchaser is entitled to the land remains to be resolved by comparing their equitable interests. The relevance of the failure to caveat by the first purchaser, the holder of the first equitable interest, has varied from State to State and within States, from time to time.[315] To be assured of protection as against a subsequent purchaser of the same land a purchaser under a contract of sale should lodge a caveat.

[5.103] A further priority dispute concerns the situation where a person claiming the earlier equitable interest is in possession of the land, either alone or together with the holder of the legal estate. The basis of the equitable interest may vary. It could, for example, arise pursuant to a tenancy or pursuant to a resulting or constructive trust. An issue arises as to whether possession alone is sufficient to provide protection for the equitable interest as against a subsequent equitable interest holder such as a mortgagee. Alternatively, is it incumbent upon the holder of the earlier equitable interest to lodge a caveat in order to ensure a full protection? Under the general law, it seems that possession per se would provide protection. Where the equitable interest arises pursuant to a tenancy or other transaction which would be protected under the express

313. *Person-to-Person Financial Services Pty Ltd v. Sharari* [1984] 1 N.S.W.L.R. 745.
314. See **[6.61]-[6.62]**. Recently introduced provisions relating to disclosure by a vendor have cut across, and perhaps reduced the significance of general principles here.
314a. See e.g. *Sale of Land Act* 1962 (Vic.), ss 24, 25, 27.
315. E.g. *Osmanoski v. Rose* [1974] V.R. 523. Cf. *Jacobs v. Platt Nominees Pty Ltd* [1990] V.R. 146.

statutory exceptions to indefeasibility of title, it is suggested that the possession per se would ensure that the earlier equitable interest prevails over the later equitable interest. The holder of a subsequent equitable estate could not be placed in a better position than the holder of a subsequent legal or registered estate. Where, however, the earlier equitable interest arises pursuant to a transaction which is not so specifically protected, the position is less clear and possession may not provide the necessary protection. It seems that the holder of such an interest should lodge a caveat in order to strengthen her or his position in relation to subsequently created equitable interests. Of course, in some cases, possession may provide the requisite degree of protection.[316]

The lodgment of a caveat is dependent upon the person who can so lodge knowing that he or she has an interest in the land and knowing that protection is available. As discussed earlier (see above [5.19]), this may often not be the case. This lack of knowledge, however, does not in itself improve the position of the unregistered interest holder.

(ii) The relevant authorities

[5.104]   It is intended here to review the most important cases and to attempt to reach some tentative conclusions. In Butler v. Fairclough[317] Griffith C.J. took the view that a caveat has the effect of giving notice to the world that the caveator has an equitable interest in the land. His Honour held that there was a positive duty on the holder of an equitable interest to lodge a caveat. In a dispute between two equitable interests where the holder of the first interest fails to caveat and the holder of the second has searched the Register, the failure would be considered to be postponing conduct such that priority in time would be displaced. In the language of Rice v. Rice, this would be a case where all other things were not equal. Griffith C.J. thus placed great importance on the caveat in the issue of priority between unregistered interests. The strong view of Griffith C.J. has been criticised[318] and has not been wholly accepted in later cases.[319]

[5.105]   In Abigail v. Lapin,[320] the Lapins were the registered proprietors of certain pieces of land. Although there was considerable dispute as to the facts, it was found by the court that the Lapins had executed transfers of the land in favour of Mrs Heavener but that the transfers were executed by way of security for costs owed by the Lapins to Mrs Heavener. They were not intended as absolute transfers and the Lapins were to have a right to redeem upon repayment. Mrs Heavener became the registered

---

316. *Taddeo v. Catalano* (1975) 11 S.A.S.R. 492.
317. (1917) 23 C.L.R. 78.
318. See Sykes, pp. 463-471. Cf. Sackville, "Competing Equitable Interests in Land under the Torrens System" (1971) 45 A.L.J. 396 and "Competing Equitable Interests in Land—A Postscript" (1972) 46 A.L.J. 344.
319. Cf. *Osmanoski v. Rose* [1974] V.R. 523.
320. [1934] A.C. 491.

proprietor and subsequently created a mortgage over the land in favour of Abigail.[321]

The dispute between the Lapins and Abigail was between two equitable interests: the Lapins' right to redeem and the subsequent equitable mortgage of Abigail. The Privy Council held in favour of Abigail on the grounds that the Lapins had armed Mrs Heavener with the means of dealing with the estate as the absolute legal and equitable owner. They had provided Mrs Heavener with the indicia of title and "clothed her to go into the world under false colours as the absolute owner". Abigail had been misled and entered the mortgage on the basis of Mrs Heavener's representations that she was the unencumbered owner. Although the Lapins had not made a direct representation to Abigail, the Lapins had placed Mrs Heavener in a position to make the representation and were thus bound by the natural consequences of their acts. The conduct of the holders of the first equitable interest, the Lapins, led the Privy Council to displace the priority the Lapins would usually have enjoyed as "first in time".

The Lapins did not lodge a caveat when their right to redeem came into existence and had not done so by the time Abigail took its interest.[322] There was no evidence to show that Abigail had searched the Register before taking its interest and thus no evidence to show that it had relied upon the Lapins' failure to caveat. The Privy Council considered that the Lapins' failure to caveat was relevant but in a subsidiary way. According to the Privy Council if the Lapins had lodged a caveat it would have "disarmed" Mrs Heavener and neutralised their earlier arming conduct. The failure to caveat was the final factor in the postponement of the Lapins' prior interest.

Although the non-lodgment of the caveat was a relevant factor in the decision, the comments of the Privy Council in relation to the importance of the caveat in a priority dispute placed less importance on the caveat than the comments of Griffith C.J. in *Butler v. Fairclough.* The Privy Council did not state that there was a positive duty to caveat and in the circumstances had no need to address the issue of whether a mere failure to lodge a caveat would be a sufficient omission to lead to postponement. Nevertheless, the Privy Council clearly took the view that depending upon the circumstances a failure to caveat could be an important factor. Two majority members of the High Court in the same case implied that a failure to caveat per se would be sufficient postponing conduct.[323] On the facts, Abigail's failure to search meant there had not been the necessary reliance upon the absence of a caveat.[324]

---

321. Abigail lodged a caveat and later lodged the mortgage for registration. In the meantime, the Lapins had lodged a caveat which prevented the registration of Abigail's mortgage. This led to the dispute.

322. The sequence of events is described above fn. 321.

323. *Lapin v. Abigail* (1930) 44 C.L.R. 166 at 183 per Knox C.J. and at 188-190 per Isaacs J.

324. Cf. the judgment of Dixon J. in *Lapin v. Abigail* (1930) 44 C.L.R. 166 at 205-206. Dixon J. would have been reluctant in any circumstances to hold that a failure to caveat results in postponement.

[5.106]   The implication of the Privy Council decision in *Abigail v. Lapin* was that a failure to caveat by the holder of the first equitable interest may be a relevant factor in a priority dispute and must be considered in light of the circumstances of each case. In most subsequent decisions relating to competitions between equitable interests, this view has been adopted. The courts have tended to consider factors such as whether it is reasonable to lodge a caveat in the circumstances and whether it is common practice to lodge a caveat in the circumstances in order to determine whether or not a failure to caveat is to be viewed as postponing conduct. Thus, in *I.A.C. (Finance) Pty Ltd v. Courtenay*[325] where the Courtenays, the purchasers, expected the transfer in their favour to be lodged for registration by the mortgagee, their failure to caveat to protect their equitable interest arising under the contract of sale was held not to constitute postponing conduct. They had followed established conveyancing practice in not lodging a caveat in the circumstances and in permitting the mortgagee to lodge the transfer for registration. In *J. & H. Just (Holdings) Pty Ltd v. Bank of New South Wales*[326] the failure to caveat did not constitute postponing conduct in the circumstances. In this case, there was a priority dispute between two equitable mortgagees, the bank's interest being first in time and J. & H. Just's interest being second in time. The bank did not lodge a caveat to protect its interest but it took possession of the duplicate certificate of title as a means of protecting its security. When J. & H. Just was negotiating to take an equitable mortgage, Josephson the registered proprietor informed it that the duplicate certificate of title was with the bank for safekeeping. The High Court held that at least in these circumstances, where the subsequent equitable interest was another mortgagee, the bank had adequately protected its interest by taking the duplicate certificate of title and that the failure to lodge a caveat could not be viewed as postponing conduct. Again, it was established conveyancing practice for a mortgagee not to lodge a caveat where the duplicate certificate had been retained as security. Further, the court was of the opinion that it would be common practice for a prospective mortgagee, such as J. & H. Just, to ensure in a case where it would not be holding the duplicate, that the duplicate was not lodged with another party as security for another loan. If the subsequent equitable interest had arisen pursuant to a contract of sale, the result may not necessarily have been the same.[327]

[5.107]   The discussion above does not suggest that the courts in *Abigail v. Lapin* and the *J. & H. Just* case were applying different principles in relation to the importance of the caveat in priority disputes between the holders of unregistered interests. However, Barwick C.J. (with whom McTiernan, Windeyer and Owen JJ. expressed agreement) in the *J. & H. Just* case, after demonstrating that it was not mandatory for the Registrar-General in New South Wales to make notations of caveats on title,[328] stated that the failure to lodge a caveat by the first equitable

325. (1963) 110 C.L.R. 550. See also *Person-to-Person Financial Services Pty Ltd v. Sharari* [1984] 1 N.S.W.L.R. 745; *Avco Financial Services Ltd v. White* [1977] V.R. 561.
326. (1971) 125 C.L.R. 546; [1972] A.L.R. 323.
327. See, however, the comments in *Jacobs'* case [1990] V.R. 146: see **[5.110]**.
328. See now Torrens statutes: N.S.W.: s. 74G.

interest holder should not be a relevant factor in deciding priority between the holders of equitable interests. In the view of his Honour, the fact that it was not mandatory for the Registrar-General to note the caveat on title made it clear that caveats were not intended to operate as notice to the world. Barwick C.J. took the view that the Privy Council's statements in *Abigail v. Lapin* about the consequences of a failure to lodge a caveat were obiter dicta.[329] There is a retreat towards the end of the judgment where Barwick C.J. suggests that in some circumstances a failure to lodge a caveat may combine with other circumstances to justify a conclusion that the conduct of the prior interest holder should lead to postponement. In turn, this suggests that it may be possible to reconcile the cases even if in a strained manner. Nevertheless, a basic difference remains, for in one decision the caveat as such is providing a form of notice to the world and in the other, it is seen simply as a direction to the Registrar.

In the subsequent High Court decision of *Breskvar v. Wall*,[330] Barwick C.J. (with whom Owen and Windeyer JJ. agreed) reiterated his views. McTiernan, Menzies and Gibbs JJ., however, relied upon the Privy Council's formulation in *Abigail v. Lapin* and may be seen as supporting the view that a failure to lodge a caveat is a factor which must be taken into consideration.[331] Walsh J. supported more strongly the notion of the relevance of the caveat in a priority dispute.[332]

[5.108]   The comments of at least two and arguably all of the High Court justices in *Heid v. Reliance Finance Corporation Pty Ltd* lend more support to the view of the caveat adopted in *Abigail v. Lapin*. Heid signed a contract of sale and transfer of his land in favour of Connell Investments and gave Gibby, an employee of Connell Investments, an authority to collect the duplicate certificate of title. Although the transfer acknowledged receipt of the purchase moneys, Heid had not received the whole of the moneys and thus held an equitable lien over the land.[333] Subsequently, Connell Investments became the registered proprietor and created an equitable mortgage in favour of Reliance Corporation. In an ensuing priority dispute between the equitable interests of Heid and Reliance Corporation, Heid's prior interest was postponed. According to Gibbs C.J. and Wilson J., the conduct of Heid enabled Connell Investments to represent itself as the unencumbered owner and Reliance had thereby suffered detriment. Heid's failure to lodge a caveat was not

---

329. A further reason for decision had been provided by the Privy Council in *Abigail v. Lapin*. A principal is bound by the actions of the agent who exceeds her or his authority but acts within her or his apparent authority: see [1934] A.C. 491 at 507-509. See also *Brocklesby v. Temperance Permanent Building Society* [1895] A.C. 143; *Perry-Herrick v. Attwood* (1857) 2 De G. & J. 21; 44 E.R. 895. The Privy Council made it clear, however, that this was not its primary reason for decision. It is difficult, therefore, to justify the view of Barwick C.J.

330. (1971) 126 C.L.R. 376; [1972] A.L.R. 205.

331. (1971) 126 C.L.R. 376; [1972] A.L.R. 205 at 393-394 and 213 per McTiernan J.; at 413 and 224-225 per Gibbs J.; at 398-399 and 216-217 per Menzies J.

332. (1971) 126 C.L.R. 376 at 409; [1972] A.L.R. 205 at 222-223.

333. Cf. *Real Property Act* 1861 (Qld), s 97, which provides that no vendor of Torrens land has any equitable lien by reason of non-payment of part or all of the purchase moneys.

in itself fatal to his case but the lodgment of the caveat would have neutralised the earlier arming conduct and disarmed Connell Investments.[334]

As in cases such as *I.A.C. (Finance) Pty Ltd v. Courtenay* and the *J. & H. Just* case, an argument was raised by Heid that his conduct in handing over the signed transfer to Gibby (purportedly his solicitor and the transferee's solicitor) before settlement, was in accord with established conveyancing practice and that, therefore, was not conduct which should result in the postponement of his interest. As it transpired, Gibby was not a solicitor at all. The court held that whilst it may be in accord with common practice and unexceptional practice to hand an executed transfer acknowledging receipt of the moneys before settlement to one's own independent solicitor, it was not acceptable conduct to hand such a document to an employee of the transferee even if the employee was a solicitor. Further it would probably be unacceptable to hand such a document to a solicitor acting for both parties even where the solicitor was not an employee of either party.

[5.109] In some cases, the failure to lodge a caveat by the holder of the prior equity may be the only possible postponing conduct. The Victorian decision of *Osmanoski v. Rose*[335] was such a case. The registered proprietor contracted to sell his land to Osmanoski and subsequently he contracted to sell the same land to Rose. Thus, Osmanoski and Rose both held equitable interests in the land and in a priority dispute between them, Rose argued that Osmanoski should lose priority in time because of his postponing conduct in failing to lodge a caveat. Rose had searched the Register and relied upon the clear title of the vendor before entering the contract. Gowans J. upheld the argument of Rose relying upon the principle set out by the Privy Council in *Abigail v. Lapin*. His Honour attempted to reconcile all the decisions concerning a failure to lodge a caveat and reached the conclusion that all supported the view that a failure to lodge a caveat may be a postponing factor. In commenting on the *J. & H. Just* case, Gowans J. pointed to the different fact situation, to the different caveat provisions in Victoria pursuant to which it is mandatory for the Registrar to note caveats on title and to the retreat in the judgment of Barwick C.J. in the *J. & H. Just* case.

Osmanoski v. Rose was a case where, *in the circumstances*, a failure to caveat was sufficient to constitute postponing conduct. It cannot be argued however, that Gowans J. intended to lay down as a general proposition that a mere failure to caveat is sufficient to postpone the earlier equity.

[5.110] In another recent Victorian case, *Jacobs v. Platt Nominees Pty Ltd*[336] a priority dispute again arose between the holders of equitable

---

334. Note that the argument by Heid that no estoppel existed because he had followed established conveyancing practice in handing over the signed transfer acknowledging receipt of moneys to the transferee before settlement was rejected on the facts. Gibby was not a solicitor at all and further he was an employee of the transferee.

335. [1974] V.R. 523.

336. [1990] V.R. 146. Cf. the earlier case *Dralter Pty Ltd v. Channel Land Co. Pty Ltd* (1988) V. Conv. R. 54-324, decision of O'Bryan J.

interests arising under separate contracts of sale. More specifically, the holder of the first equity held under an option to purchase which had been exercised. The decision has cast considerable doubt on the implication from *Osmanoski v. Rose* that in a dispute between the holders of equitable interests arising pursuant to contracts of sale, a failure to caveat by the holder of the prior interest will result in loss of priority if there is reliance on the clear title. In the circumstances of the *Jacobs* case, the failure to caveat by the holder of the earlier equity, Jacobs, was found to be reasonable and Jacobs retained her natural priority in time. Reference has been made earlier to the Full Court analysing the priority dispute in the *Jacobs* case on the estoppel by representation principle and alternatively, on the broader principle enunciated by Mason and Deane JJ. in the *Heid* case: see above [3.47]. When the facts were analysed by using the estoppel by representation principle, it was found that the idea of a representation having been made by Jacobs was "wholly inapposite".³³⁷ According to the Full Court, the purpose of the caveat is not to give notice to the world at large and thus, it is difficult to view a failure to lodge a caveat as a "representation" of the equitable interest holder.³³⁸ In addition, although the evidence supported the existence of a normal practice of lodging caveats to protect options immediately upon the grant of the option, this was not invariably done. The evidence also demonstrated that neither was there an invariable practice pursuant to which purchasers searched the title before entering a contract of sale.

Further, the 1982 amendments to the *Sale of Land Act* 1958 (Vic.) requiring a vendor to provide information regarding encumbrances and rights affecting the land results in a purchaser expecting to discover information concerning restrictions over the land from the vendor in the required statement rather than from a caveat. Thus the Full Court reasoned, these statutory obligations of the vendor "further weakened the force of any argument as to the creation of any assumption" about a failure to lodge a caveat.³³⁹

In view of all of the above factors, the Full Court was of the opinion that it is difficult to view the holder of an equitable interest as having made a representation as to the state of the title merely pursuant to a failure to lodge a caveat. Even if a representation had been proven, there was no evidence of detriment, the entry into the contract being insufficient.³⁴⁰

In considering the second possible method of resolving the priority dispute, the Full Court relied upon the joint judgment of Mason and Deane JJ. in the *Heid* case. As has been discussed earlier³⁴¹ the judgment reiterated the general principle that priority in time will decide the matter if all other things are equal. Consideration must be given primarily to the

---

337. [1990] V.R. 146 at 159.
338. Relying on the *J. & H. Just* case.
339. [1990] V.R. 146 at 159. As to vendors' statements in other States see below [6.61]-[6.62].
340. Presumably a loan of money by a mortgagee would constitute a detriment (which money could not be recouped except by exercising the security over the land).
341. Discussed in [5.97].

conduct of the first equitable interest holder and aspects of estoppel and negligence are relevant to such an analysis. In the *Jacobs* case, the evidence supported the contention of Jacobs that it was reasonable in the circumstances for her not to lodge a caveat. This was because on the facts it was inconceivable that her mother (a director of the company which was the registered proprietor and vendor) would be a party, in any way, to a sale to a third party in breach of the option.[342] In the language of the joint judgment in the *Heid* case: "It was . . . not reasonably foreseeable that her failure to lodge a caveat exposed herself or others to a risk of later sale."[343] This conclusion is strengthened by the finding referred to above that there was not an invariable practice that a purchaser searches the title before entering a contract.

[5.111] There are many situations where, quite apart from the issue of the lodgment or non-lodgment of a caveat, there has been postponing conduct by the holder of the prior equitable interest. Cases such as *Abigail v. Lapin*, *Breskvar v. Wall* and *Heid v. Reliance (Finance) Corporation Pty Ltd* all involved situations where the conduct of the holder of the prior equitable interest enabled another party to hold out that he or she had an unencumbered title. The issue of the relevance of the caveat in these circumstances is important. If the view is taken that an effect, even if an indirect effect, of the lodgment of a caveat is to give notice to the world, the lodgment of a caveat may be sufficient to neutralise the earlier postponing conduct. That is, in the language of estoppel, there would be no representation and in the language of negligence, there would be no conduct by which it would be reasonably forseeable that a subsequent equity may be created.[344] In contrast, if the view (expounded strongly in the *J. & H. Just* case and in *Jacobs'* case) is taken that the main purpose of the caveat is to give a direction to the Registrar it could not be said that the caveat has a "disarming" effect. In a practical sense, however, even on this view, the lodgment of a caveat may serve a useful purpose. If the holder of the subsequent equity does actually search before taking her or his interest and finds a caveat protecting a prior equity, the holder of the prior equity would not lose her or his natural priority in time. If the holder of the subsequent equity actually knows of the prior equity before taking her or his interest, neither the estoppel principle nor the broad principle incorporating elements of both estoppel and negligence would lead to postponement.

[5.112] There remains considerable doubt as to whether the caveat can constitute even indirectly a notice to the world of a claimed equitable interest. Thus there is no clear consensus as to the importance of the caveat in a priority dispute. The recent Victorian Full Court decision in *Jacobs v. Platt Nominees Pty Ltd* supports the view of the *J. & H. Just* case and minimises the importance of the caveat. It is clear, however, that the

---

342. This happened because at an earlier time the mother had signed a document giving her son the power to sign company documents on her behalf.
343. [1990] V.R. 146 at 160. Note that detriment or loss, other than entry into the contract is not essential under the Mason and Deane JJ. principle. Nevertheless it is a relevant circumstance: see [1990] V.R. 146 at 152.
344. *Abigail v. Lapin* [1934] A.C. 491.

relevance of the caveat must be considered in light of the facts of each particular case.

(b) Section 43A of the New South Wales Act

[5.113] The courts have interpreted the "paramountcy" and "notice" provisions in such a manner as to make it clear that it is only upon actual registration that the registered proprietor gains indefeasibility of title.[345] The period between settlement of the transaction and actual registration is one in which the purchaser is liable to lose priority for her or his interest to a prior equitable interest. Of course, upon registration of the transfer, the purchaser is not subject to any prior unregistered interests even if he or she had notice of them.

[5.114] Section 43A of the New South Wales Act attempts to give the purchaser some further protection in the hiatus between settlement and registration. Subsection (1) provides:

> "For the purpose only of protection against notice, the estate or interest in land under the provisions of this Act, taken by a person under a dealing registrable, or which when appropriately signed by or on behalf of that person would be registrable under this Act shall, before registration of that dealing, be deemed to be a legal estate."

Although there has been some dispute surrounding the interpretation of this provision[346] its meaning and import now appear to be settled.[347] The protection afforded to a purchaser after settlement but before registration is the same as the protection afforded to a bona fide purchaser of a legal estate under the general law. Thus, if the purchaser of Torrens land is a bona fide purchaser for value without notice of prior equitable interests, he or she is not subject to those interests. As the section provides, the purchaser is deemed to have a legal estate.

[5.115] The dealing under which the purchaser takes must be a "registrable" dealing and one under which the purchaser takes directly from the registered proprietor. Thus, if A, the registered proprietor executes a transfer in favour of B and B grants a mortgage in registrable form in favour of C, B but not C, can take advantage of s. 43A. The dealing in favour of C is not immediately registrable as it requires first that the dealing in favour of B be registered.[348] There is, however, some measure of protection for a person in C's position. The protection is provided by applying the principle in *Wilkes v. Spooner*[349] to the person in C's position. If B is a bona fide purchaser for value without notice and can thus enjoy the protection of s. 43A before registration, C, a person claiming through the purchaser B, can shelter behind the protection

---

345. *Templeton v. The Leviathan Pty Ltd* (1921) 30 C.L.R. 34.
346. Cf. e.g. the judgments of Kitto J. and Taylor J. in *I.A.C. (Finance) Pty Ltd v. Courtenay* (1963) 110 C.L.R. 550 at 573 per Kitto J. and at 584 per Taylor J.
347. See e.g. *Meriton Apartments Pty Ltd v. McLaurin and Tait (Developments) Pty Ltd* (1976) 133 C.L.R. 671. See generally Butt, pp. 509-510.
348. *Jonray (Sydney) Pty Ltd v. Partridge Bros Pty Ltd* (1969) 89 W.N. (Pt 1) (N.S.W.) 568.
349. [1911] 2 K.B. 473. This decision is discussed above **[3.40]**.

s. 43A affords B.[350] This is the case even if C has notice of prior equitable interests. C "succeeds" to the protection afforded to B. If B has taken through a void instrument, it is arguable that B does not obtain the protection of s. 43A between settlement and registration. Although B would obtain an indefeasible title in the absence of fraud once registered, there is authority to support the view that registration of such an instrument may be prevented at the behest of the true proprietor.[351] If B cannot gain the protection of s. 43A in these circumstances, neither can C for there is no protection to which she can "succeed".

[5.116] There are a variety of statutory provisions in which an attempt is made to provide some solution to the problems which may arise as a result of the time lag between settlement and registration. The basis of these varying provisions is for the transferee to secure a period of time between the final check of title and lodgment of the dealing for registration within which no other dealing may be registered.[352] Apart from the relevant Tasmanian provision, the provisions are little used as they are considered impractical. In Victoria and Western Australia, for example, the stay order can provide for a stay of only 48 hours.

(c) Other statutory provisions capable of affecting priority between unregistered interests

[5.117] The Torrens legislation in each State contains a provision which has the potential to affect priority between the holders of unregistered interests. In fact, it has been argued that this provision and not the general equitable principles discussed above, was intended to be used to resolve such priority disputes under the Torrens system.[353] Although the relevant provisions vary slightly in detail from State to State,[354] s. 34 of the Victorian Act is typical of the provisions. It provides:

"(1) Save as otherwise expressly provided every instrument lodged for registration shall be registered in the order in which and as from the time at which it is produced for that purpose, and instruments purporting to affect the same estate or interest shall be entitled to priority as between themselves according to order of lodgment for registration and not according to the date of the instrument or any other factor.

(2) If two or more instruments signed by the same proprietor and purporting to affect the same estate or interest are at or about the same time lodged for registration, the Registrar shall register and endorse that instrument which is lodged by the person producing the duplicate Crown grant certificate of title mortgage charge or lease (as the case may be)."

350. *Jonray (Sydney) Pty Ltd v. Partridge Bros Pty Ltd* (1969) 89 W.N. (Pt 1) (N.S.W.) 568.
351. See Butt, pp. 512-513.
352. See e.g. Torrens statutes: N.S.W.: ss 96A-96I; Vic.: ss 92-93; Qld: *Real Property Act* 1877, s. 48; W.A.: ss 146-150; Tas.: s. 52.
353. Robinson, pp. 51-56.
354. Torrens statutes: N.S.W.: s. 36(5) but see s. 36(4); Vic.: s. 34(1); Qld: *Real Property Act* 1877, s. 12; S.A.: s. 56; W.A.: s. 53; Tas.: s. 48.

Pursuant to s. 34(1), the person who first lodges a registrable instrument for registration has priority. Priority is not to be decided according to the date of the dealing or "any other factor" (which phrase presumably includes equitable principles)[355] but according to the date of lodgment for registration. Thus, issues as to conduct would be irrelevant unless the conduct constituted fraud. It is important to read s. 34(1) in conjunction with s. 29(1) which provides that the Registrar must enter in the Register "in such manner as to preserve their priorities a memorandum of all dealings and matters affecting the land . . . required or permitted to be registered notified or entered thereon".

[5.118] It might be argued that the s. 34 provision can only affect priorities where both or at least one of the competing parties have lodged documents for registration. This would leave unaffected by s. 34 priority disputes between the holders of unregistered interests where neither had lodged for registration. This may occur where for instance, the parties hold their interests pursuant to contracts of sale or mortgages not in registrable form. Even this scenario, however, is denied by Robinson who fashions a coherent and logical argument to demonstrate the applicability of s. 34 to this type of dispute.[356]

[5.119] A qualification to s. 34(1) provides that if two instruments are lodged at the same time, the person who lodged the instrument with the duplicate certificate of title is to have priority.[357]

[5.120] Despite the potential of this type of provision to resolve more simply at least some priority disputes between unregistered interests, the provisions have been largely ignored by the courts and their possible importance minimised. Once it had been accepted that equitable interests could exist under the Torrens system, the courts very quickly adopted the view that disputes between the holders of equitable, unregistered interests should be decided by the application of general equitable principles.

The New South Wales equivalent to s. 34(1)[358] was considered briefly in *I.A.C. (Finance) Pty Ltd v. Courtenay*[359] a case involving a competition between the holders of unregistered instruments both of whom had lodged dealings for registration. The dispute arose in the following way. The transfer in favour of the holders of the first equitable interest, the Courtenays, was lodged for registration but before registration, was invalidly withdrawn by the mortgagee's solicitor. The Courtenays subsequently lodged a caveat and this caveat prevented the registration of the dealing in favour of the holder of the second equitable estate. The High Court used the general equitable principle set out in *Rice v. Rice* to decide the dispute.[360] On the facts it was found that there had not been

---

355. Note that the Queensland provision is more specific "notwithstanding any express implied or constructive notice".
356. Robinson, p. 57.
357. See generally Robinson, pp. 54-57.
358. Formerly New South Wales Act, s. 36(1). See now New South Wales Act, s. 36 (4), (5).
359. (1963) 110 C.L.R. 550.
360. Sections 43 and 43A were also considered in detail.

any postponing conduct by the Courtenays, the holders of the first
equitable estate: they had followed established conveyancing practice in
leaving the transfer in their favour to be lodged by the mortgagee's
solicitor. Further, the holder of the second equitable estate had been
aware of the existence of the first estate when taking the subsequent
interest.

Kitto and Taylor JJ. both took the view that the general equitable
principle was the appropriate one to decide the dispute. Taylor J.
remarked that in determining a dispute between two equitable interests,
"it is immaterial which was first lodged for registration".[361] In contrast
it is arguable that Dixon C.J. supported a wider scope for the operation
of the statutory priority provision. His Honour commented:[362]

> "I agree that no conduct on the part of the Courtenays . . . occurred
> [pursuant to which the holder of the second equitable interest was
> misled] into adopting any prejudicial step. But I am not disposed to
> think that under the Torrens system a priority giving a right to
> registration under the statute can be lost on equitable grounds of such
> a character."

Despite the possible implications which may be drawn from this brief
settlement by Dixon C.J. and the convincing arguments of Robinson, the
weight of authority supports the view that priority disputes between
unregistered interest holders are to be determined by an application of the
general equitable principles discussed earlier.

V.   MISCELLANEOUS IMPORTANT PROVISIONS

1. State Guarantee of Title

[5.121]   When the Torrens system of land registration was first
introduced, a provision enabling a person suffering loss to seek
compensation from a guarantee fund was considered vital. The fear of loss
of title without compensation, a fear engendered largely by South
Australian lawyers opposed to the system, resulted in such a provision
being important in order to assuage the concern and to ensure the
successful passage of the legislation: see above [5.05]. A further, less
pragmatic reason for including a State guarantee of title, was to give those
administering the system some flexibility to ensure the smooth running of
the system. More specifically, it seems the provisions were designed to
ensure that persons who suffered loss because of the new concept of
indefeasibility or because of the error or misfeasance of the Registrar or
the Registrar's officers should be able to obtain compensation from an
assurance fund.[363]

---

361. (1963) 110 C.L.R. 550 at 558.
362. (1963) 110 C.L.R. 550 at 568. See Sackville, "Competing Equitable Interests
      in Land under the Torrens System" (1971) 45 A.L.J. 396 at 408-414. See also
      Vincent, "Some Practical Reflections on Courtenay v. Austin" (1964)
      38 A.L.J. 204.
363. Note that the term "Assurance Fund" is no longer universally applicable. See
      below [5.122].

[5.122]   When the Torrens system was introduced, the idea was that the guarantee schemes would be funded by contributions from particular users of the system. Thus, for example, in New South Wales persons who wished to convert their general law titles to Torrens title were required to make contributions into the fund. A compulsory contribution was also required upon the transfer of the land after the death of a registered proprietor. In Victoria contributions were required upon various risk related transactions such as conversion to Torrens title and registration of title based on adverse possession. The contributions were paid into a separate fund, the Assurance Fund. Because of the rate of payments out in comparison to contributions, the Assurance Funds became very well endowed. In turn this had lead to contributions being abolished in some States[364] and to the separate Assurance Funds being abolished in some States.[365] For example, in Victoria the Assurance Fund was abolished in 1983 and claims are paid out of Consolidated Revenue. The terms ''Assurance Fund'' and ''the Fund'' are used in the following discussion for ease of expression.

[5.123]   Recently, the right to compensation has been questioned[366] by the Law Reform Commission of New South Wales and Victoria in a joint discussion paper. In the paper it is stated that there is no evidence to prove that the concept of indefeasibility of title has caused significant loss and that errors by the Registrar or her or his officers resulting in loss could be dealt with adequately under the ordinary principles of tort law. The Commissions reason that the State does not pay compensation to innocent persons who suffer loss in other areas of registration of property interests (for example motor vehicle registration). The New South Wales Law Reform Commission took the view there was ''a case for abolishing the State compensation scheme for losses arising from operation of the Torrens system''.[367]

There remain strong arguments, however, for the retention of the compensation scheme. As it was when the Torrens system was first introduced it is still the case that innocent persons may suffer loss under the Torrens system which they would not have suffered under the general law system of conveyancing. For example, a forged conveyance has no effect under the general law whereas under the Torrens system registration of a forged transfer may operate to deprive an owner of her or his land and to confer a good title on the transferee providing the forgery was not perpetrated by the transferee.[368] One of the aims of the compensation provisions was to compensate persons who would not have been deprived of an interest but for the introduction of the Torrens

---

364.   E.g.: New South Wales.
365.   In New South Wales and Victoria.
366.   N.S.W.L.R.C. and Vic. L.R.C. *Torrens Title: Compensation for Loss*, Discussion Paper (June 1989), p. 11. Discussed in Butt, ''Reforming the Torrens title assurance fund'' (1990) 64 A.L.J. 78. See now N.S.W.L.R.C., *Torrens Title: Compensation for Loss*, Issues Paper (December 1989).
367.   N.S.W.L.R.C. and Vic. L.R.C. Discussion Paper, p. 11. By inference, it seems that the Vic. L.R.C. did not agree with this proposal.
368.   Cf. Torrens statutes: S.A.: s. 69II.

system. Despite the arguments against the retention of the scheme, on balance it is thought the compensation scheme should be retained in order to provide protection for such innocent persons. In Victoria, a further, if short-term reason exists for retention of the scheme. The provisions introduced in 1986 to encourage the more rapid conversion of general law titles to Torrens title require a less thorough analysis of a general law chain of title and are partly predicated on compensation being freely available for persons who suffer loss as a result of the conversion: see below [5.139].

[5.124] A person who is deprived of all or part[369] of her or his estate or interest in the land and thus suffers loss or damage may have a claim for compensation.[370] In all States except Victoria the loss or damage must comprise deprivation of an estate or interest in the land. In Victoria, the loss or damage may be by deprivation of land or otherwise.[371] In order to sustain a claim for compensation, the loss or damage must arise out of one of a number of listed circumstances set out in the statutes. These circumstances vary from State to State.

[5.125] First, in all States except Victoria, a person who has been deprived of an estate or interest in land in consequence of fraud may make a claim for compensation.[372] Fraud in this context has the same meaning as the fraud which is an exception to indefeasibility of title. It is not confined to particular types of fraud, such as forgery, which relate directly to the registration system. "As a consequence of fraud" is given its natural meaning and any person who loses an interest in land because of the fraud of another person who takes a registered interest, is entitled to compensation.[373] Although the Victorian Act does not have a specific provision relating to fraud, there are other listed circumstances in s. 110 under which a defrauded person could demonstrate a claim. For example, s. 110(3) provides that a person sustaining loss by reason of the registration of any other person as proprietor is entitled to be indemnified.[374]

[5.126] Secondly, in all States a person who is deprived of her or his interest and thereby suffers loss as a consequence of the bringing of the

369. A person may be deprived of part of her or his estate if, e.g., a mortgage is registered on the title.
370. Torrens statutes: N.S.W.: s. 126; Vic.: s. 110; Qld: s. 126; S.A.: s. 203; W.A.: s. 201; Tas.: s. 152.
371. The case of *Oakden v. Gibbs* (1882) 8 V.L.R. 380 discussed in Whalan, p. 347 demonstrates the possible difficulty of a requirement that the loss must be by deprivation of an interest in the land.
372. Torrens statutes: N.S.W.: s. 126; Qld: s. 126; S.A.: s. 203; W.A.: s. 201; Tas.: s. 152.
373. See *Parker v. Registrar-General* [1977] 1 N.S.W.L.R. 22 at 25 per Glass J.A. and at 30 per Mahoney J.A. See also *Heid v. Connell Investments Pty Ltd* (1989) 16 N.S.W.L.R. 629—in earlier proceedings it had been found that the registered proprietor had not been deprived of his legal estate by the fraud of Connell Investments. This created an issue estoppel and Heid was thus prevented from claiming from the assurance fund under s. 126 of the *Real Property Act* for damages for deprivation of his interest.
374. Cf. the view of Sackville and Neave, p. 402.

land under the Torrens system is entitled to compensation.[375] If it is shown that the person seeking compensation had notice of the application and had failed to act upon it, compensation is not payable.[376]

[5.127] Thirdly, in all States a loss suffered through any error, omission or misdescription in the Register is compensable.[377] In *Trieste Investments Pty Ltd v. Watson*[378] it was held that an error, omission or misdescription conveyed "the concept of something lacking from the Register Book which would be expected to be in it".[379] Thus, where there was no duty on the Registrar-General to note on the Register a resumption which effectively deprived the registered proprietor of part of its land, the Register could not be said to contain an error or misdescription.[380] This interpretation of the provision seems to be unduly restrictive. Ferguson J. in dissent, in the same case, took a broader view of the provision and held that if the Register does not reflect the true situation, innocent persons who thereby suffer loss should be entitled to compensation.[381]

Fourthly, in all States loss sustained through the registration of any other person as proprietor gives rise to a claim for compensation. This provision will often overlap with other circumstances giving rise to a claim for compensation.

[5.128] Finally, there are several other situations which in Victoria give rise to a claim for compensation. Again there is considerable scope for overlap between the provisions. The circumstances as set out in s. 110(3) are:

"(aa) a solicitor's failure to disclose in a solicitor's certificate a defect in title or the existence of an estate or interest in land; . . .

(d) any payment or consideration given to any other person on the faith of any entry in the Register Book;

(e) the loss or destruction of any document lodged at the Office of Titles for inspection or safe custody or any error in any official search; . . .[382]

(g) the exercise by the Registrar of any of the powers conferred on him in any case where the person sustaining loss or damage has not been a party or privy to the application or dealing in connexion with which such power was exercised . . ."

---

375. Torrens statutes: N.S.W.: s. 126(1)(b); Vic.: s. 110(1)(a); Qld: s. 126; S.A.: s. 203; W.A.: s. 201; Tas.: s. 152(1)(b).

376. Torrens statutes: N.S.W.: s. 130; S.A.: s. 216; W.A.: s. 211; Tas.: s. 158. Quaere whether ss 12, 110(3)(a) produce the same result in Victoria. Quaere Queensland where there is no specific provision.

377. Torrens statutes: N.S.W.: s. 126; Vic.: s. 110; Qld: s. 126; S.A.: s. 203; W.A.: s. 201; Tas.: s. 152. Note the differences in wording in these provisions.

378. (1963) 64 S.R. (N.S.W.) 98.

379. (1963) 64 S.R. (N.S.W.) 98 at 109.

380. See also *Mayer v. Coe* (1968) 88 W.N. (Pt 1) (N.S.W.) 549. Cf. the generally broader view of compensation taken in *Parker v. Registrar-General* [1977] 1 N.S.W.L.R. 22.

381. *Trieste Investments Pty Ltd v. Watson* (1963) 64 S.R. (N.S.W.) 98 at 107.

382. See also Torrens statutes: N.S.W.: s. 96I; Tas.: s. 170(2)(b).

Under provisions introduced in 1986 in Victoria,[383] a new simplified procedure was introduced to convert general law titles to Torrens title. Instead of the painstaking and extensive investigation of the general law title being undertaken by the Registrar, the scheme provides that the Registrar may issue a Torrens title if satisfied as to certain matters and if a solicitor certifies that the person seeking title has acquired a good safe holding and a marketable title to the land. Paragraph (aa) of s. 110(1) was inserted to ensure that any person who suffered loss as a result of the solicitor's certificate is entitled to compensation. Paragraph (d) of s. 110(1) seems to give considerable protection and may include, for example, compensation for a person who searches the Register, enters into a contract on the faith of the Register and then suffers loss because the Register was incorrect.

[5.129]   In all States except Victoria, the person who has suffered the loss must first bring an action against the individual who was responsible for the loss. Thus for example, if the loss is caused by fraud, the action is brought against the person who has registered through fraud.[384] A claim may only be made on the Fund if the first action does not result in the person suffering loss being compensated or if the bringing of such an action is not possible in the circumstances. Thus if the person liable for damages is dead, bankrupt or insolvent or cannot be found within the jurisdiction, damages may be recovered out of the Fund by way of action against the Registrar as nominal defendant.[385] Further, except in Queensland the person liable for damages ceases to be so liable when he or she transfers the land bona fide for value and in such a case, compensation may be obtained from the Fund by way of action against the Registrar as nominal defendant.[386] Except in Queensland, there is a further general provision permitting direct action against the Registrar as nominal defendant where the rights of action against the wrongdoer discussed above are inapplicable.[387]

In Victoria, proceedings do not have to be taken against the wrongdoer first but may be taken directly against the Registrar as nominal defendant.[388] The Registrar can then join any person as a co-defendant. In view of the fact that the scheme is intended to provide a form of insurance and in view of the difficulties claimants face in the other States, it has been suggested that the Victorian scheme is preferable.

---

383. *Transfer of Land (Conversion) Act* 1986, discussed below **[5.128]** and **[5.139]**.
384. Torrens statutes: N.S.W.: s. 126(2)(c); Qld: s. 126; S.A.: s. 203; W.A.: s. 201; Tas.: s. 152(2)(b)(iii).
385. Torrens statutes: N.S.W.: s. 126(5)(b); Qld: s. 127; S.A.: s. 205; W.A.: s. 201; Tas.: s. 152(8)(b), (c). See also *Registrar-General v. Behn* [1980] 1 N.S.W.L.R. 589.
386. Torrens statutes: N.S.W.: s. 126(5)(a); S.A.: s. 205; W.A.: s. 201; Tas.: s. 152(8)(a).
387. Torrens statutes: N.S.W.: s. 127; S.A.: s. 208; W.A.: s. 205; Tas.: s. 153(1)(b). Note the discussion in Sackville and Neave, p. 401 where it is suggested that the strong defence of claims is defeating the purpose of the funds and that the claims should be treated as ordinary insurance claims.
388. Torrens statutes: Vic.: s. 110(2).

[5.130]   In all States, it is provided that any person who suffers loss or damage through the omission, mistake or misfeasance of the Registrar or her or his officers in the execution of their duties, may seek damages from the Registrar as nominal defendant.[389] Under this head, the loss suffered does not have to be pursuant to the loss of an estate or interest in the land.

[5.131]   There are a number of restrictions on the payment of compensation from the Funds. Compensation is not payable for loss occasioned by a breach of trust.[390] Further, except in Queensland, compensation is not payable in any case in which the same land has been included in two or more Crown grants,[391] or in any case in which loss has been suffered by the land being included in the same certificate of title with other land through misdescription of boundaries or parcels of land, unless it is proved that the person liable is dead or bankrupt or has absconded or is unable to pay the full amount in any action for recovery of such compensation and damages.[392] There are further various restrictions which differ from State to State.[393] Another important restriction on access to the Fund exists in Victoria. No indemnity is payable where the claimant or her or his solicitor or agent caused or substantially contributed to the loss by fraud, neglect or wilful default or where the claimant derives title (otherwise than under a registered disposition) from a person whose solicitor or agent has been guilty of such fraud, neglect or wilful default.[394] Solicitors are required to have professional indemnity insurance and thus a claimant who sues her or his solicitor for negligence is very likely to have the claim met. If a solicitor's fraud has caused the loss, the Solicitors' Guarantee Fund covers the loss.[395] In both these instances, however, the claimant must prove the negligence or fraud of the solicitor and it has been argued that the claimant should be entitled to claim from the Fund and then to subrogate the rights against the fraudulent or negligent solicitor to the Fund.[396]

[5.132]   The Victorian provision discussed above states that the compensation is not payable if the claimant has caused or substantially contributed to the loss. This provision is broad and may prevent the recovery of compensation in a number of cases. In the other States except Queensland, there are some specific provisions which prevent compensation in particular instances where some blame may be attached

389. Torrens statutes: N.S.W.: s. 127; Vic.: s. 110; Qld: s. 128; S.A.: s. 208; W.A.: s. 205; Tas.: s. 153(1).
390. Torrens statutes: N.S.W.: s. 133; Vic.: s. 109(2); Qld: s. 42 (quaere whether constructive and implied trusts included); S.A.: s. 211; W.A.: s. 196; Tas.: s. 151(1).
391. Torrens statutes: N.S.W.: s. 133; Vic.: s. 109(2)(b); W.A.: s. 196; Tas.: s. 151(1)(b). Cf. S.A.: s. 214 (fund not liable but can proceed against nominal defendant); Qld: no provision.
392. Torrens statutes: N.S.W.: s. 133; Vic.: s. 109(2)(c); S.A.: s. 212; W.A.: s. 196; Tas.: ss 151(1)(d), 151(2).
393. See e.g. Torrens statutes: N.S.W.: s. 31A, s. 130(3), (4); Vic.: s. 56; S.A.: ss 211, 216; W.A.: ss 196, 211; Tas.: ss 127-128.
394. Torrens statutes: Vic.: s. 110(3)(a).
395. See *Legal Profession Practice Act* 1958 (Vic.), s. 88A.
396. See Sackville and Neave, pp. 402-403.

to the applicant. Thus, where a person knows of an application to bring land under the Torrens statute and omits to caveat or allows a caveat to lapse, compensation is not payable.[397] Apart from such specific provisions, the relevance of contributory negligence of an applicant remains an area of doubt.[398]

[5.133] In some States, the limitation statutes operate to bar the claim of a person with a right to seek compensation from the Fund. In Victoria, Queensland, Western Australia and Tasmania, the action must be commenced within six years of the date of the deprivation and in South Australia within 20 years.[399] In New South Wales, there is no limitation period and it has been suggested that this is the position which should be adopted.[400] If the complete absence of a limitation period is not acceptable in the other States it seems at least that the cause of action should not arise until the person suffering loss knew, or ought reasonably to have known the facts. The case of *Breskvar v. Wall*[401] provides an example of how the presence of a limitation period may operate inequitably to prevent access to the Fund. The applicant succeeded in an application for damages but the judgment could not be satisfied against the fraudulent person. By the time access to the Fund was sought six years had elapsed from the date of the deprivation and access to the Fund was denied.

[5.134] Once an applicant has been able to overcome the many possible difficulties of gaining access to the Fund, the question arises as to the *amount* of compensation which may be claimed. It seems that the aim is to place the applicant in the same position he or she would have been in had the mistake or the fraud, for example, not occurred.[402] Where the loss comprises a fixed amount such as would be the case where a registered proprietor has to pay out a mortgage he or she did not create, the measure of damage is clear. The value of improvements which have been erected on land after the loss is suffered should not be included in assessing the compensation.[403]

In cases where the loss is by a deprivation of an estate or interest in the land, such estate not comprising a fixed and certain sum, the time at which the value of the land is assessed may be very important. Inflation may increase the value of land considerably over a period of time. In Victoria, it is provided specifically that the value of the interest in the land is assessed at the date of the loss.[404] Although the same position appeared

---

397. Torrens statutes: N.S.W.: s. 130; S.A.: s. 216; W.A.: s. 211; Tas.: s. 158. Further in New South Wales and Tasmania if a person knows of a possessory application and does nothing, compensation is not payable.
398. Discussed in Whalan, p. 363.
399. Torrens statutes: Qld: ss 126-127; S.A.: s. 215; W.A.: s. 211; Tas.: s. 158(1); Vic.: *Limitation of Actions Act* 1958, s. 5(1)(d). Note the extended period where person with the cause of action is under a disability: see below **[15.54]-[15.56]**.
400. See e.g. Whalan, p. 361.
401. (1971) 126 C.L.R. 376; [1972] A.L.R. 205. See *Breskvar v. White* [1978] Qd R. 187.
402. *Parker v. Registrar-General* [1977] 1 N.S.W.L.R. 22.
403. Torrens statutes: S.A.: s. 209; W.A.: s. 201; Tas.: ss 152(9), 153(2).
404. Torrens statutes: Vic.: s. 110(4).

to be accepted elsewhere, more recent authority suggests that in some circumstances the value of the land and thus the amount of the loss, is to be assessed at the date of the trial.[405]

2. Conversion of Title

[5.135] All land alienated from the Crown since the introduction of the Torrens statutes automatically falls under the operation of the Torrens system of land registration.[406] Further, provisions were enacted to enable general law land to be brought voluntarily under the Torrens system. There are also a variety of provisions in most jurisdictions providing for the compulsory conversion of general law title to Torrens title. There is now very little general law land in Queensland and South Australia.

(a) Voluntary conversion

[5.136] The provisions allowing for voluntary conversion to Torrens title permit particular persons to apply to bring the land under the Torrens system.[407] For example, the fee simple owner entitled at law and in equity, a life tenant and some long-term lessees may apply. A mortgagor cannot apply without the mortgagee's consent but in particular circumstances, the mortgagee may so apply. The application must be in the approved or prescribed form and should contain a description of the land, a list of the documents in the chain of title, a note of any encumbrances over the land and the names of the owner and occupier of the land and of the owners and occupiers of any adjoining land.[408] The applicant must surrender the documents of title to the Registrar. Before proceeding with the application, the Registrar is required to give various notices of the intention to bring the land under the Torrens system. The nature and extent of these notices vary from State to State.[409] The notices include advertisements in newspapers, physical notices on the property and direct notices to adjoining landowners and persons who hold interests in the land. In some States, the more doubtful the title, the more vigorous is the advertising required.

[5.137] In all States, there is provision for the lodgment of caveats against bringing the land under the Torrens statute.[410] The person lodging the caveat must have some interest in the land: see above [5.81]-[5.83]. Thus, for example, a person claiming an easement over the land

---

405. See e.g. *Registrar-General v. Behn* [1980] 1 N.S.W.L.R. 589.
406. Crown leaseholds are often under the Torrens system (see below [19.25]) and land which is compulsorily acquired is brought under the Torrens system: see Torrens statutes: N.S.W.: s. 31A(2); Vic.: s. 54; S.A.: s. 115a; Tas.: s. 126; *The Real Property (Commonwealth Titles) Act* 1924 (Qld), s. 3.
407. Torrens statutes: N.S.W.: s. 14(2); Vic.: s. 9; Qld: s. 16; S.A.: s. 27; W.A.: s. 20; Tas.: s. 11.
408. Torrens statutes: N.S.W.: s. 14(4); Vic.: s. 9; Qld: ss 16-17; S.A.: ss 27-30; W.A.: s. 20; Tas.: s. 11(1).
409. Torrens statutes: N.S.W.: ss 12(1), 12(1A), 17(1), 17(3); Vic.: s. 11; Qld: ss 19-22, S.A.: ss 33-35; W.A.: ss 22-24; Tas.: ss 12-13.
410. Torrens statutes: N.S.W.: ss 74B-74E; Vic.: s. 12; Qld: ss 23-26; S.A.: ss 39-40; W.A.: ss 30-32; Tas.: s. 14.

which is the subject of the application would be entitled to lodge a caveat. The land cannot be brought under the Torrens statute whilst the caveat remains on the title. The Registrar notifies the person who has made the application. The caveator has a set period of time after lodging the caveat within which to institute court proceedings to establish her or his interest and notify the Registrar of this fact or at least to have obtained an interim injunction against the Registrar to prevent the application proceeding. The caveat lapses and the application may proceed if the caveator has failed to take such action within the set period. Once a caveat against an application for bringing the land under the Act has lapsed, no further caveat may be lodged on the same facts by the same person. The only remaining course of action for a person wishing to prevent the registration would be an application to the court seeking an injunction.

[5.138] After completion by the Registrar of required formalities, the Registrar may proceed to examine the title. Although the Registrar has a broad discretion to decide whether or not to bring the land under the Torrens system, this discretion has traditionally been exercised in a very conservative manner. Generally, Registrars have demanded a very clear chain of title before proceeding to bring the land under the Act. This approach has limited the number of voluntary conversions and thus hindered the aim of converting all general law title to Torrens title. In view of the existence of the Assurance Fund and of the aim of bringing all land under the Torrens system, the extremely rigorous approach adopted by the Registrars in this area was perhaps unnecessary and seems to have been relaxed a little in recent years. In Victoria, it is specifically provided that a title may be registered even if the claim is imperfect, provided a contribution is made to the assurance fund. The contribution is in such a sum as the Registrar considers will provide a proper indemnity.[411]

[5.139] Various other measures have been introduced in some jurisdictions to facilitate the conversion of general law title. In Victoria, for example, the *Transfer of Land (Conversion) Act* 1986 permits the Registrar to register a title under the Torrens system upon receipt of a solicitor's certificate verifying the title.[412] In these circumstances, further examination of the title by the Registrar is not required.

Whenever general law land is sold or mortgaged, the solicitor for the purchaser or the mortgagee thoroughly investigates the title of the vendor or mortgagor in order to ensure her or his client receives a good title or security. The purpose of the 1986 amendment was to make use of such searches by permitting the solicitor to certify as to the state of the title and by permitting registration under the Torrens system on reliance on such certification (providing the certification demonstrates a good safe holding and a marketable title to the land) without the need for further and expensive investigation by the Registrar. As conversion would be less

411. Torrens statutes: Vic.: s. 108(3).
412. Torrens statutes: Vic.: ss 26A-26P. See Note, "How General Law Land is being Converted" (1987) 61 L.I.J. 162.

expensive to the holder of the general law title, it was hoped that conversions would occur regularly upon the sale or mortgage of general law land. Thus far, it seems that this is happening.[413]

[5.140] In New South Wales and Tasmania, there is provision for qualified Torrens titles to be issued where there is doubt about the general law title.[414] In New South Wales, the Registrar-General may issue a qualified folio where the applicant has made a primary application but is prepared to withdraw it. The aim is to permit the general law land to be brought under the Torrens system even where the Registrar-General would not in view of the material presented in the application, be prepared to issue an unqualified title. The qualified title is subject to any subsisting interests[415] which would have been enforceable against the person being registered as proprietor had the qualified Torrens title not been created. The issue as to whether such an enforceable subsisting interest exists at the time of the issue of the qualified title requires an analysis of the relevant priority rule. Thus, for example, where the interest is a prior equitable interest, it is not a "subsisting interest" if the applicant for conversion was a bona fide purchaser of the legal estate for value without notice of the prior equitable interest.[416] Any "subsisting interest" is enforceable against the proprietor whether or not it appears on the title and a note or "caution" to this effect is placed on the title.[417] There are various provisions for the lapsing of cautions. Some lapse at the expiration of six years from the creation of the qualified title or upon a bona fide purchaser becoming registered whichever is the later.[418] Others do not lapse until six years after a bona fide purchaser has become registered or a further person has become registered whichever is the later.[419] Any caution which has not lapsed under these provisions lapses 12 years from the date of the issue of the qualified title even if there have not been any dealings with the land.[420] The lapsing of the caution frees the title from the formerly subsisting interests. Of course, interests which are recorded on the folio remain enforceable. There is also provision in the New South Wales Act for the issue of limited titles where precise definition of the boundaries is not possible.[421] Ordinary or qualified titles may be issued subject to the limitation caveat stating that the physical boundaries have not been investigated by the Registrar-General. If a plan of survey is subsequently lodged and registered, the limitation may be cancelled.[422] Although not always the case, it is now possible for a dealing to be registered without the removal of the limitation caveat.[423]

---

413. Discussion with P. Burn, Land Titles Office (Vic.), 15 March 1990. See also Law Institute of Victoria, *Property Law Bulletin* (No. 6 April 1990), p. 15.
414. Torrens statutes: N.S.W.: s. 28B; Tas.: s. 21.
415. Defined in s. 28A.
416. *Pilcher v. Rawlins* (1872) 7 Ch. A. 259. This example leaves out of consideration the registration of deeds legislation.
417. Torrens statutes: N.S.W.: ss 28I, 28J.
418. Torrens statutes: N.S.W.: s. 28M(3)(a), cf. s. 28J(1A)(1B).
419. Torrens statutes: N.S.W.: s. 29M(3)(b).
420. Torrens statutes: N.S.W.: s. 28M(8).
421. Torrens statutes: N.S.W.: s. 28T.
422. Torrens statutes: N.S.W.: ss 28s(1), 28v. See generally Butt, p. 546.
423. Torrens statutes: Tas.: ss 21, 25.

In Tasmania, there is provision for the issue of a qualified certificate of title if the Recorder is not satisfied that the title of the applicant for conversion is sufficiently certain and clear.[424] The qualified certificate of title contains a caution relating to the defects in the title and the caution does not lapse until 20 years after the qualified certificate was issued.[425]

[5.141] In Victoria and Western Australia, where an application is made to bring land under the Torrens Act by a description different from that in the title deeds, the Registrar may grant the application as to the land in the occupation of the applicant if the discrepancy appears to be due to the inaccuracy of any survey or plan.[426]

(b) Compulsory extension of Torrens system

[5.142] Over the years, and in some jurisdictions more than others, voluntary conversion has proved to be a slow method of achieving the aim of bringing all land under the Torrens system of registration. A number of schemes for compulsory conversion have been mooted and some of these have been adopted. For example, land which is to be subdivided or used under a strata title scheme must be brought under the Torrens system.[427] Some other forms of dealing require the land to be brought under the Torrens system before the dealing can take place. For example, in Tasmania, the Recorder may convert general law titles to Torrens titles every time a conveyance on sale or mortgage is lodged for registration under the deeds registration system. When such a document is lodged a statement as to ownership and all instruments affecting the title must be given to the Registrar of Deeds by the person seeking registration. The Registrar of Deeds passes these documents on to the Recorder who may bring the land under the Torrens system by the issue of an ordinary or qualified certificate of title.[428] Although it is unlikely that the aim of converting of all general law titles within ten years of the appointed day will be met, much progress has been made in the past decade.

[5.143] Another form of compulsory registration is where the Registrar has the power to initiate and to proceed with the process of converting general law titles. All States except Western Australia provide in various ways for this form of compulsory registration. The Victorian and South Australian provisions are similar and provide for the Registrar to bring general law land under the Torrens system with all convenient speed.[429]

424. *Real Property (Conversion of Title) Amendment Act* 1984 (N.S.W.).
425. Unless it has earlier ceased to have effect.
426. Torrens statutes: Vic.: s. 10(3); W.A.: s. 27. These provisions are discussed in Whalan, pp. 60-61. See also Vic.: s. 102; W.A.: ss 28-29—power to remove discrepancies by allocating between allotments.
427. Torrens statutes: N.S.W.: ss 28c, 28ea; S.A.: s. 223 1d(6); Tas.: s. 18. See also *Local Government Act* 1962, s. 464(12)(b); *Subdivision Act* 1988 (Vic.), s. 22(1)(e); *Sale of Land Act* 1970 (W.A.), s. 13.
428. Torrens statutes: Tas.: s. 17. In 1981, two sevenths of the alienated land remained under general law title. This provision and others have reduced this figure but conversion will not be completed within the ten year time frame: discussion with J. Morison, Land Titles Office (Tas.), 15 March 1990.
429. Torrens statutes: Vic.: Pt II, Div. 2, ss 17-26; *Real Property (Registration of Titles) Act* 1945 (S.A.).

The Registrar proceeds as if a voluntary application had been made and may issue a certificate of title if satisfied that such a certificate would have been issued on a voluntary application and that there is no person in adverse possession. In cases where the Registrar is not wholly satisfied with the general law title, he or she may issue a limited certificate which is limited as to the description of the land or as to the title (or both). The limitation lapses at the expiration of 30 years in Victoria or 12 years in South Australia or earlier if the Registrar is of the view that the defect no longer affects the land. A limitation as to a description of the land only lapses upon the completion of a survey. A lack of resources has resulted in these provisions being little used in Victoria. In contrast, very little general law land remains in South Australia.

[5.144]   In Queensland, very little general law land remained in 1974. In that year, the legislature introduced new provisions to speed up the completion of the conversion process.[430] In outline, the scheme provides for unregistered land to be registered in the name of the Public Curator if no person makes a claim to the land after appropriate advertisement notices have been issued by the Registrar. Even after such registration, there is provision for a person claiming to be entitled to the land to apply to the Registrar to have the land registered in her or his name. If no person has established title to the land within 12 years, the land vests in the Crown absolutely.

[5.145]   In New South Wales and Tasmania, the Registrar has the power upon her or his own initiative to convert general law land into Torrens land by the issue of ordinary or qualified certificates of title.[431] The Registrar is empowered by notice to require any person to inform the Registrar as to whether he or she claims any interest in the land. If the person claims an interest by way of an assurance, the assurance and all documents in the chain of title must be produced to the Registrar. Alternatively, if the person claims by way of adverse possession, the relevant evidence must be produced. The Registrar may then bring the land under the Torrens system by the issue of an ordinary or qualified title. The nature and operation of qualified titles in New South Wales and Tasmania have been discussed above. Various amendments have been made in New South Wales to improve the operation and effectiveness of these provisions but their ultimate success depends upon the resources available to the Registrar.

3. Interrelationship of General Property Statutes with Torrens Statutes

[5.146]   In all States, some attempt is made to deal with the issue of the interrelationship of the Torrens statutes and the general law statutes. In most States, however, many areas of doubt remain.

---

430. *Property Law Act* 1974 (Qld), ss 250-254. It is expected that the last remaining pieces of general law land will be converted to Torrens title by mid 1990: discussion with G. Topfer, Land Titles Office (Qld), 15 March 1990.

431. Torrens statutes: N.S.W.: ss 28E, 28EA; Tas.: ss 19, 21. See above **[5.140]** as to ordinary and qualified certificates.

[5.147] In New South Wales, s. 6(1) of the *Conveyancing Act* 1919 provides that the Act "so far as inconsistent with the Real Property Act 1900, shall not apply to lands, whether freehold or leasehold, which are under the prima facie provisions of that Act". This provision seems to require an analysis as to whether a particular provision in the *Conveyancing Act* is inconsistent with the Torrens statute. Despite this general provision, however, many provisions in the *Conveyancing Act* specifically provide whether or not they apply to Torrens land[432] thus obviating the need to determine whether or not there is an inconsistency.

[5.148] In Victoria, s. 3(1) of the *Transfer of Land Act* 1958 provides:

"Except so far as is expressly enacted to the contrary no Act or rule of law, so far as inconsistent with this Act, shall apply or be deemed to apply to land under the Operation of this Act; but save as aforesaid any Act or rule of law relating to land, unless otherwise expressly or by necessary implication provided by this or any other Act, shall apply to land under the operation of this Act whether expressed so to apply or not."

Thus, in Victoria, prima facie, the *Property Law Act* applies to Torrens land. However, the issue of inconsistency must be addressed for if there is an inconsistency the relevant provision in the *Property Law Act* 1958 is inapplicable. There are specific provisions in the *Property Law Act* which state clearly that certain sections do not apply to Torrens land[433] and although it may seem unnecessary in view of the prima facie position, there are certain provisions which state positively that particular sections do apply to Torrens land.[434] There are, nevertheless, a number of provisions in the *Property Law Act* where applicability to the Torrens system remains unclear. Section 62 of the *Property Law Act* is one example of a provision that has been in the "realm of uncertainty" for many years.[435] Often it is a difficult task to determine definitively whether a particular provision in the *Property Law Act* 1958 is inconsistent with the *Transfer of Land Act* 1958.[436]

[5.149] In Queensland, s. 5(1)(b) of the *Property Law Act* 1974, provides:

"Except where otherwise provided, this Act shall—

. . .

(b) apply to land under the provisions of the Real Property Acts, including any lease of such land, but subject to the provisions of those Acts."

Unless there is a specific exclusion, the provisions of the general law statute apply to Torrens land. Importantly, however, it is provided that

---

432. See e.g. ss 19(3), 19A(3), 55(5), 56(3), 60(2), 88A(3), 97(3), 106(17), 107(12). A more detailed list is provided in Whalan, p. 25.
433. See e.g. *Property Law Act* 1958, ss 198(6), 200(3).
434. See e.g. *Property Law Act* 1958, s. 273.
435. Discussed in Bradbrook and Neave, p. 190. See also below **[16.26]-[16.27]**.
436. Barton, "The Applicability of Section 62 of the Property Law Act (1958) (Vic.), to a Transfer of Torrens System Land" (1987) 61 A.L.J. 214; Wallace, "Property Law Reform in Australia" (1987) 61 A.L.J. 174.

the provisions of the *Property Law Act* are subject to the provisions of the Torrens statute.

[5.150]   In South Australia and Western Australia, the Torrens statutes provide that any law which is inconsistent with the Torrens statute is inapplicable to Torrens land.[437] The general law statutes provide that in so far as their provisions are inconsistent with the Torrens statutes, they are inapplicable to Torrens land.[438] This suggests that where there is no inconsistency the general property law statutes are applicable to Torrens land. Although there are some specific provisions which expressly exclude or include the operation of the general property statute to Torrens land,[439] in many cases the inconsistency principle must be applied.

[5.151]   In Tasmania, the position is much clearer than in the other States. Section 91 of the *Conveyancing and Law of Property Act* 1884 provides that particular listed sections do not apply to Torrens land and that all other provisions, so far as they are applicable, do apply to Torrens land. Uncertainties existing in the other States could be removed if the Tasmanian approach were adopted.

---

437. Torrens statutes: S.A.: s. 6: see *South-Eastern Drainage Board (South Australia) v. Savings Bank of South Australia* (1939) 62 C.L.R. 603; W.A.: s. 3.
438. General law statutes: S.A.: s. 6; W.A.: s. 6(a).
439. See e.g. General law statutes: S.A.: s. 56.

6

Dispositions

I. ORIGINAL ACQUISITION AND ACQUISITION BY SUCCESSION

[6.01]   Previous Chapters have examined the nature of interests in land and the means of establishing ownership of land. These issues arise most commonly because a purchaser seeks to ensure that he or she has acquired an unchallengable title. Conversely the right of disposition is one of the basic features of ownership and thus any owner is a potential vendor. Property law provides for the passing of interests in land from one person to another. Often this process has involved a role for legal practitioners though the need for this involvement with its inherent costs is a matter of public debate.

The transfer of land from one person to another is a process of succession. The purchaser succeeds to the interest of the vendor. Commonly succession involves the conclusion of an agreement between strangers. The agreement results from the operation of the free market process in our society: the owners desiring to sell may hold an auction of the property or may simply advertise their intention and negotiate with potential buyers. Again in our society it is common for the owners to employ an intermediary—a real estate or land agent—to assist with the process of sale. But succession may not involve contracts. An owner may wish to exercise beneficence in favour of a family member or close associate or in favour of charity. The transfer of land may thus occur to give effect to a gift.

Both sales and gifts result from voluntary acts of the parties, at least in the sense that the parties willingly entered the transaction: a vendor for instance may however feel that this voluntary act was forced upon her or him by economic circumstances. Subject to this qualification the sales and gifts can be classified as consensual transactions. However there are situations in which an interest in land may be transferred without the consent of the parties or at least without the consent of the person who is being deprived of ownership. Non-consensual transactions occur on the death of an owner without a will, or when an owner is deprived of assets to meet debts, or on compulsory acquisition by public authorities.

[6.02]   Death terminates ownership because the person who was the owner no longer exists. The deceased is given a measure of control over arrangements following death and medical advances mean that even decisions with respect to the use of body organs are significant. The law balances the wishes of the deceased (with procedures to record those

206

wishes) alongside those of relatives and legal representatives. With respect to land the issue is as to the power of the deceased to direct the future ownership of the land. In so far as such power is recognised the disposition of the land may be regarded as consensual even if the occurrence of death may not be regarded as consensual. The power to direct the disposition of land on death was totally denied by the common law in the period following the Norman conquest. Until the *Statute of Wills* of 1540 land passed to the deceased's heir.[1] That statute gave the power to direct the transfer after death. In the case where there is no direction or no direction meeting the formal requirements of a will, land is transferred non consensually—until the 19th century to the heir and since that time to next of kin.[2] Only in the absence of a will or next of kin does land pass to the Crown as bona vacantia.[3]

Where the phrase "land passes to the person nominated in the will" is used, the assumption is that the deceased held a fee simple interest and strictly speaking that interest passes to the beneficiary. Other interests are capable of being transmitted on death. However not only did the common law restrict the disposition of fee simple interests on death but the common law in combination with statute recognised the fee tail estate and it was a feature of this estate that on death there was no interest remaining for the deceased to dispose of.[4] Even today a life estate may have been granted so that on the life tenant's death a remainder vests in those holding the interest pursuant to the instrument which created the life estate (or a reversion in favour of those entitled at the time of the instrument).[5]

[6.03]   Although the law recognises a power to dispose of land on death and ultimately it is likely that full ownership will be placed in the hands of the beneficiary, the vesting of title is subject to procedural complications. No assets will pass to beneficiaries until debts have been paid and the gathering together and transmission of the deceased's assets can involve significant burdens. Thus all land and other property passes to the deceased's legal representatives.[6] Beneficiaries are therefore

---

1. As explained above **[2.17]**, the concept of an heir involved a preference for males over females and amongst males for the eldest or elder over younger brothers. The general power of disposal by the holder of fee simple estate is discussed above **[2.17]**.
2. N.S.W.: *Wills, Probate and Administration Act* 1898, Pt II, Div. 2A; Vic.: *Administration and Probate Act* 1958, Pt I, Div. 6; Qld: *Succession Act* 1981, Pt III; S.A.: *Administration and Probate Act* 1919, Pt IIIA; W.A.: *Administration Act* 1903, Pt II; Tas.: *Administration and Probate Act* 1935, Pt V.
3. N.S.W.: *Wills, Probate and Administration Act* 1898, s. 61B(7); Vic.: *Administration and Probate Act* 1958, s. 55; Qld: *Succession Act* 1981, Second Schedule, Pt II; S.A.: *Administration and Probate Act* 1919, s. 72g(e); Tas.: *Administration and Probate Act* 1935, s. 45. In Western Australia the principle of escheat still applies: *Escheat (Procedure) Act* 1940.
4. The fee tail estate is explained above **[2.18]**.
5. The life estate is explained above **[2.24]**.
6. N.S.W.: *Wills, Probate and Administration Act* 1898, s. 44; Vic.: *Administration and Probate Act* 1958, s. 13; Qld: *Succession Act* 1981, s. 15; S.A.: *Administration and Probate Act* 1919, s. 46; W.A.: *Administration Act* 1903, s. 8; Tas.: *Administration and Probate Act* 1935, s. 4.

properly regarded as acquiring only an equitable interest in land on the death of the former owner.[7]

Once a person has died it appears self-evident that that person can no longer own land or anything else. The person's wishes as to future ownership may or may not be respected. However with respect to land the basic principle of the Torrens system is that title depends upon registration. In a sense the register of titles needs to be altered to transfer the deceased's title. In most cases the occurrence of death without immediate alteration to the register causes only a theoretical awkwardness as to the analysis of ownership whilst procedures are carried out. However in some instances these procedures are never put into operation. Times of economic decline or changes in the environmental conditions may lead to a parcel of land becoming worthless. Civil instability such as wartime may focus attention away from the land. In such cases many years later interest in ownership may be revived. The law may recognise claims based on possession and in all jurisdictions a possessor may seek a Torrens title where no claim is made on behalf of the apparent registered owner.[8] If there is no possessor, someone seeking to acquire the land may have to instigate the administration of the estate of the person registered as owner and deal with that estate.[9]

[6.04] There is but one qualification to the proposition that an owner of land has complete power to direct the disposition of land after the person's death. The disposition may be challenged by dependants of the owner who can establish that inadequate provision has been made for their maintenance.[10] The power of disposition is in effect probably greater than at any other time in the history of the common law because of the absence of any demands by the State. The only demands apart from the debts of the deceased are those of capital gains taxation. The abolition of death duties throughout Australia in recent times means that persons do stand to gain the land of their parents. The social impact of this situation will merit examination and analysis.

II.   CONTRACTS AND TRANSFERS

1. The Land Transfer Process

[6.05] A contract for the sale of land is subject to the general rules of the law of contract which control such matters as the capacity of the

7. *Re Beavis; Beavis v. Beavis* (1906) 7 S.R. (N.S.W.) 66; *Re Campion* [1908] S.A.L.R. 1; *In the Will of Malin* [1912] V.L.R. 259; *Barrett v. Barrett* (1918) 18 S.R. (N.S.W.) 637.
8. In Victoria, Western Australia and Tasmania, the adverse possessor is protected even against the registered proprietor: Torrens statutes—Vic.: s. 42(2)(6); W.A.: s. 68; Tas.: s. 117. In New South Wales, Queensland and South Australia the adverse possessor may apply for a registered title: Torrens statutes—N.S.W.: Pt VIA; Qld: s. 46; S.A.: Pt VIIA. These principles are explained below **[15.82]**.
9. Cf. *Spark v. Meers* [1971] 2 N.S.W.L.R. 1.
10. N.S.W.: *Family Provision Act* 1982; Vic.: *Administration and Probate Act* 1958, Pt IV; Qld: *Succession Act* 1981, Pt IV; S.A.: *Inheritance (Family Provision) Act* 1972; W.A.: *Inheritance (Family and Dependents Provisions) Act* 1972; Tas.: *Testator's Family Maintenance Act* 1972. See generally, Hardingham, Neave and Ford, Chap. 35.

parties to make a contract, the degree of finality and essential contents before a contract is regarded as concluded, and the consequences of deliberate deceit by one party. Contracts for the sale of land were, however, regarded as more serious than most other contracts and this approach affected required formalities, the impact of non-deliberate misrepresentation and the duties of inquiry by a purchaser.

[6.06] Whilst a number of contracts were required by the *Statute of Frauds* of 1667 to be evidenced in writing, today the significant contract still subject to these restrictions is that for the sale of land. The traditional provision states: "No action shall be brought upon any contract for the sale or other disposition of land or of any interest in land, unless an agreement upon which such action is brought, or some memorandum or note thereof, is in writing and signed by the party to be charged or by some person thereunto by him lawfully authorised."[11] This provision is one which relates to the enforceability of agreements and requires not a written agreement but a memorandum signed by the party against whom enforcement is sought. Moreover the doctrine of part performance allows the enforcement of some unwritten contracts. The scope of the *Statute of Frauds* and the doctrine of part performance are examined later in this Chapter.

[6.07] Apart from remedies for fraud, the remedy of rescission was developed by courts of equity with respect to innocent misrepresentation. However one of the bars to the remedy was that the contract was executed: a contract for the sale of land was regarded as executed once legal title vested in the transferee.[12] Moreover the remedy of rescission was the only remedy for innocent misrepresentation. Some of the equitable rules have been modified by statute but a most significant change has been wrought by the national *Trade Practices Act* 1974 and the State Fair Trading Acts.[13] Under s. 53A of the *Trade Practices Act* and the equivalent provisions of the Fair Trading Acts it is an offence to make a false or misleading representation, in trade or commerce, in connection with the sale or grant of an interest in land. This prohibition has civil consequences in that any person who suffers loss or damage by conduct in contravention of the section may recover the amount of the loss or damage.[14] Moreover a person who has suffered loss or damage may apply to the court which may make such orders as it considers appropriate.[15]

---

11. Property Law statutes: N.S.W.: s. 54A; Vic.: *Instruments Act* 1958, s. 126; Qld: s. 59; S.A.: s. 26; Tas.: s. 36. The original statute remains in force in Western Australia, as amended by the *Law Reform (Statute of Frauds) Act* 1962. The statute has been held to apply to Torrens system land: *Wallis v. Moreton* (1932) 32 S.R. (N.S.W.) 659.

12. This result follows from the rule in *Seddon's* case: *Seddon v. North Eastern Salt Co. Ltd* [1905] 1 Ch. 326; Cheshire and Fifoot, pp. 292-294.

13. N.S.W.: *Fair Trading Act* 1987; Vic.: *Fair Trading Act* 1985; Qld: *Fair Trading Act* 1989; S.A.: *Fair Trading Act* 1987; W.A.: *Fair Trading Act* 1987. In Tasmania an equivalent Trading Standards Bill 1989 had been introduced but at the time of writing not passed.

14. *Trade Practices Act* 1974 (Cth), s. 82.

15. *Trade Practices Act* 1974 (Cth), s. 87.

Today therefore a misrepresentation in relation to the sale of an interest in land may give rise to an action in damages under these provisions or an appropriate order may amount in effect to rescission or some other remedy. A private seller of land would not ordinarily be subject to this liability which is confined to representations in trade or commerce. However the private seller commonly employs an agent who is in business and any representations are likely to be made by the agent whose actions are subject to the statutes. Relevant reported decisions involving actions under the sections have been most common with respect to statements by developers of shopping centres.[16] In these cases the interest involved is a leasehold interest. The consequences of the statutes has been to expand markedly the remedies available to the purchaser—particularly in that completion of the contract is no longer a significant barrier.

[6.08] The principle of caveat emptor has been applied with especial rigour to purchasers of interests in land. From the mid 19th century the common law developed implied terms by which the seller of goods gave guarantees to the purchaser—these terms became the implied conditions of merchantable quality and fitness for purpose of the Sale of Goods Acts. The root of modern negligence law, *Donoghue v. Stevenson*,[17] involved duties of care upon a seller of goods. No implied contractual terms as to the quality of premises have developed at common law even in relation to leases of flats where the condition of the premises could not be discovered by a purchaser of a leasehold interest and was beyond that purchaser's power to take corrective action.[18] The courts stated that there was no law against letting a tumble-down house.[19] Similarly the existence of a duty of care by a seller of a freehold interest in land to the buyer was denied even when that seller was the builder.[20] These principles were applied to excuse the seller of a leasehold interest who failed to block the gas after removing a gas heater.[21] Statutory obligations to maintain premises in a habitable condition were imposed by slum control legislation of the 1930s;[22] residential tenancies legislation has required premises be maintained in a reasonable state of repair;[23] a duty of care has been imposed upon builders, architects and building supervisors in respect of

---

16. The leading case is *Mister Figgins Pty Ltd v. Centrepoint Freeholds Pty Ltd* (1981) 36 A.L.R. 23. See also *Pavick v. Bobra Nominees Pty Ltd* (1988) A.S.C. 55-684 and *Munchies Management Pty Ltd v. Belperio* (1989) A.S.C. 40-926.
17. [1932] A.C. 562.
18. *Cruse v. Mount* [1933] Ch. 278. The only exception was in the case of furnished premises and there the implied condition was only as to the condition of the premises at the commencement of the lease: *Smith v. Marrable* (1843) 11 M. & W. 5; 152 E.R. 693; *Pampris v. Thanos* [1968] 1 N.S.W.R. 56 (this case is one where on the facts it would seem that a dangerous condition existed on commencement—loose wiring—which subsequently manifested itself—electrocution of a member of tenant's family). For the landlords' obligations to repair see below [10.25].
19. *Robbins v. Jones* (1863) 15 C.B. (N.S.) 221 at 240.
20. *Otto v. Bolton* [1936] 2 K.B. 46.
21. *Davis v. Foots* [1940] Ch. 751.
22. Bradbrook, MacCallum and Moore, pp. 39-40.
23. Bradbrook, MacCallum and Moore, pp. 359-419.

buildings and is owed even by a builder/seller of a freehold interest to a buyer.[24]

Many sellers of land are private persons who have had no involvement in the building of any structures on that land. There is no obvious superiority of knowledge or skill or commercial activity by which the seller should be taken to assume responsibility for the quality of the structures in relation to the buyer. No implied terms (excludable or otherwise) relating to the quality of structures are imposed in a contract for the sale of a freehold interest and no duty of care is owed towards the purchaser with respect to the structural safety of buildings on the land.[25]

[6.09] The process of the sale of land commonly involves a significant period between a contract and completion of the sale. In the case of Torrens system land completion involves the registration of the purchaser as the proprietor of the fee simple estate. This space of time is primarily designed to allow the buyer to satisfy her or himself that the seller has a good title to the land. The time period is also often allowed so that the buyer may arrange finance for the purchase. Completion then involves the grant of a mortgage to the provider of finance. The period today also allows the seller to fulfil various statutory obligations as to the provision of information and includes a time for reconsideration (or cooling-off) by the buyer.

Although no promises as the quality of premises are implied, the seller has an obligation to show and prove that the seller has a good title to the land contracted to be sold.[26] If the seller cannot establish that the seller will be able to transfer a title free of all encumbrances except those disclosed in the contract, the buyer is under no obligation to complete the contract. In relation to the Torrens system the buyer should search the register of title and be satisfied as to the seller's identity, the description of the land and the absence of any interests affecting the land.

The search of title is commonly one for which the buyer employs a legal practitioner. This employment is not compulsory and the task may be performed by the buyer personally. In recent times various "do-it-yourself" kits have been produced to assist such a buyer. However the preparation of documents for the transfer of land is regarded as part of legal practice and may not be performed by someone who is not a qualified legal practitioner. The monopoly of the legal profession in relation to land transfer work has been seriously challenged in recent times. In South Australia the role is shared by lawyers and land brokers. This South Australian practice does not however stem from any modern scheme to restrict the impact of licensing but from the legal profession's refusal to co-operate with the introduction of the Torrens system.[27] The

24. *Anns v. Merton B.C.* [1978] A.C. 728; *Sutherland S.C. v. Heyman* (1985) 59 A.L.J.R. 564.
25. *Bottomley v. Bannister* [1932] 1 K.B. 458. Some statutory obligations now exist, see below [6.61].
26. *Bell v. Scott* (1922) 30 C.L.R. 387; *Re Ridgeway and Smith's Contract* [1930] V.L.R. 111; *Re Roe and Eddy's Contract* [1933] V.L.R. 427.
27. See Pike, "Introduction of the Real Property Act in South Australia" (1961) 1 Adel. L.R. 169 at 182. Land brokers also operate in Western Australia.

profession refused to handle any dealings under the system: consequently another group—land brokers—were licensed to handle those dealings.

2. Formalities

[6.10]   The Torrens system requires the registration of an instrument before any legal interest may pass.[28] Under the general law a deed is required to pass a legal interest in land.[29] Furthermore under the *Statute of Frauds* a contract for the sale of an interest in land is unenforceable unless evidenced in writing.[30]

In Queensland a signed document is now sufficient to pass a legal interest in land under the general law.[31] In all other States a deed remains essential.[32] Originally a deed was a document which was sealed and delivered. In all Australian States a deed must now be signed.[33] In addition in New South Wales, South Australia and Western Australia a deed must be attested by at least one witness not being a party to the deed.[34]

Sealing involves the placing on the document of some mark intended as a seal.[35] Commonly a plain red wafer has been used but the courts have liberally accepted almost any impression inscribed on the document.[36] In all States except Tasmania a document not sealed in the traditional sense may in some circumstances be deemed to be sealed. In New South Wales, Queensland and South Australia a document expressed to be an indenture or a deed or to be sealed, and signed and attested by one witness not a party to the deed is deemed to be sealed.[37] In Victoria a document signed and expressed to be sealed is deemed to be sealed.[38] In Western Australia a deed does not have to be sealed—it is enough that it is intended to be a deed.[39]

Delivery is constituted not by a physical handing over but by an act evincing an intention to be bound.[40] If a party unilaterally reserves the

---

28. Torrens statutes: N.S.W.: s. 41; Vic.: s. 40(1); Qld: s. 43; S.A.: s. 67; W.A.: s. 58; Tas.: s. 49(1).
29. Property Law statutes: N.S.W.: ss 14, 23B, 23D; Vic.: ss 51, 52, 54; Qld: ss 8, 10 (signed document now sufficient); S.A.: ss 8, 28, 30; W.A.: ss 32, 33, 35; Tas.: ss 59, 60.
30. Property Law statutes: N.S.W.: s. 54A; Vic.: *Instruments Act* 1958, s. 126; Qld: s. 59; S.A.: s. 26; Tas.: s. 36. In Western Australia s. 4 of the *Statute of Frauds* 1667 remains in force as amended by the *Law Reform (Statute of Frauds) Act* 1962.
31. Qld: *Property Law Act* 1974, ss 8, 10.
32. See above, fn. 29.
33. Property Law statutes: N.S.W.: s. 38; Vic.: s. 73; Qld: s. 45; S.A.: s. 41; W.A.: s. 9(1)(c); Tas.: s. 63.
34. Property Law statutes: N.S.W.: s. 38(1); S.A.: s. 41(2); W.A.: s. 9(1)(b).
35. *Re Sandilands* (1871) L.R. 6 C.P. 411.
36. *First National Securities Ltd v. Jones* [1978] 2 W.L.R. 475; cf. Vann, "To Deed or Not To Deed" (1980) 54 A.L.J. 424.
37. Property Law statutes: N.S.W.: s. 38; Qld: s. 45; S.A.: s. 41.
38. Property Law statutes: Vic.: s. 73A.
39. Property Law statutes: W.A.: s. 9(2).
40. *Xenos v. Wickham* (1867) L.R. 2 H.L. 296.

right to recall or revoke a deed there is no delivery.[41] Delivery may not occur for example if a document is not intended to have effect until a formal exchange.[42] Although delivery may occur then, delivery may be conditional or what is described as "in escrow". Delivery in escrow occurs when the effectiveness of the deed depends on the occurrence of an event not referred to in the deed. Normally the deed is deposited with a third party pending the happening of the event. The condition upon which the deed is to take effect cannot be the grantor's death[43] and must be beyond the unilateral control of the grantor.[44]

[6.11] The requirement of registration for the passage of a legal interest under the Torrens system means that both parties are commonly involved in the process of effecting a transfer. The transferor hands registrable documents (an executed memorandum of transfer together with the duplicate certificate of title) to the transferee. Securing the registration is then a matter for the transferee who is at risk so long as the documents are not lodged for registration in that someone else could lodge documents for registration. Priority depends upon the time of lodgement of documents rather than the time of execution of the documents,[45] so that the transferee is at risk from an undisclosed prior document or a later but more speedily lodged document. The priority according to the timing of lodging rule does eliminate any risk from quirks within the Land Titles Office. At the time the documents are handed over the transferee does not have legal title but is in a position to secure for her or himself that legal title. The Acts in Queensland and South Australia describe the transferee at this point as having a right to registration.[46] Whether this right changes the position resulting from the law of sale or gifts will be considered later.

A registered document under the Torrens system is deemed to be a deed[47] and thus property rules as to implications from the execution of a deed apply to the registration of a transfer. However a deed does not suffice to transfer an interest under the Torrens system. Under the common law a deed has special significance in that a transaction expressed in a deed is enforceable whether or not there is consideration;[48] this significance did not however attach in equity. Under the Torrens system a deed will still create at common law binding personal obligations in the absence of consideration but it will not have any proprietary effect because of the need for registration to pass legal title and the need for consideration to pass any equitable interest.

---

41. *Beesly v. Hallwood Estates Ltd* [1961] 1 Ch. 105.
42. *Hooker Industrial Developments Pty Ltd v. Trustees of the Christian Brothers* [1977] 2 N.S.W.L.R. 109.
43. *Foundling Hospital (Governors and Guardians) v. Crane* [1911] 2 K.B. 367.
44. *Beesly v. Hallwood Estates Ltd* [1961] 1 Ch. 105.
45. Torrens statutes: N.S.W.: ss 36(5), (9); Vic.: s. 34(1); Qld: s. 12; S.A.: s. 56; W.A.: s. 53; Tas.: s. 48. *Farrier-Wamak Ltd v. Bank of New Zealand* [1965] A.C. 376.
46. Qld: *Real Property Act* 1877, s. 48; S.A.: *Real Property Act* 1886, s. 246.
47. Torrens statutes: N.S.W.: s. 36(11); Vic.: s. 40(2); Qld: s. 35; S.A.: s. 57; W.A.: s. 85; Tas.: s. 48(7).
48. See Cheshire and Fifoot, pp. 3-4.

The Torrens system does recognise some situations where registration is not required. Short-term leases are in all jurisdictions exempt from the requirement of registration and the interests of tenants in possession are protected against subsequent registered proprietors.[49] In most jurisdictions easements are recognised as arising by implication from a transfer[50] and in most jurisdictions from a course of conduct over a period of time.[51] In most jurisdictions a person in possession adversely to the registered proprietor for a period of 12 years is regarded as obtaining a title to the land.[52] These rights are not registered but are recognised by statute and not the result of equitable doctrine and are enforceable against all third parties. It is therefore probably accurate to describe these rights as legal interests even though the general tendency is to equate registered with legal interests and unregistered with equitable interests.[53]

The Torrens system statutes deny any proprietary effect to documents until registration. The High Court recognised that equitable interests flowed from unregistered transactions.[54] There was a division of opinion[55] as to whether this result flowed from an implied exception within the Torrens system statutes themselves or because equitable interests were created by the transaction not the document, the document being the thing denied proprietary effect. Both rationalisations appear sound. The caveat system in particular has no meaning unless unregistered dealings create equitable interests and the theoretical position that equitable rights stem from the transaction not the document is strongly supported.

[6.12] The enforceability of a contract is significant both for the capacity to take legal action and as an element towards equitable proprietary interests. Even though unenforceable, a contract not sufficiently evidenced to satisfy the *Statute of Frauds* remains valid and a justification for actions by parties in performance of that contract. To satisfy the statute not all the terms of the contract must be set out in writing but only the essential elements—a description of the land, identification of the parties and a statement of the transaction.[56] Separate documents may be read together so long as there is some cross reference between them.[57] Signature involves some mark of the party against whom the contract is to be enforced.[58]

49. Torrens statutes: N.S.W.: s. 42(1)(d); Vic.: s. 42(2)(e); Qld: s. 11; S.A.: s. 69(viii); W.A.: s. 68; Tas.: s. 40(3)(d).
50. New South Wales is the State where acquisition by such means is most doubtful. See *Hi-Fi Publications Pty Ltd v. Gehl* [1979] 2 N.S.W.L.R. 619 for the enforceability of easements arising in such cases against subsequent registered proprietors. See below **[16.40]**.
51. South Australia and possibly New South Wales are the States where easements do not arise in such circumstances: *Anthony v. Commonwealth* (1973) 47 A.L.J.R. 83. For the recognition of easements arising from conduct, see below **[16.31]**.
52. Torrens statutes: N.S.W.: s. 45D; Vic.: s. 42(2)(b); W.A.: s. 68; Tas.: s. 117.
53. See Whalan, pp. 21-23.
54. *Barry v. Heider* (1914) 19 C.L.R. 197.
55. Between Griffith C.J. and Isaacs J. in *Barry v. Heider.*
56. *Toogood v. Mills* (1896) 23 V.L.R. 106; see Voumard, pp 84-91.
57. *Harvey v. Edwards Dunlop & Co. Ltd* (1927) 39 C.L.R. 302; cf. *Thomson v. McInnes* (1911) 12 C.L.R. 562.
58. *Clohesy v. Maher* (1880) 6 V.L.R. (L.) 357.

III. GIFTS AND WILLS

1. Proprietary Effect of Gifts

[6.13] A transaction without consideration would not be enforced in equity although a voluntary deed would create personal obligations at common law. However once executed, that transaction cannot be revoked simply because it was without consideration. A perfected gift thus passes a proprietary interest. What equity does not enforce is the expression of intention to make a gift.

The essential question with respect to a transaction without consideration is what steps are necessary to complete that transaction. In relation to a legal transfer of land at common law the maxim "signed, sealed and delivered" applies: the transferor must execute and hand over a deed of transfer. Under the Torrens system the requirement of registration means that the documents must be lodged with and acted upon by the Land Titles Office. Similarly a transfer of equitable property could be effected by a dealing without consideration. An equitable interest in land could be transferred by a written document (the writing being required by the *Statute of Frauds*); a trust could similarly be declared by a written document.[59]

2. Proprietary Effect of Wills

[6.14] The transfer of an interest in land on death by will is similar to a gift in that the beneficiaries do not provide consideration for their interests. Traditionally wills have required formality. Different rules applied to wills with respect to freehold land and those with respect to other property. In England in 1837 a uniform rule was established: signature by the testator in the presence of two witnesses who must also sign the document.[60] Even at common law some exceptions to the formalities were recognised for example in the case of soldiers on active duty.[61] Recently several jurisdictions have experimented with the relaxation of the formal requirements.[62]

Once a will has been properly executed and is not revoked it is given legal recognition on the death of its maker. Until death a will has no operation and named beneficiaries have only a potential interest or expectancy, they certainly do not have even a contingent interest in the property. Even after death their interest may be displaced by the prior claims of creditors or by an application by a dependent of the testator for maintenance. Under the Torrens system a legal interest will only pass on registration. The first transfer is not to the beneficiaries but to the person

---

59. Property Law statutes: N.S.W.: ss 23C, 23D, 23E; Vic.: ss 53-55; Qld: ss 11, 12; S.A.: ss 29-31; W.A.: ss 34-36; Tas.: s. 60.
60. *Wills Act* 1837, s. 3.
61. See Hardingham, Neave and Ford, Chap. 4.
62. N.S.W.: *Wills, Probate and Administration (Amendment) Act* 1988, s. 3; Qld: *Succession Act* 1981, s. 9; S.A.: *Wills Act* 1936, s. 12(2); W.A.: *Wills Act Amendment Act* 1987, s. 9. See Palk, "Informal Wills: From Soldiers to Citizens" (1976) 5 Adel. L.R. 382; Lang, "Formality v. Intention—Wills in an Australian Supermarket" (1985) 15 M.U.L.R. 82.

responsible for the management of the deceased estate. This position applies whether or not there is a valid will. Except in New South Wales, the Torrens system statutes provide that the estate of a registered proprietor shall on death be transmitted to the executor, administrator or Public Trustee and that party is directed to make application to become the registered proprietor.[63] When entry of title is made, that title is expressed in three jurisdictions to relate back to and take effect from the date of death.[64] The interest of a beneficiary under a will and apparently that of a relative entitled on intestacy is, on the death of the former registered proprietor, an equitable interest in that land[65] which should be sufficient to support a caveat. The person may apply for an order for the transfer of land by the executor, administrator or Public Trustee. In New South Wales, the person entitled under a will may apply for a direct transfer to her or him without intervening registration of the personal representative.[66]

[6.15]   The rights of a remainderman after a life tenant or of a co-owner holding an interest as a joint proprietor derive from the instrument creating the successive interests or the co-ownership. These interests cannot be affected by any purported disposition on death by the life tenant or joint owner. In the case of the Torrens system the successive interests or the co-ownership may be registered. On death the remainderman or surviving co-owner should establish the fact of death to the satisfaction of the Registrar of Titles and an appropriate entry is then made in the register.[67]

3. Gifts and Equitable Intervention

[6.16]   The standard starting point for analysis of the equitable approach to transactions without consideration is that of Turner L.J. in *Milroy v. Lord*:[68]

> "I take the law of this court to be well settled, that, in order to render a voluntary settlement valid and effectual, the settlor must have done everything which, according to the nature of the property comprised in the settlement, was necessary to be done in order to transfer the property and render the settlement binding upon him. He may of course do this by actually transferring the property to the persons for whom he intends to provide, and the provisions will then be effectual, and it will be equally effectual if he transfers the property to a trustee for the purposes of a settlement, or declares that he holds out in trust

---

63. Torrens statutes: Vic.: s. 49; Qld: *Real Property Act* 1877, s. 32; S.A.: ss 176-178; W.A.: s. 187; Tas.: s. 99.
64. Torrens statutes: Vic.: s. 49; S.A.: s. 178; W.A.: s. 187.
65. *Re Beavis; Beavis v. Beavis* (1906) 7 S.R. (N.S.W.) 66; *Re Campion* [1908] S.A.L.R. 1; *In the Will of Malin* [1912] V.L.R. 259; *Barrett v. Barrett* (1918) 18 S.R. (N.S.W.) 637.
66. Torrens statutes: N.S.W.: s. 93. Cf. Whalan, pp. 203-213.
67. Torrens statutes: N.S.W.: s. 101; Vic.: s. 50; S.A.: s. 188; W.A.: s. 227; Tas.: s. 100. There appears to be no corresponding provision in Queensland.
68. (1862) 4 De G.F. & J. 264; 45 E.R. 1185.

for those purposes; and if the property be personal, the trust may, as I apprehend, be declared either in writing or by parol; but, in order to render the settlement binding, one or other of these modes must, as I understand the law of this court, be resorted to, for there is no equity in this court to perfect an imperfect gift.''

Applied strictly this passage would provide a relatively simple means of analysing dealings without consideration. There must be a transfer of the property to the desired donee or to a trustee for that donee or a declaration of a trust. Importantly equity will not attempt to give effect to the settlor's intention by treating an incomplete transfer as a declaration of trust. The temptation to implement intention in this way occurs because a complete transfer of a legal interest requires the execution of a deed and in the case of the Torrens system registration of the memorandum of transfer whereas a trust can be declared by writing. However whilst the settlor's intention is to confer a benefit upon another it is often clear that the intended means of implementing this beneficence is a transfer of the complete legal interest. At the same time it is possible to declare an immediate trust with the intention of subsequently transferring legal title. Furthermore a settlor may only have an equitable interest in which case an equitable transfer in writing is all that is possible for the transfer of that interest. It is possible that a legal owner intends to deal only with the equitable interest but this action is indistinguishable from a declaration of trust which is a transfer of the equitable title without transfer of the legal title.

[6.17] A transfer of property may require some formality but that formality may be something which can be effected only by actions of the transferor. A conveyance of land under the general law requires the execution and handing over of a deed—acts that can be performed only by the transferor. In such cases the sole issue arising from the absence of the formality is whether a court is prepared to give effect to a less formal act as sufficient for an equitable dealing. In the case of land under the general law a writing not constituting a deed may be the basis of a claim as to the declaration of a trust.

However where the transfer involves a series of steps of which only some are within the exclusive power of the transferor, issues arise as to what may be done once the steps within the exclusive power of the transferor have been completed. The transfer of land under the Torrens system is a typical example of this transfer process. The transferor must execute a memorandum of transfer and normally hands it and the duplicate certificate of title to the transferee. Normally the transferee takes the documents to the Land Titles Office to have them registered. In the case of a sale the purchaser exchanges the purchase price for the documents and bears the costs associated with transfer. In the case of a gift the transferor may carry out these steps her or himself. But if the documents are handed over to the intended transferee no legal title has passed but the transferee seems to be in a position to secure that legal title. If at this point the transferor has a change of mind the transferor has no apparent power to prevent the transferee from completing the gift. The death of the transferor may affect the position in that the document of transfer may not be effective after death.[69]

[6.18]   The issues were considered by the High Court in *Brunker v. Perpetual Trustee Company*.[70] Robert Sellar had been the registered proprietor of a piece of land subject to a mortgage. Arthur Fuller was a friend of Robert Sellar and by occupation a law stationer. Bessie Brunker was a housekeeper for Robert Sellar. The day before his death Robert Sellar signed a transfer of the land to Bessie Brunker. This transfer was handed to Arthur Fuller. Subsequently Arthur Fuller handed the transfer to Bessie Brunker's solicitor who entered particulars of the mortgage on it. Robert Sellar's executor entered a caveat against registration of the transfer and brought an action to have the transfer declared to be void.

In the dissenting judgment Latham C.J. stated firstly the principle that equity would do nothing to perfect an imperfect gift and secondly his conclusion that the execution and delivery of the transfer (if there was a delivery) did not give Bessie Brunker any estate in the land, legal or equitable. However he pointed out that she had possession of an executed transfer and was prima facie entitled to attempt to procure registration. The principle that equity would not assist a volunteer only applied if the donee was seeking assistance. On the other hand a person who has made a gift cannot recall it simply because it is a gift. The addition of the reference to the mortgage was not an unauthorised material alteration as the alteration only expressed the effect of the transfer as it originally stood. The possession of the duplicate certificate of title by the mortgagee was not decisive as the Registrar of Titles could require its production. Bessie Brunker was therefore entitled to attempt to register the document which she had in her possession.

On the other hand Dixon J. considered that whilst the intended donee was the owner of neither a legal nor an equitable estate in the land, the Torrens system allowed a volunteer to acquire an indefeasible right to registration of an instrument in that person's favour. This was a right of a new description arising under the statute. However the existence of this right required more than the mere execution of the transfer by the donor. Dixon J. inclined to the view that a person did not require a right to obtain registration without the duplicate certificate of title. But he held that Bessie Brunker certainly had no such right, first, because possession of the transfer was held by Arthur Fuller as bailee for Robert Sellar and his authority to hold it was revoked by Sellar's death and secondly, because the instrument at Sellar's death was not in registrable form because it did not contain a memorandum referring to the mortgage. McTiernan J. agreed that Arthur Fuller's possession was as bailee for Robert Sellar.

The Torrens system statutes in Queensland and South Australia do state that an unregistered instrument signed by the registered proprietor does confer upon the intended transferee a right or claim to registration.

---

69.   A point suggested by Kitto and McTiernan JJ. in *Cope v. Keene* (1968) 118 C.L.R. 1 at 7.
70.   (1937) 57 C.L.R. 555.

Nonetheless there is much attraction to Latham C.J.'s approach that the donee is in a position where the donee might or might not complete the gift but the courts will neither assist nor prevent the donee from taking any legal steps desired.

[6.19] One point upon which the judgments in *Brunker's* case are unanimous is that Bessie Brunker may have had the right to registration but did not have a legal or equitable interest in the land. The transfer of Torrens system land has not been the sole situation where only some of the steps in the process of transfer are within the exclusive power of the transferor. Any property for which title depends upon registration will present a similar situation. Thus the question whether a transaction without consideration has any effect in equity has arisen in other contexts. The courts have seized upon the words in *Milroy v. Lord* that the settlor must have done everything which according to the nature of the property was necessary to be done. It is difficult to read these words as propounding any independent property effect but rather they appear to introduce the succeeding sentence whereby either property is transferred or a trust declared. Nonetheless courts have said that an equitable interest passes when the transferor has done all that must be done by the transferor.

This approach was advanced by the High Court in 1907 in *Anning v. Anning*,[71] a case involving dealings with a range of types of property. Griffith C.J. stated that a gift is complete when all that remains to be done can be done by the donee himself. Higgins J. stated that equity would compel completion of a gift where the donor had done all that was in the donor's power to do. Isaacs J. held to the stricter interpretation of *Milroy v. Lord* that where property was transferable at law, equity would not intervene if the transfer was not complete at law. Subsequently the English Court of Appeal in *Re Rose*[72] held that a purported gift of shares would be complete in equity when the donor had done all that was necessary for the donor to do. Kitto J. in *Cope v. Keene*[73] seems to have accepted this equitable transfer theory in the case of Torrens system land but cites the judgment of Dixon J. in *Brunker* as authority for the proposition.

IV. RESULTING AND CONSTRUCTIVE TRUSTS

1. Types of Trusts

[6.20] An express trust arises where the parties intend a separation of the legal and equitable proprietary interests. The trust arises from a transfer to another who is to hold on trust or from the expression that a current owner is to hold for the benefit of another.[74] An express trust of

71. (1907) 4 C.L.R. 1049.
72. [1952] Ch. 499.
73. (1968) 118 C.L.R. 1. See also *Re Ward; Gillet v. Ward* [1968] W.A.R. 33; *Taylor v. Deputy Federal Commissioner of Taxation* (1969) 123 C.L.R. 206; Seddon, "Imperfect Gifts of Torrens Title Land" (1974) A.L.J. 13. This issue was further considered in *Corin v. Patton* (1990) 92 A.L.R. 1; this case is referred to in fn. 124 in **[9.45]**.
74. See Ford and Lee, p. 16; Snell, p. 106.

land requires written evidence: a declaration of trust must be evidenced in writing; the transfer of an equitable interest must be evidenced in writing.[75]

[6.21] A resulting trust arises when the legal title to property is transferred to someone but that person is not intended to be the beneficial owner of the property.[76] The person is intended to hold for the transferor or for a person who has advanced the money for the purchase or for a third party. A resulting trust does not require written evidence — either because of an express exception to the *Statute of Frauds* or an exception implied on the necessity to overcome fraud.

[6.22] A constructive trust on the other hand arises whenever a trust must be imposed by the courts to do justice between the parties.[77] It is a remedial device and operates independently of intention. Again because it operates to prevent fraud it is outside the writing requirement. Traditionally it has been applied where an existing trustee makes a profit out of the trust but the circumstances in which a trust will be imposed have not been defined. The Australian High Court has shown an inclination to impose a constructive trust whenever it would be unconscionable for someone to retain the beneficial interest in property.

2. Transfer to a Volunteer

[6.23] A simple transfer of land from one party to another without any consideration being provided by the transferee would appear to be such a common situation that the relevant legal principles should be well established. In the earlier section it was stated that a transaction cannot be recalled simply because it is a gift. Once a gift has been perfected the donee can enforce the rights conferred by it. A gift of land requires the transfer of the legal estate. Consequently at common law once an executed deed has been handed to the donee or under the Torrens system the donee has become registered as the proprietor of the land, the donee can claim that a gift has been completed. However the earlier discussion was concerned with situations where there was a clear intention to make a gift and the issue was whether effect had been given to that intention. The difficulty now under consideration is where the legal estate has been transferred but the intention is unclear.

Probably because some evidence as to intention will always exist, situations in the absence of intention have not been clearly analysed. The issue is whether there is a presumption against a gift: whether in the absence of evidence of intention the transferor is to be taken to intend to retain the beneficial ownership. A presumption against a gift leaves the beneficial ownership with the transferor: the transferee acquires legal title subject to a trust in favour of the transferor. Such a situation is one to which the term resulting trust is most appropriately applied. However the presumption of a resulting trust is most clearly established in cases where the purchase price is provided not by the transferee but by a third party

75. See above, fn. 34.
76. See Ford and Lee, pp. 951-985; Snell, pp. 176-191.
77. See Ford and Lee, pp. 989-1039; Snell, pp. 192-196.

and a trust results in favour of that third party. This situation is discussed in the next section. At that point a competing presumption—the presumption of advancement—is also discussed. The presumption is that, prima facie, a gift is intended in cases of dealings with close relatives and that presumption also applies to voluntary transfers to close relatives.

[6.24]   The question of a presumption against a gift was considered by Cussen J. in the Full Court of the Victorian Supreme Court in *House v. Caffyn*.[78] In that case a deceased person transferred land under the Torrens system to his brother and the brother became the registered proprietor of the land. The transfer was expressed to be in consideration of 950 pounds paid by the defendant to the intestate. The deceased's administrator claimed a beneficial interest in the land on the basis that a presumption of a resulting trust arose from non-payment of the expressed consideration. Cussen J. referred to dicta that an implication of a resulting trust does not arise on a voluntary conveyance of land under the general law. Cussen J. considered that the statements were limited to situations where a trust in favour of the transferee was expressed and that no further trust would be implied. Under the general law this express trust would be executed by the *Statute of Uses*. Consequently a statement "To and unto the use of X and his heirs" set out the express though nominal trust. However a memorandum of transfer under the Torrens system would not set out such a trust. Cussen J. therefore inclined to the view that a presumption of a resulting trust applied to voluntary transfers of land under the Torrens system. However the presumption could be negatived and the expression of a substantial consideration would exclude the presumption. Therefore he concluded that the transfer passed the legal and beneficial title to the brother.

[6.25]   The issue came before the High Court in *Wirth v. Wirth*.[79] In that case an engaged couple had purchased as joint tenants a parcel of land. Subsequently but prior to the marriage the male partner transferred his interest to his fiancee. A consideration of 100 pounds was expressed in the transfer. Dixon J. (with whom McTiernan J. agreed in the result) referred to what he described as the "valuable and important judgment" in *House v. Caffyn*. He indicated some doubt about the proposition that by reason of the expression of a substantial consideration there was no resulting trust. Dixon J. pointed out the expression would be either true or false. A true statement of consideration would mean that if no consideration was paid the transferor held a lien for the unpaid price. If the expression was false, the reason for its inclusion would provide an indication as to actual intention. However Dixon J. concluded that the fact that the transfer was made in contemplation of the marriage for which the parties had agreed was sufficient reason to exclude the presumption of a resulting trust. Dixon J. conceded that the presumption of advancement (a presumption in favour of a gift) had not been applied in cases of engaged persons but considered that it would be paradoxical to treat a transfer to an intended spouse differently from a transfer to recently joined spouse. He therefore concluded that the legal and equitable title had passed.

78. [1922] V.L.R. 67; cf. *Law of Property Act* 1974 (Qld), s. 7(3).
79. (1956) 98 C.L.R. 228.

[6.26] It can therefore be stated that a transfer of land under the Torrens system to a stranger without consideration and without any expression of consideration, and in the absence of any evidence of intention, passes a legal estate subject to a resulting trust in favour of the transferor. However this conjunction of factors seems to be more remote than the combination of numbers needed to succeed in a game of Cross Lotto.

3. Purchase in the Name of Another

[6.27] The real world does have people buying land in the name of another. In these cases the law is clear that a resulting trust arises in favour of the person providing consideration. Similarly joint owners may provide contributions of the purchase price in unequal proportions. In these cases the owners hold in trust for themselves as tenants in common in shares proportionate to their contributions. The presumption of a resulting trust in these cases is displaceable by a common intention to the contrary or a presumption of advancement. The presumption of advancement is that where the dealing is between close relatives a gift is intended.

[6.28] The operation of the presumption of a resulting trust and the scope of the presumption of advancement came before the High Court in *Calverley v. Green*.[80] In that case a couple had in 1968 commenced to live together without marriage. They lived in a house whose legal title was vested in the male partner. He made some contribution to living expenses but the female partner bore the major share of the expenses necessary for household provisions. In 1973 they decided to move to another house. The male partner indicated that finance was only available on a joint application. They both joined in the application. They became the joint owners subject to a mortgage under which they were both jointly and severally liable. The balance of the purchase price was provided from part of the proceeds of the sale of the former home. The male partner thereafter paid the instalments due under the mortgage; the female partner paid the bulk of the household expenses.

Two factual matters cloud the application of the presumptions. First, the money was provided substantially through a joint loan but that joint loan was repaid by one of the partners. Secondly the parties' intentions were not made express. The High Court concluded that the case was one of unequal contributions of the price. The male provided a payment plus half the loan; the female provided half the loan. As to intention, if there is a sole contributor that person's subjective view as to whether or not a gift was intended, would be relevant. Where there are joint purchasers contributing unequally the search is for common intention. Each party's intention is what was reasonably understood by the other to be manifested by that party's words or conduct. From this perspective most actions are equivocal. For example, the fact that the female partner's name was added as purchaser and mortgagor to facilitate the arrangement of finance can be viewed as an explanation of her acquisition of a beneficial interest

80. (1984) 59 A.L.J.R. 111.

or as an explanation of her being a trustee for the male partner. The understanding that the male partner would pay the bulk of the mortgage could be viewed as part of the arrangements as to how expenses would be shared.

The High Court therefore concluded that under the presumption of resulting trust the parties held on trust for themselves in proportion to their original contributions to the price. The husband was credited with the payment plus half the loan, the wife was credited with half the loan. The material on intention did not provide any clear common intention so that the resulting trust presumption was not rebutted.

The issue of law to be clarified was the scope of the presumption of advancement. In *Wirth v. Wirth* Dixon J. had argued for a flexible approach and applied the presumption to parties who had agreed to be married. He indicated that the presumption should be applied when the relationship between the parties is such that it is more probable than not that a beneficial interest was intended to be conferred. In *Calverly v. Green*, Gibbs C.J. accepted Dixon J.'s approach as governing the matter, He pointed out that the case was one where the relationship had an apparent permanence, and in which the parties lived together, and represented themselves to others, as man and wife. Gibbs C.J. concluded that it was natural that as between such a man and a woman property would be put in the woman's name because she was intended to have a beneficial interest and a presumption of advancement was raised. Mason and Brennan JJ. disagreed as to this factual inference. They considered that where a man and a woman are cohabiting though unmarried, an assumption that the parties intend to retain independent control of assets is more likely than a presumption of beneficience. Deane J. pointed out that originally the presumption of advancement applied in cases where the person making the transfer of legal title owed obligations of support to the transferee: a man to his child or other person to whom he stood in loco parentis; a husband to his wife. He recognised that the categories had been extended to an intended wife and modern notions of equality should extend them to the wife vis-a-vis a husband. He considered that there were convincing reasons of logic or analogy to deny the extension to persons in a de facto relationship but in any event previous decisions of the High Court precluded the extension of the presumption to such a relationship. Murphy J. rejected the approach of determining the property rights by reference to the presumptions.

The conclusion of the case was that the presumption of a resulting trust applied so that the property was held on trust for the parties in proportion to their contributions to the purchase price and there was no application of the presumption of advancement.

[6.29] The position in Australia is that the presumption of a resulting trust arises from provision of the purchase price by someone other than the transferee or by unequal contributions between joint owners. These contributions are assessed at the time of purchase. The presumption of a resulting trust may be rebutted by evidence of intention to make a gift but this intention must be that of the party contributing the whole of the purchase price or in the case of unequal contributions their common and revealed intention. Again the intention is judged at the time of the purchase. The presumption of a resulting trust may also be rebutted by the presumption of advancement which extends beyond cases of father benefitting a child and husband benefitting a wife but does not extend to couples in a de facto relationship. Later actions may indicate a dealing with the equitable interests but any transfer is subject to formality requirements.

4. Fraud or Unconscionable Conduct by the Transferee

[6.30] Where one party accepts a transfer of property but does so on the understanding that the whole or part of the property will be held for someone else, the transferee would gain an unintended advantage if the transferee were to retain the property but deny the understanding. To overcome this result a constructive trust has been imposed upon the transferee. The trust is imposed in favour of the intended beneficiary of the understanding whether or not that party was the transferor even though the party defrauded will normally be the transferor. The person in whose favour the trust is constructed may therefore be a bystander to the dealing. The lack of writing for the understanding is regarded as rendered irrelevant by the fraud: the *Statute of Frauds* should not be an instrument of fraud.

The longest-established applications of this principle are cases of secret trusts attached to wills.[81] If a named beneficiary under a will agrees with the testator that the named benefit is meant for another, the named beneficiary will be held subject to a trust in favour of the other. A similar result occurs where a person declines to make a will on the basis that the next of kin who take on intestacy will hold for an intended beneficiary. In these cases even if the subject matter is not land, formalities are required for the making of a valid will and the trust is enforced in the absence of any writing.

The principle has been applied to transfers of land. It is the assertion that a transfer was absolute when there was an understanding that the land be held for another, that gives rise to the fraud. It is not essential that there have been a malevolent intention at the time of transfer.

[6.31] In *Bannister v. Bannister*[82] the defendant agreed to sell two cottages to the plaintiff on the plaintiff's undertaking that the defendant would be allowed to live in one of the cottages rent free for as long as she desired. The price reflected this arrangement but the undertaking was not included in the formal conveyance. Thereafter the defendant lived in a room in one of the cottages until the plaintiff brought an action for recovery of possession. The Court of Appeal ruled that the plaintiff held the property on trust for the defendant during the defendant's lifetime to permit her to occupy the cottage for as long as she desired. The court

81. See Davies, "Constructive Trusts, Contract and Estoppels: Proprietary and Non Proprietary Remedies for Informal Arrangements Affecting Land (1981) 7 Adel. L.R. 200 at 206.
82. [1948] 2 All E.R. 133; see also *Hodgson v. Marks* [1971] Ch. 892; *Binion v. Evans* [1972] Ch. 359; *Hussey v. Palmer* [1972] 1 W.L.R. 1286.

stated that equity would not allow the transferee to set up the apparent absolute nature of the conveyance as to do so was of itself fraud and it was enough that there was some sufficiently defined beneficial interest in the property to be taken by another.

[6.32]   An arrangement between two co-owners brought the principle into operation in the New South Wales case of *Last v. Rosenfeld*.[83] The co-owners had had various social and business dealings with one another and had purchased a residential property for investment purposes. Ultimately it was agreed that one co-owner should buy out the other and a contract and transfer were duly executed. The selling owner however claimed that the agreement was made as a favour to the buying owner so that the buying owner could live on the property. The property was sold for its cost price. The selling owner alleged an agreement whereby the buying owner was to retransfer the half share at the sale price if the buying owner did not live on the property within one year. The selling owner's account was accepted and the New South Wales Supreme Court held that the retention of title by the buying co-owner would amount to a fraud. The trust arose upon the failure of the buying owner to live on the property within 12 months and it did not matter that the selling owner had to pay an agreed figure for the return of the property. The court rejected the argument that the selling owner was trying to enforce an oral collateral agreement.

[6.33]   In these cases the transferee holds land on trust for another and the beneficiary's interest is at least fashioned in the form of a recognised proprietary interest—a conditional life estate, a right to purchase a half share. The nature of this interest flowed from the agreement of the parties. In *Muschinski v. Dodds*[84] the obligation of the transferee could not be translated into such an interest. The two parties (a man and a woman) became the joint owners of a property purchased from funds provided by the woman. It was the parties' understanding that the man would renovate a cottage on the land and purchase a prefabricated house for it. The parties separated without these tasks being undertaken. Deane and Mason JJ. held that the woman had advanced the purchase price on the basis of the planned joint venture. That venture collapsed without attributable blame. In those circumstances it was unconscionable for the man to retain his half interest. They declared that the parties held their joint interests on trust to repay to each that person's respective contribution and as to the residue in equal shares. Brennan and Dawson JJ. on the other hand rejected the imposition of a constructive trust on the basis that to do so was merely to contend that as the circumstances unfolded it was unfair for the man to retain his half interest without any contribution. They argued that a gift could be subject to conditions of two kinds: one involving forfeiture for non-fulfilment, the other creating a personal obligation to fulfil. The woman had not imposed the condition in defeasance of the interest. In the result Gibbs C.J. reached the same conclusion as Deane and Mason JJ. but on the ground

83. [1972] 2 N.S.W.L.R. 923.
84. (1984) 160 C.L.R. 583.

(rejected by all other members of the court) that the woman's payment of the whole of the purchase price for a property in joint names created a lien for a contribution to that price.

[6.34] The failure of a joint enterprise again came before the High Court this time in the context of domestic aspects of a de facto relationship in *Baumgartner v. Baumgartner*.[85] The parties pooled their earnings to meet their expenses and outgoings which included the acquisition of land and the building of a house and furniture payments. When they separated, the man attempted to rely upon his sole legal title to the land. The High Court ruled that the contributions were made for the purpose of the relationship and were not intended as a gift. The assertion of sole title by the man was unconscionable and a constructive trust would be imposed. The parties held on trust for themselves in proportion to their contributions which the court determined as 55 per cent and 45 per cent by the man and woman respectively.

[6.35] It is fairly clear that for an owner to go back on an undertaking which has been the basis of the acquisition of ownership is unfair and that person should be held to the undertaking. A constructive trust is imposed to enforce the undertaking. But the circumstances in which it is unconscionable to assert title beyond the failure of a joint enterprise await elucidation. Furthermore where the basis of the trust is not an undertaking the terms of the constructive trust are similarly indeterminate.

[6.36] The place of the denial of undertaking cases within the Torrens system was considered by the High Court in *Bahr v. Nicolay*.[86] That case produced no clear majority one way or the other. Mason C.J. and Dawson J. took the view that the fraud exception to indefeasibility extended to cases of a subsequent repudiation of a preregistration undertaking. Wilson and Toohey JJ. denied this view of the fraud exception but concluded that the denial of the undertaking gave rise to a constructive trust which was enforceable against the registered proprietor because of the "in personam" exception to indefeasibility. Brennan J. decided the case on the basis of an express trust but inclined to the wide view of the fraud provision. The result seems clear whatever the justification. It should be pointed out that some of the statutory language refers to an obtaining of title by fraud—an expression difficult to reconcile with the wide view.

V. INFORMALITY AND INEQUITY

1. Part Performance

[6.37] The impact of the *Statute of Frauds* is that a purely oral contract for the sale of any interest is unenforceable no matter how compelling the

---

85. (1987) 62 A.L.J.R. 29. See also *Cooke v. Cooke* [1987] V.R. 625; *Glouftis v. Glouftis* (1987) 44 S.A.S.R. 298.
86. (1988) 78 A.L.R. 1.

evidence is as to its existence or how complete the agreement is as to its terms. The devices of resulting and constructive trusts have been in part developed to overcome formality issues—not those for contracts but the similar requirements for the creation of express trusts in relation to land. In the situations discussed above the basis for non-application of the writing requirements has been expressed to be fraud on the part of the person denying the existence of the trust though more recent High Court decisions have adopted the broader concern of unconscionability. In the resulting and constructive trust cases the parties have executed some dealing with the land on the basis of an undertaking or understanding as to future events. The courts in these cases have not simply returned the parties to their original position but, because of the changed circumstances, enforced the undertaking or understanding.

The *Statute of Frauds* makes a contract for the sale of an interest in land not invalid but merely unenforceable. In the absence of a dispute this unenforceability will not be of concern to the parties. Consequently the purely executory contract will often be put into effect. Again, once the contract has been fully executed the parties will have no cause for concern and in the case of contracts for the sale of an interest in land it is difficult to contemplate how execution would not involve sufficient writing for the *Statute of Frauds*. Thus, the difficult cases are those where the contract has been partly executed. Just as in the resulting and constructive trust cases, a point is reached when the parties have changed position on the basis of the contract to the extent that the courts are not prepared to allow denial of the contract.

[6.38]   The doctrine of part performance allows the enforcement of an oral contract for the sale of an interest in land when the contract has been sufficiently acted upon. The basis of equitable intervention in part performance cases can be clouded because the party seeking enforcement is often asserting simply that the contract should be enforced. The *Statute of Frauds* is often described as an evidentiary rule but it is clear that part performance does not avoid the impact of the statute because there is some independent evidence of the contract. Rather the actions done in execution of the contract make it unjust to deny enforcement of the contract. As was said by the Earl of Selbourne in the seminal case of *Maddison v. Alderson*:[87]

> "In a suit founded on such part performance, the defendant is really 'charged' upon the equities resulting from the acts done in execution of the contract, and not (within the meaning of the statute) upon the contract itself."

If part performance is a doctrine relating to the inequity to a party who has changed position on the basis of a contract, then focus should seemingly turn to the definition of a sufficient detriment to require enforcement of the contract. However, in defining sufficient acts of part performance the courts have reintroduced evidentiary concerns. The acts of part performance must provide some evidence of the contract. Again the words of the Earl of Selbourne:[88]

87. (1883) 7 A.C. 467 at 475.
88. Ibid. at 479.

"All the authorities show that the acts relied upon as part performance must be unequivocally, and in their own nature, referable to some such agreement as that alleged."

In *Maddison v. Alderson* a woman served as a housekeeper without wages for many years on the basis of a promise that a will would be made leaving her a life estate in land. A will to this effect was in fact signed but not properly witnessed. The court refused to enforce the agreement: her actions were equivocal.

"There have not been wanting recorded cases in which time and care have been bestowed by one person upon another, even from a vague anticipation that the affection and gratitude so created would, in the long run, ensure some indefinite reward. And legal tribunals have refused in those cases to turn courtesy into contract and compel any payment although such service had been performed."[89]

[6.39] Attention has therefore turned to the definition of acts of unequivocal referability. Payment of money is argued never to be a sufficient act of part performance because it is always equivocal: it never points to any particular kind of contract. The House of Lords has however concluded that the payment of a deposit and the forwarding of a deed of transfer were sufficient acts of part performance.[90]

[6.40] In Australia the authoritative pronouncement of the doctrine of part performance has come from the High Court in *Regent v. Millett*.[91] In that case a couple purchased a house for $4,500 including a loan for $3,500 secured by a mortgage. Subsequently they agreed with their daughter and son-in-law that in consideration of the children agreeing to pay off the mortgage, the children could go into possession and have the house transferred to them when the mortgage was paid off. The children went into possession, began paying off the mortgage and effected repairs. The High Court held that there were sufficient acts of part performance.

The High Court ruled that it was sufficient that the acts unequivocally and in their own nature were referable to some contract of the general nature of that alleged. The acts did not have to be compelled by the contract but should be pursuant to the contract. Entry into possession alone, or the taking of possession coupled with the expenditure of money by one party on the improvement of the property, with the cognisance of the other party, constituted in many cases sufficient part performance. The taking of possession could be explained as referable to some authority other than the contract alleged but in the absence of such explanation was the act of part performance par excellence.

VI.   INCOMPLETENESS AND INEQUITY

1.   Estoppel

[6.41] If parties act upon unenforceable agreements to their detriment, they also act upon understandings which have not been sufficiently

89. Ibid. at 486 per Lord O'Hagen.
90. *Steadman v. Steadman* [1976] A.C. 536.
91. (1976) 133 C.L.R. 679.

complete to constitute contracts. Incompleteness may also arise because of a lack of reciprocity of consideration: consideration represents a quid pro quo however, and actions in consequence of but not in return for, an undertaking will not amount to consideration.[92] Lack of consideration for an undertaking has commonly been present in cases where a party agrees to make a concession in relation to an existing contractual obligation: the concession confers a benefit on the other party who provides nothing in return. In contract analysis attention has focused on the doctrine of estoppel and the extent to which a promise is enforceable once it is acted upon.

In *Regent v. Millett*[93] the children undertook to pay off the mortgage in return for the promise of a future transfer. Consideration was provided by this undertaking. However, the situation could readily be one where an interest in land is promised not in return for a reciprocal undertaking but simply in return for performance of some desired action. "If you look after the land, I will transfer it to you." It is possible to analyse such undertakings in contractual terms: a promise is given in return for performance, and performance constitutes both acceptance and consideration. The contract is a unilateral one in that the promisee does not undertake to perform but is given an undertaking in return for performance. Revocability of the offer once performance has been commenced but not completed causes conceptual difficulty.[94] Since any benefit can amount to consideration an advantage such as children living nearby can be a sufficient return for a promise to convey to them that nearby land.[95]

[6.42] In relation to undertakings about land,[96] authority has always existed for the proposition that where an owner of land creates or encourages an expectation in another that the other will have an interest in the land, and the other acts upon that expectation, then the owner will be compelled to give effect to it.[97] The Privy Council applied the principle in 1884 in a case where an individual constructed a jetty at the instigation of the New Zealand government. The expenditure at the encouragement of the landowner gave rise to an equity which would be satisfied by the grant of a perpetual licence.[98]

This doctrine has been distinguished from contractual estoppel generally though titles such as proprietary estoppel and the equity of acquiescence. The subject matter of land has provided a special circumstance. The doctrine has been applied to situations where children have been encouraged to develop land in return for a promise of an

92. *Australian Woollen Mills Pty Ltd v. Commonwealth* (1954) 92 C.L.R. 424; Cheshire and Fifoot, p. 76.
93. (1976) 133 C.L.R. 679.
94. Cf. *Errington v. Errington* [1952] 1 K.B. 290; *Abbott v. Lance* (1860) Legge 1283; Cheshire and Fifoot, pp. 56-58.
95. *Raffaele v. Raffaele* [1962] W.A.R. 29.
96. See Finn (ed.), *Essays in Equity* (1985), Chap. 4; Bennett, "Equitable Estoppel and Related Estoppels" (1987) 61 A.L.J. 540.
97. *Ramsden v. Dyson* (1866) L.R. 1 H.L. 129.
98. *Plimmer v. Wellington Corporation* (1884) 9 A.C. 699.

interest in the future.[99] It has been applied in commercial situations where parties may be thought to have foolishly committed themselves before details were finalised. In *Crabb v. Arun District Council*[100] a landowner sought from a council a second access point and right of way along a private road. He believed this access would be granted and constructed appropriate gates. He then sold off part of his land so that this second access point was the sole access point for the remaining land. The Court of Appeal held that the council had encouraged the landowner to act to his detriment thereby raising an equity in his favour and this equity would be satisfied by the grant of a right of access and right of way. In *Re Basham*[101] the plaintiff worked for her mother's second husband for many years and stayed on in return for a promise that she would get a cottage on her stepfather's death. He died intestate. It was held that the plaintiff's belief that she would inherit the cottage had been encouraged by the stepfather and she had acted to her detriment on the basis of this understanding. She was held entitled to the cottage on the basis of proprietary estoppel. If the promise had been sufficiently certain to form a contract, the facts would be difficult to distinguish from *Maddison v. Alderson*.[102] It would seem anomolous that the vaguer undertaking gives rises to obligations but the more defined does not.

[6.43] The place of proprietary estoppel in Australian law was settled by the High Court in *Waltons Stores (Interstate) Ltd v. Maher*.[103] In that case the owners of land and a business operator negotiated for the lease of land. It was envisaged that the landowner would demolish an existing building on the land and replace it. The new building was designed for the business operator. The parties realised negotiations had to be concluded. Solicitors for the business operator wrote to solicitors for the landowner enclosing documents for the lease. The solicitors for the business operator intimated that some changes had been made without their client's authority but if they were not agreed that fact would be conveyed the following day. Four days later the documents were returned executed by the landowners. They were never executed by the business operator and returned some months later with an expression of intention not to proceed. By this point demolition was finished and the new building 40 per cent completed.

The High Court held that an equity may be brought into existence by a person whose conduct creates or lends force to an assumption by another that the other will obtain an interest in the first person's land and on the basis of that expectation the other person alters that person's position or acts to that person's detriment. An equity arises in favour of the other person, the nature and extent of the equity depending on the circumstances. In the current case the landowner was encouraged to believe that completion was a formality and that in a context of urgency nothing was done for some time and demolition allowed to proceed. It was

---

99. *Dillwyn v. Llewelyn* (1862) De G.F. & J. 517; 45 E.R. 1285; *Inwards v. Baker* [1965] 2 Q.B. 29.
100. [1976] 1 Ch. 179.
101. [1987] 1 All E.R. 405.
102. (1883) 8 A.C. 467.
103. (1987) 76 A.L.R. 513.

unconscionable for the business operator, knowing the landowners were exposed to detriment by acting on the basis of a false assumption, to adopt a course of inaction.

The High Court held that the business operator could not deny the existence of the contract. However, damages were awarded in lieu of specific performance. Furthermore the *Statute of Frauds* was dismissed as irrelevant. The business operator was estopped from denying not just the existence of contract but that of a formally executed contract. Alternatively the action was not one on the contract but on the equities arising from the parties' actions.

[6.44] The High Court does make clear that the remedy in cases of proprietary estoppel depends on what best satisfies the justice of the situation. In some cases the remedy will be the formal transfer of the interest promised. But particularly where the promise has been vague the courts have a greater discretion to shape a remedy. The understandings of the parties may genuinely have not coincided so that there is no equity to enforce one party's version of affairs.[104] An obvious alternative to a transfer is to allow a charge on the land for the value of work and money expended.

[6.45] The principle of proprietary estoppel is now clearly applicable in cases of encouragements or expectations acted upon to the detriment of the other party. An estoppel in relation to assertion of an interest in land has long been established in cases of action upon a mistake encouraged by another. Thus a person (believing land to be her or his) building on that land will estop a real owner who allows that building to proceed.[105] This doctrine requires knowledge of the mistake by the true owner.[106] These cases have been explained as ones of estoppel without reference to remedy. If they should be analysed as cases of proprietary estoppel then there is a flexibility of remedy. Mistake will often arise as to the position of a boundary: estoppel could provide a remedy in place of adverse possession or the encroachments legislation[107] of some States. The relations between the parties may fall short of mutual mistake. They may simply be ignorant of the true position of a boundary and agree to act upon an approximation. These cases may also be analysed as action on the basis of a representation.

[6.46] The doctrine of proprietary estoppel provides a remedy which can lead to a proprietary interest. A party could be compelled to execute a document registerable under the Torrens system. However, even though an equity is said to arise in favour of a party acting to that party's detriment, the right seemingly has limited proprietary impact upon

---

104. Cf. the dissenting analysis of Cox J. in *Jackson v. Crosby (No. 2)* (1979) 21 S.A.S.R. 280. That case involved representations by a woman to a man as to the transfer of land on which the man was doing building work. The woman, on Cox J.'s view, was giving an undertaking on the basis of marriage, the man had no understanding of the marriage condition.
105. *Willmott v. Barber* (1880) 15 Ch. D. 96.
106. *Brand v. Chris Building Society* [1957] V.R. 625.
107. The encroachment legislation is discussed below **[14.25]**.

subsequent transferees under the Torrens system. The protection of indefeasibility should accrue to someone who becomes the registered proprietor in good faith and for value in succession to the party creating the estoppel. Possible protection for good faith volunteers further weakens the scope of the right.[108]

If the equity is only satisfied by the grant of a proprietary interest, the person in whose favour the equity is created does seem to have a proprietary interest and thus possibly sufficient basis to lodge a caveat.[109] On the other hand if the equity can be satisfied without the grant of a proprietary interest (and the subject matter of a constructive trust could be a personal obligation), then the existence of any proprietary interest and thus capacity to caveat, at least prior to an action, becomes more doubtful. Remedies such as personal occupation of premises[110] are hard to sustain in proprietary terms though they may be explained as conditional life estates.

One situation in which a subsequent party could be bound despite indefeasibility is that of mutuality of arrangements: a concession in relation to drainage is made in return for a concession in relation to access. In such a situation a subsequent owner would not be allowed to claim the benefit without accepting the burden.[111]

[6.47] The High Court in *Walton Stores v. Maher*[112] denied that the doctrine of proprietary estoppel had any effect upon that of part performance. But in both cases there is an undertaking acted upon by another. In the part performance cases that undertaking must satisfy contractual criteria (certainty, finality, intention to be bound, consideration) and the consequent action must be referable to a contract of the kind alleged. In proprietary estoppel cases however, there need be only a creation of an expectation and a consequent detriment. It is difficult to envisage any situation in which the proprietary estoppel elements will not be easier to establish than the part performance elements. The only drawback of a proprietary estoppel argument is that the appropriate remedy to satisfy the equity is discretionary whereas part performance leads to the enforcement of the contract in toto.

VII.   PROPRIETARY EFFECTS OF CONTRACTS

[6.48]   In terms of the express intention of the parties, the proprietary dealing occurs upon the transfer of legal title, the declaration of a trust or the transfer by an equitable owner of an equitable interest. The doctrines of resulting and constructive trusts and proprietary estoppel impose proprietary remedies to counter unconscionable conduct. However the

---

108. See above **[5.64]** as to the protection for volunteers.
109. On the other hand *Re Pile's Caveats* [1981] Qd R. 81 suggests the claim to an equity to set aside a transaction for fraud is not sufficient to support a caveat. See above **[5.83]** as to the capacity to caveat.
110. Cases such as *Errington v. Errington* [1952] 1 K.B. 290 and *Binion v. Evans* [1972] 1 Ch. 359.
111. *E.R. Ives Investment Ltd v. High* [1967] 2 Q.B. 379.
112. (1987) 76 A.L.R. 513.

range of proprietary interests and thus remedies is considerably expanded by the equitable doctrine of conversion. Under this doctrine a specifically enforceable contract for the sale of an interest in land transfers that interest in equity at the time of the contract. This equitable transfer occurs whether the parties intend that there should be a subsequent formal transfer of the interest, whether the parties intend that there be an immediate formal transfer or whether no formality at all is envisaged. As has been explained earlier the conveyancing process commonly involves a time lag between contract and transfer to allow a purchaser to substantiate the vendor's proposals but minor transactions could be put into formal effect immediately or concluded by a simple oral exchange. Subject to the formality requirements for an enforceable contract, the equitable doctrine of conversion applies in all these situations. The doctrine has a number of consequences but its precise operation cannot be defined with confidence and a philosophical and practical base for the doctrine beyond its establishment throughout the centuries becomes evasive.

The classic statement of the doctrine is the passage of Jessell M.R. in *Lysaght v. Edwards*:[113]

> "It appears to me that the effect of a contract for sale has been settled for more than two centuries; certainly it was completely settled before the time of Lord Hardwicke, who speaks of the settled doctrine of the court as to it. What is that doctrine? It is that the moment you have a valid contract for sale the vendor becomes in equity a trustee for the purchaser of the estate sold, and the beneficial ownership passes to the purchaser, the vendor having a right to the purchase-money, a charge or lien on the estate for the security of that purchase-money, and a right to retain possession of the estate until the purchase-money is paid, in the absence of express contract as to the time of delivering possession. In other words, the position of a vendor is something between what has been called a naked or bare trustee, or a mere trustee (that is, a person without beneficial interest), and a mortgagee who is not, in equity (any more than a vendor), the owner of the estate, but is, in certain events, entitled to what the unpaid vendor is, viz. possession of the estate and a charge upon the estate for his purchase-money."

Equitable interests can arise through express declarations of trusts, the remedial doctrines previously discussed or because some interests are recognised only in equity (today substantially only restrictive convenants fall within this category). The doctrine of conversion means that equitable interests arise whenever a dealing has not been formally effected. This position remains true under the Torrens system though the equitable interests are more vulnerable to the subsequent registered proprietor. As well as the interest of the purchaser of a freehold interest, there are equitable mortgages, leases, easements, profits a prendre, charges and whatever other proprietary interests are recognised by our legal system.

113. (1876) 2 Ch. D. 499.

[6.49] The doctrine of conversion has a number of effects. Fundamentally the vendor becomes a trustee of the vendor's interest for the purchaser. The contract creates an equitable proprietary interest vested in the purchaser. Because the purchaser is regarded as the equitable owner, the property is regarded as at the risk of the purchaser so that if in any way it is accidentally damaged the loss falls on the purchaser.[114] The purchaser has the responsibility of taking out insurance if protection against loss is desired. The doctrine means that the rights under the contract are proprietary rights. The contract thus survives the death of either party. The vendor's interest is characterised as personalty (a right to payment) whereas the purchaser's interest is realty (the land). Consequently on the death of either party the devolution of that party's interest will reflect this characterisation so that if a will provides for the testator's realty to go to one person and personalty to another, an interest as a purchaser would pass to the first person, one as a vendor would pass to the second. Because the purchaser becomes the beneficial owner a trust relationship arises between vendor and purchaser and the parties' rights and remedies reflect this relationship. Many priority disputes come about because of the doctrine. The purchaser has more than rights against the vendor alone and these equitable rights may come into conflict with other equitable rights created by other informal dealings by the vendor. It is even possible that because equity treats the purchaser as the owner that purchaser may have some rights of a legal owner.

[6.50] The doctrine of conversion is connected with the equitable maxim that equity treats as done that which ought to be done. However this maxim does not explain why equity should intervene when a later formal transfer is intended and the parties are working towards the passage of the legal proprietary interest at that time. The absence of an intended legal dealing does gives scope for the maxim and the question arises as to the extent to which equity will treat the equitable owner in the same way as a legal owner. In *Walsh v. Lonsdale*[115] an agreement was made for the lease of a factory for a period of seven years. The parties intended that a lease (in the form of a deed) would be drawn up but it was not. However the tenant took possession. The landlord brought an action for distress for rent. Distress is a legal remedy entitling a landlord to seise chattels of tenants in arrears with rent payments. The Court of Appeal upheld the landlord's action: the parties were to be treated as if a formal lease had been drawn up.

The extent of the maxim remains of some doubt. The decision in *Walsh v. Lonsdale* occurred shortly after the enactment of the Judicature Acts and some retreat from the view that law and equity are fused has occurred. However the Australian High Court has recently shown an impatience with the strict separation of legal rights and remedies and equitable rights and remedies.[116] It has for instance even suggested that once an interest

---

114. The position has been changed by statute in New South Wales so that risk, prima facie, does not pass until the transaction is completed: *Conveyancing Act 1919*, ss 66J-66O.

115. (1882) 21 Ch. D. 9. See *Chan v. Cresdon Pty Ltd* (1990) 64 A.L.J.R. 111.

116. Particularly by Deane J. in *Walton Stores (Interstate) Ltd v. Maher* (1987) 76 A.L.R. 513.

has been established by way of equitable doctrine, the legal remedy of damages may be available for infringement of that interest.

The application of *Walsh v. Lonsdale* could be significant in determining the rights of parties to common transactions. Thus a legal mortgagee has long been regarded as having rights not possessed by an equitable mortgagee—in particular the power of sale. If the notion that the parties are to be treated as if a formal mortgage had been executed is strictly applied then a power of sale could be extended to an equitable mortgagee. Similarly the enforcement of convenants between landlord and tenant has traditionally been regarded as dependent on the execution of a formal lease. Again it can be argued that the parties should be treated as if a formal lease had been executed.

[6.51] The doctrine of conversion was expressed in *Walsh v. Lonsdale* to arise whenever there is a valid contract. However, even an unenforceable contract is valid and equitable intervention is normally regarded as dependent upon a specifically enforceable contract. As stated by Mason J. in *Chang v. Registrar of Titles*:[117] "It is accepted that the availability of the remedy of specific performance is essential to the existence of the constructive trust which arises from a contract of sale." The availability of specific performance may not be apparent at the time of the contract. In *Bahr v. Nicolay*[118] the difficulty with specific performance was whether the purchaser was ready and willing to perform. The other parties sought to withdraw not because of any competing attractions but because they believed that the purchaser lacked the financial resources to complete. The issue of capacity and willingness to perform could only be resolved as the time for completion which was some three years after the contract at the time. If conversion operates only when specific performance is available its meaning is very different from what appeared from *Lysaght v. Edwards*[119] to be an immediate creation of an equitable interest on conclusion of a contract.

[6.52] Completion of contracts commonly involves more than the willingness and ability of the parties to perform. Conditions may be inserted whereby the actions of a third party are required: the grant of finance to allow the purchaser to complete; the approval of a planning authority for subdivision of land; the consent of a minister or licensing authority for a transfer. Furthermore statutes today as a matter of consumer protection allow a purchaser cooling-off rights.

The courts have said that no equitable proprietary interest exists prior to the satisfaction of conditions such as ministerial consent or planning approval.[120] It would seem that here reference is being made to conditions that relate to the existence of the contract rather than those relating to performance of obligations but the distinction is not easily drawn. The lack of a proprietary interest has the impact under the Torrens system of

---

117. (1976) 137 C.L.R. 177.
118. (1988) 78 A.L.R. 1.
119. (1876) 2 Ch. D. 499.
120. *McWilliam v. McWilliams Wines Pty Ltd* (1964) 114 C.L.R. 656; *Brown v. Heffer* (1967) 116 C.L.R. 344; *Shanahan v. Fitzgerald* [1982] 2 N.S.W.L.R. 513.

an insufficiency of interest to sustain a caveat and the courts have said that a purchaser under a conditional contract lacks the capacity to lodge a caveat.[121] The ramifications of such qualifications to the doctrine of *Lysaght v. Edwards*[122] are immense as conditional contracts are most common.

VIII. AUCTIONS

[6.53] Surprisingly there are few statutory provisions governing the conduct of auction sales of land.[123] Cases in which the effect of conduct at an action was in dispute are also rare. The best statement of general principles is contained in the Sale of Goods legislation. The common provision states:

"In the case of a sale by auction—

(1) where goods are put up for sale by auction in lots, each lot is *prima facie* deemed to be the subject of a separate contract of sale;

(2) a sale by auction is complete when the auctioneer announces its completion by the fall of the hammer, or in other customary manner. Until such announcement is made any bidder may retract his bid;

(3) where a sale by auction is not notified to be subject to a right to bid on behalf of the seller, it shall not be lawful for the seller to bid himself or to employ any person to bid at such sale, or for the auctioneer knowingly to take any bid from the seller or any such person. Any sale contravening this rule may be treated as fraudulent by the buyer;

(4) a sale by auction may be notified to be subject to a reserved or upset price, and a right to bid may also be reserved expressly by or on behalf of the seller.

Where a right to bid is expressly reserved, but not otherwise, the seller, or any one person on his behalf, may bid at the auction."[124]

[6.54] When applied to auctions of land three issues arise from these rules: first, the enforceability of what appears to be an oral contract at the fall of the hammer; secondly, the rights flowing from an auction with or without a reserve; thirdly, the legality of the practice of bids by the vendor or dummy bidding.

[6.55] The difficulty of the lack of any written memorandum is overcome by the implied authority of the auctioneer. The auctioneer has authority to sign the contract concluded at the fall of the hammer on behalf of either the purchaser or the vendor. Commonly the auctioneer

121. *Re C.M. Group Pty Ltd's Caveat* [1986] 1 Qd R. 381; see note (1987) 61 A.L.J. 195.
122. (1876) 2 Ch. D. 499.
123. See generally Lang, *Estate Agency Law and Practice in New South Wales* (3rd ed., 1988), Chap. 13.
124. N.S.W.: *Sale of Goods Act* 1923, s. 60; Vic.: *Goods Act* 1958, s. 64; Qld: *Sale of Goods Act* 1896, s. 59; S.A.: *Sale of Goods Act* 1895, s. 57; W.A.: *Sale of Goods Act* 1895, s. 57; Tas.: *Sale of Goods Act* 1896, s. 62. See Sutton, *Sales and Consumer Law in Australia and New Zealand* (3rd ed., 1983), pp. 447-453.

will get the parties to sign themselves but if either party refuses to do so, the auctioneer has authority to sign on that person's behalf. Furthermore it is clear that the authority arises not on any part performance such as the payment of a deposit but on the fall of the hammer itself. In *Phillips v. Butler*[125] an auctioneer signed on behalf of the vendor and the purchaser signed in person. However the documents were not exchanged as it was agreed that the purchaser could post a cheque the following day in payment of the deposit. Before receipt of the cheque the vendor communicated to the auctioneer an instruction not to exchange contracts and not to receive the deposit. Romer J. held that the auctioneer had validly concluded an enforceable contract before the question of payment of the deposit arose and therefore any lack of authority to accept delayed payment was irrelevant to the existence of a contract. The court did refer to the qualification to the auctioneer's authority in that the auctioneer can only sign in connection with the auction but the precise time limits involved in this qualification were left open.

[6.56]   Queensland legislation states that: "a sale may be notified in the conditions of sale to be subject to a reserved or upset price."[126] This section does not seem to depart from the common law in that any auction may be subject to a reserve and the legislation does not appear to make the imposition of a reserve by way of notification in the conditions of sale mandatory. A mandatory means of announcement would be a change to the common law whereby any form of communication of a reserve is sufficient and any forms of words to the effect that there is a reserve is sufficient.[127] Once a reserve is announced any purported sale below that reserve is unenforceable against the vendor because of lack of authority and does not give rise to an action against the auctioneer for breach of warranty of authority as the existence of the reserve puts any prospective bidder on notice as to the auctioneer's lack of authority to sell for less.[128]

[6.57]   The position of an auction expressed to be without reserve is more difficult. It has been suggested that once such an auction has commenced, the auctioneer is liable in damages to the highest bidder if the auctioneer refuses to knock the property down to that bidder.[129] This suggestion is based on the theory that an auctioneer who puts a property up for sale without reserve makes an offer to sell to the highest bidder and the highest bidder accepts that offer by making the highest bid. On the other hand the suggestion faces some difficulties. The bid is only complete upon acceptance by the auctioneer and possibly upon the fall of the hammer and thus it can be argued that the offer to put the property up

---

125.   [1907] 2 K.B. 1. In Victoria s. 126 of the *Instruments Act* 1958 requires the appointment of an agent to be in writing so that the traditional analysis does not appear to apply in that State: see *Futuretronics International Pty Ltd v. Gadzhis* (Unreported, Vic. Sup. Ct, 1990).

126.   *Property Law Act* 1974 (Qld), s. 60(1)(b).

127.   *Torrance v. Bolton* (1872) L.R. 8 Ch. A. 118; see Butt, "Sale of Land by Auction in New South Wales" (1980) Law Soc. J. (N.S.W.) 720.

128.   *McManus v. Fortescue* [1907] 2 K.B. 1.

129.   *Warlow v. Harrison* (1859) 1 El. & El. 295 at 316; 120 E.R. 925 at 928; *Harris v. Nickerson* (1873) L.R. 8 Q.B. 286 at 288-289; *Johnston v. Boyes* [1899] 2 Ch. 73 at 77; Butt (1980), op. cit., pp. 721-722.

for sale can be withdrawn until that time. It is generally accepted that a
bidder can withdraw a bid before the fall of the hammer and this
argument concerns the reciprocal right of the auctioneer or vendor. But
in addition the question of the highest bid cannot be resolved without the
fall of the hammer. Until that time it is open to anyone else to make a
higher bid and so prior to the fall is it difficult to see how anyone can
establish that that person is the highest bidder.[130]

[6.58]   With respect to bids by the vendor, the statement in the *Sale of
Goods Act* represents a change to the common law. The position is best
summarised by Cooper J. in the New Zealand Supreme Court:[131]

> "At common law a sale by auction where the vendor had puffed the
> price by his own bidding was, unless the right to bid was reserved to
> him, a fraudulant sale, and could be avoided by the purchaser.
> Section 59 of subsection 3 (sic) of the *Sale of Goods Act* not only enables
> the purchaser to avoid the sale, but makes the bidding by the vendor
> unlawful."

Bidding by the vendor in relation to auctions of land is one practice which
has been subject to statutory regulation. However that regulation is not
universal and often does not spell out civil consequences. The common
law rules therefore remain important. Any undisclosed bidding by the
vendor means that the contract is voidable at the option of the purchaser.
It seems to follow that where bidding by the vendor exceeds what is
disclosed or what is authorised the contract is similarly voidable.
Furthermore it has been established that the reservation of the right to bid
does not mean that the auctioneer may pluck fictitious bids out of the air
in an attempt to create an atmosphere of competitive bidding;[132] again
such conduct renders the contract voidable.

In New South Wales, Queensland, Western Australia and Tasmania
statutory provisions[133] follow the *Sale of Goods Act* example to make
undisclosed bidding by the vendor unlawful. In Queensland the
consequence that the contract is regarded as fraudulent is also restated.
In all four States it is an offence to make unlawful bids or for the
auctioneer to receive them. In New South Wales and Western Australia
the terms of sale must reserve the right to make a specified number of
bids. In Queensland the terms of sale must reserve the right for the vendor
or any one person to bid. Subject to these additional requirements the
terms of sale must reserve the right for the vendor or persons acting on
behalf of the vendor to bid. Bidding not authorised by these provisions
would render any contract voidable at the option of the purchaser;
similarly in Victoria and South Australia as a result of common law
principles undisclosed bidding by the vendor renders any contract
voidable.

---

130. Slade, "Auction Sales of Goods Without Reserve" (1952) 68 L.Q.R. 238;
      (1953) 69 L.Q.R. 21.
131. *Christie v. Quaite* (1906) 26 N.Z.L.R. 495 at 496.
132. *Heatley v. Newton* (1881) 19 Ch. D. 326 at 327.
133. N.S.W.: *Auctioneers and Agents Act* 1941, s. 49; Qld: *Property Law Act* 1974, s. 60;
      W.A.: *Auction Sales Act* 1973, s. 29; Tas.: *Auctioneers and Estate Agents Act* 1959,
      s. 19.

[6.59] Auctions are conducted by an auctioneer. In all States except South Australia an auctioneer must have a licence.[134] Generally an applicant for a licence must be a person of good character and licences may be suspended or cancelled for illegal activity or failure to keep proper records. The licensing regime for auctioneers can be traced from an order issued by the Governor of the colony of New South Wales on 15 January 1801. This order imposed a duty of one half of one per cent on the proceeds of sale by auctions and prohibited persons from acting as auctioneers unless they were licensed. The good character of auctioneers has been a matter of concern from that time onwards. The licensing function has been entrusted to Magistrates Courts on the basis of the special knowledge of magistrates of the characters of local residents. The licensing systems have generally not been updated as part of the fair trading and consumer protection functions which have assumed significance in the past 20 years. The licensing regimes have included various rules as to the conduct of auctions such as prohibitions on auctions at night and given various powers, immunities and responsibilities to auctioneers. In South Australia the deregulation movement resulted in the repeal of the licensing system for agents from 1 April 1982.[135]

IX. STATUTORY REGULATION OF LAND SALES

1. Basis of Regulation

[6.60] The application of the *Statute of Frauds* has until recently been the only respect in which contracts for the sale of land required anything other than the application of the normal rules of contracts based on the concept of freedom of contract. Even the *Statute of Frauds* tended to create problems more for dealings in limited interests such as leases for a term of years rather than dealings involving fee simple interests which were not only set out in writing but expressed in detailed terms. In relation to contractual formation the issue to be resolved has tended to be the point at which the parties intended to be bound. Phrases such as "subject to contract" have been subject to extensive analysis.[136] The significant implied term in contracts for the sale of land was that of the vendor to make good title.[137] The construction of terms has presented difficulties and the courts have struggled with conditions such as those relating to finance and consent from government agencies.[138] One special damages rule was that which limited liability for failure to make good title;[139] this rule was developed because of the complexity of title under the general law and does not comfortably apply to the Torrens system.[140]

134. N.S.W.: *Auctioneers and Agents Act* 1941, s. 20; Vic.: *Auction Sales Act* 1958, s. 4; Qld: *Auctioneers and Agents Act* 1971, s. 14; W.A.: *Auction Sales Act* 1973, s. 6; Tas.: *Auctioneers and Estate Agents Act* 1959, s. 13.

135. *Appraisers Act and Auctioneers Act Repeal Act* 1980.

136. *Masters v. Cameron* (1954) 91 C.L.R. 353.

137. *Bell v. Scott* (1922) 30 C.L.R. 387; Voumard, pp. 347-350.

138. *Meehan v. Jones* (1982) 149 C.L.R. 571; *Perri v. Coolongatta Investments Pty Ltd* (1982) 149 C.L.R. 537; Cheshire and Fifoot, Chap. 22.

139. Voumard, pp. 467-473.

140. *Godfrey Constructions Pty Ltd v. Kanangra Park Pty Ltd* (1972) 128 C.L.R. 529.

The principle of freedom of contract has allowed the parties' scope to frame agreements as they see fit. Invariably practices develop amongst lawyers specialising in the conveyancing area and associated persons particularly real estate (or land) agents. In each State standard contracts of sale have been developed.[141] One significant divergence in practice has been the willingness of parties to sign a binding contract before reference to legal advisers. In New South Wales in particular it has been common for the parties to conclude an agreement subject to the preparation of formal documents by lawyers. Such an agreement does not create binding obligations and leaves the vendor free to accept a subsequent higher offer—a practice described as gazumping.[142] At the other end of the scale immediate entry into a binding agreement has been very common in South Australia (with consequent emphasis upon preperformance conditions) and land brokers have had a long established role in preparing all documents to enable title to be transferred.

Over the past 30 years—dating from the *Victorian Sale of Land Act* 1962—regulation of the contractual process has become extensive except in Western Australia and Tasmania. The legislation can be described as having four major points of concern. First although the common law implied an obligation that the vendor provide good title and registration under the Torrens system generally provided immunity from unregistered interests, purchasers found themselves subject to a range of unexpected burdens and obligations. The problem arose because government authorities availed themselves of the privilege to override the registered title in the imposition of a range of burdens on the land [143] and because the increasing controls on land use (such as the zoning requirements of planning laws) were not regarded as a matter relating to title.[144] Secondly, entry into a contract imposes marked responsibilities on ordinary home purchasers (on one view they all become petty capitalists, on another they exchange freedom for serfdom to the banks). The magnitude of these obligations may not be fully realised until subsequent reflection free from the blandishments of the real estate agent. Thirdly, the common law provided that risk passed on formation of the contract.[145] Any accidental loss thereafter must be borne by the purchaser. Insurance against such losses is today widespread and the passing of risk rule forces the purchaser to insure from the time of the contract whilst the vendor is unable to relinquish her or his insurance until performance of the contract is completed. Fourthly, completion of the contract involves the exchange of title for payment in full. Some time between contract and transfer of title is usually allowed to enable legal details to be attended to but in some cases the vendor is providing finance. It is possible for the vendor to accept a promise from the purchaser to pay by instalments over a number of years. Such a purchaser was vulnerable because the vendor's obligation

141. Butt, *The Standard Contract for Sale of Land in New South Wales* (1985); Duncan and Weld, *The Standard Land Contract in Queensland* (2nd ed., 1984).
142. Butt, "New Anti-Gazumping Laws in New South Wales" (1988) 62 A.L.J. 707.
143. *South-Eastern Drainage Board v. Savings Bank of Australia* (1939) 62 C.L.R. 603.
144. *Yammouni v. Condidono* [1959] V.R. 479; Voumard, pp. 410-413.
145. *Lysaght v. Edwards* (1876) 2 Ch. D. 499; *Fletcher v. Manton* (1940) 64 C.L.R. 37.

was to provide title only at the time of completion[146] and in the event of default the purchaser had little protection: see below [6.68].

2. Disclosure by the Vendor

[6.61]   In Victoria, New South Wales and South Australia a vendor of land is required to provide information about the land to the purchaser and if that information is not correct, the purchaser is given rights to rescind the contract. In Queensland the obligation on a vendor to provide good title is statutorily restated and remedies for breach given to the purchaser.

The matters to be disclosed in the three States requiring information disclosure cover aspects of title, planning controls, charges of government authorities and details of the vendor's insurance.[147] The relevant lists set out title information to be disclosed (including details of mortgages, easements and covenants), the form of description of planning controls and the inquiries of government agencies. The range of government authorities obviously reflects bureaucratic arrangements in each State but compliance with the disclosure requirements has necessitated a procedure for the obtaining of certificates from each of the authorities. This necessity has in turn helped to promote interest in a register not just of land title details but for all relevant data about each parcel of land.[148]

[6.62]   In Victoria and New South Wales the information must be provided before entry into a contract by the purchaser.[149] In South Australia the information must be provided at least ten days before settlement; cooling-off rights are related to the date on which information is provided.[150] If the information is inaccurate the purchaser is generally entitled to rescind up until acceptance of title but some qualifications to the right of rescission are imposed. In Victoria rescission may be denied if the court is satisfied both that the vendor has acted honestly and reasonably and ought fairly to be excused for the contravention and secondly that the purchaser is substantially in as good a position as if all the requirements had been met[151] In New South Wales the vendor is taken to provide warranties as to the accuracy of the information provided and the purchaser is given a right to rescind for breach of warranty.[152] In South Australia the remedy is at the discretion of the court which may award damages by way of compensation or avoid the contract as it sees fit.[153]

146.   *Rands Development Co. Ltd v. Davis* (1975) 133 C.L.R. 26; *Mitchell v. Colgan* [1922] V.L.R. 372; *Miller v. Kavanagh* [1932] V.L.R. 391.
147.   N.S.W.: *Conveyancing Act* 1919, s. 52A; *Conveyancing (Vendor Disclosure and Warranty) Regulation* 1986, reg. 4(1); Vic.: *Sale of Land Act* 1962, s. 32(2); S.A.: *Land Agents, Brokers and Valuers Act* 1973, s. 90(1).
148.   Lang, "Computerised Land Title and Land Information" (1984) 10 Mon. U.L.R. 196.
149.   Vic.: *Sale of Land Act* 1962, s. 32(1); N.S.W.: *Conveyancing Act* 1919, s. 52(1).
150.   S.A.: *Land Agents, Brokers and Valuers Act* 1973, s. 90(1).
151.   Vic.: *Sale of Land Act* 1962, s. 32(5) and (7).
152.   N.S.W.: *Conveyancing (Vendor Disclosure and Warranty) Regulation* 1986, reg. 5.
153.   S.A.: *Land Agents, Brokers and Valuers Act* 1973, s. 90(6), (7).

The Queensland provisions relate much more to details of the vendor's common law duty to provide good title. They cover the provision by the vendor of particulars of title, payment by bank cheque and substitution for performance due on a Saturday, Sunday or public holiday.[154] Any qualification to liability for failure by the vendor to make good title is removed by the imposition of liability for all damages reasonably foreseeable and the loss liable to result.[155]

3. Cooling-Off Rights

[6.63] A purchaser of land is given an opportunity to reconsider her or his position in Victoria, New South Wales and South Australia. In Victoria and South Australia this opportunity flows from direct cooling-off rights. In New South Wales conferral of a right to reconsider is made part of a process to prevent the vendor from exploiting the non-binding nature of an agreement "subject to contract". Consequently a system of preliminary and later agreements has been introduced.

In Victoria after a purchaser signs a contract for the sale of land that purchaser may give notice at any time before the expiration of three clear business days that he or she wishes to terminate the contract.[156] In South Australia the period is two days but because information disclosure may take place after the contract and as late as ten days before settlement time runs from the day of provision of information.[157] The exercise of the cooling-off rights frees the purchaser from all liability except loss of a preliminary deposit which is a small amount of $50 to $100 or as prescribed.[158] There is a monetary limit on the contracts to which the Victorian rights apply (originally $125,000).[159] The cooling-off rights are excluded in a range of situations the most significant being sales at auction and cases where the purchaser has received independent legal advice before signing the contract.[160]

[6.64] The New South Wales system[161] of preliminary agreements applies to sale of residential property[162] subject to various prescribed exceptions one of which is sales at auction.[163] The system requires the entry into a preliminary agreement which must be in a prescribed form and which must have attached to it the proposed contract (the later agreement which binds both parties).[164] Again the purchaser's only liability on signing this agreement is with respect to a preliminary deposit.[165] Once a preliminary agreement has been made the purchaser has a choice either to do nothing or to enter a later agreement. The vendor

154. Qld: *Property Law Act* 1974, s. 61. The right to refuse to compete, see *Foran v. Wright* (1990) 64 A.L.J.R. 1.
155. S. 68.
156. Vic.: *Sale of Land Act* 1962, s. 31(1); *Lebdeh v. Smith* [1985] V.R. 807.
157. S.A.: *Land Agents, Brokers and Valuers Act* 1973, s. 88(1).
158. Vic.: s. 31(4); S.A.: s. 88(1b).
159. Vic.: s. 31(2).
160. Vic.: s. 31(5); S.A.: s. 88(4).
161. See generally Butt (1988), op. cit.
162. N.S.W.: *Conveyancing Act* 1919, s. 66X.
163. S. 66X(4).
164. S. 66Q.
165. S. 66W(1)(e).

however must provide to the purchaser before the end of five days from the preliminary agreement, a contract in the form of the proposed contract with details of the purchaser and the price added.[166] The purchaser has five days from service of the later agreement in which to execute that agreement; if the purchaser does so the vendor must also execute the later agreement on the following business day.[167] The vendor has five days from the preliminary agreement to serve a later agreement but may do immediately or nearly so; if the later agreement is concluded within two days of the preliminary agreement the purchaser may withdraw up to five days from the preliminary agreement.[168] The vendor however is under a liability from the time of the preliminary agreement and must provide the purchaser with the opportunity of entering a later agreement. Breach of the preliminary agreement by the vendor leaves the vendor open to an action for specific performance or damages to enforce the proposed agreement.[169]

4. Passing of Risk

[6.65]   The time at which risk passes to the purchaser is a matter for the parties to stipulate in the sale contract. The common law only provides that risk prima facie passes at the time of the contract. In fact in Western Australia both the Real Estate Institute and the Law Society contracts have provided that risk will remain with the vendor until completion. The rules as to passing of risk have been modified in New South Wales. The impact of passing of risk is that any accidental loss falls on the purchaser but this consequence has been modified in Victoria and Queensland where the loss involves the destruction of a dwelling-house. The impact of loss is affected by insurance and national legislation and legislation in Victoria and Queensland gives the purchaser the benefit of insurance cover held by the vendor.

New South Wales legislation has postponed the passing of risk to the purchaser. Risk is not to pass until completion of the sale or an earlier time stipulated by the parties but only if that earlier time is one by which the purchaser has become entitled to possession.[170] This rule cannot be varied in the case of the sale of a dwelling-house.[171] If before risk passes to the purchaser the land is substantially damaged the purchaser has at least 28 days from becoming aware of the damage in which to rescind the contract.[172] If before risk passes to the purchaser the land is damaged (whether or not that damage is substantial) the purchase price is reduced by the amount which is just and equitable.[173] If before risk passes to the purchaser the land is substantially damaged the vendor may be relieved

---

166. S. 66w(1)(d).
167. S. 66w(1)(g).
168. S. 66R(2).
169. S. 66s.
170. S. 66K.
171. S. 66o.
172. S. 66L.
173. S. 66M.

from performance where it would be unjust or inequitable to require performance.[174]

[6.66]   In Victoria and Queensland the passing of risk remains a matter to be determined by the parties but limited rights of rescission are given to the purchaser in the case of accidental loss. The rights exist in relation to contracts for the sale of land on which there is a dwelling-house and the dwelling-house is destroyed or damaged so as to be unfit for occuptation before the purchaser becomes entitled to possession. In that event the purchaser may rescind in Victoria within 14 days of becoming aware of the damage[175] and in Queensland not later than the date for completion or taking possession.[176]

[6.67]   Whilst an insurance policy held by the vendor may provide cover against accidental loss that policy is one between the vendor and the insurance company. On traditional analysis the policy can only be enforced by the vendor and the vendor may be unable to establish any loss if the purchaser can be forced to complete the contract. The *Commonwealth Insurance Contracts Act* 1984 gives the purchaser rights under the vendor's insurance policy. Where a purchaser agrees to purchase a building which the purchaser will have a right to occupy, the purchaser is deemed to be insured under the vendor's insurance policy for loss or damage to the building in respect of which the risk passed to the purchaser.[177] This right exists only in relation to such insurance cover as the vendor has. Similar rights to the benefit of the vendor's insurance cover have been given to purchasers of land generally by legislation in Victoria and Queensland.[178]

5. Terms Contracts

[6.68]   Where the purchase price under a contract for the sale of land is to be provided by instalments over a period of time completion may be delayed until all instalments have been met. During that period the purchaser has equitable rights, is not entitled to call upon the vendor to show title until the time of completion and may be adversely affected by a subsequent dealing by the vendor particularly the grant of a mortgage. In South Australia the vulnerability of the purchaser's position has led to a prohibition upon instalment contracts for the sale of land.[179] Any vendor providing finance and wishing to have a legal proprietary interest in the land must therefore take a mortgage back from the purchaser.

Translation from a purchaser under a terms contract to a fee simple owner subject to a mortgage to the vendor is not compulsory in Victoria[180] New South Wales[181] and Queensland[182] but may be insisted upon by the

---

174.   S. 66N.
175.   Vic.: *Sale of Land Act* 1962, s. 34.
176.   Qld: *Property Law Act* 1974, s. 64.
177.   *Insurance Contracts Act* 1984 (Cth), s. 50.
178.   Vic.: *Sale of Land Act* 1962, s. 35; Qld: *Property Law Act* 1974, s. 63.
179.   S.A.: *Land Agents, Brokers and Valuers Act* 1973, s. 89.
180.   Vic.: *Sale of Land Act* 1962, s. 4.
181.   N.S.W.: *Land Sales Act* 1964, s. 13.
182.   Qld: *Property Law Act* 1974, s. 75.

purchaser. In New South Wales the right to call for a transfer subject to a mortgage back for the unpaid purchase price is limited to a purchaser who has paid 15 per cent of the price; in Queensland it is limited to a purchaser who has paid one third of the price. In Victoria[183] and Queensland[184] a vendor who has entered a terms contract may not grant a mortgage over the land; in New South Wales[185] a vendor must give notice of any proposed mortgage or charge over the land. In Western Australia where there is no right to call for a transfer subject to a mortgage, the vendor may not grant a mortgage without the consent of the purchaser or leave of the court.[186]

[6.69]   So long as a terms contract continues, the right of the vendor to terminate for breach by the purchaser (commonly failure to pay the instalments due) depends on the terms of the contract and subject to the power of the court to grant relief against forfeiture.[187] In Queensland and Western Australia the vendor must give written notice of breach before exercising the right to terminate.[188]

---

183. Vic.: s. 7.
184. Qld: s. 73; see *Coast Securities No. 9 Pty Ltd v. Bondoukou* (1986) 69 A.L.R. 385.
185. N.S.W.: s. 14.
186. W.A.: *Sale of Land Act* 1974, s. 8.
187. *Legione v. Hateley* (1983) 152 C.L.R. 406; *Stern v. McArthur* (1988) 81 A.L.R. 463.
188. Qld: *Property Law Act* 1974, s. 72; W.A.: *Sale of Land Act* 1974, s. 6.

7

Future Interests

I. INTRODUCTION

[7.01] The concept of estates and the various estates developed under the feudal systems of land tenure and recognised at common law have been discussed in the preceding Chapter. Each one of these estates may be created so as either to grant the holder of the estate an immediate right to physical possession of the land or to withold the right of possession until some event has occurred or a possessory estate has expired. All corporeal rights in land which do not give the holder the right of immediate possession are said to be "future interests". A future interest in land has been described as "an interest which confers a right to enjoyment of the land at some future time, in that it follows on the expiry or termination of a present but limited interest".[1]

Various complex and rigid rules were developed at common law governing the validity and enforceability of future interests. As will be shown in this Chapter, the stubbornness and unreasonable attitude of the common law was responsible for the intervention of equity in this area of law and the enactment of landmark legislation in the *Statute of Uses* 1535 and the *Statute of Wills* 1540. Although these developments all occurred in the United Kingdom long before the first white settlement in Australia, an understanding of this historical background is necessary in order to appreciate the development of real property law in this country. It will be seen that certain aspects of the common law and equitable rules concerning future interests still apply in some States. An understanding of future interests is also an essential prerequisite to the modern law of perpetuities, discussed in the next Chapter.

II. POSSESSION, REVERSION AND REMAINDER

All freehold estates may be held in possession, in reversion or in remainder.[2]

1. Possession

[7.02] An estate in possession by its very nature entitles the holder to immediate possession and is accordingly classified as a present rather than

---

1. Woodman, p. 68.
2. Blackstone, *Commentaries*, Bk II, p. 163.

a future interest. A gift "to A for life, remainder to B" will give A a life estate in possession. Possessory estates must be contrasted with reversions and remainders, both of which class as future interests.

2. Reversion

[7.03] A reversion arises by operation of law rather than by express grant. It arises whenever the holder of a freehold estate grants a lesser estate to a third party and thus does not dispose of his entire interest in the property.[3] For example, if A, the fee simple owner, makes a gift "to B for life", A will automatically retain the fee simple estate in reversion. A is commonly described as "the reversioner". Accordingly, on B's death the possessory right will automatically revert to A. The situation is unaltered if A should predecease B; in this event, the possessory right will revert to A's legal personal representative. We can contrast the situation of a gift by A, the fee simple owner, "to B and his heirs". In this case, by giving B the fee simple estate, A has disposed of his entire estate and no reversion exists. The same rules have been said to operate in respect of equitable as well as legal freehold estates.[4]

A different analysis applies if the fee simple owner conveys a leasehold rather than freehold estate. If A, the fee simple owner, grants to B a term of years, A will not be said to have the fee simple estate in reversion, but rather to have the fee simple estate in possession subject to the term. The reason for this is that the grant of seisin determines whether an estate is held in possession, reversion or remainder, and leasehold estates were not recognised as affecting seisin under the feudal system of land tenure.[5] In the above illustration, A is often said to have a leasehold reversion, but this does not class as a future interest.

3. Remainder

[7.04] A remainder occurs in respect of a gift designed to take effect on the natural termination of an earlier freehold estate.[6] Thus, in a gift by A "to B for life, then to C and her heirs", C will receive a fee simple estate in remainder. The estate will continue in remainder until B's death, whereupon it will vest in possession by operation of law. B will receive a life estate in possession and A will have nothing. If C should predecease B, the remainder estate will automatically vest in C's legal personal representative.

There is no limit to the number of remainders that can be created. Thus A could make a gift "to B for life, then to C for life, then to D for life, then to E". In this case, C and D would each have a life estate in remainder and E would have a fee simple in remainder. C, D and E are commonly called "remaindermen". As with reversions, the same rules have been said to apply to equitable estates as well as legal estates.[7]

---

3. See Co. Litt., 142b.
4. Woodman, p. 69.
5. See *Wakefield and Barnsley Union Bank Ltd v. Yates* [1916] 1 Ch. 452 (C.A.); *De Gray v. Richardson* (1747) 3 Atk. 469; 26 E.R. 1069 (Ch.).
6. See Cheshire and Burn, p. 288.
7. Woodman, p. 70.

There are four major restrictions on remainders.

1. Both the prior lesser estate in possession on which the remainder is expectant (sometimes called the "prior particular estate") and the remainder must be created in the same instrument.[8]

2. Because of the notion of seisin (see above [7.03]), the prior particular estate must be a freehold rather than a leasehold estate. Thus, a gift "to B for a term of years, then to C" will give C an estate in possession rather than in remainder.

3. No remainder can exist which is expectant upon a fee simple estate.[9] A gift "to B and his heirs, then to C and his heirs" will give B a fee simple estate in possession and C nothing. The reason is that if B receives a fee simple estate, which is the greatest possible estate, there is nothing left for C to receive. This rule is not restricted to fees simple absolute, but also applies to determinable fees simple and fees simple subsequent to a condition subsequent. The rights expectant upon these estates (a possibility of reverter and a right of entry, respectively) are sui generis and are not classed as either remainders or reversions.[10]

4. As mentioned above, a remainder must be designed to take effect upon the natural termination of an earlier freehold estate. Thus, a gift "to B for life, then one year after B's death, to C", or "to B, but if she remarries then to C" would not classify as reminders. As will be shown later, in both illustrations C would be regarded as having an "executory interest".

III. VESTED AND CONTINGENT INTERESTS

[7.05]   In addition to classifying estates as being in possession, reversion or remainder, it is also necessary to determine in each case whether they are vested or contingent. The major reason why this additional classification is essential is that the rule against perpetuities (discussed in Chapter 8) is based upon this distinction and specifically employs the concept of "vesting". A further reason is that the common law legal remainder rules required a remainder to vest within a particular period of time or else it was treated as void, although, as explained (see below [7.17]ff.), this situation is now remedied by State legislation.

Stated simply, a vested interest is one that is bound to take effect in possession at some future date, while a contingent interest may never fall into possession.[11] If the answer to the question, "Is there anything preventing the estate in question from falling into possession other than the death of the holder or holders of one or more earlier life interests?" is "No", the estate in question is vested; if the answer is "Yes", the estate is contingent. The test is sometimes put as follows: an interest is vested

---

8. Co. Litt., 49a, 143a; Challis, *The Law of Real Property* (3rd ed., by Sweet, 1911), pp. 77-79.
9. Blackstone, *Commentaries*, Bk II, p. 164.
10. See Megarry and Wade, p. 237. For determinable fees simple and fees simple subject to a condition subsequent, see above [2.41]ff.
11. See Blackstone, *Commentaries*, Bk II, p. 169.

provided that the identity of the persons taking the interest is known and provided that there is no condition precedent to the interest falling into possession other than the regular determination of the prior particular estate or estates.[12]

Some illustrations may assist comprehension. If A makes a gift "to B for life, then to C", the gift to C is vested as it is bound to fall into possession on B's death. Conversely, if A makes a gift "to my first-born child", the gift will be contingent if at the date of execution he has no children, but it will be vested if at that time he has one or more children. A gift "to B for life, then to C if she should survive B" will give C a contingent interest (provided that at the date of execution B is still alive) as C has to fulfil the condition precedent of outliving B before she is entitled to take the fee simple estate. If she fails to outlive B, the fee simple estate will revert to A on B's death. A gift "to B if he should graduate in law at Melbourne University" will also be a contingent rather than a vested interest as there is a condition precedent (viz. graduating in law) still to be satisfied.

[7.06] A contingent interest will become vested by operation of law on the satisfaction of the condition precedent. Thus, a gift "to my first-born child" will automatically vest as soon as the donor produces her or his first child. A gift "to B for life, then to C if C should outlive B" will vest in C if she is still alive at B's death, and a gift "to B if he should graduate in law at Melbourne University" will also vest as soon as B actually graduates.

Conditions precedent must be carefully distinguished from conditions subsequent. A gift "to B on condition that she moves to New South Wales", would give B a contingent interest which would become vested as soon as B satisfies the condition precedent of moving to New South Wales. Conversely, a gift "to B on condition that she does not move out of New South Wales" would give B a vested fee simple subject to later divestment if she should ever move out of New South Wales. Thus, the rule is simple: all gifts subject to conditions precedent are contingent, and all gifts subject to conditions subsequent are vested.

Sometimes the wording of the grant is ambiguous. Here, the court will try to establish the intention of the donor and in cases of genuine doubt will lean in favour of deeming the gift to be vested.[13] An interesting illustration is *Permanent Trustee Co. of New South Wales Ltd v. D'Apice*.[14] In this case, the court had to interpret a will "to B for life, and after the decease of the said B, to C in fee simple", where C predeceased B. The words "after the decease of" could have been construed as requiring C to outlive B before C's remainder could fall into possession; this interpretation would make the remainder contingent. Alternatively, the words could be construed as mere surplusage and the gift could be

12. See Sackville and Neave, p. 166; Woodman, p. 71; Megarry and Wade, pp. 231-232; *Pearson v. I.R.C.* [1981] A.C. 753 at 772 (H.L.), per Viscount Dilhorne.
13. *Duffield v. Duffield* (1829) 2 Bl. N.S. 260 at 331; 4 E.R. 1334 at 1358 (H.L.), per Best C.J.
14. (1968) 118 C.L.R. 105.

construed as in effect "to B for life, then to C"; this interpretation would make the gift vested. The majority of the Full Court of the High Court adopted the latter interpretation and held that the person entitled to the estate on B's death was the devisee under C's will.

Merely because a gift is couched in the form of a condition precedent does not mean that it will be construed as contingent if in reality there is no condition to be fulfilled. The courts are not blinded by the terminology that the donor adopts in his gift, but will examine the true effect of the instrument.[15] A gift "to B for life, but if B should die, then to C" appears at first glance to give C a contingent, rather than a vested, remainder, but in reality it would be held to be a vested remainder as C's estate is bound to take effect in possession on B's death. Conversely, a gift "to B (a bachelor) for life, then to the first-born child of B, then to C" appears to give C a vested remainder, but in reality would be held to be a contingent remainder as C's estate is subject to the implied condition precedent that C will only take the fee simple in possession if B remains childless throughout his life.

[7.07] Three other propositions may be deduced from the authorities.

1. All reversionary estates are vested.[16]

2. A gift which follows a contingent fee simple is itself contingent.[17]

3. A gift which follows a determinable fee simple or fee simple subject to a condition subsequent is always contingent.[18] These propositions are illustrations of the basic distinction between vested and contingent interests, explained above.

It is possible for estates to be vested, but subject to divestment. The classic illustration of this is a gift "to B for life, then to all of his children who shall attain the age of majority". If at the date of execution B either has no children or has children, but only under age of 18, the remainder is contingent. As soon as the eldest child reaches 18 the remainder vests solely in him, but the eldest child will be partially divested each time a younger child reaches 18. Thus, when the second child reaches 18, the eldest child is divested of half his share and the estate is vested in both of them in equal shares. When the third child reaches 18, each of the older children are partially divested so that all three hold a vested interest in a one third share.[19]

Occasionally, the divestment may be total. In *Re Master's Settlement*,[20] a sum of money was settled "upon trust for C for life, and after her death, upon trust for M for life, or until he should become bankrupt, and subject

---

15. See e.g. *Smith d. Dormer v. Packhurst* (1740) 3 Atk. 135; 26 E.R. 881 (Ch.); *Maddison v. Chapman* (1858) 4 K. & J. 709; 70 E.R. 294 (V.-C.) (affd (1859) 3 De G. & J. 536; 44 E.R. 1375).
16. Challis, p. 67.
17. *Luddington v. Kime* (1697) 1 Ld. Raym. 203; 91 E.R. 1031 (K.B.).
18. Gray, *Perpetuities* (4th ed., 1942), s. 114, n. 3.
19. See e.g. *Baldwin v. Rogers* (1853) 3 De G.M. & G. 649; 43 E.R. 255 (Ch.); *Brackenbury v. Gibbons* (1876) 2 Ch. D. 417; *Re Lechmere and Lloyd* (1881) 18 Ch. D. 524.
20. [1911] 1 Ch. 321. See also *Cunningham v. Moody* (1748) 1 Ves. Sen. 174; 27 E.R. 965 (Ch.); *Lambert v. Thwaites* (1866) L.R. 2 Eq. 151.

as aforesaid the trustees are to stand possessed of the said sum and the income thereof in trust for the children or other issue of the intended marriage, as the spouses should by deed jointly, or as the survivor should by deed or will, direct or appoint, and in default of appointment for all the children of the marriage who, being sons, should attain 21, or, being daughters, should attain that age or marry, in equal shares". Eve J. held that the children's interests in the settled fund were vested interests subject to divestment by the exercise of the power of appointment.

IV. REMAINDERS AT COMMON LAW

1. Legal Remainder Rules

[7.08]   In the 16th century the common law developed very rigid rules (usually referred to as the "legal remainder rules") concerning the enforceability of remainders.[21] The major reason for these rules was the need to preserve the continuity of seisin. This was considered essential for two major reasons: first, to ensure that some person remained seised of the land at all times so that feudal incidents of tenure would always be payable;[22] and secondly, to ensure that an owner dispossessed of land could always bring an action for recovery, which could only lie against a freeholder. A further factor was the refusal of common law to permit a grantor to alter the duration or extent of earlier interests by successively adding future interests.[23]

Stated briefly, the legal remainder rules were as follows.

1. Any remainder limited after a fee simple estate (including determinable and conditional fees simple) was void.[24]

2. Any remainder designed to vest in possession before the natural determination of the prior particular estate was void.[25] An illustration of this is a gift by A "to B for life, but if she remarries, then to C". Such a gift to C was void as an illegal attempt to cut short B's life estate. B would retain the life estate in possession and A would have the fee simple in reversion. The remainder would have been valid if the grantor had phrased the gift so as to make the prior particular estate determinable, such as "to B for life or until remarriage, then to C".[26]

3. A remainder was void unless it followed a prior particular estate created by the same instrument.[27] An illustration is a gift by A "to B and his heirs effective one year after the date of execution of this instrument". This gift was void and A retained the fee simple in possession.

21. See *Colthurst v. Bejushin* (1550) 1 Plow. 23; 75 E.R. 36 (K.B.).
22. *Freeman d. Vernon v. West* (1763) 2 Wils. K.B. 165; 95 E.R. 745.
23. For a discussion of the origin of the rules, see Sackville and Neave, pp. 168-169.
24. *Duke of Norfolk's Case* (1681) 3 Ch. Ca. 1 at 31; 22 E.R. 931 at 949-950 (Ch.); *Earl of Stafford v. Buckley* (1750) 2 Ves. Sen. 170; 28 E.R. 111 (Ch.).
25. *Blackman v. Fysh* [1892] 2 Ch. 209 (C.A.).
26. *Rochford v. Hackman* (1852) 9 Hare 475; 68 E.R. 597 (V.-C.); *Brandon v. Robinson* (1811) 18 Ves. Jun. 429; 34 E.R. 379 (Ch.).
27. *Goodlittle d. Dodwell v. Gibbs* (1826) 5 B. & C. 709; 108 E.R. 264 (K.B.); *Boddington v. Robinson* (1875) L.R. 10 Ex. 270; *Barwick's Case* (1597) 5 Co. Rep. 93b; 77 E.R. 199 (K.B.). Way C.J. held in *Re Campion* [1908] S.A.L.R. 1 that the rule that

4. There could never be an abeyance of seisin.[28] The remainder in a gift by A "to B for life, remainder to such of B's children who graduate in law after B's death" was void at common law as there was bound to be an abeyance of seisin. The life estate to B was regarded as valid, and A would be held to have a fee simple in reversion. This gift should be contrasted with one "to B for life, remainder to such of B's children who have graduated in law by the time of B's death". In this gift, there may or may not be an abeyance of seisin depending on whether any of B's children graduate prior to B's death. Where such uncertainty existed, the common law took a "wait-and-see" approach in determining whether the remainder was valid or void.

2. The Rule in Shelley's Case

[7.09] Another anomolous common law rule affecting remainders was the rule in *Shelley's Case*,[29] which applied to both deeds and wills. The rule is stated in the original text as follows:[30]

> "It is a rule in law, when the ancestor by any gift or conveyance[31] takes an estate of freehold,[32] and in the same gift or conveyance an estate is limited either mediately or immediately to his heirs in fee or in tail; that always in such cases, "the heirs" are words of limitation of the estate, and not words of purchase."

The classic illustration of the rule is a gift by A "to B for life, then to heirs of B".[33] The effect of *Shelley's Case* is that the gift is construed as bestowing a fee simple estate in possession on B and giving B's heirs nothing, regardless of the obvious intention of the donor to benefit the heirs. Another illustration is the facts in *Hordern v. Permanent Trustee Co.*,[34] where Owen C.J. in Eq. of the New South Wales Supreme Court held that a limitation "to B for life and the heirs of her body" gives B a fee tail. On many occasions the courts emphasised that the rule is one of law, not one of construction,[35] and thus would override even the clearest statement of intention to the contrary.[36]

---

27. *Continued.*
    contingent remainders must have a prior particular estate to support them does not apply to Torrens land which by virtue of the provisions of the *Real Property Act* 1886 (S.A.) becomes vested upon the death of the registered proprietor in his executors or administrators.
28. For illustrations of the operation of this rule, see *Miles v. Jarvis* (1883) 24 Ch. D. 633; *Dean v. Dean* [1891] 3 Ch. 150; *White v. Summers* [1908] 2 Ch. 256.
29. (1581) 1 Co. Rep. 93b; 76 E.R. 206 (K.B.).
30. Ibid. at 104a; at 234.
31. The rule also applies to devises: see e.g. *Hayes d. Foorde v. Foorde* (1770) 2 Bl. W. 698; 96 E.R. 410 (K.B.).
32. The rule did not apply when the ancestor held only a leasehold estate: *Harris v. Barnes* (1768) 4 Burr. 2157; 98 E.R. 125 (K.B.).
33. For reported illustrations of the rule, see e.g. *Sheppard v. Gibbons* (1742) 2 Atk. 441; 26 E.R. 666 (Ch.); *Ambrose v. Hodgson* (1781) 3 Bro. P.C. 416; 1 E.R. 1405 (H.L.); *Van Grutten v. Foxwell* [1897] A.C. 658 (H.L.).
34. (1894) 10 W.N. (N.S.W.) 190.
35. See e.g. *Roddy v. Fitzgerald* (1858) 6 H.L.C. 823; 10 E.R. 1518 (H.L.).
36. *Van Grutten v. Foxwell* [1897] A.C. 658 at 662 (H.L.), per Lord Herschell.

The rule was also held to apply where an intermediate freehold estate was interposed between a purported life estate to a person and a remainder to that person's heirs.[37] An illustration is "to B for life, then to C for life, then to the heirs of B". In this situation, B would receive a life estate in possession and a fee simple in remainder, while her heirs would again receive nothing. C's life estate in remainder was unaffected, but subject to this B was free to alienate her future interest.

The justifications for this anomolous rule have been variously stated, and were examined by Lord Macnaghten in *Van Grutten v. Foxwell*.[38] According to his Lordship, one argument is that the rule was designed to protect the property from abeyance of seisin with its subsequent loss of the incidents of feudal tenure. Other justifications are that the rule was designed to facilitate the alienation of property and the ancestor's debts, and that its object was to exclude the possibility of creating "an amphibious species of inheritance", designed to introduce confusion into the legal system.

Although the rule applied to both deeds and wills, it did not apply equally. In the case of deeds, the rule only applied where the words "heirs" or "heirs of his body" were included,[39] and would not apply where "heir" or "heir of his body" was used as the latter words did not constitute common law words of limitation.[40] In the case of wills, words of limitation were not necessary at common law; accordingly, the rule applied regardless of whether "heir" or "heirs" was used.[41]

It was held by McLelland C.J. in Eq. of the Supreme Court of New South Wales in *Mabey v. Ramsey*[42] that although the rule is capable of applying to equitable estates as well as legal estates, it does not apply where one limitation is legal and the other equitable. His Honour accordingly refused to apply the rule where on the facts he interpreted the prior life estate to be equitable and the subsequent remainder to be legal. As a matter of principle this is a curious decision as there is no logical reason for the distinction. As argued by Sackville and Neave, however, the decision should be viewed as a pragmatic one designed to avoid the application of the rule whenever possible.[43]

3. Destructibility of Legal Contingent Remainders

[7.10] Even if contingent remainders managed to avoid the operation of the legal remainder rules, they were still liable to destruction. Common

---

37. See *Ambrose v. Hodgson* (1781) 3 Bro. P.C. 416; 1 E.R. 1405 (H.L.).
38. [1897] A.C. 658 at 668ff. See also Hargreaves, "Shelley's Ghost" (1938) 54 L.Q.R. 70.
39. *Waker v. Snowe* (1621) Palm. 359; 81 E.R. 1123 (K.B.).
40. See above **[2.32]**ff. for a discussion of the common law rules relating to words of purchase and words of limitation.
41. See *Van Grutten v. Foxwell* [1897] A.C. 658 (H.L.); *Re Routledge* [1942] Ch. 457.
42. [1963] N.S.W.R. 599. See also *Re Fergusson* (1882) 3 L.R. (N.S.W.) 43.
43. Sackville and Neave, p. 159. *Shelley's Case* was also held not to be applicable in *Re Barber* (1937) 37 S R. (N.S.W.) 470 and *Goodwin v. Baylis* (1875) 13 S.C.R. (N.S.W.) Eq. 27; cf. *Andrew v. Morgan* (1923) 19 Tas. L.R. 36. There are a number of Australian cases where the application of the rule appears to have been overlooked: see e.g. *Bouel v. Cooktown Municipality* (1885) 2 Q.L.J. 93.

law classified the methods of destruction under two heads: natural destruction and artificial destruction.

Natural destruction occurred when the prior particular estate determined naturally before the contingent remainder vested. Where this occurred, the contingent remainder was held to be void.[44] Thus, for example, in a gift "to B for life, and then to C if C should move to New South Wales", if B died before C moved to New South Wales, the remainder to C was void and C could not revive it by moving at a later date.[45] The only exception recognised by common law to the operation of the natural destruction rule was that a gift to an unborn child would be saved if the child was en ventre sa mere at the time of the determination of the prior particular estate.[46]

Destruction of a contingent remainder would also occur when the prior particular estate was determined artificially prior to the vesting of the remainder. The common law methods of artificial destruction were surrender, merger, forfeiture and disclaimer. Surrender occurred when the holder of the prior particular estate surrendered her or his interest to a person with a vested remainder. This would nullify any intermediate contingent remainders.[47] Thus, in a gift "to B for life, then to C for life if she should move to New South Wales, then to D", B could at any time convey her life estate to D and by doing so automatically destroy C's interest. The same result would ensue by merger of the prior particular estate with a vested remainder. An illustration of this is the rule in *Purefoy v. Rogers*[48]: see below [7.12]. Forfeiture would occur when the holder of the prior particular estate purported to convey her or his life estate to a third party; this event was referred to as a "tortious conveyance" and had the effect of destroying any contingent remainder.[49] At common law, the contingent remainderman was powerless to prevent such a forfeiture. The final method of artificial destruction, disclaimer, would arise whenever the holder of the prior particular estate disclaimed her or his interest, which could occur at any time.[50]

The rules relating to artificial destruction were later circumvented in the 17th century by the use of a trust to preserve the contingent remainder. As explained by Sackville and Neave,[51] in a gift "to A for life, provided that if A's estate should be determined by forfeiture or otherwise

44. This is based on the rule that there cannot be an abeyance of seisin: see above [7.08]. See also Preston, *An Elementary Treatise on Estates* (2nd ed., Vol. 1), pp. 217, 249.
45. For reported illustrations, see e.g. *Doe d. Mussell v. Morgan* (1790) 3 Term. Rep. 763; 100 E.R. 846 (K.B.); *Fuller v. Chamier* (1866) L.R. 2 Eq. 682.
46. Statute 10 Will. 3 c. 22 (1698) (deeds); *Reeve v. Long* (1695) 1 Salk. 227; 91 E.R. 202 (K.B.) (wills).
47. Challis, op. cit., p. 136.
48. (1671) 2 Wms. Saund. 380; 85 E.R. 1181 (K.B.). See also *Egerton v. Massey* (1857) 3 C.B. (N.S.) 338; 140 E.R. 771 (C.P.).
49. See e.g. *Chudleigh's Case* (1595) 1 Co. Rep. 113b; 76 E.R. 261 (K.B.); *Archer's Case* (1597) 1 Co. Rep. 66b; 76 E.R. 146 (K.B.).
50. See e.g. *Re Sir Walter Scott* [1911] 2 Ch. 374.
51. Sackville and Neave, p. 172. See also Holdsworth, *A History of English Law*, (1925), Vol. VII, p. 112.

in his lifetime remainder to T and his heirs during the life of A in trust
for A and to preserve the contingent remainder next following, remainder
to A's first son to attain 21 and his heirs'', the remainder to the trustee,
T, could not be destroyed by the artificial destruction of A's life estate as
the remainder was held to be vested rather than contingent.[52] If A's estate
were destroyed, T was said to have a life estate pur autre vie held in trust
for A, and on A's death his first son would acquire the estate if his interest
had meanwhile become vested. This system of circumventing the
destructibility rules had no application to cases of natural destruction,
however, and contingent remainders remained liable to destruction in this
manner until the later intervention of legislation: see below [7.19].

V. THE ROLE OF EQUITY[53]

1. The Law Prior to 1535

[7.11]   It should not be thought that the role of equity was limited to
preserving contingent remainders from artificial destruction. As will be
shown, this was merely one illustration of the chancellor's dissatisfaction
with the operation of the common law rules regarding future interests.

Because of the unyielding approach of the common law to its legal
remainder rules, persons were deprived of interests which donors had
intended them to receive. Many of these persons petitioned the chancellor
for a remedy. The chancellor devised a system of uses whereby interests
could be created as valid in equity which would have been regarded as
invalid at common law. The device of uses was extremely simple; all that
equity required was the addition at the beginning of a gift of words such
as ''to X to the use of . . . ''. Whereas, for example, a gift by A ''to B
for life, but if she remarries, then to C'' would have been regarded at
common law as void as infringing the rule against remainders designed
to vest in possession before the natural determination of the prior
particular estate, a gift ''to X to the use of B for life, but if she remarries,
then to use of C'' would be held to be valid in equity.

By the device of uses, all the restrictive common law rules could be
avoided. The major effect of the device was to secure the recognition in
equity of three new types of interests which had previously not been
recognised at common law. The first of these interests is a ''springing
use''.[54] This type of use flouts the common law rule against the abeyance
of seisin and allows gifts to be made in futuro. An illustration is a gift ''to
X to the use of B when B reaches the age of 25 years''. The second of these
interests is the ''shifting use''.[55] This type of use flouts both the rule
against remainders limited after a fee simple estate and the rule against
remainders   designed   to   vest   in   possession   before   the   natural

52. *Duncomb v. Duncomb* (1695) 3 Lev. 437; 83 E.R. 770 (K.B.); *Smith d. Dormer v.
     Packhurst* (1940) 3 Atk. 135; 26 E.R. 881 (Ch.).
53. For a general discussion of the role of equity in the development of modern trusts
     and real property law, see above [2.51]ff.
54. See e.g. *Roe d. Wilkinson v. Tranmer* (1757) 2 Wils. K.B. 75; 95 E.R. 694 (K.B.).
55. See Megarry and Wade, p. 1180.

determination of the prior particular estate. An illustration is a gift "to B and his heirs, but if C qualifies as a medical practitioner then to C and his heirs". Both springing and shifting uses have been designated as "executory interests". These are distinguishable from contingent remainders in that contingent remainders are interests intended to operate from the natural determination of an earlier estate, while executory interests are intended to operate on the occurrence of one or more events regardless of whether the event or events take place upon the natural determination of the earlier estate.

The final of the three interests is the "executory devise". This phrase encompasses any devise which, if it had been couched as a gift inter vivos, would have constituted an "executory interest".[56] By employing a use, the common law rule against wills could be circumvented. Thus a testator was given by equity similar powers to a donor to make a devise provided that he commenced the devise with the phrase "to X to the use of . . .".

2. The Statute of Uses 1535

[7.12]   This situation continued until well into the 16th century, when it was eventually changed by the enactment of the *Statute of Uses* 1535. The relevant parts of the text of this legislation and the reasons for its introduction are cited: see above **[2.61]**ff.[57]

The purpose of the statute was to ensure that the traditional feudal incidents of tenure applied to estates created in equity behind a use. The effect of the statute was to execute the use. By this process the legal estate was taken from the feoffee to uses and vested in the cestui que use, with the result that gifts and devises subject to the use, which had previously only been enforceable at equity, were automatically converted into legal interests. In relation to inter vivos gifts, it was soon held that the effect of the statute was to execute all uses regardless of whether they were consistent with the common law legal remainder rules. The most significant result of this was that springing and shifting uses were for the first time recognised as valid legal future interests. All that was required to create a legal executory interest was to preface the gift with the words: "to X and his heirs to the use of . . ."[58] The statute was also held to execute resulting uses as well as express uses.[59] Thus, for example, in a gift by A "to X to the use of B for life", the *Statute of Uses* passed the legal estate from X to both B and A; A would be held to have the legal fee simple in reversion.

The overall effect of the creation of legal executory interests by the *Statute of Uses* could have been to render the legal remainder rules entirely redundant. Unfortunately, this did not occur. Following the Statute, the

---

56. See e.g. *Taylor v. Bydall* (1677) 1 Freem. K.B. 243; 89 E.R. 173 (K.B.); *Gulliver v. Wickett* (1745) 1 Wils. K.B. 105; 95 E.R. 517 (K.B.).
57. See generally Sanders, *Uses and Trusts* (5th ed., by Sanders and Warner, 1844).
58. For illustrations of the operation of the Statute of Uses, see Woodman, pp. 85-88. See also *Baker v. White* (1875) L.R. 20 Eq. 166; *Re Bostock's Settlement* [1921] 2 Ch. 469 (C.A.); *Silvester d. Law v. Wilson* (1788) 2 T.R. 444; 100 E.R. 239 (K.B.); *Doe d. Lloyd v. Passingham* (1827) 6 B. & C. 305; 108 E.R. 465 (K.B.).
59. Woodman, pp. 97, 101.

common law developed a restriction known as the rule in *Purefoy v. Rogers*.[60] Simply stated, the rule is that if a limitation of a legal estate is capable of existing as a contingent remainder it must be regarded as a contingent remainder rather than as an executory interest, with the result that it may be destroyed by the application of the legal remainder rules. The reason for the rule has been said to be the desire of the common law to prevent land owners from controlling the disposition of their lands for indefinite periods into the future.[61] An additional factor was the stubborn reluctance of the common law judges to depart from the legal remainder rules. The rule in *Purefoy v. Rogers* soon became entrenched and was stated by Lord St Leonards in *Cole v. Sewell*[62] to be a "sacred rule of law".

[7.13] The key to understanding the rule is to recognise that it only applies where the limitation *is capable of* existing as a contingent remainder.[63] A gift by A "to X and her heirs, then to the use of B for life, then to the use of C when C is admitted as a medical practitioner" is capable of existing as a contingent remainder and is therefore subject to the rule. The effect of the rule would be that the gift to C is void as it breaches the legal remainder rules. This should be contrasted with a gift "to X and her heirs, then to the use of B for life, then to the use of C one year after B's death". This was incapable of existing as a contingent remainder because of the abeyance of seisin, and the rule in *Purefoy v. Rogers* would accordingly have no application. The rule was also applied to class gifts (discussed in Chapter 8). Thus, for example, a gift "to X and his heirs, to the use of B for life, then to the use of such of C's children who shall have qualified as medical practitioners on B's death" would be subject to the rule, and the effect would be to vest the property exclusively in those children who had qualified for medical practice before B's death and to exclude any children who might so qualify at a later date.

The rule in *Purefoy v. Rogers* has been held to be a rule of law rather than a rule of construction and accordingly operates regardless of the intention of the donor or testator.[64] There is, however, one method available to a donor or testator to avoid the operation of the rule, namely to create alternative gifts, one as an executory interest and the other as a contingent remainder. This exception was recognised by Parker J. in *White v. Summers*.[65] The drafting of the gift or devise assumes great importance here. If the donor or testator wishes to make a gift or bequest to B for life, then to C if he is admitted to practice as a medical practitioner, the use of those words without modification would cause the gift to C to fail as the gift to C is capable of taking effect as a contingent remainder. To avoid the rule in *Purefoy v. Rogers*, however, A could phrase the gift or devise either "to X and his heirs to the use of B for life, then to the use of C whether C is admitted to practice before or after B's death", or "to

60. (1671) 2 Wms. Saund. 380; 85 E.R. 1181 (K.B.). See also *Chudleigh's Case* (1595) 1 Co. Rep. 113b; 76 E.R. 261 (K.B.); *Festing v. Allen* (1843) 12 M. & W. 279; 152 E.R. 1204 (Ex.); *White v. Summers* [1908] 2 Ch. 256.
61. Sackville and-Neave, p. 182.
62. (1843) 4 Dr. & War. 1 at 27.
63. For illustrations of the operation of the rule, see Woodman, pp. 91-92.
64. *White v. Summers* [1908] 2 Ch. 256 at 267.
65. Ibid.

X and his heirs to the use of B for life, then to the use of C if he is admitted
to practice as a medical practitioner, but if C is not admitted to practice
as a medical practitioner by the date of B's death then to C when he is
so admitted to practice".[66]

3. The Statute of Wills 1540

[7.14] Although devises of land were impossible under the feudal
system of land tenure, the effect of the doctrine of uses established prior
to 1535 was to make it possible to make a devise which would be
enforceable at equity. Thus, if A wished to devise her property to B, she
could make a gift "to X and her heirs, to the use of B on A's death".

This form of devise became comparatively common during the 15th
and early 16th centuries, but the effect of the *Statute of Uses* 1535 was to
abolish the power to devise land. This proved to be a very unpopular
reform and was one of the reasons for the Pilgrimage of Grace in 1536.
Pressure to allow devises of land finally led to the enactment of the *Statute
of Wills* 1540.

The 1540 statute created a broad power to devise land, so broad that
it was held to be unnecessary to create a prior particular estate. Thus if
A wished to bequeath land to B, he could simply make a devise "to X and
his heirs to the use of B" and the use would be executed by the *Statute of
Uses*. At a later stage, it was held to be unnecessary even to include an
express use, as one would be implied at law if it were omitted. In this
respect, the law treated devises far less rigidly than gifts inter vivos.

VI. THE CURRENT AUSTRALIAN LAW

[7.15] The earlier sections of this Chapter have discussed the historical
development of the laws relating to future interests which Australia and
the United Kingdom share in common. More recent developments have
caused the present laws in Australia and the United Kingdom to diverge.
The introduction of the Torrens system of land title in this country led to
a certain reappraisal of the old law of future interests. More influential has
been the feeling that the old law, based as it is on the feudal system, was
inappropriate to modern society. These factors have led to several changes
in the law, primarily statutory; unfortunately, in many instances uniform
legislation between the States has not been adopted.

1. The Relevance of Torrens Legislation to Future Interests

[7.16] As a general proposition, the law discussed above applies equally
to Torrens land as to general law land. The only exception to that
proposition is that the rule in *Shelley's Case*[67] has never applied to Torrens

---

66. See e.g. *Dean v. Dean* [1891] 3 Ch. 150 at 155-156; *Re Caraher* (1904) 21 W.N.
    (N.S.W.) 213 at 215-216.
67. (1581) 1 Co. Rep. 93b; 76 E.R. 206 (K.B.).

land.[68] The reason for this is that the rule is based on the common law distinction between words of purchase and words of limitation, neither of which have ever had any application or relevance under the Torrens legislation.

The means of creating future interests in Torrens land is subject to the following provision of the Torrens legislation in each State and Territory:[69]

"The registered proprietor of any estate or interest in land may, by any of the forms of transfer provided by this Act, modified as may be necessary, transfer such estate or interest, or any part thereof, to the wife or husband of such registered proprietor, or to such registered proprietor, and any other person or persons as joint tenants or tenants in common, and may limit any estates by remainder or otherwise, without limiting any use, or executing any re-assignment; and upon the registration of any such transfer the estate or interest thereby dealt with or transferred shall vest in the transferee or transferees, according to the intent and meaning appearing in and expressed by such instrument."

The Torrens legislation in New South Wales, South Australia, Tasmania and the Northern Territory permits the Registrar of Titles to create and issue separate certificates of title in respect of future interests.[70] The legislation in New South Wales and Tasmania is similar. The *Real Property Act* 1900 (N.S.W.), s. 100(2) and (3) read as follows:

"(2) Subject to subsection (3), where persons are entitled to be registered as proprietors of a life estate and an estate in remainder in, or as tenants in common of shares in, land under the provisions of this Act . . ., the Registrar-General may, in respect of the life estate and estate in remainder or, as the case may be, the shares—

(a) create separate folios of the Register and issue separate certificates of title;

(b) create a folio or folios of the Register and issue such certificate or certificates of title as he thinks proper; or

(c) deliver any existing certificate of title after making thereon and in the Register such recording as may be required by this Act.

(3) The Registrar-General shall not refuse to act in accordance with subsection (2) (a) if he is requested so to act and his expenses for so acting are paid."

The Tasmanian legisation is similar except that its scope includes "any other future estate in land under the Act" in addition to persons holding a life estate or an estate in remainder.

---

68. Note, however, Queensland Law Reform Commission, *Working Paper on a Bill to Consolidate, Amend, and Reform the Law Relating to Conveyancing, Property, and Contract* . . . , Working Paper 10 (1971), pp. 19-20.
69. Torrens legislation: N.S.W.: s. 99; *Property Law Act* 1958 (Vic.), s. 19; Qld: s. 82; S.A.: s. 111; W.A.: s. 84; *Conveyancing and Law of Property Act* 1884 (Tas.), ss 62, 80; A.C.T.: s. 79; N.T.: s. 111. This is the wording of the South Australian provision. The form of the legislation differs slightly between the jurisdictions but is to similar effect.
70. N.S.W.: s. 100(2); S.A.: s. 75; Tas.: s. 33(6)(8); N.T.: s. 75.

The South Australian and Northern Territory legislation is expressed more simply, but is to similar effect. The *Real Property Act* 1886 (S.A.), s. 75 states:

> "The proprietor of an estate of freehold in remainder or reversion in land, for a life estate in which a certificate has already been issued, may have his estate registered on the certificate issued for the life estate, or may receive a separate certificate for his estate, which shall refer to the certificate of the particular estate."

In the remaining jurisdictions, the question whether the Registrar may create and issue separate certificates of title in respect of future interests must be considered uncertain in the absence of any reported authorities. In New Zealand, where the legislation is similarly silent on the issue, Edwards J. held in *Re The Land Transfer Act 1908; Ex parte Matheson*[71] that holders of future interests are entitled to require that they be shown in the body of the certificate of title, rather than in a memorial indorsed upon the certificate of title issued to the holder of the possessory interest, as having a future estate in the property. This case is persuasive authority suggesting that the Registrar may be required to issue a separate certificate of title in respect of future interests in Victoria, Queensland, Western Australia and the Australian Capital Territory even without express legislation.

2. General Statutory Reforms

(a) Alienability of future interests

[7.17]   Historically, common law permitted vested future interests to be alienated, but not contingent remainders.[72] This rule was partially relaxed in the 18th century by decisions enabling alienation to take place by fine or recovery as a form of estoppel and by the suggestion that estoppel might take effect upon a purported conveyance under seal.[73] Alienation of contingent remainders was held to be permissible in equity.[74]

Today legislation exists in all Australian jurisdictions permitting the alienation of both vested and contingent future interests in all situations regardless of whether the interests are created by deed[75] or by will.[76] By way of illustration, the *Law of Property Act* 1936 (S.A.), s. 10 states:

> "All rights and interests in land may be disposed of, including—
>
> (a) a contingent, executory, or future interest in any land, or a possibility coupled with an interest in any land, whether or not the object of the gift or limitation of such interest or possibility be ascertained;

---

71. (1914) 33 N.Z.L.R. 838.
72. *Lampet's Case* (1612) 10 Co. Rep. 46b; 77 E.R. 994 (K.B.).
73. See *Caraher v. Lloyd* (1905) 2 C.L.R. 480.
74. See e.g. *Crofts v. Middleton* (1856) 8 De G.M. & G. 192; 44 E.R. 364 (Ch.).
75. Conveyancing legislation: N.S.W.: s. 50(1); Vic.: s. 19(1); Qld: s. 31; S.A.: s. 10; Tas : s 80(1); A C.T.: s. 3.
76. Wills legislation: N.S.W.: s. 5; Vic.: s. 5; Qld: s. 7(2); S.A.: s. 4; W.A.: s. 6; Tas.: s. 1, Sched. cl. 3; A.C.T.: s. 7(2).

(b) a right of entry, into or upon land whether immediate or future, and whether vested or contingent."

(b) Abolition of rule in Shelley's Case

[7.18] The rule in *Shelley's Case*[77] has been expressly repealed by legislation in New South Wales, Victoria, Queensland and Western Australia.[78] For example, s. 130 of the *Property Law Act* 1958 (Vic.) states:

"Where by any instrument coming into operation after the commencement of this Act an interest in any property is expressed to be given to the heir or heirs or issue or any particular heir or any class of the heirs or issue of any person in words which, but for this section would, under the rule of law known as the Rule in Shelley's case, . . . have operated to give to that person an interest in fee-simple or an entailed interest, such words shall operate as words of purchase and not of limitation, and shall be construed and have effect accordingly, and in the case of an interest in any property expressed to be given to an heir or heirs or any particular heir or class of heirs, the same person or persons shall take as would in the case of freehold land have answered that description under the general law formerly in force."

The legislation in these jurisdictions does not operate retrospectively, and any conveyance executed before the commencement date of the relevant sections is still subject to the operation of the rule in *Shelley's Case*. The relevant dates are: New South Wales, 1 July 1920; Victoria, 12 February 1929; Queensland, 1 December 1975; and Western Australia, 1 August 1969.

There is no equivalent legislation in South Australia, Tasmania and the Northern Territory, and in these jurisdictions the rule in *Shelley's Case* continues to apply.

(c) Destruction of contingent remainders

[7.19] In the United Kingdom, natural and artificial destruction of contingent remainders were abolished by statute in the 19th century. The *Real Property Act* 1845 (U.K.), s. 8 abolished artificial destruction by surrender, merger and forfeiture in the following manner:

"a contingent remainder is and shall be deemed to have been capable of taking effect notwithstanding the destruction or determination by forfeiture, surrender or merger of any preceding estate of freehold in the same manner and in all respects as if the destruction or determination had not happened."

The rules of natural destruction and artificial destruction by disclaimer were unaffected by this legislation. These methods of destruction were later repealed by s. 1 of the *Contingent Remainders Act* 1877 (U.K.) which stated:

---

77. (1581) 1 Co. Rep. 93b; 76 E.R. 206 (K.B.).
78. Conveyancing legislation: N.S.W.: s. 17; Vic.: s. 130; Qld: s. 28; W.A.: s. 27.

"Every contingent remainder which would have been valid as a
springing or shifting use or executory devise or other limitation had
it not had a sufficient estate to support it as a contingent remainder
shall in the event of the particular estate determining before the
contingent remainder vests be capable of taking effect in all respects
as if the contingent remainder had originally been created as a
springing or shifting use of executory devise or other executory
limitation."

The intended effect of this legislation was to abolish the rule in *Purefoy
v. Rogers*[79] and to overturn the rule which declared a contingent remainder
void if it failed to vest before the natural determination of the prior
particular estate. As noted by Megarry and Wade,[80] however, some doubt
remains as to whether this intended effect has been achieved as the section
does not deal expressly with class gifts and does not seem to cover the
obvious situation of a contingent remainder created by deed without a
use: for example, in a gift by deed by A "to B for life, then to his first
child to reach the age of 21", the contingent remainder to the first son
would have been invalid without the existence of the prior particular
estate. The effect of the legislation has never been tested in a reported
case.

In Australia, the abolition of the rules of natural and artificial
destruction of contingent remainders and the rule in *Purefoy v. Rogers* has
been achieved in all jurisdictions by three different methods.

Victoria, Western Australia and Tasmania[81] have copied the English
approach and have incorporated into their conveyancing legislation the
wording of the two U.K. statutes discussed above without amendment.
The consequence of this is that lingering doubt expressed by Megarry and
Wade as to the effectiveness of the *Contingent Remainders Act* 1877 (U.K.)
in achieving its intended goal applies also in these three States.

In New South Wales and South Australia, the same result appears to
have been achieved by the following legislation:[82]

"A contingent remainder existing at any time after the
commencement of this Act shall be capable of taking effect
notwithstanding the want of a particular estate of freehold to support
it in the same manner as it would take effect if it were a contingent
remainder of an equitable estate supported by an outstanding legal
estate in fee simple."

Finally, s. 30(1) of the *Property Law Act* 1974 (Qld) adopts the more
fundamental approach of declaring that future interests shall henceforth
only exist as equitable interests. The subsection reads:

79. (1671) 2 Wms. Saund. 380; 85 E.R. 1181 (K.B.).
80. Megarry and Wade, p. 1184.
81. Conveyancing legislation: Vic.: ss 191, 192; W.A.: s. 26(1)(2); Tas.: ss 80(2), 81.
82. Conveyancing legislation: N.S.W.: s. 16(1); S.A.: s. 25.

"A future interest[83] in land validly created after the commencement of this Act shall take effect as an equitable and not a legal interest."[84]

One consequence of this is the abolition of the rules of natural and artificial destruction and the rule in *Purefoy v. Rogers*.[85]

(d) Avoidance of legal remainder rules

[7.20] There is a provision in the conveyancing legislation in New South Wales, Western Australia and the Australian Capital Territory, which states:[86]

"Every limitation which may be made by way of use operating under the Statute of Uses or this Act may be made by direct conveyance without the intervention of uses."

The legislation is relevant to any interest that could exist as an equitable executory interest or (following the *Statute of Uses* 1535) as a legal executory interest if it had been created behind a use. The effect of the legislation is that a legal executory interest will henceforth be valid pursuant to the legislation even if no use is employed. Thus, the purpose of the legislation is to make uses unnecessary and to preserve as valid interests which would otherwise be void.

In New South Wales, this analysis has been complicated by the repeal of the *Statute of Uses* as from 1 January 1971: see below **[7.22]**. On one analysis, on a literal interpretation of the legislation s. 44(2) could be argued to have been impliedly repealed as from 1971 as no limitation may now be made "by way of use operating under the Statute of Uses". Alternatively, it can be argued that s. 44(2) applies to every limitation which could be made by way of use at the time when s. 44(2) came into operation (1 July 1920). If this latter approach is correct, the subsequent repeal of the *Statute of Uses* in New South Wales will have no effect on the operation of s. 44(2). The matter has not been tested in the courts. In the absence of authorities, the preference of the writers is for the latter interpretation, which preserves the operation of s. 44(2).

(e) Restriction on executory limitations

[7.21] All States except South Australia possess legislation in the following form:[87]

"Where there is a person entitled to—

(a) land for an estate in fee-simple or for any less interest; or

83. Section 30(4) defines "future interest" as meaning a legal contingent remainder and a legal executory interest.
84. The section does not apply to any future interest created before the commencement of the Act (1 December 1975). Legal executory interests created prior to this date in Queensland are still subject to the rule in *Purefoy v. Rogers* and contingent remainders created prior to this date are still subject to the common law legal remainder rules.
85. See *Berry v. Berry* (1878) 7 Ch. D. 657.
86. Conveyancing legislation: N.S.W.: s 44(2); W.A.: s. 39; A.C.T.: s. 3.
87. Conveyancing legislation: N.S.W.: s. 29B; Vic.: s. 132; Qld: s. 32; W.A.: s. 28; Tas.: s. 79.

(b) any interest in other property—

with an executory limitation over on default or failure of all or any of his issue, whether within or at any specified period of time or not, that executory limitation shall be or become void and incapable of taking effect, if and as soon as there is living any issue who has attained the age of [eighteen] years[88] of the class on default or failure whereof the limitation over was to take effect.''

The effect of this provision is to render void any executory limitation following a possessory interest where, according to the terms of the deed or will establishing the limitation, the possessory interest may be defeated by the death of the holder of the interest without issue, once any of the holder's children attain the age of 18. Thus, if A makes a gift "to B in fee simple, but if B should die without issue then to C and her heirs", the limitation to C will be treated as void by the legislation once any of B's children first reaches 18. The fact that the child who reaches 18 later dies and B is left childless at the time of her death will be of no avail to C.

This provision only applies where the executory limitation is contained in an instrument coming into operation after the following dates: New South Wales, 1 July 1920; Victoria, 31 January 1905; Queensland, 1 December 1975; Western Australia, 1 August 1969; and Tasmania, 1 January 1884.[89]

(f) The repeal of the Statute of Uses

[7.22]   In New South Wales, Victoria and Queensland, the *Statute of Uses* has been abolished by State legislation.[90] The effective dates for the operation of this repeal are: New South Wales, 1 January 1971; Victoria, 2 July 1980; and Queensland, 1 December 1975.

The effect of this reform is to return the law to its pre 1535 condition. Thus, for example, a gift "to B and his heirs to the use of C and his heirs" will henceforth give C an equitable rather than a legal estate as the use is no longer executed. The practical effect of this is that trusts can now be created without employing a use upon a use. It also follows from the repeal of the *Statute of Uses* that legal executory interests can no longer be created in New South Wales, Victoria and Queensland. The repeal has no effect, however, on legal contingent remainders, which may still be created in New South Wales and Victoria (although not in Queensland, by virtue of s. 30(1) of the *Property Law Act* 1974 (Qld): see above [7.19]).

In Victoria, an additional provision was added to the *Property Law Act* 1958 at the time of the repeal of the *Statute of Uses*. Section 19A reads:

"(1) Interests in land which under the *Statute of Uses* could before the commencement of this section have been created as legal interests

---

88. The original legislation specified 21 years. This was changed to 18 years in all States following the reduction in the age of majority: see e.g. *Minors (Property and Contracts) Act* 1970 (N.S.W.), Pt II.
89. Conveyancing legislation: N.S.W.: s. 29B(2); Vic.: s. 132(2); Qld: s. 32(2); W.A.: s. 28(2); Tas.: s. 79(2).
90. *Imperial Acts Application Act* 1969 (N.S.W.), s. 8; *Imperial Acts Application Act* 1980 (Vic.), s. 5; *Property Law Act* 1974 (Qld), s. 7.

shall after the commencement of this section be capable of being created as equitable interests.

(2) Notwithstanding sub-section (1) an equitable interest in land shall after the commencement of this section only be capable of being validly created in any case in which an equivalent equitable interest in property real or personal could have been validly created before such commencement."

The reasons for the inclusion of this section are puzzling. It is suggested by Sackville and Neave[91] that the section was designed to ensure that interests drafted as legal executory interests created after the repeal of the *Statute of Uses* now take effect as equitable interests. If this is correct (and it is difficult to contemplate any other justification) the provision appears to be unnecessary as it has always been possible to create as equitable interests those interests which are capable of creation as legal interests. Thus, the legislation appears to be superfluous.

The *Statute of Uses* still continues in effect in the remaining Australian jurisdictions.

---

91. Sackville and Neave, p. 189.

8
The Rule Against Perpetuities[1]

I. BACKGROUND

[8.01] One of the fundamental principles of English law which has been inherited in Australia is that land must be freely alienable. The origin of this principle is disputed.[2] Some ascribe it to the statute *Quia Emptores* of 1290, which gave holders of fee simple estates the right to alienate their estate either partially or wholly. Others argue that the origin lies in the judicial acceptance of the idea that a restraint on alienation is contrary to the nature of an estate of inheritance.[3] Despite its doubtful origins, it is generally agreed that significant restraints upon alienation should be outlawed for reasons of public policy, in that land should be freely marketable and that it is inappropriate for the law to permit persons to tie up land for generations by the terms of their settlement or will.[4]

The history of English real property law contains many illustrations of attempts to prevent land from being alienated: see above **[2.46]**. The most common situation was a testator who sought to prevent land from being sold outside the family. The usual method of achieving this was the creation of a fee tail estate: see above **[2.18]-[2.23]**. Eventually in the late 15th century the common law intervened to allow the conversion of a fee tail into a fee simple by the process of barring the entail.[5]

The rule developed at common law, which is still applicable today, is that a clause in a will or other instrument preventing the alienation of land is void as contrary to public policy. Numerous settlements and wills have been set aside over the years by virtue of this rule. In recent times, a partial relaxation of this rule has been allowed by the judiciary and it is now accepted that partial restraints on alienation may be valid. The relevant authorities are discussed above **[2.46]**.

In addition to the common law rule of voidness based on public policy, two other areas of law assist today in circumventing attempted restraints on the alienation of land. One is the State settled land legislation, which is discussed in Chapter 6. The other is the rule against perpetuities, which in Australia is a combination of common law principles and statutory

---

1. The authors wish to thank Mary Heath, a Research Officer at Adelaide Law School, for her research assistance in this area of law.
2. See Jenks, "An Inalienable Fee Simple?" (1917) 33 L.Q.R. 11.
3. See e.g. *Mildmay's Case* (1605) 6 Co. Rep. 40a; 77 E.R. 311.
4. The policy arguments are canvassed in Schnebly, "Restraints upon the Alienation of Legal Interests" (1935) 44 Yale L.J. 961.
5. See e.g. *Mary Portington's Case* (1614) 10 Co. Rep. 35b; 77 E.R. 976.

rules. This is by far the most significant and effective of the current legal restraints on alienation of land in Australia.

Historically, there have been two separate rules against perpetuities. One of these was the rule in *Whitby v. Mitchell*.[6] Pursuant to this rule, where an interest in land was conveyed to an unborn person, any remainder to the issue of that person, and any subsequent limitation, was void. Take, for example, a gift "to X for life, remainder to X's eldest child, remainder in fee simple to the children of the eldest child". If X had a child at the time of the gift, the rule was not infringed. However, if X had at that time not produced any children, the gift to the eldest child would be valid, but the remainder to the children of that eldest child would be void.[7] This rule, which was sometimes misleadingly referred to as "the rule against double possibilities", applied to both legal and equitable estates,[8] but not to personal property.[9] In Australia, the rule in *Whitby v. Mitchell* has been abolished by legislation in New South Wales, Victoria, Queensland and Western Australia,[10] but remains in effect in South Australia, Tasmania and the Territories. It was specifically held to be applicable in Tasmania in two reported cases.[11]

The present rule against perpetuities, which will form the remainder of the discussion in this Chapter, is sometimes referred to as the "modern" perpetuities rule.[12] It dates from a series of cases determined between 1682 and 1833.[13] Its origin lies in the basic common law principle that land should be freely alienable, and it arose in response to a specific threat to this principle. Following the *Statute of Uses* 1535 and the *Statute of Wills* 1540, a new category of executory interests became possible. When these interests were rendered indestructible by the decision in *Pells v. Brown*,[14] the possibility emerged of an infinite series of indestructible contingent interests. The rule against perpetuities was designed to prevent this occurrence.

The Privy Council first considered the application of the rule against perpetuities in Australia in 1889 in *Cooper v. Stuart*.[15] The court

6. (1890) 44 Ch. D. 85. The rule has its origin in *Perrot's Case* (1594) Moo. K.B. 368, 72 E.R. 634.
7. For illustrations of the operation of the rule, see *Re Mortimer* [1905] 2 Ch. 502; *Brudenell v. Elwes* (1801) 1 East 442; 102 E.R. 171.
8. *Re Nash* [1910] 1 Ch. 1.
9. *Re Bowles* [1902] 2 Ch. 650.
10. *Conveyancing Act* 1919 (N.S.W.), s. 23A; *Perpetuities and Accumulations Act* 1968 (Vic.), s. 12; *Property Law Act* 1974 (Qld), s. 216; *Property Law Act* 1969 (W.A.), s. 114.
11. *Re Hume's Estate* (1939) 34 Tas. L.R. 22; *Re Lawrence* [1943] Tas. S.R. 33.
12. Sometimes referred to as the rule against remoteness of vesting.
13. *Duke of Norfolk's Case* (1682) 3 Ch. Cas. 1; 22 E.R. 931; *Cadell v. Palmer* (1833) 1 Cl. & Fin. 372; 6 E.R. 956.
14. (1620) Cro. Jac. 590; 79 E.R. 504.
15. (1889) 14 A.C. 286. The Privy Council held that the common law rule against perpetuities does not bind the Crown. This position has been reversed by the modern perpetuities legislation, except in respect of dispositions made by the Crown: *Perpetuities Act* 1984 (N.S.W.), s. 5(1); *Perpetuities and Accumulations Act* 1968 (Vic.), s. 1(2); *Property Law Act* 1974 (Qld), s. 1(4); *Property Law Act* 1969 (W.A.), s. 99(2).

emphasised the continued need to safeguard the free alienability of land and to ensure that ultimate ownership of land was not deferred for lengthy periods. It stated:[16]

"The rule against perpetuities, . . . is, in its principle, an important feature of the common law of England. To that extent it appears to be founded upon plain considerations of policy, and, in some shape or other, finds a place in most, if not in all, complete systems of jurisprudence. Their Lordships see no reason to suppose that the rule . . . is not required in New South Wales by the same considerations which led to its introduction here."

The rule has been held to apply to Torrens land as well as general law land.[17] However, Young J. in *Consolidated Development Pty Ltd v. Holt*[18] has recently held that if a person achieves registration of an interest which would be void at common law for infringing the rule, the Torrens legislation will override the rule and make the interest indefeasible. The effect of this is that the Registrar of Titles will need to ensure that by the act of registration he or she does not create an interest which would otherwise be invalid.[19]

While the rule made sense at the time of its formulation in England several centuries ago, its continued application in the 20th century has been regarded by most commentators as an absurd anachronism.[20] Belated recognition of this fact has led the New South Wales, Victorian, Queensland and Western Australian legislatures to introduce legislation amending the common law to remove some of the problems and difficulties associated with the common law rule.[21] The common law rule still applies in South Australia and Tasmania, in the first-mentioned case

16. *Cooper v. Stuart* (1889) 14 A.C. 286 at 293.
17. *Kauri Timber Co. (Ltd) v. District Land Registrar, Auckland* (1902) 21 N.Z.L.R. 84 (reversed on other grounds, (1902) 22 N.Z.L.R. 260).
18. (1986) 6 N.S.W.L.R. 607.
19. Ibid. at 617.
20. For example, Leach refers to "the hobgoblins, leprechauns, and gremlins that have infested the Rule in the nearly three hundred years of its existence: see "Perpetuities Reform: London Proposes, Perth Disposes" (1964) 6 U.W.A.L.R. 11 at 12. In another article ("Perpetuities: Staying the Slaughter of the Innocents" (1952) 68 L.Q.R. 35), Leach states that the rule is: "so abstruse that it is misunderstood by a substantial percentage of those who advise the public, so unrealistic that its 'conclusive presumptions' are laughable nonsense to any sane man, so capricious that it strikes down in the name of public order gifts which offer no offence except that they are couched in the wrong words, [and] so misapplied that it sometimes directly defeats the end it was designed to further." The rule does have some modern relevance, however: see Allan, "The Rule Against Perpetuities Restated" (1964) 6 U.W.A.L.R. 27 at 30-33.
21. The present legislation is contained in the *Perpetuities Act* 1984 (N.S.W.); *Perpetuities and Accumulations Act* 1968 (Vic.); *Property Law Act* 1974 (Qld), Pt XIV; *Property Law Act* 1969 (W.A.), Pt XI. In the case of Queensland and Western Australia, the perpetuities legislation was first introduced in the *Perpetuities and Accumulations Act* 1972 (Qld) and the *Law Reform (Property, Perpetuities and Succession) Act* 1962 (W.A.). The New South Wales legislation is based in part on a 1976 Report of the New South Wales Law Reform Commission: Report No. 26 (1976). Similar legislation was enacted in New Zealand and the United Kingdom: *Perpetuities Act* 1964 (N.Z.); *Perpetuities and Accumulations Act* 1964 (U.K.).

despite a recommendation of the Law Reform Committee of South Australia[22] that legislation is required. The relevance of the common law is not confined to South Australia and Tasmania, however. The perpetuities legislation in the other jurisdictions in each case states that it applies only to instruments taking effect after either the commencement of the Act or after an appointed day.[23] The relevant dates are 31 October 1984 (New South Wales), 10 December 1968 (Victoria), 1 December 1975 (Queensland),[24] and 6 December 1962 (Western Australia). Thus, the common law rule against perpetuities continues to apply to all instruments taking effect in these jurisdictions before the relevant date.

As the perpetuities legislation differs significantly between the various States and from the common law, a separate discussion of the common law position and each Act will be required in respect of the various aspects of the rule against perpetuities.

II. THE RULE ITSELF

[8.02]   The essence of the rule against perpetuities is the imposition of a limit on the amount of time which may elapse between the creation of a future interest and the ultimate vesting of that interest. The date of ultimate vesting is the date at which the final owner of the interest is identifiable and the only thing preventing her or him from taking possession of the property is the regular termination of any prior estate. The purpose behind the imposition of such a time limit is to strike a balance between the interests of those making wills or gifts to dispose of their assets as they wish during their lifetimes, and the public interest in preventing land and other assets from being tied up for indefinite periods during which no one has the power of disposition. The rule applies to all contingent interests in real property, both legal and equitable, however created.[25] However, it has no application to vested interests.[26]

1. The Common Law Position

[8.03]   The classic statement of the common law rule is Gray's formula:[27]

22. South Australian Law Reform Committee, *Report Relating to the Reform of the Law of Perpetuities*, 73rd Report (1984).
23. N.S.W.: s. 4(1); Vic.: s. 3(1); Qld: s. 207(1); W.A.: s. 99(1). Various exceptions are specified in certain cases in respect of the administrative powers of trustees, the remuneration of trustees, and superannuation and other funds. In these cases, the legislation operates retrospectively.
24. The now repealed *Perpetuities and Accumulations Act* 1972 (Qld) applied to instruments taking effect after 1 April 1973.
25. The rule applies to all types of proprietary interests. See e.g. *Dunn v. Blackdown Properties Ltd* [1961] Ch. 433, where the rule was applied to an easement in fee simple to use drains under the grantor's land.
26. See Chapter 7 for a discussion of vested and contingent interests.
27. Gray, *The Rule Against Perpetuities* (Little, Brown & Co., Boston, 1942), p. 191. See also *Hancock v. Watson* [1902] A.C. 14 at 17-18. Note that a person attains a particular age on the day preceding the anniversary of the relevant birthdate: *Re Shurey* [1918] 1 Ch. 263.

"No interest is good unless it must vest, if at all, not later than 21 years after some life in being at the creation of the interest."

Each section of this statement will now be considered in detail.

(a) "Vest"

[8.04]   Morris and Leach list three requirements which must be fulfilled for an interest to vest within the meaning of the rule:[28]

(a) the taker must be ascertained;

(b) any condition precedent attached to the interest must be satisfied, subject only to the termination of any prior estates; and

(c) where the interest is part of a class gift, the exact amount or fraction to be taken by each beneficiary must be determined.

The effect of requirement (b) is that it is sufficient to satisfy the rule if the disposition is vested in interest, and it is irrelevant whether or not the disposition vests in possession within the perpetuity period.[29] The effect of requirement (c) is discussed below **[8.25]**.

(b) "21 years"

[8.05]   This is an arbitrary figure based upon the age of majority at the time the rule was created.[30] This period, together with the "life in being", was designed to allow parents to leave gifts to their children which would vest upon the child's majority. In the absence of any "lives in being" the perpetuity period is only 21 years.[31]

(c) "Life in being"

[8.06]   The life or lives in being relevant to determining the perpetuity period are those upon which the vesting of the gift has been made to depend, provided that they are in existence at the creation of the interest. It is not fatal to a gift if the life or lives in being are not ascertained at that time, provided that such lives are definitely in existence and they do not form part of a class which may increase in number.[32] The life or lives in being may be expressly mentioned in the terms of the gift (for example, "to X on the 21st anniversary of my great-aunt's death"), or may be included in the gift by necessary implication. For example, the mention of a child necesarily implies the existence of parents, and a gift "to my granddaughters" necessarily implies the existence of "my child" or "my children".

---

28. Morris and Leach, *The Rule Against Perpetuities* (Stevens, London, 1962), p. 38.

29. See e.g. *Re Hargreaves* (1890) 43 Ch. D. 401.

30. In Australia, the 21 year perpetuity period is unaffected by the reduction in the age of majority to 18 years.

31. *Re Raphael; Permanent Trustee Co. of New South Wales Ltd v. Lee* (1903) 3 S.R. (N.S.W.) 196; *Re Hooper* [1932] 1 Ch. 38; *Palmer v. Holford* (1828) 4 Russ. 403, 38 E.R. 857.

32. *Hardebol v. Perpetual Trustee Co. Ltd* [1975] 1 N.S.W.L.R. 221.

The perpetuity period also includes any actual periods of gestation, since a child en ventre sa mere[33] is treated as a life in being for the purposes of the rule.[34] It must be noted, however, that only *actual* periods of gestation can be used to extend the period, as nine months cannot simply be added to the perpetuity period unless the child was actually born nine months from the date the period began to run.[35]

The lives in being according to which the perpetuity period is measured need not be connected to the interest other than by being mentioned in the instrument which creates it.[36] Efforts to postpone vesting as long as possible have produced devices such as the "royal lives clause", which typically provides that the property concerned is not to vest until the expiration of 21 years from the death of the last survivor of all the lineal descendants of a named monarch living at the time that the instrument takes effect.[37]

Any number of lives may be taken provided they are not so numerous as to make it impossible to calculate the survivors upon the testator's death. In such a case, the gift would be held to be void for uncertainty.[38] The lives must be human lives, not those of animals[39] or legal entities. As stated by Morris and Leach,[40] it is therefore (arguably) not possible to postpone vesting "until the death of the survivor of all the tortoises in the zoo, or even (perhaps) of all oak trees in Hyde Park".[41]

(d) "At the creation of the interest"

[8.07] At common law, the perpetuity period begins to run "at the creation of the interest". This date differs for various types of gifts. If the gift is made by will, the period will run from the testator's death.[42] In

---

33. An unborn child in the mother's womb: *Royal College of Nursing of the United Kingdom v. Department of Health & Social Security* [1981] 1 All E.R. 545 at 554.
34. *Long v. Blackall* (1797) 7 T.R. 100; 101 E.R. 875; *Thellusson v. Woodford* (1799) 4 Ves. Jun. 227 at 255; 31 E.R. 117 at 130; *Blackburn v. Stables* (1814) 2 V. & B. 367; 35 E.R. 358; *Re Wilmer's Trusts* [1903] 2 Ch. 411; *Re Stern* [1962] Ch. 732.
35. *Cadell v. Palmer* (1833) 1 Cl. & Fin. 372; 6 E.R. 956.
36. *Thellusson v. Woodford* (1805) 11 Ves. Jun. 112; 32 E.R. 1030; *Cadell v. Palmer* (1833) 1 Cl. & Fin. 372; 6 E.R. 956.
37. *Re Villar* [1929] 1 Ch. 243; *Re Leverhulme (No. 2)* [1943] 2 All E.R. 274; *Pownall v. Graham* (1863) 33 Beav. 242; 55 E.R. 360.
38. See e.g. *Re Moore* [1901] 1 Ch. 936, where a gift in a will "21 years from the death of the last survivor of all persons who shall be living at my death" was held to be void for uncertainty. See also *Re Villar* [1929] 1 Ch. 243 at 255.
39. *Re Kelly* [1932] I.R. 255. Cf. *Re Dean* (1889) 41 Ch. D. 552.
40. Morris and Leach, op. cit., p. 63.
41. For a recent discussion of how to determine who is a relevant life in being, see Dukeminier, "Wait-and-See: The Causal Principle" (1986) 102 L.Q.R. 250. Cf. *Re Dean* (1889) 41 Ch. D. 552.
42. *Abbiss v. Burney* (1881) 17 Ch. D. 211; *Re Mervin* [1891] 3 Ch. 197 at 204; *Vanderplank v. King* (1843) 3 Hare 1 at 17; 67 E.R. 273 at 279. See Sappideen and Butt, p. 20.

respect of an inter vivos gift, the period commences when the instrument takes effect, and in respect of interests created by deed, the period commences on delivery of the deed.[43] If the gift is revocable, the period runs from the date when the right to revoke terminates. This will normally be upon the settlor's death, but if the settlor releases her or his power of revocation at any earlier time, the period will begin to run from the earlier date.[44] This rule is a manifestation "of the general principle that the perpetuity period does not being to run as long as any one person either is sole beneficial owner of the property or can at will make himself the sole beneficial owner thereof".[45]

(e) "Must vest, if at all"

[8.08] This clause indicates the requirement of the rule against perpetuities that there is absolute certainty of vesting within the vesting period (the life or lives in being plus 21 years). It is not sufficient for the rule that the gift is extremely likely to vest within the period, or that it is virtually certain to vest therein. It is not even enough that the slender possibility that the gift will vest outside the period has been eliminated by the time the matter reaches court. The rule requires that it must be absolutely certain at the time the perpetuity period begins to run that the gift will vest within the perpetuity period. If that is not certain, then the fact that the gift actually vested well within the perpetuity period will not save it.[46]

The insistence by the common law on the certainty of vesting requirement has produced some bizarre and inequitable decisions. The following are the best known situations and illustrations.

(i) The fertile octogenarian cases

[8.09] In a line of cases beginning with *Jee v. Audley*,[47] the courts have held that there is a conclusive presumption of fertility, according to which persons of any age are capable of bearing children, even women over the

---

43. *Robinson v. Hardcastle* (1788) 2 T.R. 241; 100 E.R. 131; *Routledge v. Dorril* (1794) 2 Ves. Jun. 357; 30 E.R. 671.
44. Morris and Leach, op. cit., p. 57; Sappideen and Butt, p. 49; Ford and Lee, pp. 282-283.
45. Morris and Leach, op. cit., p. 57.
46. As Leach states ((1964) op. cit. at 12), the high degree of certainty required by the rule against perpetuities is not required by any other branch of the law, whether civil or criminal. See *Re Watson's Settlement Trusts* [1959] 1 W.L.R. 732 at 739.
47. (1787) 1 Cox 324; 29 E.R. 1186. See also *Re Gaite's Will Trusts* (1949) 65 T.L.R. 194; *Re Dawson* (1888) 9 Ch. D. 155.

age of 70.[48] Further, evidence to establish physical impossibility is inadmissible.[49] Dean J. stated in *Re Fawaz (decd)*:[50]

"The attitude of the law on this matter would scarcely commend itself to an intelligent layman. It is prepared to concede that a deceased person cannot have children, but it will concede no more. The fact that by a surgical operation a woman's organs of generation have been removed or the fact that she is of advanced age will not, in the eyes of the law, exclude the possibility of further children being born to her."

A recent Australian illustration of this aspect of the law is *Teague v. Trustees, Executors & Agency Co. Ltd.*[51] In this case, the High Court refused to assume that no further grandchildren could be born to the testator, even though his only surviving child was a woman aged 69 who the court admitted was beyond the age of childbearing.

(ii) The precocious toddler

[8.10] Similarly, for the purposes of the rule against perpetuities children of any age are conclusively presumed to be capable of childbearing. For example, in *Re Gaite's Will Trusts*,[52] Pennycuick V.-C. stated that he could not deny the possibility that the gift might fail to vest because it was possible that the testator's widow (aged 65 at his death) could remarry and bear a child, who in turn could marry and bear a child, all within five years of the testator's death. In this case, the gift was saved only because the marriage of a person under the age of 16 would have been void at law. This meant that the hypothetical grandchild could not be legitimate so as to take under the will.

48. *Ward v. Van der Loeff* [1924] A.C. 653 is a particularly absurd application of the rule. In that case, a testator left his residuary estate to his wife for life (or until she should marry someone who was not a natural born British subject) and upon her death, to the children of any of his siblings then living. The residuary gift was held to infringe the rule set down in *Jee v. Audley* and it therefore failed for remoteness. Lord Blanesburgh stated (at 677-678):
    "If we consider matters as they stood at the testator's death, . . . it was necessary before anything obnoxious to the rule could take place in connection with this residuary gift, that the following remarkable conjunction of events should supervene. The testator's father and mother were then each upwards of 66 years of age; to them, . . . no child had been born for more than 30 years. It was, nevertheless, necessary that they should have another child. Alternatively it was necessary that their marriages should be dissolved otherwise than by the death of the father, and that he should marry again, and have a child by the second marriage. That child, in turn, had to have a child born after the death of the testator's widow—one born in her lifetime would not have been excluded by the rule. And even a child so born would have brought about an infraction of the rule, only if it had also eventuated that no one of the already substantial and apparently increasing families of the testator's four living brothers and sisters had survived his widow having married or attained 21."
49. *Jee v. Audley* (1787) 1 Cox 324; 29 E.R. 1186.
50. [1958] V.R. 426 at 431.
51. (1923) 32 C.L.R. 253.
52. (1949) 65 T.L.R. 194. See also *Re Atkins' Will Trusts* [1974] 1 W.L.R. 761.

(iii) The unborn widow(er)

[8.11] In *Re Frost*,[53] a testator devised his estate to the use of his sons and heirs upon trust for his daughter Emma (a spinster at the date of the will) during her life, and upon her death to any husband Emma might marry, for life, and upon his death, to any children of the marriage. In this case the gift to Emma was valid, as was the gift to her widower, since he must be ascertained at the time of Emma's death. However, the gift to their children was held to be invalid because it was possible that Emma could marry a man not born at the testator's death, who might die more than 21 years after Emma (the only life in being), causing the gift to the children to vest outside the perpetuity period (Emma's life plus 21 years).

In a situation such as occurred in *Re Frost*, it would make no difference that at a time of litigation the person to whom such a bequest was made had died a widow with children of full age.[54] The validity of any gift must be decided according to all the possibilities, no matter how remote, in existence at the time the perpetuity period begins to run.

(iv) The magic gravel pits

[8.12] If a testator leaves property to beneficiaries upon a contingency which is virtually certain to occur within 21 years, but there is a theoretical possibility that it may take longer, the gift will be void. The classic example is *Re Wood*.[55] In that case, a testator bequeathed his freehold gravel pits to his children, instructing the trustees to carry on the business until the gravel pits were worked out, and then to sell them and to hold the proceeds of sale on trust for his children in equal shares. The pits had in fact been worked out six years after the testator's death and before the matter was litigated. However, both at first instance and in the English Court of Appeal, it was held that the gift failed for remoteness because it could not be certain that the pits would be worked out within the perpetuity period.[56] The fact that the court had the power to force the trustees to work the pits out before the end of the period was apparently not considered.[57] In an analogous American case, a covenant to build an auditorium in good faith and with due diligence did not affect a finding that a lease in respect of the building was void because the building might not be completed within 21 years.[58]

(v) Alternative contingencies

[8.13] There is one partial exception to the common law requirement of certainty of vesting. As explained by Morris and Leach:[59]

---

53. (1889) 43 Ch. D. 246. Cf. *Re Garnham* [1910] 2 Ch. 413.
54. As occurred in *Harris v. King* (1936) 56 C.L.R. 177.
55. [1894] 2 Ch. 310 (first instance); [1894] 3 Ch. 381 (C.A.).
56. For other examples, see *Re Jones (decd)* (1950) 66 T.L.R. (Pt 2) 51; *Belyea v. McBride* [1942] 3 D.L.R. 785 (P.C.); *Re Bewick* [1911] 1 Ch. 116; *Re Stratheden and Campbell* [1894] 3 Ch. 265; *Haggerty v. City of Oakland* 161 Cal. App. 2d 407, 326 P. 2d 957 (1958).
57. See Leach (1964) op. cit. at 12; Leach (1952) op. cit. at 45.
58. *Haggerty v. City of Oakland* 161 Cal. App. 2d 407, 326 P. 2d 957 (1958).
59. Morris and Leach, op. cit., p. 181. See also Megarry and Wade, p. 274; Sappideen and Butt, p. 67ff.

"Where a gift is made upon either of two expressed contingencies, one of which must occur, and the other of which may not, the gift is valid if the first contingency occurs although it is invalid if the second contingency occurs."[60]

In this specific case, the court will wait and see what actually happens within the perpetuity period before deciding upon the validity of a gift. However, for the rule to apply, the two contingencies must be clearly expressed in the gift, and not merely implicit in it.[61] As stated by Cotton L.J. in *Re Harvey*:[62]

"It is not enough that you can separate the gift over so as to make it an alternative gift on two contingencies—the testatrix must herself have separated it so as to make it take effect on the happening of either of two events."

This rule appears particularly bizarre since it pays more attention to the way in which the gift is worded than to the actual intention of the testator or settlor, making the validity of the gift depend on the words chosen by the testator rather than on any intention to violate the spirit of the rule against perpetuities.[63] It also seems quite contrary to reason to invalidate the gift because a contingency which might have happened outside the perpetuity period actually comes to pass within it. Since no perpetuity resulted from the condition, it seems almost spiteful to defeat the testator's intention by rendering her or him intestate when all the conditions for carrying out her or his wishes have taken place within the perpetuity period.

(vi) Construction

[8.14] The issue whether or not a gift is vested is always a matter of construction. The traditional common law rules concerning the construction of gifts have been described by Morris and Leach as "remorseless".[64] As stated by Parke B. in *Dungannon v. Smith*:[65]

---

60. See e.g. *Longhead d. Hopkins v. Phelps* (1770) 2 Wm. Bl. 704; 96 E.R. 414; *Leake v. Robinson* (1817) 2 Mer. 363; 35 E.R. 979; *Cambridge v. Rous* (1858) 25 Beav. 409; 53 E.R. 693; *Miles v. Harford* (1879) 12 Ch. D. 691, *Re Bowles* [1905] 1 Ch. 371; *Re Davey* [1915] 1 Ch. 837; *Mainwaring v. Mainwaring* (1923) 23 S.R. (N.S.W.) 531; *Caldwell v. Fleming* [1927] N.Z.L.R. 145; *Re Curryer's Will Trusts* [1938] Ch. 952.

61. *Re Harvey* (1888) 39 Ch. D. 289; *Re Bence* [1891] 3 Ch. 242; *Harris v. King* (1936) 56 C.L.R. 177; *Attorney-General v. Cahill* [1969] 1 N.S.W.R. 85; *Proctor v. Bishop of Bath & Wells* (1947) 2 H. Bl. 358; 126 E.R. 594.

62. (1888) 39 Ch. D. 289 at 298.

63. For illustrations of the capricious nature of this rule, see Morris and Leach, op. cit., p. 182; Megarry and Wade, p. 275.

64. Morris and Leach, op. cit., p. 247.

65. (1846) 12 Cl. & Fin. 546 at 599; 8 E.R. 1523 at 1545. See also *Pearks v. Moseley* (1880) 5 A.C. 714 at 719, per Lord Selborne L.C.; *Tidex v. Trustees Executors & Agency Co. Ltd* [1971] 2 N.S.W.L.R. 453 at 458, per Street J.; *Re Turney* [1899] 2 Ch. 739 at 744; *Re Atkinson* [1916] 1 Ch. 91 at 95-96; *Re Burnyeat* [1923] 2 Ch. 52 at 57; *Re Leigh's Settlement Trusts* [1930] Ch. 39 at 47-48; *Lindsay v. Miller (No. 2)* [1949] V.L.R. 154 at 157-158; *Re Murphy, (decd)* [1958] Qd R. 456 at 466 and 471; *Re Harding* [1956] N.Z.L.R. 482 at 487.

"Our first duty is to construe the will; and this we will do, exactly in the same way as if the rule against perpetuity had never been established, or were repealed when the will was made; not varying the construction in order to avoid the effect of that rule, but interpreting the words of the testator wholly without reference to it."

Despite this so-called remorselessness, the courts have endeavoured to mitigate the rigour and harshness of the rule against perpetuities where the words of the instrument under construction permit. Over the years, where possible the courts have inclined towards holding a gift to be vested in order to save the gift.[66] For example, a gift "to X when he or she attains the age of 21"[67] will always be held to be contingent. On the other hand, however, a gift "to X, to be paid when he or she attains the age of 21"[68] may be held to confer a vested interest with rights of enjoyment postponed. Similarly, if the testator directs that payments of trust income should go to the beneficiaries prior to the ostensible date of vesting, the court may imply that the gift vested at birth but that the principal is not available until the beneficiary reaches 25.[69] However, a mere discretionary power to pay income to potential beneficiaries which might or might not be exercised by trustees will not give rise to any such implication.[70]

There are also cases where the courts purport to follow the remorseless rules of construction but nevertheless conclude that the gift can be saved despite all indications to the contrary.[71] Two notable Australian cases are *Re Hobson's Will*[72] and *Brownfield v. Earle*.[73] In *Re Hobson's Will*, Cussen J. announced his intention not to depart from the "relentless" interpretation required by Lord Selborne's judgment in *Pearks v. Moseley*,[74] but drew attention to a passage in that case which he believed indicated that the remorseless approach is required only when the testator's words are clear and unambiguous. Where the court is dealing with words which are obscure and ambiguous, however, Cussen J. concluded that a judge is entitled to give some weight, in a question of remoteness, to the consideration that it is better to make effectual than to destroy the intention of the testator or settlor.[75] The reasoning of Barton J. in *Brownfield v. Earle*[76] was very similar. Both judges concluded that there was

66. See e.g. *Bickersteth v. Shanu* [1936] A.C. 290; *Hume v. Perpetual Trustees Executors & Agency Co. of Tasmania Ltd* (1939) 62 C.L.R. 242.
67. *Stapleton v. Cheales* (1711) Prec. Ch. 317; 24 E.R. 150; *Hanson v. Graham* (1801) 6 Ves. Jun. 239; 31 E.R. 1030. See Megarry and Wade, p. 244.
68. *Re Couturier* [1907] 1 Ch. 470; *Clobberie's Case* (1677) 2 Vent. 342; 86 E.R. 476; *Re Bartholemew* (1849) 1 Mac. & G. 354; 41 E.R. 1302; *Will of Bickerdike* [1918] V.L.R. 191; *Re Croser (decd)* (1973) 6 S.A.S.R. 420.
69. See Ford and Lee, p. 280.
70. *Barrett v. Barrett* (1918) 18 S.R. (N.S.W.) 637.
71. See Morris and Leach, op. cit., p. 251ff.
72. [1907] V.L.R. 724. Cf. *White v. Commissioner for Stamps* (1908) 8 S.R. (N.S.W.) 287; *Re Fawaz* [1958] V.R. 426.
73. (1914) 17 C.L.R. 615.
74. (1880) 5 A.C. 714 at 719.
75. [1907] V.L.R. 724 at 737.
76. (1914) 17 C.L.R. 615.

sufficient ambiguity in the words of the instrument before them to allow
a construction which came far closer to carrying out the testator's wishes
than would be possible under the remorseless approach.

1. Examples of the Application of the Common Law Rule

[8.15]   1. An inter vivos disposition: "To such of my grandchildren
who reach the age of 21." This gift will be void as it infringes the rule.
The only relevant life in being is the grantor. The grantor's children
(if any) cannot count as lives in being as their number is capable of
increase so long as the grantor is alive. This remains true at common
law regardless of the age of the grantor. The perpetuity period is thus
the life of the grantor plus 21 years. The gift clearly fails as the
perpetuity period may be exceeded prior to vesting.

2. A bequest: "To such of my grandchildren who reach the age of 21."
The bequest is valid. As the bequest will not take effect until the
testator's death, the testator's children will class as lives in being as
their number is not capable of increase. The gift must vest (if at all)
within the lives of the testator's children plus 21 years.[77]

3. A bequest: "To such of my grandchildren who reach the age of 25
years." This bequest is void. As in example 2, the lives in being are
the testator and her or his children. However, if all the testator's
children die prior to the oldest grandchild attaining the age of four
years, the gift will not vest until more than 21 years after the death of
the lives in being.

4. An inter vivos gift or bequest: "To the first child of Mary who
marries."[78] The gift or bequest is void, unless at the time of the
disposition one of Mary's children has already married. The only life
in being is Mary. It is possible that none of Mary's children will marry
within 21 years of her death.

2. New South Wales and the Australian Capital Territory

(a) The perpetuity period

[8.16]   The New South Wales Act sets a mandatory 80 year perpetuity
period,[79] which replaces the complex "life in being" common law period.
Unlike other jurisdictions which have enacted perpetuities legislation,[80]

---

77. As a result of modern day sperm and ova banks, it is no longer necessarily true
that a child must reach the age of 21 within 21 years of her or his parents' death.
For the legal difficulties in this context associated with advancing medical
technology, see Sappideen, "Sperm Banks, Wills and Perpetuities" (1979) 53
A.L.J. 311; Leach, "Perpetuities in the Atomic Age: The Sperm Bank and the
Fertile Decedent" (1962) 48 Am. Bar Assoc. J. 942.
78. A child includes an ex-nuptial child: *Children (Equality of Status) Act* 1976 (N.S.W.),
s. 7(4); *Status of Children Act* (Vic.), s. 3(2); *Status of Children Act* 1978 (Qld), s. 3(2);
Family Relationships Act 1975 (S.A.), s. 6(1); *Wills Act* 1970 (W.A.), s. 31; *Status
of Children Act* 1974 (Tas.), s. 3(2).
79. N.S.W.: s. 7(1).
80. Vic.: s. 5; Qld: s. 209; W.A.: s. 101.

New South Wales does not provide for the common law period to be used as an alternative to the statutory period. It is not yet settled whether gestation periods may be added to the 80 year period in order to save a settlement.[81] The better answer would appear to be that actual periods of gestation should be added to the 80 year period, as this is consistent with the common law position (see above [8.06]) and allows gifts to the children of males and gifts to the children of females to be treated equally.[82] In addition, Sappideen and Butt state that this would accord "with the general policy of the law to treat a child en ventre sa mere as living where it is for the benefit of that child".[83]

The mandatory 80 year period seems certain to render the drafting and administration of gifts a far simpler process than it was at common law.[84] In addition, the fixed period is more appropriate to commercial transactions than the common law period with its inclusion of elements as variable as a "life in being".[85]

Section 3(2) (N.S.W.) enacts the common law rule that a will is deemed to take effect upon the death of the testator. The Act makes no specific provision for the commencement of the perpetuity period with respect to other forms of disposition. It is therefore assumed that, as at common law, in respect of an inter vivos gift the period commences when the instrument takes effect, and in respect of interests created by deed, the period commences on delivery of the deed: see above [8.07].

(b) Certainty of vesting

[8.17]   The common law requirement of certainty of vesting as at the date the disposition takes effect has been completely reformed by the perpetuities legislation, which replaces it with a "wait-and-see" system.[86] Instead of determining the validity of the gift by assessing all the possibilities, no matter how extravagant or remote, as they stand at the date the perpetuity period begins to run, the court now examines what actually happens. Under the New South Wales legislation, if a gift must vest within the 80 year period fixed by the Act, it is valid. If it is incapable of vesting inside the 80 year period, it is necessarily invalid. In either of these cases, the gift is unaffected by the wait-and-see provisions.[87] However, if the gift is capable of vesting within the period but not certain to do so, instead of being required to invalidate the gift, the court must wait and see if the gift actually vests within the 80 year period. If it does, it is valid. If it does not, it is invalid. If at any time it becomes certain

---

81. Cf. *Perpetuities and Accumulations Act* 1985 (A.C.T.), s. 8(3). A certificate from a medical practitioner who has examined a woman stating that she is pregnant is required: s. 8(4).
82. See Morris and Leach, op. cit., pp. 64-65.
83. Sappideen and Butt, p. 48.
84. Ibid., p. 47
85. See Sappideen and Butt, p. 47; Morris and Leach, op. cit., pp. 68-69.
86. N.S.W.: s. 8. For illustrations of the operation of the N.S.W. and A.C.T. provision relating to certainty of vesting, see Sappideen and Butt, p. 60ff.
87. See Sappideen and Butt, p. 62.

that the gift cannot vest within the period, wait-and-see ceases to operate and the gift fails.

The absurdities of the common law presumption of fertility have not been dealt with in the New South Wales Act, despite the New South Wales Law Reform Commission's recommendation that statutory presumptions should be enacted,[88] as in the other jurisdictions.[89] Sappideen and Butt suggest that this is because the implementation of an 80 year perpetuity· period coupled with a system of wait-and-see was thought to make such presumptions unnecessary.[90] However, the failure to provide statutory presumptions as to the ages outside which the court may assume someone to be incapable of bearing children may result in administrative inconvenience, forcing trustees and executors to wait-and-see longer than is really necessary. In the absence of presumptions, it is possible that the old cases concerning fertile octogenarians, unborn widows, and similar oddities will be imported into the reformed rule as a hurdle serving to unnecessarily prolong the wait-and-see period.

(c) Alternative contingencies

[8.18]   The common law rules concerning gifts conditional on either of two contingencies are also unnecessary under the new law.[91] Under the wait-and-see system, the issue of the validity of a gift or will is deferred until it becomes clear whether either of the contingencies occurs within the perpetuity period. If one of the contingencies happens, the gift is valid. If neither happens, it fails.

3. Victoria

(a) The perpetuity period

[8.19]   In contrast to the New South Wales legislation, the *Perpetuities and Accumulations Act* 1968 (Vic.)[92] gives the disponor a choice between a statutory period and the common law formula. By s. 5(1), the statutory period is the number of years not exceeding 80 as is specified in the instrument as the perpetuity period applicable to the disposition. Section 5(1) must be read together with s. 5(3), which states:

> "If no period of years is specified in an instrument by which a disposition is made as the perpetuity period applicable to the disposition but a date certain is specified in the instrument as the date on which the disposition shall vest the instrument shall, for the purposes of this section, be deemed to specify as the perpetuity period applicable to the disposition a number of years equal to the number of years from the date of the taking effect of the instrument to the specified vesting date."

88. New South Wales Law Reform Commission, Report No. 26 (1976), Report on Perpetuities and Accumulations Pt 10.
89. Vic.: s. 8; Qld: s. 212; W.A.: s. 102.
90. Sappideen and Butt, pp. 65-66.
91. Ibid., p 68.
92. For a detailed discussion of the Victorian perpetuities legislation, see Hogg and Ford, "Victorian Perpetuities Law in a Nutshell" (1969) 7 M.U.L.R. 155; Doane and McCredie, "Perpetuities Reform in Victoria" (1969) 43 A.L.J. 366.

The common law formula is slightly altered by s. 6(4), which increases the number of persons who may be held to be lives in being. The subsection states that in the disposition to a class of persons or to one or more members of a class, any person living at the date of the disposition whose life is so expressed or implied as relevant for any member of the class may be reckoned a life in being when ascertaining the perpetuity period.

Like the New South Wales legislation (see above [8.16]ff.), the Victorian Act does not contain a specific provision stating when the perpetuity period begins to run. In the absence of such a provision, it may be presumed that the common law rules continue to apply on this point: see above [8.07].

(b) Certainty of Vesting

[8.20]   Section 6(1) of the Victorian Act creates a wait-and-see system analogous to that provided by the New South Wales perpetuities legislation. The subsection states:

> "Where apart from the provisions of this section and of section 9 a disposition would be void on the ground that the interest disposed of might not become vested until too remote a time the disposition shall be treated until such time (if any) as it becomes established that the vesting must occur, if at all, after the end of the perpetuity period as if the disposition were not subject to the rule against perpetuities; and its becoming so established shall not affect the validity of anything previously done in relation to the interest disposed of by way of advancement, application of intermediate income or otherwise."

The reference to s. 9 is to the provision similar to s. 9 (N.S.W.) authorising the reduction of age and the exclusion of class members in order to avoid the application of the rule against perpetuities: see below [8.28].

Unlike the New South Wales legislation (see above [8.17]), the Victorian Act contains presumptions designed to abrogate the common law conclusive presumption of fertility, and to avoid the harsh effects of the "unborn widow(er)" cases. Section 8(1) provides that, subject to evidence that a living person was or was not capable of having a child at the time in question, a male is incapable of having a child if he is under the age of 12, and a female is presumed capable of bearing children between the ages of 12 and 55, but not otherwise. By s. 8(4), these provisions apply not only to begetting and giving birth, but also to having a child by "adoption, legitimation or other means". If someone has a child outside the ages indicated by the statute after a perpetuities case has been decided according to the presumption, s. 8(2) allows the court to make whatever order it thinks fit in order to place that person in the position which he or she would have held if the case had not been determined according to the presumption. Section 10 attempts to overcome the unborn widow(er) cases by deeming the widow or widower of a person who is a life in being under the terms of a gift to be a life in being in two circumstances: in the case of a disposition in favour of that widow or widower, or in the case of a gift to a third party, the vesting of which is expressed to be dependent upon the death of the widow(er) or some contingency occurring during her or his lifetime.

4. Western Australia[93]

(a) The perpetuity period

[8.21] The *Property Law Act* 1969 (W.A.) provides for a choice between a period of years and the common law "lives in being plus 21 years". By s. 101, any period of years not exceeding 80 may be specified in the disposition, and if none is specified, the common law period will apply. Unlike s. 6(4) of the Victorian Act (see above **[8.19]**), the Western Australian Act does not alter the common law rules which determine which lives may be classified as lives in being for the purposes of the rule against perpetuities.

(b) Certainty of vesting

[8.22] Section 103 creates a wait-and-see system. Subsection (1) reads in part:

> "A limitation shall not be declared or treated as invalid, as infringing the rule against perpetuities, unless and until it is certain that the interest that it creates cannot vest within the perpetuity period."

The Act also contains in s. 102(1) and (2), presumptions governing the legal capacity to procreate, bear or adopt a child. These presumptions may be rebutted by evidence tendered at the time the matter comes before the court, but not subsequently. Medical evidence of capacity or incapacity of procreating or bearing a child is admissible under s. 102(3). It is presumed that a female over the age of 55 is incapable of bearing a child, and that she will not adopt a child after the age of 55. Both females and males are presumed incapable of having children until they attain the age of 12 years.

Section 102(4) provides for the situation in which any of the presumptions are applied or where evidence as to capacity or incapacity to reproduce is accepted, but one of the persons concerned has a child nonetheless. In such a case, the decision of the court is to remain effective notwithstanding the subsequent birth or adoption of a child. However, provided that the limitation concerned is not itself invalid, a right to any property conferred upon that child or her or his spouse (including any right to follow or trace the property) is to be unaffected by the court's decision.

Section 108 contains a deeming provision similar to that contained in s. 10 of the Victorian Act (see above **[8.20]**) which is designed to prevent gifts being invalidated in a hypothetical unborn widow(er) situation.

---

93. See Simes, "Reform of the Rule Against Perpetuities in Western Australia" (1963) 6 U.W.A.L.R. 21; Allan, "The Rule Against Perpetuities Restated" (1963) 6 U.W.A.L.R. 27.

5. Queensland

(a) The perpetuity period

[8.23] Sections 210(4) and 209(1) of the *Property Law Act* 1974 (Qld) increase the number of persons who may be reckoned lives in being at common law and provide for an alternative power to specify the perpetuity period, in terms identical to those of ss 6(4) and 5(1) of the Victorian Act respectively: see above **[8.19]**.

(b) Certainty of vesting

[8.24] Section 210 of the Act institutes a wait-and-see system identical to that provided for by s. 6 of the Victorian Act: see above **[8.20]**. Sections 212 and 214 provide for presumptions as to future parenthood and to cover the unborn widow(er) situation in the same manner as ss 8 and 10 of the Victorian Act, respectively: see above **[8.20]**.

III. CLASS GIFTS

1. The Common Law Position

[8.25] Sir Denys Buckley, of the English Court of Appeal, in *Re Drummond's Settlement* recently described a class gift as:[94]

> "a limitation in favour of a number of persons which is uncertain in number when the limitation is created and is to be ascertained in the future, such persons all coming within a common classification or description, taking one divisible subject matter in specified proportions dependent on the number of takers, all of whose interests must, it seems, vest at the same time."

As this dictum indicates, the common law rules concerning gifts to classes of persons deal with situations where the amount to be received by each member of a group depends upon the total number of persons within that group. An illustration is: "My estate is to be divided equally among my nieces." This type of gift must be contrasted with separate gifts made to each of a group of persons. An illustration of this is: "I bequeath the sum of $500 per week for life to each of my children." This latter type of gift is not affected by the law relating to class gifts, as the number of children cannot vary after the testator's death.[95]

The rule applicable to class gifts is known as the "all or nothing" rule. It states that the precise proportion of the gift which is to vest in each member of the class of beneficiaries must be sure to be known within the

---

94. [1988] 1 All E.R. 449 at 453. His Honour added (at 455) that although he was not prepared to decide that a requirement that all takers should satisfy the same qualifications is an essential feature of every class gift, it is, where it exists, a strong indication that the gift may be a class gift, and its absence is a contrary indication.

95. See e.g. *Wilkinson v. Duncan* (1861) 30 Beav. 111; 54 E.R. 831. Other illustrations of gifts falling inside and outside the class gifts rules are given in Megarry and Wade, p. 261; Morris and Leach, op. cit., p. 106.

perpetuity period. If the class is capable of increase outside the period, the gift will fail, not merely in its application to any additional members who may be born after the perpetuity period ends, but for all members of the class.[96] Thus, in effect, the size of the grantee's share is itself a contingency unless it is incapable of variation.[97]

2. Class-Closing Rules

[8.26] In 1791, the "rule of convenience" commonly known as the rule in *Andrews v. Partington*[98] emerged. This rule allows the closure of a class of people at the date when the first member of the class becomes entitled to take, irrespective of whether the class is capable of further growth. Take as an illustration the devise: "To my grandchildren upon attaining the age of 21 years." In this situation, the class closes upon the first grandchild's 21st birthday, even if the children of the testator are still of childbearing age (in fact or at law). All grandchildren born at the death of the testator are included in the class and may collect their shares upon their 21st birthdays. If any of the younger grandchildren should fail to reach 21, those remaining will obtain an augmented share.

There are two important effects of the rule in *Andrews v. Partington*. First, once the class closes, no one born subsequently can enter the class. Thus, in a bequest "To my grandchildren upon attaining the age of 21 years", once one grandchild has attained 21 and the class closes, any grandchildren born later will be excluded from acquiring a share. Secondly, in certain circumstances the rule can save a gift from being declared void under the rule against perpetuities. Megarry and Wade cite as an illustration a devise "to all of A's grandchildren", where A is living at the testator's death and has a living grandchild.[99] This gift, which would otherwise be void, will be saved as the class will close immediately upon the testator's death since the first member of the class is entitled to her or his share.

As the class-closing rule is premised on the assumption that the testator or settlor would prefer an early distribution of the gift to an indefinite waiting period for those who have qualified for the gift (even at the cost

---

96. See e.g. *Re Hooper's Settlement Trusts* [1948] 1 Ch. 586 at 589; *Pearks v. Moseley* (1880) 5 A.C. 714; *Re Lord's Settlement* [1947] 2 All E.R. 685; *In the Will of Deane, Earle v. Deane* [1913] V.L.R. 272; *Ker v. Hamilton* (1880) 6 V.L.R. (Eq) 172; *In the Will of Breheney* [1915] V.L.R. 242; *Re Whiteford* [1915] 1 Ch. 347; *Tidex v. Trustees Executors & Agency Co.* [1971] 2 N.S.W.L.R. 453.

97. Although the size of the grantee's share is critical for the rule against perpetuities, the amount or value of the share is irrelevant: *Re Cassel* [1926] Ch. 358; *Beachway Management Ltd v. Wisewell* [1971] Ch. 610.

98. (1791) 3 Bro. C.C. 401; 29 E.R. 610. As stated by Sir Denys Buckley in *Re Drummond's Settlement* [1988] 1 All E.R. 449 at 454, the rule in *Andrews v. Partington* is in reality a rule of construction rather than a rule of convenience. The rule is discussed in Ford and Lee, p. 292; Morris and Leach, op. cit., p. 110ff., Megarry and Wade, p. 263ff.; Morris, "The Rule Against Perpetuities and the Rule in *Andrews v. Partington*" (1954) 70 L.Q.R. 61; Bailey, "Class-Closing, Accumulations and Acceleration" [1958] C.L.J. 39. For a modern illustration, see *Re Wernher* [1961] 1 All E.R. 184.

99. Megarry and Wade, p. 264.

of excluding some possible beneficiaries),[100] the rule can be excluded by the expression of a contrary intention.[101]

If the gift depends upon a contingency (for example, marriage, or the attainment of 21 years), the class closes when the first member of the class qualifies (that is marries or turns 21). Where the gift is preceded by a life estate, the class closes at the death of the life tenant. An illustration is: "To my husband for life, and upon his death, to the children of X in equal shares." In this case, the class closes at the death of the husband.

If the vesting of the gift is also preceded by a contingency, the class closes at the death of the life tenant, or upon the first class member satisfying the contingency thereafter. An illustration is a gift "To my husband for life, and upon his death, to the children of X who shall attain the age of 21 years". Here, if X has one or more children aged 21 or over at the death of the husband, the class will close upon his decease. If X has only infant children at the death of the husband, the class will close when the first of them reaches 21 years.

The rule in *Andrews v. Partington* does not apply to a situation where the class members are to take at birth, and there are no members of the class at the date of the distribution of the property. In such a case, the class remains open indefinitely, encountering all the difficulties the rule in *Andrews v. Partington* was designed to avoid.[102]

Examples of the Application of the Common Law Class-Closing Rule

[8.27]   1. A gift or bequest: "to my trustees on trust for A for life, and then to the children of B." Assume that at the date of the disposition B is alive and has two children (B1 and B2). Assume also that A is alive. The class (B's children) will remain open until A's death. During this time none of B's children can call for a distribution of assets. On the closure of the class at A's death, any children of B alive at that time will qualify as a beneficiary. This will include B1 and B2, and if a third child, B3, has been born after the disposition but before A's death, that child will also be beneficiary. However, if a fourth child, B4, is born after A's death, that child will be excluded.

2. A gift or bequest: "To the children of Mary who marry." If at the date of disposition Mary is dead, the gift is valid under the rule against perpetuities, as Mary's children are lives in being and they must clearly marry within their own lifetimes. Each child who marries will qualify as a beneficiary. This situation does not give rise to the class-closing rule. The class-closing rule will apply, however, if at the date of the disposition Mary is still alive. Without the class-closing rule, the gift would be void as infringing the rule against perpetuities. However,

100. *Re Charters* [1927] 1 Ch. 466 at 474; *Re Drummond's Settlement* [1988] 1 All E.R. 449 at 454.
101. *Bateman v. Foster* (1844) 1 Coll. 118; 63 E.R. 346; *Re Courtenay* (1905) 74 L.J. Ch. 654; *Re Bukowski (decd)* [1954] St.R.Qd 286; *Re Chapman's Settlement Trusts* [1977] 1 W.L.R. 1163; *Re Clifford's Settlement Trusts* [1981] Ch. 63; *Re Cockle's Will Trusts* [1967] Ch. 690; *Re Ketby-Fletcher's Will Trusts* [1969] 1 Ch. 339.
102. *Shepherd v. Ingram* (1764) Amb. 448; 27 E.R. 296; *Re Ransome* [1957] Ch. 348; *Weld v. Bradbury* (1715) 2 Vern. 705; 23 E.R. 1058.

under the class-closing rule the gift will be saved if at the date of the disposition one or more of Mary's children have already qualified as beneficiaries by being married. Assume that at the date of disposition Mary has two children, C1 and C2. C1 is married, and C2 is single. Assume further that after the date of disposition, Mary produces a third child, C3. The class will close immediately upon the disposition and the gift will be valid as C1 has a vested interest. C2 may also become a beneficiary by marrying at a later date. However, C3 cannot become a beneficiary as he or she was not in existence at the time the class was closed.

3. New South Wales

[8.28]   The "all or nothing" common law rule has been abolished by s. 8 of the *Perpetuities Act* 1984. In addition to the "wait-and-see" provisions in s. 8(1) (see above [8.17]), a number of provisions dealing with class gifts replace the all or nothing rule. These provisions are commonly referred at as "remedial" provisions in that they endeavour to prevent a gift from being declared void by the perpetuity rule. Section 9(4) provides for the exclusion of actual or potential class members where that is necessary to prevent a gift from infringing the rule, unless such exclusion would exhaust the class completely.[103] Section 9(1) further provides for the ages of potential beneficiaries to be reduced to allow them to take if they are prevented from doing so only by reason of an age contingency. The order of application of the remedial provisions is specified in s. 10 as s. 8, then s. 9(1), and finally s. 9(4).

Section 10 does not appear to have resolved all disputes regarding the application of the remedial provisions. As discussed in detail by Sappideen and Butt,[104] the exact mode in which these provisions will be applied is debatable. In the case of a class gift which must fail without the benefit of a reduction of the ages of beneficiaries, it is unclear whether the age contingency should be reduced once and for all, to ensure that all potential beneficiaries may take, or whether it should be reduced by stages, each one allowing us to wait-and-see a little longer.[105] It is also debatable whether the age reduction provisions should be applied to the whole class of beneficiaries to reduce the age of qualification for all

103. N.S.W., s. 3(3) defines the meaning of "member of a class": "A person shall be treated as a member of a class if in that person's case each and every condition identifying a member of the class is satisfied". N.S.W., s. 3(3) defines the meaning of "potential member of a class": "A person shall be treated as a potential member of a class if in that person's case only one or some of the conditions identifying a member of the class is or are satisfied but there is a possibility that the remainder of those conditions will in time be satisfied."

104. Sappideen and Butt, p. 93. See also Sappideen, "Perpetuities—Age Reduction and the Application of the 80 Year Period: Some Unexpected Problems" (1986) 60 A.L.J. 471; Megarry and Wade, p. 269; and Prichard, "Two Petty Perpetuities Puzzles" (1969) 27 C.L.J. 284 concerning the equivalent U.K. legislation.

105. Effectively, this allows each child to come as close to the age contingency as possible. Each may then take at a different age.

members of the class, or whether it should be reduced only for those members of the class who would otherwise be unable to take.[106] This dilemma cannot be solved by reference to the disponor's intentions.

4. Victoria

[8.29] Section 9 of the *Perpetuities and Accumulations Act* 1968 enacts reduction of age and exclusion of class members provisions in terms similar to those contained in the New South Wales legislation. Similar uncertainties exist in relation to the age reduction provisions as in New South Wales: see above **[8.28]**. Section 9 specifies that wait-and-see is to be the first remedy applied, followed by age reduction and finally the exclusion of class members, if necessary.

5. Western Australia

[8.30] Reduction of age provisions in order to save a class gift are contained in s. 105(1) of the *Property Law Act* 1969. Section 105(3) specifically provides that s. 105(1) applies without prejudice to any provision whereby the absolute vesting either of capital or income of property, or the ascertainment of a beneficiary or class of beneficiaries, is also made to depend upon the marriage of any person, or any other event which may occur before the age stated in the instrument has been reached.

Section 106 allows for the exclusion of class members who do not attain a vested interest within the perpetuity period, for the purpose of ensuring that the whole class gift is not declared void by the rule against perpetuities. Section 107 specifies the order of application of the remedial provisions, in terms substantially similar to s. 10 (N.S.W.). Pursuant to s. 107, the exclusion of class members is a last resort only after wait-and-see and the reduction of age provisions have failed to save the gift.

6. Queensland

[8.31] Reduction of age and exclusion of class members provisions are contained in s. 213 of the *Property Law Act* 1974 (Qld), and are to be applied in the same order required by the other States.

IV.   THE EFFECT OF INFRINGING THE RULE AGAINST PERPETUITIES[107]

1. The Common Law Position

[8.32] The effect of a violation of the rule against perpetuities at common law varies depending on the sequence of interests concerned.

---

106. Sappideen and Butt, p. 98; Prichard, op. cit. at 291.
107. The issue is discussed in Morris and Leach, op. cit., p. 164ff.; Megarry and Wade, p. 270ff.

If a particular contingency in an instrument is rendered void because it infringes the rule, any prior interest takes effect just as it would have done if the void contingency had not been inserted in the gift.[108] An illustration is a bequest: "To such of my grandchildren as attain the age of 21 years, but upon the birth of my first great-grandchild, to that great-grandchild." The bequest to the great-grandchild is void for remoteness since the child may be born more than 21 years after the death of all the testator's children. The bequest to the grandchildren takes effect absolutely.

In the case of a void disposition following upon a valid interest for a limited time, when the prior interest comes to an end the property goes to the heir (in the case of realty) or the residuary legatee (in the case of personalty) just as it would if the gift were held to be void for any other reason. An illustration is a bequest: "To Richard for life, and then to such of Richard's children as attain the age of 30 years." Upon the death of Richard the property passes to the heir or residuary legatee of the testator.

In the absence of any prior interest created by the will or settlement, the property concerned passes as it would on intestacy (if a will) or, in the case of a gift inter vivos, on a resulting trust for the settlor.

The situation with respect to subsequent interests following void dispositions must also be considered. The rule is that any limitation dependent or expectant upon a prior limitation which is void for remoteness is invalid.[109] Note, however, that limitations valid in themselves, which follow but are not dependent upon limitations which offend the rule against perpetuities, are not affected by the invalidity of the prior limitations.[110] A dependent limitation is one that is designed to take effect only if the prior limitation takes effect, whereas an independent limitation is one that is intended to take effect in all eventualities.[111] If the prior disposition is a fee simple estate, any subsequent limitation must automatically constitute a dependent limitation as it is contingent upon the failure of the prior dispositions. In other situations, the issue of dependence is a question of construction, where the courts will endeavour to ascertain the intentions of the grantor from the terms of the disposition. Megarry and Wade give as an illustration of an independent limitation the gift: "to A for life, remainder for life to A's first son to marry, remainder in fee simply to B (an infant) at 21." Here, the first remainder will be void at common law unless at the time of the disposition one of A's sons has already married, but regardless of whether this is so, B's contingent

---

108. *Garland v. Brown* (1864) 10 L.T. 292 at 294.

109. *Re Abbott* [1893] 1 Ch. 54 at 57, per Stirling J. See also *Robinson v. Hardcastle* (1788) 2 T.R. 241; 100 E.R. 131; *Routledge v. Dorril* (1794) 2 Ves. Jun. 357; 30 E.R. 671; *Beard v. Westcott* (1822) 5 B. & Al. 801; 106 E.R. 1383; *Monypenny v. Dering* (1852) 2 De G.M. & G. 145; 42 E.R. 826; *Re Buckton's Settlement Trusts* [1964] Ch. 497; *Re Hubbard's Will Trusts* [1963] Ch. 275.

110. *Re Canning's Will Trusts* [1936] Ch. 309; *Re Coleman* [1936] Ch. 528.

111. See the discussion in Morris, "Ulterior Limitations and the Rule Against Perpetuities" (1950) 10 C.L.J. 392. For cases on the meaning of "dependent" and "independent" gifts, see and cf. *Re Backhouse* [1921] 2 Ch. 51; *Re Canning's Will Trusts* [1936] Ch. 309; *Re Coleman* [1936] Ch. 528; *Macpherson v. Maund* (1937) 58 C.L.R. 341.

interest is valid. The issue involving the validity of the limitation to A's son has no relevance to the gift to B. The authors contrast this with the gift: "to A for life, remainder in fee simple to A's first son to marry, but if there is no such son then remainder to B for life." Unless one of A's sons has already married, both remainders will be void. B's gift is void as it is dependent on the failure of the limitation to A's son.[112]

If the prior disposition is held void for remoteness and the subsequent disposition is held to be dependent upon it, it makes no difference that the subsequent disposition would have been valid if it had stood separately. Even where the subsequent disposition is one to a living person which must vest within the perpetuity period, it will be invalid.[113] In contrast, if the dispositions are held to vest independently, the subsequent disposition will be valid.[114]

The apparent reasoning behind the rule is that if the testator or settlor expresses the dispositions as dependent upon each other, the second cannot take effect until the first is exhausted. If the first is void it cannot take effect at all, and therefore cannot be exhausted.[115] However, if this was the disponor's intention it seems strange logic to assume that if the disponor had been able to see the possibility that the rule against perpetuities would thwart her or his plans, he or she would have preferred to die intestate rather than allow the second gift to take effect without the first.[116]

Whether a subsequent contingency is dependent or independent of a prior void contingency is always a matter of construction. The attitude of the courts in construing such provisions varies from time to time, sometimes appearing quite relentless and at other times upholding the provisions as valid by finding that a subsequent limitation is independent of a prior void limitation.[117]

2. New South Wales, Victoria, Queensland and Western Australia

[8.33] Section 17 of the *Perpetuities Act* 1984 (N.S.W.) deals with dependent interests. It states:

"(1) Where a provision of a settlement creates an interest, the provision is not rendered invalid by the rule against perpetuities or the rule against perpetual trusts by reason only that the interest is ulterior to and dependent upon an interest which is so invalid.

(2) Where a provision of a settlement creates an interest which is ulterior to another interest and the other interest is rendered invalid

112. Megarry and Wade, p. 272.
113. *Beard v. Westcott* (1813) 5 Taunt. 393; 128 E.R. 741; *Re Thatcher's Trusts* (1859) 26 Beav. 365; 53 E.R. 939.
114. *Re Canning's Will Trusts* [1936] Ch. 309; *MacPherson v. Maund* (1937) 58 C.L.R. 341.
115. *Re Abbott* [1893] 1 Ch. 54 at 57, per Stirling J.
116. Morris and Leach, op. cit., p. 179.
117. See Megarry and Wade, p. 273; Morris and Leach, op. cit., p. 176ff.

by the rule against perpetuities or the rule against perpetual trusts, the acceleration of the vesting of the ulterior interest shall not be affected by reason only that the other interest is so invalid."

Similar provisions exist in the other Australian jurisdictions.[118]

This provision is designed to save dependent subsequent limitations otherwise void at common law, provided that they would have been valid if they had stood alone. It is submitted that this represents a rationalisation of the common law rule which is more likely to make effectual the grantor's intentions.

V. EXCEPTIONS TO THE RULE AGAINST PERPETUITIES

1. The Common Law Position

There are a number of common law proprietary interests to which the application of the rule against perpetuities is either definitely inapplicable or remains questionable. The most significant of these possible common law exceptions is as follows.

(a) Possibilities of reverter

[8.34]   As discussed above [2.42], a possibility of reverter is the interest remaining in a grantor after he or she has conveyed property on terms whereby the grantee's interest is to end upon the occurrence of a determining event. In such a case, the estate will automatically revert to the grantor if the determining event occurs.

There is some disagreement as to whether the rule against perpetuities applies to possibilities of reverter. One argument is that it should apply to possibilities of reverter (where there is an effective gift over to the grantor) just as it would apply if the gift over was to any other person.[119] The policy of the rule, to protect the free alienability of land, is surely violated by a gift over to the grantor which tends to a perpetuity just as much as a gift over to another person conditioned upon an event which may not happen for hundreds of years. Another line of reasoning is that the interest is vested, not being subject to any contingency other than the regular termination of the prior estate, and that the rule against perpetuities therefore has no application.[120]

The weight of authority suggests that the rule does not operate to invalidate possibilities of reverter which may take effect outside the perpetuity period.[121] The leading case is *Re Chardon*,[122] in which Romer J. stated:[123]

---

118. *Perpetuities and Accumulations Act* 1968 (Vic.), s. 11; *Property Law Act* 1974 (Qld), s. 215; *Property Law Act* 1969 (W.A.), s. 109.
119. See Ford and Lee, p. 302.
120. See Ford and Lee, p. 302. Cf. Leach (1952) op. cit. at 57.
121. Ford and Lee, p. 302; Megarry and Wade, p. 276.
122. [1928] Ch. 464.
123. Ibid. at 468.

"The rule against perpetuities is not dealing with the duration of interests but with their commencement, and so long as the interest vests within lives in being and 21 years it does not matter how long that interest lasts."

Despite the policy reasons in favour of applying the rule to possibilities of reverter, *Hopper v. Corporation of Liverpool*[124] is the only reported case where this result has occurred. Although the case has attracted much comment,[125] it is clear that it does not state the current law for England or (presumably) for Australia.[126]

(b) Rights of entry

[8.35]   The right of entry for condition broken attached to a fee simple estate, which is the interest remaining in a grantor who conveys a fee simple estate subject to a condition subsequent (see above **[2.43]**), is treated by the courts differently to a possibility of reverter. The traditional distinction between a right of entry and a possibility of reverter is that in the former case if the condition giving rise to the destruction of the estate of the grantee occurs, the grantee's interest does not determine automatically (as in the case of a possibility of reverter), but only upon an entry or claim by the grantee, or her or his heirs or assigns. Although this appears to be a technical and trivial distinction, it was held to be sufficient for the common law to apply the rule against perpetuities differently and to ensure its application to rights of entry. The application of the rule to rights of entry for condition broken attached to a fee simple estate was established in *Re Trustees of Hollis' Hospital and Hague's Contract*[127] and in *Re Da Costa.*[128] These English decisions have been cited with approval in several Australian cases,[129] and where applied in *Re Smith (decd)*[130] and by Street J. (at first instance) in *Perpetual Trustee Co. v. Williams.*[131] Note that a right of entry reserved in a lease to the landlord in a forfeiture clause, exercisable where the tenant commits a breach of covenant, is treated differently and is not subject to the rule against perpetuities.[132]

124. (1944) 88 Sol. J. 213.
125. *Hopper* is criticised in (1946) 62 L.Q.R. 222 and (1957) 21 Conv. (N.S.) 213, but cited with approval by Leach (1952) op. cit. at 56, and Morris and Leach, op. cit., p. 212.
126. Australian commentators have assumed that *Re Chardon* states the Australian law on this issue: see Sappideen and Butt, p. 125; Ford and Lee, p. 302; Sackville and Neave, p. 617.
127. [1899] 2 Ch. 540.
128. [1912] 1 Ch. 337. See also *Re Macleay* (1875) L.R. 20 Eq. 186; *Imperial Tobacco Co. (of Great Britain & Ireland) Ltd v. Wilmott* [1964] 1 W.L.R. 902.
129. See e.g. *Williams v. Perpetual Trustee Co. Ltd* (1913) 17 C.L.R. 469 at 485, per Barton A.C.J. See also *In the Will of Brett* [1947] V.L.R. 483 at 485, per Herring C.J.
130. [1967] V.R. 341.
131. (1913) 13 S.R. (N.S.W.) 209 at 213-214.
132. *Re Tyrrell's Estate* [1907] 1 I.R. 292.

(c) Options and contracts

[8.36]   Options and contracts also constitute an exception to the rule against perpetuities at common law in certain circumstances.[133] Because the rule is a proprietary concept, it has no application to purely contractual obligations. Contracts creating proprietary interests are enforceable between the contracting parties under normal contract law regardless of whether or not a time limit exists for the performance of the contract. Thus, if A grants B an option without a time limit to purchase land, B can enforce the contract at any time against A by way of damages or specific performance.[134] The rule against perpetuities will not apply as the option is based on contract. B can assign the benefit of the option to C and C may enforce the option at any time.[135] However, if A sells the land to D, then B or C cannot enforce the option against D as the remedy would be proprietary. In this latter situation, the option will be subject to the rule.[136]

Where the rule applies, the courts will endeavour to safeguard the option, where possible. Thus, the courts may imply a term that the option must be exercised within a reasonable time, which is less than the perpetuity period.[137] If the option is contained in a lease, it will be valid provided that the fixed term is for no longer than 21 years.[138]

(d) Other common law exceptions

[8.37]   1. No limitation following an estate in tail (still valid in South Australia and Tasmania (see above **[2.22]**)) is void as the holder of such an estate can bar any subsequent interests.[139]

2. Any grant of a future easement is void, unless the easement must take effect within a 21 year period.[140]

3. Although a gift to a charity is subject to the normal operation of the perpetuity rule,[141] an exception exists in respect of a limitation transferring a proprietary interest from one charity to another upon a contingency. Such a limitation has been held to be valid even if it may

---

133. See the discussion in Sackville and Neave, pp. 618-619; Rossiter, "Options to Acquire Interests in Land-Freehold and Leasehold (Part II)" (1982) 56 A.L.J. 624 at 632-633.

134. *Trustees Executors & Agency Co. Ltd v. Peters* (1960) 102 C.L.R. 537 at 546. Cf. *Headland Developments Pty Ltd v. Bullen* [1975] 2 N.S.W.L.R. 309.

135. *Hutton v. Watling* [1948] Ch. 26.

136. *Woodall v. Clifton* [1905] 2 Ch. 257. B or C may, however, have a remedy against A for breach of contract: see *Worthing Corporation v. Heather* [1906] 2 Ch. 532.

137. *Headland Developments Pty Ltd v. Bullen* [1975] 2 N.S.W.L.R. 309.

138. See *McMahon v. Swan* [1924] V.L.R. 397; *Longmuir v. Kew* [1960] 1 W.L.R. 862.

139. *Nicolls v. Sheffield* (1787) 2 Bro. C.C. 215; 29 E.R. 121; *Heasman v. Pearse* (1871) L.R. 7 Ch. App. 275.

140. *Dunn v. Blackdown Properties Ltd* [1961] Ch. 433; *Newham v. Lawson* (1971) 22 P. & C.R. 852.

141. *Re Stratheden and Campbell* [1894] 3 Ch. 265; *Re Mander* [1950] Ch. 547; *Re Kagan* [1966] V.R. 538.

not occur until some indefinite date in the future.[142] It is established law that a gift to a charity is valid despite the fact that the interest created may remain subject to the charitable trust indefinitely.[143]

2. New South Wales, Victoria, Queensland and Western Australia

[8.38]   Notwithstanding the common law position discussed above, the legal commentators generally agree that considerations of policy favour the application of the rule against perpetuities to both rights of entry and possibilities of reverter.[144] The event upon which a possibility of reverter or right of re-entry is conditional may not come to pass for hundreds of years in some cases, so that the task of finding the grantor's heirs to return the land to them, or obtaining information as to whether the grantor's heirs will re-enter if the condition is broken, may be so arduous as to inhibit or prevent appropriate use of the land. In the case of a possibility of reverter, the grantor's heirs may be so numerous and widespread that the task of distributing the proceeds of any sale may not be viable financially.[145]

All jurisdictions with perpetuities legislation have recognised the logic of these arguments and the incongruity of the common law position by subjecting possibilities of reverter to the rule against perpetuities in the same manner as rights of entry. For example, the *Perpetuities Act* 1984 (N.S.W.), s. 14(2) states:

> "The rule against perpetuities applies to render invalid the provision for determination of a determinable interest created by a settlement in the same manner as the rule would apply to render invalid a condition subsequent in the settlement for defeasance of the determinable interest on the same contingency, and where that rule does so apply—
>
> (a) the determinable interest shall not be so determinable; and
>
> (b) a subsequent interest not itself rendered invalid by that rule shall be postponed or defeated to the extent necessary to allow the determinable interest to have effect free from the provision for determination."

The effect of this is that a possibility of reverter will remain effective until the end of the 80 year perpetuity period. After this period is completed, if the contingency upon which the possibility of reverter depends has still not occurred, the fee simple will become absolute and any subsequent interests will be defeated to the extent necessary to achieve this result.

---

142. *Re Tyler* [1891] 3 Ch. 252; *Christ's Hospital v. Grainger* (1849) 1 Mac. & G. 460; 41 E.R. 1343; *Royal College of Surgeons of England v. National Provincial Bank Ltd* [1952] A.C. 631.
143. *Goodman v. Saltash Corporation* (1882) 7 A. C. 633; *Re Bowen* [1893] 2 Ch. 491.
144. See e.g. Leach (1952) op. cit. at 55; Allan, op. cit. at 61-63. This was the recommendation of the New South Wales Law Reform Commission: Report No. 26 (1976).
145. Leach (1952) op. cit. at 56ff. gives some awesome examples: see e.g. *Brown v. Independent Baptist Church of Woburn* 325 Mass. 645, 91 N.E. 2d 922 (1950).

Similar, although not identical, provisions exist in the other jurisdictions.[146]

The legislation of all jurisdictions exempts certain options from the rule against perpetuities. Section 15 of the *Perpetuities Act* 1984 (N.S.W.) reads:

"The rule against perpetuities does not apply to—

(a) any option to renew a lease of property;

(b) any option to acquire a reversionary interest in property comprised in a lease;

(c) any right of pre-emption given for valuable consideration or by will in respect of property; or

(d) any other option given for valuable consideration or by will to acquire an interest in property".

Similar, although not identical, legislation exists elsewhere.[147]

The legislation of all jurisdictions also reaffirms the common law rule that the rule against perpetuities does not apply to a gift over from one charity to another.[148]

3. Miscellaneous Statutory Exceptions: Victoria, Queensland and South Australia

[8.39] Certain minor statutory exceptions to the rule against perpetuities exist in the *Law of Property Act* 1936 (S.A.). Section 59 states:

"For removing doubts, it is hereby declared that the rule of law relating to perpetuities does not apply and shall be deemed never to have applied—

(a) to any power to distrain on or to take possession of land or the income thereof given by way of indemnity against a rent, whether charged upon or payable in respect of any part of that land or not; or

(b) to any rentcharge created only as an indemnity against another rentcharge, although the indemnity rentcharge may arise or become payable only on breach of a condition or stipulation; or

(c) to any power, whether exercisable on breach of a condition or stipulation or not, to retain or withhold payment of any instalment of a rentcharge as an indemnity against another rentcharge; or

(d) to any grant, exception, or reservation of any right of entry on, or user of, the surface of land or of any easements, rights, or privileges over or under land for the purpose of—

(i) winning, working, inspecting, measuring, converting, manufacturing, carrying away and disposing of mines and minerals;

146. Vic.: s. 16; Qld: s. 219; W.A.: s. 111.
147. Vic.: s. 15; Qld: s. 218; W.A.: s. 110.
148. N.S.W.: s. 14(4); Vic.: s. 16(2); Qld: s. 219(2); W.A.: s. 111(2).

(ii) inspecting, grubbing up, felling, and carrying away timber and other trees, and the tops and lops thereof;

(iii) executing repairs, alterations, or additions to any adjoining land, or the buildings and erections thereon;

(iv) constructing, laying down, altering, repairing, renewing, cleansing, and maintaining sewers, watercourses, cesspools, gutters, drains, water pipes, gas pipes, electric wires or cables, or other like works.''

Section 62a(2) also provides that the rule does not apply to the trusts of any employees' benefit fund (defined in s. 62a(1)), whether created before or after the enactment of that section.

Similar legislation to s. 59 of the South Australian Act exists in Victoria and Queensland.[149]

149. Vic.: 13; Qld: s. 217.

9

The Nature of Co-ownership

[9.01] Where two or more persons are entitled to the simultaneous enjoyment of land, they hold their interests in co-ownership. Apart from the term "co-ownership", the terms "concurrent interests" and "estates and interests in community" can be used to denote this form of ownership. Co-ownership can exist at law or in equity, and in possession or in remainder in both freehold and leasehold estates. Traditionally, four types of co-ownership were recognised: joint tenancy, tenancy in common, coparcenary and tenancy by entireties. Although there is an unlikely possibility that a coparcenary may still arise (see below **[9.14]**) for all practical purposes it is extinct. A tenancy by entireties can no longer be created:[1] see below **[9.15]**. Thus, the two main forms of co-ownership which arise today are the joint tenancy and the tenancy in common. It should be noted that the word "tenancy" in the terms "joint tenancy" and "tenancy in common" is not used to connote a leasehold interest.

The essential characteristic of any form of co-ownership is that each co-owner has the right to possession of the whole of the land: no co-owner has an exclusive right to possession of any part.

I. TYPES OF CO-OWNERSHIP

1. Joint Tenancy

[9.02] A joint tenant has been described as one who totum tenet et nihil tenet, that is he or she holds the whole and yet nothing. Each joint tenant is seised of the whole of the estate or interest. Each is entitled to the use, possession and enjoyment of the whole, subject only to the rights of the other joint tenants. Thus, at common law, one joint tenant could not transfer her or his interest to another joint tenant by a conveyance of the interest: the joint tenant had nothing to convey for the other co-owner was already seised of the whole. Such a transaction had to be by way of release of the estate. In one sense, however, it is incorrect to speak of a joint tenant owning the entirety of the land for one joint tenant cannot alone deal with the land so as to bind the other joint tenants.[2]

[9.03] The two principal features or characteristics of the joint tenancy are the "four unities" and the right of survivorship. If one of the unities

---

1. *Registrar-General (N.S.W.) v. Wood* (1926) 39 C.L.R. 46.
2. See Mendes da Costa, "Co-Ownership under Victorian Land Law" (1961) 3 M.U.L.R. 137 at 149.

of interest, title or time is missing, or if there can be no right of survivorship, the co-owners are tenants in common. If unity of possession is absent, there is no co-ownership at all, for unity of possession is common to all forms of co-ownership. The fact that all of the four unities are present does not automatically mean that the co-ownership is capable of being a joint tenancy and whether or not it is depends upon several factors, the most relevant being the terms in which the land was conveyed to the co-owners.[3]

(a) The four unities

(i) Unity of possession

[9.04] Every co-owner is entitled concurrently to possession of the whole of the land. In order for co-ownership to exist, whether it be a joint tenancy or a tenancy in common, there must be unity of possession. A co-owner is not entitled exclusively to any one part of the land for if he or she were, separate ownership, not co-ownership, would exist. One practical consequence of the unity of posession is that a co-owner who occupies the whole of the land is not subject to an action for trespass by the other co-owner. Each co-owner is entitled to possession of the whole and an exercise of that right by one co-owner will not give rise to any right of action by a co-owner not exercising the right. However, if one co-owner destroys part of the subject matter of the tenancy or wrongfully excludes another co-owner from possession, remedies are available.[4] A further consequence of the unity of possession at common law was that a co-owner who received the whole of the rents and profits from the land was not liable to account to the other co-owners. In some States, legislation now ensures that a co-owner who receives more than her or his share of rents and profits must account to the other co-owners: see below [9.37].

(ii) Unity of interest

[9.05] In order for unity of interest to exist, the interest of each joint tenant must be the same in nature, extent and duration. Thus, there can be no unity of interest when the interests are of a different type or nature, as for example, between a freeholder and a leaseholder or a tenant in possession and a tenant in remainder. A grant, "To A for life and to B for 50 years" cannot create a joint tenancy between A and B for their interests are different in nature and also in duration. Similarly, a grant "to A in fee simple as to a three quarter share and to B in fee simple as to a one quarter share" does not satisfy the unity of interest requirement for the interests of A and B are different in extent. It should be noted that in both of these examples A and B are co-owners because they are simultaneously entitled to possession of the whole of the land. They take, however, as tenants in common.

---

3. See generally, Riddall, *Introduction to Land Law* (3rd ed., Butterworths, London, 1983), p. 143.
4. An action for trespass would lie in the first instance, and equity would order payment of an occupation rent in the second instance: see Megarry and Wade, p. 419.

Where a grant is made to A and B as joint tenants, the fact that the grant also provided for A or B to take as a remainderman does not destroy the joint tenancy. The subject matter of the joint tenancy is an estate and in this instance A and B are jointly seised of the life estate.

(iii) Unity of title

[9.06] Unity of title exists if all the joint tenants derive their interests from the same document or the same act. Thus, if all the tenants acquired their title by virtue of the same conveyance or if they simultaneously took possession and subsequently acquired title through adverse possession, the requirement of unity of title is satisfied. For example, if X, the holder of a fee simple estate conveys the land to A and B, unity of title exists between A and B. However, if A subsequently conveys her interest to C, C and B hold the land in co-ownership, but not as joint tenants for there is no unity of title, B having acquired her interest in a conveyance from X and C having acquired her interest in a conveyance from A.

(iv) Unity of time

[9.07] The requirement of unity of time is satisfied if the interest of each tenant vested in interest or possession at the same time and by virtue of the same common event. The fact that unity of title is present does not necessarily mean that unity of time also exists. The following situation provides an example of where unity of title may be present and yet there is no unity of time. A grant is made "To A for life, remainder to B and C when they attain 21 years". At the time of the grant, B and C are 20 years and 19 years respectively. B and C subsequently attain 21 years and A then dies. Their remainders vested at different times, and they take as tenants in common not as joint tenants, for although there is unity of possession, interest and title, there is no unity of time.

There are two exceptions to the requirement that there must be unity of time for a joint tenancy to exist. From early times it was accepted that in a conveyance to uses and in a disposition in a will, a joint tenancy could arise despite the fact that the requirement of unity of time was not satisfied.[5] In modern terminology any conveyance executed to a trustee for beneficiaries or any disposition in a will may give rise to a joint tenancy in the grantees even where unity of time does not exist.

(b) The right of survivorship: the jus accrescendi

[9.08] Upon the death of a joint tenant, the interest of that joint tenant passes by the right of survivorship to the remaining joint tenants. Indeed to state that the interest of the deceased joint tenant "passes" to the others is not strictly correct for each joint tenant is already seised of the whole estate. The surviving joint tenants simply remain seised of the whole estate on the death of one joint tenant. "[T]he totality of their seisin cannot be affected by the death of one of their number."[6] The process continues until there is one joint tenant left and he or she is seised of the whole of the land for her or his own use and benefit. The right of

---

5. *Kenworthy v. Ward* (1853) 11 Hare 196; 68 E.R. 1245; *McGregor v. McGregor* (1859) 1 De G.F. & J. 63 at 73; 45 E.R. 282 at 286.
6. Butt, p. 188.

survivorship cannot be affected by any purported disposition in the will of a joint tenant or by intestacy: the interest of a joint tenant cannot pass in her or his will or under an intestacy. For example, if A and B are joint tenants of Blackacre and A leaves a will in which she purports to devise her interest in Blackacre to C, C takes nothing under A's will because upon A's death, A's interest in Blackacre automatically accrues to B.[7]

[9.09]   If there is no right of survivorship, there can be no joint tenancy.[8] The common law rule was that a corporation could not die and therefore could never be a joint tenant. In the 19th century, banks and other corporations began acting as trustees. It is important for trustees to be joint tenants because the trust property automatically passes to the other trustees when one trustee dies: there is no need for a conveyance from the personal representatives of the deceased trustee to the surviving trustees as there would be if the trustees held as tenants in common. Legislation was introduced to enable corporations to hold property as joint tenants in the same manner as if they were individuals.[9]

[9.10]   Except in South Australia and Western Australia, where joint tenants die in circumstances rendering it uncertain which of them survived the other or others, their deaths, for purposes affecting the title to property are presumed to have occurred in order of seniority.[10] In other words, the older is presumed to have predeceased the younger. The presumption can be rebutted by evidence that the deaths did not occur in order of seniority.[11]

[9.11]   It is important to note that for the purposes of capital gains tax, joint tenants are treated as tenants in common. Section 160ZN(1)(a) of the *Income Tax Assessment Act* 1936 (Cth) provides that where an asset is owned by persons as joint tenants, Pt IIIA (the capital gains tax provisions) applies as if they owned the asset as tenants in common in equal shares.[12]

---

7. Note that the right of survivorship could not be defeated by a widow's claim to dower before dower was abolished. See Butt, p. 188.
8. *Re Robertson* (1944) 44 S.R. (N.S.W.) 103 at 105 per Roper J.
9. General law statutes: N.S.W.: s. 25; Vic.: s. 28; Qld: s. 34; S.A.: s. 24C; W.A.: s. 29; Tas.: s. 62. See *Bodies Corporate (Joint Tenancy) Act* 1899 (U.K.).
10. *Conveyancing Act* 1919 (N.S.W.), s. 35; *Property Law Act* 1958 (Vic.), s. 184; *Succession Act* 1981 (Qld), s. 65; *Presumption of Survivorship Act* 1921 (Tas.), s. 2. See *Hickman v. Peacey* [1945] A.C. 304; *Re Brush* [1962] V.R. 596; *Re Plaister* (1934) 34 S.R. (N.S.W.) 547; *Re Zappullo* [1967] V.R. 390. Cf. *Property Law Act* 1969 (W.A.), s. 120(d) where if there is a doubt as to which joint tenant survived the other(s), the property devolves as though the joint tenants had held the property as tenants in common in equal shares and the position in South Australia where there is no provision covering the matter.
11. *Re Plaister* (1934) 34 S.R. (N.S.W.) 547.
12. Problems may arise with respect to jointly owned property where an exemption from capital gains tax is sought on the "principal residence" exemption when the property is not the principal residence of all joint owners. If the provisions on one sole principal residence per family are inapplicable (s. 160ZZ(9), (10)), it seems the exemption is only available to the joint owner who occupied the property as her or his principal residence in respect of her or his share of the dwelling: see Income Taxation Ruling 2485 (14 July 1988).

[9.12]   Although the right of survivorship renders invalid any purported dispositions in a will of a joint tenant's interest, the joint tenant can alienate or deal with her or his interest during her or his lifetime: see below **[9.42]**. Of course, the aliquot part which a joint tenant can deal with is dependent upon the number of joint tenants. For example, if there are three joint tenants, any one joint tenant can deal with a one third share of the property. There is, however, an exception to the general proposition that joint tenants are able to deal freely with their interests inter vivos. In all States except New South Wales and Tasmania, the Torrens statutes provide that the words "no survivorship" may be entered on the Register if there are two or more joint proprietors who hold the land as trustees.[13] Despite the notation of such words on the Register, the joint proprietors continue to hold as joint tenants and as the right of survivorship is an integral part of the joint tenancy, it remains applicable between the joint tenants. What then is the effect of the words "no survivorship" appearing on the Register? Once such an entry has been made, it is not lawful for less than the full number of the registered proprietors to transfer or otherwise deal with the land without obtaining an order of the Supreme Court.[14] It seems that these provisions are intended to provide some protection for beneficiaries. Even the registration of a transmission in favour of the surviving joint proprietors would need the sanction of the court.[15] In deciding whether to sanction a dealing, the court must make orders as the court considers just for the protection of persons beneficially entitled.[16] Thus in a case where there are two trustees registered as joint proprietors and one trustee dies, the court may take the view that the interests of the beneficiaries require the maintenance of two trustees and thus, may only sanction the transmission to the surviving trustee on the basis that there is then a transfer to the surviving trustee and a new trustee.

Of course, the "no survivorship" entry does not provide beneficiaries with complete protection for their interests. All the joint proprietors/trustees can join together and transfer the estate to a third party. If such a third party registers without fraud, the interests of the beneficiaries in the land will be defeated: see above **[5.30]-[5.31]**. However, the likelihood of all trustees acting fraudulently to deprive the beneficiaries of their interests is far less than the likelihood of one trustee doing so.[17] The "no survivorship" entries ensure that the latter possibility is excluded.

13. Torrens statutes: Vic.: s. 38(1) and (2) (not confined to trustees); Qld: ss 80, 81; S.A.: s. 163; W.A.: s. 61 (not confined to trustees). In Queensland this may only be done upon a grant or transfer. In the other States, persons already registered as proprietors may apply for the notation to be made—Vic.: s. 38(3); S.A.: s. 164; W.A.: s. 61. Until 1970, the notation "no survivorship" could be made in New South Wales. Whalan suggests that "no survivorship" notations created before that date in New South Wales are treated in the same way as the other States: see Whalan, p. 123.
14. Torrens statutes: N.S.W.: s. 84; Vic.: s. 38(4); Qld: s. 80; S.A.: s. 165; W.A.: s. 61. In Victoria and Western Australia the Registrar may grant the order.
15. *Re Robertson* (1943) 44 S.R. (N.S.W.) 103.
16. See e.g. Vic.: s. 38(6).
17. See Adams, "No Survivorship Titles" (1941) 17 N.Z.L.J. 137 referred to in Whalan, p. 126.

2. Tenancy in Common

[9.13] If two or more persons are entitled simultaneously to possession of the whole of the land and yet are not joint tenants, they will today (apart from the unlikely possibility of coparcenary) (see below **[9.14]**) hold the land as tenants in common. Although all four unities may exist, only the unity of possession is essential for a tenancy in common to arise.

A tenant in common is said to hold a distinct yet undivided share in the land. Each tenant in common is deemed to own an individual share, a part of all the rights involved in ownership. It is this reference to "shares" which distinguishes the tenancy in common from the joint tenancy. Although a tenant in common holds a distinct share, the land itself is not divided physically and no one tenant in common can claim any particular portion of the land as her or his own. Each tenant in common is entitled to physical possession of the whole of the land. If this were not the case separate ownership, not co-ownership, would exist.

There is no right of survivorship between tenants in common. Each tenant's share is fixed and cannot be enlarged by the death of another tenant in common.

3. Coparcenary

[9.14] Coparcenary was a type of co-ownership dependent upon the common law rules relating to descent upon intestacy. The rule was that land descended to the "heir" who was usually the deceased person's eldest son. If, however, the deceased person had no male heir but had more than one female heir in the same degree (for example, daughters), the female descendants held as coparceners. Coparcenary could also arise pursuant to the custom of gavelkind (applicable only to land in Kent, England) if a person died intestate leaving more than one son: the sons took a coparceners. Descent to the heir upon intestacy was abolished over a century ago[18] (see above **[6.02]**) and thus coparcenary became irrelevant. It may still be possible for coparcenary to arise where the holder of an unbarred fee tail dies intestate leaving no male heir and more than one female heir in the same degree. However this is most unlikely as in most Australian States it has not been possible to create an entail since the end of the 19th century: see above **[2.22]**.

Coparcenary resembled the tenancy in common in that there was no right of survivorship and the interests of the coparceners could be different in size. On the other hand, it was similar to the joint tenancy as the four unities were often present and one coparcener could release her share to the others thus suggesting they were jointly seised.

4. Tenancy by Entireties

[9.15] At common law, a husband and a wife were regarded as one person and the tenancy by entireties resulted from this unity of the husband and wife. If land were conveyed to a husband and wife in such a manner that had they been strangers they would have taken as joint

---

18. See *Property Law Act* 1974 (Qld), s. 33(2) which specifically abolishes coparcenary.

tenants, they took the land as tenants by entireties. The tenancy by entireties was a species of joint tenancy which could exist only between a husband and wife but which neither spouse could sever. Further, if property was conveyed to a husband, a wife and a stranger as joint tenants or tenants in common, the husband and wife took only a half share and held that half share as between themselves as tenants by entireties.

Legislation permitting married women to own property separately and independently from their husbands resulted in the disappearance of the tenancy by entireties.[19]

II. CREATION OF CO-OWNERSHIP

[9.16]   As Gray and Symes have stated:[20]

> "The vital secret in the understanding of concurrent interests in land law lies in the maintenance of a rigid distinction between ownership *at law* and ownership *in equity* . . . The same persons may be simultaneously joint tenants at law and tenants in common in equity."

Although the legal title is vital in that it binds the whole world, the persons with bare legal title have only nominal ownership. The holders of the legal title are trustees who must exercise fiduciary duties but they have no right to the beneficial enjoyment of the land. The persons who hold the equitable ownership derive the use and enjoyment from the land. It is they who are entitled to the occupation of the land or the rents and profits flowing from the land and it is they who are entitled to the proceeds upon a sale of the property. It is quite possible for A and B to hold the land as joint tenants at law but as tenants in common in equity. In such a case if A dies, the right of survivorship operates at law so that B becomes the sole legal owner. However, he holds the legal estate on trust for himself and the estate of A. The estate of A is entitled to the use and enjoyment of the land with B and to the proceeds of sale equivalent to the value of A's beneficial interest if the property is sold. Thus, it is most important to distinguish between co-ownership at law and co-ownership in equity.

1. Co-ownership at Law

(a) Common law

[9.17]   The common law leaned in favour of the joint tenancy for a number of reasons. The enforcement of feudal services by feudal lords was likely to be simpler and more effective because the right of survivorship made it more likely that the land would vest in one tenant from whom feudal dues could be exacted. The investigation of title by purchasers was

---

19. *Married Women's Property Act* 1901 (N.S.W.), s. 3(1); *Marriage Act* 1958 (Vic.), s. 156; *Married Women's Property Act* 1890 (Qld), ss 8-9; *Law of Property Act* 1936 (S.A.), s. 92; *Married Women's Property Act* 1895 (W.A.), s. 1(1); *Married Women's Property Act* 1935 (Tas.), ε. 3(1).
20. Gray and Symes, *Real Property and Real People Principles of Land Law* (Butterworths, London, 1981), p. 238.

easier because joint tenants held a single title whereas each tenant in common had a separate title. Further, if a joint tenant died there remained only one title whereas if a tenant in common died, his share might be left to a number of persons thereby proliferating the number of titles to be searched before the land could be sold as a whole. The presumption at law, therefore, was in favour of a joint tenancy.[21] Although the historical reasons for the common law presumption in favour of the joint tenancy have long since disappeared, the presumption remains; where land is conveyed to two or more persons as co-owners, they take their interests as joint tenants at law unless one of the four unities is absent or words of severance are used in the deed of conveyance.

Nevertheless, for many years "(b)ecause of the somewhat arbitrary and often unintended consequences of creating a joint tenancy, particularly the incident of survivorship, the courts in construing dispositions to two or more persons . . . have tended to seize upon the slightest indication that a tenancy in common was intended".[22] In *Williams v. Hensman*, Sir William Page Wood V.-C. commented:[23]

> "In these questions of joint-tenancy the court has frequently been driven to rely on minute grounds for holding a severance to have taken place, by the unfortunate circumstances that the Legislature has not thought fit to interpose by introducing the rule that express words shall be required to create a joint-tenancy in place of the contrary rule which is established."

Despite the inappropriateness of this rule of construction in modern times, the common law presumption in favour of the joint tenancy remains. However courts require only slight evidence of severance or an absence of one of the unities in order to determine that the co-ownership is a tenancy in common.

(i) Absence of unities

[9.18] The four unities have been discussed above: see above **[9.04]**-**[9.07]**. If unity of possession is present but one or more of the other unities is missing, the parties take their interests as tenants in common not as joint tenants. If unity of possession is absent, the parties do not take as co-owners but as separate owners.

(ii) Words of severance

[9.19] Any words in a grant which indicate that the grantees are to take distinct shares are words of severance and their presence prevents the creation at law of a joint tenancy between the grantees. The grantees take as tenants in common provided there is unity of possession. Words which have been held to be words of severance include "equally", "between",

---

21. *Morley v. Bird* (1798) 3 Ves. 628; 30 E.R. 1192.
22. Qld L.R.C., *A Report of the Law Reform Commission on a Bill to Consolidate, Amend and Reform the Law Relating to Conveyancing, Property and Contract and to Terminate the Application of Certain Imperial Statutes*, No. 16 (1973), p. 25. See e.g. *Williams v. Hensman* (1861) 1 John & H. 564; 70 E.R. 862; and *Re Rose (decd)* [1962] Q.W.N. 4.
23. (1861) 1 John & H. 546 at 557; 70 E.R. 862 at 866.

"amongst", "to be divided between", "in equal shares", "share and share alike", "to be distributed amongst them in joint and equal propositions", and "respectively".[24]

In *Robertson v. Fraser*[25] the testator by his will appointed Johnson and Fraser to be his executors. He provided for the payment of debts and certain legacies and left the residue of his estate to Johnson and Fraser for their own absolute use and benefit. In a codicil to his will, the testator appointed Warren to be an additional executor and provided that Warren was to be a further beneficiary of the residuary estate "so that the said J. Warren shall and may participate in such bequest" with Johnson and Fraser. Johnson died in the lifetime of the testator. A question arose as to whether the residuary estate was given to Johnson, Fraser and Warren as joint tenants or tenants in common. If the effect of the devise was to give a tenancy in common, an intestacy as to one third share would result and the next of kin of the testator would be entitled to the share.

The Court of Appeal held that the effect of the will and codicil was to create a tenancy in common between Johnson, Fraser and Warren. Lord Hatherley L.C. stated:[26]

> "[A]nything which in the slightest degree indicates an intention to divide the property must be held to abrogate the idea of a joint tenancy, and to create a tenancy in common . . . I have no doubt that the word 'participate' is sufficient to indicate an intention to divide . . . [T]he testator [was] not contented with inserting the name of the new legatee (in his codicil but expressed his reason for doing so) that the new legatee may participate with the two other legatees—in other words, that there may be a sharing of the bequest."

[9.20] The gift itself may indicate that a sharing was envisaged even where there are no clear words of severance in the deed or will. If this is the case a tenancy in common rather than a joint tenancy results.[27] For example, if a settlement to children contains provisions permitting the use of income or capital for the maintenance and advancement of each particular child, the children must hold as tenants in common for any advance to a child would have to be debited against her or his "share" and this can only be achieved if the child has a different share.[28]

---

24. *Denn d. Gaskin v. Gaskin* (1777) 2 Cowp. 657; 98 E.R. 1292 ("equally"); *Lashbrook v. Cock* (1816) 2 Mer. 70; 35 E.R. 867 ("between"); *Richardson v. Richardson* (1845) 14 Sim. 526; 60 E.R. 462 ("amongst"); *Peat v. Chapman* (1750) 1 Ves. Sen. 542; 27 E.R. 1193 ("divided between"); *Payne v. Webb* (1874) L.R. 19 Eq. 26 ("equal shares"); *Heathe v. Heathe* (1749) 2 Atk. 121; 26 E.R. 476 ("share and share alike"); *Ettricke v. Ettricke* (1767) Amb. 656; 27 E.R. 426 ("distributed in joint and equal proportions"); *Stephens v. Hide* (1734) Talb. 27; 25 E.R. 641. See Megarry and Wade, p. 425 for detailed list.
25. (1871) 6 Ch. A. 696.
26. (1871) 6 Ch. A. 696 at 699.
27. See e.g. *Surtees v. Surtees* (1871) L.R. 12 Eq. 400
28. See e.g. *L'Estrange v. L'Estrange* [1902] 1 I.R. 64 and see generally Megarry and Wade, p. 426.

[9.21] In general, therefore, it seems that any indication of an intention to divide gleaned from either the words used or from the grant as a whole, will give rise to a tenancy in common. The preference of the courts in favour of the tenancy in common where there is any doubt as to the nature of the co-ownership appears to be based on the fact that in most instances the weight of convenience favours the creation of a tenancy in common.[29] Where, however, expediency favours the creation of a joint tenancy in a given fact situation, the courts have sometimes been prepared to hold that the intention was to create a joint tenancy and a joint tenancy has resulted despite the use of words of severance. Most notably this has occurred when contradictory expressions such as "to A and B to share and share alike as joint tenants" are used in the grant or the will and the intention of the grantor or testator, determined from contextual factors, indicates a joint tenancy was intended.[30]

In *Re Barbour*[31] the testator left property to a sister and two brothers "to share and share alike as joint tenants". One of the brothers predeceased the testator. If the grant had been construed as a tenancy in common, the small share of the deceased beneficiary would have been divisible amongst 16 beneficiaries on an intestacy. Wanstall J. reviewed the facts of the case and determined that the property's real value lay in its availability for use in conjunction with other land worked by the beneficiaries surviving the testator. His Honour took the view that the testator's natural intention was: "to keep his land in the family aggregation, and that this intention was reflected in his choosing as beneficiaries of his disposition of the land in specie those who were managing and working the aggregation."[32]

[9.22] If the court cannot reconcile the use of contradictory expressions in a deed or a will (one suggesting a tenancy in common and the other suggesting a joint tenancy) the conflict is resolved by the rule that the first word prevails in a deed but the last word prevails in a will.[33] For example, the expression "to A and B equally as joint tenants" would create a tenancy in common if appearing in a deed, but a joint tenancy if appearing in a will.[34]

(b) Statutory position

(i) General law land

[9.23] In all States except New South Wales and Queensland there has been no statutory intervention and the common law position favouring a joint tenancy at law prevails.

[9.24] In New South Wales and Queensland provisions in the general property statutes appear to have reversed the common law presumption

---

29. See above **[9.17]** and *Re Rose (decd)* [1962] Q.W.N. 4.
30. See e.g. *Joyce v. Barker Bros (Builders) Ltd* (1980) 40 P. & C.R. 512—"fee simple as beneficial joint tenants in common equal shares" held to be a joint tenancy.
31. [1967] Qd R. 10.
32. Note also, those who would take on intestacy were not concerned about the result. See also *Armstrong v. Eldridge* (1791) 3 Bro. C.C. 215; 29 E.R. 497.
33. *Perkins v. Baynton* (1781) 1 Bro. C.C. 118; 28 E.R. 1022; *Forbes v. Git* [1922] 1 A.C. 256. The principle is discussed in Megarry and Wade, p. 529.
34. For further special cases, see Megarry and Wade, p. 426.

in favour of the joint tenancy.[35] Sections 26 and 27 of the *Conveyancing Act* 1919 (N.S.W.) provide:

"26. (1) In the construction of any instrument coming into operation after the commencement of this Act a disposition of the beneficial interest in any property whether with or without the legal estate to or for two or more persons together beneficially shall be deemed to be made to or for them as tenants in common, and not as joint tenants.

(2) This section does not apply to persons who by the terms or by the tenor of the instrument are executors, administrators, trustees or mortgagees and in any case where the instrument expressly provides that persons are to take as joint tenants or *tenant by entireties*.

27. Where two or more persons entitled beneficially as tenants in common to an equitable estate in any property are or become entitled in their own right whether as joint tenants or tenants in common to the legal estate in such property equal to and co-extensive with such equitable estate both the legal and equitable estates shall be held by them as tenants in common unless such persons otherwise agree."

At first reading, the wording of s. 26(1) suggests the creation of a presumption of a tenancy in common with respect to the beneficial interest rather than the legal interest. Nevertheless, it seems that the intention of the legislature was to effect a reversal of the common law presumption in favour of the joint tenancy.[36]

Mr Justice Hutley commented on s. 26(1) in 1939:[37]

"The words 'whether with or without the legal estate', placed as they are in close connection with the words 'the beneficial interest', indicate that the rule is intended to be the same for both legal and equitable interests."

Recently, Gibbs C.J. in *Delehunt v. Carmody*[38] stated:[39]

"(S)ince s. 26 of the Conveyancing Act, in New South Wales the effect at law of a disposition in favour of A and B is that they will take as tenants in common. In New South Wales a conveyance to two

35. General law statutes: N.S.W.: s. 26; Qld: s. 35 (the Queensland provision is not confined to "instruments").

36. The provisions were introduced in 1919 as a result of a Royal Commission inquiry into conveyancing and the law of property set up by the New South Wales goverment. In referring to cl. 26, Mr Justice Harvey, the Commissioner, stated in his explanatory memorandum accompanying the draft of the Bill:
    "Clause 26 is a clause which, so far as I am aware, is entirely novel. At present the presumption of law is that if *property is conveyed or devised to persons they take as joint tenants*. Probably in the majority of cases in which the instrument is silent as to whether the donees are to take in joint tenancy or as tenants in common this defeats the intention. The courts of equity have recognised that is so, and have always laid hold of slight indications to negative the legal presumption. The clause as drawn raises a presumption the other way and presumes a tenancy in common unless otherwise indicated."

37. Note, (1939) 13 A.L.J. 230 at 231.

38. (1986) 161 C.L.R. 464; 61 A.L.J.R. 54.

39. (1986) 161 C.L.R. 464 at 472; 61 A.L.J.R. 54 at 56.

purchasers who have contributed equally to the purchase price of the property will now give the purchasers a beneficial interest as tenants in common.''

It is submitted that these statements support the view that where there is a simple disposition by way of conveyance to A and B as purchasers, pursuant to s. 26(1) they hold the estate as tenants in common at law and in equity whether they contributed equally or unequally to the purchase price. In this type of example, it is not strictly correct to state that they hold the legal and equitable interests as tenants in common for until an equitable interest is carved out of the legal interest, the estate is held as one whole interest.

Where the legal and equitable estates are disposed of to different persons and thereby separated, it can be argued that s. 26(1) does not have the effect of rendering the co-owners tenants in common of the legal estate. If this view is correct, a question arises as to why it was then necessary for the legislature to include the first part of s. 26(2): "This section does not apply to persons who by the term or tenor of the instrument are executors, administrators, trustees, or mortgagees.''

In normal circumstances, persons taking in their capacity as executors, administrators, trustees or mortgagees, take only the legal estate and would not, on the view expounded above, take the legal interest as tenants in common pursuant to s. 26(1). It is submitted that this part of s. 26(2) was added as a matter of caution on the part of the draftsman and to cover any situation where it might be argued that a person falling within one of these categories holds part or all of the beneficial interest for a time.

Section 26(2) provides further that where an instrument expressly provides that persons are to take as joint tenants, s. 26(1) shall not apply.[40]

Section 27(1) was included to overcome the principle enunciated in *Re Selous*.[41] In this case, it was held that if two persons were beneficially entitled to a property as tenants in common and they subsequently acquired the legal estate as joint tenants, the equitable estate merged in the legal and they became joint tenants both at law and in equity. Section 27(1) overcomes this decision by providing that where two or more persons hold the beneficial interest as tenants in common and are or become entitled to the legal estate equal to or co-extensive with such beneficial interest, the legal and beneficial interests shall be held as tenants in common unless the persons otherwise agree. Section 27(1) accords with the concept behind s. 26(1).

[9.25] Sections 35 and 36 of the *Property Law Act* 1974 (Qld) correspond closely to ss 26 and 27 of the New South Wales Act.[42] They differ,

40. *Mole v. Ross* (1950) 1 B.P.R. 9101. Discussed in (1951) 24 A.L.J. 356.
41. [1901] 1 Ch. 921. See also *Selby v. Aston* (1797) 3 Ves. 339; 30 E.R. 1042.
42. It should be noted that the words ''legal interest'' are used in the Queensland provision, in place of the words ''legal estate'' used in the New South Wales legislation. The Queensland Law Reform Commission took the view that the provision was intended to apply to real and *personal* property, and that as the use of the words ''legal estate'' may not be appropriate to all forms of personalty, the words ''legal interest'' should be used. Further, the Commission took the view

however, from the New South Wales sections in two important respects. First, s. 35(1) is not confined to interests created by instruments. A second difference concerns disposition of property for partnership purposes. In order to avoid difficulties which may arise upon the death of a member of a partnership where the legal title is held by the partners as tenants in common, s. 35(2)(b) was inserted. It provides that s. 35(1) (in similar form to s. 26(1) of the New South Wales Act) is inapplicable to "a disposition for partnership purposes in favour of persons carrying on business in partnership". Section 35(3) explicitly deals with such dispositions.[43] The position would have been clearer had s. 36 been made subject to s. 35(3).

(ii) Torrens system land

[9.26] In New South Wales, Victoria, South Australia and Western Australia, it is provided that where two or more persons are registered as joint proprietors of an estate or interest in Torrens land, they are deemed to be entitled to the estate or interest as joint tenants.[44] In Queensland, s. 40(1) of the *Real Property Act* 1861 provides that two or more persons who are registered jointly as proprietors of land shall, in the absence of an entry in the Register indicating that they hold as tenants in common, be entitled as joint tenants at law. In Tasmania, s. 44 of the *Land Titles Act* 1980 provides that two or more persons who are named as transferees or proprietors of an estate or interest shall, in the absence of words of severance, be entitled as joint tenants.

The drafting of these provisions in all States except Queensland and Tasmania creates uncertainty for, as is stated in Baalman, it is unclear whether the words "persons who may be registered" (words used in the New South Wales and Western Australian provisions) are meant to describe: "(a) persons who have become registered and who have been described in the Register as 'joint proprietors'; or (b) persons who have the qualifications necessary for a joint tenancy, but no indication as to the form of co-ownership can be formed by inspecting the dealing whereby they acquired registered status."[45]

A further explanation of these provisions[46] is that the drafters of the Torrens statutes intended to follow the common law position and favour the creation of a joint tenancy with respect to the registered title. On this analysis, the relevant provisions, such as s. 100(1) of the New South Wales Act contained the medium for applying the common law presumption in favour of the joint tenancy to Torrens land.

---

42. *Continued*
   that as the provision applies to personalty, the section should not be confined to "instruments". In dispositions of personalty, an instrument may not be used and thus the section should apply to "a disposition" and not simply an instrument: see Qld L.R.C., Report No. 16 (1973), p. 25.
43. Quaere whether s. 35(3) would in all instances be consistent with s. 36.
44. Torrens statutes: N.S.W.: s. 100(1); Vic.: s. 30(2); S.A.: s. 74; W.A.: s. 60.
45. Baalman, *The Torrens System in New South Wales* (2nd ed., Law Book Co. Ltd, Sydney, 1974), p. 349.
46. See Whalan, p. 102.

In order to avoid the inherent difficulties created by the wording of these provisions, Registrars have required that instruments presented for registration under which two or more persons are to take concurrent interests must state whether the co-owners are to take as joint tenants or tenants in common. That is, the Registrars have avoided registering documents in which the term ''joint proprietors'' is used unless the parties are clearly intended to take as joint tenants. Where, however, a document is registered in which the term ''joint proprietors'' is used the question as to its effect must be resolved.

In *Hircock v. Windsor Homes (Development No. 3) Pty Ltd*,[47] the Supreme Court of New South Wales in considering s. 100(1) of the New South Wales Act took the view that the draftsman of the Torrens statute intended such provisions to have the effect of simply applying the body of common law already in existence in relation to the term ''joint tenancy'', to the new statutory expression ''joint proprietorship'', Hutley J.A. stated:[48]

> ''The subsection means: 'If two or more persons are registered as joint proprietors of an estate or interest in land under the provisions for this Act, they shall have the same rights as if they were joint tenants of a similar estate or interest at common law'.''

Hutley J.A. referred to the fact that the authors of the Torrens statutes had been reluctant to use the old ''terminology in describing the new statutory titles''. Thus, the term ''joint proprietorship'' was used instead of the term ''joint tenancy''. Nevertheless, it was convenient for the draftsman to adopt the law relating to joint tenancy to the joint proprietorship and thus provisions such as s. 100(1) of the New South Wales Act were inserted. However, apart from the use of the new expression, the statutes have ''left the incidents of joint tenancy to be determined by the common law and any other relevant statute''.[49]

The position appears to be as follows. If co-owners are designated ''joint proprietors'' in the registered document, prima facie, they will be viewed as persons having the rights of joint tenants and third parties will be entitled to deal with them as if they were joint tenants. It may be possible, however, to demonstrate from the registered document that the proprietors are not joint tenants for the statutory provisions do not provide that they are joint tenants but that they ''deemed to be entitled as joint tenants''. For instance, if the document provides that A and B are joint proprietors in the shares two thirds and one third respectively, the presumption in favour of the joint tenancy would be rebutted.[50]

[9.27] In New South Wales there is a further difficulty and this arises in relation to the interaction of s. 26 of the *Conveyancing Act* 1919 (N.S.W.) with s. 100(1) of *Real Property Act* 1900 (N.S.W.). At first reading, the Torrens provision may appear to be inconsistent with the general property statute provision for the former presumes a joint tenancy whilst

47. [1979] 1 N.S.W.L.R. 501.
48. [1979] 1 N.S.W.L.R. 501 at 506.
49. *Wright v. Gibbons* (1949) 78 C.L.R. 313 at 324 per Latham C.J.
50. Note that it is most unlikely that a document in such a form would be registered.

the latter presumes a tenancy in common. In the *Hircock* case, however, the Supreme Court of New South Wales took the view that there was no inconsistency between s. 26 and s. 100(1). In this case, the defendant agreed to grant the Hircocks a lease of a unit at a fixed rental for a term lasting for the lifetime of the survivor. Subsequently, a lease in registrable form was executed under which the lease was granted to the Hircocks for ten years with an option to renew for a further ten years but subject to the proviso that the lease and any extension would determine upon the death of the survivor of the lessees. The lease was registered. Mrs Hircock died during the ten year term and at the expiration of the term, Mr Hircock sought to exercise the option. A question arose as to whether he was entitled to do so as the surviving joint lessee or whether the personal representative of Mrs Hircock's estate had to join with him in exercising the option. Mr Hircock argued that upon registration of the lease, he and his wife held the lease as joint tenants pursuant to s. 100(1) of the *Real Property Act*. He argued that s. 26(1) of the *Conveyancing Act*, deeming them to be tenants in common, was inapplicable to documents registered under the Torrens statute as it was inconsistent with s. 100(1). As s. 26(1) was not expressly stated to apply to Torrens land, it would not do so pursuant to s. 6 of the *Conveyancing Act* if it were inconsistent with a Torrens statute provision.

In the Supreme Court of New South Wales, Hutley J.A. was of the opinion that no inconsistency existed between these provisions. Section 100(1) simply applied the incidents of the joint tenancy to the term "joint proprietorship": it did not deem all co-owners to be joint tenants. Therefore, s. 26 could operate and under s. 26(1) the parties were presumed to hold the beneficial estate as tenants in common. On the facts of the case, however, the presumption was rebutted, and the lease fell within s. 26(2) and the parties held as joint tenants. In determining that the lease fell within s. 26(2), the court took into account the context of the lease and all the surrounding circumstances. As Hutley J.A. stated: "[In order for s. 26(2) to operate] it is not necessary that it should be expressly stated that the intention was to create a joint tenancy."[51] It should be noted that the court took the view that even had the Hircocks been regarded as tenants in common the option could still have been exercised by Mr Hircock alone.[52]

In Queensland, the position is made clear by s. 40(3) of the *Real Property Act* 1861. Section 40(3) provides that nothing in the Torrens Act affects the operation of s. 35 of the *Property Law Act* 1974.

2. Co-ownership in Equity

(a) In Victoria, South Australia, Western Australia and Tasmania

[9.28] Equity preferred the certainty and equality of the tenancy in common.[53] Co-owners who are tenants in common at law are always

---

51. [1979] N.S.W.L.R. 501 at 506.
52. [1979] N.S.W.L.R. 501 at 507 per Hutley J.A., and at 508 per Samuels J.A.
53. See e.g. *Re Woolley* [1903] 2 Ch. 206 at 211.

presumed to hold as tenants in common in equity. Further, in three particular situations equity deems certain co-owners to be tenants in common even where they hold as joint tenants at law.[54]

(i) Unequal contributions to purchase price

[9.29] Purchasers who take the legal estate as joint tenants are deemed to be tenants in common in equity if they have contributed in unequal proportions to the purchase price. Each co-owner holds her or his share in equity proportionate to the contribution to the purchase price.[55] Thus, if A and B take a conveyance of land as joint tenants but A has contributed two thirds and B has contributed one third of the purchase price, equity deems A and B to be tenants in common of the land in the proportions of two thirds to A and one third to B. Further, if A alone had taken the conveyance in the example above and was, therefore, the sole owner at law, equity would still deem A and B to be tenants in common proportionate to their contributions.[56] If purchasers take a conveyance of land as joint tenants and provide the purchase money in equal shares, they are presumed in equity to hold as joint tenants. It is unclear why in this instance equity has been content to consider such purchasers joint tenants but as Megarry and Wade have commented "it has long been the established law".[57]

These presumptions can be rebutted. For example, if there is evidence showing that the purchasers who provided the purchase money in unequal contributions intended to take beneficially as joint tenants, they will take as joint tenants in equity.[58]

Historically, this equitable rule was applicable to property disputes which arose in the context of the family.[59] With respect to disputes arising between parties to a de facto relationship, the rule remains important although the developments in the law of constructive trusts have opened other avenues under which the beneficial interest may be distributed in a manner which takes account of factors other than direct contributions to the purchase price.[60] With respect to property disputes between parties to a marriage, this equitable rule and the above-mentioned developments in constructive trusts remain relevant but only as a starting-point for establishing the existing legal and equitable interests held by the husband and wife. Pursuant to s. 79 of the *Family Law Act* 1975 (Cth), the Family Court has the power, in proceedings with respect to the property of the parties, to alter the existing proprietary interests of the parties in order to achieve a just and equitable result: see above **[1.53]-[1.57]**.

54. See *Malayan Credit Ltd v. Jack Chia M.P.H. Ltd* [1986] 1 All E.R. 711 where it is suggested the categories may be extended.
55. *Lake v. Gibson* (1792) 1 Eq. Ca. Abr. 290 at 291; 21 E.R. 1052; *Robinson v. Preston* (1858) 4 K. & J. 505; 70 E.R. 211.
56. *Bull v. Bull* [1955] 1 Q.B. 234. See **[6.27]-[6.29]**.
57. Megarry and Wade, p. 427.
58. See e.g. *Pink v. Lawrence* (1977) 36 P. & C.R. 98.
59. The presumption of advancement is also relevant: see above **[6.27]-[6.28]**.
60. See e.g. *Baumgartner v. Baumgartner* (1987) 164 C.L.R. 137; 62 A.L.J.R. 29. For a discussion of these developments see Dodds, "The New Constructive Trust: An Analysis of its Nature and Scope" (1988) 16 M.U.L.R. 482. The developments extend beyond the family context. See **[1.58]** and **[6.30]-[6.36]**.

(ii) Mortgagees

[9.30]   Where two or more persons advance money on the security of a mortgage, whether in equal or unequal shares, equity presumes the mortgagees to hold their interests as tenants in common even though they may be joint tenants at law.[61] The reason for this rule was expressed succinctly in the case of *Morley v. Bird*:[62]

> "[I]f two people join in lending money upon a mortgage, Equity says, it could not be the intention, that the interest in that should survive. Though they take a joint security, each means to lend his own and take back his own."

The presumption that mortgagees hold as tenants in common in equity can be rebutted by evidence demonstrating that the parties intended to hold in law and equity as joint tenants.

The fact that mortgagees were deemed to be tenants in common in equity caused a practical problem for the mortgagor. In order to redeem the property, the mortgagor had to obtain a receipt from all the tenants in common: further, if one of the tenants in common had died, the mortgagor had to obtain a receipt from all the remaining tenants in common and from the personal representative of the deceased tenant. In order to overcome this difficulty, it became common practice to insert a "joint account clause" in mortgages where there were two or more mortgagees. The joint account clause states that in law and equity the money belongs jointly to the mortgagees. In many instances, this statement is incorrect but it results in the mortgagor being able to repay the money to one of the mortgagees and to obtain from the mortgagee a valid receipt for repayment of the whole of the mortgage moneys. The joint account clause, therefore, has the effect of making the mortgagees joint tenants vis-à-vis third parties. It does not alter the position of the mortgagees inter se and a mortgagee who receives repayment of the whole of the mortgage moneys holds all but her or his own share on trust for the other mortgagees in proportion to their contributions to the original loan moneys.

In all jurisdictions, a joint account clause is now implied by statute.[63]

(iii) Partners

[9.31]   Where partners acquire land for the purpose of a business enterprise and as part of their partnership assets, they are presumed in equity to hold the land as tenants in common although at law they may be joint tenants.[64] As was the case with mortgagees, equity considered that it would be unfair for the right of survivorship to operate in this business context as a partner who died first would lose her or his investment.

---

61. *Re Jackson* (1887) 34 Ch. D. 732.
62. (1798) 3 Ves. 628 at 631; 30 E.R. 1192 at 1193 per Arden M.R.
63. General law statutes: N.S.W.: ss 96A, 99; Vic.: ss 112-113; Qld: s. 93; S.A.: ss 54-55; W.A.: ss 67-68; Tas.: s. 30.
64. *Lake v. Gibson* (1729) 1 Eq. Ca. Abr. 290; 21 E.R. 1052 *Lake v. Craddock* (1732) 3 P. Wms. 158; 24 E.R. 1011; *Spence v. Federal Commissioner of Taxation* (1967) 121 C.L.R. 273. See also Megarry and Wade, p. 428.

Even if there is no formal partnership but parties have entered into a joint enterprise and purchased land with a view to profit, equity deems the parties to hold the land so purchased as tenants in common.[65]

(b) In New South Wales and Queensland

[9.32] Pursuant to the statutory provisions discussed above (s. 26(1) of the New South Wales Act and s. 35 of the Queensland Act:[66] see **[9.24]**-**[9.25]**), any disposition of the beneficial interest in property whether with or without the legal estate and to two or more persons is deemed to be made to them as tenants in common. By s. 26(2), s. 26(1) is inapplicable if the instrument expressly provides that the parties are to take as joint tenants. Although it is not necessary that the words "as joint tenants" be used in order for s. 26(2) to operate, it must appear clearly from the language of the instrument that the parties are intended to take as joint tenants.[67]

In *Mitchell v. Arblaster*[68] the Supreme Court of New South Wales considered s. 26 of the *Conveyancing Act* 1919 (N.S.W.). In his will, the testator named Harry Mitchell and Nellie Mitchell as his executors and left his residuary estate to Harry Mitchell and Nellie Mitchell. Harry Mitchell predeceased the testator and upon the testator's death, the question arose as to whether Nellie Mitchell took the whole of the beneficial residuary estate. If the devise of the residuary estate was considered to have created a joint tenancy, Nellie Mitchell would be entitled to the whole of the estate: if the devise was considered a tenancy in common, there would be an intestacy as to one half share which the testator's next of kin would take. Hardie J. held that s. 26(1) had the effect of creating a tenancy in common between Harry Mitchell and Nellie Mitchell with respect to the residuary estate. The fact that the beneficiaries were also executors and took their interests in their capacity of executors as joint tenants under s. 26(2), did not affect the position with respect to the beneficial estate.[69] *Mitchell v. Arblaster* provides a clear example of a situation where the beneficiaries would have taken as joint tenants but for the provision contained in s. 26(1): the devise contained no words of severance and there was no other indication in the will of an intention to divide.

In the *Hircock* case, discussed above, the trustees were held to be joint tenants pursuant to s. 26(2) although it was not expressly stated in the instrument that they were to take as such. The deed pursuant to which the lease was expressly executed provided that the lease should contain

65. *Lake v. Gibson* (1729) 1 Eq. Ca. Abr. 290; 21 E.R. 1052.
66. Note s. 35(3) of the Queensland Act.
67. *Mole v. Ross* (1950) 1 B.P.R. 9101 discussed in (1951) 24 A.L.J. 356.
68. [1964-65] N.S.W.R. 119.
69. If the gift to Harry Mitchell and Nellie Mitchell had been considered a class gift, Nellie Mitchell would have been entitled to the whole of the residue as being the sole member of the class surviving at the date of death of the testator: *Knight v. Gould* (1833) 2 My. & K. 265 at 298; 39 E.R. 956 at 957-958. Hardie J. rejected the contention that this was a class gift to the Mitchells in their official capacity as executors: the language of the will gave the residuary estate to the beneficiaries as named persons.

conditions whereby the lessees could continue in occupation for the life of
the tenants, and if one died, the life of the survivors. This factor, together
with the terms of the lease itself, convinced the Court of Appeal that the
parties intended the lessees to take as joint tenants. In contrast, in *Mole
v. Ross*[70] the use of the words ''as joint legatees'' was held to be insufficient
to create a joint tenancy.

An issue arises as to the relationship between the statutory
presumptions under s. 26 of the New South Wales Act and s. 35 of the
Queensland Act, and the equitable presumptions discussed above: see
[9.29]-[9.31]. For example, if persons purchase property as a business
venture and take the transfer as joint tenants so that the primary statutory
presumption of tenancy in common is inapplicable, can the equitable
presumption expressed in *Lake v. Craddock* (see above **[9.31]**) apply so that
as between themselves the partners take as tenants in common? In
Queensland, the issue is resolved by s. 35(2)(b) (see above **[9.25]**) which
provides that s. 35(1) is inapplicable to such a situation. In New South
Wales, the matter is unresolved. On one view, a statement in the title
documents that the partners are to take as joint tenants precludes the
operation of equitable presumptions. Alternatively, it may be that such a
statement will not preclude the creation of a tenancy in common if it
appears that a tenancy in common was the intention of the parties or that
a tenancy in common would prevent an unconscionable distribution as
between the partners.

The same issue as to the relationship between the statutory
presumptions and the equitable presumptions arises if purchasers provide
the purchase money in unequal shares but they are named as joint tenants
in the title documents. This difficulty does not arise in the case of the
mortgage: see above **[9.24]**.

[9.33] The High Court decision in *Delehunt v. Carmody*[71] demonstrates
that, indirectly, s. 26 may have the effect of creating a tenancy in common
in equity even where the beneficial interest is created without an
instrument. In this case, Mr Carmody was the sole registered proprietor
of the property in dispute. The property had been purchased, however,
by equal contributions to the purchase price from Mr Carmody and his
de facto wife, Miss Delehunt. It was accepted by the judge at first
instance, Wootten J., that the parties contributed equally on the basis of
an express oral agreement that they would own the property in equal
shares, and that in due course, it would be placed in the names of both
of them. Subsequently, Mr Carmody died and the respondent in the
action, Mr Carmody's legal wife, obtained letters of administration and
she became the registered proprietor of the property. Miss Delehunt
claimed that she was entitled to the whole of the beneficial interest by
survivorship as she and Mr Carmody had held the equitable interest as
joint tenants.

---

70. Discussed in Note, (1951) 24 A.L.J. 356.
71. (1986) 161 C.L.R. 464; 61 A.L.J.R. 54. See Note, (1987) 61 A.L.J. 307.

The fact that Mr Carmody and Miss Delehunt were co-owners in equity was not in issue in the High Court. The Court of Appeal in the Supreme Court of New South Wales took the view that the property was held on a resulting trust for Mr Carmody and Miss Delehunt as tenants in common in equal shares. The Court of Appeal held that there was neither an express trust nor a concluded contract. This was because an essential term, that dealing with the question of survivorship or no survivorship, had not been settled between the parties. Whilst this matter was not in issue before the High Court, Gibbs C.J. disagreed with the analysis of the Court of Appeal on this point.[72] The High Court took the view that the failure of the parties to consider and to agree upon the issue of survivorship should not lead to the conclusion that there was no valid contract and no binding trust. A simple contract to convey to A and B, which makes no reference to the form of co-ownership, will vest equitable title in A and B and it is then a matter for the law, according to relevant statute and precedent, to determine what type of co-ownership is to follow. On the facts of the case, Mr Carmody and Miss Delehunt were co-owners in equity anyway by virtue of a resulting trust.[73]

Special leave to appeal to the High Court was limited to the ground "that the Court of Appeal erred in holding that s. 26 of the *Conveyancing Act* 1919, as amended (N.S.W.) displaced the equitable presumption that where two persons advance equally the purchase moneys for a property, they held as equitable joint tenants".

The High Court, in taking a similar view to the Court of Appeal, found that Mr Carmody and Miss Delehunt held the property as tenants in common in equity. Gibbs C.J. referred to the fact that although equity had demonstrated a dislike for the joint tenancy and had in many instances held joint tenants at law to be tenants in common in equity, equity had "followed" the law and held there to be a joint tenancy in equity where contributions to the purchase price were equal. His Honour commented, however, that since the introduction of s. 26, the effect at law of a disposition to A and B is that they will take as tenants in common, unless there is a clear intention to create a joint tenancy. He stated:[74]

> "It would be indeed surprising if the rules of equity required the courts to follow a rule of the common law that no longer existed and in doing so to reach a result which equity generally tried to avoid. However, the doctrines of equity are not so inflexible. If equity follows the law, it will follow the rules of law in their current state. Where, as a result of following the law a beneficial joint tenancy would formerly have been created, now a beneficial tenancy in common will (in N.S.W.) come into existence. In other words, although s. 26 of the *Conveyancing Act* has no direct application to the present case, its indirect effect is to require it to be held that there was a resulting trust for the purchasers in an interest of the same kind as that which would have resulted if the land had been conveyed to them at law, that is, as tenants in common."

72. (1986) 161 C.L.R. 464; 61 A.L.J.R. 54 at 55. Wilson, Brennan, Deane and Dawson JJ. agreed with Gibbs C.J. on this point.
73. (1986) 161 C.L.R. 464 at 470; 61 A.L.J.R. 54 at 55 per Gibbs C.J.
74. (1986) 161 C.L.R. 464 at 473; 61 A.L.J.R. 54 at 56-58.

(c) Torrens system land

[9.34] The principles described above apply equally to Torrens land. The Torrens provisions (see above **[9.26]-[9.27]**) setting out that joint proprietors are deemed to be joint tenants affect only the registered title. The equitable title of the co-owners will still be determined according to the principles set out above:[75] see above **[9.28]-[9.33]**. Thus, as between the co-owners themselves, the right to beneficial use and enjoyment of the land is determined according to equitable principles.

Third parties are entitled to rely upon the registered title. If the registered title shows the co-owners to be joint tenants and a purchaser relying upon the title pays the purchase moneys to the co-owners in equal shares and subsequently becomes the registered proprietor, he or she will not be liable with respect to any claim one of the co-owners might make that the co-owner was entitled to, for example, three quarters of the purchase moneys. Once registered, the purchaser except in the case of fraud gains an indefeasible title and is not subject to any prior equitable interests even if he or she has notice of them: see above **[5.25]-[5.26]**.

Nevertheless, as between co-owners, an accounting is made. A co-owner who receives from a purchaser more than her or his share is bound to account to the other co-owner or co-owners for the purchase moneys received over and above the value of her or his own share. Until the co-owner does so account, such a co-owner holds the proceeds to which he or she is not entitled in equity on trust for the other co-owner or co-owners.

III. RIGHTS OF ENJOYMENT AS BETWEEN CO-OWNERS

[9.35] There are a number of areas where problems may arise between co-owners. For example, disputes relating to the occupation of property, to the right to rents and profits flowing from the property, to the right of a co-owner to encumber the property and to rights and duties relating to repairs and improvements are all potential problem areas. The first two of these issues are dealt with below. The remaining issues are dealt with in detail in Chapter 12.

1. Occupation Rent

[9.36] As set out above, the unity of possession means that each co-owner has the right to the use and enjoyment of the whole of the land.[76] Because each co-owner is entitled to possession of the whole, an exercise of that right by one co-owner will not give rise to any right of action by a co-owner not exercising the right. Thus, the general rule is that a

---

75. See *Re Foley (decd); Public Trustee v. Foley* [1955] N.Z.L.R. 702 discussed in Whalan, p. 103.
76. See *Thrift v. Thrift* (1975) 10 A.L.R. 332—this includes the right to invite other persons to live on the premises.

co-owner in sole occupation is under no obligation at law or in equity to pay occupation rent to the non-occupying co-owners.[77]

There are however three situations in which a co-owner in sole occupation may be obliged to pay occupation rent to the other co-owners.[78] First, if the occupying co-owner has wrongfully excluded the other co-owner or co-owners from possession, occupation rent is payable. Such exclusion or "ouster" includes exclusion because of violence or the threat of violence. In *Dennis v. McDonald*,[79] the husband and his de facto wife were tenants in common. The husband's violence resulted in the wife leaving the property: in these circumstances the husband was required to pay occupation rent to his de facto wife. Secondly, if there is an agreement between the co-owners that occupation rent is to be paid by the occupying co-owner to the co-owner or co-owners not in occupation, occupation rent is payable.[80] Thirdly, where a co-owner who has been in sole occupation claims from the other co-owners an allowance for improvements he or she has made to the property, the occupying co-owner will only get that allowance if he or she submits to being charged with an occupation rent.[81]

2. Rents and Profits

[9.37]   The principle that a co-owner has the right to the use and enjoyment of the whole of the land also resulted in a co-owner who took more than her or his share of the rents and profits emanating from the land not being accountable to the other co-owners. Co-ownership per se does not give rise to any relationship of agency, partnership or of a fiduciary nature. Effectively, an action for account could only be maintained by one co-owner against another if the co-owner in receipt of the rents had been appointed a bailiff for that purpose by the other co-owner, that is only if there were an agreement between the parties. This common law position was changed by a 1705 *Statute of Queen Anne*.[82] This statute provided that an action for account could be brought and maintained by one co-owner against another for receiving more than "his just share or proportion". In the case of *Henderson v. Eason*,[83] it was held that this statutory provision covers only the case where one co-owner receives money paid by a third party in respect of the land (for example, rent). It does not extend to the case where one co-owner receives more than another as a result of her or his own exertions. Thus under this provision a co-owner must account to the other co-owners for benefits received from a third party but not for benefits taken from the soil as a result of her or his own exertions.

---

77. *Luke v. Luke* (1936) 36 S.R. (N.S.W.) 310; *Scapinello v. Scapinello* [1968] S.A.S.R. 316.
78. Ibid.
79. [1982] 1 All E.R. 590; [1982] 2 W.L.R. 275, discussed in Annand, "The Tenant in Common as Tenant" (1982) 132 New L.J. 526.
80. See e.g. *Leigh v. Dickeson* (1884) 15 Q.B.D. 60
81. See e.g. *Brickwood v. Young* (1905) 2 C.L.R. 387, discussed further below [12.14].
82. Statutes 4 & 5 Anne c. 16, s. 27.
83. (1851) 17 Q.B. 701; 117 E.R. 1451.

Apart from the common law position as altered by the *Statute of Anne*, it seems to be generally accepted that equity has always[84] permitted accounting between co-owners where one co-owner has received more than her or his share.[85] In fact, it has been stated that the suit in equity was preferred because of the complex and expensive nature of the proceedings for account under the *Statute of Anne*.[86] The position may be however, that in the absence of an agreement between the parties the bill for an account in equity is only available when sought as part of a bill for partition,[87] or possibly when all the criteria for a legal action for account have been satisfied.[88] An authority favouring the general and independent availability of the suit in equity for accounting between co-owners is the ancient case of *Strelly v. Winson*,[89] a case concerning co-ownership of a ship. In *obiter dicta* it was held that there was a liability to account between the co-owners when the ship profits. It can be argued, however, that the *Strelly* case was an example of a bailiff relationship existing between the co-owners. That is, it was a case where one tenant in common managed by the mutual agreement of all for their mutual benefit.[90] In at least two subsequent decisions, the view has been taken that the *Strelly* case was not authority for the proposition that a suit in equity for account between co-owners lies whenever one co-owner receives more than her or his share or proportion.[91] The position is unclear.[92]

The proceedings for account under the *Statute of Anne* provision were complex, expensive and little used and were repealed in England as part of the wide-ranging changes made to property law in England in the mid 1920s. A related and important change to the holding of land in co-ownership ensured that the repeal of this provision did not remove the

84. At least since 1685: see *Strelly v. Winson* (1685) 1 Vern. 297; 23 E.R. 480.
85. Meagher, Gummow and Lehane, para. 2512; Butt, p. 196; Kewley, *Report on the Imperial Acts Application Act* 1922 (Victoria Government Printer, 1974), pp. 16-17.
86. See Kewley, op. cit., p. 17.
87. See Langdell, "A Brief Survey of Equity Jurisdiction" (1889) II Harv. L.R. 241 at 263. See *Hill v. Hickin* [1897] 2 Ch. 579; *Lorimer v. Lorimer* (1820) 5 Madd. 363; 56 E.R. 934; *Hill v. Fulbrook* (1822) Jac. 574; 37 E.R. 967.
88. *Denys v. Shuckburgh* (1840) 4 Y. & C. Ex. 43 at 52; 160 E.R. 912 at *Re Tolman's Estate* (1928) 23 Tas. L.R. 29 does not support the general availability of the action in equity. It was held that equity could order an accounting where the parties did not know the *state* of the accounts.
89. (1685) Vern. 295; 23 E.R. 480. It seems the same case was reported as *Anon. in Chancery* (1728) Skinner 230; 90 E.R. 106.
90. In *Henderson v. Eason*, Parkes B. referred to *Anon. in Chancery* and stated that the court was referring to a case where there was an agreement between the parties concerning management. His Honour stated: "for [the court] gives it as an illustration of the rights of a part owner of a ship to an account when the voyage is undertaken by his consent, express or implied." Further, in *Horn v. Gilpin* (1755) Amb. 255; 27 E.R. 170, the court stated that Vernon's report of *Strelly's* case was misstated. See Charles Lord Tenterden, *Abbott on Shipping* (10th ed., 1856) where co-ownership in shipping is discussed. In the shipping cases agreement between co-owners as to management for the mutual benefit of all was very readily inferred in order to ensure as great a productivity as possible.
91. *Henderson v. Eason* (1851) 17 Q.B. 701; 117 E.R. 1451; *Horn v. Gilpin* (1755) Amb. 255; 27 E.R. 170.
92. The independent availability of the action in equity is generally accepted. See e.g. Butt, p. 196; semble, *Encyclopaedia of the Laws of England*, Vol. 1, 71.

liability to account between co-owners.[93] In all jurisdictions except New South Wales, Victoria and Queensland the 1705 *Statute of Anne* still applies. The statutory provision was part of the law in New South Wales until 1969 and in Victoria until 1980 when the *Imperial Acts Application Act 1969* (N.S.W.) and the *Imperial Acts Application Act 1980* (Vic.) respectively, repealed the provision for these States.[94] The view was taken that the proceedings for account "were lengthy, complicated and expensive, and therefore it was a form of action seldom resorted to . . . a suit in equity being commonly preferred. [Further, the provision had] been repealed as obsolete or unnecessary in England."[95]

The analysis above suggests that the suit in equity may not be generally applicable. Whilst the 1705 provision was rendered unnecessary in England, it is possible to argue that its repeal in New South Wales and Victoria has resulted in there being no general liability to account between co-owners where one co-owner receives more than her or his just share or proportion in rents paid by a third party. A co-owner may, however, make a claim for account when making an application for partition:[96] see below **[12.16]-[12.18]**. As under the *Statute of Anne* provision, a co-owner is only liable for amounts received from a third party as a result of the third party's use or occupation of the land.[97] In some instances a co-owner may make a claim from the other co-owners for improvements he or she has made to the property: see below **[12.13]-[12.14]**. The amount which can be claimed is not necessarily as great as the amount expended by the co-owner effecting the improvement.[98] There is, however, at least one instance where the whole of the amount expended may be taken into account. If the co-owner not responsible for the improvements makes a claim against the improving co-owner for rents and profits accruing from the improvements made, the whole of the amount expended on improvements is set off against the rents and profits.[99]

93. Effectively, a trust relationship is set up between the co-owners. Specifically, the co-owners hold the land on trust for themselves and upon "statutory trusts" which Megarry and Wade, pp. 438-439 describe as "upon trust to sell the land, and stand possessed of the net proceeds of sale and of the net rents and profits until sale upon such trusts and subject to such powers and provisions as may be requisite for giving effect to the rights of those interested in the land". Thus it is clear that a co-owner who receives more than her or his share of rents and profits from the land is accountable to the other co-owners for the excess.

94. A strained argument may be made that the saving provision, s. 5 of the *Imperial Acts Application Act 1980* (Vic.) has the result of ensuring that the action for account remains in effect. This, however, seems very unlikely for if the provision were given such an effect many of the benefits of the Act would be lost. See also Kewley, op. cit., pp. 16-17 where it is made clear that the intention was to repeal the *Statute of Anne* provision.

95. Kewley, op. cit., pp. 16-17. Cf. fn. 87.

96. See *Supreme Court Rules* (N.S.W.), Pts 48 and 49 and *Supreme Court Rules* (Vic.), O. 52. See Butt, p. 196 for a discussion of the operation of this method of a co-owner making a claim for profits from another co-owner. See also **[15.52]**.

97. *Squire v. Rogers* (1979) 39 F.L.R. 106 at 124.

98. *Squire v. Rogers* (1979) 39 F.L.R. 106. Discussed in Note (1989) 63 A.L.J. 631.

99. *Squire v. Rogers* (1979) 39 F.L.R. 106 at 126-127. See Butt, p. 196. If the co-owner claiming a share of the rents was unaware of the making of the improvements this result may not ensue.

In Queensland, s. 43 of the *Property Law Act* 1974 provides for accounting between co-owners in a similar manner to the 1705 *Statute of Anne*.[100]

In circumstances where an account can be taken, a co-owner is only liable for the rents he or she has received and not for rents and profits that could have been accumulated if the property had, for example, been better managed.[101]

3. Trespass

[9.38] As each co-owner is entitled to the use and possession of the whole of the land, trespass cannot lie between co-owners unless one co-owner has ousted the other.[102] If there has been such an ouster, the ousted co-owner may be entitled to mesne profits. If the actions of a co-owner amount to a complete destruction of the commonly held property, the other co-owners can maintain an action in trespass.[103]

IV. SEVERANCE

[9.39] Although the term "severance" strictly includes partition,[104] it is generally used, and will be used here, for the purpose of describing the means by which a joint tenancy is converted into a tenancy in common. It is often stated that severance is effected by the destruction of one of the unities.[105] Although unity of time cannot be destroyed and destruction of the unity of possession renders co-ownership impossible, severance of the unity of title or of interest converts a joint tenancy into a tenancy in common.[106]

100. Unlike the New South Wales Law Reform Commission, the Queensland Law Reform Commission took the view that the old Imperial statute of 1705 should not be repealed without a substituting provision. The view was expressed that such a provision was necessary as a means of providing a privity relationship between the cotenants: without such a provision a cotenant could not point to a bailiff relationship on which to base an action in law or a suit in equity. See Q.L.R.C., Report No. 16 (1973), pp. 29-30.
101. *Thrift v. Thrift* (1975) 10 A.L.R. 332.
102. *Murray v. Hall* (1849) 7 C.B. 441; 137 E.R. 175.
103. *Wilkinson v. Haygarth* (1847) 12 Q.B. 837; 116 E.R. 1085; *Murray v. Hall* (1849) 7 C.B. 441; 137 E.R. 175; *Oates v. Oates* [1949] S.A.S.R. 37. Where there is partial destruction, the law of waste may be applicable: see *Murray v. Hall* (1849) 7 C.B. 441; 137 E.R. 175. See generally below [12.09]-[12.12]; Mendes da Costa, op. cit. at 140; and Teh and Dwyer, p. 149.
104. Megarry and Wade, p. 430.
105. Ibid.
106. In a seminal article on co-ownership in Victoria, Mendes da Costa raised the possibility of severance occurring in equity notwithstanding the continuance of the unities. He suggested that with respect to severance by agreement, at least, the severance may be based on intention rather than destruction of a unity. He drew an analogy with the *creation* of the joint tenancy, where by the inclusion of words of severance, a grantor can create a tenancy in common despite the presence of the four unities: Mendes da Costa op. cit. at 433-434. See now *Corin v. Patton* (1990) 92 A.L.R. 1, discussed in fn. 124.

Severance may be effected by the act or acts of one or more of the joint tenants inter vivos or by act of law. The former is the more common form of severance.

1. Severance by One or More of the Joint Tenants Inter Vivos

[9.40] A joint tenant cannot dispose of her or his interest by will as the right of survivorship is a characteristic of the joint tenancy. However, a joint tenant does have the right to sever the joint tenancy during her or his lifetime. Severance, however, may only be effected in a manner sanctioned by the law.

The classic statement on severance of joint tenancies in this manner is set out in the judgment of Sir W. Page-Wood V.-C. in *Williams v. Hensman*:[107]

> "A joint-tenancy may be severed in three ways; in the first place, an act of any one of the persons interested operating upon his own share may create a severance as to that share. The right of each joint-tenant is a right by survivorship only in the event of no severance having taken place of the share which is claimed under the *jus accrescendi*. Each one is at liberty to dispose of his own interest in such manner as to sever it from the joint fund—losing, of course, at the same time, his own right of survivorship. Secondly, a joint-tenancy may be severed by mutual agreement. And, in the third place, there may be a severance by any course of dealing sufficient to intimate that the interests of all were mutually treated as constituting a tenancy in common. When the severance depends on an inference of this kind without any express act of severance, it will not suffice to rely on an intention, with respect to the particular share, declared only behind the backs of the other persons interested. You must find in this class of cases a course of dealing by which the shares of all the parties to the contest have been effected."

Sir Page-Wood V.-C. envisaged, therefore, three methods of severance. It appears clear from this statement that the only way in which a joint tenant can sever unilaterally a joint tenancy is by the first method, an act of any party operating on her or his own share.[108] Each of the methods of severance will be analysed.

(a) Act of a party operating upon her or his own share

[9.41] The accepted means pursuant to which the first method of severance is satisfied is by a joint tenant alienating her or his interest or by a joint tenant acquiring a greater interest in the land than the other joint tenants.

---

107. (1861) 1 J. & H. 546; 70 E.R. 862.
108. However, see the judgment of Lord Denning in *Burgess v. Rawnsley* [1975] Ch. 429 where his Honour suggests that rule three may also operate on the basis of the unilateral intention of one joint tenant.

(i) Alienation

[9.42]   It should be noted that if all joint tenants together alienate by for example selling, leasing or mortgaging the joint property, there is no severance at law or in equity.[109] However, where land is held in joint tenancy by two persons and one of the joint tenants alienates her or his interest to a stranger, the joint tenancy is severed and the grantee and the remaining tenant hold as tenants in common. Unity of title does not exist. If land is held by three or more joint tenants and one joint tenant alienates her or his interest to another, the grantee holds the interest acquired as a tenant in common with the other joint tenants. As between themselves, the remaining tenants continue to hold as joint tenants. The following is a simple example of the principle. A, B and C are joint tenants in fee simple of Blackacre. A conveys her interest to X. X is a tenant in common with B and C. B and C continue to hold two thirds as joint tenants between themselves.

It is necessary to draw a distinction between alienation at law and alienation in equity. This is obvious where the joint tenants hold only the legal interest or only the equitable interest. However, even where the joint tenants hold the whole estate, it may be important to differentiate between legal and equitable interests for severance may have been effected in equity but not at law.

[9.43]   There is an effective alienation at law if there is compliance with the requirements for the passing of a legal interest in land. With respect to land falling under the general law land system, all States except Queensland require the proper execution of a deed in order for legal title to pass.[110] In relation to Torrens land, registration of a transfer is required before legal title passes to the grantee.[111] An effective alienation of the legal interest by a joint tenant results in a severance of the joint tenancy at law.

In *Wright v. Gibbons*,[112] the High Court considered whether there had been a severance of a joint tenancy. Two sisters, Olinda and Ethel Gibbons and their sister-in-law, Bessie Gibbons were registered as joint tenants of a fee simple estate. The land in question fell under the Torrens system of land registration. Olinda and Ethel wished to sever the joint tenancy and purported to do so by executing a document which provided that Olinda transferred her one third share to Ethel and Ethel transferred her one third share to Olinda. The document of transfer was registered

---

109. See *Re Allingham; Allingham v. Allingham* [1932] V.L.R. 469—where there was a sale by all joint tenants to a stranger, the joint tenants of the land became joint tenants of the proceeds of sale; *Ex parte Railway Commissioners (N.S.W.)* (1941) 41 S.R. (N.S.W.) 92—resumption of land owned by joint tenants where the former joint tenants of the land were held to have a joint claim for compensation; *Doe d. Aslin and Finch v. Summersett* (1830) 1 B. & Ad. 135 at 140; 109 E.R. 738 at 739—lease of the fee simple by all joint tenants does not effect a severance.
110. See e.g. *Property Law Act* (Vic.) 1958, s. 52(1). For the other statutory provisions, see above **[6.10]**.
111. See e.g. *Transfer of Land Act* (Vic.), s. 40(1). For the other relevant statutory provisions, see above **[6.11]**.
112. (1949) 78 C.L.R. 313.

and the former joint tenants, Olinda, Ethel and Bessie, were registered as tenants in common in equal shares. Bessie survived Olinda and Ethel and sought a declaration in the Supreme Court that the joint tenancy had not been severed.

The High Court held that the joint tenancy had been effectively severed. Each of the judges discussed the effect of a transaction pursuant to which a joint tenant transferred her or his interest to another joint tenant, rather than to a stranger. Latham C.J. stated:[113]

> "Where one joint tenant transfers his interest to another joint tenant the transfer (which at common law was effected by release because each joint tenant is conceived as holding every part and the whole of the land . . .) does not operate by way of extinguishment of the estate. A mere extinguishment would enure in favour [of all remaining joint tenants and it is clear that a joint tenant can transfer his interest to one, some or all of the remaining joint tenants] . . . [A]lthough such a transaction should be carried out by release, a grant is interpreted as a release."

The complicating factor in *Wright v. Gibbons* was that the relevant transfers were contained within the one document and the document came into effect at a particular time, the time of registration. Latham C.J., Rich J. and Dixon J. all took the view for varying reasons that upon registration, the document had the effect of severing the joint tenancy at law.[114]

[9.44] Even if there has been no severance at law, an effective alienation of the equitable interest by one of the joint tenants will result in severance of the joint tenancy in equity. Equitable interests may be alienated in a number of ways: see Chapter 6 generally. In this context, the two most relevant methods are the declaration of trust and the contract of sale.[115] First, where a joint tenant declares her or himself a trustee of the interest for another, equity will enforce the trust providing there has been compliance with the statutory requirements in relation to declarations of trust.[116] The declaration of trust severs the joint tenancy in equity.[117] Secondly, where a joint tenant enters into an enforceable contract to sell her or his interest, equity will deem as done that which ought to be done and regard the purchaser as the owner of the interest in equity.[118] Severance occurs in equity as soon as an enforceable contract of sale

---

113. (1949) 78 C.L.R. 313 at 323.
114. Latham C.J. stated that the document should be construed in accordance with the principle ut res magis valeat qum pereat. It is better for a thing to have effect than to be made void. Rich and Dixon JJ. took the view that the system for transferring and registration of interests under the Torrens system permitted such an effect (i.e. severance). It should be noted that, if the same fact situation arose under the general law land system, separate deeds of conveyance would be required to effect a severance: see Dixon J. and Rich J.
115. For further examples see Mendes da Costa, op. cit. at 444-445.
116. See e.g. *Property Law Act* 1958 (Vic.), s. 53(1)(b).
117. *Re Sorensen and Sorensen* (1977) 90 D.L.R. (3d) 26; *Ogilvie v. Littleboy* (1897) 13 T.L.R. 399, aff. 15 T.L.R. 294 sub nom. *Ogilvie v. Allen*.
118. *Walsh v. Lonsdale* (1882) 21 Ch. D. 9; *Lysaht v. Edwards* (1876) 2 Ch. D. 499; *Chan v. Cresdon Pty Ltd* (1989) 89 A.L.R. 522.

exists.[119] In practice, severance at law will usually occur later upon the execution of a deed (general law land) or upon the registration of a properly executed transfer (Torrens land).

[9.45] Some difficult questions relating to severance have arisen in relation to the situation of a gift by a joint tenant of her or his interest in Torrens land. Upon registration of a voluntary transfer from a joint tenant in favour of the grantee, the joint tenancy is clearly severed at law and in equity. The issue which has arisen is whether it is possible for there to be a severance in equity before the registration of the transfer. That is, will equity regard the grantee/volunteer as being the owner in equity before the legal title has passed? Generally, equity does not assist a volunteer, or perfect an imperfect gift. However, in *Milroy v. Lord*,[120] a case concerning the transfer of shares by way of gift, it was held that if the donor has done "everything which, according to the nature of the property comprised in the settlement, was necessary to be done [by him] in order to transfer the property"[121] equity will view the gift as being complete and perfect and hold that equitable title has passed to the volunteer. The settlor retains the legal estate holding it on trust for the donee. In *Brunker v. The Perpetual Trustee Co. Ltd*,[122] the High Court held that the principle enunciated in *Milroy v. Lord* does not apply to Torrens land.[123] Therefore, even where a joint tenant has executed a transfer of her or his interest by way of gift in favour of the grantee and physically delivered the transfer and the duplicate certificate of title to the grantee, the equitable interest does not pass to the grantee. Severance of the joint tenancy does not result until registration of the transfer. Such registration vests title (legal and equitable) in the grantee and it is at the time of registration that severance occurs.

Although the High Court in the *Brunker* case was not prepared to apply the *Milroy v. Lord* principle to Torrens land and thus view the volunteer as having an equitable interest before registration, Dixon J. took the view that the volunteer may obtain a right to have the transfer registered, a right which the donor or her or his executors could not defeat: see above [6.18]-[6.19]. Recently, the question has been raised as to whether such a right to be registered, given to a person by a joint tenant, could in itself operate to cause a severance of the joint tenancy.[124] If alienation in law

119. *Barry v. Heider* (1914) 19 C.L.R. 197 at 216 per Isaacs J.
120. (1862) 4 De G.F. & J. 264; 45 E.R. 1185.
121. (1862) 4 De G.F. & J. 264 at 274; 45 E.R. 1185 at 1189.
122. (1937) 57 C.L.R. 555.
123. See also *Re Ward* [1968] W.A.R. 33; *Taylor v. Deputy Federal Commissioner of Taxation* (1969) 123 C.L.R. 206; *Golding v. Hands* [1969] W.A.R. 121; *In the marriage of Badcock* (1979) 5 Fam. L.R. 672; *Caratti v. Grant* (1978) 3 A.C.L.R. 322. See also MacCallum, "Severance of a Matrimonial Joint Tenancy" (1980) 7 Mon. L.R. 17 at 25-29. For a detailed discussion, see above [6.16]-[6.19]. However, see *Corin v. Patton* (1990) 92 A.L.R. 1 discussed in fn. 124.
124. *Corin v. Patton* (1988) 13 N.S.W.L.R. 15 at 26 per Hope J.A. See *Corin v. Patton* (1990) 92 A.L.R. 1 where Mason C.J. and McHugh and Deane JJ. held that if a donor has done everything necessary to pass legal title, the gift is complete in equity: equitable title will have passed to the donee (contra Brennan J.; quaere Toohey J.). The majority thus took the view that the formula of Dixon J. in the *Brunker* case (see above [9.45]) no longer represents a correct statement

or equity is insisted upon in order for severance to occur, the existence of a right to be registered would not per se constitute a severance. Nevertheless, in most cases a right to be registered will lead to registration and thus a severance.

[9.46] The discussion above assumes total alienation of the interest of a joint tenant. In some instances, partial alienation by a joint tenant is sufficient to effect a severance of the joint tenancy; the partial alienation should be one that destroys the unity of title or of interest. Generally it has been accepted that the grant of an estate by a joint tenant does effect a severance but that the grant of an encumbrance by a joint tenant does not do so.[125] Thus, either the grant of a life estate by a joint tenant[126] or the grant of a mortgage of general law land by a joint tenant would effect severance of the joint tenancy as the partial alienation amounts to the grant of an estate.

As McInerney J. commented in *Lyons v. Lyons*[127] with respect to the mortgage by a joint tenant of general law land:[128]

"under the general law the mortgagor conveys his estate in the mortgaged land to the mortgagee. There is thus vested in the mortgagee all the estate and interest formerly vested in the joint tenant mortgagor: but the mortgagee obtains that estate and interest under a different instrument or judicial act than the other joint tenant or tenants, and there is thus no unity of title between the mortgagee and them."

The grant of an easement or of a rentcharge by a joint tenant does not effect a severance as the grant of an encumbrance only is involved.

For some time, it was unclear whether two types of partial alienation by a joint tenant, namely the mortgage of Torrens land[129] and the lease, would effect a severance of the joint tenancy. In 1967, the matter was resolved with respect to the mortgage by a joint tenant of Torrens land when McInerney J. delivered his judgment in *Lyons v. Lyons*.[130] His Honour took the view that such a mortgage does not sever the joint tenancy. Unlike the mortgage of general law land, the mortgage of Torrens land operates by way of a charge, not by way of a transfer of the interest of the mortgagor to the mortgagee. Although it is clear that the mortgagee of Torrens land acquires an interest in the land,[131] such an interest is separate from the fee simple interest retained by the mortgagor.

---

124. *Continued*
        of the law. In the context of severance of the joint tenancy, alienation in equity may occur when a joint tenant has done everything necessary to make a gift to a third party of her or his interest in Torrens land.
125. Mendes da Costa, op. cit. at 433, 446.
126. Mendes da Costa, op. cit. at 447.
127. [1967] V.R. 169 at 173.
128. [1967] V.R. 169 at 173.
129. There had been some doubt as to whether the Torrens mortgage operated as a security or transfer. This is discussed by McInerney J. in *Lyons v. Lyons* [1967] V.R. 169 at 174.
130. [1967] V.R. 169.
131. [1967] V.R. 169 at 175.

Thus, according to the reasoning of McInerney J., the four unities remain intact as between the joint tenants after one joint tenant mortgages her or his interest. It has been argued that a finding that a mortgage of Torrens land does not effect a severance may lead to unfair results.[132] If the joint tenant who mortgaged her or his interest dies first, the land vests in the surviving joint tenant or tenants free of the mortgage.[133] The mortgagee is, therefore, at risk of losing the security. In view of this possible scenario, mortgagees do not and should not accept as a viable security, a mortgage by one joint tenant.[134]

In *Frieze v. Unger*,[135] Sholl J. reviewed exhaustively the authorities on the issue of severance where one joint tenant had granted a lease. It is submitted that the view expressed by his Honour and set out below is the law applicable to the situation where one joint tenant in fee simple leases her or his interest.[136]

His Honour stated:[137]

"[A] demise for a term of years by one of two joint tenants in fee does not, according to the preferable view, work a severance of the whole fee; at most it effects a 'severance for the time' or 'suspends' the joint tenancy *pro tem* . . . [This] doctrine involves the proposition that the reversion expectant on the term will pass to the survivor of the joint tenants, so that any 'severance' or 'suspension' is such only as is necessary to procure for the lessee the enjoyment during the term of grantor's moiety both after as well as before the grantor's death."

In the case of joint tenants of a leasehold estate, it appears to be well accepted that the grant of a sublease by one joint tenant effects a complete severance of the joint tenancy.[138]

[9.47] Alienation by a joint tenant to her or himself. In order to avoid the consequences of the jus accrescendi, joint tenants may wish to alter their ownership from a joint tenancy to a tenancy in common. If all the joint tenants *agree*, it is a simple matter to convert the joint tenancy into a tenancy in common: see below **[9.49]-[9.51]**. However, if for

132. Mendes da Costa, op. cit. at 448 and cf. *Cedar Holdings Ltd v. Green* [1979] 2 All E.R. 517.
133. The opposite applies too. If the joint tenant who mortgaged her or his interest survives the other joint tenants, the mortgage is effective against the whole estate.
134. *Re Shannon's Transfer* [1967] Tas. S.R. 245 per Nease J. approved *Lyons v. Lyons* [1967] V.R. 169. See Preece, "The Effect of Partial Alienation by a Co-owner of Land" (1981) 55 L.I.J. 115.
135. [1960] V.R. 230.
136. See Mendes da Costa, op. cit. at 454.
137. [1960] V.R. 230 at 242-243. See also *Wright v. Gibbons* (1949) 78 C.L.R. 313 at 330 per Dixon J. The statement of Sholl J. assumes the grant of a lease for a term of years. Quaere the situation where a joint tenant grants a periodic tenancy from year to year, month to month or week to week. Contrary to the submission of counsel in *Frieze v. Unger*, it is suggested that the principle expressed by Sholl J. with respect to a lease for a term of years, should similarly apply to such tenancies.
138. *Frieze v. Unger* [1960] V.R. 230 at 243; Mendes da Costa, op. cit. at 454; Megarry and Wade, p. 431 even to another joint tenant.

example, one of two joint tenants wishes to sever the joint tenancy and the other does not, a question arises to how the joint tenant wishing to sever can do so and still retain beneficial ownership. As mentioned above, such a joint tenant can effect a severance by conveying or transferring the legal estate to a trustee. The trustee holds the estate on trust for the joint tenant.

A possible alternative method, and one by which the joint tenant retains legal and equitable ownership, involves a conveyance by the joint tenant to her or himself. This method of severance depends upon the existence of a statutory provision permitting a person to assure land to her or himself. The general property statutes in all States contain such provisions.[139] Despite some initial hesitation[140] it appears that this method of severance is permissible and effective.[141] In order for the severance to be effected, the legal interest must have passed. With respect to general law land, the proper execution of a deed suffices; in relation to Torrens land, registration of a transfer must have taken place.[142] A further alternative and one by which the joint tenant would retain beneficial ownership, involves a conveyance or transfer of the legal title to a trustee who in turn holds it on trust for the joint tenant. In order to effect the severance, it is necessary for the legal title to be effectively transferred to the trustee:[143] see above [9.45]. In the case of Torrens land, a voluntary transfer by a joint tenant does not effect a severance at law or in equity until registration.[144]

(ii) Acquisition by a tenant of another interest in the land

[9.48] If one of the joint tenants subsequently acquires a greater interest in the land than the other joint tenants, the joint tenancy is severed.[145] For example, if A and B are joint tenants for life and A subsequently acquires the fee simple remainder, the joint tenancy is severed. The subsequent acquisition is said to destroy the unity of interest and thus, the joint tenancy. However, if the original grant is to A and B for life as joint tenants and then to A in fee simple in remainder, the joint tenancy between A and B is valid and operative. Although the distinction is a curious one, it is firmly entrenched. It is based on the fact that unity of

139. General law statutes: N.S.W.: ss 24, 44(2); Vic.: s. 72(3); S.A.: s. 40(3); W.A.: s. 39; Tas.: s. 62(2). Cf. Qld: s. 14(3).

140. *Rye v. Rye* [1962] 2 W.L.R. 361; see Mendes da Costa, op. cit. at 457.

141. See e.g. *Samuel v. District Land Registrar* [1984] 2 N.Z.L.R. 673; *Re Murdoch and Barry* (1975) D.L.R. (3rd) 222; *McNab v. Earle* [1981] 2 N.S.W.L.R. 673 (no registration of the transfer and thus, no severance); *Freed v. Taffel* [1984] 2 N.S.W.L.R. 322 (as in *McNab's* case, no registration of a transfer and so no severance).

142. Registration of a transfer might be impeded by, e.g., a mortgagee refusing to produce the duplicate certificate of title.

143. *Corin v. Patton* (1988) 13 N.S.W.L.R. 15.

144. But see *Corin v. Patton* (1990) 92 A.L.R. 1 discussed in fn. 124.

145. *Morgan's Case* (1590) 2 And. 202; 123 E.R. 620; *Wiscot's Case; Giles v. Wiscot* (1599) 2 Co. Rep. 60b; 76 E.R. 555. See Mendes da Costa, op. cit. at 443.

SEVERANCE 327

interest is destroyed in the first instance but exists in the second instance.[146]

There is a further example of severance of a joint tenancy under this category. Where the land is held by A, the life tenant, with remainder in fee simple over to B and C as joint tenants, and A conveys his life estate to B, the joint tenancy between B and C is severed.[147]

It should be noted that severance does not occur under this heading unless the estate acquired differs from the estate held in joint tenancy. For example, if A, B and C are joint tenants in fee simple and A conveys his interest to B, B holds the one third share conveyed by A, as a tenant in common with himself and C who hold the remaining two thirds as joint tenants.

(b) Agreement to Sever

[9.49]   The second method of severance set out in *Williams v. Hensman*[148] is severance by mutual agreement between the joint tenants. Such a severance is one in equity and it is clear that all joint tenants must be party to the agreement to sever before it can be concluded that the co-owners hold as tenants in common.

There is some uncertainty as to whether the agreement must be a specifically enforceable one in order to effect a severance. In *Lyons v. Lyons*, McInerney J. took the view that there could be no severance in equity under this second head "unless there is a note or memorandum in writing sufficient to satisfy the *Statute of Frauds* or circumstances giving rise to the doctrine of part performance". As interests in land are affected, the view of McInerney J. appears logical.[149] However, there are a number of cases including an early Australian decision and a relatively recent English Court of Appeal decision, which suggest that the agreement need not be specifically enforceable in order to effect a severance.[150] These decisions emphasise that the important criterion for severance by mutual agreement is that the agreement, whether or not specifically enforceable, demonstrates that the parties were of one mind in that they intended, from the time of agreement, to hold as tenants in common.[151] Despite the

---

146. Mendes da Costa, op. cit. at 443 finds the distinction, and the reason for the distinction, strange. The reason for the distinction is that in the latter instance both the interests of A are created by the same instrument and are therefore not separate estates—thus merger does not operate. In the former instance, the interests of A are separate estates as they are separately acquired and so A's life estate merges with the remainder and destroys the unity of interest. In fact, Mendes da Costa argues that the distinction may no longer be upheld.
147. Cf. the situation where A. surrenders the life estate to B. Such a surrender extinguishes the life estate, both B and C benefit and the joint tenancy continues. See Megarry and Wade, p. 433.
148. (1861) 1 J. & H. 546; 70 E.R. 862.
149. See Butt, p. 576
150. *Gebhardt v. Dempster* [1914] S.A.S.R. 287; *Burgess v. Rawnsley* [1975] Ch. 429. See also *Abela v. Public Trustee* [1983] 1 N.S.W.L.R. 308.
151. See also Mendes da Costa, op. cit. at 440-443.

persuasiveness of the reasoning of McInerney J., it is suggested that severance will result even if the agreement is not capable of specific performance. As has been suggested the severance in equity may be justified on the basis of a constructive trust: the mutual agreement to sever may result in equity requiring that the joint tenants hold the legal estate on trust for themselves as tenants in common.[152]

[9.50]   The mutual agreement to sever may be an express one. It is clear, however, that the agreement to sever may be implied from the conduct of the joint tenants in relation to the property.[153] For example, married persons who hold property in joint tenancy may, upon separation, enter into negotiations and make agreements which demonstrate directly or indirectly that they intend to hold separate and distinct shares in the jointly owned property. If the court is satisfied that there is such a concluded agreement between the parties, severance will be effected.[154]

Where the parties make a joint application under s. 79 of the *Family Law Act* 1975 (Cth) to the Family Court for settlement of their jointly owned property, such application alone is insufficient to effect a severance.[155] If, however, it can be shown that behind the application there was an agreement between the parties that they intended to hold separate and distinct shares from the time of the agreement, even if there was no agreement as to the proportions, it is submitted that a severance

---

152. Butt, p. 576.
153. *Williams v. Hensman* (1861) 1 J. & H. 546 at 557; 70 E.R. 862 at 866-867. See Mendes da Costa, op. cit. at 441.
154. *Re Pozzi* [1982] Qd R. 499—after dissolution of their marriage, the husband and wife, joint tenants of the matrimonial home, executed an agreement pursuant to which the wife was to have sole use and occupancy of the matrimonial home until a particular event and then the property was to be sold and the proceeds divided in the manner stated. The agreement was registered under s. 86 of the *Family Law Act* 1975 (Cth). The husband died. The Supreme Court of Queensland held that there had been a severance of the joint tenancy. *Calabrese v. Miuccio (No. 2)* [1985] 1 Qd R. 17—after dissolution of their marriage, the husband and wife agreed that jointly held funds should be divided in a particular manner such that the wife would receive more than the husband and that agreement was sanctioned pursuant to s. 87 of the *Family Law Act* 1975 (Cth). The husband then withdrew consent for the sanctioning of the agreement, and the wife died. On the issue as to whether the joint tenancy had been severed, the Full Court of the Supreme Court held that the joint tenancy had been severed when the agreement was made. In *Public Trustee v. Pfeiffle* (1990) F.L.C. 92-123 (Full Ct of Vic. Sup. Ct) an agreement under s. 87 of the *Family Law Act* 1975 (Cth) was approved by the Family Court. Inter alia it provided that jointly owned property was to be sold and the proceeds divided upon either party remarrying. It was held that the common intention of the joint tenants to sever as evidenced by their mutual agreement and the severance took place immediately. The mechanism for sale did not fix the time of severance. See also *Abela v. Public Trustee* [1983] 1 N.S.W.L.R. 308; *Burgess v. Rawnsley* [1975] Ch. 429; *Public Trustee v. Grivas* [1974] 2 N.S.W.L.R. 316.
155. *Perstoulis and Perstoulis* (1980) F.L.C. 90,823—the court took the view that as the parties may withdraw their applications at any time before an order of the court is made, there is no concluded agreement between them.

has been effected. It is the agreement rather than the application or the court order which severs the joint tenancy.[156]

If the parties seek a court order with respect to the settlement of their jointly owned property and the court order obtained requires any form of dealing with the property, the joint tenancy is severed in equity from the date of the court order.[157] Severance at law does not occur until the relevant legal title is effectively passed.

[9.51] An unusual method of severance by agreement is where the joint tenants agree to make mutual wills and then carry out that intention by making the wills.[158] Although one joint tenant cannot overcome the jus accrescendi by the making of a will, if all joint tenants agree and do make mutual wills, the joint tenancy can be severed.[159]

(c) Course of Dealing

[9.52] Page-Wood V.-C. in *Williams v. Hensman* stated that there may be a severance "by any course of conduct sufficient to intimate that the interests" of all joint tenants are to be treated as interests under a tenancy in common. Although this third method of severance may appear to be simply a sub category of severance by agreement and although there may often be overlap between the two methods, severance by a course of dealing and yet not by agreement may result when negotiations or a "course of dealing" make it clear that the interests of all joint tenants are treated by all as being held in tenancy in common.

A course of dealing such that the interests be mutually treated as held in common implies that all joint tenants must be parties to negotiations constituting the course of dealing. Thus, a declaration of unilateral intention to sever by one joint tenant whether communicated or not to the other joint tenants does not, in Australia, constitute a severance of the joint tenancy pursuant to this third method of severance.[160]

---

156. Once the agreement is made the joint tenancy is severed finally. If one of the parties subsequently changes her or his mind, it appears that the joint tenancy cannot be revived: see *Burgess v. Rawnsley* [1975] Ch. 429; Butt, pp. 576-578; *Re Shannon's Transfer* [1967] Tas. S.R. 245 where the concept of "suspension" of the joint tenancy in these circumstances is discussed.

157. *Re Johnstone* [1973] Qd R. 347; *Public Trustee v. Grivas* [1974] 2 N.S.W.L.R. 316; cf. *McKee v. McKee* (1986) 10 Fam. L.R. 754; *Corry v. Corry* (1983) F.L.C. 91-343 where it was held there was no severance because the order was subject to conditions precedent; *McVey v. Dennis* (1984) F.L.C. 91-521 where it was held that there was no severance by order of the court because the wife died before the decree was made absolute.

158. *Re Wilford's Estate; Taylor v. Taylor* [1934] V.L.R. 129; *Szabo v. Boros* (1967) 64 D.L.R. (2d) 48; see Mendes da Costa, op. cit. at 443; Butt, pp. 587-588.

159. The joint tenants may agree not to sever—as to the effectiveness of such an agreement, see Mendes da Costa, op. cit. at 440.

160. Neither does it constitute an effective method pursuant to the first method of severance. See also *Golding v. Hands* [1969] W.A.R. 121; *Davies v. Davies* (1982) 8 Fam. L.R. 188; *Patzak v. Lytton* [1984] W.A.R. 353 which all followed this view as expressed by Walton J. in *Nielson-Jones v. Fedden* [1975] Ch. 222; [1974] All E.R. 38. Cf. the English decisions of *Hawksley v. May* [1956] 1 Q.B. 304; *Re Draper's Conveyance* [1968] 2 W.L.R. 166 and *Burgess v. Rawnsley* [1975] Ch. 429.

Thus, although an application to court by a joint tenant seeking sale and distribution of the proceeds may be a declaration of an intention to sever, it is not such an action as will sever the joint tenancy.[161]

(d) Declaration of Intention to Sever

[9.53]   In England, there is legislation which allows for severance of a joint tenancy by notice in writing given by one joint tenant to the other joint tenants.[162] There is no similar legislation in Australia and it has been suggested above that the common law does not recognise severance by mere declaration of intention either under the first or third methods of severance described in *Williams v. Hensman*.[162a] It may be argued that a declaration of intention to sever should be an acceptable means of severing a joint tenancy.[163] At present, a joint tenant, by the unilateral action of alienating her or his interest may sever the joint tenancy without the approbation or knowledge of the other co-owner or co-owners.

2. Severance other than by the Act of the Party

(a) Involuntary alienation

[9.54]   The joint tenancy is severed if the interest of a joint tenant is alienated by operation of law. For example s. 58 of the *Bankruptcy Act* 1966 (Cth) provides that upon sequestration, the property of the bankrupt vests in the trustee in bankruptcy. Thus, if A and B are joint tenants in fee simple and A is declared bankrupt, A's interest vests in the trustee in bankruptcy and B and the trustee in bankruptcy holds as tenants in common in equal shares.[164]

(b) Public policy/homicide

[9.55]   In *Rasmanis v. Jurewitsch*[165] A and B were joint tenants of a fee simple estate. A unlawfully killed B. Although at law the jus accrescendi

---

161. See *Patzak v. Lytton* [1984] W.A.R. 353. Cf. *Badcock and Badcock* (1979) F.L.C. 90-723; (1979) 5 Fam. L.R. 672.
162. *Law of Property Act* 1925 (Eng.), s. 36(2).
162a. See *Corin v. Patton* (1990) 92 A.L.R. 1.
163. MacCallum, op. cit. at 33.
164. *Re Holland; Ex parte Official Trustee in Bankruptcy* [1985] Aust Conv. R. 158 decision of Federal Court of Australia, 15 February 1985, where a question arose as to the precise time severance occurs when a joint tenant is bankrupted. The Federal Court held that when the husband/joint tenant was declared bankrupt, there was a "disposal" of the husband's share and his interest thereupon vested in the trustee in equity: see s. 58(2) of the *Bankruptcy Act* 1966 (Cth). Severance at law cannot be effected until the transmission in favour of the Official Trustee has been registered. The court in *Re Francis; Ex parte Official Trustee in Bankruptcy* (1988) 82 A.L.R. 333 followed *Re Holland*. Cf. *Re Oswald* [1985] A.C.L.D. 645. *Ex parte the Official Trustee in Bankruptcy* (1985) 61 A.L.R. 339.
165. [1968] 2 N.S.W.R. 166. See also *Re Thorp and the Real Property Act* [1962] N.S.W.R. 889; *Re Stone* [1989] 1 Qd R. 351; *Public Trustee v. Evans* [1985] 2 N.S.W.L.R. 188; cf. *Re Barrowcliff* [1927] S.A.S.R. 147; *Kemp v. Public Curator of Queensland* [1969] Qd R. 145 where the notion of enforcing principles of public policy by resort to equity was rejected. The act of killing effected a severance of the joint tenancy.

operated so that the legal estate vested in A, this was subject to the imposition of a constructive trust on A. A held the legal estate on a constructive trust for himself and the estate of B as tenants in common in equal shares. The court took the view that whilst public policy considerations required that the felon should not gain by what he had done, they did not require that either compensation be paid to the victim or that the felon be punished by loss of property.

With respect to a block of land held by A, B and C as joint tenants, it was held that A and C held the legal estate on a constructive trust for C as to one third and for A and C as joint tenants as to two thirds. In this instance, the court had to reach a decision as to whether C, the third joint tenant, or the estate of B, would be the more suitable recipient for the enhancement in value of which the felon had to be deprived. As the idea of public policy was to ensure that the felon did not gain by the felony and was not to compensate the victim, and as C should not be deprived of the enjoyment of such enhancement as would flow from the victim's death, C was considered the more suitable recipient.[166]

166. See the analysis in Mendes da Costa, op. cit. at 437 where a different solution is suggested, and at 488 where it is stated that these principles clearly should not apply to justifiable or excusable homicide or to a tortious non-criminal killing. Quaere, the crime of manslaughter. See Re Stone [1989] 1 Qd R. 351 where the charge was reduced from murder to manslaughter on the ground of diminished responsibility and the principle of Rasmanis was still applied.

10

The General Law of Landlord and Tenant

I. BACKGROUND TO THE PRESENT LAW

1. Scope of the General Law

[10.01] Until comparatively recently, landlord and tenant law in Australia has constituted one body of laws applying to all types of tenancies. This body of laws is based predominantly on the common law, coupled with certain statutory provisions in the Torrens legislation of each State and certain other universally applicable provisions contained in State landlord and tenant legislation.[1]

The application of the general law of landlord and tenant has been subject for a considerable period both to special provisions for farm tenancies in New South Wales, Queensland and South Australia[2] and to certain rent control and security of tenure provisions in New South Wales and Victoria affecting limited classes of residential premises introduced originally during the Second World War.[3] In the past decade, however, far more significant exceptions have been introduced in respect of residential tenancies and certain commercial tenancies. In respect of residential tenancies, landlord and tenant law has now been codified under *Residential Tenancies Acts*[4] in New South Wales, Victoria, South Australia and Western Australia. Less comprehensive residential tenancies legislation also exists in Queensland.[5] The law in respect of certain types of retail shop leases is also now codified in Victoria, Queensland, South Australia and Western Australia.[6] These laws will be

---

1. The relevant legislation is the *Landlord and Tenant Act* 1899 (N.S.W.); *Conveyancing Act* 1919 (N.S.W.), ss 119-130; *Landlord and Tenant Act* 1958 (Vic.); *Property Law Act* 1974 (Qld); *Landlord and Tenant Act* 1936 (S.A.); *Property Law Act* 1969 (W.A.); *Landlord and Tenant Act* 1935 (Tas.); *Supreme Court Act* 1986 (Vic.), ss 79-85; *Common Law Procedure Act* 1854 (Tas.), ss 183-185; *Conveyancing and Law of Property Act* 1884 (Tas.), ss 15-16.
2. *Agricultural Holdings Act* 1941 (N.S.W.); *Property Law Act* 1974 (Qld), ss 153-167; *Agricultural Holdings Act* 1891 (S.A.).
3. *Landlord and Tenant (Amendment) Act* 1948 (N.S.W.); *Landlord and Tenant Act* 1958 (Vic.), Pt V.
4. *Residential Tenancies Act* 1987 (N.S.W.); *Residential Tenancies Act* 1980 (Vic.); *Residential Tenancies Act* 1978 (S.A.); *Residential Tenancies Act* 1987 (W.A.).
5. *Residential Tenancies Act* 1975 (Qld).
6. *Retail Tenancies Act* 1986 (Vic.); *Retail Shop Leases Act* 1984 (Qld); *Landlord and Tenant Act* 1936 (S.A.), Pt V; *Commercial Tenancy (Retail Shops) Agreements Act* 1985 (W.A.).

discussed in Chapter 11. This Chapter will examine the general law of landlord and tenant which applies to all premises other than those subject to the specific legislation referred to in the ensuing Chapter.

2. Historical Development of the Leasehold Estate[7]

[10.02] During the 12th to the 16th centuries (the period of formulation of principles upon which the present landlord-tenant law is based), the tenant's interest began as a "status", later became contractual, and ultimately became regarded as a property interest.

The 12th century counterpart of the modern tenant was the villein. According to Pollock and Maitland, "villeinage" was considered a status as well as a tenure.[8] Very little legal protection was available to the villein over his interest in the land allotted him by the lord of the manor: he was regarded as a tenant at will and his tenure was not protected in the king's courts.[9] However, following manorial custom the manor courts improved the status of the villein by regarding him as holding a permanent and frequently heritable interest.

A tenant was first offered legal protection by the common law during the 13th century. However, leases did not fall within the system of feudal tenure and estates, and were regarded as merely personal property. The effect of this was that the only remedy available to a tenant was an action for damages based on trespass. The possessory remedy available to freeholders, the assize of novel disseisin, was not granted to tenants for a term of years;[10] accordingly, a tenant who was dispossessed was unable to recover possession and merely had an action against his landlord based on breach of contract.

The courts were slow to rectify the obvious deficiencies in the tenant's legal position. In 1235, the action quare ejecit infra terminum was formulated which allowed the tenant to recover possession of rented premises from which he had been dispossessed, but this could only be used against the landlord or his successors-in-title and had no application where the tenant was dispossessed by a third party. It was not until the late 15th century that the action of trespass de ejectione firmae became available to tenants, which granted tenants a universal remedy to recover possession.[11]

By the late 15th century, therefore, the tenant became regarded as the holder of an interest in land rather than merely the holder of a contractual interest. However, leases were still regarded as personal rather than real property because the old real actions were inapplicable. Leasehold estates were described as "chattels real" to indicate their classification as personal property and also to recognise their close practical link to real

---

7. For a general discussion of the historical development of landlord-tenant law, see Pollock and Maitland, *History of English Law* (2nd ed., 1968), Bk I, pp. 356-362, Bk II, pp. 35-38 and pp. 106-117; Plucknett, *A Concise History of the Common Law* (5th ed., 1956), pp. 373-374 and pp. 570-574.
8. Pollock and Maitland, op. cit., p. 358.
9. Ibid., p. 360
10. Ibid., p. 36.
11. Plucknett, op. cit., p. 373.

property. For many centuries, the effect of the common law classification of leases was that whereas freehold land passed on death to the eldest son, under the feudal principle of primogeniture, leases passed on intestacy to all the children of the deceased equally as next of kin. During the 19th century, State legislation in Australia intervened to apply the rules concerning the intestate succession of personal property to real property.[12] Since that time the common law classification of leasehold estates as personal property has had no practical significance.

3. Terminology

[10.03] A preliminary discussion of terminology peculiar to landlord and tenant law is warranted in light of potential confusion caused by misleading and overlapping terms.

The person granting a leasehold interest is referred to as the "lessor" or the "landlord", while the grantee of the interest may be described as the "lessee" or the "tenant". According to some sources,[13] "lessor" and "lessee" should be used to describe the original contracting parties, while the parties who are in the de facto position of landlord and tenant should be described by the latter terms.[14] This, however, is a matter of practice, not of law, and is frequently not followed. At law, "lessor" and "landlord" are synonymous, as are "lessee" and "tenant".

The agreement entered into by a landlord and a tenant may be variously described as a "demise", "lease", "tenancy" or a "tenancy agreement". "Lease" and "demise" were more commonly used historically. In modern practice, "demise" is seldom encountered, long-term agreements are frequently referred to as "lease", while "tenancy" and "tenancy agreement" are usually found in respect of short-term leases, especially of residential property. Most modern statutes tend to favour the expression "tenancy agreement". At law, there is no distinction between the terms. A landlord is usually said to "let" or "demise" the rented premises when creating a lease. Once again, these terms are synonymous and interchangeable.

A lease will usually (although not always) be granted for a term certain. Where this occurs, a "fixed-term" lease or lease for a "term of years" is said to arise. The latter term is found more commonly, although the former term is beginning to gain sway. "Term of years" may be easily confused, as the expression may refer to a fixed-term lease of any duration, even for a period of less than a year.

Once a lease has been created, the interest held by the landlord is the "leasehold reversion". If the landlord sells the fee simple estate in the property during the term of the lease, the purchaser is the "assignee of the reversion". The tenant may also dispose of his possessory interest to a third party before the expiry of the lease, either by an "assignment" or

---

12. See e.g. *Real Estate of Intestates Distribution Act* 1862 (N.S.W.) and *Probate Act* 1890 (N.S.W.).
13. See e.g. Megarry and Wade, p. 632.
14. See *R. v. Tottenham & District Rent Tribunal; Ex parte Northfield (Highgate) Ltd* [1957] 1 Q.B. 103.

a "sublease". Careful attention must be given to the basic distinction between these terms. If the tenant disposes of the whole of her or his interest, the tenant will be held to have assigned the interest, notwithstanding that the conveyance may be described as a sublease.[15] The practical legal effect of this is that the assignee substitutes for the tenant in relation to the enforceability of the parties' rights and duties.[16] In this situation the landlord and the assignee will be in privity of estate with one another. However, if the tenant does not dispose of the whole interest, he or she will be held to have created a sublease.[17] In this case, the tenant's rights and duties vis-a-vis the landlord will be unaffected, and there will be no privity of estate between the landlord and the subtenant. Where this occurs, there will be two concurrent, separate leases, one between the landlord and the tenant, the other between the tenant and the subtenant. In this situation the lease between the landlord and the tenant is often referred to as the "head lease" and the tenant as the "mesne lessor". Consider the situation where A grants a fixed-term lease to B expiring on 31 December 1990. If, prior to that date, the tenant enters into an agreement with C whereby she disposes of her interest until 31 December 1990, an assignment will have been created. Conversely, if she disposes of her interest until any day up to and including 30 December 1990, a sublease will have been created. The courts will look at the substance rather than the form of the document. Thus, if the tenant does not dispose of the whole of her or his interest, the grantee will be held to be a subtenant even if the document is expressed to be an assignment.[18]

[10.04] There is no limit to the number of assignments and subleases which may be made during the term of a lease. Where a number of transactions occur, the fact situation may be clarified by the use of a diagram. The diagram would be drawn as follows:

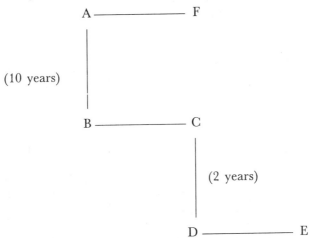

15. See *White v. Kenny* [1920] V.L.R. 290; *Beardman v. Wilson* (1868) L.R. 4 C.P. 57.
16. *Richardson v. Landecker* (1950) 66 W.N. (N.S.W.) 236.
17. Note that there may be a valid argument where the tenant delivers up her or his whole interest in part of the rented premises: *G. J. Coles & Co. Ltd v. F.C.T.* (1975) 132 C.L.R. 242.
18. *409 Lonsdale Pty Ltd v. Carra* [1974] V.R. 887. For the converse situation, see *Milmo v. Carreras* [1946] K.B. 306.

A hypothetical example will illustrate the point. A executes a ten year fixed-term lease with B. B later assigns his interest to C, who sublets the premises for two years to D. D later assigns his interest to E, and A sells the property to F.

In cases of this complexity, where one party commits a breach of covenant the question of enforceability will arise; in other words, who can sue whom? The common law rule is that before one party can sue another, the parties must be in either privity of contract or privity of estate with one another: see below **[10.41]**ff. Privity of contract in this case exists between A and F, A and B, B and C, C and D, and D and E. Privity of estate exists where the parties stand in the position of landlord and tenant vis-a-vis each other; in other words, it exists between F and C and between C and E. The major effect of the common law rule is to deny that a legal relationship exists between a landlord and subtenant (that is, between F and E).[19] Thus, if the head lease is validly determined by the effluxion of time, forfeiture or a notice to quit, the sublease will automatically terminate at the same time.[20] The subtenant has no standing to maintain her or his right of possession in these circumstances. By virtue of this common law rule, if the head tenant breaches a term of the tenancy agreement the subtenant as well as the head tenant is subject to eviction through no fault of her or his own.[21]

II.   TYPES OF LEASES

[10.05]   The basic division of leases is between those enforceable at law and those enforceable at equity. Further necessary distinctions are between fixed-term leases, periodic leases, tenancies by estoppel and concurrent leases. This section of the Chapter will discuss the essential features of each of these types of leases.

1. Legal and Equitable Leases

[10.06]   Legislation in each State deriving from the British *Statute of Frauds* 1677 states that all conveyances of land or any interest in land are void for the purpose of conveying or creating a legal estate unless made by deed.[22] However, an exception to this rule applies to certain types of leases in every State.[23] The State legislation, which is uniform throughout Australia, states:

---

19. *Fuller's Theatre & Vaudeville Co. Ltd v. Rofe* [1923] A.C. 435 (P.C.).
20. *Great Western Rly Co. v. Smith* (1876) 2 Ch. D. 235 at 253 (C.A.); *Metropolitan Trade Finance Co. Pty Ltd v. Coumbis* (1973) 131 C.L.R. 396.
21. Subject to the statutory right of the subtenant to seek relief from forfeiture: see below **[10.64]**.
22. General law statutes: N.S.W.: s. 23B(1); Vic.: s. 52(1); Qld: s. 10(1); S.A.: s. 28(1); W.A.: s. 33(1); Tas.: s. 60(1). In Queensland, the requirement of a deed has been replaced by the rule that there must be merely a written document signed by the person making an "assurance of land". Note that, except in Tasmania, a deed need not be sealed: N.S.W.: s. 38(3); Vic.: s. 73A; Qld: ss 45(2), 47; S.A.: s. 41(4); W.A.: s. 9(2)(4).
23. General law statutes: N.S.W.: s. 23D(2); Vic.: s. 54(2); Qld: s. 10(2); S.A.: s. 30(2); W.A.: s. 35(2); Tas.: s. 60(4).

"Nothing in the foregoing provisions of this Division shall affect the creation by parol of leases taking effect in possession for a term not exceeding three years (whether or not the lessee is given power to extend the term) at the best rent which can be reasonably obtained without taking a fine."

The effect of this exception is that oral leases for a fixed-term of three years or less may exist at law. The exception also applies to all types of periodic leases created orally.

The only effective qualification to the enforceability of short oral leases is the legislative requirement that they must "take effect in possession". Historically, it was considered that this phrase merely required that the tenant took possession of the property. As such, the phrase would have little practical significance. However, in *Haselhurst v. Elliot*,[24] Herring C.J. held that the phrase should be construed literally and excludes all leases taking effect at some date in the future. Thus, unless the lease commences the same day as the agreement to create it, it must be in deed form to be enforceable at law. A lease designed to commence "next Monday" or "on the first of the next month" will not fall within the statutory exception in favour of leases for three years or less. This restriction can be argued to be unnecessary and contrary to the intention of Parliament,[25] but at the present time *Haselhurst v. Elliot* appears to represent good law.

If a lease fails to satisfy the statutory requirements cited above and so is unenforceable at law, it may nevertheless be enforceable at equity. Based on the maxim that equity deems as done that which ought to have been done, a lease that is not in deed form or fails to take effect in possession will in certain circumstances be enforceable at equity. This rule is sometimes referred to as the rule in *Walsh v. Lonsdale*.[26] In this case, there was an agreement to grant a future seven year lease of a weaving shed and certain other buildings and machinery. The agreement stated that the formal lease, when drafted, would contain a covenant that on any given day the landlord could demand that the tenant pay one year's rent in advance. No formal lease was ever drafted. The tenant went into possession, paying rent quarterly in arrears. Eighteen months later the landlord demanded a year's rent in advance, and when it was not paid, exercised his common law right of distress. The tenant sued for damages for illegal distress and for an injunction to restrain the distress. His argument was that the seven year agreement was unenforceable at law and that at common law he was merely a yearly periodic tenant holding the property on such terms as were consistent with a yearly tenancy: as the payment of a year's rent in advance is clearly inconsistent with a

---

24. [1945] V.L.R. 153.
25. See the criticism in Harrison, *Cases on Land Law* (Law Book Co. Ltd, 1958), pp. 165-166.
26. (1882) 21 Ch. D. 9 (C.A.). For recent applications of the rule, see *Industrial Properties (Barton Hill) Ltd v. Associated Electrical Industries Ltd* [1977] Q.B. 580 (C.A.); *Tottenham Hotspur Football & Athletic Co. Ltd v. Princegrove Publishers Ltd* [1974] 1 W.L.R. 113; and *Noyes v. Klein* (1985) 3 B.P.R. 9216 (N.S.W. Sup. Ct). See also *O'Dwyer v. Butts* (1952) 69 W.N. (N.S.W.) 198; (1952) 87 C.L.R. 267 (H.C.).

yearly tenancy, distress was illegal. The English Court of Appeal rejected this argument, holding that as the parties had entered into a binding contract to grant a lease, that contract will be enforced at equity according to its terms in all respects even though no formal lease was ever executed. Thus, as the remedy of distress would have applied at law if the lease had been executed, it would be applied at equity on the facts at bar.

[10.07] A contract for a lease enforceable under the rule in *Walsh v. Lonsdale* is usually referred to as an "agreement for a lease". The rule will not apply unless the agreement is specifically enforceable at equity and constitutes a binding contract under normal common law principles.[27] Thus, the parties must have reached final agreement on the essential details of the lease, viz. the property to be leased, the rent payable, the names of the parties and the commencement and maximum duration of the term.[28] The other terms of the agreement do not have to be specified in detail, however, and where necessary will be implied by the courts.[29] The major difficulty confronting the court is to determine whether the contract is intended to be final.[30] Before the contract will be enforced as an agreement for a lease, the court must be of the opinion that the execution of the future lease contemplated by the contract will merely formally embody the terms of the contract already agreed upon.[31] If the court forms the opinion that certain essential features of the agreement are still open to negotiation prior to the signing of the lease, the contract for a lease will be held to be unenforceable at both law and equity. An agreement for a lease expressed to be "subject to contract" has been held to be unenforceable on the ground that such a term indicated the parties' intention to hold further negotiations on the contents of the lease.[32] The issue is one of construction for the courts in each case. In *Chipperfield v. Carter*,[33] the clause in the contract for a lease, "lease to be approved in the customary way by my solicitor" was held not to preclude the enforceability of the contract as an agreement for a lease. This case can be neatly contrasted with *Lockett v. Norman-Wright*,[34] where the clause "subject to suitable arrangements being arranged between your solicitors and mine" was held to vitiate the contract.

In addition to proof of a binding contract, before the rule in *Walsh v. Lonsdale* will apply, State legislation deriving from s. 4 of the *Statute of*

27. *Euston Centre Properties Ltd v. H. & J. Wilson Ltd* (1982) 262 E.G. 1079 at 1081; *Brownsea v. National Trustees Executors & Agency Co. of Australasia Ltd* [1959] V.R. 243 at 244; *Walpole v. Orford* (1797) 3 Ves. Jun. 402 at 420; 30 E.R. 1076 at 1085 (Ch.).
28. *Harvey v. Pratt* [1965] 2 All E.R. 786 (C.A.); *Bishop v. Taylor* (1968) 118 C.L.R. 518; *Beattie v. Fine* [1925] V.L.R. 363.
29. See e.g. *Liverpool C.C. v. Irwin* [1977] A.C. 239 (H.L.); *Karaggianis v. Malltown Pty Ltd* (1979) 21 S.A.S.R. 381.
30. See e.g. *Geftakis v. Maritime Services Board of New South Wales* [1988] A.N.Z. Conv. R. 36.
31. *South Coast Oils (Qld & N.S.W.) Pty Ltd v. Look Enterprises Pty Ltd* [1988] 1 Qd R. 680.
32. *D'Silva v. Lister House Development Ltd* [1971] 1 Ch. 17; *Masters v. Cameron* (1954) 91 C.L.R. 353.
33. (1895) 72 L.T. 487.
34. [1925] 1 Ch. 56. See also *Ratto v. Trifid Pty Ltd* [1987] W.A.R. 237.

Frauds 1677 must be complied with. The legislation is uniform between the States and reads:[35]

> "No action shall be brought . . . upon any contract or sale of lands tenements or hereditaments or any interest in or concerning them or upon any agreement that is not to be performed within the space of one year from the making thereof unless the agreement upon which such action shall be brought or some memorandum or note thereof shall be in writing and signed by the party to be charged therewith or some other person thereunto by him lawfully authorized."[36]

This legislation applies to both general law and Torrens land.[37]

[10.08] The equitable doctrine of part performance is an exception to the rule requiring a written memorandum or note of the contract for a lease. This doctrine arises wherever an unenforceable agreement at law is susceptible to a decree of specific performance and has been partly performed. To constitute a sufficient act of part performance, the act must be unequivocally, and of its own nature, referable to some such agreement as that alleged.[38] What constitutes a sufficient act of part performance in the leasehold context? The most obvious illustration is where the tenant enters into possession of the premises and pays rent.[39] Alternatively, the handing over of keys or the payment of a security deposit will usually suffice.[40] In *Kaufman v. Michael*,[41] the alleged contract for a five year fixed-term lease provided, inter alia, that the tenant would make certain alterations to the premises including rewallpapering. After carrying out the alterations, the tenant sought to escape from the agreement and argued that it was unenforceable at equity. It was held that the making of the alterations constituted a sufficient act of part performance inasmuch as it tended to suggest that a binding contract for a lease had been entered into. This conclusion was reached despite the fact that the tenant had not entered into possession or paid rent.

If a contract is construed as an agreement for a lease, it will have the same legal status as other equitable interests in land. It is sometimes said that an agreement for a lease is as good as a lease.[42] This is incorrect,

---

35. *Conveyancing Act* 1919 (N.S.W.), s. 54A; *Instruments Act* 1958 (Vic.), s. 126; *Property Law Act* 1974 (Qld), s. 59; *Law of Property Act* 1936 (S.A.), s. 26; *Conveyancing and Law of Property Act* 1884 (Tas.), s. 36. In Western Australia, s. 4 of the *Statute of Frauds* 1677 remains in effect, subject to the *Law Reform (Statute of Frauds) Act* 1962 (W.A.).
36. In Victoria, s. 127 of the *Instruments Act* 1958 states that any agent who signs the agreement must himself be authorised in writing to do so.
37. See e.g. *Conveyancing Act* 1919 (N.S.W.), s. 54A(3).
38. *Maddison v. Alderson* (1883) 8 App. Cas. 467 at 477 (H.L.); *McMahon v. Ambrose* [1987] V.R. 817; *Geftakis v. Maritime Services Board N.S.W.* [1988] A.N.Z. Conv. R. 36. See generally Cheshire and Fifoot, pp. 186-189.
39. *Brough v. Nettleton* [1921] 2 Ch. 25; *Colman v. Golder* [1957] V.R. 196. Note that the payment of rent under these circumstances will lead to an inference at common law of a periodic lease: see below **[10.10]**.
40. *McMahon v. Ambrose* [1987] V.R. 817.
41. (1892) 18 V.L.R. 375. See also *Darcy v. Ryan* (1882) 8 V.L.R. (Eq.) 36.
42. See e.g. *Re Maughan* (1885) 14 Q.B.D. 956 at 958.

however, as there are five fundamental differences between the effect of a legal and an equitable lease. These are as follows:

1. A tenant under an agreement for a lease has to rely on the remedy of specific performance which, like all equitable remedies, is discretionary.[43] Based on the "clean hands" doctrine,[44] the courts have declined to enforce an agreement for a lease specifically where the agreement required the tenant to carry out repairs before the formal lease was signed and the tenant had failed to do so,[45] and where the tenant, who was seeking specific performance, was himself in breach of his duty to keep the premises in repair.[46]

2. The holder of an agreement for a lease will always lose in a dispute concerning priority of interests to a purchaser for valuable consideration who obtains a legal estate at the time of his purchase without notice of the existence of the prior equitable agreement.[47]

3. Different rules apply in a priority dispute between the holder of an agreement for a lease and the purchaser of a prior or subsequent equitable interest such as an equitable mortgagee or the holder of an equitable fee simple under an estate contract. Under the rule in *Rice v. Rice*,[48] the earlier equitable interest will apply where the equities are equal. Kindersley V.-C. stated:[49]

> "In examining into the relative merits (or equities) of two parties having adverse equitable interests, the points to which the court must direct its attention are obviously these: the nature and condition of their respective equitable interests, the circumstances and manner of their acquisition, and the whole conduct of each party with respect thereto. And in examining into these points it must apply the test, not of any technical rule or any rule of partial application, but the same broad principles of right and justice which a court of equity applies universally in deciding upon contested rights."[50]

4. An easement cannot be implied in favour of a tenant under an agreement for a lease on the basis of the uniform State legislation copied from s. 62 of the *Law of Property Act* 1925 (U.K.), which was designed to

43. See Snell, p. 569.
44. For a discussion of the equitable maxim, "He whom comes into Equity must come with 'Clean Hands' ", see Meagher, Gummow and Lehane, paras 322-327; Snell, pp. 32-33.
45. *Cornish v. Brook Green Laundry Ltd* [1959] 1 Q.B. 394 (C.A.).
46. *Swain v. Ayres* (1888) 21 Q.B.D. 289 (C.A.). Cf. *Baxton v. Kara* [1982] 1 N.S.W.L.R. 604.
47. *Pilcher v. Rawlins* (1872) 7 Ch. App. 259. See *Powell v. Cleland* [1948] 1 K.B. 262 (C.A.) for a discussion of the meaning of "purchaser". For cases on the meaning of "notice", see *Smith v. Jones* [1954] 2 All E.R. 823; *Hunt v. Luck* [1902] 1 Ch. 428 (C.A.); *Caunce v. Caunce* [1969] 1 All E.R. 722; *Hodgson v. Marks* [1971] Ch. 892; *Williams and Glyn's Bank Ltd v. Boland* [1981] A.C. 487 (H.L.). See also the general law statutes: N.S.W.: s. 164; Vic.: s. 199; Qld: s. 256; S.A.: s. 177; Tas.: s. 5.
48. (1853) 2 Drew. 71; 61 E.R. 646 (Ch.).
49. Ibid. at 78-79; 648.
50. *Rice v. Rice* is discussed above [3.42]ff. See also *Re King's Settlement* [1931] 2 Ch. 294; cf. *Capell v. Winter* [1907] 2 Ch. 376; *Coleman v. London County & Westminster Bank Ltd* [1916] 2 Ch. 353; *B. S. Lyle Ltd v. Rosher* [1959] 1 W.L.R. 8 (H.L.).

shorten conveyances by enacting that a conveyance of land shall be deemed to include certain specified rights.[51] This legislation is cited in full: see below [16.27]. The conclusion in this paragraph results from the fact that the State legislation only applies to create implied easements on a "conveyance" of land.[52] An agreement for lease does not constitute a conveyance.

5. An equitable tenancy agreement does not create privity of estate. The significance of this relates to the enforceability of covenants on an assignment of the term by the tenant or on an assignment of the reversion by the landlord. This matter is discussed below [10.41]ff.

Despite some earlier doubts,[53] it is now recognised that the doctrine in *Walsh v. Lonsdale* applies equally to Torrens land as to general law land.[54]

2. Fixed-Term Leases

[10.09] Fixed-term leases, or leases for a term of years, may only be created expressly. Unlike periodic leases, they are never implied by operation of law. Fixed-term leases may be of any length, provided that at the time the agreement is entered into, the exact date of termination is either known or ascertainable by the parties. This is known as the rule in *Lace v. Chandler*,[55] where a purported fixed-term lease entered into in 1940 for the duration of the war was held to be invalid on the ground that at that time the length of the war was unknown. The fact that the termination date of the war was later ascertained was held to be irrelevant. On the other hand, a lease made "until Easter Sunday 1995" would be valid, as the calendar date on which Easter Sunday falls in that year is ascertainable at any time even if at the time of signing the agreement the parties are unaware of the date. It is not essential that the fixed-term be one continuous period: for example, it was held in *Smallwood v. Sheppards*[56] that a lease for three successive public holidays is valid. It is not inconsistent with the nature of a fixed-term lease to provide for its possible determination prior to the effluxion of the term. Thus, for example, a fixed-term lease for three years could validly be made subject to the proviso that it could be determined on six months' notice given by either party.[57]

---

51. General law statutes: N.S.W.: s. 67; Vic.: s. 62; Qld: s. 239; S.A.: s. 36; W.A.: s. 41; Tas.: s. 6.
52. "Conveyance" is statutorily defined in the general law statutes (N.S.W.: s. 7(1); Vic.: s. 18(1); Qld: s. 4; S.A.: s. 7; W.A.: s. 7; Tas.: s. 2) as follows:
    " 'Conveyance' includes a mortgage, charge, lease, assent, vesting declaration, disclaimer, release, surrender, extinguishment and every other assurance of property or an interest therein by any instrument except a will."
53. *Macky v. The Cafe Monico Ltd (in liq.)* (1905) 25 N.Z.L.R. 689 at 706 (S.C. in banco).
54. See e.g. *Ahern v. L. A. Wilkinson (Northern) Ltd* [1929] St. R. Qd 66; *De Luxe Confectionery Ltd v. Waddington* [1958] N.Z.L.R. 272 (C.A.); *Miller v. Jenner* [1921] N.Z.L.R. 841.
55. [1944] K.B. 368 (C.A.). See also *Bishop v. Taylor* (1968) 118 C.L.R. 518; *Anthony v. Stanton* [1943] V L.R. 179.
56. [1895] 2 Q.B. 627.
57. See e.g. *Porter v. Williams* (1914) 14 S.R. (N.S.W.) 83.

Statutory provisions exist in New South Wales, Victoria and Tasmania permitting the residue of long fixed-term leases to be enlarged into fee simple estates by an established procedure.[58] The legislation states that fixed-term leases of at least 300 years' duration may be enlarged into fee simple estates by declaration in deed form where the unexpired residue of the term is at least 200 years. The application of this provision in Australia is extremely rare.

3. Periodic Leases

[10.10] A periodic lease is a common law leasehold estate which may arise in any one of four situations. First, it may be created by express agreement between the parties in deed form. Secondly, it may be created orally at the commencement of the agreement. This latter situation arises very commonly in practice. A typical illustration would be an oral arrangement whereby the tenant is allowed to enter into possession on agreeing to pay the rent weekly, fortnightly, or monthly on specified dates. Thirdly, a periodic lease may exist at common law where the tenant enters into possession of the rented premises and pays rent[59] pursuant to a fixed-term lease which is invalid at common law or for any other reason.[60] Such a tenant may also hold a fixed-term agreement at equity (under the rule in *Walsh v. Lonsdale*)[61] and a periodic tenancy at law;[62] in this case, the rules of equity will prevail. Finally, a periodic lease may arise where a fixed-term lease expires and the tenant remains in possession of the premises with the consent of the landlord and pays rent in respect of the overholding period.[63]

At first glance, a periodic lease might appear to infringe the basic rule as to the distinction between freehold and leasehold estates, namely that the maximum duration of the lease must be specified or be ascertainable at the commencement of the agreement. This is not the case, however, as a periodic lease is treated at common law as a succession of terms, which in retrospect are deemed under a fiction to have been part of the original term. Thus, for example, a monthly periodic lease which has continued in effect for ten years will be treated in retrospect as a ten year term.[64]

Periodic leases may be subclassified into yearly periodic leases (or leases from year to year), monthly and weekly periodic leases. These are the most commonly encountered types of periodic leases, although it is

---

58. *Conveyancing Act* 1919 (N.S.W.), s. 134; *Property Law Act* 1958 (Vic.), s. 153; *Conveyancing and Law of Property Act* 1884 (Tas.), s. 83. See Note (1962) 35 A.L.J. 408. This legislation may be used in the context of freehold covenants to avoid the rule in *Austerberry v. Oldham Corporation* (1885) 29 Ch. D. 750 (C.A.) that the burden of a covenant will not run at common law: see below [17.05].
59. Prior to paying rent, he would be classified as a tenant at will: see below [10.12].
60. See *Atler Pty Ltd v. C.D.F.C. Australia Ltd* (1982) 103 L.S.J.S. 70.
61. (1882) 21 Ch. D. 9 (C.A.).
62. *Moore v. Dimond* (1929) 43 C.L.R. 105.
63. Ibid.
64. See e.g. *Cattley v. Arnold* (1859) 1 J. & H. 651; 70 E.R. 905 (V.-C.); *Oxley v. James* (1844) 13 M. & W. 209; 153 E.R. 87 (Exch.).

possible to have a daily[65] or fortnightly[66] periodic lease or a lease for any designated period.[67]

It is important to understand the methods by which the courts determine which type of periodic lease exists in any given situation. The issue is one of fact, and the court will make its decision on the basis of the intention of the parties.[68] Where there is no direct evidence of the parties' intention, the courts may infer the type of periodic lease from the manner in which the rent is paid. For example, if the rent is paid weekly, the court will infer a weekly periodic lease,[69] and if it is paid monthly, the court will infer a monthly periodic lease.[70] The method of payment of the rent is not legally conclusive of the issue and is only evidential, but according to Dixon J. in *Turner v. York Motors Pty Ltd*,[71] depending on the circumstances any other conclusion may be held to be unreasonable. Occasionally the parties may calculate the rent on a different basis from the manner in which the rent is payable. For example, instead of demanding a monthly rental of $300 the landlord may require the tenant to pay rent of $3,600 per annum payable at the rate of $300 per month. In both cases, the quantum of rent is identical, but the calculation of the rental by reference to an annual sum may suggest that a yearly rather than a monthly periodic lease is intended. In this situation, the courts have opted for a periodic lease commensurate with the length of the period of calculation rather than the period of payment.[72]

[10.11] The problem of determining the type of periodic lease also arises when the tenant holds over at the end of a fixed-term lease and pays rent in respect of the overholding period.[73] In this situation, different rules appear to apply. Frequently the expired lease will stipulate the nature of the tenancy which is to arise in the event of the tenant remaining in possession. Where this occurs, the courts will follow the terms of the lease. In other cases, however, the courts look to other means to determine the presumed intention of the parties. The major Australian authority on this issue is *Moore v. Dimond*.[74] In this case, the tenant remained in possession at the end of a fixed-term lease of five years and eight months at a weekly rental and negotiated for the grant of a further five year lease. The negotiations later broke down, and the landlord claimed one week's rent on the basis, inter alia, of an alleged yearly periodic tenancy which was

---

65. *Butcher v. Bowen* [1964] N.S.W.R. 36.
66. *Foenander v. Dabscheck* [1954] V.L.R. 38; *Munro v. Dare* [1934] St. R. Qd 332 (F.C.).
67. A periodic lease of periods of 364 days was held to exist in *Land Settlement Association Ltd v. Carr* [1944] 1 K.B. 657 (C.A.).
68. *Fitzgerald v. Button* (1891) 17 V.L.R. 52 at 53.
69. *Burnham v. Carroll Musgrove Theatres Ltd* (1928) 41 C.L.R. 540.
70. *Precious v. Reedie* [1924] 2 K.B. 149.
71. (1951) 85 C.L.R. 55 at 66.
72. See e.g. *Ladies' Hosiery & Underwear Ltd v. Parker* [1930] 1 Ch. 304 (C.A.).
73. Prior to paying rent, the tenant will be a tenant at will if he or she receives the landlord's consent to remain in the rented premises, and a tenant at sufferance if he or she remains without the consent or dissent of the landlord: see below [10.12] and [10.13].
74. (1929) 43 C.L.R. 105. See also *Atler Pty Ltd v. C.D.F.C. Australia Ltd* (1982) 103 L.S.J.S. 70.

argued to exist between the parties. The High Court held that in the case of overholding tenancies, a presumption arises that a yearly periodic lease is created once rent has been paid. The presumption is rebuttable, but is nevertheless very strong. The contention that the type of periodic lease should be determined by a reference to the method of payment of the rent under the expired fixed-term lease was held to be irrelevant. Knox C.J., Rich and Dixon JJ. stated:[75]

> "When the parties agree for a five years' holding with weekly payments of the compensatory rent, their intention is not that each week's rent shall represent a distinct and therefore terminable holding of a week. The weekly rent is part of the compensation for the entire period. Where the intention of the parties is to hold for a greater duration than a yearly tenancy would give them, and this intention fails because of its want of appropriate expression or of formal demise, the presumption or assumption that a general holding is from year to year supplies the term."

The presumption of a yearly periodic lease on overholding clearly applies where the term of the original fixed-term lease exceeded one year. However, some doubt exists as to whether it applies where the fixed term is one year or less and where a weekly rent is reserved. In *Bank of Victoria v. M'Hutchison*[76] and *Box v. Attfield*,[77] a yearly periodic lease was presumed where the original leases were for one year and six months (respectively). However, more recently there is dicta by Cussen J. in *Beattie v. Fine*[78] suggesting that a yearly lease will only be presumed where the original lease is of one year's duration or more. In addition, there are several authorities to the effect that the rent must be paid by reference to a year before a yearly periodic lease will be presumed. An illustration of this approach is *Adler v. Blackman*,[79] where the English Court of Appeal refused to infer a yearly lease where the rent was calculated and payable on a weekly basis rather than calculated on a yearly basis and payable on a weekly basis.

In New South Wales, Queensland and Western Australia, the common law rules discussed above concerning the creation of periodic leases have been modified by the following legislation:[80]

> "No tenancy from year to year shall, after the commencement of this Act, be implied by payment of rent; if there is a tenancy, and no agreement as to its duration, then such tenancy shall be deemed to be a tenancy determinable at the will of either of the parties by one month's notice in writing expiring at any time."

75. Isaacs J. stated (at 119) that a yearly periodic lease will not be presumed to arise unless the rent paid has a yearly character.
76. (1881) 7 V.L.R. (L.) 452.
77. (1886) 12 V.L.R. 574 (F.C.).
78. [1925] V.L.R. 363 at 374.
79. [1953] 1 Q.B. 146 (C.A.). See also *Ball and Huntley v. Laffin* (1876) 10 S.A.L.R. 6; *Solomon v. Bray* (1873) 7 S.A.L.R. 128. Cf. *Edwards v. Horrigan; Ex parte Horrigan* [1923] St. R. Qd 8 (F.C.); *Bank of Victoria v. M'Hutchison* (1881) 7 V.L.R. (L.) 452.
80. General law statutes: N.S.W.: s. 127(1); Qld: s. 129(1); W.A.: s. 71. The exact wording of the provision differs from State to State.

This section has been held to be applicable only where a yearly periodic lease would have applied at common law, and has no application where the payment of rent would have led to the implication of a weekly, monthly or other periodic lease.[81] Where the section applies, the court will imply into the monthly periodic lease such terms as are applicable under general law to such a lease.[82]

In the case of all periodic leases, in the absence of express agreement between the parties the courts will imply such terms into the agreement as are necessary to give business efficacy to the lease and which are consistent with the nature of the lease created.[83] In the case of overholding tenancies, the courts will apply all the terms of the expired lease or agreement for a lease provided that they are not inconsistent with the nature of the yearly (or other) periodic lease implied by law.[84]

The reason why it is essential to subclassify every periodic lease into its correct subclassification arises by virtue of the common law rules as to the termination of periodic leases. These are discussed in detail: see below [10.53].

4. Tenancy at Will

[10.12] A tenancy at will may occasionally arise by express agreement,[85] although more commonly it will be implied at law.[86] A tenancy at will arises whenever the tenant enters or remains in possession of property with the consent of the landlord without paying rent. Thus, it often arises when a tenant under a formally invalid lease enters into possession or when a fixed-term lease expires and the tenant remains in possession with the express permission of the landlord.[87] In both cases, the payment of rent by the tenant and its acceptance by the landlord will convert the tenancy at will into a periodic lease. Note, however, that the reservation of rent does not prevent there being a tenancy at will,[88] and that the giving and receiving of rent does not of itself necessarily import the existence of a tenancy:[89] all will depend on the terms of the agreement.

---

81. *Burnham v. Carroll Musgrove Theatres Ltd* (1928) 41 C.L.R. 540; *Willshire v. Dalton* (1948) 65 W.N. (N.S.W.) 54 (S.C. in banco); *Rowston v. Sydney C.C.* (1954) 92 C.L.R. 605.

82. *Dockrill v. Cavanagh* (1944) 45 S.R. (N.S.W.) 78 (S.C. in banco).

83. *Moore v. Dimond* (1929) 43 C.L.R. 105.

84. *Lee v. Smith* (1854) 9 Exch. 662; 156 E.R. 284; *Felnex Central Properties Ltd v. Montague Burton Properties Ltd* (1981) 260 E.G. 705. Cf. *Bradbury v. Grimble & Co.* [1920] 2 Ch. 548.

85. See e.g. *Hagee (London) Ltd v. A. B. Erikson and Larson* [1976] Q.B. 209 (C.A.); *Manfield & Sons Ltd v. Botchin* [1970] 2 Q.B. 612.

86. *Wheeler v. Mercer* [1957] A.C. 416 (H.L.).

87. See e.g. *Meye v. Electric Transmission Ltd* [1942] Ch. 290.

88. *Cardiothoracic Institute v. Shrewdcrest Ltd* [1986] 3 All E.R 633.

89. *Clarke v. Grant* [1950] 1 K.B. 104; *Cardiothoracic Institute v. Shrewdcrest Ltd* [1986] 3 All E.R. 633.

A tenancy at will may more accurately be described as a type of licence than a "tenancy".[90] Such a tenant may not be sued for trespass until the tenancy is revoked. A tenant at will has been held to have the right to emblements.[91]

This type of tenancy may be determined without notice on demand at any time by either party.[92] Where the demand is given by the landlord, the tenant is allowed a reasonable time to remove her or his goods from the property, and the tenant may re-enter the property for this purpose. The tenancy will also terminate automatically when either party dies[93] or does an act incompatible with the nature of the tenancy. This may arise, for example, where the landlord enters the property and uses it for her or his own purposes[94] or where the tenant commits voluntary waste.[95]

5. Tenancy at Sufferance

[10.13]   This type of leasehold estate is described by Bradbrook and Croft as a "mere fiction",[96] in that it lacks the essential features of all tenancies. It arises whenever a tenant overholds after the expiration of a fixed-term lease without the express consent or dissent of the landlord and does not pay rent.[97] If the landlord later gives consent, a tenancy at will will arise, and payment of rent will lead to the implication of a periodic lease: see above [10.12]. A tenant at sufferance differs from a trespasser in that her or his original entry into the property was lawful. The very nature of the estate dictates that it cannot be created by express grant.

A landlord can sue for possession at any time without giving notice.[98] A tenant at sufferance cannot be sued for rent, although he is liable to an action for use and occupation of the property.[99] Unlike a tenant at will, there is no right to emblements.[100] Because of the lack of consent of the landlord, by virtue of the State limitation of actions legislation, if he or she remains in possession for 12 years (15 years in Victoria and South Australia) without the consent of the landlord and without paying rent, the landlord's right to recover possession of the land will be extinguished.[101]

90. See *Dougal v. McCarthy* [1893] 1 Q.B. 736 (C.A.). Note, however, that the limitation of actions legislation draws a clear distinction between a licence and a tenancy at will by making special provision for the latter: see N.S.W.: s. 34(2); Vic.: s. 13; Qld: s. 18; S.A.: ss 15, 16; W.A.: ss 9, 10; Tas.: s. 15.
91. Litt. 68.
92. *Commonwealth Life (Amalgamated) Assurance Ltd v. Anderson* (1945) 46 S.R. (N.S.W.) 47 at 49 (S.C. in banco).
93. *James v. Dean* (1805) 11 Ves. Jun. 383 at 391; 32 E.R. 1135 at 1138 (Ch.).
94. *Turner v. Doe d. Bennett* (1842) 9 M. & W. 643; 152 E.R. 271 (Exch.).
95. *Countess of Shrewsbury's Case* (1600) 5 Co. Rep. 13b; 77 E.R. 68 (K.B.).
96. Bradbrook and Croft, para. 2.20.
97. *Wheeler v. Mercer* [1957] A.C. 416 (H.L.); *Anderson v. Bowles* (1951) 84 C.L.R. 310.
98. *Natural Gas & Oil Corporation Ltd (in liq.) v. Byrne and Boyle* (1951) 68 W.N. (N.S.W.) 207.
99. *Bayley v. Bradley* (1848) 5 C.B. 396 at 406; 136 E.R. 932 (C.P.); *Leigh v. Dickeson* (1884) 15 Q.B.D. 60 (C.A.).
100. *Doe d. Bennett v. Turner* (1840) 7 M. & W. 226; 151 E.R. 749 (Exch.).
101. See below Chapter 15 for the relevant State legislation.

6. Tenancy by Estoppel[102]

[10.14] A tenancy by estoppel is a misnomer as no legal or equitable interest is passed to the tenant. Under the principle of estoppel, each party is prevented from denying each other's title. Thus, if after entering into a lease a tenant discovers that the landlord's title is deficient or non-existent, the tenant cannot use the lack of title as an excuse for not paying the rent or not complying with any of the other covenants contained in the lease. Similarly, the landlord is unable to evict a tenant by virtue of her or his own lack of title.

The principle of estoppel has been held to bind the successors-in-title to both parties.[103] After earlier doubts,[104] the English Court of Appeal has held in *Industrial Properties (Barton Hill) Ltd v. Associated Electrical Industries Ltd*[105] that the principle even applies once the tenant has given up possession and extends to the whole period during which the tenant was in possession. The only exception to this rule arises where a tenant is evicted by title paramount, which applies where a third party asserts a superior title to the property.[106]

A tenancy by estoppel arises most commonly on a fee simple conveyance of land, where the purchaser leases the property to a tenant prematurely before he or she acquires the legal or equitable title to the land. In this situation, and in other cases, if the landlord later acquires the legal fee simple estate, the tenant will automatically acquire a legal tenancy by operation of law under the principle of "feeding the estoppel".[107]

7. Concurrent Leases

[10.15] Concurrent leases will arise where a landlord lets rented premises to one tenant and then later leases the same premises to a second tenant either for the same term or for a shorter term. In this situation the second lease does not grant a possessory interest, but instead amounts to a lease of the landlord's reversionary interest.[108] The effect of this is to create a landlord-tenant relationship between the first and the second tenants, the latter as landlord and the former as tenant.[109]

Any covenants entered into by the tenant in the first lease may be enforced by and against the second tenant in his or her capacity as lessee of the reversion.[110] If the term of the second lease was for a longer period

---

102. See generally Prichard, "Tenancy by Estoppel" (1964) 80 L.Q.R. 370; Spencer Bower and Turner, *Estoppel by Misrepresentation* (3rd ed., 1977), pp. 191ff.
103. *Cuthbertson v. Irving* (1859) 4 H. & N. 742; 157 E.R. 1034 (Exch.).
104. See e.g. *Harrison v. Wells* [1967] 1 Q.B. 263 (C.A.).
105. [1977] Q.B. 580.
106. *Wilson v. Anderton* (1830) 1 B. & Ad. 450; 109 E.R. 855 (K.B.).
107. See e.g. *Bucknell v. Mann* (1862) 2 S.C.R. (N.S.W.) 1. For other circumstances where estoppel may arise, see *Noyes v. Klein* (1985) 3 B.P.R. 9216 (N.S.W. Sup. Ct).
108. See *Land v Clyne* (1968) 92 W.N. (N.S.W.) 134.
109. *Buckby v. Speed* [1959] Qd R. 30 (F.C.); *Birch v. Wright* (1786) 1 T.R. 378 at 384.
110. *Horn v. Beard* [1912] 3 K.B. 181; *Cole v. Kelly* [1920] 2 K.B. 106 (C.A.); *Noone v. Traynor* (1952) 69 W.N. (N.S.W.) 33 (S.C. in banco).

than the first lease, the second tenant will be entitled to possession of the rented premises on the expiration of the first lease. If, however, the term of the second lease is the same or shorter than the first lease, possession in these circumstances will vest in the landlord.[111]

In New South Wales, Victoria, Queensland and Western Australia, the common law rule in relation to concurrent leases is partially affirmed by State legislation, which reads:[112]

> "Nothing in this Part shall affect the rule of law that a legal term, whether or not being a mortgage term, may be created to take effect in reversion expectant on a longer term, which rule is hereby confirmed."

III. THE CHARACTERISTICS OF A LEASE

1. Exclusive Possession

[10.16]   At common law, exclusive possession is the distinguishing feature between leases and licences. The applicable legal propositions can be stated quite simply: first, the grant of a right of exclusive possession automatically creates a lease;[113] and secondly, no lease can exist unless the tenant is granted the right of exclusive possession.[114]

For many years a rival test, sometimes referred to as the "intention test", was adopted by the English courts. This new test only partially contradicts the exclusive possession test. Under this test a lease cannot exist unless the tenant is granted the right of exclusive possession. However, under the intention test the existence of exclusive possession does not automatically imply a lease; rather it is necessary to find the true relations of the parties.

The intention test was largely the work of Denning L.J., who gave a series of judgments in favour of the intention test in *Marcroft Wagons Ltd v. Smith*,[115] *Cobb v. Lane*,[116] *Errington v. Errington and Woods*[117] and *Facchini v. Bryson*.[118] The best known English case supporting the intention test is *Somma v. Hazelhurst*.[119] In this case, an unmarried couple each separately

---

111. See *Re Moore and Hulm's Contract* [1912] 2 Ch. 105; *Neale v. Mackenzie* (1836) 1 M. & W. 747; 150 E.R. 635 (Exch. Ch.).
112. General law statutes: N.S.W.: s. 120A(5); Vic.: s. 149(5); Qld: s. 102(5); W.A.: s. 74(5).
113. *Glenwood Lumber Co. v. Phillips* [1904] A.C. 405 at 408 (P.C.); *Landale v. Menzies* (1909) 9 C.L.R. 89 at 100-101 per Griffith C.J., at 111 per Barton J.; *Radio Theatres Pty Ltd v. City of Coburg* [1948] V.L.R. 84 at 86 (F.C.).
114. *Francis Longmore & Co. v. Stedman* [1948] V.L.R. 322 at 323; *Robert John Pty Ltd v. Fostar's Shoes Pty Ltd* [1963] N.S.W.R. 419 (F.C.); *Commonwealth v. K. N. Harris Pty Ltd* [1965] N.S.W.R. 63.
115. [1951] 2 K.B. 496 (C.A.).
116. [1952] 1 All E.R. 1199 (C.A.).
117. [1952] 1 K.B. 290 (C.A.).
118. [1952] 1 T.L.R. 1386 (C.A.).
119. [1978] 1 W.L.R. 1014 (C.A.). Discussed in (1979) 42 M.L.R. 331 and (1980) 124 Sol. J. 367. See also *Walsh v. Griffiths-Jones* [1978] 2 All E.R. 1002. Cf. *Chandler v. Kerley* [1978] 2 All E.R. 942 (C.A.); *Hardwick v. Johnson* [1978] 2 All E.R. 935 (C.A.).

entered into a "licence" agreement in respect of a furnished room in a house. Each agreement specified that the licensor was entitled to use the room in common with the licensees and could authorise a third person to share the room. The licensees argued that the agreement should be regarded as a joint interest and should be treated as a grant of a right of exclusive possession on the basis that the reference to the possibility of a third party sharing the room was merely a device to avoid the operation of the Rent Acts. They submitted that a lease had been created. This line of reasoning was successful at first instance, but was unanimously rejected by the Court of Appeal based on an application of the intention test. The court reasoned that provided that an agreement entitled a "licence" is not a lease masquerading as a licence and provided that the parties intended to create a licence, which was clear on the facts of this case, the agreement will be upheld as a licence.

Somma v. Hazelhurst has recently been overruled by the unanimous decision of the House of Lords in *Street v. Mountford*.[120] In this case, the occupant was granted exclusive possession of a furnished room under a written licence stating, inter alia, that the occupant had a duty to pay a "licence fee" of £37 per week, and that the licence "does not and is not intended to give [the licensee] a tenancy protected under the Rent Acts". The court held that a lease exists whenever there is a grant of exclusive possession for a fixed or periodic term at an agreed rent. The stated intention contained in the written agreement, that only a licence was to be created and that the Rent Acts should not apply, was held to be irrelevant. Lord Templeman stated:[121]

> "The only intention which is relevant is the intention demonstrated by the agreement to grant exclusive possession for a term at a rent. Sometimes it may be difficult to discover whether, on the true construction of an agreement, exclusive possession is conferred. Sometimes it may appear from the surrounding circumstances that the right to exclusive possession is referable to a legal relationship other than a tenancy. . . . But where as in the present case the circumstances are that residential accommodation is offered and accepted with exclusive possession for a term at a rent, the result is a tenancy."

120. [1985] A.C. 809. Discussed in (1987) 14 U.Q.L.J. 167; [1987] Conv. 137; [1986] Conv. 344; [1986] Conv. 39; [1985] C.L.J. 351.

121. Ibid., at 826. It is unclear at present whether this principle applies to commercial tenancies: see *Dresden Estates Ltd v. Collinson* (1987) 281 E.G. 1321 (C.A.), discussed in [1987] Conv. 220. *Street v. Mountford* has also been distinguished in *Brooker Settled Estates Ltd v. Ayers* (1987) 282 E.G. 325 (C.A.) and *Smith v. Northside Developments Ltd* (1987) 283 E.G. 1211 (C.A.). *Street v. Mountford* has been applied in *Royal Philanthropic Society v. County* (1985) 129 Sol. J. 854 (C.A.), discussed in (1986) 278 E.G. 63; *Dellneed Ltd v. Chin* (1986) 53 P. & C.R. 172; *Ashburn Anstalt v. W. J. Arnold & Co.* [1988] 2 W.L.R. 706 (C.A.), discussed in (1988) 47 C.L.J. 353; [1988] Conv. 201; *A G Securities v. Vaughan; Antoniades v. Villiers* [1988] 3 All E.R. 1058, discussed in (1988) 62 A.L.J. 450; [1989] Conv. 128; [1989] C.L.J. 19. See also *Hadjiloucas v. Crean* [1987] 3 All E.R. 1008 (C.A.).

[10.17]   The major Australian authority in this context is *Radaich v. Smith*.[122] This case concerned a deed entitled a "licence", which stated that "the Licensors hereby grant to the Licensee for a term of five years . . . the sole and exclusive License [sic] and privilege to supply refreshments to the public admitted to" a certain shop and to carry on the business of a milk bar therein. The High Court unanimously agreed that despite the fact that the document was referred to as a licence, the court should examine the substance of the document rather than its form.

The court held that a lease had been created. Apart from Dixon C.J., who agreed with the reasons prepared by the other members of the court, each judge issued a separate judgment. McTiernan and Menzies JJ. gave unqualified support to the conclusiveness of the test of exclusive possession. Unlike Menzies J., who merely stated that this test was "decisive",[123] McTiernan J. attempted to reconcile the earlier English authorities. His Honour referred[124] to the dictum of Denning L.J. in *Errington v. Errington and Woods*,[125] that "the test of exclusive possession is by no means decisive", but based on the dictum of Jenkins L.J. in *Addiscombe Garden Estates Ltd v. Crabbe*[126] that "the law remains that the fact of exclusive possession, if not decisive against the view that there is a mere licence, as distinct from a tenancy, is at all events a consideration of the first importance", stated[127] that the exclusive possession test has survived intact the criticism it received in *Errington v. Errington and Woods*. This case did not doubt that exclusive possession was an important consideration; it merely doubted whether it was the critical test. As already shown, the intention test does not treat exclusive possession as an irrelevant factor, but recognises that it is an important factor in determining the true intention in each case. By citing the dictum of Jenkins L.J. in *Addiscombe Garden Estates Ltd v. Crabbe*,[128] McTiernan J. indicates his belief that the adoption of the intention test makes exclusive possession irrelevant. As McTiernan J.'s judgment is based on a misunderstanding of the differences between the two competing tests, it is submitted that it should not be treated as an indorsement of the exclusive possession test.

Taylor J., like Menzies J., regarded the factor of exclusive possession as "decisive", but qualified this remark by stating that: "This, however, does not deny that exceptional cases may arise in which it will be seen that a right to exclusive occupation or possession has been given without the grant of a leasehold interest."[129] This qualification implies that the intention test has at least been partially accepted by Taylor J. Any situation falling within an "exceptional case" (for example, that the transaction was motivated by family ties) would be based on the fact that the parties could not be said to have intended to create a lease.

122. (1959) 101 C.L.R. 209.
123. Ibid. at 220.
124. Ibid. at 214.
125. [1952] 1 K.B. 290 at 297 (C.A.).
126. [1958] 1 Q.B. 513 at 528 (C.A.).
127. (1959) 101 C.L.R. 209 at 214.
128. [1958] 1 Q.B. 513 at 528 (C.A.).
129. (1959) 101 C.L.R. 209 at 217. See also *Facchini v. Bryson* [1952] 1 T.L.R. 1386 (C.A.).

Windeyer J. attempted to reconcile the two competing tests, and stated:[130]

" 'Whether when one man is allowed to enter upon the land of another person pursuant to a contract he does so as licensee or as tenant must', it has been said, 'be in the last resort a question of intention', per Lord Greene M.R. in *Booker v. Palmer*.[131] But intention to do what?—Not to give the transaction one label rather than another.—Not to escape the legal consequences of one relationship by professing that it is another. Whether the transaction creates a lease or a licence depends upon intention, only in the sense that it depends upon the nature of the right which the parties intend the person entering upon the land shall have in relation to the land . . . And how is it to be ascertained whether such an interest in land has been given? By seeing whether the grantee was given a *legal right of exclusive possession* of the land for a term or from year to year or for a life or lives. If he was, he is a tenant. And he cannot be other than a tenant, because a legal right of exclusive possession is a tenancy and the creation of such a right is a demise. To say that a man who has, by agreement with a landlord, a right of exclusive possession of land for a term is not a tenant is simply to contradict the first proposition by the second."

Issue can be taken with the correctness of the final four sentences of this dictum. His Honour cites no authority for his statement that "the legal right of exclusive possession is a tenancy and the creation of such a right is a demise" and, with respect, is begging the question. This analysis would not admit of the exceptional class of cases adverted to by Taylor J. and by earlier English cases.[132] More importantly, however, Windeyer J. appears to misunderstand the meaning of the intention test propounded in *Errington v. Errington and Woods*[133] and subsequent cases. In these cases the English courts make it clear that the intention test is entirely separate from the exclusive possession test, which it treats as a competing test to be rejected in favour of the intention test. On the other hand, Windeyer J. regards the intention test in the English cases as subordinate to the exclusive possession test and one that is capable of reconciliation. Thus, Windeyer J., like McTiernan J., has failed to recognise the significance of the earlier English decisions.

[10.18] *Radaich v. Smith*[134] is commonly cited as the major authority for the proposition that the exclusive possession test applies in Australia. However, of the four judges who issued separate judgments, only that of Menzies J. can be treated as giving unqualified support to the exclusive possession test. The remaining judges either misunderstood the intention test or gave only qualified support to the exclusive possession test. Despite this fact, however, in recent years the Australian courts have followed *Radaich v. Smith* and have done so by adopting the reasoning of

130. (1959) 101 C.L.R. 209 at 221-222.
131. [1942] 2 All E.R. 674 at 676.
132. *Facchini v. Bryson* [1952] 1 T.L.R. 1386 (C.A.).
133. [1952] 1 K.B. 290 (C.A).
134. (1959) 101 C.L.R. 209.

Windeyer J.[135] who reconciled the intention test and the exclusive possession test by concluding that the question of intention is merely a subsidiary aspect of the exclusive possession test. The first judge to adopt this approach was Maguire J. in *Metcalfe and Morris Pty Ltd v. Reekie.*[136] The importance of exclusive possession has been emphasised in all the later Australian cases.[137]

These decisions compel the conclusion that the judgment of Windeyer J. in *Radaich v. Smith*[138] is good law in Australia, despite the criticisms that can be made of its reasoning, and that exclusive possession is the critical test; if intention is relevant, it must be treated as merely one aspect of the exclusive possession test, not as a separate test.

2. Commencement of the Lease

[10.19]   A lease may be expressed to commence from a past date,[139] although more commonly it will take effect from the present or a future date. Where the lease does not specify a commencement date, in the absence of evidence to the contrary it will be presumed to commence on the date the lease is executed or the oral lease is agreed to.[140] The date of commencement must be certain when the lease is agreed to, or if not, it must become certain before the lease comes into effect.[141] This latter rule allows for conditional leases to be entered into. An illustration of this would be a lease beginning on the admission of the tenant as a student of the University of Melbourne. Once such an event occurs, the lease is binding.[142]

A lease taking effect in the future is referred to at common law as a "reversionary lease". At common law, the lease could take effect at any time in the future, however distant.[143] However, legislation in New South Wales, Victoria, Queensland and Western Australia now provides that a lease stated to take effect more than 21 years from the date of the instrument purporting to create it shall be void and any contract to create such a term shall likewise be void.[144] It has been held that the 21 year

---

135. Ibid. at 221-222. See also Windeyer J.'s judgment in *Chelsea Investments Pty Ltd v. F.C.T.* (1966) 115 C.L.R. 1.
136. [1963] N.S.W.R. 459 at 463.
137. See e.g. *Goldsworthy Mining Ltd v. Federal Commissioner of Taxation* (1973) 128 C.L.R. 199; *I.C.I. Alkali (Aust.) Pty Ltd (in vol. liq.) v. Federal Commissioner of Taxation* [1977] V.R. 393; *Lapham v. Orange C.C.* [1968] 2 N.S.W.R. 667; *General Discounts Pty Ltd v. Crosbie* [1968] Qd R. 418; *Hayes v. Seymour-Johns* (1981) 2 B.P.R. 9366 (N.S.W. Sup. Ct).
138. (1959) 101 C.L.R. 209.
139. See *James v. Lock* (1978) 264 E.G. 395; *Bradshaw v. Pawley* [1980] 1 W.L.R. 10. In these circumstances a lease will not have a retrospective effect: a lease executed today for two years effective six months ago will be construed as a fixed-term lease for 18 months.
140. Cf. *Sandill v. Franklin* (1875) L.R. 10 C.P. 377.
141. *Harvey v. Pratt* [1965] 1 W.L.R. 1025 (C.A.).
142. See *Brilliant v. Michaels* [1945] 1 All E.R. 121; *Terry v. Tindale* (1882) 3 L.R. (N.S.W.) 444; *Swift v. Macbean* [1942] 1 K.B. 375.
143. See e.g. *Mann, Crossman and Paulin Ltd v. Registrar of the Land Registry* [1918] 1 Ch. 202.
144. General law statutes: N.S.W.: s. 120A(3); Vic.: s. 149(3); Qld: s. 102(3); W.A.: s. 74(3).

period refers to the date of the lease rather than the contract. Thus, a 35 year lease containing an option to renew for a further 35 years on giving 12 months' notice is valid; the fact that at the date of the initial lease it is more than 21 years until the option is exercised is irrelevant.[145]

3. Maximum Duration

[10.20]   The essential characteristic of a fixed-term lease is that it must be of a specified maximum duration.[146] This rule, which does not apply to periodic leases,[147] is discussed in detail: see above **[10.10]**. The duration has to be certain at the time the lease takes effect, not necessarily at the date the lease is executed. For example, a lease by L to T for the length of term chosen by X (a third party) will be valid provided that under the terms of the lease X has to make the choice before the lease takes effect.

If the maximum duration is specified in the lease, it is irrelevant that the lease permits the agreement to be terminated prior to that date on the occurrence of an uncertain event. Thus, for example, a lease granted by L to T for a period of three years subject to prior determination at any time on one month's notice if T is transferred to another location by his employer would be valid.[148]

4. Other Characteristics

[10.21]   The names of the contracting parties and the identity of the demised premises must be clear if the lease is to be valid. These matters are seldom contentious, but disputes have occasionally arisen concerning the latter point. Mason J. held in *Goldsworthy Mining Ltd v. F.C.T.*[149] that a lease of part of the sea bed is valid where the boundary is described by reference to the surface, and where the boundary may occasionally move. It thus appears to be sufficient where the description of the demised premises is not accurate provided that it enables the boundaries to be defined.

Contrary to popular belief, rent is not an essential feature of a lease.[150] For this reason, for example, a tenancy at will may arise in circumstances where no rent has been paid. However, except where the lease is in deed form, under normal contractual rules some consideration must be provided by the tenant in return for the grant of a lease. Although rent is usually payable in money, this is not necessarily the case. Rent may be

---

145. See *Re Strand and Savoy Properties Ltd* [1960] Ch. 582. See also *Weg Motors Ltd v. Hales* [1962] 1 Ch. 49 (C.A.).

146. *Lace v. Chantler* [1944] K.B. 368 (C.A.); *Morison v. Edmiston* [1907] V.L.R. 191; *Bishop v. Taylor* (1968) 118 C.L.R. 518.

147. *Re Midland Rly Co.'s Agreement* [1971] Ch. 725 (C.A.); *Centaploy Ltd v. Matlodge Ltd* [1974] Ch. 1.

148. See e.g. *Porter v. Williams* (1914) 14 S.R. (N.S.W.) 83.

149. (1973) 128 C.L.R. 199.

150. *Hayes v. Seymour-Johns* (1981) 2 B.P.R. 9366 (N.S.W. Sup. Ct); *Francis Longmore & Co. Ltd v. Stedman* [1948] V.L.R. 322; *Bagust v. Rose* (1963) 80 W.N. (N.S.W.) 604; *Knight's Case* (1588) 5 Co. Rep. 54b; 77 E.R. 137 (K.B.).

in kind[151] or may be paid by the provision of services[152] (as in the case of a caretaker of a building who lives in part of it). Rent, where it is reserved, need not be specified as a precise figure provided that the relevant clause contains a means of quantification of the amount: for example, rent may be calculated by reference either to a percentage of the gross receipts of a business[153] or to variations in the consumer price index.[154]

IV. THE RIGHTS AND DUTIES OF LANDLORDS AND TENANTS

1. Express Terms

[10.22]   Based on the principle of freedom of contract, subject to certain statutory exceptions[155] the parties may incorporate as many terms into a lease as they mutually agree upon. These terms may be phrased as covenants or conditions. If they are phrased as covenants, the remedy for a breach will be an action for damages and/or an injunction, whereas if they are phrased as conditions, a right of rescission exists at common law in favour of the injured party.[155a] It should be noted, however, that even if the terms are expressed as covenants, the majority of leases expressly permit the landlord to determine the lease in the event of a breach committed by the tenant. Such a clause is commonly referred to as a "forfeiture clause".

The terms of a lease will vary from lease to lease. However, a lease will almost invariably contain the following covenants:

a. a covenant by the tenant to pay rent;

b. a covenant by either the tenant or the landlord to repair the premises;

c. a covenant by the tenant not to assign or sublet the premises without the prior consent of the landlord;

d. a covenant as to the user of the premises.

The courts will resolve any dispute as to the meaning of any of the terms of a lease in accordance with the normal common law rules concerning the construction of documents. First, in the event of a forfeiture resulting from a breach of covenant, any ambiguity will be resolved in favour of the tenant.[156] Secondly, any term of the lease will be interpreted in light of the contents of the whole lease,[157] and the court may also have regard to

---

151. *Pitcher v. Tovey* (1692) 4 Mod. 71; 87 E.R. 268 (K.B.); *Lanyon v. Carne* (1669) 2 Wms. Saund. 161; 85 E.R. 910 (K.B.).
152. *Montagu v. Browning* [1954] 1 W.L.R. 1039 (C.A.); *Duke of Marlborough v. Osborn* (1864) 5 B. & S. 67; 122 E.R. 758 (K.B.).
153. *Aarons v. Lewis* (1877) 3 V.L.R. (E.) 234.
154. *Tanner v. Stocks & Realty (Premises) Pty Ltd* [1972] 2 N.S.W.L.R. 722 (C.A.). See also *Daniel v. Gracie* (1844) 6 Q.B. 145; 115 E.R. 56; *United Scientific Holdings Ltd v. Burnley B.C.* [1978] A.C. 904 (H.L.).
155. See the State legislation discussed in Chapter 11 for numerous exceptions.
155a. Modern cases refer to the distinction between essential and non-essential terms of contract: see e.g. *Associated Newspapers Ltd v. Bancks* (1951) 83 C.L.R. 322.
156. *Downie v. Lockwood* [1965] V.R. 257.
157. *Iggulden v. May* (1806) 7 East. 237; 103 E.R. 91 (K.B.).

surrounding circumstances.[158] Finally, as a last resort, in the event of ambiguity a covenant will be construed against the covenantor in favour of the covenantee.[159]

Occasionally, the lease may expressly state that the performance by one party of one or more of the covenants is conditional upon the performance by the other party of one or more of her or his covenants. The terms of such an agreement are enforceable at common law. However, in the absence of such an express agreement, the courts will treat each covenant as independent of the others[160] and will not apply the doctrine of mutuality of covenants.[161] Thus, for example, if the landlord breaches the covenant of quiet enjoyment, the tenant is not entitled to withhold rent in order to bring pressure to bear on the landlord but must sue for damages for breach of covenant.[162]

Occasionally, the parties may state in a lease that the lease is subject to the "usual covenants". The question thus arises as to the meaning of this term. The same issue may arise in other contexts by virtue of the rule that an agreement for a lease is subject to the usual covenants where the parties do not state which terms are to be included in the formal lease.[163]

Based on *Hampshire v. Wickens*,[164] the following covenants are said to be "usual covenants":

a. a covenant by the landlord for quiet enjoyment;

b. covenants by the tenant;

* To pay the rent;

* To pay rates and taxes, except for those expressly the duty of the landlord;

* To keep and deliver up the premises in good and tenantable repair;

* To permit the landlord to enter the rented premises to inspect its condition.

In addition, a right of re-entry for breach of the covenant to pay rent (but not for other covenants) will be a "usual" term.[165]

---

158. *Downie v. Lockwood* [1965] V.R. 257.
159. *New South Wales Sports Club Ltd v. Solomon* (1914) 14 S.R. (N.S.W.) 340 (F.C.); *Webb v. Plummer* (1819) 2 B. & Ad. 746 at 751; 106 E.R. 537 at 539 (K.B.).
160. There is no presumption of mutuality of covenants: *Bishop v. Moy* [1963] N.S.W.R. 468.
161. Sometimes referred to as the doctrine of interdependence of covenants. For a general discussion of this doctrine, see Cheshire and Fifoot, para. 2306ff.; *Chitty on Contracts* (24th ed., 1977), para. 1494ff.; Stoljar, "Dependent and Independent Covenants" (1957) 2 Syd. L.R. 217.
162. See e.g. *Chatfield v. Elmstone Resthouse Ltd* [1975] 2 N.Z.L.R. 269; *Taylor v. Webb* [1937] 2 K.B. 283 (C.A.).
163. See e.g. *Propert v. Parker* (1832) 3 My. & K. 280; 40 E.R. 107 (Ch.).
164. (1878) 7 Ch. D. 555. See also *Sharp v. Milligan (No. 2)* (1857) 23 Beav. 419; 53 E.R. 165 (Rolls Ct); *Charalambous v. Ktori* [1972] 1 W.L.R. 951.
165. *Hodgkinson v. Crowe* (1875) L.R. 10 Ch. App. 622; *Re Lander and Bagley's Contract* [1892] 3 Ch. 41.

In addition to these covenants, other covenants may be held to be "usual" depending on the facts of the case.[166] Proof may be led as to whether a particular covenant is commonly found in leases of similar premises in similar areas; if so, a covenant will be held to be "usual". As this is a question of fact, the issue as to whether a covenant is "usual" may vary between commercial, residential and agricultural leases, and may differ from one location to another.[167]

2. Implied Terms

[10.23] If an agreement for a lease is silent as to the terms of the formal lease, it is implied that the lease will be subject to the "usual" covenants.[168]

If covenants are not included in a lease, or if the terms of the express covenants are inadequate in light of the nature of the lease and the surrounding circumstances, as many covenants will be implied at common law as are necessary to give "business efficacy" to the contract. The major authority on this issue is *Liverpool C.C. v. Irwin*.[169] In this case, the tenants of a high-rise block of flats owned by the Council withheld their rent in protest against the conditions in the building, and in an action for possession counter-claimed that the Council had breached an implied covenant to maintain the common parts of the building, including lifts, staircases and rubbish chutes. These common facilities had been in constant disrepair for many years. The House of Lords held that the Council was under an implied covenant to keep the common parts of the building in repair and that on the facts the Council had been in breach of that duty. Their Lordships stated that the decision must not be construed too widely, and emphasised that courts do not have the power to imply terms into leases merely because it seems reasonable to do so.[170]

The most recent Australian authority is *Karaggianis v. Malltown Pty Ltd*.[171] In this case, a tenant of commercial premises leased part of the sixth floor of a high-rise building. Access to the premises was provided by four lifts and two escalators. One year after the commencement of the lease, the landlord ceased operating the escalators and reduced the lift services. The tenant applied for a declaration that the landlord had breached an implied covenant in the lease to maintain and operate the lifts and escalators, and for a mandatory injunction to compel him to restore the services. Wells J. held that a covenant should be implied in the lease that the landlord would maintain and operate the lifts and escalators in

---

166. The issue was held to be a question of fact in, e.g. *Sweet & Maxwell Ltd v. Universal News Services Ltd* [1964] 2 Q.B. 699 (C.A.); *Blake v. Lane* (1876) 2 V.L.R. (L.) 54 (F.C.); *Chester v. Buckingham Travel Ltd* [1981] 1 All E.R. 386.
167. See especially *Flexman v. Corbett* [1930] 1 Ch. 672 at 677ff. per Maugham J.
168. *Propert v. Parker* (1832) 3 My. & K. 280; 40 E.R. 107 (Ch.).
169. [1977] A.C. 239 (H.L.). See also *Bournemouth & Boscombe Athletic Football Club Co. Ltd v. Manchester United Football Club Ltd, The Times*, 22 May 1980; *Western Electric Ltd v. Welsh Development Agency* [1983] 2 All E.R. 629 (C.A.); *Duke of Westminster v. Guild* [1984] 3 W.L.R. 630 (C.A.), discussed in [1985] Conv. 66; *Barrett v. Lounova (1982) Ltd* [1989] 1 All E.R. 351 (C.A.).
170. *Liverpool C.C. v. Irwin* [1977] A.C. 239 at 262.
171. (1979) 21 S.A.S.R. 381.

the same condition and to the same effect as at the commencement of the lease. He based his decision on the ground, inter alia, that the covenant was necessary to give business efficacy to the transaction between the parties, and stated:[172]

> "Prima facie that which in any contract is left to be implied and need not be expressed is something so obvious that it goes without saying; so that, if, while the parties were making their bargain, an officious bystander were to suggest some express provision for it in their agreement they would testily suppress him with a common 'Oh, of course!'."

In Australia, terms have also been implied that the tenant is entitled to use a lift for the carriage of such goods and passengers as is reasonably necessary for the conduct of his business,[173] that the tenant can have access through premises retained by the landlord to the only lavatory on the property,[174] and that the rented premises should be supplied with electricity.[175] On the other hand, the Federal Court has refused to imply a term that the floor of the rented premises is of a sufficient standard and quality that it is able to withstand industrial use associated with the business of a printer,[176] and the New South Wales Supreme Court has refused to imply a term that in the event of damage by fire to the demised premises, the landlord would use the proceeds of the insurance policy to reduce or extinguish the tenant's liability under an express covenant to repair.[177]

In addition to this general rule concerning implied terms, certain specific covenants are implied under State legislation and at common law.

(a) Covenants implied by legislation

[10.24]   Five statutory covenants are implied in leases pursuant to the *Conveyancing Act* 1919 (N.S.W.), *Transfer of Land Act* 1958 (Vic.), *Property Law Act* 1974 (Qld), *Real Property Act* 1886 (S.A.), *Transfer of Land Act* 1893 (W.A.) and the *Land Titles Act* 1980 (Tas.). The covenants vary slightly in their terms from one jurisdiction to another, but are uniformly designed to safeguard the landlord's interest. The covenants apply to rented premises of both general law land and Torrens land in New South Wales and Queensland, but elsewhere they apply only to Torrens land.

(i) Covenant by tenant to pay rent, rates and taxes

[10.25]   In all States, legislation implies a covenant by the tenant that he or she will pay the rent reserved by the lease at the times therein mentioned and all rates and taxes payable in respect of the rented premises, except for those charges payable exclusively by the landlord under any State or local government legislation. An exception applies in

---

172. Ibid. at 392.
173. *Dikstein v. Kanevsky* [1947] V.L.R. 216.
174. *Dillon v. Nash* [1950] V.L.R. 293.
175. *Jenkins v. Levinson* (1929) 29 S.R. (N.S.W.) 151 (F.C.)
176. *Bradford House Pty Ltd v. Leroy Fashion Group Ltd* [1983] A.T.P.R. 44,162.
177. *Linden v. Staybond Pty Ltd* [1986] N.S.W. Conv. R. 55-308.

New South Wales and Queensland where the premises are destroyed by fire, flood, lightning, storm, tempest or war damage. In these circumstances the rent is abated.[178]

The State legislation does not alter the common law rule that in the absence of an express covenant to the contrary, rent is not payable in advance but rather in arrears, at the end of each period specified for payment.[179]

Other common law rules also remain in effect. It is the duty of the tenant to seek out the landlord to pay rent to her or him.[180] Even if a third party pays any arrears of rent pursuant to a guarantee contract, the rent remains payable by the tenant and may justify the forfeiture of the lease.[181] If the tenant wrongfully abandons the rented premises, the landlord is not under a duty to mitigate his losses; instead, the landlord may elect to leave the premises vacant rather than to relet them and may sue the tenant for rent as it falls due.[182] Except where the rented premises are requisitioned by government authority[183] or where the tenant is evicted by title paramount,[184] the duty to pay rent ceases if the tenant is evicted by the landlord or anyone claiming under her or him from any part of the rented premises. Finally, pursuant to State limitation of actions legislation a maximum of six years' rent may be sued for by the landlord in Victoria, Queensland and Tasmania, 12 years' rent in New South Wales and Western Australia, and 15 years' rent in South Australia.[185]

(ii) Covenant by tenant to repair

[10.26] Except in Queensland, the legislation in all jurisdictions uniformly states that there is an implied term in every instrument of lease that the tenant will keep and yield up the leased property in good and tenantable repair, accidents and damage from storm and tempest and reasonable wear and tear excepted.[186] In Queensland, a similar covenant exists but is restricted to fixed-term leases exceeding three years.[187] In respect of fixed-term leases of three years or less and in respect of all periodic leases, two statutory terms are implied: a covenant by the landlord to provide and maintain the premises in good repair, and a covenant by the tenant to care for the premises in the manner of a reasonable tenant and to repair damage caused by any person coming onto the premises with her or his permission.[188]

178. N.S.W.: s. 84(1)(a); Vic.: s. 67(1)(a); Qld: s. 105(a); S.A.: s. 124(1); W.A.: s. 92(i).
179. *Coomber v. Howard* (1845) 1 C.B. 440; 135 E.R. 611 (C.P.); *Collett v. Curling* (1847) 10 Q.B. 785; 116 E.R. 298.
180. *Harrison v. Petkovic* [1975] V.R. 79.
181. *London & County (A. & D.) Ltd v. Wilfred Sportsman Ltd* [1971] Ch. 764 (C.A.).
182. *Maridakis v. Kouvaris* (1975) 5 A.L.R. 197; *Boyer v. Warbey* [1953] 1 Q.B. 234 (C.A.).
183. *Commissioners of Crown Lands v. Page* [1960] 2 Q.B. 274 (C.A.).
184. *Neale v. Mackenzie* (1836) 1 M. & W. 747; 150 E.R. 635 (Exch. Ch.).
185. Limitation statutes: N.S.W.: s. 27(1) and definition of "land" in s. 11(1); Vic.: s. 19; Qld: s. 25; S.A.: s. 4; W.A.: s. 4; Tas.: s. 22.
186. N.S.W.: s. 84(1)(b); Vic.: s. 67(1)(b); S.A.: s. 124(2); W.A.: s. 92(ii); Tas.: s. 66(b).
187. Qld: s. 105(b).
188. Qld: s. 106(1)(a)(b).

"Good tenantable repair" was defined by Lopes L.J. in *Proudfoot v. Hart* as:[189]

> "such repair as, having regard to the age, character, and locality of the house, would make it reasonably fit for the occupation of a reasonably minded tenant of the class who would be likely to take it."

The following common law propositions would appear to be relevant to the interpretation of the scope of the tenant's statutory duty to repair:

1. Before the tenant is in breach of the duty to repair, the damage must be of a substantial character, as distinguished from a mere fanciful injury.[190]

2. In order to comply with the duty to maintain premises, the tenant may be obliged to carry out repair work in anticipation of the likely defects rather than wait for the defects to occur.[191]

3. The tenant must maintain the premises in repair at all times during the lease. If the premises are at any time out of repair, the tenant will be in breach of the legislation.[192]

4. Cases at common law concerning the interpretation of a covenant by either party to "keep" the premises in repair have held that this includes the requirement of putting the premises into repair at the commencement of a lease.[193] It is submitted that these cases can be used by analogy to support the conclusion that the tenant's duty to repair the premises includes the duty to put them into repair initially.

5. The court will measure the extent of the duty to repair according to the age, locality and character of the premises.[194]

6. The obligation to repair does not involve an obligation to renew or improve the premises, although replacement of the structure from time to time may be necessary depending on the facts of the case. It appears to be a question of degree whether the amount of work required can properly be described as repair.[195]

7. The repair of buildings with inherent structural or design defects has caused the courts difficulty. The English Court of Appeal has recently held that disrepair connotes a deterioration from a former better

---

189. See also *Lurcott v. Wakely and Wheeler* [1911] 1 K.B. 905 at 923ff. (C.A.), per Buckley L.J.; *Payne v. Haine* (1847) 16 M. & W. 541; 153 E.R. 1304 (Exch.).
190. *Julian v. McMurray* (1924) 24 S.R. (N.S.W.) 402.
191. *Day v. Harland and Wolff Ltd* [1953] 2 All E.R. 387 at 388 (C.A.); *London & North-Eastern Rly Co. v. Berriman* [1946] A.C. 278 at 307 (H.L.).
192. *Luxmoore v. Robson* (1818) 1 Barn. & Ald. 584; 106 E.R. 215 (K.B.).
193. *Chatfield v. Elmstone Resthouse Ltd* [1975] 2 N.Z.L.R. 269 at 272; *Beaumont v. Whitcombe and Tombs* (1897) 16 N.Z.L.R. 133 at 136 (S.C. in banco); *Lurcott v. Wakely and Wheeler* [1911] 1 K.B. 905 at 919 (C.A.).
194. *Anstruther-Gough-Calthorpe v. McOscar* [1924] 1 K.B. 716 (C.A.); *Proudfoot v. Hart* (1890) 25 Q.B.D. 42 (C.A.); *Bailey v. J. Paynter (Mayfield) Pty Ltd* [1966] 1 N.S.W.R. 596.
195. *Graham v. Market Hotels Ltd* (1943) 67 C.L.R. 567 at 579; *Smedley v. Chumley and Hawke Ltd* (1982) 126 S.J. 33 (C.A.); *Elite Investments Ltd v. T. I. Bainbridge Silencers Ltd* (1986) 280 E.G. 1001; *Clowes v. Bentley Pty Ltd* [1970] W.A.R. 24. See also Wilkinson, "Major Structural Repairs" (1982) 132 N.L.J. 677.

position.[196] Thus, if a tenant leases a building erected with an inherent defect, the tenant is not required to remedy that defect. However, if a defective building deteriorates in some way, this will constitute disrepair.[197] In this latter situation, the duty to repair may include the duty to improve the property to eliminate the original inherent defect if there is no other way of remedying the problem.[198]

8. The duty to repair binds the tenant to rebuild the premises if they are destroyed. This duty arises in all cases, regardless of the cause of the destruction.[199]

(iii) The landlord's right of entry for inspection[200]

[10.27] In all jurisdictions the landlord is allowed the right to enter the rented premises to view its state of repair.[201] The terms of the legislation differ markedly, however. In Victoria and Western Australia, the landlord may enter the premises once a year at a reasonable time of the day; there is no requirement for notice to be given.[202] In New South Wales, the landlord may enter twice a year on two days' notice.[203] In Queensland, the landlord may enter at any time on two days' notice,[204] while in South Australia and Tasmania he or she may enter at all reasonable times.[205]

Apart from this statutory right of entry, unless more extensive rights of entry are reserved in the lease, the landlord is not permitted to enter the rented premises without the permission of the tenant, as this would conflict with the tenant's right to exclusive possession.[206]

(iv) Landlord's right of re-entry for non-payment of rent

[10.28] As discussed below **[10.54]**, at common law in the absence of an express covenant to the contrary the landlord is unable to determine a lease for non-payment of rent: This common law rule has been superseded by State legislation granting a statutory right of re-entry for

---

196. *Post Office v. Aquarius Properties Ltd* (1986) 281 E.G. 798 (C.A.); discussed in (1987) 281 E.G. 1207; (1987) 61 A.L.J. 250; [1987] Conv. 224.

197. Ibid.

198. *Elmcroft Developments Ltd v. Tankersley-Sawyer* (1984) 270 E.G. 140 (C.A.); *Stent v. Monmouth D.C.* (1987) 282 E.G. 705 (C.A.).

199. *Paradine v. Jane* (1647) Aleyn. 26; 82 E.R. 897 (K.B.); *Redmond v. Dainton* [1920] 2 K.B. 256; *Matthey v. Curling* [1922] 2 A.C. 180 (H.L.).

200. Note that in New South Wales (s. 85(1)(b)) and Queensland (s. 107(c)), there is also an implied statutory covenant that the landlord may enter the rented premises in order to carry out any repair work ordered to be undertaken by public authorities.

201. This statutory covenant, where it applies, appears to impliedly repeal the common law implied covenant by a tenant to allow the landlord to inspect the property wherever the landlord is under a duty to repair: *Mint v. Good* [1951] 1 K.B. 517 (C.A.). This common law implied covenant presumably continues to apply to general law land in Victoria, South Australia, Western Australia and Tasmania.

202. Vic.: s. 67(1)(c); W.A.: s. 93(i).

203. N.S.W.: s. 85(1)(a).

204. Qld: s. 107(a).

205. S.A.: s. 125(2); Tas.: s. 67(a).

206. See *Stocker v. Planet B.S.* (1879) 27 W.R. 877.

the landlord in these circumstances.[207] A right of re-entry is allowed the landlord where the rent is at least three months in arrears in South Australia and Tasmania, but in the remaining jurisdictions such a right can be exercised as soon as the rent is one month in arrears.

(v) Landlord's right of re-entry for breach of covenants other than the covenant to pay rent

[10.29]   As in the case of non-payment of rent, a statutory right of re-entry for breach of all other covenants is now granted to landlords.[208] This right may be exercised in the case of any breach or non-observance of any of the covenants implied by law or expressed in the lease where the breach or non-observance has continued for the minimum period of one month in Victoria and Western Australia, two months in New South Wales and Queensland, and three months in South Australia and Tasmania.

Except in Queensland, any or all of the statutory terms can be modified or excluded by express declaration in the instrument of lease.[209] In Queensland, however, the statutory obligations contained in s. 106 of the *Property Law Act* 1974 concerning the repair of rented premises where the lease does not exceed three years are stated to apply notwithstanding any agreement to the contrary.

In addition to the statutory covenants implied in leases, in respect of Torrens land in Victoria, Western Australia and Tasmania there is an implied covenant in every sublease that the sublessor will during the term of the sublease pay the rent and perform and observe the covenants and agreements contained in the original lease.[210]

(b) Covenants implied at common law

[10.30]   At common law, a number of specific covenants on the part of one or other of the parties are implied. These will now be considered individually.

(i) Implied condition of fitness of habitation by the landlord

[10.31]   At common law, the landlord had no general duty towards the tenant to do repairs during the term of the lease or to put the premises into repair at the commencement of the lease, however poor the condition of the premises might be.[211] The prevailing principle was that of caveat emptor. There are two exceptions: first, a warranty of fitness is implied where a lease is executed prior to the completion of the erection of the building;[212] and secondly, there is an implied condition, established in

207. N.S.W.: s. 85(1)(d); Vic.: s. 67(1)(d); Qld: s. 107(d); S.A.: s. 125(3); W.A.: s. 93(ii); Tas.: s. 67(b).
208. N.S.W.: s. 85(1)(d); Vic.: s. 67(1)(d); Qld: s. 107(d); S.A.: s. 125(3); W.A.: s. 93(ii); Tas.: s. 67(b); A.C.T.: s. 120(d).
209. N.S.W.: s. 74(1); Vic.: s. 112; S.A.: s. 262; W.A.: s. 131; Tas.: s. 57(1).
210. Torrens statutes: Vic.: s. 71(4); W.A.: s. 103; Tas.: s. 69(3).
211. *Gott v. Gandy* (1853) 2 El. & Bl. 845; 118 E.R. 984 (K.B.); *Collins v. Winter* (1924) 43 N.Z.L.R. 449 (S.C. in banco); *Wilchick v. Marks and Silverstone* [1934] 2 K.B. 56.
212. *Miller v. Cannon Hill Estates Ltd* [1931] 2 K.B. 113.

Smith v. Marrable,[213] that in the case of furnished premises the premises are fit for habitation at the commencement of the lease.[214]

Smith v. Marrable involved a lease of a furnished summer house to one Sir Thomas Marrable for six weeks. After only one week's occupation, Sir Thomas vacated the premises on the ground that they were infested by bugs, and refused to pay the balance of the rent owing. Parke B. held that authority existed for the proposition that although slight grounds would not suffice, serious reasons might exist that would justify a tenant's quitting the rented premises at any time. *Hart v. Windsor*,[215] a case involving a similar situation, arose the following year. In this case Parke B. stated that he was now satisfied that the two cases he relied upon in reaching his decision in *Smith v. Marrable* could not be supported. However, instead of holding that *Smith v. Marrable* was wrongly decided, he distinguished it[216] on the ground that that case involved furnished premises while the premises in the case at bar were unfurnished.[217] Later cases further limited the application of *Smith v. Marrable* to situations where the defect existed at the commencement of the lease,[218] and have refused to apply the rule in the case of defective furniture or appliances.[219]

(ii) Implied covenant of quiet enjoyment by the landlord

[10.32]   The covenant for quiet enjoyment, which is implied into all leases in the absence of an express covenant for quiet enjoyment, is commonly misunderstood. In this context, "quiet" means "peaceful" or "freedom from interruption" rather than "without noise". This implied term imposes an obligation on the landlord to put the tenant into possession and allow the tenant to remain peacefully in possession during the term of the lease free from interruption.[220]

It is sometimes said that this covenant provides the tenant with a legal remedy in all cases of harassment. Some instances of harassment are undoubtedly within the scope of the covenant: thus, for example, the covenant has been held to be breached where the landlord removed the doors and windows to the premises[221] and cut off the gas and electricity supplies[222] in order to induce the tenant to vacate the premises. Unfortunately, however, this statement is too broad-ranging to be

213. (1843) 11 M. & W. 5; 152 E.R. 693 (Exch.).
214. The meaning of "fit for habitation" was considered by McCardie J. in *Collins v. Hopkins* [1923] 2 K.B. 617 at 620-621.
215. (1843) 12 M. & W. 67; 152 E.R. 1114 (Exch.).
216. Ibid. at 86-87; 1122.
217. *Collins v. Hopkins* [1923] 2 K.B. 617 and *Wilson v. Finch Hatton* (1877) 2 Ex. D. 336 held that the rule in *Smith v. Marrable* still applies to furnished premises. *Cruse v. Carr* [1933] Ch. 278 and *Penn v. Gatenex Co. Ltd* [1958] 2 Q.B. 210 (C.A.) held that the rule does not extend to unfurnished premises.
218. *Penn v. Gatenex Co. Ltd* [1958] 2 Q.B. 210 (C.A.); *Sarson v. Roberts* [1895] 2 Q.B. 395 (C.A.).
219. *Pampris v. Thanos* [1968] 1 N.S.W.R. 56 (C.A.).
220. See e.g. *Jaeger v. Mansions Consolidated Ltd* (1903) 87 L.T. 690 (C.A.); *Markham v. Paget* [1908] 1 Ch. 697.
221. *Lavender v. Betts* [1942] 2 All E.R. 72. See also *Drane v. Evangelou* [1978] 1 W.L.R. 455.
222. *Perera v. Vandiyar* [1953] 1 All E.R. 1109.

accurate; while some acts of harassment undoubtedly breach the covenant of quiet enjoyment, other acts are outside the scope of the covenant.

There are at least two and possibly three limitations on the scope of the implied covenant. First, the covenant does not amount to a guarantee of title. The landlord is not liable for acts of her or his predecessors-in-title or grantees of rights or interests created by predecessors-in-title.[223] The landlord is only liable for a breach of the covenant if he or she personally disturbs the tenant's peaceful possession or authorises a third party claiming under her or him to commit a disturbance.[224] Thus, for example, if the landlord lets premises adjoining the tenant to other persons who engage in unruly behaviour and disturb the tenant's peaceful possession, there will only be a breach of the implied covenant if the tenant can prove that the landlord either authorised or encouraged the other persons to commit the disturbance. In the absence of such authorisation or encouragement, the tenant's only remedy would be to sue the unruly persons in nuisance.

Secondly, there is no remedy under the implied covenant where the tenant's possession is disturbed by a person claiming through title paramount.[225] The most common illustration of this arises in the case of subleases. Take the case where X leases premises to Y and Y sublets the premises to Z. If Y breaches one of the covenants of the head lease and X exercises a right of re-entry under the express or implied terms of the lease, the sublease to Z will be determined automatically and the remedy of quiet enjoyment will be regarded by the courts as inoperative.

A third possible limitation on the scope of the implied covenant is that it applies only in cases of direct physical interference with the tenant's peaceful possession. The major authority supporting this limitation is *Browne v. Flower*,[226] where the tenant of the upper floors of a building obtained the landlord's permission to erect a staircase outside the plaintiff tenant's flat on the ground floor. The fact that this constituted an invasion of privacy was held to be irrelevant to the covenant of quiet enjoyment and a remedy for breach of this covenant was refused. A more recent authority is *Gordon v. Lidcombe Developments Pty Ltd*,[227] where the landlord erected a wall on his property partially obscuring from sight a coffee shop previously leased to a tenant and causing the profitability of the shop to decline. In this case it was held, inter alia, that there was no breach of the covenant of quiet enjoyment. However, in *Owen v. Gadd*,[228] the obstruction of the window of the rented premises by scaffolding was held to amount to a breach of the covenant of quiet enjoyment, and there are dicta in *Kenny v. Preen*[229] by Pearson L.J. with whose judgment

223. *Celsteel Ltd v. Alton House Holdings Ltd (No. 2)* [1987] 2 All E.R. 240 (C.A.).
224. See e.g. *Sanderson v. Mayor of Berwick-on-Tweed* (1884) 13 Q.B.D. 547 (C.A.); *Malzy v. Eichholz* [1916] 2 K.B. 308 at 318 (C.A.). For the meaning of "claiming under", see *Celsteel Ltd v. Alton House Holdings Ltd (No. 2)* [1987] 2 All E.R. 240 (C.A.).
225. *Jones v. Lavington* [1903] 1 K.B. 235 (C.A.); *Kenny v. Preen* [1963] 1 Q.B. 499 (C.A.).
226. [1911] 1 Ch. 219.
227. [1966] 2 N.S.W.R. 9.
228. [1956] 2 Q.B. 99 (C.A.).
229. [1963] 1 Q.B. 499 at 513 (C.A.).

Ormrod L.J. agreed, that there can be a breach of the covenant even where physical interference is absent. In the most recent Australian case, *J. C. Berndt Pty Ltd v. Walsh*,[230] Walsh J. applied *Owen v. Gadd*, although holding on the facts of the case that the covenant for quiet enjoyment had not been breached. In summary, the issue as to whether the covenant applies in cases where there is no direct physical interference by the landlord of the tenant's peaceful possession must be regarded as unsettled.

(iii) Implied covenant of non-derogation from grant by the landlord

[10.33] There is a general principle of real property law that a grantor must not derogate from her or his grant. The application of this principle in the landlord-tenant context is merely one illustration of its operation.[231]

The meaning of the principle has been explained in various ways. Bowen L.J. stated in *Birmingham, Dudley & District Banking Co. v. Ross*[232] that "a grantor having given a thing with one hand is not to take away the means of enjoying it with the other", while Stirling J. stated in *Aldin v. Latimer, Clark, Muirhead & Co.* that:[233]

> "Where a landlord demises part of his property for carrying on a particular business, he is bound to abstain from doing anything on the remaining portion which would render the demised premises unfit for carrying on such business in the way in which it is ordinarily carried on."

The doctrine can best be understood by way of illustrations. In *Lend Lease Development Pty Ltd v. Zemlicka*,[234] the New South Wales Court of Appeal held that a reduction in security for a tenant caused by demolition work undertaken by the landlord around the demised premises may constitute a breach of the implied covenant. In *Cable v. Bryant*,[235] where the landlord had granted a lease of a stable, it was held that he could not derogate from his grant by erecting hoardings which adversely affected the supply of ventilation to the stable. Similarly in *Aldin v. Latimer, Clark, Muirhead & Co.*[236] it was held to be a derogation from grant where the landlord had leased property to the tenant for the purpose of carrying on a timber business and the landlord's successors-in-title erected equipment on adjoining land for the purpose of supplying electricity to neighbouring districts which interfered with the access of air to the drying sheds used in the timber business. In *Harmer v. Jumbil (Nigeria) Tin Areas Ltd*,[237] the landlord leased certain premises to a tenant for the purposes of an explosive magazine. Pursuant to legislation, the tenant's licence for storing explosives would be withdrawn if buildings were erected on the landlord's adjoining property within a certain distance from the

---

230. [1969] S.A.S.R. 34.
231. Another illustration is the law of easements, where the principle of non-derogation from grant is one method of creating an implied easement: see Bradbrook and Neave, at paras 446ff.
232. (1888) 38 Ch. D. 295 at 313 (C.A.).
233. [1894] 2 Ch. 437 at 444.
234. (1985) 3 N.S.W.L.R. 207 (C.A.).
235. [1908] 1 Ch. 259.
236. [1894] 2 Ch. 437.
237. [1921] 1 Ch. 200 (C.A.).

magazine. The landlord later leased the adjoining land to another tenant for different purposes, and that tenant proceeded to erect buildings within the prohibited distance of the explosive magazine. It was held that a breach of the landlord's obligation not to derogate from his grant had occurred. In contrast, the obligation will not be breached where the landlord lets adjoining premises for a purpose which competes with the business carried on by another tenant of the same landlord, even if reduced profitability can be proved.[238] In addition, no remedy will lie where the use to which the tenant puts the demised premises is particularly sensitive, and the landlord was unaware of the sensitivity at the time he or she granted the lease.[239]

The principle of non-derogation from grant partially overlaps in its operation with the covenant of quiet enjoyment. According to Woodfall,[240] the real distinction is that non-derogation from grant is concerned with user of the retained part which makes the demised premises less fit for the purpose for which they were let, while the covenant for quiet enjoyment is concerned with the enjoyment of the premises and any disturbance of such enjoyment.

(iv) Implied covenant to use the premises in a tenant-like manner by the tenant

[10.34]   The existence of this implied covenant has long been settled, but its exact scope is still uncertain.[241] Lord Denning stated in *Warren v. Keen*:[242]

> "But what does to 'use the premises in a tenant-like manner' mean? It can, I think, best be shown by some illustrations. The tenant must take proper care of the place. He must, if he is going away for the winter, turn off the water and empty the boiler. He must clean the chimneys, where necessary, and also the windows. He must mend the electric light when it fuses. He must unstop the sink when it is blocked by his waste. In short, he must do the little jobs about the place which a reasonable tenant would do. In addition, he must, of course, not damage the house, wilfully or negligently, and he must see that his family and guests do not damage it: and if they do, he must repair it. But apart from such things, if the house falls into disrepair through fair wear and tear or lapse of time, or for any reason not caused by him, then the tenant is not liable to repair it."

The tenant's implied covenant will not be extended beyond the bounds of this dictum. Thus, in *Wycombe Health Authority v. Barnett*[243] the English Court of Appeal dismissed the landlord's action for damages against a

---

238. See e.g. *Port v. Griffith* [1938] 1 All E.R. 295.
239. *Robinson v. Kilvert* (1889) 41 Ch. D. 88 (C.A.).
240. *Woodfall's Law of Landlord and Tenant*, Vol. 1, p. 544.
241. It was held by Cussen A.C.J. in *City of Ballarat v. Waller* [1924] V.L.R. 115 at 119 that the implied covenant by a tenant to use the premises in a tenant-like manner is not necessarily excluded by the inclusion of an express covenant to repair in a lease.
242. [1954] 1 Q.B. 15 at 20 (C.A.).
243. (1984) 47 P. & C.R. 394 (C.A.).

tenant where a hot water tank and pipes in the rented premises had burst during freezing weather. Watkins L.J. stated that it is going much too far to say that a prudent tenant can be expected, whenever a cold spell of weather occurs and when contemplating being away from home for a night or two, to turn off the stop-cock and drain the water system.[244]

The precise ambit of the implied covenant remains unclear. Other courts have referred to an obligation of the tenant to "keep the premises wind and watertight", and an obligation to make "fair and tenantable repairs".[245] Although it has generally been assumed that these phrases are synonymous with "tenant-like manner", this has never been settled.[246]

In relation to agricultural land, there is an implied covenant by the tenant to cultivate the property in a husband-like manner.[247] The meaning of the covenant has not been judicially considered in detail, but appears to be analogous to the implied covenant to use the premises in a tenant-like manner.

(v) Implied duty by the tenant not to commit waste

[10.35]   Waste is a tortious rather than a contractual doctrine which was originally devised to regulate the respective rights of a life tenant and the remainderman concerning the use which the former can legitimately make of property during the existence of a life tenancy. Its application in that context and the various categories of waste are discussed in detail below **[12.09]**ff. The doctrine of waste also applies to leasehold estates, although it is seldom invoked today in light of the statutory and common law duties established under landlord-tenant law in respect of repairs.

The liability of a tenant for waste turns on the particular classification of leasehold estate into which the tenant happens to fall. Although all tenants are liable under voluntary waste if they commit a positive act causing injury to the land,[248] their liability under permissive waste if they fail to keep the property in a satisfactory state of repair depends on whether they are tenants for a term of years or periodic tenants, and within this latter category whether they fall under the subcategory of weekly, monthly or yearly tenants. It is unclear from the authorities

---

244. Ibid. at 399.
245. See e.g. *Wedd v. Porter* [1916] 2 K.B. 91 (C.A.); *Gregor v. Mighell* (1811) 18 Ves. 328 at 331; 34 E.R. 341 at 342 (Ch.).
246. The authors of *Halsbury's Laws of England* (4th ed.), Vol. 27, para. 275, believe that it is doubtful whether the tenant's liability extends beyond the duty to use the premises in a tenant-like manner.
247. *Williams v. Lewis* [1915] 3 K.B. 493.
248. In respect of fixed-term leases, the *Statute of Marleberge* (1267) applies except in New South Wales. The Statute stipulates that a tenant for a fixed term of years is liable for voluntary waste. In New South Wales, the position is similar: see *Imperial Acts Application Act* 1969 (N.S.W.), s. 32(1). *Marsden v. Heyes Ltd* [1927] 2 K.B. 1 (C.A.) held that a tenant from year to year is liable for voluntary waste. *Regis Property Co. Ltd v. Dudley* [1959] A.C. 370 (H.L.) and *Warren v. Keen* [1954] 1 Q.B. 15 (C.A.) held that tenants from month to month and week to week, respectively, are also liable for voluntary waste.

whether a tenant for a term of years[249] or a tenant from year to year[250] is liable for permissive waste, but it is settled that monthly or weekly periodic tenants are not liable under that heading.[251]

(vi) The tenant's duty to yield up possession to the landlord at the end of the lease

[10.36] This implied covenant requires the tenant not merely to vacate the premises but to ensure that the landlord is able to retake possession. Thus, for example, the covenant will be breached if a caretaker or a subtenant installed by the tenant during the term of the lease fails to vacate at the end of the lease. Loss of rent and other expenses may be claimed by the landlord in these circumstances.[252]

V. ASSIGNMENTS AND SUBLEASES

1. Covenants Prohibiting Assignments and Subleases

[10.37] In the absence of an express covenant to the contrary, at common law both the landlord and the tenant have the right to dispose of all or part of their respective interests to a third party during the term of a lease by way of assignment (in the case of the landlord) or either assignment or sublease (in the case of the tenant).[253] The only exceptions to this rule are in respect of tenancies at will and tenancies at sufferance,[254] where any attempt to assign or sublet by the tenant will automatically determine the lease and will create no interest in the third party.[255]

249. Lord Coke considered that a tenant for a term of years was liable for permissive waste (2 Co. Inst. 145) and the same view was expressed in *Davies v. Davies* (1888) 38 Ch. D. 499 and *Reihana Terekuku v. Kidd* (1885) N.Z.L.R. 4 S.C. 140. Cf. *In re Cartwright; Avis v. Newman* (1889) 42 Ch. D. 532; *Brian Stevens Pty Ltd v. Clarke* (1965) 83 W.N. (Pt 1) (N.S.W.) 32. The editors of *Halsbury's Laws of England* have accepted that this seems to be the better opinion (4th ed.); Vol. 27, para. 282. Bradbrook and Croft also accept that the better view is that a tenant for a term of years is liable for permissive waste: para. 10.03. The authors of *Woodfall on Landlord and Tenant* doubt the correctness of this early view and say that "there must be considerable doubt whether a tenant for years would be found liable for permissive waste if the matter were thoroughly tested at the present day": Vol. 1, paras 1-1526.
250. The authors of *Woodfall on Landlord and Tenant* state that tenants from year to year are not generally liable for permissive waste: para. 750. Bradbrook and Croft also consider that they are probably not liable: para. 10.03. The editors of *Halsbury's Laws of England*, on the other hand, consider that tenants from year to year are liable for permissive waste to a limited extent: *Halsbury's Laws of England* (4th ed.), Vol. 27, para. 282.
251. *Regis Property Co. Ltd v. Dudley* [1959] A.C. 370 (H.L.); *Warren v. Keen* [1954] 1 Q.B. 15 (C.A.); *Gallo v. St Cyr* (1983) 144 D.L.R. (3d) 146.
252. *Henderson v. Squire* (1869) L.R. 4 Q.B. 170.
253. *Commonwealth Life (Amalgamated) Assurance Ltd v. Anderson* (1945) 46 S.R. (N.S.W.) 47; *Keeves v. Dean* [1924] 1 K.B. 685 (C.A.).
254. *Picone v. Grocery & General Merchants Ltd* [1964] N.S.W.R. 1018 (F.C.); *Martin v. Elsasser* (1878) 4 V.L.R. (L.) 481.
255. Note that this exception does not apply to tenancies at will arising under the *Conveyancing Act* 1919 (N S W.), s. 127(1); *Property Law Act* 1974 (Qld), s. 129(1); and *Property Law Act* 1969 (W.A.), s. 71. See above **[10.11]** for a discussion of this legislation.

Most modern leases contain a covenant by the tenant prohibiting or restricting the tenant's common law right to assign or sublet her or his interest. The drafting of the covenant varies from lease to lease, but the following form is typical:

"The tenant covenants with the landlord not to assign over nor in any way dispose of or part with possession of the said premises or any part thereof and not to sublet lend license or install a caretaker in the said premises or any part thereof either furnished or unfurnished unless written permission has first been obtained from the landlord."

The basic rule of interpretation of such covenants is that they are construed against the landlord.[256] Thus, for example, it has been held that a covenant against subletting is not infringed where the tenant sublets part of the premises,[257] a covenant against assigning is not breached where the tenant sublets the premises,[258] and a covenant against assigning or subletting is not infringed where the tenant parts with possession pursuant to a revocable licence.[259] Note, however, that a covenant against subletting or parting with possession of the premises will be breached where the tenant assigns the term.[260]

Regardless of the wording of the covenant, it will only be breached where there is a voluntary dealing by the tenant with her or his interest. Thus, at common law there is no breach where the interest involuntarily vests in a trustee in bankruptcy if the tenant becomes bankrupt.[261] It has further been held that a bequest of the lease[262] and an equitable mortgage created by the deposit of the title deeds[263] did not breach the covenant. In New South Wales and Queensland, this matter is partially dealt with by legislation, which reads:[264]

"Neither the assignment nor the underletting of any leasehold by the official assignee of a bankrupt, or by the liquidator of a company (other than a liquidator in a voluntary winding-up of a solvent company), nor the sale of any leasehold under an execution, nor the bequest of a leasehold, shall be deemed to be a breach of a covenant, condition, or agreement against the assigning, underletting, parting with the possession, or disposing of the land leased."

The meaning of an assignment and a sublease and the distinction between these two concepts have been discussed in detail: see above [10.03]. The meaning of "part with possession" must also be considered. The authorities suggest that possession in this context should be limited

---

256. *Field v. Barkworth* (1986) 277 E.G. 193.
257. *Cook v. Shoesmith* [1951] 1 K.B. 752 (C.A.).
258. *Sweet & Maxwell Ltd v. Universal News Services Ltd* [1964] 2 Q.B. 699 (C.A.).
259. *Stening v. Abrahams* [1931] 1 Ch. 470. See also *Chaplin v. Smith* [1926] 1 K.B. 198; *Re Smith's Lease* [1951] 1 All E.R. 346.
260. *Marks v. Warren* [1979] 1 All E.R. 29.
261. *Marsh v. Gilbert* (1980) 256 E.G. 715; *Re Riggs; Ex parte Lovell* [1901] 2 K.B. 16; *Re Farrow's Bank Ltd* [1921] 2 Ch. 164 (C.A.).
262. *Doe d. Goodbehere v. Bevan* (1815) 3 M. & S. 353; 105 E.R. 644 (K.B.).
263. *Doe d. Pitt v. Hogg* (1824) 4 Dow. & Ry. 224; 171 E.R. 1144 (N.P.). See also *Gentle v. Faulkner* [1900] 2 Q.B. 267 (C.A.).
264. *Conveyancing Act* 1919 (N.S.W.), s. 133; *Property Law Act* 1974 (Qld), s. 122.

to legal possession.[265] Thus, a tenant who merely parts with the right to use and occupy the premises but retains legal possession, cannot be said in this context to have "parted with possession".[266] The major authority is the Privy Council decision in *Lam Kee Ying Sdn Bhd v. Lamb Shes Tong.*[267] This case involved a lease of commercial premises. During the term of the lease, the tenant formed a company which took over his business. Amongst other things, the tenant erected a signboard with the company's name outside the premises, transferred the electricity and telephone accounts into the company's name, and paid the rent with the company's cheques. The landlord claimed that the tenant had breached an express covenant in the lease against assigning, subletting or parting with possession, arguing that on the facts the tenant had parted with possession in favour of the new company. The Privy Council regarded the evidence of the signboard and the electricity and telephone accounts as equivocal, but upheld the landlord's contention on the basis that the payment of rent by a company cheque indicated that the tenant regarded the company as entitled to legal possession. While each case will be decided on its facts, it thus appears that the payment of the rent by the occupier will prima facie be regarded as proof of possession in him.

[10.38] A covenant against assignments or subleases may absolutely prohibit assignments and subleases in all cases or (more commonly) will state that there must be no assignment or sublease unless the prior consent in writing of the landlord has been obtained. The former is usually referred to as an "absolute" covenant and the latter as a "qualified" covenant.

In respect of both absolute and qualified covenants, an assignment or sublease in breach of the covenant will be effective to convey the legal estate. The remedy for the landlord is an action for damages against the tenant and the exercise of the right of forfeiture of the lease if the lease contains a forfeiture clause.[268] Alternatively, if the landlord is sufficiently prompt, he or she may obtain an injunction to restrain any proposed assignment or sublease prior to its occurrence.[269]

Under an absolute covenant, the landlord has an unchallengeable right to refuse to consent to an assignment or a sublease regardless of her or his motive for doing so or any other circumstances.[270] However, the landlord may allow a particular assignment or sublease to take place if he or she so wishes. At common law, the rule in *Dumpor's Case*[271] held that one act of waiver would render the covenant void, but this has since been repealed

---

265. See e.g. *Stoyles v. Job* (1954) 73 W.N. (N.S.W.) 41; *Watson Holdings Pty Ltd v. Hodinott* (1957) 75 W.N. (N.S.W.) 168; *Scala House and District Property Co. Ltd v. Forbes* [1974] Q.B. 575 (C.A.).
266. Note, however, that this situation would amount to the grant of a licence, which may also be prohibited under the terms of an express covenant.
267. [1975] A.C. 247 (P.C.).
268. *Massart v. Blight* (1951) 82 C.L.R. 423; *Old Grovebury Manor Farm Ltd v. W. Seymour Plant Sales & Hire Ltd (No. 2)* [1979] 1 W.L.R. 1397 (C.A.); *Morison v. Hale* [1923] V.L.R. 93.
269. *McEachern v. Colton* [1902] A.C. 104 (P.C.).
270. *Tredegar v. Harwood* [1929] A.C. 72 (H.L.).
271. (1601) 4 Co. Rep. 119b; 76 E.R. 1110 (K.B.).

by legislation in all States specifically stating that any waiver of a covenant or condition by a landlord or persons deriving title under her or him shall not operate as a general waiver of the benefit of any such covenant or condition.[272] In addition, at common law the acceptance of rent by the landlord from the assignee or subtenant would amount to a waiver of the right to insist on the covenant and would be treated as an implied consent by the landlord to the assignment or sublease.[273]

In relation to qualified covenants against assignment or subletting by the tenant, legislation exists in New South Wales, Victoria, Queensland and Western Australia which states that it is implied into such a covenant that the landlord shall not unreasonably withhold her or his consent.[274] In New South Wales and Queensland, the implication applies notwithstanding any express agreement to the contrary, but in Victoria and Western Australia the implication may be excluded by an express provision to the contrary. In Tasmania, the legislation is silent on this issue, while in South Australia the only safeguard for tenants is the statutory power of the courts to grant relief against forfeiture where the landlord vexatiously withholds consent to the assignment or sublease.[275] The effectiveness of the statutory safeguard in New South Wales, Victoria, Queensland and Western Australia has been drastically reduced by decisions in both Australia and England upholding the validity of an express covenant requiring a tenant who wishes to assign or sublet her or his interest to first offer to surrender the lease to the landlord, whereupon the landlord may require payment for agreeing to the assignment or sublease.[276]

[10.39]   There are numerous authorities concerning the circumstances in which a landlord will be said to have withheld consent unreasonably.[277] The English Court of Appeal once held that the landlord was permitted to withhold consent based on the personality of the proposed assignee or subtenant or based on the nature of the proposed user of the premises, but that refusal to consent on any other ground would be unreasonable.[278] This proposition received support in later English and Australian cases,[279] but has been rejected as too narrow by recent English decisions.[280]

---

272. General law statutes: N.S.W.: ss 120, 123; Vic.: ss 143, 148; Qld: s. 119; *Landlord and Tenant Act* 1936 (S.A.), s. 47; W.A.: ss 73, 79; Tas.: s. 16.
273. *Hyde v. Pimley* [1952] 2 Q.B. 506 (C.A.).
274. General law statutes: N.S.W.: s. 133B(1); Vic.: s. 144(1); Qld: s. 121; W.A.: s. 80(1).
275. *Landlord and Tenant Act* 1936 (S.A.), s. 12(4).
276. *Creer v. P. & O. Lines of Australia Pty Ltd* (1971) 125 C.L.R. 84; *Bocardo S.A. v. S. & M. Hotels Ltd* [1979] 3 All E.R. 737 (C.A.).
277. See Annand, " 'Reasonable' Grounds for Landlord's Refusal to Certain Consents" (1983) 127 N.L.J. 247; Kodilinye, "Refusal for Consent to Assign: The Unreasonable Landlord" [1988] Conv. 45.
278. *Houlder Brothers & Co. Ltd v. Gibbs* [1925] Ch. 575 (C.A.).
279. *Lee v. K. Carter Ltd* [1949] 1 K.B. 85 (C.A.); *Colvin v. Bowen* (1958) 75 W.N. (N.S.W.) 262; *Bambury v. Chapman* (1959) 77 W.N. (N.S.W.) 191; *Cominos v. Rekes* (1979) 2 B.P.R. 9619 (N.S.W. Sup. Ct).
280. *Bickel v. Duke of Westminster* [1977] Q.B. 517 (C.A.); *West Layton Ltd v. Ford* [1979] Q.B. 593 (C.A.); *Bromley Park Garden Estates Ltd v. Moss* [1982] 2 All E.R. 890 (C.A.).

Although the matter has not been finally resolved in Australia, the better view appears to be that the court can take account of any relevant factors when determining whether the landlord has been unreasonable in withholding his consent. In each case, the issue is one of fact.[281] In England, the Court of Appeal in *International Drilling Fluids Ltd v. Louisville Investments (Uxbridge) Ltd*[282] recently expounded the following propositions:

1. A landlord is not entitled to refuse consent on grounds which are designed to achieve a purpose unconnected with, or collateral to, the terms of the lease.

2. It is not necessary for the landlord to show that her or his reasons for refusing consent were *justified*, so long as they could have been given by a reasonable landlord.

3. A landlord may reasonably refuse consent to an assignment on the basis of the proposed user, even if that user is permitted under the terms of the lease. However, this will not apply where only one specific use is permitted by the lease.

4. While a landlord can in normal circumstances only consider her or his own interests, in cases where a substantial disproportion exists between the benefit to the landlord and the detriment to the tenant, this can be a ground for treating the refusal of consent as unreasonable.

[10.40] Illustrations of situations where the landlord's refusal to consent has been declared unreasonable are: (a) where the assignee might intend to breach the covenant as to user, but where the assignment would not necessarily lead to a breach of the covenant;[283] (b) where the tenant was a respectable and responsible person and had purchased the tenant's business;[284] (c) where the landlord's motive was to force the tenant to offer to surrender the lease;[285] (d) where the sole purpose of the refusal was to give the landlord a new advantage not originally contemplated in the lease;[286] and (e) where the proposed use of an office block was not a conventional office use and would be less attractive to institutional investors.[287] Illustrations of situations where the landlord's refusal to consent has been declared reasonable are: (a) where the assignee would be able to claim the benefit of legislation conferring rent control and security of tenure;[288] (b) where the use to which the assignee intends to put the rented premises might injure other neighbouring property

281. *International Drilling Fluids Ltd v. Louisville Investments (Uxbridge) Ltd* [1986] 1 Ch. 513 (C.A.).
282. [1986] 1 Ch. 513 (C.A.); discussed in (1986) 277 E.G. 419. See also *Ponderosa International Development Inc. v. Pengap Securities (Bristol) Ltd* (1986) 277 E.G. 1252.
283. *Killick v. Second Covent Garden Property Co. Ltd* [1973] 1 W.L.R. 658 (C.A.).
284. *McKenzie v. McAllum* [1956] V.L.R. 208.
285. *Bates v. Donaldson* [1896] 2 Q.B. 241 (C.A.); *Colvin v. Bowen* (1958) 75 W.N. (N.S.W.) 262.
286. *Bromley Park Garden Estates Ltd v. Moss* [1982] 2 All E.R. 890 (C.A.).
287. *International Drilling Fluids Ltd v. Louisville Investments (Uxbridge) Ltd* [1986] 1 Ch. 513 (C.A.).
288. *Lee v. K. Carter Ltd* [1949] 1 K.B. 85 (C.A.); *Re Cooper's Lease* (1968) 19 P. & C.R. 541.

belonging to the landlord;[289] (c) where the terms of the proposed sublease were such that the covenant as to user in the head lease would clearly be breached;[290] (d) where the landlord had real doubts as to the proposed assignees' financial ability to meet the obligations under the lease;[291] and (e) where insufficient details are available upon which the landlord can make a reasonable decision.[292]

The burden of proving that the landlord has acted unreasonably uniformly rests on the tenant.[293] The tenant's task is made more difficult by the rule that the landlord is not obliged to give any reasons for her or his decision, although in these circumstances the court may be willing to infer that he or she has been unreasonable.[294] Where the tenant believes that the landlord is acting unreasonably, the tenant has two possible courses of action: he or she can either apply for a declaration from the court that the landlord is acting unreasonably, or he or she may assign or sublet her or his interest without the landlord's consent and take the risk that if the landlord later sues for damages the court will determine that the landlord was unreasonable.[295]

Where a landlord grants consent to a proposed sublease or assignment by the tenant pursuant to the terms of a qualified covenant, the landlord may lawfully require the payment of a reasonable sum in respect of any legal or other expenses incurred in relation to the granting of the consent. In South Australia and Tasmania, where no legislation exists on this issue, the landlord may also impose a general fee or payment as a precondition to the granting of his consent. In the remaining States, however, legislation[296] states that no fine or sum of money in the nature of a fine shall be payable for the landlord's consent.[297]

2. The Enforceability of Covenants By and Against Assignees or Subtenants

[10.41]   Where a tenant assigns the lease to a third party, he or she remains liable to the landlord for breaches of covenant committed while a tenant.[298] It has recently been held that the landlord's liability to the

---

289. *Governors of Bridewell Hospital v. Fawkner and Rogers* (1892) 8 T.L.R. 637.
290. *Barina Properties Pty Ltd v. Bernard Hastie (Australia) Pty Ltd* [1979] 1 N.S.W.L.R. 480 (C.A.).
291. *British Bakeries (Midlands) Ltd v. Michael Testler & Co. Ltd* (1986) 277 E.G. 1245.
292. *Daventry Holdings Pty Ltd v. Bacalakis Hotels Pty Ltd* [1986] Qd R. 406; discussed in (1986) 16 Qd L. Soc. J. 185.
293. *Shanly v. Ward* (1913) 29 T.L.R. 714 (C.A.); *Mills v. Cannon Brewery Co. Ltd* [1920] 2 Ch. 38; *International Drilling Fluids Ltd v. Louisville Investments (Uxbridge) Ltd* [1986] 1 Ch. 513 (C.A.).
294. *Frederick Berry Ltd v. Royal Bank of Scotland* [1949] 1 K.B. 619.
295. See *Yared v. Spier* [1979] 2 N.S.W.L.R. 291.
296. General law statutes: N.S.W.: s. 132; Vic.: s. 44(1); Qld: s. 121(1); W.A.: s. 80(1).
297. Under similar United Kingdom legislation, the Court of Appeal held in *Andrew v. Bridgman* [1908] 1 K.B. 596 that any money paid by the tenant cannot be recovered by later court action as the legislation does not declare the payment to be unlawful.
298. Megarry and Wade, p. 750; Woodfall, para. 1-1095.

tenant for existing breaches survives the assignment of the lease, in the same way as the tenant's liability to the landlord.[299]

In addition, regardless of whether the landlord assigns or the tenant assigns or sublets her or his interest,[300] based on the principle of privity of contract each party will remain liable for the remainder of the term for the performance of the various covenants contained in the lease.[301] Thus, for example, if the tenant assigns her or his interest and the assignee fails to pay the rent, the landlord may sue the original tenant for the rent as an alternative to the assignee.[302] Similarly, if the landlord disposes of her or his interest and the assignee fails to fulfil a covenant to repair, the original landlord may be sued for damages.[303] In these circumstances, the injured party cannot recover double damages. Thus, in the case of failure to pay rent, the landlord cannot recover damages from the original tenant if the landlord has already successfully sued the assignee.[304]

The liability of a third party to the lease, whether an assignee or a subtenant, will depend on the principle of privity of estate, as privity of contract will be irrelevant in this context. The meaning of privity of estate has already been discussed above **[10.04]**. The major conclusion reached therein is that whereas privity of estate exists between the landlord and the tenant's assignee, and between the tenant and the landlord's assignee, it does not exist between the landlord and a subtenant. Neither the landlord nor the subtenant may sue or be sued by the other for breach of covenant.[305] For this reason, further discussion will be limited to the enforceability of covenants by and against assignees.

Before an assignee of either party can sue or be sued for breach of covenant, in addition to proving that privity of estate exists between the parties it must be shown that the covenant "touches and concerns" the demised land and that the detailed common law and statutory rules concerning the passing of the benefit and burden of covenants are satisfied.

---

299. *City & Metropolitan Properties Ltd v. Greycroft Ltd* [1987] 1 W.L.R. 1085.

300. The difference between an assignment and a sublease is discussed above **[10.03]**.

301. In England, the Law Commission has recommended that the liability of the original contracting parties for post-assignment breaches of covenant should be abrogated in most situations: English L.C., Report No. 174 (1988).

302. *Re Teller Home Furnishers Pty Ltd (in liq.)* [1967] V.R. 313; *195 Crown Street Pty Ltd v. Hoare* [1969] 1 N.S.W.R. 193 (C.A.); *Warnford Investments Ltd v. Duckworth* [1979] Ch. 127; *Bel Madelyn Investments Pty Ltd v. Briscoes Charter Service* (1988) 146 L.S.J.S. 30.

303. *Stuart v. Joy* [1904] 1 K.B. 362 (C.A.); *Eccles v. Mills* [1898] A.C. 360 (P.C.).

304. See *Brett v. Cumberland* (1619) Cro. Jac. 521; 79 E.R. 446 (K.B.).

305. Note, however, that the landlord may possibly be able to obtain an injunction against a subtenant protecting a restrictive covenant under the principle in *Tulk v. Moxhay* (1848) 2 Ph. 774; 41 E.R. 1143 (Ch.): discussed below **[17.06]**. See *Hall v. Ewin* (1888) 37 Ch. D. 74, where the Court of Appeal held that a restrictive covenant in a head lease can be enforced against *any* occupier of the land who enters into possession with knowledge of the covenant, regardless of whether privity of estate exists.

3. The Covenant Must "Touch and Concern" the Demised Land

[10.42]   The phrase "touch and concern" is a common law expression, which technically only applies where the tenant rather than the landlord assigns her or his interest: see below **[10.44]**ff. As discussed see below **[10.46]**-**[10.47]** where the landlord assigns her or his interest, the liability of the assignee to sue or be sued is governed by legislation in each State, copied from ss 141 and 142 of the *Law of Property Act* 1925 (U.K.), which employs the term "having reference to the subject matter [of the lease]" instead of "touching and concerning" the land. In practice, however, the meaning of touching and concerning is relevant wherever either party disposes of their interest, as it has been held that the meaning of "touching and concerning" and "having reference to the subject-matter [of the lease]" is identical.[306]

There have been numerous attempted definitions of touch and concern. The best known is that of Scott L.J., who stated in *Breams Property Investment Co. Ltd v. Stroulger* that a covenant touches and concerns the land if it affects either the landlord qua landlord or the tenant qua tenant.[307] In other words, as expresed by Cheshire and Burn, the covenant must affect the landlord in her or his normal capacity as landlord or the tenant in her or his normal capacity as tenant.[308] According to Bayley J. in *Mayor of Congleton v. Pattison*,[309] an assignee cannot sue or be sued unless:

> "the covenant . . . either affect[s] the land itself during the term, such as those which regard the mode of occupation, or it . . . [is] such as per se, and not merely from collateral circumstances, affects the value of the land at the end of the term."

The most recent guide for determining the meaning of touching and concerning is that of Lord Oliver of Aylmerton in *P. & A. Swift Investments v. Combined English Stores Group Plc*:[310]

> "[I]t seems to me that, without claiming to expound an exhaustive guide, the following provides a satisfactory working test for whether, in any given case, a covenant touches and concerns the land: (1) the covenant benefits only the reversioner for time being, and if separated from the reversion ceases to be of benefit to the covenantee; (2) the covenant affects the nature, quality, mode of user or value of the land of the reversioner; (3) the covenant is not expressed to be personal (that is to say neither being given only to a specific reversioner nor in respect of the obligations only of a specific tenant); (4) the fact that a covenant is to pay a sum of money will not prevent it from touching and concerning the land so long as the three foregoing conditions are satisfied and the covenant is connected with something to be done on, to or in relation to the land."

---

306. *Davis v. Town Properties Investment Corporation Ltd* [1903] 1 Ch. 797 (C.A.).
307. [1948] 2 K.B. 1 at 7 (C.A.)
308. Cheshire and Burn, p. 430.
309. (1808) 10 East 130 at 138; 103 E.R. 725 at 728 (K.B.). See also *Horsey Estate Ltd v. Steiger* [1899] 2 Q.B. 79 and 89 (C.A.) per Lord Russell C.J.
310. [1989] A.C. 632 at 642. See also *Kumar v. Dunning* [1989] Q.B. 193.

It is clear from these definitions that the purpose of the requirement that the covenant touches and concerns the land is to prevent personal covenants affecting third parties. Such covenants are enforceable between the original contracting parties, but not otherwise. Also excluded from the scope of the definition are covenants which may relate to the land, but not to the parties in their capacity as landlord and tenant. Covenants of this nature are sometimes referred to a collateral covenants. An illustration is a covenant giving the tenant an option to purchase the land at a certain price during the term of the lease. This covenant has been held not to run in favour of the tenant's assignee as it does not affect the contracting parties in their relationship as landlord and tenant.[311]

The phrase "touch and concern" can perhaps best be understood by the use of illustrations in reported cases. The following covenants, inter alia, have been held to touch and concern the rented premises: (a) covenants by the tenant to repair the premises,[312] to pay rent,[313] not to assign or sublet without the landlord's prior consent,[314] to insure the premises against fire,[315] to use the premises as a private dwelling only,[316] to sell fixtures,[317] and not to advertise upon the rented premises;[318] (b) covenants by the landlord not to serve a notice to quit in respect of a periodic lease for a period of three years,[319] not to build on certain parts of neighbouring property,[320] to renew the lease,[321] to consent to the assignment of a lease,[322] and to supply the rented premises with good water;[323] (c) a covenant by a surety guaranteeing that a tenant's covenants which touched and concerned the land would be performed and observed.[324] These covenants should be contrasted with the following covenants which, inter alia, have been held not to satisfy the touching and concerning test: (a) covenants by the tenant to pay rates assessed in respect of other property[325] and to pay a sum of money not reserved as rent to a third party;[326] (b) covenants by the landlord not to open another

---

311. *Charles Frodsham & Co. Ltd v. Morris* (1972) 229 E.G. 961. See also *Re Hunter's Lease* [1942] Ch. 124; *Collison v. Lettsom and Whitton* (1815) 6 Taunt. 224; 128 E.R. 1020 (C.P.).
312. *Williams v. Earle* (1868) L.R. 3 Q.B. 739; *Martyn v. Clue* (1852) 18 Q.B. 661; 118 E.R. 249.
313. *Parker v. Webb* (1699) 3 Salk. 5; 91 E.R. 656 (K.B.).
314. *Cohen v. Popular Restaurants Ltd* [1917] 1 K.B. 480; *Goldstein v. Sanders* [1915] 1 Ch. 549; *McEachern v. Colton* [1902] A.C. 104 (P.C.).
315. *Vernon v. Smith* (1821) 5 B. & Ald. 1; 106 E.R. 1094 (K.B.).
316. *Wilkinson v. Rogers* (1864) 2 De G.J. & S. 62; 46 E.R. 298 (Ch.).
317. *Malmsbury Confluence Gold Mining Co. Ltd v. Tucker* (1877) 3 V.L.R. (L.) 213.
318. *White v. Kenny* [1920] V.L.R. 290.
319. *Breams Property Investment Co. Ltd v. Stroulger* [1948] 2 K.B. 1 (C.A.).
320. *Ricketts v. Enfield Churchwardens* [1909] 1 Ch. 544.
321. *Weg Motors Ltd v. Hales* [1961] Ch. 176; *Muller v. Trafford* [1901] 1 Ch. 54.
322. *Re Rakita's Application* [1971] Qd R. 59 (F.C.).
323. *Jourdain v. Wilson* (1821) 4 B. & Ald. 266; 106 E.R. 935 (K.B.).
324. *P. & A. Swift Investments v. Combined English Stores Group Plc* [1989] A.C. 632; discussed in (1989) 63 A.L.J. 294. See also *Coronation Street Industrial Properties Ltd v. Ingall Industries Plc* [1989] 1 W.L.R. 304.
325. *Gower v. Postmaster-General* (1887) 57 L.T. 527.
326. *Mayho v. Buckhurst* (1617) Cro. Jac. 438; 79 E.R. 374 (K.B.); *Flight v. Glossopp* (1835) 2 Bing. N.C. 125; 132 E.R. 50 (C.P.).

public house within half a mile of the demised premises,[327] to pay the tenant a fixed sum of money at the end of the lease unless a renewal is offered and accepted,[328] to purchase buildings erected by the tenant,[329] and to repay a security deposit (even though the events to which it relates are contained in covenants which do touch and concern the land).[330]

4. The Passing of the Burden and Benefit of Leasehold Covenants[331]

[10.43]   Assuming that the threshold test that the covenant must touch and concern the rented premises is satisfied, the liability of an assignee to sue and be sued for breach of covenant will depend on the detailed common law and statutory rules concerning the passing of the benefit and burden of leasehold covenants.

It is instructive to discuss the law on this issue separately in the context of five quite different fact situations:

Situation 1: During the term of the lease, the tenant (T) assigns his interest to an assignee (A). Is A able to enforce covenants binding the landlord (L), such as the covenant of quiet enjoyment or an express covenant to repair?

Situation 2: As in situation 1, T assigns her interest to A. Is L able to enforce against A covenants contained in the original lease between L and T, such as the covenant to pay rent or a covenant relating to the user of the premises?

Situation 3: During the term of the lease, L assigns his interest to a third party (L1). Is L able to enforce against T covenants binding T (such as the covenant to pay rent) contained in the original lease between L and T?

Situation 4: As in situation 3, L assigns her interest to L1. Is T able to enforce against L1 covenants binding L (such as the covenant of quiet enjoyment) contained in the original lease between L and T?

Situation 5: In situations 1-4, it is assumed that the transaction between L and T created a legal rather than an equitable interest in T. Would any of the answers posed in situations 1-4 be different if in fact the original transaction is construed as an agreement for a lease rather than a lease, or if the assignment is equitable even though the original lease is legal?

Each of these five situations will now be considered individually. It should be noted first, however, that these situations may sometimes arise in combination. Thus, for example, L and T may respectively assign their interests to L1 and A, and the question may arise whether L1 can sue A for breach of the covenant to pay rent. In this case, A will only be liable if the legal requirements relevant to both situations 2 and 3 are satisfied:

---

327. *Thomas v. Hayward* (1869) L.R. 4 Ex. 311.
328. *Re Hunter's Lease* [1942] Ch. 124; *Doe d. Solomon v. Purves* (1846) 1 R.J. 38.
329. *Lee v. Close* (1870) 10 S.C.R. (N.S.W.) 86; *Cheyne v. Moses* [1919] St. R. Qd 74 (F.C.).
330. *Hua Chiao Commercial Bank Ltd v. Chiapua Industries Ltd* [1987] A.C. 99 (P.C.).
331. For a recent interesting discussion of this area of law, see Gordon, "The Burden and Benefit of the Rules of Assignment" [1987] Conv. 103.

in other words, both the benefit of the covenant must pass with the landlord's reversion and the burden of the covenant must pass with the tenant's interest.

[10.44] *Situation 1: Does the benefit of a covenant pass with the tenant's interest?*

This situation is governed by common law. The rule, stipulated originally in *Spencer's Case*,[332] is that wherever T assigns his interest to A, A will be able to sue L for breach of covenant provided that the covenant touches and concerns the land. There are no exceptions or qualifications to this rule.

[10.45] *Situation 2: Does the burden of a covenant pass with the tenant's interest?*

This situation is also governed by the rule in *Spencer's Case*. Wherever T assigns her interest to A, L will be able to sue A for breach of covenant provided that the covenant touches and concerns the land. A's liability as assignee is limited to breaches of covenant which occur while the possessory interest is vested in her. Unlike T, who is liable for any breach occurring at any time during the lease, A is not liable for breaches which occur before the assignment or after A has reassigned the property to a third party.[333] Note, however, that in the case of continuing breaches, A will be liable even though the breach first occurred before T assigned the possessory interest to A.[334] Furthermore, A's liability for a breach of covenant occurring during her entitlement to possession will continue even if A later reassigns the property to a third party.[335]

Tichborne v. Weir[336] establishes the proposition that a squatter who extinguishes the tenant's title by adverse possession does not class as an assignee at common law due to the lack of a contractual relationship between the squatter and the tenant. For this reason, L is unable to sue a squatter for damages for breach of the tenant's covenants.

In relation to both situations 1 and 2, the rule in *Spencer's Case* originally only applied to covenants in esse, and not to covenants in posse. Covenants in esse were covenants relating to an object already in existence, such as a covenant to repair a house, whereas covenants in posse were covenants relating to an object not yet in existence, such as a covenant to build a house. This anomalous distinction has now been abolished by legislation in all States,[337] and the rule in *Spencer's Case* is capable of applying to all types of covenants.

332. (1583) 5 Co. Rep. 16a; 77 E.R. 72 (K.B.).
333. *Renshaw v. Maher* [1907] V.L.R. 520; *Paul v. Nurse* (1828) 8 B. & C. 486; 108 E.R. 1123 (K.B.); *Grescot v. Green* (1700) 1 Salk. 199; 91 E.R. 179 (K.B.).
334. *Granada Theatres Ltd v. Freehold Investment (Leytonstone) Ltd* [1959] Ch. 592; *Rankin v. Danby* (1883) 9 V.L.R. (L.) 278.
335. *Valliant v. Dodemede* (1742) 2 Atk. 546; 26 E.R. 728 (Ch.).
336. (1892) 67 L.T. 735 (C.A.).
337. *Conveyancing Act* 1919 (N.S.W.), s. 70A; *Property Law Act* 1958 (Vic.), s. 79; *Property Law Act* 1974 (Qld), s. 53(2); *Real Property Act* 1886 (S.A.), s. 151; *Property Law Act* 1969 (W.A.), s. 48(2); *Conveyancing and Law of Property Act* 1884 (Tas.), s. 71A(2). As the *Real Property Act* 1886 (S.A.) applies only to Torrens land, the distinction between covenants in posse and in esse appears still to apply in respect of general law land in South Australia. However, the amount of general law land remaining in that State is minimal: see above **[4.05]**.

[10.46]   *Situation 3: Does the benefit of a covenant pass with the landlord's interest?*

At common law, unlike in the situation where the tenant assigned his interest, the benefit and burden of a covenant did not pass to an assignee of the landlord (L1). This situation was reversed in England by the *Grantees of Reversions Act* 1540 (Imp.), which introduced in the present context a similar rule to that in *Spencer's Case*.

In every State except South Australia, legislation has been introduced re-enacting in modern form the terms of the 1540 statute. In relation to the passing of the benefit of a covenant with the landlord's interest, the legislation, which is identical in each State, reads:[338]

"(1) Rent reserved by a lease, and the benefit of every covenant or provision therein contained,[339] having reference to the subject-matter thereof, and on the lessee's part to be observed or performed, and every condition of re-entry and other condition therein contained, shall be annexed and incident to and shall go with the reversionary estate in the land, or in any part thereof, immediately expectant on the term granted by the lease, notwithstanding severance of that reversionary estate, and without prejudice to any liability affecting a covenantor or his estate.

(2) Any such rent, covenant or provision shall be capable of being recovered, received, enforced and taken advantage of, by the person from time to time entitled, subject to the term, to the income of the whole or of any part as the case may require, of the land leased.

(3) Where that person becomes entitled by conveyance or otherwise, such rent, covenant or provision may be recovered, received, enforced or taken advantage of by him notwithstanding that he becomes so entitled after the condition of re-entry of forfeiture has become enforceable, but this sub-section shall not render enforceable any condition of re-entry or other condition waived or released before such person becomes entitled as aforesaid."

Subsection (1) refers to covenants "having reference to the subject-matter [of the lease]" and makes no reference to the need for the covenant to touch and concern the land. This difference of terminology appears to be inconsequential, however, as it has been held that the statutory and common law expressions have a similar meaning.[340]

The effect of this modern legislation is to extend its scope beyond leases created by deed under seal so as to include all types of leases valid at law, including oral periodic leases and oral leases for a term not exceeding three years.[341] The position in relation to equitable leases is less certain, and is discussed below.

---

338. General law statutes: N.S.W.: s. 117; Vic.: s. 141; Qld: s. 117; W.A.: s. 77; Tas.: s. 10.
339. *Cole v. Kelly* [1920] 2 K.B. 106 (C.A.) held that the phrase "therein contained" includes implied as well as express covenants.
340. *Davis v. Town Properties Investment Corporation Ltd* [1903] 1 Ch. 797 (C.A.).
341. The scope of the 1540 statute did not extend to oral leases: *Blane v. Francis* [1917] 1 K.B. 252 (C.A.).

In South Australia, in the absence of State legislation, the terms of the *Grantees of Reversions Act* 1540 (Imp.) continue to apply. Although the scope of this statute is limited to leases created by deed under seal, the requirement for a deed to be sealed has since been abolished by s. 41(4) of the *Law of Property Act* 1936 (S.A.). Despite this reform, however, a written deed is still required,[342] and it appears that the benefit of the tenant's covenants will not pass with the landlord's reversionary interest in respect of oral periodic leases or oral leases for a fixed period not exceeding three years. The position in relation to equitable leases is discussed below.

Under the modern State legislation, once L assigns his reversion to L1, it has been held that L is henceforth unable to sue T for past breaches of covenant. The right to sue vests solely in L1, regardless of whether the breach is a continuing breach and regardless of whether it occurred prior to the assignment of L's interest.[343] This conclusion was reached by virtue of the use by the legislatures of the words "go with" in addition to "shall be annexed and incident to". The only exception to this is where L expressly reserves his right to sue for past breaches of covenant in the deed of assignment.[344]

Prior to modern legislative changes, under the 1540 Imperial legislation, it was not possible for the assignee of part only of the landlord's reversion to enforce a covenant agreed to between the landlord and the tenant. This limitation has now been rectified by legislation in all States (including South Australia) apportioning any conditions in the case of a part assignment of the landlord's interest. In the case of part assignment, where the lease contains a right of entry the legislation also allows the assignee to exercise the right against the tenant in respect of that part of the land assigned to him, but where this occurs the legislation also gives the tenant the right within one month to determine the lease in regard to the rest of the land by giving the owner of the reversionary estate a counter-notice expiring at the same time as the original notice.[345]

[10.47] *Situation 4: Does the burden of a covenant pass with the landlord's interest?*

As in situation 3, the answer at common law was in the negative but was reversed by the *Grantees of Reversions Act* 1540 (Imp.), which introduced in the present context a similar rule to that in *Spencer's Case.*

Every State except South Australia has re-enacted the essential terms of the 1540 legislation in the following form:[346]

342. *Blane v. Francis* [1917] 1 K.B. 252 (C.A.).
343. *London & County (A. & D.) Ltd v. Wilfred Sportsman Ltd* [1971] Ch. 764 (C.A.); *Re King* [1963] Ch. 459 (C.A.).
344. *Re King* [1963] Ch. 459 (C.A.).
345. General law statutes: N.S.W.: s. 119; Vic.: s. 140; Qld: s. 116; *Landlord and Tenant Act* 1936 (S.A.), s. 50; W.A.: s. 76; Tas.: s. 12. See *Nevill Long & Co. (Boards) Ltd v. Firmenich & Co.* (1981) 261 E.G. 461; *Jelley v. Buckman* [1974] Q.B. 488 (C.A.).
346. General law statutes: N.S.W.: s. 118; Vic.: s. 142; Qld: s. 118; W.A.: s. 78; Tas.: s. 11.

"The obligation under a condition or of a covenant entered into by a lessor with reference to the subject-matter of the lease shall, if and as far as the lessor has power to bind the reversionary estate immediately expectant on the term granted by the lease, be annexed and incident to and shall go with that reversionary estate, or the several parts thereof, notwithstanding severance of that reversionary estate, and may be taken advantage of and enforced by the person in whom the term is from time to time vested by conveyance, devolution in law, or otherwise; and, if and as far as the lessor has power to bind the person from time to time entitled to that reversionary estate, the obligation aforesaid may be taken advantage of and enforced against any person so entitled."

The various observations made in the light of situation 3 regarding the scope and meaning of this legislation and the position in South Australia apply equally in this context.

[10.48] *Situation 5: The passing of the benefit and burden of covenants in the case of equitable leases or equitable assignments*

This final situation involves a reconsideration of the answers given in situations 1-4 in two separate cases: first, where the original lease between L and T is valid only in equity rather than in law; and secondly, where although the original lease is valid, the assignment is only effective in equity.

Neither of these cases will have any bearing on the liability of L and T, the original contracting parties. Each party may sue and be sued by the other throughout the term of the lease for breach of covenant based on the principle of privity of contract.[347] The result in situations 3 and 4 would also appear to be unaffected by either of these cases. The State legislation cited earlier in this paragraph refers to "leases". It appears to be beyond doubt that "leases" in this context includes equitable leases. This conclusion is reached by virtue of other sections in the same State statutes. The legislation varies from State to State. In Victoria, for example, the *Property Law Act* 1958 states that: " 'lease' includes so far as circumstances will admit any instrument of letting whether under seal or not."[348]

[10.49] This leaves for consideration situations 1 and 2, those governed by common law rules. Where the original lease is equitable, or where the original lease is legal but the assignment is equitable, no privity of estate is created between the assignee and the original contracting party as privity of estate is a common law concept. In these circumstances, the operative rule is the contractual principle that the benefit of a covenant can be assigned, but not the burden.[349] Thus, as in situation 1, it appears that an equitable assignee of the tenant's interest would be able to sue the

---

347. See above, fns 298-299.
348. *Property Law Act* 1958 (Vic.), ss 136, 154. For the interrelationship of these sections, see *Thomson v. Cross* [1954] V.L.R. 635. Cf. *Conveyancing Act* 1919 (N.S.W.), s. 128; *Property Law Act* 1974 (Qld), s. 123(2); *Property Law Act* 1969 (W.A.), s. 81(5). There appears to be no equivalent legislation in South Australia and Tasmania.
349. See Cheshire and Fifoot, Chap. 17.

landlord for a breach of any of the landlord's covenants, but unlike in situation 2, an assignee of the landlord's reversion would not be able to enforce any of the tenant's covenants contained in the original lease. Authority for this latter proposition is *Purchase v. Lichfield Brewery Co.*,[350] where after an assignment of the term of the lease it was held that the assignee was not liable to the landlord for breach of the covenant to pay rent contained in the original lease.

Despite *Purchase v. Lichfield Brewery Co.* and other authorities to similar effect, the principle that a landlord cannot sue the tenant's assignee for breach of covenant has been critically questioned in recent times. Denning L.J. argued in *Boyer v. Warbey*[351] that since the fusion of law and equity an equitable assignee can be sued. His Lordship stated:[352]

> "I know that before the *Judicature Act* 1873, it was said that the doctrine of covenants running with the land only applied to covenants under seal and not to agreements under hand . . . But since the fusion of law and equity, the position is different. The distinction between agreements under hand and covenants under seal has been largely obliterated. There is no valid reason nowadays why the doctrine of covenants running with the land—or with the reversion—should not apply equally to agreements under hand as to covenants under seal; and I think we should so hold, not only in the case of agreements for more than three years which need the intervention of equity to perfect them, but also in the case of agreements for three years or less which do not."[353]

As similar legislation to the *Judicature Act* 1873 (U.K.) now exists in all States,[354] this argument is equally relevant to Australia. A quite separate argument has been advanced elsewhere that the entry into possession and payment of rent by the assignee may be sufficient to give rise to the implied creation of a periodic tenancy between the landlord and the assignee on the same terms as the lease between the landlord and the tenant.[355] If this is correct, the landlord would be able to enforce the covenants against the assignee on the principle of privity of contract. The validity of these arguments has yet to be fully explored or finally resolved in Australia. In the meantime, the more likely conclusion is that an assignee of the tenant where the original lease is equitable or where the original lease is legal but the assignment is equitable cannot be sued by the landlord for breach of covenant. If this is correct, it exposes a serious deficiency in the law. Note, however, that the covenant which the landlord would most commonly wish to enforce against the tenant's assignee would be the covenant to pay rent. While the covenant itself

350. [1915] 1 K.B. 184. See also *Elliott v. Johnson* (1866) L.R. 2 Q.B. 120; *The Marquis Camden v. Batterbury* (1860) 7 C.B. (N.S.) 864; 141 E.R. 1055 (C.P.).
351. [1953] 1 Q.B. 234 (C.A.).
352. Ibid. at 245-246. Romer L.J. concurred on this point: at 247.
353. Ibid. at 247.
354. See e.g. *Supreme Court Act* 1970 (N.S.W.).
355. See *Buckworth v. Simpson and Benner* (1835) 1 Cr. M. & R. 834; 149 E.R. 1317 (Exch.); *Birch v. Wright* (1786) 1 T.R. 378; and the discussion in Smith, "The Running of Covenants in Equitable Leases and Equitable Assignments of Legal Leases" (1978) 37 C.L.J. 98 at 105ff.

appears not to be capable of enforcement against the assignee, the assignee would presumably be liable for an action for use and occupation as soon as he takes possession: see below **[10.77]**. Thus, any hardship to the landlord based on the rule in *Purchase v. Lichfield Brewery Co.*[356] would be alleviated in these circumstances.

Indemnity by assignees

[10.50] As discussed above **[10.03]**, at common law where T assigns her or his interest to A and A breaches any of the covenants in the lease, L may sue either A or T for damages. Although L has an unfettered discretion as to which party to sue, the primary debtor is A as the right of exclusive possession is vested in him at the time of the breach of covenant.[357] If T is sued by L, this gives rise at common law to a quasi-contractual action by T for reimbursement against A.[358] In the event that A reassigned to A1 and A1 breached the covenant, the quasi-contractual action would lie on behalf of T directly against A1. However, if A sublet the premises to ST and ST breached the covenant, the quasi-contractual claim would not lie against ST but A; in these circumstances, the question whether A also has a right of reimbursement against ST will depend on the terms of the sublease.[359]

As an alternative to this quasi-contractual action, the tenant may claim reimbursement from her or his assignee under a covenant to indemnify contained in the deed of assignment. An express covenant of this nature will usually be included in deeds of assignment. If no such covenant is expressed, in Victoria, South Australia and Western Australia it will be implied by legislation.[360] In Victoria, the legislation states that the covenant shall be in the following terms:[361]

> "That the assignees or the persons deriving title under them, will at all times, from the date of the conveyance or other date therein stated, duly pay all rent becoming due under the lease creating the term or interest for which the land is conveyed, and observe and perform all the covenants, agreements and conditions therein contained and thenceforth on the part of the lessees to be observed and performed. And also will at all times, from the date aforesaid, save harmless and keep indemnified the conveying parties and their estates and effects, from and against all proceedings, costs, claims and expenses on account of any omission to pay the said rent or any breach of any of the said covenants, agreements and conditions."

---

356. [1915] 1 K.B. 184.
357. *Moule v. Garrett* (1872) L.R. 7 Ex. 101; *Humble v. Langston* (1841) 7 M. & W. 517; 151 E.R. 871 (Exch.).
358. See e.g. *Wolveridge v. Steward* (1833) 1 Cr. & M. 644; 149 E.R. 557 (Exch. Ch.); *Murphy v. Harris* [1924] Q.S.R. 187.
359. *Bonner v. Tottenham & Edmonton Permanent Investment Building Society* [1899] 1 Q.B. 161 (C.A.).
360. *Property Law Act* 1958 (Vic.), s. 77(1)(c); *Real Property Act* 1886 (S.A.), s. 152; *Transfer of Land Act* 1893 (W.A.), s. 95. See *Johnsey Estates Ltd v. Lewis and Manley (Engineering) Ltd* (1987) 54 P. & C.R. 296 (C.A.).
361. *Property Law Act* 1958, Pt IX of Fourth Schedule.

Where there have been multiple assignments of the term by T to A and then from A to A1, the statutory covenants enable T to join A and for A to join A1 as a party to the action. Indemnity will be awarded against the assignee who was entitled to possession at the time when the breach of covenant occurred.

VI. DETERMINATION OF LEASES

[10.51]   Six methods of determining leases are provided for in Australia by common law and State legislation. These methods will now be considered individually in decreasing order of their incidence in practice.

1. Natural Expiration of the Term

[10.52]   At common law, a fixed-term lease automatically determines at the expiration of the fixed-term. No notice to quit is required. This rule, which differs from that in effect in civil law jurisdictions,[362] is subject to a number of exceptions contained in State residential and retail tenancies legislation, where a notice to vacate is required.[363]

A sublease will automatically determine on the expiration of the term of the head lease even if the sublease is expressed to continue beyond that date.[364]

2. Notice to Quit

[10.53]   At common law either party may terminate the lease by giving a notice to quit of a minimum duration commensurate with the length of the period of the lease. Thus, one week's notice is necessary for a weekly tenancy[365] and a month's notice is necessary for a monthly tenancy.[366] The only common law exception is that a yearly periodic tenancy may be determined by six months' notice by either party expiring at the end of the completed year.[367] In Victoria, s. 32(4) of the *Landlord and Tenant Act* 1958, which applies only to dwelling-houses,[368] states that in the case of periodic leases the recurring period of which does not exceed one month, a notice to quit given by a landlord shall be at least 14 days except where

362. See *Report of the Committee on the Rent Acts* (1971), H.M.S.O. Cmnd 4609, at 161.
363. See Chapter 11 generally.
364. *Weller v. Spiers* (1872) 26 L.T. 866.
365. *Precious v. Reedie* [1924] 2 K.B. 149; *Gleeson v. Richey* [1959] V.R. 258; *Amad v. Grant* (1947) 74 C.L.R. 327. Note that some authorities exist to the effect that "reasonable notice" is required in the case of a weekly tenancy, which depending on the facts may be less than one week: see *Carter v. Aldous* [1921] V.L.R. 234; *Mornane v. All Red Carrying Co. Pty Ltd* [1935] V.L.R. 341 at 346-347; *Dikstein v. Kanevsky* [1947] V.L.R. 216 at 224-225. Bradbrook and Croft (para. 20.03) conclude that it is unlikely that less than one week's notice would be acceptable.
366. *Willshire v. Dalton* (1948) 65 W.N. (N.S.W.) 54 (S.C. in banco); *Turner v. York Motors Pty Ltd* (1951) 85 C.L.R. 55.
367. *Sidebotham v. Holland* [1895] 1 Q.B. 378 (C.A.); *Landale v. Menzies* (1909) 9 C.L.R. 89 at 101.
368. "Dwelling-houses" is defined in s. 29.

the tenant is in arrears of rent for at least four weeks. In all cases, the notice to quit must expire at the end of one of the recurring periods of the tenancy.[369] Thus, for example, in the case of a monthly periodic lease where the recurring periods commence on the first day of each month, a notice to quit given on 15 February will not expire until 31 March.[370] As an alternative to the notice to quit procedure, a periodic lease may be determined by forfeiture or by any of the other methods referred to below [10.54]ff. However, in view of the simplicity and effectiveness of the notice to quit procedure, these other methods are seldom invoked in the case of periodic leases.

Although the general rule is that a fixed term lease cannot be prematurely terminated prior to the end of the term by a notice to quit, this rule only applies in the absence of an express provision to the contrary. Thus, it is possible, for example, for the parties to stipulate in the instrument of lease that the ten year fixed term can be terminated after three years by either party on giving six months' notice.[371]

There is no requirement that a notice to quit should be formal.[372] At common law, the notice can be oral,[373] and if written, need not correspond with any particular form.[374] In contrast, the rules as to the contents of the notice are more strict. It has been held that the notice must be expressed clearly and unequivocally.[375] In addition, while the notice need not refer to the specific date on which possession is required, if no date is mentioned the notice must contain a method by which the tenant can calculate the date.[376] In general, although the courts will not declare a notice void for breach of a technicality, the courts will determine the validity of a notice according to whether the notice would be likely to mislead the tenant.[377] The onus of proving that a notice is valid is on the party who serves the notice.[378]

A notice may be given by or to an agent of the other party, provided that the agent has been given the necessary authority.[379] If either party is a corporation, the notice must be addressed to the name of the corporation rather than any of its officers.[380]

---

369. *Amad v. Grant* (1947) 74 C.L.R. 327; *Lemon v. Lardeur* [1946] K.B. 613 (C.A.).
370. This rule does not apply under State residential tenancies legislation. See Chapter 11.
371. *Hankey v. Clavering* [1942] 2 K.B. 326.
372. *W. H. Tuckett & Sons v. Ransom* [1914] V.L.R. 8.
373. *Roe ex d. Dean and Chapter of Rochester v. Pierce* (1809) 2 Camp. 96; 170 E.R. 1093.
374. *Marshall v. Burman (No. 2)* [1961] V.R. 161; *Love v. Chryssoulis* (1977) 16 A.C.T.R. 1.
375. *Gardner v. Ingram* (1889) 61 L.T. 729.
376. See e.g. *Addis v. Burrows* [1948] 1 K.B. 444 (C.A.).
377. *Carradine Properties Ltd v. Aslam* [1976] 1 All E.R. 573.
378. *Lemon v. Lardeur* [1946] K.B. 613 (C.A.).
379. *Freeman v. Hambrook* [1947] V.L.R. 70; *Heyward v. Miles* [1944] V.L.R. 155.
380. *Doe d. Carlisle v. Woodman and Forster* (1807) 8 East. 227; 103 E.R. 329 (K.B.). Cf. *Ex parte Palmer* (1912) 12 S.R. (N.S.W.) 756.

3. Forfeiture

(a) The nature of the right of forfeiture

[10.54]   A right of forfeiture is the right of a landlord in certain circumstances to terminate a lease on the ground that the tenant or her or his assignee has committed a breach of one or more of the terms of the lease.

In the absence of an express provision in the lease, there is a right at common law to forfeit the lease where the tenant breaches one of its express or implied conditions.[381] However, in relation to covenants, at common law there is no such right of forfeiture, the only remedy for the landlord in these circumstances being an action for damages and/or an injunction.[382] This common law rule is subject to two exceptions. First, a right of re-entry for breach of covenant will be implied by equity in agreements for a lease, although only in respect of the non-payment of rent.[383] Secondly, statute law has since intervened and has partially redressed the situation at common law.[384] The extent of these statutory reforms is discussed below. Note in particular that these reforms have no application to general law land in Victoria, South Australia, Western Australia and Tasmania.

Because of the absence of an automatic right of forfeiture in all cases for breach of covenant, most fixed-term leases contain an express forfeiture clause, sometimes referred to as a proviso for re-entry. One commonly found illustration is as follows:

> "If the tenant shall commit a breach of or fail to observe and/or perform any of the conditions or agreements contained or implied in this agreement or fail to pay the rent herein reserved as herein provided whether formally demanded or not notwithstanding the waiver of any previous breach the landlord and/or his agent may re-enter upon the said premises or any part thereof (and for such purpose may break open any inner or outer door or windows without thereby becoming liable for damage trespass assault or otherwise) and expel and remove all persons therefrom and to put an end to this tenancy agreement and in the latter case this agreement may be produced by the landlord or his agent to any person on the premises as a notice to quit duly given and expired."

Such a clause is occasionally also found in periodic leases, where it has a similar effect.[385] The reason why it is used less commonly in respect of periodic leases is that it is usually much simpler and quicker for a landlord

381. *Doe d. Lockwood v. Clarke and Brown* (1807) 8 East. 185; 103 E.R. 313 (K.B.). Modern cases refer to the distinction between essential and non-essential terms of a contract: see e.g. *Associated Newspapers Ltd v. Bancks* (1951) 83 C.L.R. 322.
382. *Bashir v. Commissioner of Lands* [1960] A.C. 44 (P.C.); *Whall v. Bulman* [1953] 2 Q.B. 198 (C.A.); *Sanders v. Wadham* (1870) 4 S.A.L.R. 73.
383. Gray and Symes, p. 406; *Re Brain* (1874) L.R. 18 Eq. 389.
384. See *Conveyancing Act* 1919 (N.S.W.), ss 74, 84, 85; *Transfer of Land Act* 1958 (Vic.), ss 67, 112; *Property Law Act* 1974 (Qld), ss 105-107; *Real Property Act* 1886 (S.A.), ss 124, 125, 262; *Transfer of Land Act* 1893 (W.A.), ss 92, 93, 131; *Land Titles Act* 1980 (Tas.), ss 57, 66, 67.
385. See e.g. *Maley v. Fearn* (1947) 176 L.T. 203 (C.A.).

to terminate a periodic lease by giving a notice to quit than to rely on forfeiture. The only exception to this is in respect of yearly periodic leases which require a minimum of six months' notice.[386]

Forfeiture clauses, however drafted, will be treated as valid provided that they are couched in clear and unambiguous terms.[387] The clause will be construed strictly at common law[388] and no forfeiture will arise unless the terms of the clause are complied with fully.[389]

[10.55] The effect of a forfeiture clause is to render the lease voidable, not void, when a breach of the lease occurs.[390] Thus, the lease remains in effect even after the breach until the landlord exercises his right of re-entry. The lease will be treated as voidable even if the forfeiture clause states that the lease shall be void as soon as the breach occurs.[391] Where a breach occurs and the landlord decides to exercise the right of re-entry, the lease terminates at the time when the landlord unequivocally decides to forfeit the lease. Henceforth, the tenant is regarded at law as a trespasser and is liable to mesne profits rather than rent.[392]

Where the landlord becomes entitled to a right of re-entry, he or she has the right at common law either to exercise a right of peaceful re-entry or to commence an action for possession. In the latter case, re-entry will not occur until the writ is both issued and served. Rent may be claimed up to and including the date of service.[393]

The right of peaceful re-entry has been abolished in respect of residential premises in New South Wales, Victoria, South Australia and Western Australia,[394] but remains available in respect of all other leases. This right entitles the landlord to use self-help to expel a tenant rather than to invoke a remedy from the courts. Pursuant to this right, the landlord may use as much force as is reasonably necessary in order to remove the tenant and his goods from the rented premises, and in so doing the landlord is protected from liability for trespass and/or assault. The major authority on this issue is *Hemmings v. Stoke Poges Golf Club*.[395] In this case, the plaintiff was formerly an employee of the defendant.

---

386. *Sidebotham v. Holland* [1895] 1 Q.B. 378 (C.A.); *Landale v. Menzies* (1909) 9 C.L.R. 89 at 101.
387. See *Richard Clarke & Co. Ltd v. Widnall* (1976) 33 P. & C.R. 339 (C.A.) concerning the absence of any formal requirements as to the drafting of a forfeiture clause.
388. *Doe d. Lloyd v. Powell* (1826) 5 B. & C. 308; 108 E.R. 115 (K.B.); *Doe d. Abby v. Stevens* (1823) 3 B. & Ad. 299; 110 E.R. 112 (K.B.).
389. *Hamilton v. Warne* (1907) 4 C.L.R. 1293.
390. *Massart v. Blight* (1951) 82 C.L.R. 423; *MacIntosh v. Bebarfalds Ltd* (1922) 22 S.R. (N.S.W.) 371; *Quesnel Forks Gold Mining Co. Ltd v. Ward* [1920] A.C. 222 (P.C.).
391. *Roberts v. Davey* (1833) 4 B. & Ad. 664; 110 E.R. 606 (K.B.); *Davenport v. R.* (1877) 3 App. Cas. 115 (P.C.).
392. *Wilson v. Kelly* [1957] V.R. 147; *Elliott v. Boynton* [1924] 1 Ch. 236 (C.A.).
393. *Canas Property Co. Ltd v. K.L. Television Services Ltd* [1970] 2 Q.B. 433 (C.A.).
394. *Landlord and Tenant Act* 1899 (N.S.W.), s. 2AA; *Residential Tenancies Act* 1980 (Vic.), s. 109; *Residential Tenancies Act* 1978 (S.A.), s. 80; *Residential Tenancies Act* 1987 (W.A.), s. 80.
395. [1920] 1 K.B. 720. See also *Housing Commission (N.S.W.) v. Allen* [1967] 1 N.S.W.R. 776 (C.A.); *Aglionby v. Cohen* [1955] 1 All E.R. 785.

When the plaintiff resigned, his licence to occupy a cottage on the defendant's property was determined. On the refusal of the plaintiff to vacate the cottage, the defendant's agent, accompanied by several men, gently pushed the plaintiff from the cottage and carried his wife outside. The agent also removed the plaintiff's furniture and stored it in the adjoining garage. The plaintiff unsuccessfully claimed damages for trespass and assault. The Court of Appeal upheld the existence of the right of peaceful re-entry and held on the facts that no more force had been used than was reasonably necessary to expel the plaintiff from the premises.

The right of peaceful re-entry is seldom invoked in modern times as the landlord, by exercising such a right, although immune from civil liability for damages provided that excessive force is not used, may incur criminal liability for a breach of the peace. The State legislation is similar from State to State and is based on the *Statute of Forcible Entry* 1381 (Imp.). For example, the *Crimes Act* 1958 (Vic.), s. 207, states:[396]

> "No person except where entry is given by the law shall make an entry upon the land in a manner likely to cause a breach of the peace or reasonable apprehension of breach of the peace. Except as aforesaid it is immaterial whether he is entitled to enter upon the land or not."

A maximum penalty of $5,000 or imprisonment for one year or both is prescribed. Lord Denning M.R. stated in *McPhail v. Persons, Names Unknown*[397] that a landlord would always incur criminal liability under the *Statute of Forcible Entry* 1381, however the right of peaceful re-entry was effected and regardless of the degree of force used.

If a landlord institutes an action for possession, he or she may not later curtail the proceedings by exercising a right of peaceful re-entry. This proposition emerges from *Argyle Art Centre Pty Ltd v. Argyle Bond & Free Stores Co. Pty Ltd.*[398] In this case, Needham J. stated that where a landlord has taken proceedings to establish the right to possession, he or she is not entitled, before the right has been upheld in the proceedings, to exercise a right of peaceful re-entry at common law, which depends for its existence upon an affirmative answer to the question whether the former tenant's right to possession has been determined. In so concluding, his Honour distinguished earlier cases where a right of peaceful re-entry was held to be lawful where the landlord's right of possession had been proven and a warrant for possession had already been obtained.

(b) Waiver

[10.56] As a breach of a covenant entitling the landlord to exercise a right of forfeiture will render the lease voidable rather than void, it follows that the landlord has a right of election in each case whether to exercise the right of re-entry. The election does not have to comply with any

---

396. See also *Criminal Law Consolidation Act* 1935 (S.A.), s. 243. In New South Wales, the 1381 U.K. Act is expressly preserved by the *Imperial Acts Application Act* 1969 (N.S.W.), s. 18.
397. [1973] Ch. 447 at 459 (C.A.). See also *R. v. Robinson* [1971] 1 Q.B. 156 (C.A.).
398. [1976] 1 N.S.W.L.R. 377.

formalities; it can be oral or in writing.[399] If the landlord elects not to enforce the right, he or she is said to have waived the breach. At common law under the rule in *Dumpor's Case*[400] a waiver by the landlord of one breach amounted by operation of law to a general waiver of all breaches. However, legislation in modern times has since abrogated this rule, and any waiver nowadays applies only to the particular breach.[401]

A waiver may be made expressly. More commonly, however, it will be implied. Implied waiver has been held to arise where the landlord becomes aware of a breach of covenant entitling her or him to forfeit the lease and where he or she does an unequivocal act recognising the continuance of the relationship of landlord and tenant.[402] The acts of the landlord are not relevant for determining whether waiver has occurred until the landlord becomes aware of the breach, even if this knowledge of the breach does not arise for a long period after the actual breach.[403]

When determining whether on the facts the landlord has waived the right of forfeiture, the courts lean in favour of the conclusion that waiver has occurred. This is because forfeiture is regarded at common law as stricti juris.[404] A well-known illustration of this point is *Moore v. Ullcoats Mining Co. Ltd.*[405] This case concerned a fixed-term lease of certain iron ore mines. The lease contained a covenant by the tenant to allow the landlord and his agents to inspect the mines at all reasonable times, and a proviso for re-entry in the usual form. The successors-in-title of the lessor were refused permission to inspect the mines, whereupon they issued a detailed writ claiming, inter alia, possession, mesne profits and damages. In addition, claim 4 in the writ sought an order permitting inspection of the mines. The inclusion of this clause was held to constitute an equivocal rather than an unequivocal demand for possession. Warrington J. stated:[406]

> "I think the real question that I have to consider is whether this writ is in such a form that it would not have been open to the plaintiffs thereafter, if they had considered that their most convenient course, to ask for relief on the footing of the lease being in existence, and to abandon their claim for possession. I think I am bound to come to the conclusion that this writ was equivocal . . . It seems to me, therefore, that the writ was not an unequivocal demand for possession. I think the writ was so framed that it might have been possible for the plaintiffs, if they had been so minded, to say: 'We will go for the other relief expressed in the writ; we will not go for possession': in other words, I think that the claim for possession and the claim for an injunction and for the order expressed in claim 4 are

---

399. *Brikom Investments Ltd v. Carr* [1979] Q.B. 467 (C.A.).
400. (1601) 4 Co. Rep. 119b; 76 E.R. 1110 (K.B.).
401. General law statutes: N.S.W.: ss 120, 123; Vic.: ss 143, 148; Qld: s. 119; *Landlord and Tenant Act* 1936 (S.A.), s. 47; W.A.: ss 73, 79; Tas.: s. 16.
402. *Matthews v. Smallwood* [1910] 1 Ch. 777; *Fuller's Theatre & Vaudeville Co. Ltd v. Rofe* [1923] A.C. 435 (P.C.); *Davenport v. Smith* [1921] 2 Ch. 270.
403. See Woodfall, para. 1-1108.
404. *Doe d. Lloyd v. Powell* (1826) 5 B. & C. 308; 108 E.R. 115 (K.B.).
405. [1908] 1 Ch. 575.
406. Ibid. at 585.

inconsistent, and therefore the plaintiffs cannot obtain possession in this present action.''

Note, however, that once the landlord has unequivocally treated the lease as forfeited, no subsequent act will constitute a waiver. Thus, for example, in *N.G.L. Properties Pty Ltd v. Harlington Pty Ltd*,[407] the lease was held to be forfeited once the landlord had issued and served a writ of possession; the fact that the landlord later discontinued the action was held to be irrelevant.

[10.57] There are many authorities on the issue as to what constitutes waiver. Delay has been held not to constitute a waiver,[408] nor does mere inaction on the part of the landlord[409] or the service of a notice under s. 146(1) of the *Property Law Act* 1958 (Vic.): see below **[10.60]**.[410] On the other hand, waiver has been held to occur where the landlord executes a lease with knowledge that previous breaches have occurred,[411] where the landlord describes the lessee as her or his tenant,[412] if the landlord issues and serves a notice to quit,[413] or if the landlord institutes any legal proceedings which imply that the lease has not been determined.[414] The most common example of implied waiver is where the landlord accepts or demands rent after he or she has knowledge of a breach of covenant entitling her or him to forfeiture.[415] Waiver will occur by operation of law in this latter situation even if the rent is accepted or demanded without prejudice[416] or if the demand and acceptance occurred as a result of a clerical mistake.[417] In the case of rent payable in advance, however, the receipt of such payment has been held not to deprive the landlord of the right to forfeit the lease if a right of forfeiture later arises during the period for which payment has been made.[418] Further exceptions are where the landlord has already issued and served on the tenant a writ or summons for possession,[419] and where the landlord has merely given the tenant a statement of the amount of rent owing.[420] The parties may agree that the demand and acceptance of rent shall not constitute a waiver; where this

---

407. [1979] V.R. 92. See also *Civil Service Co-operative Society Ltd v. McGrigor's Trustee* [1923] 2 Ch. 347.
408. *Selwyn v. Garfit* (1888) 38 Ch. D. 273 (C.A.).
409. *Perry v. Davis* (1858) 3 C.B. (N.S.) 769; 140 E.R. 945 (C.P.).
410. *Church Commissioners for England v. Nodjoumi* (1986) 51 P. & C.R. 155.
411. *Carson v. Wood* (1884) 10 V.L.R. (L.) 223.
412. *Green's Case* (1582) Cro. Eliz. 3; 78 E.R. 269 (K.B.).
413. *Doe d. Nash v. Birch* (1826) 1 M. & W. 402; 150 E.R. 490 (Exch.).
414. *Evans v. Davis* (1878) 10 Ch. D. 747.
415. See e.g. *Segal Securities Ltd v. Thoseby* [1963] 1 Q.B. 887; *M'Goun v. Smith* (1886) 12 V.L.R. 244. Cf. *Chrisdell Ltd v. Johnson* (1987) 283 E.G. 1553 (C.A.). See also Wilkinson, ''Acceptance of Rent as Surrender'' (1988) 138 N.L.J. 95.
416. *Oak Property Co. Ltd v. Chapman* [1947] K.B. 886 (C.A.); *Davenport v. R.* (1877) 3 App. Cas. 115 (P.C.).
417. *Central Estates (Belgravia) Ltd v. Woolgar (No. 2)* [1972] 1 W.L.R. 1048 (C.A.).
418. *Toogood v. Mills* (1896) 23 V.L.R. 106.
419. *Civil Service Co-operative Society Ltd v. McGrigor's Trustee* [1923] 2 Ch. 347; *Grimwood v. Moss* (1872) L.R. 7 C.P. 360; *Lidsdale Nominees Pty Ltd v. Elkharadly* [1979] V.R. 84.
420. *Inner City Businessmen's Club Ltd v. James Kirkpatrick Ltd* [1975] 1 N.Z.L.R. 636.

occurs, waiver will not occur automatically by operation of law but may still be held to have occurred on the facts at bar.[421]

In the case of continuing breaches of covenant, waiver only applies to past acts of the tenant and those occurring during the period of time in which the landlord knew that the breaches would continue.[422] Any breaches which occur after this time will lead to a further right of forfeiture.

In recent cases, it has been decided that waiver will occur where rent is demanded and accepted by the landlord's agent,[423] even if the landlord instructed the agent not to do so[424] and even if the landlord himself was unaware that a breach of covenant giving rise to a right of forfeiture had occurred.[425] In these circumstances, the landlord would have a remedy in negligence against the agent.

Finally, it should be noted that the issue whether the landlord has waived the right of forfeiture in any particular situation does not affect the right of the landlord in all cases to sue for damages for breach of covenant.[426]

(c) Forfeiture for breach of the covenant to pay rent[427]

[10.58]   A proviso for re-entry in the event of the failure of the tenant to pay rent is expressly included in most leases. If such a clause is not included, no right of forfeiture arises except in the case of agreements for a lease[428] and where the statutory implied covenant discussed above **[10.28]** applies.

At common law, a right of re-entry cannot be exercised unless the landlord first makes a formal demand for the rent.[429] Under this doctrine,[430]

> "the landlord or his authorised agent must demand the exact sum due on the day when it falls due at such convenient hour before sunset as will give time to count out the money, the demand being made upon the demised premises and continuing until sunset."

This common law rule has been modified by statute throughout Australia, as all States have introduced legislation stipulating that re-entry may be effected without formal demand where one half year's rent is in

---

421. *Owendale Pty Ltd v. Anthony* (1967) 117 C.L.R. 539.
422. *Segal Securities Ltd v. Thoseby* [1963] 1 Q.B. 887.
423. *Argyle Art Centre Pty Ltd v. Argyle Bond & Free Stores Co. Pty Ltd* [1976] 1 N.S.W.L.R. 377.
424. *Central Estates (Belgravia) Ltd v. Woolgar (No. 2)* [1972] 1 W.L.R. 1048 (C.A.).
425. *David Blackstone Ltd v. Burnetts (West End) Ltd* [1973] 1 W.L.R. 1487.
426. *Wilson v. Stewart* (1889) 15 V.L.R. 781 (F.C.).
427. Rent may include royalties: *Pioneer Quarries (Sydney) Ltd v. Permanent Trustee Co. of N.S.W. Ltd* (1970) 2 B.P.R. 9562 (N.S.W. Sup. Ct).
428. See above fn. 383 and accompanying text.
429. *Gallic Pty Ltd v. Cynayne Pty Ltd* (1986) 83 F.L.R. 31 (N.T. Sup. Ct); *Hill v. Kempshall* (1849) 7 C.B. 975; 137 E.R. 386.
430. Megarry and Wade, p. 675; referring to 1 Wms. Saund. (1871) pp. 434ff, being Notes to *Duppa v. Mayo* (1669). See also *Gleeson v. Richey* [1959] V.R. 258; *Lo Giudice v. Biviano (No. 1)* [1962] V.R. 412.

arrears.[431] In New South Wales no demand is necessary where the rent is more than one month in arrears.[432] In practice, the doctrine is of little relevance as most forms of lease exempt its operation by including the words "whether formally demanded or not" in the proviso for re-entry.

Provided that the formal demand requirement is satisfied, a right of forfeiture for non-payment of rent may be exercised in all cases where it is available by law or where a proviso for re-entry exists. It has been held that the right may be exercised where the non-payment of rent is due to the tenant's bankruptcy.[433] Once the landlord has exercised the right of re-entry, the tenant will remain liable for any accrued rent owned prior to the forfeiture; this rule applies regardless of the working of the forfeiture clause.[434]

Relief against forfeiture

[10.59] Even though a landlord is entitled to forfeiture or has exercised the right of forfeiture, in certain circumstances the tenant may claim relief against forfeiture. If relief is granted, the landlord will be restrained from regaining possession; if the landlord has already regained possession, the tenant may be reinstated into the premises. Relief in this context was originally the prerogative of equity. The Court of Chancery regarded a forfeiture clause as security for the payment of rent and would usually grant relief against forfeiture wherever the landlord received accrued arrears and costs prior to the making of an order for possession.[435] As stated by Jenkins L.J. in *Gill v. Lewis*:[436]

> "save in exceptional circumstances, the function of the court in exercising this equitable jurisdiction is to grant relief when all that is due for rent and costs has been paid up, and (in general) to disregard any other causes of complaint that the landlord may have against the tenant. The question is whether provided all is paid up, the landlord will not have been fully compensated; and the view taken by the court is that if he gets the whole of his rent and costs, then he has got all he is entitled to so far as rent is concerned, and extraneous matters of breach of covenant, and so forth, are, generally speaking, irrelevant."

The equitable rules have now been consolidated into legislation in each Australian State.[437] This legislation follows the terms of an earlier British enactment and is similar from State to State. Where the tenant pays all

431. *Landlord and Tenant Act* 1899 (N.S.W.), s. 9; *Supreme Court Act* 1986 (Vic.), s. 79; *Property Law Act* 1974 (Qld), s. 108; *Landlord and Tenant Act* 1936 (S.A.), s. 4; *Supreme Court Civil Procedure Act* 1932 (Tas.), s. 11(14).
432. *Conveyancing Act* 1919 (N.S.W.), ss 85(1)(d), 85(2).
433. *Ezekiel v. Orakpo* [1976] 3 All E.R. 659.
434. See *Hartshorne v. Watson* (1838) 4 Bing. N.C. 178; 132 E.R. 756 (K.B.).
435. See *Chandless-Chandless v. Nicholson* [1942] 2 K.B. 321 at 323 (C.A.); *Jam Factory Pty Ltd v. Sunny Paradise Pty Ltd* [1989] V.R. 584 at 590; *Hayes v. Gunbola Pty Ltd* [1986] A.C.L.D. 523 (N.S.W. Sup. Ct).
436. [1956] 2 Q.B. 1 at 13 (C.A.).
437. *Landlord and Tenant Act* 1899 (N.S.W.), ss 8-10; *Supreme Court Act* 1986 (Vic.), ss 79, 80, 85; *Property Law Act* 1974 (Qld), ss 123-128; *Landlord and Tenant Act* 1936 (S.A.), ss 4, 5, 7, 9; *Common Law Procedure Act* 1854 (Tas.), ss 103-185; *Supreme Court Civil Procedure Act* 1932 (Tas.), s. 11(14).

arrears of rent and costs into court or to the landlord at any time before the hearing for the recovery of possession, all further proceedings in the action shall cease. This is a mandatory provision and is not subject to the court's discretion. If the tenant does not pay all rent arrears and costs prior to the hearing, the legislation gives the court a discretion to grant relief on equitable grounds to the tenant within six months after the judgment of the court is executed.[438] After the six month period, relief may not be granted in any circumstances.[439]

Where the court is granted a discretion in this matter, it is usually exercised in the tenant's favour.[440] However, following normal equitable principles, in exceptional circumstances relief against forfeiture may be denied. Past instances have occurred where the six month period after re-entry has almost expired and the landlord had agreed to let the premises to a third party,[441] where the tenant was shown to be unable to make future rental payments even if the present rental could be paid,[442] where the tenant was found to be insolvent,[443] and where the tenant had failed in the past to take care of the premises.[444] In appropriate circumstances, relief may be granted only on specified terms or conditions.[445]

The statutory rules as to relief against forfeiture for non-payment of rent appear to have a wide application. It has been held that relief against forfeiture extends to tenants holding possession pursuant to an agreement for a lease rather than a lease[446] and to cases where the landlord exercises the right of peaceful re-entry.[447]

The final issue is the relevance of the above rules to Torrens land. In each State, the legislation requires the Registrar of Titles to enter a memorandum in the register book where a right of re-entry is exercised. For example, the *Transfer of Land Act* 1958 (Vic.), s. 70 states:[448]

"The Registrar upon proof to his satisfaction—

(a) of recovery of possession of the leased premises by the lessor or by any legal proceeding;

(b) that the lessor has re-entered upon the leased premises in strict conformity with the provisions for re-entry contained or implied in the lease; or

---

438. At equity, prior to the legislation, there was no six month limitation: *Bowser v. Colby* (1841) 1 Hare 109; 66 E.R. 969 (V.-C.).
439. See *Dennis and Copley v. Eddie* [1952] V.L.R. 92.
440. *Jam Factory Pty Ltd v. Sunny Paradise Pty Ltd* [1989] V.R. 584.
441. *Re Catholic Supplies Ltd and Jones* [1922] N.Z.L.R. 196 (S.C. in banco); *Stanhope v. Haworth* (1886) 3 T.L.R. 34 (C.A.).
442. *Direct Food Supplies (Vic.) Pty Ltd v. D.L.V. Pty Ltd* [1975] V.R. 358.
443. *Inner City Businessmen's Club Ltd v. James Kirkpatrick Ltd* [1975] 2 N.Z.L.R. 636. Cf. *Greenwood Village Pty Ltd v. Tom the Cheap (W.A.) Pty Ltd* [1976] W.A.R. 49.
444. *Stieper v. Deviot Pty Ltd* (1977) 2 B.P.R. 9602 (N.S.W.C.A.).
445. See e.g. *Belgravia Insurance Co. Ltd v. Meah* [1964] 1 Q.B. 436; *Newbolt v. Bingham* (1895) 72 L.T. 852 (C.A.).
446. *Greenwood Village Pty Ltd v. Tom the Cheap (W.A.) Pty Ltd* [1976] W.A.R. 49.
447. *Howard v. Fanshawe* [1895] 2 Ch. 581.
448. See also Torrens statutes: N.S.W.: s. 55; S.A.: s. 126; Qld: s. 72; W.A.: ss 96, 104; Tas.: s. 68.

(c) that the lessee has abandoned the leased premises and the lease and that the lessor has thereupon re-entered upon and occupied the premises by himself or tenants undisturbed by the lessee—

shall enter a memorandum thereof in the Register Book, whereupon the lease shall determine without prejudice to any action or cause of action previously commenced or accrued in respect of any breach or non-observance of any covenant expressed or implied in the lease.''

The issue arises whether relief against forfeiture for non-payment of rent may be granted where a memorandum has already been entered. The issue was answered in the affirmative in New South Wales in *Brooker's Colours Ltd v. Sproules*,[449] although in respect of the South Australian legislation the Privy Council stated in *Laffer v. Gillen*[450] that once a memorandum had been entered in the register book the validity of the forfeiture cannot be questioned, for the statute provides that the estate of the tenant shall thereupon determine. In the absence of further authority, the matter must be considered unresolved. Whalan[451] cites a New Zealand authority, *Maori Trustee v. Kahuroa*,[452] as authority for the proposition that relief cannot be granted if the notification of re-entry is followed by the registration of a new lease to a third party.

(d) Forfeiture for breach of covenants other than the convenant to pay rent

[10.60] The proviso for re-entry commonly found in most leases applies equally to covenants other than the covenant to pay rent. If such a clause is not included, no right of forfeiture arises except in the case of agreements for a lease and where the statutory implied covenant discussed above **[10.29]** applies.

Unlike in the case of forfeiture for non-payment of rent, no formal demand is necessary before the right of forfeiture can be exercised. However, based on legislation in all States, the landlord must first serve a notice containing specified particulars on the tenant. The legislation is based on earlier United Kingdom legislation and is similar (although not identical) in all States. For example, the *Property Law Act* 1958 (Vic.), s. 146(1) states:[453]

''A right of re-entry or forfeiture under any proviso or stipulation in a lease for a breach of any covenant or condition in the lease shall not be enforceable, by action or otherwise, unless and until the lessor serves on the lessee a notice—

(a) specifying the particular breach complained of; and

(b) if the breach is capable of remedy, requiring the lessee to remedy the breach; and

449. (1910) 10 S.R. (N.S.W.) 839.
450. (1927) 40 C.L.R. 86. See also *Hill v. Short* [1910] S.A.S.R. 141.
451. Whalan, p. 201.
452. [1956] N.Z.L.R. 713.
453. See also general law statutes: N.S.W.: s. 129(1); Qld: s. 124(1); *Landlord and Tenant Act* 1936 (S.A.), s. 10; W.A.: s. 81(1); Tas.: s. 15(1).

(c) in any case, requiring the lessee to make compensation in money for the breach—

and the lessee fails, within a reasonable time thereafter, or the time not being less than fourteen days fixed by the lease to remedy the breach, if it is capable of remedy, and to make reasonable compensation in money, to the satisfaction of the lessor, for the breach.''

This requirement for a notice acts as a form of protection for the tenant in that it enables the tenant to consider the issue before a right of re-entry is exercised and to determine whether he or she wishes to make compensation in order to avoid the landlord prematurely terminating the lease.[454] Where there are two or more tenants, the statutory notice must be served on each one.[455]

There are a number of exceptions to the operation of this legislation. Excepted from its scope in all States are covenants relating to the non-payment of rent[456] and (in New South Wales, Victoria and Queensland) covenants in a mining lease allowing the landlord to have access to or to inspect books and accounts or to enter or inspect the mine or its workings.[457] In all States except South Australia conditions of forfeiture on the bankruptcy of the tenant or on taking in execution of the tenant's interest as specified leases are also excepted.[458] This latter exception recognises that on the bankruptcy of the tenant or where the tenant's interest is taken in execution, in respect of certain leases it is vital for the landlord to recover her or his interest. The relevant specified leases are leases of (a) agricultural or pastoral land, (b) mines or minerals, (c) a home used or intended to be used as licensed premises, (d) a house let as a dwelling-house with the use of any furniture, books, works of art or other chattels not being in the nature of fixtures, and (e) any property with respect to which the personal qualifications of the tenant are of importance for the preservation of the value or character of the property, or on the ground of neighbourhood to the landlord, or to any person holding under her or him.

The legislation in all States operates notwithstanding any provision to the contrary in the lease.[459] A number of past attempts by landlords to circumvent the requirement for a notice have been thwarted by the courts. For example, in *Holden v. Blaiklock*[460] the fixed-term lease gave the landlord an option to convert the lease into a periodic lease in the event of a breach by the tenant of any of the covenants. It was held that the exercise by the landlord of this option would amount to a forfeiture within

---

454. *Horsey Estate Ltd v. Steiger* [1899] 2 Q.B. 79 at 91 (C.A.), per Lord Russell C.J.
455. *Blewett v. Blewett* [1936] 2 All E.R. 188 (C.A.).
456. N.S.W.: s. 129(8); Vic.: s. 146(12); Qld: s. 124(7); *Landlord and Tenant Act* 1936 (S.A.), s. 12(5); W.A.: s. 81(9); Tas.: s. 15(7).
457. N.S.W.: s. 129(6)(d); Vic.: s. 146(8); Qld: s. 124(6)(d).
458. N.S.W.: s. 129(6)(e); Vic.: s. 146(9); Qld: s. 124(6)(c); W.A.: s. 81(8)(b); Tas.: s. 15(6).
459. N.S.W.: s. 129(10); Vic.: s. 146(13); Qld: s. 124(9); *Landlord and Tenant Act* 1936 (S.A.), s. 12(6); W.A.: s. 81(10); Tas.: s. 15(8).
460. [1974] 2 N.S.W.L.R. 262.

the meaning of the legislation. A further illustration is *Plymouth Corporation v. Harvey*.[461] In this case, the tenant was required to execute a deed of surrender to be held in escrow by a solicitor on the condition that he would deliver it to the landlord if the tenant had not performed certain obligations under specified covenants within an agreed time. Plowman J. held that the deed was void in that it infringed the legislation, and should be regarded as a forfeiture in the guise of a surrender.

[10.61] There are many authorities concerning the contents of a notice. In general, the purpose of the legislation is to inform the tenant as to what he or she is required to do, and the notice must give the tenant sufficient details of the alleged breach of covenant in order to fulfil this purpose.[462] The major Australian authority is *Gerraty v. McGavin*,[463] where the High Court, in the case of an alleged breach of covenant to repair, held that it is not sufficient for the notice merely to state that there has been a breach of the covenant; rather, the notice must state the condition of the premises. Any ambiguity in the notice will result in it being declared void. Thus, for example, a notice was held void where it required the tenant to remove a structure without referring to which of two possible structures it concerned.[464] A fortiori, a notice referring to a breach of the wrong covenant or to a breach of a covenant not included in the lease will be invalid.[465]

Section 146(1)(b) of the *Property Law Act* 1958 (Vic.) (and its equivalent in the other States)[466] requires the court to determine which breaches are capable of remedy. The English Court of Appeal has recently held that this question depends on whether the harm suffered by the landlord by the relevant breach is capable of being remedied in practical terms.[467] A breach of a positive covenant, whether continuous or once and for all, is distinguishable from a breach of a negative covenant, and is ordinarily capable of remedy provided that the remedy is carried out within a reasonable time. What is a reasonable time depends on the circumstances of each case.[468] According to one view, all negative covenants are incapable of remedy.[469] However, this view has been disapproved and appears to be expressed too widely.[470] Again, each case must be determined on its facts. In the past, the following breaches of covenant have been held to be incapable of remedy: using the premises as a gaming

---

461. [1971] 1 W.L.R. 549.
462. *Fox v. Jolly* [1916] 1 A.C. 1 (H.L.); *Fletcher v. Nokes* [1897] 1 Ch. 271.
463. (1914) 18 C.L.R. 152.
464. *Davenport v. Smith* [1921] 2 Ch. 270. Cf. *Guillemard v. Silverthorne* (1908) 99 L.T. 584.
465. *Jacob v. Down* [1900] 2 Ch. 156.
466. See above, fn. 453.
467. *Expert Clothing Service & Sales Ltd v. Hillgate House Ltd* [1986] 1 Ch. 340 (C.A.).
468. Ibid. at 355.
469. See e.g. *Hoffman v. Fineberg* [1949] Ch. 245 at 254 per Harman J.; *Rugby School (Governors) v. Tannahill* [1934] 1 K.B. 695 (at first instance).
470. *Rugby School (Governors) v. Tannahill* [1935] 1 K.B. 87 (C.A.); *Bass Holdings Ltd v. Morton Music Ltd* [1988] 1 Ch. 493.

house,[471] or for immoral purposes,[472] breaching the licensing laws,[473] and (after earlier doubts) assigning or subletting without obtaining the landlord's prior consent.[474] Where the breach is irremediable, the notice need not require the tenant to remedy the breach, although the remainder of the procedure must be followed.[475]

The final requirement of the notice is the compensation requirement. Regardless of whether the breach of covenant is capable of remedy, it has been held that a notice will never be void for failure to include a reference to the payment of compensation as the landlord need not claim compensation if he does not require it.[476]

In all States, the legislation states that the tenant must be given "a reasonable time" after the service of the notice to remedy the breach, if it is capable of remedy, and to make reasonable compensation.[477] In Victoria, the legislation contains the additional words "or the time being not less than fourteen days fixed by the lease". The effect of this additional clause appears to be that the necessary period of time will be that specified in the lease, provided that it is a minimum of 14 days, regardless of whether it is a reasonable time;[478] if a lease does not fix a period of time, the time will be what the court considers to be "a reasonable time". The courts have held that where the breach is capable of remedy, a "reasonable time" will usually be three months.[479] Where the breach is not capable of remedy, the tenant is allowed a certain time to consider her or his position; in these circumstances, 14 days has been held to be sufficient[480] and two days has been held to be insufficient.[481] The courts will resist any attempt by the landlord to reduce the time considered reasonable; thus, in *Dogan v. Morton*,[482] where a notice required a breach of covenant to be remedied within a reasonable time "which is seven days from the date hereof" the seven day period was disregarded as surplusage.

471. *Hoffman v. Fineberg* [1949] Ch. 245.
472. *British Petroleum Pension Trust Ltd v. Behrendt* (1986) 52 P. & C.R. 117 (C.A.); *Egerton v. Esplanade Hotels London Ltd* [1947] 2 All E.R. 88; *Borthwick-Norton v. Romney Warwick Estates Ltd* [1950] 1 All E.R. 798; *Rugby School (Governors) v. Tannahill* [1935] 1 K.B. 87 (C.A.). Cf. *Dunraven Securities Ltd v. Holloway* (1982) 264 E.G. 709 (C.A.).
473. *Bickerton's Aerodromes Ltd v. Young* (1958) 108 L.J. 218.
474. *Scala House & District Property Co. Ltd v. Forbes* [1974] Q.B. 575 (C.A.); *Johnson v. Senes and Berger* [1961] N.S.W.R. 566. Cf. *Batson v. De Carvalho* (1948) 48 S.R. (N.S.W.) 417.
475. *Central Estates (Belgravia) Ltd v. Woolgar (No. 2)* [1972] 1 W.L.R. 1048 (C.A.); *Hoffman v. Fineberg* [1949] Ch. 245; *Horsey Estate Ltd v. Steiger* [1899] 2 Q.B. 79 (C.A.).
476. *Rugby School (Governors) v. Tannahill* [1935] 1 K.B. 87 (C.A.).
477. N.S.W.: s. 129(1); Vic.: s. 146(1); Qld: s. 124(1); *Landlord and Tenant Act 1936* (S.A.), s. 10; W.A.: s. 81(1); Tas.: s. 15(1).
478. See *Re Automotive & General Industries Ltd's Lease* (unreported, Vic. Sup. Ct, Adam J., 1 May 1970).
479. *Penton v. Barnett* [1898] 1 Q.B. 276 (C.A.).
480. *Civil Service Co-operative Society Ltd v. McGrigor's Trustee* [1923] 2 Ch. 347; *Scala House & District Property Co. Ltd v. Forbes* [1974] Q.B. 575 (C.A.).
481. *Horsey Estate Ltd v. Steiger* [1899] 2 Q.B. 79 (C.A.).
482. (1935) 35 S.R. (N.S.W.) 142.

Relief against forfeiture

[10.62] As in the case of non-payment of rent, relief against forfeiture may be granted by the courts in respect of all leases falling within the scope of s. 146 of the *Property Law Act* 1958 (Vic.) (or its equivalent in the other States). This relief also extends to subtenants (see below **[10.64]**). The relevant legislation in each State reads as follows:[483]

> "Where a lessor is proceeding, by action or otherwise, to enforce or has enforced without the aid of the Court or the county court such a right of re-entry or forfeiture, the lessee may, in the lessor's action (if any) or in any action brought by himself, or upon summons apply to the Court or a judge thereof for relief; and the Court or judge may grant or refuse relief, as the Court or judge, having regard to the proceedings and conduct of the parties under the foregoing provisions of this section, and to all the other circumstances thinks fit; and in case of relief may grant it on such terms (if any) as to costs, expenses, damages, compensation, penalty or otherwise, including the granting of an injunction to restrain any like breach in the future, as the Court or judge, in the circumstances of each case, thinks fit."

The argument that in addition to this legislation the court still has an equitable jurisdiction to grant relief in any circumstances in which the statutory jurisdiction is not available has recently been rejected in England by Walton J. in *Smith v. Metropolitan City Properties Ltd.*[484] In Australia, however, the Full Court of the Supreme Court of Western Australia has held to the contrary in *Esther Investments Pty Ltd v. Cherrywood Park Pty Ltd.*[485] The Australian court relied for its decision on English authorities which were distinguished by Walton J.[486] As the Australian court gave its decision prior to the most recent English case, the issue must be considered to be unsettled.

As the relevant legislation refers to forfeiture "under any proviso or stipulation in a lease", it follows that relief against forfeiture is not available where the tenant denies the landlord's title.[487] For a similar reason, adverse possessors cannot claim relief against forfeiture.[488]

Different time limits during which relief may be sought apply to breaches of covenants other than the covenant to pay rent. The rule in the present context is that the tenant must seek relief against forfeiture prior to the court order for possession.[489] The court is unable to grant relief after actual re-entry by the landlord. This conclusion follows from the relevant wording: "Where a lessor *is proceeding* . . . to enforce . . . such a right of re-entry or forfeiture" (emphasis added).

483. N.S.W.: s. 129(2); Vic.: s. 146(2); Qld: s. 124(2); *Landlord and Tenant Act* 1936 (S.A.), s. 11; W.A.: s. 81(2); Tas.: s. 15(2).
484. *Smith v. Metropolitan City Properties Ltd* (1986) 227 E.G. 753; discussed in (1986) 130 Sol. J. 136.
485. [1986] W.A.R. 279.
486. *Shiloh Spinners Ltd v. Harding* [1973] A.C. 691 (H.L.); *Abbey National Building Society v. Maybeech Ltd* [1985] Ch. 190.
487. *Warner v. Sampson* [1958] 1 Q.B. 404.
488. *Tickner v. Buzzacott* [1965] Ch. 426.
489. *Rogers v. Rice* [1892] 2 Ch. 170 (C.A.); *Lock v. Pearce* [1893] 2 Ch. 271; *Quilter v. Mapleson* (1882) 9 Q.B.D. 672.

Earlier attempts by the courts to lay down guidelines or principles which the courts should follow in determining how to exercise their jurisdiction have been disapproved,[490] and it has been held that the discretion is wide and unfettered.[491] In practice, it is a rare case where relief is denied to a tenant who applies within the specified time period provided that the tenant remedies the breach and pays the landlord's costs.[492] The courts appear to be even more willing to grant relief in these circumstances than in respect of a breach of the covenant to pay rent.[493] Relief has been refused in the past in respect of negative covenants, such as a breach of the covenant not to use the premises for immoral purposes.[494] Even here, however, relief has occasionally been granted in the past.[495] Relief was also refused in *Earl Bathurst v. Fine*[496] on the basis that the lease was one in which the personal qualifications of the tenant were important for the preservation of the value of the property and the tenant had been shown to be an unfit person to be a tenant of the property.

It is usual for the court to make relief against forfeiture conditional on the tenant paying all the landlord's costs.[497] Although rarely done, it is possible for the courts to impose other conditions upon the tenant when granting her or him relief against forfeiture.[498] It is a matter for the tenant whether to accept the terms. The tenant may withdraw the claim for relief if he or she is unwilling to abide by the conditions.[499]

(e) Denial of title

[10.63] If at any stage during the term of a lease a tenant denies the landlord's title, the lease is determinable by way of forfeiture at the election of the landlord.[500] This ground of forfeiture does not apply in respect of oral denials of title by tenants holding under a fixed-term lease,[501] but appears to apply in respect of all categories of periodic leases.[502] As in respect of all other grounds of forfeiture, the landlord may waive the disclaimer, in which case the right of forfeiture will be lost.[503]

490. See the general principles enunciated by Cozens-Hardy M.R. in *Rose v. Spicer* [1911] 2 K.B. 234 at 241-242 (C.A.).
491. *Hyman v. Rose* [1912] A.C. 623 (H.L.).
492. See e.g. *Earl Bathurst v. Fine* [1974] 1 W.L.R. 905 (C.A.).
493. See e.g. *Central Estates (Belgravia) Ltd v. Woolgar (No. 2)* [1972] 1 W.L.R. 1048 (C.A.).
494. *Borthwick-Norton v. Romney Warwick Estates Ltd* [1950] 1 All E.R. 362.
495. *Central Estates (Belgravia) Ltd v. Woolgar (No. 2)* [1972] 1 W.L.R. 1048 (C.A.).
496. [1974] 1 W.L.R. 905 (C.A.).
497. *Langley v. Foster* (1909) 10 S.R. (N.S.W.) 54.
498. See e.g. *Platt v. Ong* [1972] V.R. 197; *Duke of Westminster v. Swinton* [1948] 1 K.B. 524; *McIvor v. Donald* [1984] 2 N.Z.L.R. 487 (C.A.).
499. *Talbot v. Blindell* [1908] 2 K.B. 114.
500. See e.g. *Re Teller Home Furnishers Pty Ltd* [1967] V.R. 313; *Scanlon v. Campbell* (1911) 11 S.R. (N.S.W.) 239. Cf. *Australian Safeway Stores Pty Ltd v. Toorak Village Development Pty Ltd* [1974] V.R. 268.
501. *Doe d. Graves v. Wells* (1839) 10 Ad. & E. 427; 113 E.R. 162 (K.B.).
502. See *Wisbech St Mary Parish Council v. Lilley* [1956] 1 W.L.R. 121 (C.A.).
503. *Warner v. Sampson* [1959] 1 Q.B. 297 (C.A.); *Sydney Real Estate & Investment Co. Pty Ltd v. Rich* (1957) 74 W.N. (N.S.W.) 427; *Douglas & Co. (Insurance) Pty Ltd v. Economic Insurance Co. Ltd* (1951) 68 W.N. (N.S.W.) 225.

The State legislation cited above **[10.60]** providing for relief against forfeiture for breach of covenant is expressed to apply to forfeiture "under any proviso or stipulation in a lease". Accordingly, as denial of title is a common law concept, no relief against forfeiture is available in this context.[504]

(f) Protection of subtenants and mortgagees

[10.64] At common law, whenever a head lease is determined the sublease is simultaneously determined by operation of law.[505] In modern times, however, State legislation has intervened to safeguard the position of subtenants in certain circumstances where the head lease is determined.[506] The legislation, which is similar although not identical in each State, stipulates that where a landlord is proceeding by action or otherwise to enforce or has enforced a right of re-entry or forfeiture for breach of any covenant, including the covenant to pay rent, the court may, on the application of a subtenant, make an order vesting in the subtenant a leasehold estate for the whole term of the lease or any less term.[507] The leasehold estate may be granted on such conditions as the court may think fit in the circumstances of each case. In no case shall the subtenant be entitled to require a lease to be granted to her or him for any longer term than the subtenant had under the original sublease. This provision is sufficiently wide to include a mortgagee, if the mortgage is by sublease or legal charge.[508] Relief will not be granted to a subtenant in the absence of proof that he or she has acted reasonably and has not participated in the tenant's breach of covenant.[509] In general, the court's discretion will be granted sparingly because it thrusts upon the landlord a person whom he or she has never accepted as tenant and creates in invitum a privity of contract between them.[510] Thus, for example, in *Hill v. Griffin*[511] the court refused relief to the subtenant as he was unwilling to enter into a similar covenant to repair as under the forfeited head lease.

A further form of protection for subtenants applicable in all jurisdictions is the common law rule that if the head tenant is granted relief against forfeiture, the sublease is revived in its entirety by operation of law. The court does, however, retain a discretion to grant relief to a tenant without reviving a sublease if the court is satisfied that the breach of covenant was caused by the subtenant.[512]

504. *Warner v. Sampson* [1959] 1 Q.B. 297 (C.A.).
505. *Great Western Rly Co. v. Smith* (1876) 2 Ch. D. 235 (C.A.). See also *G.M.S. Syndicate Ltd v. Gary Elliott Ltd* [1982] Ch. 1 at 10 per Nourse J.
506. N.S.W.: s. 130; Vic.: s. 146(4); Qld: s. 125; W.A.: s. 125; Tas.: s. 15(3). Cf. *Landlord and Tenant Act* 1936 (S.A.), s. 12.
507. *Hammersmith & Fulham London B.C. v. Top Shop Centres Ltd* [1989] 2 All E.R. 655.
508. *Re Good's Lease* [1954] 1 W.L.R. 309; *Grand Junction Co. Ltd v. Bates* [1954] 2 Q.B. 160; *Chelsea Estates Investment Trust Co. Ltd v. Marche* [1955] Ch. 328.
509. *Imray v. Oakshette* [1897] 2 Q.B. 218 (C.A.).
510. *Creery v. Summersell and Flowerdew & Co. Ltd* [1949] Ch. 751 at 767 per Harman J.; *Hill v. Griffin* (1987) 282 E.G. 85 at 86 (C.A.) per Slade L.J.
511. (1987) 282 E.G. 85 (C.A.).
512. *G.M.S. Syndicate Ltd v. Gary Elliott Ltd* [1982] Ch. 1.

In *Ladup Ltd v. Williams and Glyn's Bank*,[513] relief was granted to an equitable chargee, who had no interest in the lease entitling him to possession. The rationale for this decision was that there is no fetter on the jurisdiction of courts of equity to grant relief against forfeiture where the object of the right to forfeit was to secure the payment of money. Thus, the principle that relief against forfeiture will be granted in equity if it is unconscionable for the landlord to insist on the right to forfeit a lease applies regardless of the identity of the person to whose detriment the forfeiture would operate. Note that this decision is only valid on the assumption that the court still has an equitable relief to grant relief against forfeiture in any circumstances in which the statutory jurisdiction is not available. This issue is discussed above [10.62].

4. Surrender

[10.65]   Surrender has been described as "a species of merger which occurs when a lessee gives up his leasehold interest to his immediate lessor and the lessor accepts it".[514] The essential elements are the offer by the tenant to terminate the lease and the acceptance of that offer by the landlord. Where this occurs, the lease is extinguished.

A surrender may be created expressly or may arise by operation of law. In respect of express surrenders, the State legislation requires a deed or assurance to be executed, even in the case of oral leases.[515] However, under the rule in *Walsh v. Lonsdale*,[516] (see above [10.06]) where the surrender is oral and value is given, the surrender will be effective if the tenant can adduce evidence of part performance or an informal written agreement.

Surrender by operation of law is based on estoppel by conduct[517] and arises wherever the parties, by their conduct, show an intention to treat the lease as terminated, and where it would be inequitable for them to continue to treat the lease as valid.[518] The most obvious illustration of this is where the landlord, with the existing tenant's consent, grants a new lease of the premises to a third party.[519] This situation must be distinguished from an assignment of the lease by the existing tenant, where surrender is an irrelevant issue.[520] Other illustrations are where the

---

513. [1985] 2 All E.R. 577.
514. Helmore, *The Law of Real Property in New South Wales* (2nd ed., Sydney, 1966), p. 107.
515. General law statutes: N.S.W.: s. 23B(1); Vic.: s. 52(1); Qld: s. 10(1); S.A.: s. 28(1); W.A.: s. 33(1); Tas.: s. 60(1).
516. (1882) 21 Ch. D. 9 (C.A.).
517. *Robinson v. Kingsmill* (1954) 71 W.N. (N.S.W.) 127; *Wallis v. Hands* [1893] 2 Ch. 75; *Lyon v. Reed* (1844) 13 M. & W. 285; 153 E.R. 118 (Exch.).
518. *Steve Christenson & Co. Ltd v. Furs & Fashions (N.Z.) Ltd* [1971] N.Z.L.R. 129; *Foster v. Robinson* [1951] 1 K.B. 149 (C.A.); *Nickells v. Atherstone* (1847) 10 Q.B. 944; 116 E.R. 358 (K.B.). There is no requirement for a deed in respect of surrenders by operation of law: N.S.W.: s. 23B(2)(c); Vic.: s. 52(2)(c); Qld: s. 10(2)(b); S.A.: s. 28(2)(c); W.A.: s. 33(2)(c); Tas.: s. 60(1)(c).
519. *Metcalfe v. Boyce* [1927] 1 K.B. 758; *Wallis v. Hands* [1893] 2 Ch. 75; *Maridakis v. Kouvaris* (1974) 5 A.L.R. 197.
520. See e.g. *Ahern v. L. A. Wilkinson Ltd* [1929] St. R. Qd 66.

landlord grants a fresh lease during the term of the lease for a shorter or longer fixed-term period,[521] or where the tenant abandons the premises or leaves by agreement and the landlord re-enters the premises.[522] Note, however, that mere abandonment by the tenant without re-entry by the landlord will not constitute surrender.[523] The mere giving up of the keys to the premises to the landlord,[524] and the signing by the tenant of a contract to purchase the reversion[525] have also been held not to amount to a surrender by operation of law.

Surrender has been held to apply to both fixed-term and periodic leases, although not to tenancies at will, as although these may be abandoned, there is no term which can be surrendered.[526] In the absence of authority, tenancies at sufferance presumably cannot be surrendered for the same reason.

Leek and Moorlands Building Society v. Clark[527] is authority for the proposition that in the case of two or more joint tenants, all the tenants must join in the surrender before the surrender will be valid. Any purported act of surrender by one tenant without the authority of the others will be insufficient to determine the lease.

Even where a surrender occurs the tenant will remain liable for any breach of covenant which has occurred prior to that time. All future liability under the covenants is extinguished, however.[528]

Finally, the application of the doctrine of surrender to Torrens land must be considered.[529]

A universal feature of the Torrens statutes is that except in the case of the bankruptcy of the tenant, no lease subject to a mortgage or charge can be surrendered without the written consent of the mortgagee, encumbrancee or chargee.[530] Subject to this rule, surrender of a registered lease can be effected as follows. In Victoria, Queensland and Western Australia, the Torrens statutes state that "a registered lease may be surrendered and determined by the word 'surrendered' and the date being endorsed on the duplicate and signed by the lessee and lessor".[531] In New South Wales and South Australia[532] surrender will occur on the

---

521. *Knight v. Williams* [1901] 1 Ch. 256; *Fenner v. Blake* [1900] 1 Q.B. 426.
522. *Buchanan v. Byrnes* (1906) 3 C.L.R. 704; *Robinson v. Kingsmill* (1954) 71 W.N. (N.S.W.) 127.
523. *Spinks v. Mundy* [1957] St. R. Qd 234; *Andrews v. Hogan* (1952) 86 C.L.R. 223.
524. *Siggers v. Scott* (1951) 68 W.N. (N.S.W.) 131; *Oastler v. Henderson* (1877) 2 Q.B.D. 575 (C.A.).
525. *Nightingale v. Courtney* [1954] 1 Q.B. 399 (C.A.).
526. *Chelsea Investments Pty Ltd v. F.C.T.* (1966) 115 C.L.R. 1.
527. [1952] 2 Q.B. 788 (C.A.). See also *Greenwich London B.C. v. McGrady* (1983) 46 P. & C.R. 223 (C.A.).
528. *Richmond v. Savill* [1926] 2 K.B. 530 (C.A.); *Dalton v. Pickard* [1926] 2 K.B. 545n (C.A.).
529. See generally Whalan, pp. 195ff.
530. Torrens statutes: N.S.W.: s. 54(5); Vic.: s. 69(1); Qld: s. 54; S.A.: s. 123; W.A.: s. 98; Tas.: s. 65(3). In New South Wales and Queensland, the legislation does not require the consent to be in writing, but according to Whalan, p. 196 it is required in practice.
531. Vic.: s. 69(1); Qld: s. 54; W.A.: s. 98.
532. N.S.W.: s. 54(1); S.A.: s. 120.

registration of a surrender and in Tasmania[533] the registration of a memorandum of surrender.[534] In all States the legislation provides that the Registrar shall enter in the Register Book and on the duplicate lease (if any) a memorandum of the surrender, whereupon the tenant's interest shall vest in the landlord.[535]

The provisions relating to the application of the doctrine of surrender by operation of law to Torrens land are less clear. The most straightforward provision is the *Transfer of Land Act* 1893 (W.A.), s. 98, which states in part that "a lease made under this Act may be surrendered and determined as well by operation of law". In Victoria, the provision relating to express surrender commences "[w]ithout affecting any other method of determining the operation thereof",[536] which is presumably referring indirectly to surrender by operation of law. A similar implication appears to arise in New South Wales and Queensland,[537] where the section on express surrender of a registered lease uses the words "and the surrender thereof is effected otherwise than through the operation of a surrender in law". The only real doubt is in respect of South Australia and Tasmania where no direct or indirect mention is made of surrender by operation of law; in these States the relevance of the principle to Torrens land is unsettled.

5. Merger

[10.66] A merger arises where the leasehold estate and the leasehold reversion become vested in the same person in the same right.[538] Wherever this occurs, the lease is immediately determined at common law by operation of law. The most obvious illustrations of merger are where the tenant acquires the reversion in the property or where the landlord acquires the lease. Note that merger will not occur where the lease and the reversion are held by one person but in different capacities.[539] An illustration of this is where the lease is held by the one person in a personal capacity and the reversion in his capacity as executor (or vice versa). Merger will also fail to occur where there is an intervening estate between the lease and the reversion, regardless of the length of this estate.[540]

Each State has similar but not identical legislation relating to the interrelationship of legal and equitable rules relating to merger. The Victorian legislation reads:[541]

> "There shall be no merger by operation of law only of any estate the beneficial interest in which would not be deemed to be merged or extinguished in equity."

533. Tas.: s. 65.
534. See the additional alternative procedure stipulated in S.A.: s. 121.
535. N.S.W.: ss 54(2), (3); Vic.: s. 69(2); Qld: s. 54; S.A.: ss 120, 122; W.A.: s. 98; Tas.: s. 65(2).
536. Vic.: s. 69(1).
537. N.S.W.: s. 54(1); Qld: s. 54.
538. *Rye v. Rye* [1962] A.C. 496 (H.L.); *Herman v. Gill* (1921) 24 W.A.L.R. 10.
539. *Chambers v. Kingham* (1878) 10 Ch. D. 743.
540. *Burton v. Barclay and Perkins* (1831) 7 Bing. 745; 131 E.R. 288 (C.P.).
541. General law statutes: N.S.W.: s. 10; Vic.: s. 185; Qld: s. 17; S.A.: s. 13; W.A.: s. 18. There does not appear to be a similar provision in Tasmania.

The effect of this provision is to allow the court to determine whether the parties intended a merger to occur as a result of their actions. The legislation effectively abolishes the common law rule pursuant to which merger occurred regardless of intention, and substitutes the equitable rule that merger is a matter of intention, and will not be held to have occurred in the absence of direct evidence of intention if it is to the interest of the party acquiring both the lease and the reversion that the merger should not take place.[542]

Further legislation in each State reads:[543]

> "Where a reversion expectant on a lease of land is surrendered or merged, the estate or interest which as against the lessee for the time being confers the next vested right to the land shall be deemed the reversion for the purpose of preserving the same incidents and obligations as would have affected the orginal reversion had there been no surrender or merger thereof."

This legislation effectively ensures that the rights and duties of a subtenant are unaffected where the head lease and the leasehold reversion merge.

The issue whether the principle of merger applies in respect of Torrens land must be considered. On the current authorities, it appears that a registered leasehold interest will not be held to have merged as long as it remains registered as a separate interest. Before a merger will occur, it is necessary for the person acquiring the lease and the reversion to apply to the Registrar of Titles to extinguish the lease and remove the interest from the register.[544] This conclusion is consistent with dicta by Dixon C.J., Fullagar and Taylor JJ. in *Cooper v. F.C.T.*[545] and with the decision of the New South Wales Court of Appeal in *Shell Co. of Australia Ltd v. Zanelli*.[546] The decision in both cases was stated to be justified on the basis that it was more consistent with the Torrens system and that full weight should be given to the Register.

6. Frustration[547]

[10.67] Under this doctrine, if a contract becomes incapable of performance because of unforeseen circumstances both parties are relieved from their obligations under the contract.[548] At common law, however, this doctrine was considered inapplicable to landlord-tenant

542. See *Capital & Counties Bank v. Rhodes* [1903] 1 Ch. 631 (C.A.); *Re Fletcher* [1917] 1 Ch. 339 (C.A.).
543. This is the text of the Victorian and Western Australian provision. General law statutes: N.S.W.: s. 122; Vic.: s. 139(1); Qld: s. 115(1); W.A.: s. 75(1); Tas.: s. 82. The exact wording of this legislation varies slightly in some States.
544. The Registrar is given the express power to deal with such applications pursuant to the *Real Property Act* 1900 (N.S.W.), s. 12(1)(i). There is no similar provision in the Torrens statutes in the other States, but Registrars deal with such applications as a matter of practice throughout Australia: see Whalan, p. 199.
545. (1958) 100 C.L.R. 131.
546. [1973] 1 N.S.W.L.R. 216 (C.A.).
547. For a general discussion of this doctrine, see Cheshire and Fifoot, Chap. 25; Chitty, op. cit., Chap. 23.
548. See *Davis Contractors Ltd v. Fareham Urban D.C.* [1956] A.C. 686 at 729 (H.L.).

law.[549] Thus, at common law, in the absence of an exculpatory clause in the lease, if the rented premises are destroyed by fire, flood or storm or are expropriated by a government authority during the term of the agreement, the tenant remains bound by her or his covenant to pay the rent even though the premises are incapable of occupation. This result occurs because the land upon which the premises are situated is, of course, still in existence, and it is this legal estate in the land with which the law is historically concerned.[550]

The Australian courts have consistently rejected the application of the contractual doctrine of frustration to the landlord-tenant relationship. The major authority is the High Court decision in *Minister of State for the Army v. Dalziel*.[551] In that case the Commonwealth, acting under wartime powers conferred on it by the National Security (General) Regulations, requisitioned premises being rented by a weekly tenant. It was held that as the tenant was not evicted by title paramount he remained liable to pay rent according to the terms of the lease despite the fact that he was dispossessed. Williams J. stated that the doctrine of frustration does not apply to leases.[552]

It is probable in the future that Australian courts will change their position on this issue in light of the House of Lords decision in *National Carriers Ltd v. Panalpina (Northern) Ltd*.[553] By a four to one majority (Lord Russell of Killowen dissenting) the court held that frustration is capable of applying to leases, although it was emphasised that its application in this context would be rare.[554] Lord Wilberforce dismissed the traditional argument against the applicability of the doctrine, namely that the estate in land still exists despite the occurrence of the frustrating event, on the basis that the grant of the estate was not realistically speaking the main consideration for the transaction: it was merely a means to an end, not an aim or an end of itself.[555] In reaching this conclusion, the court was influenced by various decisions of United States' and Canadian courts applying the doctrine of frustration to leases.[556] This case marks a significant shift in judicial opinion since *Cricklewood Property & Investment*

---

549. See e.g. *Cricklewood Property & Investment Trust Ltd v. Leighton's Investment Trust Ltd* [1945] A.C. 221 (H.L.); *London & Northern Estates Co. v. Schlesinger* [1916] 1 K.B. 20; *Swift v. Macbean* [1942] 1 K.B. 375.

550. The other reason is that the contractual obligations of the parties are only incidental to the creation by the lease of an estate in land: see *Lobb v. Vasey Housing Auxiliary (War Widows Guild)* [1963] V.R. 239 at 247 per Hudson J. For the rationale of the common law rule, see *Paradine v. Jane* (1647) Aleyn 26; 82 E.R. 897 (K.B.).

551. (1944) 68 C.L.R. 261.

552. Ibid. at 302. See also *Thearle v. Keeley* (1958) 76 W.N. (N.S.W.) 48.

553. [1981] A.C. 675 (H.L.). Discussed in (1981) 55 A.L.J. 115; and (1981) 40 C.L.J. 217. See also Wilkinson, "Frustration of Leases" (1981) 131 N.L.J. 189; and Dickson, "Leases as Contracts" (1981) 32 N. Ireland L.Q. 162.

554. On the facts of this case, it was held that a fixed-term lease for ten years in respect of a warehouse was not frustrated by the closure of the only street giving vehicular access to it for a likely period of 20 months.

555. [1981] A.C. 675 at 695.

556. See e.g. *Highway Properties Ltd v. Kelly, Douglas & Co. Ltd* (1971) 17 D.L.R. (3d) 710 (S.C.C.); *Capital Quality Homes Ltd v. Colwyn Construction Ltd* (1976) 61 D.L.R. (3d) 385 (Ont. C.A.).

Trust Ltd v. Leighton's Investment Trust Ltd,[557] in which only two members of the court (Lord Simon and Lord Wright) were of the opinion that the doctrine is capable of application to leases.

No case on the application of frustration in landlord-tenant law has reached the Full High Court of Australia since the *National Carriers* case, but the analogous decisions in *Shevill v. Builders' Licensing Board*,[558] *Progressive Mailing House Pty Ltd v. Tabali Pty Ltd*[559] and *Laurinda Pty Ltd v. Capalaba Park Shopping Centre Pty Ltd*[560] (discussed above [10.73]ff.), where the High Court held that the principles of termination of contract, including the doctrine of repudiation, apply to leases, point to the probable acceptance of the doctrine of frustration in the present context.

7. Enlargement into a Fee Simple Estate

[10.68]   In New South Wales, Victoria and Tasmania, legislation exists which permits fixed-term leases of at least 300 years' duration to be enlarged into fee simple estates by declaration in deed form where the unexpired residue of the term is at least 200 years.[561] This legislation is based on an earlier British enactment and is seldom invoked in Australia. As explained below [17.05], its main practical purpose may be as a method of avoiding the rule in *Austerberry v. Oldham Corporation*,[562] pursuant to which the burden of a freehold covenant will not run at common law to an assignee of the covenantor.

VII.   REMEDIES OTHER THAN DETERMINATION

1. Landlord's Remedies

[10.69]   The major remedy available to landlords for breach of covenant or condition by the tenant is determination of the lease. In addition to determining the lease, the landlord has the following remedies in appropriate circumstances:

(a) Damages and/or injunction

[10.70]   The landlord may apply for damages as compensation for past breaches of covenant by the tenant and may seek an injunction to restrain the tenant from committing similar breaches in the future. The common law and equitable principles upon which damages and injunctions are awarded are discussed in detail elsewhere.[562a] The same principles apply in the present context.

---

557. [1945] A.C. 221 (H.L.).
558. (1982) 149 C.L.R. 620.
559. (1985) 157 C.L.R. 17. See also *Wood Factory Pty Ltd v. Kiritos Pty Ltd* (1985) 2 N.S.W.L.R. 105 (C.A.).
560. (1989) 63 A.L.J.R. 372.
561. *Conveyancing Act* 1919 (N.S.W.), s. 134; *Property Law Act* 1958 (Vic.), s. 153; *Conveyancing and Law of Property Act* 1884 (Tas.), s. 83. See Note (1962) 35 A.L.J. 408.
562. (1885) 29 Ch. D. 750 (C.A.).
562a. Cheshire and Fifoot, Chap. 24; Meagher, Gummow and Lehane, Chaps 21, 23.

(b) Action for arrears of rent

[10.71]   An action for arrears of rent is available wherever the tenant breaches the covenant to pay rent. Pursuant to the State limitation of actions legislation, the landlord is limited to a maximum period of six years for recovery of arrears in Victoria, Queensland and Tasmania, 12 years in New South Wales and Western Australia and 15 years in South Australia.[563]

(c) Repudiation and damages for prospective loss

[10.72]   The traditional common law position was that contractual principles are not necessarily applicable to tenancy disputes and that leases are different from other contracts. In the context of the doctrine of anticipatory breach of contract, Lord Denning stated in *Total Oil Great Britain Ltd v. Thompson Garages (Biggin Hill) Ltd*:[564] "A lease is a demise. It conveys an interest in land. It does not come to an end like an ordinary contract on repudiation and acceptance." Thus, at common law a landlord was restricted to one of the following three remedies when a tenant abandoned the rented premises:

1. The landlord could do nothing to alter the relationship of landlord and tenant, but could simply insist on performance of the terms and sue for rent or damages on the footing that the lease remained in force.

2. The landlord could elect to terminate the lease, retaining the right to sue for accrued rent, or for damages to the date of termination for previous breaches of covenant.

3. The landlord could advise the tenant that he or she proposed to relet the property on the tenant's account and enter in possession on that basis.

In the landmark case of *Highway Properties Ltd v. Kelly, Douglas & Co. Ltd*[565] the Supreme Court of Canada determined that the contractual doctrine of anticipatory breach applies to leases. Laskin J. stated:[566]

> "It is no longer sensible to pretend that a . . . lease . . . is simply a conveyance and not also a contract. It is equally untenable to persist in denying resort to the full armoury of remedies ordinarily available to redress repudiation of covenants, merely because the covenants may be associated with an estate in land."

The effect of this decision is to give a landlord a further possible remedy where the tenant abandons the rented premises, namely to terminate the lease but with notice to the defaulting tenant that damages will be claimed on the footing of a present recovery of damages for losing the benefit of the lease over its unexpired term.

563. Limitation statutes: N.S.W.: s. 27(2) and definition of "land" in s. 11(1); Vic.: s. 19; Qld: s. 25; S.A.: s. 4; W.A.: s. 4; Tas.: s. 22.
564. [1972] 1 Q.B. 318 at 324 (C.A.).
565. (1971) 17 D.L.R. (3d) 710. See Sustrik, "Highway Properties—Look Both Ways Before Crossing" (1986) 24 Alberta L.R. 477. See also *Toronto Housing Co. Ltd v. Postal Promotions Ltd* (1981) 128 D.L.R. (3d) 51 (Ont. H.C.J.); *North Bay T.V. & Audio Ltd v. Nova Electronics Ltd* (1984) 4 D.L.R. (4th) 88 (Ont. H.C.J.); *Acadian Properties Ltd v. R. & T. Foods Ltd* (1984) 59 N.B.R. (2d) 285 (N.B.Q.B.).
566. (1971) 17 D.L.R. (3d) 710 at 721.

[10.73]   After several earlier conflicting decisions,[567] the position in Australia has recently been clarified by the Full High Court in three cases.[568] In *Shevill v. Builders' Licensing Board*,[569] after the tenant had consistently been in arrears of rent over several months, the landlord elected to terminate the lease, and sued in addition to the rent due prior to the recovery of possession, for prospective damages for loss of future rent. The Full High Court unanimously held that the doctrine of repudiation is applicable to leases, but overturned a monetary order in favour of the landlord made at first instance on the grounds that on the facts the tenant, by merely being in arrears of rent, had not repudiated the lease or committed a breach of an essential term of the lease, and that the lease did not expressly confer on the landlord the right to sue for damages for prospective loss. The effect of this decision is to place a heavy onus on legal practitioners to draft leases expressly stating that the covenant to pay rent is an essential term of the lease and/or that the landlord is entitled to sue for loss of future rent wherever a lease is terminated for failure to pay rent.[570] The standard forfeiture clauses found prior to this decision were held to be inadequate to justify a claim for future rent. In essence, the decision allows future rent to be sued for in any of the following situations:

1. Where the tenant commits the breach of an essential term of the lease and termination is based on that ground.

2. Where the tenant has repudiated the lease, although this "is a serious matter and is not to be lightly found or inferred".[571]

3. Where the lease expressly entitles the landlord to recover damages for prospective loss. The onus here is on the landlord to show a "clear expression of intention".[572]

The second case is *Progressive Mailing House Pty Ltd v. Tabali Pty Ltd*.[573] In this case, the tenant company had breached its covenants relating to repairs and subletting, and was four months in arrears of rent. The Full High Court held that these breaches constituted a repudiation of the contract of lease, and that by virtue of this repudiation the landlord was entitled to terminate the lease and sue for damages for loss of the benefit of the covenant to pay rent.

567. See and cf. *Maridakis v. Kouvaris* (1975) 5 A.L.R. 197 (N.T. Sup. Ct); *Buchanan v. Byrnes* (1906) 3 C.L.R. 704; *Leitz Leeholme Stud Pty Ltd v. Robinson* [1977] 2 N.S.W.L.R. 544 (C.A.).
568. See Carter, "Repudiation of Leases" [1985] Conv. 289; Carter and Hill, "Repudiation of Leases: Further Developments" [1986] Conv. 262; Morgan, "Damages for Loss of Benefit of Covenants in Leases" (1985) 59 L. Inst. J. 719.
569. (1982) 149 C.L.R. 620. See also *Ripka Pty Ltd v. Maggiore Bakeries Pty Ltd* [1984] V.R. 629. Both cases are discussed in [1985] Conv. 289.
570. See Drafting Comments, "Lease Drafting after Shevill's Case" (1983) A.N.Z. Conv. R., Issue 34, pp. 35.
571. (1982) 149 C.L.R. 620 at 633, per Wilson J.
572. Ibid. at 637.
573. (1985) 157 C.L.R. 17. This case was followed and applied in *Wood Factory Pty Ltd v. Kiritos Pty Ltd* (1985) 2 N.S.W.L.R. 105 (C.A.); *Findlay v. Nut Farms of Australia Pty Ltd* [1989] A.N.Z. Conv. R. 40; *Nangus Pty Ltd v. Charles Donovan Pty Ltd* [1989] V.R. 184 (F.C.); *J. & C. Reid Pty Ltd v. Abau Holdings Pty Ltd* [1989] A.N.Z. Conv. R. 44.

Mason J. stated that the ordinary principles of contract law relating to termination for repudiation or for fundamental breach apply to leases.[574] His Honour stated the following formula for determining when a contract has been repudiated:[575]

> "What needs to be established in order to constitute a repudiation is that the party evinces an intention no longer to be bound by the contract or that he intends to fulfil the contract only in a manner substantially inconsistent with his obligations and not in any other way."

This formula effectively overrules the earlier test applied by the High Court in *D.T.R. Nominees Pty Ltd v. Mona Homes Pty Ltd*[576] pursuant to which the court determines whether the clause in the contract is so important to the innocent party that he would not have entered into the contract in its absence.

[10.74] The following significant matters also emerge from the *Progressive Mailing House* case:

1. "The well recognised distinction between common law rescission and termination pursuant to a contractual power provides no reason in principle why damages are recoverable by the innocent party in one case and not in the other, provided that the exercise of the power is consequent upon a breach or default by a defendant which would attract an award for such damages."[577]

2. The existence in the lease of an express proviso for re-entry does not exclude any other right of termination of the lease by the landlord.[578]

3. The ordinary principles of contract law apply to leases. This proposition, which was enthusiastically indorsed by the New South Wales Court of Appeal in *Wood Factory Pty Ltd v. Kiritos Pty Ltd*,[579] has wide-ranging ramifications for the development of the common law of landlord and tenant. In particular, it follows that the doctrines of frustration of contract (discussed above **[10.67]**), mitigation of damages and mutuality of covenants will apply to landlord-tenant law in the future.[580]

---

574. (1985) 157 C.L.R. 17 at 29.
575. Ibid. at 33. This formula was originally propounded by Gibbs C.J. in *Shevill v. Builders' Licensing Board* (1982) 149 C.L.R. 620 at 625-627. Note that Mason J. specifically rejected (at 34) the submission that abandonment of possession is necessary to constitute a case of repudiation by a tenant.
576. (1978) 138 C.L.R. 423.
577. (1985) 157 C.L.R. 17 at 31.
578. Ibid. at 29-30.
579. (1985) 2 N.S.W.L.R. 105. See also *Gallic Pty Ltd v. Cynayne Pty Ltd* (1986) 83 F.L.R. 31 (N.T. Sup. Ct); *Nangus Pty Ltd v. Charles Donovan Pty Ltd* [1989] V.R. 184 at 193 (F.C.).
580. For a general discussion of the application of these principles to landlord-tenant law, see Bradbrook, MacCallum and Moore, pp. 122-129; Bradbrook, "The Role of the Judiciary in Reforming Landlord and Tenant Law" (1976) 10 M.U.L.R. 459.

[10.75]   The third case is *Laurinda Pty Ltd v. Capalaba Park Shopping Centre Pty Ltd.*[581] The relevant facts were that the landlord company was dilatory in registering the lease granted to the tenant company. The tenant company eventually wrote to the landlord requiring the lease to be registered within 14 days and reserving its rights in respect of default. The landlord failed to register within the stipulated period, whereupon the tenant terminated the lease, claiming repudiation had occurred. The issue was whether the lease had been validly terminated. The High Court held in the affirmative, and expanded as follows on the meaning and application of repudiation in the context of leases:

1. Mason C.J. stated in relation to repudiatary conduct:[582]

   "There is a difference between evincing an intention to carry out a contract *only* if and when it suits the party to do so and evincing an intention to carry out a contract as and when it suits the party to do so. In the first case the party intends not to carry out the contract at all in the event that it does not suit him. In the second case the party intends to carry out the contract, but only to carry it out as and when it suits him. It is much easier to say of the first than of the second case that the party has evinced an intention no longer to be bound by the contract or to fulfil it only in a manner substantially inconsistent with his obligations and not in any other way. But the outcome in the second case will depend upon its particular circumstances, including the terms of the contract. In some situations the intention to carry out the contract as and when it suits the party may be taken to such lengths that it amounts to an intention to fulfil the contract only in a manner substantially inconsistent with the party's obligations and not in any other way.

2. Repudiation may occur in relation to the whole contract or in relation to a particular term of the contract if sufficiently important.[583]

3. Repudiation is not ascertained by an inquiry into the subjective state of mind of the party in default, but rather in the conduct of the defaulting party which conveys to the other party the defaulting party's inability to perform the contract or promise, or his or her intention not to perform it or to fulfil it only in a manner substantially inconsistent with his or her obligations and not in any other way.[584]

4. The question whether an inference of repudiation should be drawn merely from continued failure to perform requires an evaluation of the delay from the standpoint of the innocent party. Would a reasonable person in the shoes of the innocent party clearly infer that the other party would not be bound by the contract or would fulfil it only in a manner substantially inconsistent with that party's obligations?[585]

---

581. (1989) 63 A.L.J.R. 372.
582. Ibid. at 376.
583. Ibid. at 380 per Brennan J.
584. Ibid. at 382 per Deane and Dawson JJ.
585. Ibid. at 382-383 per Deane and Dawson JJ.

5. Repudiation may be established without proof of an effective notice to complete. The absence of an effective notice means that the other evidence must be examined to determine whether a clear inference of repudiation should be drawn, but it does not preclude the drawing of that inference.[586]

(d) Distress for rent (South Australia and Tasmania only)

[10.76] At common law, the landlord could seek to recover arrears of rent by distraining on the goods found in the rented premises as an alternative to or in addition to suing for the arrears. Originally this remedy was available throughout Australia, but has now been abolished by legislation in New South Wales, Victoria, Queensland, Western Australia,[587] and (in respect of residential premises only) in South Australia.[588] The remedy thus applies only in Tasmania and (in respect of commercial premises) in South Australia.

The remedy of distress empowers the landlord to enter the rented premises and to seize and sell sufficient goods found therein to satisfy the rent arrears and any expenses incurred.[589] The landlord is not restricted to seizing goods belonging to the tenant but may take any goods found on the premises regardless of their ownership.

The harshness of the common law rule was responsible for its abolition in four States. Even in South Australia and Tasmania, where it still survives, there are many statutory restrictions on the exercise of the remedy designed to make it more equitable.[590] In outline, these restrictions are as follows. Certain goods are absolutely exempted from distress: money, animals ferae naturae, perishable items, goods actually in use by the tenant or another person, goods falling within trade privilege (that is, goods belonging to third parties delivered to the tenant in the course of a trade carried on by the tenant), and specified goods of the tenant which are regarded as necessary for everyday living (for example, clothes, cooking utensils and tools of trade up to a specified value). Certain other goods are conditionally exempted from distress (that is, they can only be seized and sold if there are insufficient other goods on the premises to satisfy the rent arrears and expenses). Illustrations are tools and instruments of trade and (in Tasmania) sheep, cattle and beasts of the plough. Special protection is also afforded to goods belonging to subtenants and lodgers and goods on hire purchase.[591] There is also a prescribed procedure for protecting all goods belonging to third parties.

---

586. Ibid. at 383 per Deane and Dawson JJ.
587. *Landlord and Tenant Amendment (Distress Abolition) Act* 1930 (N.S.W.), s. 2; *Landlord and Tenant Act* 1958 (Vic.), s. 12; *Property Law Act* 1974 (Qld), s. 103; *Distress for Rent Abolition Act* 1936 (W.A.), s. 2.
588. *Residential Tenancies Act* 1978 (S.A.), s. 41.
589. *Lyons v. Elliott* (1876) 1 Q.B.D. 210 at 213.
590. These restrictions are contained in the *Landlord and Tenant Act* 1936 (S.A.), Pt II, and the *Landlord and Tenant Act* 1935 (Tas.), Pt V.
591. Special provisions as to hire-purchase goods are contained in the *Landlord and Tenant Act* 1935 (Tas.), s. 66. In South Australia, hire purchase has now been abolished pursuant to the *Consumer Transactions Act* 1972.

By virtue of these restrictions, distress for rent is seldom exercised by landlords in modern times.[592]

(e) Action for use and occupation

[10.77] An action for use and occupation will lie in either of two situations: first, wherever the tenant has entered into possession under an agreement to pay rent, but the exact amount of the rent was never settled by the parties; and secondly, wherever there is an oral agreement to pay rent or an agreement not in deed form. In this latter situation, an action for use and occupation is an alternative to an action for rent. In England, the law was codified in s. 14 of the *Distress for Rent Act* 1737. In some States, similar although not identical legislation has been enacted. For example, the *Landlord and Tenant Act* 1958 (Vic.), s. 8 states:[593]

> "Where the agreement between the landlord and tenant is not by deed, the landlord may recover a reasonable satisfaction for the lands tenements or hereditaments held or occupied by the defendant in an action for the use and occupation of what was so held or enjoyed. And if in evidence on the trial of such an action any parol demise or any agreement (not being by deed) whereon a certain rent was reserved shall appear, the plaintiff in such action shall not be non-suited but may make use thereof as an evidence of the *quantum* of the damages to be recovered."

In both situations, it is essential that the landlord prove that an express or implied agreement was made with the tenant to the effect that the tenant would occupy the rented premises and pay rent,[594] and that the tenant actually entered into the premises.[595]

The quantum of the order will be the amount that the court considers that the occupation is worth on the evidence.[596] Wherever the rent is specified in an unenforceable agreement, the sum specified may be used as evidence of the value of the occupation and will be persuasive although it is not conclusive on the issue.[597]

As this remedy is based on use and occupation, rent payable in advance cannot be sued for by the landlord.[598]

---

592. See *Abingdon Rural D.C. v. O'Gorman* [1968] 2 Q.B. 811 at 819 (C.A.) per Lord Denning M.R.

593. See also *Landlord and Tenant Act* 1935 (Tas.), s. 8.

594. *Specktor v. Lees* [1964] V.R. 10; *Sanders v. Cooper* [1974] W.A.R. 129 (F.C.); *Australian Provincial Assurance Association Ltd v. Rogers* (1943) 43 S.R. (N.S.W.) 202 (S.C. in banco).

595. *Woodhouse v. Ah Peck* (1900) 16 W.N. (N.S.W.) 166 (S.C. in banco); *Cooper v. Dick* (1862) 1 S.C.R. (N.S.W.) 127.

596. *Thetford Corporation v. Tyler* (1845) 8 Q.B. 95; 115 E.R. 810; *Gibson v. Kirk* (1841) 1 Q.B. 850; 113 E.R. 1357.

597. *Murdock v. Kennedy* (1952) 69 W.N. (N.S.W.) 191 (S.C. in banco).

598. *Angell v. Randall* (1867) 16 L.T. 498.

(f) Actions for double rent and double value against overholding tenants[599]

[10.78] The actions for double rent and double value originated in the *Landlord and Tenant Act* 1730 (Imp.), s. 1 and the *Distress for Rent Act* 1737 (Imp.), s. 18. These ancient statutes were later incorporated into the Australian States by virtue of the reception of imperial laws legislation.[600] It would appear that the actions are still available in all Australian States except New South Wales, where they have been abolished by s. 8(1) of the *Imperial Acts Application Act* 1969.[601] In Queensland, Victoria and Tasmania, State legislation in modern times has replaced the necessity for reliance on the British legislation.[602] This State legislation has modernised the language of the U.K. legislation but has adhered to the substance of its provisions. For example, ss 138 and 139 of the *Property Law Act* 1974 (Qld) read:

"Where any tenant for years, including a tenant from year to year or other person who is or comes into possession of any land by, from or under or by collusion with such tenant, wilfully[603] holds over any land after—

(a) determination of the lease or term: and

(b) after demand made and notice in writing has been given for the delivery of possession thereof by the lessor or landlord or the person to whom the remainder or reversion of such land belongs to his agent thereunder lawfully authorized—

then the person so holding over shall, for and during the time he so holds over or keeps the person entitled out of possession of such land, be liable to the person so kept out of possession at the rate of double the yearly value of the land so detained for so long as the land shall have been so detained, to be recovered by action in any court of competent jurisdiction.

. . .

Where a lessee who has given notice of his intention to quit the land held by him at a time specified in such notice does not accordingly deliver up possession at the time so specified, then he shall thereafter be liable to the lessor for double the rent or sum which would have been payable to the lessor before such notice was given.

599. See Bradbrook, "The Action for Double Rent and Double Value Against Overholding Tenants" (1978) 13 U.W.A.L.R. 420.
600. *Australian Courts Act* 1828 (U.K.), s. 24; *Constitution Act* 1867 (Qld), s. 33; *Acts Interpretation Act* 1918 (S.A.), s. 48; *Imperial Laws Application Act* 1922 (Vic.); *Interpretation Act* 1918 (W.A.), s. 43.
601. Section 8(1) reads: "In addition to the repeals effected by subsection two of section five of this Act all other Imperial enactments (commencing with the Statute of Merton, 20 Henry III A.D. 1235-6) in force in England at the time of the passing of the Imperial Act 9 George IV Chapter 83 are so far as they are in force in New South Wales hereby repealed."
602. *Landlord and Tenant Act* 1958 (Vic.), ss 9, 10; *Property Law Act* 1974 (Qld), ss 138, 139; *Landlord and Tenant Act* 1935 (Tas.), ss 9, 10.
603. For the meaning of "wilfully", see *French v. Elliott* [1959] 3 All E.R. 866 at 874; *Richards v. Golden Fleece Petroleum Pty Ltd* (1983) 49 A.L.R. 337 at 345.

Such lessee shall continue to be liable for such double rent or sum during the time he continues in possession as aforesaid, to be recovered by action in any court of competent jurisdiction.''

In South Australia and Western Australia no specific State legislation covering this matter exists, and reliance is still placed on the United Kingdom legislation.

A number of illogical distinctions exist in the scope and operation of the present laws. While the double rent penalty applies universally regardless of the nature of the lease, the double value penalty appears not to extend to periodic leases other than yearly periodic leases.[604] While it may be true to argue that there is no real justification for extending the double value penalty to short periodic leases as they are generally of less valuable premises and can be readily determined,[605] the same arguments could be applied to the double rent penalty. Similarly inexplicable is the fact that although a landlord must give the tenant written notice before he can sue for the double value penalty,[606] in the case of the double rent penalty the notice given by the tenant can be either written or oral.[607] Again, the requirement in the 1730 Act that the tenant hold over "wilfully" before being liable for the double value penalty does not appear in the 1737 Act. A further illogicality is that at common law the double rent penalty, but not the double value penalty, can be enforced by distress.[608] While conceptually this latter distinction can be justified as the double value penalty is in the nature of unliquidated damages rather than rent, the distinction makes no sense on policy grounds.

[10.79]   Problems also exist in the calculation of the double value penalty. Although in the Queensland case of *Public Curator v. L.A. Wilkinson (Northern) Ltd*[609] double yearly value was calculated by doubling single rent, it has been held before and since that case that "double yearly value and double rent are two entirely different things, and you cannot ordinarily estimate the former by doubling a single rent, for this might not afford an equivalent compensation".[610] Despite the assumption by some

---

604. The action for double value does not lie against a weekly tenant: *Lloyd v. Rosbee* (1810) 2 Camp. 453; 170 E.R. 1216 (N.P.); *Sullivan v. Bishop* (1826) 2 Car. & P. 359; 172 E.R. 162 (N.P.). Quaere whether a quarterly tenant is liable under this action: *Wilkinson v. Hall* (1837) 3 Bing. N.C. 508; 132 E.R. 506 (C.P.). The action definitely applies to tenancies from year to year: *Ryal v. Rich* (1808) 10 East. 48; 103 E.R. 693 (K.B.).

605. See Queensland Law Reform Commission, *Relief from Forfeiture of an Option to Renew and Certain Aspects of the Law Relating to Landlord and Tenant*, Report No. 1 (Q.L.R.C. 1; 1970), p. 10.

606. Woodfall, para. 1-2094. See also *French v. Elliott* [1959] 3 All E.R. 866.

607. *Johnstone v. Hudlestone* (1825) 4 B. & C. 922; 107 E.R. 1302 (K.B.); *Timmins v. Rowlison* (1765) 1 Wm. Bl. 533; 96 E.R. 309 (K.B.).

608. *Humberstone v. Dubois* (1842) 10 M. & W. 765; 152 E.R. 681 (Exch.); *Timmins v. Rowlison* (1765) 1 Wm. Bl. 533; 96 E.R. 309 (K.B.). The remedy of distress has been abolished in Victoria, New South Wales, Queensland and Western Australia: see above **[10.53]**.

609. [1933] Q.W.N. 28.

610. *Trivett v. Hurst* [1937] Q.S.R. 265 at 271 per Blair C.J. See also *Doe d. Matthews v. Jackson* (1779) 1 Doug. 175; 99 E.R. 115 (K.B.).

judges that the double value penalty is more favourable to landlords than the double rent penalty, this is not universally correct. The double value penalty must be calculated on the yearly value of the premises, and must not include the value of incidental advantages. Thus, in *Robinson v. Learoyd*,[611] where the landlord, the owner of a woollen mill and steam-engine, let to the tenant a room in the mill together with a supply of power from the steam-engine, it was held that the value of the power supplied could not be included in the calculation of the double value penalty. In addition, according to Keith J. in *Yonge-Rosedale Developments Ltd v. Levitt*, the value of the land means "the pecuniary value to the particular landlord having regard to his own special circumstances. In other words, the true test is subjective."[612] In this case, despite evidence that the landlord could have let the premises at a rental of between $3,000 and $4,000 per month on a medium to long-term lease, this would have conflicted with the intention of the landlord to keep the lease subject to termination on short notice. Accordingly, the double value was assessed on the rental of $2,000, the value of the premises let on a short-term lease.

There is a dispute between the authorities as to whether the acceptance by the landlord of the normal rent will constitute an implied waiver of the right to apply for the double value remedy. According to one line of authorities, acceptance of rent is not necessarily fatal to a later claim for double value. For example, according to Blair C.J. in *Trivett v. Hurst*:[613]

"If after [the double value penalty] has accrued [the landlord] accepts the single rent, it is a question of fact whether such rent has been received in part satisfaction of the claim to double value or as a waiver of it. What acts on either side amount to a waiver of a notice after its expiration is ordinarily a mixed question of law and fact, the intention with which the act was done being for the jury and its legal effects for the court to decide."

However, Woodfall and other authors have found cases to support the proposition that the acceptance of single rent, accrued due subsequently to the notice to quit, is always a waiver of the landlord's right to double value.[614] Proponents of this proposition regard the receipt of rent as inherently inconsistent with a claim for double value. The matter must be regarded at present as unsettled.

2. Tenant's Remedies

The remedy of damages and/or an injunction (see above [10.70]) is available to tenants wherever the landlord has breached a covenant or

611. (1840) 7 M. & W. 48; 151 E.R. 673 (Exch.).
612. (1978) 82 D.L.R. (3d) 263 at 270.
613. [1937] Q.S.R. 265 at 273. Ellenborough C.J. expressed the same view in *Ryal v. Rich* (1808) 10 East. 48; 103 E.R. 693 (K.B.).
614. Woodfall, para. 1-2099. See also Evans, *The Law of Landlord and Tenant* (1974) p. 219. Cases supporting this proposition are *Doe d. Cheny v. Batten* (1775) 1 Cowp. 243; 98 E.R. 1066 (K.B.) and *Davenport v. R.* (1877) 3 A.C. 115 (H.L.). See also the arguments of counsel for the respondent in *Public Curator v. L. A. Wilkinson (Northern) Ltd* [1933] Q.W.N. 28.

condition of the lease. In addition, the tenant has the following remedies in certain circumstances:

(a) The right of set-off

[10.80] Although a specific right of rent withholding was never recognised at common law or equity where the landlord breached any of the terms of the lease, in most circumstances rent may be withheld by tenants pursuant to the right of set-off.[615] This situation arises most commonly where the tenant defends an action for arrears of rent on the ground that the landlord has neglected the duty to repair. At common law, if the landlord breaches the covenant to repair, the tenant may carry out the work her or himself and set off the cost of the repairs against her or his liability for rent due in the future. The only two qualifications to this common law right of set-off are that the tenant must notify the landlord of the need for repair before the set-off can arise, and that the set-off must be for a sum which is not to be regarded as unliquidated damages.[616] The basis of this right is that the money spent by the tenant is regarded as having been paid to the use of the landlord. The common law right originates from *Taylor v. Beal*,[617] which held that a right of set-off could be applied in appropriate cases even though it was denied on the facts of that case.[618] The first case in modern times to recognise this right in the context of repairs in landlord-tenant law was *Lee-Parker v. Izzet*,[619] a case where the plaintiff mortgagee was seeking a decree to enforce a registered charge on certain properties. These properties were in disrepair. Two of the defendants carried out repairs at their own expense and claimed the right to set-off this cost against their liability for rent which was payable by them as tenants of the plaintiff mortgagee. Goff J. held that this claim was valid.

This common law remedy was of limited use to tenants in that being restricted to liquidated damages it only applied where the tenant was able to carry out the repairs her or himself. However, *Knockholt Pty Ltd v. Graff*[620] and *British Anzani (Felixstowe) Ltd v. International Marine Management (U.K.) Ltd*[621] have held that based on equity a right of set-off will now apply where there is a claim by the tenant to unliquidated damages and that the right of set-off for money spent on repairs may apply in respect of arrears of rent.[622] In the *British Anzani* case, the landlords agreed to build two warehouses on the demised land and to remedy any defects in

615. See generally Meagher, Gummow and Lehane, Chap. 37. See also Waite, "Disrepair and Set-Off of Damages Against Rent: The Implication of British Anzani" [1983] Conv. 373.
616. *British Anzani (Felixstowe) Ltd v. International Marine Management (U.K.) Ltd* [1980] Q.B. 137 at 147-148 per Forbes J. For a detailed discussion of the circumstances in which set-off is available, see *Hanak v. Green* [1958] 2 Q.B. 9 at 17-25 (C.A.) per Morris L.J.
617. *Taylor v. Beal* (1591) Cro. Eliz. 222; 78 E.R. 478 (K.B.).
618. Cf. *Waters v. Weigall* (1795) 2 Anst. 575; 145 E.R. 971 (Exch.).
619. [1971] 3 All E.R. 1099.
620. [1975] Qd R. 88.
621. [1980] Q.B. 137.
622. See also *Melville v. Grapelodge Developments Ltd* (1980) 39 P. & C.R. 179 (Q.B. Div.).

them within two years of their completion. In a later action brought by the landlords for arrears of rent, the tenant argued in defence a right of set-off as the buildings were in a state of disrepair. Forbes J. held that although the right of set-off at common law was unavailable in that no money had been spent on repairs by the tenant, at equity a right of set-off would be applied against the arrears of rent in respect of the unliquidated damages claimed for the landlord's breach of his duty to repair. Thus, equity has significantly improved the position of the tenant in that unlike at common law the tenant is now able to use this remedy even if he or she pays no money in respect of the repairs. The only restriction on the availability of the equitable right of set-off is that as at common law it will not apply unless the tenant has given the landlord notice of the need for repair.

(b) Statutory repair orders

[10.81] In each State, legislation exists empowering either State government instrumentalities or local councils (or both) to impose orders requiring landlords to repair rented premises. The legislation is restricted to residential premises and has no application in the commercial context. The legislation is not a part of landlord-tenant legislation and is not designed to cover solely the plight of a tenant in an inadequately maintained dwelling; instead, the purpose is to upgrade the quality of the housing stock in the State. In most instances the legislation is employed against owner-occupiers; however, as the legislation also extends to rented premises it is incidentally helpful to tenants in poor quality housing.

The legislation differs from State to State. Victoria and South Australia will be used as illustrations.[623] In Victoria, the *Housing Act* 1983 grants express powers to the Director of Housing. Where the Director is satisfied that any house does not comply with the *Housing (Standard of Habitation) Regulations* 1984 he may serve on the owner and the occupier a copy of a declaration to that effect setting out the particulars in respect of which the house fails to comply with the regulations: s. 64. The owner has a right of appeal to a magistrates' court against this declaration: s. 65. If the appeal is lost or no appeal is lodged, the Director may serve on the owner and occupier a direction, inter alia, that he undertake all necessary repairs to make the house comply with the Regulations: s. 66. If this direction is not complied with, the Director may make arrangements for the repairs to be undertaken and may recover the necessary expenses from the owner: s. 67. Any prospective purchaser is protected by the requirement in s. 69(1) that the owner of a house to which a declaration relates must not sell or enter into any contract to sell the land on which the house is erected without first serving the purchaser with a copy of a s. 70 certificate specifying the existence of a direction to repair. A breach of s. 69(1) is an offence punishable by 50 penalty units[624] and entitles the purchaser at any time before he or she has executed a transfer or conveyance of the land

---

623. For the relevant legislation in the other States, see *Public Health Act* 1902 (N.S.W.); *Health Act* 1937 (Qld); *Health Act* 1911 (W.A.); *Substandard Housing Control Act* 1973 (Tas.).

624. See *Penalties and Sentences Act* 1981 (Vic.), s. 5. A penalty unit is currently $100.

to her or himself to rescind the contract and claim a repayment of any sum paid to the owner: s. 69(2)(a). If the purchaser has already executed the transfer or conveyance, he or she is entitled to recover damages from the owner for any loss suffered as a result of the wilful concealment of the defect in the title: s. 69(2)(b).

A further duty to repair on the landlord in Victoria exists in the *Health Act* 1958. Under s. 45(1) any person can complain to the local council that a nuisance exists. This subsection can be invoked by any tenant or other occupier in respect of substandard accommodation. A tenant wishing to complain about the condition of the rented premises would base her or his complaint on s. 39A, which states:

"This Part applies to nuisances which are, or are liable to be, dangerous to health or offensive and in particular to nuisances arising from or constituted by:—

(a) any building or structure;

. . .

which is, or is liable to be, dangerous to health or offensive."

If the local council regards the tenant's complaint as valid and is of the opinion that a nuisance exists, it will serve a notice of abatement on the owner pursuant to s. 44(1) requiring her or him to improve the standard of the premises. Under s. 44(2), if the owner fails to comply with s. 44(1), the local council shall cause a complaint to be made before a justice who may summon the owner to appear before a magistrates' court. In this event, under s. 44(4) if the magistrates' court is satisfied that the alleged nuisance exists, or that although removed it is likely to recur, the court may make an order, inter alia, requiring the owner to comply with all or any of the requirements of the notice or otherwise to abate the nuisance within a time specified in the order and to do any works necessary for that purpose. In addition, pursuant to s. 44(5) the court may impose a maximum penalty of 100 penalty units against the owner and may give directions as to the payment of all costs and expenses. The other major remedy available to the local council is to do the repairs itself and recover the expenses from the owner: s. 44(9). If the tenant is dissatisfied with the action taken by the local council he or she may complain to a justice: s. 45(1). If the magistrates' court is satisfied that the tenant had reasonable grounds for making a complaint under s. 45(1) it may order the local council to pay her or his costs and expenses: s. 45(3).

In South Australia, the *Housing Improvement Act* 1940 provides that if premises are declared to be undesirable for human habitation, the owner may be directed to carry out certain repairs within a specified time: s. 23. The primary duty of imposing repair orders is performed by the local boards of health. They act pursuant to s. 23(1), which states:

"Where a local board, after making due inquiries and obtaining such reports as it deems necessary, is satisfied that any house is undesirable for human habitation or is unfit for human habitation, the local board may declare that the house—

(a) is undesirable for human habitation; or

(b) is unfit for human habitation."

[10.82]   Whenever a local board declares a house to be undesirable for human habitation or unfit for human habitation, it must serve on the owner a copy of the declaration together with a statement in writing setting out the particulars in respect of which the house is deficient: s. 23(2). The local board must also direct the owner to comply within a specified time with the directions contained in the statement designed to restore the use to a satisfactory condition. This specified time must be at least one month after the service of the declaration: s. 23(2)(a).[625] Under s. 25, the South Australian Housing Trust is empowered to require the relevant local board to exercise its powers contained in s. 23 if the Trust is of the opinion that a house is undesirable for human habitation or unfit for human habitation. If the local board fails to comply with any notice given to it under s. 25 by the Housing Trust, the Trust may exercise any of the powers given by s. 23 to the local board: s. 25(2).

If the rented premises are in such a state of disrepair as to constitute an "insanitary condition", the tenant also will have a remedy against the landlord under the *Health Act* 1935 (S.A.) provided that the tenant was not responsible for creating the insanitary condition. This remedy is in addition to the provisions of s. 23 of the *Housing Improvement Act* 1940 (*Housing Improvement Act* s. 23(7)). A duty is placed on each local board of health to investigate any complaint establishing reasonable grounds for suspicion of the existence of any insanitary condition: s. 53. If the health surveyor believes that the insanitary condition should be removed immediately, he or she has the power to serve upon the occupier or owner a notice to rectify the condition, specifying the work required to be done and a time limit for compliance: s. 56. No minimum or maximum time limit is specified in the legislation. In less urgent cases, the health surveyor will report the circumstances to the local board, which under s. 58 may serve a similar notice to that served by the health surveyor under s. 56. Again, no minimum or maximum time limit is specified by the legislation. The Act places the primary responsibility for effecting the necessary repairs on the landlord, by providing in s. 60 that the notice given by the local board shall be served on the owner except in cases where the owner is unknown or if, in the opinion of the local board, the insanitary condition is caused by the act or neglect of the occupier. In the latter circumstances, the notice may be served on the tenant. Three methods of enforcement are available to the local board of health against a landlord who fails to comply with a notice served under ss 60 or 56 of the *Health Act*. First, failure to comply constitutes an offence punishable by a penalty not exceeding $200: s. 61. Secondly, the local board may itself carry out the requirements of the notice and remove the insanitary condition: s. 62. In this event, the local board may recover the expenses from the landlord: s. 66. All expenses incurred by any local board are a charge upon the premises and may be recovered as if they were rates in arrears: s. 69. Thirdly, the local board may institute summary proceedings against the landlord: s. 64. Under s. 65(1), the court, if satisfied that an insanitary condition exists or is likely to recur on the same premises, may by order require the landlord to remove or amend the condition, or to prevent its

625. "Month" means calendar month, not lunar month: *Acts Interpretation Act* 1915 (S.A.), s. 4.

recurrence within a time to be specified in the order. It may also specify
the necessary work to be undertaken. If the landlord fails to comply with
this order, he or she is guilty of an offence against the Act and liable to
a penalty not exceeding $200 for every day during which the default
continues: s. 65(2).

(c) Statutory rent control orders (South Australia and Tasmania only)[626]

[10.83]   Where residential rented premises are in disrepair, in certain
circumstances the South Australian Housing Trust and the Tasmanian
Director of Housing are statutorily empowered to subject the premises to
rent control.

Under s. 52 of the *Housing Improvement Act* 1940 (S.A.), where the
Housing Trust is satisfied that premises are undesirable or unfit for
human habitation it may serve a notice on the owner stating that after the
expiration of one month (to allow the owner time to make representations
to the Trust) the premises will be declared substandard. The Trust may
then publish the declaration in the *Gazette*, and after the expiration of a
further month may fix the maximum rental per week which shall be
lawfully payable in respect of the premises: s. 54. The owner is permitted
a right of appeal to the nearest local court against a Trust declaration, in
which case any fixed maximum rental is suspended until the appeal is
heard: s. 53(1)(3). In the event that some improvements to the premises
are made by the owner, the Trust is empowered to increase the maximum
rental (s. 55(1)), and if satisfied that the premises have ceased to be
undesirable or unfit for human habitation, it may by notice in the *Gazette*
revoke the declaration made pursuant to s. 52 (s. 55(2)).

The relevant legislation in Tasmania is the *Substandard Housing Control
Act* 1973. Pursuant to s. 4, where the Director of Housing is satisfied that
a house is undesirable or unfit for human habitation he or she may serve
notices on the interested parties stating an intention to declare the house
substandard and inviting them to submit representations on this matter.
A minimum of 30 days must be allowed for these representations from the
date of the service of the notices, after which the Director may declare by
notice in the *Gazette* that the house is substandard. This declaration will
continue in force until the Director, pursuant to s. 7(1), publishes a
further notice in the *Gazette* declaring that the house has ceased to be
substandard. Under s. 9, the Director may by publication in the *Gazette*
fix a maximum rental for a declared substandard house, and by virtue of
s. 11(3), notwithstanding any agreement to the contrary any rent in excess
of the maximum specified is irrecoverable. When a notice of intention has
been served under s. 4(1), any notice to quit given by or on behalf of a
landlord is ineffective unless either the tenant has failed to pay the rent
or the notice to quit is confirmed by a magistrate as not having been
served in retaliation for the initial complaint by the tenant: s. 17.
Similarly, once the premises are controlled, the legislation prohibits
recovery of possession by a landlord except under certain defined
circumstances: s. 18(1).

626. See Bradbrook, "The Role of State Government Agencies in Securing Repairs
     to Rented Housing" (1977) 11 M.U.L.R. 145.

VIII.   LEASES AND THE TORRENS SYSTEM

[10.84]   The application and relevance of the common law doctrines of surrender, merger and re-entry to Torrens land have been discussed earlier: see above [10.65], [10.66] and [10.59] respectively. The following issues arise for consideration:

(a)   the registration of leases;

(b)   the registration of subleases;

(c)   leases as a statutory exception to indefeasibility of title; and

(d)   leases falling outside the statutory exception to indefeasibility of title.

1. The Registration of Leases

[10.85]   In every State, the Torrens legislation specifically authorises leases for any term exceeding three years to be created in the approved form and registered. The only exception is South Australia, where a one year period is specified.[627] In all cases, upon registration a legal leasehold interest will be created in the tenant. In order to fall within the three year or one year designated period, the lease must be for a fixed period; thus, periodic leases are excluded. A lease exceeding the designated period but determinable within that period is covered by the section,[628] but a lease less than the designated period containing an option to renew which taken together with the original period would exceed the designated period is excluded from the section.[629]

A more controversial issue is whether it is possible to register a lease for a term of less than three years (one year in South Australia). The position appears to vary from State to State. The Queensland and South Australian legislation[630] expressly permit such leases to be registered, while the Tasmanian legislation states the opposite.[631] Elsewhere the legislation is silent on this issue. In New South Wales, the Supreme Court has held that leases for a term less than three years may be registered.[632] In Victoria, the practice of the Registrar of Titles is not to register such leases.[633] In the remaining jurisdictions the issue appears to be unresolved. In jurisdictions where the registration of short-term leases is permitted, upon registration full legal protection is afforded the tenant against subsequent dealings by the landlord with the property.

Once a lease is registered, it does not follow automatically that all the covenants contained in the lease are protected by the principle of indefeasibility. In *Mercantile Credits Ltd v. Shell Co. (Aust.) Ltd*[634] the issue arose whether a covenant to renew a lease, which had been registered,

---

627.   Torrens statutes: N.S.W.: s. 53(1); Vic.: s. 66(1); Qld: s. 52; S.A.: s. 116; W.A.: s. 91; Tas.: s. 64(1).

628.   *Kushner v. Law Society* [1952] 1 All E.R. 404.

629.   *Roberts v. Birkley* (1888) 14 V.L.R. 819; *Hand v. Hall* (1877) 2 Ex. D. 355 (C.A.).

630.   Torrens statutes: *Real Property Act* 1877 (Qld), s. 18; S.A.: s. 116.

631.   Tas.: s. 64(2).

632.   *Parkinson v. Braham* (1961) 62 S.R. (N.S.W.) 663 (S.C. in banco).

633.   Robinson, p. 269.

634.   (1976) 136 C.L.R. 326. Cf. *Friedman v. Barrett; Ex parte Friedman* [1962] Qd R. 498.

prevailed over the title of the mortgagee. The argument advanced by the mortgagee was that although the lease was entitled to priority over the mortgage based on prior registration, the right of renewal was not an integral part of the lease, and was not registrable, and that priority was given by the Torrens statute only to the term of the lease and not to the right of renewal or to any extended term resulting from the exercise of that right. The Full High Court, although deciding in favour of the lessee, held that the registration of a lease does not in all cases give priority or the quality of indefeasibility to every right which the lease creates. Gibbs J. drew a distinction between collateral covenants, not affecting the estate in land granted by the lease, which would not obtain priority, and covenants so intimately connected with the term granted to the tenant that they should be regarded as part of the estate obtained by the tenant under the lease. Stephen J. based his decision on the specific enforceability of the right of renewal, if exercised. In *Travinto Nominees Pty Ltd v. Vlattas*,[635] the Full High Court held that a covenant which was illegal when made, obtained no validity or protection from the registration of the instrument in which it was found because its illegality denied the possibility of its specific performance.

2. The Registration of Subleases

[10.86] In Victoria, Western Australia and Tasmania, the Torrens legislation expressly permits the landlord to create and register a sublease.[636] Where this occurs, the provisions in the legislation affecting landlords and tenants are stated to apply equally to sublessors and subtenants. The issue whether subleases may be registered in the remaining jurisdictions is unresolved by the legislation. Whalan[637] appears to be correct in his analysis that registration is permitted in these jurisdictions on the basis that the provisions relating to leases apply whenever "land" is intended to be leased, and "land" is defined in each jurisdiction as including all tenements and hereditaments corporeal and incorporeal of every kind and every estate or interest therein.[638]

3. Leases as a Statutory Exception to Indefeasibility of Title

[10.87] As shown above, in certain situations leases may be unregistrable. Moreover, a tenant who is entitled to register her or his lease may fail to do so. Is a tenant holding under an unregistrable or registrable but unregistered lease protected against any subsequent dealings by the landlord with the title to the property? Despite the principle of indefeasibility of title, an exception to indefeasibility exists in all jurisdictions in favour of leases in certain circumstances. As the scope of the statutory exception to indefeasibility differs in each Torrens statute, it is necessary to consider the legal protection afforded to tenants under an unregistered lease separately in each State.

635. (1973) 129 C.L.R. 1.
636. Torrens statutes: Vic.. s. 71; W.A.: ss 99-101; Tas.: s 69(1).
637. Whalan, p. 191.
638. Torrens statutes: N.S.W.: ss 3, 53(1); Qld: ss 3, 52; S.A.: ss 3, 116.

Victoria

The scope of the statutory exception in favour of leases is very wide. The *Transfer of Land Act* 1958, s. 42(2)(e) reads: "the interest (but excluding any option to purchase) of a tenant in possession of the land." The word "tenant" is wide enough to include a tenant holding under an agreement for a lease,[639] a life tenant[640] and a purchaser of land under a contract of sale.[641] In *Downie v. Lockwood*,[642] Smith J. held that s. 42(2)(e) is not limited to the actual interest of the tenant but extends to the tenant's equity of rectification arising from the lease.[643] Thus a lease as rectified will bind any successor-in-title of the landlord. The only effective limitation is that the tenant's interest must be "in possession" before the statutory exception will apply. Because of the wide scope of the exception, there is little incentive for any tenant to register a lease in Victoria.

New South Wales

In New South Wales the statutory exception in favour of leases is much more restricted. The *Real Property Act* 1900, s. 42(1)(d) couches the exception in the following terms:

"a tenancy whereunder the tenant is in possession or entitled to immediate possession, and an agreement or option for the acquisition by such a tenant of a further term to commence at the expiration of such a tenancy, of which in either case the registered proprietor before he become registered as proprietor had notice against which he was not protected: Provided that—

(i) The term for which the tenancy was created does not exceed three years; and

(ii) in the case of such an agreement or option, the additional term for which it provides would not, when added to the original term, exceed three years."

Thus, unlike in Victoria, a tenant's interest under an unregistered lease only applies to leases for a fixed term of three years or less. Moreover, the landlord's successor-in-title as registered proprietor is only bound by the lease if prior to registration he or she had notice of the tenant's interest. "Notice" has been held to include constructive notice as well as actual notice.[644] The relevant time for considering "notice" was determined by the New South Wales Court of Appeal in *United Starr-Bowkett Co-operative Building Society v. Clyne*.[645] In that case, the court referred to *I.A.C. (Finance) Pty Ltd v. Courtenay*,[646] where the High Court stated that "notice" in s. 42(d) should be read in the light of s. 43A of the same Act, and held

---

639. *National Trustees, Executors & Agency Co. of Australasia Ltd v. Boyd* (1926) 39 C.L.R. 72.
640. *Black v. Poole* (1895) 16 A.L.T. 155.
641. *Sandhurst Mutual Permanent Investment Building Society v. Gissing* (1889) 15 V.L.R. 329 (F.C.).
642. [1965] V.R. 257.
643. It may extend also to other interests held by the tenant (for example, an option to renew the lease).
644. *Clyne v. Lowe* (1968) 69 S.R. (N.S.W.) 433 (C.A.).
645. [1968] 1 N.S.W.R. 134.
646. (1963) 110 C.L.R. 550 at 584.

that: "notwithstanding registration, the purchaser holds subject to a tenancy for a term not exceeding three years created by a previous registered proprietor . . . if he had notice of that tenancy before he obtained a registered instrument, or one which when appropriately signed by him or on his behalf would be registrable, that is, before completion of his purchase."[647]

South Australia

The relevant statutory exception to indefeasibility is restricted to leases "[w]here at the time when the purchaser becomes registered a tenant shall be in actual possession of the land under an unregistered lease or an agreement for a lease or for letting for a term not exceeding one year".[648] This section is complemented by a further section reading: "Every registered dealing with land shall be subject to any prior unregistered lease or any agreement for lease or for letting for a term not exceeding one year to a tenant in actual possession thereunder."[649] The latter provision appears to add nothing to the earlier section.

Queensland

The *Real Property Act* 1877, s. 11 excepts from indefeasibility of title "any tenancy from year to year or for any term not exceeding three years".[650]

Western Australia

The *Transfer of Land Act* 1893, s. 68 excepts from indefeasibility of title, inter alia, "any prior unregistered lease or agreement for lease or for letting for a term not exceeding five years to a tenant in actual possession."

Tasmania

Pursuant to the *Land Titles Act* 1980, s. 40(3), the title of a registered proprietor of land is not indefeasible,

"(d) so far as regards the interest of a tenant under—

    (i) a periodic tenancy;

    (ii) a lease taking effect in possession for a term not exceeding 3 years (whether or not the lessee is given power to extend the term) at the best rent that can be reasonably obtained without taking a fine; and

    (iii) a lease capable of taking effect in equity only, except as against a *bona fide* purchaser for value without notice of the lease who has lodged a transfer for registration;"

647. [1968] 1 N.S.W.R. 134 at 142 per Sugerman J.A.
648. S.A.: s. 69 VIII.
649. S.A.: s. 119.
650. Leases not exceeding three years executed after the registration of a mortgage are not binding on a registered mortgagee: *English, Scottish & Australian Bank Ltd v. City National Bank Ltd* [1933] St. R. Qd 81.

4. Leases Falling Outside the Statutory Exception to Indefeasibility of Title

[10.88]   Occasionally a lease may be unregistered and outside the statutory exception to indefeasibility. This is a comparatively rare occurrence, though based on the wording of the statutory exceptions to indefeasibility (see above [10.87]) it may occur, for example, where the tenant is not in actual possession of the property. In this situation the lease cannot constitute a legal interest[651] but is still capable of existing as an equitable interest.[652] Based on the rule in *Walsh v. Lonsdale* (see above [10.06])[653] an equitable periodic or fixed-term lease will exist in these circumstances. Thus, an unregistered lease which is outside the statutory exception to indefeasibility is still enforceable between the contracting parties although it cannot be enforced by the tenant against a subsequent registered proprietor.[654] In those jurisdictions where short-term leases are unregistrable (Victoria, Tasmania and (possibly) Western Australia (see above [10.85])), a tenant may protect her or his interest against subsequent dealings with the landlord by lodging a caveat.[655]

IX.   TRADE PRACTICES LEGISLATION

[10.89]   A number of provisions exist in Pts IV and V of the *Trade Practices Act* 1974 (Cth) (hereafter referred to as "the Act") which directly affect the parties' legal relationship and (in some instances) give additional remedies to tenants.[656]

For constitutional reasons, the relevant provisions are limited in their scope to actions by a "corporation".[657] In the present context, it thus follows that the landlord must constitute a "corporation" before the tenant may invoke any of the provisions of the Act. However, subject to this limitation, the Act will extend to all types of commercial tenancies, including retail tenancies. In the latter situation, the provisions of the Act will apply in addition to those in the State retail tenancies legislation[658] in the absence of any inconsistency between the various sections.

The relevant provisions of Pts IV and V of the Act will be considered separately.

651. Torrens statutes: N.S.W.: s. 41; Vic.: s. 40(1); Qld: s. 43; S.A.: s. 67; W.A.: s. 58; Tas.: s. 49(1).
652. *Barry v. Heider* (1914) 19 C.L.R. 197.
653. (1882) 21 Ch. D. 9 (C.A.).
654. See *R. M. Hosking Properties Pty Ltd v. Barnes* [1971] S.A.S.R. 100.
655. Vic.: s. 89(1); Tas.: s. 133; W.A.: s. 137.
656. Consumer protection measures available to tenants are also available under certain State legislation: see e.g. *Fair Trading Act* 1985 (Vic.), *Fair Trading Act* 1987 (N.S.W.), *Fair Trading Act* 1987 (S.A.), *Consumer Affairs Act* 1972 (Vic.).
657. For a discussion of the constitutional aspects of the Act, see e.g. Taperell, Vermeesch and Harland, *Trade Practices and Consumer Protection* (3rd ed., Butterworths, Sydney, 1983), Chap. 2.
658. See Chapter 11 for a discussion of the State retail tenancies legislation.

1. Restrictive Trade Practices: Trade Practices Act, Pt IV

[**10.90**]   The relevance of Pt IV to commercial leases is that many such leases contain covenants which restrain the tenant's freedom to trade on the demised premises as he or she sees fit. The most notorious and one of the most ancient of such covenants effects a tie of trade, compelling the tenant to purchase stock from the landlord or a supplier nominated by her or him. There are, of course, other covenants which affect directly and indirectly the tenant's ability to conduct business on the demised premises in her or his chosen manner. For example, commercial leases often seek to regulate:

(a) the type of business that the tenant is permitted to carry on;

(b) the hours during which he or she may or must trade;

(c) the advertising signs which must be displayed inside and outside the premises;

(d) the tenant's contribution towards the costs of advertising schemes which relate to the whole of a shopping centre;

(e) the insurance that is to be provided by the tenant; and

(f) the lessee's membership of a merchant's association.

When the Act was first introduced, there was considerable doubt as to whether Pt IV applied to covenants contained in leases. These doubts proved to be well-founded in light of the decision of the Full Court of the High Court in *Quadramain Pty Ltd v. Sevastopol Investments Pty Ltd.*[659] This case concerned the application of s. 45 of the Act, as originally drafted, to restrictive covenants contained in a contract for the sale of land. The Court held that on a grant of land it cannot be said, whatever the terms of the covenants, that it is in restraint of trade for conditions to be attached to the grant. The rationale for this decision is that prior to the sale the purchaser had no rights in relation to the land, and regardless of the severity of the conditions, after the grant the purchaser will inevitably have greater rights in the land. In this regard, the High Court followed the reasoning of the House of Lords in *Esso Petroleum Co. Ltd v. Harper's Garage (Stourport) Ltd.*[660] Although the decision in *Quadramain* did not relate to the landlord-tenant relationship, there is a direct parallel between the sale of land and the grant of a leasehold estate, and it was universally accepted that leases were outside the scope of Pt IV.

Following *Quadramain*, the *Trade Practices Act* was extensively amended in 1977. Some of the changes were designed to ensure the future application of the Act to leases. For example, a new s. 4H was inserted which states, inter alia, that a reference to a contract shall be construed as including a reference to a lease of, or a licence in respect of, land or a building or part of a building. Section 47, relating to exclusive dealing, was repealed and replaced. The new provision specifically defines "exclusive dealing" as including the situation where a corporation refuses to grant or renew a lease or exercise a right to terminate a lease where

659. (1976) 133 C.L.R. 390.
660. [1968] A.C. 269.

another party to the lease has acquired goods or services directly from a competitor of the corporation.

Section 45B: Covenants Affecting Competition

[**10.91**]   Section 45B(1) states:

> "A covenant, whether the covenant was given before or after the commencement of this section, is unenforceable in so far as it confers rights or benefits or imposes duties or obligations on a corporation or on a person associated with a corporation if the covenant has, or is likely to have, the effect of substantially lessening competition in any market in which the corporation or any person associated with the corporation supplies or acquires, or is likely to supply or acquire, goods or services or would, but for the covenant, supply or acquire, or be likely to supply or acquire, goods or services."

Subsection (2) prohibits a corporation from requiring the giving of a covenant, or giving a covenant, if the proposed covenant has the purpose, or would have or be likely to have the effect of substantially lessening competition in any market for the supply or acquisition of goods or services in which the corporation is involved. A person is deemed to require the giving of a covenant, within the meaning of s. 45B(2), where he or she issues an invitation or an offer to another person to enter into a contract containing a covenant, or makes it known that he or she will not enter into a contract of a particular kind unless the contract contains a covenant of a particular kind or in particular terms: s. 45B(3). By s. 45B(9), the section does not apply to any covenant if the sole or principal purpose for which it is required to be given is to restrict the use of the relevant land to residential purposes. The section also has no application where the person requiring the covenant to be given is a religious, charitable or public benevolent institution or its trustees.

"Covenant" is defined in s. 4(1) as meaning a covenant

> "annexed to or running with an estate or interest in land (whether at law or in equity and whether or not for the benefit of other land)."

Thus, s. 45B only applies to those covenants running with the land.[661] This is not an important restriction since most provisions in a lease which could affect competition, including covenants as to user and ties, run with the land. In addition, it is important to note that all covenants run with the land in respect of Torrens land.[662]

Section 47: Exclusive Dealing

[**10.92**]   Section 47(1) states that a corporation shall not, in trade or commerce, engage in the practice of exclusive dealing. The relevance of this provision to landlord-tenant law is explained in s. 47(8) and (9). Section 47(8) states:

> "A corporation also engages in the practice of exclusive dealing if the corporation grants or renews, or makes it known that it will not

---

661. See above [**10.42**] for covenants which run with the land.
662. Torrens statutes: N.S.W.: ss 36, 51, 52; Vic.: s. 45(2); Qld: ss 3, 44, 65, 66, 68; W.A.: s. 95; Tas.: ss 3, 60.

exercise a power or right to terminate, a lease of, or a licence in respect of, land or a building or part of a building on the condition that another party to the lease or licence or, if that other party is a body corporate, a body corporate related to that body corporate—

(a) will not, or will not except to a limited extent—

    (i) acquire goods or services, or goods or services of a particular kind of description, directly or indirectly from a competitor of the corporation or from a competitor of a body corporate related to the corporation; or

    (ii) re-supply goods, or goods of a particular kind or description, acquired directly or indirectly from a competitor of the corporation or from a competitor of a body corporate related to the corporation;

(b) will not supply goods or services, or goods or services of a particular kind or description, to any person, or will not, or will not except to a limited extent, supply goods or services, or goods or services of a particular kind or description—

    (i) to particular persons or classes of persons or to persons other than particular persons or classes of persons; or

    (ii) in particular places or classes of places or in places other than particular places or classes of places; or

(c) will acquire goods or services of a particular kind or description directly or indirectly from another person not being a body corporate related to the corporation.''

Section 47(9), which was held by the High Court to be constitutionally valid in *Trade Practices Commission v. Tooth & Co. Ltd*,[663] deals with the converse situation and includes within the meaning of ''exclusive dealing'' a refusal by a corporation to grant or renew, or exercise a power or right to terminate a lease on the ground that the tenant is engaged in one or more of the practices referred to in s. 47(8). Section 47(11) contains similar exemptions to these granted by s. 45B(9) in favour of trustees for religious, charitable or public benevolent institutions. None of the conduct of the corporation referred to in subss (8) and (9) constitutes an infringement of s. 47(1) unless it has the purpose, or has or is likely to have the effect, of substantially lessening competition: s. 47(10).

Redfern and Cassidy[664] give a number of illustrations of the operation of s. 47 in the landlord-tenant context. Useful examples are a condition in the lease that the tenant shall acquire some or all of his stock only from the landlord or from a company associated with the landlord, or the fact that the landlord takes into account when granting, renewing or terminating a lease the source from which the tenant has acquired its stock. In fact, the section is sufficiently wide-embracing to include within its scope any tie requiring the tenant to deal with the landlord or an associated person or to refrain from dealing with another specified person.

---

663. (1979) 142 C.L.R. 397.
664. Redfern and Cassidy, para. 1512.

If a company proposes to engage in conduct which amounts or may amount to exclusive dealing, it can lodge a notification with the Commission under s. 93. If the Commission is satisfied that the engaging by the company in the proposed conduct is likely to have a substantial anti-competitive effect and that in all the circumstances the conduct is not likely to result in a benefit to the public or that any such benefit would not outweigh the detriment to the public constituted by any lessening of competition, the Commission may give notice in writing to the company stating that it is so satisfied. Before it can lawfully give such a notice, however, the Commission is required by s. 93A to afford the company the opportunity to confer with it about the proposed conduct. Once the company notifies the Commission of its intention to engage in the proposed conduct, then it can lawfully engage in that conduct until the expiration of 30 days from the date of the service upon it of the Commission's notice. This means that in practical terms, a company can engage in conduct which is or may amount to exclusive dealing immediately after it has given to the Commission the requisite notice and may continue to do so until at least 30 days after the holding of a compulsory conference: s. 93(7)(b). The authorisation procedures were retained in the 1977 Amendment, but a new test has been substituted for the one that was set out in the original 1974 legislation. The test now is whether the public benefit flowing from the agreement outweighs the detriment of its anti-competitive provisions: s. 90(7). In other words, it seems that it may no longer be necessary for the applicant to demonstrate that the agreement will have a "substantial" public benefit or that such a benefit was "not otherwise available". As in the case of the notification procedure, before the Commission finally determines an application for an authorisation adversely to the applicant, it must afford the applicant an opportunity to hold a conference with it. The Commission's refusal to grant an authorisation may be reviewed by the Trade Practices Tribunal.

Other Provisions

[10.93]   Sections 45B and 47 are the only substantive provisions in Pt IV of the Act specifically referring to leases. Despite this, however, as a lease is included within the meaning of a "contract" by virtue of s. 4H, other provisions may occasionally be applicable to the landlord-tenant relationship. Thus, the anti-monopolisation law in s. 46 and the provisions in s. 45 against contracts which constitute an exclusionary provision or have the purpose, or have or are likely to have the effect, of substantially lessening competition may sometimes apply in the present context.[665]

Declarations as to Act

[10.94]   It is now possible to apply for a declaration under s. 163A as to the operation of the relevant provisions of the Act. The application may be made to the Federal Court or to the State Supreme Court.

---

665. For a detailed discussion of these provisions, see Redfern and Cassidy, paras 1513-1514.

2. Consumer Protection: Trade Practices Act, Pt V

[10.95] Part V of the Act contains a number of consumer protection measures which are concerned with the supply of goods or services. "Services" is defined in s. 4(1) as including rights in relation to, and interests in, real property. Leases are thus clearly within the scope of this Part of the legislation. The following remedies may be available to tenants:

Section 52

[10.96] A general proscription of misleading or deceptive conduct engaged in by a corporation in trade or commerce is contained in s. 52. Section 52(1) states:

"A corporation shall not, in trade or commerce, engage in conduct that is misleading or deceptive or is likely to mislead or deceive."

The purpose of this section was explained by Barwick C.J. in *Hornsby Building Information Centre Pty Ltd v. Sydney Building Information Centre Ltd*:[666]

"Section 52 is concerned with conduct which is deceptive of members of the public in their capacity as consumers of goods or services: it is not concerned merely with the protection of the reputation or goodwill of competitors in trade or commerce."

The phrase "engaging in conduct" is defined in s. 4(2) as follows:

"In this Act a reference to engaging in conduct shall be read as a reference to doing or refusing to do any act, including the making of, or the giving effect to a provision of, a contract or arrangement, the arriving at, or the giving effect to a provision of, an understanding or the requiring of the giving of, or the giving of, a covenant."

Surprisingly, however, there is no definition of "misleading" and "deceptive" contained in the *Trade Practices Act*. In interpreting these words, Franki J. stated in *Weitmann v. Katies Ltd*:[667]

"The most appropriate meaning for the word 'deceive' in the Oxford Dictionary is: 'To cause to believe what is false; to mislead; as to a matter of fact, to lead into error, to impose upon, delude, take in'. The most appropriate definition in that dictionary for the word 'mislead' is: 'To lead astray in action or conduct; to lead into error, to cause to err'."

The reported cases on s. 52 establish several propositions of law:

1. According to Northrop J. in *Keehn v. Medical Benefits Fund of Australia Ltd*,[668] a statement is misleading "if it would lead one ordinary member of the public, likely to read the statement or be influenced by it, into error".[669] This seems to suggest that the correct test of liability under

666. (1978) 140 C.L.R. 216 at 220.
667. (1977) 29 F.L.R. 336 at 343.
668. (1977) 14 A.L.R. 77 at 81.
669. *Taco Co. of Australia v. Taco Bell Pty Ltd* (1982) 42 A.L.R. 177. See also *Global Sportsman Pty Ltd v. Mirror Newspapers Ltd* (1984) 2 F.C.R. 82 at 88; *Bill Acceptance Corporation Ltd v. G.W.A. Ltd* (1983) 78 F.L.R. 171; *Parkdale Custom Built Furniture Pty Ltd v. Puxu Pty Ltd* (1982) 149 C.L.R. 191; *C.R.W. Pty Ltd v. Sneddon* (1972) A.R. (N.S.W.) 17 at 28.

s. 52 is to ascertain whether the conduct complained of has a misleading or deceptive tendency; if so, the section will be infringed without the need for proof of further facts.

2. Section 52 will be breached even in circumstances where a corporation did not intend to deceive or believe that its conduct was not misleading or deceptive. In other words, mens rea on the part of the corporation is irrelevant: *Hornsby Building Information Centre Pty Ltd v. Sydney Building Information Centre Ltd.*[670]

3. Section 52 will not be breached if the only result of the conduct is to confuse the public. The major authority on this point is *McWilliam's Wines Pty Ltd v. McDonald's System of Australia Pty Ltd*,[671] where the Full Court of the Federal Court held that the confusion caused by the appellants in advertising one of its table wines as "Big Mac", the same title as given to the respondent's hamburgers, did not amount to misleading conduct within the meaning of s. 52(1).

4. As stated by Stephen J. in *Hornsby Building Information Centre Pty Ltd v. Sydney Building Information Centre Ltd*:[672] "nothing in [s. 52(1)] suggests that a statement made which is literally true . . . may not at the same time be misleading and deceptive." It thus appears that s. 52 extends to cases of failure to disclose relevant information where the suppression of facts will mislead a person. Two relevant cases interpreting the American legislation equivalent to s. 52(1) are *Aronberg v. F.C.T.*[673] and *Tashof v. F.C.T.*[674] *Aronberg's* case held that the section will be breached where a corporation fails to identify an inherently dangerous feature of goods or services, while in *Tashof's* case it was decided that a breach occurs where there is a failure to disclose an essential term of a transaction.

5. Mere exaggeration of the capabilities of goods or services is permissible provided that the corporation does not make specific claims for the product that cannot be substantiated. Legally permissible exaggeration is usually referred to as "puffing". Each case is decided on all the facts in light of the surrounding circumstances: see for example, *Lyndon v. Coventry Motors Retailers Pty Ltd.*[675]

There are several reported illustrations of the application of s. 52 to the landlord-tenant relationship. For example, in *Mister Figgins Pty Ltd v. Centrepoint Freeholds Pty Ltd*,[676] Northrop J., of the Federal Court, held that the section was infringed by representations by the landlord's agent relating to the appearance of the shopping complex, the nature of the tenants of the other shops and the rate of occupancy of the rented premises within the complex. A further illustration is *Brown v. The Jam Factory Pty Ltd*,[677] where the tenant successfully argued for the application of s. 52 where the landlord's agent had falsely misrepresented to him that all but

670. (1978) 140 C.L.R. 216.
671. (1980) 33 A.L.R. 394.
672. (1978) 140 C.L.R. 216 at 217.
673. (1943) 132 F. 2d 165.
674. (1970) 473 F. 2d 707.
675. (1975) 11 S.A.S.R. 308.
676. (1981) 36 A.L.R. 23.
677. (1981) 53 F.L.R. 340.

one of the shops within the shopping centre had been leased and that all the shops would be opened when the shopping centre itself was opened.[678]

A breach of s. 52 is not treated as an offence punishable by a fine. Section 79(1), which creates offences for breaches of Pt V of the Act, expressly excepts s. 52 from the scope of its operation. The major remedy for a breach of s. 52 is for the Minister for Business and Consumer Affairs, the Trade Practices Commission or any other person to apply to the court for an injunction restraining a person from engaging in conduct that constitutes a breach of s. 52: s. 80(1). In addition, a tenant of commercial premises who proves that a landlord corporation has infringed s. 52 may bring an action for damages: s. 82(1), and may also seek rectification under the general discretionary power of the court contained in s. 87(1) to make "such order or orders as it thinks appropriate against the person who engaged in the conduct".

Section 53A(1)

[10.97] Pursuant to s. 53A(1)(b), a corporation must not, in trade or commerce, in connection with the actual or possible sale or grant of an interest in land, or in connection with the promotion of such sale or grant, make a false or misleading representation concerning the nature of the interest in the land, the price payable for the land, the location of the land, the characteristics of the land, the use to which the land is capable of being put or may lawfully be put or the existence or availability of facilities associated with the land.

The majority of cases concern the sale of freehold land, where a number of convictions under s. 53A(1)(b) have occurred.[679] In the landlord-tenant context, most actions brought against corporations under this provision have been unsuccessful. For example, a tenant who had leased premises to store printing materials failed to prove a breach of s. 53A(1)(b) where the floor proved inadequate and the premises became unsuitable for its business: *Bradford House Pty Ltd v. Leroy Fashions Group Ltd.*[680] See also *Brown v. The Jam Factory Pty Ltd.*[681] Both actions in these cases appear to have failed because the false or misleading representation did not on the facts relate to a "characteristic" of the land.

Section 53A(2)

[10.98] This subsection proscribes the use of physical force, undue harassment or coercion in connection with the grant of an interest in land

678. For further cases on s. 52 involving the landlord-tenant relationship, see *A.D.C. Centres Pty Ltd v. Kilstream Pty Ltd* (1979) 25 A.L.R. 549; *Cohen v. Centrepoint Freeholds Pty Ltd* (1982) 66 F.L.R. 57; *Maniero Pty Ltd v. El Barador Holdings Pty Ltd* (1982) 1 T.P.R. 437; *Lyons v. Kern Konstructions (Townsville) Pty Ltd* (1983) 47 A.L.R. 114. For s. 52 cases involving service station leases, see e.g. *George MacGregor Auto Service Pty Ltd v. Caltex Oil (Australia) Pty Ltd* (1980) 51 F.L.R. 458; *Dinyarrak Investments Pty Ltd v. Amoco Australia Ltd* (1982) 45 A.L.R. 214; *Steedman v. Golden Fleece Petroleum Ltd* (1986) A.T.P.R. 40-060.

679. *Given v. Pryor* (1980) 30 A.L.R. 189; *Sackville v. Mansard Developments Pty Ltd* (1981) A.T.P.R. 40-222; *Videon v. Barry Burroughs Pty Ltd* (1981) 53 F.L.R. 425; *Latella v. L. J. Hooker Ltd* (1985) 5 F.C.R. 146.

680. (1983) 46 A.L.R. 305.

681. (1981) 53 F.L.R. 340.

or the payment of an interest in land. The most obvious illustration of the use of this subsection in the present context is harassment or force used in the collection of arrears of rent. To date, there are no relevant authorities on this subsection relating to the landlord-tenant relationship.

Section 55A

[10.99] Pursuant to this section, a corporation must not, in trade or commerce, engage in conduct that is liable to mislead the public as to the nature, the characteristics, the suitability for their purpose or the quantity of any services. This section could be infringed where the landlord publishes a misleading brochure or prospectus concerning premises to be leased.

To date, there are no reported cases concerning the application of this section to the sale or grant of an interest in land. For cases where a travel agent and an insurance agent were held guilty of breaches of s. 55A(1), see *Doherty v. Traveland Pty Ltd*[682] and *Adams v. Anthony Bryant & Co. Pty Ltd*,[683] respectively.

Other Sections

[10.100] It is possible for a landlord corporation to be guilty of one of a number of specific offences contained in s. 53. Several of these overlap with s. 52. In this regard, it must be remembered that whereas s. 52 creates only civil liability, a breach of s. 53 is regarded as an offence.

Section 53 creates 11 separate offences, of which the following five may be applicable in the landlord-tenant context in the appropriate circumstances. The relevant parts of the section read:

"A corporation shall not, in trade or commerce, in connexion with the supply or possible supply of goods or services or in connexion with the promotion by any means of the supply or use of goods or services—

. . .

(aa) falsely represent that services are of a particular standard, quality or grade;

. . .

(bb) falsely represent that a particular person has agreed to acquire goods or services;

. . .

(d) represent that the corporation has a sponsorship, approval or affiliation it does not have;

(e) make a false or misleading representation with respect to the price of goods or services;

. . .

(g) make a false or misleading representation concerning the existence, exclusion or effect of any condition, warranty, guarantee, right or remedy."

682. (1982) A.T.P.R. 40-323.
683. (1987) A.T.P.R. 40-784.

Like s. 52, it appears that s. 53 is based on strict liability. Authority for this proposition is *Given v. C.V. Holland (Holdings) Pty Ltd*[684] where the defendant argued unsuccessfully that the words "falsely represent" require the plaintiff to prove in the case of a corporation that a person of sufficient seniority to bind the company knew that the representation was false. Franki J. stated:[685]

> "if a representation is in fact not correct it comes within the words of the section, even if it is not false to the knowledge of the person making the representation, and even if the person making the representation is a servant of the company of insufficient significance in the company for his knowledge, according to the ordinary principles of common law, to be deemed to be the knowledge of the company. There is nothing novel in equating 'false' with 'contrary to fact'."

Section 59(2) may also possibly be of relevance. This subsection reads:

> "Where a corporation, in trade or commerce, invites, whether by advertisement or otherwise, persons to engage or participate, or to offer or apply to engage or participate, in a business activity requiring the performance by the persons concerned of work, or the investment of moneys by the persons concerned and the performance by them of work associated with the investment, the corporation shall not make with respect to the profitability or risk or any other material aspect of the business activity, a representation that is false or misleading in a material particular."

As discussed by Redfern and Cassidy,[686] the subsection arguably includes within its scope an invitation contained in an advertisement or brochure to take a tenancy of business premises, particularly if either a premium is to be paid, or investment in plant, fixtures or stock is required. A further possible illustration is a general offer for the sale of a business conducted on the rented premises.

At first glance, s. 52A, added in 1986, appears to be significant to landlord-tenant law. Pursuant to s. 52A(1), a corporation must not, in trade or commerce, in connection with the supply of possible goods or services to a person, engage in conduct that is, in all the circumstances, unconscionable. Section 52A(5) states, however, that a reference to goods and services is a reference to goods and services of a kind ordinarily acquired for personal, domestic or household use or consumption. The effect of this is to make the section irrelevant to commercial leases in all but the most exceptional circumstances.

Remedies

[10.101] Except for s. 52, a breach of any of the clauses of Pt V of the Act discussed above constitutes an offence punishable by a maximum fine of $20,000 (in the case of a person) or $100,000 (in the case of a body corporate): s. 79(1). Section 85(1) states that it is a defence if the

684. (1977) 29 F.L.R. 212.
685. Ibid. at 217.
686. Redfern and Cassidy, para. 1614.

defendant establishes one or more of three factors: first, that the contravention was due to a reasonable mistake; secondly, that the contravention was due to reasonable reliance on information supplied by another person; or thirdly, that the contravention was due to the act or default of another person, to an accident or to some other cause beyond the defendant's control and that the defendant took reasonable precautions and exercised due diligence to avoid the contravention.[687]

687. For a discussion of s. 85, see Duggan, "The Criminal Liability of Corporations for Contravention of Part V of the Trade Practices Act" (1977) 5 Aust. Bus. L. Rev. 221.

11
Statutory Tenancies

[11.01] In addition to the general law of landlord and tenant, discussed in the preceding Chapter, there exists in Australia four different types of legislation regulating certain classes of premises:

(a) residential tenancies legislation (in all States except Tasmania);

(b) retail tenancies legislation (in all States except New South Wales and Tasmania);

(c) rent control legislation (in New South Wales and Victoria); and

(d) farm tenancies legislation (in New South Wales, Queensland and South Australia).

These Acts either totally or partially replace the general law of landlord and tenant in respect of premises to which they apply.

I. RESIDENTIAL TENANCIES LEGISLATION

[11.02] Comprehensive legislation regulating residential tenancies was initially introduced in South Australia[1] and Victoria,[2] and later in New South Wales[3] and Western Australia.[4] In these States, landlord and tenant law has now been codified in respect of those residential tenancies within the scope of the legislation. In Queensland,[5] less comprehensive residential tenancies legislation exists which merely supplements the general law.

The content of the residential tenancies legislation varies significantly between the States. In no State does the *Residential Tenancies Act* apply to all residential leased premises. In each State, the Act expressly exempts a variety of miscellaneous types of premises from the scope of the legislation.[6] It achieves this result by stating that the Act applies to a "tenancy agreement" entered into on or after the commencement of the legislation, and by then declaring that the Act does not apply to certain designated tenancy agreements. The lists of exemptions vary slightly between the States, but include the following categories: where the premises form part of a farm, tenancy agreements arising pursuant to a

1. *Residential Tenancies Act* 1978 (S.A.).
2. *Residential Tenancies Act* 1980 (Vic.).
3. *Residential Tenancies Act* 1987 (N.S.W.). As at April 1989, this legislation has not yet been proclaimed in effect.
4. *Residential Tenancies Act* 1987 (W.A.).
5. *Residential Tenancies Act* 1975 (Qld).
6. N.S.W.: ss 5-6; Vic.: ss 6-7; S.A.: ss 7, 7a; W.A.: ss 5-6. Cf. Qld: s. 5.

contract of sale or mortgage, tenancy agreements created or arising under
the terms of a contract of employment, fixed-term agreements exceeding
five years in duration, agreements in respect of premises that immediately
before the agreement was entered into constituted the landlord's principal
place of residence, holiday premises, club premises, hotels, motels,
educational institutions, and hospitals, nursing homes and homes for the
disabled. There is also a power included within the legislation to designate
other premises as exempted from the operation of the legislation. Other
important exceptions are boarders and lodgers and occupiers of mobile
homes. In South Australia,[7] although not in the remaining States,[8] public
housing tenancies are also exempted.

Undoubtedly the most wide-ranging reform achieved by the residential
tenancies legislation was the establishment of a Residential Tenancies
Tribunal with powers to hear and determine all disputes arising within the
scope of the *Residential Tenancies Act*.[9] The legislation gives the Tribunal
extensive powers, including the power to make monetary compensation
orders (up to a specified limit), orders for possession, orders requiring
either party to undertake designated work, restraining orders, orders
reducing rent declared to be excessive, ancillary or incidental
determinations, and (in Victoria) the power to shorten the term of fixed-
term tenancy agreements in certain circumstances.

Numerous changes to the substantive law of landlord and tenant were
effected by the residential tenancies legislation.

1. Repairs and Cleanliness

[11.03]　　The legislation imposes for the first time a basic duty on the
landlord to repair the premises.[10] The landlord's duty is subject to a
statutory duty on the tenant to ensure that care is taken to avoid damaging
the rented premises.[11] Thus, the landlord will be liable to repair any
damage caused intentionally, recklessly or negligently by the tenant or her
or his invitees. The landlord's duty to repair is also subject to an
obligation on the tenant to give notice of any damage to the landlord.[12]
As a basic rule, the tenant is required to obtain an order for repairs from
the Tribunal, if he or she believes that the premises are substandard.[13]
However, in certain circumstances the legislation allows the tenant to
undertake urgent repairs and to seek reimbursement from the landlord for
the reasonable costs incurred.[14] This provision, which was strongly
opposed by landlords and developers, is severely limited in its operation

---

7.　S.A.: s. 6(2).

8.　N.S.W.: s. 4 (but see also s. 132); Vic.: s. 10; W.A.: s. 4.

9.　The provision relating to the constitution and establishment of the Tribunal are
　　contained in N.S.W.: ss 80-85; Vic.: ss 14-48; S.A.: ss 14-29. In Western
　　Australia, disputes are determined by a referee of the Small Claims Tribunal: see
　　s. 12.

10.　N.S.W.: s. 25(1); Vic.: s. 97; Qld: s. 7(a)(ii); S.A.: s. 46(1)(b); W.A.: s. 42(1)(b).

11.　N.S.W.: s. 30; Vic.: s. 102(b); Qld: s. 7(b)(ii); S.A.: s. 42(1)(c); W.A.: s. 38(1)(c).

12.　N.S.W.: s. 26(1)(b); Vic.: s. 90; S.A.: s. 42(1)(b); W.A.: s. 38(1)(b).

13.　N.S.W.: s. 85(1); Vic.: s. 100; S.A.: s. 22(1).

14.　N.S.W.: s. 28(1); Vic.: s. 99; S.A.: s. 46(1)(c); W.A.: s. 43.

in New South Wales and Victoria by legislative restrictions on the maximum amount of reimbursement which can be sought and by limitations on the type of repairs which fall within the scope of the "urgent repairs" provision.[15]

In contrast to the law on repairs, the new legislation imposes the primary duty relating to cleanliness on the tenant. The legislation requires a tenant to keep the rented premises in a reasonably clean condition.[16] However, although the tenant is under a duty to *keep* the premises in a reasonably clean condition, he or she is not under a duty to *put* it in such a condition at the commencement of the lease. This falls within the statutory duties of the landlord.[17]

2. Excessive Rents

[11.04] Except in Queensland, the legislation has introduced a new system of controlling excessive rents. This new system enables any tenant who considers that the rent payable is excessive having regard to the fact that the landlord has reduced or withdrawn any goods, services or facilities provided with the rented premises, or who has received notice from the landlord of a rent increase and considers that the increase is excessive, to apply to the Tribunal for an order declaring that the rent, or proposed rent, is excessive.[18] If the Tribunal makes such an order, it may determine the maximum amount of rent payable in respect of the premises. This order will continue in effect for 12 months after the day on which the order comes into operation.[19] In Victoria, the procedure is complicated by a statutory requirement that the matter cannot be determined by the Tribunal until the Director of Consumer Affairs has investigated and reported on the matter.[20] In South Australia, the legislation is broader and permits a tenant to challenge the original rent as excessive before the Tribunal.[21] In all States, the legislation lists a number of factors which the Tribunal must take into account when determining whether the rent is excessive.[22]

3. Rent Increases

[11.05] The relevant provisions vary between the States. For example, in Victoria, any provision in a tenancy agreement under which the landlord may exercise a right to review, or to increase, the rent at intervals of less than six months, is void. Where a tenancy agreement contains a provision under which a landlord may exercise a right to review, or to increase, the rent at intervals of not less than six months, a landlord shall

---

15. N.S.W.: s. 28(1); Vic.: ss 99(1)(b), 99(3). Cf. S.A.: s. 46(1a); W.A.: s. 43(1).
16. N.S.W.: s. 26(1)(a); Vic.: s. 102(a); S.A.: s. 42(1)(a); W.A.: s. 38(1)(a). Cf. Qld: s. 7(b)(i).
17. N.S.W.: s. 25(1)(b); Vic.: s. 91; S.A.: s. 46(1)(a); W.A.: s. 42(1)(a).
18. N.S.W.: ss 46-47; Vic.: s. 63(1); S.A.: s. 36(1); W.A.: s. 32(1). This legislation is based on the now-repealed *Excessive Rents Act* 1962 (S.A.).
19. N.S.W.: s. 49(4); Vic.: s. 64(5); S.A.: s. 36(4); W.A.: s. 32(5) (six months only).
20. Vic.: ss 63(1), 64(1).
21. S.A.: s. 36(1).
22. N.S.W.: s. 48; Vic.: s. 63(2); S.A.: s. 36(2); W.A.: s. 32(3).

not exercise a right to increase the rent unless he or she gives the tenant at least 60 days' notice in writing of the increase.[23]

4. Security Deposits

[11.06]　No common law rules existed on security deposits, and there was no statutory regulation of the taking of deposits. Thus, prior to the new legislation, there was no maximum limit imposed on the amount of deposit which could lawfully be demanded, there were no rules as to the entitlement of either party to interest, and no rules as to the use of the deposit during the lease.[24] Although the landlord was obliged to return the deposit at the end of the lease, the expense and time involved for the tenant in pursuing her or his claim before a magistrates' court was out of proportion to the amount of money in dispute.

The new legislation aims to establish a system of control over the important issues of security deposits, while at the same time endeavouring to minimise the occurrence of disputes in the future. The major reform in this area is the requirement that the deposit must be paid into the Tribunal,[25] and will be held by the Tribunal during the term of the lease.[26] At the end of the lease, the deposit will be returned in full to the tenant unless the landlord proves her or his entitlement to all or part of the deposit by lodging an application with the Tribunal and having the issue determined. In Victoria, a less satisfactory procedure applies whereby the landlord pays the deposit into an approved trust account maintained by her or him at an approved institution before the end of the third business day after the day on which the deposit is received.[27] As in other States, in Victoria the deposit must be returned to the tenant unless the Tribunal, on application by the landlord, otherwise determines.[28] The objection to the Victorian legislation is that it still allows for the possibility of default by the landlord.

In most States, the legislation regulates the maximum amount of any security deposit which may be demanded.[29] No interest is paid to either party. The interest is retained by the State Government and is used to defray the costs of the Tribunal and its staff; any excess is used for general housing purposes.[30] Unlike the other States, the Victorian Act contains an interesting provision whereby the tenant may elect to pay, in lieu of the

---

23. Vic.: ss 62(1)(2). Cf. N.S.W.: s. 45; S.A.: ss 34(1)(2); W.A.: s. 30(1).
24. The status of the deposit was stated by Barwick C.J. in *N.L.S. Pty Ltd v. Hughes* (1966) 120 C.L.R. 583 at 589, to be "an earnest of performance which on default, may be retained and credited against the damage suffered".
25. In New South Wales and Queensland, security deposits must be paid into a separate authority, the Rental Bond Board (N.S.W.) and the Rental Bond Authority (Qld).
26. *Landlord and Tenant (Rental Bonds) Act* 1977 (N.S.W.), s. 8; *Rental Bond Act* 1989 (Qld), s. 19; S.A.: s. 32(4); W.A.: s. 29(4) and Sched. 1.
27. Vic.: s. 67.
28. Vic.: s. 77.
29. *Landlord and Tenant (Rental Bonds) Act* 1977 (N.S.W.), s. 9(2); Vic.: s. 70; S.A.: s. 32(1); W.A.: s. 29(1).
30. *Landlord and Tenant (Rental Bonds) Act* 1977 (N.S.W.), s. 9(2); Vic.: ss 54, 68; S.A.: ss 84, 86; W.A.: s. 29(4) and Sched. 1.

security deposit, an amount in respect of a contract of insurance relating to the performance of the tenant's obligations in respect of the tenancy agreement, being a contract under which the amount of the sum assured is the amount of the security deposit demanded by the landlord.[31] The unsatisfactory nature of this provision has been commented upon in the past.[32] In this context, it is sufficient to note that the provision is in effect redundant, as neither the State Insurance Office nor any private insurance company is presently offering insurance of this nature. It is understood that damage caused by tenants to rented premises is regarded as an uninsurable risk.

5. The Tenant's Right to Assign or Sublet

[11.07] The residential tenancies legislation has replaced the common law rules by a new section detailing the rights and duties of both parties.[33] This section imposes two major changes in the law. First, except in New South Wales any assignment or sublease without the consent of the landlord is void, rather than valid but subject to forfeiture as under common law. Secondly, every tenancy agreement is subject to a term that the consent of the landlord shall not be unreasonably withheld. Thus, there is no further scope for the principle of freedom of contract in this matter.

6. Statutory Standard Form of Tenancy Agreement

[11.08] In Victoria, it is an offence, punishable by a penalty of $200, to prepare or authorise to be prepared a written tenancy agreement which is not in or to the effect of the prescribed standard form.[34] The form is prescribed by reg. 9 of the *Residential Tenancies Regulations* 1981. The form is very short and merely incorporates the rights and duties of the parties as specified in the Act itself. In South Australia, the Act states that the regulations may prescribe the form of written residential tenancy agreements and authorise or require the use of such form.[35] Although no form has been prescribed to date, a form has been prepared and is distributed by the Residential Tenancies Branch of the Department of Public and Consumer Affairs. Unlike the Victorian form, the South Australian form is lengthy and repeats the majority of the legislative provisions. The overall effect of the legislation is to abolish the "adhesive" standard forms of tenancy agreement in circulation prior to the new Acts.[36]

31. Vic.: s. 70(2).
32. Bradbrook, "The Rights and Duties of Landlords and Tenants under the Victorian Residential Tenancies Act" (1981) 13 M.U.L.R. 159 at 176-178.
33. N.S.W.: s. 33; Vic.: s. 108; Qld: s. 15; S.A.: s. 52; W.A.: s. 49.
34. Vic.: s. 85(1)(2).
35. S.A.: s 95(2)(f). Cf. N.S.W.: s. 8. No standard form has been prescribed in New South Wales. There is no relevant provision in Western Australia.
36. See Kessler, "Contracts of Adhesion—Some Thoughts About Freedom of Contract" (1943) 43 Columbia L. R. 629.

7. Termination of Tenancy Agreements

[11.09] The residential tenancies legislation has departed fundamentally from the common law principles in a number of different
respects. For the first time, different periods of notice are required from
the landlord and the tenant.[37] In general, the periods of notice required
of the tenant are shorter than those required of the landlord. The
justification for this change is the dislocating effect that eviction has on the
tenant and the need to give the tenant adequate time to find alternative
accommodation. Another change is that the length of the statutory notice
to vacate varies according to the reason for the termination of the lease.
In Victoria, for example, the specified periods of notice required of a
landlord range from six months, where no reason is given for
termination,[38] to immediate notice, where the rented premises are unfit
for human habitation, where the tenant causes malicious damage to the
premises or threatens the safety of occupiers of neighbouring premises, or
where the rented premises have been destroyed totally or to such an extent
as to be rendered unsafe.[39]

Numerous other changes have been made in this regard to the common
law. Limited protection is given to tenants whose leases are terminated by
landlords in retaliation for the exercise of any right conferred by the
residential tenancies legislation.[40] The Tribunal is empowered to nullify
or modify the application to the agreement of any provision of the
Residential Tenancies Act.[41] This provision may be used by the Tribunal to
prevent or delay orders for possession on the ground of hardship to
tenants. In Victoria, the legislation goes further and specifically empowers
the Tribunal, on the application of either party, to make an order
reducing the term of a fixed-term agreement by a period stated in the
order and to make such variations in the terms of the agreement as are
necessary because of the reduction of the term where it is satisfied that,
because of an unforeseen change in the applicant's circumstances, the
severe hardship which the applicant would suffer if the term of the lease
were not reduced would be greater than the hardship which the other
party to the agreement would suffer if the term were reduced.[42] A further
feature of the legislation of some States is the abrogation of the common
law rule that a fixed-term lease will expire due to the effluxion of time.
Under this legislation a notice to vacate must be served in accordance with
the terms of the legislation before the lease will come to an end.[43]

8. Miscellaneous Rights and Duties of the Parties

[11.10] The residential tenancies legislation contains a variety of
provisions affecting the rights and duties of landlords and tenants. Three
illustrations may be offered. First, the landlord's right to enter the rented

---

37. N.S.W.: ss 56-70; Vic.: ss 114-123; Qld: s. 17; S.A.: ss 63-72; W.A.: ss 60-75.
38. Vic.: s. 123.
39. Vic.: s. 118.
40. N.S.W.: s. 65(2); Vic.: ss 124, 148(b); S.A.: ss 66(1), 73(3); W.A.: s. 65(2).
41. N.S.W.: s. 126; Vic.: s. 71(1); S.A.: s. 91; W.A.: s. 84.
42. Vic.: s. 113.
43. N.S.W.: s. 60; Vic.: s. 109(1). Cf. S.A.: s. 61(1)(ab); W.A.: s. 72.

premises during the term of the lease, which was previously a matter for individual negotiations between the parties, is now heavily circumscribed by the terms of the new legislation.[44] Secondly, it is no longer possible for the parties to negotiate as to additional charges, other than the rent and security deposit, to be paid at the commencement of the lease. Thus, application deposits must be returned to the tenant in all cases, holding deposits and other charges are outlawed, and the costs of preparing a written lease cannot be charged by the landlord to the tenant.[45] Finally, except in New South Wales the legislation adds to other State and Commonwealth anti-discrimination laws by making it an offence, except in exceptional specified circumstances, for a landlord or an estate agent to refuse to let premises to another person under a lease on the ground that the tenant intends to live on the premises with a child.[46]

II. RETAIL TENANCIES LEGISLATION

[11.11]   Legal protection for certain types of retail tenancies was first introduced in Queensland in the *Retail Shop Leases Act* 1984 (Qld).[47] Similar, though not identical, legislation has since been enacted in Victoria (*Retail Tenancies Act* 1986 (Vic.)),[48] in South Australia (*Statutes Amendment (Commercial Tenancies) Act* (S.A.), which adds a new Pt IV to the *Landlord and Tenant Act* 1936 (S.A.)) and in Western Australia: *Commercial Tenancy (Retail Shops) Agreements Act* 1985 (W.A.).[49]

Although constituting a significant legal reform, the retail tenancies legislation is of less fundamental significance than the new residential tenancies legislation. Unlike the Residential Tenancies Acts, none of the States' retail tenancies legislation constitutes a code. For this reason, there is still significant scope for the application of common law principles and general property law legislation to retail tenancies. Thus, for example, common law and existing general property law legislation continue to apply to retail tenancies in respect of repairs, cleanliness, rent increases and security deposits[50] in the absence of any express provisions relating

44. N.S.W.: s. 24; Vic.: s. 95; S.A.: s. 49; W.A.: s. 46.
45. N.S.W.: ss 36-39, 42-43; Vic.: ss 80, 81, 83; S.A.: ss 30, 57; W.A.: ss 27, 28.
46. Vic.: s. 88; S.A.: s. 58; W.A.: s. 56.
47. See generally Tarlo, "The Great Shop Lease Controversy" (1984) 13 U.Q.L.J. 7; Tarlo, "The Retail Shop Leases Act 1984 (Queensland)" [1984] A.C.L. 36069; Tarlo, "Pioneering in the Deep North: Tinkering with Shop Leases" (1985) 8 Qd Lawyer 67; Preece, "Property: The Retail Shop Leases Act 1984" (1984) 14 (No. 2) Q.L.S.J. 25; Preece, "Legislative Regulation of Leases of Business Premises" (1985) 1 Q.I.T.L.J. 139; Bradbrook and Croft, Chap. 24.
48. Bradbrook and Croft, Chap. 23; Redfern, "The Victorian Retail Tenancies Act 1986" (1988) 62 L.I.J. 37; Paine, "Advanced Conveyancing and Property Law—Retail Tenancies Act 1986", B.L.E.C., *Seminar Paper* (May 1987); Best, "Ambit of the Arbitration Provisions of the Retail Tenancies Act" (1989) 63 L.I.J. 367.
49. Bradbrook and Croft, Chap. 26.
50. Except in South Australia, where ss 59-61 of the *Landlord and Tenant Act* 1936 regulate many aspects of the taking of security deposits.

to these issues in the retail tenancies legislation. In addition, the scope of the legislation is very limited.[51]

The most significant restrictions on the scope of the legislation are the statutory exclusion of premises that have a floor area exceeding 1,000 square metres,[52] and the exclusion of premises where the lease is held as a tenant by a corporation or a subsidiary of a corporation which would not be eligible under the State *Companies Code* to be incorporated as a proprietary company. Both limitations were inserted in order to exclude national retail chains of stores from the application of the Act, and can be justified on the basis that the owners of larger stores possess sufficient bargaining power and negotiating skills to conduct their legal relationship with their landlords on an equal footing, and do not require the statutory forms of protection required by small business tenants.

Thus, numerous retail tenancies are excluded from the scope of the legislation. Interestingly, however, the Act is not restricted to leases of premises in shopping centres, even though most of the arguments in favour of legal reform resulted from the nature of shopping centre standard form leases and various restrictions placed on the individual retailers by the owners or developers of the centres. The Act is worded to apply to all retail situations, regardless of the nature of the land development.[53] Except in Queensland, the Act is also stated to apply to the Crown in all its capacities.[54]

Perhaps the most significant feature of the legislation is the mechanism for the determination of disputes. In this regard, the legislation differs between the States. In Victoria, any dispute other than the payment of rent or a dispute which is capable of being determined by a registered valuer must be referred to arbitration.[55] The Victorian legislation empowers the Governor-in-Council, on the nomination of the Minister, to appoint members of a panel of arbitrators for the purposes of the Act.[56] This simple procedure should be compared with Queensland, where the legislation establishes a two-tiered system of mediation and determination by a specialist tribunal.[57] The Queensland Act seeks to ensure that, wherever possible, disputes are resolved by a member of a panel of mediators appointed under the terms of the legislation. Where mediation fails, however, the dispute is determined by the Retail Shop Lease Tribunal, which is constituted by three persons—a District Court judge, a person representative of landlords under retail-shop leases and a person representative of tenants under such leases. This Tribunal has general jurisdiction over disputes relating to retail-shop leases, but is not empowered to make an order that requires the payment of rent arrears or to make an order as to the amount of rent payable under a retail-shop

---

51. See the definition of "retail premises" or "retail shop" in Vic.: s. 3(1); Qld: s. 4(1); S.A.: s. 54; W.A.: s. 3(1).
52. This restriction does not exist under the South Australian legislation.
53. Vic.: s. 3(1); Qld: s. 4(1); S.A.: ss 54-55; W.A.: s. 3(1).
54. Vic.: s. 6; S.A.: s. 36; W.A.: s. 5.
55. See Vic.: ss 20-22 and the *Commercial Arbitration Act* 1984 (Vic.).
56. Vic.: s. 20(1).
57. See Qld: ss 17-50.

lease.[58] It is further provided that where a provision of a retail-shop lease requires or permits any issue to be submitted to arbitration it is not competent for a mediator to refer a dispute involving that issue to a Tribunal so far as it involves that issue.[59] In South Australia and Western Australia, disputes are resolved by the previously established State Commercial Tribunal.[60] However, it is provided in both States that when determining retail tenancy disputes, the Tribunal must consist, in addition to the Chairman or a Deputy Chairman of the Tribunal, of a member of a panel established under the retail tenancy legislation containing suitable persons to represent the interests of landlords under commercial tenancy agreements, and a member of a similar panel containing suitable persons to represent the interests of tenants under such agreements.[61]

The major provisions of the legislation reforming the common law of landlord and tenant are as follows.

1. Minimum Term of Lease

[11.12] Except in South Australia, the legislation bestows on each tenant the right to a lease of at least five years' duration.[62] This is presumably in recognition of the substantial period of time taken to establish goodwill in a business.

The relevant section in each State stipulates that a retail-premises lease gives the tenant an option to renew the lease for a term beginning immediately after the end of the current term and continuing until the day specified in the notice, that is five years after the beginning of the period when the premises were first occupied by the tenant as retail premises. Several exceptions are granted to the application of this section, the most significant being:[63]

1. The landlord holds the premises under a head lease and renewal of the retail-premises lease, or renewal of the retail-premises lease for a longer term than that provided for in an option to renew contained in it, would be inconsistent with the head lease.

2. The lease is not the first retail-premises lease entered into by the tenant as a tenant.

3. Not less than 90 days before the current term ends the landlord gives notice to the tenant in the prescribed form that at the end of the term the premises are to be demolished, or substantially repaired, renovated or reconstructed and the repair, renovation or reconstruction cannot be carried out practicably without vacant possession.

58. Qld: s. 36(2).
59. Qld: s. 36(3).
60. See S.A.: s. 56 and *Commercial Tribunal Act* 1982 (S.A.); W.A.: ss 16-27 and *Commercial Tribunal Act* 1984 (W.A.).
61. S.A.: Schedule, cll. 2-3; W.A.: s. 23.
62. Vic.: s. 13; Qld: s. 13; W.A.: s. 13.
63. The following represents the Victorian legislation. The equivalent legislation in Queensland and Western Australia differs slightly.

The legislation further provides that the statutory option is exercisable not less than 90 days before the current term ends and only if the tenant has remedied any default under the lease about which the landlord has given the tenant written notice. With certain specified exceptions, the terms and conditions upon which a lease is renewable under the statutory option are the same as those upon which the lease is held at the time the tenant gives notice of exercising the option.

2. Options to Renew (Victoria only)

[11.13] In addition to creating a statutory option to renew a lease, discussed above, the Victorian legislation regulates options to renew created by the parties.[64]

It is provided that any lease containing an option exercisable by the tenant to renew the lease for a further term must state the date until which the option is exercisable, the manner in which the option is to be exercised, the terms and conditions upon which the lease is renewable, and the manner in which the rent payable during the term for which the lease is renewed is to be determined. It is further provided that the only circumstances in which an option contained in a retail-premises lease is not exercisable is if the tenant has not remedied any default under the lease about which the landlord has given the tenant written notice, or if the tenant has persistently defaulted under the lease throughout its term and the landlord has given the tenant written notice of the defaults.

If a retail-premises lease contains an option exercisable by the tenant to renew the lease for a further term, the landlord must notify the tenant in writing of the date after which the option is no longer exercisable at least three months before that date. If a lease does not provide for an option to renew the lease, at least three months before the lease ends the landlord must give the tenant written notice as to whether he or she wishes to renew the lease, and if so, under which terms and conditions. In all such cases, if the landlord fails to give the requisite notice, the tenant is statutorily entitled to three months notice, and the lease or the right to exercise the option will continue for the declared three months period by virtue of the legislation.

3. Rent

[11.14] The common law right of the parties to negotiate freely as to the method of calculating the rent or as to increasing the rent has been severely compromised by various provisions in the retail-tenancies legislation.

Detailed provisions, which vary slightly between the States, have been prescribed affecting rent review.[65] In Victoria, the following clauses contained in a retail-premises lease have been declared to be void:

(a) a provision for a review of the rent to the extent that it states that the rent payable after the review must exceed or be not less than the rent payable immediately before the review;

64. Vic.: s. 14.
65. Vic.: s. 10; Qld: s. 10; S.A.: s. 62(1)(a); W.A.: s. 11.

(b) a provision that the rent is to be wholly or partly determined by reference to any index of prices, costs or wages; and

(c) a provision for a review of the rent, unless the lease specifies how the review is to be made.

Wherever a provision about rent is declared void by the statute, the rent must be agreed in writing between the landlord and tenant, or failing agreement within 30 days, will be determined by a registered valuer appointed jointly by the parties.

Except in South Australia, the legislation also strictly controls rent based on turnover.[66] It is stipulated that a provision in a retail-premises lease that the rent is to be determined either wholly or partly by reference to the turnover of the business is void unless the lease specifies how the rent is to be determined. If a rent clause is made void by this provision and the lease makes no other provision for determining the rent, the rent is to be as agreed in writing between the landlord and tenant. Failing such agreement, the rent is as determined by a registered valuer appointed jointly by the parties. If a rent clause is not made void by the provision controlling rent based on turnover, the tenant is obliged to provide monthly turnover statements to the landlord within a specified period, and also an annual audited turnover statement prepared by an independent accountant. Tenants are protected by a statutory definition of "turnover", which includes the amount recovered of a credit account previously written off by the tenant, but excludes various amounts which might otherwise be included to the detriment of the tenant. These include, for example, the net amount of discounts allowed to customers in the usual course of business, the amount of losses incurred in the resale or disposal of goods purchased from customers as trade-ins, the amount of uncollected credit accounts written off by the tenant, the amount of any cash or credit refunds allowed if merchandise is returned and the sale is cancelled, the amount of delivery charges, and the price of merchandise returned to shippers, wholesalers or manufacturers.

4. Statutory Covenants

[11.15] Except in South Australia, the retail-tenancies legislation retreats from the principle of freedom of contract by providing that every lease is taken to include certain specified covenants by the landlord, regardless of the parties' intention.[67] For example, the Victorian legislation specifies the following six covenants: not to inhibit the access of the tenant to the retail premises in any substantial manner; except with the tenant's consent, not to take any action that would substantially alter or inhibit the flow of customers to the premises; if the premises are situated in a retail shopping centre, not to cause, or to fail to make reasonable efforts to prevent or remove, any disruption to trading within the centre; to rectify any breakdown of plant or equipment under the landlord's care and maintenance; to comply with any requirement of a public statutory authority or government department if it is the landlord's

66. Vic.: s. 11; Qld: ss 6, 9; W.A.: s. 7.
67. Vic.: s. 17; Qld: s. 15; W.A.: s. 14.

responsibility to do so; and, if the premises are situated in a retail shopping centre, to adequately clean, maintain, repair or repaint any common area. The legislation provides for reasonable compensation to be paid to the tenant if any of these covenants are breached.

Collectively, these covenants protect the tenant far more effectively than the previously applicable common law rules, which allowed the parties to reach their own agreement as to each matter.

5. No Additional Charges to be Imposed on Tenants

[11.16] Like the residential-tenancies legislation, the retail-tenancies legislation seeks to prevent the imposition on tenants of charges other than rent and security deposits. It achieves this aim in a number of separate sections. In each State, the Act declares that a provision in a retail-premises lease is void if it entitles the landlord or a person claiming through the landlord to obtain from the tenant any key-money or any consideration for the goodwill of the business.[68] Certain exceptions are allowed. These allow the landlord to recover from the tenant, inter alia, costs which the landlord reasonably incurred in investigating a proposed assignee or subtenant of the premises, costs which the landlord reasonably incurred in connection with the documentation of the lease, an assignment or a sublease, and goodwill in relation to the sale of a business which the landlord operated from the retail premises immediately before its sale, if the lease was granted to the tenant in the course of the sale of the business.[69]

In Victoria, the legislation goes further and declares void any provision in a retail-premises lease to the extent that it purports to indemnify or require the tenant to indemnify the landlord against any action, liability, penalty, claim or demand for or to which the landlord would otherwise be liable or subject, and requires the landlord to indemnify the tenant for any amount recoverable from the tenant in respect of retail premises for charges, rates or taxes. Exceptions are specified in favour of charges for excess water rates, and any charges, rates or taxes for which, under the terms of the retail-premises lease, the tenant is liable.[70]

6. The Tenant's Right to Assign or Sublet

[11.17] The retail-tenancies legislation has substantially copied the form of the residential-tenancies legislation in replacing the common law rules in respect of assignments and subleases by a new section detailing the rights and duties of both landlords and tenants.[71] Two minor, yet significant, differences exist between the terms of the retail-tenancies and

68. Vic.: s. 9; Qld: s. 8; S.A.: ss 57, 63; W.A.: s. 9. In South Australia, a penalty of $400 is prescribed against landlords who require or receive from tenants or prospective tenants any monetary consideration for or in relation to entering into, extending or renewing a commercial tenancy agreement other than rent and a security deposit: s. 57(1).
69. This is the wording of Vic.: s. 9(2). Cf. Qld: s. 8(2); S.A.: s. 57(2); W.A.: s. 9(2).
70. Vic.: s. 19.
71. Vic.: s. 16; Qld: s. 11; S.A.: s. 64; W.A.: s. 10.

residential-tenancies legislation on this subject. First, the retail-tenancies legislation does not contain a provision that any assignment or sublease entered into by the tenant without the consent of the landlord is void. The effect of this is that, in respect of retail tenancies, the common law rule, that an assignment or sublease in these circumstances is valid but subject to forfeiture, continues to apply.[72] Secondly, the legislation states that if the tenant has requested the landlord in writing to consent to an assignment or a sublease of the premises and has provided the landlord with the name and address of the proposed assignee or subtenant, together with specified references and a copy of the proposed deed of assignment or sublease, the landlord is taken to have consented if he or she fails to give the tenant notice in writing consenting or withholding consent within 42 days.[73]

7. Additional Ground for Determination of Leases (Victoria and Western Australia only)

[11.18] In Victoria and Western Australia, the retail-tenancies legislation prescribes an additional ground available to tenants to terminate leases. This ground relates to the need for the tenant to be fully acquainted prior to entering into a retail-premises lease with certain relevant details of the lease.[74] A Schedule to the legislation prescribes a "disclosure statement", which refers to a variety of miscellaneous information concerning the lease including, for example, rent details, shopping-centre details, details as to the interest of the landlord in the premises, details as to agreements or representations made by either party in respect of the premises, and details as to the lease itself.

The legislation does not formally require the landlord to complete the disclosure statement and to give a copy of it to the tenant, but states that if a tenant has not been given a disclosure statement at least seven days before entering into a retail-premises lease, or if a disclosure statement given to a tenant is misleading, contains false information, or does not contain all the required information, the tenant may give the landlord a written notice of termination at any time within 28 days after entering into the lease. Exceptions are provided for on the assignment or renewal of the lease. If a tenant gives the landlord a notice of termination under this provision, the lease terminates 14 days after the notice is given.

III.   RENT CONTROL LEGISLATION

[11.19]   The advent of the Second World War led to the enactment of Australia-wide rent control legislation, enacted by the Commonwealth pursuant to its defence power under s. 51(vi) of the Constitution.[75] Following the repeal of the Commonwealth controls at the end of 1948,

---

72. See *Massart v. Blight* (1951) 82 C.L.R. 423.
73. Vic.: s. 16(1). Cf. Qld: s. 11(1); W.A.: s. 10.
74. Vic.: s. 7 and Sched.; W.A.: s. 6.
75. See *National Security Act* 1939 (Cth); *National Security (Landlord and Tenant) Regulations* 1941 (Cth).

all States enacted legislation designed to continue the operation of the
same system of rent control as before.

The legislation in Queensland, South Australia, Western Australia and
Tasmania was allowed to expire during the 1950s and early 1960s. In
Victoria and New South Wales, the former Commonwealth controls (as
re-enacted under State legislation) remain in effect, although they only
apply to a rapidly dwindling number of premises.

1. Victoria

[11.20]   In Victoria, the controls are now contained in Pt V of the
Landlord and Tenant Act 1958 (as amended by the *Residential Tenancies Act*
1980). This legislation restricts the application of the rent control
provisions to prescribed premises. Pursuant to s. 43, "prescribed
premises" means all premises (with certain exceptions)[76] leased between
31 December 1940 and 1 February 1954 which have not been relet to the
same tenant by a lease in writing for three years or over, nor have been
relet at any time to another tenant, nor have become excluded from the
protection of Pt V by an Order of the Governor-in-Council published in
the *Government Gazette*. The number of premises subject to the Act has been
decreasing over the years as premises are vacated, relet to a third party,
or as the tenant dies.[77]

Rents for prescribed premises were originally determined by the Fair
Rents Board, either on application by a landlord or a tenant (s. 57) or on
its own motion: s. 61. This power has now been transferred to the
Residential Tenancies Tribunal.[78] Pursuant to s. 64(1), the Tribunal
must have regard to the following matters when determining the fair rent:
the capital value of the premises;[79] annual rates, insurance premiums,
land tax and real estate agent's commission; the estimated annual cost of
repairs, maintenance and renewals; annual depreciation in the value of
the premises; the rents of comparable premises in the locality;[80] the rate
of interest charged upon overdrafts by the Commonwealth Trading Bank
of Australia; any services provided by the landlord or tenant in connection
with the lease; any obligation on the part of the tenant to make repairs;
the justice and merits of the case and the circumstances of the parties; and
any hardship which would be caused to either party by raising or lowering

---

76. The major exception is premises which are the property of any municipality,
    including the City of Melbourne and the City of Geelong, or of any waterworks
    trust under the *Water Act* 1958 (Vic.).
77. All tenants falling within the scope of s. 43 would now be aged pensioners. The
    Victorian Minister for Consumer Affairs reported in October 1982 that the
    average age of protected tenants within Pt V of the *Landlord and Tenant Act* 1958,
    was 74 years: Victoria, *Parliamentary Debates* (1982), p. 681. See also Community
    Committee on Tenancy Law Reform, *Reforming Victoria's Tenancy Laws*
    (Melbourne, 1978), p. 27.
78. *Residential Tenancies Act* 1980 (Vic.), s. 154(c).
79. When determining the capital value of the premises, prime consideration must be
    given to comparable sales in the locality: *Bourke v. Gow* [1961] V.R. 76; *Hume
    Investments Pty Ltd v. Zucker* [1958] V.R. 623; *Beresford v. Ward* [1961] V.R. 632.
80. "Comparable" does not mean "identical". *Sandhurst and Northern District Trustees
    Executors & Agency Co. Ltd v. Auldridge* [1952] V.L.R. 488 at 497.

the rent.[81] Once the fair rent has been determined, s. 73(1) prohibits any further proceedings to determine the fair rent until six months have elapsed. The only exceptions to this section are where by an error or omission any injustice has been occasioned, substantial alterations or additions have been made to the premises, or a substantial decrease has occurred in the goods provided for in the lease.

Actions for recovery of possession under the Victorian legislation must be brought before the Residential Tenancies Tribunal: s. 89. Section 82(6) provides that a landlord may not evict a tenant except on one or more of 25 specified grounds. The most significant and the most often used of these grounds are the following: (a) that the tenant is a minimum of four weeks in arrears of rent; (b) that the tenant has failed to perform or observe a term of the lease; (c) that the tenant has failed to take reasonable care of the premises; (d) that the tenant or any other person residing with her or him or visiting the premises has been guilty of conduct which is a nuisance to neighbours; (e) that the tenant has used the premises for some illegal purpose; (f) that the tenant has indicated her or his willingness or intention to vacate, as a result of which the landlord has agreed to sell or let the premises; (g) that the premises within 12 months will be reasonably required by the landlord for her or his own occupation or that of her or his immediate family; (n) that the landlord has sold the premises and the purchaser reasonably requires the premises within 12 months for her or his own occupation or that of her or his immediate family; (o) that the premises are reasonably required by the landlord for reconstruction, demolition, or removal; (q) that the tenant has sublet the premises in part or whole without the express or implied consent of the landlord; (x) that the financial circumstances of the tenant are such that he or she could without undue financial hardship purchase or lease other uncontrolled premises; and (y) that the tenant has other adequate and suitable premises presently available for occupation.

The Tribunal is obliged by s. 92 to consider in all applications for possession under s. 82(6) any hardship that would result to the landlord or tenant by making or refusing to make an order for possession. In addition, if the application is brought under certain of the grounds the Tribunal must consider the availability of reasonably suitable alternative accommodation and may, in its discretion, refuse to make the order for possession if such accommodation is not available.

2. New South Wales

[11.21] In New South Wales, similar (but not identical) legislation exists in the *Landlord and Tenant (Amendment) Act* 1948. The vast majority of residential premises are excluded from control by s. 5A, which automatically excludes the following premises:

(a) Where a dwelling house was in course of erection at, or erection commenced after 16 December 1954.

---

81. The Tribunal is not required to fix a monetary value in each case on every consideration, but must merely bear all the relevant matters in mind when making its determination: *De Iacovo v. Lacanale (No. 3)* [1958] V.R. 628 (F.C.).

(b) Where a residential unit came into existence on or after 1 January 1969.

(c) Where the dwelling house or residential unit was on 1 January 1969 already the subject of a current lease registered under the section that this section replaces.[82]

In addition, s. 5A allows further categories of premises to be excluded from control under the 1948 Act by registration of a lease with the Rent Controller on payment of a $10 fee. The premises requiring registration before they can be excluded are as follows:

"(a) Dwelling houses or residential units of which vacant possession was obtained on or after 1 January 1969 or where vacant possession was obtained before 1 January 1969 and the premises had remained vacant until 1 January 1969.

(b) Dwelling houses or residential units which were occupied by the landlord or his predecessor on or after 1 January 1969.

(c) Dwelling houses or residential units of which vacant possession was obtained before 1 January 1969 and are the subject of leases executed before that date but are not registered until after 1 January 1969."

The determination of the fair rent can be conveniently discussed under four headings:

(a) Determination on 1939 values.

Unless a landlord of prescribed premises can fit her or his case under any of the other headings discussed later, the fair rents determination will be based on the rent payable on 31 August 1939, the date prescribed under the Act, or at the date the premises were erected, whichever date is later: s. 20(4).

In assessing the fair rent, s. 21(1) of the 1948 Act provides that the Board must have regard to a list of 11 factors: the capital value of the premises at the prescribed date; the landlord's liability for annual rates and insurance premiums; the estimated cost of repairs, maintenance and renewals; the estimated amount of annual depreciation in the premises and the estimated time per annum during which the premises may be vacant; the fair rents determined for similar prescribed premiums in the same locality; the rate of interest charged upon overdrafts by the Commonwealth Trading Bank; any services provided by the landlord or tenant; the value of any goods leased with the premises; any repair obligation on the tenant; the conduct of the parties; and the amount, if any, that the Fair Rents Board is satisfied was necessarily expended by the landlord upon the improvement or structural alterations of the premises. In addition, any real estate agent's commission is taken into account: s. 21(1AB).

Thus, in effect, a determination of the fair rent is reached by assessing the rental value of the premises as at 31 August 1939 and adding to it the increase in outgoings since 1939 in respect of rates, insurance, repairs, depreciation and the estate agent's commission.

82. For a recent decision on s. 5A, see *Muscolino v. Ranim* (1984) 5 N.S.W.L.R. 385.

(b) Determination on current values.

A new Division 4AA was added to the 1948 Act by virtue of a 1968 Amendment which permits a landlord to apply to a fair rents board for a determination based on current rental values under the so-called "wealthy tenants" provision.

As a first step towards an application, the landlord is empowered under s. 31MBA to serve a notice on the tenant requiring that he or she furnish a statutory declaration detailing particulars of income for the preceding financial year together with particulars of all relatives ordinarily resident in the premises. The landlord may then serve a notice requiring a similar statutory declaration from each of the other residents. If the total income of the tenant and the resident relatives is $15,000 or more (s. 31MAA), the Board must determine a fair rent based on current value rental rather than the 1939 value: s. 31MDA. In this case, the fair rent is assessed by adding one ninth to the assessed annual value last determined by the Valuer-General: s. 31MAA.

(c) Rent of prescribed premises by agreement.

Section 17A permits the landlord and the tenant to agree upon a fair rent for the premises and so avoid taking the case before the Fair Rents Board or the Rent Controller. An agreement will supersede any previous fair rent determination by the Board: s. 17A(1).

A fair rent agreement may be varied by the Fair Rents Board or Rent Controller in three situations: first, at the instigation of the tenant where he or she considers that the agreement was harsh or unconscionable, or that the agreement was obtained by fraud, duress, intimidation or improper means (s. 17A(12)); secondly, in a normal application before the Controller to have the fair rent increased (s. 17A(13)); and thirdly, on an application under Div. 4AA (ss 31MCA, 31MDA).

(d) Determination of rents for shared accommodation.[83]

Unlike Victoria, New South Wales has special Divisions in its rent control legislation covering shared accommodation.[84] Shared accommodation is deemed to exist where a kitchen or cooking recess, bathroom, toilet or other rooms are shared in common with other premises,[85] but under s. 8(2A) of the 1948 Act a shared laundry does not have the effect of bringing the premises within the category of shared accommodation.

Division 4 of Pt II of the 1948 Act vests the jurisdiction to determine fair rents of shared premises in the Sydney metropolitan area in the Rent Controller (s. 27(1)), with a right of appeal to the Fair Rents Board:

---

83. "Shared accommodation" is defined by s. 8 as "any prescribed premises leased, or intended to be leased, for the purpose of residence and forming part of other prescribed premises, but does not include any prescribed premises forming a complete residence in themselves".
84. Divs 3A and 4 of Pt II.
85. See *Ex parte Jordans; Re Rent Controller* [1964] N.S.W.R. 564 (F.C.); *Parker v. Richards* [1954] Q.S.R. 325 (F.C.); *Oliffe v. Ryan* [1949] V.L.R. 314.

s. 30(1). Application for a rental determination can be made by either a landlord or a tenant (if he or she is not more than seven days in arrears of rent): s. 27(1). The Controller may also, of his own motion, determine the rents of this type of accommodation, although in practice this is never done: s. 27(3).

Recovery of possession.

The statutory requirements that the landlord must satisfy in order to recover possession are specified in s. 62(5) of the Act. A total of 26 grounds are specified, the most significant and most often used being the following: (a) that the tenant is a minimum of four weeks in arrears of rent (two weeks in arrears when the tenant's period of occupation does not exceed 12 months); (b) that the tenant has failed to perform or observe a term of the lease; (c) that the tenant has failed to take reasonable care of the premises; (d) that the tenant or any other person residing with her or him or visiting the premises has been guilty of conduct which is a nuisance to neighbours; (e) that the tenant has used the premises for some illegal purpose; (f) that the tenant has indicated her or his willingness or intention to vacate, as a result of which the landlord has agreed to sell or let the premises; (g) that the premises are reasonably required by the landlord for her or his own occupation or that of her or his immediate family; (l) that the landlord has agreed to sell the premises and the purchaser reasonably requires the premises within 12 months for her or his own occupation, or that of her or his immediate family; (m) that the premises are reasonably required by the landlord for reconstruction, demolition, or removal; (o) that the tenant has sublet the premises in part or whole without the express or implied consent of the landlord; and (u) that the tenant has other reasonably suitable alternative premises presently available for her or his occupation.

IV. FARM TENANCIES LEGISLATION

[11.22] Certain farm tenancies in New South Wales, Queensland and South Australia are subject to separate legislation designed to increase the rights of tenant farmers. The relevant legislation is the *Agricultural Holdings Act* 1941 (N.S.W.),[86] the *Property Law Act* 1974 (Qld), ss 153-167, and the *Agricultural Holdings Act* 1891 (S.A.).

1. Scope of Legislation

[11.23] In New South Wales, the Act applies to any rented parcel of land greater than 0.8 hectares which is used for agricultural or pastoral purposes, but does not apply to land cultivated as a garden: s. 4(1). The Act extends to share-farming agreements, whereby the owner and the share-farmer agree that the produce of the land, derived during the currency of the lease, or the proceeds of sale of such produce, shall be

---

86. See Carter, "Compensation for Landlords and Tenant Farmers" (April, 1987) 25 Law Soc. J. 24; New South Wales Department of Agriculture, *Farm Tenancy in New South Wales*, Legal Branch Bulletin 3 (5th ed., 1978).

divided between the parties in specified proportions or shares: s. 5.[87] The Queensland Act is stated to apply to any rented parcel of agricultural land, including land suitable for dairying purposes, of a minimum area of five acres: s. 154. Leases of Crown land are exempt: s. 153. The South Australian Act applies regardless of land size to all rented land which is agricultural or pastoral (or both) (s. 4), but does not apply to any lease for a term longer than 21 years at a fixed rent: s. 5.

2. Tenant's Compensation

[11.24] Each Act provides for compensation to be paid to tenant farmers in certain circumstances. The provisions differ slightly between the States. In the following account, the New South Wales legislation will be used by way of illustration.[88]

The legislation provides for the payment of compensation by the landlord to the tenant in four circumstances: for improvements on holdings (ss 7-12); in respect of increased value of holding (s. 13); for disturbance (s. 15); and in case of tenancy under mortgagor: s. 16. Compensation is also payable by the tenant to the landlord in respect of diminished value of holding: s. 14. The First Schedule to the Act contains the improvements for which the tenant is entitled to compensation. The Schedule is divided into three Parts. Part I lists those improvements which require prior written notice by the tenant to the landlord, and which allow the landlord either to dispute the work before an agricultural committee or to do the work her or himself. Illustrations are the reclamation of waste land, and the making of irrigation works. Part II improvements also require prior written notice by the tenant. The landlord has the right to carry out the work her or himself but may not object to the work. Illustrations are drainage and domestic water supply. Part III improvements may be carried out by the tenant without the need for notice or the landlord's consent. Such improvements include the laying down of permanent pastures and the making of permanent subdivision fences.

In each State the issue of compensation is determined by arbitration[89] conducted (in New South Wales) according to the general commercial arbitration legislation.[90]

3. Minimum Term of Tenancy

[11.25] Under the New South Wales legislation (only), a fixed-term lease of less than two years entered into prior to 18 April 1989 is automatically extended to two years: s. 22. The only exception is a holding for a term not exceeding one year for the sole purpose of stock agistment. This provision does not apply to periodic leases, which are not extended. Section 22 has recently been repealed by the *Agricultural Holdings*

---

87. A share-farming agreement may fall within the *Industrial Arbitration Act* 1940 (N.S.W.), s. 88F: *Barham v. Stevenson* [1975] 1 N.S.W.L.R. 31 (C.A.).
88 Cf. Qld: ss 156-166; S.A.: ss 6-22.
89. N.S.W.: ss 17-19 and Second Schedule; Qld ss 159 and Fifth Schedule; S.A.: ss 13-19.
90. *Commercial Arbitration Act* 1984 (N.S.W.).

(Amendment) Act 1989, but pursuant to the Third Schedule continues to apply to a contract of tenancy of a holding that was either in force immediately before its repeal, or which commenced or is renewed after its repeal because of the exercise of an option granted before its repeal.

4. Notices to Quit

[11.26] In Queensland and South Australia, the general law rules as to the service of notice to quit apply: see above **[10.53]**. In New South Wales, special rules apply. Pursuant to s. 23(1), either party must give a minimum notice of one year and a maximum notice of two years to terminate a fixed-term lease. If no such notice is given, the lease will continue on after its expiration date as a yearly periodic lease.

5. Right of Entry

[11.27] In New South Wales and Queensland (but not in South Australia), the landlord is given a statutory right to enter the holding at all reasonable times in order to view the state of the holding.[91]

6. Tenant's Right to Sell Holding

[11.28] In South Australia (only), the tenant may, notwithstanding any covenant, condition or agreement to the contrary, and without incurring any forfeiture or other penalty by so doing, sell her or his tenancy, subject to certain specified conditions: s. 23. Where this occurs, the landlord is given the right to purchase the tenancy for the consideration agreed to be paid by the proposed purchaser, or the landlord may refer the question as to the amount to be paid by her or him for the tenancy to arbitration: s. 23(c).

91. N.S.W.: s. 26; Qld: s. 167.

12

Management Where Ownership is Divided

I. MULTIPLE DECISION MAKERS

[12.01] Conflicts as to the responsibility for the repair, maintenance and improvement of buildings and land areas can arise whenever the rights of ownership and occupation are not all vested in a single person. Landlord and tenant agreements confer rights of occupation of limited duration and the rules as to management responsibility have already been discussed (see above [10.22]): members of tenancy tribunals quickly learn about such things as the quality of carpet cleaning and the capacity of glass shower screens to withstand hot water. This Chapter is concerned with disputes which occur because of the division of ownership of freehold estates. The simplest situation is that of the fee simple ownership vested in two or more persons. Division of the legal and beneficial ownership because of a trust, and the existence of successive interests as a result of estates less than a fee simple, present further complications. Often there will be both a trust and successive interests as a trustee holds for a life tenant and then on a trust for the holders of remainder interests.[1] In such cases as well as mere differences of opinion as to what is best for the land there are obvious advantages and disadvantages between the parties as to whether work is charged against income or capital. Further, in such cases an enforceable consensus may be impossible because of the lack of contractual capacity of some of the parties. Even the existence of a mortgage can create management differences as a mortgagee has an interest in the maintenance of buildings to the fullest extent possible.

[12.02] Management decisions relating to repair, maintenance and improvement tend to revolve around two questions: What is best for the land? How should work be paid for? Payment for work on the land raises questions as the ability to compel contributions from persons having similar or different interests in the land. The value of the land itself is another source of payment as money may be raised by a mortgage over the land—the mortgage imposes liability for repayment. Damage to the land can result from a particular event such as flood, fire or earthquake and insurance to cover such events is common but again divided ownership presents scope for argument as to responsibility for and the appropriate level of insurance.

---

1. See the discussion of future interests above [2.13].

The extreme management decision is disposal of the property itself. A property may become unsuited to the needs of those with interests in it or may present potential for considerable profit from redevelopment by others. With today's shortage of urban land and urban consolidation principles, sale of part of the land is a further possibility. Holders of limited interests can only dispose of what they have. As already mentioned, not all holders may have full contractual capacity but that problem aside they may simply disagree. A life tenant can transfer only estate for the transferor's life.[2] Even a more limited disposal by a life tenant, such as a fixed-term lease, cannot be transferred except subject to termination on the transferor's death.

[12.03] The common problems of repairs, maintenance and improvement, exploitation of the land, sale and other dispositions can be identified as applying to co-ownership, settlements and trusts. However, the legal rules for the resolution of those problems have developed quite separately in relation to the three forms of divided ownership. It is necessary therefore to examine the legal framework relevant to each of the three forms and then consider how that framework copes with the common problems. The emphasis upon the common problems suggests that rather than separate off the forms of ownership the writers should concentrate on those problems. However the answers are so heavily dependent upon the framework that such an arrangement becomes overly disjointed.

Before the three forms of divided ownership and their solutions to the problems are considered there are two background matters. The first such matter is the development of settlements and trusts for sale. There is a considerable overlap between settlements and trusts generally and the division is only important because of the retention of statutory law relating to settlements. This law is (as will be explained later, see below [12.22]) really only significant today in Victoria and Tasmania. The second background matter is the law of waste. This doctrine has been most significant in relation to settlements but has some potential as a restraint upon present exploitation in the interests of future owners.

II.   SETTLEMENTS AND TRUSTS FOR SALE

[12.04] Traditionally divided ownership in English law arose from what were known as strict settlements. These settlements were used to preserve land within families. The fee tail estate of itself provides a means for such preservation but strict settlements were more complicated arrangements providing for a succession of interests. Most commonly the successive interests were established by a formal arrangement entered into by a living grantor but that fact reflected the ability to impose the greatest restrictions rather than the legal impossibility of creating a settlement by a will. Again interests tended to be legal rather than equitable because of the status desired for the holders of interests.

---

2. The estate per autre vie: see above [2.24].

The creation of such interests not only restricted the disposition of land subject to a settlement but also what could be done with the land. Increasing environmental awareness has led today's society at least to the point where the need to balance development and conservation is appreciated. Consequently, the preservation purpose should be treated with less scorn today than it was by 19th century jurists and text writers. The doctrine of waste which set out most of the restrictions may therefore repay renewed consideration. Of course the fact that preservation was an incidental result of settlements does not mean that the landed classes were concerned so much with the environment as the preservation of power which was the express purpose of the settlement.

[12.05] The fact that the fee simple estate was recognised by statute[3] rather than by the common law is an early reflection of the fact that what might appear technical legal argument is concerned with the balance between preservation of the status quo and development. The common law recognition of devices whereby a fee tail owner could bar the entail or effectively pass a fee simple interest weakened the preservation effects of settlements.[4] At the same time the efforts of conveyancers were directed towards adaptations of settlements to prevent destructive endeavours. Consequently, settlements took the form of a life estate in favour of the settlor's eldest son, followed by estates in tail to that son and other sons and an ultimate remainder to the heirs in general of the eldest son. Such settlements have not featured in Australian property dealings. The continued recognition of the fee tail estate in some States seems only to reflect a perverse legislative desire not to interfere with antiquities.[5]

[12.06] However, the term settlement at least in a property context[6] covers any disposition by which property is held for different persons in succession. Thus a simple devise of land to a spouse for the spouse's lifetime followed by a remainder to the devisor's children is a settlement. It is still possible in most States, even under the Torrens system, that the spouse and children could be registered legal owners of their interests. In Queensland future interests must be equitable.[7] Even in the other States it is more common but not essential for a trust to be employed for such a settlement. Whereas the strict settlement was the product of much legal thought and that thought extended to provision for most conceivable (and sometimes barely conceivable) eventualities, the simple devise to the spouse and children may ignore altogether possible complications in their future. Reliance on rules of law rather than the terms of settlement may therefore be greater in the cases of the simple devise.

---

3. *De Donis Conditionalibus* 1285 discussed above **[2.19]**.
4. These devices are discussed above **[2.20]**.
5. The fee tail estate has been abolished in New South Wales, Victoria, Queensland and Western Australia; in South Australia and Tasmania the tenant in tail in possession is empowered to dispose of a fee simple interest by transfer inter vivos or by will: see above **[2.22]**.
6. The *Bankruptcy Act* 1966 (Cth), s. 120 uses the term in a broader sense to cover any transfer of property whereby the transferee is intended to retain that property. See Rose, *Lewis' Australian Bankruptcy Law* (9th ed., 1990), p. 157.
7. *Property Law Act* 1974 (Qld), s. 30.

A further impact upon settlements has been the development of death duties. A settlor could expose the estate to greater duties than would otherwise be payable as a result of the form of that settlement. Whilst such duties have been abolished in Australia today, the form of disposition on death may affect other taxation imposts—principal of which at the time of writing is the capital gains tax.

[12.07]   Once a settlement of any sort has been created, a dealing with the land as a whole is impossible unless all parties entitled to an interest are alive, have legal capacity and concur in the proposed course of action. In the mid 19th century these restrictions on the development of land were tackled by English legislation. The comprehensive reform came in the 1882 *Settled Land Act*. This Act entitled the life tenant, despite that person's limited estate, to sell the fee simple and provided the life tenant with extensive powers of management. That legislation was followed in Queensland, Victoria, Western Australia and Tasmania. New South Wales and South Australia adopted earlier legislation which requires the concurrence of the courts for the exercise of the powers. More recently Queensland and Western Australia have repealed their settled land legislation and assimilated settled land with trust property so that the powers are exercised by the trustees.

[12.08]   The settlement envisaged the use of the land itself by the holders of the successive interests. The land could provide for those persons by conversion into money. Therefore, land could be left to trustees for these beneficiaries but on the basis that the land was to be sold and the proceeds invested for the beneficiaries. Wherever trustees are directed to sell trust property there is a trust for sale. A trust for sale does not impede development in the same way as a settlement because the trustees had the capacity, indeed a duty, to transfer a fee simple interest. Powers of management may not however be addressed in the settlement particularly as emphasis is upon sale. By 1925, the English *Settled Land Act* did not apply to trusts for sale. Thus trusts for sale could be used where it was desired that the powers of sale and management vest in trustees rather than the tenant for life. The trustees could be chosen because they were indeed less likely to sell than the life tenant. Similarly, consent for the exercise of powers could be required from someone unlikely to consent. One author gives the example of a trust for sale subject to the consent of the holder of a contingent remainder entitled only if the property is unsold at the life tenant's death.[8] In all cases where there is a trust, trustees may seek powers to dispose of or manage the land. There is a potential for conflict between trustees and life tenants.

In Australia the relationship between settled land legislation and trusts for sale varies between the four States which retain settled land legislation. The relationship between the powers of life tenants and those of trustees similarly varies. Even though Victoria and Tasmania have fairly comprehensive settled land legislation, the continued value of that legislation must be questioned. Academic opinion leans strongly in support of the Queensland and Western Australian initiatives vesting

---

8. See Harvey, *Settlements of Land* (1973), p. 79, citing *Re Inns* [1947] Ch. 576.

powers in the trustees.[9] The Queensland position which makes future interests equitable and confers statutory powers overriding the settlement seems best to enable the land to be dealt with responsibly and to protect beneficiaries of the settlement.

III. DOCTRINE OF WASTE

[12.09] Because of the general doctrine that persons can only dispose of such interests as they have, owners of estates less than freehold cannot as a rule deal with the whole interest in the land. However, the owner of a lesser estate will at some point be entitled to possession—the person is then described as holding an interest in possession. The use of the land can significantly affect its longer-term value. In Australia, land degradation because of an absence of proper soil conservation measures is a major environmental harm.[10] Even the absence of regular painting may cause serious building decay. The exercise of the right of possession can therefore cause injury to the interests of the holders of future interests. To protect their interests the common law developed the doctrine of waste whereby the owners of limited interests are limited in their use of the land. The doctrine is also applicable as between tenants (periodic or fixed-term) and landlords and is also discussed in that context.[11]

[12.10] Traditionally there have been said to be four categories of waste: voluntary waste, permissive waste, ameliorating waste and equitable waste. Voluntary waste is the commission of acts harming the property. The simplest form is damage to the fabric of improvements on land.[12] But, because the doctrine of waste is concerned with long-term preservation of the land some acts of exploitation are regarded as waste and if intentionally undertaken as voluntary waste, in particular the opening of a mine[13] and the cutting of timber.[14] Permissive waste occurs where harm is allowed to occur—typically a failure to repair.

Ameliorating waste is an alteration to the land which constitutes an improvement to the land.[15] There is therefore some doubt whether ameliorating waste amounts to waste at all. As was said by Jessell M.R.:[16]

> "The erection of buildings on land which improve the value of the land is not waste. In order to prove waste you must prove an injury to the inheritance."

9. Harvey, op. cit. at 80.
10. Bradsen, "Land Degradation—Current and Proposed Legal Controls" (1987) 4 E. & P.L.J. 113.
11. The application of the doctrine varies according to the duration of the tenancy: see above [10.35].
12. *Marsden v. Edward Heyes Ltd* [1927] 2 K.B. 1.
13. *Saunder's Case* (1599) 5 Co. Rep. 12a; 77 E.R. 66; *Spotswood v. Hand* (1874) 5 A.J.R. 85; *Dashwood v. Magniac* [1891] 3 Ch. 306. Working an already opened mine would not constitute waste as the grantor has shown an intention that it is to be worked and its profits enjoyed.
14. *Re Hart* [1954] S.A.S.R. 1.
15. *Doherty v. Allman* (1878) 3 A C 709; *Meux v. Cobley* [1892] 2 Ch. 253; *Hockley v. Rendell* (1909) 11 W.A.L.R. 170.
16. *Jones v. Chappell* (1875) L.R. 20 Eq. 539 at 542.

The more traditional view seems to be that any alteration to the nature of the land constitutes waste and that if the alteration benefits the land, technically, ameliorating waste has been committed. However, such waste does not give rise to any remedy by way of injunction[17] or in damages.[18] It has been suggested[19] that modernisation of an historic building could constitute ameliorating waste and could well be the subject of concern. The acts of modernisation might result in an increase in value of the land but different opinions exist as to whether the land is improved. The issue then is whether the courts would restrain the modernisation. That issue seems to be moving towards a judgment as to the merits of modernisation against the merits of preservation. The courts would have little by way of legal guidelines for such a judgment. In the only case in which the issue arose (in a co-ownership context) the court resolved the matter by asserting that the works amounted to a betterment and would not be restrained.[20] This conclusion does seem to be a value judgment as to the merit of the works and to take the law of waste into the realm of aesthetics and similar considerations.

The fourth class of waste is equitable waste which clearly is a subspecies of voluntary waste, in that it occurs when intentional and serious harm is done to the property. Examples of equitable waste have been stripping a building of lead, iron, glass, doors and boards[21] and secondly, the removal of trees providing ornament or shelter.[22] In the Australian rural environment the destruction of vegetation essential for soil conservation could be an act of equitable waste. Equitable waste has been developed because of limits on liability for voluntary waste.

[12.11]   The categories of waste have been developed to differentiate the levels of responsibility owed by owners of limited interests in land. These levels have largely depended upon the provisions of the instrument creating the limited interest. Liability for permissive waste exists only if the instrument imposes a liability to repair.[23] If the instrument is silent there is no liability for permissive waste. An owner is, however, liable for voluntary waste unless exempted by the instrument.[24] An exempted owner is said to be unimpeachable for waste. However, even an owner unimpeachable for waste is liable for equitable waste.[25] But again the instrument could confer an exemption for this liability.

[12.12]   The rules as to waste govern the ability to cut timber without liability to holders of future interests. If the instrument is silent as to

---

17. *Doherty v. Allman* (1878) 3 A.C. 709; *Meux v. Cobley* [1892] 2 Ch. 253.
18. *Hockley v. Rendell* (1909) 11 W.A.L.R. 170.
19. Butt, p. 116.
20. *Ferguson v. Miller* [1978] N.Z.L.R. 819.
21. *Vane v. Barnard* (1716) 2 Vern. 738; 23 E.R. 1082.
22. *Turner v. Jackson* (1856) 1 V.L.T. 127; *Weld-Blundell v. Wolseley* [1903] 2 Ch. 664.
23. *Re Cartwright* (1889) 41 Ch. D. 532.
24. *Woodhouse v. Walker* (1880) 5 Q.B.D. 404.
25. This common rule is now restated by statute in all States except Tasmania. The provisions appear to impose an obligation at common law for what was equitable waste and thus probably make available legal as well as equitable remedies. Property Law Statutes: N.S.W.: s. 9; Vic.: s. 133; Qld: s. 25; S.A.: s. 12; W.A.: s. 17.

liability for waste, the owner will be impeachable and thus liable if he or she cuts timber. If the instrument makes the owner unimpeachable he or she will be able to cut timber without liability unless what is to be cut comprises trees providing ornament or shelter. However, not all trees are classified as timber. In England, the traditional timber trees were oak, elm and ash.

The issue of the liability in Australia of a life tenant cutting down trees arose in *Re Hart*.[26] In that case, land was left by will in 1951 to trustees on trust for life interests. The land comprised a rural property in the south-east of South Australia on which there was a house, an orchard and a number of pinus radiata trees; part of the land was used for grazing. The trustees sold 713 trees and netted over 4,000 pounds. The issue was whether this sum was income or capital and that issue depended on whether the trees could have been cut by the life tenants without liability. Reed J. pointed out that although oak, ash and elm were the traditional timber trees, even in England other trees could be classified as timber if by the custom of the district the trees were used for building. Reference was made to the practice in some parts of South Australia of building houses from mallee posts stopped with clay and with mallee rafters carrying the roof. In such places, mallee would be regarded as timber. However, in the area of the land pinus radiata trees were not used for the construction or repair of buildings and therefore they were not timber. A life tenant could therefore cut such trees and keep the proceeds. Reference was made to further rights of life tenants to cut even timber. First, young trees could be cut to allow the proper growth of other trees. Secondly, trees planted as a timber estate could be cultivated and cut in the regular course of management.

The relevance in Australia of the use for building test as to what constitutes timber must be questioned. At the same time categorisation as timber only imposes liability if the owner is impeachable for waste. The interests of future owners probably depends more classifying the cutting of timber significant for soil conservation as equitable waste.

IV. MANAGEMENT BETWEEN CO-OWNERS

1. Repair, Maintenance and Improvements

[12.13] All co-owners are regarded by the common law as entitled to use each and every part of the land co-owned so long as they do not exclude other co-owners from the land.[27] The right of user extends to the exploitation of the land and whilst cases have involved the growing of crops[28] the carrying on of a business would seem to be equally justified. The co-owner who exploits the land is entitled to keep personally the profits of this exploitation unless the exploitation has involved an arrangement which properly accrues for the benefit of all co-owners such

26. [1954] S.A.S.R. 1.
27. *Luke v. Luke* (1936) 36 S.R. (N.S.W.) 310; *McCormick v. McCormick* [1921] N.Z.L.R. 384; *Dennis v. McDonald* [1982] 2 W.L.R. 275.
28. *Rees v. Rees* [1931] S.A.S.R. 78.

as a lease of the land.[29] No obvious mechanism exists for the resolution of differences as to how the land should be exploited and the absence of any mechanism places pressure on the co-owners to reach agreement.

[12.14]   Exploitation of the land may involve the expenditure of money on the land. No differences appear to be drawn as to whether the expenditure is for repair, maintenance or improvements. A spending co-owner cannot claim contributions for improvements until the co-ownership is brought to an end. Normally this termination has occurred through the disposition of the land by all co-owners to a third party. It is unclear whether the estate of spending joint tenant co-owner has a claim against a surviving co-owner when the death of the spender terminates the co-ownership through survivorship. The claim has been allowed in actions involving the general adjustment of rights in the property such as distributions of the proceeds after compulsory acquisition[30] or after a judicial sale.[31]

Expenditure of money on the land creates an equitable lien in favour of the spending co-owner over the interests of the other co-owners.[32] The lien exists for the amount of the outlay to the extent that the value of the shares of the owners has been improved.[33] No allowance seems to be made for inflation so that the effluxion of time will substantially detract from the worth of the lien. Furthermore, because the expenditure has to be reflected in an increase in value of the property, improvements which add to the property rather than maintenance works[34] are likely to the expenditures whereby the lien has significant value.

In *Squire v. Rogers*[35] the plaintiff and defendant were joint holders of a perpetual lease of a Darwin caravan park. The plaintiff had not occupied the land for 16 years. During this time the defendant made substantial improvements to the land. However, Cyclone Tracey to a significant extent destroyed these improvements. Consequently, an expenditure of $100,000 resulted in an increase in value of only $15,000. The claim for compensation was limited to this amount. The court was clear that if the figures were reversed so that $15,000 expenditure produced an increased value of $100,000 the claim is again limited to the $15,000.

The claim for compensation is an equitable right in favour of the spending co-owner against the other co-owners. It is an equitable lien on the interests of the other owners in favour of the spending owner.[36] The

---

29. *Henderson v. Eason* (1857) 17 Q.B. 701. This case gave such a narrow interpretation to the statute 4 Anne c. 3, s. 27 (1705), that the repeal of that statute in Victoria, New South Wales and Queensland would appear to have little effect.
30. *Brickwood v. Young* (1905) 2 C.L.R. 387.
31. *Boulter v. Boulter* (1898) 19 L.R. (N.S.W.) (Eq.) 135; *Squire v. Rogers* (1979) 27 A.L.R. 330.
32. *Brickwood v. Young* (1905) 2 C.L.R. 387.
33. *Squire v. Rogers* (1979) 27 A.L.R. 330.
34. There is a dispute as to whether mere repairs can be the subject of a claim for contributions. They were allowed in *Noack v. Noack* [1959] V.R. 137 but not in *McMahon v. Public Curator* [1952] St. R. Qd 197.
35. (1979) 27 A.L.R. 330.
36. *Brickwood v. Young* (1905) 2 C.L.R. 387 at 396.

interest passes to successor in title of the spending co-owner and is enforceable against successors in title of the other owners. This consequence is subject to the fact that as it is an equitable charge, a successor in title may not be subject to the equitable interest because of the bona fide purchaser rule or the indefeasibility principle of the Torrens system.

Moreover the situation where a claim for compensation for improvements is made is one of the exceptions to the rule that a co-owner who enjoys sole occupation is under no liability for an occupation rent to a co-owner out of possession. Liability for rent is said to be based on the maxim that he who seeks equity must do equity. The accounts are reciprocal: equitable assistance to get part of the expenditure requires a willingness to be charged for what is not otherwise chargeable.[37]

2. Exploitation of the Land

[12.15] The absence of any mechanism to resolve differences as to the exploitation of the land means that a co-owner who wishes to leave land undeveloped cannot prevent another from developing it so long as the other is prepared to rely upon that other's own money. However a co-owner cannot destroy or substantially injure the property.[38] This obligation has been expressed in terms of rules of good husbandry and to forbid the cutting down of ornamental trees or the removal of valuable turf and peat.[39]

More recently the restraints of the law of waste which apply between life tenants and remaindermen have been applied by a New Zealand court as between co-owners. In *Ferguson v. Miller*[40] the owners of three adjoining parcels of land were in turn co-owners of a strip of land providing access to the land. One of the co-owners sought to restrain a scheme whereby a 15 foot wide concrete or asphalt carriageway was to be laid on this strip. This carriageway would replace an existing surface but would be 50 per cent wider and slightly longer than that surface. The objector considered that the improvement would detract from the existing amenity by destroying the country-lane appearance and atmosphere. The claim to restrain the work on the basis of the doctrine of waste was rejected. McMullin J. considered that the resealing of the existing surface would be merely an act of repair and its extension would be an act of betterment. On the other hand an alternative proposal which would have involved the removal of some trees was considered to be likely to amount to waste. The application of the doctrine of waste as between co-owners was argued to flow from the *Statute of Westminister II* (1285).

3. Sale

[12.16] At common law, any dealing with the land as a whole, either to divide it between the co-owners or to dispose of it to a third party,

37. *Re Jones; Farrington v. Forrester* [1893] 2 Ch. 461; *Teasdale v. Sanderson* (1864) 33 Beav. 534; 55 E.R. 476.
30. *Durham and Sunderland Ry Co. v. Wawn* (1840) 3 Beav 119 at 123; 49 E.R. 47 at 48.
39. *Wilkinson v. Haygarth* (1847) 12 Q.B. 837 at 845; 116 E.R. 1085 at 1088.
40. [1978] 1 N.Z.L.R. 819.

required the agreement of all co-owners. The first statutory power enabling one co-owner to compel action was conferred in the 16th century whereby partition could be compelled. Physical division of the land might not be able to be carried out so as to produce a fair distribution between the co-owners and might not be practicable. Indeed, in Australia today subdivision of land is subject to stringent statutory controls, and partition is thus an outmoded remedy.[41]

[12.17] From the second half of the 19th century the courts have been empowered to order sale in lieu of partition and statutory provisions to this effect[42] exist in all jurisdictions except New South Wales and Queensland. These provisions contain three distinct powers: one in the case of special circumstances; the second in the case of an application by the holder or holders of a half share or more; the third in any other circumstance.[43] In the case of special circumstances the court has a general discretion to act as it thinks fits in the interests of the co-owners. In the case of an application by the holder of a half share, a sale shall be ordered unless there is good reason to the contrary. In *Peek v. Peek*[44] a husband brought an action for the sale of a home owned jointly with his wife. The wife argued that she had been deserted by her husband and the sale would deprive her of her residence. This argument is held to be an insufficient reason to deny sale. In circumstances other than special circumstances or applications by the holders of the half share or more, the court has a discretion whether to order sale. However, in these cases the remaining co-owners have a right to buy out the applicant. Because the three powers are distinct the right to buy out does not extend to cases of special circumstances or applications by half share holders; though it is difficult to see why such an offer should be refused.

[12.18] In New South Wales and Queensland, a different procedure has been enacted.[45] One or more co-owners may apply to the court for the appointment of trustees. These trustees may be appointed under a statutory trust for sale or a statutory trust for partition.[46] Appointment on the trust for partition may be ordered if the court is satisfied that partition is more beneficial than sale for the holders of a half share or more.[47] Where trustees for sale are appointed they hold on trust for sale and hold the proceeds and income prior to sale upon trust to give effect to the rights

---

41. Nonetheless, it has been held that where a request for partition is made and neither party requests a sale the court is obliged to order partition: *De Campo Holdings Pty Ltd v. Cianciullo* [1977] W.A.R. 56. Apparently the order for partition is made without regard to the restrictions on subdivision and subject to the ability of the parties to apply for alternative orders if partition is not possible.
42. Vic.: *Property Law Act* 1958, Pt IV; S.A.: *Law of Property Act* 1936, Pt VIII; W.A.: *Property Law Act* 1969, Pt XIX; Tas.: *Partition Act* 1869; see Cock, "Co-Ownership: Back to the Partition Act" [1982] Conv. R. 415.
43. *Perman v. Maloney* [1939] V.L.R. 376.
44. [1965] S.A.S.R. 293; see also *Bray v. Bray* (1926) 38 C.L.R. 542.
45. N.S.W.: *Conveyancing Act* 1919, Pt IV Div. 6; Qld: *Property Law Act* 1974, Pt V Div. 2.
46. N.S.W.: s. 66G(1).
47. N.S.W.: s. 66G(4).

of the co-owners.[48] In the case of either trust, the trustees should consult the beneficiaries and give effect to their wishes so far as practicable and consistent with the general interest of the trust.[49]

This legislation means that in principle and not merely because of practicalities emphasis has shifted from partition as the primary right with sale in special circumstances to sale as the primary right with partition in special circumstances.[50] Even where partition is shown to be more beneficial than sale to the majority co-owners the court retains a discretion. Hardship on the minority is a ground for refusal of partition.[51]

On the other hand if sale is sought, it will ordinarily be granted.[52] Unfairness is not sufficient to refuse an order for sale. There must be special circumstances which make it inappropriate for the applicant co-owner to be granted sale. Such circumstances would be an agreement not to sell without unanimous consent or some other obligation on the applicant.[53] A stay of proceedings may be appropriate where other proceedings are in progress, in particular where family law proceedings have been commenced as those proceedings involve a broader range of considerations.[54]

4. Other Dispositions

[12.19] Every co-owner has an interest which can be dealt with. The issue commonly arising in the cases of grants of rights of possession, security interests or other encumbrances is the relationship between the grantee and the non-granting co-owners. Where the grantor is a joint tenant rather than a tenant in common the grant may effect a severance of the joint tenancy. In the absence of severance the grantee's rights may be affected by survivorship on the death either of the grantor or of the other co-owners.

[12.20] A co-owner may grant a lease of that owner's interest and the grantee will gain the co-owner's right to enjoy possession of each and every part of the land but in common with the non-granting co-owners. Consequently, a co-owner who is not a party to the lease may occupy the land but may not interfere with the tenant's concurrent occupation. In *Cantazarri v. Whitehouse*[55] a wife left a jointly owned home. Her husband granted a lease of the premises for a period of 12 months. Subsequently, the wife moved back onto the premises and interfered with the tenant's personal effects. In was held that whilst entry by the wife onto the land

48. N.S.W.: s. 66F(2).
49. N.S.W.: s. 66H.
50. *Re Cordingley* (1948) 48 S.R. (N.S.W.) 248.
51. *Hayward v. Skinner* [1981] N.S.W.L.R. 590; *Pannizutti v. Trask* (1987) 10 N.S.W.L.R. 531.
52. *Re Tettell* (1952) 52 S.R. (N.S.W.) 221.
53. *Re McNamara and the Conveyancing Act* (1961) 78 W.N. (N.S.W.) 1068; *Stephens v. Debney* (1959) 60 S.R. (N.S.W.) 460; *Ex parte Eimbart Pty Ltd* [1982] Qd R. 398.
54. *Norris v. Norris* [1985] 1 N.S.W.L.R. 472.
55. (1981) 55 F.L.R. 426.

was not wrongful as against the tenant, she could not prevent the tenant from exercising the right of use and occupation. Therefore damage to the personal effects was an actionable wrong.

It is unclear whether a lease by a joint tenant severs the joint tenancy. However, the lease does operate as a suspension of the joint tenancy for its duration.[56] Thus even if the joint tenant who has granted the lease dies, the tenant's rights continue until termination of the lease. Survivorship does not operate during the term of the lease.[57] However, where the lease may be terminated by notice, any one of the co-owners probably can give notice to terminate the lease.[58]

[12.21]   Where an encumbrance is granted by one co-owner that encumbrance will be enforceable against the other co-owners if it does not interfere with the rights of the others to possession of the land. In *Hedley v. Roberts*[59] one co-owner granted an easement to use a toilet on the co-owned land. Harris J. considered that this right would not subject the other co-owner to any undue interference with the right to use the land.

In that case the granting co-owner was a tenant in common. There was thus no question of cessation of the interest on the death of the grantor. Harris J. indicated that an encumbrance granted by a joint tenant would cease on the death of the joint tenant before the death of the other joint tenant. The principle of survivorship meant that the grantor's interest ceased and the encumbrance granted over that interest ceased with it. Similarly a mortgage granted by a joint tenant binds only the granting co-owner[60] and ceases to have effect on the death of the joint tenant.[61] Under the Torrens system a mortgage as a charge over the land can be granted by a joint tenant without severance of the joint tenancy; a common law mortgage will sever the joint tenancy because there is a transfer of the interest of the joint tenant.[62]

One co-owner may grant a right to occupy premises which does not confer any proprietary interest upon the grantee, such as a licence to occupy premises, or a contract to provide board or lodgings. The nature of the interest means that the grantee's remedies exist only against the grantor and would not exist against the other co-owners. Furthermore, it has been held that a co-owner other than the grantor can give notice to terminate a licence without the authority or consent of the grantor.[63]

56. *Frieze v. Unger* [1960] V.R. 230.
57. Ibid.
58. *Doe d. Aslin and Finch v. Sommersett* (1830) 1 B. & Ad. 135; 109 E.R. 738. Complications may arise in the case of statutory regulations of tenancies, cf. Bradbrook, MacCallum and Moore, pp. 625-627.
59. [1977] V.R. 282.
60. *Fulton v. 523 Nominees Pty Ltd* [1984] V.R. 200.
61. *Lyons v. Lyons* [1967] V.R. 169.
62. Ibid.
63. *Annen v. Rattee* (1985) 273 E.G. 503; Slatter, "Co-owners and Licensees: Not So Simple" (1985) 135 New L.J. 885.

V. MANAGEMENT AND THE SETTLED ESTATES

1. Scope of the Settled Land Legislation

[12.22]   The differences between the settled land legislation[64] in the four States in which it is retained are such that whereas in Victoria and Tasmania a life tenant gains significant powers from the legislation, in New South Wales and South Australia the powers are so limited that other means of coping with the situation involved are likely to be preferable. Furthermore only in Victoria and Tasmania does the existence of the life tenant's statutory powers impinge upon the exercise of powers by trustees. In New South Wales and South Australia, resort is likely to be had to the powers of trustees which will be available except in the rare situation where the successive estates are legal rather than behind a trust. In Queensland and Western Australia, the repeal of the settled land legislation means that the trustees are the holders of powers. In Queensland, successive interests cannot be created without a trust as future interests must be equitable.

Although there are parallels between the Victorian and Tasmanian legislation and between the New South Wales and South Australian legislation, the parallels are only at the general level as to whether the life tenants have significant powers of their own motion and not at the level of the details of these powers. These powers are to sell, lease, cut timber and to effect repairs and maintenance including the raising of funds by mortgage for this purpose. In Tasmania, the life tenant may exercise these powers but must give notice of intention to the trustees who may bring any difference before the court. In Victoria, the powers can be exercised by the life tenant with the concurrence of the trustees or the court. The management powers (repairs, improvements) are greater than in Tasmania. In New South Wales and South Australia, the life tenant has limited powers to grant short-term leases but otherwise may sell or lease only with court approval. In these two States, applications for approval require the consent of all persons beneficially entitled; the need for this consent may be dispensed with.[65] In South Australia, court approval may be sought to cut timber but in neither New South Wales nor South Australia are any management powers conferred.

2. Key Terms Under The Settled Land Acts

[12.23]   The fundamental concept so far as the application of the Settled Land Acts is concerned is that of a settlement. A settlement is defined in all four jurisdictions to exist where an instrument provides that any land is limited to or in trust for any persons by way of succession.[66] In Victoria, Tasmania and New South Wales a settlement is deemed to exist where a minor is entitled in possession even to a fee simple interest.[67] In Victoria the term is extensively defined and includes instances where a person is

---

64. N.S.W.: *Conveyancing and Law of Property Act* 1898, Pt IV; Vic.: *Settled Land Act* 1958; S.A.: *Settled Estates Act* 1880; Tas.: *Settled Land Act* 1884.
65. Settled land legislation: N.S.W.: ss 55, 57-60; S.A.: ss 23-27.
66. Settled land legislation: N.S.W.: s. 37; Vic.: s. 8; S.A.: s. 2; Tas.: s. 2.
67. Settled land legislation: N.S.W.: s. 37(7); Vic.: s. 8(1)(b)(iv); Tas.: s. 54.

entitled to a conditional fee simple and where land is charged with the payment of any sum to a person for life or other period.[68] Land which is the subject of a settlement is described as settled land.

[12.24]   The operation of the legislation depends upon the life tenant, the trustees and the court. The person for the time being beneficially entitled to possession of settled land for life is the life tenant. In New South Wales and South Australia that person must be entitled to an estate.[69] Where two or more persons are entitled to a life interest jointly or in common they together constitute the life tenant. In Victoria, the powers of the life tenant are conferred on a range of persons (the list reflecting the list of arrangements deemed to be settlements).[70] A person entitled to the income of land for life is amongst those upon whom the powers are conferred. In Victoria and Tasmania, the trustees of the settlement are the persons who are for the time being under the settlement the trustees with power to sell or to consent to sale or who are appointed trustees for the purpose of the Settled Land Act.[71] In New South Wales and South Australia, trustees have a far lesser role and the only reference to trustees is to all persons who are trustees under the settlement.[72] In all jurisdictions the court is the Supreme Court.[73]

The most troublesome situation with respect to the application of the legislation has been where a personal right of residence has been conferred upon one person and subject to this right the land has been left to another. The definition of settlement is in terms of a limitation by way of succession.[74] The concept of succession has been held not to have any technical force though it has been suggested that it contemplates succession on death.[75] Consequently, a mere personal right to reside on premises during a person's lifetime provided that the person has control of the premises has been held to be a sufficient interest to found a succession.[76] Even where land is held on trust to pay from the rents and profits a nominated sum to one person for life and subject to that payment to pay the balance of the income to another for life there was a sufficient succession to constitute a settlement.[77] The concept of succession and thus the meaning of settlement seems equally broad in all jurisdictions.

However, the definition of life tenant is broadest in Victoria. In Victoria and Tasmania, the definition includes persons entitled by way of succession; in Victoria various others are also included.[78] As previously pointed out in New South Wales and South Australia, the life tenant must be entitled to an estate. It therefore seems that a person who has a

68. Settled land legislation: Vic.: s. 28.
69. Settled land legislation: N.S.W.: s. 54; S.A.: s. 22
70. Settled land legislation: Vic.: s. 16.
71. Settled land legislation: Vic.: s. 30; Tas.: s. 2(8).
72. Settled land legislation: N.S.W.: ss 55, 61; S.A.: s. 29.
73. Settled land legislation: N.S.W.: s. 37(8); Vic.: s. 3(1); S.A.: s. 3; Tas.: s. 10(2)(e).
74. Settled land legislation: N.S.W.: s. 37(7); Vic.: s. 8(1)(b)(iv); Tas.: s. 54.
75. Re Hoppe [1961] V.R. 381 at 402-3.
76. Ibid.
77. Re Joseph; Joseph v. Equity Trustees Executors & Agency Co. Ltd [1960] V.R. 550.
78. Settled land legislation: Vic.: s. 8; Tas.: s. 2.

personal right of residence is a life tenant in Victoria and Tasmania at least unless that right of residence has been declined.[79] On the other hand the holder of such an interest has been held not to be a life tenant under the New South Wales legislation.[80] It is possible that the right could be construed as a determinable life interest and thus there would be an estate even in New South Wales and South Australia. Not only does the Victorian Act not require an estate but it deems various persons to be the life tenant and confers the powers of the life tenant on other persons. In the case referred to above[81] of a payment of a fixed sum to one person from the rent and profits and the balance to another, it was suggested that the two recipients together had the powers of the life tenant in that they were together entitled to the income of the land and the powers of the life tenant are conferred upon the person entitled to the income of land under a trust or direction.

3. Role of Life Tenant and Trustees

[12.25] In Victoria and Tasmania the life tenant is given wide powers—in Victoria with the concurrence of the trustees, in Tasmania subject to the power of the trustees to refer matters to the court. However, the policy of the Act is to increase the alienability of land and not to affect the interests of the parties between themselves. The rights of the parties are transferred from land to the proceeds of the land. Whilst the life tenant is given powers, those powers are to be exercised in the interests of all persons entitled under the settlement. The life tenant is therefore deemed to be in the position of and have the duties and liabilities of a trustee for all persons entitled under the settlement.[82] The life tenant is subject to directions from the court as to the exercise of her or his powers because of the nature of the life tenant's position.

The life tenant in *Chirnside v. Chirnside*[83] was the defendant to an action seeking directions with respect to his intended exercise of his powers. The property had been settled by will and the defendant was the settlor's brother. He had resided in California and not visited Victoria for over 40 years. Another brother, his wife and their two sons had long occupied the property. After that brother's death a lease had been granted to the widow and one of the sons. The two sons were beneficially entitled to the property on the life tenant's death. At the time of the application the life tenant was 70. When the lease to the widow and son expired the life tenant proposed to grant a new lease to another. This action was based on an accusation of failure to look after the property. However, it was found that the two sons had obtained experience as graziers and pastoralists and the property and many improvements thereon were in good condition. The court held that it would control a life tenant in the same way as it would control the exercise by an ordinary trustee of any power the trustee had. A trustee would be prevented from exercising a power in any way which

79. *Re Hoppe* [1961] V.R. 381.
80. *Stevenson v. Myers* (1929) 47 W.N. (N.S.W.) 94.
81. *Re Joseph; Joseph v. Trustees Executors & Agency Co. Ltd* [1960] V.R. 550.
82. Settled land legislation: Vic.: s. 107; Tas.: s. 48.
83. [1947] V.L.R. 183.

was wrong or unreasonable. The judgment on which the life tenant based his proposed exercise of discretion was founded on a complete misconception of the facts. From the point of view of what is best for the property the persons interested in the inheritance should be preferred as tenants to any outsider. Furthermore, it was unreasonable to eject the widow and the sons from what had been their home for 28 years. The life tenant had shown a capricious disregard for the interests and wishes of the widow and sons. The life tenant would be directed not to lease without first offering a lease on like terms to the sons.

In *Re O'Shea*[84] the life tenants purported to lease hotel premises to a company owned by themselves. The remaindermen were all minors. The trustee of the settlement opposed the lease and brought an action to have the grant of the lease declared an invalid exercise of the life tenants' powers. The court held that the lease savoured of a grant by the life tenants to themselves. There was a conflict of interest and duty with respect to the enforcement of covenants by the life tenants. The life tenants had little experience of hotel management. There were misgivings as to their suitability as lessees. The tenant company's financial position was insecure. Therefore the purported lease was declared invalid.

[12.26] On the other hand the legislation seeks to remove any impediments to the proper exercise by the life tenant of her or his powers. Any provision in any instrument which attempts to induce the life tenant to abstain from exercising her or his powers under the *Settled Land Act* is declared to be void.[85] Any contract by a life tenant not to exercise her or his powers is declared to be void.[86] Any interest which is limited to continue so long as the life tenant abstains from exercising any power is freed from determination on that event.[87] The exercise by the life tenant of any of the statutory powers is declared not to occasion a forfeiture.[88]

The powers of the life tenant are not capable of assignment or release. Consequently, if the life tenant transfers the life interest (which is the interest the tenant has in most cases, though not all), the transferee will acquire an estate per autre vie but the transferor will retain the powers under the *Settled Land Act*. That transferee's right can be significantly affected by the exercise of the life tenant's powers, particularly sale or lease. Victoria and Tasmania split as to their solutions to this happening. In Victoria since the coming into operation of the *Settled Land Act* 1928 the original life tenant may exercise the statutory powers without the consent of the assignee and the assignee's rights are transferred to whatever property represents the land.[89] In Tasmania, on the other hand, the assignee's rights may not be affected without consent except that consent to a lease is necessary only if the assignee is in actual possession.[90]

84. [1957] V.R. 353.
85. Settled land legislation: Vic.: s. 106(1); Tas.: s. 46(1).
86. Settled land legislation: Vic.: s. 104(2); Tas.: s. 45(2).
87. Settled land legislation: Vic.: s. 106(3); Tas.: s. 46(2).
88. Settled land legislation: Vic.: s. 106(3); Tas.: s. 47.
89. Settled land legislation: Vic.: s. 105.
90. Settled land legislation: Tas.: s. 45(3).

[12.27] The protection for the freedom of the life tenant to exercise the statutory powers may mean that an attack may be made on common provisions conferring ancillary benefits in addition to life interest. The situation is illustrated by the case of *Re Patten, Westminster Bank Ltd v. Carlyon.*[91] There a woman was left the use of a house and furniture for her life or so long as she required them. A power to sublet was denied. The house and furniture were to be sold on termination of occupation. A capital sum was set aside for the payment from the interest of taxes, rates and repairs of the house. The direction against subletting was regarded as obviously deemed void. Furthermore, the provision for sale of the house on termination of occupation was avoided so far as it would operate in the event of the exercise of the statutory powers. Therefore should the woman exercise the power to sell or lease she was entitled during her life to receive the interest on the proceeds of sale or rent. The gift over the furniture also had the tendency to induce the woman to abstain from the exercise of her powers. Consequently, she was entitled to the furniture during her life or until she ceased to occupy the house for any reason other than the exercise of the statutory powers. The argument with respect to the interest on the capital sum was that on a lease or sale she would lose a benefit. Consequently, there was an inducement not to lease or sell and she should be entitled to have the payments continue or on sale to a sum equivalent to the value of the rates, taxes and repairs. Romer J. accepted that on a lease the woman would lose and that loss was an inducement; therefore the payment of the amounts should continue despite a lease. But his honour declined to grant a benefit on sale. The trust for the payment of outgoings was an extra benefit enabling residence without the expenses but was not a provision tending to induce the woman to abstain from exercising the power of sale.

[12.28] The life tenant's powers may be extended by the instrument creating the interest and the statutory powers are cumulative upon any provisions of that instrument.[92] However, in the case of a conflict between the provisions of the instrument and those of the Act relative to the statutory powers, the provisions of the Act prevail.[93] Similarly the trustees of a settlement may be given additional powers.[94] But where the trustees or any other person is given any power exercisable by the life tenant under the *Settled Land Act*, the consent of the life tenant to the exercise of that power is necessary.[95] This proviso significantly affects the balance of powers between the life tenant and trustees and is the major reason why the Settled Land Acts in Victoria and Tasmania retain significance whatever the powers of the trustees happen to be. Further reference to this relationship is made below **[12.38]**.

[12.29] In Victoria, the position of the trustees of the settlement is central in that their consent is necessary for the exercise of most of the statutory powers. They are directed to have regard to the interests of all parties under the settlement and not to withhold their consent

---

91. [1929] 2 Ch. 276.
92. Settled land legislation: Vic.: s. 108(1); Tas.: s. 51(1).
93. Settled land legislation: Vic.: s. 108(2); Tas.: s. 51(2).
94. Settled land legislation: Vic.: s. 109(1); Tas.: s. 51(1).
95. Settled land legislation: Vic.: s. 108(2); Tas.: s. 51(2).

arbitrarily.[96] The life tenant may apply to the court if dissatisfied at the withholding of consent.[97] In both Victoria and Tasmania, notice must be given to trustees of any intended exercise of statutory powers.[98] If any difference between the life tenant and the trustees arises either party may refer the matter to the court.[99] The trustees are given various protections with respect to the exercise of their powers.[100]

4. Repairs, Maintenance and Improvement

[12.30]   The carrying out of repairs, maintenance and improvements on settled land is addressed only in the Victorian and Tasmanian legislation. The Victorian Act is much more facilitative of such work in that it allows money for improvements to be raised by way of mortgage of the settled land.[101] The Tasmanian Act restricts the raising of money for work on the land to cases of the erection of dwelling-houses and outbuildings and other buildings for agricultural or horticultural purposes.[102] However, capital money may otherwise exist—either as a result of the original settlement or the exercise of the statutory powers of the Acts. Both Victoria and Tasmania allow for the expenditure of capital money on listed improvements.[103] Capital money includes the money which may be raised by the mortgages authorised by the Acts.

[12.31]   In Victoria the lists of authorised improvements are set out in the Second Schedule of the Act. That Schedule is divided into three parts: Pt I lists improvements, the costs of which are not liable to be replaced by instalments; Pt II lists improvements, the cost of which the trustees or the court may require to be replaced by instalments; Pt III lists improvements, the costs of which the trustees or the court must require to be replaced by instalments. The Tasmania Act simply authorises the expenditure of capital money on works listed in the Act.[104] The Tasmanian list closely resembles Pt I of the Victorian Second Schedule.

The works set out in Pt I of the Victorian Second Schedule and in the Tasmanian Act are generally substantial and reflect a holding of a substantial piece of land. They include drainage, bridges, irrigation, roads, cottages, farmhouses and reservoirs. Both lists do include additions or alterations to buildings reasonably necessary to enable them to be let. Part II of the Victorian Schedule includes structural additions to or alterations in buildings reasonably required whether the buildings are intended to be let or not, or are already let.

[12.32]   The operation of the powers to authorise improvements was reviewed by Sholl J. in *Equity Trustees Executors & Agency Co. Ltd v. Riddell*.[105] He pointed out that there may be overlaps between items in the

96. Settled land legislation: Vic.: s. 93(a).
97. Settled land legislation: Vic.: s. 93(b).
98. Settled land legislation: Vic.: s. 101; Tas.: s. 42.
99. Settled land legislation: Vic.: s. 93; Tas.: s. 41.
100. Settled land legislation: Vic.: ss 97-99; Tas.: ss 38-39.
101. Settled land legislation: Vic.: s. 71(1)(b).
102. Settled land legislation: Tas.: s. 9 of the amending Act of 1911.
103. Settled land legislation: Vic.: ss 83-89; Tas.: s. 23.
104. Settled land legislation: Tas.: s. 23, as added by s. 11 of the 1911 Act.
105. *Equity Trustees Executors & Agency Co. Ltd v. Riddell* [1954] V.L.R. 161.

various parts. However, any item which could fairly be regarded as failing under Pt I should be regarded as covered by that Part rather than the others so costs were not liable to replacement. He further considered that building additions or alterations to enable letting were not confined to structural additions or alterations. With regard to items in Pt II where a discretion existed as to replacement he considered repayment of cost should normally be required over the period for which the benefit of the work ensued. Items which were merely repairs should be paid for out of income.

The relationship of the lists to the provisions of the settlement was considered again by Sholl J. in *Re Joseph; Joseph v. Equity Trustees Executors & Agency Co. Ltd.*[106] In that case the will creating the interests had provided for all improvements and repairs to be paid for from income. Sholl J. pointed out that the life tenant could insist on items in the first part of the Second Schedule being paid for from capital. There was therefore a conflict between the Act and the settlement, and the Act prevailed. Similarly the life tenant was entitled to an exercise of judgment as whether items in Pt II should be paid for out of capital. He considered that a major roof replacement was a structural alteration within Pt II and because of the significance of the work and the advanced years of the life tenant should be chargeable to capital. The other item—unblocking and recementing of drains—was not properly classified as drainage (a permanent improvement) or a structural alteration, therefore fell outside the Schedule and should be charged to income.

5. Exploitation of the Land

[12.33] As between life tenant and remainder, the doctrine of waste clearly applies and controls any action which might be regarded as detrimental to the land. The instrument creating the settlement remains important as the life tenant is liable for voluntary waste unless made unimpeachable for waste and even then is liable for equitable waste unless such liability is removed.

The right to carry out improvements (discussed in the previous section) may arguably involve the commission of ameliorating waste but the right given by the statute would override common law restraints. The other significant addition to the life tenant's powers is in relation to the cutting of timber. Some authorisation is given to do what would not otherwise be allowed especially if the life tenant is impeachable for waste and thus unable to cut timber.

[12.34] In Victoria, Tasmania and South Australia, express provision is made for the cutting and sale of timber. In South Australia, the court's power to authorise sale is simply extended to sales of timber.[107] In New South Wales the equivalent provision may extend to timber as the timber would be part of the land.[108] In Victoria, the power to cut and sell timber is conferred upon the life tenant with the concurrence of the trustees or

106. [1960] V.R. 550.
107. Settled land legislation: S.A.: s. 15.
108. Settled land legislation: N.S.W.: s. 48.

the court.[109] Similarly in Tasmania the power is conferred on the life tenant with the concurrence of the trustees or the court:[110] this qualification is unusual in that State's legislation as the life tenant has even the power to sell without the need for consent. In both Victoria and Tasmania the power exists where the life tenant is impeachable for waste, if unimpeachable the tenant in most instances could cut timber without liability. In Victoria and Tasmania, the proceeds of sale are divided one quarter to rents and profits and three quarters to capital. The Victorian Act alone then defines timber to include trees of any species which have a market value for their wood for any use or purpose whatsoever.[111] This definition is considerably broader than the common law which confines timber to that used for buildings. The broader definition seems to limit the life tenant's power as the life tenant could otherwise cut and sell non-timber trees without liability even if impeachable for waste. Although s. 108(1) of the Victorian Act states that the statutory powers are cumulative upon other powers, s. 108(2) states that in case of conflict as to the exercise of statutory powers the Act prevails.

6. Sales and Other Dispositions

[12.35]   A power to sell settled land is conferred by statute in all jurisdictions. But this power is one where the authorisation processes differ. In Victoria, concurrence of the trustees or the court is necessary;[112] in Tasmania, the life tenant has the power;[113] in New South Wales[114] and South Australia,[115] sale requires a court order. In Victoria and Tasmania, the sale must be for the best consideration reasonably obtainable. In New South Wales and South Australia, the sale must be in accordance with the rules and practice of sale under an order of the court. In all jurisdictions, provision is made for what amounts to a scheme of subdivision of land to be sold with the dedication of streets, establishment of public reserves and provision of drainage.

[12.36]   The power to lease is the one power which in all jurisdictions can be exercised by the life tenant without the concurrence of other parties or the court. The powers are broadest in Tasmania but in the other jurisdictions the life tenant's limited powers may be extended if the relevant consent is obtained. In all jurisdictions reference is made to various types of leases. The common lease today whereby possession is taken for residential, commercial or industrial purpose is described in New South Wales and South Australia as an occupation lease and forms the residual category in Victoria and Tasmania. The special types of leases referred to—building, mining and repairing leases—involve work on the land by the tenant. In all jurisdictions formal requirements are imposed.

109. Settled land legislation: Vic.: s. 66.
110. Settled land legislation: Tas.: s. 32.
111. Settled land legislation: Vic.: s. 66(3).
112. Settled land legislation: Vic.: ss 38-40.
113. Settled land legislation: Tas.: ss 14-18.
114. Settled land legislation: N.S.W.: ss 48-53.
115. Settled land legislation: S.A.: ss 15-21.

In Tasmania, the life tenant can lease for a period not exceeding 21 years or in the case of a building lease 99 years.[116] In Victoria, the life tenant can lease for up to a 21 year term provided the tenant is impeachable for waste.[117] In New South Wales, the period is only ten years again subject to a requirement as to waste.[118] In South Australia, the period is 21 years also, so long as the tenant is not unimpeachable for waste.[119]

In Victoria, the life tenant has wider powers with the concurrence of the trustees or the court. In the case of an ordinary lease the period remains 21 years but the waste requirement is not essential. In the case of a building lease the maximum period is 50 years and in the case of a mining lease 60 years.[120] In New South Wales, the court may authorise leases beyond the power of the life tenant. In the case of occupation or agricultural leases the maximum term is ten years but again without the waste requirement. A maximum term of 40 years is established for mining leases, 15 years for repairing leases, and 30 years for building leases. The court may authorise any individual lease or give powers to trustees to grant authorisations.[121] The South Australian provisions follow those of New South Wales except that the maximum terms are longer: 21 years for occupation or agricultural leases; 40 years for mining leases; 60 years for repairing leases; and 90 years for building leases.[122]

VI. MANAGEMENT AND TRUSTS AND TRUSTS FOR SALE

1. Impact of Settled Land Legislation

[12.37] The New South Wales and South Australian settled land legislation gives very limited powers to the life tenant and makes no impediment from the existence of these powers upon powers of trustees. The only relevance of the life tenant's powers could be that a court could decline to exercise contested powers on the basis of the existence of the settled land powers. But since the life tenants powers of their own initiative are so limited and the court's powers are limited to sale or lease, settled land powers are unlikely to impact upon trustees' powers in those States.

[12.38] In Victoria and Tasmania, as mentioned earlier, the powers of the life tenant are protected. The settled land legislation was attempting to ensure that powers did reside in the life tenant whatever limitations may have been desired by the settlor or other beneficiaries. Accordingly, both States provide that if someone other than the life tenant seeks to exercise powers which could have been exercised by the life tenant then the consent of the life tenant to that exercise is necessary.

116. Settled land legislation: Tas.: ss 6-13.
117. Settled land legislation: Vic.: s. 42(5).
118. Settled land legislation: N.S.W.: ss 68, 69.
119. Settled land legislation: S A.; ss 4-14.
120. Settled land legislation: Vic.: ss 41-47.
121. Settled land legislation: N.S.W.: ss 38-47.
122. Settled land legislation: S.A.: ss 44-45.

Section 52(2) of the Tasmanian *Settled Land Act* 1884 states:

"but, in case of conflict between the provisions of a settlement and the provisions of this Act, relative to any matter in respect whereof the tenant for life exercises or contracts or intends to exercise any power under this Act, the provisions of this Act shall prevail, and accordingly, notwithstanding anything in the settlement, the consent of the tenant for life shall, by virtue of this Act, be necessary to the exercise by the trustees of the settlement or other person of any power conferred by the settlement exercisable for any purpose provided for in this Act."

Section 108(2) of the Victorian *Settled Land Act* 1958 is in similar terms.

The consequence is that trustees in Victoria and Tasmania will often need the consent of the life tenant for the exercise of powers that otherwise are clearly possessed by them. However, the scope of this qualification is greater in Tasmania because even trusts for sale are subject to the *Settled Land Act*. In Victoria, trusts for sale are specifically exempted from the operation of the *Settled Land Act*.[123]

2. General Powers of Trustees

[12.39] The role of trustees is a matter to be addressed in the instrument setting up the trust. Their role may vary from a purely nominal ownership for the benefit of others, to management responsibilities which can include the running of a business, to discretionary duties not just as to looking after property but as to sale and purchase and the allocation of benefits between a class of potential beneficiaries. In the case of discretionary trusts the potential beneficiaries have no entitlement to any particular property until the discretion is exercised. This feature has been relied upon as part of schemes for tax minimisation and the form of these interests have developed in response to taxation legislation. On the other hand a bare trust may result from a simple provision in a will to provide for a spouse and children. Whilst the trustees in such a case may appear to have a purely nominal role, the condition of specific property may call for action and the trustees may face a lack of any enabling powers in the will and beneficiaries lacking legal capacity to authorise any action.

Trustees have been able to appeal to the general supervisory power over trusts exercised by courts of equity but more importantly today in all States the trustees are given powers by legislation.[124] Some of these powers are confined to trustees under a trust for sale. Some of the powers may be exercised by the trustees of their own motion. Other powers may be exercised upon application to the court. Today trustees may in general receive authorisation for any action which is beneficial for the trust. The court's powers extend to variations of the trust itself but this section of the text is concerned with management of land.

---

123. *Settled Land Act*, 1958 (Vic.), s. 9.
124. N.S.W.: *Trustee Act* 1925; Vic.: *Trustee Act* 1958; Qld: *Trusts Act* 1973; S.A.: *Trustee Act* 1936; W.A.: *Trustees Act* 1962; Tas.: *Trustee Act* 1898.

[12.40] The statutory powers have generally been drafted to supplement those of the instrument creating the trust. They enable the trustee to look after the property where no provision has been made in the instrument. That instrument may however express intention that the trustees are to have only limited powers. In Victoria, Western Australia and Tasmania, these limitations usually prevail as the statutory powers are expressed as a general rule to be subject to the trust instrument.[125] Similarly in New South Wales and South Australia, most powers are individually expressed to be subject to the trust instrument though in South Australia some powers are stated to override any contrary provision in the trust instrument and in both States some powers are set out without any statement of their relationship with the instrument. In Queensland on the other hand, whilst a few powers are made subject to the trust instrument, the usual position is that the statutory powers apply whether or not a contrary provision is made in the trust instrument.[126] The Queensland position seems to reflect a policy to override restrictions on land management which was an aim of the life tenant's powers under the settled land legislation which has been repealed in that State.

There are some instances in which the contrary intention referred to is an express contrary intention. Otherwise a contrary intention may flow from the overall purport of the trust instrument.[127]

[12.41] Whilst there are many specific powers conferred by statute upon trustees, in all States the courts are given general powers to authorise dealings by trustees.[128] It is the breadth of these powers that leads to the proposition that the trustees may receive court authorisation for any action in the interests of the trust. The Victorian provision is as follows:

"Power of Court to authorize dealings with trust property.

63.(1) Where in the management or administration of any property vested in trustees, any sale, lease, mortgage, surrender, release or other disposition, or any purchase, investment, acquisition, expenditure or other transaction, is in the opinion of the Court expedient, but the same cannot be effected by reason of the absence of any power for that purpose vested in the trustees by the trust instrument (if any) or by law, the Court may by order confer upon the trustees, either generally or in any particular instance, the necessary power for the purpose on such terms and subject to such provisions and conditions (if any) as the Court thinks fit and may direct what manner any money authorized to be expended, and the costs of any transaction are to be paid or borne as between capital and income.

(2) The Court may from time to time rescind or vary any order made under this section, or may make any new or further order.

---

125. Trustee legislation: Vic.: s. 2(3); W.A.: s. 5(3); Tas.: s. 64.
126. Trustee legislation: Qld: s. 7A.
127. *Re Gertsman* [1966] V.R. 15.
128. Trustee legislation: N.S.W.: s. 81; Vic.: s. 63; Qld: s. 94; S.A.: s. 59b; W.A.: s. 89; Tas.: s. 47.

(3) An application to the Court under this section may be made
by the trustees, or by any of them, or by any person beneficially
interested under the trust.''

The Queensland and Tasmanian provisions are very close to this
section; the Western Australian provision states that an order may be
made not only when considered expedient but also if it would be in the
best interests of the persons, or the majority of the persons, beneficially
interested under the trust; the New South Wales and South Australian
provisions are more extensive but to the same effect.

The provision draws from the inherent powers traditionally exercised
by courts of equity. However, those powers were exercised with great
caution and based more upon emergency (often referred to as the salvage
jurisdiction) rather than expediency. The language of the section is that
of expediency and a conservative construction of this language was
rejected by the Australian High Court in *Riddle v. Riddle*.[129] The issue of
the scope of the court's power to authorise dealings by trustees has arisen
not in relation to management of land but in relation to investment of
moneys. The challenge of inflation led trustees to seek authorisation for
investment in stocks or shares rather than more secure but less profitable
government bonds and securities. The courts have approved broader
investment proposals though in the exercise of their discretion imposed
safeguards such as a spread of investments and investigation of company
history.[130]

The general approach was stated by Williams J. in *Riddle v. Riddle*:[131]

"The one and only test is the expediency of the act or thing which
the court is asked to authorise the trustees to do or abstain from
doing. The court has only to be of opinion that the trust property as
a whole will in fact benefit from the making of the order."

3. Repairs, Maintenance and Improvements

[12.42]   The powers of trustees with respect to repairs or maintenance
have traditionally been dependent on the classification of their
relationship with the property. The distinction between bare trustees and
those with active powers of management has been emphasised.[132]

"The result of the authorities is that a bare trustee who has no
mandate under the trust instrument to expend moneys in repairs has
no power to do and should apply to the court if the repairs considered
necessary are to salvage the property."

The absence of power is declared even in those cases where the repair
is essential for the maintenance of the property because those cases are
stated to be ones where assistance might be gained from the courts

---

129. (1952) 85 C.L.R. 202.
130. *Re Baker* [1961] V.R. 641; *Re Dehnert* [1973] V.R. 449; *National Trustees, Executors
    & Agency Co. of Australasia Ltd v. Attorney-General for Victoria* [1973] V.R. 610; *Re
    Sykes* [1973] 1 N.S.W.L.R. 597.
131. (1952) 85 C.L.R. 202 at 222.
132. *Re Dawes* [1954] V.L.R. 76.

through the salvage doctrine. Since a power to preserve is denied, an upgrading of the property would seem to be out of the question. The distinction between repairs and improvements has been made in the interpretation of powers conferred by the settlement with the general consequence that repairs are chargeable to income and improvements to capital.[133] One of the factors apparently relevant to the denial of power to repair is the supposed policy of the *Settled Lands Act* that the life tenant had the powers of management. As has been seen in Australia only the Victorian *Settled Lands Act* makes any meaningful provision for repairs and thus only in that State can the *Settled Land Act* provide a starting-point for an argument against trustees' powers. The concession of court authorisation in emergency situations is based upon the now discarded view of the court's general powers of authorisation. Today the test as to what may be authorised is what is in the interests of the trust property as a whole. Therefore, the court would seem to have power to authorise both repairs and improvements and to be able to do so if the work is in the best interests of the trust even if no emergency exists.

[12.43] Even the narrow statement of the powers of bare trustees to effect repairs or improvements has been subject to qualification where the nature of the property has been such that work by trustees must have been intended by the settlor. In *Harkness v. Harkness*,[134] a testatrix left her property to her husband upon trust to convert but with a full discretionary power to postpone conversion. In her lifetime the testatrix had carried on a business as a builder and contractor. She bought vacant land, built on it and sold or leased the buildings. She raised money for the ventures by way of mortgage. Part of the estate consisted of lands bought for such a venture. The land could not advantageously be dealt with as vacant land and some existing leased buildings were in a state of disrepair and required renovation. The husband sought a declaration that he was entitled to build and renovate and raise money for these purposes by mortgage. He was held to be entitled to do so because of the use of the land by the testatrix and the implied continuation of that use.

Similarly the nature of a vineyard was relied upon by the High Court in *Cousins v. Cousins*[135] to justify borrowing by way of mortgage. The jurisdiction relied upon there was that relating to the administration of real estate of infants where the court acted parens patriae but again with emphasis on the salvage doctrine. O'Connor J. argued that the children were intended to enjoy the benefit of the vineyard as a going concern. The property could not be so enjoyed unless the vines were restored. The principle would seem today even more strongly to be applicable when the court exercises its general powers to approve what is expedient.

[12.44] In all States except Tasmania, trustees are given specific statutory powers with respect to repairs and maintenance.

In Victoria, trustees for sale are given the powers of the life tenant under the *Settled Land Act*. Those powers have been discussed earlier.[136]

133. *O'Neill v. Cottill* (1920) 20 S.R. (N.S.W.) 264.
134. (1904) 20 W.N. (N.S.W.) 269.
135. (1906) 3 C.L.R. 1198.
136. *Property Law Act* 1958 (Vic.), s. 58.

In New South Wales, a trustee may expend moneys on repairs on improvements which may include construction and repair of buildings, dams and fences, restocking with livestock and replacement of machinery. Money may be raised by mortgage. A private trustee may spend only the lesser sum of $1000 or one third of the value of the land. The Public Trustee or a statutory trustee may spend $10,000 or a larger sum if all beneficiaries are legally competent and agree. The court may authorise expenditure of larger sums. Trustees for sale and trustees for infants may construct, renovate or repair houses, dams and fences.[137]

In Queensland[138] and Western Australia,[139] trustees are given general powers of repair whether or not the work is necessary for salvage. They may also spend money on the improvement or development of the property but they require the sanction of the court for amounts over $10,000 (in Western Australia for any one purpose). They may also spend money without limit on works relative to the subdivision of land (in Western Australia provided they have a power of sale). The expenditure may be apportioned between income and capital sources as the trustees consider equitable.

In South Australia,[140] trustees are authorised to carry out such repairs as they consider necessary or proper for the preservation of any building, erection or fixture and apportion expenditure as between income and capital as they consider equitable. They may be authorised by the court to spend money on building or repair or alteration or improvement and to raise money for the purpose by way of mortgage. Again expenditure may be apportioned as considered just.

4. Exploitation of the Land

[12.45]   The issue of restraint upon exploitation of the land has not been addressed as such. The cases have concentrated upon the presence or absence of powers of trustees. The issue could have arisen in Re Hart[141] the previously discussed (see above [12.12]), South Australian case involving the cutting of timber. There the land was held on trust for life interests and then on trust for remainder interests. The trustees cut and sold 713 pinus radiata trees. The case was fought on the question of whether the proceeds were income or capital. It was accepted that the trees were not classified as timber and could be cut by the life tenant without liability. On this basis the proceeds were treated as income. The powers of the trustees were thus linked to the powers of the life tenant. Thus the actions of the trustees are restricted by the rules of waste.

The general fiduciary relationship provides a broader basis for respect for future concerns in the exploitation of land. Clearly trustees must have regard to the interests of all beneficiaries in reaching decisions as to what

137. Trustee legislation: N.S.W.: ss 82, 82A.
138. Trustee legislation: Qld: s. 33(1).
139. Trustee legislation: W.A.: s. 30(1).
140. Trustee legislation: S.A.: ss 25a, 25b.
141. [1954] S.A.S.R. 1.

to do with the land. Consequently, any action which makes the land markedly less valuable for holders of future interests would amount to a breach of duty.

5. Sales and other Dispositions

[12.46] Whilst a single parcel of land could be subject to arrangements for use by family members and thus the subject of settlement, where arrangements are made with respect to an individual's assets generally, those arrangements would normally provide for the conversion of the assets into money and the investment of that money. Thus, the duty or trust for sale is often referred to as a "trader's settlement"[142] in that its subject is a collection of mixed assets and where substantial, normally produced by commercial activity. Trusts for sale are commonly regarded as artificial devices in that they provided a means to avoid the powers of the life tenant under the *Settled Land Act* to sell the land.[143] If these trusts are so used then, as already explained, only in Victoria does the purpose have any meaning.

[12.47] If a settlor creates a trust for sale, the trustees have as their primary duty the sale of the land. Since their duty is to sell, the question arises as to the time within which that duty must be exercised. That question flows into that of postponement and the power to postpone may be express or implied. If there is a power to postpone then the question is as to the extent of that power.

Where there is no power of postponement the trustees are not obliged to sell the property immediately without regard to economic circumstances. They have a responsibility to serve the best interests of the beneficiaries and to ensure that the sale provides the best practicable return for the beneficiaries. As the High Court has stated:[144]

"A trust for sale for whatever purpose with no special power of postponement must be exercised within a reasonable time. It does not imperatively oblige the trustees to sell at once, or at any precise, definite, or particular time; they are entitled to use a reasonable discretion . . . but the courts have had no difficulty in holding that where there is a trust for sale unqualified by a power of postponement no one would regard it as within the limits of a reasonable discretion to retain the property unsold for as long as 21 years."

It is impossible to glean how this passage suggests (as asserted by authors of the leading text) that a period of 21 years is a reasonable time.[145] The only reason for the nomination of 21 years as too long was that there was no possibility of infringing the perpetuity period. The passage does not even imply 20 years is a reasonable time.

[12.48] Since a duty to sell does not mean an immediate sale the duty of itself implies some power to postpone. In all jurisdictions, except South

142. Butt, p. 178.
143. Ford and Lee, p. 548.
144. *Cox v. Archer* (1964) 110 C.L.R. 1 at 7.
145. See Ford and Lee, p. 550.

Australia and Tasmania, an express power to postpone sale is conferred by statute subject to differing restrictions.[146] Trustees should be able to gain court authorisation for postponement in appropriate cases even if that power is not given by the settlement or statute.

Even the power of postponement does not mean that the property may be retained indefinitely. In *Re Morish*[147] a residuary estate was left to trustees upon trust to convert with power to postpone conversion for as long as they should think fit and to pay the income to the widow for life and then to the children. Part of the estate was the business of a furniture manufacturer. The testator died in 1905 and the trustees carried on the business until the action in 1939. Not surprisingly the years 1930 to 1937 showed an aggregate loss which amounted to 34,306 pounds. Murray C.J. held that even with a power of postponement trustees could not postpone realisation for an unlimited time. The business should properly have been sold as a going concern and thus the trustees properly had to operate it until they found a purchaser. But their duty was to seek a purchaser and they had a reasonable time to find one. The trustees had received court authorisation to postpone sale until the end of 1926. Thereafter they had made no effort to find a purchaser as they assumed no one would be prepared to buy. They were held to be in breach of their duty and liable for losses incurred from the beginning of 1929.

The High Court's statement of the matter is that a power to postpone does not extend to an arbitrary postponement for an indefinite period.[148]

[12.49] Whereas a trust for sale imposes a duty to sell (even where sale is not regarded as imperative), a power of sale given to trustees extends the trustees' options with respect to the management of the property. The Settled Lands Acts at least provide a mechanism whereby the land may be sold even though by the life tenant rather than the trustees. In Queensland, the trustees have a power of sale[149] and this power cannot be excluded or modified;[150] in Western Australia, trustees again have a power of sale[151] but that power is subject to a contrary provision in the settlement.[152] In Western Australia, the trustees may be directed to sell by the persons at the time of the direction entitled to an interest in possession.[153] This power of direction is effectively vested in the life tenant but it is unclear whether it is subject to a contrary provision in the settlement. Certainly the court has an express power[154] to override provisions of the settlement.

A power of sale may arise from the nature of a settlement. In *Pagels v. MacDonald*[155] a testator left his real and personal property for a life interest

146. Trustee legislation: N.S.W.: s. 27B; Vic.: s. 13; Qld: s. 32; W.A.: s. 27.
147. [1939] S.A.S.R. 305.
148. *Cox v. Archer* (1964) 110 C.L.R. 1 at 7.
149. Trustee legislation: Qld: s. 32(a).
150. Trustee legislation: Qld: s. 7A.
151. Trustee legislation: W.A.: s. 27(1)(a).
152. Trustee legislation: W.A.: s. 5(3).
153. Trustee legislation: W.A.: s. 27(4).
154. Trustee legislation: W.A.: s. 89.
155. (1935) 54 C.L.R. 519.

and thereafter to be equally divided between his youngest son and his six youngest daughters. The High Court rejected the view that the property was to be transferred to the beneficiaries to be held as co-owners. The natural construction of the direction to divide and the direction for equality of shares was that the property should be sold and the proceeds divided.

[12.50]   One impediment to sale may be the need for consent. Indeed, it has already been suggested (see above [12.08]) that one method to frustrate the policies promoting alienability is to create a trust for sale but subject to the consent of someone with an incentive not to agree to sale.

A distinction is drawn between fiduciary and non-fiduciary powers to consent to the exercise of powers by a trustee. Powers to consent granted for the benefit of the person granting consent are non-fiduciary. Powers to consent for the benefit of other persons are fiduciary. Fiduciary powers cannot be delegated and must be exercised in the interests of the beneficiaries.[156] Where a settlement created a life estate and a remainder and empowered the trustees to sell but required the consent of the life tenant to a sale during his lifetime, the power to consent was held to be non-fiduciary.[157] The person affected by sale was the life tenant and the provision for consent was inserted solely for his benefit. As a non-fiduciary consent, the power could be delegated.

[12.51]   If trustees are to retain property the production of income from the property may involve leasing of the property. Again the court's general powers would include the authorisation of leases. The power to lease may also be implied. Thus in *Re Burgess*[158] a business was to be retained by trustees until a child reached the age of 21. Way C.J. held that to make the most of the goodwill of the business until the specified time it was proper that the trustees were impliedly empowered to lease.

Implied powers to lease are conferred by statute in all States except Tasmania.

In Victoria, trustees for sale have all the powers to lease of life tenants and trustees of the settlement under the *Settled Land Act*.[159] These powers have been set out above.

In New South Wales and South Australia, a trustee with a power to manage and a trustee for sale with a power to postpone sale may lease for a period not exceeding five years in New South Wales or ten years in South Australia.[160] Other trustees may lease for three years in New South Wales or five years in South Australia.[161]

---

156. *Commonwealth v. Colonial Combing Spinning & Weaving Co. Ltd* (1922) 31 C.L.R. 421.
157. *Re Callen* (1918) 18 S.R. (N.S.W.) 219.
158. [1899] S.A.S.R. 145
159. *Property Law Act* 1958 (Vic.), ss 35(1) and 40.
160. Trustee legislation: N.S.W.: s. 36; S.A.: s. 25C.
161. Ibid.

In Queensland and Western Australia trustees may lease for a term not exceeding 30 years in the case of a building lease or 21 years in other cases.[162] In addition trustees may lease for any term not exceeding one year or on a yearly or shorter periodic basis.[163]

162. Trustee legislation: Qld: s. 32; W.A.: s. 27.
163. Ibid.

13

Schemes for Unit Ownership

I. PROBLEMS OF SHARED SPACE

[13.01] Intensity of urban development is not a new phenomenon. The industrial revolution pushed masses into the urban areas. Buildings were used to house large numbers of persons—often the conditions in which these persons lived did little to provide for health or happiness. Provision of occupation for these persons did not however create demands for new forms of property rights—the occupants had little power and the owners of the buildings were pleased to adapt existing categories of property rights to meet the situation. The strongest position the occupants were likely to be in was that of tenants. That status conferred rights enforceable against third parties but as explained in Chapter 10 the feudal origins of landlords' obligations provided little in the way of legal entitlement to enforce standards of shelter and the common law was in no mood to create new standards for the urban environment. The occupants might not have achieved even the status of tenants but have been regarded as boarders, lodgers or some other form of licensees. Such occupants did not have rights against third parties and their rights against their landlords depended upon contract law in an era which emphasised freedom of contract.

[13.02] Crowding in Australian cities was of concern particularly at the turn of this century[1] and during the depression. The period since the Second World War has however been marked by the suburban sprawl of the urban capitals. Ownership of the quarter acre block was not only the dream but the reality for the majority of the population.[2] Occupation as tenants was the common alternative, and for significant numbers this occupation was as tenants of government agencies which fulfilled welfare and entrepreneurial housing roles.[3] Boarding-homes and guest houses tended to provide for the most disadvantaged—often persons not only economically deprived but also with personal problems. One social reform, the movement of mentally handicapped from institutions, has added to the problems likely to be faced in this part of the housing market.

---

1. See Tregenza, "Charles Reade: Town Planning Missionary" in Hutchings and Bunker (eds), *With Conscious Purpose: A History of Town Planning in South Australia* (1986), pp. 45-59; Sandercock, *Cities for Sale* (1976), pp. 7-28.
2. See Hutchings, "Adelaide: Suburbia Triumphant" in Hutchings and Bunker (eds), op. cit., pp. 35-44.
3. Bradbrook, MacCallum and Moore, pp. 46-48, 66-69.

A reasonable degree of affluence was enjoyed by a considerable proportion of the population. Investment of this affluence in housing was encouraged, in part as a way of enhancing social stability and conservatism. Thus Commonwealth-State Housing Agreements of the 1950s directed government assistance towards home buyers even at the expense of government housing which would seem to have assisted the less advantaged.[4] Certainly assistance was provided for home-buyers in the absence of any assistance for private tenants. Demand for privately owned dwellings was met by the continued outward expansion of the major cities. Concentration of wealth opportunities in the major cities as opposed to other towns and rural areas added to the demand for expansion. Much of the Australian population is concentrated in Melbourne and Sydney and to a lesser extent the other capitals.

At first, the more affluent moved to the outer suburbs with greater space and higher building standards. By about the mid 1960s, however, the appeal of the outer suburbs commenced to wane and access to employment, educational, social and transport facilities of established areas was prized. The crassness of much post Second World War development came to be realised. The gentrification of the inner suburbs led to marked declines in the population of these areas as older buildings which had served as multiple dwelling-units were restored for single family occupation. Thus pressure mounted for new dwellings at a more intensive level than the homes on quarter acre allotments.[5] The 1970s also saw a decline of the medium sized family of four to six persons which had occupied the suburban dwelling. The *Family Law Act* 1974 removed fault-based divorce and is blamed for an increase in marriage breakdown, though it may well have been rather a reflection of the social phenomenon. But it is clear that the number of persons occupying separate dwelling-units (whether or not those units are separate buildings) declined significantly and that decline has continued to the present time. To add to the pressure, demographic trends have produced an aging population in a society in which multiple-generational sharing of dwellings has been uncommon.

[13.03] One solution to the pressures on urban land was the construction of large blocks of high-rise accommodation for the poor. In fact such buildings increase interdependence of occupants and matters such as security, respect for one another and maintenance of common areas are far greater problems for the poor than for other groups. Whilst high-rise apartments for the poor soon increased the urban blight they were supposed to relieve and were generally abandoned, other forms of more intensive housing succeeded.[6] In real estate parlance it has been common to distinguish between home units and flats. This distinction is based not on building form but on ownership arrangements—home units

---

4. Bradbrook, MacCallum and Moore, pp. 62-64.
5. Troy (ed.), *Urban Redevelopment in Australia* (1967), pp. 403-412.
6. Bradbrook, MacCallum and Moore, p. 47.

are parts of a building for which separate title has been granted. Often these units are single storey but they do not have their own allotment. The system that has provided ownership for these units is that of strata title— that system must deal with the interaction of the individual owners.[7] The system of strata title has in turn proved attractive as a means of providing separate ownership within buildings used for commercial and industrial purposes.

As well as the spread of the strata title system, other forms of multiple occupancy with ownership have been created. Beach shacks have long been in Australia a form of dwelling devoted to holiday or recreational use. Often these shacks would be used for only a few weeks in the year. Consequently developers recognised that rights of enjoyment of substantial recreational dwellings could be divided not only spatially but also temporally. The process of time-sharing allows the purchase of ownership for a number of weeks each year.[8]

Since the mix of generations has been uncommon in Australia, the aged are one group who do not have a need for large areas of buildings or grounds. Many of the aged desire peaceful surroundings, freedom from the need to work on buildings or gardens, and access to nursing care. Again efforts have been made to meet these demands through retirement villages where persons without children and without daily work routines can gather together, and where greater services are available. Again rights of occupation will often be purchased rather than leased, but the relationship between residents has features outside those of ordinary strata titled dwellings.

II. DEVELOPMENT OF STRATA TITLES

[13.04]   A system of strata title to interests in land was introduced in Victoria and New South Wales in 1960-1961 and extended to other Australian states in following years. The system was designed to facilitate acquisition of a Torrens system title to individual dwellings in a building consisting of multiple dwellings. The Australian system has had a considerable influence overseas.[9] Although first designed for residential application, strata titles have become common in industrial and commercial settings. What is owned can be identified by reference to a building plan. Areas not set aside for individual use—not only grounds but staircases and other common property—are vested in a specially created corporation in which all the individual owners hold joint interests. Mutual rights and obligations stem from the legislation and rules which the corporation is empowered to make.

---

7. Bugden, *Strata Title Management and Practice in New South Wales* (5th ed., 1988), pp. 2-3.
8. Ryan, *Urban Development Law and Policy* (1987), pp. 89-90.
9. Pavlich, *Condominium Law in British Columbia* (1983), pp. 31-32.

The common law allowed vertical and horizontal division of land so the concept that someone owns a cubic space situated between say 3 metres and 6 metres over ground level is not alien.[10] Precise definition of boundaries could nonetheless be difficult. The law of easements would allow for access for persons and utilities and drainage and for rights of support and protection from the weather. The law of covenants could ensure the preservation of grounds but positive obligations to contribute towards maintenance of common areas are not so readily expressed as proprietary interests. The whole property could be the subject of concurrent ownership but neither joint tenants nor tenants in common have any right to exclusive enjoyment of any part of the land. Contributions to improvements can only be demanded from co-owners on termination of co-ownership.

[13.05]   A variety of common law techniques could be combined to overcome some of these limitations. Co-ownership does not allow the partition of separate areas of use for individual co-owners, but these rights of enjoyment can be conferred by lease and positive undertakings enforced by leasehold covenants. However, the grant of leasehold interests came to be controlled by subdivision regulations. Moreover the leasehold structure would commonly mean that the co-owners as lessors granted a lease of particular portions to individual co-owners. This structure created a problem of decision making between the joint lessors. On the other hand a company form provides a mechanism for this decision making; rights of enjoyment of individual areas can be attached to particular shareholdings and contributions imposed upon shareholders. However, this model means that the individuals own shares in a company and the company is the legal and beneficial owner of the land. Ownership of land has been important for the purpose of borrowing money, as security over land has a special significance for moneylenders. Title to individual living units was difficult although not impossible to create.

The strata title system was based on techniques adopted by conveyances using a combination of common law techniques. In particular, it uses the company form to provide for ownership of common areas, the enforcement of maintenance contributions and for a decision-making process to balance the interests of the individuals involved. However, the statutory scheme does confer upon individuals a title to that part of the building to be occupied by the individuals.[11] They thus have a registered title which can be used as security and dealt with in the same way as any other title to land.

Strata titles have not been the only form of ownership of units within a multiple unit area. Essentially strata titles have required the completion of all buildings before the issue of title: title is defined by reference to the building. Such titles have been limited to cases where different parts of a building are to be separately owned: there may be more than one building and there need not be any vertical as opposed to horizontal division so that

---

10. *Bursill Enterprises Pty Ltd v. Berger Bros Trading Co. Pty Ltd* (1971) 124 C.L.R. 73. See above **[5.39]**.
11. Moore, "Regulation of Housing" (1986) 3 E. & P.L.J. 208 at 214-216.

all buildings might be single storey. However, sometimes it is desired to combine common areas with individually owned buildings on separate parcels of land. Some planners favour such schemes as the common area can provide more than the traditional backyard. In some instances, strata title cannot be conferred for such schemes; in others, title requires completion of all buildings. The schemes have some popularity in holiday areas and individuals may wish to purchase their building allotments and their share in the common area before committing the finance for building construction. In some cases, a separate system of cluster titles has been introduced for cases where all buildings are individually owned but there is a common area in joint ownership. In Victoria there has been a recent attempt to bring together these systems as far as possible with a single system of subdivision approval with flexibility in the grant of title and the form of corporate ownership of common property.

[13.06]   Strata titles have sometimes been used to achieve separate titles for what have been designed as individual building spaces. These individual spaces commonly arise in relation to maisonettes or row dwellings where although buildings have common walls the space around them is distinct. Separate title has been prevented by rules prescribing minimum sizes for allotments. Historically separate rights of occupation were achieved by co-ownership of the whole area subject to long-term leases of the parts. In the case of maisonettes this arrangement has been commonly referred to as a moiety title. Later planning legislation prevented even these arrangements by deeming a long-term lease of part of land to be a subdivision. Strata titles could only be produced for such cases by the artificial creation of common property. Today the minimum allotment sizes have been reduced and a discretion has been given to planning authorities to waive the requirements. Since more intensive use of urban land now receives favourable response from governments, the exercise of discretion to allow separate title for what are already in fact existing individual building spaces can be strongly supported.[12]

III.   CREATION AND ADMINISTRATION OF STRATA SCHEMES[13]

1. Creation of Strata Titles

[13.07]   Strata titles for units flow from the deposit with the Land Titles Office of a strata plan.[14] If the plan is accepted, existing certificates of title must be cancelled and new strata titles issued for each unit and the common property. In Queensland, South Australia and Tasmania, the strata plan must contain at least two units and common property.[15] In

---

12. Moore, "Power and the Planning System" (1988) 5 E. & P.L.J. 226 at 228.
13. On strata titles generally see Bugden, op. cit.; Collins and Robinson, *Strata Title Units in New South Wales* (2nd ed., 1982); Ilken, *Strata Title Management and the Law* (1989); Moses and Tzannes, *Strata Titles* (1978).
14. Strata title legislation: N.S.W · s 54(1); Vic.: s. 28; Qld: s. 27(1); S.A.: s. 8(2)(1); W.A.: s. 32(1); Tas.: s. 75Q(1).
15. Strata title legislation: Qld: s. 7(1); S.A.: s. 5; W.A.: s. 3; Tas.: s. 75E.

New South Wales there need not be any common property so long as there are two units superimposed on one another; in Western Australia there need only be two units.[16] In Victoria the concept of a strata plan has been abolished, but whenever there is common property a body corporate must be created; moreover more than one body corporate may be created.[17]

Under a strata plan a unit must comprise the whole or part of a building. A unit may be on one or more levels of the building. The plan must delineate the boundaries of all buildings and the boundaries of all units. It is possible for each unit to comprise the whole of the separate building so long as there is common property shared by the unit holders. There may be an additional area set aside for the separate use of the occupier of a unit. Rather than units comprising separate buildings more commonly units comprise only part of a building. The common property consists of all land or space not within a building and common areas within building and such items as pipes, cables, wires, ducts or drains not for the exclusive use of a unit.

A strata plan must set out the unit entitlement of each unit.[18] The significance of this figure is that it determines the proportion of liability for common maintenance and repairs. In Queensland, South Australia and Western Australia, the allocation of unit entitlements is controlled by the legislation. In those States the unit entitlements must represent the proportionate value of each unit compared to all units and the plan must be accompanied by a certificate from a licensed valuer to the effect that the requirement has been met.[19] In New South Wales the Strata Titles Board is empowered to adjust unit entitlements on application from a unit holder or the strata corporation.[20]

[13.08] Before the strata plan may be deposited with the Land Titles Office, it must receive planning approval. In South Australia this approval is expressly confined to the appropriateness of strata titles for the units as the question of construction of the buildings will have been considered prior to commencement of construction. The crucial matters for planning approval are thus that the buildings are of sufficient substance or quality and each unit is suitable for separate occupation.[21]

The issue of strata title normally follows completion of construction.[22] In Queensland provision is made for group titles—these titles can be issued where they are two or more units and common property but unit boundaries are not defined by reference to buildings.[23] In Victoria the

16. Strata title legislation: N.S.W.: s. 8; W.A.: s. 3.
17. Strata title legislation: Vic.: s. 27(2). In relation to Victoria therefore a reference to a strata title means a title on which there is common property and therefore a body corporate.
18. Strata title legislation: N.S.W.: s. 8A; Qld: s. 19(2); S.A.: s. 6; W.A.: s. 14(1); Tas.: s. 75U(1).
19. Strata title legislation: Qld: s. 19(3); S.A.: s. 7(4)(e); W.A.: s. 14(2).
20. Strata title legislation: N.S.W.: s. 119.
21. Strata title legislation: S.A.: s. 14; *Holiday Investments Pty Ltd v. Wallaroo Corporation* [1971] S.A.P.R. 11; *Hartley v. East Torrens D.C.* P.A.T. No. 553, 1988.
22. Strata title legislation: N.S.W.: ss 8(1), 37(1); Vic.: s. 6(1); Qld: s. 9(1), (8); S.A.: ss 7, 14; W.A.: ss 5, 23; Tas.: s. 75F.
23. Strata title legislation: Qld: s. 9(2).

processes of subdivision and building construction may proceed as the developer thinks fit. However where unit boundaries are specified by reference to a building, building works must have reached the stage where the boundaries of the units can be accurately determined before a title will be issued.[24] In New South Wales a system for individual land titles together with shared interests in community land was introduced by the Community Land Development Act 1989.

[13.09] Because strata titles can normally be issued only on completion of the buildings, dealings in relation to proposed units are likely to be desired by owners seeking financial contributions from prospective purchasers and by such purchasers seeking to secure desired units. Legislation controlling subdivision prevents the sale, transfer or mortgage of less than a whole allotment. Parties have sought to make contracts for the sale of part of an allotment subject to the obtaining of appropriate approvals. The form of such contracts has not been without difficulty. Legislation has allowed for conditional contracts, and more recently to make it clear that there is a binding contract subject to the condition, legislation has allowed contracts subject to a condition that performance of the contract will not be effected without appropriate approval.[25] It seems that a purchaser under such a contract has a caveatable interest with respect to the title of the undivided land.[26]

[13.10] Upon the deposit of a strata plan new certificates of title must be issued for the units and common property and a strata corporation is created. The title for the units is issued in the name of the registered proprietor of the former undivided land and that of the common property in the name of the strata corporation.[27] The common property is held on trust by the strata corporation for the unit holders and this equitable property cannot be dealt with separately from the unit.[28] Easements are created between the units and the common property for support and shelter and access for such services as water and electricity, communications cables and drainage access.[29]

2. Administration of Strata Schemes

[13.11] The strata corporation is not only the owner of the common property but it is the organ by which matters of mutual concern of unit holders are dealt with. Regulations and the articles of the strata corporation spell out the obligations of unit holders with respect to the

24. Strata title legislation: Vic.: s. 6(1)(g).
25. This matter has been addressed in the recent Victorian legislation: *Subdivision (Amendment) Act* 1989, s. 44(6); *Sale of Land (Amendment) Act* 1989, s. 9AA; cf. *Real Property Act* 1886 (S.A.), s. 2231b(4).
26. *Ovenden v. Palyaris Construction Pty Ltd* (1974) 11 S.A.S.R. 65.
27. Strata title legislation: N.S.W.: s. 18(2); Vic.: s. 28(c); Qld: s. 20(2); S.A.: s. 8(3); W.A.: s. 4(4); Tas.: s. 75L(2). In Western Australia no separate title is issued for the common property.
28. Strata title legislation: N.S.W.: ss 18, 20; Vic.: s. 28(d); Qld: s. 20; S.A.: s. 10(1); W.A.: s. 17(1); Tas.: s. 75L(1).
29. Strata title legislation: N.S.W.: s. 7; Vic.: s. 12; Qld: ss 15-18; S.A.: s. 9; W.A.: s. 11-13; Tas.: ss 75G, 75H, 75L, 75K.

property.[30] The strata corporation is responsible for the maintenance of the common property and to ensure unit holders fulfill their responsibilities with respect to individual holdings. It has the duty to arrange insurance of all property and is empowered to borrow money for capital works. It has the responsibility to convene meetings of the members of the corporation.

The members of the corporation are the unit holders and the affairs of the corporation can be carried out through general meetings of the members. The corporation must have responsible officers—normally a presiding officer, secretary and treasurer.[31] Between meetings the day to day affairs are normally handled by a committee or council and in most States it is mandatory for the strata corporation to appoint such a management committee whose constitution and organisation are matters to be determined by the corporation.[32] The corporation may also employ a person to assist the office bearers of the corporation.[33] In New South Wales, in particular, professional managing agents are used to handle the affairs of strata corporations and such a service is offered by some firms of land agents; managing agents must hold a licence under s. 23 of the *Auctioneers and Agents Act*.[34]

[13.12]   Both the appointment of office bearers and decisions as to how the strata corporation is to operate are actions which require an initial meeting of members. Until persons are appointed to them, offices are commonly held by the original registered proprietor and that proprietor is empowered to call an initial meeting.[35] An annual general meeting must be held in every calendar year and not more than 15 months after the last meeting.[36] Thus the original registered proprietor has the responsibility for convening the initial meeting within the first year.

As well as annual general meetings which must be held, other general meetings may be desired by residents. The power to convene a general meeting depends upon the articles of the strata corporation. In South Australia the power to convene is conferred by legislation upon the

30. Strata title legislation: N.S.W.: s. 80; Sched. 1, By-law 12; Vic.: *Subdivision (Body Corporate) Regulations*, reg. 504; Qld: s. 51A; Third Schedule, By-law 1; S.A.: s. 20; Third Schedule, By-laws 1 and 2; W.A.: Sched. 1; By-law 1; Tas.: Sched. 7.

31. Strata title legislation: N.S.W.: s. 57(2); Vic.: *Subdivision (Body Corporate) Regulations*, regs 608, 615; Qld: s. 27(2)(d); S.A.: s. 23; W.A.: s. 45; no such provision seems to exist in Tasmania.

32. Strata title legislation: N.S.W.: s. 71 (mandatory); Vic.: *Subdivision (Body Corporate) Regulations*, reg. 613(2) (committee mandatory where more than 13 members of the body corporate); Qld: s. 42 (mandatory); S.A.: s. 35; W.A.: s. 44 (mandatory); Tas.: Sched. 7, reg. 4 (mandatory).

33. Strata title legislation: N.S.W.: s. 78; Vic.: *Subdivision (Body Corporate) Regulations*, reg. 616; Qld: s. 50; S.A.: ss 23, 35; W.A.: Sched. 1, Pt I, cl. 8(2)(b); Tas.: Sched. 7, Pt I, cl. 4(8)(b).

34. Strata title legislation: N.S.W.: s. 78 (1AA).

35. Strata title legislation: N.S.W.: s. 57(1); Vic.: *Subdivision (Body Corporate) Regulations*, reg. 201; Qld: s. 29; S.A.: s. 33(1)(d); W.A.: s. 49; Tas.: Sched. 7.

36. Strata title legislation: N.S.W.: Sched. 2, Pt 1, cl. 1(1); Vic.: *Subdivision (Body Corporate) Regulations*, reg. 601; Qld: s. 29A; S.A.: s. 33(4); W.A.: s. 49(1); Tas.: Sched. 7, Pt I, cl. 5(2).

secretary of the corporation or any two members of the management committee or if there is no committee upon unit holders representing at least one fifth of the units.[37] A quorum is again a matter for the articles; requirements vary from persons entitled to exercise the voting power in respect of a quarter of the units in Queensland,[38] to those entitled in respect of a half in South Australia.[39] Again it is commonly provided that if a quorum is not formed within half an hour of the time set for the meeting, the meeting is adjourned for exactly one week when if a quorum is not formed within half an hour a quorum is constituted by the members present.[40] Normally at general meetings each unit carries with it one vote towards ordinary resolutions though in relation to commercial or business premises votes are often weighted according to unit entitlements.[41]

3. Rules and Regulations of Strata Schemes

[13.13] Responsibilities for neighbourliness between individual land-owners take legal form from the law of nuisance supplemented by duties of care in negligence and public duties largely imposed by by-laws of local councils. The indeterminate nature of these branches of private law and the court procedures needed for their enforcement inhibit their utility in dealing with day to day matters such as barking dogs and overhanging and underground spreading of trees. Thus local government regulations are often relied upon to resolve what are essentially private disputes. More recently, informal neighbourhood dispute resolution centres have been established to bring neighbours to the conference table.

Residents of buildings subject to a strata scheme are typically in much closer contact with one another. The articles of the strata corporation impose rules of behaviour for the use of units and common property. In all States except Victoria and Tasmania, these rules are binding upon the strata corporation and unit holders and in so far as they affect the use of units or the common property, occupiers of units who are not unit holders. Unit holders and occupiers must take reasonable steps to ensure that any occupiers who are not unit holders comply with the articles.[42] In Victoria the rules are expressed only to bind the unit holders though in Victoria a unit holder is obliged to ensure any tenant obeys any negative rules.[43]

The articles or by-laws of a strata corporation are in the absence of any provision to the contrary those set out in schedule to the statutes. Subject to some restrictions, which are extensive in New South Wales, the strata

---

37. Strata title legislation: S.A.: s. 33(5).
38. Strata title legislation: Qld: Sched. 2, Pt II, cl. 3(2).
39. Strata title legislation: S.A.: s. 33(5).
40. Strata title legislation: Qld: Sched. 2, Pt II, cl. 3(3); S.A.: s. 33(6).
41. Strata title legislation: N.S.W.: Sched. 2, Pt I; Vic.: *Subdivision (Body Corporate) Regulations*, regs 603, 609, 611; Qld: Sched. 2, Pt II; S.A.: ss 33, 34; W.A.: Sched. 1, Pt I, cl. 11; Tas.: s. 75Y; Sched. 7.
42. Strata title legislation: N.S.W.: s. 80, Sched. 1, By-laws 12-29; Qld: Third Sched., By-laws 1-11; S.A.: s. 20(1); W A : s. 42(6) By-laws, Pt I, cl. 10.
43. Strata title legislation: Vic.: *Subdivision (Body Corporate) Regulations*, reg. 509; Tas.: s. 75R(6).

corporation may adopt different articles or by-laws. Similarly, it may amend the by-laws.[44] The adoption of substitute by-laws or amendment of by-laws must be done by an extraordinary resolution (unanimous or special) of the corporation. Special resolutions commonly require a 75 per cent majority; in Victoria, Western Australia and Tasmania votes are weighted according to unit entitlement.[45]

IV.   DUTIES OF STRATA OWNERS

1. Contributions

[13.14]   Enforcement of obligations to contribute a share of costs of upkeep of premises and grounds was a significant factor in the adoption of corporate forms of prelegislative arrangements. The common law does not provide for compulsory contributions between co-owners and does not allow the enforcement of positive covenants beyond contracting parties except in the terms of a lease. On the other hand the level of maintenance costs is of central concern to owners within a strata scheme. Complexities of management may induce a strata corporation to employ a professional manager and managers naturally tend to employ properly trained persons to undertake tasks in situations where needs of economy might incline an individual owner constrained only by statutory controls and possible tortious liability to undertake a task in person. Therefore although strata titles allow ownership of more compact housing and thus commonly cheaper housing, the more compact form and management complexities often involve higher ongoing costs.

[13.15]   A strata corporation is entitled to raise such funds as it thinks necessary and these funds may include reserves for future capital expenditure.[46] The decision as to what optional work as opposed to necessary maintenance is to be done rests with the strata corporation. Funds may come from levies on all strata owners. Contributions must be proportional to unit entitlements. The level of contributions may be fixed by an ordinary resolution of the corporation. Contributions owed by a unit holder may be recoverable as a debt by the strata corporation and may be recovered from any successor in title to the unit holder.

[13.16]   Repair work will not uncommonly relate more to some unit holders than to others. Thus in *Proprietors of Strata Plan No. 159 v. Blake*[47]

44. Strata title legislation: N.S.W.: s. 58(2)—by-laws 1 to 11 in Sched. 1 cannot be amended; Vic.: *Subdivision (Body Corporate) Regulations*, reg. 407; Qld: s. 30(2); S.A.: 19(2); no amendment may prevent or restrict alienation by a unit holder, or the lease or grant of rights of occupation by a unit holder, or the keeping of a guide-dog by a person who is blind or deaf: s. 19(4); W.A.: s. 42(1); by-laws in Sched. 1 Pt 1 can be amended only by unanimous resolution; Tas.: s. 75R(1); by-laws other than those in Pt II may be amended by ordinary resolution.
45. Strata title legislation: N.S.W.: s. 5; Vic.: *Subdivision (Body Corporate) Regulations*, reg. 105; Qld: s. 7(1); S.A.: s. 3 (third thirds rather than 75 per cent); W.A.: s. 3(1); Tas.: Sched. 7, Pt I, cl. 10.
46. Strata title legislation: N.S.W.: s. 59; Vic.: *Subdivision (Body Corporate) Regulations*, regs 401(6)(c), 508; Qld: ss 32, 33; S.A.: s. 27; W.A.: s. 36; Tas.: s. 75Q(6).
47. Unreported, N.S.W. Sup. Ct, 1986, No. 110264.

the property involved was a shopping and office arcade on three floors of which only the ground floor was airconditioned. Repairs were needed to the air conditioning system which was part of the common property. Yeldham J. held that the strata corporation was under a duty to maintain the common property and in the absence of any statutory qualifications contributions were to be levied according to unit entitlement and not subject to any comparative benefit calculation. Consequently the upper floor unit holders would be contributing to work which was of no benefit to them.

This principle has been reversed in Victoria and South Australia. There the contrary principle has been established: in the words of the Victorian regulation, the unit which benefits more pays more.[48] This statement indicates that even amongst a group of units which are specially benefitted contributions may be adjusted to reflect the degree of benefit. In this respect the Victorian rule seems to go further than that in South Australia. In that State costs of work which wholly or substantially benefit one unit or a group of units may be recovered from the owners of those units but where more than one unit is specially benefitted as between the units, liability is apportioned according to unit entitlement.[49]

As well as special items of repair the strata corporation is under a duty to carry out regular maintenance of common property.[50] Again some units may impose greater ongoing demands on common property than others but no qualification exists to the principle that contributions are to be levied according to unit entitlement. In *Jacklin v. Proprietors of Strata Plan No. 2975*[51] the strata property consisted of one single storey block and a tower block. The tower block required greater maintenance costs because of some items as the lifts. Holland J. ruled that the common property could not be divided in two classes—that relating to the tower block and that relating to the single storey block. All common property was to be treated alike. The current Victorian Act does allow for more than one body corporate for a strata plan (see above [13.07]) and that scheme would allow the division attempted in *Jacklin's* case.

2. Maintenance by Unit Holders

[13.17] The strata corporation is responsible for the common property. Responsibility for individual units rests with the unit owner. What is common property and what is within a unit depends on the definition of boundaries discussed later (see below [13.23]). The articles or by-laws of the corporation impose a duty on the unit owner to maintain her or his unit in good repair.[52]

---

48. Strata title legislation: Vic.: *Subdivision (Body Corporate) Regulations*, reg. 401(g).
49. Strata title legislation: S.A.: s. 27(6), (7).
50. Strata title legislation: N.S.W.: s. 68(1)(b); Vic.: *Subdivision (Body Corporate) Regulations*, reg. 401(b); Qld: s. 38A; S.A.: s. 25(a); W.A.: s. 36(1)(9); Tas.: s. 76Q(6)(a).
51. [1975] 1 N.S.W.L.R. 15.
52. Strata title legislation: N.S.W.: s. 80A; Vic.: *Subdivision (Body Corporate) Regulations*, reg. 504; Qld: s. 51(1)(a); S.A.: Sched. 3, By-law 1; W.A.: Sched. 1, Pt 1, cl. 1(1); Tas.: Sched. 7.

The fulfillment of the duty to care for the individual unit commonly affects other unit owners. Consequently the duty may be enforced by the strata corporation. The corporation may serve notice on a unit holder requiring the holder to carry out specified work.[53] If the notice is not complied with, the corporation may authorise persons to carry out the work and such persons are entitled to enter the unit for the purpose. Any cost reasonably incurred in carrying out the work may be recovered from the unit holder.[54]

[13.18] Work by an individual owner may have an impact on other units. Consequently any construction, demolition or alteration of a building or structure or any alteration to the external appearance of a building or structure must be approved.[55] A person who acts without approval may be required to remedy any structural deficiency caused by the work or to restore the unit to its previous state. In Victoria and Western Australia a specific right to interior decoration is conferred.[56]

5. Duties to Neighbours

[13.19] The sharing of buildings and common areas requires restraint in consideration of the enjoyment of others. Duties in relation to common property are discussed later. Duties in relation to others are imposed by the statutory by-laws or articles. As mentioned previously, in all States except Victoria and Tasmania these by-laws or articles are not only binding on unit holders but in so far as they affect the use of units or common property, are binding upon occupiers of units.[57] The by-laws or articles do not directly require observance by the persons not bound by them but require persons bound to control their customers, clients and visitors.

The by-laws or articles essentially impose obligations of good neighbourliness.[58] Consequently unit holders are required to refrain from undue noise and to refrain from interference with others in the enjoyment of their rights in relation to units or common property. Furthermore a person must not keep an animal in, or in the vicinity of, a unit without the consent of the strata corporation. This restriction does not operate so as to prevent the keeping of a guide dog at a unit by an occupier who is blind or deaf, or so as to restrict the uses of a guide dog by such a person.

53. Strata title legislation: Vic.: *Subdivision (Body Corporate) Regulations*, reg. 401(e); S.A.: s. 28(1); W.A.: s. 39; Tas.: Sched. 7. No notice seems to be required in New South Wales or Queensland.
54. Strata title legislation: N.S.W.: s. 60(2); Vic.: *Subdivision (Body Corporate) Regulations*, reg. 401(f); Qld: s. 33(2); S.A.: s. 28(2); W.A.: s. 38; Tas.: Sched. 7.
55. Strata title legislation: N.S.W.: Sched. 1, By-laws 28, 29; Vic.: *Subdivision (Body Corporate) Regulations*, reg. 505; Qld: Third Sched., By-laws; S.A.: s. 29(6); W.A.: Sched. 1, Pt I, cl. 2; Tas.: Sched. 7.
56. Strata title legislation: Vic.: *Subdivision (Body Corporate) Regulations*, reg. 507; W.A.: Sched. 1, Pt I, cl. 2.
57. See above fns 34 and 35.
58. Strata title legislation: N.S.W.: Sched. 1; Vic.: *Subdivision (Body Corporate) Regulations*, reg., Sched. 1; Qld: Third Sched.; S.A.: Sched. 3; W.A.: Sched. 1, Pt II; Tas.: Sched. 7.

New South Wales has perhaps the most demanding by-laws in that washing should not be hung to be visible from other units or common property and windows must be kept clean.

V. PROPERTY RIGHTS UNDER STRATA SCHEMES

1. Rights of Disposal and Enjoyment

[13.20]   A feature of the strata scheme is that unit holders are given a registered title to their unit and hold an equitable interest as tenants in common of the common property for which legal title is vested in the strata corporation. These proprietary rights are therefore prima facie freely alienable or may be used as security for the loan of money. Furthermore the rights of enjoyment may be transferred to others by way of lease or contractual licence. The unit holders are however bound by the articles of association of the strata corporation of which unit holdings create membership. However the controlling statute provides that the articles cannot prevent or restrict the alienation of a unit by a unit holder or the leasing or granting of rights of occupation in respect of a unit by a unit holder.[59]

The use of any unit is governed by the articles of the strata corporation. The range of permissible uses may well be restricted in accordance with the purpose for which the strata units are established. A building divided into strata units may be constructed for any of the range of residential, commercial or industrial purposes pursued in our society: often the general type of use will be prescribed by planning controls. The statutory articles commonly provide only that a unit may not be used for any unlawful purpose and that the display of any sign or similar object requires the consent of the corporation.

2. Subsidiary Interests

[13.21]   The holder of a unit is entitled to the exclusive enjoyment of part of a building and to share the use of the common property. The use of part of the building may be supplemented by other exclusive rights. In a residential context a private garage for storage, parking or similar use is the most likely supplement. Spatial considerations make exclusive rights to a tennis court or swimming pool unlikely but a private spa is conceivable.

These supplementary entitlements are specifically described in the New South Wales and South Australian legislation as utility lots or unit subsidiaries. These lots or subsidiaries must be for the separate use of the occupier of a unit and appurtenant to the unit. Since the unit subsidiary is included within the unit, dealings with it are subject to the controls on dealings with part of a unit. The use of this separate area must be subject to restrictions.

59. Strata title legislation: N.S.W.: ss 58(6), 122; Qld: s. 31(6); S.A.: s. 19(4); W.A.: s. 42(3); Tas.: s. 75R(3). The right seems not be explicit in the Victorian legislation.

[13.22]   An equitable share in the common property vests in each unit holder in proportion to the unit entitlement of the unit. This beneficial ownership cannot be alienated or dealt with separately from the unit.[60] As the unit holders are co-owners of the common property they are all entitled to enjoy each and every part of it and cannot exclude any other co-owner from such enjoyment. But again private use of a particular parking site or a clothes line might be desired. A unit holder may be granted an exclusive right to occupy part of the common property for a specified period but only by a unanimous resolution of the corporation.[61]

3. Common Property

[13.23]   As already stated, the common property vests beneficially in the unit holders and cannot be dealt with separately from the units. Use of the common property is governed by the by-laws or articles of the corporation. The statutory by-laws or articles commonly forbid the obstruction of any lawful use of the common property and any use of the common property that unreasonably interferes with the use and enjoyment of the common property by other members of the strata community and their customers, clients or visitors.

The common property is not confined to the land surrounding the buildings but includes all space not within a unit and all pipes, cables, wires, ducts or drains not for the exclusive use of a unit. In New South Wales, South Australia and Western Australia, subject to any contrary statement in the strata plan, where a wall, fence, floor, ceiling or roof forms a boundary, the boundary is the inner surface of that wall, fence, floor, ceiling or roof.[62] Since the substance of the structure is not within the unit, it is part of the common property. In Victoria, Queensland and Tasmania, subject to any contrary statement in the strata plan, the boundary is the centre of the structure.[63]

One of the functions of the strata corporation is to administer and maintain the common property for the benefit of the unit holders and other members of the strata community. Because of the definitions this function extends to the grounds, common stairs and passages, common drains and similar inlets and outlets, and in New South Wales, South Australia and Western Australia the exterior of buildings. Even in Victoria, Queensland and Tasmania many matters of repair relate to the outer surface of walls or roofs.

[13.24]   In *Allen v. Proprietors of Strata Plan No. 2110*[64] a dampness problem became evident in a ground floor unit in a home unit building. Damage was caused to carpeting, furnishings, a wall and flooring.

60. Strata title legislation: N.S.W.: s. 24; Qld: s. 20(3); S.A.: s. 10; W.A.: s. 19; Tas.: s. 75M. Again this restriction is not explicit in the Victorian legislation.
61. Strata title legislation: N.S.W.: s. 58(7); Qld: s. 30(7); S.A.: s. 26(4); W.A.: s. 42(8). There is nothing explicit on this matter in the Victorian or Tasmanian legislation.
62. Strata title legislation: N.S.W.: s. 5(1), (2); S.A.: s. 5; W.A.: s. 3(2)(a).
63. Strata title legislation: Vic.: *Subdivision (Body Corporate) Regulations*, reg. 902; Qld: s. 9(5)(a); Tas.: s. 75F(2).
64. [1970] 3 N.S.W.R. 339.

Street J. concluded that the dampness was caused by the blocking of weepholes in the external skin of the walls which precluded the water from escaping. Since the problem related to the outer surface and was thus part of the common property, responsibility for ensuring the escape of water rested with the strata corporation. Water penetration was the problem in *Proprietors of Strata Plan No. 6522 v. Furney.*[65] Needham J. concluded that water was entering a unit because of the lack of proper flashings and similar items in the process of construction. Again these items should have been part of the exterior surface. The duty to repair included not just restoration but a making good. The result in both cases would be maintained in all States as the exterior surface is clearly part of the common property.

In *Simons v. Body Corporate of Strata Plan No. 5181*[66] again defective construction of a wall allowed the entry of water and damp into a unit. However in this case it was the construction of the wall as a whole which was defective and Lush J. could not apportion the problem between the outer and inner half. In that case the boundary was the median of the wall. The wall therefore was the joint property of the unit holder and the strata corporation. Lush J. concluded that there was a joint responsibility to repair the wall and thus share the costs. In New South Wales, South Australia and Western Australia the wall would be totally owned by the strata corporation and responsibility for repair fall on the corporation.

VI.   DISPUTES AND TERMINATION

1. Procedures to Resolve Disputes

[13.25]   The unit holders as members of the strata corporation are entitled to put forward their point of view at meetings of the corporation. The purchase of additional real estate requires a unanimous resolution of the corporation. A decision to undertake improvements on the property could be made by a resolution of the corporation. The maintenance of the common property is a function of the corporation; insurance of all buildings at their replacement value and public liability insurance must be taken out by the corporation. The maintenance of each unit is a duty imposed on each unit holder by the statutory articles; similarly duties of neighbourliness are imposed on unit holders and occupiers by the articles. The enforcement of the articles is a function of the corporation.

Consequently the corporation has some discretion as to what it will do. In many instances the corporation is entrusted with a responsibility. The responsibilities include the enforcement of obligations by unit holders. A unit holder may seek to compel the corporation to carry out the corporation's duties or to compel the corporation to enforce other unit holders responsibilities. On the other hand, a unit holder may feel that a decision of the corporation is oppressive to that unit holder or that the corporation is behaving oppressively in compelling the unit holder to do something. The legislation provides no express remedy to deal with these situations.

65. [1976] 1 N.S.W.L.R. 412.
66. [1980] V.R. 103.

[13.26] There is considerable diversity as to the remedies by way of action available to a strata corporation or a unit owner. In New South Wales there is a Strata Titles Commissioner and a Strata Titles Board.[67] In Queensland there is a Strata Titles Referee and a Strata Titles Tribunal.[68] In Western Australia there is a Strata Titles Referee and appeals from the referee go to the District Court.[69] In Victoria application may be made to the Magistrates Court but that court may refer the matter to the County Court having regard to the general importance, complexity and amount involved in the dispute.[70] In South Australia applications may be made to the Supreme Court.[71] The Tasmanian legislation says nothing about any legal actions relating to its provisions though the contract between the body corporate and the unit owners could presumably be enforced by ordinary action.

The New South Wales Strata Commissioner may make an order for the settlement of a dispute or the performance of duties imposed by the Act or by-laws.[72] Application may be made by a strata corporation, a managing agent, an owner or a person with any interest in a unit.[73] Appeals from the Commissioner may be made to the Board.[74] The Commissioner and the Board are given specific power to modify, waive or vary requirements of the Act. The Queensland provisions are very similar to those in New South Wales.[75] The Western Australian Referee has a similar jurisdiction to that of the New South Wales Commissioner and the Queensland Referee;[76] however the role of the District Court is limited to appeals from the Referee;[77] all powers to modify, vary or waive are vested in the Referee.

In Victoria application may be made to the Magistrates Court by the body corporate or a unit owner for a declaration or order determining a dispute or matter.[78] The dispute or matter must be one arising between the strata corporation and a unit owner or between unit owners.[79] In South Australia application to the Supreme Court may be made by a strata corporation, a unit owner or a unit occupier.[80] The court may make an order enforcing the performance of the articles or restraining a breach

---

67. Strata title legislation: N.S.W.: Div. V.
68. Strata title legislation: Qld: Pt V.
69. Strata title legislation: W.A.: Pt VI.
70. Strata title legislation: Vic.: s. 38.
71. Strata title legislation: S.A.: s. 20.
72. Strata title legislation: N.S.W.: s. 105(1).
73. Strata title legislation: N.S.W.: s. 105(1).
74. Strata title legislation: N.S.W.: s. 128.
75. Strata title legislation: Qld: ss 77, 106.
76. Strata title legislation: W.A.: s. 83.
77. Strata title legislation: W.A.: s. 105.
78. Strata title legislation: Vic.: s. 38.
79. Strata title legislation: Vic.: s. 38.
80. Strata title legislation: S.A.: s. 20.

of them.[81] In addition the court is given some specific powers to modify, vary or waive requirements of the Act.[82]

2. Termination

[13.27] It is possible to terminate a strata scheme and return the land to undivided ownership. Termination takes effect by cancellation of a strata plan. An application for cancellation must be approved by all unit holders and all other persons with registered interests in a unit or the common property. Alternatively cancellation may be ordered by the Supreme Court on application by the strata corporation, a unit holder or any other person who has a registered interest in a unit.[83]

Upon cancellation of a strata plan the fee simple of the undivided land vests in the former unit holders as tenants-in-common.[84] The co-owners hold in proportions equal to their previous unit entitlements. Any co-owner's interest is subject to any registered interest previously existing against that owner's unit. The liabilities of the strata corporation are transferred to the unit holders subject to a right of contribution in proportion to the unit entitlements. The assets of the corporation are divided amongst the unit holders again in proportion to their entitlements.

VII. TIME-SHARING

1. Nature of Arrangements

[13.28] Time-sharing has to date been an arrangement in relation to holiday resorts.[85] Purchasers acquire rights to a certain number of weeks at a particular resort. The weeks of the year are classified according to levels of demand. Purchasers may acquire fixed or floating weeks; rules must exist for the weeks to become settled in any one year. Purchasers may acquire rights to use common facilities and rights to a particular unit or rights to any unit or any unit of a particular class.

A common feature of time-share arrangements has been the availability of swapping the right to use the facilities of the site purchased for those of other developments subject to similar schemes. This exchange

---

81. Strata title legislation: S.A.: s. 20. Most obligations between unit holders will arise from the articles and thus be subject to action in the Supreme Court under this section. However some of the financial liabilities stem from the Act itself and are deemed by the Act to create debts. These debts would appear to be recoverable in whatever court has jurisdiction for the amount in question.
82. The court may deem support for a resolution requiring unanimous support to have been sufficient where two thirds of the possible votes had been obtained: s. 46(1); the court may also authorise payments by the corporation to members: s. 22(1).
83. Strata title legislation: N.S.W.: s. 51(1); Vic.: s. 31(1); Qld: s. 25(1); S.A.: s. 17(1); W.A.: ss 30(1), 31(1); Tas.: s. 75v(1)(c).
84. Strata title legislation: N.S.W.: s. 54; Vic.: s. 31(7); Qld: s. 26(3); S.A.: s. 17(7); W.A.: ss 30(3), 31(9); Tas.: s. 75v(1)(c).
85. Cf. Tarlo, *The March of Time* (A.U.L.S.A. Conference Paper, 1981): Jones, "Time Sharing Practice and Operation" (1983) 27 Val. 700.

programme is a service provided by management agencies and extends to all continents. Ultimately the availability of this exchange depends upon demand for the facilities at the site purchased.

The entry into the purchase of a time-share interest fulfils the same purposes as any real estate purchase in that the holder owns an interest which can be used without cost and which is an asset which can be sold. Just as strata ownership imports obligations to neighbouring holders, so time-sharing ownership involves obligations to neighbours who are both spatial and temporal. The divisions are so great that control effectively passes to the management agency. Similarly the asset to be sold is a limited one. It has been asserted that the same increase in value as with an ordinary real estate purchase cannot be expected in the case of a purchase of a time-share interest. This lack of appreciation is attributed to the fact that between 30 and 50 per cent of the initial retail cost is taken up with marketing and promotion costs.[86] At the same time the purchaser is paying only for time likely to be used rather than the full price of a holiday home which may be unused for much of the year.

By 1989 there were 46 time-share resorts in Australia: 27 in Queensland, 14 in New South Wales, 12 in Victoria, six in Western Australia and two in Tasmania. Internationally over 2,000 time-share resorts exist in 51 countries.

[13.29]   Developers have drawn upon experience in the development of strata systems to devise arrangements for time-share interests in Australia. There are two major models;[87] one involving a proprietary interest in land, the other shares in a company. Under the proprietary model the purchaser acquires an interest as a tenant in common either in the resort as a whole or in a particular unit. The tenants in common lease on a long-term (of normally 99 years) rights of occupation to the whole of the resort to a management company. The shareholders in this company are in turn the tenants in common. The shareholding confers rights of occupation for the defined time. The alternative scheme simply vests title in the company and the purchasers acquire shares in that company. In both cases the right of occupation stems from the company shareholding. The proprietary model has been more widespread largely it seems because of the psychological advantage of the land title rather than because of any substance of that interest.

2. Regulation: The Role of the Developer

[13.30]   Often time-share interests are offered to the public at a stage when the development is at planning or part-completed point. In such cases risks exist as to the employment of money contributed for shares towards the completion of the development. Because of these risks, offers of these interests have been the subject of scrutiny by corporate affairs regulators.

---

86. *The Weekend Australian*, 6 May 1989, p. 55.
87. Butt, pp. 567-570. A further variation is a unit trust scheme whereby title to the resort is vested in trustees who hold for the use and enjoyment of interest holders: see *Costa and Duppe Properties Pty Ltd v. Duppe* [1986] V.R. 90.

The common agreements involve rights of occupation of land owned or leased by a company. Consequently the offer of sale of those rights amounts to the offer of a prescribed interest as defined by s. 5(1) of the *Companies Code*. It was held that an offer of such rights amounted to an invitation to purchase an interest in the assets of a business undertaking and thus subject to the *Companies Code*: *Wade v. A Home Away Pty Ltd*.[88] The current definition of prescribed interest specifically includes any right to participate in a time-sharing scheme. Such schemes are defined as those whereby a participant is entitled to the use, occupation or possession for two or more periods during the duration of the scheme of property to which the scheme relates. The duration must be not less than three years.

The consequence of the classification of the interest as a prescribed interest is that only public companies may offer time-share interests for sale to the public.[89] The offer must be by way of a registered prospectus.[90] In addition there must be a trust deed which has been approved by the National Companies and Securities Commission and which contains the prescribed contents.[91] The deed will set up a trustee for the holders of time-share interests. The deed will seek to protect the holders by safeguarding investments until the time when the resort is completed.

[13.31] The role of the developer is to establish the resort and sell off all the time-share interests. Once the interests are sold management becomes the responsibility of the time-share company whose shareholders are the time-share interest holders. As pointed out earlier, management is likely to be complicated as there are common areas, relations between individual units and relations between holders of different time-rights in individual units. A management company is likely to be employed and shareholding involves liability for management fees.

The holder of a time-share interest normally has a fee simple interest as tenant in common in the resort as a whole (effectively a reversionary interest) and shares in the lessee company. Those interests are likely to be freely alienable. However the offer of even an existing time-share interest to the public is subject to the *Companies Code* and information must be provided to prospective purchasers.[92]

VIII. LEGAL STRUCTURES AFFECTING RETIREMENT VILLAGES

1. Nature of Retirement Village Arrangements

[13.32] Retirement villages essentially comprise a group of dwellings in which occupation is restricted to persons above a particular age or who are not actively employed. Persons are drawn to such establishments not

---

88. [1981] V.R. 475.
89. *Companies Code*, ss. 164, 169.
90. Sections 99, 170.
91. Section 160. Exemptions from the requirements of this section may be granted by the Commission but are granted only where protections for purchasers are similarly guaranteed.
92. *Companies Code*, s. 552.

only through the commonality of interests and outlook but because of the prospect of particular services—especially nursing care. The problems associated with residence in such villages has been regarded as sufficiently different from those of other group dwellings (such as strata title units or leasehold units) that separate legislation for retirement villages has been introduced in South Australia, Victoria, New South Wales and Queensland.

[13.33]   South Australia and Victoria were the first States to legislate[93] on a parallel with their pioneering work in relation to residential tenancy agreements. Their legislation can be regarded as covering four general areas: first, disclosure prior to entry into an agreement; secondly, matters concerning the management of the village and conduct by residents; thirdly, financial matters which include maintenance and capital contributions, saleability of interests and recovery of any admission charges; and fourthly, the rights of eviction of residents. Protection given to residents' rights of residence means that what may not otherwise be properly classified as a proprietary interest has achieved that status.

Legislation has also followed in Queensland and New South Wales.[94] The Queensland legislation is much along the lines of the Victorian and South Australian legislation. The New South Wales legislation on the other hand concentrates almost exclusively on protection for residents facing eviction. This legislation is supplemented by a Code of Practice under the *Fair Trading Act*; the Code governs disclosure and bargaining practices.

Prohibitions upon deceptive, misleading and unconscionable conduct will apply to offers to the public of interests in retirement villages as a result of the *Trade Practices Act* and the Fair Trading Acts (in all States except Tasmania). The Victorian *Retirement Villages Act*[95] specifically provides that services or goods provided under a residence contract are to be regarded as contracts for the supply of services or goods even though the services or goods are provided under a contract of service.

[13.34]   Just as with time-sharing arrangements, the offer of rights of residence in a retirement village may take the legal form of an offer of rights of occupation of land owned by a company. The issue then arises whether there is an offer of a prescribed interest as defined by s. 5(1) of the *Companies Code*. However, from 1 July 1987 interests in retirement village schemes have been exempted from the operation of the *Companies Code*. From that date nothing in Div. 6 of Pt IV applies to a prescribed interest that is constituted by a right to participate in a retirement village scheme.[96] A retirement village scheme is defined as one undertaken or carried out with the intention that the participants or a majority of the participants be provided with the residential accommodation within a

---

93. Vic.: *Retirement Villages Act* 1987; S.A.: *Retirement Villages Act* 1987; Moore, "Retirement Villages—Victoria and South Australia" [1989] N.Z.C.L. 312.
94. N.S.W.: *Retirement Villages Act* 1989; Qld: *Retirement Villages Act* 1988.
95. Retirement villages legislation: Vic.: s. 18.
96. *Companies Code*, s. 215D.

retirement community. The exemption does not however extend to Western Australia where the *Companies Code* remains the basis of regulation.

The protection of the *Companies Code* is limited. It regulates explanations of what was being offered. It has no impact on the substance of these rights, the performance of on-going obligations or the means of resolving disputes.

[13.35] Developers of a residential village have some flexibility as to how to set up the legal status and classification of occupants of a retirement village. In the case of separate dwelling-units occupants could be granted title to their units through a strata title scheme under the legislation discussed earlier in this Chapter: see above [13.07]. Matters relating to the physical upkeep of the property could be set out in articles of the strata title corporation. If the developers are to maintain an ongoing role in the provision of services a separate service agreement between the developers and the strata title corporation would be needed.

If ownership remains with the developer or a subsequent operator, residents may be granted leasehold interests or some lesser rights. Status as a tenant depends on the grant of control over a specific dwelling-unit.[97] Control may be absent because of the on going management role of the operator or simply because a resident may be moved from one unit to another. Moreover the provision of services normally indicates that an occupant is not a tenant but a boarder. Traditionally a distinction has been drawn between provision of a cup of tea and provision of a full breakfast: the former being insufficiently significant to alter the legal classification of the relationship, the latter effecting a change.[98] Presumably provision of medical or nursing services beyond a minimal or insignificant level would also result in the status of a boarder rather than a tenant.

2. Scope of Retirement Village Legislation

[13.36] Because of the variety of possible legal structures governing occupation of retirement villages and because the association of problems with particular features is only just emerging, definition of a retirement village is not easy. The definitions of the Acts in the four States all require that an initial charge be imposed in order that the village constitute a retirement village subject to the legislation. In Victoria and Queensland a regulated village is one in which services are provided in addition to accommodation. In New South Wales, South Australia and Queensland a village in which a permanent interest without any restriction on disposition is granted to residents would not be subject to the legislation. The Victorian Act defines a village by reference to a community, the other three Acts by reference to a physical structure.

---

97. *Radaich v. Smith* (1959) 101 C.L.R. 209; *Street v Mountford* [1985] 2 W.L.R. 877.
98. *Holiday Flat Co. v. Kuczera* [1978] S.L.T. 47; Bradbrook, MacCallum and Moore, p. 86.

The Victorian Act[99] defines retirement village as "a community: (a) the majority of which is retired persons who are provided with accommodation and services; and (b) at least one of whom, before or on becoming a member of the community, pays or is required to pay, an in-going contribution". Thus grants of rights of residence without any services are not subject to the Act—they are most likely to fall under the Residential Tenancies Act. Further grants of accommodation and services without any initial payment are outside the Act and probably confined to the boarders and lodgers wasteland.

The New South Wales and South Australian definitions are similar. In New South Wales[100] a retirement village is defined as

"a complex containing residential premises (whether or not including hostel units) predominantly or exclusively occupied, or intended to be predominantly or exclusively occupied, by retired persons in pursuance of—

(a) a residential tenancy agreement or any other lease or licence; or

(b) a right conferred by shares; or

(c) the ownership of residential premises subject to a right or option of repurchase or conditions restricting the subsequent disposal of the premises; or

(d) any other scheme or arrangement prescribed for the purposes of this definition,

and for the right to occupy which those persons are or will be required to pay or donate money."

In South Australia[101] a retirement village is "a complex of residential units or a number of separate complexes of residential units occupied or intended for occupation under a retirement village scheme". A retirement village scheme is one established "for retired persons and their spouses or predominantly for retired persons and their spouses, under which: (a) residential units are occupied in pursuance of lease or licence; (b) a right to occupation of residential units is conferred by ownership of shares; (c) residential units are purchased from the administering authority subject to a right or option of repurchase; or (d) residential units are purchased by prospective residents on conditions restricting their subsequent disposal, but does not include any such scheme under which no resident or prospective resident of a residential unit pays a premium in consideration for, or in contemplation of, admission as a resident under the scheme". In neither State is it necessary that services be provided in addition to accommodation but there must be an initial payment and the definition would exclude situations where residents purchase, for example, a freely alienable strata title interest.

The Queensland definition[102] is not dissimilar to that in New South Wales and South Australia except that it does not include villages where

99. Retirement villages legislation: Vic.: s. 3(1).
100. Retirement villages legislation: N.S.W.: s. 3.
101. Retirement villages legislation: S.A.: s. 3.
102. Retirement villages legislation: Qld: s. 6.

services are not provided in addition to accommodation. A retirement village is defined as

"premises conducted or promoted as suitable for the use (exclusively or primarily) by elderly or retired persons in respect of which premises—

(a) a person acquires, in consideration of the payment of an in-going contribution—
a right of residence, from whatever right, title or interest the right of residence may accrue; and
a right to receive a service,
pursuant to one contract or more than one contract if, in the case of more than one contract, the making of each contract is dependent on the making of each other contract; and

(b) the person who has the right of residence either—
cannot validly dispose of that right to another; or
is subject to a restriction as to the manner in which or the person to whom he may dispose of that right during his lifetime to another;"

All Acts apply to existing as well as future villages.[103] In all States except New South Wales the Acts allow for exemptions to be made by the Minister for specified religious or charitable organisations or particular retirement villages.[104] In New South Wales exemptions may be granted pursuant to regulation.[105]

[13.37] The Victorian Act specifically provides that the *Residential Tenancies Act* does not apply to a residence right.[106] A residence right is one to use residential hostel or hospital accommodation or other services provided for a retirement village.[107] In New South Wales the *Retirement Villages Act* is expressed to apply in addition to and not in derogation of any other law of the State[108] and nothing in the Act is to limit the operation of the *Contracts Review Act* 1980.[109] However a residence contract in a retirement village can only be terminated in accordance with the *Retirement Villages Act*.[110] In Queensland the problem of overlap does not arise to the same extent because of the lack of extensive residential tenancies legislation. However in South Australia the potential for overlap is considerable and nothing about it is said in the *Retirement Villages Act*. However that Act's statement of termination rights[111] is clearly inconsistent with that of the *Residential Tenancies Act*. Furthermore the *Retirement Villages Act* contemplates residence rules[112] which are defined as

---

103. Retirement villages legislation: N.S.W.: s. 5; Vic.: s. 4; Qld: s. 15; S.A.: s. 4(1).
104. Retirement villages legislation: Vic.: s. 6; Qld: s. 12; S.A.: s. 4(2).
105. Retirement villages legislation: N.S.W.: s. 46.
106. Retirement villages legislation: Vic.: s. 15.
107. Retirement villages legislation: Vic.: s. 3.
108. Retirement villages legislation: N.S.W.: s. 6.
109. Retirement villages legislation: N.S.W.: s. 42.
110. Retirement villages legislation: N.S.W.: s. 15.
111. Retirement villages legislation: S.A.: s. 7.
112. Retirement villages legislation: S.A.: s. 6(3).

the rules with which residents of a retirement village are expected by the administering authority to comply.[113] This definition implies a contractual freedom to frame rules and that freedom is inconsistent with the detailed statement of rights of obligations of landlord and tenant in the *Residential Tenancies Act.* Finally the formalities of s. 6 of the *Retirement Villages Act* exclude any other formality provisions. In the end it is difficult to see how any part of the South Australian *Residential Tenancies Act* could apply to a retirement village and even more difficult to understand why this point was not made express.

3. Administration of Retirement Village Legislation

[13.38] The history of prescribed interests under the companies code resulted in major administrative functions being entrusted in Victoria and South Australia to the corporate affairs authorities. In Victoria there is no general statutory provision as to administration of the Act but particular powers such as those to grant exemptions or to enforce charges over the land are conferred upon the Commissioner for Corporate Affairs. In South Australia the Corporate Affairs Commission is responsible to the Minister for the administration of the Act.[114]

The New South Wales emphasis upon protection of rights of residence led to assimilation with residential tenancies administration. The Tenancy Commissioner established under the *Residential Tenancies Act* 1987 is entrusted with the general administrative functions under the *Retirement Villages Act.*[115] The Commissioner's functions include the investigation and attempted resolution of complaints and the taking of proceedings in defined circumstances. The Queensland Act establishes the office of the Registrar of Retirement Villages.[116] Whilst the Registrar has extensive powers to investigate conduct by operators of villages,[117] the functions do not extend to complaint negotiation.

[13.39] In Victoria, applications under the Act or actions for the enforcement of rights or obligations conferred by the Act must be made to the courts of competent jurisdiction. Specific provision is made for arbitration.[118] If a dispute or difference arises between residents, between a resident and a manager, or between a resident and an owner, the resident, owner or manager may refer the matter to an independent arbitrator. In Queensland a resident whose residence rights are under threat of termination or curtailment may apply to the Supreme Court for an injunction.[119] Otherwise no special rights of action are conferred.

New South Wales places stress on dispute resolution machinery. The Tenancy Commissioner's role has already been addressed. In addition a resident or an administering authority of a village may make application

---

113. Retirement villages legislation: S.A.: s. 3.
114. Retirement villages legislation: S.A.: s. 5.
115. Retirement villages legislation: N.S.W.: ss 7-10.
116. Retirement villages legislation: Qld: s. 7.
117. Retirement villages legislation: Qld: s. 52.
118. Retirement villages legislation: Vic.: s. 35.
119. Retirement villages legislation: Qld: s. 42.

to the Residential Tenancies Tribunal where that person claims that there is a dispute between a resident and the authority or between residents.[120] The Tribunal is empowered to make a range of orders and there is no monetary limit on its jurisdiction.

Similarly in South Australia applications may be made to the Residential Tenancies Tribunal.[121] Either party to a dispute may apply to the Tribunal for resolution of the matters in dispute where a dispute arises between the administering authority and a resident. Disputes between residents are thus not within the jurisdiction of the Tribunal. Disputes as to repayments of premiums are excluded from the jurisdiction.[122] The jurisdiction is not exclusive.[123]

In both Victoria and South Australia jurisdiction is conferred in relation to disputes and this term is not confined to actions for the enforcement of rights. Thus a disagreement between residents and management as to the appropriate form of a boundary fence could be referred to an arbitrator in Victoria or the Tribunal in South Australia: *Re Pineview Village*.[124] In New South Wales on the other hand the orders which can be made by the Tribunal are limited to those relating to the enforcement or setting aside of provisions of a residence contract or a residence rule.

4. Establishment of a Retirement Village

[13.40]   The forms taken by retirement villages vary from a group of dwelling-units sharing a common purpose, to more of an institutional structure providing a range of services on a communal basis. The impact of planning controls thus varies according to the form. The group of dwelling-units would properly be classified as a residential building and be appropriate for residential zones.[125] An institutional building is more difficult to classify as it does not fall readily into the traditional categories of boarding-house, hospital or welfare institution. It may nonetheless be appropriate for more intensive residential zones particularly if the density of the building is not great.[126] Differing opinion as to the design of retirement villages led to the defamation action in *Harry Seidler & Associates Pty Ltd v. John Fairfax & Sons Pty Ltd*.[127]

[13.41]   Institutional facilities may be subject to regulation of their management if they fall within the categories of nursing homes or private hospitals.[128] Regulation of the establishment and management of such facilities occurs primarily through State government agencies. In Victoria

120. Retirement villages legislation: N.S.W.: s. 14.
121. Retirement villages legislation: S.A.: s. 14.
122. Retirement villages legislation: S.A.: s. 14(5).
123. Retirement villages legislation: S.A.: s. 14(6).
124. Unreported, S.A. Residential Tenancies Tribunal, 1989.
125. Cf. *Hornsby S.C. v. Malcolm* (unreported, N.S.W. Sup. Ct, 1986, C.A. 38); *Webb v. Morris* (unreported, Vic. Sup. Ct, 1983, No. м 293).
126. Cf. *Walkerville v. Adelaide Clinic Holdings Pty Ltd* (1985) 119 L.S.J.S. 239.
127. N.S.W. Sup. Ct, C.A. 292, 1984.
128. Cf. Moore and Tarr, *Entrepreneurial Medicine* (1988) 16 A.B.L.R. 4 at 32.

the construction and operation of private hospitals and nursing homes is subject to extensive controls under the *Health Act* 1958.[129] These controls apply to any physical facility so long as care of a prescribed kind is offered.[130] In South Australia no health services may be provided by a private hospital except at premises in respect of which a licence from the Health Commission is in force.[131] A hospital is defined as a body of persons by which health services are provided being health services provided to persons on a live-in basis.[132] Variations on these models occur in all States.

Institutions seeking financial assistance from the Commonwealth government for themselves or their patients are subject to some regulation if funding is to be gained. Under the Commonwealth *National Health Act* 1953 nursing homes and private hospitals must be approved if patients are to continue to receive Commonwealth benefits. In addition specific government assistance is available under the *Nursing Homes Assistance Act* 1974, the *Aged or Disabled Persons Homes Act* 1954 and the *Aged Persons Hostels Act* 1972. A private hospital is defined as any premises declared to be such by the Minister pursuant to s. 23EA(1) of the *Health Insurance Act* 1973. The Commonwealth Department of Health formerly carried out regular inspections of private hospitals. However these inspections ceased as a result of the Commonwealth's decision to abolish the bed day subsidy and repeal its control over the approval and categorisation of private hospitals. A nursing home is defined by the *Nursing Homes Assistance Act* as premises in which patients are received and lodged exclusively for the purpose of nursing home care. Nursing homes may be approved under s. 4(1) of the *Nursing Homes Assistance Act* or s. 40AB of the *National Health Act*.

129. *Health Act* 1958 (Vic.), Div. 3.
130. *Health Act* 1958 (Vic.), s. 178. Under Div. 3, institutions may be classified as hospitals or nursing homes at the discretion of the Chief General Manager of the Health Department: s. 179. The building of any facility and any addition to or alteration or extension of any facility must be approved by the Chief General Manager: s. 182. Records are required to be kept and certain diseases must be notified. Certificates of character and fitness to operate a private hospital must be provided by every person named as an operator of a hospital including any shareholder or beneficial owner of a share in any corporation named. Any Director of Nursing or Deputy Director of Nursing must be approved. Approval for any works in a private hospital may be withheld if the Department of Health considers that works would result in more than adequate facilities becoming available for the provision of care of a prescribed kind or kinds to the population of the area in which the works are proposed: s. 182(4).
131. South Australian *Health Commission Act*, s. 57b. Approval for a licence will take into account, amongst other factors:
    (d) the location of the premises and their proximity to other facilities for the provision of health services; and
    (e) the adequacy of existing facilities for the provision of health services to persons in the locality; and
    (g) the requirements of economy and efficiency in the provision of health services within the State: s. 57d.
    Under regulations standards to be observed in the provision of health services and records to be kept by private hospitals are established. These requirements extend to nursing homes because of the width of the definition of hospital.
132. South Australian *Health Commission Act*, s. 6.

IX. REGULATION OF RETIREMENT VILLAGES

1. Disclosure and Formalities

[13.42] Often arrangements with respect to residence in a retirement village involve considerable commitments by the resident and fall outside established legal protections. Controls in all States seek to ensure that prospective residents are given detailed information as to their position and they enable residents to withdraw even after making a contract.

In Victoria documents relating to the retirement village must be given to a prospective resident at least 21 days before a resident enters into a residence contract.[133] Residence documents include the residence contract, the management contract, the undertaking to observe by-laws and to pay any service charge, a disclosure statement, a checklist in a prescribed form and the by-laws.[134] The checklist contains a number of questions and the owner is obliged to answer them if asked.[135] The owner must also provide all information about the village reasonably required by the resident.[136] Any failure to respond or provision of inaccurate information confers a right to rescind.[137] The resident is entitled to rescind a residence contract without any ground within three business days after the signing of the contract.[138] The existence of this right must be conspicuously notified in the residence contract.[139]

In New South Wales the disclosure requirements come from the Code of Practice adopted under the *Fair Trading Act*. This Code similarly requires information to be made available about charges, fees and services and a checklist and the village rules. The legal basis of occupancy and the type and length of tenure must be fully disclosed. A ten day cooling-off period applies.

In Queensland no invitation to any person to reside in a retirement village may be made until a scheme for the village has been approved by the Registrar.[140] Approval cannot be given until the Registrar is satisfied as to disclosure of tenure, services, contractual provisions and by-laws.[141]

In South Australia listed documents must be given prior to the signing of a residence contract.[142] The documents include the residence rules and a checklist in the prescribed form.[143] The cooling-off period is ten days.[144]

---

133. Retirement villages legislation: Vic.: s. 19.
134. Retirement villages legislation: Vic.: s. 3.
135. Retirement villages legislation: Vic.: s. 20(2).
136. Retirement villages legislation: Vic.: s. 20(3).
137. Retirement villages legislation: Vic.: s. 22.
138. Retirement villages legislation: Vic.: s. 24(2).
139. Retirement villages legislation: Vic.: s.24(5).
140. Retirement villages legislation: Qld: s. 16.
141. Retirement villages legislation: Qld: ss 17, 18.
142. Retirement villages legislation: S.A.: s. 6(2).
143. Retirement villages legislation: S.A.: s. 6(3).
144. Retirement villages legislation: S.A.: s. 6(4).

2. Rules of Conduct and Management

[13.43] In all States residents will enter a residence contract which governs the financial arrangements and rights of tenure and agree to residence rules or by-laws which govern the general quality of life within the village. In Victoria and Queensland residents are given a statutory right to alter the by-laws by a special resolution of a meeting of residents.[145] Such a resolution must be notified in advance and carried by a threequarters majority. The New South Wales Code of Practice says nothing about alteration of such rules. In South Australia residence rules are defined as those with which residents of a village are expected by the administering authority to comply.[146] This definition implies that the rules are set by the administering authority and it seems that they may be changed by the authority as notice of any alteration must be given.[147] No power of alteration by the residents' committee is mentioned in the Act. However in New South Wales and South Australia harsh or unconscionable rules may be set aside by the Residential Tenancies Tribunal.[148]

[13.44] In all States there are provisions for residents' committees.[149] Election to this committee is carried out by the residents and membership of the committee is confined to residents. The committees are empowered to determine their own procedures and to appoint subcommittees. The New South Wales Code is most detailed about resident interaction. The committee is described as a residents' forum with authority to consider any issues relevant to the operation of the village. In addition there should be a village planning and budgeting committee and a disputes committee.

3. Financial Matters

[13.45] A primary concern of residents of a retirement village is liability for charges for services provided. These services will commonly extend beyond the property maintenance services associated with most multiple-dwelling-unit buildings to meals, nursing and medical care. Central to the regulation of charges for these services is the annual meeting which must be convened by the manager or administering authority.[150] The manager must present a financial statement to that meeting setting out performance for the past year and a budget for the year ahead.[151] The statement of performance must set out income by way of charges for the provision of goods and services and expenditure of that income. Future expenditure may include provision for major works.

---

145. Retirement villages legislation: Vic.: s. 36; Qld: s. 50.
146. Retirement villages legislation: S.A.: s. 3.
147. Retirement villages legislation: S.A.: s. 12(2).
148. Retirement villages legislation: N.S.W.: s. 14(6); S.A.: s. 11.
149. Retirement villages legislation: N.S.W.: Code of Practice; Vic.: s. 36; Qld: s. 49; S.A.: s. 13.
150. Retirement villages legislation: N.S.W.: Code of Practice; Vic.: s. 33; Qld: s. 47; S.A.: s. 10.
151. Retirement villages legislation: N.S.W.: Code of Practice; Vic.: s. 34; Qld: s. 48; S.A.: s. 10(5).

Increases in maintenance charges are restricted. In Victoria a maintenance charge may not exceed the adjusted maintenance charge.[152] The adjusted charge is one indexed in accordance with regulations.[153] An increase above the index may be approved by the majority of residents[154] and may be justified by increases in rates and taxes or award wages.[155] In New South Wales the budget must be presented to the residents' forum and if the forum disagrees with any item contained in the budget it must notify the management accordingly and thereupon a dispute will be deemed to exist.[156] In Queensland the maintenance charge must not be increased beyond an amount provided for by a formula set out in the Act and similar to that applicable in Victoria.[157] In South Australia maintenance charges must be justified by estimates of expenditure presented to a residents' meeting.[158]

[13.46] Additional property works or exceptional building upgrading require special levies. In Victoria and Queensland a special levy can only be imposed if authorised by special resolution of residents, or if expenditure is required by a legislative or judicial pronouncement, or is provided for pursuant to the residence contract or management contract or by-laws.[159] In South Australia special levies may only be imposed if authorised by a special resolution[160] and even then only (it seems) if they are provided for by the residence contract. In New South Wales any such proposal should where possible be included in the annual budget and in any event requires the consent of the residents' forum.[161]

[13.47] Substantial sums have been demanded for the right to enter a retirement village. The issues that arise in relation to those sums are first, their use prior to entry into residence, secondly, the rights to a refund on leaving the village or on death, and thirdly, the relationship with financial investors in the village.

The dissipation of ingoing contributions or premiums on building or other costs without the capacity to provide the residential unit is sought to be avoided by the placement of such funds in a form of trust. In Victoria the money must be held by an estate agent or solicitor as stake-holder until the happening of the listed events.[162] These events are the satisfying of any preconditions to the right or entitlement to enter the village, completion of any building work and a refund to any previous resident entitled to a refund. In Queensland payment into a trust account where work is incomplete may be required by the Registrar as part of the conditions for approval of a village scheme.[163] In South Australia the

---

152. Retirement villages legislation: Vic.: s. 38(3).
153. Retirement villages legislation: Vic.: s. 38(1).
154. Retirement villages legislation: Vic.: s. 38(4).
155. Retirement villages legislation: Vic.: s. 38(5).
156. Retirement villages legislation: N.S.W.: Code of Practice.
157. Retirement villages legislation: Qld: s. 51.
158. Retirement villages legislation: S.A.: s. 10(8).
159. Retirement villages legislation: Vic.: s. 38(6); Qld: s. 51(7).
160. Retirement villages legislation: S.A.: s. 10(9).
161. Retirement villages legislation: N.S.W.: Code of Practice.
162. Retirement villages legislation: Vic.: s. 25(2).
163. Retirement villages legislation: Qld: s. 18(2).

money must be held in trust in a bank or trustee investment.[164] The money must be held until entry into occupation by the resident. In New South Wales the Code simply provides that where proposed facilities or services are referred to, an unequivocal assurance of implementation must be given.

[13.48] It is not uncommon for ingoing contributions to be designated as contributions to the organisation setting up or managing the village particularly where that organisation is a religious or charitable body. No Act confers any right to return of the contribution unless that return was part of the arrangements between the parties. The Victorian Act does however give effect to any oral representation of a right to a refund in precedence to any provision of the formal written agreement. The right to a refund arises where an owner or manager or person acting on behalf of, or with the knowledge of, the owner or manager, makes a statement to the resident during negotiations leading to the signing of a residence contract. The statement must be one to the effect that all or part of the contribution will be refunded to the resident if the resident leaves the village or be refunded to the resident's estate if the resident dies. In these circumstances the resident has a right to the refund on the happening of the event specified subject to any other specified conditions being fulfilled.[165]

Apart from this provision the right to a refund depends entirely upon the residence contract. The right to a refund if conferred is given greater force through a statutory charge on the land in the village but this right is relevant to the enforceability of the right against third parties not to the existence of the right. Even where rights to a refund are conferred they may be subject to conditions such as the subsequent purchase of residence rights to the resident's unit. That sale may lead to a considerable time-lag. Similarly the right to sell or otherwise dispose of the rights of occupation in the village depends solely on the contract conferring those rights. Since the rights will commonly not amount to recognised proprietary rights the common law presumption in favour of alienability will be inapplicable. Furthermore in South Australia the jurisdiction of the Residential Tenancies Tribunal does not extend to disputes in relation to premiums.[166]

[13.49] In Victoria, Queensland and South Australia some protection is given to any right to a refund where that right otherwise exists. The Retirement Villages Acts in those three States give the right to a refund a special status and that status is of greatest significance in disputes with third parties claiming an interest in the land.

In the three States the fact of the existence of a retirement village must be notified to the Land Titles Office.[167] The fact of the existence of the village is then notified on the title to the land.[168] Within a retirement

---

164. Retirement villages legislation: S.A.: s. 8(1).
165. Retirement villages legislation: Vic.: s. 26.
166. Retirement villages legislation: S.A.: s. 14(4); the jurisdiction also does not extend to claims by the estate because of the definition of resident in s. 3.
167. Retirement villages legislation: Vic.: s. 9(1); Qld: s. 33(1); S.A.: s. 15(2).
168. Retirement villages legislation: Vic.: s. 11; Qld: s. 33(4); S.A.: s. 15(1).

village the right of residents to a refund of an ingoing contribution or premium is (amongst other rights) given force as a charge on the land.[169] In Victoria and Queensland the charge has priority over all encumbrances created after the noting of the fact of the village on the title.[170] In South Australia no rules are prescribed as to the priority of the charge for a refund. However its enforcement is entrusted to the discretion of the Supreme Court.[171]

4. Protection from Eviction

[13.50]   In all four States security of tenure for residents of retirement villages is obtained by restrictions on eviction. In Victoria, New South Wales and South Australia termination of residence can only occur on grounds specified in the Acts. In Queensland a threatened eviction can be challenged. In New South Wales and South Australia termination other than by the resident can only occur pursuant to an order of the Residential Tenancies Tribunal.

[13.51]   In Victoria termination can be effected by notice on the basis of breach, incapacity or expiration of the term of a periodic tenancy. Notice on the basis of breach involves two notices. The first notice must require that within 28 days of service the resident remedy the breach or if the breach is not capable of being remedied the resident cease committing the breach.[172] If this notice is not complied with and the breach is substantial the owner may serve notice requiring the resident to leave by a date not earlier than 60 days from the second notice.[173]

In Victoria notice on the basis of incapacity may be served requiring the resident to leave within 14 days.[174] This notice must include a certificate signed by two legally qualified medical practitioners stating that the resident needs care of a kind not available at the village. One of the doctors must be nominated or agreed to by the resident. Notice on this basis is only available if provided for by the residence contract. Notice on the basis of expiration of the term may be given where the right of residence is conferred by way of a periodic tenancy.[175] The notice must be not less than six months and must not cut short the period of the tenancy. Nothing appears to forbid even weekly tenancies and thus residence terminable on six months notice can apparently be created. If a fixed-term tenancy were created, there appears to be no power to terminate at the end of that term.

[13.52]   In New South Wales application to the Residential Tenancies Tribunal for termination may be made on the grounds of physical or mental incapacity, breach, serious damage or injury or undue hardship to the administering authority. In the case of termination for incapacity

---

169. Retirement villages legislation: Vic.: s. 29(1); Qld: s. 34; S.A.: s. 4.
170. Retirement villages legislation: Vic.: s. 29(3); Qld: s. 35.
171. Retirement villages legislation: S.A.: s. 9(5).
172. Retirement villages legislation: Vic.: s. 16(2).
173. Retirement villages legislation: Vic.: s.16(2).
174. Retirement villages legislation: Vic.: s. 16(5).
175. Retirement villages legislation: Vic.: s. 16(4).

or for breach, the Tribunal must be satisfied that procedures for notice of intention to terminate have been complied with. In the case of termination for incapacity the Tribunal must be satisfied that the premises are unsuitable because of the resident's physical or mental incapacity and that termination is otherwise appropriate.[176] In the case of termination for breach the Tribunal must be satisfied that the breach or breaches justify termination or that termination is otherwise justified.[177] In the case of termination because of serious damage or injury, the Tribunal must be satisfied that the resident has or is likely to cause serious damage to the premises or injury to an employee of management or to a resident.[178] Termination may be granted because of undue hardship to the administering authority which must be justified by special circumstances.[179]

[13.53] In Queensland a resident who is (amongst other things) threatened with removal or actually removed from a village may apply to the Supreme Court for an injunction.[180] The Supreme Court may grant an injunction preventing removal if it is satisfied that the removal would be in breach of the residence contract and not in the interests of the resident or is not justified for any adequate reason.[181] The court may have regard to the rights and interests of all persons affected.

[13.54] In South Australia termination may be granted only by the Residential Tenancies Tribunal and only after notice on the basis of breach or incapacity. An administering authority may give notice of termination on the basis of any breach of the residence contract or the residence rules.[182] The administering authority must then make application to the Residential Tenancies Tribunal and satisfy it that the breach is sufficiently serious to justify termination of the right of occupation.[183] If the Tribunal is satisfied it must fix a period within which the resident must leave and may grant an order for ejectment of the resident at the expiration of that period.[184] Alternatively the authority may give notice of termination on the basis that the premises have become an unsuitable place of residence for the resident because of the resident's mental or physical incapacity.[185] Again the administering authority must satisfy the Residential Tenancies Tribunal that proper grounds for termination exist.[186] Whereas termination on the basis of breach is likely to involve issues of conduct determinable by hearing the accounts of the parties in the normal manner of the Residential Tenancies Tribunal,

---

176. Retirement villages legislation: N.S.W.: s. 16.
177. Retirement villages legislation: N.S.W.: s. 17.
178. Retirement villages legislation: N.S.W.: s. 20.
179. Retirement villages legislation: N.S.W.: s. 21.
180. Retirement villages legislation: Qld: s. 42.
181. Retirement villages legislation: Qld: s. 43.
182. Retirement villages legislation: S.A.: ss 7(1)(c), 7(8).
183. Retirement villages legislation: S.A.: s. 7(3).
184. Retirement villages legislation: S.A.: ss 7(6), 7(7).
185. Retirement villages legislation: S.A.: ss 7(1)(d), 7(8).
186. Retirement villages legislation: S.A.: s. 7(4).

applications on the basis of mental or physical incapacity may well involve detailed and conflicting expert evidence. A fee of $400 is imposed for an application, no restrictions are imposed upon legal representation, and appeals lie to the Supreme Court.[187]

187. Retirement villages legislation: S.A.: s. 20(1); *Retirement Villages Regulations 1987* (S.A.), Sched. II.

14

The Scope and Meaning of Real Property

[14.01] This Chapter will examine a number of miscellaneous legal doctrines which separately consider the limits to land. First, we will consider the doctrine of fixtures, which determines when and in which circumstances an item of personal property which is attached to land loses its identity as a chattel and merges with the land. This will be followed by a discussion of the rules relating to the ownership of airspace and minerals. As will be shown, the traditional common law estates and interests in land are concerned primarily with legal rights in respect of the land surface; rights vested in a person in relation to the surface do not always extend to the airspace above the surface or the minerals below the surface. A discussion of land boundaries then follows. This investigates, inter alia, the rights of a landowner adjoining a river or road to the river bed or the soil under the highway, rules as to the ownership of the seashore, and the legal effects of the advance or retreat of the sea or rivers over adjacent or riparian land over the years. This discussion leads logically to a consideration of the common law and statutory rules relating to the encroachment of buildings across boundary lines. Finally, consideration will be given to the State legislation concerning the rights and duties of neighbouring landowners concerning the construction and maintenance of boundary fences.

I. FIXTURES

1. Introduction

[14.02] The issue as to the circumstances in which personal property becomes part of the realty to which it is attached pursuant to the doctrine of fixtures is relevant in the following relationships:

(a) landlord and tenant;
(b) vendor and purchaser of land;
(c) mortgagor and mortgagee;
(d) life tenants and remaindermen or reversioners; and
(e) devisees and personal representatives.

In each of these situations, a dispute may arise as to the ownership of particular chattels. Thus, for example, there may be a dispute between a vendor and purchaser of land as to whether certain curtains or objects in the house at the time of the signing of the contract of sale remain the property of the vendor or pass to the purchaser. Similarly, disputes as to ownership may arise between landlords and tenants in respect of items attached to the property by the tenant during the lease. In each situation the issue is one of law for the judge[1] and the answer will depend on the application of the doctrine of fixtures. The effect of the operation of the doctrine on each of the relationships identified above will be considered after a discussion of the general law of fixtures.

2. The Relevant Tests

[14.03] Based on normal contractual principles, if a dispute involving the ownership of fixtures arises between two persons who are parties to a contract, the question of ownership may be determined by an express term of the contract. Thus, in such cases the court's first duty is to examine any such term and to apply it if the normal laws of contract are satisfied.[2] The following discussion presupposes that no such express term exists, and that the general law will therefore be applicable.

The starting point is the common law maxim, quicquid plantatur solo, solo cedit, (whatever is attached to the land forms part of the land).[3] Like most legal maxims, however, this is a gross over-simplification of the state of the law. The two factors regarded at common law as relevant to the resolution of disputes over fixtures have been identified in the cases as the degree of annexation and the object of annexation.

The so-called degree of annexation test looks to the manner in which the chattel is attached to the land. There appear to be two relevant legal presumptions. First, if a chattel is attached to the land other than by its own weight (for example, by screws or bolts), prima facie it is a fixture.[4] This presumption applies even if the degree of attachment is very slight.[5] The greater the degree of attachment, the stronger the presumption appears to be.[6] Secondly, if a chattel is only attached by its own weight, prima facie the chattel is not a fixture even if it has become embedded in the soil.[7] An illustration of the first presumption is *Buckland v. Butterfield*,[8] where a verandah attached to a house was held to be a fixture. Illustrations of the second presumption are *Elwes v. Maw*,[9] where a Dutch barn attached to the land by wooden upright posts inset into the ground was held not to be a fixture, and *Hulme v. Brigham*,[10] where a printing press attached merely by its own weight was similarly held not to be a fixture.

1. *Reynolds v. Ashby & Son* [1904] A.C. 466 (H.L.).
2. *Montague v. Long* (1972) 24 P. & C.R. 240; *Simmons v. Midford* [1969] 2 Ch. 415.
3. See *Minshall v. Lloyd* (1837) 2 M. & W. 450 at 459; 150 E.R. 834 at 838 (Exch.) per Parke B.
4. See e.g. *Jordan v. May* [1947] K.B. 427 (C.A.); *Australian Provincial Co. Ltd v. Coroneo* (1938) 38 S.R. (N.S.W.) 700 (F.C.).
5. *Holland v. Hodgson* (1872) L.R. 7 C.P. 328 at 335.
6. *Spyer v. Phillipson* [1931] 2 Ch. 183 (C.A.).
7. *Hamp v. Bygrave* (1983) 266 E.G. 720; *Monti v. Barnes* [1901] 1 Q.B. 205 (C.A.); *H.E. Dibble Ltd v. Moore* [1970] 2 Q.B. 181 (C.A.); *Australian Provincial Co. Ltd v. Coroneo* (1938) 38 S.R. (N.S.W.) 700 (F.C.).
8. (1820) 2 Brod. & B. 54; 129 E.R. 878 (C.P.).
9. (1802) 3 East 38; 102 E.R. 510 (K.B.) See also *Wiltshear v. Cottrell* (1853) 1 El. & Bl. 674; 118 E.R. 589 (K.B.).
10. [1943] K.B. 152.

Originally, the doctrine of fixtures consisted solely of the degree of annexation test. However, by the turn of this century, the so-called "object of annexation test" had been added by the courts as an additional relevant consideration on the ground that the degree of annexation test was unnecessarily rigid.[11] Pursuant to the object of annexation test, the courts will examine whether the object was affixed to the land, on the one hand, as a temporary measure or for the purpose of displaying it as a chattel, or, on the other hand, in order to benefit the real estate; in the former case, the chattel will be held not to be a fixture even if it is attached to the building other than by its own weight.[12]

The traditional opinion is that the courts will infer the object of annexation from the surrounding circumstances and the nature of the chattel and will apply an objective test. Thus, the test is what the reasonable person would consider to be the reason for attaching the object to the land;[13] the actual intention of the parties is merely one piece of relevant evidence.[14] Kaye J. stated in *Belgrave Nominees Pty Ltd v. Barlin-Scott Airconditioning (Aust.) Pty Ltd*:[15]

> "Whether the intention of the party fixing the chattel was to make it a permanent accession to the freehold is to be inferred from the matters and circumstances including the following: the nature of the chattel; the relation and situation of the party making the annexation vis-a-vis the owner of the freehold or the person in possession; the mode of annexation; and the purpose for which the chattel was fixed."

Another relevant factor might be the nature of the estate or interest held in the land by the owner of the chattel. Thus, for example, the court is less likely to infer an intention to benefit the real estate by a person with only a limited interest in the real estate (such as a tenant).

The seminal case on the object of annexation test is *Leigh v. Taylor*.[16] In this case, the tenant for life attached valuable tapestries to the wall of the drawing room of a house. The tapestries were attached to canvas by tacks, the canvas was nailed to wooden supports and the supports were nailed to the wall. The House of Lords held that the tapestries were not fixtures and could be removed by the executors of the life tenant. The case was determined on the basis that the affixing of the tapestries by nails to the wall was the only method by which the tapestries could be effectively displayed as chattels and that there was no intention to benefit the real estate by attaching the tapestries. A similar conclusion was reached by the English Court of Appeal in *Spyer v. Phillipson*[17] in relation to oak panelling

11. See *Re De Falbe* [1901] 1 Ch. 523 at 534-535 (C.A.) per Vaughan Williams L.J.
12. See e.g. *Bradshaw v. Davey* [1952] 1 All E.R. 350; *Vaudeville Electric Cinema Ltd v. Muriset* [1923] 2 Ch. 74; *Hamp v. Bygrave* (1983) 266 E.G. 720.
13. *Hobson v. Gorringe* [1897] 1 Ch. 182 (C.A.); *Re De Falbe* [1901] 1 Ch. 523 (C.A.); *London C.C. v. Wilkins* [1957] A.C. 362 (H.L.).
14. *Love v. Bloomfield* [1906] V.L.R. 723; *London C.C. v. Wilkins* [1957] A.C. 362 (H.L.).
15. [1984] V.R. 947 at 951. See also *Reid v. Shaw* (1906) 3 C.L.R. 656 at 667 per Griffiths C.J.
16. [1902] A.C. 157 (H.L.).
17. [1931] 2 Ch. 183 (C.A.).

nailed by a tenant to the walls of the rented premises. Before a chattel will escape the classification as a fixture under the object of annexation test if it is attached to the land, it must be shown that the annexation was "absolutely necessary".[18]

It has been frequently stated by academic writers that the doctrine of fixtures turns both on the application of the degree of annexation and the object of annexation tests.[19] This, however, appears to be misleading as the object of annexation test has assumed far greater significance than the degree of annexation test in recent times.[20] The degree test is still relevant in a negative sense in that if a chattel is only attached by its own weight it is most unlikely to be a fixture.[21] It is also relevant in that, as already stated, if a chattel is affixed to land, the onus of proof will shift to the person who affixed it to prove on the balance of probabilities why the object should not be regarded as a fixture. Subject to these exceptions, however, it appears that the case will be resolved purely on the application of the object of annexation test, that is, the intention of the person who annexed the chattel to the land as inferred from the surrounding circumstances.[22]

3. Recent Cases

[14.04]   Despite the application of the above-mentioned rules, cases on fixtures largely depend on their facts and are often difficult to reconcile. The following are a representative sample of recent cases on this area of law:[23]

Attorney-General (Cth) v. R. T. Co. Pty Ltd (No. 2).[24] The High Court held that two printing presses were not fixtures even though they were attached to the building by nuts and bolts, since the sole purpose of the annexation was to hold the presses steady so that they could be used properly.

Berkley v. Poulett.[25] Large paintings screwed into the wall of a building were held by the English Court of Appeal not to be fixtures as the purpose

---

18. *Re De Falbe* [1901] 1 Ch. 523 at 537 (C.A.).
19. See e.g. Megarry and Wade, pp. 732ff.
20. See e.g. *Palumberi v. Palumberi* [1986] A.N.Z. Conv. R. 592 at 596 per Kearney J.; *Adele Holdings Ltd v. Westpac Finance Ltd* [1988] A.N.Z. Conv. R. 20 at 21 per Doogue J.; *Neylon v. Dickens* (1979) 2 N.Z.L.R. 714.
21. *Berkley v. Poulett* (1976) 242 E.G. 39; *H.E. Dibble Ltd v. Moore* [1970] 2 Q.B. 181 (C.A.).
22. Note the decision in *Goulburn C.C. v. McIntosh* (1985) 3 B.P.R. 9367 (N.S.W. Sup. Ct), where Carruthers J. decided that when determining whether an item had become a fixture, the court must have regard to *all* the circumstances, including the intention with which the item was installed, the degree of annexation and the relationship which existed between the parties when the item was installed.
23. See also *Waige & Co. Constructions Pty Ltd v. Suburban Timbers Pty Ltd* [1976] A.C.L.D. 387 (N.S.W.C.A.); *Chateau Douglas Hunter Valley Vineyards Ltd v. Chateau Douglas Hunter Valley Winery & Cellars Ltd* [1978] A.C.L.D. 258 (N S W. Sup. Ct).
24. (1957) 97 C.L.R. 146.
25. [1977] E.G. Dig. 754.

of their attachment was to enjoy them as paintings and not to complement the architectural design of the room.

N. H. Dunn Pty Ltd v. L. M. Ericcson Pty Ltd.[26] A private automatic branch telephone exchange hired to a tenant and installed by him in the rented premises was held by the New South Wales Court of Appeal not to be a fixture.

Wellesmore v. Ratford.[27] A fibreglass house was installed at a building materials exhibition centre. It was annexed to the land by steel spikes inserted into the ground and welded to steel base plates on the legs which supported the house. Despite the fact that the building was only intended to remain at the exhibition centre for one year, the house was held to be a fixture.

Anthony v. Commonwealth.[28] Water pipelines from Manton Dam to Darwin were held to be fixtures. The pipelines, which were partly below and partly above the land, consisted of concrete-lined steel pipes supported on cradles set in concrete.

Belgrave Nominees Pty Ltd v. Barlin-Scott Airconditioning (Aust.) Pty Ltd.[29] Airconditioning plants, together with chillers, were installed on the roofs of two buildings. The chillers stood by their own weight on a platform specially constructed to hold them. The chillers were connected by bolts to the water reticulation system, and water pipes were connected to water pumps which were affixed to the platforms on which the chillers rested. Kaye J. of the Victorian Supreme Court held that the airconditioning plant was a fixture.

Royal Bank of Canada v. Saskatchewan Telecommunications.[30] Various buildings, which were designed to house diesel engines and radio equipment, were either bolted to timber embedded in the ground or were constructed on treated skids which could be affixed to the ground by anchor rods. The Saskatchewan Court of Appeal held that the buildings were not fixtures as the degree of annexation was slight and the intention was that the buildings could be moved if the need arose.

Dean v. Andrew.[31] The English Court of Appeal held that a large prefabricated greenhouse which was bolted to a concrete plinth which rested on the ground by its own weight was not a fixture.

Hynes v. Vaughan.[32] Scott J. held, inter alia, that seven piles of rubbish consisting mostly of soil, rotting vegetation and bonfire residue merged with and became part of the real property by virtue of the law of fixtures.

26. [1980] A.C.L.D. 082 (N.S.W.C.A.).
27. (1973) 23 F.L.R. 295 (A.C.T. Sup. Ct).
28. (1973) 47 A.L.J.R. 83.
29. [1984] V.R. 947. Cf. *Pan Australian Credits (S.A.) Pty Ltd v. Kolim Pty Ltd* [1981] A.C.L.D. 398 (S.A. Sup. Ct).
30. (1985) 20 D.L.R. (4th) 415.
31. *The Times*, 25 May 1985.
32. (1985) 50 P. & C.R. 444 (Ch. D.).

4. The Effect of the Doctrine of Fixtures on Various Relationships

(a) Vendor and purchaser of land

[14.05] The relevant time for the consideration of the issue of fixtures is the date of the contract of sale.[33] All fixtures attached to the land at that date pass with the land to the purchaser,[34] unless they are expressly exempted in the contract of sale or unless the court is satisfied that the purchaser bought with notice (whether in writing or orally) that specified fixtures would not pass with the land.[35] Legislation in each State designed to shorten conveyances uniformly specifies that a conveyance of land is deemed to include fixtures;[36] for this reason there need be no express mention of fixtures in the conveyance.

(b) Mortgagor and mortgagee

[14.06] All fixtures annexed to land subject to mortgage are automatically included within the scope of the mortgage and form part of the security.[37] This rule applies to both legal and equitable mortgages.[38] The mortgagor has no right to remove any fixtures (in the absence of express agreement to the contrary) installed either before or after the date of the mortgage,[39] and cannot take advantage of exceptions admitted in favour of tenants: see below **[14.10]**ff.[40]

(c) Devisee and personal representative

[14.07] In the case of a bequest of land, at common law all fixtures pass with the devise, and the testator's personal representatives have no right to remove them.[41] This rule also applies in the case of intestacies.[42]

---

33. *Phillips v. Lamdin* [1949] 2 K.B. 33; *Colegrave v. Dias Santos* (1823) 2 B. & C. 76; 107 E.R. 311 (K.B.).
34. *Phillips v. Lamdin* [1949] 2 K.B. 33; *Gibson v. Hammersmith and City Rly Co.* (1863) 32 L.J. Ch. 337; 62 E.R. 748; *Meehan v. N.Z. Agricultural Co. Ltd* (1907) 26 N.Z.L.R. 766.
35. *Isaacs v. Lord* [1920] V.L.R. 274.
36. General law statutes: N.S.W.: s. 67; Vic.: s. 62; Qld: s. 239; S.A.: s. 36; W.A.: s. 41; Tas.: s. 6.
37. See legislation in fn. 36 above. A mortgage classes as a "conveyance" for the purposes of this legislation: N.S.W.: s. 7(1); Vic.: s. 18(1); Qld: s. 4; S.A.: s. 7; W.A.: s. 7; Tas.: s. 2. See also *Vaudeville Electric Cinema Ltd v. Muriset* [1923] 2 Ch. 74; *Cockburn v. Cockburn* [1921] N.Z.L.R. 652; *Adele Holdings Ltd v. Westpac Finance Ltd* [1988] A.N.Z. Conv. R. 20.
38. *Meux v. Jacobs* (1875) L.R. 7 H.L. 481.
39. *Longbottom v. Berry* (1869) L.R. 5 Q.B. 123; *Re New South Wales Co-operative Ice & Cold Storage Co.* (1891) 12 L.R. (N.S.W.) Eq. 87; *Australian Joint Stock Bank v. Colonial Finance, Mortgage, Investment & Guarantee Corporation* (1894) 15 L.R. (N.S.W.) 464 (F.C.).
40   *Climie v. Wood* (1869) L.R. 4 Ex. 328 (Exch. Ch.); *Monti v. Barnes* [1901] 1 Q.B. 205 (C.A.).
41. *Re Whaley* [1908] 1 Ch. 615; *Re Lord Chesterfield's Settled Estates* [1911] 1 Ch. 237.
42. *Norton v. Dashwood* [1896] 2 Ch. 497.

(d) Disputes involving third parties

[14.08]   At common law, despite the maxim nemo dat quod non habet, title to chattels may be lost if they are attached to real property by someone other than the owner of the chattels.[43] As stated by Megarry and Wade,[44] if X steals Y's bricks and builds them into a house on Z's land, Z not Y becomes the owner of the land. Y's remedies (if any) will lie in contract and/or tort.

An interesting problem arises where chattels subject to a chattel mortgage or hire-purchase agreement are attached to real property and repossession is sought by the original owner following a repayment default. At common law, the problem would be resolved in the following manner. If A hires goods to B and B installs them in his own property which is subject to mortgage to C, the goods will become subject to the mortgage.[45] However, A will be regarded as having an equitable interest in the land if the hire-purchase agreement entitles A to enter B's property and seize the goods on default. This is referred to as a "right of entry" and, like other equitable interests in land, prevails against every person except a bona fide purchaser of a legal estate for value without notice.[46]

In many circumstances, this problem would now be resolved by State legislation. The legislation controlling hire-purchase agreements in the various States contains the following section:[47]

"(1) Goods comprised in a hire purchase agreement which, at the time of the making of the agreement, were not fixtures to land shall not in respect of the period during which the agreement remains in force be treated as fixtures to land.

(2) Notwithstanding anything contained in the last preceding subsection, the owner shall be entitled to repossess goods which have become affixed to a dwelling house or residence if after the goods have become so affixed any person other than the hirer has bona fide acquired for valuable consideration an interest in the land without notice of the rights of the owner of the goods."

The legislation is still in effect in Queensland, Tasmania, Victoria and Western Australia.[48]

---

43. See e.g. *Crossley Bros Ltd v. Lee* [1908] 1 K.B. 86; *Gough v. Wood & Co.* [1894] 1 Q.B. 713 (C.A.). See also *Reliance Corporation Ltd v. Swindon Nominees Pty Ltd* [1989] A.C.L.D. 41 (W.A. Sup. Ct).
44. Megarry and Wade, p. 738.
45. *Reynolds v. Ashby & Son* [1904] A.C. 466 (H.L.); *Holland v. Hodgson* (1872) L.R. 7 C.P. 328 (Exch. Ch.); *Hobson v. Gorringe* [1897] 1 Ch. 182 (C.A.).
46. See e.g. *Kay's Leasing Corporation Pty Ltd v. C.S.R. Provident Fund Nominees Pty Ltd* [1962] V.R. 429; *Re Morrison, Jones and Taylor Ltd* [1914] 1 Ch. 50 (C.A.).
47. *Hire Purchase Act* 1959 (Vic.), s. 27; *Hire Purchase Act* 1959 (Qld), s. 32; *Hire Purchase Act* 1959 (W.A.), s. 27; *Hire Purchase Act* 1959 (Tas.), s. 36. See *Stanley Thompson Investments Pty Ltd v. Nock and Kirby Finance Co. Pty Ltd* [1969] 1 N.S.W.R. 345 (C.A.) for a discussion of the meaning of the phrase "goods which have become affixed" in subs. (2). See Else-Mitchell, *Hire Purchase Law 1960 to 1965*, 4th ed., 1968, pp. 187-189 for a discussion of the effect of the phrase "during which the agreement remains in force" in s. 27(1).
48. In Victoria and Western Australia, the hire purchase legislation does not apply to contracts regulated by the *Credit Act*.

In South Australia, the *Consumer Transactions Act* 1972 governs the position with respect to all credit transactions involving chattels with a maximum value of $20,000. Section 5 states that credit transactions must take the form of either a consumer lease or a consumer mortgage, and s. 33 states that goods subject to a consumer mortgage or a consumer lease that were not at the time of the creation of the mortgage or lease fixtures to land, shall not in respect of the period for which the mortgage or lease remains in force for the purpose of any Act or law be treated as fixtures to land. Where the 1972 Act is inoperative because the $20,000 limit is exceeded, disputes will be resolved in South Australia on the application of common law principles. Common law principles will also apply in all cases in New South Wales. The new credit legislation introduced into this jurisdiction[49] makes no mention of fixtures, and as the hire-purchase legislation was repealed with the introduction of the credit legislation, the common law principles re-emerge as relevant.

In Victoria, the *Chattel Securities Act* 1987 applies to all chattels subject to a security interest. Section 6 states:

"(1) If, after a security interest attaches, goods subject to the security interest are affixed to land and become fixtures, the fixtures, for the purposes of the exercise of the secured party's right to take possession of, remove or sell the goods, shall be deemed not to have become fixtures.

(2) A secured party who removes fixtures to which sub-section (1) applies is liable to make good damage done to the land in removing the fixtures.

(3) If, after a lease of goods is made, goods subject to the lease are fixed to land and become fixtures, the fixtures, for the purposes of the exercise of the lessor's right to take possession of the goods, shall be deemed not to have become fixtures.

(4) A lessor who removes fixtures to which sub-section (3) applies is liable to make good damage done to the land in removing fixtures.

(5) If, after a hire-purchase agreement is made, goods subject to the agreement are affixed to land and become fixtures, the fixtures, for the purposes of the exercise of the owner's right to take possession of the goods, shall be deemed not to have become fixtures.

(6) An owner who removes fixtures to which sub-section (5) applies is liable to make good damage done to the land in removing the fixtures.

(7) Despite this section, a secured party is not entitled to take possession of goods that have become affixed to land and become fixtures if, after the goods have become so affixed, a person other than the secured party has acquired an interest in the land for value in good faith and without notice of the security interest of the secured party.

(8) If goods subject to a security interest were affixed to land after an offer to enter into the agreement giving rise to the interest was

49. *Credit Act* 1984 (N.S.W.); *Credit (Administration) Act* 1984 (N.S.W.),

made, but before the offer was accepted, the goods, for the purposes of this section, shall be deemed to have been affixed to the land after the agreement was made."

This section applies to all security transactions and ensures that goods which are installed before the credit agreement is entered into remain chattels. As the *Hire Purchase Act* 1959 (Vic.) has not been repealed, its provision in relation to fixtures may still apply where: (a) the price of the goods exceeds $20,000, unless the goods comprise a commercial vehicle or farm machinery; or (b) the hirer is a body corporate.

The position in the remaining jurisdictions (Western Australia, Queensland and Tasmania) is that the hire-purchase legislation cited above continues to apply.

5. Modified Rules Affecting Landlords and Tenants

(a) The installation of fixtures

[14.09]   At common law, there is no implied covenant prohibiting a tenant from installing fixtures in the rented premises. However, a tenant who installs fixtures without the landlord's consent may in certain circumstances be in breach of the implied covenant to use the premises in a tenant-like manner: see above [10.34]. In addition, the doctrine of waste is applicable and a tenant who reduces the value of the rented premises by installing fixtures will have committed voluntary waste and will be liable in damages to the landlord: see above [12.10].

(b) The removal of fixtures

[14.10]   Public policy appears to demand that tenants be given a limited right to remove chattels which they have attached to the rented premises during the lease even though the objects may class as fixtures under ordinary common law principles.[50] As stated in 1801 by Lord Kenyon C.J.:[51]

> "The old cases upon this subject leant to consider as realty whatever was annexed to the freehold by the occupier: but in modern times the leaning has always been the other way in favour of the tenant, in support of the interests of trade which has become the pillar of the State. What tenant will lay out his money in costly improvements of the land, if he must leave everything behind him which can be said to be annexed to it. Shall it be said that the great gardeners and nurserymen in the neighbourhood of this metropolis, who expend thousands of pounds in erection of greenhouses and hothouses, etc. are obliged to leave all these things upon the premises, when it is notorious that they are even permitted to remove trees, or such as are

50.   In the case of trade fixtures, the rationale is to encourage industry: *Poole's Case* (1703) 1 Salk 368; 91 E.R. 320 (K.B.). The issue is discussed generally in Kodilinye, "Time for Removal of Tenant's Fixtures" [1987] Conv. 253.
51.   *Penton v. Robart* (1801) 2 East 88 at 91; 102 E.R. 302 at 303 (K.B.).

likely to become such, by the thousand, in the necessary course of their trade. If it were otherwise, the very object of their holding would be defeated.''

Based on such considerations, modified rules have been adopted by common law in respect of tenant's fixtures. Chattels annexed by a tenant to the rented premises may become fixtures under ordinary principles and legal title will vest in the landlord. However, as will be explained later, in certain circumstances (subject to express agreement to the contrary) the tenant is given a limited right to remove the fixtures he or she has installed. In these circumstances, during the term of the lease the landlord is treated as the owner of the fixture subject to the tenant's right of removal. Legal title will not revert to the tenant unless and until the tenant actually exercises her or his right of removal and severs the object from the rented premises.[52]

The tenant is only entitled to remove certain categories of fixtures. At common law, the tenant may only remove trade, ornamental and domestic fixtures. In certain States, the tenant is also permitted by legislation to remove agricultural fixtures: see below [14.12].

There are numerous cases concerning the scope of trade fixtures. This exception has been held to include petrol pumps installed at a garage,[53] salt pans,[54] engines and boilers,[55] shelves and counters,[56] a milking plant with oil engine and accessories,[57] the fittings of a public house[58] and shrubs planted by a market gardener.[59] Ornamental and domestic fixtures have been held to include ranges and ovens,[60] ornamental chimney-pieces,[61] looking glasses,[62] panelling[63] and blinds.[64] In all cases, before a chattel can class as a tenant's fixture, in addition to proving that it falls within one of the recognised categories, the tenant must also prove that the object was affixed temporarily and was not intended to be a permanent improvement.[65]

It is unclear from the authorities whether the tenant is permitted at common law to remove trade fixtures if significant damage is caused to the rented premises by the removal.[66] In such cases, the tenant will be liable to repair the damage caused by the removal pursuant to the doctrine

---

52. *Crossley Bros Ltd v. Lee* [1908] 1 K.B. 86; *Bain v. Brand* (1876) 1 A.C. 762 (H.L.).
53. *Smith v. City Petroleum Co. Ltd* [1940] 1 All E.R. 260.
54. *Earl of Mansfield v. Blackburne* (1840) Bing. N.C. 426; 133 E.R. 165 (C.P.).
55. *Climie v. Wood* (1869) L.R. 4 Ex. 328 (Exch. Ch.); *Lawton v. Lawton* (1743) 3 Atk. 13; 26 E.R. 811 (Ch.).
56. *Harding v. National Insurance Co.* (1871) 2 A.J.R. 67.
57. *Booth v. Goodwin* [1923] N.Z.L.R. 703; *Johnson v. International Harvester Co. (N.Z.) Ltd* [1925] N.Z.L.R. 529 (C.A.).
58. *Elliott v. Bishop* (1854) 10 Exch. 496; 156 E.R. 534.
59. *Wardell v. Usher* (1841) 3 Scott N.R. 508; 10 L.J.C.P. 316.
60. *Winn v. Ingilby* (1822) 5 B. & Ald. 625; 106 E.R. 1319 (K.B.).
61. *Leach v. Thomas* (1835) 7 C. & P. 327; 173 E.R. 145 (N.P.).
62. *Beck v. Rebow* (1706) 1 P. Wms 94; 24 E.R. 309 (Ch.).
63. *Spyer v. Phillipson* [1931] 2 Ch. 183 (C.A.).
64. *Colegrave v. Dias Santos* (1823) 2 B. & C. 76; 107 E.R. 311 (Ch.).
65. See e.g. *Spyer v. Phillipson* [1931] 2 Ch. 183 (C.A.).
66. Cf. *Fisher v. Dixon* (1845) 12 Cl. & Fin. 312; 8 E.R. 1426 (H.L.); *Climie v. Wood* (1869) L.R. 4 Ex. 328 (Exch. Ch.).

of waste and the implied covenant to use the premises in a tenant-like manner.[67] Ornamental and domestic fixtures have been held to be removable only if they can be removed without substantial injury to the premises.[68]

[14.11]   The basic common law rule is that the tenant must exercise his right of removal prior to the termination of the tenancy agreement.[69] However, a number of modifications to this rule have been recognised. Thus, the tenant under a fixed-term lease whose agreement has expired by the effluxion of time (rather than forfeiture or surrender) is allowed a reasonable time after the termination of the lease to remove the fixtures.[70] A similar extension may also be granted to tenancies of uncertain duration (tenancies at will and periodic tenancies) where the court considers that the tenant has not had a reasonable time to remove the fixtures.[71] There is no extension, however, where the lease is determined by a surrender[72] or forfeiture.[73] The validity of the proposition that a tenant has the right to remove trade fixtures within a reasonable time after the determination of the lease in all cases regardless of the manner of the determination is uncertain.[74]

These latter propositions must be reassessed in light of two recent decisions. In *Concepts Property Ltd v. McKay*,[75] the status of the defendant tenant had been in doubt as the tenant claimed the benefit of a fixed-term tenancy pursuant to a disputed equitable assignment. The plaintiff landlord regarded the defendant as merely a monthly periodic tenant and served a notice to quit, which had duly expired by the time of the trial. At the trial the landlord was successful in proving that the claimed equitable assignment was ineffective. The landlord also sought an injunction to prevent the removal of the fixtures by the tenant, arguing that the tenant should have removed the fixtures at the end of the periodic tenancy. The court refused to grant t' ~ injunction, and stated that a tenant should have the right to remove ʃxtures wherever he or she remained in possession under a genuine colour of right to remain there as a tenant; in such cases, the tenant would be allowed a reasonable time to remove his fixtures after the legal issue was resolved. This decision is

---

67. See e.g. *Mancetter Developments Ltd v. Garmanson Ltd* [1986] 1 All E.R. 449 (C.A.); discussed in (1986) 83 L. Soc. Gaz. 3661.
68. *Spyer v. Phillipson* [1931] 2 Ch. 183 (C.A.); *Martin and Coles v. Roe* (1857) 7 El. & Bl. 237; 119 E.R. 1235 (K.B.).
69. *Hooper v. Rawson* [1920] N.Z.G.L.R. 476; *D'Arcy v. Burelli Investments Pty Ltd* (1987) 8 N.S.W.L.R. 317.
70. *Ex parte Brook; Re Roberts* (1878) 10 Ch. D. 100 (C.A.).
71. *Smith v. City Petroleum Co. Ltd* [1940] 1 All E.R. 260; *Braidwood v. Dunn* [1917] N.Z.L.R. 269; *D'Arcy v. Burelli Investments Pty Ltd* (1987) 8 N.S.W.L.R. 317.
72. *Leschallas v. Woolf* [1908] 1 Ch. 641; *Re British Red Ash Collieries Ltd* [1920] 1 Ch. 326 (C.A.); *Slough Picture Hall Co. Ltd v. Wade* (1916) 32 T.L.R. 542.
73. *Pugh v. Arton* (1869) L.R. 8 Eq. 626; *Ex parte Brook; Re Roberts* (1878) 10 Ch. D. 100 (C.A.).
74. See *Clarke v. Tresider* (1867) 4 W.W. & a'B(L) 164; *Bacchus Marsh Brick & Pottery Co. Ltd (in liq.) v. Federal Building Society (in liq.)* (1895) 22 V.L.R. 181.
75. [1984] 1 N.Z.L.R. 560. See also *Weeton v. Woodcock* (1840) 7 M. & W. 14; 151 E.R. 659 (Ex.).

consistent with *New Zealand Government Corporation v. H.M. & S. Ltd,*[76] where the English Court of Appeal held that a tenant remains entitled to remove "tenant's fixtures" in all situations so long as he or she remains in possession.

The common law rules discussed above relating to trade, ornamental and domestic fixtures no longer apply in Victoria, where the tenant's right of removal is now codified by s. 28(2) of the *Landlord and Tenant Act* 1958 (Vic.). This subsection reads:[77]

> "If any tenant holding lands by virtue of any lease or agreement . . . . at his own cost and expense erects any building either detached or otherwise or erects or puts in any building fence engine machinery or fixtures for any purpose whatever (which are not erected or put in in pursuance of some obligation in that behalf) then, unless there is a provision to the contrary in the lease or agreement constituting the tenancy, all such buildings fences engines machinery or fixtures shall be the property of the tenant and shall be removable by him during his tenancy or during such further period of possession by him as he holds the premises but not afterwards."

The subsection goes on to require the tenant to restore the landlord's property to its original condition if damage is caused by the removal of a fixture.

[14.12] Common law did not permit the tenant to remove agricultural fixtures.[78] This rule still applies in South Australia and Western Australia. In the remaining jurisdictions, the position has been altered by State legislation.[79] The position differs slightly from State to State. In each State enactment it is provided[80] that the tenant of farm lands who installs specified categories of farm equipment shall retain title to the equipment and is entitled to remove it for such time as he retains possession of the premises[81] provided that the removal does not damage the landlord's property, or if it does, that the tenant restores the property to its original condition. Pursuant to this legislation, the tenant's right of removal cannot be exercised until the landlord has been given one month's written notice of removal. At any time prior to the expiry of the notice the landlord may elect to purchase the equipment at a value determined by two referees. In New South Wales the provision extends only to land of a minimum size of 8,000 square metres which is used wholly or partly for agricultural or pastoral purposes, and land cultivated as a garden is expressly excluded.[82] In this State, farms outside the scope of the

---

76. [1982] Q.B. 1161 (C.A.).
77. For an illustration of a case containing a "provision to the contrary", see *Dawson v. Stevenson* [1920] V.L.R. 564.
78. *Elwes v. Maw* (1802) 3 East 38; 102 E.R. 510 (K.B.).
79. *Agricultural Holdings Act* 1941 (N.S.W.); *Landlord and Tenant Act* 1958 (Vic.); *Property Law Act* 1974 (Qld); *Landlord and Tenant Act* 1935 (Tas.).
80. N.S.W.: s. 21; Vic.: s. 28(1); Qld: s. 155; Tas.: s. 26.
81. In New South Wales, the property is removable by the tenant within a reasonable time after the termination of the tenancy (s. 21), and in Queensland the property is removable within two months after the termination of the tenancy. s. 155.
82. N.S.W.: s. 4.

legislation are subject to common law rules. In New South Wales, Queensland and South Australia the legislation allows the tenant a limited right to claim compensation at the termination of the tenancy from the landlord for certain specified types of improvement to the extent to which the improvement fairly represents the value of the improvement to an incoming tenant.[83]

If a fixture is classed as irremovable according to the rules discussed above, but the tenant removes the fixture illegally, the landlord may sue the tenant for damages under the doctrine of waste.[84] If the landlord anticipates an illegal act of removal by the tenant, the landlord may obtain an injunction to restrain such removal.[85]

The above-mentioned rules concerning tenant's fixtures presupposes that the tenant wishes to remove all fixtures he or she has installed during the lease. In fact, however, the tenant is not under a legal obligation to remove any of the fixtures.[86]

Except for agricultural fixtures, tenants for life have the same rights in this area of law as enjoyed by tenants of leasehold estates. Thus, on the death of a life tenant, the personal representatives may remove trade, ornamental and domestic fixtures within a reasonable time of the death.[87]

II.   OWNERSHIP OF AIRSPACE

[14.13] Two issues arise for consideration: first, can airspace be regarded in its own right as real property or "land" and be conveyed separately from the soil; and secondly, does the owner of the land surface have a sufficient proprietary interest in the airspace above the land to ground an action for trespass or nuisance against any person who infringes the airspace?

The most common example of the conveyance of airspace is the subdivision and sale of strata title units. This practice is sanctioned and regulated by legislation in each State: see above Chapter 13. Can airspace be conveyed in other circumstances? There appear to have been objections to this in medieval times, but by the time of Coke the right of a person to dispose of her or his holding by horizontal subdivision in a similar manner to vertical subdivision was entrenched at common law. As stated by Coke: "A man may have an inheritance in an upper chamber though the lower buildings and soil be in another, and seeing it is an

---

83. N.S.W.: ss 7-12; Qld: ss 153-167; *Agricultural Holdings Act* 1891 (S.A.), ss 6-22.
84. *Hitchman v. Walton* (1838) 4 M. & W. 409; 150 E.R. 1489 (Ex.); *Smith v. Render* (1857) 27 L.J. Ex. 83.
85. See *Woodfall on Landlord and Tenant*, Vol. 1, para. 1-1577.
86. *Never-Stop Rly (Wembley) Ltd v. British Empire Exhibition (1924) Inc.* [1926] Ch. 877.
87. *Registrar of Titles v. Spencer* (1909) 9 C.L.R. 641; *Leigh v. Taylor* [1902] A.C. 157 (H.L.); *Chateau Douglas Hunter Valley Vineyards Ltd v. Chateau Douglas Hunter Valley Winery & Cellars Ltd (Rec. App.)* [1978] A.C.L.D. 258 (N.S.W. Sup. Ct).

inheritance corporeal it shall pass by livery."[88] This dictum has been cited with approval by both Australian and English courts.[89]

The most recent Australian authority is *Bursill Enterprises Pty Ltd v. Berger Bros Trading Co. Pty Ltd.*[90] In this case, an easement of carriage way was granted "together with all buildings at present erected on said road or gateway and the right to pull down such buildings and to rebuild others at a height of not less than 12 feet from the ground . . . and for any of such purposes to use and to build upon the walls to the extent aforesaid". It was argued, inter alia, that these various rights could not constitute an easement because they purported to confer on the dominant owner the exclusive use of part of the servient tenement. McLelland C.J. in Eq. rejected this argument on the ground that no rights were granted in respect of the land beneath the surface of the soil, and held that a valid easement to maintain an existing building had been created.[91] On appeal, the High Court varied in part the decision of the trial judge and held by a two to one majority (Menzies J. dissenting) that the transfer and grant in respect of the buildings was not of an easement but of a fee simple estate in the defined stratum occupied by the building. This decision turned on the construction of the instrument of transfer and clearly indicates the implicit acceptance by the court of the possibility at law of conveying airspace outside the scope of the strata titles legislation.

Re Lehrer and the Real Property Act[92] is further authority for this proposition. In this case, Jacobs J. held that the airspace contained within the upper floor of a building can be conveyed separately at common law from the soil on which the building stands and classes as real property. His Honour stated:[93]

> "It has not been argued on behalf of either the Registrar-General or any of the applicants for registration of the leases now being considered that there cannot be a good conveyance or transfer in fee simple of air space or of the upper floor of a building. It would appear that the possibility of such a fee has long been stated in English law . . .
>
> It appears that there could be a feoffment of such a part of a building; but the part of a building could be regarded as a tenement and hereditament at common law and could be dealt with in the same manner as could the actual soil upon which the building rested. There have not been many occasions upon which this question has been dealt with directly in the cases, but the little authority that there is appears to be all the one way."

---

88. Co. Litt. 48b; Sheppard's Touchstone 206.
89. See e.g. *Re Lehrer and the Real Property Act* (1961) 61 S.R. (N.S.W.) 365 at 369; *Bursill Enterprises Pty Ltd v. Berger Bros Trading Co. Pty Ltd* (1970) 124 C.L.R. 73 at 91.
90. (1969) 91 W.N. (N.S.W.) 521 (McLelland C.J. in Eq.); (1970) 124 C.L.R. 73 (H.C.). The case is discussed in (1971) 45 A.L.J. 157 and (1972) 46 A.L.J. 39.
91. (1969) 91 W.N. (N.S.W.) 521 at 525.
92. (1961) 61 S.R. (N.S.W.) 365.
93. Ibid. at 369.

Reference should also be made to *Resumed Properties Department v. Sydney M.C.*,[94] where Roper J. stated that "land" may be defined by horizontal as well as vertical boundary and that an estate in fee simple may exist in respect of land so defined where it is held by a private person.

[14.14] The issue arises whether a person who claims title to airspace may apply to the Registrar of Titles to bring her or his interest under the Torrens system. The issue is not expressly dealt with by the Torrens legislation in each State and Territory, but the wording of the enactments strongly suggest that such a right exists. The legislation states that "land" already alienated in fee by the Crown and not under the operation of the Act may be brought under the operation of the Act on the application, inter alia, of the person claiming to be the owner of the fee simple either at law or in equity.[95] "Land" is described in the various Torrens enactments as including any estate or interest in land.[96] As (except in New South Wales) this definition is not exhaustive, the general definition of "land" in the interpretation of legislation enactments would also apply. The New South Wales enactment states that "land" shall include messuages, tenements, hereditaments, corporeal and incorporeal, of any tenure or description and whatever may be the estate or interest therein.[97] In other States, the statutory definition is similar, although not identical.[98] Based on this legislation, it is submitted that a person claiming title to airspace may claim registration. This conclusion is consistent with *Re Lehrer and the Real Property Act*,[99] where Jacobs J. held that the lease or conveyance of an upper chamber of a building would undoubtedly come within the wide definition of "land" contained within s. 21(e) of the *Interpretation Act* 1897 (N.S.W.). Note, however, that this conclusion only applies if the person claiming title to airspace has complied with the terms of local government legislation concerning the subdivision of land. In *Re Lehrer*, the applicant for registration had not lodged a plan of subdivision in accordance with the *Local Government Act* 1919 (N.S.W.). Jacobs J. held that the Registrar-General is not bound to register an instrument which, although otherwise classing as a registrable document, effects an unapproved subdivision.

The ancient maxim, cujus est solum ejus est usque ad coelum et ad inferos, is the starting point for determining the circumstances in which the owner of the land surface has a cause of action against persons who

---

94. (1937) 13 L.G.R. (N.S.W.) 170. See also *Glentham Pty Ltd v. City of Perth* [1986] W.A.R. 205; *Harris v. Ryding* (1839) 5 M. & W. 60; 151 E.R. 27 (Exch.); *Reilly v. Booth* (1890) 44 Ch. D. 12 (C.A.); *Batten Pooll v. Kennedy* [1907] 1 Ch. 256.
95. Torrens statutes: N.S.W.: s. 14(2); Vic.: s. 9; Qld: s. 16; S.A.: s. 27; W.A.: s. 20; Tas.: s. 11(1).
96. Torrens statutes: N.S.W.: s. 3; Vic.: s. 4(1); Qld: s. 3; S.A.: s. 3; W.A.: s. 4(1); Tas.: s. 3(1).
97. *Interpretation Act* 1897 (N.S.W.), s. 21(e).
98. *Interpretation of Legislation Act* 1984 (Vic.), s. 38; *Acts Interpretation Act* 1954 (Qld), s. 36; *Acts Interpretation Act* 1915 (S.A.), s. 4; *Interpretation Act* 1984 (W.A.), s. 5; *Acts Interpretation Act* 1931 (Tas.), s. 46.
99. (1961) 61 S.R. (N.S.W.) 365.

infringe her or his airspace.[100] Loosely translated, the maxim means that
the person who owns the surface of the land also owns both the skyspace
above the surface stretching to the limits of the atmosphere and the soil
beneath the surface down to the centre of the earth. The maxim is
commonly attributed to Coke, although its real origin is lost in history and
may have emanated from Roman law or Jewish law.[101] Its earliest
reference in English law is in *Bury v. Pope*[102] in 1586, a case involving a
claimed prescriptive easement of light.

There is considerable doubt whether the wide application of the maxim
represents the current position at common law. The major case in recent
times supporting the wide application is *Kelsen v. Imperial Tobacco Co. (of
Great Britain & Ireland) Ltd.*[103] In this case, the plaintiff sought an
injunction based on a claim of trespass to airspace to require the defendant
to remove an advertising sign which projected into the airspace above the
plaintiff's shop. McNair J. held that the plaintiff, as tenant, had the right
to use the airspace and that the interference by the sign constituted a
trespass. His conclusion was influenced by the terms of the *Civil Aviation
Act* 1949 (U.K.), s. 40(1), which states:

"No action shall lie in respect of trespass or in respect of nuisance,
by reason only of the flight of an aircraft over any property or height
above the ground, which, having regard to wind, weather and all the
circumstances of the case is reasonable."

His Lordship reasoned that the enactment of this legislation implies that
the legislature considered that the maxim applies in respect of all aircraft
or else such legislation would be unnecessary. As there is legislation in the
Australian States similar to the *Civil Aviation Act* 1949 (U.K.), s. 40(1),[104]
Kelsen's case is a highly persuasive authority in this country.

[14.15]   Other authorities, however, suggest a different result. The best-
known case limiting the scope of the maxim is *Lord Bernstein of Leigh v.
Skyviews & General Ltd.*[105] In this case, the defendants had flown over the
plaintiff's land and had taken an aerial photograph of it with the intention
of selling it to him. The plaintiff unsuccessfully sued the defendants in
trespass on the basis of his alleged unrestricted ownership of the airspace
above his land. Griffith J. distinguished the earlier cases in favour of the

100. On this subject, see also Morgan, "The Law Relating to the Use of Remote
Sensing Techniques in Mineral Exploration" (1982) 56 A.L.J. 30; McKendrick,
"Trespass to Air Space and Property Development" (1988) 138 N.L.J. 23.
101. See Note, (1931) 47 L.Q.R. 14; McNair, *The Law of the Air* (3rd ed., 1964)
App. 1.
102. (1586) Cro. Eliz. 118; 78 E.R. 375 (K.B.).
103. [1957] 2 Q.B. 334. See also *Gifford v. Dent* [1926] W.N. 336. Note, however, that
Morgan, op. cit. at 36, argues that *Kelsen's* case was decided on the basis that
the defendant had deliberately exploited the airspace above the plaintiff's land
and had derived a material benefit for himself by the occupation of the airspace.
There is a dictum by Stamp J. in *Woollerton and Wilson Ltd v. Richard Costain Ltd*
[1970] 1 W.L.R. 411 at 413 supporting this view.
104 See, e.g. *Wrongs Act* 1958 (Vic.), s. 30; *Damage by Aircraft Act* 1952 (N.S.W.),
s. 2(1); *Damage by Aircraft Act* 1963 (Tas.), s. 3; *Air Navigation Regulations* 1920
(Cth), reg. 90.
105. [1978] Q.B. 479.

broad application of the maxim on the ground that they concerned the rights in the airspace immediately adjacent to the surface of the land. His Honour rejected the claim that a landowner's rights extend to an unlimited height, and stated:[106]

> "The problem is to balance the rights of an owner to enjoy the use of his land against the rights of the general public to take advantage of all that science now offers in the use of air space. This balance is in my judgment best struck in our present society by restricting the rights of an owner in the air space above his land to such height as is necessary for the ordinary use and enjoyment of his land and the structures upon it and declaring that above that height he has no greater rights in the air space than any other member of the public."

A further authority in favour of a narrow scope for the maxim is *Graham v. K.D. Morris & Sons Pty Ltd.*[107] In this case, the jib of a crane infringed the airspace of the neighbouring property at certain times when the wind blew from the north. On these occasions the jib was suspended 20 metres over the neighbour's house. On these facts Campbell J. held that there was a trespass to land. Although purporting to apply *Kelsen v. Imperial Tobacco Co. Ltd*, his Honour stated that the plaintiff succeeded because the defendant "interfere[d] with that part of the airspace above her land which is requisite for the proper use and enjoyment of that land".[108] The judge indicated that the proper use and enjoyment was affected inasmuch as the overhanging of the jib could adversely affect the market value of the property. By inference the judgment suggests that there would be no trespass if the infringement of the airspace did not adversely affect the use and enjoyment of the land.

The most recent authority on this issue in *Anchor Brewhouse Developments Ltd v. Berkley House (Docklands Development) Ltd.*[109] The issue in this case was whether trespass to airspace was committed by the boom of a crane oversailing the plaintiff's land. The defendants, although admitting that oversailing regularly occurred both when the crane was operational and when left free-swinging, denied liability on the basis that the operations complained of constituted nuisance rather than trespass and did not cause actual damage. Scott J. held for the plaintiffs and granted an injunction to restrain the continuing trespass. His Lordship stated:[110]

> "A landowner is entitled, as an attribute of his ownership of the land, to place structures on his land and thereby to reduce into actual possession the air space above his land. If an adjoining owner places a structure on his (the adjoining owner's) land that overhangs his neighbour's land, he thereby takes into his possession air space to which his neighbour is entitled. That, in my judgment, is trespass. It does not depend upon any balancing of rights."

---

106. Ibid. at 488.
107. [1974] Qd R. 1. Cf. *Clifton v. Bury* (1887) 4 T.L.R. 8.
108. Ibid. at 4.
109. (1987) 284 E.G. 625. Discussed in (1988) 138 N.L.J. 385.
110. Ibid. at 629.

This appears to represent a shift in judicial thinking from other recent authorities, and a return to a wide view of the cujus est solum doctrine. Scott J. referred to the view in the *Bernstein* case that the critical question is whether the invasion of airspace interfered with the ordinary use and enjoyment of land, and stated that he was not satisfied that this represents a permissible application of Griffiths J.'s approach in *Bernstein*,[111] nor that it would be workable in practice. His Lordship then proceeded to distinguish cases of trespass to airspace caused by structures from trespass to airspace as a result of other cases. He continued:

> "The difficulties posed by overflying aircraft or balloons, bullets or missiles seem to me to be wholly separate from the problem which arises where there is invasion of air space by a structure placed or standing upon the land of a neighbour. One of the characteristics of the common law of trespass is, or ought to be, certainty. The extent of proprietary rights enjoyed by landowners ought to be clear. It may be that, where aircraft or overflying missiles are concerned, certainty cannot be achieved. I do not wish to dissent at all from Griffiths J.'s approach to that problem in the *Bernstein* case. But certainty is capable of being achieved where invasion of air space by tower cranes, advertising signs and other structures are concerned. In my judgment, if somebody erects on his own land a structure, part of which invades the air space above the land of another, the invasion is trespass."[112]

In the light of the existing authorities, the law concerning the aerial extent of the scope of the cujus est solum doctrine must be considered to be unsettled.

III. OWNERSHIP OF MINERALS

[14.16]   In order to determine whether the owner of the land surface also owns the minerals beneath the land, it is first necessary at common law to examine the terms of the original Crown grant and also any subsequent conveyance to determine whether the right to minerals has been reserved in favour of the Crown or any other party. As will be shown later, even if there is no reservation at common law in favour of the Crown, pursuant to State legislation many mineral rights over private land today are vested in the Crown by statutory authority. Thus, having examined the common law position, it is always necessary to examine the extent to which the common law minerals regime has been affected by State legislation.

1. The Common Law Position

[14.17]   Based on the maxim, cujus est solum ejus est usque ad coelum et ad inferos (see above [14.13]), at common law the owner in fee simple

---

111. [1978] Q.B. 479.
112. (1987) 284 E.G. 625 at 629.

of the land surface owns all the subsoil, including minerals,[113] down to the centre of the earth.[114] However, it has always been possible to exclude minerals from the scope of a conveyance, either by express grant or reservation,[115] and common law has always recognised the possibility of separate ownership of the subsoil and/or any minerals lying beneath the surface.[116]

Separate title to minerals is recognised under the Torrens system. In each jurisdiction, the Torrens statute defines "land" widely as including, inter alia, all corporeal and incorporeal hereditaments and/or any estate or interest in land.[117] In *Chirnside v. Registrar of Titles*,[118] the registered proprietor of the land transferred the land surface to a third party but expressly reserved all minerals beneath the land. The Full Court of the Supreme Court of Victoria held that the transfer was registrable and that the transferor was entitled to have issued a separate certificate of title in respect of the minerals. The Court relied on the wide definition of "land" contained in s. 4 of the *Transfer of Land Act* 1915 (Vic.).

The only common law exception to the rule that the owner in fee simple of the land surface owns the minerals beneath the surface relates to precious metals (that is, gold and silver). The *Case of Mines*[119] established that precious metals lying beneath private land belongs to the Crown, together with the right to enter, dig and remove the ores and such other powers as are necessary to effect this purpose. Such minerals were held to pass into private ownership only where "apt and precise words" were contained in the original Crown grant. Initial doubts as to whether this prerogative mineral right applies in Australia were resolved in *Woolley v. Attorney-General (Vic.)*,[120] where the Privy Council held that the prerogative extends to Victoria as part of the common law. The Privy Council stated that it is open to the legislature to curtail or abolish this prerogative right by statute, but this could be achieved only by express words or necessary implication, and no Victorian statute had done so.[121] The decision applies generally to other Australian jurisdictions.

113. It has been held at common law to be a question of fact in each case whether a substance is a mineral (*Waring v. Foden* [1932] 1 Ch. 276 (C.A.)). On this issue, see also Forbes and Lang, *Australian Mining and Petroleum Laws* (2nd ed., Butterworths, Sydney, 1987), para. 407.

114. *Wade v. N.S.W. Rutile Mining Co. Pty Ltd* (1969) 121 C.L.R. 177; *Wilkinson v. Proud* (1843) 11 M. & W. 33; 152 E.R. 704 (Exch.).

115. *Williamson v. Wootton* (1855) 3 Drew. 210; 61 E.R. 883 (V.-C.).

116. *Cox v. Glue* (1848) 5 C.B. 533; 136 E.R. 987 (C.P.). See also *Re Haven Gold Mining Co.* (1882) 20 Ch. D. 151 (C.A.).

117. Torrens statutes: N.S.W.: s. 3(a); Vic.: s. 4(1); Qld: s. 3; S.A.: s. 3; W.A.: s. 4(1); Tas.: s. 3(1). The exact wording of the legislation differs slightly from State to State.

118. [1921] V.L.R. 406.

119. (1568) 1 Plow. 310; 75 E.R. 472 (K.B.). See also *Attorney-General v. Morgan* [1891] 1 Ch. 432 (C.A.); *Attorney-General v. Great Cobar Copper Mining Co.* (1900) 21 N.S.W.R. 351 (F.C.).

120. (1877) 2 App. Cas. 163.

121. Ibid. at 167-168.

2. Statutory Reservation of Minerals[122]

[14.18] The general pattern which developed in each State was to progressively reserve various minerals from Crown grants by legislation. In most cases, such legislation does not apply retrospectively. Thus, the dates of the original Crown grant and the various enactments assume great significance in determining in each instance whether a landowner owns a particular mineral beneath her or his land. It is necessary to consider each State separately.

(a) New South Wales

[14.19] Pursuant to the *Crown Lands Alienation Act* 1861 (N.S.W.), land could be purchased from the Crown either at two pounds per acre, in which case the only reservation was in favour of gold, or at one pound per acre, where all minerals were reserved. "Minerals" were left undefined pursuant to this Act. Regulations dated 13 October 1865 made pursuant to the 1861 Act permitted purchasers to convert their holdings into mineral purchases on payment of the greater amount. A general policy in favour of mineral reservation to the Crown was introduced by the *Crown Lands Act* 1884, which states that all grants of land issued under the Act shall contain a reservation of all minerals.

The 1884 Act has since been replaced by the *Crown Lands Consolidation Act* 1913, which continues the policy in favour of reservation of all minerals.[123] Section 5 states:[124]

> " 'Minerals' means and includes coal kerosene shale and any of the following metals and any ore containing the same, viz—gold silver copper tin iron antimony cinnabar galena nickel cobalt platinum bismuth and manganese and any other substance which may from time to time be declared a mineral within the meaning of this Act by proclamation of the Governor published in the Gazette."

It appears that any proclamations will only apply to grants made after their respective dates and have no retrospective application.

The overall position in New South Wales is that private ownership of minerals will only exist if the Crown grant was dated prior to the 1884 Act and minerals were not expressly exempted prior to that date by the terms of the express grant or the 1861 statute.[125] Two exceptions have recently been created to this position. First, s. 5 of the *Coal Acquisition Act* 1981 (N.S.W.) vests all coal in the State in the Crown and abolishes private ownership of this mineral. Secondly, s. 45(2) of the *Aboriginal Land Rights Act* 1983 (N.S.W.) states that notwithstanding any other Act, where land

---

122. The following discussion is based in part on Forbes and Lang, op. cit., paras 204ff.
123. Miscellaneous provisions reserving minerals are also contained in the *Western Lands Act* 1901 (N.S.W.), the *Prickly-Pear Act* 1924 (N.S.W.) and the *Closer Settlement Act* 1904 (N.S.W.).
124. See Forbes and Lang, op. cit., para. 205 for the details of various proclamations.
125. Note that the right of conversion allowed by the 1865 regulations survived despite the introduction of the 1884 Act and continued to apply until 1909 to minerals other than coal, and 1913 for coal.

is transferred to an Aboriginal land council or where a council otherwise acquires land, any mineral resources which were previously vested in the Crown shall become vested in the Aboriginal land council.

(b) Victoria

[14.20] A similar scheme of progressive reservation of minerals in favour of the Crown was applied in Victoria. However, the effect of the *Mines (Amendment) Act* 1983 (Vic.) is that all privately owned minerals in the State have reverted to the Crown on the expiration of 12 months from the date of commencement of s. 291 of the *Mines Act* 1958 (30 October 1984). Section 291 states in part:

"(1) On and from the day (in this section called "the appointed day") on which a period of twelve months from the date of commencement of this section expires, all minerals (other than gold, silver, uranium, thorium and oil shale) whether on or below the surface of land alienated from the Crown on or before 1 March 1892 are and shall be and remain the property of the Crown.

(2) Gold, silver, uranium and thorium and oil shale, whether on or below the surface of any land whatever in Victoria, whether alienated or not alienated from the Crown, and if alienated whenever alienated, are and shall be and remain the property of the Crown.

(3) All minerals other than minerals which are already the property of the Crown by virtue of sub-section (2) on or below the surface of land alienated from the Crown after 1 March, 1892, whether before or after the commencement of this section are and shall be and remain the property of the Crown.

(4) Where a substance is declared to be a mineral for the purposes of this Act the substance shall be and remain the property of the Crown.

(5) This section has effect notwithstanding anything to the contrary in any other Act."

Section 3(1) of the 1958 Act (as amended) defines "mineral" as:

"(a) any substance (excluding water) which occurs naturally as part of the earth's crust;

(b) any substance which may be extracted from a substance to which paragraph (a) applies; and

(c) a substance that is declared to be a mineral or is included in a class of substances declared to be minerals for the purposes of this interpretation, to the extent to which and in the circumstances in which the declaration is expressed to apply—

other than—

(d) petroleum within the meaning of the Petroleum Act 1958;

(e) stone within the meaning of the Extractive Industries Act 1966;

(f) living matter; and

(g) a substance declared not to be a mineral for the purposes of this interpretation, to the extent to which and in the circumstances in which the declaration is expressed to apply.''

(c) Queensland

[14.21]　Section 110(2) of the *Mining Act* 1968 (Qld) states the basic rule that all minerals (except coal) are vested in the Crown except those contained in grants made under the *Crown Lands Alienation Act* 1860, the *Crown Lands Alienation Act* 1868 and the *Minerals Lands Act* 1870. Section 7(1) defines ''mineral'' as:

''Any substance which occurs naturally as part of the earth's crust and any substance which may be extracted from such a substance: Save where otherwise expressly included the term does not include—

(a) living matter;

(b) petroleum within the meaning of the *Petroleum Act* 1923-1982;

(c) soil, sand, gravel, rock or water to be used or to be supplied for use as such, whether intact or in a broken form;

(d) to the extent it is so declared, any other substance for the time being declared by the Governor in Council not to be a mineral for the purposes of this Act either generally or in the circumstances so declared.

The term includes and, in the case of substances referred to in provisions (e), (f) or (g), it is declared always did include—

(e) shale from which mineral oil may be extracted or produced;

(f) mineral oil extracted or produced from shale or coal or other rock by some chemical or thermal process;

(g) hydrocarbons and other substances or matter occurring in association with shale or coal and necessarily mined, extracted, produced or released by or in connexion with mining for shale or coal or the extraction or production of mineral oil therefrom;

(h) to the extent it is so declared, any substance (including any substance referred to in provisions (a), (b) or (c) of this definition) for the time being declared by Order in Council to be a mineral for the purposes of this Act either generally or in the circumstances so declared.''

Section 110(1) confirms the Crown prerogative in respect of gold, and the better view appears to be that the prerogative in favour of silver is also preserved. The ownership of coal is determined by s. 110(3), which vests ownership in the Crown in respect of all land alienated after 1 March 1910, plus limited rights in respect of other land.

(d) South Australia

[14.22]　Pursuant to s. 16 of the *Mining Act* 1971 (S.A.), property in all minerals belongs to the Crown. ''Minerals'' is defined in s. 6 as:

"(a) any naturally occurring deposit of metal or metalliferous ore, precious stones, or any other mineral (including sand, gravel, stone, shell, shale and clay);

(b) any metal, metalliferous substance, or mineral recoverable from the sea or a natural water supply;

or

(c) any metal, metalliferous ore, or mineral, dumped or discarded in the course of mining operations, or operations incidental thereto."

The definition goes on to exclude soil and petroleum.

Section 19 safeguards persons who were divested of minerals pursuant to the 1971 Act. Where a private mine has been established, a person divested of her or his property in minerals may apply to the Minister for the right to receive royalty collected upon minerals recovered after the date of the application: s. 19(17). Any dispute may be referred to the Land and Valuation Court: s. 19(19). No application may be made in respect of "extractive minerals" (s. 19(18)), which are defined in s. 6 as "sand, gravel, stone, shell, shale or clay but does not include fire clay, bentonite or kaolin".

(e) Western Australia

[14.23] Pursuant to s. 9(1) of the *Mining Act* 1978 (W.A.), "all gold, silver and any other precious metal" belong to the Crown. Other minerals not alienated in fee simple prior to 1 January 1899 are Crown property. Section 9 of the 1978 Act is in identical form to s. 138 of the now-repealed *Mining Act* 1904. However, the definition of "minerals" differs. Section 8(1) of the 1978 Act (as amended), defines "minerals" as including:

"all naturally occurring substances, not being soil or a substance the recovery of which is governed by the *Petroleum Act* 1967 or the *Petroleum (Submerged Lands) Act* 1982, obtained or obtainable from any land by mining operations carried out on or under the surface of the land, including evaporites, limestone, rock, gravel, shale (whether or not oil shale) sand and clay except that where—

(a) limestone, rock or gravel;

(b) shale, other than oil shale;

(c) sand, other than mineral sands, silica sand or garnet sand; or

(d) clay, other than kaolin, bentonite, attapulgite, or montmorillonite,

occurs on private land, that limestone, rock, gravel, shale, sand or clay shall not be taken to be minerals."

In contrast, "minerals" in the 1904 Act are defined in s. 3 as "all minerals other than gold, and all precious stones". The issue thus arises whether the 1978 Act has expropriated from Crown grants prior to 1978 the wider range of minerals encompassed within the more modern definition. The issue awaits judicial resolution, but as a matter of statutory interpretation it appears that the 1978 Act has effected an expropriation.

(f) Tasmania

[14.24] Legislative reservation of minerals from Crown grants dated from 14 November 1893. This results from s. 25 of the *Mining (Amendment) Act* 1911 (Tas.), which states that all minerals except gold and silver in lands alienated since 14 November 1893 are Crown property.

Crown grants made since 1905 are also subject to the *Crown Lands Act* 1976 (Tas.). Section 16(3) reserves to the Crown all "gold, silver, copper, tin, or other metals, ore, mineral, or other substances containing metals, or gems or precious stones, or coal or mineral oil" in any grant, deed or transfer of any Crown land. Pursuant to s. 54(1), all Crown land sold shall be deemed to have been sold as regards the surface and to a depth of 15 metres below the surface unless the Minister otherwise determines. The reservation to the Crown in the 1976 Act is copied from the terms of both the *Crown Lands Act* 1905 and the *Crown Lands Act* 1911.

3. Petroleum and Helium

[14.25] All the States have legislated to ensure complete Crown ownership over petroleum and helium under private land regardless of when the relevant Crown grant was made. For example, s. 6 of the *Petroleum Act* 1955 (N.S.W.) states:[126]

"(1) Notwithstanding anything to the contrary in any Act or in any grant, lease, licence or other instrument of title or tenure or other document, all petroleum and helium existing in a natural state on or below the surface of any land in the State whether alienated from the Crown or not and, if alienated, whether the alienation took place before or after the commencement of this section, shall be and shall be deemed at all times to have been the property of the Crown.

No compensation shall be payable by the Crown for any such petroleum or helium which before the commencement of this section was vested in any person other than the Crown.

(2) All Crown grants and leases and every licence and other instrument of title or tenure under any Act relating to lands of the Crown (other than petroleum exploration licences, petroleum prospecting licences and petroleum mining leases) shall, whether granted before or after the commencement of this section, be deemed to contain a reservation to the Crown of all petroleum and helium existing in a natural state on or below the surface of the land comprised therein or demised thereby."

---

126. See also *Petroleum Act* 1958 (Vic.), s. 5; *Petroleum Act* 1923 (Qld), ss 5, 6; *Petroleum Act* 1940 (S.A.), s. 4; *Petroleum Act* 1967 (W.A.), s. 9; *Mining Act* 1929 (Tas.), s. 28.

The legislation in the other States differs slightly in its wording, but is to similar effect.

Each statute defines "petroleum". The following definition in s. 3 of the *Petroleum Act* 1955 (N.S.W.) is typical:[127]

> " 'Petroleum' means naturally occurring hydrocarbons in a free state, whether in the form of natural gas or in a liquid or solid form, but does not include—
>
> (a) helium occurring in association with petroleum; or
>
> (b) coal or shale or any substance which may be extracted from coal, shale or other rock by the application of heat or by a chemical process."

4. Atomic Substances

[14.26] Part III of the *Atomic Energy Act* 1953 (Cth) reserves to the Commonwealth powers over "prescribed substances". These powers shall only be exercised for the purposes of defence or in relation to substances situated, or things done or proposed to be done, in a Territory: s. 34. "Prescribed substance" means "uranium, thorium, plutonium, neptunium or any of their respective compounds, and includes any other substance that is specified in the regulations as a substance that is or may be used for or in connection with the production of atomic energy or for research into matters connected with atomic energy".

Section 41 vests power in the Commonwealth to mine "prescribed substances". Section 41(1) states:

> "Where it appears to the Minister that a prescribed substance, or minerals from which, in the opinion of the Minister, a prescribed substance can be obtained, is or are present on or under the whole or a part of an area of land, either in a natural state or in a deposit of waste material obtained from an underground or surface working, the Minister may, by writing under his hand, authorize a person to carry on, on behalf of the Commonwealth, operations in accordance with this section on that land."

Pursuant to s. 41(3), all prescribed substances and minerals mined pursuant to this power are by force of this section vested in the Commonwealth. Any person who suffers loss or damage as a result of the exercise of the powers contained in s. 41 or who had a right, title or interest in the prescribed substance or minerals may claim compensation: s. 42.

In Victoria and Tasmania, atomic substances are automatically vested in the Crown. Section 508(1) of the *Mines Act* 1958 states:

> "Notwithstanding anything in this Act or any other Act or in any grant lease licence or other instrument of title or tenure or other document, all uranium and thorium on or below the surface of all land in Victoria, whether alienated or not alienated from the Crown,

___
127. See also Petroleum statutes: Vic.: s. 3(1); Qld: s. 3; S.A.: s. 3(1); W.A.: s. 5(1); Tas.: s. 2(1) (definition of "oil").

and if alienated whensoever alienated, are and shall be deemed always to have been the property of the Crown."

Section 2B of the *Mining Act* 1929 (Tas.) is to similar effect except that in addition to uranium and thorium it includes any other substance declared by the Minister to be an atomic substance. There is no similar legislation in the other Australian States.

IV. LAND BOUNDARIES[128]

1. Land Adjoining the Seashore

[14.27] Where there is a Crown grant describing the land conveyed as abutting the seashore, unless it is expressly stated to the contrary it is presumed that the boundary line is the mean high water mark.[129] This is the level reached by the ordinary high tide, which is taken as the average between the spring and neap tides.[130] The Supreme Court of New South Wales held in *Verrall v. Nott*[131] that this rule applies to Torrens land as well as general law land and applies even if a certificate of title is issued containing a plan marking the boundary.[132] In Western Australia, the law is partially modified by s. 16(3) of the *Land Act* 1933, which states:

> "The boundaries of any lands fronting on the ocean, or any sound, bay, or creek, or any part thereof affected by the ebb or flow of the tide, or on any lake, lagoon, swamp, river or main stream, shall be limited in every case where possible by straight lines, as near to the high water mark as the Minister shall decide, and such lines shall be marked on the ground, and the land between such lines and the water shall vest in the Crown."

The property in the soil of the seashore below the high water mark belongs to the Crown in right of the State.[133] This common law rule is reaffirmed in Queensland by s. 77(1) of the *Harbours Act* 1955, which states that all foreshores shall, unless and until the contrary is proved, be deemed to be Crown property. Despite the fact that ownership in the seashore is in the Crown, the public has a right of navigation,[134] which

---

128. See generally Moore, "Land by the Water" (1968) 41 A.L.J. 32; and Jackson, "Alluvio and the Common Law" (1983) 99 L.Q.R. 412.
129. *Hill v. Lyne* (1893) 14 N.S.W.L.R. 449 (F.C.); *Attorney-General v. Chambers* (1854) 4 De G.M. & G. 206; 43 E.R. 486 (Ch.); *Fowley Marine (Emsworth) Ltd v. Gafford* [1967] 2 All E.R. 472.
130. *Attorney-General v. Chambers* (1854) 4 De G.M. & G. 206; 43 E.R. 486 (Ch.); *Tracey Elliot v. Earl of Morley* (1907) 51 Sol. J. 625.
131. (1939) 39 S.R. (N.S.W.) 89. See also *Auty v. Thompson* (1903) 5 N.Z.G.L.R. 541.
132. The principle of indefeasibility of title in the Torrens legislation does not extend to measurements included in a certificate of title. Extrinsic evidence may be adduced to prove the intended land boundaries. See Moore, op. cit., at 533.
133. *Blundell v. Catteral* (1821) 5 B. & Ald. 268; 106 E.R. 1190 (K.B.); *Attorney-General v. Emerson* [1891] A.C. 649 (H.L.); *Malcolmson v. O'Dea* (1863) 10 H.L.C. 593; 11 E.R. 1155 (H.L.).
134. *R. v. Ward* (1836) 4 Ad. & El. 384; 111 E.R. 832 (K.B.).

extends to the rights of trade and commerce as well as the right of passage, and includes the right to fix moorings and to anchor.[135]

By virtue of the doctrine of accretion, land which is gained gradually and imperceptibly from the sea is the property of the owner of the adjoining land.[136] This doctrine has been held to apply to cases where the adjacent land is Torrens land as well as to general law land.[137] "Imperceptible" has been held to mean imperceptible in day to day progress; the fact that the result after a long period of time is clearly perceptible is irrelevant.[138] It appears that the doctrine does not operate without qualification, and may be excluded by express words contained in the conveyance of transfer document. This might arise, for example, if the conveyance referred to the foreshore as it was from time to time, rather than the foreshore as it was at the time of the conveyance.[139] Such a grant is referred to as a "movable freehold".[140] The doctrine is not limited to cases of accretion due to the action of water. Thus, the Privy Council held in *Southern Centre of Theosophy Inc. v. South Australia*[141] that accretion can apply to an increase in land area caused solely by the advance of sand dunes caused by the wind.

Where the increase in land is perceptible, pursuant to the doctrine of avulsion the land boundary does not change and the land gained is the property of the Crown.[142]

The fact that the owner of adjoining land contributes to the natural process of accretion by conducting artificial works does not prevent the doctrine of accretion applying provided that there was no intention by the landowner of assisting the natural process.[143] However, the doctrine of accretion will not apply where the additional land is formed solely due to artificial reclamation; in this case, the land will belong to the Crown.[144] Thus, for example, in *Attorney-General v. Reeve*[145] the Divisional Court of the Queen's Bench held that land gained from the sea which resulted from harbour works and the removal of sand and shingle authorised by legislation was the property of the Crown. This matter is still governed by common law throughout Australia. The only relevant statutory provision is in Queensland, where the common law position is reaffirmed

135. *Attorney-General v. Wright* [1897] 2 Q.B. 318 (C.A.).
136. *Gifford v. Lord Yarborough* (1828) 5 Bing. 163; 130 E.R. 1023 (H.L.).
137. *Southern Centre of Theosophy Inc. v. South Australia* [1982] A.C. 706 (P.C.).
138. *R. v. Lord Yarborough* (1828) 2 Bli. N.S. 147; 4 E.R. 1087 (H.L.); *Gifford v. Lord Yarborough* (1828) 5 Bing. 163; 130 E.R. 1023 (H.L.).
139. See *Baxendale v. Instow P.C.* [1981] 2 All E.R. 620.
140. This phrase is used by Bailey J. in *Scratton v. Brown* (1825) 4 B. & C. 485 at 498; 107 E.R. 1140 at 1145-1146. See generally Howarth, "The Doctrine of Accretion: Qualifications, Ancient and Modern" [1986] Conv. 247; Annand, "Movable Fees" [1982] Conv. 208.
141. [1982] A.C. 706; discussed in (1983) 99 L.Q.R. 412.
142. *Gifford v. Lord Yarborough* (1828) 5 Bing. 163; 130 E.R. 1023 (H.L.); *Doe d. Seebkristo v. East India Co.* (1856) 10 Moo. P.C. 140; 14 E.R. 445 (P.C.).
143. *Verrall v. Nott* (1939) 39 S.R. (N.S.W.) 89; *Brighton and Hove General Gas Co. v. Hove Bungalows Ltd* [1924] 1 Ch. 372.
144. *Attorney-General (Southern Nigeria) v. John Holt & Co. (Liverpool) Ltd* [1915] A.C. 599 at 615 (P.C.).
145. (1885) 1 T.L.R. 675.

by s. 78 of the *Harbours Act* 1955, which states that any land raised or reclaimed, whether imperceptibly or otherwise, as a result of the construction of any harbour works belongs to the Crown.

Where land is gradually and imperceptibly lost as a result of encroachment by the sea, property in the land covered belongs to the Crown and is lost to the adjoining landowner.[146] Property remains in the adjoining landowner, however, where there is an avulsive change and the original marks of ownership remain (for example, where the sea encroaches suddenly as a result of a storm).[147] The landowner's title is not extinguished in these circumstances by the passage of time, and he or she may seek at any time to regain the land by reclamation works. The adjoining landowner also has the right at common law to undertake any work necessary to prevent the loss of her or his land by erosion.[148]

Sudden encroachment by the sea may lead to the formation of islands. Where the island was part of the mainland at the time of the Crown grant, property in the island will belong to the adjoining landowner.[149] Where, however, islands are created by other means (for example, volcanic activity), property vests in the Crown.[150]

The above rules relating to accretion and encroachment have been justified on the grounds of convenience and fairness. The Privy Council stated in *Southern Centre of Theosophy Inc. v. South Australia*:[151]

"Except in cases where a substantial and recognisable change in boundary has suddenly taken place (to which the doctrine of accretion does not apply), it is manifestly convenient to continue to regard the boundary between land and water as being where it is from day to day or year to year. To do so is also fair. If part of an owner's land is taken from him by erosion, or diluvion (that is, advance of the water) it would be most inconvenient to regard the boundary as extending into the water: the landowner is treated as losing a portion of his land. So, if an addition is made to the land from what was previously water, it is only fair that the landowner's title should extend to it. The doctrine of accretion, in other words, is one which arises from the nature of land ownership from, in fact, the long-term ownership of property inherently subject to gradual processes of change."

2. Land Adjoining Tidal Navigable Rivers

[14.28] As in the case of land adjoining the seashore, in the case of a Crown grant describing land as abutting a tidal, navigable river it is

146. *Re Hull and Selby Rly* (1839) 5 M. & W. 327; 151 E.R. 139 (Ex.); *Humphrey v. Burrell* [1951] N.Z.L.R. 262 (C.A.).
147. Coulson and Forbes, *The Law of Waters and Land Drainage* (6th ed., Sweet and Maxwell, 1952), p. 42.
148. *R. v. Commissioners of Sewers for Pagham (Sussex)* (1828) 8 B. & C. 355; 108 E.R. 1075 (K.B.).
149. Hale, *De Jure Maris*, cap. VI; Fleta lib. 3, c. 2, s. 6.
150. *Secretary of State (India) v. Chelikani Rama Rao* (1916) 85 L.J.P.C. 222.
151. See also *Re Hull and Selby Rly* (1839) 5 M. & W. 327, 151 E.R. 139 (Ex.); *Attorney-General (Southern Nigeria) v. John Holt & Co. (Liverpool) Ltd* [1915] A.C. 599 (P.C.).

presumed in the absence of express words to the contrary that the mean high water mark is the boundary.[152]

Title to the bed of a tidal, navigable river (the alveus) is treated differently at common law to non-tidal and tidal but non-navigable rivers. Whether a particular river is tidal is a question of fact in each case. Presumably tidal will be given its normal meaning of waters caused to ebb and flow periodically as a result of the gravitational effect of the moon and the sun.[153] Note, however, that tidal rivers have been held not to be limited to salt water, but will include fresh water ponded back.[154] There is no exhaustive statutory definition of "tide", "tidal river" or "tidal water" in any Australian jurisdiction, although s. 4 of the *Local Government Act* 1919 (N.S.W.), defines "tidal waters" as including "the waters of the sea or of any lake, estuary, harbour, river, bay or lagoon in which the tide ebbs and flows".[155] If a river is found to be tidal, it is deemed to be navigable at common law; conversely, non-tidal rivers, even though navigable in fact, are deemed not to be navigable in law.[156]

The common law rule is that title to the alveus of a tidal, navigable river vests in the Crown as far as the mean high water mark.[157] Crown ownership in the alveus does not affect the common law public rights of fishery and navigation, which apply to all tidal waters unless modified by statute.[158] In Western Australia and Queensland, the common law rule has been affected by s. 16(3) of the *Land Act* 1933 (W.A.) (see above [14.27]) and s. 77 of the *Harbours Act* 1955 (Qld) (see above [14.27]), both of which apply equally to tidal rivers and the seashore.

The common law rules concerning the effect of accretion, avulsion and encroachment on title to land apply to land adjoining tidal navigable rivers as well as to land adjoining the seashore.

3. Land Adjoining Non-Tidal Rivers

[14.29]   If a non-tidal river flows through private land, the alveus belongs to the landowner.[159] If, however, a non-tidal river marks the boundary between two blocks of land, there is a presumption at common law that each adjoining landowner separately owns the alveus ad medium filum.[160] This presumption applies regardless of the breadth of the river. The middle line will be determined in line with the position of the banks

---

152. *Hill v. Lyne* (1893) 14 N.S.W.L.R. 449 (F.C.); *Attorney-General v. Chambers* (1854) 4 De G.M. & G. 206; 43 E.R. 486 (Ch.).
153. See *Earl of Ilchester v. Rashleigh* (1889) 5 T.L.R. 739.
154. *R. v. Smith* (1780) 2 Doug. 441; 99 E.R. 283 (K.B.); *Hume v. MacKenzie* (1839) 6 Cl. & Fin. 628; 7 E.R. 834 (H.L.).
155. See also the definition of "tidal waters" in *Fisheries and Oyster Farms Act* 1935 (N.S.W.), s. 4(1).
156. *Re Waldron* (1893) 3 L.C.C. 144 at 159 (N.S.W. Land App. Ct).
157. *Attorney-General v. Earl of Lonsdale* (1868) L.R. 7 Eq. 377.
158. *Mayor of Colchester v. Brooke* (1845) 7 Q.B. 339; 115 E.R. 518 (K.B.); *Williams v. Wilcox* (1838) 8 Ad. & E. 314; 112 E.R. 857 (K.B.); *Malcolmson v. O'Dea* (1862) 10 H.L.C. 593; 11 E.R. 1155 (H.L.).
159. *Orr Ewing v. Colquhoun* (1877) 2 A.C. 839 (H.L.).
160. *Hesketh v. Willis Cruisers Ltd* (1968) 19 P. & C.R. 573 (C.A.); *Blount v. Layard* [1891] 2 Ch. 681n; *Micklethwait v. Newlay Bridge Co.* (1886) 33 Ch. D. 133 (C.A.).

at either side of the river when the river is in its normal condition (that is, not in flood or drought).[161] The common law ad medium filum presumption was held to be applicable to Crown grants in New South Wales[162] (and presumably elsewhere in Australia) and to land held under the Torrens system. Authority for the latter proposition is *Lanyon Pty Ltd v. Canberra Washed Sands Pty Ltd*,[163] where the High Court held that the ad medium filum rule applied to a certificate of title issued pursuant to the *Real Property Act* 1925 (A.C.T.), which made no mention of the common law. The argument that the common law rule was inappropriate in respect of Torrens land, was rejected.[164]

Gradual and imperceptible changes in the course of a river lead to progressive alteration of the adjacent land boundaries at common law. However, in the case of avulsive change, the land boundaries are unaffected and the original central point in the river continues to be the boundary even if the effect of this is that the river runs entirely through the land of one of the original adjoining owners.[165]

The ad medium filum rule has been either abrogated or restricted in its operation in many jurisdictions. In Victoria, it has been abrogated by s. 5 of the *Water Act* 1958 (Vic.) in the following terms:

"Where any river creek stream or water-course or any lake forms the boundary or part of the boundary of an allotment of land alienated before the commencement of the Water Act 1905 by the Crown the bed and banks thereof shall be deemed to have remained the property of the Crown and not to have passed with the land so alienated.

Where any river creek stream or water-course or any lake lagoon swamp or marsh forms the boundary or part of the boundary of an allotment of land alienated after the commencement of the said Act by the Crown the bed and banks thereof shall notwithstanding such alienation remain the property of the Crown and shall not pass with the land so alienated.

In any case whether of land alienated before or after the commencement of the said Act by the Crown such bed and banks shall be and remain the property of the Crown notwithstanding that one and the same person has been or is the owner of the lands adjacent to both banks or holds or obtains a consolidated certificate under the Transfer of Land Act 1958 or any corresponding enactment previously enforced in respect of such lands."

Similar, although not identical, legislation exists in Queensland and Western Australia.[166] The legislation in all these jurisdictions gives the

---

161. *Kingdon v. Hutt River Board* (1905) 25 N.Z.L.R. 145 (S.C. in banco); *Hindson v. Ashby* [1896] 2 Ch. 1 (C.A.).
162. *Lord v. Commissioners (Sydney)* (1859) 12 Moo. P.C. 473; 14 E.R. 991; *Attorney-General v. White* (1925) 26 S.R. (N.S.W.) 216.
163. (1966) 115 C.L.R. 342.
164. Cf. *Rotter v. Canadian Exploration Ltd* (1959) 23 D.L.R. (2d) 136 (B.C.C.A.).
165. See e.g. *Mayor of Carlisle v. Graham* (1869) L.R. 4 Exch. 361; *Ford v. Lacy* (1861) 7 H. & N. 151, 158 E.R. 429 (Ex.). See also *Dickinson v. Brown* [1989] A.C.L.D. 144 (Vic. Sup. Ct).
166. *Water Act* 1926 (Qld), s. 5; *Rights in Water and Irrigation Act* 1914 (W.A.), s. 15(1).

owner of the land adjacent to the watercourse access thereto and a remedy in trespass.[167]

In New South Wales, s. 235A(8) of the *Crown Lands Consolidation Act* 1913, states:

> "Where under the Crown Lands Act the bed of any river has been reserved from sale or lease no person shall by reason of his being the owner of any land adjoining the river which has been subsequently alienated as bounded by or by reference to or by the margin or bank of the river be entitled to any rights of access over or to the user of any part of the bed of the river other than to such rights as are or have been acquired either before or after the commencement of the Crown Lands (Amendment) Act, 1931, under or pursuant to the Water Act, 1912."

This section operates retrospectively upon Crown grants in the Eastern and Central Divisions of New South Wales as from 3 May 1918 and in the Western Division as from 31 May 1935.[168] While this section does not directly affect the ad medium filum rule, the overall effect is to remove all practical benefits from the right of ownership of the alveus.

There is no relevant legislation in the remaining jurisdictions.[169] Thus, the common law ad medium filum rule applies unabated in South Australia and Tasmania.

4. Land Adjoining Lakes and Pools

[14.30] Lakes and pools in this context mean standing fresh water not subject to a current. The terms do not extend to salt water lagoons.

At common law, the ad medium filum rule determined the ownership of the alveus of lakes and pools equally to that of non-tidal rivers.[170] This rule, however, has been expressly abrogated by legislation in respect of all lakes and pools in New South Wales, Victoria, Queensland and Western Australia.[171] In these jurisdictions, title to the alveus vests in the Crown. In the remaining jurisdictions, the common law continues to vest title in the adjoining landowners.

---

167. Vic.: s. 7; Qld: s. 7; W.A.: s. 16.
168. Woodman, p. 33.
169. Section 5 of the now-repealed *Control of Waters Act* 1919 stated:
> "Where any watercourse to which this Act applies forms the boundary, or part of the boundary, of any land which after the date of the passing of this Act is alienated by the Crown, the bed and banks of such watercourse shall, notwithstanding such alienation, remain the property of the Crown and shall not pass with the land so alienated."

This Act was repealed by the *Water Resources Act* 1976 (S.A.), which contains no provision relating to title to the alveus. Accordingly, the common law ad medium filum rule appears to apply in South Australia.
170. Coulson and Forbes, op. cit., p. 124.
171. *Crown Lands Consolidation Act* 1913 (N.S.W.), s. 235A(3); *Water Act* 1958 (Vic.), s. 5; *Water Act* 1926 (Qld), s. 5; *Rights in Water and Irrigation Act* 1914 (W.A.), s. 15(1). In relation to the position in South Australia, see fn. 169 above.

Despite earlier English authority to the contrary,[172] the Privy Council held in *Southern Centre of Theosophy Inc. v. South Australia*[173] that the doctrine of accretion is capable of being applied to land adjoining lakes as well as to land adjoining rivers and the seashore. In this case, the doctrine was applied to an inland lake in South Australia in the absence of any State legislation modifying the common law position. This decision will be applicable in all other Australian jurisdictions except New South Wales, where s. 235A(6) of the *Crown Lands Consolidation Act* 1913 states that the doctrine of accretion shall not apply and shall be deemed never to have applied to a non-tidal lake.

5. Land Adjoining Artificial Watercourses

[14.31] Title to the alveus of artificial watercourses constructed by a private landowner over her or his own land will remain the property of the landowner. Where such a watercourse is constructed on the land of another person, title to the alveus will depend on the terms of the relevant instrument.[174] Where a watercourse is constructed pursuant to legislation (for example, a canal), title to the alveus will be dependent upon the terms of the legislation.

6. Land Adjoining Public Roads

[14.32] In Australia, the common law principle that the owners of land adjoining a public road own the soil of the road usque ad medium filum viae has not gained judicial acceptance. Authority for this proposition is *Garibaldi Mining & Crushing Co. v. Cravens New Chum Co. N.L.*,[175] where Williams J. stated:[176]

> "The doctrine of ad medium filum viae is one that is founded in the mother country on the presumption that the fee in the soil of the road belongs to the owners of the adjoining lands on either side. That presumption has arisen in England from the fact of the antiquity of the roads. It is a presumption of convenience on account of the impossibility in a great many cases, and the difficulty in others, of going back through a series of centuries to ascertain the title to the soil of the road, or in many cases the title to the adjoining land. . . . That reason does not apply to the roads in this country. We know that the soil of the roads in Victoria is vested in the Crown, so that the reason for the presumption does not exist here."

The only exception recognised in this country is in respect of roads created by a private individual.[177]

---

172. *Trafford v. Thrower* (1929) 45 T.L.R. 502.
173. [1982] A.C. 706 at 715.
174. See e.g. *Badger v. South Yorkshire Rly and River Dun Navigation Co.* (1858) 28 L.J.Q.B. 118 (Exch. Ch.).
175. (1884) 10 V.L.R. (L.) 233 (F.C.). See also *Barker v. Adelaide C.C.* [1900] S.A.L.R. 29 (S.C. in banco); *Tierney v. Loxton* (1891) 12 L.R. (N.S.W.) 308 (F.C.).
176. (1884) 10 V.L.R. (L.) 233 at 239-240.
177. *Harris v. Sydney M.C.* (1910) 10 S.R. (N.S.W.) 860 (F.C.).

Legislation enacted in each Australian jurisdiction now affirms that the ownership in the soil of public roads vests in the Crown and that the ad medium filum rule has no application. For example, s. 518 of the *Local Government Act* 1958 (Vic.), states:[178]

> "It is hereby declared and enacted that notwithstanding any presumption of law to the contrary the absolute property in the land hereto before or hereafter reserved or proclaimed under the Land Act 1958 or any corresponding previous enactment as a road street or highway is and shall be registered in the Crown."

7. Incorrect Description of Boundaries

[14.33]   In Victoria, a margin of error is allowed in the description of boundaries. By virtue of the *Property Law Act* 1958 (Vic.), s. 272, unless there is an express agreement to the contrary, no action shall be brought · if the margin of difference between a boundary line as stated in a document and as measured on the ground is less than 50 millimetres irrespective of its length where its length does not exceed 40.3 metres. Where the length of a boundary exceeds 40.3 metres, the maximum margin is one in five hundred computed on the total length of the boundary line. This rule applies to all land, regardless of whether it is registered under the Torrens system: *Property Law Act* 1958, s. 273. No similar legislation appears to exist in the other States.

V.   ENCROACHMENTS

1. Buildings Erected Under Mistake of Title

[14.34]   The situation may arise that a person builds on land belonging to another person. The resolution of the questions of ownership and compensation between the builder and the landowner turns on State legislation in Queensland and Western Australia, but in the remaining Australian jurisdictions is based on common law principles.

The position at common law is as follows if B builds on A's land. Prima facie ownership of the building will vest in A pursuant to the doctrine of fixtures[179] and B will be unable to claim compensation. However, in certain circumstances B will be able to raise equitable estoppel or the equity of acquiescence[180] (sometimes referred to as the rule in *Ramsden v. Dyson*)[181] as a defence to prevent A from asserting his title against him. If the equity of acquiescence applies, B will also have a cause of action

---

178. See also *Local Government Act* 1919 (N.S.W.), s. 232; *Local Government Act* 1934 (S.A.), s. 306(1); *Local Government Act* 1960 (W.A.), s. 286(1); *Roads and Jetties Act* 1935 (Tas.), s. 8(1). In Queensland, there appears to be no statutory declaration of ownership of public roads; however, the *Local Government Act* 1936 refers to encroachments, so by implication the local councils must own the roads: see e.g. s. 35(8)(ix).
179. See above **[14.02]**ff. for a discussion of the doctrine of fixtures.
180. For a general discussion of this difficult area of law, see Meagher, Gummow and Lehane, Chap. 17.
181. (1866) L.R. 1 H.L. 129.

against A. Fry L.J. in *Russell v. Watts* detailed five essential elements for the application of acquiescence:[182]

1. The plaintiff (B) must have made a mistake as to her or his legal rights.
2. The plaintiff must have expended some money, or must have done some act (not necessarily upon the defendant's land) on the faith of her or his mistaken belief.
3. The defendant (A), the possessor of the legal right, must know of the existence of her or his own right which is inconsistent with the right claimed by the plaintiff.
4. The defendant must know of the plaintiff's mistaken belief of her or his rights.
5. The defendant must have encouraged the plaintiff in her or his expenditure of money or in the other acts which he or she has done, either directly or by abstaining from asserting her or his legal right.[183]

If B fails to satisfy all five elements, A may assert title to the building and is not liable to compensate B for her or his loss. An illustration is *Brand v. Chris Building Society Pty Ltd*,[184] where Hudson J. of the Supreme Court of Victoria held that this result applies regardless of the seeming injustice and that the doctrine of unjust enrichment has no application in this context. Conversely, if B satisfies all five elements, the court will have a wide-ranging discretion as to the appropriate remedy; it may choose to vest title in A, subject to the award of full compensation to B, or in exceptional cases it may vest title in the whole or part of A's land in B if such a result appears equitable.

The law relating to adverse possession of land is also applicable in this context. Thus, if the essential elements of the doctrine (discussed in Chapter 15) are satisfied and A does not assert her or his right to possession of the land occupied by B's building within the requisite 12 year statutory period (15 years in Victoria and South Australia), A's title will be extinguished and B will be entitled to retain possession of the land occupied by her or his building without the need to compensate A.

Pursuant to the *Property Law Act* 1974 (Qld), s. 196 and the *Property Law Act* 1969 (W.A.), s. 123(1), in Queensland and Western Australia an application may be made to the court for relief where a person makes a lasting improvement on land owned by another in the genuine[185] but mistaken belief that such land is her or his property, or such land is the property of a person on whose behalf the improvement is made or intended to be made.[186] Where this occurs, if the court believes that it is

---

182. (1883) 25 Ch. D. 559 at 586 (C.A.). See also *McBean v. Howey* [1958] N.Z.L.R. 25 at 29.
183. Cf. *McDonald v. Peddle* (1923) 42 N.Z.L.R. 987 at 1002, per Reed J.; Snell, pp. 565-567.
184. [1957] V.R. 625.
185. The word "genuine" connotes that the test is essentially a subjective one in determining the existence of the required belief: *Ex parte Karynette Pty Ltd* [1984] 2 Qd R. 211.
186. This is the wording of the Queensland section. The Western Australian section is similar, except that there is no reference to a "genuine but mistaken belief".

just and equitable that relief should be granted to the applicant or to any other person, the court may make any of the following orders: (a) an order vesting in any person the whole or any part of the land on which the improvement has been made; (b) an order requiring any person to remove the improvement from the land; (c) an order for the payment of compensation in respect of any land or any improvement; or (d) an order that any person have or give possession of the land or improvement for such period and upon such terms and conditions as the court may specify.[187] In making such an order, the court may, inter alia, order any person to execute any instrument or to produce any title deed, instrument or document relating to any land.[188]

2. Encroachment by Buildings onto Adjoining Land

[14.35] The situation where one landowner erects a building which encroaches onto adjoining land must be analysed separately. In Victoria and Tasmania there is no relevant legislation governing this issue. In these jurisdictions, the matter will be resolved on the same principles discussed above **[14.34]**. The result is that if B's building encroaches onto A's land, A may assert title provided that he or she has not acquiesced in the encroachment. In this situation, the court will have a discretion to award damages and/or an injunction requiring the part of the building encroaching across the boundary to be removed. However, if B satisfies the essential elements of the equity of acquiescence the court may, in its discretion, vest title to part of A's land in B or award B compensation if the building is ordered to be removed or modified. Adverse possession may also apply: see above **[14.34]**.

In the remaining jurisdictions (New South Wales, Queensland, South Australia and Western Australia), the situation under discussion is specifically provided for by legislation.[189] The legislation enables either an adjacent owner (the owner of land over which an encroachment extends) or an encroaching owner to apply for relief in respect of any encroachment.[190] "Encroachment" is statutorily defined (except in Western Australia) as meaning "encroachment by a building, and includes encroachment by overhang of any part as well as encroachment by intrusion of any part in or upon the soil".[191]

Where an application is made, the court may make such orders as it considers just with respect to the payment of compensation to the adjacent owner, the removal of the encroachment, the conveyance, transfer or lease of the subject land to the encroaching owner, or the grant to the encroaching owner of any estate or interest in the subject land or any

---

187. Qld: s. 197(1); W.A.: s. 123(2).
188. Qld: s. 197(2); cf. W.A.: s. 123(5).
189. *Encroachment of Buildings Act* 1922 (N.S.W.); *Property Law Act* 1974 (Qld), ss 182-194; *Encroachments Act* 1944 (S.A.); *Property Law Act* 1969 (W.A.), s. 122.
190. N.S.W.: s. 3(1); Qld: s. 184(1); S.A.: s. 4(1); W.A.: s. 122(1).
191. N.S.W.: s. 2; Qld: s. 183; S.A.: s. 2.

easement right or privilege in relation thereto.[192] The court is empowered to make such order as it deems proper in the circumstances of the case, and may consider all relevant factors concerning the encroachment and the circumstances surrounding it.[193]

The legislation (except in Western Australia) states that the maximum compensation to be paid to the adjacent owner in respect of any conveyance, transfer, lease or grant to the encroaching owner shall, if the encroachment was not intentional and did not arise from negligence, be the unimproved capital value of the subject land. In other cases, the minimum compensation is three times the improved capital value.[194] Unless the court orders otherwise, the order for the payment of compensation operates upon registration as a charge upon the land of the encroaching owner in priority to any charge created by her or him or by the predecessor-in-title.[195]

Finally, the legislation in New South Wales, Queensland and South Australia permits either of the owners of two contiguous parcels of land to apply to the court for the determination of the true boundary wherever any question arises whether an existing building encroaches or a proposed building will encroach beyond the boundary. On such applications, the court may make any order it deems proper for determining, marking and recording the true boundary.[196]

3. Other Encroachments

[14.36]   Damages and/or an injunction based on trespass or nuisance may be sought by a landowner in respect of any other form of encroachment onto the land surface of her or his property.

Similar remedies may also be sought where there is a temporary or permanent encroachment into the airspace above the land or into the subsoil beneath the land. In these circumstances, the landowner's title depends on the usque ad coelum et ad inferos principle: see above [14.14]. As explained at [14.13], in respect of encroachments into airspace it appears likely that the landowner is not entitled to assert title to the airspace beyond the height which can be reasonably claimed to be within her or his effective control. Thus, for example, a landowner is entitled to assert title in respect of overhanging branches from a tree

---

192. N.S.W.: s. 3(2); Qld: s. 185(1); S.A.: s. 4(2); W.A.: s. 122(2). See *Re W.H. Marsh* (1941) 42 S.R. (N.S.W.) 21; *Kostos v. Devitt* (1979) 1 B.P.R. 9231 (N.S.W. Sup. Ct); and *Ward v. Griffiths* (1987) 9 N.S.W.L.R. 458, for illustrations where the court held that the appropriate order was the granting of an easement.

193. N.S.W.: s. 3(3); Qld: s. 185(2); S.A.: s. 4(3); cf. W.A.: s. 122(4).

194. N.S.W.: s. 4(1); Qld: s. 186(1); S.A.: s. 5(1). In Western Australia, there is no minimum compensation specified; it is within the discretion of the court: s. 122(4). See *Gesmundo v. Anastasiou* (1975) 1 B.P.R. 9297 (N.S.W. Sup. Ct) and *Re Melden Homes No. 2 Pty Ltd's Land* [1976] Qd R. 79 concerning the award of compensation.

195. N.S.W.: s. 5(1); Qld: s. 187(1); S.A.: s. 6(1).

196. N.S.W.: s. 9; Qld: s. 191; S.A.: s. 10.

growing on adjoining property,[197] wires passing over land at the height of 9 metres,[198] and an advertising sign projecting into her or his airspace by 20 centimetres from the second storey of an adjoining building.[199] On the other hand, there has been stated to be no remedy in trespass where a balloonist passes over land[200] or where bullets pass at a height of 25 metres over the land.[201]

There are no direct Australian authorities concerning the limitation on the circumstances in which a landowner can sue in trespass for trespass to the subsoil, but it is assumed that as in the case of trespass to airspace, the landowner has a right to assert title to the subsoil within her or his effective control. The top layers of soil are clearly within the landowner's control, and this has been judicially recognised as giving rise to damages for trespass in respect of encroaching tree roots.[202] The landowner's title clearly goes beyond this depth, however, as evidenced by *Bulli Coal Mining Co. v. Osborne*,[203] where a person who exploited a coal seam beneath a private landowner's property was held to have trespassed. A similar remedy has also been granted in the United States where a neighbour exploited a cave 110 metres below the surface of the adjoining land where coal mining operations were conducted.[204] These latter cases may arguably no longer represent good law in light of more recent decisions in the context of trespass to airspace which are more restrictive of the application of the usque ad coelum et ad inferos principle.[205]

VI.   FENCING OBLIGATIONS

1. Common Law

[14.37]   At common law, a landowner has no obligation to erect or maintain fences around her or his property on its adjoining boundaries or its road frontage.[206] A number of exceptions to this rule came to be recognised. First, a landowner is under an obligation to prevent her or his

---

197. *Lemmon v. Webb* [1895] A.C. 1 (H.L.); *Davey v. Harrow Corporation* [1958] 1 Q.B. 60 (C.A.).
198. *Wandsworth District Board of Works v. United Telephone Co. Ltd* (1884) 13 Q.B.D. 904 (C.A.).
199. *Kelsen v. Imperial Tobacco Co. (Great Britain & Ireland) Ltd* [1957] 2 Q.B. 334. See also *John Trenberth Ltd v. National Westminster Bank Ltd* (1979) 39 P. & C.R. 104.
200. *Pickering v. Rudd* (1815) 4 Camp. 219 at 220-221; 171 E.R. 70 at 70-71 (N.P.) per Lord Ellenborough. Cf. *Kenyon v. Hart* (1865) 6 B. & S. 251 at 252; 122 E.R. 1188 at 1189 (K.B.) per Blackburn J.
201. *Clifton v. Bury* (1887) 4 T.L.R. 8. Cf. *Davies v. Bennison* (1927) 22 Tas. L.R. 52 at 56.
202. *Morgan v. Khyatt* [1964] 1 W.L.R. 475 (P.C.); *Butler v. Standard Telephones & Cables Ltd* [1940] 1 All E.R. 121.
203. [1899] A.C. 351 (P.C.).
204. *Edwards v. Sims* (1929) 24 S.W. 2d 619.
205. See e.g. *Lord Bernstein of Leigh v. Skyviews & General Ltd* [1978] Q.B. 479; *Graham v. K.D. Morris & Sons Pty Ltd* [1974] Qd R. 1. See above **[14.13]**.
206. *Noarlunga D.C. v. Coventry* [1967] S.A.S.R. 71; *Churchill v. Evans* (1809) 1 Taunt. 529; 127 E.R. 939 (C.P.); *Star v. Rookesby* (1710) 1 Salk. 335; 91 E.R. 295 (K.B.).

cattle trespassing on adjoining land, and as a practical matter this may only be achieved by fencing.[207] Secondly, the parties may enter into an express agreement to fence,[208] which will be enforceable at common law on basic contractual principles. Thirdly, a duty to fence may be created by prescription or the implied grant or reservation of an easement.[209] This latter right was sometimes referred to as a quasi-easement or a spurious easement, inasmuch as (unlike other easements) it imposes a positive duty on the owner of the servient tenement.

In Australia, fencing easements may still be created, although they are rarely found. Fencing covenants may also be created, although being positive in nature the burden of such a covenant will not be enforceable against a successor-in-title of the covenantor: see below **[17.05]**. In all other respects, however, the common law has been replaced by legislation controlling the rights and duties of neighbouring landowners concerning the construction and maintenance of dividing fences.[210] This legislation preserves the right of adjoining landowners to make their own covenant or agreement relating to fencing,[211] but in the absence of such an agreement establishes certain rules concerning the construction, maintenance and repair of dividing fences. The form and content of the legislation differs slightly between the jurisdictions, but the following represents an outline of the essential features of the various enactments.

2. Dividing Fences Legislation—Construction

[14.38] In New South Wales, Queensland and Western Australia the legislation states that the owners of adjoining lands not divided by a sufficient fence[212] shall be liable to join in or contribute in equal proportions to the construction of a dividing fence between their properties.[213] In Victoria, the extent of each landowner's liability depends in part on the type of use to which each block of land is put.[214] In South Australia, any dispute as to the adjoining owners' respective liabilities for the cost of fencing is determined according to the benefit that each of them derives from the performance of the fencing work, and in the absence of

---

207. *Egerton v. Harding* [1975] Q.B. 62 (C.A.).
208. *Hilton v. Ankesson* (1872) 27 L.T. 519 (Exch.); *Jones v. Price* [1965] 2 Q.B. 618 (C.A.).
209. See Bradbrook and Neave, Chap. 10. See also *Crow v. Wood* [1971] 1 Q.B. 77 (C.A.); *Lawrence v. Jenkins* (1873) L.R. 8 Q.B. 274; *Sutcliffe v. Holmes* [1947] K.B. 147 (C.A.). Note that in South Australia a fencing easement cannot be created by prescription: *Fences Act* 1975 (S.A.), s. 21.
210. *Dividing Fences Act* 1951 (N.S.W.); *Fences Act* 1968 (Vic.); *Dividing Fences Act* 1953 (Qld); *Fences Act* 1975 (S.A.); *Dividing Fences Act* 1961 (W.A.); *Boundary Fences Act* 1908 (Tas.).
211. N.S.W.: s. 6; Vic.: s. 30; Qld: s. 5; W.A.: s. 6; Tas.: s. 43. Cf. S.A.: s. 7.
212. For the meaning of "sufficient fence", see *R. v. Hutchinson; Ex parte Jessell* (1884) 10 V.L.R. (L.) 332; *Hose v. Cobden* [1921] V.L.R. 617. A retaining wall on the boundary line of adjoining properties is not a "dividing fence" and is not within the scope of the legislation: *Carter v. Murray* [1981] 2 N.S.W.L.R. 77.
213. N.S.W.: s. 7; Qld: s. 7; W.A.: s. 7.
214. Vic.: s. 4(1).

proof to the contrary it is presumed that the parties derive equal benefit.[215] The joint liability may be varied by court order (in Victoria) or by the ruling of an arbitrator (in Tasmania).[216]

Any owner desiring to compel an adjoining owner to join in or contribute to the construction of a dividing fence may serve her or him with a notice in writing to fence which must specify the boundary to be fenced, contain a proposal for fencing it, and specify the type of fence proposed to be constructed.[217]

Where the adjoining landowners do not agree as to the construction of the fence, the relevant court of summary jurisdiction[218] may, upon application of either person, make an order determining the type of fence to be constructed, what portion shall be constructed by each person, the time within which it shall be constructed and, if necesssary, the boundary or line upon which the fence is to be constructed and the compensation to be paid in consideration of loss of occupation of any land.[219] In Victoria, the magistrates' court may refer the determination of the issues to an arbitrator appointed by court order.[220] In Tasmania, any dispute must be referred to two arbitrators appointed by the parties.[221] The court (or arbitrator) must take into consideration the kind of fence usual in the locality and the purposes for which the adjoining lands are used.[222]

If one party fails to comply with the terms of the court order or a fencing agreement within a specified time, the other party may construct the whole fence and may recover from the person in default half the cost of the construction.[223]

Where a landowner satisfies the court that he or she has made reasonable inquiries and has been unable to ascertain the whereabouts of the adjoining landowner for the purpose of serving a notice to fence, the court may, upon application, make an ex parte order authorising the applicant to construct a fence of a specified type on the boundary line. Any person who constructs a fence in compliance with such an order may, if he or she later ascertains the whereabouts of the adjoining landowner, serve the landowner with a copy of the order and shall, after a specified period, be entitled to recover half the original cost of the fence.[224]

215. S.A.: s. 12(6).
216. Vic.: s. 4(1)(b); Tas.: s. 8(2).
217. N.S.W.: s. 8; Vic.: s. 6; Qld: s. 8; S.A.: s. 5(1); W.A.: s. 8; Tas.: s. 9(1).
218. Court of Petty Sessions (New South Wales, Western Australia); Magistrates' Court (Victoria, Queensland); Local Court (South Australia). In New South Wales, jurisdiction is also vested in the local Land Board constituted under the *Crown Lands Consolidation Act* 1913 (N.S.W.) or the *Western Lands Act* 1901 (N.S.W.). In Queensland disputes up to $1,500 may be resolved by the Small Claims Tribunal, or in South Australia (up to $2,000) by the small claims division of the Local Court.
219. N.S.W.: s. 9(1); Vic.: s. 7(1); Qld: s. 9(1); S.A.: s. 12(1); W.A.: s. 9(1).
220. Vic.: s. 7(2).
221. Tas.: Pt IV.
222. N.S.W.: s. 9(4); Vic.: s. 7(6); Qld: s. 9(4); W.A.: s. 9(3). Cf. Tas.: s. 36. There is no equivalent provision in South Australia.
223. N.S.W.: s. 10; Vic.: s. 8(1); Qld: s. 10; S.A.: ss 8(3), 12(2); W.A.: s. 10; Tas.: s. 13.
224. N.S.W.: s. 11; Vic.: s. 9; Qld: s. 11; W.A.: s. 11. Cf. S.A.: s. 9. There is no equivalent provision in Tasmania.

The legislation (except in Tasmania) apportions the contributions between landlords and tenants where any fence is constructed which divides any lands held by any person as tenant of any landlord from any adjoining lands.[225] The apportionment depends on the nature of the tenant's interest at the time of the construction of the fence. In New South Wales, Queensland and Western Australia, if the tenant's interest is less than for a term of five years, the whole contribution is payable by the landlord; if the interest is between five and seven years, three fourths is payable by the landlord and one fourth by the tenant; if the interest is between seven and 12 years, one half is payable by each party; and if the interest is 12 years or upwards, the whole of the contribution is payable by the tenant. In Victoria and South Australia, if the tenant's interest is less than for a term of three years, the whole contribution is payable by the landlord; if the interest is between three and six years, three fourths is payable by the landlord and one fourth by the tenant; if the interest is between six and 12 years, one half is payable by each party; and if the interest is 12 years or upwards, the whole cost is payable by the tenant. In all jurisdictions (except South Australia), if either the landlord or the tenant pays more than her or his proper proportion of the contribution, he or she may recover the excess from the other party; in addition, any tenant may set off any such sum against any rent payable to the landlord.[226]

Every person engaged in constructing a fence, together with her or his agents and servants, may at all reasonable times enter upon adjoining lands, and do such acts as are necessary or reasonably required to carry into effect the construction of the fence.[227]

3. Dividing Fences Legislation—Repair

[14.39] Wherever any dividing fence is out of repair, the adjoining landowners are liable to join in or contribute in equal proportions to the repair of the fence.[228] In Victoria, each landowner is liable to join in or contribute in such proportions as are agreed upon or, in the absence of agreement, as determined by a magistrates' court.[229] In South Australia, the liability of each landowner is determined according to the benefit that each of them derives from the repair work, and in the absence of proof to the contrary it is presumed that they derive equal benefit.[230]

An adjoining landowner may serve on her or his neighbour at any time a notice requiring her or him to assist in repairing the dividing fence.[231]

225. N.S.W.: s. 18(1); Vic.: s. 10(1); Qld: s. 20(1); S.A.: s. 14(1); W.A.: s. 19(1).
226. N.S.W.: s. 18(2); Vic.: s. 10(2); Qld: s. 20(2); W.A.: s. 19(2). Cf. Tas.: s. 37(2).
227. N.S.W.: s. 20; Vic.: s. 32; Qld: s. 22; S.A.: s. 18; W.A.: s. 21; Tas.: s. 44.
228. N.S.W.: s. 13; Qld: s. 15; W.A.: s. 14; Tas.: s. 22(1). Cf. S.A.: s. 12(2)(6). In *Stacey v. Meagher* [1978] Tas. S.R. 56, Neasey J. held that the liability to contribute in equal proportions is not absolute and can be modified in arbitration. "Repair" includes a case where an existing fence is entirely replaced by a new fence: *Palmer v. Lincott* [1981] W.A.R. 157.
229. Vic.: s. 14.
230. S.A.: s. 12(6).
231. N.S.W.: s. 14(1); Vic.: s. 15(1); Qld: s. 16(1); S.A.: s. 5(3); W.A.: s. 15(1); Tas.: s. 23(1).

Where a person served with the notice does not within a specified period assist in repairing the fence it is lawful for the person serving the notice to repair the fence and demand and recover from the person on whom the notice has been served one half of the cost of the repairs.[232] Various exceptions are provided for in the legislation. The most common are: (a) if the fence has been constructed partly by one owner and partly by another owner, each shall bear the cost of the part constructed by her or him; (b) if the fence is damaged or destroyed by flood, fire, lightning, storm, tempest or accident, either owner may repair it without notice to the other and is entitled to recover half the expenses from the neighbour; and (c) if the fence is damaged or destroyed by fire or the falling of any tree, the landowner through whose neglect the damage occurred is bound to repair the fence, and if he or she fails to do so, the adjoining landowner may repair it and recover from the liable owner the whole cost of the repairs.

The legislation (referred to in [14.38]) apportioning the contributions between landlords and tenants for the construction of fences dividing land held by any person as tenant of any landlord from any adjoining land applies equally to the repair of fences as well as to their construction. The legislation (referred to above [14.38]) entitling every person engaged in constructing a fence to enter adjoining lands also applies to situations where repair work is undertaken.

4. Miscellaneous Fencing Legislation

[14.40]   A variety of miscellaneous statutes other than the dividing fences legislation impose on landowners a duty to fence their property boundaries. Many of these statutes relate to the construction and repair of vermin-proof fences. In some instances, the types of vermin are not specified: see *Wire Netting Act* 1958 (Vic.) and *Fences Act* 1958 (Vic.), Pt III. In other cases, the type of vermin is specified: rabbits (*Rabbit Destruction Act* 1919 (A.C.T.) and *Boundary Fences Act* 1908 (Vic.), Pt II); dogs (*Dog Fence Act* 1946 (S.A.)); rabbits, marsupials and dogs (*Pastures Protection Act* 1934 (N.S.W.), Pt VII); dingoes and other vermin (*Barrier Fences Act* 1954 (Qld) and *Rural Lands Protection Act* 1985 (Qld)). The *Land Act* 1962 (Qld), ss 324-332 contains a unique provision requiring in certain circumstances the joint construction by adjoining landowners of a communal ring fence around their properties against vermin. In many instances, the legislation specifies the type of materials to be used in the construction and the method of the construction: for example, s. 17 of the *Fences Act* 1968 (Vic.). Other statutes require the construction of fences in certain cases to secure the eradication or control of weeds (for example, *Noxious Weeds Act* 1964 (Tas.)) and to protect or improve reserves for the use of travelling stock: *Pastures Protection Act* 1934 (N.S.W.), s. 126, *Rural Lands Protection Act* 1985 (Qld) and the *Stock Routes and Travelling Stock Act* 1954 (N.T.).

232. N.S.W.: s. 14(2); Vic.: s. 15(2)(3); Qld: s. 16(2); W.A.: s. 15(7); Tas.: s. 23(2).
      There is no equivalent provision in South Australia.

15

Adverse Possession, Merger and Extinguishment

I. INTRODUCTION

[15.01] A person unlawfully dispossessed of land has a right to bring an action against the wrongdoer to recover possession of the land. The common law regarded this right, and other types of rights of action, as subsisting forever. Most systems of law, however, embrace the principle of "limitation", the principle of fixing a finite time in which an action may be instituted. Legislation in various forms[1] in England has for a long time adopted a limitation principle. The most recent revision and consolidation of the English legislation is contained in the *Limitation Act* 1980 (U.K.). All Australian States have statutes of limitation in various forms.[2] The legislation in New South Wales was comprehensively revised and consolidated in 1969 pursuant to the recommendations of the New South Wales Law Reform Commission[3] and the revised legislation in Queensland and Tasmania incorporates some provisions which are similar to the provisions in the New South Wales Act. The Victorian Act is based on the 1939 English legislation[4] and the West Australian and South Australian legislation draw largely from early Imperial statutes.

[15.02] A number of reasons of policy have been advanced in favour of the principle of limitation. Sir Thomas Plumer M.R. in *Marquis Cholmondeley v. Lord Clinton* took the view that the community at large benefits if the status quo is eventually recognised. His Honour stated:[5]

> "The public have a great interest, in having a known limit fixed by law to litigation, for the quiet of the community, and that there may be a certain fixed period, after which the possessor may know that his title and right cannot be called into question. It is better that the negligent owner who has omitted to assert his right within the prescribed period, should lose his right than that an opening should be given to interminable legislation."

1. For a brief outline of the English limitation statutes, see Megarry and Wade, p. 1031.
2. *Limitation Act* 1969 (N.S.W.); *Limitation of Actions Act* 1958 (Vic.); *Limitation of Actions Act* 1974 (Qld); *Limitation of Actions Act* 1936 (S.A.); *Limitation Act* 1935 (W.A.); *Limitation Act* 1974 (Tas.).
3. New South Wales Law Reform Commission, *Report on the Limitation of Actions*, Report No. 3 (1967) (L.R.C. 3).
4. *Limitation Act* 1939 (U.K.).
5. (1820) 2 Jac. & W. 1 at 139-140; 37 E.R. 527 at 577.

More specifically, it has been suggested that the community as a whole benefits from a limitation principle as the principle encourages the use and development of land and makes more certain the validity of title, thereby encouraging the alienability of land.[6] "[I]t is in the public interest that a person who has long been in undisputed possession should be able to deal with the land as owner."[7] In a detailed article on limitation, Professor Jackson advanced three possible reasons for having a scheme of limitation of actions.[8] These were as follows: first, holders of rights should not sleep on their rights; secondly, problems of proof become more difficult the longer the period of time between the dispute arising and the action being heard, and finally, the status quo should be recognised at some stage, and there should be a certain end to litigation. Professor Jackson concludes that the basic principle behind the idea of limitation of actions is the third—recognition of the status quo and a certain end to litigation. The rationale accords with that described by Lord Plumer M.R. Professor Jackson takes the view that the other two possible reasons for the principle are more relevant in determining the various lengths of limitation periods with respect to different causes of action.

The "morality", and consequently the existence of, a limitation principle in relation to actions for the recovery of land has been questioned. In one sense, the existence of such a principle sanctions the act of the person who has taken possession of another's land: it sanctions what some may call "land stealing"[9] by providing that the lawful right of another to bring proceedings to eject the "thief" will be lost after a finite period of time. Despite the apparent validity of the morality argument, it is suggested that the reasons in favour of having a limitation period in relation to actions for the recovery of land outweigh such an argument. Certainty of title, pursued and gained by eventual recognition of the status quo, and the greater emphasis in modern times on residential security[10] are aided and enhanced by the existence of a principle of limitation of actions. Of course, with respect to Torrens system land, the register is intended to provide "certainty of title" and it may be argued that the concept of adverse possession contraverts a basic aim of the Torrens system. Nevertheless, even under the Torrens system, there may be situations where uncertainty exists. For example, where a registered proprietor has died and no successor has claimed the land, there may, after a number of years, be some uncertainty as to who is entitled to the land. The principle of adverse possession may well have a legitimate place, even in the Torrens system, in providing certainty of title in such

6. Butt, p. 571; Goodman, "Adverse Possession of Land—Morality and Motive" (1970) 33 Mod. L.R. 281 at 281-283; see also Dockray, "Why Do We Need Adverse Possession?" [1985] Conv. 272 where he argues that simplification of conveyancing procedures has been, and remains, an important reason for having a limitation principle.
7. Megarry and Wade, p. 1030.
8. Jackson, "The Legal Effects of the Passing of Time" (1970) 7 M.U.L.R. 407 at 409.
9. Goodman, op. cit. at 281-282.
10. See Gray and Symes, *Real Property and Real People Principles of Land Law* (Butterworths, London, 1981), p. 93.

instances. The States have dealt with the issue of the interaction of Torrens statutes and the limitation statutes in varying ways: see below **[15.82]-[15.86]**.

[15.03] The limitation principle enshrined in the English and Australian limitation legislation operates in a negative way by eliminating the claim of a person with a better title. Thus, although a person who has a right to bring an action to recover land loses that right after a set period of time, the prospective defendant to the action, the possessor of the land, does not acquire thereby the exact interest in the land formerly held by the person with the right of action. Rather, the right to the land is enhanced as a result of the extinguishment of a better right. It should be noted that each of the limitation statutes in Australia provide that at the expiration of the statutory period, the title of the person dispossessed is extinguished in addition to the cause of action being lost.[11] The extinguishment of title is important. Before 1833 in England, the statute of limitations did not provide for the loss of *title* and therefore, if the title holder managed to obtain possession again, her or his title would prevail over that of the previous possessor. The principle of limitation is to be contrasted with the concept of *prescription*. Prescription is a doctrine of the common law but it has been altered and extended by statute. The idea of prescription is that a right may be acquired through long use: if a person has enjoyed a right over a long period of time, it will be presumed that there was a grant of the right to the user.[12] In contrast to the principle of limitation which operates negatively by extinguishing rights, prescription operates *positively* by presuming an actual grant of the right. In English law the operation of prescription has been confined to incorporeal hereditaments, in particular easements and profits à prendre.

II. LENGTH OF LIMITATION PERIOD

[15.04] The Australian limitation statutes divide various types of actions into categories. The statutes provide for these principal limitation periods.

The limitation period with respect to actions to recover land is the longest: in New South Wales, Queensland, Western Australia and Tasmania, the period is 12 years[13] and in Victoria and South Australia, the period is 15 years.[14]

III. ADVERSE POSSESSION AND THE CROWN

[15.05] The legislative approach in relation to adverse possession against the Crown varies from State to State. In Victoria, Queensland and

11. Limitation statutes: N.S.W.: s. 65; Vic.: s. 18; Qld: s. 24; S.A.: s. 28; W.A.: s. 30; Tas.: s. 21.
12. See Megarry and Wade, pp. 869ff., 1030; Cheshire and Burn, p. 824. See below Chapter 16.
13. Limitation statutes: N.S.W.: s. 27(2); Qld: s. 13; W.A.: s. 4; Tas.: s. 10(2).
14. Limitation statutes: Vic.: s. 8; S.A.: s. 4.

Western Australia, the limitation statutes provide that the right and title of the Crown in any land cannot be affected by the possession of such land adverse to the Crown, whether or not the adverse possession has exceeded 60 years.[15] In New South Wales and Tasmania, the limitation statutes provide that an action by the Crown with respect to recovery of Crown land, is barred after 30 years adverse possession.[16] Despite the provision in the limitation statute in New South Wales, s. 170 of the *Crown Lands Act* 1989 effectively provides that title to Crown land may not, on the basis of adverse possession, be asserted or established against the Crown. Various transitional provisions and exceptions are set out.[16a] In South Australia, there is no specific statutory provision relating to adverse possession against the Crown. It appears, therefore, that the *Crown Suits Act* 1769 (Imp.), sometimes referred to as the *Nullum Tempus Act* is the applicable law.[17] Pursuant to this provision the Crown's right to bring an action is lost after 60 years possession by the adverse possessor or her or his "ancestors or predecessors". Unlike the general provisions relating to adverse possession where the right of action and title of the owner are lost if the land has been in continuous adverse possession for the relevant limitation period, a title by adverse possession may only be alleged and gained under the *Nullum Tempus Act*, if the applicant can prove that he or she has adversely possessed the land for 60 years or that he or she has a good documentary title to the possessory interest. Further it is important to note the interaction of the limitation statutes and the Torrens statutes: see below **[15.82]**ff.

The justification for giving the Crown a longer limitation period, or for providing that there can be no adverse possession against the Crown at all, appears to be that the Crown cannot be expected to check and monitor all Crown lands for adverse possessors. The justification clearly has validity if the Crown land is land which has never been alienated and which would rarely, if ever, be checked for adverse possessors. The

15. Limitation statutes: Vic.: s. 7; Qld: s. 6(4); W.A.: s. 36. The *Crown Suits Act* 1769 (Imp.), more often referred to as the *Nullum Tempus Act* 1769 (Imp.), which provided for the Crown's right to be barred after 60 years adverse possession *was* part of the law (see *Delohery v. Permanent Trustee Co. (N.S.W.)* (1904) 1 C.L.R. 283; *Attorney-General (N.S.W.) v. Love* [1898] A.C. 679) but is of no effect in Victoria, Queensland and Western Australia in view of the specific provisions mentioned above. Note that the provisions of these limitation statutes generally bind the Crown. Vic.: s. 32; Qld: s. 6; cf. W.A.: s. 48.

16. Limitation statutes: N.S.W.: s. 27(1) specifically repealing *Crown Suits Act* 1769 (Imp.); Tas.: s. 10(1). It is important to note that in Tasmania, there are particular fact situations where no period of adverse possession, however long, will extinguish the Crown's title: see Tas.: s. 10(4)-(6). For example s. 10(4) provides that there can be no adverse possession against the Crown where the Crown land has been reserved as a road under an Act.

16a. See *Crown Lands Act* 1989 (N.S.W.), s. 170. See also the *Real Property Act* 1900 (N.S.W.), s. 45D(3) which provides that a possessory application with respect to Torrens land may not be made in relation to an estate in land of which the Crown, Minister of the Crown, a statutory body representing the Crown, particular public corporations or a local council is the registered proprietor.

17. *Attorney-General (N.S.W.) v. Love* [1898] A.C. 679; *Delohery v. Permanent Trustee Co. (N.S.W.)* (1904) 1 C.L.R. 283; *South Australian Co. v. Port Adelaide C.C.* [1914] S.A.L.R. 16.

reasoning has less validity where the Crown owns the land through it being vested in a minister of a government department or a public corporation. In most instances, the land would be used for a particular purpose and it would be unlikely that possession by an adverse possessor would remain unnoticed for a longer period.[18] Despite this reasoning, the recent trend appears to prohibit adverse possession against the Crown.[19]

[15.06] Problems may arise if a person takes adverse possession of Crown land, and subsequently, the Crown transfers its interest in the land. In Victoria, where a right of action to recover land first accrues to the Crown and the Crown subsequently conveys the land to another person, the proviso to s. 8 of the *Limitation of Actions Act* 1958 ensures that the transferee has 15 years to bring an action to recover the land from the date the land was conveyed to the transferee. The effect of the proviso appears to be that no matter how long someone has been in adverse possession of Crown land, the person to whom the land is conveyed or any person who claims the land through that person has 15 years from the date of the conveyance to bring an action to recover the land.

The Victorian position is to be contrasted with the position in Tasmania where a 30 year period bars the Crown. The right of action of a person to whom the Crown land is conveyed is barred at the expiration of 30 years from the date of the original dispossession or 12 years from the conveyance, whichever is the shorter. Thus, in this case the assignee from the Crown is entitled to 12 years from the date of the conveyance, unless at that time there was less than 12 years of the Crown period of 30 years unexpired: in this case, the assignee has the residue of that period.[20]

Although the limitation statutes in Queensland and Western Australia mirror the Victorian Act in providing that no period of adverse possession can bar the Crown, neither of them contains a proviso dealing with the Crown similar to the proviso in s. 8 of the Victorian Act. Where the Crown land is conveyed and time has commenced to run against the Crown before the conveyance, then the operation of the adverse possession provisions depend on whether the Crown is a "person" to whom the right of action accrues. On balance, it is suggested that the Crown is a person for this purpose.[21] If the Crown is a person, the 12 year period applying in these States will commence to run against the Crown and continue to run after the conveyance against the assignee from the Crown, notwithstanding that no period of adverse possession could ever bar the Crown. If the Crown is deemed to be a person for the purpose of this provision, the Crown would be in a position to convey land which had

18. In the N.S.W.L.R.C., Report No. 3 the Commissioner recommended that the normal period, i.e. 12 years, should apply to land alienated by the Crown or to, e.g., Ministers and public corporations. Nevertheless, the Bill drafted by the Commission did not give effect to the recommendation as it was thought that further research should be undertaken before such a change was made.
19. See e.g. s. 170 of *Crown Lands Act* 1989.
20. Limitation statutes: N.S.W.: see generally *Crown Lands Act* 1989, s. 170; Tas.: s. 10(1) (3).
21. See Hogg, *Liability of the Crown in Australia, New Zealand and the United Kingdom* (Law Book Co. Ltd, Melbourne, 1971).

been adversely possessed for over 12 years and the assignee would have her or his title extinguished from the date of purchase.

IV. COMMENCEMENT OF THE LIMITATION PERIOD

1. Present Interests

[15.07] The limitation period commences from the time the cause of action accrues. In relation to land, the limitation statutes set out specifically when a person's right to bring an action to recover land accrues. There are two ways in which a cause of action may accrue to the holder of a present interest. First, such a person may have been in possession and then discontinued possession or been dispossessed or, secondly, although entitled to possession under a will or deed for instance, the holder of a present interest may never have obtained possession.

(a) In possession and then discontinued or dispossessed

[15.08] With the exception of the South Australian legislation, the relevant provisions on this type of case are substantially the same in all jurisdictions. They provide that a person's right to bring an action to recover land accrues when first, the person entitled to possession has discontinued possession or has been dispossessed;[22] and secondly, adverse possession has been taken by some other person.[23] In South Australia, the relevant statutory provision states simply that a cause of action accrues when a person entitled to possession has discontinued possession or has been dispossessed. It is clear, however, that despite the lack of a specific statutory provision in South Australia, the cause of action arises only if another person has taken adverse possession of the land.[24]

The provisions encompassing this principle are poorly drafted and confusing. For example, the two matters referred to above which must exist before a cause of action can be said to arise are contained in quite separate provisions in the limitation statutes.[25] Section 9(1) of the *Limitation of Actions Act* 1958 (Vic.) for instance, provides simply that:

> "Where the person bringing an action to recover land or some person through whom he claims—
>
> (a) has been in possession thereof; and

---

22. Limitation statutes: N.S.W.: s. 28; Vic.: s. 9(1); Qld: s. 13; S.A.: s. 6; W.A.: s. 5; Tas.: s. 11.
23. Limitation statutes: N.S.W.: s. 38; Vic.: s. 14(1); Qld: s. 19; W.A.: s. 5; Tas.: s. 16.
24. As stated above, the South Australian legislation is drawn directly from the *Real Property Limitation Act* 1833 (U.K.). As in South Australia, this Act stated simply that the cause of action accrued upon dispossession or discontinuance of possession. In *Smith v. Lloyd* (1854) 9 Exch. 562; 156 E.R. 240, the court had to consider this legislation and it was held "that the statute applies not to cases of want of actual possession by the plaintiff, but to cases where he had been out of and another in possession for the prescribed time".
25. Note that this is not the case in Western Australia: see s. 5.

(b) has while entitled thereto been dispossessed or discontinued his possession—

the right of action shall be deemed to have accrued on the date of the dispossession or discontinuance.''

A reading of such a provision alone, suggests that a right of action accrues either on the date of dispossession or discontinuance. It is clear, however, from a thorough perusal of the statute that s. 9(1) must be read in conjunction with s. 14(1) which provides that no right of action shall be deemed to accrue ''unless the land is in the possession of some person in whose favour the limitation period can run (adverse possession)''.

[15.09] Before undertaking an analysis of the meaning of the various terms, it is important to note that in all jurisdictions where a true owner who has been dispossessed or discontinued her or his possession subsequently assigns inter vivos or devises the land to another person, the assignee or devisee can be in no better position than the former true owner. Although the principle of nemo dat quod non habet alone might ensure such a result, the general provisions in each jurisdiction equivalent to s. 9(1) of the Victorian Act extracted above[26] provide that this is so. The assignee or devisee ''claims through'' the grantor and the right of action dates from the dispossession or discontinuance of a person through whom the assignee or devisee claims.

In Victoria, Queensland, Western Australia and Tasmania there is a further specific provision relating to this situation.[27] In these jurisdictions, it is provided that where a cause of action has accrued to a person and that person assures the land to another, the person taking under the assurance may only bring the action during the period which the person by whom the assurance was made could have brought such an action.[28]

[15.10] Apart from the confusing manner of the presentation of the statutory provisions, resort must be had to the case law in order to ascertain the legal meaning of the terms used in these provisions. An integration of the relevant statutory provisions suggests that a person's right to bring an action to recover possession of land may occur in one of two ways.[29] First, the cause of action may arise at the date the person entitled to the land is ''dispossessed'' or ousted from possession by the adverse possessor. Secondly, and perhaps more usually, the cause of action may arise at the date of the taking of adverse possession following an earlier ''discontinuance'' of possession by the person then entitled to possession. Thus, for example, if A, the owner of land, abandons the land or, in the terminology of the statutes ''discontinues possession'', and five

---

26. Limitation statutes: N.S.W.: ss 27(2), 11(2)(a); Vic.: ss 9(1), 3(4); Qld: ss 14(1), 5(4); S.A.: ss 6, 3(1); W.A.: ss 5(a), 3; Tas.: ss 11(1), 2(4), (5).
27. Limitation statutes: Vic.: s. 10(3); Qld: s. 15(3); W.A.: s. 7; Tas.: s. 12(5).
28. It appears that these provisions were drawn from the *Limitation Act* 1939 (U.K.). The mirror provision in the English Act related to future interests created in settlements (post 1925 future interests are equitable in England).
29. See *Treloar v. Nute* [1976] 1 W.L.R. 1295 at 1300 per Sir John Pennycuick and generally Gray and Symes op. cit., p. 96.

years later S enters into adverse possession, A's right of action does not accrue until S takes possession.

How are these terms interpreted by the courts? Although brief descriptions of the terms "discontinuance" and "dispossession" are given below, the need to discuss the meaning of each of these terms individually and at length is minimal. The aim of the statutes is that time should start running against the true owner only when another person has taken *adverse possession of the land*. Whether the taking of adverse possession follows a discontinuance by the true owner or arises by virtue of a dispossession is not important. Further, what constitutes a discontinuance or a dispossession depends upon the facts of the individual case. Basically, "discontinuance" means that the true owner, or a person with a possessory interest, has abandoned possession. The law assumes that the true owner has possession of her or his land,[30] but it is possible for a "discontinuance" to occur. "Dispossession" means that the true owner, or a person with a possessory interest has been driven out of possession by another.[31]

[15.11] The term "adverse possession" bore a complex, technical meaning in the early 19th century and before.[32] Under the current Australian legislation, the term "adverse possession" connotes simply, actual possession of the land without the licence of the true owner. The adverse possessor must be able to show that he or she has taken possession and that the true owner no longer enjoys possession. The difficult question is as to what constitutes "possession" in any given instance.

At common law, possession comprises two elements: first, there must be factual possession which "signifies an appropriate degree of physical control of the land in question",[33] and secondly, the animus possidendi, the intention to possess, must be present.[34] The courts have not formulated specific rules or definitions that can be applied to any given fact situation such that it is possible to say that the presence or absence of particular factors demonstrate the existence or absence of "possession". "Acts, implying possession in one case, may be wholly inadequate to prove it in another."[35] Although each case must be decided on its own facts, the courts have laid down guidelines which may be used when the issue arises of whether adverse possession of particular land has been taken and these are discussed below.

---

30. Megarry and Wade, p. 42. See, however, Western Australia, s. 5 which appears to provide that unless someone has taken adverse possession the true owner or any other person with a right to possession shall be deemed to be in possession.
31. All of these terms, "discontinuance", "dispossession" and "adverse possession" concern the presence or absence of possession in the relevant parties.
32. See Megarry and Wade, p. 1034 and *Staughton v. Brown* (1875) 1 V.L.R. (L) 150 at 158-159.
33. See Gray and Symes op. cit., p. 97.
34. Note that there are some inconsistencies with respect to the actual meaning of the animus possidendi in the context of adverse possession. See below **[5.18]-[5.25]** and Dockray, "Adverse Possession and Intention—1" [1982] Conv. 256.
35. *Lord Advocate v. Lord Lovat* (1880) 5 A.C. 273 at 288. See also *Riley v. Penttila* [1974] V.R. 547.

(i) Factual possession—nature of the land

[15.12]   Factual possession denotes an appropriate degree of physical control. In order to determine whether there is a sufficient degree of exclusive control, the particular and peculiar circumstances of the case in hand must be analysed closely. The character and value of the property, the suitable and natural mode of using it having regard to all the circumstances, and the course of conduct which a proprietor might be expected reasonably to follow with due regard to her or his own interests should all be taken into account in determining whether adverse possession of the land has been taken.[36] As was stated by Slade J. in *Powell v. McFarlane*,[37] the issue of possession must be determined having regard to "the nature of the land and the manner in which land of that nature is commonly used or enjoyed".[38] Effectively, "the alleged possessor (must have) been dealing with the land in question as an occupying owner might have been expected to deal with it and [show] that no one else has done so".[39]

Many cases emphasise that the type of factual possession which is necessary for a cause of action to accrue, has to be determined in light of the facts of the particular case. In *Red House Farms (Thorndon) Ltd v. Catchpole*[40] it was held that shooting over marshy land, which was of no use for agriculture, constituted adverse possession. In contrast, the tethering of ponies and the playing by children on land were held to be, in the circumstances, too trivial to constitute acts of adverse possession.[41] In *Riley v. Penttila*[42] the enclosure of land and its use first as a tennis court and then as a garden by a person already holding an easement for recreational and garden purposes over the land in dispute, was held not to constitute adverse possession in the circumstances.

[15.13]   Where the land comprises a large area, acts of possession performed on one part of the land may provide evidence of possession of the whole.[43] Further, where land is farmed on a rotational or peripatetic basis, adverse possession of the whole may be claimed.[44] It is important to note that an owner and an alleged possessor cannot both be in

36. See *Littledale v. Liverpool College* [1900] 1 Ch. 19; *Murnane v. Findlay* [1926] V.L.R. 80; *Riley v. Penttila* [1974] V.R. 547. All these matters are relevant in considering whether there has been a "discontinuance" or a "dispossession".
37. (1977) 38 P. & C.R. 452.
38. (1977) 38 P. & C.R. 452 at 471.
39. Ibid. Cf. *Buckinghamshire C.C. v. Moran* [1989] 2 All E.R. 225 at 237-238 per Slade L.J. where it is stated in relation to the intention element that it is the intention to possess, *not* the intention to own, which is the relevant criterion: see below **[15.24]**.
40. [1977] 244 *Estates Gazette* 295; 121 Sol. J. 136.
41. *Tecbild Ltd v. Chamberlain* (1969) 20 P. & C.R. 633.
42. [1974] V.R. 547.
43. *Staughton v. Brown* (1875) 1 V.L.R. (L) 150 at 163. Cf., however, the situation where land is divided on a strata basis. The adverse possessor may well take possession only of the stratum occupied: see e.g. *Rains v. Buxton* (1880) 14 Ch. D. 537 (a cellar).
44. *Higgs v. Nassauvian Ltd* [1975] A.C. 464. Cf. *Ocean Estates Ltd v. Pinder* [1969] 2 A.C. 19.

possession at the same time. Possession is single and exclusive.[45] In cases where neither can demonstrate a "single and exclusive possession" the owner will be held to have possession.[46]

[15.14]   It has been stated in a number of cases that in order for time to start running, the acts of user should be inconsistent with the rights of the true owner and with the use he or she intends to make of the land.[47] Whether the acts of user constitute such an inconsistency must necessarily vary with each fact situation. Satisfaction of a criterion which demands that the alleged possessor demonstrate acts of user inconsistent with the purpose to which the true owner intends to put the land may prove difficult where the true owner has no present use but a future intended purpose regarding the land or where the true owner has no particular present or future intended use. Thus, for example, in *Leigh v. Jack*[48] where the test was first stated by Bramwell L.J., the alleged possessor failed to prove adverse possession: his act of placing refuse on the plaintiff's land for the statutory period was not inconsistent with the plaintiff's intention of dedicating the land in the future to the public as a roadway. A question arises as to whether any use could have been inconsistent with the true owner's purpose. Arguably, no use, even the erection of a building, would have been inconsistent in the appropriate sense: the building could have been demolished.[49] Similarly, in *Williams Bros Direct Supply Ltd v. Raftery*[50] where the plaintiffs intended to use their land for development purposes in the future, the Court of Appeal held that Raftery's acts of user were not inconsistent with the purpose for which the plaintiffs intended to use the land. The cultivation of land, the erection of sheds and lines of bricks and the use of the land for the purpose of rearing greyhounds were insufficient to satisfy the criterion.

Although it had been suggested that the decision in *Raftery's* case was a high water mark in the tide against recognition of titles acquired by adverse possession, two further Court of Appeal decisions reiterated the importance of the *Leigh v. Jack* formulation and expanded upon it. In both *Wallis' Cayton Bay Holiday Camp Ltd v. Shell-Mex & B.P. Ltd*[51] and in *Gray v. Wykeham-Martin*,[52] it was suggested that where the true owner had no particular present purpose but had a future intended use for the land, a licence from the true owner to the alleged possessor was to be implied, thus precluding completely any suggestion that the alleged possessor was in adverse possession. According to these decisions such a licence was to be implied without any factual basis for the implication. Lord Denning in

45. Dockray, "Adverse Possession and Intention—II" [1982] Conv. 345 at 346.
46. Ibid.
47. *Leigh v. Jack* (1879) 5 Ex. D. 264; *Williams Bros Direct Supply Ltd v. Raftery* [1958] 1 Q.B. 159; *Wallis's Cayton Bay Holiday Camp Ltd v. Shell-Mex & B.P. Ltd* [1975] Q.B. 94; *Treloar v. Nute* [1976] 1 W.L.R. 1295; *Riley v. Penttila* [1974] V.R. 547.
48. (1879) 5 Ex. D. 264.
49. Cf. the judgment of Ormrod L.J. in the *Shell-Mex* case [1975] Q.B. 94 at 117.
50. [1958] 1 Q.B. 159.
51. [1975] Q.B. 94.
52. Unreported, Court of Appeal, 17 January 1977, No. 10A, referred to in *Powell v. McFarlane* (1977) 38 P. & C.R. 452.

the *Shell-Mex* case[53] and the Court of Appeal in the *Gray* case suggested that such a licence was also to be implied where the true owner had no particular present or future use for the land.[54]

Stamp L.J., in dissent, in the *Shell-Mex* case conceded the greater difficulty in finding adverse possession where the true owner is not using the land for the purpose for which it was acquired. Nevertheless, his Honour stated:[55]

"I find it impossible to regard those cases as establishing that so long as the true owner cannot use his land for the purpose for which he acquired it, the acts done by the squatter do not amount to possession of the land."

On the facts, his Honour took the view that the plaintiffs had dispossessed the defendants and remained in adverse possession for the requisite period. The acts of the plaintiffs could not be said to have been performed under an implied licence from the defendants. Slade J. in *Powell v. McFarlane*,[56] expressed strong reservations about the interpretations given to the relevant provisions in the limitation statute by the majority of Court of Appeal in the *Shell-Mex* case and the Court of Appeal in the *Gray* case and doubted whether the authorities relied upon by the Court of Appeal justified their findings. His Honour took the view that the terms "possession" and "dispossession" should be given their ordinary meaning and that the implication of a licence for the purpose of defeating the plain provisions of the Act was not justified. Further, and more specifically, Slade J. cast doubt on the basic criterion expounded in *Leigh v. Jack, Raftery's* case and the *Shell-Mex* and *Gray* cases. His Honour took the view that "possession" comprises the two elements of factual possession and the animus possidendi and that any requirement of proof of an additional third factor was unjustified.

Slade J. was of the opinion that the failure of the purported adverse possession in cases such as *Leigh v. Jack* and *Raftery's* case were explicable on the basis that such a person had failed to prove the relevant animus possidendi. The fact that the claimant could not demonstrate acts of user inconsistent with the purpose to which the true owner intended to put the land helped to show "the defendant's acts as not being those of a man who *intended* to dispossess the owner".[57]

[15.15] The English Law Reform Committee considered the situation and suggested legislation to prevent the implication of a licence in the

---

53. Ormrod L.J. also held that the plaintiffs had not dispossessed the defendants as the farming activities of the plaintiffs were not inconsistent with the defendants' future plans for the land. His Honour suggested that if the plaintiffs had built chalets or other structures, this may have jeopardised the proposed development for the land and thus constituted adverse possession: [1975] Q.B. 94 at 117.

54. Cf. *Treloar v. Nute* [1976] 1 W.L.R. 1295 at 1301. Even here, however, Sir John Pennycuick took the view that a special rule may apply where the true owner has no present purpose for the land but only a future intended use.

55. [1975] Q.B. 94 at 110.

56. (1977) 38 P. & C.R. 452 at 484-485.

57. (1977) 38 P. & C.R. 452 at 473.

manner suggested in the *Shell-Mex* and *Gray* cases. The *Limitation Act* 1980 (U.K.), s. 15(6), Sched. 1, para. 8(4) now provides:

> "For the purpose of determining whether a person occupying land is in adverse possession of the land it shall not be assumed by implication of law that his occupation is by permission of the person entitled to the land merely by virtue of the fact that his occupation is not inconsistent with the latter's present or future enjoyment of the land.
>
> This provision shall not be taken as prejudicing a finding to the effect that a person's occupation of any land is by implied permission of the person entitled to the land in any case where such a finding is justified on the actual facts of the case."

The provision may not have wholly achieved its purpose as the way is still open for the courts to imply a licence if "such a finding is justified on the actual facts of the case". Nevertheless, the English legislature has declared its distaste for the contrived views of the Court of Appeal in the *Shell-Mex* and *Gray* cases. Slade J. in *Powell v. McFarlane* attempted to rationalise the earlier cases in a manner which would, for all practical purposes, remove altogether the criterion of acts of user inconsistent with the purpose to which the true owner intended to use the land.

[15.16]   The Court of Appeal, of which Slade L.J. was a member, in the case of *Buckinghamshire C.C. v. Moran*[58] took a similar view of the earlier cases. The *Moran* case concerned yet another example of a fact situation where the true owner, the council, had no particular present use but only a future intended purpose for the land. The intention was that the land would be used in the future to construct a road. Moran's predecessors in title and then Moran, owned and lived on land adjoining the council's land in dispute and had used this land in dispute as a garden for the statutory period. They had enclosed the land with a fence and a locked gate. Although there could be no question of an implied licence in view of the amendment to the limitation statute the council argued that the basic proposition expounded first in *Leigh v. Jack* and reiterated by many justices including Sir John Pennycuick in *Treloar v. Nute*[59] remained good. That is, the council argued that the alleged possessor must show acts of user inconsistent with the purpose to which the true owner intends to put the land and such proof will not be forthcoming where the owner has only some future intended purpose.

The Court of Appeal rejected this argument. Slade L.J. repeated the remarks he had made in *Powell v. McFarlane* and Nourse and Butler-Sloss L.JJ. agreed with Slade L.J. Slade L.J. reiterated that legal possession comprises the elements of factual possession and the animus possidendi and that proof of acts of user inconsistent with the purpose to which the true owner intends to put the land is unnecessary. All members of the Court of Appeal conceded that it may be more difficult to prove the requisite intention where the true owner has only a future intended purpose and no present use and the alleged possessor is aware of this fact:

58. [1989] 2 All E.R. 225.
59. [1976] 1 W.L.R. 1295 at 1300-1301.

see below [15.18]ff. The judgment of Nourse L.J. clarifies the point by stating that in any question of adverse possession, it is the intention of the alleged possessor not the true owner, which is relevant.[60] The criterion of acts of user inconsistent with the purpose to which the true owner intends to use the land directs attention to the true owner's intentions. Nourse L.J. suggests that the only way in which the intention of the true owner to use the land for a particular purpose at a future date may become relevant is if the alleged possessor knows of such an intention and thus does not, in light of this knowledge, form the requisite intention her or himself to possess the land and exclude others.

[15.17] Although many cases, both Australian and English,[61] have referred to the criterion of acts of user inconsistent with the purpose to which the true owner intends to use the land, its validity in the adverse possession area must now be seriously doubted in both England and Australia. It was the formulation of Bramwell L.J. in *Leigh v. Jack* which provided the basis for the criterion and the Court of Appeal in *Buckinghamshire C.C. v. Moran* did not accept his observations to be a correct statement of the law. Whilst it is the case that special difficulties may exist in proving adverse possession where the true owner has a specific future purpose but no present use for the land, it seems that an alleged possessor no longer has to prove acts of user inconsistent with the purpose to which the true owner intends to use the land. Even if the criterion were still to form part of the law relating to adverse possession in Australia, it is suggested that it will not be interpreted in a strict sense.

(ii) Animus possidendi

[15.18] The second material consideration in determining whether adverse possession of the land has been taken, concerns intention. The person claiming to have taken adverse possession must have the relevant animus possidendi.[62] Especially where the acts relied upon as constituting adverse possession are equivocal, the intention with which they are done is important.[63] The person claiming to have taken adverse possession must be more than a persistent trespasser; that person must have the intention to use the land as her or his own (see below [15.24]), and to exclude all others including the true owner so far as is practicable and so far as the law permits.[64]

[15.19] The issue of proof of the requisite intention is a vexed and difficult one. It has been suggested that the enclosure of an area of land is as unequivocal as an act of adverse possession can be and prima facie

---

60. *Buckinghamshire C.C. v. Moran* [1989] 2 All E.R. 225 at 239.
61. See fn. 47 above.
62. *Littledale v. Liverpool College* [1900] 1 Ch. 19; *Williams Bros Direct Supply Ltd v. Raftery* [1958] 1 Q.B. 159; *George Wimpey & Co. Ltd v. Sohn* [1967] Ch. 487; *Murnane v. Findlay* [1926] V.L.R. 80; *Riley v. Penttila* [1974] V.R. 547.
63. See particularly, *Riley v. Penttila* [1974] V.R. 547.
64. *Murnane v. Findlay* [1926] V.L.R. 80; *Riley v. Penttila* [1974] V.R. 547; *Powell v. McFarlane* (1977) 38 P. & C.R. 452 at 470-471; *Buckinghamshire C.C. v. Moran* [1989] 2 All E.R. 225 at 236. See also Dockray, op. cit. I, at 257-261; and see below [15.23].

demonstrates the requisite intention.[65] However, even where there is enclosure, the intention must be considered in light of the facts of the particular case: despite enclosure, the requisite intention may be absent. In *Riley v. Penttila*[66] a plan of subdivision provided for the purchasers of lots adjoining a common reserve to have the right to use and enjoy the reserve for the purposes of recreation or as a garden or a park. The right was held to amount to an easement. A predecessor in title of the defendant erected a fence around a part of the land adjoining his lot for the purpose of enclosing a tennis court he built.

The evidence showed that the person who erected the tennis court and the fence around it, intended to use the easement he possessed for a specific recreational purpose and that he invited other lot owners, who enjoyed the benefit of the same type of easement, to use the tennis court. Therefore, the evidence did not support the proposition that the defendant's predecessor intended to take actual possession adverse to the possession of the true owner. Rather, the evidence suggested that he simply wished to gain a special enjoyment from the liberty already granted to him.

[15.20] In *Powell v. McFarlane*, Slade J. stated that not only must the intention to possess be present but that that intention should be made clear to the world.[67] As has been stated in another case, the intention should be clear from the acts themselves.[68] The statement of Slade J. also suggests that certain acts may be so obvious as to satisfy such a test: the cultivation of agricultural land and the fencing of land are examples of this.[69] Many acts, however, are more equivocal and it would be difficult to prove that it was "perfectly plain to the world at large [that he] intended to exclude the true owner".[70] Australian cases such as *Clement v. Jones*[71] and *Riley v. Penttila*[72] suggest that in Australia, the intention to possess adversely to the true owner is an essential element in establishing that a cause of action has accrued. Whether the animus must be made clear to the whole world, as is suggested in *Powell's* case, is less clear. No Australian decision has stated the test in such a specific and strict manner, and yet the implication from cases such as *Clement v. Jones* is that the intention should be made clear to the world at large.

[15.21] A question arises as to the relative value of the evidence of the adverse possessor in determining whether the requisite intention has been proved. Direct evidence from an adverse possessor of a lack of the requisite intention clearly proves that the animus possidendi did not exist and prevents the squatter from being in possession for the purpose of a limitation statute. For example, in *Williams Bros Direct Supply Ltd v.*

65. *Seddon v. Smith* (1877) 36 L.T. 168 at 169; *George Wimpey & Co. Ltd v. Sohn* [1967] Ch. 487 at 511.
66. [1974] V.R. 547.
67. (1977) 38 P. & C.R. 452 at 472.
68. *Tecbild Ltd v. Chamberlain* (1969) 20 P. & C.R. 633.
69. See Jackson, "The Animus of Squatting" (1980) 96 L.Q.R. 333 at 334.
70. *Powell v. McFarlane* (1977) 38 P. & C.R. 452 at 472.
71. (1909) 8 C.L.R. 133.
72. [1974] V.R. 547.

Raftery,[73] Raftery's evidence that he was entitled to use the strip of land at the back of his rented premises, that he was "[n]ot trying to take over land, not really" and that he had done nothing to keep the true owners off the land revealed a lack of the relevant intention and was one reason for the Court of Appeal deciding that he had not taken possession. The Court of Appeal appeared to apply a subjective intention test but it seems that such a test may only be used in the very unusual situation of a squatter directly denying the requisite intention. Where there is no such denial of intention by the squatter, an objective based intention test must be used.

In contrast to the situation where the alleged possessor specifically denies having the requisite intention as in *Raftery's* case, it appears that statements or declarations of intention made by the claimant indicating possession of the requisite intention, should be accorded little weight in determining whether or not the animus possidendi exists. Such statements are capable of being "merely self-serving"[74] and may be very difficult to refute. This is not only the case where the statement is made at the time of any hearing but also where the statement relied upon was purportedly made at the time when the squatter took factual possession.

[15.22] A consideration, not necessarily relevant to every fact situation, has been referred to and used in a number of cases, both Australian and English.[75] In *Murnane v. Findlay* Cussen J. of the Victorian Supreme Court described this consideration as follows:[76]

> "where an act done is given a more limited effect than otherwise might have been the case by reason of the fact that it may be taken in the circumstances not as indicating an intention to exclude the true owner, but as indicating an intention merely to produce a particular special benefit to the person doing it."

For example, a person claiming rights through adverse possession may be held not to have dispossessed the true owner because the claimant was merely doing something in furtherance of rights of enjoyment already conferred on her or him by the true owner. In *Riley v. Penttila*, it was held that the act of erecting a fence and enclosing the disputed area showed an intention to produce a special benefit rather than an intention to exclude everyone including the true owner.[77]

[15.23] Two specific questions arise in a consideration of the exact nature of the requisite intention. First, the issue as to whether or not it is necessary to have an intention to exclude the true owner specifically must be addressed. The Australian and English authorities referred to above are clear in their definition of the animus possidendi in the

73. [1958] 1 Q.B. 159.
74. (1977) 38 P. & C.R. 452 at 476.
75. *Murnane v. Findlay* [1926] V.L.R. 80; *Riley v. Penttila* [1974] V.R. 547; *Littledale v. Liverpool College* [1900] 1 Ch. 19; *Leigh v. Jack* (1879) 5 Ex. D. 264; *Philpot v. Bath* (1904) 20 T.L.R. 589, (1905) 21 T.L.R. 634; *George Wimpey & Co. Ltd v. Sohn* [1967] Ch. 187.
76. [1926] V.L.R. 80 at 88.
77. [1974] V.R. 547 at 564.

limitation context. The traditional view taken in these cases, first in *Littledale v. Liverpool College*[78] and followed in a number of subsequent cases, requires that the person claiming to be in adverse possession must intend, not only to exclude strangers and exercise control over the land, but also to exclude the true owner specifically.[79] It has been argued that this seemingly entrenched view of the animus possidendi is not part of the common law's concept of possession of land.[80] The more common meaning ascribed to the term animus possidendi is that it comprises an intention to exercise control and to exclude strangers. The English Court of Appeal in *Ocean Estates v. Pinder*[81] adopted this meaning. There seems to be little merit in the insistence upon an unlimited intention to exclude the true owner specifically: the owner is not placed in any better position,[82] and the adverse possessor is not required to prove any further or more substantial facts with respect to user than if the usual definition of animus possidendi were adopted. Further, it fails to take account of the situation, which has been accepted as constituting adverse possession, where the adverse possessor uses the land believing her or himself to be the owner.[83] The interpretation of the animus possidendi which requires an intention to exclude the true owner "seems to be an artificial obstacle; it appears to require little more than a private intention to do something which a squatter is not actually required to attempt and which, in most cases, he could not lawfully or practically do".[84]

It should be noted that many of the cases in which the purported adverse possessor failed, and in which the court took the view that an intention to exclude the true owner was necessary, could have been resolved against the adverse possessor upon a more liberally based intention test. For example, in *Riley v. Penttila*, the adverse possessor had no intention to control the area enclosed and exclude others; rather, he erected the fence as a means of better enjoying the easement already granted. A return to the ordinary and simple meaning of the animus possidendi in the limitation context is to be encouraged.

[15.24] A second issue is whether the adverse possessor needs to demonstrate an intention to exclude the true owner for all time and in all future circumstances. Several decisions suggest that an intention to *own* the land must be present and thus indicate that the above intention must

---

78. [1900] 1 Ch. 19 at 23.
79. See e.g. *Clement v. Jones* (1909) 8 C.L.R. 133; *Riley v. Penttila* [1974] V.R. 547 at 563; *Powell v. McFarlane* (1977) 38 P. & C.R. 452 at 471ff.; *Buckinghamshire C.C. v. Moran* [1989] 2 All E.R. 225 at 236, 238-9. See Dockray, op. cit. I, 257ff.
80. Dockray, op. cit. I, at 258 and the texts he cites supporting his argument— Pollock and Wright, *Possession*, p. 17; Lightwood, *Possession*, p. 23; Holmes, *The Common Law*, p. 220.
81. [1969] 2 A.C. 19.
82. Such an intention does not give the owner any greater knowledge of the adverse possessor's possession as it does not require the adverse possessor to "inform" the owner of her or his presence on the land.
83. *Bligh v. Martin* [1968] 1 W.L.R. 804.
84. Dockray, op. cit. I at 261.

be present.[85] However, the better view is that the requisite intention is an intention to possess to the exclusion of all others rather than an intention to own.[86] In the *Moran* case, statements by the adverse possessor that impliedly acknowledged that he would have to leave the land in dispute if the council, the true owner, decided to go ahead with plans to construct a new road, showed that he did not have an intention to exclude the true owner in all future circumstances. Nevertheless, the adverse possessor intended to possess the plot to the exclusion of all persons including the council, unless and until the road was constructed. On these facts, the Court of Appeal found that the requisite intention was present.

[15.25] The requirement that an adverse possessor has a particular intention or motive has been the subject of some criticism.[87] The question has been asked as to whether deliberate "land stealers" should be placed in a better position than those mistakenly using the land believing they have a right to do so. The limitation statutes do not require any particular motive. However, the interpretation of the term "possession" by the courts, particularly in limitation cases, has ensured that the requisite intention is a vital element. One commentator, Goodman, suggests that the intention of an adverse possessor should be irrelevant. He argues that there should be a rebuttable presumption that long continued possession is adverse to the true owner. More recently, it has been suggested that: "[C]onsideration should be given to changing the whole basis of acquisition of title by possession and limiting it to cases where possession was acquired in *good faith* but, for one reason or another, no valid legal title passed."[88] The suggestion of Goodman is based upon the notion that the common law concept of prescription would be a better doctrine with which to deal with this area of law. In contrast to the statutory principle of limitation, prescription presumes a grant after long use and only operates where the possession is taken as of right—without permission, without stealth and without force. As Nourse L.J. remarked in *Buckinghamshire C.C. v. Moran*: "[t]hat is the antithesis of what is required for limitation, which perhaps can be described as possession as of wrong."[89] Unlike the principle of limitation, the intention of the true owner in prescription is very important for no grant may be presumed if the true owner's intention is shown to be against such a grant. The limitation statutes ensured that prescription did not develop except in the area of incorporeal hereditaments such as easements and profits à prendre.

85. E.g. *Littledale v. Liverpool College* [1900] 1 Ch. 19 at 23; *George Wimpey & Co. Ltd v. Sohn* [1967] Ch. 487 at 511 per Russell L.J.; *Powell v. McFarlane* (1977) 38 P. & C.R. 452.
86. *Buckinghamshire C.C. v. Moran* [1989] 2 All E.R. 225 at 238 per Slade L.J.
87. See e.g. Goodman, op. cit. at 281, passim; Dockray, op. cit. I at 263 and passim; Jackson, "The Animus of Squatting" (1980) 96 L.Q.R. 333 at 336. See also the judgments in *Hayward v. Chaloner* [1968] 1 Q.B. 107.
88. Jackson, "The Animus of Squatting" (1980) 96 L.Q.R. 333 at 336. Emphasis added.
89. [1989] 2 All E.R. 225 at 238.

(iii) Two common examples

[15.26] The most important point which should emerge from the analysis above, is that the issue as to whether or not adverse possession exists, depends heavily upon the facts of each case and the nature of the land involved. Because of this, it is perhaps inappropriate to analyse separately two particular acts that are often relied upon to aid in proof in cases concerning adverse possession. Nevertheless, as the acts in question are so often referred to and relied upon, it is intended to consider them briefly below.

[15.27] **Fencing**. The enclosure of an area of land by fencing is clearly a method by which a person can demonstrate that he or she intends to dispossess and has taken possession of the land. In fact, enclosure has been said to be the strongest possible evidence of adverse possession.[90] Nevertheless, as stated above (see above **[15.19]**), in order to determine if adverse possession has been taken, the erection of a fence must be considered in light of all the circumstances.[91] In *Clement v. Jones*,[92] two blocks of land belonging to two different owners were enclosed within the one ring fence erected by the plaintiff. The plaintiff grazed his cattle over both blocks of land and eventually brought an action claiming to have extinguished the defendants' title. The High Court held in favour of the defendants. Griffith C.J. took the view that the running of cattle on the defendants' land and the erection of the one ring fence around both properties were equivocal acts. Therefore, to determine if there had been dispossession by the plaintiff, the intention of the parties, and in particular the plaintiff, was very important. In view of the fact that the property comprised large areas of grazing land, the acts relied upon by the plaintiff were insufficient to demonstrate that he intended to take exclusive possession and to exclude the defendants.[93]

[15.28] **Payment of Rates**. The payment of rates by a person who is not the true owner, but is in occupation, may be significant in relation to the issue of adverse possession. In *Bank of Victoria v. Forbes*,[94] it was held that such a payment of rates constituted very strong evidence to show that the claimant had a deliberate purpose to create a title in himself and intended to do whatever acts might be necessary to effect that purpose.[95]

90. *Seddon v. Smith* (1877) 36 L.T. 168 at 169.
91. See in particular, *Littledale v. Liverpool College* [1900] 1 Ch. 19; *Riley v. Penttila* [1974] V.R. 547.
92. (1909) 8 C.L.R. 133.
93. Isaacs J. approached the problem by holding that the defendants had not *discontinued* their possession. In view of the type of land, their actions in cutting down timber on the property several times during the relevant period and checking and replacing boundary pegs were evidence of assertion of title and continuing possession. The actions of the plaintiffs were insufficient to demonstrate "dispossession" in these circumstances.
94. (1877) 13 V.L.R. 760.
95. Higinbotham C.J. further held that the payment of rates by a person in occupation who is not the true owner is conclusive to show that the true owner is not in possession. See also *Bree v. Scott* (1904) 29 V.L.R. 692 where the court stated that there should be a strong inference in favour of adverse possession when the person in occupation pays the rates.

The payment of rates by a person who is not in occupation, and who is not the true owner, will not constitute adverse possession save in exceptional circumstances.[96] In *Kirby v. Cowderoy*,[97] the land in dispute comprised wild and unusable bushland. The payment of rates was the only act of possession of which the land was capable and, thus in the circumstances, the payment was considered to constitute an act of adverse possession.

The payment of rates by a true owner who is out of possession, provides only very slight evidence in her or his favour that the occupier of the land is not holding in adverse possession for her or himself.[98]

(b) Entitled to possession but never obtained possession

[15.29] The second type of case may be divided according to whether the title arose upon death or by an assurance inter vivos.

(i) Deceased person in possession at date of death

[15.30] In order for a cause of action to accrue there must be a plaintiff who can sue and a defendant who can be sued. That is, there must be persons who can legally take the position of plaintiff and defendant. When a person entitled to land dies while still in possession, the limitation statutes provide that the cause of action of a person entitled to the land pursuant to a will or an intestacy, accrues at the date of death.[99] This statutory provision ensures that on an intestacy, the cause of action can date from death rather than from the date of the grant of letters of administration. Without such a provision, no cause of action could accrue until the date of the grant of letters of administration for it is only such a grant which confers title on the administrators: the status of the administrator does not automatically date back to the date of death.[100] An executor derives title from the will and thus at the date of death the executor would be competent as a plaintiff or defendant. The grant of probate is simply an affirmation of this. Although perhaps unnecessary, the statutory provision ensures that there can be no argument at all that the right of action does not accrue until the grant of probate.

The rule is subject to the overriding proviso that a right of action will only accrue if there is some other person in whose favour time can run; that is, there is some other person who is in adverse possession of the land.[101]

---

96. *Kirby v. Cowderoy* [1912] A.C. 599; *Ferguson v. Registrar of Titles* [1919] V.L.R. 509.
97. [1912] A.C. 599.
98. *Bree v. Scott* (1904) 29 V.L.R. 692.
99. Limitation statutes: N.S.W.: s. 29; Vic.: s. 9(2); Qld: s. 14(2); S.A.: s. 7; W.A.: s. 5(6); Tas.: s. 11(2). The same rule applies to a rentcharge created by will or taking effect on death.
100. See e.g. *Douglas v. Forrest* (1828) 4 Bing. 686; 130 E.R. 933; *Chetty v. Chetty* [1916] 1 A.C. 603 (P.C.); *Finnegan v. Cementation Co.* [1953] 1 Q.B. 688 (C.A.).
101. See Voumard, p. 346 where he discusses the position of an administrator of the estate of a person dying intestate, where the administrator wishes to institute an action.

(ii) Grant of present interest

[15.31] Where land is assured (other than by will) by a person who was in possession at the time of the assurance and the person to whom the land is assured does not take possession, her or his right to bring an action to gain possession accrues on the date the assurance took effect.[102] Again, the overriding rule is that no right of action accrues unless there is some person in adverse possession in whose favour the limitation period can run.

2. Future Interests

[15.32] The general rule is that the right of action of the holder of a future interest accrues on the date on which the estate becomes one in possession.[103] Thus, for example, if X grants to A for life and to B in fee simple remainder, B's right to bring an action accrues on the date of A's death. That is, the right accrues at the moment her interest changes from a future to a present interest. As in the situations above, the relevant provisions setting out this principle must be read together with the overriding rule that no cause of action shall be deemed to accrue unless there is a person in adverse possession in whose favour the limitation period can run.

[15.33] In Victoria, Queensland, Western Australia and Tasmania, if the land has been adversely possessed whilst the present interest is on foot, the holder of the future interest may not have the full limitation period to bring an action from the time the interest becomes one in possession. Section 10(2) of the *Limitation of Actions Act* 1958 (Vic.) is typical of the statutory provisions on this point.[104] It provides that if the holder of the preceding estate were not in possession at the date her or his estate determined, the holder of the succeeding estate has 15 years from the date on which the right of action accrued to the holder of the preceding estate *or* six years from the date her or his own right of action accrued,[105] whichever is the longer. Assume that in the example of the grant given by X to A for life and to B in fee simple remainder, the grant was made in 1980 and in 1982, A was dispossessed by S. If A died in 1985, B would have until 1997, that is 15 years from when the right of action accrued to A, to bring an action to recover the land from S.[106] The qualification cannot be circumvented by creating new interests in land by way of assurance.[107] For example, if A transferred her life estate to Z in 1983, no

---

102. Limitation statutes: N.S.W.: s. 30; Vic.: s. 9(3); Qld: s. 14(3); S.A.: s. 8; W.A.: s. 5(c); Tas.: s. 11(3). The same rule applies with respect to rent charges.
103. Limitation statutes: N.S.W.: s. 31; Vic.: s. 10(1); Qld: s. 15(1); S.A.: s. 9; W.A.: s. 7; Tas.: s. 12(1).
104. Limitation statutes: Qld: s. 15(2); W.A.: s. 7; Tas.: s. 12(2).
105. That is, the date of death of the holder of the preceding estate, assuming the land was held in adverse possession by another person.
106. B's own right of action accrued in 1985 and the six years from that date is the shorter period.
107. Limitation statutes: Vic.: s. 10(3); Qld: s. 15(3); W.A.: s. 7; Tas.: s. 12(5). Note that "assurance" in the context of these particular provisions presumably includes assurance by way of will: no specific exemption is made for wills as is made, e.g., in s. 9(3) of the Victorian Act. See above **[15.31]**.

fresh right of action arises. Z would have 15 years from when A's cause of action accrued and B the holder of the future interest, would be in the same position as if A had not transferred her interest: that is, B would have 15 years from when the right of action accrued to A or six years from when her own right of action accrued, whichever is the longer, to institute an action.

[15.34] Where a person is entitled to both a present interest and a future interest in the land (successive interests) and the right to recover the estate or interest in possession is barred, no action may be brought in respect of the future estate unless in the meantime possession has been recovered by a person entitled to an intermediate estate.[108] Thus, if the grant is to A for life, to B for life in remainder and then to A in fee simple remainder, and A, during the currency of the life estate is dispossessed for the statutory period, she and her successors lose the right of action with respect to both the life estate and the fee simple remainder. If, however, B recovered possession subsequently, the estate of A would have a right to recover in respect of the fee simple upon B's death.[109]

3. Land Held on Trust

[15.35] The limitation statutes make clear that the provisions of the statutes apply to equitable interests in like manner as they apply to legal interests.[110] There are two situations where a beneficiary may be affected by the wrongful possession of another: first, where a right of action accrues to the beneficiary as against the trustee, and secondly, where a right of action accrues to the beneficiary or the trustee as a result of adverse possession being taken by a stranger. Further, consideration must be given to the question of whether a beneficiary can ever bar the title of the trustee.

(a) Adverse possession by the trustee

[15.36] Despite the general provision described above, a trustee cannot obtain a title to the land by way of adverse possession against the beneficiaries. No period of limitation applies to an action by a beneficiary in respect of any fraud or fraudulent breach of trust to which the trustee was privy *or to recover from the trustee, trust property or the proceeds thereof in the possession of the trustee or previously received by the trustee and converted to his use.*[111]

108. Limitation statutes: N.S.W.: s. 67; Vic.: s. 10(4); Qld: s. 15(4); S.A.: s. 22; W.A.: s. 20; Tas.: s. 12(6).
109. Ibid.
110. Limitation statutes: N.S.W.: s. 36; Vic.: s. 11(1); Qld: s. 16; S.A.: ss 31 and 32; W.A.: s. 24; Tas.: s. 13(1). See also the definition sections in the limitation statutes which provide that "land" includes equitable interests: N.S.W.: s. 11(1); Vic.: s. 3(1); Qld: s. 5(1); Tas.: s. 2(1).
111. Limitation statutes: Vic.: s. 21(1); Qld: s. 27(1); S.A.: s. 32(1); W.A.: s. 47(1); Tas.: s. 24(1). See *Re J. Flavelle (decd), Moore v. Flavelle* [1969] 1 N.S.W.R. 361 for an interpretation of this type of provision. Helsham J. took the view that the terminology "an action by a beneficiary to recover from the trustee trust property or the proceeds thereof in the possession of the trustee" must be interpreted strictly: on the facts, the action for the taking of accounts could not

In New South Wales alone, the trustee is entitled to the benefit of limitation periods.[112] Section 47 of the New South Wales Act provides that a beneficiary has 12 years from the time he or she discovered, or could with reasonable diligence have discovered, that he or she had a cause of action to recover the land.

(b) Adverse possession by a stranger

[15.37]   Where a stranger takes adverse possession of the trust property, the normal limitation periods apply and apply equally to legal and equitable interests. However, generally the limitation statutes provide that adverse possession by a stranger for the statutory period will not bar the trustee's legal title until the interests of all the beneficiaries have been extinguished.[113] For example, if T holds property on trust for A for life and for B in fee simple remainder, and S takes adverse possession and remains in possession for the statutory limitation period, A's right of action would be barred. T's legal estate however, is not extinguished until B's right of action is extinguished. B's right to bring an action does not arise until A's death.

In effect, once A's equitable life interest is extinguished, S gains an equitable interest pur autre vie.[114] Upon A's death, B's interest becomes one in possession and his right to bring an action accrues. There is provision for the trustee to bring an action on behalf of a person who holds a beneficial interest in possession. In the example given, therefore, T could bring an action on behalf of B.

---

111. *Continued*
      be construed as an action for the recovery of trust property, although the ultimate aim of the beneficiaries in instituting the action was to recover trust property. See also *Dalton v. Christofis* [1978] W.A.R. 42.

      In England pursuant to s. 91(2) of the *Limitation Act* 1980 (U.K.), an exception is made for a trustee who is also a beneficiary where the trustee acts honestly and reasonably in distributing the property. In this instance the trustee's liability to restore the property or its proceeds is limited to any excess over her or his own proper share.

      There is a general limitation period of six years to recover trust property or in respect of breach of trust, in cases where no other limitation period is prescribed: N.S.W.: s. 48; Vic.: s. 21(2); Qld: s. 27(2); S.A.: ss 32, 35; W.A.: ss 47, 38(1); Tas.: s. 24(2). It does *not* apply to the circumstances set out in the provisions such as s. 21(1) of the Victorian Act.

112. The New South Wales Law Reform Commission took the view that trustees, even fraudulent ones, should gain some protection from the limitation legislation: N.S.W.L.R.C., Report No. 3, paras 230-6.

113. Limitation statutes: N.S.W.: s. 37; Vic.: s. 11(2), (3); Qld: s. 16(2), (3); Tas.: s. 13(3), (4). Cf. the situation in South Australia and Western Australia where there are no such provisions.

114. B has no right to bring an action until her estate is one in possession, that is, upon A's death. T has no right to bring an action on B's behalf until B's estate is one in possession. See Limitation statutes: N.S.W.: s. 37(1); Vic.: s. 11(4); Qld: s. 16(3); Tas.: s. 13(4).

(c) Adverse possession by a beneficiary

[15.38]   By inference, the limitation statutes provide that a beneficiary may, in certain circumstances, extinguish the title of the trustee.[115] In the case of land held on *trust for sale* or *settled land*,[116] time may run against the trustee if the beneficiary is in possession of the land and is solely and absolutely entitled to the beneficial interest.[117]

It is suggested that where land is held on any other type of trust, the beneficiary is in at least as strong a position as if he or she were a beneficiary under a trust for sale or settled land.[118] In referring to this matter, Harman J. in *Bridges v. Mees*[119] quoted with approval from *Underhill on Trusts*:[120]

> "[I]t is apprehended that any other trustee, including a constructive trustee (as, for example, a vendor under an uncompleted contract), is liable to be divested of the legal estate by possession of a person entitled in equity in exactly the same way as if the latter were 'a stranger'."

Therefore, where a purchaser is in possession under an uncompleted contract of sale and has paid the whole of the purchase price and the vendor thereby holds on a constructive trust for the purchaser, time will run in favour of the purchaser-beneficiary who is solely and absolutely entitled and will run against the vendor-trustee. Of course, it must be shown that the beneficiary is not there by the licence of the legal owner.[121] Even where the purchaser has not paid the whole of the purchase moneys, it is suggested the result may be the same provided the purchaser-

---

115. Limitation statutes: N.S.W.: s. 37(2), (3); Vic.: s. 11(3), (5); Qld: s. 16(4); Tas.: s. 13(5).
116. In South Australia and Western Australia there is no provision to suggest otherwise. See Chapter 12 for discussion of the terms "trust for sale" and "settled land".
117. Limitation statutes: N.S.W.: s. 37(2), (3); Vic.: s. 11(3), (5); Qld: s. 16(4); Tas.: s. 13(5). In *Murdoch v. Registrar of Titles* [1913] V.L.R. 75 it was held that time does not run against a legal owner of land until he or she has an effective right of action for recovery. Thus, provided the person in possession is entitled in equity to possession, time would not run against the legal owner because the possession is not adverse. It is submitted that this case is no longer good law in view of the implications to be drawn from the specific statutory provisions such as s. 11(3) and (5) of the Victorian Act.
118. Voumard, p. 348. Cf. *Hyde v. Pearce* [1982] 1 W.L.R. 560.
119. [1957] Ch. 475. The case of *Bridges v. Mees* was referred to with approval by the House of Lords in *Williams and Glyn's Bank Ltd v. Boland* [1981] A.C. 487.
120. See now Underhill and Hayton, *Law of Trusts and Trustees* (14th ed., Butterworths, London, 1979), p. 390.
121. The statutory provisions governing the case in *Bridges v. Mees* were equivalent to the Victorian provisions on this point. In *Bridges v. Mees*, the purchaser originally entered the premises by the permission of the vendor who retained a vendor's lien. Once the whole of the purchase moneys had been paid, the lien disappeared and, prima facie, the vendor with the legal title had a right to enter possession. The fact that the trustee could not have brought an effective action to recover the land because the whole beneficial estate was vested in the purchaser, was considered to be irrelevant: see [1957] Ch. 475 at 485—relying upon *Re Cussons* (1904) 73 L.J. Ch. 296.

beneficiary is not viewed as being there by the licence of the vendor-trustee.[122]

(d) The doctrine of laches

[15.39] Although the general rule now is that the provisions of the limitation statutes apply to equitable interests, there are some examples where these provisions do not apply to equitable claims. For instance, as set above, in all States except New South Wales, a trustee's possession is not considered to be adverse to the beneficiary: see above **[15.36]**. Further, in most States the statutory bars do not apply to claims for equitable relief such as specific performance or an injunction unless they can be applied by analogy to the statutes.[123]

[15.40] However, a person who has a right of action to which no statutory bar applies cannot delay indefinitely the bringing of the action. Courts of equity have always required the plaintiff to use due diligence in proceeding with a claim and have discouraged laches which means literally "negligent inactivity"[124] or more specifically, a failure to proceed with a claim within a reasonable time after becoming aware of the right. The term "acquiescence" is important in a consideration of the doctrine of laches. In the general sense acquiescence is an equitable defence available where the plaintiff has allowed her or his rights to be violated and has sought no redress. The conduct of the plaintiff has no specific relationship to a lapse of time but amounts to an abandonment of rights such that the plaintiff is estopped from enforcing these rights at a later time. However, acquiescence may be inferred if there is an unreasonable delay in the bringing of an action and this inferred acquiescence is the principal criterion in the doctrine of laches.

[15.41] The operation of the doctrine of laches may arise in two different sets of circumstances: first, where the equitable remedy corresponds to a legal remedy for which there is a statutory bar, and secondly, where there is no corresponding claim at common law, or even if there is, the equitable claim has been specifically excluded from any statutory bar. If the equitable remedy being sought corresponds to an action at law that is within a statute of limitation, the courts have applied by analogy the statutory bar applicable to the legal right of action.[125] That

---

122. Voumard, p. 385 and the interpretation given there of s. 11(3) and (5) of the Victorian Act. Cf. *Hyde v. Pearce* [1982] 1 W.L.R. 560 where a purchaser under an uncompleted contract of sale, who had not paid the whole of the purchase price, was held not to have extinguished the title of the legal owner. The Court of Appeal appeared to take the view that a beneficiary cannot establish adverse possession against her or his trustee. The court was not referred to the decision in *Bridges v. Mees*. If it could be shown that the purchaser had been in possession without the licence of the vendor (query this on the facts), it is suggested the decision should have been different. See Thompson "Establishing Adverse Possession" (1983) 127 Sol. J. 210 at 212.

123. Limitation statutes: N.S.W.: s. 23; Vic.: s. 5(8); Qld: s. 10(6)(b); W.A.: s. 38(3); Tas.: s. 9 *Cohen v. Cohen* (1929) 42 C.L.R. 91. See below **[15.41]**.

124. *Partridge v. Partridge* [1984] 1 Ch. 351 at 360.

125. See e.g. *Beckford v. Wade* (1805) 17 Ves. Jun. 87 at 97; 34 E.R. 34 at 38.

is, in applying the doctrine of laches the courts of equity attempt to mirror the statutory bar for a corresponding legal action. This principle of application by analogy of a statutory bar is less relevant now the limitation statutes specifically provide for their provisions to apply to most equitable claims.

Where such analogy cannot be used, equity is forced to find its own definition of what constitutes unreasonable delay. The basic inquiry is whether acquiescence in the state of affairs can be inferred from the plaintiff's delay. The plaintiff must be aware of the relevant facts.[126] Apart from examining the plaintiff's conduct, the court will consider whether the plaintiff's delay has prejudiced the defendant. If there is prejudice to the defendant, this will be a factor in refusing to permit the plaintiff to proceed.[127] So, for example, where a beneficiary seeks to recover trust property from the trustee (an equitable claim which has been specifically excluded from a statutory bar), that right may be barred by the operation of the doctrine of laches if there is "unreasonable delay" by the beneficiary.

4. Limitation and Leasehold Estates

(a) As between the landlord and tenant

(i) Land comprised in lease

[15.42]   The landlord's right to recover possession of the land from the tenant accrues at the end of the term of the lease. Thus, with respect to a fixed-term lease, time starts running against the landlord when the term of the lease has expired.[128]

[15.43]   The fact that any due rent has not been paid by the tenant, does not affect the landlord's title to the land.[129] The landlord is barred from bringing an action to recover any particular instalment of rent, six years from the date on which the rent became due but this has no effect on her or his title to the land.[130] A failure to pay rent may give rise to the landlord having a right to recover the land. This occurs where the lease contains a forfeiture clause for breach of condition, for example non-payment of rent. In all States, except New South Wales and Tasmania, the right to recover possession of the land pursuant to such a clause accrues at the time of the forfeiture.[131] In New South Wales and Tasmania, the right of action accrues when the lessor could with reasonable diligence have discovered

---

126. *Life Association of Scotland v. Siddal* (1861) 3 De G.F. & J. 58 at 73; 45 E.R. 800 at 806; *Lindsay Petroleum v. Hurd* (1874) L.R. 5 P.C. 221 at 241; *Allcard v. Skinner* (1887) 36 Ch. D. 145 at 188 (C.A.).

127. *Gresley v. Mousley* (1859) 4 De G. & J. 78; 45 E.R. 31; *Turner v. Collins* (1871) 7 Ch. App. 329; *Allcard v. Skinner* (1887) 36 Ch. D. 145 at 192 (C.A.).

128. See Megarry and Wade, p. 1037.

129. *Doe d. Davy v. Oxenham* (1840) 7 M. & W. 131; 151 E.R. 708.

130. Limitation statutes: N.S.W.: s. 24; Vic.: s. 19; Qld: s. 25; S.A.: s. 37(f); W.A.: s. 34, but see also s. 38(1); Tas.: s. 22.

131. Limitation statutes: Vic.: s. 12; Qld: s. 17; S.A.: s. 10; W.A.: ss 5(e), 6. Account must also be taken of statutory regimes affecting some types of tenancies (e.g. residential, retail tenancies in some States: see Chapter 11).

the facts giving rise to the right to forfeiture.[132] The failure by the landlord to bring an action pursuant to the forfeiture has no effect on the landlord's quite separate right of action to recover the land at the natural expiration of the term of the lease. This right of action will not be barred until the limitation period has expired.[133]

[15.44]   Special provision is made in the limitation statutes with respect to the accrual of the landlord's right of action against the tenant where the tenancy is, periodic and not in writing, or, is one at will.

[15.45]   With respect to the tenancy at will, the limitation statutes provide that a tenancy at will is deemed to be determined at the expiration of one year from its creation, unless it has previously been determined, and that, accordingly the right of action of the person entitled to the land subject to the tenancy is deemed to accrue on the date of the determination.[134] Thus, in the absence of actual determination by the landlord, time begins to run against the landlord at the end of one year after the creation of the tenancy. Licensees are not provided with the same advantages as tenants at will. If it can be shown that a person has a licence, rather than a leasehold interest,[135] the statutory provisions have no effect and the owner's title cannot be extinguished. The only way in which time can start running against the true owner is if the licence has been actually terminated. Upon revocation of the licence, the true owner has a right to bring an action to recover the land. Failure to exercise that right within the limitation period results in the true owner's title being extinguished.

The anomalous distinction between the position of a tenant at will and a licensee has been removed from the limitation legislation in the United Kingdom.[136] It is suggested that similar amendments to the Australian limitation statutes should be made in order to provide that the limitation period commences to run only upon an *actual*, rather than deemed, termination of a tenancy at will.

[15.46]   In the case of a periodic tenancy without a lease in writing,[137] it is provided that the tenancy shall be deemed to be determined at the

132. Limitation statutes: N.S.W.: s. 32; Tas.: s.14.
133. A fresh right of action accrues each time the tenant breaches the condition. With respect to continuing breaches, forfeiture may be used at any time because time runs anew continually: see Megarry and Wade, p. 837.
134. Limitation statutes: N.S.W.: s. 34; Vic.: s. 13(1); Qld: s. 18; S.A.: s. 15; W.A.: s. 9; Tas.: s. 15.
135. See above [10.16-10.18] for a discussion of the lease/licence distinction. Quaere whether it is correct to define a tenancy at will as a leasehold estate: see the discussion above [10.12].
136. *Limitation Amendment Act* 1980 (U.K.), s. 3(1), repealed itself by the *Limitation Act* 1980 (U.K.). See now *Limitation Act* 1980 (U.K.), ss 17, 29(5), (6). The change was made in response to the English Law Reform Committee's recommendation: see *Final Report on Limitation of Actions* (Cmnd 6923, 1977), paras 3.54-3.56. The Committee also recommended the abolition of the provision discussed below relating to periodic tenancies but this recommendation was not acted upon by the legislature.
137. For interpretations of these terms, see *Moses v. Lovegrove* [1952] 2 Q.B. 533; *Jessamine Investment Co. v. Schwartz* [1978] Q.B. 264.

end of the first year or other period and the right of action of the person entitled to the land shall be deemed to have accrued at the date of the determination. If rent is subsequently received, the right of action is deemed to accrue on the date of the last receipt of rent.[138]

As Megarry and Wade state, the result of such a provision is that[139] "[a]n oral tenancy will . . . in time ripen into ownership if rent is not paid." Although the English Law Reform Committee suggested the repeal of the English statutory provision covering this matter, the legislature retained the provision, but abolished the provision relating to the tenancy at will. It is suggested that a valid distinction can be drawn between the periodic tenancy and the tenancy at will. Under a periodic tenancy, rent has been paid and the landlord expects and is entitled to regular payments of the relevant periodic sums. A landlord who does not receive a rental payment which is due has some notice of a change in the circumstances of the relationship. This is not the case with respect to a tenancy at will where the landlord has granted a tenancy at will to the tenant usually upon the basis that no rent will be paid. Logically, therefore, a statutory "deemed" termination of a tenancy seems patently less fair to the landlord in the case of a tenancy at will than in the case of a periodic tenancy. Further, it can be argued that the specific statutory provision concerning deemed termination of the periodic tenancy is simply a recognition of the fact that periodic tenancies are treated as a series of fixed-term tenancies: in a fixed-term tenancy, a right of action accrues to the landlord at the expiration of the fixed term.

[15.47]   The provisions discussed above with respect to the accrual of rights of actions (see above **[15.08]-[15.11]** and **[15.30]-[15.32]**), demonstrate that no right of action shall arise unless the land is in the possession of some person in whose favour the period of limitation can run (that is, unless some person is in adverse possession). Thus, although for example s. 9(1) of the *Limitation of Actions Act* 1958 (Vic.) provides that a right of action arises when a person has been dispossessed of land or has discontinued her or his possession, s. 14(1) makes it clear that no right will so arise unless another person is in adverse possession of the land.

The provisions relating to the accrual of rights of action in particular tenancy situations (such as in s. 13(1) and (2) of the Victorian Act), *deem* that in particular circumstances a right of action will accrue in relation to certain tenancies in the same way as s. 9(1), relating to present interests, *deems* a right of action to accrue in particular circumstances. If s. 9(1) is to be read in conjunction with s. 14(1), as it undoubtedly is, it is suggested that so too should s. 13(1) and (2) be read in conjunction with s. 14(1). In most instances where a tenant does not pay rent and continues in possession, it would be difficult to deny that he or she was in adverse possession pursuant to s. 14(1). Nevertheless, there may be special facts indicating that there was no adverse possession by the tenant, no person in whose favour the limitation period could run and thus, pursuant to

138. Limitation statutes: N.S.W.: s. 34; Vic.: s. 13(2); Qld: s. 18; S.A.: s. 16; W.A.: s. 10; Tas.: s. 15.
139. Megarry and Wade, p. 1039.

s. 14(1), no accrual of a right of action. For instance, a tenant under a periodic tenancy may not ever have taken possession[140] pursuant to the tenancy. Although prima facie failure to pay rent would give rise, pursuant to s. 13(1), to a right of action in the landlord, it is suggested that s. 14(1), providing that no right of action will accrue unless some person has adverse possession would apply and negative the accrual of a right of action.

The above analysis has been placed in the realm of supposition as a result of the English Court of Appeal decision in *Hayward v. Chaloner*.[141] In this case, the English provisions equivalent to ss 13(2) and 14(1) of the *Limitation of Actions Act* 1958 (Vic.) were considered. The majority of the Court of Appeal took the view that the s. 14(1) provision bore no further on the s. 13(2) provision. As Russell L.J. stated:[142]

> "I have no doubt that the possession of a tenant is to be considered adverse once the period covered by the last payment of rent has expired, so that s. 10(1) [(s. 14(1) of the Victorian Act)] does not bear further on s. 9(2) [s. 13(2) of the Victorian Act]."

Although of persuasive authority, the decision in *Hayward v. Chaloner* is not binding in Australia. A subsequent English Court of Appeal, although bound by *Hayward's* case, by inference doubted the correctness of the decision.[143]

It is suggested that, in Australia, no cause of action should accrue in the tenancy examples unless the tenant is in adverse possession. It is important to reiterate that in most fact situations the tenant relying upon the s. 13(1) or s. 13(2) type of provision will also satisfy s. 14(1).[144]

(ii) Land of landlord or a stranger not included in the lease

[15.48] If the tenant encroaches on to other land of the landlord, on to waste land or on to the land of a third person, "the encroachment must be considered as annexed to the holding, unless it clearly appears that the tenant made it for his own benefit".[145] As the land encroached upon forms part of the demised premises, it is subject to the terms of the tenancy and must be surrendered to the landlord at the expiration of the term of the lease.[146] Thus, if the land encroached upon is that of a third party, any

140. That is, physical possession or receipt of rent.
141. [1968] 1 Q.B. 107.
142. [1968] 1 Q.B. 107 at 122. See the judgment of Lord Denning, in dissent, where his Honour took the view that the ss 13(2) and 14(1) type provisions should be read together.
143. *Jessamine Investment Co. v. Schwartz* [1978] Q.B. 264.
144. It is interesting to note that although *Williams Bros Direct Supply Ltd v. Raftery* (see above [15.14] and [15.21]) was a case concerning a dispute between a landlord and a tenant, the principle discussed in this section was not referred to in argument by counsel or by the court. This point is taken up by Pennycuick V.-C. in *Smirk v. Lyndale Developments* [1975] 1 Ch. 317 at 332.
145. *Kingsmill v. Millard* (1855) 11 Exch. 313 at 318 per Parke B. Approved in *Smirk v. Lyndale Developments* [1975] 1 Ch. 317 at 324 per Pennycuick V.-C. and by the Court of Appeal.
146. *J. F. Perrott & Co. Ltd v. Cohen* [1951] 1 K.B. 705; *Smirk v. Lyndale Developments* [1975] 1 Ch. 317.

rights arising pursuant to a limitation statute, enure for the benefit of the landlord.[147] The presumption that the tenant holds the land encroached upon as part of the demised premises can only be rebutted by strong and clear proof that the tenant intends to take for her or his own benefit and the tenant must communicate this intention to take for her or his own use and benefit to the landlord.[148] For instance, if the tenant conveyed the land to a third party during the tenancy and informed the landlord of the action, the presumption would be rebutted.[149]

(b) As between landlord and stranger

[15.49] Where a tenant is dispossessed of the demised land by a stranger, a right to bring an action to recover the land accrues to the tenant. The landlord, however, holds a reversion and no right of action accrues to the holder of a future interest until the interest falls into possession.[150] The interest becomes one in possession at the termination of the lease. In Victoria and Tasmania, the landlord has the full limitation period from when her or his own cause of action arose in which to bring the action.[151] Although the tenant's right to recover the land is lost at the expiration of the limitation period, the landlord's right to recover the land does not even arise until the expiration of the term.

[15.50] The only way in which the landlord's title to the land can be extinguished during the term of the lease is if "adverse possession" of the rent is taken by a stranger. If the tenant pays the rent to a third party, time runs against the landlord from the time the rent is paid to the third party provided the rent is not a nominal sum.[152]

5. Limitation and Mortgages

(a) Right to redeem

[15.51] The mortgagor's right to redeem the land[153] is lost if the

147. *Kingsmill v. Millard* (1855) 11 Exch. 313; *Tabor v. Godfrey* (1895) 64 L.J. Q.B. 245; *Smirk v. Lyndale Developments* [1975] 1 Ch. 317.
148. Ibid.
149. *Smirk v. Lyndale Developments* [1975] 1 Ch. 317. Cf. *Lord Hastings v. Saddler* (1898) 79 L.T. 355.
150. Limitation statutes: N.S.W.: s. 31; Vic.: s. 10(1); Qld: s. 15(1); S.A.: s. 9; W.A.: s. 7; Tas.: s. 12(1).
151. See above **[15.42]**. The proviso relating to future interests contained in s. 10(2) of the Victorian Act and s. 12(2) of the Tasmanian Act under which the limitation period may be shortened, is inapplicable to leasehold reversions. However, it appears to be applicable to leasehold reversions in Western Australia (s. 7) and Queensland: s. 15(2).
152. Limitation statutes: Vic.: s. 13 ($2 a year); Qld: s. 16(3); S.A.: s. 17; W.A.: s. 11; Tas.: s. 15(3). Cf. N.S.W.: s. 33, where it is provided that in order for a cause of action to accrue to the landlord a further condition must be satisfied: the term of the lease must have become liable to determination by virtue of forfeiture or breach of condition.
153 In New South Wales, Victoria, Queensland and Tasmania, it is clear that the mortgagor's title also is extinguished at the expiration of the limitation period. Limitation statutes: N.S.W.: s. 65 and 4th Schedule; Vic.: s. 18; Qld: s. 24;

mortgagee remains in possession[154] of the mortgaged land for the limitation period,[155] and neither gives a written acknowledgment of the mortgagor's title or equity of redemption, nor receives any money from the mortgagor on account of principal or interest.[156] Receipt of rent whilst in possession is not considered to be receipt of principal or interest.[157]

(b) Mortgagee's rights

The mortgagee's rights to foreclose,[158] to claim possession[159] and to sue for the principal sum[160] accrue when repayment becomes due under the mortgage. The mortgagee loses those rights after the relevant limitation period has elapsed. Time runs anew if the mortgagor makes a written acknowledgment or he or she, or the person in possession of the land, makes any payment of principal or interest.[161]

6. Limitation and Co-ownership

[15.52]   At common law, each co-owner is entitled to the use and possession of the whole of the land: see above [9.01]. Thus, possession by one co-owner cannot be considered to be adverse vis-à-vis the other co-owners. In the absence of wrongful exclusion and of statutory

---

153. *Continued*
    Tas.: s. 21. Quaere the position in South Australia and Western Australia: see Sykes, p. 903. If the land is Torrens land, however, the position may be different. In New South Wales and Tasmania, the extinction of title would occur when the register is altered upon application by the mortgagee: see below [15.84] and [15.86] and see Sykes, p. 908. In Victoria and Western Australia, it has been argued that the title of the mortgagor is extinguished in the same way as it is under general law land and would be effected even before an alteration to the register: see Sykes, pp. 913-914. In Queensland, the mortgagor's title may not be extinguished despite the loss of the right to redeem: see Sykes, p. 914 and in South Australia it is arguable that neither the right to redeem nor title are lost: see Sykes, p. 914.

154. See *Park v. Brady* [1976] N.S.W.L.R. 119; [1976] 2 N.S.W.L.R. 329 (C.A.) where is was held that "possession" in this context means possession in the capacity as mortgagee.

155. Limitation statutes: N.S.W.: s. 41 (12 years); Vic.: s. 15 (15 years); Qld: s. 20 (12 years); S.A.: s. 27 (15 years); W.A.: s. 29 (12 years); Tas.: s. 18 (12 years). Note that formal entry does not constitute possession: N.S.W.: s. 39; Vic.: s. 16; Qld: s. 21; S.A.: s. 18; W.A.: s. 12; Tas.: s. 19.

156. Limitation statutes: N.S.W.: ss 41 and 54; Vic.: ss 24(2), 26; Qld: ss 35, 37; Tas.: ss 29, 31. See generally *Young v. Clarey* [1948] Ch. 191. Cf. the position in South Australia (s. 27) and Western Australia (s. 29) where an acknowledgment of title must be given. See Sykes, pp. 902-904.

157. *Harlock v. Ashberry* (1882) 19 Ch. D. 539. Further see the relevant provisions referred to above for the effect of acknowledgment or part payment on persons other than the maker or recipient.

158. See Sykes, pp. 878-885.

159. See e.g. s. 3(5) of the Victorian Act which provides that a right of action to recover land shall include a reference to a right to enter into possession of the land. See Sykes, pp. 878-885.

160. See e.g. Victorian Act s. 20(1). See Sykes, pp. 889-902.

161. See Sykes, pp. 889-902.

intervention, possession by one co-owner for however long a period would not bar the right and title of the co-owners out of possession.

In all Australian States, however, the limitation statutes provide that a co-owner who takes possession of more than her or his share is deemed to be in adverse possession. The right and title of the co-owner or co-owners out of possession is barred after the relevant statutory period.[161a]

V. POSTPONEMENT OF COMMENCEMENT OF THE LIMITATION PERIOD AND EXTENSION OR SUSPENSION OF THE LIMITATION PERIOD

[15.53] In certain circumstances, the limitation statutes provide for an effectively extended limitation period, either by postponing the time at which the cause of action is deemed to accrue or by suspending the running of the limitation period for a particular time. The extended limitation period may apply where there is disability, fraud, fraudulent concealment, and in some cases, mistake. In South Australia, there is a general power to extend periods of limitation.[162]

1. Disability

(a) Definition

[15.54] Each of the limitation statutes defines the term "disability" for the purposes of the legislation. In all States, a person is deemed to be under a disability if the person is an infant or is of unsound mind.[163] In New South Wales, Queensland and Tasmania, a person undergoing a sentence of imprisonment is deemed to be under a disability.[164] Further, in New South Wales a person is deemed to be under a disability if, for

---

161a. See *Paradise Beach Transportation Co. Ltd v. Price-Robinson* [1968] A.C. 1072; [1968] 1 All E.R. 530 (P.C.). At **[9.37]** it was suggested that in the absence of a relevant statutory provision, there may be no general liability to account between co-owners where one co-owner receives more than her or his joint share or proportion. Quaere, however, whether this right must be deemed to exist in view of these statutory provisions in the limitation statutes discussed here. If a co-owner's title can be barred by a failure to claim her or his just share or proportion, a right to claim must surely exist.

162. S.A.: s. 48. Before exercising such a power the court must be satisfied as to one of two matters: first, material facts were not ascertained by the plaintiff until some time occurring within the 12 months before the expiration of the limitation period *or* occurring after the expiration of the limitation period and that the action was instituted within 12 months of the plaintiff ascertaining those facts; or secondly, that the plaintiff failed to institute the action because of representations or conduct of the defendant and that the failure was reasonable in view of the representations or conduct. Further, it must be just in all the circumstances to grant the extension.

163. Limitation statutes: N.S.W.: s. 11(3)(a), (b); Vic.: s. 3(2); s. 3(3) defines "unsound mind"; Qld: s. 5(2); s. 5(3) defines "unsound mind"; S.A.: s. 45(2); W.A.: s. 16; Tas.: s. 2(2); s. 2(3) defines "unsound mind".

164. Limitation statutes: N.S.W.: s. 11(3)(b)(ii); Qld: s. 5(2); Tas.: s. 2(2)(c).

a period of 28 days or more he or she is incapable of, or substantially impeded in, the management of her or his affairs in relation to the cause of action by reason of, inter alia, a physical disease, and war or warlike operations or circumstances arising therefrom.[165]

The aim of the provisions permitting an extended limitation period for persons under a disability is to ensure that persons with a valid cause of action have the opportunity to initiate a claim when they become fully aware of their rights. There seems no valid reason for confining the definition of disability to cover infancy and lunacy alone. As the legislature of New South Wales has recognised, a person's disability and resulting inability to institute a cause of action may arise from other causes equally as disabling as infancy and insanity.

(b) Application of extended time periods

[15.55]   In Victoria, Queensland, Western Australia and Tasmania, a person who is under a disability at the time the cause of action accrues does not automatically have the right of action barred at the expiration of the normal limitation period. In such a case, the action may be brought at any time before the expiration of six years from the date the person ceased to be under a disability or died.[166] In all of these jurisdictions there is an absolute limit of 30 years where the action is to recover land or money charged on land.[167] It is clear from the wording of the statutory provisions in these States, that the disability must exist at the time the cause of action accrues: a disability arising during the limitation period does not give rise to any extension of time. This position is to be contrasted with the more equitable position in New South Wales and South Australia: see below [15.56].

If a person under a disability becomes subject to another disability before the first has ceased, the extended period of six years from the cessation of the disability applies to both disabilities: that is, such a person would have six years from when he or she ceased to be under a disability at all, subject to the maximum period of 30 years. If, however, the first disability ends before the second disability arises the extended period of six years is computed from the date the first disability ends.[168] Similarly, if the person under a disability is succeeded by another person under a disability, no further extension of time is permitted pursuant to the disability of the second person.[169]

---

165. Limitation statutes: N.S.W.: s. 11(3)(b)(i), (iii) and (iv). See below [15.56] for suspension of limitation periods in the event of war in other jurisdictions. See also Western Australia, s. 16 where coverture (except in the case of a married woman entitled to make such entry or distress or bring such action) is deemed to be a disability.

166. Limitation statutes: Vic.: s. 23(1); Qld: s. 29(1); W.A.: s. 16; Tas.: s. 26(1).

167. Limitation statutes: Vic.: s. 23(1)(c); Qld: s. 29(2)(b); W.A.: s. 18; Tas.: s. 26(4).

168. The wording of the provisions makes these conclusions clear.

169. Limitation statutes: Vic.: s. 23(1)(b); Qld: s. 29(2)(a); W.A.: s. 19; Tas.: s. 26(3). Note also, that where the right of action accrues first to a person not under a disability and another person who *is* under a disability succeeds to the interest of the first person, no extension of time is granted: Vic.: s. 23(1)(a); Qld: s. 29(3)(a); W.A.: s. 16; Tas.: s. 26(2).

[15.56] In New South Wales and South Australia, the running of the limitation period is suspended while the person with a cause of action is under a disability.[170] In both jurisdictions it is provided that no period of limitation may be extended to more than 30 years from when the cause of action first arose.[171] Unlike the position in the other jurisdictions, it is immaterial whether the person with the cause of action suffered from the disability at the time the cause of action arose or whether the disability arose at a later date. Whilst the person with the right is under a disability, time does not run.

Further, in New South Wales if the limitation period would expire within three years of the date the person with the right of action ceases to be under a disability or dies, the limitation period is extended so as to provide for expiration three years after the disability ceases or death occurs.[172] Section 52(2) of the *Limitation Act* 1969 (N.S.W.) provides specifically that the section applies whenever a person is under a disability, whether or not that person is under the same or another disability during the limitation period. Although the *Limitation of Actions Act* 1963 (S.A.) does not contain such a provision, it is suggested that the wording of the general provision on this point, s. 45(1), ensures that the same principle is applicable.

The limitation statutes in some jurisdictions provide for the suspension of the running of the limitation period when the person with the right of action is prevented from exercising that right as the result of involvement in a war. The New South Wales provision has been discussed above: see above **[15.54]**. In Victoria and Tasmania, the limitation statutes provide that any time during which it was not reasonably practicable for a person to commence an action by reason of a war in which Australia was or is engaged, is to be excluded in computing the limitation period. Further, the limitation period is deemed not to expire before the end of 12 months from the date on which it was reasonably practicable to commence an action.[173]

2. Fraud and Fraudulent Concealment

[15.57] Despite some insubstantial differences in wording, the provisions relating to the extension of the limitation period in the case of fraud and fraudulent concealment are the same in Victoria, Queensland and Tasmania. The provision in New South Wales is very similar to the provisions in these jurisdictions.[174] For example, s. 27 of the *Limitation of Actions Act* 1958 (Vic.) provides:

170. Limitation statutes: N.S.W.: s. 52; S.A.: s. 45(1).
171. Limitation statutes: N.S.W.: s. 51; S.A.: s. 45(3).
172. Limitation statutes: N.S.W.: s. 52(1)(e).
173. Limitation statutes: Vic.: s. 23(2); Tas.: s. 28. Section 48 of the *Limitation of Actions Act* 1936 (S.A.) contains a general power to extend periods of limitation subject to the court being satisfied as to a number of matters. It is doubtful, however, whether this provision could be used in all cases of inability to institute an action by reason of war. The matters of which the court must be satisfied pertain to non-ascertainment of material facts and failure to institute the action because of representations by the defendant.
174. Limitation statutes: N.S.W.: s. 55; Vic.: s. 27; Qld: s. 38; Tas.: s. 32.

"Where, in the case of any action for which a period of limitation is prescribed by this Act—

(a) the action is based upon the fraud of the defendant or his agent or of any person through whom he claims or his agent; or

(b) the right of action is concealed by the fraud of any such person as aforesaid;

. . .

the period of limitation shall not begin to run until the plaintiff has discovered the fraud . . . or could with reasonable diligence have discovered it:

Provided that nothing in this section shall enable any action to be brought to recover or enforce any charge against or set aside any transaction affecting any property which—

(i) in the case of fraud, has been purchased for valuable consideration by a person who was not a party to the fraud and did not at the time of the purchase know or have reason to believe that any fraud had been committed."

[15.58]   The provisions have their origins in the *Real Property Limitation Act* 1833 (U.K.) and are substantially the same as the fraud provisions in the now repealed *Limitation Act* 1939 (U.K.). It should be noted, however, that the fraud provisions in earlier legislation applied only to actions in relation to land whereas the fraud provisions in the 1939 legislation applied generally to all types of actions. The English decisions interpreting the English legislation are therefore, of direct relevance. In order to demonstrate that the "action is based on fraud", fraud must be an essential criterion of the cause of action. For example,[175] "an action for damages for deceit and an action claiming rescission of a transaction brought about by fraud" are actions pursuant to which fraud is an essential criterion and are, therefore, actions based on fraud. More specifically, the fraud must be such as would give rise to an independent cause of action. It is unlikely that an extension of the limitation period would be obtained with respect to actions for the recovery of land.

[15.59]   The second ground, fraudulent concealment of a cause of action, has not been interpreted as strictly. In fact, it has been stated that fraudulent concealment has[176] "been carried far beyond its natural meaning and dishonesty and moral turpitude [are] not indispensable elements". Fraudulent concealment does not necessarily involve fraud which would be sufficient to give rise to an independent cause of action:[177] rather, it involves a situation where the defendant knowing to whom a right of action belongs, conceals the circumstances giving rise to the right

---

175. *Beaman v. A.R.T.S. Ltd* [1949] 1 K.B. 550 at 558.
176. Megarry and Wade, p. 1047. In England, the term "fraudulent concealment" was considered so inappropriate that s. 32(1) of the *Limitation Act* 1980 (Eng.) refers to deliberate concealment instead of fraudulent concealment.
177. *Beaman v. A.R.T.S. Ltd* [1949] 1 K.B. 550 at 559 per Lord Greene M.R.

of action.[178] In commenting upon the meaning of concealment by fraud, Lord Evershed M.R. in *Kitchen v. Royal Air Force Association* stated:[179]

"But it is now clear that the word 'fraud' in the section . . . is by no means limited to common law fraud or deceit. Equally, it is clear, . . . that no degree of moral turpitude is necessary to establish fraud. . . . What is covered by equitable fraud is a matter which (is not capable of definition) . . . but it is, I think, clear that the phrase covers conduct which, having regard to some special relationship between the two parties concerned, is an unconscionable thing for the one to do towards the other."

There have been a number of cases concerning fraudulent concealment in the context of actions for the recovery of land.[180] Clearly, a person who conceals from the ultimate plaintiff that he or she had a right to the land and has by such concealment enabled her or himself or some other person to hold the land in adverse possession, has concealed by fraud a right of action. Most specifically, it has been held that a right of action has been fraudulently concealed where title deeds to the property showing the plaintiff to have an interest, have been withheld or destroyed.[181]

[15.60] In South Australia and Western Australia, the relevant provisions are confined to equitable actions concerning the recovery of land or rent.[182] The provisions are drawn directly from the 1833 English limitation legislation. Effectively, these provisions have the same effect in the context of actions for the recovery of land as do the more recently drafted provisions in the other jurisdictions. Actions for the recovery of land will rarely fall within the terminology of "an action based on fraud". "Fraudulent concealment" of a right of action is more likely to give rise to a claim for an extended limitation period where the action concerns land. The term "concealed fraud" is interpreted in the same way as the terms "fraudulent concealment" or "concealed by fraud".[183]

[15.61] In all States, the defences of fraud and fraudulent concealment may not be used to extend the limitation period if the defendant is or claims through a purchaser for valuable consideration who was not a party to the fraud and did not know at the time of the purchase or have reason to believe that any fraud had been committed.

178. *Petre v. Petre* (1853) 1 Drew 371 at 397-398; 61 E.R. 493 at 504.
179. (1958) 1 W.L.R. 563 at 572-573.
180. See generally Cheshire and Burn, p. 846. Megarry and Wade, p. 1047.
181. *Lawrence v. Lord Norreys* (1890) 15 App. Cas. 210. Other examples of fraudulent concealment include the obtaining of a conveyance from a person under a disability such as insanity (*Lewis v. Thomas* (1843) 3 Hare 26; 67 E.R. 283); the concealment of a title deed or deeds which showed the plaintiff to have an interest (*Re McCallum* [1901] 1 Ch. 143). Cf. *Rains v. Buxton* (1880) 14 Ch. D. 537 where the occupation of subterranean land without the knowledge of the owner did not amount to fraudulent concealment. See also *Vane v. Vane* (1873) 8 Ch. A. 383; *Applegate v. Moss* [1971] 1 Q.B. 406 (agent/independent contractor); *Bulli Coal Mining Co. v. Osborne* [1899] A.C. 351.
182. Limitation statutes: S.A.: s. 25(1); W.A.: s. 27.
183. *Bulli Coal Mining Co v. Osborne* [1899] A.C. 351; *Crown v. McNeil* (1922) 31 C.L.R. 76. See also *Clark v. Clark* (1882) 8 V.L.R. (E) 303; *Montgomeries Brewery Co. Ltd v. Blyth* (1901) 27 V.L.R. 175.

3. Mistake

[15.62] In all jurisdictions except South Australia and Western Australia, similar provisions as those discussed above in relation to fraud and fraudulent concealment, apply to actions "for relief from the consequences of a mistake". In *Phillips-Higgins v. Harper*[184] it was held that the provision had a very narrow operation and that relief is only available under this provision "where the mistake is an essential ingredient of the cause of action". An action for the recovery of money paid under mistake of fact is an example of the mistake being an essential criterion of the cause of action.[185] In contrast, there is no general rule that a mistake prevents time from running: for example, an owner of land who permits a neighbour to take adverse possession of part of her land because of a "mistake" about the boundary, may not rely on the provision to prevent time from running.

Prior to 1939, the limitation legislation concerning land in England did not contain a mistake provision. It seems clear that the mistake provision was not included in the 1939 English limitation statute for the purpose of dealing with actions relating to land. As Megarry and Wade state, claims for relief against mistake concerning land are most often based on equitable grounds (for example, a claim for rectification) and such equitable claims are not subject to specific limitation periods anyway.[186] There appears to be little, if any, scope for the operation of "the relief from mistake" provisions with respect to actions for the recovery of land. Therefore it is suggested that the absence of such provisions from the South Australian and Western Australian legislation has no practical significance.[187]

VI.   RUNNING OF THE LIMITATION PERIOD

[15.63] A person's right to bring an action to recover land will not be barred unless it is proved that adverse possession of the land has continued unbroken for the limitation period. The limitation statutes provide specifically that no cause of action accrues until adverse possession is taken of the land, and that a cause of action which has accrued will be deemed not to have accrued if the land ceases to be in adverse possession.[188] Thus, it is clear that there must be a continuous, uninterrupted period of adverse possession for the whole of the limitation period before the owner's right to recover the land is lost.

For various reasons the person who originally takes adverse possession may not complete the full period of adverse possession her or himself.

---

184. [1954] 1 Q.B. 411.
185. *Phillips-Higgins v. Harper* [1954] 1 Q.B. 411.
186. Megarry and Wade, pp. 1047-1048.
187. Note the general power, subject to specific conditions to extend the limitation period in South Australia: s. 48(1), (2), (3).
188. Limitation statutes: N.S.W.: s. 38(3); Vic.: s. 14(2); Qld: s. 19(2); W.A.: s. 5; Tas.: s. 16(2). Effect obtained by implication in South Australia: see above **[15.08]**.

1. Alienation by Adverse Possessor

[15.64] The possessor of land has a proprietary interest in the land, a title based on possession.[189] This right is enforceable against the whole world except someone with a superior right to possession (the true owner or a person with a prior possessory interest, such interest not having been abandoned). The possessory interest of the adverse possessor is capable of being disposed of to another person. The adverse possessor can sell, give or devise her or his title and the recipient of the interest has an interest in the land which is the same as that of the adverse possessor. For example, if S has been in adverse possession of A's land, Blackacre, for six years, and S dies leaving her possessory interest in Blackacre to Z; Z, who goes into possession of Blackacre, may add S's period of adverse possession to her own. Therefore, if the action arose in Victoria where the limitation period is 15 years, A's title would be extinguished at the end of a further nine year period of adverse possession by Z. Z, who is S's devisee, can add the two periods together. It is important to remember that if Z does not take adverse possession herself, time stops running against A, the owner, and no fresh right of action accrues to A until adverse possession of the land is taken again.[190]

[15.65] In order for the true owner's title to be lost in these circumstances, it is not essential that the adverse possessor formally conveys the interest by appropriate documentation.[191] Provided there has been continuous adverse possession for the statutory period, the true owner's right of action is lost.

[15.66] Nevertheless, in a dispute between two persons each claiming under possessory titles, the presence or absence of formal documentation may be important.[192] Assume that S took adverse possession of O's land, remained there for ten years and then conveyed the possessory title to X. Assume further that Y, not X, took adverse possession at the time S left the land and stayed there for the remainder of the statutory period. As between X and Y, X has the better possessory interest because X can rely on the prior possession of S: the possessory title had been conveyed to him.[193] Without proof of the formal conveyance from S to X, X would

---

189. For earlier discussion of this matter, see above **[2.05]-[2.12]**. See *Asher v. Whitlock* (1865) L.R. 1 Q.B. 1; *Allen v. Roughley* (1955) 94 C.L.R. 98. Cf. *Nicholas v. Andrew* [1920] 20 S.R. (N.S.W.) 178 where there were periods of up to three months in duration when the land was not occupied, and yet, it was held the requirement of continuous adverse possession for the statutory period had been satisfied.

190. *Trustees Executors & Agency Co. Ltd v. Short* (1888) 13 App. Cas. 793.

191. *Mulcahy v. Curramore Pty Ltd* [1974] 2 N.S.W.L.R. 464 at 471. Cf. the position under the *Nullum Tempus Act* discussed above **[15.05]**.

192. *Mulcahy v. Curramore Pty Ltd* [1973] 1 N.S.W.L.R. 737 at 746 per Helsham J.; *Kirk v. Sutherland* [1949] V.L.R. 33.

193. Note that in New South Wales, the effect of s. 50(2) of the *Conveyancing Act* 1919 deriving from the *Pretenced Titles Act* 1540 (32 Hen. VIII c. 9) may have the effect of preventing a person in X's position from ejecting a person in Y's position. By s. 50(2) the conveyance or the agreement to convey of a right of entry is void against the person in possession.

have no right against Y. O's position, however, does not depend on the existence of formal documentation: continuous adverse possession for the statutory period extinguishes O's title.

2. Successive Adverse Possessors

[15.67] If the adverse possessor is dispossessed by another, the second adverse possessor can add the first period of adverse possession to her or his own for the purpose of barring the true owner's right of action.[194] For example, if S takes adverse possession of A's land, remains there for six years and is then in turn dispossessed by T, A's title to the land would be extinguished after a further nine years' adverse possession by T.[195] In fact, the limitation period may comprise adverse possession by any number of unrelated adverse possessors. The only proviso is that there must be continuous and uninterrupted adverse possession for the duration of the relevant limitation period. As Bowen C.J. in *Mulcahy v. Curramore Pty Ltd* stated:[196]

"Where there have been a series of trespassers, not deriving title from each other, who have been in adverse possession for [the limitation period, the statute] will operate to extinguish the true owner's title. It is emphasised that possession by successive trespassers must be continuous to have this effect."

This principle is now expressly statutorily enacted in New South Wales.[197]

In the example above, A's right of action is barred and his title is extinguished at the end of the limitation period. The question then arises as to whether S or T has a better right to the land. Possession is prima facie evidence of title. S, whilst in possession, was dispossessed by T. S, who had the prior possessory interest, has a right to bring an action against T to recover the land from the wrongdoer.[198]

It is important to note that S's right to bring an action will in turn be barred if T remains in adverse possession for the limitation period.

3. Abandonment by the Adverse Possessor

[15.68] An adverse possessor whose only title to the land is based on possession, loses any interest in the land upon the abandonment of possession before the full limitation period has run. The true owner of the land, or any other person who had a right to recover the land from the adverse possessor, is in the same position as if the land had never been adversely possessed.[199] Thus, when the land is taken into adverse

---

194. *Mulcahy v. Curramore Pty Ltd* [1974] 2 N.S.W.L.R. 464 at 476; *Willis v. Earl Howe* [1893] 2 Ch. 545; *Salter v. Clarke* (1904) 4 S.R. (N.S.W.) 280.
195. In jurisdictions with a 12 year limitation period, A's title would be extinguished after a further six years' adverse possession by T.
196. [1974] 2 N.S.W.L.R. 464 at 476.
197. Limitation statute: N.S.W.: s. 38(2).
198. See *Allen v. Roughley* (1955) 94 C.L.R. 98 at 110 per Dixon C.J.
199. *Allen v. Roughley* (1955) 94 C.L.R. 98; *Mulcahy v. Curramore Pty Ltd* [1974] 2 N.S.W.L.R. 464; *Trustees Executors & Agency Co. Ltd v. Short* (1888) 13 App. Cas. 793.

possession again after an abandonment, the two separate periods of adverse possession cannot be added together.[200]

> "[Upon abandonment the adverse possessor] leaves no cloud on the true owner's title, which is then restored to its pristine force, and another person . . . who later enters into adverse possession of the property, cannot add the period of [the first adverse possessor's] possession to his own so as to extinguish the title of the true owner."

The issue of what constitutes abandonment is a question of fact. Guidance on this matter is gained from looking at the materials on adverse possession covered earlier: see above **[15.12]-[15.28]**. The question as to whether or not there has been an abandonment, must be determined by deciding whether or not the adverse possessor is still in "possession" of the land. Whether the adverse possessor has retained possession in any given instance will depend upon matters such as the nature and character of the land, the usual and natural mode of using it and the animus possidendi.[201]

As stated above, the adverse possessor who abandons the land before the expiration of the limitation period, thereby loses the interest in the land. The title of the adverse possessor is based upon possession: the abandonment of possession means the loss of title.[202] Thus, if S takes adverse possession of A's land, remains for six years and then abandons the land, his possessory title is lost. If T subsequently goes into adverse possession, S has no right of action against T to recover the land. However, a fresh right of action in favour of the owner of the land, A, accrues when T takes adverse possession.

[15.69] The matter is not as simple if the adverse possessor remains in adverse possession for the limitation period, and subsequently, "abandons" possession. Several cases support the view that in this case, the rights of the adverse possessor are not lost by abandonment.[203] Once the statutory limitation period has expired, the adverse possessor acquires a title in fee simple to the land which is good against the whole world, including the true owner.[204] The clear inference to be elicited from this principle is that the adverse possessor has an interest which "extends beyond his actual possession".[205] In *Kirk v. Sutherland*,[206] H enclosed part of the land of his neighbour, B. B knew of the enclosure but did not assert title to the land or demand any rent from H. The area of land remained enclosed by H for a period in excess of the statutory limitation period. Subsequently, H sold the land of which he was the registered proprietor

---

200. *Mulcahy v. Curramore Pty Ltd* [1974] 2 N.S.W.L.R. 464 at 476.
201. See *Nicholas v. Andrew* (1920) 20 S.R. (N.S.W.) 178 at 184 non-user per se is not irrefutable proof of abandonment.
202. *Allen v. Roughley* (1955) 94 C.L.R. 98.
203. *Perry v. Clissold* [1907] A.C. 73; *Ferguson v. Registrar of Titles* [1919] V.L.R. 509; *Kirk v. Sutherland* [1949] V.L.R. 33; *Allen v. Roughley* (1955) 94 C.L.R. 98; *Mulcahy v. Curramore Pty Ltd* [1974] 2 N.S.W.L.R. 464. See generally the position regarding Torrens land **[15.82]**ff.
204. *Allen v. Roughley* (1955) 94 C.L.R. 98; *Asher v. Whitlock* (1865) L.R. 1 Q.B. 1.
205. *Kirk v. Sutherland* [1949] V.L.R. 33 at 37.
206. [1949] V.L.R. 33.

to X and, several years later, X sold the land to the plaintiffs. B sold the land of which he was the registered proprietor to the defendant. Seven years after the sale of his land to X, H purported to convey to the defendant that portion of B's land enclosed by the fence. H claimed that he had acquired a title through adverse possession and that he had not transferred this title at the time he sold the land of which he was the registered proprietor. The plaintiffs brought an action seeking a declaration that they were entitled to be registered as proprietors of the strip of B's land enclosed by the fence.

The Supreme Court of Victoria refused to grant the declaration. Although H had acquired a title through adverse possession, that title had not been transferred to his successors in title. Further, it was held that possessory rights which have endured for the limitation period are not lost if possession no longer continues. The title gained by the adverse possessor, although not the same as that lost by the true owner, is good against the whole world including the true owner. Although B had been in possession of the land for some seven years, H retained "title" to the land and was able to transfer his interest to the defendant.[207]

VII. THE EFFECT OF TIME LAPSING

1. Person Dispossessed

[15.70]   Limitation statutes originally operated to bar the remedy, but not to extinguish the title, of the person dispossessed.[208] Therefore, a person whose right of action to recover land had been barred, and who regained possession of the land peaceably, could reassert title against the adverse possessor. As discussed above, the limitation statutes in all Australian States now provide that both the right of action and the title of the claimant are extinguished at the end of the limitation period.[209]

The extinguishment of title, however, is not as complete and wide-ranging as the above analysis tends to suggest. In a straightforward fact situation, the extinguishment of title *is* final. For example, where S dispossesses A of her land and remains there for the limitation period, A loses her right of action and her title is finally extinguished against S: there is no method by which she can revive her title so as to defeat S.

It is important to note, however, that the title of the dispossessed person is extinguished only against the adverse possessor.[210] In the uncomplicated example above, extinguishment of title as against the

---

207. It should be noted that had B not transferred his interest, his "title" to the land could in turn have been extinguished.
208. For a discussion of this historical point see Cheshire and Burn, p. 840; Megarry and Wade, p. 1050; Sackville and Neave, p. 509.
209. As discussed above **[15.37]**, the right of action and the title of the trustee are not lost until the rights of action of all beneficiaries have been barred. As to land under the Torrens system of land registration: see below **[15.82]**ff. As to the situation concerning mortgages see above **[15.51]-[15.52]** and Sykes, pp. 878ff.
210. *Fairweather v. St Marylebone Property Co. Ltd* [1963] A.C. 510 (H.L.); *Taylor v. Twinberrow* [1930] 2 K.B. 16. Cf. *Re Field* [1918] 1 I.R. 140.

adverse possessor results in the true owner, A, losing the land finally and completely. The extinguishment of the fee simple as against the adverse possessor is effectively the same as extinguishment of title per se: there is no method by which the person dispossessed can reassert title. However, where the person dispossessed is a lessee, the position is different. Although the lessee's right of action and title are extinguished as against the adverse possessor, the lessee's title remains good as against the lessor. Thus, the lessee can go back into possession under the lease if the adverse possessor leaves the land.[211] The corollary is that even after her leasehold title is extinguished as against the adverse possessor, the lessee remains liable on the covenants in the lease.[212]

2. The Title of the Adverse Possessor

[15.71]   The adverse possessor holds a title in the land based on possession. Even before the limitation period has expired, the adverse possessor holds an interest in the land, based on possession, which is enforceable against the whole world except a person with a better legal right to possession. Once the limitation period has expired, the adverse possessor does not "acquire" or have transferred to her or him, the estate or title of the person whose title has been extinguished. The interest in the land remains based upon possession. Lord Radcliffe in *Fairweather v. St Marylebone Property Co. Ltd* commented as follows upon the title of the adverse possessor:[213]

> "He is not at any stage of his possession a successor to the title of the man he has dispossessed. He comes in and remains in always by right of possession, which in due course becomes incapable of disturbance as time exhausts the one or more periods allowed by statute for successful intervention. His title, therefore, is never derived through but arises always in spite of the dispossessed owner."

The interest of an adverse possessor is capable of "progressive improvement".[214] The following examples demonstrate the meaning of this phrase. First, if S takes adverse possession of A's land and remains there for eight years before being dispossessed himself by T, S has a title which, at the time of his dispossession, is good against the whole world except A. If T remains in adverse possession for a further seven years (assuming the limitation period to be 15 years), A's title is barred and S has the best title to the land. S's interest in the land has progressively improved. Secondly, if S takes adverse possession of leased land and bars the interest of the tenant, he has an interest in the land which is good against everyone except the landlord. S's interest may "improve" into one which is enforceable against everyone, including the landlord, if the landlord fails, when his own cause of action has arisen, to bring an action to recover the land within the relevant limitation period.

---

211. See Cheshire and Burn, p. 841.
212. See *Taylor v. Twinberrow* [1930] 2 K.B. 16, discussed below [15.73].
213. [1963] A.C. 510 at 535.
214. Megarry and Wade, p. 535.

(a) Rights of third parties

[15.72]   The adverse possessor by dispossessing the true owner of the fee simple and retaining adverse possession for the relevant limitation period does not extinguish the title of a third party who has a proprietary interest in the land.[215] The adverse possessor is bound by easements or restrictive covenants affecting the land.[216] By express provision, the limitation statutes do not apply to easements[217] and the majority of the English Court of Appeal in Re Nisbet and Potts' Contract[218] took the view that the benefit of a restrictive covenant was not a right which could be barred by the operation of the limitation statute.[219]

(b) Adverse possession of leased land

[15.73]   When a person takes adverse possession of leased land and remains for the relevant limitation period, the right of action of the tenant is barred. The landlord's title remains valid, however, and upon the expiration of the lease, the landlord will have a full limitation period in which to bring an action to recover the land.

The fact that the adverse possessor extinguishes the right of action and the title of the tenant does not result in a positive transfer of the leasehold estate to the adverse possessor. As explained above (see above [15.03]), the limitation statutes operate negatively: the adverse possessor's title is founded on possession. The interest is best described as a legal fee simple interest subject to the landlord's right of entry at the end of the term of the lease.

As there is no "transfer" of the leasehold estate from the lessee to the adverse possessor, it is clear that there is no privity of estate between the landlord and adverse possessor and that, therefore, the adverse possessor is not liable on the covenants in the lease.[220] The adverse possessor is directly liable only with respect to covenants that are enforceable as restrictive covenants.[221] Nevertheless, if the lease contains a forfeiture clause for breach of condition, the landlord may effectively force the adverse possessor to comply with the covenants. Although there is no privity of estate, a clause giving a right of re-entry is proprietary in nature

---

215. Re Nisbet and Potts' Contract [1906] 1 Ch. 386.
216. If the interest is legal in nature, it binds the whole world. If it is equitable in nature, it binds the adverse possessor because the adverse possessor is not a bona fide purchaser of the legal estate for value without notice.
217. See the definitions of "land" which do not include incorporeal hereditaments: Limitation statutes: N.S.W.: s. 11(1); Vic.: s. 3(1); Qld: s. 5(1); S.A.: s. 3(1); W.A.: s. 3; Tas.: s. 2(1)2.
218. [1906] 1 Ch. 386.
219. Cf. the judgment of Collins M.R. who took the view the statute may operate to bar such a right if the right were infringed. It should be noted that easements and restrictive covenants may be extinguished in the usual ways: see Chapters 16 and 17.
220. Tichborne v. Weir (1892) 67 L.T. 735.
221. Re Nisbet and Potts' Contract [1906] 1 Ch. 386.

and binds successors in title, including adverse possessors.[222] If the adverse possessor is forced to pay rent to the landlord in order to prevent the landlord from exercising the right of forfeiture, the adverse possessor becomes a periodic tenant.[223] The adverse possessor must not take advantage of the previous tenant's lease in order to avoid a finding that he or she is estopped from denying that she is holding under the lease.[224] Mere payment of rent does not give rise to any such estoppel.[225]

It should be noted that the tenant whose title has been extinguished as against the adverse possessor, remains liable on the covenants of the lease. Privity of contract exists between the landlord and the tenant. Even if the dispossessed tenant is an assignee of the lease rather than the original tenant, it is suggested liability on the covenants remains. Although the tenant's title is extinguished as against the adverse possessor, privity of estate remains as between the landlord and the tenant.[226]

(c) **Effect of surrender of lease and acquisition of reversion where the leasehold interest has been extinguished by an adverse possessor: means by which a lessee may become entitled to possession again despite extinguishment of title**

(i) Surrender

[15.74] A tenant, whose title has been extinguished by the adverse possession of another, may surrender the leasehold interest to the landlord, and thereupon, the landlord may recover the land from the adverse possessor.[227] In *Fairweather v. St Marylebone Property Co. Ltd*,[228] the owner of the land, A, granted a 99 year lease to the tenant, B. A neighbouring landowner, S, took adverse possession of a shed at the back of the leased land and in time barred the tenant's right to bring an action to recover the land. Subsequently, B surrendered the lease to A. The issue to be decided was whether A could resume possession immediately or whether he had to wait until the lease determined by the effluxion of time, that is, until the expiration of the 99 year term.

The House of Lords held that A, the owner of the land, had the right to possession of the land upon surrender of the lease. Although the adverse

---

222. See Chapter 10 for a discussion of forfeiture clauses in leases. Note that the landlord would also have a right of re-entry against the adverse possessor if the lease can be determined by notice. Further, Megarry and Wade pp. 709 and 1054 argue that the adverse possessor may be liable to distress in the event of failure to pay rent: in this context, note that distress is no longer a remedy available in New South Wales, Victoria, Queensland or Western Australia (see below **[10.76]**) and is a limited remedy in South Australia and Tasmania: see below **[10.76]**.

223. The type of periodic tenancy is determined by the way in which the rent is paid: e.g. weekly, monthly, yearly. See Chapter 10.

224. A person who claims the benefits of a deed, must accept the burdens: see Megarry and Wade, p. 1054.

225. *Tichborne v. Weir* (1892) 67 L.T. 735 Cf. *Ashe v. Hogan* [1920] 1 I.R. 159.

226. *Fairweather v. St Marylebone Property Co. Ltd* [1963] A.C. 510 (H.L.).

227. Ibid.

228. [1963] A.C. 510 (H.L.).

possession of S barred B's right of action and extinguished B's leasehold interest as against S, the landlord and tenant relationship between A and B continued. As against A, although not S, B had a right to possession.[229] When B surrendered the lease, he gave up this right to possession and the leasehold interest merged with the freehold and thus, was extinguished.[230] As the lease was no longer in existence, A had an immediate right to recover the land.[231] The result of the decision in *Fairweather's* case is that the landlord and tenant may work together to defeat the interest of the adverse possessor who has extinguished the tenant's title. The tenant surrenders the term of the lease thereby giving the landlord the right to regain possession from the adverse possessor. After recovering possession, the landlord may grant a new lease to the tenant.[232] The decision in *Fairweather's* case and its possible unpalatable consequences were discussed by the English Law Reform Committee[233] but in the final analysis, no change was recommended.[234]

It has been argued strongly that *Fairweather's* case was incorrectly decided.[235] Megarry and Wade argue that the decision infringes the principle of nemo dat quod non habet. They argue that even if it is accepted that the title of the tenant is extinguished only as against the adverse possessor, the tenant in the *Fairweather* fact situation is still giving the landlord something the tenant has not got—the right to recover the land from the adverse possessor.[236] The logic of this argument appears straightforward and simple. However, if it is accepted that the tenant's title is lost only as against the adverse possessor, it is suggested that the scenario in the *Fairweather* fact situation is inevitable.[237] The tenant has an interest to surrender to the landlord and upon surrender, that interest is extinguished: it merges with the freehold. The landlord, in seeking to recover the land from the adverse possessor, relies upon the immediate right to possession arising from the freehold title.[238]

---

229. This right is evidenced by the fact that the tenant would have been able to resume possession under the lease had the adverse possessor vacated the land.
230. A person cannot have rights against her or himself.
231. See *Fairweather v. St Marylebone Property Co. Ltd* [1963] A.C. 510 where the House of Lords overruled *Walter v. Yalders* [1902] 2 K.B. 304 and approved *Taylor v. Twinberrow* [1930] 2 K.B. 16 on this point.
232. The House of Lords, and in particular Lord Denning, understood that its decision left scope for such collusion and yet did not take the view that this possibility should alter its decision.
233. *Final Report on Limitations of Actions* (Cmnd 6923, 1977), paras 3.44-3.46.
234. See Sackville and Neave, p. 530.
235. Megarry and Wade, p. 1052; Wade, "Landlord, Tenant and Squatter" (1962) 78 L.Q.R. 541. See also the judgment of Lord Morris in dissent: [1963] A.C. 510 at 548.
236. Megarry and Wade concede that it would be different if the landlord had an independent right to recover.
237. See Sackville and Neave, p. 529.
238. *Fairweather's* case has been applied in *Tickner v. Buzzacott* [1965] Ch. 426 and in *Jessamine Investment Co. v. Schwartz* [1978] Q.B. 264. Note however, that in the latter case, there was no question of the principle of nemo dat quod non habet being infringed.

Despite criticism of the decision in *Fairweather's* case, there is no suggestion that it would not apply in Australia.[239]

(ii) Acquisition of reversion

[15.75] A tenant, whose title has been extinguished by the adverse possession of another, is able to recover possession of the land if he or she acquires the reversion from the landlord.[240] Upon such an acquisition, the lease merges in the freehold and is extinguished in the same way as the lease is extinguished if the tenant surrenders the leasehold interest to the landlord.

3. Proof of Title

[15.76] In most cases, a contract for the sale of land provides that the purchaser is entitled to a title evidenced wholly by proper documentary title.[241] Where the contract has such a provision, the vendor cannot force the purchaser to accept a title based on adverse possession.[242]

Even where the contract of sale does not contain such a provision, a purchaser is not required to accept a title based purely on evidence of possession for the relevant limitation period. The simple fact of possession for the limitation period does not show that the titles of all persons with interests in the land have been barred. For example, the true owner might be a person who has granted a lease for a long period and is entitled to a reversion.

In order to be in a position to force the purchaser to accept a possessory title, the vendor must prove the title of the former owner and prove that it has been extinguished in the vendor's favour.[243] This will often be a difficult task for a vendor. In practice, the purchaser may agree to accept an imperfect title.[244]

VIII. METHODS BY WHICH TIME IS STOPPED FROM RUNNING

[15.77] Time stops running if the owner asserts her or his right or if the adverse possessor admits that the owner has a superior right.

1. Asserting Right

[15.78] Time may be stopped from running if the person with the right of action asserts the right by instituting an action to recover the land or

239. See e.g. Sackville and Neave, p. 530. Cf. however, the situation with respect to Torrens land: see below **[15.82]**ff.
240. *Taylor v. Twinberrow* [1930] 2 K.B. 16.
241. See e.g. the general conditions of sale in Table A of the *Transfer of Land Act* 1958 (Vic.), note condition no. 12.
242. *Re Brine and Davies* [1935] 1 Ch. 388. See generally Voumard, pp. 380-381.
243. *Re Atkinson and Horsell's Contract* [1912] 2 Ch. 1; *Ferguson v. Registrar of Titles* [1919] V.L.R. 509; *Allen v. Roughley* (1955) 14 C.L.R. 98; *Maguire v. Browne* (1913) 17 C.L.R. 363. See generally Voumard, pp. 380-381.
244. *Re Nisbet and Potts' Contract* [1906] 1 Ch. 386.

by making a peaceable but effective entry on the land. A mere formal entry is insufficient.[245] In order to stop time from running, the entry must amount to a resumption of possession.[246] Paper claims are not effective to amount to a resumption of possession.[247] Whether there has been a resumption of possession is a question of fact in each case.[248] It is clear that it is immaterial how short the resumed possession may be.[249] In *Robertson v. Butler*, Beckett A.-C.J. stated:[250]

> "The legal effect of acts relied upon as disturbances of possession must in every case depend upon the character of the possession which they are said to disturb. That which would be an interruption of possession evidenced by continuous acts done upon a small area might be no interruption of possession evidenced by intermittent acts of ownership done at different places over a wide area. Having regard to the extent of the land in the possession of the defendant when the plaintiff made his visits to the land in dispute, and to the use which the defendant was then making of it, I think that what was done was not at any time enough to divest the possession out of the defendant."

2. Admission

(a) Acknowledgement and part payment

[15.79]   Where any right of action[251] to recover land has accrued and the person in possession acknowledges the title of the person with the right of action, the right of action is deemed to accrue on and not before the date of acknowledgement.[252] The acknowledgement must be in writing and signed by the person making the acknowledgement or by his agent.[253] There need not be any intention to make the acknowledgement and no special form is required. For instance, in *Edgington v. Clark*[254] it was held that an offer to purchase the land in dispute made by the adverse possessor to the true owner would constitute an acknowledgement of the title of the true owner.[255]

---

245. Limitation statutes: N.S.W.: s. 39; Vic.: s.16; Qld: s. 21; S.A.: s. 18; W.A.: s. 12; Tas.: s. 19.
246. *Symes v. Pitt* [1952] V.L.R. 412.
247. *O'Neil v. Hart* [1905] V.L.R. 107; *Robertson v. Butler* [1915] V.L.R. 31; *Symes v. Pitt* [1952] V.L.R. 412 at 430.
248. *Randall v. Stevens* (1853) 2 E. & B. 641; 118 E.R. 908; *Worssam v. Vandenbrande* (1858) 17 W.R. 53, where the true owner took down a fence erected by the adverse possessor and placed a sign claiming the right to let the land (he was only on the land for three quarters of an hour but it was held that he had effectively resumed possession); *Scanlon v. Campbell* (1911) 11 S.R. (N.S.W.) 239.
249. *Symes v. Pitt* [1952] V.L.R. 412 at 430.
250. [1915] V.L.R. 31 at 37.
251. This includes a foreclosure action.
252. Limitation statutes: N.S.W.: s. 54(1); Vic.: s. 24(1)(a); Qld: s. 35(1)(a); S.A.: s. 21(b); W.A.: s. 15; Tas.: s. 29.
253. Limitation statutes: N.S.W.: s. 54(4); Vic.: s. 25(1), (2); Qld: s. 36; S.A.: s. 21; W.A.: s. 15; Tas.: s. 30.
254. [1964] 1 Q.B. 367.
255. This depends upon the form of words used.

Where a right to recover land has accrued to a mortgagee, and the person in possession or the person liable for the mortgage debt, makes any payment of principal or interest, the right of action is deemed to accrue on, and not before, the date of the payment.[256]

If a right of action has accrued to recover any debt or other liquidated pecuniary claim, such as rental payments, and the person liable acknowledges the claim or makes a payment in relation to it, the right is deemed to have accrued on the date of the acknowledgement or payment.[257] Payment of part of the rent does not, however, extend the time for claiming the rest of the rent due.

(b) Persons bound

[15.80] An acknowledgement of title to land by any person in possession is binding on all other persons in possession during the ensuing period of limitation. Thus, a successor-in-title to the adverse possessor or, indeed, a person who dispossesses the first adverse possessor, would be bound by the acknowledgement: time is deemed to run only from the date of the acknowledgement.[258] An acknowledgement of a debt or other pecuniary claim binds the person making the acknowledgement and her or his successors, but no other person.[259]

Payment in respect of a debt or other liquidated pecuniary claim, however, binds all persons liable in respect thereof.[260]

(c) Acknowledgement or part payment when time has run

[15.81] Once the full period of limitation has run, an acknowledgement or payment has no effect.[261]

IX.   ADVERSE POSSESSION AND THE TORRENS SYSTEM

[15.82] A basic aim of the Torrens system of land registration is that the registration of an interest provides complete security for that interest: the very basis of the Torrens system is to provide certainty of title. The concept of acquisition of title by adverse possession militates against the main philosophy behind the Torrens system. Nevertheless, unpalatable and unfair results may ensue if the limitation legislation were to be totally inapplicable to Torrens system land. For example, if the registered owner abandons the land and another takes possession and remains for a long

---

256. As to acknowledgments and part payments see generally Limitation statutes: N.S.W.: s. 54; Vic.: ss 24-26; Qld: ss 35-37; S.A.: ss 21, 42; W.A.: ss 15, 38, 44; Tas.: ss 29-31.
257. Ibid.
258. See e.g. Limitation statute: Vic.: s. 26(1).
259. See e.g. Limitation statute: Vic.: s. 26(5).
260. See e.g. Limitation statute: Vic.: s. 26(6).
261. See e.g. Limitation statute: Vic.: s. 24.

period of time, perhaps paying the rates and effectively utilising and improving the land, there should be some means by which the status quo can be recognised.[262]

There has not been a consistent legislative response by the Australian legislatures to these conflicting policy considerations. In fact, the legislatures have taken a number of different approaches when determining how to integrate the limitation of actions legislation into the Torrens system of land registration. In all States there is some recognition of the concept of acquisition of title by adverse possession.[263] It should be noted, however, even if the effect of particular provisions is that the adverse possessor cannot defeat the interest of the registered proprietor, the adverse possessor does have interest based on her or his possession. Such an interest gives the adverse possessor a better right to the land than any person who dispossesses her or him.[264]

1. Victoria and Western Australia

[15.83]   In Victoria and Western Australia, the concept of acquisition of title by adverse possession applies fully to Torrens land. The Torrens statutes create an express exception to the indefeasibility of the title of the registered proprietor by providing that the registered proprietor holds the land subject to any rights subsisting under any adverse possession of the land.[265] Further, there is provision for the adverse possessor to apply to obtain registration of title if the possession has extinguished the registered proprietor's title.[266] Even without such formal registration, however, the interest of a person who by adverse possession has extinguished the title of the registered proprietor, prevails against the registered proprietor.

There has been some discussion as to the precise meaning of s. 42(2)(b) of the *Transfer of Land Act* 1958 (Vic.) and s. 68 of the *Transfer of Land Act* 1893 (W.A.). Arguably, the clause "any rights subsisting under any adverse possession of the land" may not include the inchoate possessory rights an adverse possessor has before the expiration of the full limitation

---

262. Alternatively where the land was sold many years before, but the formalities of registration were not attended to, there may be a need to recognise the right and title of an adverse possessor.

263. Cf. the position in the Australian Capital Territory and the Northern Territory where the title of the adverse possession cannot be extinguished: see *Real Property Act* 1925 (A.C.T.), s. 69; *Real Property Act* 1886 (N.T.), s. 251.

264. *Spark v. Meers* [1971] 2 N.S.W.L.R. 1; *Spark v. Three Minute Car Wash (Cremorne Junction) Pty Ltd* [1970] 92 W.N. (N.S.W.) 1087.

265. *Transfer of Land Act* 1958 (Vic.), s. 42(2)(b); *Transfer of Land Act* 1893 (W.A.), s. 68.

266. *Transfer of Land Act* 1958 (Vic.) ss 60-62; *Transfer of Land Act* 1893 (W.A.), ss 222-225. It is important to note that in practice, the adverse possessor is usually unable to obtain a registered title until 30 years have elapsed. This is because the registered proprietor may have been under a disability and thus have a maximum of 30 years to bring an action: see above [15.54]-[15.56]. If the registered proprietor is a corporation, the disability provisions are inoperative and 15 years' adverse possession should suffice. If there is proof that the registered proprietor is of full age and capacity when the limitation period commenced, 15 years may suffice: *Lambourne v. Hosken* [1912] V.L.R. 395.

period. Pursuant to this argument, the registered proprietor's "title" is subject only to the interest of an adverse possessor where the full limitation period has run. The better view is that the legislatures in these two States intended that an adverse possessor of Torrens land should be in the same position as an adverse possessor of general law land: the words "any rights subsisting under any adverse possession of land" should be given their natural meaning and would include, therefore, inchoate possessory rights and possessory rights which have developed with the effluxion of time into the best interests in the world. Thus, a purchaser becoming the registered proprietor of land takes subject to any rights subsisting under adverse possession. For example, if S has been in adverse possession of A's land (A being the registered proprietor) for seven years and A sells the land to B who becomes the registered proprietor, B takes the land subject to S's possessory rights. If the limitation period is 15 years, this effectively means that B has only eight years in which to bring an action against S to recover possession of the land. If S had been in adverse possession of the land for 15 years, A's title, and consequently, B's title, would be extinguished.

2. Tasmania

[15.84] As in Victoria and Western Australia, the principle of acquisition of title by adverse possession applies fully to Torrens land in Tasmania. The relevant statutory provisions are, however, in a different form. Section 117 of the *Land Titles Act* 1980 (Tas.) provides that the limitation statute applies to Torrens land in the same way as it does to general law land. As a corollary, s. 40(3)(h) provides that the registered proprietor's title is not indefeasible "so far as regards rights acquired, or in the course of being acquired under a statute of limitations".

Although the limitation statute in general applies to Torrens land, it is specifically provided that the registered proprietor's title is not to be extinguished by the limitation legislation. Once the limitation period has expired, the registered proprietor holds on trust for the adverse possessor and the adverse possessor may apply to the Recorder for an order vesting the legal estate in her or him.[267]

3. Queensland and South Australia

[15.85] It has been stated that:[268]

"the Queensland and South Australian provisions strike a balance between absolutely securing the title to a person's estate or interest and the competing principle that public interest demands that if a person chooses to abandon those rights for a long period of time there should be a method of clearing the title to the land so that it can be utilised for public benefit."

267. *Land Titles Act* 1980 (Tas.) s. 117. It should be noted that the registered proprietor holds the land on trust for the adverse possessor without any prejudice to any interest that would not have been extinguished by adverse possession had the land been unregistered.

268. Whalan, p. 328.

The Torrens statutes in both of these States provide that title by adverse possession may not be obtained over Torrens land except pursuant to the specific provisions for doing so set out in the statutes.[269] Under these provisions, a person who would have extinguished the title of the true owner had the land been general law land may apply to the Registrar seeking title to the land.[270] The application is advertised. A person claiming an estate or interest in the land may lodge a caveat. If the Registrar is satisfied that the person lodging the caveat is the registered proprietor, or a person claiming through the registered proprietor, the Registrar must refuse the application of the adverse possessor.[271] If the caveator is the holder of an estate or interest of less than the fee simple in Queensland,[272] or, of an easement in South Australia,[273] the Registrar may issue a certificate of title to the adverse possessor subject to the estate or easement.[274] If there are no caveats or the caveators cannot substantiate their claims, and if the Registrar is satisfied that the claimant has been in adverse possession for the requisite period, the Registrar may cancel the current certificate of title and issue a new one in the name of the claimant.[275]

Section 69VI of the *Real Property Act* 1886 (S.A.) provides that a certificate of title is void as against the title of a person adversely in occupation of, and rightfully entitled to, the land at the time it was brought under the Act and continuing in occupation at the time of issue of any subsequent certificate of title.[276] The words "adversely in actual occupation of and rightfully entitled to" do not carry the same meaning as the term "adverse possession". The provision is intended to cover the situation where a person has an interest in the land and is in actual occupation but, for some reason, this interest is not reflected in the certificate of title issued. The term "adversely" means adversely to the certificate of title,[277] and the words "rightfully entitled" connote an occupation which, but for the certificate of title, would have given an interest or ownership in the land.[278] For example, A brings her land under the Torrens system. By an error in survey, part of B's land is included

---

269. *Real Property Acts Amendment Act of 1952* (Qld), s. 46; *Real Property Act* 1886 (S.A.), ss 80a-80i, 25l.
270. *Real Property Acts Amendment Act of 1952* (Qld), s. 50 (see s. 48 which provides that no title may be acquired against a Crown corporation or instrumentality); *Real Property Act* 1886 (S.A.), s. 80a. In practice it appears that the Registrars require proof of 30 years' adverse possession. If the period is less than 30 years, evidence must be adduced to prove that the disability or other extension of time provisions do not apply in relation to the land in issue.
271. Torrens statutes: Qld (1952): s. 56(2); S.A.: s. 80f(3).
272. Torrens statutes: Qld (1952): s. 56(2).
273. Torrens statutes: S.A.: s. 80f(3).
274. Torrens statutes: Qld (1952): ss 57, 58; S.A.: s. 80f(3).
275. Torrens statutes: Qld (1952): ss 57, 58; S.A.: ss 80g, 80h.
276. The Northern Territory has the same provision and Tasmania has a similar provision with respect to the situation where land is first brought under the Act or where a certificate of title is created pursuant to an adverse possession application: *Land Titles Act* 1980 (Tas.), s. 46.
277. *Franklin v. Ind* (1883) 17 S.A.L.R. 133.
278. See *Zachariah v. Morrow and Wilson* (1915) 34 N.Z.L.R. 855; *Gallash v. Schutz* (1882) 16 S.A.L.R. 129. For a discussion of this point see Whalan, pp. 329-330.

within the certificate of title issued to A. If B is in actual occupation of the land wrongly included in A's certificate of title, B may rely successfully on s. 69VI to defeat A: B is adversely in occupation (adversely to the certificate of title), and she is rightfully entitled. That is, but for the certificate of title, she would have owned the land.

In some circumstances, it may be possible for an adverse possessor to use s. 69VI. If an adverse possessor has barred the right of action of the true owner and yet, the true owner succeeds in bringing the land under the Torrens system, s. 69VI may apply to render the registered proprietor's title defeasible as against the adverse possessor. At the time the certificate of title was issued, the adverse possessor was adversely in actual occupation and rightfully entitled to the land when it was brought under the Torrens system.[279]

4. New South Wales[280]

[15.86] Before the *Real Property (Possessory Titles) Amendment Act* 1979 (N.S.W.)[281] came into operation in 1979, the concept of acquisition of title acquired through adverse possession was wholly inapplicable to Torrens land in New South Wales. The amending Act has made it possible, within specific and narrow confines, to acquire title through adverse possession. Under the provisions, a person who has been in adverse possession of Torrens land in circumstances under which had the limitation statute applied to Torrens land the title of the registered proprietor would have been extinguished, may apply to the Registrar-General to be registered as proprietor of the land.[282] In order to prevent applications with respect to small areas of land, such an application may only be made with respect to a "whole parcel of land".[283] However, where the adverse possessor has occupied the land up to an "occupational boundary"[284] but such boundary is inside the true boundary, the adverse possessor may claim the strip of land up to the true boundary even though he or she has not occupied it.[285] Conversely, a person who takes adverse possession of a whole parcel of land and at the same time occupies a strip of land beyond the true boundary and up to an occupational boundary cannot apply for title by adverse possession to the extra strip of land.[286] It should be noted that no application may be made with respect to Crown land.[287]

279. See Whalan, p. 330.
280. See Butt, pp. 589-592 and Woodman and Butt, "Possessory Title and the Torrens system in New South Wales" (1980) 54 A.L.J. 79 for a critique of the position in New South Wales.
281. This Act inserted Pt VIA into the *Real Property Act* 1900 (N.S.W.).
282. *Real Property Act* 1900 (N.S.W.), s. 45D(1).
283. *Real Property Act* 1900 (N.S.W.), s. 45B(1). Butt, p. 591 states that s. 45B(1) refers to land which accords with minimum town planning standards.
284. *Real Property Act* 1900 (N.S.W.), see s. 45D(6): e.g. a fence, a ruler. See Woodman and Butt, op. cit. at 85.
285. *Real Property Act* 1900 (N.S.W.), s. 45D(2).
286. Thus claims for small pieces of land along boundaries are prohibited. These may be dealt with under the *Encroachment of Buildings Act* 1922 (N.S.W.): see Woodman and Butt, op. cit at 85.
287. S. 45D(3) provides that an application cannot be made where the registered proprietor is the Crown or a Minister of the Crown, a statutory body representing the Crown, particular public corporations or a council or county council.

As explained above, the relevant provisions of the *Real Property Act* 1900 (N.S.W.) are very specific about the type of Torrens land that may be the subject of an application for title acquired by adverse possession. Further, the Act provides that it is not possible for an applicant to be registered as proprietor of the land unless the whole limitation period of adverse possession has run against the person who is the registered proprietor.[288] In order to take advantage of this provision, the registered proprietor must have become registered without fraud and for valuable consideration. Clearly this provision is intended to prevent a registered proprietor, against whom the limitation period has run, from colluding with another person and transferring the property to that person in order to defeat the rights of the adverse possessor.[289] It is important to note that "fraud" in this context presumably carries the same meaning as it does in other parts of the Act: therefore, mere notice by the purchaser that a full period of adverse possession had run against the vendor/registered proprietor would not constitute fraud. Upon registration such a purchaser could resist a claim for registration by the adverse possessor.[290]

By s. 45E(4), easements and covenants affecting the land continue to have the same force after an adverse possessor has become the registered proprietor.

The provisions of Pt VIA of the *Real Property Act* 1900 (N.S.W.) contain a number of inherent problems and inconsistencies, some of which have been referred to above.[291] Further amending legislation may be necessary in order to solve these problems.

X. OTHER RELEVANT LEGISLATION

[15.87] Apart from the limitation statutes, there are other statutory provisions which pertain to the general issue of use of another's land. For example, a building or part thereof may be erected or lasting improvements may be made on another's land. Several jurisdictions have legislation dealing with these matters,[292] and providing for relief where

---

288. S. 45D(4).
289. If there is fraud in the new registered proprietor, presumably any period of adverse possession can be "counted against" the new registered proprietor: see Woodman and Butt, op. cit. at 86. This scenario suggests that the adverse possessor does have some "interest" in the land as against the registered proprietor *before* the application for registration has been made successfully to the Registrar. This goes against s. 45(c) which provides that no title adverse to the registered proprietor can be acquired by any length of possession except pursuant to Pt VIA.
290. See Woodman and Butt, op. cit. for a discussion of this point.
291. Ibid.
292. *Property Law Act* 1974 (Qld), ss 195-198. Under these provisions where a person makes a lasting improvement on another's land in the mistaken belief that the land is her or his own, application may be made to the court for relief. The court has wide powers to grant varying forms of relief. For example, the court may order that the land be vested in the applicant, that compensation be paid to any person or that the improvement be removed. *Property Law Act* 1969 (W.A.), s. 123 is similar to the Queensland provision but covers only buildings and not

such encroachment has taken place. Further, in Victoria[293] the dimensions of the boundaries of a piece of land in any document of title are construed, unless expressly negatived, as though the phrase "a little more or less" followed immediately the dimensions stated.[294] The phrase is deemed to cover any difference between the dimensions so stated and the actual, physical dimensions of the boundaries where the difference does not exceed particular limits. These are a limit of 50 millimetres for one boundary line irrespective of length where the length does not exceed 40.30 metres and where the boundary line does exceed 40.30 metres, a limit equivalent to one in 500 computed on the total length is imposed. By s. 273 of the *Property Law Act* 1958 (Vic.), the above provisions apply to both general law land and Torrens land. In South Australia, s. 220(4) of the *Real Property Act* 1886 (S.A.) contains a similar provision. It seems that the general powers of the Registrars to amend the Register Book, including amendment to boundaries, are not intended to be used where there is a *dispute* between parties as to boundaries.[295] With respect to s. 99 of the *Transfer of Land Act* 1958 (Vic.), Robinson argues that a person who thinks he or she has acquired title by adverse possession would need to use s. 60. To have "bona fide" occupation within s. 99(1) the applicant must have a legal basis to justify the occupation.

XI. MERGER AND EXTINGUISHMENT

[15.88] Merger and extinguishment are the two common law doctrines relating to the destruction of interests in land. Merger occurs where a greater and lesser estate in land vest in the same person in the same right without any intervening estate. The estates merge. Effectively, the lesser estate ceases to exist. For example, if land is granted to A for life and to B in fee simple remainder and A acquires the remainder from B, the life estate merges in the remainder and A holds a fee simple estate. However, if the grant had been to A for life, remainder to X for life, remainder to B in fee simple and A had acquired the interest of B, no merger would result because of the intermediate estate of X. Although merger originally applied only where the one person held two freehold estates, it applies now to where the one person holds a leasehold and a freehold estate or two leasehold estates.[296]

Provided the basic criteria are satisfied, there is a merger at common law despite any contrary intention of the parties. On the other hand,

---

292. *Continued*
   lasting improvements. Further, the Western Australian provision applies to the encroachment of buildings generally in addition to mistakes as to the identity of the land. New South Wales, Queensland and South Australia all have general provisions relating to the encroachment of buildings: see *Encroachment of Buildings Act* 1922 (N.S.W.), *Property Law Act* 1974 (Qld), Pt XI and *Encroachments Act* 1944 (S.A.). See above **[14.36]-[14.38]**.

293. Note that in South Australia, the provision similar to this Victorian provision applies only to Torrens land.

294. *Property Law Act* 1958 (Vic.), s. 272.

295. Robinson, p. 395.

296. *Ingle v. Vaughan Jenkins* [1900] 2 Ch. 368; *Lea v. Thursby* [1904] 2 Ch. 57.

equity considers the intention of the parties. A clear and declared intention that the lesser estate be retained prevents merger in equity.[297] Further, equity will imply such an intention if merger is disadvantageous to the person who has the two estates.[298] It seems that the equitable position now prevails.[299]

[15.89] Whereas the doctrine of merger applies to the situation where one person holds two estates in land, extinguishment applies where one person holds an estate in land and a collateral interest, such as a mortgage, charge, easement, profit à prendre or restrictive covenant over the land.[300] In fact, however, the destruction of mortgages and charges has developed and been dealt with under the doctrine of merger. Thus at common law a mortgage or charge "merges" in the estate out of which it was created when the estate and the mortgage or charge vest in the one person in the same right. In equity, the issue of whether merger occurs depends upon intention: see above **[15.88]**. In fact, it was in the area of mortgages and charges that equity developed its principle that merger should not occur if such a merger were not intended.[301]

[15.90] Collateral rights such as easements and profits à prendre are extinguished when there is unity of ownership and possession in the one person.[302] With respect to restrictive covenants, where one person has both the benefited and burdened land vested in her or him, the covenant is clearly unenforceable. It seems that unity of ownership extinguishes the restrictive covenant unless the covenant forms part of a building scheme: in this case, the restrictive covenant is merely suspended during the period when the burdened and benefited land is in common ownership.[303] The very basis of the building scheme is to ensure that the restrictive covenants are enforceable by and against all lot owners in the scheme. It is, therefore very important that the restrictive covenant is not extinguished for all time when the benefited and burdened lands are in common ownership for a time.[304]

297. *Ingle v. Vaughan Jenkins* [1900] 2 Ch. 368; *Golden Lion Hotel (Hunstanton) Ltd v. Carter* [1965] 1 W.L.R. 1189; *Re Fletcher* [1971] 1 Ch. 330.
298. *Re Fletcher* [1971] 1 Ch. 330.
299. It seems that the equitable position now prevails: see General Law Statutes: N.S.W.: s. 10; Vic.: s. 185; S.A.: s. 13; W.A.: s. 18; Qld: *Judicature Act* 1876, s. 5; *Supreme Court Civil Procedure Act* 1932 (Tas.), s. 11. See Boros, "Merger and Extinguishment of Interests in Land" (1986) 10 Adel. L.R. 427 at 434.
300. See Boros, op. cit. at 427.
301. E.g. *Forbes v. Moffatt, Moffatt and Hammond* (1811) 18 Ves. Jun. 384; 34 E.R. 362. See also Boros, op. cit. at 435.
302. See Boros, op. cit. at 439ff. where the issue of the circumstances in which there is a suspension of rights, rather than an extinguishment of rights, is discussed. There appears to be no clear differentiation between the common law and equitable requirements for extinguishment. Provided there is unity of ownership and possession, (see Boros, op. cit. at 439-445 for a detailed analysis of the requirements) the easement is extinguished without regard to the intention of the owner. This seems to be a reasonable result while the tenements are held in common ownership: see Boros, op. cit. at 445. Quaere whether an extinguished easement can be brought back into existence: this may occur by use of the doctrine in *Wheeldon v. Burrows*. See below **[16.38]**.
303. Boros, op. cit. at 447 and see below **[17.27]**.
304. Ibid.

[15.91] A difficult but important issue arises when the application of the doctrines of merger and extinguishment to Torrens land is considered. The concept of the register being conclusive as to title in Torrens land does not fit easily with the concept of automatic destruction of interests pursuant to the doctrines of merger and extinguishment. For example, if a mortgage of Torrens land is transferred to the registered proprietor of the fee simple, does the mortgage merge and disappear in the fee simple despite the fact that both the registered fee and the registered mortgage remain registered as separate interests on the certificate of title? Any law which is inconsistent with the provisions of the Torrens statutes does not apply to land falling under the operation of the Torrens statutes.[305] Thus, the issue to be addressed is whether the doctrines of merger and extinguishment are inconsistent with the relevant provisions of the Torrens statutes.[306]

Although some early cases lent support to the applicability of the doctrine of merger to Torrens land,[307] in more recent decisions it has been concluded that the doctrine of merger is inapplicable to Torrens land. Thus, it has been held that registered mortgages[308] and leases[309] survive even when vested in the registered proprietor of the estate out of which the lesser interests were created.[310] As Jacobs P. remarked in *Shell Co. of Australia Ltd v. Zanelli*:[311]

> "[S]o long as the lease remains on the title as a distinct interest, it must be regarded as a separate estate or interest . . . [I]t could not be assumed from the unity of title that there had been a merger . . . It is better to give full weight to the Register."

Where a merger is intended, it seems that such a merger must be registered.[312]

It is unclear whether an easement is extinguished when the same person becomes the registered proprietor of both dominant and servient tenements.[313] In New South Wales and Tasmania, specific legislation ensures that extinguishment of an easement does not occur where ownership of the dominant and servient tenements vests in the same person.[314] Perhaps these provisions suggest that extinguishment *will* occur on a unity of seisin unless statutorily reversed.

---

305. See above **[5.146]-[5.151]** and Whalan, pp. 23-26.
306. See Boros, op. cit. at 483 and Francis, *Torrens Title in Australasia* (Butterworths, 1973), Vol. 1, pp. 289-290.
307. *Bevan v. Dobson* (1906) 26 N.Z.L.R. 69; *Lewis v. Keene* (1936) 36 S.R. (N.S.W.) 493.
308. *The English, Scottish & Australian Bank Ltd v. Phillips* (1937) 57 C.L.R. 302.
309. *Cooper v. Federal Commissioner of Taxation* (1958) 100 C.L.R. 131; *Shell Co. (Australia) Ltd v. Zanelli* [1973] 1 N.S.W.L.R. 216.
310. Quaere easements see below and see **[16.38]**.
311. [1973] 1 N.S.W L.R. 216 at 221.
312. See Whalan, p. 199. Also see Boros, op. cit. at 458-462 where the author discusses difficulties which may be involved in registering a merger.
313. *Re Standard and the Conveyancing Act* 1919 (1970) 92 W.N. (N.S.W.) 953.
314. Torrens statutes: N.S.W.: s. 47(7); Tas.: s. 109.

As restrictive covenants are at best only noted on the register[315] it is difficult to reach any clear conclusion as to the applicability of the principle of extinguishment to restrictive covenants where the same person holds both benefited and burdened land.[316] In New South Wales and Tasmania, it is specifically provided that the covenant is not extinguished upon the benefited and burdened land being vested in the same person.[317]

---

315. See below [17.11].
316. Discussed in Boros, op. cit. at 467.
317. General law statutes: N.S.W.: s. 88B; Torrens statutes: Tas.: s. 103.

16

Easements, Profits and Rentcharges

[16.01] Previous Chapters have considered rights in land which common law classes as corporeal hereditaments, namely rights which entitle their owner to exclusive possession. This Chapter will examine those rights in land which do not entitle their owner to possession and which are designated as incorporeal hereditaments at common law.

There have been numerous definitions of incorporeal hereditaments coined over the centuries. Perhaps the best known is that of Blackstone, who described an incorporeal hereditament as:[1]

> "a right issuing out of a thing corporate, whether real or personal, or concerning or annexed to, or exercisable within, the same. It is not the thing corporate itself, which may consist in lands, house, jewels, or the like; but something collateral thereto, as a rent issuing out of those lands or houses."

Historically, under English law a variety of miscellaneous rights have been classified as incorporeal hereditaments, such as seigniories, franchises, advowsons, titles, rights of common and various inheritable offices or titles of honour which are not necessarily connected with land. None of these rights are applicable in Australia. In this country, the only relevant incorporeal hereditaments are easements, profits à prendre and rentcharges. This Chapter will consider each of these three rights separately.

I. EASEMENTS

1. Introduction

[16.02] According to Barton J. in *Concord M.D. v. Coles*, an easement is:[2]

> "a privilege without profit, which the owner of one neighbouring tenement has of another . . . by which the servient owner is obliged to suffer or not to do something on his own land, for the advantage of the dominant owner."

Another useful definition is provided by Halsbury, who describes an easement as:[3]

---

1. Blackstone, *Commentaries on the Laws of England* (Kerr, 4th ed.), Vol. 2, p. 16, cited and applied by Cotton L.J. in *Re Christmas* (1886) 33 Ch. D. 332.
2. (1906) 3 C.L.R. 96 at 110.
3. *Halsbury's Laws of England* (4th ed., 1975), Vol. 14, "Easements and Profits à Prendre", para. 1.

615

"a right annexed to land to utilise other land of different ownership in a particular manner (not involving the taking of any part of its soil) or to prevent the owner of the other land from utilising his land in a particular manner."

It is important to identify the distinctions between easements and various other proprietary interests in land with which easements may possibly be confused:

(a) Leases

[16.03] As discussed above **[10.16]**, the distinguishing feature between a licence and a lease is that no lease can exist unless the tenant is given the right of exclusive possession.[4] In contrast, an essential feature of an easement is that the right must not amount to exclusive use or possession of the servient tenement. An illustration of this is *Thomas W. Ward v. Alexander Bruce (Grays) Ltd*,[5] where the Court of Appeal rejected a claim for a prescriptive easement to use the silt bed alongside their wharf for the stranding of hulks for shipbreaking on the ground that such a right would involve an almost complete exclusion of the alleged servient owner. The question whether this rule applies in respect of the grant of a right involving the exclusive use by the alleged dominant owner of the airspace above the servient tenement was raised in *Berger Bros Trading Co. Pty Ltd v. Bursill Enterprises Pty Ltd*,[6] where McLelland C.J. in Eq. held at first instance that there is an exception to the rule in this situation. This distinction appears to be illogical, and the matter cannot be regarded as settled in the absence of higher authority. The only firm exception to the rule is that minimal interferences by the dominant owner with the servient owner's right of possession which are inherent in the nature of the right claimed will be disregarded.

(b) Licences

[16.04] There are certain essential differences between licences and easements:[7]

1. An easement must be created at common law by deed of grant whether actual, implied or presumed. A licence can be created without legal formalities.

2. An easement requires a dominant tenement, unlike a licence which can exist in gross.

3. Unlike a licence, an easement cannot grant a general right to occupy neighbouring land. For example, the right to occupy a room in a boarding-house may exist as a licence, but cannot constitute an easement.

4. *Radaich v. Smith* (1959) 101 C.L.R. 209; *Goldsworthy Mining Ltd v. Commissioner of Taxation (Cth)* (1973) 128 C.L.R. 199; *I.C.I. Alkali (Aust.) Pty Ltd (In vol. liq.) v. Commissioner of Taxation (Cth)* [1977] V.R. 393.
5. [1959] 2 Lloyd's Rep. 472 (C.A.). See also *Thorpe v. Brumfitt* (1873) 1 L.R. 8 Ch. App. 650; *Harada v. Registrar of Titles* [1981] V.R. 743 at 753.
6. (1969) 91 W.N. (N.S.W.) 521; discussed in (1971) 45 A.L.J. 157. On appeal the decision was varied on a different issue: (1970) 124 C.L.R. 73.
7. See above **[1.29]**ff. for a discussion of the legal nature of a licence.

4. An easement, once created, will class as either a legal or an equitable interest in land. In contrast, at the most a licence will only constitute a mere equity.

(c) Restrictive covenants

[16.05] There is a significant overlap in the scope of easements and restrictive covenants in the sense that certain rights may be equally protected under both laws. For example, a person wishing to ensure that the light reaching certain windows of his house will not be diminished by buildings erected later on neighbouring land may safeguard his position either by entering into an express easement of light with his neighbour or by entering into an agreement whereby the neighbour covenants not to erect a building above a certain height on designated portions of his land. Because of this overlap, restrictive covenants have been referred to as an extension of the doctrine of negative easements.[8] Further similarities are that there must be both a dominant and a servient tenement and that the right must "touch and concern" the land.

Despite these similarities, easements and restrictive covenants are conceptually quite distinct. In addition, whereas easements can be traced back to the origin of common law, restrictive covenants did not come into existence until the mid 19th century.[9] The following major differences exist between the two legal rights:

1. Easements may exist either at law or at equity, whereas restrictive covenants are purely equitable.

2. Easements, unlike restrictive covenants, may be acquired by prescription: see below **[16.31]**ff.

3. Easements are broader in scope in that they can give a right to enter the servient land (for example, pursuant to a right of way).

4. Restrictive covenants are broader in scope in that they can be used to safeguard certain amenities (for example, the right to a view) which cannot be protected under the law of easements: see below **[16.11]**ff.

(d) Natural rights

[16.06] There are two major natural rights which belong to a fee simple owner of land: the right of support for land by neighbouring land[10] and a right to water flowing naturally in a defined channel.[11] Both these rights have been narrowly defined. For example, it has been held that the right to water does not extend to water percolating underground or running

---

8. *London & South Western Rly Co. v. Gomm* (1882) 20 Ch. D. 562 at 583 (C.A.) per Jessel M.R.; *Re Nisbet and Potts' Contract* [1906] 1 Ch. 386 at 401 per Collins M.R.
9. *Tulk v. Moxhay* (1848) 2 Ph. 774; 41 E.R. 1143 (Ch.) established the doctrine.
10. See e.g. *Minter v. Eacott* (1952) 69 W.N. (N.S.W.) 93 (F.C.); *Public Trustee v. Hermann* [1968] 3 N.S.W.R. 94; *Economy Shipping Pty Ltd v. A.D.C. Buildings Pty Ltd* [1969] 2 N.S.W.R. 97; *Stephens v. Anglian Water Authority* [1987] 3 All E.R. 379 (C.A.).
11. *Swindon Waterworks Co. Ltd v. Wilts and Berks Canal Navigation Co.* (1875) L.R. 7 H.L. 697.

down the slopes of a hill,[12] and the right of support is limited to the support of the land itself and does not extend to buildings on the land.[13] In both these cases, a right will not exist unless it is acquired as an easement.

The significance of natural rights is that they exist by operation of law and do not have to be specifically acquired. They are protected by the law of nuisance.

Positive and negative easements

[16.07]   Easements can be subdivided into positive and negative rights. Positive easements are rights (for example, rights of way) which give the landowner a right to do a certain act on his neighbour's land, while negative easements are rights (for example, rights of light) which give a landowner the right to prevent his neighbour engaging in certain activity on his own land.

The distinction is significant because of continuing doubt as to whether new negative easements can be created. The major modern authority on this issue is *Phipps v. Pears*.[14] In this case, a house had been built with its flank wall so close to the wall of the adjoining house that it did not need to be completely weatherproofed. The owner of the adjoining house later demolished his building causing the unprotected wall to become exposed to the elements. The Court of Appeal unanimously rejected the claim for a prescriptive easement on the basis that an easement to be protected from the weather does not exist in law, Lord Denning stating that the law is very chary of creating any new negative easements.[15] His Lordship justified his conclusion on the ground that the contrary conclusion would restrict the redevelopment of property, although he appears to have overlooked the fact that this is also true of restrictive covenants and some positive easements: for example, a right of way. *Phipps v. Pears* has recently been applied in similar circumstances in *Marchant v. Capital & Counties Property Co. Ltd.*[16] Against these two decisions, however, should be compared the generality of the principle expressed by the Privy Council and the High Court of Australia in *Attorney-General (Southern Nigeria) v. John Holt & Co. Ltd*[17] and *Commonwealth v. Registrar of Titles (Vic.)*[18] (respectively) that the class of possible easements is not closed. In the latter case, Griffith C.J. stated that he saw no reason why novel negative

---

12. *Acton v. Blundell* (1843) 12 M. & W. 324; 152 E.R. 1223 (Exch.); *Bradford Corporation v. Pickles* [1895] A.C. 587 (H.L.); *Langbrook Properties Ltd v. Surrey C.C.* [1970] 1 W.L.R. 161.

13. *Dalton v. Angus & Co.* (1881) 6 App. Cas. 740 at 792 (H.L.); *Public Trustee v. Hermann* [1968] 3 N.S.W.R. 94 at 108; *Bognuda v. Upton and Shearer Ltd* [1972] 2 N.Z.L.R. 741 at 745 (C.A.). In Queensland, the *Property Law Act* 1974, s. 179 imposes liability for withdrawal of support "from any building, structure or erection".

14. [1965] 1 Q.B. 76 (C.A.); discussed in [1964] C.L.J. 203; (1964) 27 M.L.R. 614 and (1964) 80 L.Q.R. 318.

15. Ibid. at 82-83.

16. (1982) 263 E.G. 661 (first instance); (1983) 267 E.G. 843 (C.A.).

17. [1915] A.C. 599 (P.C.).

18. (1918) 24 C.L.R. 348.

easements such as an easement for the passage of the sun's rays should not be capable of existing at common law. The existence of such an easement was expressly left open by the English Court of Appeal in *Allen v. Greenwood*:[19] see below **[16.15]**.

2. Essential Characteristics of an Easement

In *Riley v. Penttila*,[20] Gillard J. approved the existence of four characteristics of an easement originally advanced by Dr Cheshire and adopted by the English Court of Appeal in *Re Ellenborough Park*:[21]

(a) There must be a dominant tenement and a servient tenement

[16.08] This requirement has been constantly reiterated by Australian and English courts,[22] and is based on the rationale that an easement over one land must benefit other land in the vicinity. Thus, an easement cannot benefit the public at large.

As a result of this requirement, common law does not recognise easements in gross.[23] An easement which is declared to be in gross on the ground that it infringes this essential characteristic will confer a mere personal licence upon the person for whose benefit the right was created.[24] The origin of the rule against easements in gross is obscure and its rationale is unclear. As stated by one commentator,[25] if A wishes to grant to B a right enforceable as an easement to land helicopters on A's property, why should this be prevented because of the lack of a dominant tenement? Similarly, if a long-distance truck driver wishes to acquire easements of parking along his routes, why should this be denied? As discussed at **[16.41]**, profits à prendre can be created in gross, and easements in gross are recognised in the United States.[26]

There are numerous statutory exceptions to the rule against easements in gross. In Victoria, the *Local Government Act* 1958, s. 509(1B) enables easements to be created without dominant tenements in favour of a council of any municipality, and the *Water Act* 1958, s. 312 gives a similar right in favour of any water authority. In New South Wales, South Australia, Western Australia and Tasmania, easements in gross are recognised in favour of the Crown or of any public or local authority.[27]

---

19. [1979] 1 All E.R. 819.
20. [1974] V.R. 547 at 557. See also *Harada v. Registrar of Titles* [1981] V.R. 744 at 749.
21. [1956] 1 Ch. 131 (C.A.).
22. See e.g. *Concord M.D. v. Coles* (1905) 3 C.L.R. 96; *Re Salvin's Indenture* [1938] 2 All E.R. 498; *Re Ridgeway and Smith's Contract* [1930] V.L.R. 111.
23. *Rangeley v. Midland Rly Co.* (1868) L.R. 3 Ch. App. 306 at 311; *Bouquey v. D.C. of Marion* [1932] S.A.S.R. 32 at 37; *Commissioner for Main Roads v. North Shore Gas Co. Ltd* (1967) 120 C.L.R. 118 at 134.
24. *Gapes v. Fish* [1927] V.L.R. 88 at 90 (F.C.).
25. McLean, "The Nature of an Easement" (1966) 5 U. Western Ontario L.R. 32 at 40. See also Sturley, "Easements in Gross" (1980) 96 L.Q.R. 557.
26. *Corpus Juris Secundum*, Vol. 28, "Easements", pp. 634ff.
27. *Conveyancing Act* 1919 (N.S.W.), s. 88A(1); *Law of Property Act* 1936 (S.A.), s. 41a; *Public Works Act* 1902 (W.A.), s. 33A; *Conveyancing and Law of Property Act* 1884 (Tas.), s. 90A(1).

The case law in Australia mkes it clear that the instrument creating an easement need not expressly identify the dominant tenement. The court may have regard to surrounding circumstances to identify the dominant tenement.[28] This rule applies to Torrens land as well as general law land despite the argument that under the Torrens system the parties should only be required to have regard to what is in the certificate of title or other relevant documents.[29] This rule operates in New South Wales despite the wording of s. 46 of the *Real Property Act* 1900. In Victoria and New South Wales, the case law must be read in the light of certain statutory amendments. The *Property Law Act* 1958 (Vic.), s. 197 makes it unnecessary in the case of a grant of a right of way for the dominant tenement to be specified. In contrast, s. 88(1) of the *Conveyancing Act* 1919 (N.S.W.) states, inter alia, that no easement expressed to be created by an instrument coming into affect after the commencement of the *Conveyancing (Amendment) Act* 1930 shall be enforceable against a person interested in the land claimed to be subject to the easement and not being a party to its creation unless the instrument clearly indicates both the dominant and the servient land.[30] Section 88(4) excepts easements acquired by or for the Crown or for any public or local authority constituted by Act of Parliament.

The dominant tenement need not necessarily be corporeal real property. It may consist solely of incorporeal property[31] or a combination of corporeal and incorporeal property.[32]

(b) An easement must accommodate the dominant tenement

[16.09]   There must be a "connexion" between the alleged easement and the dominant tenement in the sense that the dominant tenement benefits from the easement. The alleged easement must also be reasonably necessary for the enjoyment of the dominant tenement. The origin of this requirement is *Ackroyd v. Smith*,[33] where a close was conveyed together with the right for the grantee and others to pass and repass "for all purposes" along a certain road. It was held that a right in gross had been created as the grant was not only made for the purposes of the land conveyed, but also for purposes unconnected with it. Consequently, the right could not be assigned by the grantee. Cresswell J. stated that it is not in the power of a vendor to create any rights not connected with the use or enjoyment of the land and annex them to it.

28. *Re Maiorana and the Conveyancing Act* [1970] 1 N.S.W.R. 627 (discussed in (1971) 45 A.L.J. 157); *Gas & Fuel Corporation v. Barba* [1976] V.R. 755.
29. *Re Maiorana and the Conveyancing Act* [1970] 1 N.S.W.R. 627.
30. See *Papadopoulos v. Goodwin* [1982] 1 N.S.W.L.R. 413 and *Goodwin v. Papadopoulos* [1985] A.C.L.D. 775 (C.A.) for a discussion of the meaning of "clearly indicates". Extrinsic evidence, including evidence not of a written nature, may be examined for the purpose of determining whether the requirements of s. 88(1) are satisfied: *Margil Pty Ltd v. Stegul Pastoral Pty Ltd* [1984] A.C.L.D. 554 (N.S.W. Sup. Ct).
31. *Hanbury v. Jenkins* [1901] 2 Ch. 401.
32. *Re Salvin's Indenture* [1938] 2 All E.R. 498; discussed in (1938) 54 L.Q.R. 487.
33. (1850) 10 C.B. 164; 138 E.R. 68 (C.P.). See also *Bailey v. Stephens* (1862) 12 C.B. (N.S.) 91; 142 E.R. 1077 (C.P.).

Certain other legal propositions apply in relation to this characteristic of an easement:

(i) The dominant and servient tenements need not be contiguous

It appears to be sufficient if the dominant and servient tenements are so adjacent that the enjoyment of one should be evidently connected with and dependent upon the state of the other. Thus, while the tenements need not be adjoining, the tenements must be physically close to one another.[34] As stated in the earlier editions of *Gale on Easements*, "there cannot be a right of way over land in Kent appurtenant to an estate in Northumberland".[35]

(ii) An easement is limited to the needs of the dominant tenement

It is impossible to establish under the guise of an easement a business enterprise which has no normal connection with the use of the dominant tenement. Authority for this proposition is *Hill v. Tupper*.[36] In this case, ownership of a canal and certain adjoining land was vested in a company. Other land abutting the canal was owned by the defendant. The company leased a small parcel of land of approximately 19 poles on the banks of the canal to the plaintiff. The lease purported to grant to the plaintiff "the sole and exclusive right or liberty to put or use boats on the said canal, and let the same for hire for the purpose of pleasure only". The plaintiff alleged that the defendant had disturbed the exclusive right of the plaintiff of letting out pleasure boats for hire. It was held that the grant to the plaintiff did not create a sufficient estate or interest in him to enable him to maintain an action in his own name against the defendant. Pollock C.B. commented that it is not possible to create rights unconnected with the use and enjoyment of land, and annex them to it so as to constitute a property in the grantee.

The rationale of this case is disputed. Evershed M.R. in *Re Ellenborough Park*[37] stated that the dominant tenement was in reality accommodating the alleged easement, which infringes the characteristic of an easement under discussion. If this is correct, it would seem that the easement must accommodate the dominant tenement in the sense that it be subservient to it. However, Gooderson believes that this proposition would be unlikely to apply today.[38] Support for this view can be found in *R. v. Registrar of Titles; Ex parte Waddington*,[39] where the issue was whether a right of way could be said to benefit a dominant tenement as small as one square link. Hood J. held in the affirmative on the ground that although it is difficult to see what benefit can be derived from the benefit of a ti piece of land from a right of carriageway, such a benefit is not impos for example, there might be a water pipe or a letterbox erected on square link.

34. *Gas & Fuel Corporation v. Barba* [1976] V.R. 755; *Pugh v. Savage* [1 *Concord* (C.A.); *Harada v. Registrar of Titles* [1981] V.R. 743 at 751.

35. E.g. 11th ed., 1932, p. 19.   *Ch. App. 650.*

36. (1863) 2 H. & C. 121; 159 E.R. 51 (Exch.).

37. [1956] 1 Ch. 131 at 175 (C.A.).

38. Gooderson, "Easement—Ius Spatiandi" [1956] C
    M.C. v. Coles (1905) 3 C.L.R. 96.

39. [1917] V.L.R. 603. See also *Thorpe v. Brum*

(iii) People other than the dominant owner may also derive benefit from the alleged easement

As stated obiter by Evershed M.R. in *Re Ellenborough Park*,[40] a right of way may be a valid easement even though it is capable of benefiting any passer-by, wholly unconnected with the dominant tenement, who chooses to use it as a short cut.

(iv) An easement may accommodate the business carried out on the dominant tenement

In *Moody v. Steggles*,[41] an alleged prescriptive right in favour of the plaintiffs, the owners of a public house, to affix a signboard on the wall of the defendant's house was held to be a valid easement notwithstanding that it related to the business of the occupant of the tenement rather than the tenement itself. Similarly, in *Copeland v. Greenhalf*[42] an alleged easement to store vehicles awaiting repairs or collection on neighbouring land was not valid merely because it benefited the dominant owner's business as a wheelwright rather than the dominant tenement itself.

(c) The dominant and servient owners must be different persons

[16.10] This proposition is based on the rationale that no one can acquire rights against her or himself.[43] In the context of prescriptive rights, the proposition rests on the fact that there is nobody who could have prevented the user.[44] It should be noted that an easement is not invalid unless both tenements are owned *and* occupied by the same person. Thus a tenant may acquire, by express or implied grant, an easement over adjoining land belonging to the landlord, even though both tenements are vested in the landlord in fee simple.[45] However, a tenant may not acquire an easement over adjoining land belonging to her or his landlord by prescription.[46]

In Australia, two statutory modifications have been made to the common law on this characteristic. First, the *Conveyancing Act* 1919 (N.S.W.), s. 88B(3) provides that an easement may be created by registration of a plan of subdivision in the office of the Registrar-General, notwithstanding that at the time of registration both the land benefited and the land burdened are in the same ownership. Secondly, in the context of strata titles, the *Conveyancing and Law of Property Act* 1884 (Tas.) s. 75ZB states that unity of seisin in two or more flats shall not destroy easements implied or created by this Part, but on the cessation of such unity they shall continue in full force and effect as if the seisin had never been united.[47]

40. [1956] 1 Ch. 131 at 172 (C.A.). See also *Simpson v. Mayor of Godmanchester* [1897] A.C. 696 (H.L.).
41. (1879) 12 Ch. D. 261. See also *Harada v. Registrar of Titles* [1981] V.R. 743 at 751. [1952] 1 Ch. 488. Cf. *Nelson v. Hughes* [1947] V.L.R. 227.
  ~ *v. Siddons* (1888) 22 Q.B.D. 224 at 236.
      Gardiner (1838) 4 M. & W. 496 at 500; 150 E.R. 1525 at 1527 (Exch. of
  ~rges v. Bridgman* (1879) 11 Ch. D. 852 (C.A.).
          Pty Ltd v. Macy's Emporium Pty Ltd [1970] 1 N.S.W.R. 474; *Borman*
            1 Ch. 493.
              ᵔ4] 1 K.B. 457 (C.A.).
                ᵗ980 (Tas.), s. 109(1).

(d) The right must be capable of forming the subject matter of a grant

[16.11] Evershed M.R. stated in *Re Ellenborough Park*[48] that the major questions involved under this condition are whether the rights purported to be given are expressed in terms of too wide and vague a character and whether such rights constitute mere rights of recreation, possessing no quality of utility or benefit. In both situations, the rights will infringe the characteristic of an easement under discussion.

(i) Wide and vague rights

Several different types of alleged easements have been challenged on the ground that they are too wide and vague to constitute easements.

Ius spatiandi. A ius spatiandi is "a privilege of wandering at will over all and every part of another's field or park".[49] Several older authorities existed to the effect that such a right cannot constitute an easement.[50] The more recent decisions of *Re Ellenborough Park*[51] and *Riley v. Penttila*[52] suggest a contrary conclusion, however. In the former case, the land subject to the dispute was undeveloped and surrounded by houses on three sides. In 1855 the tenants in common who owned the land sold the subdivision surrounding the park for building purposes. The form of conveyance signed by each purchaser granted him "the full enjoyment . . . at all times hereafter in common with the other persons to whom such easements may be granted of the pleasure ground . . . in the centre of said square called Ellenborough Park". The Court of Appeal unanimously upheld the decision of Danckwerts J. that the right to use the pleasure ground was an easement. The court distinguished a valid easement of using a park as a garden from a mere ius spatiandi on the basis of whether, on the facts, the right of wandering is the main or merely a subsidiary purpose of the alleged grant. The court gave a narrow construction to cases suggesting that a ius spatiandi could not be a valid easement and applied *Duncan v. Louch*[53] where, according to the Court of Appeal, the reasoning of the decision, the circumstances of the case and the language used involve acceptance of a ius spatiandi as an easement. In Australia, *Re Ellenborough Park* was approved and applied in *Riley v. Penttila* on essentially similar facts. Although Gillard J. did not discuss the concept of a ius spatiandi, it is clear from his acceptance of *Re Ellenborough Park* and *Duncan v. Louch* that he recognised that a ius spatiandi is capable of ranking in law as an easement.

48. [1956] 1 Ch. 131 at 164 (C.A.).
49. Ibid. at 176.
50. See e.g. *International Tea Stores Co. v. Hobbs* [1903] 2 Ch. 165; *Attorney-General v. Antrobus* [1905] 2 Ch. 188.
51. [1956] 1 Ch. 131 (C.A.); discussed in [1955] C.L.J. 154; [1956] C.L.J. 24; (1955) 71 L.Q.R. 324; and (1956) 72 L.Q.R. 16.
52. [1974] V.R. 547.
53. (1845) 6 Q.B. 904; 115 E.R. 341.

Right of prospect. Ever since the decision in 1610 in *Aldred's* case,[54] English and Australian courts have held that the right of prospect is too indefinite to be capable of forming the subject matter of a grant.[55]

Right to an undefined flow of air. In a landmark decision, the High Court of Australia held in *Commonwealth v. Registrar of Titles (Vic.)*[56] that a right to an undefined flow of air can constitute an easement if created by express grant or reservation. The English authorities have held to the contrary.[57]

Other rights. An undefined right of way has been held to be a valid easement provided that the parties agree that the route is to be fixed later by the grantor, the grantee or any third party.[58] On the other hand, Lord Sumner stated obiter in *Pwllbach Colliery Co. Ltd v. Woodman*[59] that a colliery company cannot claim that a right to deposit coal dust on neighbouring land constitutes an easement as the burden would cover a very large and indefinite area.

(ii) Rights of recreation

The rule that rights of recreation cannot constitute easements is sometimes referred to as the rule in *Mounsey v. Ismay*.[60] Its major justification is that such rights are trivial and frivolous and cannot be said to be reasonably necessary to the use of the dominant tenement. This rule has been attacked as outmoded in light of the large financial investments made in recreational areas and the modern day emphasis on and interest in the value of recreation.[61] The Court of Appeal in *Re Ellenborough Park* refused to overrule *Mounsey v. Ismay*, but obiter confined it to its facts and gave a very narrow construction to the meaning of recreation.[62]

3. Types of Easements

(a) Rights of way

[16.12] A right of way may be granted in general terms or may be of a limited nature. The extent of the user may be limited to a particular purpose. The courts will enforce such limitations if the wording of the document is clear and unambiguous. For example, a restriction to "vehicular traffic only" has been held to exclude pedestrians.[63] The extent of the way may also be limited to particular persons, although such a limitation will be strictly construed by the courts. As stated by

---

54. (1610) 9 Co. Rep. 57b; 77 E.R. 816.
55. *Palmer v. Board of Land & Works* (1875) 1 V.L.R. (E.) 80; *Chastey v. Ackland* (1895) 11 T.L.R. 460.
56. (1918) 24 C.L.R. 348.
57. See e.g. *Harris v. De Pinna* (1885) 33 Ch. D. 238 (C.A.).
58. *Maurice Toltz Pty Ltd v. Macy's Emporium Pty Ltd* [1970] 1 N.S.W.R. 474; *Talga Investments Pty Ltd v. Tweed Canal Estates Pty Ltd* [1974] A.C.L.D. 215.
59. [1915] A.C. 634 at 648-649.
60. (1865) 3 H. & C. 486; 159 E.R. 621 (Exch.).
61. Note, (1955) 71 L.Q.R. 324 at 326; McLean, op. cit. 32 at 56-57.
62. [1956] 1 Ch. 131 at 177-179.
63. *Barry v. Fenton* [1952] N.Z.L.R. 990.

Haslam J. in *Grinskis v. Lahood*,[64] in cases where the classes of persons entitled to use the way are enumerated, prima facie such categories are by way of example only.

(i) Basic principles of construction

Despite some authorities to the contrary,[65] it appears to be settled in Australia that when construing the words of the grant the court is entitled to take into consideration the circumstances existing at the time when the grant was made and is not confined exclusively to the language used in the document.[66]

The court will consider the nature of the route where this is relevant to the interpretation of a right of way.[67] For example, the issue in *St Edmundsbury and Ipswich Diocesan Board of Finance v. Clark (No. 2)*[68] turned on whether a right of way was limited to a footpath or whether it included the right to drive vehicles along it. In deciding in favour of the former interpretation, Megarry J. examined the terminus of the route, the space in front of a church porch, and concluded that it was not large enough to permit the turning round of average-sized vehicles without the risk of damage to the adjoining grass and graves.

The court will also consider the purpose for which the way is to be used. For example, in *Elliott v. Renner*,[69] where a right of way over a laneway leading to the defendant's shop was expressly granted, the Full Court of the Supreme Court of Queensland held that as the premises were used or intended to be used for the purposes of a pastrycook's business, the right of way should be construed as including the right of bringing up vehicles to the premises and keeping them standing outside the premises while they were being loaded or unloaded.

A dispute may arise over the construction of a grant which defines or restricts the modes of user of a right of way. There have been many disputes over the meaning of a "right of carriageway". The courts have decided that the grant is not to be construed by reference to the mode of traction used at the time of the grant.[70] Bennett J. stated in *Lock v. Abercester Ltd* that the law must keep pace with the times: where proof is given of the user of a way by carriages drawn by horses for the required period so as to establish the right to an easement for a carriageway, the right so acquired is one which enables the owner of the dominant tenement to use the way with mechanically propelled vehicles.[71]

The majority of States have established a legislative definition of "right of carriageway". For example, the *Conveyancing Act* 1919 (N.S.W.),

---

64. [1971] N.Z.L.R. 502 at 509.
65. *Barry v. Fenton* [1952] N.Z.L.R. 990; *Robinson v. Bailey* [1948] 2 All E.R. 791 (C.A.).
66. *Rodwell v. G. R. Evans & Co. Pty Ltd* [1977] A.C.L.D. 510 (N.S.W. Sup. Ct); *Paterson and Barr Ltd v. University of Otago* [1925] N.Z.L.R. 191.
67. *Bond and Leitch v. Delfab Investments Pty Ltd* (1980) 90 L.S.J.S. 570; *Cannon v. Villars* (1878) 8 Ch. D. 415.
68. [1973] 1 W.L.R. 1572. See also *Cannon v. Villars* (1878) 8 Ch. D. 415.
69. [1923] St. R. Qd 172. See also *Bulstrode v. Lambert* [1953] 1 W L.R. 1064.
70. *Attorney-General v. Hodgson* [1922] 2 Ch. 429; *Kain v. Norfolk* [1949] Ch. 163.
71. [1939] Ch. 861 at 864.

s. 181A(1) and Sched. VIII and the *Conveyancing and Law of Property Act* 1884 (Tas.), s. 34A(1) and Eighth Schedule 1977, define the right as:[72]

> "Full and free right for every person who is at any time entitled to an estate or interest in possession in the land herein indicated as the dominant tenement or any part thereof with which the right shall be capable of enjoyment, and every person authorised by him, to go, pass and repass at all times and for all purposes with or without animals or vehicles or both to and from the said dominant tenement or any such part thereof."

A legislative definition of a "right of footway" exists in New South Wales and Tasmania. In New South Wales the definition applies to both Torrens system and general law land (see *Conveyancing Act* 1919, s. 6(1)), but in Tasmania it applies only to general law land. The New South Wales definition states:[73]

> "Full and free right for every person who is at any time entitled to an estate or interest in possession in the land herein indicated as the dominant tenement or any part thereof with which the right shall be capable of enjoyment, and every person authorised by him, to go pass and repass on foot at all times and for all purposes, without animals or vehicles to and from the said dominant tenement or any such part thereof."

In the absence of words of restriction, the basic rule is that the use to which a right of way may be put are as general as are compatible with the physical nature of the servient tenement.[74]

In relation to the purpose of user, the present rule is that a grantee is not confined to using a right of way for the purpose prevailing at the date of the grant, but may use the way for any different purpose.[75] However, the rule is arguably different where the changed purpose results in an increase of the user. Although the matter is by no means settled, the balance of authorities suggests that changed purpose of user will be denied if the result is to increase substantially the burden on the servient tenement. The major authority on this point is *Jelbert v. Davis*,[76] where changed purpose of user was denied where the conversion of the dominant tenement from agricultural use to a large camping park would lead to an unreasonable increase in the burden on the servient tenement.

---

72. See also Torrens statutes: Vic.: s. 72(3) and Twelfth Schedule; W.A.: s. 65 and Ninth Schedule; A.C.T.: s. 81 and Seventh Schedule.
73. *Conveyancing Act* 1919 (N.S.W.), s. 181A(1) and Sched. VIII. The definition in the *Conveyancing and Law of Property Act* 1884 (Tas.), s. 34A(1) and Eighth Schedule is similar although not identical.
74. *Elliott v. Renner* [1923] St. R. Qd 172 (F.C.).
75. *Grinskis v. Lahood* [1971] N.Z.L.R. 502; *Flavell v. Lange* [1937] N.Z.L.R. 444; *White v. Grand Hotel, Eastbourne* [1913] 1 Ch. 113 (discussed in (1966) 116 N.L.J. 1451).
76. [1968] 1 W.L.R. 589 (C.A.); discussed in (1969) 43 A.L.J. 584. See also *Rodwell v. G. R. Evans & Co. Pty Ltd* [1977] A.C.L.D. 510; *Malden Farms Ltd v. Nicholson* (1956) 3 D.L.R. (2d) 236 (Ont. C.A.). Cf. *Hurt v. Bowmer* [1937] 1 All E.R. 797; *South Eastern Rly Co. v. Cooper* [1924] 1 Ch. 211 (C.A.); *Rosling v. Pinnegar* (1986) 54 P. & C.R. 124 (C.A.).

(ii) Other Principles

Obstruction. It is possible for a right of way to be granted subject to an obstruction. In cases where a right of way is granted over land on which there exists an obstruction at the date of the grant, it is a question of interpretation of the instrument of grant whether the easement is granted subject to the obstruction or free from it.[77] In the latter event and in the absence of an express agreement to the contrary, the onus is on the grantee to remove the obstruction.[78]

Gohl v. Hender[79] has decided that the owner of the servient land subject to a right of way may lawfully erect a gate across the way, provided that the gate is left unlocked and does not substantially obstruct the way. The issue whether the grantee of a right of way has a duty to close such a gate is a question of fact depending on the circumstances of the case.[80] The New South Wales Supreme Court held in *Dunnell v. Phillips*[81] that although there is no absolute right in a servient owner to fence the common boundary if the grant is silent, nevertheless there is a natural presumption that he should be able to do so. This matter will be of considerable importance in construing the words of the grant.

The owner of the dominant tenement has a right to deviate on to another part of the servient land from the route of a right of way where it is obstructed by the grantor, although not in any other circumstances.[82]

Height and width of right of way. In the absence of an express grant to the contrary, a right of way does not extend in height "usque ad coelum", but only as far as is required by the reasonable needs of the owner of the dominant tenement. It is a question of fact in each case as to what is reasonable.[83] Similarly, the width of a right of way only extends as far as is required by the reasonable needs of the owner of the dominant tenement.[84]

Miscellaneous rights of dominant owner. The owner of the dominant tenement always has the right to stop momentarily, to set down or pick up passengers.[85] Where the dominant land is used for business purposes, the owner may allow vehicles to stand outside her or his premises for the purpose of loading or unloading them, or for other reasonable business purposes, provided that the vehicles do not cause an obstruction to other

---

77. *Spear v. Rowlett* (1924) 43 N.Z.L.R. 801.
78. Ibid. at 804.
79. [1930] S.A.S.R 158; discussed in (1930) 4 A.L.J. 94. See also *Deanshaw v. Marshall* (1978) 20 S.A.S.R. 146. Cf. *Dunell v. Phillips* [1982] A.C.L.D. 501 (N.S.W. Sup. Ct).
80. See *Powell v. Langdon* (1944) 45 S.R. (N.S.W.) 136.
81. (1982) 2 B.P.R. 9517.
82. *Selby v. Nettlefold* (1873) L.R. 9 Ch. App. 111.
83. See *Manly Properties Pty Ltd v. Castrisos* [1973] 2 N.S.W.L.R. 420; *Ex parte Purcell* [1982] Qd R. 613.
84. See *V. T. Engineering Ltd v. Richard Barland & Co. Ltd* (1968) 19 P. & C.R. 890, discussed in (1970) 44 A.L.J. 39; *Celsteel Ltd v. Alton House Holdings Ltd* [1985] 1 W.L.R. 204.
85. *Bulstrode v. Lambert* [1953] 1 W.L.R. 1064 at 1070.

persons entitled to use the right of way.[86] Where a person has a right of
way over land which is impassible to vehicles, he or she is entitled to
construct a road within the limits of the right of way and to make entry
upon the right of way for that purpose even though excavation or building
up for the purpose of constructing the right of way is an impediment to
the free use of the area by the owner of the servient tenement.[87]

The duty of repair. The duty to repair is on the grantee, even where
the right of way at the time of the grant is not physically fit for that
purpose.[88] A right to enter the servient tenement for the purpose of
effecting repairs will be implied by the courts in favour of the grantee
unless there is an express provision in the grant to the contrary.[89]

(iii) Creation of rights of way by prescription

In Queensland, the *Property Law Act* 1974, s. 198A(1) prohibits the
establishment of future prescriptive rights of way. Prescriptive rights of
way in existence prior to 1975 are preserved by virtue of s. 198A(2). In
New South Wales, no prescriptive rights of way can be claimed against
the Crown. The *Conveyancing Act* 1919, s. 178 states that no dedication or
grant of a way shall be presumed or allowed to be asserted as against the
Crown or any persons holding land in trust for any public purposes by
reason only of user. The issue whether prescriptive rights of way can be
claimed against the Crown in other States is less clear, but the answer
appears to be in the negative.[90] In other respects, except in Queensland
prescriptive rights of way can be claimed in Australia as in England.
Thus, for example, in *Byrne v. Steele*,[91] a prescriptive right of way was
recognised where the defendant admitted that the plaintiff and his
predecessors in title had continuously passed over a defined portion of the
plaintiff's land for over 70 years.

(b) Rights in relation to watercourses

[16.13] Various rights in respect of the flow of water have been
recognised at common law as amounting to easements. Illustrations of
these are the right to discharge pollution into watercourses[92] and the right
to divert watercourses.[93] In recent times, however, various State

---

86. *Grinskis v. Lahood* [1971] N.Z.L.R. 502; *Elliott v. Renner* [1923] St. R. Qd 172
    (F.C.). This right was assumed to exist in *East End Market Co. Ltd v. Garden Inn
    Pty Ltd* (1986) 132 L.S.J.S. 322 (F.C.).
87. *Lawrence v. Griffiths* [1988] A.C.L.D. 152.
88. *Stokes v. Mixconcrete (Holdings) Ltd* (1978) 38 P. & C.R. 488 (C.A.).
89. *Byrne v. Steele* [1932] V.L.R. 143; *Spear v. Rowlett* (1924) 43 N.Z.L.R. 801.
90. See *Thwaites v. Brahe* (1895) 21 V.L.R. 192 at 201; *Wheaton v. Maple & Co.* [1893]
    3 Ch. 48 (C.A.).
91. [1932] V.L.R. 143.
92. *McIntyre Bros v. McGavin* [1893] A.C. 268 (H.L.); *Ballard v. Tomlinson* (1885) 29
    Ch. D. 115 (C.A.).
93. *John White & Sons v. J. & M. White* [1906] A.C. 72 (H.L.); *Ivimey v. Stocker* (1866)
    1 Ch. App. 396.

enactments in Australia have been introduced which control the use of rivers and streams and those have largely supplanted the common law in this area.[94]

(c) Rights to support

(i) General principles

[16.14]   As stated above [16.06], the right to support by land from neighbouring land is a natural right attaching to real property and does not need to be created by easement. This natural right is still based on common law in all States except Queensland, where the *Property Law Act 1974*, s. 179 states:

> "For the benefit of all interests in other land which may be adversely affected by any breach of this section, there shall be attached to any land an obligation not to do thereon anything which will withdraw support from any other land or from any building, structure, or erection which has been placed upon it."

The natural right has been held not to give rise to liability for loss of support caused by withdrawal of water as distinguished from withdrawal of soil,[95] although it will give rise to liability where the abstraction of water is merely the agency whereby a shrinkage of soil and a consequent subsidence of land occurs. Liability was held to exist in *Todorovic v. McWatt*,[96] where the defendant simply excavated his property to a depth of 1.3 metres, which caused the side of the excavation next to the plaintiff's property to dry out and crumble through erosion and the plaintiff's house to subside.

The natural right to support does not extend to liability to support any building erected on the adjoining land.[97] Such a right of support must be created by easement. This common law rule applies in all States except Queensland, where the *Property Law Act 1974*, s. 179 imposes liability for withdrawal of support "from any building, structure or erection". The only exception to the rule is that if the adjacent support is withdrawn causing the land to subside and the subsidence has not been the result of the additional weight of the buildings on the land, the landowner may recover, in addition to damages for the land subsidence, damages for the injury to buildings notwithstanding that he or she does not have an easement of support in respect of them.[98]

The support of buildings by buildings on adjoining land is also outside the scope of the natural right and must be acquired by easement. In the absence of an easement, one party may remove her or his portion of a

---

94. See e.g. *River Murray Waters Act* 1983 (S.A.); *Rights in Water and Irrigation Act* 1914 (W.A.).
95. *Popplewell v. Hodkinson* (1869) L.R. 4 Exch. 248; *Metropolitan Water Supply & Sewerage Board v. R. Jackson Ltd* [1924] Q.S.R. 82.
96. [1927] Tas. S.R. 9.
97. *Dalton v. Angus & Co* (1881) 6 App. Cas. 740 at 792 (H.L.); *Stephens v. Anglian Water Authority* [1987] 3 All E.R. 379 (C.A.); *Kebewar Pty Ltd v. Harkin* (1987) 9 N.S.W.L.R. 738.
98. *Public Trustee v. Hermann* [1968] 3 N.S.W.R. 94 at 109.

party wall, even if the other party's house might collapse. There is no obligation on either party to shore up or underpin, or to notify the other party of an intention to remove part of the wall.[99]

(ii) Party walls

In many instances, buildings are mutually supported by means of a party wall. Unlike the other States, New South Wales and Tasmania possess legislation which defines "party wall" when this expression is contained in documents, and expressly provides for mutual cross-easements of support.[100] The *Conveyancing Act* 1919 (N.S.W.), s. 181B(1) reads:

> "Where in an assurance of land made by a person entitled to assure or create easements in respect of a wall built or to be built on the common boundary of that land and adjoining land so that the boundary passes longitudinally through the wall, the wall is described as a party wall, that expression means (unless a contrary intention appears) a wall severed vertically and longitudinally with separate ownership of the severed portions and with cross-easements entitling each of the persons entitled to a portion to have the whole wall continued in such manner that each building supported thereby shall have the support of the whole wall, and the assurance shall operate to create such easements accordingly."

This section applies to both Torrens and general law land: s. 181B(3).

In the other States, the common law operates. In *Walsh v. Elson*,[101] O'Bryan J. held that in the case of party walls, the property in the wall follows the property in the land upon which it stands; on a sale of one of the blocks of land by a person owning both properties, there is an implied grant and reservation of such cross-easements as may be necessary to carry out the common intention of the parties with regard to the user of the wall.

(iii) Strata titles

The strata titles legislation in each State except New South Wales expressly provides for a right to support for the common property and each unit in the building.[102]

(d) Rights of light

(i) Creation of easements

[16.15]   All States and Territories have enacted legislation outlawing the creation of any easement of light by prescription after a certain date.[103]

99. *Walsh v. Elson* [1955] V.L.R. 276 at 280; *Jones v. Pritchard* [1908] 1 Ch. 630 at 636; *Peyton v. Mayor etc. of London* (1829) 9 B. & C. 725 at 736ff.; 109 E.R. 269 at 273ff. (K.B.).
100. See also the definitions in *Building Act* 1970 (S.A.), s. 6 and the *Local Government Act* 1919 (N.S.W.), s. 304.
101. [1955] V.L.R. 276. See also *Jones v. Pritchard* [1908] 1 Ch. 630 at 635.
102. *Subdivision Act* 1988 (Vic.), s. 12; *Real Property Act* 1886 (S.A.), s. 223 ni(3); *Strata Titles Act* 1985 (W.A.), s. 11; *Building Units and Group Titles Act* 1980 (Qld), s. 15; *Conveyancing and Law of Property Act* 1884 (Tas.), s. 75G.
103. General law statutes: N.S.W.: s. 179; Vic.: s. 195; Qld: s. 178; S.A.: s. 22; W.A.: s. 121; *Prescription Act* 1934 (Tas.), s. 9.

The dates stipulated in the legislation are 1 December 1904 (N.S.W.), 25 August 1910 (Tas.), 1 March 1907 (Qld), 26 October 1911 (S.A.), 7 October 1907 (Vic.) and 19 February 1902 (W.A.). In New South Wales, Queensland and Tasmania, the legislation is framed so as to abolish retrospectively any easement of light obtained by prescription before the stipulated date.

In *Commonwealth v. Registrar of Titles (Vic.)*,[104] the Commonwealth acquired land "together with full and free right . . . to the uninterrupted access and enjoyment of light and air to the doors and windows of the building or buildings erected or to be erected . . . over and across all that strip of land 10 feet wide adjoining the eastern boundary of the said land". The Registrar of Titles refused to amend the certificates of title, arguing that the right to light and air through windows of any possible future building is not an existing easement. The High Court held that a right to the general flow of light could be acquired as an easement by express grant and refused to follow earlier English authorities[105] to the effect that an easement of light must be limited to existing defined apertures. The court also held that an easement of light may be appurtenant to the dominant tenement as a whole, not just to a particular building on the land.

(ii) Alteration of buildings on the dominant tenement

If a dominant owner possessing the benefit of an easement of light in favour of certain defined apertures completely rebuilds, the easement is not extinguished provided that the apertures in the new building occupy a substantial proportion of the space formerly occupied by the apertures in the old building. It does not matter that the builder has not constructed the new building in such a way as to take all the light which formerly passed through the old windows in the old building.[106]

An enlargement or reduction of the size of the windows in the dominant tenement will not affect an existing easment of light,[107] although it would seem that the dominant owner cannot demand an increase in the quantum of light by enlarging a window, as this would amount to an additional burden on the servient tenement.

(iii) Quantum of light

Not every interference with an easement of light amounts to an actionable nuisance. Lord Davey stated in *Colls v. Home & Colonial Stores Ltd*[108] that the measure of the quantity of light to which the dominant owner is entitled is that which is required for the ordinary purposes of inhabitance or business of the tenement according to the ordinary notions of mankind. The quantum of light to which the dominant owner is entitled may vary according to the nature of the building on the dominant

104. (1918) 24 C.L.R. 348.
105. See e.g. *Roberts v. Macord* (1832) 1 M. & Rob. 230; 174 E.R. 78 (N.P.).
106. *Smith v. Baxter* [1900] 2 Ch. 138; *Scott v. Pape* (1886) 31 Ch. D. 554 (C.A.).
107. *Aynsley v. Glover* (1875) L.R. 10 Ch. App. 283.
108. [1904] A.C. 179 at 204 (H.L.). See also *Lyme Valley Squash Club Ltd v. Newcastle Under Lyme B.C.* [1985] 2 All E.R. 405 at 411; *Carr-Saunders v. Dick McNeil Assoc. Ltd* [1986] 1 W.L.R. 922 at 928.

tenement. In *Allen v. Greenwood*,[109] the plaintiff, who possessed a prescriptive easement of light in favour of a greenhouse, complained of an interference caused by the erection of a nearby fence and the parking of a caravan on the servient tenement. The Court of Appeal held that the quantum of light was to be measured according to the nature of the building and the purposes for which it was normally used. As the normal use of a greenhouse required a high degree of light, the plaintiff had acquired that high standard of light and not just the amount of light required for illumination.

According to Lord Denning M.R. in *Ough v. King*,[110] a judge is entitled to have regard to the locality when assessing the quantum of light and also to the higher standards expected for comfort as the years go by.

(iv) Quality of light

When assessing whether an easement of light has been obstructed to such an extent as to amount to an actionable nuisance, the court may take into account light entering through skylights provided that the right to such light is not precarious.[111] Reflected light will be disregarded, however.[112]

An easement of indirect light, transmitted through glass, can be acquired.[113]

(e) Rights of Air

[16.16]   The landmark decision of the High Court in *Commonwealth v. Registrar of Titles (Vic.)*[114] held that a right to the general flow of air, like a right to the general access of light, can be created by express grant.

In every State except South Australia, the future creation of easements of air by prescription has been abolished by legislation with effect from a specified date.[115] The relevant dates are 1 December 1904 (N.S.W.), 1 March 1907 (Qld), 19 February 1902 (W.A.), 30 October 1924 (Vic.) and 29 January 1963 (Tas.). As in the case of the easement of light, the New South Wales and Queensland legislation abolishes retrospectively any easements of air obtained by prescription before the stipulated date.

The position in South Australia appears to be that based on English case law,[116] and a prescriptive easement of air may still be acquired. However, this right is restricted to a defined flow of air (that is, air enjoyed through a defined aperture on the dominant tenement or through

109. [1979] 1 All E.R. 819.
110. [1967] 3 All E.R. 859 at 861 (C.A.). See also *Carr-Saunders v. Dick McNeil Assoc. Ltd* [1986] 1 W.L.R. 922 at 928.
111. *Smith v. Evangilization Society (Inc.) Trust* [1933] Ch. 515 (C.A.).
112. *Dent v. Auction Mart Co.* (1866) L.R. 2 Eq. 238. Cf. *Sheffield Masonic Hall Co. Ltd v. Sheffield Corporation* [1932] 2 Ch. 17.
113. *Tisdall v. McArthur & Co. (Steel & Metal) Ltd* [1951] I.R. 228.
114. (1918) 24 C.L.R. 348.
115. General law statutes: N.S.W.: s. 179; Vic.: s. 196; Qld: s. 178; W.A.: s. 121; *Prescription Act* 1934 (Tas.), s. 10.
116. *Webb v. Bird* (1861) 10 C.B. (N.S.) 268; 142 E.R. 455; affd (1863) 13 C.B. (N.S.) 841; 143 E.R. 332 (Exch.); *Harris v. De Pinna* (1886) 33 Ch. D. 238.

a defined channel over adjoining property) and, unlike in the case of express grants, does not extend to a claim to the general flow of air across the whole of the servient tenement.[117]

(f) Fencing easements

[16.17] A fencing easement has often been referred to as a spurious easement or as a "quasi-easement" as it imposes a positive obligation on the servient owner and requires her or him to expend money.[118] However, as recently stated by Lord Denning M.R. in *Crow v. Wood*,[119] if we put aside questions of theory and turn to the practice of the courts, there seems to be little doubt that a fencing obligation can constitute an easement.

In the context of fencing to keep out animals, the obligation under a fencing easement is not absolute, but is to maintain the fence in a condition suitable for keeping out the animals usually found in the locality.[120] In all cases where a fencing easement exists, the servient owner will be liable for all damage resulting from the failure to maintain the fence, the only exceptions being an act of God or vis major.[121]

(g) Miscellaneous novel easements

[16.18] A variety of novel easements have been recognised in modern times by Australian and English Courts. The most significant of these are:

1. An easement in a windbreak of natural timber located on the servient tenement.[122]

2. An easement to create noise over adjoining land.[123]

3. An easement to pollute water and cast noxious matter onto adjoining land.[124]

4. A right to discharge surplus water from the dominant land when reasonably necessary.[125]

5. The right to use an area alongside a wharf for the loading and unloading of vessels.[126]

6. The right to enter the servient tenement to repair and maintain the wall of a cottage built on the extreme edge of the dominant tenement and to clean out the gutters.[127]

---

117. See e.g. *Newham v. Lawson* (1971) 22 P. & C.R. 852.
118. *Jones v. Price* [1965] 2 Q.B. 618 at 631 (C.A.) per Willmer L.J.
119. [1971] 1 Q.B. 77 at 84-85 (C.A.).
120. *Coaker v. Willcocks* [1911] 2 K.B. 124 (C.A.).
121. *Lawrence v. Jenkins* (1873) L.R. 8 Q.B. 274.
122. *Ford v. Heathwood* [1949] Q.W.N. 11.
123. *Re State Electricity Commission (Vic.) and Joshua's Contract* [1940] V.L.R. 121; *Auckran v. Pakuranga Hunt Club* (1905) 24 N.Z.L.R. 235.
124. *Kirkcaldie v. Wellington City Corporation* [1933] N.Z.L.R. 1101.
125. *Municipality of Waterloo v. Hinchcliffe* (1866) 5 S.C.R. (N.S.W.) 273.
126. *Thomas W. Ward Ltd v. Alexander Bruce (Grays) Ltd* [1959] 2 Lloyd's Rep. 472.
127. *Ward v. Kirkland* [1967] 1 Ch. 194.

7. The right to use an airfield for testing planes.[128]

8. The right to use a lavatory on the servient tenement.[129]

9. A right to place rocks, stones and piles on the servient land for the purpose of protecting and securing a building on the dominant land from the sea.[130]

10. A right to extend an existing party wall and the right to use the extended portion of the wall.[131]

11. An easement for the passage (but not the supply) of water through pipes located on neighbouring land.[132]

In *Commonwealth v. Registrar of Titles (Vic.)*,[133] Griffith C.J. stated obiter that it would be possible to create easements for the passage of aircraft, for the passage of electricity through wires crossing the servient land, for the free passage of the flash from a heliograph station and for the sun's rays. This latter possible easement may become of increasing significance in future years in light of the modern use of solar water and space heating systems in homes and factories. However, the existence of an easement of solar access is not yet settled, as in *Allen v. Greenwood*[134] Goff and Orr JJ. stated obiter that they were leaving open the question whether solar heating would be appropriate for the creation of a new type of easement.[135] A further possible easement which might arise in the future is an easement of wind access to wind generators. There seems to be no reason in theory why such a right would not be recognised as an easement, although the matter has yet to be tested.[136] It thus seems that the common law of easements may have a significant role to play in the practical application of alternative energy technologies.

Despite the flexibility of the law of easements, the following suggested easements have been rejected by the courts:

(a) rights of prospect;[137]

(b) rights of recreation[138] (see above **[16.11]**);

(c) the right to ground a barge on the bed of a navigable river;[139]

(d) the right to allow trees to overhang neighbouring property;[140]

128. *Dowty Boulton Paul Ltd v. Wolverhampton Corporation (No. 2)* [1976] Ch. 13 (C.A.).
129. *Hedley v. Roberts* [1977] V.R. 282; *Miller v. Emcer Products Ltd* [1956] Ch. 304 (C.A.).
130. *Philpot v. Bath* (1905) 21 T.L.R. 634 (C.A.).
131. *Rufa Pty Ltd v. Cross* [1981] Qd R. 365; discussed in (1982) 56 A.L.J. 45.
132. *Rance v. Elvin* (1985) 50 P. & C.R. 9 (C.A.).
133. (1918) 24 C.L.R. 348 at 354.
134. [1979] 1 All E.R. 819 at 828 (C.A.).
135. See generally Bradbrook, *Solar Energy and the Law* (Law Book Co. Ltd., Sydney, 1984), Chaps 3 & 4.
136. See Bradbrook, ''Access of Wind to Wind Generators'' [1984] A.M.P.L.A. Yearbook 433.
137. *Palmer v. Board of Land & Works* (1875) 1 V.L.R. (E.) 80; *Harris v. De Pinna* (1885) 33 Ch. D. 238.
138. *Mounsey v. Ismay* (1865) 3 H. & C. 486; 159 E.R. 621 (Exch.).
139. *Hawkins v. Rutter* [1892] 1 Q.B. 668 (C.A.).
140. *Lemmon v. Webb* [1895] A.C. 1 (H.L.).

(e) the right to hit cricket balls onto neighbouring property;[141]

(f) the right of protection from the weather;[142]

(g) the right to spread noxious wastes in indeterminate quantities generally over the servient land.[143]

In the case of claims for a prescriptive right, there cannot be an easement in any situation where the user is neither actionable nor capable of interruption by the servient owner.[144]

4. Legal and Equitable Easements

[16.19] As stated at **[16.22]**ff., legal easements may be created by prescription or by implied grant or reservation. In relation to the express creation of legal easements, however, the general rule throughout Australia is that a deed is essential. Except in Queensland,[145] State legislation requires that all conveyances or dispositions of legal interests in land (except by will) must be made by deed.[146] Except in New South Wales, where the *Conveyancing Act* 1919, s. 23B(3) specifically provides that the above legislation is not applicable to land under the Torrens system, the necessity for a deed also applies to Torrens land. However, this legislation is less significant in relation to Torrens land as the registration of documents takes the place of the execution of a deed. Each State has legislation stating that a registered instrument takes effect as if it were a deed.[147]

Contrary to common law, however, equity has never insisted on a formal deed for the conveyance of an interest in land. Based on the rule in *Walsh v. Lonsdale*,[148] if a deed is absent equity will treat a contract to convey an easement as effective to transfer the equitable interest to the purchaser. However, equity will only intervene where there is an enforceable contract for the creation of a legal easement: see above **[6.37]**ff. In addition, the agreement, unless it is in writing, must be evidenced either by a memorandum or note in writing signed by the party to be charged or by a sufficient act of part performance: see above **[6.37]**ff.

As an alternative to the rule in *Walsh v. Lonsdale*, equitable easements may arise under the principle of equity of acquiesence[149] and possibly also

141. *Miller v. Jackson* [1977] Q.B. 966 (C.A.); discussed in (1977) 93 L.Q.R. 481.
142. *Phipps v. Pears* [1965] 1 Q.B. 76 (C.A.).
143. *Pwllbach Colliery Co. Ltd v. Woodman* [1915] A.C. 634 (H.L.).
144. *Sturges v. Bridgman* (1879) 11 Ch. D. 852 (C.A.).
145. See *Property Law Act* 1974 (Qld), s. 10.
146. General law statutes: N.S.W.: s. 23B; Vic.: s. 52(1); S.A.: s. 28; W.A.: s. 33; Tas.: s. 60(1).
147. Torrens statutes: N.S.W.: s. 36(11); Vic.: s. 40(2); Qld: s. 35; S.A.: s. 57; W.A.: s. 85; Tas.: s. 48(7); A.C.T.: s. 48(4).
148. (1882) 21 Ch. D. 9 (C.A.).
149. See e.g. *McDonald v. Peddle* (1923) 42 N.Z.L.R. 987; *Dewhirst v. Edwards* [1983] 1 N.S.W.L.R. 34; *Crabb v. Arun D.C.* [1976] Ch. 179 (C.A.). Cf. *Brownsea v. National Trustees Executors & Agency Co. (Australasia) Ltd* [1959] V.R. 243.

under the principle of equitable or promissory estoppel.[150] This latter point is subject to controversy, however, and is not settled.[151]

Equitable easements may also arise where the grantor with only an equitable fee simple estate in land agrees to grant an easement to a neighbouring landowner. This may occur, for example, where the grantor is a beneficiary of land held under a trust or holds the property under a contract of sale. In these situations an equitable easement will be created if the grantor expressly creates an easement and complies with the relevent State legislation.[152]

Equitable easements are clearly recognised in respect of Torrens land: see above [5.78]ff. However, the issue whether such easements constitute an exception to indefeasibility is doubtful in some States. Equitable easements are expressly mentioned as an exception to indefeasibility by the *Land Titles Act* 1980 (Tas.), s. 40(3)(e)(ii). In addition, the wording of the *Transfer of Land Act* 1958 (Vic.), s. 42(2)(d), "easements howsoever acquired subsisting over or upon or affecting any land", and in the *Transfer of Land Act* 1893 (W.A.), s. 68, "easements acquired by enjoyment or user or subsisting over or upon or affecting such land" is clearly sufficiently wide to embrace equitable easements. On the other hand, the *Real Property Act* 1886 (S.A.), s. 84 clearly excludes equitable easements created by express grant or transfer. In the remaining jurisdictions, the relevant wording of the statutory exception is that the title of the registered proprietor is paramount except "in the case of the omissions or misdescription of any right of way or other easement created in or existing upon any land".[153] The meaning of this clause, which is discussed in [16.40], has not yet been sufficiently judicially clarified to determine precisely whether equitable easements are included within its scope. In the meantime, the issue must be considered unsettled.

5. Creation of Easements

(a) By statute

[16.20]   In Australia there are numerous State enactments creating easements. Most, but not all, of these Acts are designed to create easements in favour of local councils or State government authorities, the majority being granted in favour of authorities supplying essential services.[154] An easement created by statute may validly create an easement in gross in favour of a government authority even though this would not be possible in the case of an agreement inter partes.[155]

---

150. See Jackson, "Estoppel as a Sword" (1965) 81 L.Q.R. 84 (Pt I); 223 (Pt II); Sheridan, "Equitable Estoppel Today" (1952) 15 M.L.R. 325.
151. See *Dewhirst v. Edwards* [1983] 1 N.S.W.L.R. 34 at 51. Cf. *Walton Stores (Interstate) v. Maher* (1988) 62 A.L.J.R. 110.
152. General law statutes: N.S.W.: s. 23C; Vic.: s. 53; Qld: s. 11; S.A.: s. 29; W.A.: s. 34; Tas.: s. 60(2).
153. Torrens statutes: N.S.W.: s. 42(b); Qld: s. 44; S.A.: s. 69IV.
154. See e.g. *Hydro-Electric Commission Act* 1944 (Tas.), ss 11, 36(1); *Acquisition of Land Act* 1967 (Qld), ss 5, 6; *Public Works Act* 1902 (W.A.), s. 65.
155. *Newcastle-under-Lyme v. Wolstanton Ltd* [1947] 1 Ch. 92 at 103.

Where a statutory easement is created, the grantee only has such authority as is granted by the statute. If the grantee exceeds its powers, it is in the same position as a mere wrongdoer creating a public nuisance.[156]

Unlike in other States, in Queensland and Tasmania legislation has been introduced empowering the courts in limited circumstances to impose easements over servient land where this is necessary for the effective use of the dominant land. The *Property Law Act* 1974 (Qld), s. 180 states in part:

"Where it is reasonably necessary in the interests of effective use in any reasonable manner of any land (herein in this section referred to as 'the dominant land') that such land, or the owner for the time being of such land, should in respect of any other land (herein in this section referred to as 'the servient land') have a statutory right of user in respect of that land, the court may, on the application of the owner of the dominant land but subject to the succeeding provisions of this section, impose upon the servient land, or upon the owner for the time being of such land, an obligation of user or an obligation to permit such user in accordance with that order.

. . .

(3) An order of the kind referred to in subsection (1) shall not be made unless the Court is satisfied that—

(a) it is consistent with the public interest that the dominant land should be used in the manner proposed; and

(b) the owner of the servient land can be adequately recompensed in money for any loss or disadvantage which he may suffer from the imposition of the obligation; and either

(c) the owner of the servient land has refused to agree to accept the imposition of such obligation and his refusal is in all the circumstances unreasonable; or

(d) no person can be found who possesses the necessary capacity to agree to accept the imposition of such obligation."

Any order made shall, except in special circumstances, include payment for fair compensation by the applicant: s. 180(4)(a). Except in special circumstances, no order for costs shall be made against the servient owner: s. 180(6). The section does not bind the Crown: s. 180(8).

The legislation has been construed conservatively by the courts, and in practical terms a heavy onus rests on the applicant.[157] Despite this, however, the phrase in s. 180(3)(a), "consistent with the public interest" has been held not to be restricted to "in the public interest"; the onus on the applicant is not to prove that the public interest would be advanced by the proposed use of the dominant tenement, but rather that the use is not inconsistent with or contrary to the public interest.[158]

---

156 *Perth Corporation v. Halle* (1911) 13 C.L.R. 393 at 399.
157. See e.g. *Re Seaforth Land Sales Pty Ltd's Land* [1976] Qd R. 190; *Tipler v. Fraser* [1976] Qd R. 272.
158. *Ex parte Edward Street Properties Pty Ltd* [1977] Qd R. 86.

Similar powers to impose easements are vested in the Supreme Court of Tasmania by the *Conveyancing and Law of Property Act* 1884, s. 84J. Although land within a plan of subdivision is exempted from the scope of this legislation by s. 84J(7), the *Land Titles Act* 1980 (Tas.), s. 110(4)-(12) empowers the Recorder of Titles to create easements over any such land by order. Under this legislation, the Recorder must first notify every person appearing on the Register of Titles or the Register of Deeds of her or his intention to make an order imposing a statutory right of user on the land and must allow a period of 14 days from the giving of the notice within which written objections may be made to the Recorder: s. 110(6). If an objection is received, the Recorder must either vary her or his proposed order in light of the objection or must conduct a hearing. At the conclusion of the hearing the Recorder may make an order in terms of the proposed order or differing from it in light of the objections: s. 110(7). The Recorder may give effect to an order by registering it in the Registry of Deeds or recording the order upon the folio of the Register (s. 110(9)), although he or she must not take this course of action within 30 days from the making of the order; during this period a person affected by the order may appeal to the Supreme Court which may stay proceedings or quash or vary the order: s. 110(8). On completion of the registration or recording, any easement specified in the order will come into being: s. 110(10).

(b) By express grant or reservation

[16.21]   Any individual can create an easement to the extent that it is consistent with her or his power of alienation. The fact that he or she may not hold an unencumbered fee simple estate is irrelevant. Similarly, a corporation can grant an easement which is consistent with the purposes for which it holds the land.[159] In addition, legislation in all States gives trustees for sale and mortgagees (on the exercise of a power of sale) a right to grant easements.[160]

The rule at common law was that a legal easement could not be created by simple reservation. Instead, a conveyance containing a reservation had to be executed by the purchaser in which case it was held to operate as a regrant of the easement from the purchaser to the vendor. This rule still applies in South Australia and Western Australia, where the reservation still has to be included in the conveyance and signed by the purchaser. However, under the rule in *Walsh v. Lonsdale*,[161] if the purchaser fails to execute the conveyance the vendor is nevertheless entitled to an easement in equity. In the remaining States, however, the requirement of the execution of the reservation by the grantee of the legal estate out of which the reservation is made has been abolished and the common law rule appears to have been reversed.[162]

159. *British Transport Commission v. Westmoreland C.C.* [1958] A.C. 126 (H.L.).
160. *Property Law Act* 1958 (Vic.), s. 101(2); *Trustee Act* 1958 (Vic.), ss 13, 63; *Conveyancing Act* 1919 (N.S.W.), ss 109, 110; *Trustee Act* 1925 (N.S.W.), s. 26(1); *Law of Property Act* 1936 (S.A.), s. 47; *Trustee Act* 1936 (S.A.), ss 20, 59; *Property Law Act* 1969 (W.A.), s. 57; *Trustees Act* 1962 (W.A.), ss 27, 30, 31; *Conveyancing and Law of Property Act* 1884 (Tas.), s. 21; *Trustee Act* 1898 (Tas.), ss 16, 47.
161. (1882) 21 Ch. D. 9 (C.A.).
162. General law statutes: N.S.W.: s. 45A; Vic.: s. 65(1); Qld: s. 9; Tas.: s. 34C.

An alternative method of reserving easements is available in Tasmania, which has enacted legislation enabling easements to be created at law by way of uses.[163] In New South Wales, the *Conveyancing Act* 1919, s. 88(1) states, inter alia, that an easement shall not be enforceable against a person interested in the land claimed to be subject to the easement and not being a party to its creation unless the instrument clearly indicates (a) the land to which the benefit of the easement is appurtenant; (b) the land which is subject to the burden of the easement; (c) the person (if any) having the right to release, vary or modify the easement other than the persons having, in the absence of any agreement to the contrary, the right by law to release, vary or modify the same; and (d) the persons (if any) whose consent to a release, variation or modification of the easement is stipulated for. The section applies to Torrens land as well as land under the general law: s. 88(3).

(c) By implied grant or reservation

(i) Implied reservation

[16.22] Based on the duty of express reservation which is imposed at common law upon a grantor,[164] the general rule is that, on a disposition of part of the land, no reservation of any easement in favour of any part retained will be implied.[165] Exceptions to this general rule have been recognised in respect of easements of necessity and intended easements.

[16.23] Easements of necessity. Easements of necessity usually, although not necessarily, arise in the context of rights of way, where on the sale by a common owner of part of her or his land either the grantor or grantee is left without any means of access to her or his property.

This category of easements has been held to be based on the actual or presumed intention of the parties, not on a rule of public policy. The major authority is *North Sydney Printing Pty Ltd v. Sabemo Investment Corporation Pty Ltd*,[166] where the plaintiff subdivided a large block of land and sold a part of it, intending that the part retained, which was landlocked and zoned for parking, should be sold to the local council as an extension to its existing car park. Thus, there was no intention on the part of the plaintiff to retain a means of access for itself to the land retained. The plaintiff unsuccessfully sought a way of necessity on the basis of public policy after the negotiations with the council for the sale of the land broke down. The unfortunate practical effect of the conclusion that a way of necessity is not based on public policy is that the doctrine of necessity cannot be regarded as a universal remedy for providing access to landlocked land.[167]

163. *Conveyancing and Law of Property Act* 1884 (Tas.), s. 74(1).
164. *Liddiard v. Waldron* [1934] 1 K.B. 435.
165. *Bolton v. Clutterbuck* [1955] S.A.S.R. 253 at 267; *Re Webb's Lease; Sandom v. Webb* [1951] Ch. 808 at 823 (C.A.).
166. [1971] 2 N.S.W.L.R. 150; discussed in (1972) 46 A.L.J. 471. See also *Nickerson v. Barraclough* [1981] Ch. 426 (C.A.); discussed in [1981] Conv. 442 and (1982) 132 N.L.J. 224.
167. See Bradbrook, "Access to Landlocked Land: A Comparative Study of Legal Solutions" (1983) 10 Syd. L.R. 39.

Traditionally at common law, before an easement of necessity is implied a court must be satisfied that the right claimed is essential for the use of the alleged dominant tenement and is not merely a matter of convenience. The existence of an alternative means of access exercisable as of right has always been regarded as fatal to a claim of a way of necessity, even if this alternative access is very inconvenient.[168] There is a suggestion in *Parish v. Kelly*[169] and *Torrisi v. Magame Pty Ltd*,[170] however, that reasonable necessity may be all that is required. Whether this represents good law remains to be determined. At the very least, in the context of a right of way evidence must be addressed of difficulties affecting access to the alleged dominant tenement. Note that a way of necessity will be implied even if the grantee of the easement has an alternative means of access if the user of that alternative means is precarious.[171]

No way of necessity over neighbouring land will arise where a person by her or his own acts cuts off direct access to a road. Thus, in *Harris v. Flower*,[172] a claim for a way of necessity was dismissed where the defendant, who had a right of way over the plaintiff's land to certain land coloured pink on a plan, and who was also the owner of certain adjoining land coloured white, had by his own acts completely landlocked the white land so that the only access thereto was over the pink land.

An easement of necessity does not create a right to a way of necessity for all purposes for which the landlocked close may at any time be used, but only such a right of way as will enable the owner of the close to enjoy it in the condition it happened to be at the time of the grant. If, for example, the land was used for agricultural purposes at the time of the grant, the burden of a way of necessity cannot be increased (except by prescription) if the land is later used for building purposes.[173]

A way of necessity may arise even if the dominant tenement is not completely surrounded by the land of the grantor of the easement, but is surrounded partially by the land of the grantor and partially by the land of one or more other landowners.[174] In this situation, the way of necessity will always be granted over the land of the grantor, not through private lands belonging to others.[175]

It was decided in *Smith v. Christie*[176] that a way of necessity ceases on the cesser of the necessity, even though the new way may not be as convenient as the previous one. Contrary authorities exist, however, and the matter cannot be regarded as settled.

---

168. *McLernon v. Connor* (1907) 9 W.A.L.R. 141 (F.C.); *Union Lighterage Co. v. London Graving Dock Co.* [1902] 2 Ch. 557 (C.A.).
169. (1980) 1 B.P.R. 9394.
170. [1984] 1 N.S.W.L.R. 14 at 22.
171. *Barry v. Hasseldine* [1952] 1 Ch. 835.
172. (1905) 74 L.J. Ch. 127.
173. *Corporation of London v. Riggs* (1880) 13 Ch. D. 798.
174. *Barry v. Hasseldine* [1952] 1 Ch. 835.
175. *Riddiford v. Foreman* (1910) 29 N.Z.L.R. 781 at 786.
176. (1905) 24 N.Z.L.R. 561 (C.A.). See also *B.O.J. Properties Ltd v. Allen's Mobile Home Park Ltd* (1979) 96 D.L.R. (3d) 431 (N.S. Sup. Ct).

In respect of Torrens land, the doctrine has been held to apply in Queensland[177] and appears to be within the scope of the wording of the relevant legislation in Victoria, Western Australia and Tasmania.[178] It has been held not to apply in New South Wales.[179] The position in South Australia is undecided.

[16.24] Intended easements. The law will imply the reservation or grant of such easements as are required to give effect to the common intention of the parties to a grant of real property as to the manner in which the land granted or the land retained by the grantor is to be used, subject only to the qualification that the parties must intend that the land granted or retained should be used in some definite and particular manner.[180]

A common illustration of the operation of this principle is in the case of semi-detached or terraced houses where the houses are so constructed as to be mutually subservient to and dependent on each other for drainage and support, neither house being capable of standing or being enjoyed without the support it derives from its neighbour. These rights are sometimes said to be mutual cross-easements.[181] Another illustration is provided in *Re State Electricity Commission (Vic.) and Joshua's Contract*,[182] where the S.E.C.V. purchased land which, to the knowledge of the vendor, was intended to be used for the erection of an electricity substation which necessarily involved the transmission of noise over neighbouring land. Martin J. held that the Commission was entitled to have included in the transfer of the land it had purchased an easement of transmitting such noise as would arise from the proper use of an electricity substation.

There are no cases in any State or Territory relating to the applicability of this doctrine to Torrens land. In the absence of authority, it is submitted that the same position applies as in respect of easements of necessity: see above **[16.23]**.

(ii) Implied grant

[16.25] Easements of necessity and intended easements may be implied in appropriate circumstances in favour of a grantee as well as a grantor of the land. In addition, grants may be implied under the rule in *Wheeldon v. Burrows*,[183] under general words imported into conveyances by State

177. *Pryce and Irving v. McGuiness* [1966] Qd R. 591.
178. Torrens statutes: Vic.: s. 42(2)(d); W.A.: s. 68; Tas.: s. 40(3).
179. *M.C.A. Camilleri Building & Constructions Pty Ltd v. H. R. Walters Pty Ltd* [1981] A.C.L.D. 396 (N.S.W. Sup. Ct); *Torrisi v. Magame Pty Ltd* [1984] 1 N.S.W.L.R. 14.
180. *Pwllbach Colliery Co. Ltd v. Woodman* [1915] A.C. 634 at 646-647 (H.L.); *R. J. Finlayson Ltd v. Elder, Smith & Co. Ltd* [1936] S.A.S.R. 209 at 233; *Rufa Pty Ltd v. Cross* [1981] Qd R. 365 at 367-368.
181. See *Union Lighterage Co. v. London Graving Dock Co.* [1902] 2 Ch. 557 at 563 (C.A.).
182. [1940] V.L.R. 121.
183. (1879) 12 Ch. D. 31 (C.A.).

legislation, by implication from the description of the land, on simultaneous conveyances by one landowner, and by the creation of a plan of subdivision.

[16.26]   The rule in Wheeldon v. Burrows. Thesiger L.J. stated in *Wheeldon v. Burrows*:[184]

> "On the grant by the owner of a tenement of part of the tenement as it is then used and enjoyed, there will pass to the grantee all those continuous and apparent easements (by which, of course I mean quasi-easements) or, in other words, all those easements which are necessary to the reasonable enjoyment of the property granted and which have been and are at the time of the grant used by the owners of the entirety for the benefit of the part granted."

This rule has been adopted in numerous cases in Australia.[185] It applies in respect of Crown land[186] and to contracts for the sale of land[187] as well as conveyances.

There are three elements of the test propounded by Thesiger L.J.: (a) "continuous and apparent"; (b) "necessary to the reasonable enjoyment of the property granted", and (c) "at the time of the grant used by the owners of the entirety for the benefit of the part granted". An initial problem is whether the first two elements are synonymous, alternative or cumulative. Thesiger L.J. treated them as synonymous in one part of his judgment and as alternative in another part. Later courts have tended to the view that both elements must be complied with before the rule will apply.[188]

The "continuous and apparent" element has given rise to problems of interpretation. The courts have tended to ignore the need for continuity in the exercise of an easement. The cases have construed the word as meaning "permanent" and reading it together with "apparent" have concluded that there must be, on the quasi-servient tenement, a feature which would be seen on inspection and which is neither transitory nor intermittent.[189] A right of way over a made-up road or over worn tracks, an easement of watercourse and a right of light have all been held to satisfy this element.[190] On the other hand, alleged rights having no physical evidence pointing to their existence (such as a right of way along a path which was unformed or unmade and an overflow from a tank) have been held to fail the test.[191]

---

184. Ibid. at 49.
185. See e.g. *Lancaster v. Lloyd* (1927) 27 S.R. (N.S.W.) 379; *Taylor v. Browning* (1885) 11 V.L.R. 158 (F.C.); *Billiet v. Commercial Bank of Australasia Ltd* [1906] S.A.L.R. 193.
186. *Howitt v. Fitzgerald* (1898) 24 V.L.R. 387 at 398.
187. *Bowman v. Griffith* [1930] 1 Ch. 493.
188. See e.g. *Sovmots Investments Ltd v. Secretary of State for the Environment* [1979] A.C. 144 (H.L.).
189. *Stevens and Evans v. Allan and Armanasco* (1955) 58 W.A.L.R. 1 at 15; *Ward v. Kirkland* [1967] 1 Ch. 194 at 225.
190. *Hansford v. Jago* [1921] 1 Ch. 322; *Watts v. Kelson* (1871) 6 Ch. App. 166; *Phillips v. Low* [1892] 1 Ch. 47.
191. *Polden v. Bastard* (1865) L.R. 1 Q.B. 156; *Bartlett v. Tottenham* [1932] 1 Ch. 114.

The test of "necessary to the reasonable enjoyment of the property granted" is less strict than the test of necessity in an easement of necessity.[192] This element can be satisfied either by showing that the alleged easement is necessary to the enjoyment of the tenement demised or that it is necessary to the enjoyment in a reasonable manner of some permanent feature or part of the demised tenement.[193]

The application of the doctrine to Torrens land in Victoria, South Australia and Western Australia[194] is supported by judicial authority, but the doctrine has been held not to apply to Torrens land in New South Wales.[195] In Tasmania the doctrine is clearly within the scope of s. 40 of the *Land Titles Act* 1980. In Queensland the issue is unresolved, but by analogy with the decision in *Pryce and Irving v. McGuinness*,[196] decided in respect of easements of necessity, it is submitted that *Wheeldon v. Burrows* probably applies to Torrens land.

[16.27]   General words imported into conveyances. At common law it was customary to include in conveyances "general words", which operated to convey expressly easements which, before the sale, had been used for the benefit of the part granted. The Australian State legislatures, following English precedent, have endeavoured to shorten conveyances by enacting that a conveyance of land shall be deemed to include certain specified rights. Each State has introduced identical legislation. For example, the *Conveyancing Act* 1919 (N.S.W.), s. 67 states:[197]

> "(1) A conveyance of land shall be deemed to include and shall by virtue of this Act operate to convey, with the land, all buildings, erections, fixtures, commons, hedges, ditches, fences, ways, waters, watercourses, liberties, privileges, easements, rights, and advantages whatsoever, appertaining or reputed to appertain to the land, or any part thereof, or, at the time of conveyance, demised, occupied, or enjoyed with, or reputed or known as part or parcel of or appurtenant to the land or any part thereof . . .
>
> (3) This section applies only if and as far as a contrary intention is not expressed in the conveyance, and has effect subject to the terms of the conveyance and to the provisions therein contained."

This legislation only operates on a conveyance of land. "Conveyance" is statutorily defined in each State so as to exclude holders of equitable interests.[198] Thus, neither party to a contract for the sale of land[199] or an

---

192. See *Goldberg v. Edwards* [1950] 1 Ch. 247 (C.A.).
193. *National Trustees Executors & Agency Co. (Australasia) Ltd v. Long* [1939] V.L.R. 33; discussed in (1932) 48 L.Q.R. 154.
194. *Taylor v. Browning* (1885) 11 V.L.R. 158 (F.C.); *Billiet v. Commercial Bank of Australasia Ltd* [1906] S.A.L.R. 193; *Stevens and Evans v. Allan and Armanasco* (1955) 58 W.A.L.R. 1.
195. *Australian Hi-Fi Publications Pty Ltd v. Gehl* [1979] 2 N.S.W.L.R. 618 (C.A.); *Kebewar Pty Ltd v. Harkin* (1987) 9 N.S.W.L.R. 738.
196. [1966] Qd R. 591.
197. General law statutes: Vic.: s. 62; Qld: s. 239; S.A.: s. 36; W.A.: s. 41; Tas.: s. 6.
198. General law statutes: N.S.W.: s. 7(1); Vic.: s. 18(1); Qld: s. 4; S.A.: s. 7; W.A.: s. 7; Tas.: s. 2.
199. *Re Peck* [1893] 2 Ch. 315.

agreement for a lease[200] may rely on the legislation. An oral lease also appears to be outside the scope of the word "conveyance".[201]

Despite these limitations, the legislation has a very broad application. The fact that the licence which is alleged on conveyance to be converted into an easement is personal to the plaintiff does not preclude the legislation from operating,[202] nor does the fact that the owner of the quasi-servient tenement has suffered the exercise of the alleged easement voluntarily, rather than as a matter of obligation or agreement or as a result of requests.[203] The fact that the owner of the quasi-servient tenement did not intend to create an easement has been considered irrelevant.[204]

A useful illustration of the operation of this legislation is *International Tea Stores Co. v. Hobbs*,[205] where the defendant owned two adjoining blocks of land, one of which was leased to the plaintiff company. By permission of the defendant, renewed from time to time, the plaintiff used in business hours a way across the defendant's other property to a door at the back of the plaintiff's premises. The defendant later sold to the plaintiff the property which it had been leasing. No mention of any right of way was made in the conveyance. Farwell J. held that the easement passed to the plaintiff by virtue of the general words implied into the conveyance by the legislation.

There are two major limitations on the scope of the operation of the legislation. First, the legislation will only operate if the kind of user relied on could have been the subject of a legal right binding on successors-in-title. Thus, if the expectation was that the enjoyment of the easement would be only temporary, or if prior to the conveyance the right was precarious in the sense that permission had to be sought on each exercise of user, the legislation will not operate to convert a licence into an easement on a later conveyance.[206]

Secondly, the rule was developed in *Long v. Gowlett*[207] that before the legislation will operate there must be prior diversity of occupation of the quasi-dominant and quasi-servient tenements.[208] The rationale is that if the grantor not only owned but also occupied both the land sold and the land retained, then whatever he or she was accustomed to do on the land retained was attributable solely to her or his ownership and occupation of that part, and so should not be converted into an easement under the legislation. This rule has been affirmed by the House of Lords in *Sovmots*

200. *Borman v. Griffith* [1930] 1 Ch. 493.
201. *Rye v. Rye* [1962] A.C. 496 (H.L.).
202. *Goldberg v. Edwards* [1950] 1 Ch. 247.
203. *Crow v. Wood* [1971] 1 Q.B. 77 (C.A.).
204. *Wright v. Macadam* [1949] 2 K.B. 744 (C.A.).
205. [1903] 2 Ch. 165; discussed in (1966) 29 M.L.R. 573; (1966) 116 N.L.J. 941; and (1932) 48 L.Q.R. 154. See also *Graham v. Philcox* [1984] Q.B. 747 (C.A.).
206. See e.g. *Wright v. Macadam* [1949] 1 K.B. 744 (C.A.); *Phipps v. Pears* [1965] 1 Q.B. 76 (C.A.).
207. [1923] 2 Ch. 177.
208. See Jackson, "Easements and General Words" (1966) 30 Conv. 340; Harpum, "Easements and Centre Point: Old Problems Resolved in a Novel Setting" (1977) 41 Conv. 415.

Investments Ltd v. Secretary of State for the Environment.[209] Lord Wilberforce stated that when land is under one ownership one cannot speak in any intelligible sense of rights, privileges or easements being exercised over one part for the benefit of another: whatever the owner does, he or she does as owner, and until a separation of ownership or occupation occurs, the condition for the existence of rights does not exist.

In respect of Torrens land, the legislation appears to have a more limited application than the rule in *Wheeldon v. Burrows*:[210] see above **[16.26]**. The legislation has been held to apply to Torrens land in Victoria[211] and appears to apply to Torrens land in Western Australia by virtue of the similarity of the Torrens statutes. In New South Wales, Queensland and Tasmania, State legislation expressly precludes the application of the "general words" doctrine to Torrens land.[212] The issue has not been decided in South Australia.

The operation of the legislation is subject to the principle of rectification, both in respect of general law and Torrens land.[213] However, this principle has only a narrow scope. Being an equitable remedy, it is discretionary and may be refused where there is delay amounting to laches.[214] There can be no rectification unless the mistake to reserve rights in a conveyance is mutual: a unilateral mistake is insufficient.[215] What the plaintiff must prove in all cases is that there was an actual agreement antecedent to the conveyance which is sought to be rectified, and that such agreement is inaccurately represented in the instrument.[216]

[16.28] By implication from the description of the land. At common law, if, in a conveyance or a contract of sale, land is described as "bounded by" or "abutting on" a road or street the grantor will be regarded as having impliedly agreed to grant to the grantee a right of way over the land forming the road or street. An illustration of this principle is *Mellor v. Walmesley*,[217] where the English Court of Appeal held that by describing land conveyed as "situate on the seashore" the grantor was estopped from saying that some land belonging to him, intervening between the actual seashore and the land conveyed, was not itself seashore, and that the plaintiffs, the successors-in-title of the grantees, were entitled to unrestricted access over the intervening land to the sea.

209. [1979] A.C. 144 (H.L.).
210. (1879) 12 Ch. D. 31 (C.A.).
211. *National Trustees & Agency Co. (Australasia) Ltd v. Long* [1939] V.L.R. 33. See Barton, "The Applicability of Section 62 of the Property Law Act 1958 (Vic.) to a Transfer of Torrens System Land" (1987) 61 A.L.J. 215.
212. General law statutes: N.S.W.: s. 67(5); Qld: s. 234; Tas.: s. 91 and Fourth Schedule.
213. *Clark v. Barnes* [1929] 2 Ch. 368; *Braye v. Horsfall* (1908) 8 S.R. (N.S.W.) 258; *Zdrojkowski v. Pacholczak* (1959) 59 S.R. (N.S.W.) 382.
214. *Christie v. Dalco Holdings Pty Ltd* [1964] Tas. S.R. 34.
215. *Slack v. Hancock* (1912) 107 L.T. 14; *Braye v. Horsfall* (1908) 8 S.R. (N.S.W.) 258.
216. *Reid v Zoanetti* [1943] S.A.S.R. 92 at 99; *Australian Gypsum Ltd v. Hume Steel Ltd* (1930) 45 C.L.R. 54 at 63.
217. [1905] 2 Ch. 164. See also *Roberts v. Karr* (1809) 1 Taunt. 495; 127 E.R. 926 (C.P.); *Rudd v. Bowles* [1912] 2 Ch. 60.

The major Australian authority is *Dabbs v. Seaman*.[218] In this case, Seaman, the registered proprietor of Torrens land in New South Wales, sold part of his land to one Smith, describing that land as bounded on one side by a lane 20 feet wide over another part of Seaman's land. The transfer was registered and the certificate of title issued to Smith showing his land abutting the lane. Mrs Dabbs eventually acquired title to Smith's land, but her right to use the lane as an easement was disputed by Seaman. The High Court held by a two to one majority that Mrs Dabbs was entitled to have the 20 foot strip for her use as a lane, with a right of way over it. All the judges in the case gave different reasons for their decisions. Higgins J. (dissenting) rejected Mrs Dabbs' claim to an easement on the basis that under the relevant Torrens legislation the only valid method for the creation of easements is by registration of an express grant. He added that Seaman's implied representation that a lane existed on one of the boundaries of the property did not create any right of way in the absence of registration of an express grant. Starke J. held that an easement of way had been created by estoppel on the basis that such a right would be created on these facts if the land were general law land. Isaacs J. held that Mrs Dabbs was entitled to a right of way over the land as long as she remained registered proprietor of the land, but complicated the issue by rejecting the contention that the right of way in this case constituted an easement, likening it instead to natural rights in property, such as the support of land by adjoining land. Because of these differing analyses, the interpretation of *Dabbs v. Seaman* has long been a matter of controversy.[219]

In Victoria, unlike the other States, *Dabbs v. Seaman* appears not to apply to Torrens land by virtue of the *Transfer of Land Act* 1958, s. 96(2).

[16.29] Simultaneous conveyances of land by one landowner. If a landowner severs her or his property and sells both parts to different purchasers, what quasi-easements previously enjoyed by the common owner over the quasi-servient tenement will pass to the purchaser of the quasi-dominant tenement?

The doctrine of implied grant applies equally in the case of simultaneous conveyances of the whole of the property to different purchasers as when the common owner disposes of part of her or his land and retains the rest.[220] Thus each grantee of simultaneous conveyances obtains the same easements over the land of the other grantee as he or she would have obtained if the grantor had retained the remainder of the land. In other words, each grantee is in the same position as if he or she had obtained the first grant.[221]

---

218. (1925) 36 C.L.R. 538; discussed in (1944) 18 A.L.J. 186. See also *Rock v. Todeschino* [1983] 1 Qd R. 356; *Hutchinson v. Lemon* [1983] 1 Qd R. 369. Cf. *Boulter v. Jochheim* [1921] St. R. Qd 105; 29 C.L.R. 602.
219. See the detailed discussion in Bradbrook and Neave, paras 454ff.
220. *Sunset Properties Pty Ltd v. Johnston* (1985) 3 B.P.R. 9185 (N.S.W. Sup. Ct).
221. *Swansborough v. Coventry* (1832) 9 Bing. 305; 131 E.R. 629 (C.P.); *Hansford v. Jago* [1921] 1 Ch. 322.

[16.30] Plan of subdivision. The *Transfer of Land Act* 1958 (Vic.), s. 98 and the *Conveyancing and Law of Property Act* 1884 (Tas.), s. 90B provide that the proprietor of an allotment of land shown on an approved plan of subdivision shall be entitled to all such easements of way, drainage and for the supply of specified essential services as may be necessary for the reasonable enjoyment of the allotment or any building thereon as if such easements had been expressly granted. This statutory form of implied grant also extends to cases of the subdivision of a building.

The *Real Property Act* 1886 (S.A.), s. 90 provides that any proprietor may deposit with the Registrar-General a plan of subdivision showing the rights of way intended to be created over the land, and every subsequent proprietor of the whole or part of the land shall be entitled to a right of way over all the rights of way shown in the plan, unless otherwise declared in her or his certificate of title. The *Transfer of Land Act* 1893 (W.A.), s. 167A states that every right of way shown on a plan deposited with the Registrar shall, unless the contrary is stated, be deemed an easement appurtenant to the land comprised in the plan and abutting upon such right of way. The equivalent New South Wales legislation is not confined to rights of way. The *Conveyancing Act* 1919 (N.S.W.), s. 88B(3) states:[222]

"[On registration under section 196 of a plan upon which any easement is indicated], then, subject to compliance with the provisions of this division—

(a) any easement so indicated as intended to be created as appurtenant to any existing public roads shown in the plan or roads to be vested in the council upon registration of the plan shall be created and shall without any further assurance vest in the council by virtue of such registration and of this Act;

(b) any easement so indicated as intended to be created pursuant to section 88A of this Act shall be created and shall without any further assurance vest in the Crown or in the public or local authority, as the case may be, by virtue of such registration and of this Act;

(c) any other easement or restriction as to user so indicated as intended to be created shall—

(i) be created;

(ii) without any further assurance and by virtue of such registration and of this Act, vest in the owner of the land benefited by the restriction, as the case may be, notwithstanding that the land benefited and the land burdened may be in the same ownership at the time when the plan is registered and notwithstanding any rule of law or equity in that behalf."

(d) By prescription

[16.31] Prescription must be distinguished from limitation. In the case of limitation, adverse possession of land for the requisite period of time

222. See also *Conveyancing Act* 1919 (N.S.W.), s. 196(11).

operates to extinguish the existing title to land whereupon the adverse possessor has title to her or his land based on the right of possession: see above **[15.03]**. In contrast, prescription does not extinguish the landowner's title but creates an additional incorporeal right which is superimposed on the title of the servient tenement.

Statute law now declares certain easements to be incapable of acquisition by prescription. Easements of light can no longer be acquired by prescription anywhere in Australia (see above **[16.15]**), while prescriptive easements of air may only arise in South Australia: see above **[16.16]**. In Queensland, rights of way can no longer be acquired as easements since 1975.[223]

The scope of prescription is also restricted in respect of Torrens legislation. Although there is case law establishing the applicability of prescription to Torrens land in Victoria and Western Australia,[224] and although the Torrens legislation in Queensland and Tasmania is phrased sufficiently broadly to allow for prescriptive easements,[225] the position is otherwise in South Australia and New South Wales. In respect of New South Wales, Powell J. held in *Dewhirst v. Edwards*[226] that except for prescriptive easements existing before the servient tenement was brought under the *Real Property Act* 1900 but omitted from the register on registration, the Act does not recognise the existence of easements alleged to have been acquired merely by the effluxion of time. A similar conclusion appears to apply in South Australia by virtue of the wording of ss 83 and 85 of the *Real Property Act* 1886 and the decision in *Anthony v. Commonwealth*.[227]

Two separate forms of acquisition of prescriptive easements apply in Australia. The common law doctrine of lost modern grant applies throughout the country. In addition, a statutory form of acquisition based on the *Prescription Act* 1832 (U.K.) applies in Western Australia,[228] Tasmania,[229] and (probably) in South Australia.[230] In these States, an easement is frequently claimed in the alternative under both the statute and the common law.[231]

(i) Lost modern grant

[16.32]   The doctrine operates as a fiction. A grant will be presumed to have been made and lost in modern times if enjoyment of the alleged easement for 20 years can be proved. Its justification is that the alleged

---

223. *Property Law Act* 1974 (Qld), s. 198A(1).
224. *Nelson v. Hughes* [1947] V.L.R. 227; *National Trustees Executors & Agency Co. (Australasia) Ltd v. Long* [1939] V.L.R. 33; *Di Masi v. Piromalli* [1980] W.A.R. 57.
225. *Real Property Act* 1861 (Qld), s. 44; *Land Titles Act* 1980 (Tas.), s. 40(3).
226. [1983] 1 N.S.W.L.R. 34. See also *Kostos v. Devitt* (1979) 1 B.P.R. 9231. Cf. *Australian Hi-Fi Publications Pty Ltd v. Gehl* [1979] 2 N.S.W.L.R. 618 (C.A.).
227. (1973) 47 A.L.J.R. 83.
228. The United Kingdom Act was adopted by the Act 6 Will. IV No. 4 (1836) (W.A.).
229. The United Kingdom Act was substantially re-enacted in the *Prescription Act* 1934 (Tas.).
230. See *White v. McLean* (1890) 24 S.A.L.R. 97.
231. See e.g. *Diment v. N. H. Foot Ltd* [1974] 1 W.L.R. 1427.

servient owner would not have abstained from exercising her or his right of interference, knowing that 20 years' abstinence would extinguish it, unless he or she intended to permit the enjoyment; and, after the alleged dominant owner has been encouraged to rely on acquiescence, there is a strong ground to make possession the basis of right.[232] A further justification is that the state of affairs which is shown to exist is otherwise unexplained.[233]

Despite early doubts, it appears that the fiction is irrebuttable, and evidence showing that a grant was impossible or that no grant was made will be regarded as irrelevant.[234] The only exception to this is proof that the alleged grantor was under a legal incapacity to make the grant.[235]

There are numerous miscellaneous rules affecting the scope of the fiction. The fiction does not operate in respect of Crown lands[236] nor between landlords and tenants.[237] In calculating whether the prescription period has been satisfied, the alleged dominant owner may add to her or his own period of user any period of user of a predecessor-in-title, provided that there has been no interruption between the periods.[238] Where there is an increase in the user during the prescription period, no bar to prescription arises unless it is user of a different kind or for a different purpose, or unless the increase is so great that the practical burden on the servient tenement is drastically increased;[239] in any of these situations, there must be a further 20 year period before the prescriptive right will apply to the increased burden or different user.[240] There is no requirement that an easement claimed by prescription be used with any particular frequency, although in the case of an easement intermittently used, such as a right of way, the enjoyment must be of such a nature and frequency as to indicate that the dominant owner is asserting a right.[241]

To obtain an easement by lost modern grant, it must be proved that the enjoyment by the alleged dominant owner is "as of right".[242] This means that the enjoyment must be exercised not by violence, nor secretly or by stealth, nor by permission asked from time to time, on each occasion

232. *Wynstanley v. Lee* (1818) 2 Swan 333 at 340; 36 E.R. 643 at 646 (Ch.) per Plumer M.R.
233. *Hamilton v. Joyce* [1984] 3 N.S.W.L.R. 279 at 287 per Powell J. See also *Attorney-General v. Simpson* [1901] 2 Ch. 671 at 698.
234. *White v. McLean* (1890) 24 S.A.L.R. 97; *Thwaites v. Brahe* (1895) 21 V.L.R. 192 (F.C.); *Oakley v. Boston* [1976] Q.B. 270 (C.A.).
235. *Thwaites v. Brahe* (1895) 21 V.L.R. 192 (F.C.); *Tuckett v. Brice* [1917] V.L.R. 36.
236. *Thwaites v. Brahe* (1895) 21 V.L.R. 192 at 201 (F.C.).
237. *Wheaton v. Maple & Co.* [1893] 3 Ch. 48 (C.A.); *Kilgour v. Gaddes* [1904] 1 K.B. 457 (C.A.). Cf. *Rodwell v. G. R. Evans & Co. Pty Ltd* [1978] 1 N.S.W.L.R. 448 at 451.
238. *Auckran v. Pakuranga Hunt Club* (1905) 24 N.Z.L.R. 235 at 240.
239. *Cargill v. Gotts* [1980] 1 W.L.R. 521; *Nelson v. Hughes* [1947] V.L.R. 227.
240. *Johns v. Delaney* (1890) 16 V.L.R. 729.
241. *Eaton v. Swansea Waterworks Co.* (1851) 17 Q.B. 267; 117 E.R. 1282.
242. *Attorney-General v. Horner (No. 2)* [1913] 2 Ch. 140 at 178 (C.A.); *Dewhirst v. Edwards* [1983] 1 N.S.W.L.R. 34 at 49; *Fulwood Nominees Pty Ltd* [1988] A.C.L.D. 46. Cf. *Bridle v. Ruby* [1988] 3 W.L.R. 191.

or even on many occasions of using it.[243] The "stealth" requirement is justified on the basis that the enjoyment of the alleged easement must be such that an ordinary owner of the land, diligent in the protection of her or his interests, would have, or must be taken to have, a reasonable opportunity of becoming aware of that enjoyment.[244] Thus, in *Milne v. James*,[245] which concerned an alleged prescriptive easement of support, Griffith C.J. stated that the fact that the defendant's beams rested upon the plaintiffs' wall could not be discovered by an inspection of the exterior of the buildings or the plaintiff's building was fatal to a prescriptive claim.

The "permission" requirement is justified on the ground that the asking of permission is inconsistent with a claim "as of right".[246] While it is settled that consent given during a prescriptive period is fatal to a claim for an easement,[247] controversy surrounds the effect of consent given before the commencement of the prescriptive period. In *Wilkinson v. Spooner*,[248] Burbury C.J. held that permission given before the commencement of the period is irrelevant, but on the other hand, *Healey v. Hawkins*[249] decided that permission, whenever granted, is fatal to a prescriptive claim. The latter approach seems more consistent with the notion that enjoyment must always be "as of right". Payment for a right to use neighbouring land has been held to infringe the "permission" requirement.[250] On the other hand, if during the prescriptive period the neighbours compromise as to the exercise of a right claimed by one landowner, the permission requirement is not infringed. Thus, where during the 20 year period the parties agreed to alter the route of a claimed right of way, the user of the original and substituted ways were considered as one and added together for the purposes of prescription.[251]

In addition to proof that the enjoyment was "as of right", it must be proved that the servient owner acquiesced in the exercise of the alleged easement.[252] This has been held to involve actual knowledge or means of knowledge on the part of the alleged servient owner.[253] Knowledge of the basic details is sufficient: for example, in the case of an easement of support, it is unnecessary for the servient owner to possess particular information as to those details of the internal structure of the building on which the weight depends.[254] On the other hand, mere proof of common

243. See e.g. *Gardner v. Hodgson's Kingston Brewery Co. Ltd* [1903] A.C. 229 at 238 (H.L.); *Hough v. Taylor* (1927) 29 W.A.L.R. 97.
244. *Union Lighterage Co. v. London Graving Dock Co.* [1902] 2 Ch. 557 at 570 (C.A.).
245. (1910) 13 C.L.R. 168.
246. *Hyman v. Van den Bergh* [1907] 2 Ch. 516 at 530.
247. *Austin v. Wright* (1926) 29 W.A.L.R. 55.
248. [1957] Tas. S.R. 121.
249. [1968] 1 W.L.R. 1967.
250. *Gardner v. Hodgson's Kingston Brewery Co. Ltd* [1903] A.C. 229 (H.L.). Cf. *Smith v. Christie* (1904) 24 N.Z.L.R. 561 (C.A.).
251. *Davis v. Whitby* [1974] Ch. 186 (C.A.); discussed in (1974) 124 N.L.J. 576.
252. *Hamilton v. Joyce* [1984] 3 N.S.W.L.R. 279 at 288; *Dalton v. Angus & Co.* (1881) 6 App. Cas. 740 at 773 (H.L.); *Capar v. Wasylowski* [1983] 4 W.W.R. 526 (Man. Q.B.).
253. *Davies v. Du Paver* [1953] 1 Q.B. 184 (C.A.); *Diment v. N. H. Foot Ltd* [1974] 1 W.L.R. 1427.
254. *Dalton v. Angus & Co.* (1881) 6 App. Cas. 740 at 801 (H.L.).

knowledge in the local community of the exercise of the alleged easement is insufficient.[255] The requirement of acquiescence also means that there can be no prescriptive claim if either there is genuine doubt as to the boundaries of the servient land as a result of which the servient owner does not know whether the right claimed is over her or his land,[256] or the servient owner has a mistaken belief as to the ownership of the land over which the disputed easement has been exercised.[257]

(ii) Prescription Act 1832 (U.K.)[258]

[16.33] In general, the rules as to the scope and methods of acquisition of easements under the *Prescription Act* 1832 are the same as in the case of a presumption of a lost grant. However, the following differences exist.

1. The legislation provides for two different time periods. Section 2[259] provides that no claim to any easement which has been actually enjoyed by any person claiming right thereto without interruption for 20 years can be defeated by showing only that such easement was first enjoyed at any time before that period. The claim, however, remains liable to be defeated in any other way in which it could be defeated apart from the Act. If the enjoyment has continued for 40 years, the right to the easement is deemed absolute and indefeasible, unless it appears that it was enjoyed by some consent or agreement expressly given or made for that purpose by deed or writing. In practice, the 40 year period is very rarely invoked.

2. Pursuant to s. 4,[260] the period of enjoyment must immediately precede the commencement of an action in which the claim is in question. This is unnecessary in the case of lost modern grant. This rule effectively reduces the scope of the application of the *Prescription Act* 1832 in comparison with the doctrine of lost modern grant.

3. Pursuant to s. 4, no interruption is deemed to have occurred for the purposes of prescription unless the dominant owner has submitted to it or acquiesced in it for at least one year after notice of the fact of interruption and of the person responsible for causing it. This requirement does not exist under the doctrine of lost modern grant.

4. Sections 7 and 8[261] grant extensions of time to the prescriptive period of enjoyment in certain circumstances. Section 7 stipulates that, for the purposes of computing the period of enjoyment, any time during which any person otherwise capable of resisting any claim shall have been or shall be "an infant, idiot, non compos mentis, feme covert, or tenant for life" must be disregarded. This section, however, is limited to claims for prescription based on a 20 year period of prescription,

---

255. *Davies v. Du Paver* [1953] 1 Q.B. 184 at 210 (C.A.).
256. *Anthony v. Commonwealth* (1973) 47 A.L.J.R. 83 at 91; *Hamilton v. Joyce* [1984] 3 N.S.W.L.R. 279 at 290-291.
257. *Hamilton v. Joyce* [1984] 3 N.S.W.L.R. 279. This issue is discussed in [1986] Conv. 356.
258. In Tasmania, the operative legislation is the *Prescription Act* 1934.
259. In Tasmania, the relevant provision is the *Prescription Act* 1934, s. 3.
260. In Tasmania, the relevant provision is the *Prescription Act* 1934, s. 4.
261. In Tasmania, see the *Prescription Act* 1934, ss 7, 8.

and not where the enjoyment has continued for 40 years, in which case the easement is deemed absolute and indefeasible: s. 2. On the other hand, s. 8 extends the 40 year period, but not the 20 year period, in respect of any time during which the servient tenement is subject to a life interest or term of years longer than three years from the date of grant.

6. Remedies

[16.34] The dominant owner whose easement is interfered with can sometimes exercise the remedy of abatement. This remedy enables the dominant owner to enter the servient tenement and put an end to the interference.[262]

Like all self-help remedies, abatement is not encouraged by the courts.[263] For this reason, certain restrictions apply. Interference with the property of a wrongdoer in order to abate a nuisance will only be justified if the interference is considered by the court to be "positively necessary".[264] If there are two alternative methods of abating a nuisance, the least mischievous must be adopted.[265] Even if an interference with the property of the wrongdoer can be justified, abatement cannot be used if some injury would thereby be inflicted on the public or on an innocent third party.[266] Any action undertaken by way of abatement must not be excessive.[267] Finally, notice of an intended act of abatement must be given where the owner of the dominant tenement intends to pull down an inhabited dwelling or where the person possessing the land is not the person responsible for the commission of the nuisance, although not otherwise.[268]

The more common remedy is court action based on nuisance. The plaintiff may seek damages at law or a remedy of equitable damages or an injunction. The normal rules as to the availability of damages and injunctions apply in this context.[269]

7. Extinguishment or Modification of Easements

(a) By agreement

[16.35] The dominant and servient owners, if both sui juris, may extinguish or modify an easement by agreement. Although at common law an express release of an easement must be made by deed,[270] an

---

262. See e.g. *Nicol v. Nicol* (1887) 13 V.L.R. 322 (F.C.); *Roberts v. Rose* (1865) L.R. 1 Exch. 82 (Exch. Ch.).
263. *Lagan Navigation Co. v. Lambeg Bleaching, Dyeing & Finishing Co. Ltd* [1927] A.C. 226 at 244.
264. *Roberts v. Rose* (1865) L.R. 1 Exch. 82 at 89 (Exch. Ch.).
265. *Lagan v. Lambeg Bleaching, Dyeing & Finishing Co. Ltd* [1927] A.C. 226 at 245.
266. *Roberts v. Rose* (1865) L.R. 1 Exch. 82 at 89 (Exch. Ch.).
267. *Perry v. Fitzhowe* (1846) 8 Q.B. 757 at 775; 115 E.R. 1057 at 1064.
268. *Jones v. Jones* (1862) 1 H. & C. 1; 158 E.R. 777 (Exch.); *Jones v. Williams* (1843) 11 M. & W. 176; 152 E.R. 764 (Exch.).
269. See Bradbrook and Neave, paras 1811ff. See also *Grasso v. Love* [1980] V.R. 143 (F.C.).
270. *Poulton v. Moore* [1915] 1 K.B. 400.

informal agreement to release an easement will be enforceable in equity, provided that it is in writing or supported by acts of part performance. The Torrens legislation relating to the cancellation or alteration of a notification of an easement if the easement is extinguished, varied or modified by agreement of the parties differs from State to State. In New South Wales, Victoria and Tasmania the Registrar is empowered to cancel any such notification if the easement is released, varied or modified by agreement of the parties.[271] In Queensland, South Australia and Western Australia it would seem that the respective parties must obtain a court order before any notification of an easement will be removed from the Register even though the parties may have reached an agreement that the easement be extinguished.[272]

Unlike in other States, the *Land Titles Act* 1980 (Tas.), s. 110 empowers the Recorder of Titles, with the consent of all persons having registered interests in the land shown in a plan of subdivision of Torrens land, to cancel or alter easements by making an order setting forth, in respect of each lot shown in the plan, the easements to be appurtenant to the lot. Notice of intention must be given to every person appearing in the Register to have an interest in that land, and during a period of 30 days from the making of an order by the Recorder a person affected by such order may appeal to the Supreme Court. The Supreme Court may stay proceedings wholly or in part, quash or vary the order, or make any order that the Recorder might have made.

(b) By abandonment by non-user

[16.36] Abandonment is a question of intention by the owner of the dominant tenement, to be decided on the facts of each case.[273] Mere non-user of an easement is not in itself sufficient to constitute abandonment, nor is it conclusive evidence of intention to abandon. For example, in *Re Marriott*[274] Gillard J. held that, even though a right of way had not been used for over 20 years, in the absence of proof of intention this did not mean that the way had been abandoned. The only exception to this rule is where other persons acquire rights by acquiescence. For example, Shand J. held in *Boulter v. Jochheim*[275] that a right of way was abandoned where the dominant owners allowed the servient owners to erect fences and buildings across the way without protest.

It is possible for part abandonment to occur. Thus, for example, in the case of a right of way for vehicles, if there is an abandonment of the right to drive vehicles along the way the court may hold that the easement has been converted into a footpath only.[276]

271. Torrens statutes: N.S.W.: s. 47(b); Vic.: s. 73(2); Tas.: s. 108(1).
272. *Property Law Act* 1974 (Qld), s. 181; *Real Property Act* 1886 (S.A.), s. 64; *Transfer of Land Act* 1893 (W.A.), s. 129C(1)(b).
273. *Pearce v. City of Hobart* [1981] Tas. R. 334; *McIntyre v. Porter* [1983] 2 V.R. 439; *James v. Stevenson* [1893] A.C. 162 (P.C.); *Scott v. Pape* (1886) 31 Ch. D. 554; *Wolfe v. Freijahs' Holdings Pty Ltd* [1988] V.R. 1017.
274. [1968] V.R. 260. See also *Ward v. Ward* (1852) 7 Exch. 838; 155 E.R. 1189.
275. [1921] Q.S.R. 105.
276. *Proprietors Strata Plan No. 9968 v. Proprietors Strata Plan No. 11173* [1979] 2 N.S.W.L.R. 605; *Webster v. Strong* [1926] V.L.R. 509.

Unlike the case of prescription or adverse possession (see above
[16.32]-[16.33]), there is no minimum period stipulated either by statute
or common law for the extinguishment by abandonment of an easement.
The only exceptions are in relation to Torrens land in Victoria, Western
Australia and Tasmania. The *Transfer of Land Act* 1958 (Vic.), s. 73 states
that where it is proved to the satisfaction of the Registrar that any such
easement has not been used or enjoyed for a period of not less than 30
years, such proof shall constitute sufficient evidence that such easement
has been abandoned. The *Transfer of Land Act* 1893 (W.A.), s. 229A and
the *Land Titles Act* 1980 (Tas.), s. 108(3) specify a period of 20 years' non-
user.[277] The Tasmanian and Western Australian legislation do not require
the Registrar to treat an easement as abandoned after the 20 year period
in all cases, but rather give her or him a discretion in this matter.

Despite the lack of a minimum period, the length of time of non-user
is significant. The longer the non-user continues the more readily will the
courts infer that the dominant owner should be deemed to have
abandoned the easement, unless there is proof of facts or circumstances
which provide a satisfactory explanation for the non-user and which
negative any intention of abandonment.[278]

In the case of rights of way, the mere non-removal of obstructions to
the use of the easement is insufficient to show an intention to abandon.
Thus, for example, the High Court held in *Treweeke v. 36 Wolseley Road
Pty Ltd*[279] that there had been no abandonment of a right of way even
though the way was impassable becuase of sheer rock faces, an
impenetrable bamboo clump and the construction of a swimming pool
across the way.

In respect of Torrens land, *Riley v. Penttila*[280] has held that in Victoria
an easement noted on a certificate of title remains enforceable by the
dominant owner even though at common law it would be held to have
been abandoned. The easement will remain effective until it is removed
from the register as a result of a successful application under the *Transfer
of Land Act* 1958 (Vic.), s. 73. In New South Wales, by reference to the
legislative intent behind the enactment of the *Conveyancing Act* 1919
(N.S.W.), s. 89(1), which gives the courts the power to modify and
extinguish easements, such power not extending to easements under the
equivalent Victorian legislation (*Property Law Act* 1958, s. 84), it has been
held that easements over Torrens land may be abandoned.[281] As Western
Australia, Queensland and Tasmania all possess legislation equivalent to
the *Conveyancing Act* 1919 (N.S.W.), s. 89(1),[282] it is submitted that the

---

277. The relevant legislation concerning abandonment of rights of way is the *Transfer
      of Land Act* 1958 (Vic.), s. 73A and the *Transfer of Land Act* 1893 (W.A.), s. 230.
278. *McIntyre v. Porter* [1983] 2 V.R. 439 at 444; *Crossley & Sons v. Lightowler* (1867)
      L.R. 2 Ch. App. 478 at 482; *Swan v. Sinclair* [1925] A.C. 227 (H.L.).
279. (1973) 128 C.L.R. 274. See also *Proprietors Strata Plan No. 9968 v. Proprietors Strata
      Plan No. 11173* [1979] 2 N.S.W.L.R. 605.
280. [1974] V.R. 547. See also *Webster v. Strong* [1926] V.L.R. 509.
281. *Treweeke v. 36 Wolseley Road Pty Ltd* (1973) 128 C.L.R. 274; *Proprietors Strata Plan
      No. 9968 v. Proprietors Strata Plan No. 11173* [1979] 2 N.S.W.L.R. 605.
282. *Transfer of Land Act* 1893 (W.A.), s. 129C; *Property Law Act* 1974 (Qld), s. 181;
      Conveyancing and Law of Property Act 1884 (Tas.), s. 84C.

New South Wales authorities would be followed in those jurisdictions. South Australia, which has no such equivalent legislation, will probably adopt the Victorian position.

In respect of the abandonment of unregistered easements over Torrens land, although the matter is still undecided it is submitted that the common law principles on abandonment will apply.

(c) By alterations to the dominant tenement

[16.37] In certain circumstances, alterations made to the dominant tenement which significantly increase the burden imposed on the servient tenement and restrict the use to which it can be put may be treated by the courts as an extinguishment of the rights to which the dominant owner was formerly entitled. In *Ray v. Fairway Motors (Barnstaple) Ltd*,[283] the parties owned adjoining yards separated by a wall. The plaintiff erected a shed at the rear of his yard, using the dividing wall as one of the walls of the shed. The defendant later excavated its property adjacent to the separating wall, causing the wall of the shed to crack and bulge. The defendant admitted the existence of an easement of support for the wall, but argued that by attaching the shed to it the plaintiff had so increased the burden on the servient tenement as to cause the easement to be extinguished. The Court of Appeal held that an easement is extinguished when the owner of the servient tenement proves that its mode of use is altered in such a way as to prejudice the enjoyment of the servient tenement and to restrict the use to which it can be put.

In *Graham v. Philcox*,[284] however, the Court of Appeal indicated that the normal remedy for the dominant owner where alterations made to the dominant tenement significantly increase the burden imposed on the servient tenement is to obtain an injunction against excessive user.[285] An easement will only be extinguished in these circumstances in two situations: first, where the excessive burden cannot be separated from the original, permissible burden due to the nature of the dominant tenement;[286] and secondly, if the dominant owner disposes of part of her or his property and retains none of the dominant tenement for which the original easement was granted.[287]

(d) By unity of seisin

[16.38] If the same person acquires a fee simple estate in possession in both the dominant and servient tenements, the easement is extinguished. If the servient tenement is later resold, the easement will not revive and the purchaser will not be bound unless a fresh easement is taken.[288] This

283. See also *Luttrell's* case (1601) 4 Co. Rep. 86a; 76 E.R. 1063 (K.B.); *Colls v. Home & Colonial Stores Ltd* [1904] A.C. 179 at 202 (H.L.).
284. [1984] Q.B. 747 (C.A.); discussed in [1985] Conv. 60; (1985) 44 C.L.J. 15.
285. [1984] Q.B. 747 at 756 per May L.J.
286. *Ankerson v. Connelly* [1906] 2 Ch. 544 held that an easement will not be extinguished where the excessive burden can be separated from the original, permissible burden.
287. See [1985] Conv. 60 at 65.
288. *Roe v. Siddons* (1888) 22 Q.B.D. 224; *Ivimey v. Stocker* (1866) 1 Ch. App. 396.

rule has been reversed by legislation in respect of Torrens land in New South Wales and Tasmania.[289]

Occasionally, unity of title without unity of possession will occur, as when one person acquires the title of both the dominant and servient tenements but the right of possession of only one. This situation occurred in *Richardson v. Graham*,[290] where the dominant tenement was leased to the plaintiffs. Later during the lease the owner of the dominant tenement sold the reversion to the owner of the servient tenement. It was held that this conveyance did not extinguish the easement. However, after the determination of the lease the easement would be extinguished as there would then be unity of possession and title vested in the same person.

Unity of possession without unity of title occurs more commonly, usually in the case where the owner of the servient tenement is granted a leasehold estate in the dominant tenement. In these circumstances the easement will not be extinguished but will merely be suspended during the term of the lease.[291]

(e) By statute

[16.39] In Tasmania, the *Conveyancing and Law of Property Act* 1884 (Tas.), s. 84D permits the owner of a dominant tenement to apply to the Recorder of Titles for the title of all or part of the servient tenement. The Recorder may, by order, direct that the servient land, or such part of it as may be specified in the order, be vested in her or him as an addition to such of the dominant land owned by her or him, and if it does so direct, it may further direct whether or not on being so vested it shall remain or become subject to any specified easement. The section only operates where the easement concerned is a right of way; in addition, a successful applicant may be required to pay to any person divested of an estate in land by virtue of the order such compensation as the Recorder thinks just to award. A right of appeal to the Supreme Court exists in favour of any person aggrieved by a decision made by the Recorder.

In New South Wales, Queensland, Western Australia and Tasmania, jurisdiction is conferred upon the Supreme Court, or in the case of Tasmania either the Supreme Court or the Recorder of Titles, to extinguish or modify easements on certain specified grounds. These grounds are contained in the *Conveyancing Act* 1919 (N.S.W.), s. 89(1), the *Property Law Act* 1974 (Qld), s. 181, the *Transfer of Land Act* 1893 (W.A.), s. 129C and the *Conveyancing and Law of Property Act* 1884 (Tas.), Pt XVA. In Western Australia, the legislation only applies to Torrens Land, and in Tasmania it does not apply to easements which have effect by virtue of a plan of subdivision. In all cases, this legislation also permits the court to modify or discharge restrictive covenants. As the majority of

---

289. *Real Property Act* 1900 (N.S.W.), s. 47(7); *Land Titles Act* 1980 (Tas.), s. 109. See *Margil Pty Ltd v. Stegul Pastoral Pty Ltd* [1984] 2 N.S.W.L.R. 1.
290. [1908] 1 K.B. 39 (C.A.).
291. *Aynsley v. Glover* (1875) 10 Ch. App. 283; *Cuvet v. Davis* (1883) 9 V.L.R. (L.) 390 at 395 (F.C.); *McCarthy v. Cunningham* (1877) 3 V.L.R. (L.) 59 at 63-64.

applications under this legislation have been made in respect of covenants, the legislation is discussed in that context and reference should be made to [17.28]ff.

In Victoria, the *Subdivision Act* 1988, s. 36(1) states that if a municipal council decides that the economical and efficient subdivision, consolidation or servicing of any land requires that the owner of the land acquire or remove an easement over any land in the subdivision or consolidation of any land in the vicinity, the owner may apply to the Administrative Appeals Tribunal for leave to acquire or remove the easement compulsorily.

8. Easements as a Statutory Exception to Indefeasibility of Title

[16.40]   Easements may be expressly granted or reserved in respect of Torrens land and may be entered on the certificate of title of the dominant and servient tenements.[292] Where this occurs, the easement is binding on all future purchasers of the servient tenement.

This section of the Chapter considers the situation where easements are not registered. The principle of indefeasibility of title in respect of Torrens land and the various statutory exceptions to this principle have been discussed in general terms at [5.25]ff. One of the statutory exceptions recognised in each State is easements. Unfortunately, the scope of the exception varies from State to State. The scope is widest in Victoria, Western Australia and Tasmania. For example, s. 42(2)(d) of the *Transfer of Land Act* 1958 (Vic.) refers to "any easements howsoever acquired subsisting over or upon or affecting the land". The relevant Western Australian and Tasmanian sections are to similar effect.[293] The New South Wales, Queensland and South Australian legislation is phrased more narrowly. The *Real Property Act* 1900 (N.S.W.), s. 42(1)(b), substantially mirrored in Queensland and South Australia,[294] provides for an exception to indefeasibility "in the case of the omission or misdescription of any right-of-way or other easement created in or existing upon land".

In respect of the New South Wales, Queensland and South Australian legislation it is necessary to understand the meaning of the word "omission" contained in the statutory exception to indefeasibility in respect of "easements".[295] In *Papadopoulos v. Goodwin*,[296] Wootten J. held that the failure of the Registrar-General to record an easement on the folio relating to the servient tenement constituted an "omission" within the meaning of s. 42(1)(b) of the *Real Property Act* 1900 (N.S.W.). His Honour also held that the failure of the Registrar-General to record an existing easement when creating a new folio also constitutes an "omission". In

---

292. Torrens statutes: N.S.W.: ss 46, 47; Vic.: s. 72; Qld: ss 36, 51; S.A.: ss 81, 96; W.A.: ss 63A, 64, 65, 67; Tas.: ss 105, 106.
293. Torrens statutes: W.A.: s. 68; Tas.: s. 40(3).
294. Torrens statutes: Qld. s. 44; S.A · s. 69.
295. For a recent discussion of this issue, see (1987) 61 A.L.J. 660.
296. [1983] 2 N.S.W.L.R. 113.

Australian Hi-Fi Publications Pty Ltd v. Gehl,[297] the registered proprietor of Torrens land had subdivided his property into two lots. The appellant became the owner of lot 1, while the respondent company purchased lot 2. The owner of lot 1 used lot 2 in such a way that had the land been general law land an easement would have been created in favour of lot 1 under the rule in *Wheeldon v. Burrows,*[298] but no notification of any easement appeared on either certificate of title. The New South Wales Court of Appeal granted an injunction restraining the appellant from attempting to enforce the easement on the ground that the appellant could not bring his case within the statutory exception to indefeasibility. In reaching its conclusion, the court deliberately gave a narrow definition to the word "omission". The court rejected the wider interpretation of "omission" suggested by the appellant, namely that s. 42(1)(b) is not confined to what is "not there" because of the failure to discharge some form of obligation, and held that it may also extend to a case where a thing is "not there" merely because a person did not do something which he was entitled to do. The decision was justified, inter alia, on the ground that the Torrens system is based on the conclusiveness of the register and that to make the system effective any exceptions to indefeasibility should be construed narrowly. This decision has been applied in later New South Wales decisions.[299]

A similar, narrow interpretation has been given to "omission" under s. 44 of the *Real Property Act* 1861 (Qld). In *Stuy v. B. C. Ronalds Pty Ltd,*[300] at first instance Carter J. refused to follow *Gehl's* case and held that the statutory exception to indefeasibility includes easements validity created and in registrable form but not lodged for registration, and also easements howsoever created and whether in registrable form or otherwise and not recorded in the register. On appeal, however, this decision was reversed by the Full Court of the Supreme Court of Queensland, which expressly adopted the approach of the New South Wales Court of Appeal in *Gehl.* To date, there are no South Australian authorities relevant to this issue.

In all States, the statutory exception to indefeasibility appears to apply to easements created before the land is brought under the Torrens system and not recorded in the register.[301] In all States, it also appears that the statutory exception extends to easements validly created after the land is brought under the Torrens system, but which are omitted from or misdescribed in the register. This latter conclusion is based on case law in New South Wales,[302] Victoria,[303] Queensland,[304] and Western

297. [1979] 2 N.S.W.L.R. 618.
298. (1879) 12 Ch. D. 31 (C.A.).
299. *Beck v. Auerbach* (1986) 6 N.S.W.L.R. 454 (C.A.); *Papadopoulos v. Goodwin (No. 2)* [1983] 2 N.S.W.L.R. 113.
300. [1984] A.C.L.D. 098 (first instance); [1984] 2 Qd R. 578 (F.C.).
301. *Jobson v. Nankervis* (1943) 44 S.R. (N.S.W.) 277; *James v. Stevenson* [1893] A.C. 162 (P.C.); *Wilkinson v. Spooner* [1957] Tas. S.R. 121; *Stuy v. B.C. Ronalds Pty Ltd* [1984] A.C.L.D. 098 (Qld Sup. Ct).
302. *James v. Registrar-General* (1967) 69 S.R. (N.S.W.) 361; *Maurice Toltz Pty Ltd v. Macy's Emporium Pty Ltd* [1970] 1 N.S.W.R. 474 (discussed in (1971) 45 A.L.J. 157); *Berger Bros Trading Co. Pty Ltd v. Bursill Enterprises Pty Ltd* (1969) 91 W.N. (N.S.W.) 521.
303. *Nelson v. Hughes* [1947] V.L.R. 227.
304. *Rock v. Todeschino* [1983] 1 Qd R. 356.

Australia,[305] and on statutory interpretation of the relevant legislation in the remaining States.[306]

II. PROFITS A PRENDRE

1. Meaning and Nature of Profits

[16.41] A profit à prendre has been defined as "a right to take from the servient tenement of another some part of the soil of that tenement or minerals under it or some of its natural produce, or the animals ferae naturae existing upon it".[307]

Common law recognises both sole or several profits and profits in common. A profit exists in severalty if the owner of the profit enjoys her or his right to the exclusion of the owner of the servient tenement. In contrast, a profit exists in common where the servient owner is entitled to share the enjoyment of the right with the owner of the profit. Profits in common are frequently encountered in the United Kingdom, where they are now subject to the control contained in the *Commons Registration Act* 1965. However, profits in common are non-existent in Australia, and for this reason no further mention will be made of them.

At common law, both appurtenant profits and profits in gross are recognised. An appurtenant profit is one which, like an easement, benefits or accommodates the dominant tenement. A profit in gross is one where the use of the profit need have no connection with the ownership of other land.[308] In this regard, the law of profits differs markedly from the law of easements, which does not recognise rights in gross: see above **[16.08]**. Even if the profit is in gross, it is a proprietary interest which can be disposed of by the owner by sale or gift and can pass under a will or by the laws of intestacy.[309] It is essential that appurtenant profits relate to the needs and use of the dominant tenement. For example, in *Anderson v. Bostock*[310] the plaintiff's claim to an exclusive right to grazing without limit was rejected as an appurtenant right, although there would appear to be no reason why such a right could not exist as a profit in gross.

Apart from cases involving wild animals,[311] the right claimed must be part of the land itself. Thus, while the right to remove sand has been held to be a profit,[312] the right to collect objects blown onto the land is probably

---

305. *Di Masi v. Piromalli* [1980] W.A.R. 57.
306. See above **[16.19]** for a discussion of the recognition of equitable easements in respect of Torrens land.
307. *Alfred F. Beckett Ltd v. Lyons* [1967] Ch. 449 at 482 (C.A.) per Winn L.J. See also *National Executors & Trustee Co. (Tas.) v. Edwards* [1957] Tas. S.R. 182 at 187; *Manning v. Wasdale* (1836) 5 Ad. & E. 758 at 764; 111 E.R. 1353 at 1355 (K.B.).
308. See e.g. *Staffordshire & Worcestershire Canal Navigation v. Bradley* [1912] 1 Ch. 91.
309. See e.g. *Webber v. Lee* (1882) 9 Q.B.D. 315 (C.A.).
310. [1976] Ch. 312. See also *Lord Chesterfield v. Harris* [1911] A.C. 623 (H.L.).
311. See e.g. *Mason v. Clarke* [1955] A.C. 778 (H.L.); *Webber v. Lee* (1882) 9 Q.B.D. 315 (C.A.).
312. *Blewitt v. Tregonning* (1835) 3 Ad. & El. 554; 111 E.R. 524 (K.B.); *Unimin Pty Ltd v. Commonwealth* (1974) 2 A.C.T.R. 71.

not a profit because of the lack of affinity with the land.[313] A borderline case would be a right to collect coal washed up by the sea from the shore. There are dicta in *Alfred F. Beckett Ltd v. Lyons*[314] to the effect that this would be a valid profit.

The following rights have been recognised as valid profits by Australian courts:

1. A licence to operate a mine or quarry for the extraction of coal or other minerals.[315]

2. A right to take sand[316] or salt[317] from land.

3. A right to gather and burn mallee roots.[318]

4. The sale of slate and authority to the purchaser to enter land for the purpose of removing the slate.[319]

5. An agreement for participation in the commercial enterprise of planting and harvesting pine trees on the land of another.[320]

6. An agreement for the supply of nut trees growing or to be grown on the land belonging to a proprietary company, the trees to be cared for by the company for a maximum period of 25 years. The owners of the trees were given the right to have the company harvest the crop or to harvest the crop themselves.[321]

In contrast, an agreement by a purchaser of land to permit the vendor's sheep to remain on the land for a period of time after the date of settlement has been held not to be a profit.[322]

Pursuant to the *Conveyancing Act* 1919 (N.S.W.), s. 88AB, a forestry right is a profit à prendre. "Forestry right" is defined in s. 87A as "an interest in land pursuant to which a person having the benefit of the interest is entitled (a) to enter the land; (b) to establish, maintain and harvest a crop of trees on the land; and (c) to construct and use such buildings, works and facilities as may be necessary or convenient to enable the person to establish, maintain and harvest the crop".

---

313. Jackson, op. cit. at 29.

314. [1967] Ch. 449 at 476 (C.A.).

315. *Ex parte Henry; Re Commissioner of Stamp Duties* (1963) 63 S.R. (N.S.W.) 298 (S.C. in banco); *Mittagong S.C. v. Mittagong Anthracite Coal Co.* (1957) 3 L.G.R.A. 290 (A.C.T. Sup. Ct); *Emerald Quarry Industry Pty Ltd v. Commissioner of Highways* (1976) 14 S.A.S.R. 486 (S.C. in banco).

316. *Unimin Pty Ltd v. Commonwealth* (1974) 2 A.C.T.R. 71; *Australian Aggregates (N.S.W.) Pty Ltd v. Maxmin Pty Ltd* [1988] A.C.L.D. 576. Cf. *Maddalozzo v. Commonwealth* (1979) 22 A.L.R. 561 (N.T. Sup. Ct).

317. *Nicholls v. Lovell* [1923] S.A.S.R. 542.

318. *Vanstone v. Malura Pty Ltd* (1988) 50 S.A.S.R. 110.

319. *Mills v. Stockman* (1967) 116 C.L.R. 61.

320. *Australian Softwood Forests Pty Ltd v. Attorney-General (N.S.W.)* (1981) 36 A.L.R. 257 (H.C.).

321. *Warren v. Nut Farms of Australia Pty Ltd* [1981] W.A.R. 134. Cf. *Corporate Affairs Commission v. Australian Softwood Forest Pty Ltd* [1978] 1 N.S.W.L.R. 150.

322. *Beach v. Trims Investments Ltd* [1960] S.A.S.R. 5.

A profit may be granted in perpetuity or for a term of years.[323] In the latter case, a profit can still exist even if it is expressed to be determinable on a month's notice.[324]

2. Creation of Profits

[16.42] With certain exceptions, profits may be created in the same manner as easements. Thus, profits may be created by express or implied grant or reservation or by prescription: see above [16.21]ff. In relation to implied rights, the doctrine of "general words" has been held to apply to profits: see [16.27]. Although there is no authority on the point, profits may be created by mutual intention (see above [16.24]) or under the doctrine in *Wheeldon v. Burrows*[325] (see above [16.26]), although in this latter regard it might be difficult on the facts to satisfy the "continuous and apparent" requirement. By the very nature of a profit, however, it is submitted that profits cannot be created as of necessity or by implication from the description of land.

In relation to prescription, profits may be claimed after 20 years' enjoyment by lost modern grant although this occurs very rarely in practice. In South Australia, Western Australia and Tasmania, where the *Prescription Act* 1832 (U.K.) is in effect (see above [16.33]), profits may also be claimed under s. 1 of that Act,[326] although the two periods of necessary enjoyment are 30 years and 60 years, rather then the 20 year and 40 year periods applicable to easements by virtue of s. 2. A further limitation is that profits in gross cannot be acquired under the *Prescription Act* as s. 5 states that the right must have been enjoyed "by the owners of the tenement in respect whereof the same is claimed".[327] Thus, the *Prescription Act* applies only to appurtenant profits.

Like easements, profits may be created at equity under the rule in *Walsh v. Lonsdale*:[328] see above [16.19]. Australian courts have recognised equitable profits in the case of an informal written agreement[329] and in the case of part performance by entry onto the servient land pursuant to a profit granted orally.[330]

In New South Wales, pursuant to s. 88AA(1) of the *Conveyancing Act* 1919, a profit created by an instrument coming into operation after the commencement of the *Conveyancing (Forestry Rights) Amendment Act* 1987 is not enforceable against a person interested in land claimed to be subject to the profit (other than a person who is party to the instrument) unless

---

323. *A.S.C. Timber Pty Ltd & Companies (N.S.W.) Code; Corporate Affairs Commission v. A.S.C. Timber Pty Ltd* [1989] A.C.L.D. 491 (N.S.W. Sup. Ct).
324. *Unimin Pty Ltd v. Commonwealth* (1974) 2 A.C.T.R. 71 at 78. Cf. *Vanstone v. Malura Pty Ltd* (1988) 50 S.A.S.R. 110.
325. (1879) 12 Ch. D. 31 (C.A.).
326. The relevant legislation in Tasmania is the *Prescription Act* 1934, s. 2.
327. The relevant legislation in Tasmania is the *Prescription Act* 1934, s. 5.
328. (1882) 21 Ch. D. 9 (C.A.).
329. *Mills v. Stockman* (1967) 116 C.L.R. 61; *Ellison v. Vukicevic* (1986) 7 N.S.W.L.R. 104.
330. *Unimin Pty Ltd v. Commonwealth* (1977) 18 A.C.T.R. 1; *Mason v. Clarke* [1955] A.C. 778 (H.L.); *Vanstone v. Malura Pty Ltd* (1988) 50 S.A.S.R. 110.

the instrument indicates (a) the land subject to the burden of the profit; and (b) in the case of an appurtenant profit, the benefited land.

3. Remedies and Extinguishment of Profits

[16.43]   As in the case of easements (see above [16.34]), the owner of a profit may protect her or his interest by abatement or by court action based on nuisance. In the former case, the restrictions discussed earlier on the availability of abatement (see above [16.34]) apply equally in this context.

It is clearly established that profits may be extinguished by unity of seisin[331] and by agreement between the parties (if sui juris). In respect of Torrens land, the *Land Titles Act* 1980 (Tas.), s. 108(1) empowers the Recorder of Titles to cancel the registration of a profit à prendre if the profit is extinguished, varied or modified by agreement of the parties. In the other jurisdictions, it would seem that the respective parties must obtain a court order before the profit will be removed from the register.

Although at common law mere non-user of a profit for a lengthy period is not in itself sufficient to constitute abandonment, extinguishment will occur if non-user is coupled with proof of evidence that the owner of the profit never intended to exercise her or his right again.[332] This has been judicially described as a "heavy onus".[333] The only statutory modification to this is in respect of Torrens land in Tasmania, where s. 108(3) of the *Land Titles Act* 1980 states that the Recorder of Titles may treat evidence of 20 years' non-user of a profit as evidence that the profit has been abandoned. By analogy with the law of easements (see above [16.36]), even if at common law a profit would be held to have been abandoned, it is submitted that a profit under Torrens land will be enforceable in Victoria and South Australia until it is removed from the register by court order. The rule in the remaining jurisdictions is the reverse: see above [16.36].

Extinguishment of a profit may occur where the dominant tenement is altered to such an extent as to make further use of the profit impossible. However, extinguishment will not occur where the dominant tenement is altered but where it is still in such a state that it might be turned to the original purpose of the profit.[334] Thus, for example, there would be no extinguishment where grazing land subject to a profit was turned into a crop-growing area.

The final issue is whether profits may be extinguished pursuant to the legislation in New South Wales, Queensland, Western Australia and Tasmania permitting a court to modify or wholly or partially extinguish

---

331.   *White v. Taylor (No. 2)* [1969] 1 Ch. 150; *Re Yateley Common (Hampshire)* [1977] 1 W.L.R. 840.

332.   *Tehidy Minerals Ltd v. Norman* [1971] 2 Q.B. 528 at 533 (C.A.); *Re Yateley Common (Hampshire)* [1977] 1 W.L.R. 840.

333.   *Re Yateley Common (Hampshire)* [1977] 1 W.L.R. 840 at 846.

334.   *Carr v. Lambert* (1866) L.R. 1 Exch. 168.

easements and restrictive covenants in certain specified circumstances.[335]
This issue has not yet been resolved by the courts. The identical wording
of the relevant enactment in each State reads, "where land is subject to
an easement or to a restriction arising under covenant or otherwise as to
the user thereof". While the matter is not beyond dispute, it is submitted
that profits are included within the scope of this legislation as a
"restriction arising . . . otherwise".

4. Profits and the Torrens System

[16.44] The basic issue for consideration is whether profits can be
created in respect of Torrens land. Unlike in the case of easements,[336]
where all of the State Torrens statutes state expressly that easements may
be created, in the case of profits only Tasmania makes such a provision.
The *Land Titles Act* 1980, s. 107 states:

> "(1) A profit a prendre may be granted by an instrument in the
> prescribed form which shall indicate clearly the nature of the profit
> a prendre, the period for which it is to be enjoyed, and whether it is
> to be enjoyed—
>
> (a) in gross or as appurtenant to other land; and
>
> (b) by the grantee exclusively or by him in common with the
> grantor.
>
> (2) The Recorder shall register the instrument referred to in
> subsection (1)—
>
> (a) by recording it on the folio of the Register or the registered
> lease which it burdens; and
>
> (b) where it is appurtenant to registered land, by recording it
> on the folio of the Register or registered lease evidencing
> title to that land."

In Queensland,[337] the Torrens legislation empowers the Registrar of
Titles to enter a memorial of instruments creating "any easement or other
incorporeal right" in the register book. In this jurisdiction the issue is
settled as profits clearly constitute an incorporeal right.

In the remaining jurisdictions there is no reference to "other
incorporeal right", so there is genuine doubt as to the creation of profits
in respect of Torrens land.[338] Both Barwick C.J. and Menzies J.
considered in *Mills v. Stockman*[339] that profits can exist in respect of
Torrens land although neither judge analysed the issue in terms of the
legislation. Professor Whalan states that the correct analysis is that the

---

335. *Conveyancing Act* 1919 (N.S.W.), s. 89(1); *Property Law Act* 1974 (Qld), s. 181;
      Transfer of Land Act 1893 (W.A.), s. 129C; *Conveyancing and Law of Property Act*
      1884 (Tas.), Pt XVA. Cf. *Property Law Act* 1958 (Vic.), s. 84(1). This legislation
      is discussed at **[16.39]**.
336. Torrens statutes: N.S.W.: s. 46; Vic.: ss 45, 72; Qld: ss 48, 51; S.A.: s. 96;
      W.A.: ss 82, 88A; Tas.: ss 105, 106.
337. *Real Property Act* 1861 (Qld), s. 51.
338. See Note (1982) 56 A.L.J 426.
339. (1967) 116 C.L.R. 61 at 73 and 79. See also *Moreland Timber Co. v. Reid* [1946]
      V.L.R. 237 at 247.

definition of "land" in the Torrens statutes is wide enough to include profits, and as all jurisdictions permit "land" to be transferred, this should permit the use of a transfer to create a profit by grant or reservation.[340] This conclusion was supported by the recent decision of the New South Wales Supreme Court (Young J.) in *Ellison v. Vukicevic*.[341] Based on this analysis, it is submitted that profits can be created in respect of Torrens land throughout Australia.

A major distinction between profits and easements is that there is no statutory exception to indefeasibility in favour of profits. The statutory exception in favour of easements is strictly limited to easements: see above [16.40]. Thus, all profits created by express grant or reservation will not receive protection until registration, while profits arising by implied grant or reservation or by prescription must be recognised by court declaration and the court declaration must be registered; until a court order is obtained, profits may be protected by the lodging of a caveat: see above [5.81]ff.

III.   RENTCHARGES

1. Nature and Meaning of Rentcharges

[16.45]   Rent payable by a tenant to a landlord is classified at law as a "rent service". Rent services arise whenever privity of estate exists between the parties. Rent services must be distinguished from rentcharges, which may be defined as any annual or other periodic sum of money charged on or issuing out of land, except for rent reserved in a lease or any money by way of interest.[342]

Rentcharges are encountered frequently in the United Kingdom, but only rarely in Australia. Following the recommendation of the Queensland Law Reform Commission,[343] the Queensland legislature enacted in s. 176 of the *Property Law Act* 1974 that no rentcharges shall be created after the commencement of this Act. Thus, any rentcharges created after 1 December 1975 are void and of no effect. This abolition only applies in respect of general law land, however, as s. 176(2) states that the section does not apply to the creation, in respect of registered land, of an encumbrance within the meaning of the *Real Property Act* 1861 (Qld).

Apart from this Queensland provision, rentcharges appear to be recognised throughout Australia in respect of both general law and Torrens land. Except in Victoria and Western Australia, the State Torrens legislation makes specific reference to the registration of rentcharges.[344] As this term is not defined in the statutes, it presumably

340. *Ellison v. Vukicevic* (1986) 7 N.S.W.L.R. 104.
341. Whalan, p. 107.
342. This is the definition in the *Rentcharges Act* 1977 (U.K.), s. 1(1). See also *National Executors & Trustee Co. (Tas.) v. Edwards* [1957] Tas. S.R. 182 (F.C.) for a discussion of the nature and meaning of rentcharges.
343. Q.L.R.C., Report No. 10 (1972), p. 100.
344. Torrens statutes: N.S.W.: s. 56(2); S.A.: s. 128; Qld: s. 56; Tas.: s. 72(b).

has the same meaning as at common law. In Victoria and Western Australia, where the Torrens legislation makes no mention of rentcharges, the issue rises whether such interests are recognised over Torrens land. It is submitted that the answer is in the affirmative. In both States, the *Transfer of Land Act* defines "annuity" as "a sum of money payable periodically and charged on land under the operation of this Act by an instrument of charge".[345] This coincides with the common law meaning of a rentcharge. Thus, curiously, in Victoria and Western Australia, rentcharges are defined as annuities and a person who would class as a rentchargee at common law is protected as an annuitant under the Torrens legislation.

A rentcharge is an incorporeal hereditament as no possessory right is given to the rentchargee. Like profits à prendre, rentcharges may exist in gross, and no necessary connection with any land owned by the beneficiary need be proved.

The most common illustration of a rentcharge arises upon a sale of land, where the vendor reserves to her or himself and her or his heirs the payment of an annual sum of money in perpetuity. This annual sum may be in lieu of or in addition to a lump sum payment. In Australia, rentcharges have been held to exist in *Re Trusts of the Will of Foss*,[346] where the testator bequeathed an annuity of 400 pounds to his wife charged upon certain specified lands and premises with power of entry and distress in case of non-payment of the annuity within 30 days after the due date, and in *In the Will of Walmsley*,[347] where the testator devised land to his son on the condition that he pay 25 pounds per annum rent to M.E.W., the testator's widow, for the benefit of two children named in the will of his son. In the latter case, the court held that the effect of the disposition was to create a charge in favour of the two children and the survivor of them for life. In *Thompson v. Whittard*,[348] the testator bequeathed a certain property to his son and stated:

> "executors also will make provision that one mass shall be said for the repose of my soul once every week until they hand over the property to my son, when he attains the age of 30 years, when he shall take the place of the executors and have the masses said weekly forever, and these are the conditions I make."

The court held that these directions created a valid charitable trust and that in effect it imposed a charge upon the property in question.[349]

The issue arises whether rentcharges may be used to avoid the rule in *Austerberry v. Oldham Corporation*[350] (see below [17.05]), that the burden of positive freehold covenants does not run at common law. In the past a device has been used whereby a nominal rentcharge is imposed, which is

---

345. *Transfer of Land Act* 1958 (Vic.), s. 4(1); *Transfer of Land Act* 1893 (W.A.), s. 4(1).
346. (1868) 7 S.C.R. (N.S.W.) Eq. 68.
347. (1922) 18 Tas. L.R. 32.
348. (1925) 25 S.R. (N.S.W.) 430.
349. See also *Williams v. Papworth* [1900] A.C. 563 (P.C.); *Daly v. Papworth* (1906) 6 S.R. (N.S.W.) 572; *Wilson v. Whyte* (1892) 25 S.A.L.R. 46 (F.C.).
350. (1885) 29 Ch. D. 750 (C.A.).

supported by one or more positive covenants. As these covenants incidentally support the rentcharge, it may be argued that they will be enforceable. In *Blacks Ltd v. Rix*,[351] the plaintiff company registered a rentcharge as an encumbrance in order to achieve the registration of several restrictive covenants contained in the encumbrance. Napier C.J. of the Supreme Court of South Australia did not question the legitimacy of the device. Despite this favourable analogy, the device under consideration was rejected by the Full Court of the Supreme Court of South Australia in *Clem Smith Nominees Pty Ltd v. Farrelly*[352] on the basis that a covenant must be taken in favour of a corporeal rather than an incorporeal hereditament.[353]

2. Creation of Rentcharges

[16.46]   Rentcharges may be created by instrument inter vivos or by will, and may be held in fee simple, for life or for a term of years. The normal rules concerning words of limitation apply in this context.[354] In respect of Torrens land, rentcharges may be created by the execution of an instrument in the form specified in the legislation.[355]

An equitable rentcharge may be created under the rule in *Walsh v. Lonsdale*.[356] As explained above **[6.37]**ff, this may arise in the case where an informal agreement to grant a rentcharge has been signed or where there has been part performance.

The rule at common law is that a rentcharge can only be charged upon a corporeal hereditament.[357] The traditional justification for this is that the major remedy of a rentcharge is the power to distrain. Although in Australia the right of distraint has been abolished by State legislation in all jurisdictions except South Australia and Tasmania,[358] the common law rule presumably continues to operate. A partial exception to this rule exists in Victoria, where s. 127(1) of the *Property Law Act* 1958 states that a rentcharge may be granted, reserved, charged or created out of or on another rentcharge in like manner as it could have been made to issue out of land. Thus, in Victoria a rentcharge may be created on a rentcharge, but not on other incorporeal hereditaments.

3. Remedies

[16.47]   A rentchargee may enforce her or his proprietary interest in one or more of a number of ways:

351. [1962] S.A.S.R. 161.
352. (1978) 20 S.A.S.R. 227 (F.C.).
353. Ibid. at 248 per Hogarth J.
354. See above **[2.32]**ff. for a discussion of the rules relating to words of limitation.
355. Torrens statutes: N.S.W.: s. 56(2); Vic.: s. 74(1)(b); Qld: s. 56; S.A.: s. 128; W.A.: s. 105(2); Tas.: s. 72(b).
356. (1882) 21 Ch. D. 9 (C.A.). See e.g. *Jackson v. Lever* (1792) 3 Bro. C.C. 605; 29 E.R. 724 (Ch.).
357. *Re the Alms Corn Charity* [1901] 2 Ch. 750 at 759; *Earl of Stafford v. Buckley* (1750) 2 Ves. Sen. 170 at 178; 28 E.R. 111 (Ch.).
358. *Landlord and Tenant Amendment (Distress Abolition) Act* 1930 (N.S.W.), s. 2; *Landlord and Tenant Act* 1958 (Vic.), s. 12; *Property Law Act* 1974 (Qld), s. 103; *Distress for Rent Abolition Act* 1936 (W.A.), s. 2.

(a) Distress (South Australia and Tasmania only)

Distress for rent was the basic remedy given to a rentchargee at common law. Except in South Australia and Tasmania, the right of distraint has now been abolished by State legislation (see above [10.76]) and where it is still applicable, it is now subject to stringent controls.[359] For this reason, distress is seldom exercised. In New South Wales, s. 4 of the *Landlord and Tenant Amendment (Distress Abolition) Act* 1930 states that a rentchargee owed arrears of rent may recover the arrears as a debt from the person in possession of the land charged. This right was bestowed in lieu of the right of distress.

(b) Entry into possession after 40 days' arrears

State legislation in each State now gives a rentchargee the right to take possession of the landcharged once the charge is at least 40 days in arrears.[360] There is no need for a formal demand. Where this remedy is exercised, the rentchargee may hold the land charged and take the income thereof until the annual sum, all arrears due at the time of her or his entry or afterwards becoming due, and all costs and expenses are fully paid. The possession of the rentchargee is stated to be without impeachment of waste.

(c) Lease to a trustee

In similar circumstances as in the preceding remedy, the rentchargee is also given the right by State legislation,[361] whether or not he or she takes possession, to lease all or part of the land charged to a trustee for a term of years, with or without impeachment of waste, on trust, to raise and pay the annual sum, all arrears, and all costs and expenses, including the costs of the preparation and execution of the deed of lease and the costs of the execution of the trusts of that deed.

(d) Sale or mortgage of land

The court may order a sale or mortgage of the land charged, although this remedy is discretionary and depends on the circumstances of the case.[362] In addition to these non-statutory rights, the Torrens legislation in each State gives a registered rentchargee similar powers of sale by public auction to those of a registered mortgagee, although there is no power of private sale by foreclosure proceedings.[363]

---

359. Restrictions on the right of distress are contained in the *Landlord and Tenant Act* 1936 (S.A.), Pt II, and the *Landlord and Tenant Act* 1935 (Tas.), Pt V.
360. General law statutes: N.S.W.: s. 146; Vic.: ss 125, 127; Tas.: s. 56.
361. See above fn. 360.
362. See e.g. *Blackburne v. Hope-Edwardes* [1901] 1 Ch. 419; *Cupit v. Jackson* (1824) McCle. 495; 148 E.R. 207 (Exch.).
363. Torrens statutes: N.S.W.: s. 58; Qld: s. 57; S.A.: s. 133; W.A.: s. 108, Tas.: s. 78.

(e) Appointment of receiver (Victoria only)

As stated above [16.46], in Victoria it is possible to create a rentcharge charged on another rentcharge. Where this occurs, an additional remedy is given to enforce the rentcharge. Section 127(2) of the *Property Law Act* 1958 states that where the charge is at least 21 days in arrears, the rentchargee has the power to appoint a receiver of the sum charged. In this event, the provisions of Pt II relating to the appointment, powers, remuneration and duties of a receiver apply in the same manner as if the person were a mortgagee entitled to exercise her or his statutory power of sale.

4. Extinguishment of Rentcharges

[16.48]   Rentcharges may be extinguished in any one of the following ways:

(a) Natural determination

A rentcharge may be extinguished by its natural determination. Thus, for example, if the charge is created for the life of the chargee it will determine naturally on the death of the chargee.

(b) Express release

Alternatively, a rentcharge may be extinguished at any time by express release of part or all of the land charged. The rule at common law was that the extinguishment of part of the land operated to extinguish the whole of the rentcharge.[364] This harsh rule has now been replaced by legislation in all States. For example, s. 70(1) of the *Property Law Act* 1958 (Vic.)[365] states that a release from a rentcharge of part of the land charged shall operate only to bar the right to recover any part of the rentcharge out of the land released, without prejudice to the rights of any persons interested in the land remaining unreleased, and not concurring in or confirming the release.

(c) Merger

This doctrine is subject to the equitable rule that there is no merger if it is contrary to the intention of the person in whom the merged estates vest.[366]

(d) Limitation of actions

A further method of extinguishment arises under the State limitation of actions legislation. If a rentcharge remains unpaid for 12 years (15 years

---

364. Co. Litt. 147b.
365. General law statutes: Qld: s. 177; S.A.: s 38; Tas.: s. 57.
366. See e.g. *Re Fletcher* [1971] 1 Ch. 330; *Ingle v. Vaughan Jenkins* [1900] 2 Ch. 368; *Snow v. Boycott* [1892] 3 Ch. 110.

in Victoria and South Australia) and no acknowledgment of the chargee's title is made during that period, it is extinguished by operation of law.[367]

(e) Miscellaneous statutory provisions

State legislation in New South Wales, Victoria, South Australia and Tasmania provides for a discharge of encumbrances (including rentcharges) by the Supreme Court on sales or exchanges. For example, s. 50(1) of the *Property Law Act* 1958 (Vic.) states:[368]

"Where land subject to any incumbrance, whether immediately realizable or payable or not, is sold or exchanged by the Court, or out of court, the Court may, if it thinks fit, on the application of any party to the sale or exchange, direct or allow payment into court of such sum as is hereinafter mentioned, that is to say:—

(a) In the case of an annual sum charged on the land, or of a capital sum charged on a determinable interest in the land, the sum to be paid into court shall be of such amount as, when invested in Government securities, the Court considers will be sufficient, by means of the dividends thereof, to keep down or otherwise provide for that charge; and

. . .

but in either case there shall also be paid into court such additional amount as the Court considers will be sufficient to meet the contingency of further costs, expenses and interest, and any other contingency, except depreciation of investments, not exceeding one-tenth part of the original amount to be paid in, unless the Court for special reason thinks fit to require a larger additional amount."

Where this occurs, the court may, in its absolute discretion, declare the land to be freed from the rentcharge.

The settled land legislation in Victoria and Tasmania also provides for the removal of rentcharges and other encumbrances. Section 69 of the *Settled Land Act* 1958 (Vic.)[369] states that where there is an encumbrance affecting any part of the settled land, the tenant for life may, with the consent of the encumbrancer and with the consent of the trustees of the settlement or order of the court charge that encumbrance on any other part of the settled land, or on all or any part of the capital money or securities representing capital money subject or to become subject to the settlement, in exoneration of the first-mentioned part.

---

367. Limitation statutes: N.S.W.: ss 11, 27(2); Vic.: s. 20(1); Qld: s. 13; S.A.: s. 4; W.A.: s. 4; Tas.: s. 23.
368. General law statutes: N.S.W.: s. 66; S.A.: s. 27; Tas.: s. 4.
369. See also *Settled Land Act* 1884 (Tas.), s. 5.

17

Freehold Covenants

I. INTRODUCTION

[17.01] The law relating to the enforcement of leasehold covenants has been discussed earlier in Chapter 12. This Chapter will analyse the different rules of law and equity which apply where a covenant is entered into between two or more owners of freehold estates in land and where one of the parties or her or his successor-in-title seeks to enforce the covenant against another party or her or his successor-in-title.

A covenant is defined by Halsbury as "an agreement under seal whereby the parties, or some of them, are or is bound to do or not to do a specified thing".[1] This must be distinguished from a restrictive covenant, which is a covenant restricting the use or enjoyment of certain land for the benefit of other land and binding on every owner of the burdened land having notice of the covenant.[2] A restrictive covenant is a right recognised by equity since the mid 19th century, created in order to overcome the rigid common law rule that the burden of a covenant cannot be enforced against any person other than the original contracting party. The reason why it is referred to as a *restrictive* covenant is that equity will not enforce a covenant against an assignee of the covenantor where to do so would oblige the assignee to expend money.[3] Thus, any covenant must be negative in nature in that it merely requires the owner of the burdened land to refrain from doing certain activities or exercising certain rights which would otherwise be available to her or him.

Covenants represent a form of private land-use planning. By the use of covenants, for example, a subdivider of a large block of land can impose legally binding restrictions on the purchasers of each of the subdivided blocks regarding the type of building later erected and its positioning on the block. In recent decades the States have taken over the function of planning and each jurisdiction now possesses detailed legislation regulating building,[4] town planning and subdivision.[5] These modern

---

1. *Halsbury's Laws of England* (4th ed.) Vol. 12, "Deeds and Other Instruments", para. 1539.
2. See Preston and Newsom, para. 1-03 for a discussion of the meaning of "restrictive covenant".
3. *Haywood v. Brunswick Permanent Benefit Building Society* (1881) 8 Q.B.D. 403 at 409 per Cotton L.J.
4. The building controls are contained in the *Building Control Act* 1981 (Vic.); *Local Government Act* 1919 (N.S.W.); *Building Act* 1975 (Qld); *Building Act* 1970 (S.A.); *Local Government Act* 1960 (W.A.); *Local Government Act* 1962 (Tas.).
5. The town-planning and subdivision controls are contained in the *Planning and*

controls coexist with private covenants, and a landowner wishing to develop land must comply with the terms of both the State legislation and any relevant restrictive covenants which bind the land.

As discussed in **[16.05]**, there is a considerable overlap between easements and restrictive covenants. In certain circumstances, the same obligation can be imposed either as an easement or as a restrictive covenant, depending on the wording of the instrument. For example, a landowner who sells part of her or his land and wishes to ensure that the purchaser will not erect a building which severely restricts the access of light to the part of the land retained may either reserve to her or himself an express easement of light or may insist that the purchaser enter into a covenant restricting the height of the building to be erected and/or imposing restrictions on the area of the land sold which can be developed. The overlap between the scope of easements and restrictive covenants is such that covenants have frequently been referred to as an extension in equity of the doctrine of negative easements.[6] Despite this, however, easements and covenants are conceptually quite distinct, and covenants are primarily used to circumvent the refusal of the courts to recognise certain rights (for example, the right of prospect or of privacy) as capable of constituting an easement.

There is also an overlap between the law under discussion in this Chapter and the law relating to the enforcement of leasehold covenants: see above Chapter 10. For example, there is the requirement in both cases that a covenant touch and concern the land of the covenantee before the benefit will run to an assignee. In this instance, the laws applicable to freehold covenants, like those applicable to leasehold covenants, derive from the rule in *Spencer's* case.[7] In most respects, however, the laws relevant to freehold covenants have developed separately from those of leasehold covenants. The major distinction is the concept of privity of estate. This concept is the basis of the enforceability of covenants by and against persons other than the original contracting parties, and arises between two persons whenever one of them is lawfully in possession of land under a leasehold estate and the other has the leasehold reversion. The concept of privity of estate has no relevance in the freehold context, however. The reasons why the laws relating to the enforceability of freehold and leasehold covenants (other than those between the original contracting parties) developed separately appear not to have been considered. Possibly, the explanation is the late recognition of the leasehold estate as forming part of real property law on the ground that it was outside the feudal structure. Another possible explanation is that the restrictive common law rules regarding the enforceability of freehold

<hr />

5. *Continued.*
   Environment Act 1987 (Vic.); *Environmental Planning and Assessment Act* 1979 (N.S.W.); *Local Government Act* 1919 (N.S.W.); *Local Government Act* 1936 (Qld); *Planning Act* 1982 (S.A.); *Town Planning and Development Act* 1928 (W.A.); *Local Government Act* 1962 (Tas.).
6. See e.g. *London & South London Western Rly Co. v. Gomm* (1882) 20 Ch. D. 562 at 583 (C.A.) per Jessel M.R.; *Re Nisbet and Potts' Contract* [1906] 1 Ch. 386 at 401 per Collins M.R.
7. (1583) 5 Co. Rep. 16a; 77 E.R. 72 (K.B.). See above **[10.44]**.

covenants may have been influenced by the rule against unlawful restraints on alienation (see above [2.46]) which would have no relevance in the leasehold context.

The law relating to the enforceability of freehold covenants has been criticised by one commentator as "a blundering conceptualist jungle full of semantic swamps",[8] and elsewhere as "a morass of technicalities, inconsistences and uncertainties".[9] Several law reform proposals have been made, one of which, the English Law Commission's Report on the *Law of Positive and Restrictive Covenants*,[10] recommends that the existing division between covenants enforceable at law and equity should be replaced by a new legal entity entitled a land obligation. Such an obligation would be automatically enforceable by and against the owners of the respective lands at the relevant date. To date, no Australian jurisdiction has fundamentally reformed the law on this subject, and with certain exceptions the law is still based primarily on case law.

II.   PARTIES TO THE COVENANT

[17.02]   Covenants may be enforced by the original contracting parties based on the doctrine of privity of contract. Covenants may also be enforced in certain circumstances between an assignee or other successor-in-title of the covenantee and an assignee or other successor-in-title of the covenantor. Thus, if A covenants with B, and A later sells his property to A1 and B later sells his property to B1, in certain circumstances B1 may enforce the covenant against A1 even though neither of them was a party to the covenant. The detailed rules discussed below [17.10]ff. concerning the passing of the benefit and the burden of a covenant will determine the exact circumstances where B1 can successfully enforce the covenant against A1.

In certain circumstances, pursuant to State legislation, covenants may also be enforced by third parties who are neither parties to the covenant nor assignees or other successors-in-title to the parties to the covenant. The legislation in New South Wales, Victoria,[11] South Australia and Tasmania[12] follows that of the United Kingdom[13] and reads:

"A person may take an immediate or other interest in land or other property, or the benefit of any condition, right of entry, covenant or

---

8. Beuscher, *Land Use Controls, Cases and Materials* (3rd ed., 1964), p. 92.
9. Bradbrook and Neave, para. 1211.
10. English Law Reform Commission, *The Law of Positive and Restrictive Covenants*, Law Com., Report No. 127 (H.M.S.O., 1984); discussed in Edell, "Fundamental Reform of Positive and Restrictive Covenants" [1984] J.P. & E.L. 222. See also *Report of the Committee on Positive Covenants Affecting Land* (Cmnd 2719, H.M.S.O., 1965); *Final Report of the Australian Commission of Enquiry into Land Tenure* (the Else-Mitchell Commission, A.G.P.S., 1976); New Zealand Property Law and Equity Reform Committee, *Report on Positive Covenants Affecting Land* (Wellington, 1985).
11. General law statutes: N.S.W.: s. 36C; Vic.: s. 56(1).
12. General law statutes: S.A.: s. 34; Tas.: s. 61.
13. *Law of Property Act* 1925 (U.K.), s. 56(1).

agreement over or respecting land of any other property, although he is not named as a party to the conveyance or other instrument.''

The scope of this legislation has been the subject of dispute. According to Lord Denning M.R., the section completely abrogates the principle of privity of contract,[14] but this wide-ranging interpretation was rejected by the House of Lords in *Beswick v. Beswick*[15] and by the Supreme Court of Victoria in *Bird v. Trustees Executors & Agency Co. Ltd.*[16]

Although the matter is not yet settled, it appears that the legislation should be construed as merely repealing the common law rule that only a person who is expressly named as a party to a covenant may enforce the covenant. The legislation thus has only a very narrow application.[17] Consider the following three illustrations. First, if X covenants with Y to grant a benefit to Z, under the rule in *Beswick v. Beswick* Z cannot sue to enforce the covenant despite the existence of the legislation. Secondly, where X covenants with Y and Z to grant a benefit to Z, Z may enforce the agreement at common law. Finally, where X covenants with Y and the owners of adjoining land, the owners of the adjoining land may sue to enforce the covenant by virtue of the State legislation. It is only in the last-mentioned illustration that the legislation has any relevance. An important limitation on the legislation is that it will only operate in favour of persons who are in existence and identifiable at the date the covenant was entered into.[18] Thus, for example, any covenant purporting to grant a benefit to the future owners of adjoining land cannot be enforced by any future owner.

In Queensland and Western Australia, the equivalent State legislation is phrased more broadly and in both cases it abrogates the principle of privity of contract. The *Property Law Act* 1974 (Qld), s. 55(1) states that a promisor who for a valuable consideration moving from the premises, promises to do or to refrain from doing an act or acts for the benefit of a beneficiary shall, upon acceptance by the beneficiary, be subject to a duty enforceable by the beneficiary to perform that promise. By s. 55(5), the section operates with respect to an interest in land. Pursuant to s. 55(6), "beneficiary" includes a person who, at the time of acceptance is identified or in existence, although that person may not have been identified or in existence at the time when the covenant was made. Although the section has a wide application, it appears to have no effect on the passing of the burden of the covenant to the successor-in-title of the covenantor, and in this case the equitable and common law rules have to be satisfied. Note, finally, that the common law rule that the legislation will not operate in favour of persons who are not in existence and identifiable on the date the covenant was entered into, has been

14. *Beswick v. Beswick* [1966] Ch. 538 at 556 (C.A.); *Drive Yourself Hire Co. (London) Ltd v. Strutt* [1954] 1 Q.B. 250 at 274 (C.A.).
15. [1968] A.C. 58.
16. [1957] V.R. 619.
17. See *Re Ecclesiastical Commissioners for England's Conveyance* [1936] Ch. 430 for an illustration of the operation of the legislation. Cf. *White v. Bijou Mansions Ltd* [1938] Ch. 351 (C.A.).
18. *Bohn v. Miller Bros Pty Ltd* [1953] V.L.R. 354 at 358; *Bird v. Trustees Executors & Agency Co. Ltd* [1957] V.R. 619.

overturned in Queensland by s. 13(1) of the *Property Law Act*. In Western Australia, the *Property Law Act* 1969, s. 11(2) is to similar effect as the Queensland legislation except that it appears not to permit a person who was not identified or in existence at the date of the covenant to enforce the covenant against the covenantor.

III. COVENANTS AT LAW

1. Nature of the Covenant

[17.03]   At common law, a covenant is enforceable regardless of whether it relates to any land owned by the covenantor and regardless of whether the covenant is positive or negative in nature. Both points are illustrated by *The Prior's Case*[19] where a Prior covenanted that he and his convent would sing every Sunday in the chapel owned by the covenantee. It was held that the covenantee's successor-in-title could enforce the covenant at common law. A modern illustration is *Smith and Snipes Hall Farm Ltd v. River Douglas Catchment Board*,[20] where the defendant had covenanted with certain landowners whose land was prone to flooding to keep the banks of a certain river in good repair. The covenant was held to be enforceable by an assignee of the covenantee even though the covenant imposed a positive duty on the defendant and despite the fact that the covenant was unrelated to land in that the defendant owned no land in the district.

2. Passing of the Benefit

[17.04]   At common law, the following legal requirements must be satisfied before the benefit of a covenant will pass to an assignee of the covenantee:

(a) The covenant must touch and concern the benefited land

This requirement also applies in the context of leasehold estates: see above **[10.42]**ff. In essence, it means that the covenant must not be intended for the personal benefit of the covenantee but rather for the benefit of the land owned by her or him.[21] Generally speaking, the test applied by the courts will be the same for freehold as for leasehold covenants. If the covenant fails the "touching and concerning" test, its benefit may still run to an assignee of the covenantee under legislation in all Australian jurisdictions permitting the express assignment of a covenant as a chose in action.[22] The legislation requires the assignment to be written and for express written notice to be given to the covenantor.

19. (1368) Y.B. 42 Ed. III, pl. 14; Co. Litt. 384a.
20. [1949] 2 K.B. 500 (C.A.).
21. See *Rogers v. Hosegood* [1900] 2 Ch. 388 at 395 (C.A.).
22. General law statutes: N.S.W.: s. 12; Vic.: s. 134; Qld: ss 199, 200; S.A.: s. 15; W.A.: s. 20; Tas.: s. 86.

(b) The estate of the assignee of the covenantee must be legal

This ancient rule of common law was reaffirmed by the English Court of Appeal in *Rogers v. Hosegood*,[23] which held that the benefit of a covenant could only run at equity, not common law, where the covenantee had merely an equity of redemption.

(c) An assignee of the covenantee must have the same legal estate as the covenantee (South Australia only)

The effect of this rule is, for example, that a tenant cannot take the benefit of a covenant made by the owner of the fee simple estate.[24] This rule was of dubious validity and (except in South Australia) appears to have been abolished by State legislation. For example, s. 78(1) of the *Property Law Act* 1958 (Vic.) states:

> "A covenant relating to any land of the covenantee shall be deemed to be made with the covenantee and his successors in title and the persons deriving title under him or them, and shall have effect as if such successors and other persons were expressed. For the purpose of this sub-section in connection with covenants restrictive of the user of land 'successors in title' shall be deemed to include the owners and occupiers for the time being of the land of the covenantee intended to be benefited."[25]

Despite initial doubts that this was merely a consolidating provision, it has been held by the English Court of Appeal in two decisions to abolish the rule under discussion.[26]

(d) The benefit of the covenant must be intended to run (South Australia only)

This common law rule no longer applies in all jurisdictions except South Australia by virtue of the legislation cited in the preceding paragraph.[27]

3. Passing of the Burden

[17.05] Unlike in the case of leasehold estates, the inflexible rule at common law is that the burden of a freehold covenant will not run to an assignee of the covenantor. This is sometimes referred to as the rule in *Austerberry v. Oldham Corporation*.[28] It applies even if the assignee purchases the land with actual knowledge of the existence of the covenant affecting the land.

---

23. [1900] 2 Ch. 388 (C.A.).
24. See e.g. *Westhoughton U.D.C. v. Wigan Coal Co.* [1919] 1 Ch. 159 (C.A.).
25. See also general law statutes: N.S.W.: s. 70; Qld: s. 53(1); W.A.: s. 47; Tas.: s. 71.
26. *Smith and Snipes Hall Farm Ltd v. River Douglas Catchment Board* [1949] 2 K.B. 500 (C.A.); *Federated Homes Ltd v. Mill Lodge Properties Ltd* [1980] 1 All E.R. 371 (C.A.). See the discussion at [17.16]ff.
27. See *Federated Homes Ltd v. Mill Lodge Properties Ltd* [1980] 1 All E.R. 371 at 377 (C.A.).
28. (1885) 29 Ch. D. 750 (C.A.).

In order to avoid the severity of this rule, a number of methods of ensuring that the burden will run have been suggested.

(a) A chain of indemnity covenants

It is possible for the original covenantor to enter into an indemnity covenant with a purchaser of her or his land requiring her or him to indemnify the covenantor against future breaches of the covenant for which the original covenantor will always be liable under the principle of privity of contract. Each later purchaser may also be required to enter into a similar covenant. In this way, a chain of covenants may develop.[29] However, in many cases this method of avoiding the rule in *Austerberry v. Oldham Corporation* is ineffective. A commonly cited truism is that a chain is only as strong as its weakest link; thus, a chain of indemnity covenants may be rendered ineffective if one of the intermediate purchasers becomes bankrupt or cannot be traced, or if one of the intermediate vendors neglects to take an indemnity covenant from her or his successor-in-title.

(b) The rule in Halsell v. Brizell[30]

This rule, which has been applied in Australia in *Frater v. Finlay*,[31] establishes a system of mutual benefit and burden under which a person will not be permitted by the courts to accept a benefit under a deed without also accepting any obligations imposed in the same document. Thus, as in the facts in *Halsell v. Brizell*, in the case of a covenant to contribute to the maintenance of roads and various services on a building estate, the successor-in-title to the covenantor cannot rely on the rule in *Austerberry v. Oldham Corporation*[32] to avoid liability to contribute to the maintenance of the roads if he or she has to rely on the same deed for his right to use the roads.[33] The rule has since been extended to apply to parol agreements.[34]

This method of avoiding the common law rule prohibiting the burden of a covenant from passing to an assignee of the covenantor was discussed in detail by Megarry V.-C. in *Tito v. Waddell (No. 2)*.[35] This judgment distinguishes two aspects of the benefit and burden principle, the pure principle of benefit and burden and the conditional benefits principle. Under the conditional benefits principle, the burden is drafted as a specific qualification to the grant of the land so as to achieve the integration of the benefit and burden. Under this pure principle (of which *Halsell v. Brizell* is an illustration), the burden is contained in a separate covenant which will only bind a successor-in-title on proof of an intention that the benefit and burden should pass together and that the successor

---

29. See Bicknell, "Restrictive and Positive Covenants" (1969) 113 Sol. J. 238; Pritchard, "Making Positive Covenants Run" (1973) 37 Conv. (N.S.W.) 194.
30. [1957] Ch. 169. See also *Rufa Pty Ltd v. Cross* [1981] Qd R. 365 (F.C.).
31. (1968) 91 W.N. (N.S.W.) 730; discussed in (1971) 45 A.L.J. 105. See also *E.R. Ives Investment Ltd v. High* [1967] 2 Q.B. 379 (C.A.).
32. (1885) 29 Ch. D. 750 (C.A.).
33. It is unclear whether this principle applies in respect of Torrens land.
34. *E.R. Ives Investment Ltd v. High* [1967] 2 Q.B. 379 (C.A.).
35. [1977] Ch. 106.

has exercised a "sufficient benefit" under the grant. These two aspects, and the judgment of Megarry V.-C. is examined by E. P. Aughterson,[36] who concludes:

"There appear to be two clear aspects of the benefit and burden principle; namely the conditional benefits principle and the pure principle of benefit and burden. The effect is the same; if a successor takes the benefit he is bound by the burden. However, there are qualification[s] to the pure principle. First, it must be shown from the surrounding circumstances of each transaction that the successor was intended to take the independent burden upon assuming the benefit and, secondly, that he has received a sufficient benefit. Which, if either, of these principles will apply in a given case depends on the construction of the instrument. The line of demarcation between an obligation which is a condition of the grant and one which is independent of it, is not altogether clear. If, as suggested in *Tito's* case, an obligation which appears in a separate covenant can be construed as a condition of the grant, then the drafting of documents in this area must be undertaken with considerable care, in order to ensure that the desired result is achieved.

In relation to the pure principle difficulties are apparent. First, there is uncertainty as to what constitutes a sufficient benefit. Secondly, Megarry V.-C.'s observation in *Tito's* case that a mere opportunity to accept a benefit might be sufficient seems to contradict the basic tenet of the benefit and burden principle that the burden attaches only upon the assumption of the benefit, so that the burden does not run with the land."

(c) Enlargement of leasehold into fee simple estates (New South Wales, Victoria and Tasmania)

It has long been assumed by English real property textbook authors[37] that statutory provisions enlarging the residue of long-term leasehold estates into fee simple estates may be used to avoid the rule in *Austerberry v. Oldham Corporation*.[38] The British legislation has been adopted without modification in New South Wales, Victoria and Tasmania.[39] For example, s. 153 of the *Property Law Act* 1958 (Vic.) permits fixed-term leases of at least 300 years' duration to be enlarged into fee simple estates by declaration in deed form where the unexpired residue of the term is at least 200 years. If positive covenants are attached to a long-term lease which is later converted into a fee simple, the covenants will continue to bind the land after the conversion.

36. Aughterson, "Enforcement of Positive Burdens—A New Viability" [1985] Conv. 12.
37. See e.g. Megarry and Wade, p. 768.
38. (1885) 29 Ch. D. 750 (C.A.).
39. General law statutes: N.S.W.: s. 134; Vic.: s. 153; Tas.: s. 83. See Note, (1962) 35 A.L.J. 408.

(d) Covenants ancillary to a rentcharge

A device used in the past is to enter into a rentcharge to which positive covenants are attached. By this device, it is argued that the covenants would continue to be enforceable on a later sale of the burdened land. This device is unavailable in respect of general law land in Queensland, pursuant to State legislation.[40] In respect of other land in Australia, it appears that the device will be ineffective. Authority for this proposition is *Clem Smith Nominees Pty Ltd v. Farrelly*,[41] where the Full Court of the Supreme Court of South Australia held that a covenant must be taken in favour of a corporeal, rather than an incorporeal hereditament.

IV. COVENANTS IN EQUITY

1. The Intervention of Equity

[17.06] With the rapid development of urban areas in Britain during the early 19th century following the industrial revolution, and in the absence of any statutory planning controls at that stage, the need for the introduction of laws respecting private land use planning schemes became more acute. The harshness caused by the continued refusal of common law to allow the burden of a covenant to run was circumvented by the intervention of equity.

This intervention first occurred in 1848 in the landmark decision in *Tulk v. Moxhay*.[42] The facts of this case were that Tulk owned undeveloped land in the middle of Leicester Square in London and surrounding houses. He sold the undeveloped land to one Elms, who covenanted inter alia to retain the land in an open state. The land was later acquired by Moxhay, who despite taking with notice of the covenant, argued that it was unenforceable against him. The Lord Chancellor defied earlier precedents and upheld the grant of an injunction restraining Moxhay from developing the land. The decision was based on the fact that Moxhay purchased the land with notice of the covenant. This decision has since been affirmed and applied in numerous decisions in Australia.[43]

2. Essential Prerequisites

[17.07] Despite the wide-ranging nature of the decision in *Tulk v. Moxhay*, later decisions have established two essential prerequisites to the operation of the equitable doctrine. As will become clear, somewhat paradoxically in both instances equity has applied narrower rules than the common law courts. These prerequisites will now be considered.

---

40. Rentcharges have been abolished in respect of general law land pursuant to s. 176(1) of the *Property Law Act* 1974 (Qld).
41. (1978) 20 S.A.S.R. 227. Cf. *Blacks Ltd v. Rix* [1962] S.A.S.R. 161.
42. (1848) 2 Ph. 774; 41 E.R. 1143 (Ch.).
43. See e.g. *Clem Smith Nominees Pty Ltd v. Farrelly* (1978) 20 S.A.S.R. 227 (F.C.).

(a) The covenant must be negative in nature

[17.08] In 1881, the English Court of Appeal held in *Haywood v. Brunswick Permanent Benefit Building Society*[44] that equity will only enforce covenants against successors-in-title of the covenantor where the covenants are negative in nature and do not impose any expenditure on the owner of the burdened land. The court thus refused on the facts to enforce a covenant to repair against the successor-in-title of the covenantor.

In determining whether a covenant is negative or positive in nature, the courts will examine the substance rather than the form of the agreement.[45] Many covenants which appear to be positive will thus be construed as negative (and vice versa). For example, a covenant to use a dwelling as a private residence only, although it appears positive, will be construed as negative as in substance it is a covenant not to use the premises for any purposes other than a dwelling.[46] In this regard, the drafting used by the parties is not of vital significance. Where the covenant contains both positive and negative obligations, the courts will sever the obligations where possible and will enforce the negative obligations against the successor-in-title of the covenantor.[47]

(b) The covenant must relate to the land of the covenantee

[17.09] As in the case of easements (see above **[16.08]**), there must be both burdened and benefited land before equity will enforce a restrictive covenant. This was initially decided in *London C.C. v. Allen*.[48] In *Kerridge v. Foley*,[49] it was further decided that a covenant declaring that a certain restriction is appurtenant to land described in a plan is not enforceable where part of the land included in the plan has already been sold before the covenant was entered into. Thus, a covenant cannot be annexed to land which the covenantee does not own except in the case of schemes of development.

There are certain statutory exceptions to the rule under discussion. For example, the *Conveyancing Act* 1919 (N.S.W.), s. 88E states that specified statutory authorities may impose restrictive covenants as to the use of land not vested in the authority, and the restriction will be enforceable whether or not the benefit of the covenant is annexed to other land. Legislation in New South Wales and Western Australia also makes it possible for the benefit of a covenant to be annexed to an easement created in favour of the Crown or of any public or local authority.[50]

---

44. (1881) 8 Q.B.D. 403 (C.A.). See also *Marquess of Zetland v. Driver* [1939] 1 Ch. 1 (C.A.).
45. See e.g. *Shepherd Homes Ltd v. Sandham (No. 2)* [1971] 2 All E.R. 1267.
46. *German v. Chapman* (1877) 7 Ch. D. 271 (C.A.).
47. *Shepherd Homes Ltd v. Sandham (No. 2)* [1971] 2 All E.R. 1267 at 1272.
48. [1914] 3 K.B. 642 (C.A.).
49. (1964) 82 W.N. (Pt I) (N.S.W.) 293. See also *Re Mack and the Conveyancing Act* [1975] 2 N.S.W.L.R. 623.
50. *Conveyancing Act* 1919 (N.S.W.), s. 88A; *Public Works Act* 1902 (W.A.), s. 33A.

3. Passing of the Burden

(a) General law rules

[17.10] The successor-in-title of the covenantee must prove the existence of a mutual intention by the contracting parties that the burden of the covenant should run on a later disposition of the land.[51] This matter is seldom in contention in Australia, as legislation in each jurisdiction (except South Australia) now provides that a covenant relating to land shall, unless a contrary intention is expressed, be deemed to be made by the covenantor on behalf of himself, his successor-in-title and the persons deriving title under him or them.[52]

(b) Application of general law rules to Torrens land[53]

[17.11] The Torrens legislation in New South Wales, Victoria, Western Australia and Tasmania expressly authorises the Registrar of Titles to enter notification of restrictive covenants on the certificate of title of the burdened land.[54] The effect of such notification is that a purchaser of the burdened land is prevented from relying on the indefeasibility provisions of the Torrens legislation to defeat a restrictive covenant notified on her or his certificate of title. Where notification takes place, the covenant is not converted from an equitable into a legal interest. This is made clear by the wording of the relevant legislation. For example, s. 88(3) of the *Transfer of Land Act* 1958 (Vic.) states in part:

> "a notice in the Register Book of any such restrictive covenant charge or right shall not give it any greater operation than it has under the instrument or Act creating it."[55]

In Queensland and South Australia, the Torrens legislation makes no mention of a power to notify restrictive covenants on the certificate of title of the burdened land. As a basic rule, it appears that the better view is that notification of restrictive covenants is not permitted in these States.[56] However, the issue arises whether restrictive covenants may be protected by any other means.

One such possibility might be to register a restrictive covenant as an "encumbrance". This possibility is supported by *Re Arcade Pty Ltd,*[57] where Sholl J. held that the practice of the Victorian Registrar of Titles

---

51. See *Re Royal Victoria Pavilion (Ramsgate)* [1961] Ch. 581 for an illustration of a case where there was a lack of the necessary intention. See also *Re Contract between Fawcett and Holmes* (1889) 42 Ch. D. 150 (C.A.).
52. General law statutes: N.S.W.: s. 70A; Vic.: s. 79; Qld: s. 53; W.A.: s. 48; Tas.: s. 71A.
53. For a detailed discussion of this issue, see Bradbrook and Neave, paras 1706-1716.
54. *Conveyancing Act* 1919 (N.S.W.), s. 88(3)(a) (since 1930); *Transfer of Land Act* 1958 (Vic.), s. 88 (since 1954); *Transfer of Land Act* 1893 (W.A.), s. 129A (since 1950); *Land Titles Act* 1980 (Tas.), ss 102-104 (since 1962).
55. See also *Conveyancing Act* 1919 (N.S.W.), s. 88(3)(b); *Transfer of Land Act* 1893 (W.A.), s. 129A; *Land Titles Act* 1980 (Tas.), s. 102(3)(10).
56. Bradbrook and Neave, paras 1706ff.
57. [1962] V.R. 274 (F.C.). See also *Re Cashmore's Application* [1967] Tas. S.R. 217.

in registering covenants as encumbrances was justified. His Honour relied, inter alia, on the definition of "encumbrance" in s. 4(1) of the *Transfer of Land Act* 1958 (Vic.) and on the analogy between restrictive covenants and negative easements. However, a contrary approach was taken in New South Wales in *Re Martyn*[58] and *Re Pirie and the Real Property Act*,[59] where the narrower definition of "encumbrance" in s. 3 of the *Real Property Act* 1900 was held to exclude restrictive covenants. Whether the Registrar in Queensland and South Australia is entitled to register a covenant as an encumbrance has not been finally resolved, although the conclusion reached elsewhere is that the issue should be answered in the negative.[60]

Another possibility came to light in South Australia in *Blacks Ltd v. Rix*.[61] In this case, a nominal rentcharge was registered as an encumbrance as a device in order to achieve the registration of restrictive covenants contained in the encumbrance. This case concerned the sale of land in a scheme of development by the plaintiff company. Every purchaser of land in the scheme was required to accept a transfer subject to a nominal rentcharge created by an encumbrance. This encumbrance also included seven restrictive covenants. Napier C.J. assumed that this device was legitimate. This decision has been subject to trenchant academic criticism, however,[62] and has been questioned by Bray C.J. in *Clem Smith Nominees Pty Ltd v. Farrelly*.[63] A similar device was used by the plaintiffs in this case, but Bray C.J. suggested that such a device would infringe s. 97 of the *Real Property Act* 1886 (S.A.). This section reads:

"In every instrument purporting to transfer land mortgaged or encumbered there shall be implied the following covenant by the transferee with the transferor, and so long as such transferee shall remain the registered proprietor, with the mortgagee or encumbrancee, that is to say—That the transferee will pay the principal, interest, and other moneys secured by such mortgage or encumbrance, after the rate and at the time or times specified therein, and will indemnify and keep harmless the transferor from and against such principal, interest, and other moneys and from and against all liability in respect of any of the covenants contained in such mortgage or encumbrance or by this Act implied on the part of the transferor."

It should be noted that the section does not impose liability on the transferee to the mortgagee or encumbrancee to observe any covenants other than the covenant to pay the principal and interest. On Bray C.J.'s analysis, s. 97 arguably impliedly excludes all other restrictive covenants.

In Queensland, where rentcharges have been abolished,[64] the device employed in the past is to register a bill of encumbrance which binds the

58. (1965) 65 S.R. (N.S.W.) 387.
59. [1962] N.S.W.R. 1004.
60. Bradbrook and Neave, para. 1710.
61. [1962] S.A.S.R. 161. See also *Mahony v. Hosken* (1912) 14 C.L.R. 379.
62. Bradbrook and Neave, para. 1714.
63. (1978) 20 S.A.S.R. 227.
64. *Property Law Act* 1974 (Qld), s. 176(1).

land for the payment of an annual sum which is reduced if certain covenants contained in the encumbrance are adhered to. There are dicta in *Mahony v. Hosken*[65] and *Perpetual Executors & Trustees Association (Australia) Ltd v. Hosken*[66] to the effect that this device might succeed in that the Registrar may be bound to register the encumbrance even though it was clearly a device to achieve registration of a restrictive covenant. However, the validity of this device should still be regarded as unresolved.

The final possibility is that restrictive covenants may be protected in Queensland and South Australia by the use of a caveat. In South Australia, s. 191 of the *Real Property Act* 1886 permits a caveat to be lodged by "any person claimed to be interested at law or in equity, whether under an agreement, or under an unregistered instrument, or otherwise howsoever in any land". In Queensland, s. 98 of the *Real Property Act* 1861 permits a caveat to be lodged by any person claiming "an estate or interest in land".[67] In both cases, it is submitted that this legislation would encompass restrictive covenants, in that such covenants constitute an equitable interest in land.[68]

(c) New South Wales legislation

[17.12] By virtue of the *Conveyancing (Covenants) Amendment Act* 1986 (N.S.W.), positive covenants taken in favour of the Crown, statutory authorities and local councils will henceforth bind successors-in-title of the covenantee.[69] The new legislation defines "positive covenants" as follows:

> " 'positive covenant', in relation to land, includes a covenant which imposes obligations requiring—
>
> (a) the carrying out of development on or with respect to the land, within the meaning of the Environmental Planning and Assessment Act 1979;
>
> (b) the provision of services on or to the land or other land in its vicinity; or
>
> (c) the maintenance, repair or insurance of any structure or work on the land,
>   or imposes any term or condition with respect to the performance of or failure to perform any such obligation."[70]

---

65. (1912) 14 C.L.R. 379.
66. (1912) 14 C.L.R. 286 at 294.
67. See the definition of "estate" in *Acts Interpretation Act* 1954 (Qld), s. 36.
68. See e.g. *Woodbury v. Gilbert* (1907) 3 Tas. L.R. 7; *Wilkes v. Spooner* [1911] 2 K.B. 473; *Re Nisbet and Potts' Contract* [1905] 1 Ch. 391. Cf. *Staples & Co. Ltd v. Corby and District Land Registrar* (1900) 19 N.Z.L.R. 517 (C.A.); *Miller v. Minister of Mines and the Attorney-General (New Zealand)* [1963] A.C. 484. See also Bradbrook and Neave, paras 1721ff; Barber, "Restrictive Covenants and the Real Property Acts of Queensland" (1970) 2 A.C.L.R. 85.
69. This legislation is discussed in Note, "Legislation to Permit Positive Covenants" (December 1986) 24 Law Soc. J. 28. See also *Local Government (Covenants) Amendment Act* 1986 (N.S.W.); *Real Property (Covenants) Amendment Act* 1986 (N.S.W.); and *Strata Titles (Covenants) Amendment Act* 1986 (N.S.W.).
70. *Conveyancing Act* 1919, s. 87A.

Section 88F of the principal Act (*Conveyancing Act* 1919) states that any positive covenant which is imposed pursuant to the 1986 Act affects the land and persons from time to time having any estate or interest in the land in the same way as if it were a covenant imposing a restriction on the use of the land.

Any prescribed authority having the benefit of a positive covenant has certain specified rights of entry into the covenantor's land (s. 88F(2)), and may apply to have a charge registered over the land under the provisions of the *Real Property Act* 1900 where the authority obtains a judgment for an amount payable to it for a failure to comply with a positive covenant: s. 88F(4).

The Supreme Court is empowered to grant an injunction restraining a person from engaging in conduct constituting a contravention of a positive covenant whenever the court considers it desirable to do so: s. 88H(1). As a final resort, to ensure compliance with a positive covenant, the prescribed authority entitled to enforce the covenant may apply to the court for an order that the land be conveyed or transferred to the authority: s. 88I(1). Such an order may only be made in any of the following circumstances: that the continued holding of the land by the covenantor is reasonably likely to endanger the health or safety of the public; that there is no reasonable likelihood of the person complying with the obligations imposed by the covenant; that the person has previously committed frequent contraventions of restrictive or positive covenants imposed on the land; that the person has persistently and unreasonably delayed complying with the obligations of any positive covenant imposed on the land; or that the order should be made because of any other special circumstances: s. 88I(3). When making such an order, the court may impose such conditions on the conveyance or transfer of the land as it thinks fit: s. 88I(4).

4. Passing of the Benefit

(a) General law rules

[17.13] In all cases, a covenant must touch and concern the land of the covenantee before the benefit of the covenant will run.[71] The meaning of this requirement is discussed above [10.42] and [17.04]. In addition, the benefit of the covenant must have passed to the successor-in-title of the covenantee by one of the recognised methods. The doctrines clearly established are express annexation and express assignment. In addition, there is a possibility that the same result may be achieved by statutory annexation and by State legislation importing general words into conveyances. A further method of schemes of development will be considered later: see below [17.19]. Except for schemes of development, these methods will now be considered and explained:

---

71. See e.g. *Re Union of London and Smith's Bank Ltd's Conveyance* [1933] Ch. 611 (C.A.); *Re Ballard's Conveyance* [1937] Ch. 473.

(i) Express annexation

[17.14]   Annexation of a covenant will occur where a covenant is made for the benefit of specified land or where the covenant states that it is made for the benefit of the covenantee, her or his assigns and successors in her or his capacity as owner of the benefited land.[72] A covenant taken for the benefit of the vendor, her or his assigns and successors is insufficient for annexation.[73]

If the instrument contains a clear intention to annex the covenant expressly to the benefited land, but the land is referred to in descriptive terms rather than specifically, it appears that the parties may lead extrinsic evidence to identify the relevant land, and if the land is so identified, annexation will be held to exist.[74] This rule applies in all jurisdictions except New South Wales, where s. 88(1)(a) of the *Conveyancing Act* 1919 states that a restrictive covenant shall not be enforceable against any person other than the original contracting parties unless it clearly indicates, inter alia, the land to which the benefit of the covenant is appurtenant.

The separate issue whether annexation may be implied from surrounding circumstances is more controversial. The major authority in favour of this approach is obiter dicta by Wilberforce J. in *Marten v. Flight Refuelling Ltd.*[75] His Honour rejected the contention that annexation must be apparent in the terms of the covenant and stated:

> "[T]he existence and situation of the land to be benefited need not be indicated in the conveyance, provided that it can otherwise be shown with reasonable certainty, and the natural interpretation to place on these later words is first that they may be so shown by evidence dehors the deed, and secondly, that a broad and reasonable view may be taken as to the proof of the identity of the lands. This general approach would, I think, be consistent with the equitable origin and character of the enforcement of restrictive covenants."[76]

He added later that any other approach would "involve not only an injustice but a departure from common sense".[77] Wade and others have taken the view that this case establishes the principle of implied annexation,[78] but this view is criticised elsewhere on the ground, inter alia, that the dicta of Wilberforce J. are referable to the rules for assignment rather than annexation.[79] This latter viewpoint has now been accepted by Megarry and Wade.[80]

---

72. See e.g. *Drake v. Grey* [1936] Ch. 451 (C.A.); *Rogers v. Hosegood* [1900] 2 Ch. 388 (C.A.).
73. *Renals v. Cowlishaw* (1878) 9 Ch. D. 125; affd (1879) 11 Ch. D. 866 (C.A.).
74. See *Rogers v. Hosegood* [1900] 2 Ch. 388 (C.A.).
75. [1962] Ch. 115.
76. Ibid. at 131.
77. Ibid. at 133.
78. Wade, "Covenants—A Broad and Reasonable View" (1972) 31 C.L.J. 157.
79. Baker, "The Benefit of Restrictive Covenants" (1968) 84 L.Q.R. 22; Hayton, "Restrictive Covenants as Property Interests" (1971) 87 L.Q.R. 539.
80. 4th ed., 1975, p. 764, fn. 54.

The most recent case on this issue is *J. Sainsbury Plc v. Enfield London B.C.*,[81] in which Morritt J. accepted the contention that the intention to annex must be manifested in the conveyance in which the covenant was contained when construed in the light of the surrounding circumstances, including any necessary implication in the conveyance from those surrounding circumstances. His Honour rejected the contention that the intention to annex may be inferred from surrounding circumstances which fall short of those which would necessitate an implication in the conveyance itself.[82]

Once annexation has been held to exist, the benefit of the covenant will continue to run with the land automatically on future dispositions of the benefited land regardless of whether later purchasers of the burdened land are aware of the existence of the covenant.[83]

The problems caused to legal practitioners in the drafting of covenants are compounded by the rule that there will be no annexation where the benefited land is too large to benefit from the covenant. The origin of this rule is *Re Ballard's Conveyance*.[84] In this case, a restrictive covenant was made for the benefit of the owners from time to time of the Childwickbury estate, a large estate of some 800 hectares. It was held that the covenant could not be said to benefit the whole of this large estate, and as severance of the covenant was not possible, the benefit of the covenant could not run. His Honour indicated that annexation would have occurred if the covenant had been expressed to benefit the whole of the estate, or each and every part of it. This approach was adopted by the majority of the Full Court of the Supreme Court of Victoria in *Re Arcade Hotel Pty Ltd*,[85] who held that the benefit of a covenant expressed to be made for the "owners for the time being of the land marked green" is annexed to the whole of the land and will not run on a sale of certain parts of the land. Despite dicta by the English Court of Appeal in *Federated Homes Ltd v. Mill Lodge Properties Ltd*[86] that the court should construe a covenant made for the benefit of certain land as annexed to each and every part of the land, the earlier cases still appear to represent good law. Thus, there is a heavy onus on legal practitioners to ensure that the covenant is taken for the whole or any part of the benefited land.

Statutory amendments enacted to overcome the rule in *Re Ballard's Conveyance* now exist in Victoria and Western Australia. In both States, the relevant legislation reads:

"It is hereby declared that when the benefit of a restriction as to the user of or the building on any land is or has been annexed or purports to be annexed by an instrument to other land the benefit shall unless it is expressly provided to the contrary be deemed to be and always

81. [1989] 2 All E.R. 817.
82. Ibid. at 822-4.
83. *Rogers v. Hosegood* [1900] 2 Ch. 388 (C.A.).
84. [1937] Ch. 473.
85. [1962] V.R. 274. See also *Lane Cove M.C. v. H. & W. Hurdis Pty Ltd* (1955) 72 W.N. (N.S.W.) 284; *Re Roche and the Conveyancing Act* (1960) 77 W.N. (N.S.W.) 431.
86. [1980] 1 All E.R. 371 at 381.

to have been annexed to the whole and to each and every part of such other land capable of benefiting from such restriction."[87]

(ii) Express assignment

[17.15] If the wording of a covenant is insufficient to annex the benefit to the land, it is possible for the covenantee to pass the benefit to her or his successor-in-title on the future disposition of the benefited land by express assignment.

To be valid, an express assignment of a covenant must be made in writing pursuant to the requirements of State legislation.[88] The majority of the requirements, however, are based on case law. Romer L.J., delivering the judgment of the English Court of Appeal, stated in *Re Union of London and Smith's Bank Ltd's Conveyance*:[89]

"If the restrictive covenant be taken not merely for some personal purpose or object of the vendor, but for the benefit of some other land of his in the sense that it would enable him to dispose of that land to greater advantage, the covenant, though not annexed to such land so as to run with any part of it, may be enforced against an assignee of the covenantor taking with notice, both by the covenantee and by persons to whom the benefit of such covenant has been assigned, subject however to certain conditions. In the first place, the 'other land' must be land that is capable of being benefited by the covenant—otherwise it would be impossible to infer that the object of the covenant was to enable the vendor to dispose of his land to greater advantage. In the next place, this land must be 'ascertainable' or 'certain'. . . For, although the court will readily infer the intention to benefit the other land of the vendor where the existence and situation of such land are indicated in the conveyance or have been otherwise shown with reasonable certainty, it is impossible to do so from vague references in the conveyance or in other documents laid before the court as to the existence of other lands of the vendor, the extent and situation of which are undefined. In the third place, the covenant cannot be enforced by the covenantee against an assign of the purchaser after the covenantee has parted with the whole of his land."

The requirement that the land must be ascertainable will be satisfied where the land can be identified by the assistance of evidence of surrounding circumstances. In *Newton Abbot Co-operative Society Ltd v. Williamson and Treadgold Ltd*,[90] Upjohn J. went further and held that the requirement is satisfied where the identity of the benefited land is based solely on surrounding circumstances. It is an unresolved issue whether this latter case is valid law in Australia. There are dicta by Zelling J. in

---

87. *Property Law Act* 1958 (Vic.), s. 79A; *Property Law Act* 1969 (W.A.), s. 49.
88. General law statutes: N.S.W.: s. 23C; Vic.: s. 53; Qld: s. 11; S.A.: s. 29; W.A.: s. 34; Tas.: s. 60(2).
89. [1933] Ch. 611 at 631-632.
90. [1952] Ch. 286. See Elphinstone, "Assignment of the Benefit of Covenants Affecting Land" (1952) 68 L.Q.R. 353.

Clem Smith Nominees Pty Ltd v. Farrelly[91] that the *Newton Abbot* case was wrongly decided on this point, but the issue was left open by Bray C.J.[92] in the same case and by Kitto and Taylor JJ. in *Pirie v. Registrar-General*.[93] In New South Wales, this issue must be reconsidered in light of the requirements of s. 88(1)(a) of the *Conveyancing Act* 1919: see below **[17.19]**. The nub of the issue is whether the words "the benefit of which is intended to be annexed to other land" should be confined to express annexation or whether they extend to express assignment and other methods of passing the benefit. The matter is subject to considerable controversy. Baalman is of the opinion that s. 88(1) applies to all methods of passing the benefit of a covenant,[94] while the contrary view is taken by Helmore.[95] Helmore's view is supported by dicta of Jacobs J.A. in *Re Louis and the Conveyancing Act*,[96] who in the context of schemes of development in respect of general law land stated that s. 88(1) might not apply.[97]

Based on the third requirement of Romer L.J. stated above, it is clear that the assignment of the covenant must be contemporaneous with the sale of the benefited land.[98] The major justification for this rule is that the covenant was entered into to enable the covenantee to dispose of her or his property to advantage and this result will have been achieved when all that property has been sold; accordingly, there is no reason why a covenantee should be able to pass the benefit of the covenant at a later date. A further justification is that where at the date of the purported assignment of the benefit of the covenant the covenantee has disposed of the whole of her or his land, the covenant is no longer enforceable by the covenantee her or himself and he or she cannot confer any greater rights upon the assignee than he or she possessed her or himself.

A controversial issue is whether the benefit of a covenant which has been expressly annexed to land can be later expressly assigned to a third party who cannot rely on the annexation. Ungoed-Thomas J. held in the affirmative in *Stilwell v. Blackman*[99] and rejected the argument that express annexation and express assignment are mutually-exclusive categories. His Lordship stated that annexed covenants can in principle be expressly assigned to a third party, and it is a matter of construction of the wording of the covenant whether this is permissible in any given case. He added that express assignment can only be forbidden if it is positively excluded; thus, there is a presumption that assignability is permitted in the absence of clear words to the contrary. This latter point is subject to trenchant

91. (1978) 20 S.A.S.R. 227 at 255.
92. Ibid. at 236.
93. (1962) 109 C.L.R. 619 at 629, 634.
94. Para. 1399.
95. Helmore, "The Common Building Scheme and Statutory Provisions" (1963) 37 A.L.J. 81.
96. [1971] 1 N.S.W.L.R. 164 at 180 (C.A.).
97. See below **[17.23]** for a more detailed discussion of this legislation in the context of Torrens land.
98. *Chambers v. Randall* [1923] 1 Ch. 149; *Re Union of London and Smith's Bank Ltd's Conveyance* [1933] Ch. 611 at 632 (C.A.). Cf. *Lord Northbourne v. Johnston* [1922] 2 Ch. 309.
99. [1968] Ch. 508; discussed in (1968) 32 Conv. 60 and (1970) 44 A.L.J. 40.

criticism by Preston and Newsom.[100] The issue has not yet been determined in Australia or by the appellate courts in the United Kingdom.

The final issue is whether one express assignment of the benefit of a covenant will have the effect of automatically annexing the covenant to the benefited land so that further assignments are unnecessary, or whether there must be a separate express assignment each time the benefited land is sold before the benefit of the covenant will run. Despite earlier authorities and an article by Baker[101] to the effect that an assignment will annex the covenant to the land, it is assumed without argument by Wynn-Parry J. in *Re Pinewood Estate, Farnborough*[102] that a separate assignment of the benefit of the covenant is necessary on each sale of the land. Again, there are no Australian authorities on this issue. It thus appears that a complete chain of assignments must be shown before a covenant can be enforced in this situation.

(iii) Statutory annexation

[17.16] The *Law of Property Act* 1925 (U.K.), s. 78(1) contains the following provisions concerning the benefit of covenants relating to land:

> "A covenant relating to any land of the covenantee shall be deemed to be made with the covenantee and his successors in title and the persons deriving title under him or them, and shall have effect as if such successors and other persons were expressed. For the purposes of this sub-section in connexion with covenants restrictive of the user of land 'successors in title' shall be deemed to include the owners and occupiers for the time being of the land of the covenantee intended to be benefitted."

An identical provision exists in each Australian jurisdiction except South Australia.[103]

The effect of this legislation has been the subject of considerable controversy in recent years. The conventional view is that the section merely obviates the need to expressly mention the successors-in-title of the covenantee in the wording of the covenant. This view, however, was rejected by the English Court of Appeal in *Federated Homes Ltd v. Mill Lodge Properties Ltd*[104] in favour of a more wide-ranging interpretation. The case concerned an action by the successor-in-title of a covenantee to enforce a restrictive covenant against the covenantor. Despite clear evidence that the requirements of express annexation and express assignment had not been complied with, the Court of Appeal held that the benefit of the covenant passed by virtue of s. 78. Brightman L.J. explained the operation of the section in the following terms:

---

100. Preston and Newsom, pp. 43ff.
101. Baker, "The Benefit of Restrictive Covenants" (1968) 84 L.Q.R. 22.
102. [1958] Ch. 280. See also *Sutton v. Shoppee* (1964) 80 W.N. (N.S.W.) 1550 at 1554 (S.C. in banco).
103. General law statutes: N.S.W.: s. 70; Vic.: s. 78; Qld: s. 53; W.A.: s. 47; Tas.: s. 71.
104. [1980] 1 All E.R. 371; discussed in (1980) 43 Mod. L.R. 445; [1980] Conv. 216; (1981) 97 L.Q.R. 32; (1982) 98 L.Q.R. 202; [1985] Conv. 177.

"If, as the language of s. 78 implies, a covenant relating to land which is restrictive of the user thereof is enforceable at the suit of (a) a successor-in-title of the covenantee; (b) a person deriving title under the covenantee or under his successors-in-title; and (c) the owner or occupier of the land intended to be benefited by the covenant, it must, in my view, follow that the covenant runs with the land because ex hypothesi every successor-in-title to the land, every derivative proprietor of the land and every other owner and occupier has a right by statute to the covenant. In other words, if the condition precedent of s. 78 is satisfied, that is to say, there exists a covenant which touches and concerns the land of the covenantee, that covenant runs with the land for the benefit of his successors-in-title, persons deriving title under him or them and other owners and occupiers."[105]

The effect of this interpretation is quite revolutionary in that provided that the covenant touches and concerns the land, it appears that the benefit will be presumed to run with the land regardless of whether the rules relating to express annexation and express assignment are satisfied. The decision appears to achieve in one stroke a major simplification of a body of laws which has long been argued to be unnecessarily complex and legalistic.[106]

It remains to be seen whether this decision will survive in England and whether it is later adopted in Australia. For several reasons this appears to be doubtful: first, the legislative history of s. 78 indicates that it was designed to have only a narrow purpose; secondly, the narrower purpose has been accepted in relation to s. 79, the corresponding provision relating to the passing of the burden of the covenant; and finally, in many earlier cases it was assumed tacitly that s. 78 does not have the wider scope claimed for it in the *Federated Homes* case.[107]

The only case in which the *Federated Homes* case has been raised directly is *Roake v. Chadha*.[108] In this case, the restrictive covenant subject to dispute expressly stated that it would not enure for the benefit of any owner or subsequent purchaser unless the benefit of the covenant was expressly assigned. The plaintiffs, the successors-in-title of the covenantee, sought to enforce the covenant based on s. 78 in the absence of express assignment. Counsel for the plaintiff sought to rely on the *Federated Homes* case and argued that s. 78 has a mandatory operation and is not subject to contrary intention. The first instance judge considered himself bound by the earlier Court of Appeal decision, but rejected the mandatory operation which the plaintiff advanced for the section and held that it does not have the effect of annexing the benefit of the covenant in each and every case irrespective of the other express terms of the

---

105. Ibid. at 379.
106. Note, however, that on one analysis the decision in the *Federated Homes* case may have a narrower interpretation: see Todd, "Annexation After Federated Homes" [1985] Conv. 177 on this point.
107. See generally Newsom, "Universal Annexation?" (1981) 97 L.Q.R. 32.
108. [1984] 1 W.L.R. 40; discussed in [1984] Conv. 68. Other issues in respect of the *Federated Homes* decision were considered in *J. Sainsbury Plc v. Enfield London B.C.* [1989] 2 All E.R. 817.

covenant.[109] Where, as in the *Federated Homes* case, the covenant is not qualified in any way, annexation may be readily inferred, but any qualification must be given effect to.

(iv) General words imported into conveyances

[17.17] The legislation adopted in England and every Australian jurisdiction[110] shortening conveyances by enacting that a conveyance of land shall be deemed to include certain specified rights has been cited earlier and its application in detail in the context of easements has been discussed: see above **[16.27]**. In the present context, the argument is that the words in the legislation "rights and advantages whatsoever appertaining or reputed to appertain to the land, or any part thereof" are sufficiently broad-ranging to pass the benefit of a covenant to successors-in-title of the covenantee. The argument in favour of this approach is put by Wade.[111]

The relevance of the "general words" legislation to the passing of the benefit of a restrictive covenant was first considered by Farwell J. in *Rogers v. Hosegood*.[112] His Honour did not decide the issue as he determined that express annexation existed on the facts, but obiter expressed doubts as to whether the right to sue on a covenant can be said to belong, or be reputed to belong, to the land.[113] It has recently been considered in *Roake v. Chadha*,[114] the relevant facts of which are referred to above **[17.16]**. It was held that as the wording of the covenant precluded the benefit from passing unless it was expressly assigned, it could not be said to be a right "appertaining or reputed to appertain" to land within the meaning of the section. The issue whether the benefit of a covenant not annexed can ever pass under the legislation importing general words into conveyances was left open, but the judge stated obiter that the rights referred to in the legislation may be confined to legal rights rather than equitable rights.[115]

Thus, in summary, while the matter is still unresolved, it appears doubtful whether the "general words" legislation can be said to pass the benefit of a restrictive covenant. These doubts apply a fortiori in Australia, where in *Sutton v. Shoppee*,[116] the only relevant case on the point, Sugerman J. stated that the legislation is inapplicable in this context.

(b) Application of general law rules to Torrens land

[17.18] In those States where restrictive covenants may be notified on the certificate of title (New South Wales, Victoria, Western Australia and Tasmania), the issue arises whether the principles of express annexation

---

109. Ibid. at 46.
110. General law statutes: N.S.W.: s. 67; Vic.: s. 62; Qld: s. 239; S.A.: s. 36; W.A.: s. 41; Tas.: s. 6.
111. Wade, "Covenants—A Broad and Reasonable View" (1972) 31 C.L.J. 157 at 175.
112. [1900] 2 Ch. 388.
113. Ibid. at 398.
114. [1984] 1 W.L.R. 40.
115. Ibid. at 47.
116. (1963) 63 S.R. (N.S.W.) 853 at 860.

and express assignment, under which the benefit of covenants may pass, apply equally to Torrens land as to general law land.[117]

As discussed in detail in Chapter 5, the basic purpose of the Torrens system is to ensure that the certificate of title contains a full record of the state of the title and, with certain exceptions, to regard any interests in land not entered on the certificate of title as unenforceable. Thus, it should not be necessary for a prospective purchaser of land to look beyond the register to establish the nature of the title. Bearing this in mind, express annexation presents no problem as the benefited land will by the very nature of annexation be clearly identified in the documentation. For this reason, express annexation applies equally to Torrens land as to general law land.

Difficulties arise, however, with express assignment, as if they are enforceable, it would be necessary for a purchaser of land to look beyond the register to establish the nature of the title. Bray C.J. stated obiter in *Clem Smith Nominees Pty Ltd v. Farrelly*[118] that there can be no express assignment over Torrens land as the recognition of this doctrine would necessarily involve the purchaser making inquiries outside the Register. The refusal to recognise express assignments over Torrens land would also appear to follow from the reasoning of Hudson J. in *Re Dennerstein*[119] and Jacobs J.A. in *Re Louis and the Conveyancing Act*,[120] although the issue was not raised directly in either case. Thus, although the matter has not been formally decided, it is submitted that express assignment is limited in its application to general law land.

V.   SCHEMES OF DEVELOPMENT

1. General Law Rules

[17.19]   At the time of the decision in *Tulk v. Moxhay*,[121] large-scale subdivisions of land by developers were virtually unknown. Schemes of development (sometimes referred to as "building schemes") are a product of the present century. Under modern development schemes, it is common for a developer to include restrictions as to the future use which the purchasers of each of the blocks may make of the land. These restrictions are usually designed to enhance the value and amenities of the neighbourhood, and the intention behind the imposition of the restrictions is that they should bind and be capable of enforcement by all purchasers of all the blocks of land.

By the turn of the present century, it was obvious that the equitable rules as to the passing of the benefit and burden of restrictive covenants were ill-equipped to cope with the enforcement of restrictions contained in schemes of development. One problem was that of intention that the burden and the benefit should pass. Under normal equitable rules this

---

117. See Bradbrook and Neave, paras 1733ff.; Sykes, pp. 422ff.
118. (1978) 20 S.A.S.R. 227 at 236 (S.C. in banco).
119. [1963] V.R. 688.
120. [1971] 1 N.S.W.L.R. 164 (C.A.).
121. (1848) 2 Ph. 774; 41 E.R. 1143 (Ch.).

must be proved in relation to each separate transaction, while it was considered by equity that in the case of schemes of development the intention to pass the burden and benefit of the covenant should be obvious from the very nature of the scheme. A more fundamental difficulty is that technical difficulties often prevented the enforceability of covenants in schemes of development. This is best explained by an illustration. Assume that A owns a large tract of land which she subdivides. She sells three blocks to B, C and D in that chronological sequence. In each case the sale is made subject to similar restrictive covenants. B later sells her block to E, C later sells her block to F, and D later sells her block to G. Consider whether E can enforce the benefit of one or more of the covenants against F or G. Without any special law applying to schemes of development, the answer to this problem is that except where s. 56 of the *Property Law Act* 1958 (Vic.) or its equivalent in other Australian jurisdictions is applicable on the facts (see above [17.02]), E will be unable to enforce the covenants against F or G as the benefit of the covenants did not exist at the time when B (E's predecessor-in-title) purchased her land.

It was in order to overcome these difficulties that the courts developed special rules concerning the enforceability of covenants contained in schemes of development. Where these rules apply, they operate as a "local law" for the estate subject to the scheme.[122]

[17.20] The circumstances which must exist before the courts will recognise the existence of a scheme of development were expounded as follows by Parker J. in the seminal case of *Elliston v. Reacher*:[123]

> "In my judgment, in order to bring the principles of [schemes of development] into operation it must be proved (a) that both the plaintiffs and defendants derive title under a common vendor; (b) that previous to selling the lands to which the plaintiffs and defendants are respectively entitled the vendor laid out his estate, or a defined portion thereof (including the land purchased by the plaintiffs and defendants respectively), for sale in lots subject to restrictions intended to be imposed on all the lots, and which, though varying in details as to particular lots, are consistent and consistent only with some general scheme of development; (c) that these restrictions were intended by the common vendor to be and were for the benefit of all the lots intended to be sold, whether or not they were also intended to be and were for the benefit of other land retained by the vendor; and (d) that both the plaintiffs and the defendants, or their predecessors in title, purchased their lots from the common vendor upon the footing that the restrictions subject to which the purchases were made were to enure for the benefit of the other lots included in the general scheme whether or not they were also to enure for the benefit of other lands retained by the vendors."

Parker J. added that if all these four points were established, the plaintiff is entitled in equity to enforce the restrictive covenants entered into by the

---

122. *Reid v. Bickerstaff* [1909] 2 Ch. 305 at 319 (C.A.).
123. [1908] 2 Ch. 374 at 384. Cf. *Texaco Antilles Ltd v. Kernochan* [1973] A.C. 609 (P.C.).

defendants or their predecessors with the common vendor irrespective of the dates of the respective purchases.[124]

It can be seen that the doctrine both enables earlier purchasers of blocks of land in a scheme to enforce covenants against later purchasers, and enables the benefit of covenants to pass without the need to prove either express annexation or express assignment.

[17.21]   The four requirements of Parker J. stated above have been cited with approval in numerous Australian cases.[125] However, further discussion of each of these requirements is necessary in the light of subsequent court decisions.

The first requirement, that title be derived from a common vendor, must be considered of doubtful validity today in light of the decisions in *Re Dolphin's Conveyance*[126] and *Re Mack and the Conveyancing Act*.[127] In both these cases, a scheme of development was held to exist despite the lack of a common vendor. The former case held that a scheme can exist where the vendor sells some of the blocks of land and dies, and the remaining blocks are sold by the vendor's successor-in-title subject to certain restrictive covenants. In the latter case, a scheme was held to exist over land subdivided into 115 lots where 27 had never been owned by the vendor and the remaining 88 lots were distributed throughout the whole subdivision. The latter case was decided on the basis that despite the fact that there were several vendors, the vendors had intended to create a common scheme and had made an agreement to carry out this intention. Wootten J. stated:

> "[T]here is no ground of reason or justice for requiring that there be a common vendor, unless indeed that term be understood in an artificial sense to include several vendors sharing a common intention. The 'community of interest' between the purchasers is as real in the one case as the other. No doubt in cases where there is only one vendor it may be easier to infer the intention to take the covenants for the benefit of all the land in a scheme, but that is no reason for refusing to give effect to the common intention of several vendors to establish reciprocal benefits and obligations throughout an estate where such an intention is established."[128]

The second requirement, concerning the laying out of the estate for sale in lots subject to common restrictions, has also been relaxed in certain respects. Although the area of land subject to the scheme must be defined by the vendor, the area need not be defined in the various instruments if it can be identified by the wording of the documents construed in the context of surrounding circumstances.[129] It has also been held that it is not necessary to prove that the vendor laid out the land subject to the scheme

---

124. Ibid. at 384-385.
125. See e.g. *Cobbold v. Abraham* [1933] V.L.R. 385; *Langdale Pty Ltd v. Sollas* [1959] V.R. 637; *Christie v. Dalco Holdings Pty Ltd* [1964] Tas. S.R. 34. It has also been approved recently in New Zealand: *Sawyer v. Starr* [1985] 2 N.Z.L.R. 540.
126. [1970] Ch. 654.
127. [1975] 2 N.S.W.L.R. 623.
128. Ibid. at 630.
129. See e.g. *Re Dolphin's Conveyance* [1970] Ch. 654.

for sale in lots, but merely to produce evidence on the facts that the vendor intended to create a scheme.[130] Finally, Wootten J. held in *Re Mack and the Conveyancing Act*[131] that the fact that the covenants imposed on the purchasers of all the lots are not identical or that some lots are sold free from the restrictions is not fatal to a scheme of development; all that is required is an intention to create a scheme at the time when the scheme was created. In this case, the fact that nine of the 115 lots in the alleged scheme were sold free from restrictions was held not to vitiate the scheme.

The reasoning of the third requirement, that the restrictions were intended by the common vendor to be for the benefit of the lots sold, was amplified by Parker J. in *Elliston v. Reacher*[132] later in his judgment. His Honour stated that the vendor's object in imposing the restrictions must in general be gathered from all the circumstances of the case, including in particular the nature of the restrictions: if a general observance of the covenants is in fact calculated to enhance the value of the lots offered for sale, it may easily be inferred that the vendor intended the restriction to be for the benefit of all the lots. The effect of this amplification is that a scheme seldom fails by virtue of this third requirement. As a matter of practice, evidence of the intention of the vendor may be gleaned from a variety of sources: for example, the forms of contracts,[133] conveyances[134] or evidence of the vendor or her or his solicitor.[135]

Regarding the fourth requirement, Parker J. stated in *Elliston v. Reacher*[136] that this may readily be inferred, provided that the purchasers have notice of the facts involved in the first three points. In considering this question the court can draw inferences although it cannot rely on mere conjecture.[137] If the purchaser buys the land in ignorance of any material part of the facts involved in the first three points, it will be difficult, if not impossible, to satisfy the fourth point. The fourth requirement has been inferred in recent times in *Re Dennerstein*[138] and *Re Mack and the Conveyancing Act*,[139] but was not inferred in *Re Naish and the Conveyancing Act*[140] where the only evidence of knowledge of the scheme by the purchasers was that all the lots sold over a preceding 16 year period had been sold subject to similar covenants.

[17.22] The relevance in New South Wales of s. 88(1) of the *Conveyancing Act* 1919 to schemes of development must be considered. If

---

130. *Baxter v. Four Oaks Properties Ltd* [1965] 1 Ch. 816; *Re Application of Poltava Pty Ltd* [1982] 2 N.S.W.L.R. 161.
131. [1975] 2 N.S.W.L.R. 623.
132. [1908] 2 Ch. 374 at 384. For a recent application of the third requirement, see *Re 6, 8, 10 and 12 Elm Avenue, New Milton* [1984] 3 All E.R. 632 at 638.
133. See e.g. *Sutton v. Shoppee* (1963) 63 S.R. (N.S.W.) 853; *Re Dennerstein* [1963] V.R. 688.
134. See e.g. *Re Dolphin's Conveyance* [1970] Ch. 654.
135. See e.g. *Eagling v. Gardner* [1970] 2 All E.R. 838.
136. [1908] 2 Ch. 374 at 385.
137. *Re Application of Poltava Pty Ltd* [1982] 2 N.S.W.L.R. 161 at 168; *Sutton v. Shoppee* (1963) 63 S.R. (N.S.W.) 853 at 863.
138. [1963] V.R. 688.
139. [1975] 2 N.S.W.L.R. 623.
140. (1960) 77 W.N. (N.S.W.) 892.

the section applies to schemes of development, it would have the effect of rendering such schemes inoperable in New South Wales. As discussed in the context of express assignment (see above [17.15]), the issue is whether the words "the benefit of which is intended to be annexed to other land" applies only to express annexation or extends to schemes of development. The better view, supported by Helmore[141] and *Re Louis and the Conveyancing Act*,[142] appears to be that the section is inapplicable to covenants over general law land imposed under a scheme of development. The issue whether the section applies to covenants over Torrens land imposed under a scheme of development is discussed in detail: see below [17.23].

Finally, it should be noted that several cases have recognised the possibility of creating subschemes of development, where the owners of certain lots in a valid scheme agree between themselves that different or additional covenants will bind their blocks of land.[143] These different or additional covenants will be enforceable between the owners of the blocks affected by the subscheme, but cannot affect the right of the owners of the blocks of land in the head scheme not subject to the subscheme to enforce the original covenants in the head scheme as if the subscheme had not occurred.

2. Application of General Law Rules to Torrens Land[144]

[17.23] As in the case of express assignment (see above [17.15]), difficulties arise with schemes of development in respect of Torrens land, as if they are enforceable, it would be necessary for a purchaser of land to look beyond the register to establish the nature of the title. Based on the decided cases, the issue is not treated uniformly across the States.

In Victoria, the major authority is *Re Dennerstein*.[145] In this case, Hudson J. concluded that the notification of a restrictive covenant on the certificate of title would not be effective to bind a transferee of the burdened land "unless not only the existence of the scheme and the nature of the restrictions imposed thereunder, but the lands affected by the scheme (both as to the benefit and burden of the restrictions) are indicated in the notifications either directly or by reference to some instrument or other document to which a person searching the register has access". Thus, the scheme of development doctrine appears to be recognised as valid in Victoria in respect of Torrens land but is subject to more stringent limitations than apply in respect of general law land. In addition to the requirements in *Elliston v. Reacher*[146] (see above [17.20]), it must be shown that a purchaser of the burdened land could discover the existence of the scheme of development, either from the notification on the certificate of

---

141. See above fn. 95.
142. [1971] 1 N.S.W.L.R. 164 (C.A.); discussed in (1972) 46 A.L.J. 91.
143. See e.g. *Knight v. Simmonds* [1896] 1 Ch. 653; *Brunner v. Greenslade* [1971] Ch. 993; *Lawrence v. South County Freeholds Ltd* [1939] Ch. 656.
144. See Bradbrook and Neave, paras 1733ff.
145. [1963] V.R. 688. See the discussion of this case in *Sawyer v. Starr* [1985] 2 N.Z.L.R. 540 at 550-551.
146. [1908] 2 Ch. 374 at 384-385.

title or from some other document (for example, a transfer) to which the notification directly refers. On the facts in *Re Dennerstein*, the enforceability of a covenant contained in a scheme against a purchaser of the burdened land was rejected, as although the existence of a scheme at general law was proved, the additional requirements discussed above were not satisfied.

In Tasmania, *Re Dennerstein* was followed in *Re Cashmore's Application*,[147] but the issue in that State is subject to the overriding requirement in the *Land Transfer Act* 1980, s. 102(2)(a)(iv) that the burden of a covenant will only run with freehold registered land if the land intended to be benefited by the covenant is identified in the instrument containing the covenant. There are no relevant statutory or case law authorities in Western Australia, but there appears to be no reason why *Re Dennerstein* should not also apply in that State.

In New South Wales, the issue turns on s. 88(1) of the *Conveyancing Act* 1919: see above **[17.14]**. Section 88(3) gives the Registrar-General the power to record a restrictive covenant referred to in s. 88(1) on the certificate of title of the burdened land. The major authority is *Re Louis and the Conveyancing Act*.[148] In this case, the New South Wales Court of Appeal held that schemes of development could exist over Torrens land in that State and covenants contained therein are enforceable if the statutory requirements in s. 88(1) are satisfied and the covenants are created by an instrument. Jacobs J.A. emphasised that s. 88(1) does not affect the substantive rules of equity and common law concerning the creation of restrictive covenants and the passing of the benefit and the burden, but merely adds conditions for the validity of the covenant. He added that the requisite intention to annex referred to in s. 88(1) must be established, but this can be proved in the case of schemes of development by showing an intention to bind the whole and each part of the burdened land. One effect of this decision is to reverse an earlier restrictive interpretation of the wording of s. 88(1), ''intended to be annexed to other land'', under which this applied only to cases of express annexation at common law,[149] and to extend the relevance of s. 88(1) to covenants contained in schemes of development. Under this interpretation covenants imposed in schemes of development or the benefit of which could be assigned could not be identified on the Register and were therefore unenforceable in respect of Torrens land.

[17.24] In its decision in *Re Louis*, the Court of Appeal partially reversed the Full Court decision in *Re Martyn*,[150] where the majority held that a covenant contained in a scheme of development was invalid on the ground that the formal requirement in s. 88(1)(a) was not satisfied, and that the failure to specify the land benefited cannot be rectified by proof of the existence of a scheme of development. The Full Court inferred that even where s. 88(1) is satisfied, covenants imposed in a scheme of

147. [1967] Tas. S.R. 217.
148. [1971] 1 N.S.W.L.R. 164 (C.A.).
149. *Re Pirie and the Real Property Act* [1962] N.S.W.R. 1004.
150. (1965) 65 S.R. (N.S.W.) 387; discussed in (1965) 39 A.L.J. 62.

development will not be enforceable unless the existence of the scheme and the land subject to it can be found by searching the title of the burdened land.

The practical effect of *Re Louis* is that apart from the statutory requirements in s. 88(1) of the New South Wales Act the Victorian and New South Wales positions appear to be similar. Since the decision in *Re Louis* was handed down, the court in *Re Mack and the Conveyancing Act*[151] and *Jones v. Sherwood Hills Pty Ltd*[152] has assumed that schemes of development may be created in respect of Torrens land in New South Wales.

In South Australia, Napier C.J. assumed in *Blacks Ltd v. Rix*,[153] without detailed analysis of the point, that schemes of development apply equally to Torrens land as to general law land. This judicial assumption must be considered to be questionable in light of the absence of any power in the *Real Property Act* 1886 (S.A.) to notify restrictive covenants on the certificate of title of the burdened land. This difficulty also exists in respect of Queensland, where the issue under discussion appears not to have been judicially considered.

VI.   DISCHARGE AND MODIFICATION OF RESTRICTIVE COVENANTS

Restrictive covenants may be modified or discharged in any one of the following four methods:

1. By Agreement

[17.25]   As in the case of easements (see above [16.35]), the persons entitled to the benefit and burden of a covenant may agree to modify or discharge a covenant provided that they are both sui juris. Where this occurs, the Torrens legislation in New South Wales, Victoria, Western Australia and Tasmania empowers the Registrar (in Tasmania, the Recorder of Titles) to cancel or amend any notification of a restrictive covenant on the register.[154]

In New South Wales, pursuant to s. 88(1)(c) of the *Conveyancing Act* 1919 no covenant is enforceable against any person other than the original contracting parties unless, inter alia, the covenant clearly indicates "the persons (if any) having the right to release, vary or modify the . . . restrictions, other than the persons having, in the absence of agreement to the contrary, the right by law to release, vary or modify the . . . restrictions". Waddell J. held in *Jones v. Sherwood Hills Pty Ltd*[155] that this section permits the parties to impose the power to discharge or modify a

151. [1975] 2 N.S.W.L.R. 623.
152. Unreported, 8 July 1975; discussed in (1978) 52 A.L.J. 223.
153. [1962] S.A.S.R. 161.
154. *Conveyancing Act* 1919 (N.S.W.), s. 88(3)(a); *Transfer of Land Act* 1958 (Vic.), s 88(1); *Transfer of Land Act* 1893 (W.A.), s. 129B(2); *Land Titles Act* 1980 (Tas.), s. 104.
155. Unreported, 8 July 1975; discussed in (1978) 52 A.L.J. 223.

covenant upon a third party who has no interest in the benefited or burdened land. He also held that there is no requirement that such a power, if conferred, has to be exercised subject to the requirements of natural justice. In so deciding, his Honour rejected the contrary arguments advanced by Baalman[156] to the effect that the interest of a third party purportedly given a power of variation or discharge cannot amount to an interest in land.

2. By Laches or Acquiescence

[17.26]   The general equitable rules disentitling the plaintiff to relief in the discretion of the court where he or she has been guilty of laches or acquiescence are applicable in this context. Where they apply, they effectively achieve the discharge of a restrictive covenant.[157]

3. By unity of ownership

[17.27]   If the same person acquires a fee simple estate in possession in the benefited and burdened land, any restrictive covenants binding the burdened land will be discharged and will not revive if the burdened land is later sold.[158] This rule has been altered by statute in Tasmania and New South Wales. The *Land Titles Act* 1980 (Tas.), s. 103 reads in part:

> "(1) A covenant which runs with freehold registered land is not affected by the same person being the registered proprietor at any time of the lands benefited and burdened by the covenants unless the covenant is expunged from the Register as provided in subsection (2).
>
> (2) On the application of the registered proprietor of the lands benefited and burdened by a covenant, and proof to his satisfaction that the covenant would have been extinguished but for the operation of subsection (1), the Recorder shall expunge the covenant from the Register."[159]

The *Conveyancing Act* 1919 (N.S.W.), s. 88B, permits restrictive covenants to be created by lodging a plan of subdivision with the Registrar-General. Pursuant to s. 88(3)(c), the covenant will be created on the registration or the recording of the plan and will not be discharged if the owner of the benefited land holds or acquires an interest in the burdened land.[160]

The rule that a restrictive covenant will be discharged on unity of seisin of the benefited and burdened land appears not to apply to schemes of

156. Baalman, "Variation of Restrictive Covenants (N.S.W.)" (1948) 21 A.L.J. 427 (Pt 1), 461 (Pt 2).
157. See e.g. *Sayers v. Collyer* (1884) 28 Ch. D. 103; *Gaskin v. Balls* (1879) 13 Ch. D. 324 (C.A.).
158. *Re Tiltwood, Sussex* [1978] 1 Ch. 269. This issue is discussed in Bates, "Extinguishment and Revival of Restrictive Covenants in Land" (1980) 54 A.L.J. 156; Preece, "The Effect of Unity of Ownership of Benefited and Burdened Land on Easements and Restrictive Covenants" (1982) 56 A.L.J. 587.
159. See also *Conveyancing and Law of Property Act* 1884 (Tas.), s. 9A.
160. See also *Crown Lands Consolidation Act* 1913 (N.S.W.), s. 136L(7).

development. Authority for this proposition is *Texaco Antilles Ltd v. Kernochan*,[161] where the owner of one block of land in a scheme sought to enforce a covenant against the owners of one of the other blocks. The argument made by the defendants that since both they and the plaintiff had a common predecessor-in-title the covenants were discharged was rejected by the Privy Council. Lord Cross of Chelsea stated that it does not follow from the general rule under discussion that if a number of people agree that the area covered by their properties shall be subject to a "local law", the provisions of which shall be enforceable by any owner for the time being of any part against any other owner, and the whole area has never at any time come into common ownership, an action by one owner of a part against another owner of a part must fail if it can be shown that both parts were either at the inception of the scheme or at any time subsequently in common ownership.[162]

4. By State Legislation

[17.28]   In all States, piecemeal legislation exists which authorises certain State public authorities to discharge or modify restrictive covenants in a variety of specified circumstances.[163]

More importantly, in all jurisdictions except South Australia, the State Supreme Court (and in Tasmania, the Recorder of Titles) has been granted the general power to discharge or modify restrictive covenants under certain specified circumstances. Except in Victoria, this legislation also authorises that court to extinguish or modify easements.

The New South Wales, Victorian and Western Australian provisions are similar.[164] For example, the *Property Law Act* 1958 (Vic.), s. 84(1) states:

> "The Court shall have power from time to time on the application of any person interested in any land affected by any restriction arising under covenant or otherwise as to the user thereof or the building thereon by order wholly or partially to discharge or modify any such restrictions (subject or not to the payment by the applicant of compensation to any person suffering loss in consequence of the order) upon being satisfied—
>
> (a) that by reason of changes in the character of the property or the neighbourhood or other circumstances of the case which the Court deems material the restriction ought to be deemed obsolete or that the continued existence thereof would impede the reasonable user of the land without securing practical

---

161. [1973] A.C. 609 (P.C.).
162. Ibid. at 626.
163. See e.g. *Local Government Act* 1919 (N.S.W.), s. 327A; *Planning and Environment Act* 1987 (Vic.), s. 6(2); *Town and Country Planning Act* 1961 (Vic.), s. 9 and Third Schedule; *State Housing Act* 1945 (Qld), s. 22(1)(d)(i); *Housing Improvement Act* 1940 (S.A.), ss 36(1)(c), 39.
164. *Conveyancing Act* 1919 (N.S.W.), s. 89(1); *Property Law Act* 1958 (Vic.). s. 84(1); *Transfer of Land Act* 1893 (W.A.), s. 129C. The Western Australian provision applies only to Torrens land.

benefits to other persons or (as the case may be) would unless modified so impede such user; or

(b) that the persons of full age and capacity for the time being or from time to time entitled to the benefit of the restriction whether in respect of estates in fee-simple or any lesser estates or interests in the property to which the benefit of the restriction is annexed have agreed either expressly or by implication by their acts or omissions to the same being discharged or modified; or

(c) that the proposed discharge or modification will not substantially injure the persons entitled to the benefit of the restriction."

The legislation in Queensland and Tasmania has been modified in line with the reforms introduced by the English *Law of Property Act* 1969. The *Property Law Act* 1974 (Qld), s. 181 retains the grounds in paragraphs (b) and (c) of the Victorian legislation above, but adds the following grounds in substitution for paragraph (a) of the Victorian legislation:

"(a) that by reason of change in the user of any land having the benefit of the restriction, or in the character of the neighbourhood or other circumstances of the case which the Court may deem material, the . . . restriction ought to be deemed obsolete; or

(b) that the continued existence of the . . . restriction would impede some reasonable user of the land subject to the . . . restriction, or that the . . . restriction,[165] in impeding that user, either—

(i) does not secure to persons entitled to the benefit of it any practical benefits of substantial value, utility, or advantage to them; or

(ii) is contrary to the public interest,

and that money will be an adequate compensation for the loss or disadvantage (if any) which any such person will suffer from the extinguishment or modification."[166]

The *Conveyancing and Law of Property Act* 1884 (Tas.), s. 84c(1) retains paragraphs (a) and (b) of the Victorian legislation above, and adds the following ground:

---

165. It has been held in *Ex parte Melvin* [1980] Qd R. 391 and *Ex parte Proprietors of "Averil Court" Building Units Plan No. 2001* [1983] 1 Qd R. 66 that the phrase "or that the . . . restriction" should be read as "and that the . . . restriction".
166. Section 181(2) reads:
   "In determining whether a case is one falling within paragraph (a) or (b) of subsection (1), and in determining whether (in such a case or otherwise) a . . . restriction ought to be extinguished or modified, the Court shall take into account the town plan and any declared or ascertainable pattern of the local authority for the grant or refusal of consent, permission or approval to use any land or to erect or use any building or other structure in the relevant area, as well as the period at which and context in which the . . . restriction was created or imposed, and any other material circumstance."

"that the continued existence of the interest would impede a user of the land in accordance with an interim order or planning scheme, or, as the case may be, would, unless modified, so impede such a user."[167]

In addition, unlike s. 84(1)(c) of the Victorian Act which refers to *substantial* injury to the persons entitled to the benefit of the restriction,[168] the equivalent Tasmanian provision (s. 84C(1)(e)) does not include the word "substantial". Thus, any injury, whether substantial or not, must be taken into account in Tasmania.[169]

[17.29]   In all States, it appears that the scope of the legislation is confined to restrictive covenants. It has been held by the English Lands Tribunal under similar legislation that there is no power to modify or discharge positive covenants or personal covenants.[170]

The legislation in Victoria, Queensland and Tasmania confers the power on the Supreme Court to make the modification or discharge of a restrictive covenant subject to the payment of compensation.[171] This is a matter of discretion for the court on the facts of each case. No similar provision exists in the New South Wales and Western Australian legislation.

There can be no modification or discharge unless one or more of the specified legislative grounds exists on the facts.[172] Despite differing authorities, it appears that the court retains a discretion to refuse an application for modification or discharge even where one of the grounds is proved to exist.[173] This interpretation is consistent with the word "may" in the legislation in each State.

There are numerous reported cases in Australia and England interpreting the meaning of the various grounds for modification and discharge of restrictive covenants and easements. Reference should be made elsewhere for a detailed discussion of this case law.[174] The

---

167. Cf. *Property Law Act* 1974 (Qld), s. 181(2).
168. For the meaning of "substantially injure", see e.g. *Re Cook* [1964] V.R. 808; *Re R.K. Roseblade and V.M. Roseblade and the Conveyancing Act* [1964-5] N.S.W.R. 2044; *Re Markin* [1966] V.R. 494.
169. Unlike in other jurisdictions, the *Conveyancing and Law of Property Act* 1884 (Tas.), s. 84C(1) states that the power to modify or discharge restrictive covenants does not apply to covenants contained in plans of subdivision.
170. *Re Blyth Corporation's Application* (1962) 14 P. & C.R. 56; *Re Chatham B.C.'s Application* (1970) 21 P. & C.R. 661.
171. General law statutes: Vic.: s. 84(1); Qld: s. 181(4); Tas.: s. 84C(7).
172. *Re Application of Poltava Pty Ltd* [1982] 2 N.S.W.L.R. 161; *Pieper v. Edwards* [1982] 1 N.S.W.L.R. 336 at 341; *Kort Pty Ltd v. Shaw* [1983] W.A.R. 113.
173. *Kort Pty Ltd v. Shaw* [1983] W.A.R. 113; *Pieper v. Edwards* [1982] 1 N.S.W.L.R. 336 (C.A.); *Re Cook* [1964] V.R. 808; *Re Ghey and Galton's Application* [1957] 2 Q.B. 650 (C.A.). Cf. *Re Rose Bay Bowling and Recreation Club Ltd* (1935) 52 W.N. (N.S.W.) 77.
174. Bradbrook and Neave, paras 1943ff. For more recent decisions, see e.g. *Re Abbey Homesteads (Developments) Ltd's Application* (1985) 49 P. & C.R. 263; *Re Reynolds' Application* (1987) 54 P. & C.R. 121; *Re Ulman* [1986] A.N.Z. Conv. R. 475 (Vic. Sup. Ct); *Caledonian Associated Properties Ltd v. East Kilbride Development Corporation* (1985) 49 P. & C.R. 410.

remainder of this discussion will merely examine the basic principles which the courts apply.

[17.30] As a general proposition it may be stated that the applicant for modification or discharge of a covenant or easement has a heavy onus to overcome if her or his application is to succeed. There are comparatively few cases where such applications have been successful. The conservative attitude taken by the courts is typified by the following comments of Farwell J. in *Re Henderson's Conveyance*:[175]

> "I do not view this section of the Act as designed to enable a person to expropriate the private rights of another purely for his own profit. . . . [I]n my judgment this section of the Act was not designed, at any rate prima facie, to enable one owner to get a benefit by being freed from the restrictions imposed upon his property in favour of a neighbouring owner, merely because, in the view of the person who desires the restriction to go, it would make his property more enjoyable or more convenient for his own private purposes. I do not think the section was designed with a view to benefiting one private individual at the expense of another private individual. At any rate, primarily, that was not, in my judgment, the object of this section. If a case is to be made out under this section, there must be some proper evidence that the restriction is no longer necessary for any reasonable purpose of the person who is enjoying the benefit of it, or by reason of a change in the character of the property or the neighbourhood, the restriction is one which is no longer to be enforceable or has become of no value."

It has been held that there is nothing in the legislation to prevent an application for modification or discharge being brought by the original covenantor.[176] However, in this situation, the court will be slow to exercise its discretion in favour of the applicant especially if the covenant was only entered into in recent times. As stated by Gillard J. in *Re Makin*,[177] the court should entertain a strong bias against the original covenantor seeking to modify or discharge a restriction on her or his title brought about by their own voluntary act in entering into a contract with the covenantor. In this case, Gillard J. discharged the covenants but stated that the applicants would still be liable for contractual damages at common law. This latter issue has not been finally resolved in Australia, but it is submitted with respect that Gillard J. was incorrect. As stated earlier by the English Court of Appeal in *Ridley v. Taylor*,[178] it would be an extraordinary result if the covenantee could still sue the original covenantor for contractual damages although he or she had parted with all interest in the property.

---

175. [1940] Ch. 835 at 846. See also *Re Truman, Hanbury, Buxton & Co. Ltd's Application* [1956] 1 Q.B. 261 at 270 (C.A.) and *Re Ghey and Galton's Application* [1957] 2 Q.B. 650 at 659 (C.A.).
176. *Re Markin* [1966] V.R. 494 (discussed in (1967) 40 A.L.J. 357); *Ridley v. Taylor* [1965] 2 All E.R. 51 (C.A.).
177. [1966] V.R. 494 at 498.
178. [1965] 2 All E.R. 51 at 55, 57.

[17.31]   At common law, town-planning considerations will be held to be irrelevant in establishing whether a ground exists for modification or discharge of a covenant. Authority for this proposition is *Re Robinson*,[179] where the local planning scheme prohibited the use of certain land for residential purposes. An application was brought to modify a covenant that only private dwellings could be erected upon certain land covered by this planning scheme. As none of the specific grounds in s. 84(1) of the *Property Law Act* 1958 (Vic.) applied on the facts, Adam J. dismissed the application even though the continued existence of the covenants effectively prevented any development on the land. His Honour stated that town-planning considerations were quite beside the point. It is possible, however, though unresolved in Australia, that if an applicant can fit her or his case within one of the grounds for modification or discharge, the court may refuse the application based on town-planning considerations.[180] Note that the common law on this issue no longer applies in Queensland and Tasmania, where by virtue of legislative amendment the courts will take into account the local town plan in certain circumstances: see above **[17.28]**.

The discussion in the preceding paragraph is illustrative of the general criticism that can be made of the law in this area that little account is taken of public policy considerations, with far greater emphasis being given to existing proprietary interests.[181] Even in Queensland and Tasmania, where by legislative amendment public interest has been added as a ground for modification or discharge of a restrictive covenant, it must be proved that the covenant is *contrary* to the public interest.[182] It is not sufficient merely to prove that it is in the public interest that land be developed in a particular manner. The nature of the onus imposed by the legislation is such that the provision is seldom argued in practice.

In Queensland and Tasmania, the courts are statutorily empowered to impose conditions in an order modifying or discharging a covenant if it appears reasonable to do so.[183] In Queensland the power is confined to negative covenants, while in Tasmania the legislation appears to be sufficiently broad to encompass positive covenants. In the remaining jurisdictions, the issue depends on common law. The power to impose conditions was assumed without discussion in *Re R.K. Roseblade and V.M. Roseblade and the Conveyancing Act*,[184] where Else-Mitchell J. modified a covenant restricting future subdivision of the land, but imposed conditions limiting the size of the houses erected on the subdivided blocks and requiring that existing trees should not be removed. In *Manly Properties Pty Ltd v. Castrisos*,[185] a case involving easements, the court held

179. [1972] V.R. 278; discussed in (1972) 45 A.L.J. 533. See also *Perth Construction Pty Ltd v. Mount Lawley Pty Ltd* (1955) 57 W.A.L.R. 41.
180. Contrast *Re St Albans Investment Ltd's Application* (1958) 9 P. & C.R. 536 with *Re Luton Trade Unionist Club and Institute Ltd's Application* (1969) 20 P. & C.R. 1131.
181. On this point, see *Kort Pty Ltd v. Shaw* [1983] W.A.R. 113 at 115.
182. See *Re Brierfield's Application* (1978) 35 P. & C.R. 124.
183. *Property Law Act* 1974 (Qld), s. 181(3); *Conveyancing and Law of Property Act* 1884 (Tas.), s. 84C(4).
184. [1964-5] N.S.W.R. 2044.
185. [1973] 2 N.S.W.L.R. 420.

that it had the power to extinguish an easement upon specified conditions, including the grant of a new easement. This latter decision suggests in the context of covenants that the court's power at common law to impose conditions when modifying or discharging a covenant includes the power to impose positive as well as negative covenants. In the case of positive covenants, however, it is unclear whether the burden would run with the land; in the absence of authority, it is submitted that the burden would not run.

VII.   REMEDIES[186]

[17.32]   Damages may be recovered at law for breach of a covenant by the covenantee or her or his personal representative, her or his assignee or successor-in-title to whom the benefit of the covenant has run at law against the covenantor or her or his personal representative.[187]

The normal contractual principles will apply to the assessment of damages at law.[188] These would include any costs incurred in alleviating the adverse effects of the breach of covenant and any reduction in the value of the benefited land. The basic principle is that the injured party should be restored to the same position as he or she would have been in if the covenant had not been breached. A major difficulty arises where the breach of covenant does not reduce the value of the benefited land and where there is no cost incurred in alleviating the adverse effects of the breach. In this situation, Brightman J. stated in *Wrotham Park Estate Co. Ltd v. Parkside Homes Ltd*[189] that damages should not be restricted to nominal damages, and should extend to the sum of money which might reasonably have been demanded by the covenantee as the price for waiving the covenant. This principle was applied in *Bracewell v. Appleby*[190] in the context of easements. It was rejected by Megarry V.-C. in *Tito v. Waddell (No. 2)*[191] in relation to a positive contract to perform acts on the plaintiff's land, but appears to have been accepted obiter by his Honour in relation to contracts not to perform certain acts. In light of the present state of the authorities, the matter must be regarded as unsettled.

[17.33]   In most circumstances, the covenant will be enforceable only in equity. The normal rules governing equitable remedies will be applicable here. Thus, the court may grant prohibitory, mandatory, quia timet and interlocutory injunctions to restrain breaches of restrictive covenants.[192] Based on a controversial dictum by Lord Cairns in *Doherty v. Allman*,[193] it is arguable that in relation to prohibitory injunctions the court has no

---

186. For a detailed discussion of this issue, see Bradbrook and Neave, Chap. 18.
187. *Rogers v. Hosegood* [1900] 2 Ch. 388 (C.A.); *Smith and Snipes Hall Farm Ltd v. River Douglas Catchment Board* [1949] 2 K.B. 500 (C.A.).
188. See Cheshire and Fifoot, Chap. 24.
189. [1974] 2 All E.R. 321 at 339-341.
190. [1975] Ch. 408.
191. [1977] Ch. 106.
192. See Meagher, Gummow and Lehane, Chap. 21.
193. (1878) 3 App. Cas. 709 at 719.

discretion to take into account the various discretionary circumstances such as hardship to one or more of the parties, the conduct of the plaintiff, laches, acquiescence, unfairness and the balance of convenience to which the grant of equitable remedies is normally subject and will enforce the remedy as of right. The justification for this approach is that in this context the injunction merely gives the sanction of the process of the court to that which already is the contract between the parties. The better view today, however, appears to be that the grant of equitable relief to protect restrictive covenants is subject to a consideration of the circumstances generally disentitling the plaintiff to relief in equity.[194] This conclusion is based on the logic of the situation, in that it would be very strange if restrictive covenants were to be the only area of equitable jurisdiction where the court is unable to exercise its discretion, and on dicta by Wilberforce J. in *Marten v. Flight Refuelling Ltd*[195] indicating the existence of a discretion in this matter.

In addition to or in lieu of an injunction, where a breach of a restrictive covenant occurs, the court may award equitable damages under legislation enacted in all Australian jurisdictions based on s. 2 of the *Chancery Amendment Act* 1858 (U.K.) (commonly known as *Lord Cairns' Act*).[196] Despite earlier doubts, the House of Lords has held in *Johnson v. Agnew*[197] that equitable damages are assessed in the same manner as damages at common law.

As to the circumstances in which equitable damages will be awarded instead of an injunction, A. L. Smith L.J. stated in *Shelfer v. City of London Electric Lighting Co.* that:[198]

"(a) If the injury to the plaintiff's legal rights is small;

(b) And is one which is capable of being estimated in money;

(c) And is one which can be adequately compensated by a small money payment;

(d) And the case is one in which it would be appropriate to the defendant to grant an injunction—

then damages in substitution of an injunction may be given."

His Lordship stated that this should be regarded as a "good working rule". This dictum has been cited with approval on numerous occasions by Australian and English courts,[199] although it was disregarded by the

194. See Meagher, Gummow and Lehane, para. 2138. The issue is discussed in *Dalgety Wine Estates Pty Ltd v. Rizzon* (1979) 141 C.L.R. 552 and *Broken Hill Proprietary Co. Ltd v. Hapag Lloyd Aktiengesellschaph* [1980] 2 N.S.W.L.R. 572.
195. [1962] Ch. 115 at 151.
196. *Supreme Court Act* 1970 (N.S.W.), s. 68; *Supreme Court Act* 1986 (Vic.), s. 38; *Supreme Court Act* 1935 (W.A.), s. 25(10); *Supreme Court Civil Procedure Act* 1932 (Tas.), s. 11(13); *Supreme Court Act* 1935 (S.A.), s. 30; *Judicature Act* 1876 (Qld), s. 4.
197. [1980] A.C. 367 (H.L.); discussed in (1980) 96 L.Q.R. 403. See also *Domb v. Isoz* [1980] 1 All E.R. 942 (C.A.); *Ansett Transport Industries (Operations) Pty Ltd v. Halton* (1979) 25 A.L.R. 639 at 655 (H.C.).
198. [1895] 1 Ch. 287 at 322 (C.A.).
199. See e.g. *Kelsen v. Imperial Tobacco Co. etc. Ltd* [1957] 2 Q.B. 334; *Owen v. O'Connor* [1964] N.S.W.R. 1312; *Wollerton and Wilson Ltd v. Richard Costain Ltd* [1970] 1 All E.R. 483.

English Court of Appeal in *Miller v. Jackson*[200] and has been criticised elsewhere as unnecessarily rigid.[201] If the dictum still represents good law, it would seem that damages will only rarely be ordered instead of an injunction where a breach of a restrictive covenant occurs.

200. [1977] Q.B. 966 (C.A.).
201. Spry, pp. 603-605; Jolowicz, "Damages in Equity—A Study of *Lord Cairns' Act*" (1975) 34 C.L.J. 224.

18

Mortgages

I. THE NATURE OF SECURITY INTERESTS

1. Mortgages in English Law

[18.01] The term mortgage is used to describe the most common form of security interest in land recognised by the common law. The features of the mortgage were developed to reflect social conditions and restraints at the time of its development. The rights under a mortgage agreement have resulted not so much from the terms agreed by the parties as the framework developed by courts of equity to reflect what those courts considered the true intention of the parties. The term mortgage and many of the associated trappings have been retained today even though much of the form if not the substance has been altered by the Torrens system statutes.

Common law theory accepted a mortgage over chattels as much as a mortgage over land.[1] However the development of security interests in chattels was considerably affected by the bills of sale legislation of the 19th century. This legislation sought to stamp out fraudulent dealings and required public recording of (in essence) transactions transferring rights to goods not matched by an accompanying transfer of possession.[2] Unfortunately the recording processes were extremely cumbersome and were accompanied by some social stigma[3] so that a primary goal of those developing security interests in chattels was a device avoiding the need for recording as a bill of sale. In addition enforceability of property rights was restricted by the Sale of Goods Acts.[4] In Anglo-Australian commerce, financial arrangements relating to goods were from the late 19th century until very recently expressed most commonly in the hire-purchase transaction.[5] This transaction avoided the registration requirements of the Bills of Sale legislation and the restrictions on enforceability of property rights imposed by the Sale of Goods Acts.

1. Sykes, pp. 533-537.
2. Sykes, pp. 531-533.
3. The development of consumer credit and acceptance of secured borrowings beyond the mortgage for the purchase of the family home represent a major reversal of earlier attitudes. Sykes, p. 529, refers to the view that mortgages of chattels are usually indicative of serious financial embarrassment and frequently a prelude to bankruptcy.
4. In particular a buyer in possession of goods with the consent of the seller could pass good title to a subsequent buyer in good faith and for value. See Sutton, *Sales and Consumer Law in Australia and New Zealand* (3rd ed., 1983), pp. 330-353.
5. Sykes, pp. 677-682.

2. Purposes of Security

[18.02]   The purpose of a security interest is to confer property rights upon someone to whom a debt is due. Those property rights confer remedies not enjoyed by someone who has a claim against another for a debt. The creditor without any security in general can proceed against a debtor only by legal action.[6] The creditor must obtain a judgment for the sum due. A judgment can be obtained only after initiation of legal process, service of process upon the other party and proof of the claim; some short cuts are provided for. Even after judgment a creditor cannot proceed against a debtor's assets as the creditor sees fit. Procedures for the enforcement of judgments differ amongst Australian jurisdictions but all of them limit the creditor's actions. In some instances a creditor is bound to accept instalment payment; commonly a creditor must sell goods before land; the remedy of an order against wages (garnishment) is favoured in some jurisdictions and prohibited in others. A judgment creditor cannot trace assets into the hands of third parties even if those assets were purchased with funds lent by the creditor. Some tracing of assets is allowed if a debtor is declared bankrupt.[7] But bankruptcy proceedings may be initiated by any creditor or by the debtor, and upon bankruptcy the total amount of recovery is limited to the bankrupt's assets and that amount is generally divided equally amongst the creditors.

A security interest avoids many of these difficulties. Land is an ideal security. It is readily identifiable and permanent and by and large has held its value well in Australian history. The precise rights a secured creditor has against land or other property depends upon the details of her or his security interest; commonly the creditor may upon default sell the land to gain payment of the debt. The creditor is not required to take action in the courts to force a sale, though commonly some notice is required. Because the creditor has a proprietary interest, the land cannot be disposed of by the debtor to a third party taking free of that interest though there are instances in which some third parties may do so. Even if the debtor becomes bankrupt the creditor is entitled to look to the land for the debt even if that land is the bankrupt's sole asset and other creditors are left with no return. Again in some instances a security interest many be set aside in bankruptcy.

3. Forms of Security Interests

[18.03]   While it is common to speak of the classical mortgage as that produced by the application of equitable rules prior to statutory changes, the incidents of a mortgage have changed over time as a result both of social change and changes to legal rules. At no stage did the mortgage conform completely to any model of security interests. In the classic Australian text on securities, Professor Sykes[8] refers to three main forms of security interests based on Roman law models; they are security by way

---

6. Moore, "Repayment of Debts: Creditor Enforcement and Debtor Protection" (1986) 8 A.Bus.L.R. 81, 153.
7. On bankruptcy, see Rose, *Lewis' Australian Bankruptcy Law* (9th ed., 1990).
8. Sykes, pp. 14-15.

of ownership, security by possession, and security by means of a charge. Under the first form the security holder becomes the owner of the property promising to reconvey it upon repayment of the debt; under the second, the security holder obtains possession of the property but the debtor retains the general ownership; under the third, the security holder does not gain either the general ownership or possession but has rights over the property, principally the right to sell, exercisable upon default. As shall be seen the common law mortgage took the form of a security by way of ownership but in substance was closer to a charge and the Torrens system mortgage has largely adopted the substantive situation.

[18.04] Most security interests arise from agreements. The debtor borrows money and in return confers the security rights upon the creditor. The rights of the parties flow from that agreement, though to some extent the law restricts the capacity of the parties to settle particular terms between themselves, and the law does limit the range of security interests. However it is possible that security rights arise independently of any agreement of the parties. Persons who do work on land or goods are commonly given security rights over that land or those goods by operation of law.[9] These rights are described as liens and, for example, may enable possession to be retained until payment.

Security interests normally exist because of a debt that has been incurred. Security interests protect the creditor in the event of default in payment of the debt. It is however possible to burden property with payment of a sum of money even though that money is not otherwise owed to the payee. Except in Queensland, the Torrens system statutes all recognise an encumbrance over land whereby the land is subject to the payment, on a regular basis, of a sum of money.[10] Such an arrangement arose more commonly in the past when, for example, property was left to the eldest child subject to an encumbrance intended to provide for the child's siblings.

4. Charges and Liens

[18.05] This Chapter concentrates on the most common form of security over land—the mortgage. The nature of that interest is described in the next section. There are however several types of charges and liens over land.

An equitable charge differs from an equitable mortgage principally because the holder of the charge has no right to foreclosure. The principal remedies of the holder, in the absence of any express remedies, are judicial

---

9. Carriers' and innkeepers' liens are discussed by Sykes, p. 655, repairers' liens p. 655, warehouseworkers' liens p. 662, solicitors' liens pp. 662-663 and contractors' and workers' liens pp. 706-713.
10. In Queensland the rentcharge is excluded from the range of securities by *Property Law Act* 1974 (Qld), s. 176 and the *Real Property Act* 1861, s. 56. In other States the rentcharge under the Torrens system is recognised by Torrens system statutes: N.S.W.: s. 56(2); Vic.: s. 74(1); S.A.: s. 129; W.A.: s. 105; Tas.: s. 72.

sale and the appointment of a receiver. A charge may be created between parties as security for a debt or by will or a settlement in favour of a person other than the one receiving the property. Where a security transaction is entered informally it may be difficult to discern whether an equitable mortgage or an equitable charge has been created. Where there is simply an intention to grant a security, such as in the case of the deposit of title documents, an intention to create an equitable mortgage is inferred. It has been suggested that in all cases of contract such an intention is inferred but that proposition has critics.[11] Legal charges are practically unknown.[12]

A equitable lien arises not from agreement but by operation of law.[13] The lien confers the same rights upon the holder as an equitable charge. A lien arises in situations in which a debt is incurred in relation to property. The most common type of lien is the vendor's lien for unpaid purchase money in favour of a vendor of land who has parted with legal title. Liens also commonly arise in cases where a purchaser of land has paid the purchase price before receiving legal title and where a trustee spends money on land held in trust in the proper execution of her or his duties. Equity has also developed rules whereby a lien is the remedy of an injured party in cases of breach of trust, dissolution of a partnership and a mistaken expenditure on property permitted by the other party.

In Australia there are special statutory securities developed to assist primary producers.[14] The problem leading to the special provisions has been that producers wish to grant security rights over their produce. That produce may not exist when the security is granted and when it does come into existence may be legally classified as part of the land. Thus the statutes have provided for fruit and crop liens. Similar issues have seen the development of stock and wool mortgages.

5. Credit for Purchasers

[18.06]   The purpose of security was said earlier to be to confer proprietary rights upon a creditor; this statement implied ownership by a debtor of property in respect of which rights were transferred. Very commonly the debt is incurred for the purposes of purchasing residential land. The purchaser acquires title only, it seems, substantially to grant it away to the bank or building society providing the loan. Very little change to the transaction occurs if the creditor obtains title to the land directly and agrees to sell it to the would-be purchaser. The transaction is even simpler if the vendor provides the finance. The creditor-debtor relationship is translated into one of vendor and purchaser.

The legal situation of a purchaser who is paying by instalments has not in Anglo-Australian law been as protected as that of a mortgagor.[14] That is so even though the form of a common law mortgage has been close to

11. Sykes, p. 193.
12. Sykes, p. 191.
13. Sykes, pp. 592-644.
14. Sykes, pp. 356-357.

the model of a security for the creditor by way of ownership. As will be explained in the next section, equity stepped in to protect the mortgagor. Probably because the transaction was not common when equitable rules were more flexible the same protection was not accorded to an instalment purchaser. Indeed the rules in relation to land as to recovery of instalment payments and forfeiture of the purchaser's interest have only been definitively stated by the High Court in the past 20 years.[15] The lack of protection for an instalment purchaser of land has resulted in legislation in some States forcing the transaction into the form of a sale plus mortgage: see above [6.68]. The position of a purchaser of goods was equally tenuous and exposed because of the adoption of hire purchase[16] as the common form of security relating to goods. Such a purchaser had only contractual rights and those rights were dependent on due performance by the purchaser of the purchaser's obligations. The position of such a purchaser was later protected by detailed statutory regulation of hire purchaser transactions.[17] This regulation has now been replaced by consumer credit legislation which requires the use of the sale plus mortgage format.[18] This legislation applies to a defined range of transactions aimed to confine it to consumer transactions and outside its scope transactions may still adopt the hire-purchase form; in such cases some issues as to the rights of the purchaser remain unresolved.

6. Remedies

[18.07] The contrast between the secured and unsecured creditor was earlier stated to flow from the requirement that an unsecured creditor could not take action directly against a debtor or his property but had to obtain a judgment from a court, and use the procedures for the enforcement of judgments. The common law did allow one widespread remedy against a debtor's property without court action. This was the remedy of distress which allowed a landlord to seise any goods on the rented premises of a defaulting tenant.[19] As explained in the analysis of landlord and tenant law (see above [10.76]) this remedy has been substantially extinguished by statute. It remains as a remedy of non-residential landlords in South Australia and generally in Tasmania, and has been extended to local government bodies as a remedy for unpaid rates since governments are reluctant to apply to themselves rules deemed necessary for private creditors against residential landholders. Distress is a remedy that mortgagees sometimes seek for themselves by use of a notional landlord and tenant relationship between the mortgagee and the mortgagor.

---

15. The right to recover instalments other than the deposit was considered in *McDonald v. Dennys Lascelles Ltd* (1933) 48 C.L.R. 457 and the right to relief against forfeiture for failure to pay a due instalment was considered in *Legione v. Hateley* (1983) 46 A.L.R. 1 and *Stern v. McArthur* (1988) 81 A.L.R. 463.
16. Else-Mitchell and Parsons, *Hire Purchase Law* (4th ed., 1968).
17. Sutton, op. cit., pp. 40-44.
18. Duggan, Begg and Lanyon, *Regulated Credit—The Credit and Security Aspects* (1989) Chap. 1.
19. Sykes, pp. 187-189, 282-286.

II. THE NATURE OF A MORTGAGE

1. The General Law

[18.08]   The form of the general law mortgage is said to have been influenced by such factors as attitudes in the middle ages to usury and the expulsion of the Jews from England in the reign of Edward IV.[20] The form of transaction adopted was one whereby the mortgagor transferred the land to the mortgagee and the mortgagee promised to reconvey the land upon payment in full of the debt and interest. Moreover the date for repayment was commonly set at a short time after the loan—most often six months. Thereafter the mortgagor was in default with respect to the obligation and the condition for reconveyance was apparently broken.

Such a form would appear to leave the mortgagor with few, if any, legal rights. Again for historical reasons, equity stepped in to transform the substance of the transaction. Equity is said to have acted on the view it adopted that the substance of the transaction was that of a security for the mortgagee. Consequently, so long as the mortgagee received her or his money (including interest and costs) the mortgagee had no further claim against the land.

[18.09]   As a general law mortgage took the form of a transfer of the legal estate from the mortgagor to the mortgagee the formalities involved were those associated with any transfer of land. The mortgagee thus had the legal estate and the mortgagor an equitable right to get the land back. Only a first mortgage could confer legal rights on the mortgagee; since the mortgagor retained equitable rights all that could be transferred to a second or subsequent mortgagee were in turn equitable rights. In some cases a mortgagor has only equitable rights—such as a beneficiary under a trust—and therefore even a first mortgagee could acquire only equitable rights. In some cases, although a mortgagor may have legal rights, the formalities for the transfer of those rights may not be completed and thus again the mortgagee would acquire only equitable rights. In fact mortgages without any written agreement were not uncommon—a mortgagor would simply deposit title deeds with the mortgagee; that deposit is a sufficient act of part performance to enable enforceability despite the *Statute of Frauds*.

[18.10]   Essential to the equitable approach with respect to mortgages were the notions of redemption and foreclosure. Redemption is the mortgagor's right to get back the property. Foreclosure is the mortgagee's right to extinguish the right of redemption.

Even under the common form of mortgage with a provision for payment in six months, the mortgagor has a contractual right (enforceable in courts of common law if not by way of specific performance) to get this land back if payment is made within the six month period. This right can be properly described as a contractual right to redeem. The significance of equitable intervention was to entitle the mortgagor to redeem even after the contractual right had expired. This right is described as the

---

20. Megarry and Wade, pp. 913-918, Whalan, p. 167, Sykes, pp. 40-41.

mortgagor's equity of redemption. Moreover equity enforced the contractual and equitable rights against all except a bona fide purchaser of the legal estate for value and without notice. The mortgagor thus has an equitable proprietary interest. The terminology is confusing as this proprietary interest is described as the equity of redemption and includes both the contractual and equitable right to redeem.[21]

The right of foreclosure was the means whereby mortgagees could obtain the land for themselves. Despite the apparent absolute ownership, and whatever the mortgagee may have provided in the agreement, without foreclosure the mortgagee was subject to the mortgagor's right of redemption. The mortgagee could however apply to the court of chancery for an order—foreclosure—cutting off the right of redemption.[22] The mortgagee could apply whenever the mortgagor was in default under the contractual provision. The established practice was for a conditional order to be made allowing the mortgagor six months in which to repay the debt; the order becoming absolute if payment was not made. Even a foreclosure order was not absolute and redemption would still be allowed if the mortgagor was not guilty of unconscionable delay, the mortgagee had not acted to her or his detriment on the basis of the foreclosure order and provided that no innocent third party had acquired an interest in the land.[23]

[18.11] Equity intervened to allow redemption wherever the parties intended the agreement to be by way of security. Equity would look beyond any written agreement to discover this intention. It acted against a background where the standard agreement at least disguised the security nature of the transaction. In the case of doubtful transactions the court endeavoured to find that a security was intended. A transaction very similar to the standard mortgage is one whereby the land is transferred but the vendor is given an option to purchase at a future date. Equity accepted a distinction between a power to redeem and one to repurchase but it had to be convinced that the real intention was repurchase.

The High Court has indicated that today the courts will take the parties at their word unless it can be shown that the form of the transaction was adopted as a disguise. In *Gurfinkel v. Bentley Pty Ltd*[24] the plaintiff mortgagor was the registered proprietor of land subject to two mortgages. The mortgagor was in default and the mortgagees had arranged a public auction of the land. The mortgagor had been seeking finance from the defendant. Just prior to the auction the mortgagor entered an agreement for the sale of the land to the defendant for the sum of 3,760 pounds which covered the debts plus expenses. The defendant undertook to complete a building on the land at a cost of 1,240 pounds. In consideration of the payment of 10 pounds by the plaintiff, the plaintiff was given an option to repurchase the land for 5,500 pounds within 12 months. The option was not exercised. The plaintiff brought an action seeking nonetheless to

---

21. Sykes, p. 52.
22. Sykes, pp. 53-54, 124-125.
23. *Campbell v. Holyland* (1877) 7 Ch. D. 166.
24. (1966) 116 C.L.R. 98.

get the land by way of redemption. He claimed that the sum of 5,500 pounds represented the amount lent plus the cost of building plus interest calculated at 10 per cent for 12 months. He alleged that the transaction was truly one of security and thus he was entitled to redeem even after the contractual date. A majority of the High Court held that despite the surrounding circumstances there was insufficient evidence that both parties truly intended a security transaction.

2. The Torrens System

[18.12] The Torrens system form of mortgage represents a significant alteration to the position under the general law. Even if the substance of the transaction was retained, at the very least the Torrens system translated the mortgagor's equitable rights into legal rights.[25] The changes also meant that the form of the transaction could be simpler and what was set out in the agreement corresponded with the actual legal rights of the parties.

The essential change made by the Torrens system is that mortgagor does not transfer her or his legal estate but grants a charge over the estate. This concept is expressly stated in all the Torrens system statutes. Both the mortgagor and mortgagee have legal interests in the land: the mortgagor as the beneficial owner, the mortgagee as the holder of charge.[26] The significance of the charge is to confer upon the mortgagee rights in case of default by the mortgagor.

[18.13] The character of the mortgagor's interest has a consequential impact upon subsequent mortgages. As the mortgagor retains legal title he or she can confer legal rights over that interest. Consequently second, third and subsequent mortgages may all confer legal rights upon the mortgagees. These mortgages take the same form as a first mortgage and are entitled to be registered. Upon registration the mortgagee's rights are legal.

Even under the Torrens system the mortgage may still be equitable. Even if a document in registrable form is executed it will not confer a legal right until it is registered. Prior to registration the mortgagee may well gain equitable rights under the *Walsh v. Lonsdale*[27] principle. Furthermore it is possible to deposit the duplicate certificate of title with the mortgagee without any written agreement. Just as under the general law, this deposit is a sufficient act of part performance to overcome the requirements of the *Statute of Frauds* so there is an enforceable contract to grant a mortgage. This result is expressly recognised by some Torrens system statutes.[28]

A hankering for the past may induce some parties or their advisors to attempt to reproduce a general law mortgage. They are able to execute

25. Whalan, p. 167, argues that the form of mortgage under the common law was regarded by the drafters of the Torrens system as unsuitable to the needs of the colonies.
26. Torrens system statutes: N.S.W.: s. 57(1); Vic.: s. 74(2); Qld: s. 60; S.A.: s. 132; W.A.: s. 106; Tas.: s. 73. See also *Alliance Acceptance Co. Ltd v. Ellison* (1986) 5 N.S.W.L.R. 102.
27. (1882) 21 Ch. D. 9.
28. Torrens system statutes: Qld: s. 30; S.A.: s. 149.

an apparently absolute transfer to the mortgagee which will be registered and confer legal title upon the mortgagee. They may execute a separate agreement for the transfer of land back to the mortgagor on payment of the debt, interest and costs. This agreement cannot be registered but the mortgagor's rights can be protected by the lodging of a caveat. Whilst the wording of the Torrens system statutes is mandatory and requires the use of the statutory form of mortgage by way of charge whenever land is to be made the subject of a security, it has not been argued that a general law form of mortgage is illegal and confers no rights. Such an argument is likely only to hurt the mortgagor and the mortgagor is unlikely to have dictated the form adopted. A stronger argument exists that the registrar should deny registration to an apparently absolute transfer where the transfer indicates that it is a security only.[29] Practice appears to differ from State to State.

[18.14] Although the form of the Torrens system mortgage differs markedly from the general law, much of the nomenclature and trappings of the general law mortgage have been retained. Even a right of foreclosure survives though it is available only in most limited circumstances. The tension between the change in form and the retention of nomenclature surfaces when it is argued that general law doctrines apply to the Torrens system mortgage in areas upon which the Torrens system statutes are silent.

In *Perry v. Rolfe*,[30] Fullagar J. held that the rule that a mortgagee was entitled to her or his costs in a suit for redemption did not apply to an action in which a Torrens system mortgagor claimed an order that on payment of all amounts due, the mortgagee execute a discharge. Fullagar J. pointed out that the general law mortgagee's entitlement to costs reflected the absence of any legal rights once the date for legal redemption had passed. As the mortgagor was thus seeking a concession or indulgence from equity a condition of that concession or indulgence was the payment of costs. On the other hand a Torrens system mortgagor was entitled at law to have the mortgage discharged on payment of the debt and was therefore seeking to enforce his other rights. The mortgagor had such an entitlement even after default as the default did not take away the right to a discharge but was the basis of other compensatory remedies of the mortgagee.

By contrast in *Re Forrest Trust*[31] the Victorian Full Court held that the mortgagor's right to discharge the mortgage could still properly fall within the description of "a suit to redeem the mortgage". The term was used in the *Property Law Act* in reference to the limitation of actions in a situation where the mortgagee had been in possession. The Full Court pointed out that on payment the mortgagor was entitled to have the mortgage discharged and this right involved freeing the land of the interest of the mortgagee. The right thus conformed to the essence of what

29. Sykes, pp. 229-232; *Putz v. Registrar of Titles* [1928] V.L.R. 348; *Wright v. Registrar of Titles* [1979] Qd R. 523.
30. [1948] V.L.R. 297.
31. *Re Forrest Trust; Trustees, Executors & Agency Co. Ltd v. Anson* [1953] V.L.R. 869.

was understood by the concept of a right to redeem. The term "all right and equity of redemption" was used in the Torrens system statute in relation to what was taken away by foreclosure. The court concluded that the term redemption suit could apply equally to the general law and Torrens system.

The application of general law rules will depend upon an analysis of each rule and the Torrens system context. Whereas in *Perry v. Rolfe* there was good reason to displace the general law rule, in *Re Forrest Trust* no obvious alternative to the term redemption suit was used in the Torrens system statute and (given the application of the particular limitation of actions provisions to the Torrens system) no reason existed to exclude the limitation in relation to cases of mortgagees in possession.

3. Formalities for the Creation of a Mortgage

[18.15]   Under the general law the formalities necessary for the creation of a legal mortgage are therefore the same as those involved in the transfer of a legal fee simple estate. Consequently in all jurisdictions except Queensland a deed is essential; in Queensland either a deed or a signed written instrument is essential: see above [6.10].

In Victoria and Tasmania a short form of deed of mortgage is set out in a schedule to the property law statute.[32] The statute provides that such a deed is sufficient with respect to form and expression. In New South Wales and Western Australia the short form of deed of conveyance could be adopted for a mortgage by the addition of the proviso for redemption.[33]

Under the Torrens system there is express provision for the mortgage as a statutory charge. The form of the mortgage is set out in a schedule or regulations.[34] In Queensland, South Australia and Tasmania the document must contain an accurate statement of the estate or interest mortgaged and a statement of all encumbrances. In all jurisdictions the general requirements for the transfer of a legal interest under the Torrens system apply and in particular a legal interest will not pass until registration.

III.   PRIORITIES BETWEEN MORTGAGEES

1. Conflicting Mortgages

[18.16]   Priority disputes often arise in the context of mortgages because they are essentially paper transactions in which money is lent and security taken without any effect upon possession at least until default. In general the principles by which priority is determined are those by which priority between any legal or equitable interests is determined. The applicable rules will however reflect the fact that under the general law the first

---

32. Property law statutes: Vic.: s. 206, Eighth Schedule; Tas.: s. 70, Second Schedule.
33. Property law statutes: N.S.W.: s. 43; W.A.: s. 37.
34. Torrens system statutes: N.S.W.: s. 57; Vic.: s. 74; Qld: s. 60; S.A.: s. 132; W.A.: s. 106; Tas.: s. 73.

mortgage may be legal and all subsequent mortgages must be equitable and that under the Torrens system all mortgages may be legal.

Under the general law a legal mortgagee will have priority over a purported subsequent legal mortgagee and any subsequent equitable mortgagees because of her or his priority in time. The mortgagee acquires the full legal interest in the land. The only instance in which the mortgagee will be defeated by subsequent mortgagees is if he or she has been guilty of some conduct which will cause her or him to be estopped. The mortgagee will take free of prior equitable mortgagees unless he or she is regarded as having notice of their interests. As between equitable mortgages, priority according priority of time only occurs if the conduct of the parties can be regarded as equal. Priority may be upset by non-registration under the deeds registration system. In general an unregistered mortgage will lose priority to a subsequent registered mortgage where the mortgagee takes bona fide and for value.

Under the Torrens system priority amongst legal mortgagees will depend upon the order of registration. Even notice of a prior and yet unregistered mortgage will not of itself defeat a mortgagee otherwise bona fide and for value who first becomes registered.[35] Similarly a registered mortgagee has priority over prior equitable mortgages and any subsequent mortgages. As between equitable mortgages again priority in time only confers priority of interest if conduct is equal. What conduct causes postponement is a vexed question and competition between unregistered mortgages does not raise issues different from those of competition between equitable interests generally.[36]

2. Tacking

[18.17] The general law had some doctrines by which the priorities between mortgagees could be affected. These doctrines rest on established authority rather than any readily explicable principle. Their application to the Torrens system is also obscure.

[18.18] The most peculiar of the doctrines is that of "the plank in the shipwreck", a title which Professor Sykes tells us "evokes a vision of drowning equitable owners struggling for the lifebelt of the legal estate".[37] The doctrine applies where there are equitable mortgagees one of whom has advanced money without notice of a prior equitable interest but later discovers that interest. If that person subsequently acquires the legal estate he or she can rely upon that legal title to protect her or his security against the formerly prior equitable holder on the basis of the good faith purchaser without notice doctrine.

In *Bailey v. Barnes*[38] the claimant purchased what he understood to be an equity of redemption. However the holder of the equity of redemption was subject to a previous equitable interest which had arisen because the

---

35. *Zatiropoulos v. Recchi* (1978) 18 S.A.S.R. 5.
36. Priority between competing unregistered mortgages will depend upon such factors as the effect of the failure to lodge a caveat. See above [5.97].
37. Sykes, p. 325.
38. [1894] 1 Ch. 25.

power of sale under a previous mortgage had been improperly exercised. The title of the purchaser was therefore subject to this previous equitable interest which conferred a right to set aside. The holder of this right had granted a charge over his interest to the respondents. However the claimant paid out the legal mortgagee and took a conveyance of the legal estate. It was held the claimant could rely on his legal title to gain priority over the respondents.

Even this doctrine is subject to an exception in cases where the holder of the legal estate stood in the position of trustee towards the prior equitable owner. However the leading case establishing this exception is one in which the reason for a trust is on general principle difficult to discern. In *Mumford v. Stohwasser*[39] the subsequent equitable mortgage was an informal mortgage of a leasehold estate. The prior equitable interest was an informal sublease. The mortgagee took a formal legal mortgage but was held not to be entitled to priority because of a breach of trust by the lessee.

[18.19] The application of "the plank in a shipwreck" doctrine to the Torrens system has been denied by Holland J. in the New South Wales Supreme Court[40] and by Professor Whalan.[41] They argue that priority amongst mortgagees depends upon the time of registration and that the first mortgagee does not acquire the legal estate but has merely a charge. However it is possible that both a second and a third mortgage be created informally, that at the time of an advance by the third mortgagee the third mortgagee has no knowledge of the second mortgage, and that the third mortgagee then acquires the interest of the first mortgagee. Professor Sykes suggests that in this event the principle in *Bailey v. Barnes* should apply.[42] However, even without the application of the principle, in the absence of a caveat by the second mortgagee the third mortgagee could register the mortgage and thereby claim the protection of indefeasibility. Mere notice of the second mortgage before registration should not be enough to constitute a lack of good faith on the part of the third mortgagee.

[18.20] The more general tacking doctrine was that involving further advances by a prior mortgagee. It is possible under the general law for the prior mortgagee to be a first mortgagee and have the legal estate. In this case a further advance without notice of a subsequent equitable mortgage would form part of the legal interest and be protected against the claim of the subsequent mortgagee by the good faith purchaser rule. If the mortgage is equitable, assuming conduct is equal, priority depends on priority in time and a subsequent advance could not gain priority over a prior interest. The prior equitable mortgage may however require further advances. In this case the prior mortgage would cover the further advances and give them priority. It is however possible that the legal or equitable mortgagee has notice of the subsequent mortgage prior to

---

39. (1874) L.R. 18 Eq. 556.
40. *Matzner v. Clyde Securities Ltd* [1975] 2 N.S.W.L.R. 293.
41. Whalan, p. 70.
42. Sykes, pp. 461-462.

making the further advance. It has been held that once a legal or equitable mortgagee has notice of a subsequent mortgage, priority cannot be claimed for any further advance even when that advance is required by the prior mortgage.

The absence of priority for required advance was the basis of the decision in *West v. Williams*.[43] It was reasoned in that case that notice of the subsequent mortgage destroyed the obligation to make further advances. This decision was assumed to represent the law in Australia by Holland J. in *Matzner v. Clyde Securities Ltd*.[44] However Holland J. stated that it rested on a general principle of doing justice between mortgagees and held that priority for required further advances was preserved where those advances were to improve the land and thus enhanced the value of the property.

In Victoria, Queensland and Tasmania the general law rules have been displaced by statute although only the Queensland provisions expressly purport to apply to Torrens system land.[45] Under this legislation further advances may be added to a mortgage in priority to the claims of subsequent mortgagees in three instances (a) where an arrangement to that effect has been reached with subsequent mortgagees; (b) where the prior mortgagee had no notice of the subsequent mortgage when making the further advance; and (c) where the mortgagee is by virtue of the mortgage instrument under an obligation to make the advances. The major effect of these rules is to reverse the rule flowing from the decision in *West v. Williams*.[46]

[18.21] The general law approach to further advances has been applied to the Torrens system. However all the mortgages may be legal and in that event priority depends on time of registration and priority could not be claimed for a further advance not required by the mortgage instrument. Moreover as Professor Whalan points out[47] where the subsequent mortgages are registered the process of registration will involve application to the prior mortgagee for production of the duplicate certificate and thus clear notice of the subsequent registered interest will be given. If a voluntary further advance is made by a legal mortgagee where other mortgages are equitable, the variation can be registered and the varied mortgage would be protected by indefeasibility. If a further advance is made by a legal mortgagee pursuant to an obligation in the mortgage instrument it was assumed in *Matzner v. Clyde Securities Ltd*[48] that the rule in *West v. Williams*[49] would apply both to general law and Torrens system land. In Queensland the legislation altering this result expressly applies to Torrens system land; the application of the Victorian and Tasmanian legislation to Torrens system land is not clear.

---

43. [1899] 1 Ch. 132.
44. [1975] 2 N.S.W.L.R. 293.
45. Property law statutes: Vic.: s. 94; Qld: s. 82; Tas.: s. 38.
46. [1899] 1 Ch. 132.
47. Whalan, p. 173.
48. [1975] 2 N.S.W.L.R. 293.
49. [1891] 1 Ch. 132.

Where both mortgages are equitable the general law position seems to be maintained. Further advances will gain priority only if made pursuant to an obligation in the mortgage and only if made without notice of the subsequent mortgage. Again priority for required further advances even with notice will be conferred by the Queensland legislation and may be conferred by the Victorian and Tasmanian legislation.

IV. RIGHTS, OBLIGATIONS AND REMEDIES

1. Source of Obligations

[18.22]   In the case of a formal legal mortgage the rights and obligations of the parties are likely to be set out in the mortgage document itself. The position of the parties will largely depend upon these express provisions. Statutory provisions will only be relevant in so far as they set out requirements that override the express intention of the parties. However formality is not always observed; in the case of an equitable mortgage by way of deposit of title documents, no written agreement whatsoever may exist. In such cases implications to be made by the general law or by statute are most significant.

In Australia statutory terms relating to mortgages have been set out in both the property law and Torrens system statutes. To some extent the application of these statutes depends upon the nature of the instrument in which the mortgage is set out. Under both the general law and the Torrens system an informal mortgage is necessarily equitable. However it is possible that a deed be used in relation to an equitable mortgage, particularly if the property mortgaged is itself equitable.

[18.23]   Four questions arise with respect to the application of the statutory terms. First, with respect to informal mortgages under the general law the issue is to what extent the property law statutory terms apply. Secondly, with respect to Torrens system formal mortgages, the issue is whether the general law statutory implications apply. Thirdly, with respect to the informal Torrens system mortgages, the issue is whether general law statutory terms apply. Fourthly, again with respect to informal Torrens system mortgages, the issue is whether Torrens system statutory terms apply. These four questions will be considered in turn.

1. In all jurisdictions except Queensland the general law statutory implications are expressed to apply to all mortgages made by deed. In Queensland, the implications apply to all mortgages made by deed or by written instrument.

2. The application of the property law statutory terms to the Torrens system differs widely from jurisdiction to jurisdiction. In Victoria, all the mortgage provisions indicate whether they apply to instruments under the Torrens system. In New South Wales most provisions make an indication of application and where they do not it appears that the provisions do not apply. In Queensland, the provisions generally apply to Torrens system land except for instances of express inconsistency. In South Australia, the provisions generally apply to Torrens system land except for instances of

express inconsistency, and some provisions expressly do apply thus, as later provisions, presumably they override in the event of any inconsistency. In Western Australia the application of some provisions is expressed to extend to Torrens system land and that of other provisions appears to extend except for inconsistency. In Tasmania, all the mortgage provisions indicate whether they apply to Torrens system land.

3. The property law statutory terms will apply to informal mortgages under the Torrens·system if in any individual jurisdiction a positive answer is given to questions one and two. The position in Victoria however, is complicated by the statutory expression for the application of the property law terms to the Torrens system. Except for specified sections the provisions of the *Property Law Act* do not apply to mortgages under the Torrens system affected by instruments under the *Transfer of Land Act*.[50] An informal mortgage would not normally be described as effected by an instrument under the *Transfer of Land Act*. None of the property law terms are therefore excluded in relation to informal mortgages; their application therefore depends solely on the first question, viz., whether the mortgage was made by deed.

4. The Torrens system statutory implications have been asserted not to extend to informal mortgages under the system. In some instances this result seems to flow from the express reference to the exercise of a power by a registered mortgagee (New South Wales) or by the definition of "mortgagor" and "mortgagee" as the registered mortgagor and registered mortgagee (South Australia). Otherwise the proposition does not appear to be as clear as is asserted.

The matter is complicated by the potential application of the principle of *Walsh v. Lonsdale*.[51] In *Walsh v. Lonsdale* the tenant was said to be regarded in equity as holding on the same terms as if a formal lease had been granted. Because of the *Judicature Act* this interpretation of the tenant's position by equity entitled the landlord to the legal remedy of distress. If, in the case of a mortgage the mortgagee is to be treated as if a formal mortgage had been executed, this mortgage would then include the common rights of mortgagees or be deemed to include the statutory implications. On the other hand it can be argued first, that there are no common rights of mortgagees certainly not on the same lines as the statutory implications and secondly, that as the statutory implications are said to apply to actual formal documents they can be said not to apply to notional formal documents. The arguments against a broad interpretation of *Walsh v. Lonsdale* have been strengthened by the High Court decision in *Chan v. Cresdon Pty Ltd*.[52]

[18.24] A further restriction on the rights of an informal mortgagee comes from the strongly expressed view of Dean J. in the Victorian Supreme Court[53] that a mortgagee by deposit of title documents has no right to specific performance with respect to the grant of a mortgage

50. Property law statutes: Vic.: ss 86 and 102.
51. (1882) 21 Ch. D. 9.
52. (1989) 89 A.L.R. 522.
53. *Ryan v. O'Sullivan* [1956] V.L.R. 99 at 100.

generally but only to compel the vesting of legal title in the case of default. However as Professor Sykes argues[54] the act of deposit of title documents is an act of part performance making enforceable a contract and that contract must be one to grant a mortgage.

2. Promise to Pay

[18.25]   The mortgage agreement normally provides an express promise by the mortgagor to repay the loan and interest. In Victoria, Queensland and Tasmania, a promise to pay the principal and interest is in some instances implied by statute.[55] In any event, the promise to repay will be implied from the fact of the loan and the payment of interest will also be implied. Only the original mortgagor is directly liable on the covenant, as the covenant does not run with the land.

An action for the debt is regarded in equity as conditional upon the ability to reconvey the mortgaged property. Thus if the mortgagee has foreclosed and then disposed of the property, he or she is unable to sue on the personal covenant.[56] This condition does not apply where the mortgagee exercises the power of sale.

A mortgagee is able to take legal action to enforce the personal covenant. In the exercise of the remedies for enforcement of a judgment, the mortgagee may require the sale of the mortgagor's interest in the land. At such a sale, the mortgagee is able to purchase the mortgagor's interest.[57] This result seems to contradict the restrictions on the mortgagee's ability to exercise the power of sale in favour of her or himself. The result has been overturned by legislation in New South Wales and Queensland.[58]

3. Possession

[18.26]   Entitlement to possession in one right significantly affected by the difference between the forms of the general law and Torrens system mortgages. Under the general law the mortgagee is the fee simple owner of the land prima facie entitled to possession; under the Torrens system the mortgagor is the fee simple owner. The starting point of the two systems in relation to the right to possession reflects this prima facie entitlement. The right is qualified, particularly in the case of the general law.

The general law mortgagee is the fee simple owner from the time of the formal execution of the mortgage. As this ownership is the basis of entitlement to possession, the entitlement arises even before the nominal default after the six month period.[59] The courts have recognised the mortgagee's claim even where the mortgage sets out a schedule for payments and that schedule has been complied with. The only discretion

54. Sykes, p. 147.
55. Property law statutes: Vic.: s. 117; Qld: s. 78; Tas.: s. 28.
56. *Palmer v. Hendrie* (1859) 27 Beav. 349; 54 E.R. 136.
57. *Simpson v. Forrester* (1973) 132 C.L.R. 499.
58. Property law statutes: N.S.W.: s. 102; Qld: s. 97.
59. *Four-Maids Ltd v. Dudley Marshall (Properties) Ltd* [1957] Ch. 317.

has been said to be to allow a short adjournment to give the mortgagor an opportunity to pay off the mortgagee in full.[60]

[18.27] The traditional view has been challenged by the Court of Appeal decision in *Quennell v. Maltby*[61] a decision in which the leading judgment was given by Lord Denning. He framed his new rule on the basis that "in modern times equity can step in to prevent a mortgagee, or a transferee from him, from getting possession of a house contrary to the justice of the case". The mortgagee would be entitled to claim possession only where it was sought bona fide and for the purposes of enforcing the security. Claiming possession from a mortgagor not in default would not satisfy these conditions.

The case involved a most unmeritorious claim. The owner of a house had let the premises to two tenants for a period of one year. Before the expiration of the year, he granted a mortgage to a bank on terms which included a prohibition on leasing without the mortgagee's consent. After the grant of the mortgage, further one year leases were granted without the mortgagee's consent. The defendants became the tenants and stayed on after a one year lease as protected statutory tenants. The mortgagor then wished to sell but desired vacant possession to obtain a favourable price. After legal advice the mortgagor's wife paid off the balance owing to the bank and took a transfer of the mortgage. She then brought proceedings for possession claiming that as a transferee of the mortgagee she was not subject to the leases and had a general right to claim possession. For once Lord Denning was concerned to prevent widespread evasion of the Rent Acts.

[18.27] Whatever the status of *Quennell v. Maltby*[62] it has long been established that a mortgagee taking possession does so for the purposes of the security and must account for rents and profits received. This liability extends not only to actual receipts but amounts which ought to be received. The mortgagee has been said to be chargeable for the utmost value the lands are proved to be worth. If the mortgagee moves into occupation of the land and thereby decreases the income available from the land the mortgagee will be liable for the amount of income lost from the occupation. However merely because the mortgagee is in occupation he or she is not liable for a charge if that occupation does not reduce income. It is possible that an occupation essential to operate a business on the land which does decrease income will also not be chargeable to the mortgagee.

In *Fyfe v. Smith*[63] a mortgage had been granted over a hotel in the small New South Wales country town of Fifield. Upon default the mortgagees took possession. In order to run the hotel they occupied one room in the premises and used hotel facilities such as the dining room and laundry. Helsham J. held that the basis of the mortgagee's liability was to account for rents and profits received or those which would have been received but

---

60. *Birmingham Citizens Permanent Building Society v. Gaunt* [1962] Ch. 883.
61. [1979] 1 W.L.R. 318.
62. Ibid.
63. [1975] 2 N.S.W.L.R. 408.

for wilful neglect and default. As there was no evidence the room could have been let to or occupied by anyone who would pay for it, no liability arose.

[18.28]   The position of general law equitable mortgagee with respect to possession, is far less certain. An equitable mortgagee does not have the legal fee simple estate but as explained above has a promise of such an estate not a mere charge over the land. Professor Sykes points out that the difficulty faced by an equitable mortgagee seeking possession is the insufficiency of his title to support an action for possession.[64] That action is one in the nature of an action for ejectment which requires a legal title. Professor Sykes considers that for this reason an equitable mortgagee could not succeed in an action even if an express power to take possession is conferred by the mortgage agreement. He disagrees with the contrary decision of the Queensland Supreme Court in *Mercantile Credits Ltd v. Archbold*.[65] On the other hand he concludes that the equitable title would be sufficient to defend an action if possession was obtained peaceably.

[18.29]   The Torrens system legal mortgagee has no legal estate on which to base a claim for possession. Even on default by the mortgagor there is nothing inherent in the interest entitling the mortgagee to possession. However in all jurisdictions a statutory right to possession is conferred upon the mortgagee upon default by the mortgagor.[66] In New South Wales, Queensland, South Australia and Tasmania the right is limited to default by the mortgagor in payment of principal or interest and does not extend to breach of other covenants. Although in New South Wales, Queensland and Tasmania the right is expressed simply to be to receive the rents and profits; that phrase appears sufficiently broad to cover right to actual possession not merely a right to take the income from those in possession.

In Victoria and Western Australia the rights of the mortgagee are statutorily extended by a provision stating that the mortgagee shall have the same rights and remedies at law and in equity as the mortgagee would have had if the legal estate had been vested in that person as mortgagee.[67] So far as possession is concerned however, this right is expressly qualified by a right of the mortgagor to quiet enjoyment until default in payment of any principal or interest or a breach in the performance or observance of some covenant. This qualification however, means that the right of the mortgagee to possession is not limited to cases where the default relates to payment.

The rights of a Torrens system equitable mortgagee to possession are even weaker than those of a general law equitable mortgagee. They could

---

64. Sykes, pp. 155-157.
65. [1970] Q.W.N. 9.
66. Torrens system statutes: N.S.W.: s. 60; Vic.: ss 78, 86; Qld: s. 60; S.A.: s. 137; W.A.: ss 111, 116; Tas.: s. 82. In Victoria and Western Australia the mortgagee is expressed to have the same rights as if the legal estate had been vested in the mortgagee: Vic.: s. 81; W.A.: s. 116.
67. Ibid.

only arise upon default and then only upon a generous interpretation of *Walsh v. Lonsdale*.[68]

[18.30] A general law legal mortgage may confer an express right to possession upon the mortgagor until default. As the mortgagee holds the fee simple estate and the mortgagor is being granted a right to possession the mortgagor is a tenant of the mortgagee if the leasehold characteristic of certain duration is satisfied. If this requirement is not satisfied the tenant is a contractual licensee. An express landlord and tenant relationship may be created by what is described as an attornment clause. Such a clause is inserted to confer upon the mortgagee the benefit of a landlord's remedies for possession and the landlord's right to distress. Today it threatens to impose upon the landlords responsibilities under tenancy legislation. Nothing denies a mortgagee/landlord the landlord's remedies for possession or the right of distress in those situations where it is still exercisable. The Victorian, New South Wales, South Australian and Western Australian Residential Tenancies Acts expressly exclude landlords and tenants who are in a mortgagor and mortgagee relationship: see above **[11.02]**.

Under the Torrens system, the Victorian and Western Australian Acts create a landlord and tenant relationship by conferring a legal right upon the mortgagee subject to quiet enjoyment by the mortgagor until default. The tenancy is for the term of the mortgage subject to termination upon default. In other States, an attornment clause is commonly inserted. In these States a true landlord and tenant relationship cannot exist because the mortgagor has the fee simple estate. The express clause might however be considered to estop the parties from denying a landlord and tenant relationship. Professor Harrison has argued that a tenancy by estoppel cannot arise in such circumstances.[69] However there is much Australian authority to the contrary and similarly English cases concerning the parallel mortgages by deed of charge have accepted the creation of tenancies by estoppel.[70]

4. Leasing

[18.31] Under a general law legal mortgage, a mortgagor does not have any legal interest and has generally been assumed to have no right to possession. Consequently, the mortgagor cannot confer upon a tenant any rights to possession binding upon the mortgagee. As the mortgagor has no legal interest the relationship between the mortgagor and the tenant is one governed by the principle of estoppel preventing the tenant from denying his or her landlord's title. If the mortgagor has been granted a right to possession and holds as a tenant from the mortgagee, the relationship between the mortgagor and a tenant would be one of subtenancy.

68. (1882) 21 Ch. D. 9.
69. (1942) 16 A.L.J. 64 at 96.
70. Sykes, p. 246.

In Victoria, New South Wales and Tasmania, statutory powers of leasing have been conferred upon a mortgagor.[71] These powers are subject to contrary provisions in the mortgage. In New South Wales, the maximum period of such a lease is five years to take effect in possession not later than three months from execution; in Victoria, seven years taking effect within three months; in Tasmania, 21 years in the case of an agricultural or occupation lease, or 99 years in the case of a building lease taking effect within 12 months. In all States, the rent must be the best reasonably obtainable and the lease must contain a proviso for re-entry on non-payment of the rent for a period specified not exceeding 30 days. In New South Wales, the lessee's covenants under s. 84 of the *Conveyancing Act* 1919 may not be excluded. In New South Wales and Victoria, the powers are not exercisable after the appointment by the mortgagee of a receiver.

[18.32]   As legal owner, the general law legal mortgagee could grant a lease. The mortgagee could not however grant a lease binding upon the mortgagor after redemption, as it would be regarded as a clog on the equity of redemption. The New South Wales, Victorian and Tasmanian powers to lease conferred upon a mortgagor have also been conferred upon a mortgagee in possession.

[18.33]   Under the Torrens system, the mortgagor retains the registered legal estate and may execute a lease. However, the legal mortgagee also has an interest and the issue that arises is whether the mortgagor's lease restricts the exercise of the mortgagee's powers. In all jurisdictions it is provided that no lease of mortgaged land is valid and binding against the mortgagee unless he or she has given prior consent.[72] It is clear that a lease subject to this provision will not bind a mortgagee if made without her or his consent. But not all leases are necessarily subject to the section. In Victoria the section expressly relates only to registered leases; in New South Wales it has been held not to apply to oral or implied leases;[73] and in Queensland it has been held not to apply to unregistrable leases.[74] However there is significance to the question of what leases are subject to the section significant only if it can be implied that leases not subject to the section only if it can be implied that leases not subject to the section are binding upon the mortgagee even without her or his consent. There is no apparent source of a power to grant such leases and the power has been denied in the only modern Supreme Court decision on the topic.[75]

[18.34]   The Torrens system mortgagee's powers to lease are more limited than those of a general law mortgagee as the Torrens system mortgagee does not have a legal estate. Even in Victoria and Western Australia the lease would amount only to a lease of the reversion as the right to possession arises only on default. Again a lease lasting after

---

71. Property law statutes: N.S.W.: s. 106; Vic.: s. 99; Tas.: ss 19, 20.
72. Torrens system statutes: N.S.W.: s. 53(4); Vic.: s. 66(2); Qld: s. 52; S.A.: s. 118; W.A.: s. 91; Tas.: s. 64.
73. *Dancher v. Fitzgerald* (1919) 19 S.R. (N.S.W.) 260.
74. *English, Scottish & Australian Bank Ltd v. City National Bank* [1933] St.R.Qd 81.
75. *Australian & New Zealand Bank Ltd v. Sinclair* [1968] 2 N.S.W.R. 26.

redemption would be a clog on the mortgagor's equity of redemption. In New South Wales and Tasmania the powers to lease of a mortgagee in possession extend to a Torrens system mortgagee. In South Australia the mortgagee in possession is empowered to lease for a term not exceeding one year.[76]

5. Receivers

[18.35] A receiver is in effect a manager of the property who takes the income from the property and uses that income to pay off the mortgage debt. The advantages of the appointment of a receiver are that the mortgagee is not only freed from the actual responsibility of managing the property but if the receiver is stated to be the agent of the mortgagor the mortgagee is freed from legal liability for those rents and profits which he or she would have received but for wilful neglect and default.

[18.36] In all States a power to appoint a receiver is statutorily conferred upon a legal mortgagee.[77] The power extends to both general law and Torrens system mortgagees. In New South Wales, Victoria, Queensland, Western Australia and Tasmania the power is exercisable whenever the statutory power of sale given by the general law property statute or the Torrens system statute becomes exercisable. In South Australia the power is exercisable in addition when any power of sale conferred by the mortgage instrument becomes exercisable. In all jurisdictions the receiver is deemed to be the agent of the mortgagor. In New South Wales the appointment is required to be registered, in other jurisdictions except Queensland the appointment must be in writing.

In addition, as a result of statute and inherent equitable powers, a legal mortgagee may apply to court for the appointment of a receiver.[78] A judicially appointed receiver is an officer of the court and the agent of neither party. The receiver's duty is to get in the rents and profits and pay them into court. Traditionally, a legal mortgagee was denied a judicially appointed receiver because of the power to take possession. This bar to a claim has been removed but still a legal mortgagee must establish some basis for the appointment.[79]

[18.37] An equitable mortgagee would, according to the statutory terms, only have available the statutorily implied power to appoint a receiver without court action if the mortgage was granted by deed or in Queensland by instrument. However the equitable mortgagee under the general law or the Torrens system has always been entitled to apply to court for the appointment of a receiver. The reluctance to grant the remedy did not apply in cases of applications by an equitable mortgagee.[80]

76. Torrens system statutes: N.S.W.: s. 53; S.A.: s. 137; Tas.: s. 64.
77. Property law statutes: N.S.W.: s. 109(1)(c); Vic.: s. 101(1)(c); Qld: s. 83(1)(c); S.A.: s. 47(1)(c); W.A.: s. 57(1)(c); Tas.: s. 21(1)(c).
78. *Evans v. Coventry* (1854) 5 De G.M. & G. 911; 43 E.R. 1125; Sykes, p. 123.
79. Sykes, p. 123.
80. Ibid.

6. Sale

[18.38] The power of sale is today the most effective remedy of the mortgagee upon unremedied default by the mortgagor. The power however, represents a development in the form of the mortgage from its common law origins. A power may be set out in the mortgage agreement. In the case of a general law and Torrens system legal mortgage, it is implied by statute in all jurisdictions. The ability of the Torrens system mortgagee to convey a fee simple estate to a purchaser is also expressed in all jurisdictions.

The exercise of the power of sale is governed by a variety of rules. These rules specify when the power may be exercised, what notice must be given before exercise, the responsibilities of the mortgagee in carrying out a sale and the obligations of and protection for purchasers from the mortgagee. Because of the significance of the power of sale, these rules will be considered separately.

[18.39] With respect to an equitable mortgage, two questions about the power of sale arise: first when will such a power exist? Secondly, in the case of equitable mortgage of a legal estate, what power does the mortgagee have to convey a legal interest to a purchaser?

The power of sale is not inherent in a mortgage and in the case of a legal mortgagee comes about by statutory implication; consequently, an equitable mortgage will not without more confer such a power. The property law statutory implication will extend to an equitable general law mortgage where that mortgage is created by deed or in Queensland by instrument.

In the case of the Torrens system the implied power is on its face confined to registered mortgages and would extend to an equitable mortgage only on the broadest application of the *Walsh v. Lonsdale*[81] principle. The general law statutorily implied power of sale (requiring a deed, or in Queensland an instrument) does seem to extend to unregistered Torrens system mortgages in Queensland, South Australia and Western Australia. In New South Wales the power is expressed to be supplanted in the case of registered mortgages thus leaving the unregistered mortgage within its purview. In Victoria, the power does seem to apply even though the power is not one expressly applying to Torrens system mortgage since as it has been argued (see **[18.23]**) the provisions are only excluded in the case of registered mortgages under the Torrens system. In Tasmania it is specifically excluded. As well as statutory implications, a power may be conferred by the express terms of the agreement. In addition a sale may be available by court order at least in foreclosure proceedings.

The equitable mortgagee of a legal interest, if the mortgagee has a power of sale, is clearly able to convey an equitable interest to a purchaser. However the intention of the transaction will normally be that the mortgagor's legal interest was the security for the loan. It is fairly clear that the equitable mortgagee under the general law and under the Torrens

81. (1882) 21 Ch. D. 9.

system can convey a legal interest if the mortgage agreement contains an express power of attorney. It is also asserted that in the case of an express declaration of trust, the mortgagee could utilise vesting order powers of trustee legislation to have the court vest the legal estate in the purchaser.[82] It is equally asserted[83] that the purchaser's equitable interest is not of itself enough to enable the power to be utilised but is not obvious why this is so.

Where the statutorily implied power of sale is exercised, the power to convey a legal estate may be thought to be derived from the further provision that a mortgagee exercising the power of sale conferred by the statute shall have the power by deed to convey the property sold for such estate and interest therein as is the subject of the mortgage. However in *Re Hodson and Howe's Contract*[84] the Court of Appeal held that the interest, the subject of the mortgage, referred to the interest conferred upon the mortgagee, not that intended as the subject of the mortgage. In *Re White Rose Cottage*[85] Lord Denning considered that a power to convey a legal estate was conferred and dismissed the earlier decision on what seems an inconsequential change in wording adopted in England in 1925 but not in the Australian statutes. Harman L.J. was content to base the power to convey the legal estate on an express power of attorney. Salmon L.J. concurred in the two judgments. An Australian court may take the lead to a broader reading of the section. The power to convey a legal estate by deed obviously has no application to the Torrens system.

7. Foreclosure

[18.40] Foreclosure became an inherent part of the general law mortgage because of the equitable right to redeem even though the contractual right had been extinguished. Originally the power of sale was uncommon and foreclosure was the only means whereby the mortgagor could be deprived of her or his interest in the land. Foreclosure entitled the mortgagee to hold the land free from any right of redemption.

Under the general law foreclosure comes about by court proceedings. Foreclosure is available upon default, even in relation to interest only, without default in relation to the principal.[86] The proceedings involve two stages: an interim and a final order. Under the interim order the court directs that an account be taken of what is due by the mortgagor to the mortgagee and that upon payment of the amount within a time specified—usually six months—the mortgagee is to reconvey the land but that otherwise the mortgagor will be foreclosed.[87]

In all jurisdictions the court is given by statute a discretion to order a judicial sale in place of foreclosure.[88] Either the mortgagor or the mortgagee may seek such an order. The court has a discretion whether

---

82. Sykes, p. 154.
83. Ibid.
84. (1887) 35 Ch. D. 66.
85. [1965] Ch. 940.
86. *Twentieth Century Banking Corporation Ltd v. Wilkinson* [1976] 2 W.L.R. 489.
87. Sykes, p. 124.
88. Property law statutes: N.S.W.: s. 103(2), Vic.: s. 91(2); Qld: s. 99(2); S.A.: s. 44(2); W.A.: s. 55(2); Tas.: s. 27(2).

to accede to any application. The most common instance of the exercise of the discretion is where the amount of the debt is vastly exceeded by the value of the property.

Although foreclosure appears to extinguish the mortgagor's right of redemption, even it is not an absolute bar, though it is exceptional where a sale to a third party has occurred.[89] If the mortgagor can show some special circumstance leading to her or his failure to redeem and acts promptly, foreclosure may be re-opened; if a purchaser is involved, re-opening may occur if the purchaser had been aware of the circumstance justifying re-opening. If after foreclosure the mortgagee seeks to sue the mortgagor for the contractual debt, the mortgagee will be allowed to do so only if the mortgagee permits the foreclosure to be re-opened.[90] In Victoria, New South Wales and Western Australia foreclosure is deemed to discharge the mortgage debt (so that a later personal action is prohibited), and also to extinguish the right of redemption (so that re-opening is prevented).[91]

[18.41] Foreclosure is as much inherent in a general law equitable mortgage as a general law legal mortgage. It may well be more significant in such cases because of the more limited availability of other remedies for the mortgagee. Where the interest subject to the equitable mortgage is a legal one, foreclosure confers a legal title on the mortgagee. The court may direct a mortgagor to transfer the legal estate to the mortgagee. If the mortgagor is not before the court, in New South Wales there is an express power relating to such cases to make a judgment vesting the legal estate in the mortgagee.[92] In other jurisdictions the courts have to rely upon general vesting powers expressed to relate to trustees. Again as in the case of the exercise by the equitable mortgagee (see above **[18.39]**) of a power of sale, argument exists about the scope of these powers. But the effect of the foreclosure order is to vest the full beneficial ownership in the mortgagee and the vesting powers should be sufficient.

[18.42] As the Torrens system legal mortgage confers only a statutory charge upon the mortgagee and makes the power of sale fundamental to that charge, the existence of a power of foreclosure represents an adherence to historical tradition rather than an inevitable part of the transaction. However in all jurisdictions foreclosure is retained as a remedy of the Torrens system legal mortgagee even though subject to considerable restrictions.[93]

Foreclosure is available in all jurisdictions except Queensland through application to the Lands Titles Office rather than to the court. Application may be made if the following conditions have been met:

---

89. *Campbell v. Holyland* (1877) 7 Ch. D. 166.
90. *Lockhart v. Hardy* (1846) 9 Beav. 349; 50 E.R. 378; *Law of Property Act* 1936 (S.A.), s. 55b(3).
91. Property law statutes: N.S.W.: s. 100; Vic.: s. 87; W.A.: s. 53.
92. *Trustee Act* 1925 (N.S.W.), s. 77.
93. Torrens system statutes: N.S.W.: s. 61; Vic.: s. 79; Qld: s. 60; S.A.: s. 140; W.A.: s. 121; Tas.: s. 85.

1. Default in payment of principal or interest must have existed for six months.
2. The land must have been offered for sale at a public auction by a licensed auctioneer and the highest bid have been insufficient to meet the mortgage debt together with expenses of sale.
3. Notice of intention to apply for a foreclosure order must have been served on the mortgagor.

After the application is made and the Registrar is satisfied as to the matters stated, the Registrar offers the land for sale. This offer is made by a notice published for four consecutive weeks in the Government Gazette. After a time specified in the notice, not less than one month after the first publication, the Registrar may issue an order for foreclosure unless a sufficient sum has been been raised by a sale to cover the amount of the debt and the costs of the attempted sale and foreclosure. The effect of the order is to vest in the mortgagee the land free of any equity of redemption of the mortgagor and the interest of any person claiming through the mortgagor.

In Queensland, the Torrens system legal mortgagee is given a power of foreclosure but the statute is silent as to how the power is to be effected. The courts have adopted the traditional equitable procedure.[94] Upon a foreclosure order being made, they have ordered the mortgagor to execute a transfer or in the absence of the mortgagor utilised the somewhat questionable vesting powers with respect to trustees.

In Victoria, Western Australia and New South Wales the general law prohibition upon re-opening foreclosure applies to the Torrens system. In South Australia and Tasmania, the statutory statement that foreclosure vests in the mortgagee the mortgagor's interest free from all right and equity of redemption has been held to prevent re-opening.[95] It must be conceded that these statutory words are very similar to those of the traditional equitable order which did not have the effect of preventing re-opening. If foreclosure cannot thus be re-opened the mortgagee should not be able to sue on the personal covenant. In Queensland, although the common law procedure remains applicable to the Torrens system, the final effect of foreclosure is an order vesting the registered interest in the mortgagee and because there is a transfer an implied indemnity by the transferee to the mortgagor seems to prevent an action on the personal covenant by the mortgagee. However, re-opening of foreclosure does not appear otherwise to be restricted.

[18.43] The equitable mortgagee under the Torrens system has generally been regarded as not being entitled to the statutory powers of the mortgagee though the scope of the *Walsh v. Lonsdale*[96] doctrine has previously been argued to raise questions. In denying such remedies, the right to apply for a traditional court order for foreclosure has been

---

94. *Finance Corporation of Australia Ltd v. Commissioner of Stamp Duties* [1981] Qd R. 493.
95. *Campbell v. Bank of New South Wales* (1883) 16 N.S.W.L.R. (E) 285. This decision was approved in *Fink v. Robertson* (1967) 4 C.L.R. 864. The decision in *Campbell* related to New South Wales legislation since repealed but equivalent to the current South Australian and Tasmanian legislation.
96. (1882) 21 Ch. D. 9.

asserted so the remedy of foreclosure is clearly accepted. As in the case of the equitable mortgage under the general law, the courts' powers to effect a transfer in the absence of the mortgagor seem to rest on the vesting powers with respect to trustees.

8. Discharge

[18.44]   Upon payment of the mortgage debt the mortgagor will seek to hold the property free from the mortgage. Courts of equity saw this right as fundamental to implementing the concept that the mortgagee's rights were of a security nature only. The right was secured by the action of redemption. The protection for redemption extended to a number of doctrines invalidating impediments upon redemption—these are discussed in the next section of this Chapter.

Under the general law the redemption action is the means by which the mortgage can be discharged. In the case of a general law legal mortgage, redemption involves the reconveyance of legal title to the mortgagor. In the traditional form where the contractual date for redemption is artificial the mortgagor is seeking equitable assistance to procure that to which he or she has no contractual right. Consequently, the success of a redemption action was conditional not only on payment of the debt and interest but also of the costs of the action itself. Those costs were the price of the exercise of equitable indulgence or relief against forfeiture.

[18.45]   Whilst the traditional mortgage agreement in its fictional form provided for redemption after a period of only six months, a mortgage agreement may bind the parties to a programme of repayment over a number of years. The parties may seek the certainty of a fixed term and a fixed-interest rate. Movements in interest rates will mean that the parties may view their agreement as having become more or less attractive. If interest rates decline the mortgagor may seek to repay and discharge the mortgage before the contractual date for repayment. As discussed in the following sections on clogs on the equity of redemption (see below **[18.53]**) the courts upheld terms for repayment over a stated period of time.[97] In New South Wales a mortgagor is allowed to redeem early but only if he or she pays interest on the principal sum for the unexpired balance of the mortgage term.[98] Under the uniform consumer credit legislation the mortgagor may discharge a mortgage on tender of the "net balance due".[99] This term is defined so that in effect liability for future interest is extinguished. The applicability of the uniform credit legislation is considered subsequently: see below **[18.67]**.

[18.46]   On the other hand, where the mortgagor is seeking to redeem after the contractual date, the traditional rule has been that he or she should provide six months' notice of intention to repay.[100] This rule has

97. *Knightsbridge Estates Ltd v. Byrne* [1939] Ch. 441.
98. *Conveyancing Act* 1919 (N.S.W.), s. 93.
99. *Credit Acts*, s. 105.
100. *Grugeon v. Gerrard* (1840) 4 Y. & C. Ex. 119; 160 E.R. 945; *Cape v. Trustees of the Savings Bank of New South Wales* (1893) 14 N.S.W.L.R. (Eq.) 204; *McColl v. Bright* [1939] V.L.R. 204.

been asserted to rest on the indefinite time span of the traditional mortgage with an artificial repayment date. Because an indefinite mortgage was intended, the notice period enables the mortgagee to find alternative investments.[101] The application of the rule to mortgages with a fixed-repayment schedule and to Torrens system as well as general law mortgages has yet to be resolved. In the High Court Mason J. has referred to the rule but acknowledged criticisms of it.[102] In *Friend v. Mayer*[103] in the Victorian Supreme Court, Young C.J. considered the rule to be too well established even in relation to Torrens system mortgages to be overruled.[104] However Lush and Gray JJ. both expressly reserved any conclusion on the point.[105]

[18.47]   A mortgage may provide that on default interest will be payable at a higher rate, or that the total balance payable (including future interest) will become due. Such provisions may infringe the common law prohibition upon penalty clauses. The penalty doctrine has however, been subjected to some triumphs of form over substance. Whilst a higher interest rate on default may not be demanded, stipulation of a lower rate for punctual payment is acceptable. Similarly, the stipulation of liability for an entire amount subject to the acceptability of punctual periodic payments has also had some degree of acceptance.

On the whole however, acceleration of future interest on default is today unlikely to be acceptable. In *Wanner v. Carvana*[106] the balance payable, after 14 days' default with respect to any instalment, was expressed to include the balance of the principal and interest thereon at 10 per cent for the balance of the mortgage term. Street C.J. invalidated the clause as a penalty. He distinguished early cases on the basis that they had involved the form of an entire sum due whereas the case before him expressly required the calculation of unaccrued interest.

The general issue of penalties came before the High Court in the context of a fixed period leasing of goods in *O'Dea v. Allstates Leasing System (W.A.) Pty Ltd.*[107] That case involved the lease of a prime mover for 36 months. The consideration was stated in clause 1 of the agreement to be an entire rental of $39,550.32 due on the signing of the agreement with the proviso that if the lessee performed all the covenants of the lease and paid 36 instalments of $1,098.62 the lessor would not enforce payment otherwise than by instalments. Clause 12 provided that on default in any payment or performance of any covenant, the lessor might retake possession and the lessee's right to possession would thereby terminate. The lessee failed to make some instalments, the lessor repossessed, and sued for the balance of the $39,550.32.

101. Moerlin Fox, "The Redemption of Torrens System Mortgages After Default" (1950) 24 A.L.J. 311; Butt, p. 397.
102. *Hyde Management Services Pty Ltd v. F.A.I. Insurances Ltd* (1979) 144 C.L.R. 541 at 548.
103. [1982] V.R. 941.
104. Ibid. at 942-946.
105. Ibid. at 947.
106. [1974] 2 N.S.W.L.R. 301.
107. (1984) 57 A.L.J.R. 172. See also *David Securities Pty Ltd v. Commonwealth Bank of Australia* (1990) 93 A.L.R. 271 at 297-300.

The High Court held that in the circumstances the lessee's liability
under the contract amounted to a penalty and was not enforceable. The
majority of the court (Gibbs C.J., Wilson, Brennan, Deane JJ.) confined
the scope of their judgments by characterising the situation before them
as one of an action under clause 12 for money due after repossession. The
liability was therefore solely that upon breach and in such circumstances
the clause was a penalty. The majority therefore did not have to reach a
conclusion as to their attitude to clause 1. It was argued that liability
under clause 1 could not be a penalty as the liability was expressed to exist
irrespective of default. Gibbs C.J., Brennan and Deane JJ. all expressed
hesitation about such an argument, pointing out that the matter had to
be one of substance, not form, and that the argument had an air of
commercial unreality. Murphy J. took a broader ground and rejected the
traditional view that a statement of liability subject to an indulgence
would not prevent the liability from being characterised as a penalty if the
substance was that the indulgence was the liability in the absence of
default and the expressed liability operated only on default. Murphy J.'s
view would invalidate clauses allowing lower interest rates as an
indulgence for prompt payment.

[18.48]   The discharge of a mortgage under the general law would as a
matter of principle require the reconveyance of the land to the mortgagor.
In New South Wales and Victoria the necessity for reconveyance is
avoided by statutory procedures for an indorsed memorandum of
discharge and indorsed receipt under seal, respectively. In South
Australia and probably Western Australia and Tasmania if the original
mortgage has been registered under the deeds registration system a
certificate of satisfaction may be registered and operates as a discharge.
In all States except Western Australia the mortgagor may require the
transfer of the mortgage to a third person.

Under the Torrens system, the discharge of a mortgage requires
notification upon the register. In Victoria, New South Wales and Western
Australia the mortgagor must lodge a memorandum of discharge of the
mortgage. In Queensland, South Australia and Tasmania, the mortgagor
must lodge either the mortgage with a memorandum or indorsement
thereon of the discharge, or a separate discharge.

[18.49]   The discharge of the mortgage releases the land as security for
the debt; this release is separate from the discharge of the debt. The
discharge of the mortgage may not discharge the debt. However the
discharge of the mortgage may purport to do so. In *Groongal Pastoral Co.
v. Falkiner*[108] a registered discharge document did so purport. The High
Court held that the document was an instrument under the New South
Wales Torrens system statute and therefore had the effect of a deed. The
expression of full satisfaction of the debt in a deed discharged the debt.
The case clearly depends on the statement, in the document, of discharge
of the debt as well as of the mortgage, and such a statement is not required
in any jurisdiction.[109] Moreover the form of document for discharge may

108. (1924) 35 C.L.R. 157.
109. Cf. *I.A.C. v. Torulli* [1974] W.A.R. 125.

not amount to an instrument within the Torrens system statutes and therefore not amount to deed; even in New South Wales the forms have been changed.

Even the proposition that an expression of full satisfaction in deed discharges the debt has been challenged. In *Perpetual Trustees Estate & Agency Co. (N.Z.) Ltd v. Morrison*[110] the form of discharge read: "Received from the mortgagor (within named) this 2nd day of December 1974 all moneys intended to be secured by and being in full satisfaction and discharge of the within obligation." Roper J. held that the vital issue was that of estoppel—whether as a representation the receipt had induced the other party to act to their detriment. As both parties will normally be aware of the true state of facts, it is unlikely, though not impossible, that a receipt will have a prejudicial impact and thus form the basis of an estoppel. He rejected the earlier decision in *Broad v. Public Trustee*.[111]

The real issue seems to be whether a deed of discharge has effect of its own force irrespective of its force as a representation. A receipt normally has only evidentiary effect. "When the receipt in full was given, it was prima facie evidence against the plaintiff that the amount stated in it was paid. It was not conclusive evidence; because it is competent for the parties to contradict such a receipt, by shewing that the money was not in fact paid."[112] The position seems to be the same whether or not the receipt is given under seal.[113] However, whilst a receipt may come close to an implied release of a debt, it does not of itself constitute such an undertaking. A release of a debt supported by consideration is undoubtedly effective and a release under seal should be similarly effective. In some situations the doctrine of mistake may affect the validity of the release.

[18.50] Whilst some doubt exists about the scope of a receipt discharging both the mortgage and the personal debt, such a discharge is preferable for mortgagors than a mere discharge of the mortgage. Yet it is common in Australia that discharges are limited to the mortgage. Equitable protection for the right of redemption would seem satisfied by such a discharge as its concern is with the unfettered return of the property. There seems to be nothing in the equitable rules to require a statement of discharge of the debt. Consequently a mortgagor's claim seems to be no different from that of any other debtor who has fulfilled contractual obligations and any entitlement to a statement of discharge of the debt is lacking.

V. REDEEMABILITY

1. Clogs on the Equity of Redemption

[18.51] Courts of Equity overrode the stated terms of the parties' agreement (if necessary) to ensure that mortgagors got back their property

---

110. [1986] 2 N.Z.L.R. 447.
111. [1939] N.Z.L.R. 140; cf. Campbell, "Discharge of a Land Transfer Mortgage" [1942] N.Z.L.J. 173.
112. *Foster v. Dawber* (1851) 6 Ex. 839 at 843; 155 E.R. 785 at 787 788.
113. Guest, *Chitty on Contracts* (25th ed., 1983), pp. 811-812.

on payment of the debt, interest and costs. Wherever the transactions were in substance mortgages, the fundamental right of mortgagors to get back their property could not be taken away from them. Equitable intervention extends not merely to ensuring that mortgagors are able to get back the property but that any fetters associated with the property will not endure beyond redemption. At the same time, the right of redemption does not entitle mortgagors to pay off the mortgage at any time but redemption could be postponed so long as a real right to redeem was retained.

The leading Australian case of *Toohey v. Gunther*[114] provides a simple illustration of the basic prohibition upon fetters on redemption. The owner of a New South Wales hotel had entered into a mortgage agreement with the Tooth Brewery. The owner entered a further undertaking to obtain all drink supplies from Tooth Brewery until December 1935. The mortgage was discharged. A successor in title sought to sell the hotel and the purchaser declined to accept his title on the basis of the existence of this undertaking. The High Court rejected the purchaser's claim. The court held that a tie could not operate after redemption of the mortgage. The court further held that the unregistered covenant could not be enforced because of the principle of indefeasibility.

[18.52] Fetters of the sort involved in *Toohey v. Gunther* are directly attached to the mortgage property and if enforceable after redemption render the property less valuable than prior to the mortgage. The doctrine has however been extended to restrictions that have a practical effect upon the mortgaged property even though the property itself is free of restriction. In *Bradley v. Carritt*[115] shares in a tea company were mortgaged to a tea broker. The mortgagor agreed to use his best endeavours to ensure that the mortgagee would always thereafter have the sale of the company's teas and that if the teas were sold through another broker the mortgagee would have the commission he would have earned had the tea been sold through him. The loan was paid off. The company changed its broker and the mortgagee sued for breach of the agreement. The House of Lords held that enforcement of the agreement would burden the equity of redemption. The shares were of value mainly to tea brokers for the purpose of obtaining the sale of the company's teas. If the agreement were enforceable, the shares of the mortgagor after redemption would be frozen in the hands of the mortgagor as their sale would almost certainly result in his being liable for the loss of brokerage.

Covenants have however been upheld as independent from the mortgage. In *Kreglinger v. New Patagonia Meat & Cold Storage Co. Ltd*[116] a firm of woolbrokers lent 10,000 pounds to a meat preserving company secured by a floating charge over its assets. The loan was repayable on a month's notice. In the absence of default, the mortgagee could not call up the loan for five years. The parties agreed that during the five years, so long as the mortgagee was willing to buy at the best price otherwise available, the mortgagor should not sell sheep-skins to any other person;

114. (1928) 41 C.L.R. 181.
115. [1903] A.C. 253.
116. [1914] A.C. 25.

the mortgagor agreed to pay a commission to the mortgagee on all skins sold to another. The loan was repaid after two and a half years. The House of Lords held that the mortgagee was entitled to enforce the selling agreement. The court considered that the agreement was independent of, and separate from, the mortgage.

On the other hand, any artificial attempt to create separate undertakings is likely to be struck down. In *Toohey v. Gunther*[117] the mortgage and trade ties were set out in separate documents. The High Court held that wherever contemporaneous documents belonged in substance to the one transaction, equity would treat those documents as part of the mortgage transaction and apply its rules to them. In South Australia the effectiveness of the use of separate agreements is destroyed by s. 55a(2) of the *Law of Property Act* which declares that any covenant collateral to the mortgage has no effect upon extinguishment of the mortgage debt.

[18.53]   The continuation of a collateral covenant for a fixed period may be achieved by a prohibition upon redemption of the mortgage. In *Biggs v. Hoddinot*[118] a hotel was mortgaged to a brewer. The mortgage provided that the loan could not be repaid for five years and that during the continuance of the loan the mortgagors were to purchase all their beer from the brewer. The mortgagor sought to redeem before the five years and the mortgagee sought to restrain breach of the covenant. The mortgagee's injunction was granted. The postponement of the right to redeem was considered reasonable in the circumstances. The equity of redemption was not clogged or fettered as the tie ceased when the mortgage was repaid.

Postponement of the right to redeem must not render that right illusory. In *Fairclough v. Swan Brewery*[119] a mortgage for 500 pounds was granted to a brewery over a hotel lease for a term of 20 years. The mortgage was repayable by 209 monthly instalments, the last of which fell due about six weeks before the expiration of the term of the lease. The mortgage tied the hotel to the brewery. The hotelkeeper offered to redeem. The Privy Council held that the permission to redeem was a mere sham and effectively prevented any redemption. Redemption at an earlier date was therefore permitted.

Despite the statements in *Biggs v. Hoddinot*,[120] so long as there is a real right to redeem, postponement will be permitted so long as it is not unconscionable or oppressive without any judgment as to its reasonability. In *Knightsbridge Estates Trust Ltd v. Byrne*[121] the owner of substantial freeholds mortgaged them in 1931 to secure a loan of 310,000 pounds. The mortgagor was bound to pay by 80 half yearly instalments and the mortgagee bound to accept such payments. The price of money fell in the following years and the mortgagor sought a declaration that the mortgage could be redeemed prior to the expiration of the 40 years. The

117. (1928) 41 C.L.R. 181.
118. [1898] 2 Ch. 307.
119. [1912] A.C. 565.
120. [1898] 2 Ch. 307
121. [1939] Ch. 441.

Court of Appeal rejected the claim holding that the reasonableness of the postponement was irrelevant. What was essential was that there was a real right to redeem and that the transaction was not oppressive or unconscionable. It is however difficult to see that any issue of unreasonableness arose: the transaction was completed by two informed parties dealing at arms length after considerable negotiation.

2. Restraint of Trade

[18.54] The cases on the right of redemption have been subject to detailed analysis—probably to a far greater extent than their significance warrants. Meaningful reconciliation of all the decisions has so far eluded the many learned commentators. The principal cases arose in the early part of this century when the traditional interventionist role of equity ran up against the then dominant ethos of freedom of contract. Litigation in Australia was much less than in England. Today many of the issues are subject to statutory rules relating to company debentures and restraint of trade.

[18.55] Possible invalidity of provisions of company debentures because of constraints upon redemption is overcome by s. 150 of the *Uniform Companies Code*. The section applies to the provisions of any "debenture" but that term is defined in s. 5(1) of the code to cover any document evidencing or acknowledging the indebtedness of a corporation in relation to money lent to the corporation whether or not that document creates a charge on property of the corporation. Any written undertaking by a company to repay a debt would thus be subject to s. 150. The section provides that no provision of a debenture shall be invalid because the debenture is irredeemable or redeemable on the happening of a contingency, however remote, or on the expiration of a period however long. The section expressly overrides any rule of law on equity to the contrary.

[18.56] The rules as to restraint of trade are far more complex. These rules result from both common law doctrine and statute. The principal statutory provisions are sections 45 and 45B of the *Trade Practices Act* 1974 (Cth).

At common law any agreement in restraint of trade is valid only if that agreement is reasonable in the interests of the parties and the public. The common law has however, viewed ties between sellers and buyers with less suspicion than those between employers and employees. The common law has been prepared to accept exclusive dealing arrangements between seller and buyer so long as they are not too broad and provide safeguards for the buyer. Thus in *Peters American Delicacy Co. Ltd v. Patricia's Chocolates & Candies Pty Ltd*[122] the High Court upheld an agreement restricting a storekeeper to ice cream provided by the particular manufacturer. The court emphasised that the agreement was for a limited time and restricted the buyer only within a limited area and was subject to the supply by the manufacturer of ice cream at agreed prices.

122. (1947) 77 C.L.R. 574.

The application of the common law doctrine has also been restricted by an insistence that there be a restriction on a freedom previously enjoyed. Otherwise the agreement is not classified as imposing any restraint. In *Esso Petroleum Co. Ltd v. Harper's Garage (Stourport) Ltd*[123] the House of Lords held the doctrine to be inapplicable to a restrictive covenant in a petrol station lease tieing the lessee to a particular brand of petrol. The House of Lords argued that prior to the agreement the lessee had no right to sell any petrol on the premises and so was giving up no freedom in entering a lease subject to a restriction.

The *Trade Practices Act* controls originally related to contracts in restraint of trade. The High Court in *Quadramain Pty Ltd v. Stevastop Investments Pty Ltd*[124] relied upon the use of the common law phrase to import to the Act limitations inherent in the application of the common law doctrine. However after that decision the Act was changed to avoid the use of common law concepts.

Currently the two most significant provisions of the *Trade Practices Act* are sections 45 and 45B. These sections are mutually exclusive as s. 45(5) states that s. 45 does not apply where s. 45B applies. As a result of the definitions in s. 4, s. 45B applies to any covenant attached to or running with any interest in land. A covenant in a mortgage would seem therefore to be subject to s. 45B.

The substance of the two sections is very similar. Under s. 45 any contracts, arrangements or understandings which have the purpose or effect of substantially lessening competition are unenforceable. Under s. 45B any covenants which have the effect of substantially lessening competition are unenforceable. The key issue under both sections is whether the undertaking has a result of substantially lessening competition.

VI. UNCONSCIONABILITY

1. Equitable Unconscionability

[18.57]   The basic equitable protection for the mortgagor is commonly said to be related to the concept of unconscionability. "The lending of money, on mortgage or otherwise, was looked on with suspicion, and the court was on the alert to discover want of conscience in the terms imposed by lenders."[125] More particularly, the right to redeem at any time before foreclosure is linked to relief against penalties or forfeiture. The loss of the mortgagor's right to have her or his interest back because of failure to repay the loan by the named day, is seen as a penalty. Furthermore, equitable intervention was associated with ecclesiastics' concern to protect the spirit of usury laws—any advantage beyond repayment of debt, interest and costs amounted to a greater return than that allowed by usury laws.

123. [1968] A.C. 269.
124. (1976) 133 C.L.R. 390.
125. Per Viscount Haldane in *Kreglinger v. New Patagonia Meat & Cold Storage Co. Ltd* [1914] A.C. 25 at 36.

Even when the courts have restricted equitable intervention and promoted freedom of contract, they have added a clear proviso that enforcement of contractual terms is subject to unconscionability. In *Kreglinger v. New Patagonia Meat & Cold Storage Company Ltd*[126] the House of Lords indicated that after the repeal of the usury laws in 1854 a more relaxed attitude could be taken towards collateral advantages. Such advantages were to be struck down if they fettered or were inconsistent with the right to redeem. Such advantages were also subject to review for unfairness or unconscionability. In *Knightsbridge Estate Trust Ltd v. Byrne*[127] postponement of the right to redeem was upheld by the Court of Appeal. Again the court qualified contractual freedom by requiring a real and not illusory right of redemption. Again the court added the proviso that oppressive or unconscionable terms are not enforced.

The focus of these cases is to deny bases broader than unconscionability for equitable intervention in favour of a mortgagor. They therefore do not provide any analysis of what is meant by the qualification that unconscionable terms are not enforced. The *Knightsbridge Case* distinguished unconscionability from unreasonableness stating that unreasonableness was not a basis of intervention. The statements about unconscionability are made in the context of the right to redeem though the doctrine is expressed to apply to all terms of a mortgage agreement (or possibly to all terms of a loan agreement). The lack of specificity has led Professor Sykes to asset that the unconscionability doctrine is limited to two situations: those of undue influence and exploitation of expectant heirs in relation to reversionary interests.[128] Early cases applying the doctrine outside these situations are claimed by Professor Sykes to be based on protection for usury laws and to have lost force with the repeal of those laws.

[18.58]   The High Court has however, affirmed the existence of an equitable doctrine of unconscionability distinct from that of undue influence and applicable beyond contracts of mortgage and contracts of loan. The doctrine is said to apply wherever one party, by reason of some condition or circumstance, is placed at a special disadvantage vis-a-vis another and unfair or unconscientious advantage taken of the opportunity thereby created. This principle was affirmed and used as the basis of relief by the High Court in *Commercial Bank of Australia Ltd v. Amadio*.[129] The plaintiffs in that case had executed a mortgage in favour of the bank as a guarantee for the extension of credit by the bank to the plaintiffs' son. The plaintiffs had no appreciation of the perilous financial position of their son and their command of written English was limited. Without the guarantee, the bank's existing relationship with the son was markedly unprotected, the guarantee protected existing credit more than extended credit and the bank was engaged in a joint venture with the son through a subsidiary company. The bank realised that the son was the dominant

126. [1914] A.C. 25.
127. [1939] Ch. 441.
128. Sykes, pp. 49-50.
129. (1983) 57 A.L.J.R. 358.

member of the family and that the plaintiffs' understanding of the transaction was derived from him. The court held that the mortgage and guarantee should be set aside as the plaintiffs would not have entered the agreement if they had known the state of the son's account and its peculiar features.[130]

The common law doctrine of unconscionability was summed up by Mason J. in the following terms:[131]

> "Relief on the grounds of unconscionable conduct will be granted when unconscientious advantage is taken of an innocent party whose will is overborne so that it is not independent and voluntary, just as it will be granted when such advantage is taken of an innocent party, who, though not deprived of an independent and voluntary will, is unable to make a worthwhile judgment as to what is in his best interest."

2. Statutory Unconscionability

[18.59] Whilst the common law doctrine of unconscionability has been given significant effect in relation to mortgage agreements only in recent times, since the late 19th century statutory review of mortgage agreements on the basis of unconscionability has been available in some cases. This statutory review was contained in the moneylenders legislation.[132] Today there are several statutory bases for the review of mortgage agreements: consumer credit legislation; in New South Wales the *Contracts Review Act* 1980; *Trade Practices Act* 1974 (Cth), s. 52A; and in all States except Tasmania the fair trading legislation.

[18.60] The moneylenders legislation was based on English legislation and in general terms it was applicable where the loan was made by a moneylender (a person in the business of lending money). That legislation has been repealed in every State except Tasmania and replaced by consumer credit legislation.[133] Such legislation was first introduced in South Australia in 1972.[134] Subsequently, uniform legislation (referred to as the Credit Acts) was introduced in 1985 in New South Wales,[135] Victoria[136] and Western Australia[137] and in 1987 in Queensland.[138] For some time proposals have been current for further revised legislation drafted in plain English in all jurisdictions. The consumer credit legislation is slightly narrower than the moneylenders legislation in that

---

130. Cf. Meagher, Gummow and Lehane (2nd ed.), pp. 385-389.
131. (1983) 57 A.L.J.R. 358 at 363.
132. Pannam, *The Law of Moneylenders* (1965), pp. 277-302.
133. Duggan, Begg and Lanyon, *Regulated Credit—The Credit and Security Aspects* (1989), pp. 1-24.
134. *Consumer Credit Act* 1972 (S.A.).
135. *Credit Act* 1984 (N.S.W.): an earlier reform was contained in the *Consumer Credit Act* 1981. The 1984 Act was adopted in the interest of greater national uniformity.
136. *Credit Act* 1984 (Vic.): again this Act replaced *Credit Act* 1981.
137. *Credit Act* 1984 (W.A.).
138. *Credit Act* 1987 (Qld). Hereafter the references to the Credit Acts are to the four Credit Acts whose provisions are substantially uniform.

it is restricted not only to loans by persons in the business of providing credit but also to loans to consumers. The restriction to loans to consumers is achieved by excluding corporate borrowers and loans over a particular amount. The amount is low in the context of mortgage finance ($20,000 in Victoria, New South Wales, and Western Australia; $30,000 in South Australia and $40,000 in Queensland) (see below **[18.66]**) and many mortgage agreements would fall outside the legislation on this basis. Indeed it is more likely that a loan by way of second mortgage (taken out to cover a shortfall in the amount provided by a major loan) would be subject to the legislation. Because of the lesser security such loans have often contained more onerous terms.

The traditional English moneylenders legislation provided for relief where the interest was excessive and the transaction was harsh and unconscionable.[139] In Australia excessive interest has been allowed as a sufficient ground for relief as an alternative to harshness and unconscionability.[140] The traditional English requirement meant a borrower had to show both excessive interest and harshness and unconscionability. Whilst an excessive rate was accepted as evidence of harshness, to establish unconscionability a borrower had to point to some conduct by which advantage had been taken of the borrower's position. Capitalising on a desperate need for money is the most commonly cited example of such oppression.[141] Framing any agreement in a form most disadvantageous to the borrower and empty promises of future advances are other examples of oppression.[142] Oppression could be discovered in any of the circumstances relating to the formation of the agreement.[143]

In determining whether an interest rate was excessive the courts have been much influenced by the value of any security and the risk of non-payment.[144] In times of stable bank home loan interest rates the courts have looked to a lack of security and risk of non-payment to justify higher rates.[145] In an era of rapidly changing rates and a deregulated finance industry producing many sources of finance the issue of excessive rates is much more indefinite and the courts are likely to compare the rate charged with rates available for the particular transaction. Intervention is thus only likely where borrower ignorance has enabled a rate to be charged out of line with commercial rates.

[18.61]   The South Australian consumer credit legislation substantially broadened the basis for review by making excessive interest rates, harshness and unconscionability all alternatives. Any one of the grounds as opposed to a combination of all three may thus be used to justify relief.

139. Duggan, Begg and Lanyon, op. cit., pp. 79-80, 116-117.
140. "[T]ransactions may be perfectly honest, straightforward, open and above board in every respect . . . but if, notwithstanding all that, the interest is excessive, then the law enables the agreement to be re-opened": *Wilson v. Moss* (1909) 8 C.L.R. 146 at 163-164 per O'Connor J.
141. *W.F. Leane Ltd v. Dale* (1936) 39 W.A.L.R. 22.
142. *Popjak v. Finance & General Corporation Ltd* [1964] A.L.R. 340.
143. *Harrison v. Gremlin Holdings Pty Ltd* (1961) 78 W.N. (N.S.W.) 711.
144. *Bailey v. N.S.W. Mont De Piete Deposit & Investment Co. Ltd* [1918] V.L.R. 16; *Cloverdell Lumber Co. Pty Ltd v. Abbott* (1924) 34 C.L.R. 122.
145. *Popjak v. Finance & General Corporation Ltd* [1964] A.L.R. 340.

The Credit Tribunal[146] has made it clear that because the grounds for relief are alternatives, a claim may be based on either procedural or substantive unconscionability. It defined procedural unconscionability to include the use of surprise or oppression or the exercise of economic ascendancy; substantive unconscionability meant terms which were plainly unfair in the light of current trade, commercial and social conditions and existing legislation; in application substantive unconscionability meant a term which went beyond reasonable protection for the interests of one of the parties.

[18.62] This trend was substantially followed in the uniform consumer credit legislation. The Credit Tribunal is empowered by s. 146 to reopen a transaction which is unjust; injustice could be constituted by unconscionability or harshness or oppression or an excessive interest rate.[147] The Acts proceed to list matters which are to be taken into account in determining whether a transaction is unjust.[148] Those matters are:

"(a) whether or not there was any material inequality in the bargaining powers of the parties to the contract or mortgage;

(b) whether or not, at the time the contract or mortgage was entered into, its provisions were the subject of negotiation;

(c) whether or not it was reasonably practicable for the applicant to negotiate for the alteration of, or to reject, any of the provisions of the contract or mortgage;

(d) whether or not any of the provisions of the contract or mortgage impose conditions that are unreasonably difficult to comply with, or not reasonably necessary for the protection of the legitimate interests of a party to the contract or mortgage;

(e) whether or not—

(i) the debtor or mortgagor was reasonably able to protect his interests; or

(ii) a person who represented the debtor or mortgagor was reasonably able to protect the interests of the debtor or mortgagor—

because of his age or the state of his physical or mental capacity;

(f) the form of the contract or mortgage and the intelligibility of the language in which it is expressed;

(g) whether or not, and when, independent legal or other expert advice was obtained by the applicant;

(h) the extent to which the provisions of the contract or mortgage and their legal and practical effect were accurately explained to

146. *Anderson v. Shuttleworth* (unreported, South Australian Credit Tribunal, No. 03/013/75); noted Moore, "Consumer Litigation Before the Credit Tribunal" (1978) 6 Adel.L.R. 304 at 304-305.
147. Credit Acts, s. 145.
148. Credit Acts, s. 147. See *Tirant v. L.N.S Autos Pty Ltd* (1986) A.S.C. 55-470; *Roberts v. A.G.C. Ltd* (1986) A.S.C. 55-515.

the applicant and whether or not the applicant understood those provisions and their effect;

(i) whether undue influence, unfair pressure or unfair tactics were exerted on or used against the applicant—

   (i) by any other party to the contract;

   (ii) by any person acting, or appearing, or purporting, to act for any other party to the contract or mortgage; or

   (iii) by any person to the knowledge (at the time the contract was made) of any other party to the contract or mortgage, or of any person acting, or appearing or purporting to act, for any other party to the contract;

(j) the conduct of the parties to the proceedings in relation to similar contracts or mortgages, or courses of dealing, to which any of them has been a party; and

(k) the commercial or other setting, purpose and effect of the contract or mortgage.''

These matters primarily relate to procedural unconscionability and cover factors detracting from entry into a bargain of free will and with full awareness. Procedural unconscionability includes the exercise of economic ascendancy: paragraph (a). Factors of substantive unconscionability are incorporated by paragraph (d) not by reference to prevailing standards but by reference to undue burden on the complaining party or an unwarranted benefit to the other.

[18.63] The uniform credit legislation whilst compatible with the earlier South Australian credit legislation is more closely based on the New South Wales *Contracts Review Act* 1980.[149] This Act allows the re-opening of any contract considered to be unjust. In determining whether a contract is unjust a court is directed to have regard to a list of factors which (once allowance is made for the context) are identical with those of the credit legislation. The *Contracts Review Act* will only therefore be significant where the credit legislation does not apply. In the mortgage context those cases will be loans to private persons outside the financial limits of the credit legislation. This area of operation arises because the credit legislation operates upon loans for not more than $20,000, whereas the *Contracts Review Act* applies to any contract where a service is supplied to a person or entity other than a corporation and is supplied other than for the purposes of the trade, business or profession of the recipient or is supplied to a farmer.[150]

[18.64] The application of the *Contracts Review Act* to a mortgage agreement was considered by the New South Wales Court of Appeal in *West v. A.G.C. (Advances) Ltd.*[151] In that case a loan had been made to the

---

149. See Peden, *The Law of Unjust Contracts* (1982); Terry, ''Unconscionable Contracts in New South Wales: The *Contracts Review Act* 1980'' (1982) 10 A.Bus.L.R. 311.

150. *Contracts Review Act* 1980 (N.S.W.), s. 6(2).

151. (1986) 5 N.S.W.L.R. 610.

applicant (Mrs West) and a mortgage over the applicant's dwelling-house taken to secure the loan. The loan was guaranteed by the applicant's husband, a company, and three persons who were directors of that company. In fact of the loan of $68,000, $30,000 was used to discharge an existing mortgage over the applicant's home and the balance was provided for the company guarantor. The company had been in a difficult financial position and the applicant had been substantially advised by persons connected with that company.

The majority of the New South Wales Court of Appeal denied relief under the *Contracts Review Act*. They pointed out that A.G.C. had made a loan to the applicant at ordinary commercial rates to be paid over four years and took a first mortgage over the applicant's property to secure the loan. There was nothing relevant in the terms of the memorandum of mortgage or the deed or loan and guarantee which of itself was harsh, oppressive, unconscionable or unjust. Nor was it suggested that A.G.C. in any way sought to induce Mrs West to enter the deed or mortgage or applied any pressure to her.

The major argument for the applicant was that she had not received any independent legal or other expert advice before entering the agreement. The majority pointed out that there was nothing to suggest that Mrs West was incapable of protecting her interests because of age or physical or mental incapacity. Any advice she had received from directors of the company was not conduct for which A.G.C. was responsible. Nor was Mrs West without any advice. She had received independent advice from her son, an accountant, that she should not enter into the transaction at all. Moreover, she was also advised by a barrister that she should obtain more substantial guarantees from the directors of the company. The majority concluded that Mrs West ignored the advice given because she thought that the transaction was highly beneficial from her and her husband's point of view.

Kirby P. dissented. He based his dissent on the absence of independent advice. He considered that the advice Mrs West had received was from persons close to her and thus not properly independent. Kirby P. considered that there was not an absolute requirement of independent advice before mortgagors, such as the appellant, entered loan and mortgage arrangements with finance companies, such as A.G.C. However in some circumstances the finance company would take a risk that the court might subsequently decide that a contract was unjust if the mortgagee lender failed to protect itself and the mortgagor borrower, by insisting upon the interposition of appropriate independent legal or other expert advice. The case was one where a person with little experience was entering into an arrangement in which the risks were considerable and where the person's own dwelling was at risk under the contract. The finance company knew that the company to whom the money was being advanced was in a precarious financial position. Circumstances were so extraordinary that independent advice was demanded.

[18.65] A further attack upon unconscionable terms may be based on s. 52A of the *Trade Practices Act* 1974 or corresponding provisions of the

Fair Trading Acts in force in all States except Tasmania.[152] Section
52A(1) provides that a corporation shall not, in trade or commerce, in
connection with the supply or possible supply of goods or services to a
person, engage in conduct that is, in all the circumstances,
unconscionable. The *Fair Trading Act* provisions extend this prohibition to
acts of individuals. The actions must occur in trade or commerce so that
private loans are outside the sections. Services are defined to include the
rights provided under a contract for the lending of moneys. The subject
matter of the prohibition is conduct; although conduct may include the
making of a contract, the offence may occur in negotiations or in the
exercise of rights conferred by an existing contract. Relief in cases of
unconscionability includes all relief available for breaches of Pt V of the
Trade Practices Act 1974 and the equivalent parts of the Fair Trading Acts;
relief thus includes the granting of compensation or the setting aside or
variation of a contract.

The term "unconscionable" is not defined, but s. 52A(2) lists factors
which a court may take into account in determining whether conduct is
unconscionable. Those factors are:

"(a) the relative strengths of the bargaining positions of the
corporation and the consumer;

(b) whether, as a result of conduct engaged in by the corporation, the
consumer was required to comply with conditions that were not
reasonably necessary for the protection of the legitimate interests
of the corporation;

(c) whether the consumer was able to understand any documents
relating to the supply or possible supply of goods or services;

(d) whether any undue influence or pressure was exerted on, or any
unfair tactics were used against, the consumer or a person acting
on behalf of the consumer by the corporation or a person acting
on behalf of the corporation in relation to the supply or possible
supply of the goods or services; and

(e) the amount for which, and the circumstances under which, the
consumer could have acquired identical or equivalent goods or
services from a person other than the corporation."

VII.   CONSUMER CREDIT LEGISLATION

1. Impact of the Legislation

[18.66] The impact of consumer credit legislation on mortgage
agreements extends considerably beyond unconscionability review. The
legislation requires contracts to be set out in writing, with a statement of
the interest rate in a prescribed form, restricts some terms, regulates
associated contracts of insurance and guarantee, and imposes some

---

152. Vic.: *Fair Trading Act* 1985, s. 11A; N.S.W.: *Fair Trading Act* 1987, s. 43; Qld:
Fair Trading Act 1989, s. 39; S.A.: *Fair Trading Act* 1987, s. 57; W.A.: *Fair
Trading Act* 1987, s. 11.

restrictions upon the exercise of rights upon default. The uniform legislation applying in New South Wales, Victoria, Queensland, and Western Australia will be considered first and then differences in South Australia noted.

2. Scope of the Legislation

[18.67] To ascertain whether a mortgage is subject to the consumer credit legislation involves consideration of the scope of the legislation.

The uniform credit legislation does not apply to loans for more than $20,000, or in Queensland $40,000.[153] This upper limit remains whether the loan is unsecured, secured by mortgage over goods, or secured by mortgage over land. It is relaxed only in the case of loans secured by mortgage over a commercial vehicle or farm machinery. Moreover the legislation does not apply where the interest calculated as an annual percentage rate does not exceed 14 per cent per annum. Further where the lender is a credit union or a bank only the re-opening provisions apply.

3. Requirements of the Legislation

[18.68] The major impact of the uniform legislation is with respect to disclosure. Any contract subject to the legislation must be set out in full in writing and contain prescribed information.[154] The total amount of principal and interest must be set out in accordance with the requirements of Schedules; these requirements are designed, for example, to prevent disguise of interest as transaction charges. The time and place of payments must be set out. Interest must be stated as an annual percentage rate, again calculated in accordance with rules set out in s. 38 of the legislation.

The rights of a mortgagee upon default are subject to restraints from the Credit Acts.[155] These restraints operate first where the mortgagor experiences temporary difficulties. In New South Wales protection for the mortgagor in cases of temporary difficulties is extended by cognate legislation to mortgages over dwelling-houses of up to $67,500.[156] Where a mortgagor reasonably experiences a temporary inability to discharge obligations the mortgagor may seek a variation of the contract. Such a variation may be sought where inability stems from illness, unemployment or other reasonable cause. An approach must first be made to the creditor but if that is unsuccessful assistance may be sought from the Director of Consumer Affairs. If the Director cannot negotiate a variation he may refer the matter to the Credit Tribunal to determine an appropriate settlement.[157]

---

153. Credit Acts, s. 30.
154. Credit Acts, s. 36.
155. Credit Acts, s. 74.
156. *Credit (Home Finance Contracts) Act* 1984 (N.S.W.), s. 5.
157. See also *Celand v. Westpac Savings Bank Ltd* (1987) A.S.C. 55-581; *Wicks v. Wicks* (1987) A.S.C. 55-547.

The rights of the mortgagee are further restrained under the Credit Acts in that notice is made a prerequisite to the enforcement of rights. The taking of any legal action, the exercise of any remedies or the advancement of the time for payment may only proceed after default, notice of that default and the passing of a month from the notice. If the default is remedied during that time no action may be taken.[158] Furthermore, any clause resulting in default may be challenged in the re-opening proceedings referred to above.[159] Also the burdens of the mortgage may be reduced by the exercise of the right conferred by s. 105 to pay off the mortgage at any time. This payment need be only of the net balance due, a sum calculated to include only the accrued credit charge.[160]

4. South Australian Legislation

[18.69]   South Australia has its own consumer credit legislation. That legislation applies to loans secured by a mortgage over a dwelling-house for an amount not exceeding $30,000. Formality requirements similar to those applying in Victoria are imposed by s. 40 of the *Consumer Credit Act* 1972. Relief against default caused by temporary difficulties may be sought under s. 38 of the *Consumer Transactions Act* 1972. No further action may be taken with respect to any default which has been remedied.[161]

South Australia also limits the exercise of rights upon default through the *Law of Property Act*. The relevant provisions of this Act apply to any loan secured by a mortgage over a dwelling-house or property used for the purpose of primary production.[162] The provisions restrict the exercise of the remedies of sale, taking possession, foreclosure and the advancement of the time of payment of any money. The remedies must await default, notice of default and the passing of one month.[163] In addition application may be made to court for relief against the exercise of the rights.[164]

VIII.   POWER OF SALE

1. Introduction

[18.70]   The power of sale is today the most significant remedy of a mortgagee in the event of default by a mortgagor. It is regularly exercised in both commercial and consumer dealings.

2. Prerequisites to Exercise

[18.71]   The Torrens system mortgage differs fundamentally from the general law mortgage in making the power of sale central to the

---

158. Credit Acts, s. 107.
159. Credit Acts, ss 145, 146.
160. Defined in s. 11 of the Credit Acts.
161. *Consumer Credit Act* 1972 (S.A.), s. 42(3).
162. *Law of Property Act* 1936 (S.A.), s. 55a(5).
163. Section 55a(1), (2).
164. Section 55a(3).

mortgagee's security whereas under the general law it was but one of the powers of a mortgagee. The general law position is borne out by current property law statutes which incorporate the power of sale as an implied power of the mortgagee.

Under the Torrens system the mortgagee is entitled to exercise the power of sale where there has been default in payment of mortgage moneys or in observance of any other covenant for a period of one month, notice is served upon the mortgagor and the default is not rectified within one month. On the other hand the property law statutes confer a power of sale in the event of default of payment but provide that the power conferred by the statute cannot be exercised until failure within one month to comply with a notice of demand for payment, or interest is in arrears for one month or there has been breach of some other covenant.

[18.72] The Torrens system statutes expressly allow the periods of default before notice and of non-compliance after notice to be varied by the parties. That ability leaves open the question whether the mortgage may provide for sale without any notice of default at all. In Tasmania there is express provision that notice may be waived.[165] The Torrens system statutes all allow any covenant or power by the statutes implied in any instrument to be negatived or modified by express declaration. However the power of sale is not expressed as something implied in an instrument but as an inherent right flowing from the existence of the mortgage.

Consequently notice of default can be argued to be an inherent feature of the power of sale conferred by the Torrens system statutes and an instrument attempting to dispense with notice altogether is inconsistent with the basic structure of the legislation and should be denied registration.

This conclusion is supported by Professor Sykes and by recent cases. Whilst authority is not clear-cut more recent cases support this result. In an early New Zealand case *Public Trustee v. Morrison*[166] Denniston J. stated in relation to the argument advanced above that he could "see nothing in the Act warranting this contention, and the practice has certainly been to the contrary".[167] By contrast, in *Hall v. Hall*[168] the mortgage did purport to give the mortgagee the right to sell immediately upon default. Money being due and owing, the mortgagee took possession of the property. He then advertised the land for sale without any notice to the mortgagor. Matthews J. held that a mortgagee seeking to exercise the statutory power of sale had to give notice in conformity with the Torrens system statute. A similar approach was taken in the New Zealand case of *Jaffe v. Premier Motors Ltd.*[169]

---

165. *Land Titles Act* 1980, s. 80.
166. (1894) 12 N.Z.L.R. 423 at 426.
167. See also *Skinner v. Crabb* (1878) 5 Q.S.R. 131; *Campbell v. Commercial Banking Company of Sydney* (1881) N.S.W.R. 375 at 3898.
168. [1956] Q.W.N. 28.
169. [1960] N.Z.L.R. 146.

[18.73] Under the Torrens system statutes, the notice is a notice of breach—in the payment of principle or interest or the observance of any covenant. Again if this structure is regarded as an inherent part of the mortgage, exercise of the power of sale otherwise than upon breach appears not to be allowed. In Western Australia, express recognition is given to a power of sale in default of payment due on demand.[170]

3. Requirement of Notice

[18.74] Traditionally, the parties have been left free to vary the periods of notice and perhaps even to dispense with any requirement of notice. The idea of compulsory notice before repossession of goods was part of the uniform hire-purchase legislation of 1959 and has been maintained in the current consumer credit legislation. It is therefore not surprising that notice before the exercise of the power of sale be made compulsory in cases of land mortgages at least where the mortgages relate to a private dwelling-house. In Queensland and New South Wales[171] one month's notice must be given in separate forms according to whether the default is in the payment of money or compliance with other covenants. In South Australia one month's notice must be given where the mortgage relates to a dwelling or land used for the purpose of primary production.[172]

As with the prerequisites to notice, the Torrens system statutes are more specific as to the form of notice than the general law statutes. The latter simply require service of a notice requiring payment. Under the Torrens system statutes the notice is to be in writing and it is to require the mortgagor to correct the default. It is to state that sale will be effected if the default is continued. Alternative methods of service are provided for: the mortgagee may leave notice on the mortgaged land or may leave it at the last known place of abode of the mortgagor. However, details of the default and the steps necessary to correct that default are not required. Even the precise date by which the power of sale becomes exercisable does not have to be specified.

[18.75] The courts have not interpreted the notice requirements to require information for the mortgagor. In the early Victorian case of *Ewart v. General Finance Guarantee & Agency Society (Australasia)*[173] a notice stating that "the company hereby requires you to pay the money owing on mortgage from you to the company" was accepted as valid. This approach was explicitly approved in *Kay's Leasing Corporation Pty Ltd v. C.S.R. Provident Fund Nominees Pty Ltd*.[174] There the notice read: "whereas

---

170. *Property Law Act* 1969 (W.A.), s. 59(1); *Transfer of Land Act* 1898 (W.A.), s. 107.
171. *Property Law Act* 1974 (Qld), applying to both general law and Torrens system mortgages. *Conveyancing Act* 1919 (N.S.W.), s. 111, applying to general law mortgages and *Real Property Act* 1900 (N.S.W.), ss 57, 58A, applying to Torrens system mortgages. See also Butt, p. 421 and *Carr v. Finance Corporation of Australia Ltd* (1982) 56 A.L.J.R. 730. In New South Wales the notice with respect to breaches other than those for the repayment of money may be dispensed with by express agreement: *Conveyancing Act* 1919 (N.S.W.), s. 109(2).
172. *Law of Property Act* 1936 (S.A.), s. 55a.
173. (1889) 15 V.L.R. 625.
174. [1962] V.R. 429.

default has been made in the due payment of interest to [the mortgagee] . . . Take notice that if the said default continues for a period of 14 days from the date of service of this notice the said mortgagee intends to exercise the powers of sale conferred on it by s. 77 of the *Transfer of Land Act* 1958." Adam J. held that the recital of the fact of default and the notice that the power of sale would be exercised if such default continued, fulfilled the statutory requirements.

By contrast a strict construction has been given to the recent South Australian compulsory notice provisions on the basis that they serve consumer protection purposes. In *Commonwealth Development Bank of Australia Ltd v. Cormack*[175] a letter was sent by a mortgagee demanding payment and threatening action. The notice was required by statute to allege a breach and to demand its remedy within one month or a longer stipulated time. The court concluded that although a threatening letter is normally assumed to reflect a breach, there was in fact no allegation of breach. The letter therefore did not amount to a sufficient notice.

4. Erroneous Notice

[18.76]   If the statutory notice can be short of detail for the mortgagor, the courts have accepted that even an erroneous notice is not invalid. If a notice demands more than is due it may still form the basis for the exercise of the power of sale. The mortgagor can only avoid sale by tendering the correct amount due. Tender can only be excused if the mortgagor can show that such tender would not have been accepted. Explicit evidence of non-preparedness to accept tender of the correct amount has been required.

This approach was most clearly adopted in the drawn-out and bitter litigation in *Campbell v. Commercial Banking Co. (Sydney)*.[176] In an appeal to the Privy Council from the first trial of this action it was directly held that a notice is not bad because it demands more than is due. Moreover, the Privy Council held that a demand for a larger amount than that due does not do away with the necessity for tendering what is actually due, unless there is at the same time a refusal to receive the correct amount. In two subsequent appeals to the Full Court of the Supreme Court, consideration turned to what would amount to evidence of a refusal to accept a lesser sum. In the course of three trials, it emerged that the mortgagee had entered a contract of sale prior to the notice of demand, the mortgagee was in possession and had not responded to the mortgagor's request for an account, and that when asked what was owing an assistant accountant of the mortgagee had stated that the money could not be accepted because of the sale. Nonetheless the Supreme Court held that there was no evidence that the bank would have refused tender of the correct amount owing.

The case is an emphatic 19th century statement of the debtor's duty to seek out her or his creditor. It contrasts with the strict construction placed on recent notice requirements with an avowed consumer protection aim.

175. (1983) 108 L.S.J.S. 38.
176. (1881) 2 N.S.W.R. 375 at 389, 397.

However the decision was applied in the 1970 New Zealand case of *Clyde Properties Ltd v. Tasker*.[177] In that case the notice of demand specified a default of failure to pay the principal of 5,500 pounds when the principal owing was 5,000 pounds. Further it required payment of interest when interest had not been specified as in default and thus arguably, as a result of relevant legislation, could not be the basis of a power of sale. The court applied the *Campbell* principle even though there was earlier New Zealand authority which had sought to distinguish that case.

5. Nature of the Sale

[18.77]   By statute the mortgagee is given considerable flexibility in disposing of the land. The mortgagee may sell by public auction or private contract or by a combination of auction and contract. The mortgagee may sell the land altogether or in lots. The mortgagee may sell subject to such conditions as thought fit. Thus sales on credit are allowed.[178]

The mortgagee may sell the land or any part of the land. Where a mortgage covers more than one parcel the mortgagee may sell any one or more parcels, but even where there is only one parcel the sale of part in consequence of subdivision is allowed (subject to planning restrictions). However, although fixtures are part of the land and may be sold with the land they cannot be sold separately. Once severed they cease to be part of the land and therefore beyond that which the mortgagee is entitled to sell.[179]

6. Title Free From Encumbrances

[18.78]   The Torrens system mortgagee does not hold legal title and the mortgagee's ability to pass title depends upon statutory provisions. The statutes provide for an ability to make binding contracts and to pass title free from encumbrances. The statutes provide that upon registration a purchaser from the mortgagee will hold free from all mortgages and encumbrances registered after the mortgage.

The existence of a registered mortgage does not impose any restrictions, other than economic, upon the mortgagor in dealing with the land. The mortgagor may create any range of interests in the land and these interests will be valid though subject to the interest of the mortgagee. It is only if the mortgagee sells that these interests are defeated. The subsequent interests may be created by registered dealings or be the result of unregistered dealings. The statutes are clear in conferring protection for the purchaser from the mortgagee against holders of subsequent registered interests. Holders of unregistered interests should be in no better position yet the statutes are not as explicit in relation to them and particular problems may arise if the holders do as they would be well advised to do and lodge caveats.

177. [1970] N.Z.L.R. 754.
178. *Wright v. New Zealand Farmers Co-operative Assoc. of Canterbury Ltd* [1939] A.C. 439.
179. *Kay's Leasing Corporation Pty Ltd v. C.S.R. Provident Fund Nominees* [1962] V.R. 429; see also *Re Penning; Ex parte State Bank of South Australia* (1989) 89 A.L.R. 447.

[18.79] In *Forster v. Finance Corporation of Australia Ltd*[180] a registered mortgagee had, pursuant to its power of sale, entered into a contract of sale with Forster. Forster discovered the existence of caveats lodged by subsequent equitable mortgagees and sought to rescind on the basis that the vendor could not make good title. Forster's argument was upheld. The court concluded that registration of a transfer from the mortgagee would be impossible whilst the caveats remained. The purchaser would not be protected by statutory priority for the purchaser over the holder of an unregistered mortgage, charge, or encumbrance because the caveat was not an encumbrance.

The purchaser would be entitled to the benefit of provisions relating to the lapsing of caveats. If the transfer were lodged, the Registrar would be required to give notice to the caveator and the caveator would be required to take proceedings to defend the caveat or it would lapse. The caveator would have no grounds of defence. However a purchaser may be unwilling to rely upon these rights and could not be forced to accept a title involving such disputation.

Prior to any contract a mortgagee is entitled to bring proceedings for the removal of a caveat as a person adversely affected by the caveat. An early Victorian ruling that removal of a caveat will not be required simply because the caveat will interfere with some future intended dealing with the land has been overruled in *Commercial Bank of Australia v. Shierholter*.[181] The Full Court in *Shierholter* pointed out that in proceedings challenging a caveat, the court had a wide discretion and that an equitable mortgagee should not be able to interfere with the proper exercise of the power of sale of a registered mortgagee. This decision accords with single instance decisions in other States.[182] The court does have a discretion as to the approriate order and where the propriety of the exercise of the power of sale was in question could allow the caveat to remain.

[18.80] If the holder of an interest subsequent to a registered mortgage lodges a caveat forbidding all dealings in the land, it is arguable that the caveat is defective or improper in form. As argued above, such a caveat does prevent registration of a transfer from the mortgagee to a purchaser pursuant to valid exercise of the power of sale. Yet the caveator has no right to prevent such a sale. Thus the caveat can be argued to extend beyond the proper protection of the interest claimed. The caveat should take a more qualified form.

7. Mortgagee's Duties

[18.81] The exercise of the mortgagee's power of sale has a considerable impact upon the mortgagor. Not only does the mortgagor lose any interest in the land but the comparison between the price obtained and the debt owing determines whether the mortgagor remains in debt or receives some surplus. Of course the mortgagee has a financial interest to obtain

180. [1980] V.R. 63.
181. [1981] V.R. 344.
182. *Kerabee Park Pty Ltd v. Daley* [1978] 2 N.S.W.I.R. 222; *Re Stewart Fitzsimmons Projects Pty Ltd's Caveats* [1976] Qd R. 187.

a price sufficient to cover the debt especially as the mortgagor is by
definition in default. However, it has been clearly established that beyond
this financial interest the mortgagee cannot disregard the interest of the
mortgagor.

[18.82] The existence of the mortgagee's duty to act so as not to
sacrifice the mortgagor's interest was affirmed by the High Court in *Barns
v. Queensland National Bank Ltd.*[183] The issue again surfaced in *Pendlebury v.
Colonial Mutual Life Assurance Society Ltd.*[184] That case involved a mortgagee
sale of a block of 640 acres of land in the mallee country of north western
Victoria. The land was sold at an auction held in Melbourne. That
auction was advertised in two Melbourne newspapers. The advertisement
contained only a Land Titles Office reference to the land and a general
statement as to its location. The location of the land was not specified and
no indication was given of the nature of the soil, that the land was cleared,
partially under crop, divided into paddocks, within a mile of a water
channel or of the amount of the balance due to the Crown. The court
concluded that with respect to both the extent of advertising and the
content of the advertisements the mortgagee had acted in absolute
disregard of the interests of the mortgagor.

The High Court in *Pendlebury's* case concentrated upon an analysis of
the facts which all pointed to the mortgagee's attempting only to recapture
the amount of the mortgage debt. Indeed there was considerable
argument as to collusion between the mortgagee's agent and the
purchaser. The court accepted a statement of principle that a mortgagee
must not recklessly or wilfully sacrifice the interests of the mortgagor and
that if the mortgagor does so he or she is not to be regarded as having
acted in good faith.[185] Barton J. suggested that good faith included
fairness. On the other hand Isaacs J. stated that lack of good faith did not
extend to mere negligence or carelessness.

[18.83] In Australia the nature of the duty remains unresolved. On four
occasions subsequent to *Pendlebury* the High Court has dealt with the
matter inconclusively.[186] In *Forsyth v. Blundell*, Menzies J. stated that the
duty to take reasonable precautions to obtain a proper price was but part
of the duty to act in good faith. In *Commercial & General Acceptance Ltd v.
Nixon* the court had to apply the Queensland statutory duty of a mortgagee
to take reasonable care. The court held that the mortgagee did not escape
liability for improper exercise of the power merely by employing reputable
agents to conduct the sale. Aickin J. indicated however, that he
considered that the common law duty equated with that of the
Queensland statute.

183. (1906) 3 C.L.R. 925.
184. (1912) 13 C.L.R. 676.
185. (1912) 13 C.L.R. 676 at 694.
186. *Latec Investments Ltd v. Hotel Terrigal Pty Ltd* (1965) 113 C.L.R. 265; *Forsyth v.
Blundell* (1973) 129 C.L.R. 477; *Australian & New Zealand Banking Group v.
Bangadilly Pastoral Co. Pty Ltd* (1978) 52 A.L.J.R. 529; and *Commercial & General
Acceptance Ltd v. Nixon* (1981) 56 A.L.R. 130.

State courts have tended to apply a duty of good faith as opposed to a duty of reasonable care.[187] Zelling J. has argued that a duty of care is inappropriate as a mortgagee is doing something he or she is entitled to do and is justified in putting her or his interests first.[188] However all duties are limitations upon justified conduct in the interests of others. As was said by Lush J. in *Henry Roach*: "A mortgagee in exercising his powers is entitled to give first consideration to his own interests, a concept which is consistent with having regard to the interests of others or with taking reasonable care to protect the interests of others, what is reasonable being assessed in light of the fact that not only is the mortgagee entitled to give his own interest first consideration, but also that the reason for the existence of the power is to protect those interests."[189]

On the other hand the English Court of Appeal has unequivocally opted for a duty of care. In *Cuckmere Brick Co. Ltd v. Mutual Finance Ltd*[190] the court held that a mortgagee must take reasonable care to obtain a proper price for the land in the interest of the mortgagor. This duty has been extended in favour of guarantors of the mortgagor; it has been imposed upon a receiver in favour of the mortgagor and guarantor.[191] Adopting general negligence principles, Lord Denning asserted that the mortgagor and guarantor are in very close proximity to those conducting a sale and the duty of care is owing to them—even if possibly not to the general body of creditors of the mortgagor. The receiver is an agent of the mortgagor and because of this relationship owes a duty of care to the mortgagor. The duty was extended by the Court of Appeal to a guarantor who was only liable to the extent of the mortgagor.

[18.84] One of the mortgagee's rights has long been considered to be that to force an immediate sale though the market be unfavourable. The precise timing may have to be chosen with regard to the mortgagor's interest. In *Standard Chartered Bank* it was alleged that one reason for a low price was that the sale was at the wrong time of the year. Lord Denning commented: "There are several dicta to the effect that the mortgagee can choose his own time for the sale, but I do not think this means that he can sell at the worst possible time."[192]

If Australian courts impose a duty of care upon a mortgagee they must then decide whether to extend the duty as has occurred in England. They may well balance the interests of the parties more towards those of the mortgagee.

187. *Expo International Pty Ltd v. Chant* [1979] 2 N.S.W.L.R. 820; *Brutan Investments Pty Ltd v. Underwriting & Insurance Ltd* (1980) 39 A.C.T.R. 47; *Henry Roach (Petroleum) Pty Ltd v. Credit House (Vic.) Pty Ltd* [1976] V.R. 809; *Citicorp v. McLoughney and Registrar General of Deeds* (1984) 35 S.A.S.R. 375; and *Westpac Banking Corporation v. Mousellis* (1985) 37 N.T.R. 1.
188. (1984) 35 S.A.S.R. 375 at 381.
189. [1976] V.R. 309 at 313.
190. [1971] Ch. 949.
191. *Standard Chartered Bank Ltd v. Walker* [1982] 1 W.L.R. 1410.
192. [1982] 1 W.L.R. 1410 at 1415.

8. Protection of the Purchaser

[18.85]   Under the general law the mortgagee will commonly have the legal estate. The exercise of the power of sale will attempt to pass this legal estate to the purchaser. Any impropriety as against the mortgagor may give rise to rights associated with the equity of redemption. The mortgagor may seek to assert these rights against the purchaser. At the time of contract there will be competition between two equitable interests and the principal issue is likely to be whether anything associated with the mortgagor's conduct causes her or his interest to be postponed to that of the purchaser. However, once a conveyance is effected the purchaser will have legal title and be free of the mortgagor's claim unless affected by notice.

Under the Torrens system however, the mortgagor retains the legal interest. The mortgagee does however also have a legal interest. Whatever rights the mortgagor may have against the mortgagee, the mortgagee can assign an interest and thus a contract by the mortgagee will confer equitable rights upon the purchaser. At this point any competition between the mortgagor and the purchaser is one between the holder of a legal interest and the holder of a subsequent equitable interest. It will only be if the conduct of the mortgagor is such that the mortgagor is estopped from asserting her or his interest that the interest of the purchaser from the mortgagee will prevail. A transfer from the mortgagee to the purchaser is effected by the registration of the purchaser as proprietor of the land. At this point the purchaser gains the protection of indefeasibility and a mortgagor seeking to set aside the transfer would have to show a lack of good faith; notice would be insufficient.

[18.86]   These principles are subject to specific statutory provisions. The Torrens system statutes provide that any contract authorised by the statutory power of sale is as valid and effectual as if made by the mortgagor and the receipt by the mortgagee is sufficient discharge for the purchaser. The purchaser is not answerable for nor obliged to inquire as to whether there has been any default or notice given in accordance with the power of sale. Upon registration of the transfer from the mortgagee the mortgagor's interest vests in the purchaser who is deemed to be the registered proprietor of that interest.

Upon registration the protection for a purchaser who has acted in good faith appears complete. A dispute between a mortgagor complaining of some irregularity in the sale and a purchaser who has entered a contract but has not become registered, presents greater difficulty.

[18.87]   In *Forsyth v. Blundell*[193] a mortgage had been granted in March 1968 over a petrol station site for $125,000 by Blundell to Associated Securities Ltd (A.S.L.). In November 1968, a second mortgage was granted to A.S.L. for $10,000. Subsequently Blundell defaulted and A.S.L. proceeded to exercise the power of sale. In March 1970, A.S.L. entered a contract to sell the petrol station to the Shell Company for $120,000. Another petrol company had earlier indicated that it was

193.   (1973) 129 C.L.R. 477.

prepared to pay $150,000 for the site. No notice of the sale was given to Blundell or the other company. Blundell sought to redeem. The court held that A.S.L. had acted in deliberate disregard of the rights of the mortgagor and was thus not bona fide. The Shell Company however, was held to have been unaware of any impropriety.

The court concluded that on general principles there was no ground on which the right of mortgagor was postponed to that of the purchaser. Blundell had not contributed to any assumption by the purchaser that the mortgagee was acting bona fide. Even treating the matter as a dispute between competing equitable interests, Blundell's interest was prior in time and nothing in Blundell's conduct caused him to be postponed. The provisions of the Australian Capital Territory Torrens System Ordinance did not provide any additional protection for the particular purchaser prior to registration. The ordinance provided that contracts were as effectual as if made by the mortgagor. This provision was held however, merely to ensure that the mortgagee could contract to give title, even though the mortgagee did not have title. No protection against any irregularity was given to the purchaser. Some protection was given in relation to payment of the purchase money and its subsequent application by the mortgagee. Further, protection was given against failure to make inquiries with respect to the fact of any default and the giving of notice. But no protection was given from failure to make inquiry as to whether the power was otherwise being properly and regularly exercised. Blundell therefore was entitled to redeem even against the Shell Company.

[18.88] *Forsyth v. Blundell* is a case of lack of good faith on the part of the mortgagee. Lesser improprieties do lead to situations in which the purchaser is protected even before registration. Protection is given by the provisions discussed in *Forsyth's* case. In *Emerald Securities Pty Ltd v. Tee Zed Enterprises Pty Ltd*[194] the mortgagor alleged that the appropriate notice of intention to sell had not been given. The Full Court of the South Australian Supreme Court held that any deficiency of notice did not entitle the mortgagor to challenge the contract with the purchaser nor restrain a transfer to him. *Forsyth v. Blundell* was a case of lack of good faith by the mortgagee; where the attack is in relation to the notice, the purchaser was given immunity by the statute.

The purchaser depends upon the statute for protection and the issue is therefore whether the situation is one within the express terms of the statute. Only serious defaults by the mortgagee, will, prior to a transfer and registration, leave a purchaser subject to redemption by the mortgagor.

194. (1981) 101 L.S.J.S. 101.

19

Crown Lands

I. LEASEHOLD TENURE IN AUSTRALIA

[19.01] Most urban land in Australia has been granted to private persons by freehold tenure. Although the Crown retains a reversionary interest in such land, that interest is for almost any conceivable purpose purely nominal and the fee simple owner can properly be regarded as having an absolute interest in the land. Even on the death of a fee simple owner without a valid will and without any next of kin, in all jurisdictions except Western Australia the fee simple interest passes to the Crown as bona vacantia rather than the land passing through an extinguishment of the estate: see above **[6.02]**. In early Australia disputes over the use of land were matters between neighbouring land-owners to be settled according to the law of nuisance. In modern times controls on land use have been imposed by general planning and environmental statutes. But even such statutes regularly require permits for individual developments and the permits may be issued subject to a number of conditions.[1] The conditions then impose a management regime in respect of the piece of land.

[19.02] The proposition that urban Australia has been developed under freehold tenure has one significant exception—the national capital, Canberra. When the decision on the site for the national capital was made the land for the site was acquired by the national government. Of course public buildings are a feature of the capital and are naturally retained in public ownership. However from the first stages of development the decision was taken that even residential and commercial land should be retained in public ownership and individual land-holders granted leasehold interests. The issue of public ownership has been linked with the characteristic of planned development, though the planning may well be more a factor of time—the other major urban centres all commenced prior to the acceptance of comprehensive land-use planning.

The desirability of urban land generally being held on leasehold tenure came into focus in the 1970s. Reformers sought to reduce population pressures in the major cities through the establishment of new towns and new forms of tenure were considered for these towns. However tenure did not become a major innovation in the initial experiments. Within a short time economic difficulties facing the nation as a whole led to the abandonment of such large-scale initiatives as new towns. However one

---

1. On the validity of planning conditions: see *Cardwell v King Ranch Australia Pty Ltd* (1984) 58 A.L.J.R. 386.

aspect of the regulation of urban growth did result in a long-term policy change. Opposition was directed against speculators who purchased urban fringe land and then realised the increase in value from the conversion of rural to residential land. To prevent this practice much fringe land was purchased by government agencies to reap the profit for the community generally.

[19.03] If most urban land is held on freehold tenure, much rural land is held on lease or licence. In particular pastoral lands have been held on limited tenure. The relevant legislation in Victoria is the *Land Act* 1958; in New South Wales, the *Crown Lands Act* 1989 and *Western Lands Act* 1901 (as amended by the *Western Lands (Crown Lands) Amendment Act* 1989); in Queensland, the *Land Act* 1962; in South Australia, the *Crown Lands Act* 1929 and the *Pastoral Land Management and Conservation Act* 1989; in Western Australia, the *Land Act* 1933; and in Tasmania, the *Crown Lands Act* 1935.

These statutory codes of landholding introduced many novel forms of holding.[2] Leases could be annual, for a term of years (often with provisions as to renewal), or even perpetual. Licences at common law are distinguished from leases on the basis that they do not confer proprietary interests. But some of the statutory licences did confer rights against third parties and set out procedures for actions against them.[3] Rather than adapt general forms of tenure to special situations, new tenure forms were created for different situations. Often the new forms reflected peculiar local situations.

Leases and licences were granted generally for the purpose of opening up the vast interior of the country. Conditions attached commonly required the development of the land and the undertaking of improvements. But also the size of individual landholdings was sought to be controlled and the leaseholders were intended to reside on and manage the land themselves. Applications for land grants were thus scrutinised and the transfer of interests restricted.

[19.04] One of the conflicts in rural Australia has been that between the large pastoralists and the person of modest means seeking land as a source of income. In the 1860s rights of free selection were conferred by statute so that small freehold rural holdings could be acquired. However pastoral interests managed to thwart most of the aims of the selection movement. Similar movements occurred with the resettlement of war veterans but again these programmes had limited success. Large holdings have dominated Australian rural life.

Even a selection did not necessarily lead to freehold title immediately but could lead to conditional purchases under which the Crown undertook to pass freehold title on completion of a series of payments. A wide range of other rights of occupation of Crown lands have existed and continue to exist—allowing anything from grazing to beach shacks.

2. On land tenures generally, see Lang, *Crown Land in New South Wales* (1973); Fry, *Freehold and Leasehold Tenancies of Queensland* (1946); Brierley and Irish, *The Crown Lands Acts of New South Wales* (3rd ed., 1914).
3. Cf. *Victorian Land Act* 1958, s. 120; *Bourchier v. Mitchell* (1890) 16 V.L.R. 415.

[19.05]   As well as land used for commercial or residential purposes, much land is retained to be conserved for public purposes. Land such as coastal areas, rivers and lakes has been kept in public ownership. In addition all States and Territories have established extensive national parks and public ownership has again been regarded as essential for such parks. Land is held for public purposes on a more modest scale in public parks and gardens—often vested in local government. As well as for conservation purposes, government land is used for government activities such as schools, hospitals and roads. For what may be an accident of late 19th century philosophy forestry has been regarded in Australia and in many western countries as a government rather than a private commercial activity and much forest land is held by State governments.

[19.06]   This Chapter does not seek to set out the different terms attached to Crown leases and licences. The variety of tenure has been remarkable and recent efforts have been directed to some forms of standardisation. Thus, in New South Wales a radical simplification of leasehold tenure was attempted in the *Crown Lands Act* 1989. However whilst the different forms of tenure will not be analysed, the issue of tenurial relationships both in the urban and rural context will be examined. Attention then turns to the application of general property doctrines to arrangements with the Crown, and procedures for incorporation of these dealings within the land registration system. Finally, the enforceability of public purposes—especially when land has been handed over by private persons to government—will be considered.

II.   LEASEHOLD TENURE AND RURAL LAND

1. History of Rural Land Grants[4]

[19.07]   In the earliest days of settlement land was allocated by grants in fee simple. In many cases these grants occurred without any purchase price paid to the Crown but subject to a payment of an annual fee known as a "quit rent". The quit rent was in effect a tenurial incident and represented an obligation of the holder of the land to the Crown. Although only small blocks were granted at first, eventually extremely large holdings were permitted. Furthermore, despite the charge on the land, by 1831 most landholders did not pay the quit rents and no action was taken for non-payment.

The first significant change of policy came as a result of the ideas of Edward Gibbon Wakefield. He believed that persons of means should be encouraged to become land-holders. Money would become available from purchase payments for public works and for transporting further immigrants. If landholding were restricted, persons excluded for ownership would be available to work as farm labourers. These theories were particularly applied in the settlement of South Australia where

---

4.   The standard historical account is Roberts, *History of Australian Land Settlement 1788-1920* (1968); see also Castles, *An Australian Legal History* (1982), pp. 456-465 and Campbell, *The Crown Lands of Australia* (1855).

convict settlement was excluded. As a result of these ideas, throughout the colonies from 1832 free grants were abolished in favour of grants for a sufficient purchase price. In fact during the 1840s land speculation became so rife that the colonies almost collapsed financially.

During this early period most grants had taken the form of fee simple dispositions by the Crown. During the governorship of Macquarie limited-term leases and occupation licences were more common. The policy had however been to concentrate settlement and to decline to make grants beyond certain points. Individuals had, however, moved well beyond these lines and thus a class known as the squatters had emerged. In 1846 the *Imperial Sale of Waste Lands Act* was passed and in 1847, a consequential Order-in-Council was made by the Imperial Government to provide some security for the squatters. Squatters were enabled to apply for Crown leaseholds for periods from one to 14 years. Leaseholders were given the further right to purchase a fee simple from the Crown. From 1855, with the grant of self-government, land administration was exercised by the colonial governments. Those governments produced a range of land holdings from the Crown unknown in the United Kingdom.

As mentioned earlier, legislation was introduced to give potential small landholders some scope to encroach upon the squatters. From 1861, closer settlement legislation gave effect to the policy of free selection. Under this process, individuals could select a small area of farming land subject to a pastoral lease and enter an agreement for the purchase of the land by instalments through the means of a conditional purchase grant. The squatters resisted the efforts of the selectors and through manipulation of the system had much success in thwarting inroads into their holdings. The result has been that throughout much of Australia rural land is still held under various forms of pastoral lease.

[19.08] Historically, the details of legislation providing for Crown leases and licences have provoked trepidation and little attention to underlying principle. In *Re Hawkins*[5] the former New South Wales *Crown Lands Consolidation Act* 1913 was described by Jordan C.J. as "a jungle penetratable only by the initiate". If numerous tenures existed in each State, comparisons from State to State are even more difficult. But recently attempts have been made towards simplification and for a re-evaluation of legislative direction in light of current needs for land conservation.

Some features of the various land tenures merit comment:

1. Convertibility: It has been common for leaseholders to have an option to purchase a fee simple interest (or to convert from leasehold to freehold). The conditions applicable to such conversion have been subject to dramatic change often simply as a matter of Ministerial policy. Conceptually it is difficult to classify a lease with an option to convert as realty or personalty—an issue which has arisen in interpreting the will of a Crown tenant.[6]

---

5. (1948) 49 S.R. (N.S.W.) 114 at 118.
6. *Joy v. Curator of the Estates of Deceased Persons* (1895) 21 V.L.R. 620.

2. Conditional purchase: Any purchaser of land may enter a contract for payment by instalments.[7] In respect of Crown land such arrangements have been described as conditional purchases. The purchaser normally becomes a tenant until completion of the payment conditions and has a statutory right normally to a fee simple estate on completion.

3. Perpetuity: At common law a lease must be for a certain period and thus a perpetual lease could not be recognised. Nonetheless such leases have been common under the statutory regimes. In terms of duration, no differences exist between them and fee simple interests, but various conditions have been applied to the interest of a perpetual lessee.

4. Fixed duration: The demand for security has led to the grant of terms ranging from one year to commonly 42 years. In these fixed-term leases the issue of renewal becomes significant; the discretion of the granting authority is often circumscribed.

5. Licences: Short-term access to land for grazing or other purposes has been achieved by way of what are commonly annual licences. In New South Wales the concept of permissive occupancies has been used.

6. Improvements: As land policy sought to encourage development, covenants were often imposed requiring improvements. If the landholder's interest was for a term of years, the expenditure might not accrue to the landholder's long-term benefit. To overcome any discouragement, provision for compensation on resumption was common.

2. Comparison of Freehold and Leasehold Tenure

[19.09] The application of the doctrine of seisin meant that private landowners could not deal with the land so that at any one time there was no one seised of land. Consequently, there always had to be someone with a present freehold interest: that person being seised was liable to render feudal dues. Leasehold estates arose outside the prohibition on subinfeudation as they were viewed as commercial interests. But because of the co-existence of freeholder and leaseholder, leases commonly involve the payment of rent by the leaseholder to the freeholder and thus provide a means of acquiring a right of occupation without any initial capital investment. The restrictions on dealings without seisin do not fetter the Crown in its dealings and would in any event be subject to statutory countermand. However, the freeholder and leaseholder relationship between private persons has formed a guiding point for dealings by the Crown.

[19.10] Whereas a lease differed from a fee simple interest at common law by being for a limited term of years, many Crown leases in Australia are in perpetuity. The existence of any difference between a fee simple and a perpetual lease was questioned by Roper J. in *Nolan v. Wilambong S.C.*[8] On the other hand the High Court in *Fisher v. Deputy Federal*

---

7. Subject to recent sale of land legislation attempting to protect purchasers through the technique of a sale plus mortgage back.
8. (1939) 14 L.G.R. (N.S.W.) 89.

Commissioner of Land Tax[9] and *Hawkins v. Minister for Lands*[10] has emphasised that there are fundamental differences between a freehold and even a perpetual leasehold interest.

In *Hawkins* the issue arose as to whether land held on a perpetual Crown lease was classified as Crown land for the purposes of the New South Wales *Crown Lands Consolidation Act* 1913. Land held in fee simple was not so classified. Such land was distinguished from land held on perpetual lease. Dixon J. stated:[11]

> "Because it is a Crown lease in perpetuity, the land, it is claimed, is no longer vested in His Majesty within the meaning of the definition. No doubt the reversionary interest in the Crown is slight and it may be said to be technical. But a rent is reserved, there are special conditions, the interest is capable of surrender and, for non-payment of survey fees, of forfeiture."

In evaluating the differences between the forms of tenure, regard must be had to both theoretical and practical differences. One of the complications in the relationship between the Crown and landholders stems from the nature of a democracy. The executive government ultimately depends upon popular support. The class of landholders may be a significant and sometimes a major portion of the public. The actions open to the Crown will be constrained by public reaction. Some of the changes to Canberra's leasehold system have been widely considered to reflect political opportunism. A further complication is that the Crown's tenurial position in relation to freehold land has had little consequence for so long that it would today be difficult to utilise it as a basis of control. As was mentioned in the historical survey even the quit rents of the early 19th century were rarely collected.

[19.11] One common control upon the rights of the holders of leasehold interests from the Crown is a requirement that assignment take place only with the consent of the relevant Minister. This requirement parallels an equally common provision of private rental agreements. In the case of Crown leases, the concern of the Crown as landlord has not been as much with the standing of any potential tenant as with the extent of ownership of any individual. The Crown has sought to ensure that leases are held only by persons who will themselves manage the particular property and that any individual not amass what would be regarded by the Crown as excessive holdings. The effectiveness and desirability of a policy of preventing entrepreneurial non-resident ownership is open to question. The tenure system is not absolutely vital to the implementation of such a policy.

The second difference is that charges by way of rent are imposed on leaseholders. As the historical evolution has illustrated, quit rents were imposed on those acquiring fee simple interests. The feasibility of imposing rents on property already granted absolutely, would be more

9. (1915) 20 C.L.R. 242 at 248.
10. (1949) 78 C.L.R. 479.
11. Ibid. at 492.

difficult. But charges are imposed on fee simple owners by way of land rates and taxes. In Australia, rates have been imposed as a source of revenue for local government services. Some land taxes have been imposed by reference to unimproved land value so as to encourage land development. However, residential owners in particular have been successful in limiting or eliminating land taxes. Technically the rates and taxes have not been imposed by means of tenure but amounts owing for the taxes are levied as a charge on the land and are more than a personal imposition upon the landholder. Freeholders may be even less inclined to pay substantial sums for land taxes than leaseholders are to pay rent, but liability to charges can be imposed whatever the tenure and the issue of level of charges is largely political.

The third difference is the capacity to change land use and in particular to profit from changes from a less valuable to a more valuable land use. Again there is an attitude that freeholders are entitled to do whatever they please with their land within the limits of the law. These limits were traditionally the law of nuisance which protected neighbours from unreasonable interference. But planning controls have been in place since the 1920s and since the end of the Second World War have become almost universal and very restrictive. The range of land-use choices for a fee simple owner has become increasingly circumscribed. Nonetheless as urban areas continue to expand, the need arises to rezone fringe land from rural to urban use. At this point the fee simple owner has the opportunity to profit from the higher value attributed to the changed use. This profit from simply changed land use rather than land development has attracted much adverse attention. The basis of the opposition is that the gain does not come from any productive effort nor even the investment in an asset producing benefit for others. Proposals have been advanced to impose a betterment tax or to charge for windfalls to reimburse wipeouts. As mentioned earlier, in Australia the most widely used method to remove this gain from private hands has been to establish government agencies to buy fringe land at rural values and to arrange for the subsequent development of the land for urban purposes. The technique has avoided any redefinition of the landholder's interest.

The fourth difference has been the range of management conditions imposed upon leaseholders. Originally these conditions sought to ensure that the land was developed but today may be directed towards responsible land management. Conditions may relate to soil conservation, preservation of native vegetation, control of noxious plants and animals and generally the preservation of land for future generations. These requirements can be imposed by way of statutes controlling actions by land-owners rather than by way of leasehold conditions. Leasehold conditions do however promise the additional remedy for breach of forfeiture of the leasehold interest. Experience suggests that this remedy is a notional rather than a practical one. Furthermore, enforcement measures in planning and similar statutes have become much more sophisticated so that a fine is not the only alternative to forfeiture. Planning statutes are also providing techniques for assessment of individual land parcels. Land management agreements allow for the owner and a government agency to agree upon a programme of land management. These agreements are by statute given effect as encumbrances on the land binding successors in title. The advantages of leasehold tenure for land management are therefore limited.

Historically at least however it seems that the most significant factor explaining the widespread adoption of leasehold grants by the Crown has been the greater psychological acceptance of conditions and obligations attaching to leasehold rather than freehold tenure. The best statement remains that of Fry:[12]

"In many lay minds the most distinctive feature of mesne leaseholds is the number and onerous nature of the tenurial incidents binding upon the tenant, in comparison with the almost total absence of tenurial incidents binding upon freehold tenants. That this, rather than the 'length' or 'size' of the freehold and leasehold interests respectively, is an important practical basis of differentiation between them is evident from the fact that even legal minds sometimes minimise the importance of the difference in essential nature in the length of leasehold and freehold terms respectively, especially as in mesne tenures it is possible to have a freehold life estate which is in law 'larger' than any and all leasehold terms of years although in fact it is inevitably shorter in length than even a 1,000 years leasehold term; whilst even a fee simple is not actually likely to last longer in this practical world of everyday affairs than a 1,000 years leasehold term. These ideas, formulated in their minds by the Australian parliamentarians' everyday experience as mesne lessors and mesne lessees, led them to use the term 'leasehold' in legislation about Crown tenures between the Crown and its Crown tenants in capite, when they desired to indicate thereby that title was to be not only limited in duration but dependent upon due performance of many tenurial incidents imposed to prevent the anti-social use of the land. It is natural enough, and justifiable enough, to regard Crown perpetual leasehold tenures as being in some respects like those non-perpetual Crown leasehold tenures which also impose on the Crown tenant onerous incidents of tenure."

III. TENURE AND URBAN LAND

1. History of Urban Land Tenure

[19.12] The national capital, Canberra, has been developed under leasehold tenure. The land for the Australian Capital Territory was acquired by the Commonwealth from 1911 pursuant to the *Seat of Government (Administration) Act* 1910. Grants to individuals were made pursuant to City Area Leases Ordinances first enacted in 1918. Comprehensive planning of the city followed the establishment of the National Capital Development Commission in 1958. The most significant growth of the city occurred under the management of the Commission.

12. Fry, op. cit., p. 71.

With the grant of self-government in 1988 the Commission was abolished and planning responsibilities handed to the Territory government.[13]

[19.13] The history of tenure arrangements was reviewed by the Commission of Inquiry into Land Tenures in 1973:[14]

"8.7 We have seen that the form of land tenure in the Australian Capital Territory is determined by the *Seat of Government (Administration) Act* 1910, which provides that 'no Crown land in the Territory shall be sold or disposed of for any estate of freehold'. Evidence placed before the Commission indicated that leasehold tenure was adopted for Canberra in order that speculation in undeveloped land could be avoided, unearned increments could be retained for the people and the expenses of establishing the national capital defrayed; in the words of the first Prime Minister (Sir Edmund Barton): 'as a mere business proposal a system of leases with periodical re-appraisement will be about the best manner in which we can set about the meeting of any expense which we may incur in connexion with (the national capital) project.'

HISTORY OF CANBERRA LEASEHOLD TENURE

8.8   The conditions under which leases were first offered in Canberra in 1924 included the following:

(a) a distinction was made between residential and different types of business leases;

(b) lease terms were not to exceed 99 years;

(c) leases were to be disposed of either by auction or by tender, subject to reserve prices with amounts bid representing the unimproved values on which land rent was to be payable;

(d) land rent, the first year of which was payable at auction, was to be 5 per cent of the unimproved value which had been bid or the reserve price, whichever was the higher;

(e) unimproved values were to be re-appraised after the first 20 years and thence every ten years, provision being made for appeals against the re-appraised values; and

(f) leases could not normally be transferred prior to completion of approved buildings, minimum costs of which were nominated and which were required to be commenced within two years and completed within three.

8.9   Despite many vicissitudes in the intervening period, most of these features of the Canberra leasehold system were in force in 1970.

8.12   Submissions to the Commission showed that, in the face of what it believed to be legal and other difficulties in introducing more frequent re-appraisals, the Government decided in 1970 to reduce

---

13.   As a result of the *Australian Capital Territory (Planning and Land Management) Act* 1988 (Cth) and *Interim Territory Planning Act* 1988 (A.C.T.).

14.   Commission of Inquiry into Land Tenures, *First Report* (1973), pp. 169-170, 172-173.

land rent to a peppercorn value of 5 cents per annum 'if and when demanded' and to increase rates to a level which initially would be equal to the revenue previously obtained from both rents and rates, and subsequently would be increased having regard to increases in municipal expenditure in Canberra and in rates in other capital cities. New leases continued to be disposed of by auction, but reserve prices were calculated at levels to return overall the costs of land acquisition and development. Following the introduction of the new system on 1 January 1971, premiums were usually well in excess of reserve prices.

8.13   Other features of leasehold tenure, notably those relating to lease terms and improvement conditions, were preserved under the new system. In the terminology we have used earlier in the Report, it is clear that the main effect of the change was to substitute a premium leasehold system for a rental leasehold system. The Government gave up, along with land rent, its right to receive unearned increments based on the 20 year re-appraisals. It retained its right to unearned value increments arising from approved variations in purpose clauses but, as we have seen, it introduced a scheme which requires a lessee to pay to the Government a premium equal to only half the increase in market value resulting from the variation of purpose, less $1,500. Power to approve the change in purpose is vested in the Supreme Court.''

[19.14]   Current leasehold arrangements for Canberra are made pursuant to the *City Area Leases Act* 1936 (A.C.T.). Leases are granted for business or residential purposes and the class of business for which the land may be used may be specified.[15] Action may be taken in the Supreme Court to restrain use of land for an unauthorised purpose by the relevant Minister or any person resident in the Australian Capital Territory or a lessee or sublessee of land in the Territory.[16] A lessee may make application to the Supreme Court for an order varying any leasehold provision as to the purpose for which the land may be used; variation is subject to payment of a premium representing part of any increased land value flowing from the variation.[17] Procedures are established with respect to fencing obligations of lessees and between adjoining lessees; these procedures involve determinations by the Minister.[18] Where partywalls are shown on building documents the lessee is given a right of support for a partywall.[19] There is a statutory duty to keep land clean, tidy, and free from debris, dry herbage, rubbish, carcasses of animals and other unsightly or offensive matter.[20]

[19.15]   Whilst Canberra has developed under a consistent policy of leasehold tenure, policy in the Northern Territory has been subject to regular upheavals. As in the Australian Capital Territory there have been

15. *City Area Leases Act* 1936, ss 5, 6, 8.
16. Sections 9A, 9B.
17. Section 11A.
18. Section 31.
19. Section 32.
20. Section 35.

some determined efforts to implement a leasehold tenure system even for urban land. Again the best historical review is set out in the Report of the Land Tenures Commission:[21]

"THE NORTHERN TERRITORY

8.31   The Northern Territory differs from other parts of Australia in that a system of dual urban land tenure has applied during most of the Territory's history.

HISTORY OF LAND TENURE IN THE NORTHERN TERRITORY

8.32   Under South Australian administration until 1911, fee simple grants had been the basic form of urban land tenure, but after the Commonwealth assumed control of the Territory in 1911 it passed legislation which required all future grants of urban land to be in the form of perpetual leases purchased at auction on the basis of bids for annual rentals. Fee simple tenure for new grants was re-introduced in 1926 but, following the bombing and civilian evacuation of Darwin during World War II, all land in Darwin and its environs (90 square miles in area) was acquired by the Government. At the same time, legislation was passed which restricted grants of both residential and non-residential land to leasehold tenure, which provided for maximum terms of 99 years, rents based on 5 per cent of unimproved capital value (which was the basis of the initial reserve value and was to be re-appraised in 1970 and thereafter every 20 years) and, except in the case of direct grants to some privileged groups, capital premiums where amounts bid at auction exceeded the reserve value. In 1961 amending legislation provided for conversion of all Darwin town leases to perpetual leases. Few conversions were made.

8.33   In 1962 new legislation was passed which provided for conversion of urban leases to fee simple tenure on payment of the current unimproved capital value, either by lump sum or by instalments over a period not exceeding ten years. Relatively few conversions were made until 1971, presumably because rents based on earlier unimproved capital values were lower than financial costs of conversion. (In 1969, also, unimproved values and rents on new Darwin leases were pegged at 1967 values following steep increases in land prices.) More conversions were made after 1971 when, as a corollary to the introduction of a premium leasehold system, the cost of conversion to freehold was reduced to a fixed fee of $100. In May 1973, the Government suspended further conversions to fee simple at least until 30 June 1974.

8.34   On 1 January 1971 a new system of disposing of urban land was introduced for Darwin and other municipalities (Alice Springs also became a municipality in 1971). This paralleled the new system which came into force in the Australian Capital Territory in 1971, and involved the virtual abolition of land rent (on existing as well as new leases) and the auctioning of new leases on the basis of reserve

---

21.   Commission of Inquiry into Land Tenures, *First Report* (1973), pp. 184-186.

prices intended to ensure that costs of acquisition and servicing were fully recouped. As in Canberra, premiums bid could exceed the reserve price but in Darwin maximum prices were fixed for both restricted and unrestricted residential blocks. Provision was likewise made for payment of the differences by instalments when amounts bid at restricted auctions fell short of reserve prices.''

[19.16] A further dramatic change occurred after the grant of self-government for the Territory. In 1980, legislation was passed by virtue of which from 1 January 1981 any person who was the lessee or entitled to be granted a lease of described land was granted a fee simple estate in that land.[22] The described land included most urban land in the Northern Territory. The land to which a fee simple estate was thus granted was automatically brought under the provisions of the *Real Property Act*[23] and the owner became entitled without charge to a certificate of title.[24] All fee simple estates in the Territory are subject to the reservation to the Crown of all minerals.[25] The sale of land in fee simple by the Minister may be subject to an agreement as to its development and a bond required as to the performance of the development agreement.[26]

2. Desirability of Urban Land Tenure Systems

[19.17] As mentioned earlier, during the early 1970s government attention was directed to the quality of life in the cities and their infrastructures and planning. Relief from the sheer population size of the ever sprawling major centres was seen as desirable. One means to achieve this goal was the promotion of a number of growth centres throughout the country. Some initiatives were undertaken at Albury-Wodonga, plans drawn for Bathurst-Orange, and land acquired for the subsequently abandoned South Australia centre at Monarto. In planning for these centres the issue of the desirable form of land tenure was raised and some laudatory references made to the example of the leasehold system in Canberra. It was principally these concerns that led to the establishment of the Land Tenures Commission to which reference had already been made.

[19.18] The Commission however, favoured freehold rather than leasehold systems for residential land grants. It did recommend the reservation from the freehold grant of development rights. This reservation meant that a charge could be made for a change in the type of land use. The Commission favoured residential freehold title because it considered that the overriding factors were permanency and a capital payment system for home ownership. On the other hand it considered that business and industrial investment was made on a fixed-term basis and that land for these purposes could be granted by a lease of fixed duration.

---

22. *Crown Lands Amendment Act (No. 3)* 1980, s. 8(1).
23. Section 9.
24. Section 8(5).
25. Section 20.
26. Section 22.

The following passages set out the major arguments of the Land Tenures Commission:[27]

"[W]e believe that the adoption of a leasehold rental system would increase inequalities between rich and poor, and fail to treat similarly persons in similar circumstances, by:

(a) reacting adversely on the distribution of national wealth;

(b) absorbing a higher proportion of household income at the lower end of the income scale and imposing insecurity on all home owners on relatively low incomes;

(c) creating comparative injustice and insecurity for particular classes of income recipients, especially wage and salary earners, and for particular age groups, notably those in or approaching retirement;

(d) discriminating against households taking up land in the new growth centres and in favour of those who already own land in existing cities; and

(e) providing opportunities for political decisions which will have the effect both of giving windfall gains to particular groups of landholders and of destroying the stability of the land tenure system.

GRANTS IN FEE SIMPLE FOR RESIDENTIAL LAND

7.23   If, as we recommend, the case for economic rents is rejected and the case for the reservation of development rights is accepted, the question arises whether there is any need for residential land to be made available for a limited term of years. We can see no justification for restricting the period of residential tenure provided that development rights are retained by the Crown, but we believe that the desire by home owners for security of tenure provides a strong positive reason for not limiting the period of tenure. This means that, in those places where residential land continues to be made available on leasehold tenure (as we assume will be the case in Canberra) the leases should be perpetual leases (or, more accurately in the light of the possibility of resumption for redevelopment, leases of indefinite duration). In terms of the characteristics we have now specified as desirable for purposes of residential tenure, residential leases would then be purchased for capital premiums (which might be payable by instalments over a period); they would not be subject to rent; they would be for an indefinite term; and they would be restricted in the use of land to single dwelling-houses.

7.24   On the assumption that these specifications for leasehold tenure are virtually identical with the characteristics of fee simple titles with development rights removed, it is necessary to ask whether there are any other factors which warrant the continuing use of leasehold forms of residential tenure? One factor which obviously needs to be considered is the contribution which leasehold tenure

27. Commission of Inquiry into Land Tenures, *First Report* (1973), pp. 126, 135-137.

may make to the planning and control of initial development and subsequent redevelopment. It was argued before us that development controls are greatly facilitated by the leasehold system.

7.25   Effective control over initial urban development depends primarily on public acquisition of rural land prior to its conversion for residential purposes. The tenure system is not of any significance in relation to public acquisition, although leasehold tenure does provide an effective means for stipulating and enforcing the form of land use (through the purpose clause) and the time within which development must take place. But evidence placed before the Commission shows that this desirable objective may be (and is being) achieved in Australia in ways which do not involve continuing leasehold tenure when the development phase has been completed.

7.26   Leasehold tenure would give development corporations greater control over residential properties subsequent to the development period, but on balance we believe that such control would conflict with the rights of individual land-holders for security, peaceful enjoyment and privacy in the use of their land. The rights of neighbours may be protected in other ways.

7.27   Given the strong psychological attachment which most people have to so-called freehold land and the predominance of this form of tenure in existing cities, the Commission has concluded that compelling reasons would need to be advanced to justify a change to residential leasehold tenure in the new centres of urban growth. In the light of the foregoing discussion, it will be clear that we are not persuaded that such reasons exist. We therefore recommend that all grants of residential land in the new metropolitan and regional growth centres be made on the basis of fee simple title, subject to the specification of the purpose for which the land is to be used, the enforcement of improvement conditions prior to the issue of title and the reservation of development rights.''

[19.19]   The Commission's report seems to have marked the end of interest in land tenure systems. If anything, the psychological attachment to fee simple interests has strengthed and self-government in the two Territories has increased land-holder influence upon decisions. Whilst the Commission's views may influence thinking about the problems, little in the way of implementation has flowed from its recommendations. Concern about the quality of life in the cities has been drowned by macro-economic issues. Even the acquisition of fringe land by government agencies has not been without difficulties, as initially prices slumped and then holding costs increased because of climbing interest rates.

IV.   APPLICATION OF GENERAL PRINCIPLES TO CROWN TENURE

1. Rights Dependent on Statute

[19.20]   The statutes creating the variety of Crown leaseholds and licences specify the range of recognised interests and the conditions attaching to them, procedures for applications for the grant of an interest, and the consideration of and response to those applications (normally by the responsible Minister). Applications are required to pass through approval processes, conditions are specified and payment of the purchase-money and fees made. The courts have been reluctant to apply common law doctrines to the creation of interests through this process. Even though there may appear to have been an offer and acceptance no contract will come into existence. An applicant may however acquire a statutory right to the grant of an interest. Similarly conduct which might create an estoppel against a private person wi" be not held to do so against the Crown because of the statutory statement as to when rights arise.

The leading statement is that of Knox C.J. in *Davies v. Littlejohn*:[28]

> "It is abundantly clear, from the provisions of the Act and of the regulations, that the object of the legislature was, not to provide for the making of ordinary contracts for the sale of land by the Crown to its subjects, but to make Crown lands available for purposes of settlement in limited areas; not primarily to provide for raising revenue by sales of land, but to promote settlement on the land. This is illustrated by the restrictions imposed on auction sales and special sales, and by the limitation of the areas of holdings and of the rights of existing holders of land to acquire by transfer or otherwise further holdings. Reference may be made to the schedule of questions which the applicant for a conditional purchase is required to answer: see Form 9, Sched. B. The mutual rights and obligations of the Crown and the applicant for, or holder of, a conditional purchase are to be ascertained by reference to the provisions of the Act and regulations, for the Crown has no power to dispose of the land except in strict accordance therewith. The rights and obligations of the purchaser are statutory—not contractual. He does not, at any rate expressly, agree to perform the conditions or pay the purchase-money, though the statute imposes an obligation upon him to do so. There is no agreement on the part of the Crown to issue a Crown grant, though, no doubt, the purchaser could by appropriate proceedings compel the performance of the statutory obligation to issue a grant when the conditions have been complied with. These conditions lead me to think that it is unsafe to treat the rules governing ordinary sales of land by one person to another as necessarily applicable in determining the relations of the Crown to a conditional purchaser under the statute."

[19.21] In that case an individual had held land under a conditional purchase agreement. By his will he directed his trustees, until "the charges or encumbrances" on that land should be entirely liquidated, to appropriate the income of his residuary estate towards payment of those charges or encumbrances. The issue was whether the residuary estate should bear the cost of the unpaid instalments for the land. It was argued that these instalments were a charge or encumbrance because the Crown had an unpaid vendor's lien for the unpaid money. The High Court rejected the existence of such a lien as such a right was not spelt out in

28. (1923) 34 C.L.R. 174 at 183.

the statute and the remedy of sale to enforce the lien would be inconsistent with the statutory provision for forfeiture on default. Consequently, the unpaid instalments were not a charge or encumbrance.

The existence of any interest in the absence of formalities was also denied by the Full Court of the South Australian Supreme Court in *Matthews v. South-Eastern Drainage Board*.[29] In that case an individual applied for an allotment of land under the *War Service Settlement Agreement Act* 1945. The individual was informed that he had been selected for allotment of the land applied for and sent an application form which he duly completed and returned. The individual went into possession and paid rent over a substantial number of years. The issue arose as to liability for rates. These rates were imposed upon persons who were classified as "land-holders" a term defined to include lessees of land held under lease from the Crown. Liability was successfully denied on the basis that as no formal lease had been executed the individual had no rights as lessee. The court held that the status of a person who had applied for and been allotted land under perpetual lease conditions but whose tenure had not been the subject of a formal instrument could not be equated with that of a lessee. On the other hand the person may have a statutory right to a lease.

A similar absence of rights prior to the completion of procedures was asserted by the High Court in *Walsh v. Minister for Lands (N.S.W.)*.[30] There an individual held land pursuant to a lease. One of the rights of the holder of such a lease was to turn the conditional lease into a conditional purchase. The individual lodged an application to convert. Before that application was processed the land was reserved from sale as a timber reserve. The individual argued that the reservation was invalid as the land was already subject to a contract for a conditional purchase. The right conferred by the lease was claimed to constitute an offer by the Crown which was taken up by the individual by making the application. The argument was rejected and the individual's rights held to flow solely from the statute. Under the statute the holder of a conditional lease was entitled to make a conditional purchase out of a lease by following the prescribed procedures. Conversion was however only effected upon completion of the procedures. Before that time the land had been reserved and in accordance with the procedures could not thereafter be converted. The case is of particular significance in that it directly concerned the relationship between the individual and the Crown rather than some consequential issue.

More recently, Stein J. in the New South Wales Supreme Court held that the Crown's capacity to create interests was strictly circumscribed by the relevant legislation. In *New South Wales Aboriginal Land Council v. Minister for Natural Resources*[31] the Secretary of the Western Lands Commission purported in 1982 to grant a permissive occupancy to an individual. Subsequently, the Aboriginal Land Council made a claim to the land under the *Aboriginal Land Rights Act* 1983. The question whether the land was claimable depended on whether it was lawfully used or

29. [1965] S.A.S.R. 328.
30. (1960) 103 C.L.R. 240.
31. (1986) 59 L.G.R.A. 318.

occupied by an individual. Stein J. held that both the type of interest granted and the procedures by which it had been granted were invalid. He pointed out that at the time the relevant Act provided for leases and not occupancies and that the occupancy could not be justified as a tenancy at will. Furthermore, grants had to be made by the Minister and there was no proof that the Minister's powers had been lawfully delegated to the Secretary.

[19.22] This emphasis upon procedural compliance not only prevents what would normally be contractual or even equitable proprietary claims but also threatens claims based on estoppel. One of the early cases establishing the doctrine of proprietary estoppel was *Plimmer v. Wellington Corporation*.[32] The conduct giving rise to the estoppel was that of a local government authority which had allowed a pier to be established. Similarly in *Crabb v. Arun D.C.*[33] a local government authority was held not to be entitled to go back on the appearance it had created even though it was clear that no formal documents had been executed. Despite these cases, the statutory statement of procedures for dealings by the Crown may prevent the acquisition of rights where those procedures had not been complied with.

In *State of Victoria v. Rossignoli*[34] a letter was sent by an officer of the Victorian Department of Lands and Survey stating that if the named party completed the filling and levelling of certain Crown land, that party would be granted exclusive filling rights in respect of other Crown land. The party completed the required filling and levelling and then claimed the other filling rights. The Crown argued that any licence could be granted only by the Governor-in-Council or a duly authorised delegate and since no such grant had been made no rights could accrue. The argument succeeded. The Full Court of the Victorian Supreme Court held that any equity sought to be raised would establish against the Crown in respect of Crown land rights which the Crown was prevented by statute from creating except in a prescribed manner.

2. Scope of an Established Relationship

[19.23] The statutes concentrate on the procedures for the creation of a relationship between the Crown and an individual. Once that relationship has been established in accordance with the statutory procedures, the courts are less reluctant to give meaning to the relationship by reference to common law principles. Thus the implied covenants as between landlord and tenant may be applied to a Crown lease in the absence of any contrary terms or features of the arrangement.

[19.24] In *O'Keefe v. Williams*[35] a grant had been made of occupation licences of certain areas of land. By mistake a part of these lands was leased to another. The original grantee sued for damages for breach of an

32. (1884) 9 A.C. 699.
33. [1976] Ch. 179.
34. (1983) 2 V.R. 1.
35. (1910) 11 C.L.R. 171.

implied term of his lease. The High Court held that a contractual obligation would be implied that the Crown would not disturb, or authorise the disturbance, of the lessee in his occupation, and would not do anything in derogation of the rights conferred by the statutory contract. The court could see no reason why different canons of construction should apply to the construction of contracts between the Crown and a subject, and contracts between subject and subject. The court did concede that the obligation might not be co-extensive in all respects with that applicable between subject and subject. That qualification was taken up in *Commissioners of Crown Lands v. Page*.[36] There the Crown during wartime requisitioned premises which were the subject of a Crown lease. The Court of Appeal held that any covenant for quiet enjoyment must be read so as to exclude those measures affecting the nation as a whole which the Crown took for the public good.

The extent to which common law doctrines will be applied will vary according to the extent to which the terms of any arrangement are specified in the governing legislation. The mere use of terms such as lease or mortgage or transfer carries no meaning unless there are express definitions or common law definitions are applied. In *American Dairy Queen (Qld) Pty Ltd v. Blue Rio Pty Ltd*[37] the issue arose of the power of a sublessee to assign his interest in lands held by trustees as a reserve. Dealings with lands of this sort were set out in a separate part of the *Queensland Land Act 1972*. That part was silent as to the sublessee's right to assign. It was argued on the one hand that as no right to assign was conferred by the legislation, none existed; on the other hand, it was argued that at common law a sublessee could assign in the absence of any express restriction and since there was no express restriction the sublessee could assign. The High Court applied the common law position on the basis that the relevant part of the Act was so limited in its terms that meaning had to be given by reference to the common law. "The statutory scheme does not consist of a statement of new rights, powers and obligations; instead it assumes the existence of those arising under the general law and proceeds to modify them to the extent considered necessary."[38] A policy objection to this result was that the Minister's control of the land would be diminished. However, the court pointed out that restrictions on subleases could always be included in the terms of the head lease. To reinforce its position on the scope of the relevant part of the Act, the court referred to other parts dealing with tenure of different sorts of Crown lands. In these parts there were extensive provisions relating to the disposition of interests and they could well be construed to exclude general law principles.

The consistency of any common law doctrine with any form of holding of Crown lands will always depend on analysis on the basis of that doctrine and the nature of the statutory terms of the holding. In *Cooper v. Stuart*[39] a grant in fee simple had been subject to the reservation of "any quantity of land, not exceeding 10 acres, in any part of the said grant, as may be

36. [1960] 2 Q.B. 274.
37. (1981) 37 A.L.R. 613.
38. Ibid. per Mason J. at 616.
39. (1889) 14 A.C. 286.

required for public purposes''. Subsequently, a proclamation was made resuming a parcel of 10 acres for a public park. The validity of this resumption was challenged. One of the bases of the challenge was that the reservation infringed the rule against perpetuities. The Privy Council concluded that (on the assumption that the rule in England was applicable to Crown grants) the rule was inconsistent with the needs of Crown grants in an infant colony. In such a colony grants were made to attract immigrants and development. To provide prospective wants which could not be foreseen the Crown had to retain the right to resume such parts as might be found necessary for the uses of an increased population. The rule against perpetuities would inhibit this needed flexibility and so was inconsistent with the overall scope of the Crown grants. In *Hari v. Trotter*[40] claims to an easement based on the doctrines of prescription or lost modern grant were made against a conditional purchaser. The claims were held to be inconsistent with the powers of the holder of an interest under a conditional purchase agreement. That holder had a statutory right to a fee simple, but did not have a fee simple and was subject to the Crown's rights of forfeiture. The essence of the doctrines of prescription and lost modern grant was the presumption that at some time there had been a grant. The presumption could not be made against a person whose estate would not entitle that person to make a grant. Only a person holding a fee simple estate could make a grant and the holder of a conditional purchase agreement did not have a fee simple.

V.   REGISTRATION AND ALIENATION

[19.25]   In several jurisdictions the Torrens statutes make provision for the registration of leases or licences granted by the Crown.[41] In some cases these leases and licences are recorded in a separate register but that register is deemed to have the same effect as an ordinary Torrens system register. There are two major consequences of registration: any transfer by a lessee has the same effect as a transfer by an ordinary registered proprietor and thus attracts the protection of indefeasibility; any entry of forfeiture or determination is deemed to be effective to forfeit or determine the interest.

A transfer from one lessee to another is clearly assimilated to a transfer from one fee simple registered proprietor to another and as between the parties the grounds of challenge would be limited by the doctrine of indefeasibility. To set aside the transfer the transferor would have to show fraud or a personal equity or another recognised exception to indefeasibility. A second transferee taking in good faith and for value similarly will take free of any claim of the original transferor for fraud against the first transferee. The position of the original grantor from the Crown is more problematic and there may not be any protection against claims by the Crown with respect to an impropriety in the application process.

---

40.   (1959) 76 W.N. (N.S.W.) 112.
41.   N.S.W.: *Real Property Act* (1900), s. 13A et. seq.; S.A.: *Real Property Act* (1886), s. 91 et. seq.; W.A.: *Transfer of Land Act* (1893), s. 81A et. seq.

Once an entry of forfeiture or determination has been made, that entry has been held to be conclusive even if the procedures for forfeiture or determination have not been followed. In *Laffer v. Gillen*[42] a forfeiture was challenged on the basis of the sufficiency of notice after default. The Privy Council held that once the necessary entry had been made in the register, the validity of the forfeiture could not be challenged. Similarly, in *Tucker v. Minister of Lands*[43] a notice of intent to forfeit was challenged on the basis that it insufficiently described the land affected. Again that challenge was dismissed on the basis that upon registration the fact of forfeiture was conclusively established. The court pointed out that there were procedures under the Crown lands legislation for the cancellation of the certificate of title so that the land was again to be regarded as unalienated Crown land. This procedure for the reversion of the land to its former status was separate from that for the termination of the lease.

[19.26] Rights of alienation of Crown lessees are generally more limited than those of fee simple owners and much closer to those of private lessees. The position of private lessees comes as a result not of the common law which permitted alienation but of standard restrictions in lease agreements. The statutes typically provide that the sale, transfer or subletting of any lease or interest in the lease or any interest in the land comprised in the lease requires the consent of the Minister or relevant administrative authority. Whilst such a requirement is common in private leases, the effect of a transfer without consent is that the transfer is effective but the landlord has the right to forfeit for breach. The Crown lands legislation typically provides that the purported transaction has no validity without that consent.

The High Court has affirmed that a dealing without consent is invalid and has no legal effect.[44] Any sublease without consent is illegal and thus rent due cannot be claimed[45] and conversely any rent illegally paid cannot be recovered.[46] Similarly, any agency or trust must under the legislation be disclosed and approved as part of the policy against absentee landholders. Any undisclosed trust is therefore unenforceable,[47] even though because of the specific legislation the legal interest may exist until forfeited.

The prohibition upon transfers without consent applies to transfers of an interest in the lease. Thus the passing of a proprietary interest to the transferee is necessary to constitute a breach. The creation of purely personal rights (that is, rights against the lessee) does not infringe the prohibition. The scope of the rights conferred by a share-farming agreement entered into by a Crown lessee fell to be considered by the High Court in *Hill v. O'Brien*.[48] The grantee of the share-farming rights

42. [1927] A.C. 886.
43. (1982) 99 L.S.J.S. 181.
44. *Bouch v. Bickle* (1915) 20 C.L.R. 663 at 670-671.
45. *Gaudron v. Mackay* (1936) 60 W.N. (N.S.W.) 11.
46. *Marks v. Jolley* (1938) 38 S.R. (N.S.W.) 351.
47. *Orr v. Pond* [1988] 2 Qd R. 258.
48. (1938) 61 C.L.R. 96.

sought to prevent acts of an outsider interfering with the share-farmer's possession. The title to do so was denied on the basis that the share-farmer had purely personal rights. The majority of the High Court reached this characterisation purely as a matter of construction of the share-farming agreement. Latham C.J. however, held that the share-farming agreement was ineffectual so far as it purported to create any proprietary interest because any attempted alienation was prohibited and deprived of legal effect by the statutory terms of the lease.

[19.27] Transactions which might otherwise create proprietary interests have been denied such an effect because of the prohibitions. In particular, any equitable rights of a transferee have been held not to exist because equitable rights are dependent upon the availability of specific performance which would not be granted in face of the statutory prohibitions. In consequence an agreement may be viewed as purely personal and thus any breach of the prohibition on alienation avoided. In *Harrington v. Keene*[49] a valid sublease for a term of five years conferred an option to purchase on three months' notice. The option was exercised and consent granted to the exercise of the option. The validity of the transaction was attacked on the basis that consent was necessary to the grant of the option not just to its exercise. Jacobs J. in the South Australian Supreme Court held that the conferral of the option did not amount to an agreement for sale nor to an alienation of any interest. There was no agreement for sale until the option was exercised. There was no alienation even though an option ordinarily confers an equitable interest upon the holder of an option. This option, given without consent, was not specifically enforceable.

The creation of an interest by virtue of the doctrine of proprietary estoppel has also been held to fall outside prohibitions on dealings. In *Wood v. Browne*[50] a lessee had encouraged another to build on land on the basis that the individual would at all times be able to occupy the land. The individual built and claimed the right to occupy against a successor-in-title of the original lessee. The Queensland Supreme Court held that under the proprietary estoppel doctrine the individual had a right to occupy the dwelling throughout his lifetime. The court held that the grant of this right did not infringe any prohibitions on dealings in the relevant legislation. The court held that the arrangement did not amount to a transfer or sublease. This decision may turn on the narrow scope of the prohibitions on dealings in the particular statute. The court referred only to prohibitions on transfers and subleases and not a more general prohibition on the creation of interest in the land. Alternatively the doctrine of proprietary estoppel may have been viewed as creating purely personal rights though the more general current view is that the equity entitles the holder to a proprietary interest and the court did enforce the right against successors-in-title. No mention was made of any capacity of those successors to hold free of prior informal interests.

49. (1975) 11 S.A.S.R. 361.
50. [1984] 2 Qd R. 593.

VI. PUBLIC PURPOSES

1. Nature of the Public Interest in Public Land

[19.28] Much Crown land is set aside for particular public purposes. The existence of land set aside for a particular purpose may encourage individuals to purchase land in the vicinity. Furthermore members of the public may come to enjoy accustomed uses of public land or simply believe that a particular use is right and proper on grounds ranging from patriotism to conservation. Any threatened change of use may meet resistance and give rise to the issue whether the use over a period of time gives rise to any public rights. Some form of charitable trust constitutes the most readily accepted vehicle for public rights in such cases.

[19.29] Generally the public does not acquire any interest in public land even though the public purpose is set out in statutory form. In *Stow v. Mineral Holdings (Australia) Pty Ltd*[51] members of the public lodged objections to the grant of a prospector's licence in respect of Crown land. The right to lodge an objection was conferred upon persons who had any estate or interest in the land. The High Court ruled that the objections were invalid because members of the public had no estate or interest in Crown land. In the words of Aickin J.:[52]

"The first question to be considered is whether any of the objectors had an estate or interest in the land. In my opinion it is clear that none of them had an estate or interest in the land, and indeed none of them claimed to do so. The definition of the word 'estate' in the *Acts Interpretation Act* 1915 (Tas.) was relied upon. Section 46 of that Act provides that, in the absence of a contrary indication, 'Estate' used in reference to land shall include any estate or interest, easement, right, title, claim, demand, change, lien, or encumbrance in, over, to or in respect of such land.

The expression 'interest in land' is not defined in any relevant Act, nor is the compound expression 'estate or interest in land'. I do not consider that the assistance is to be derived from an attempt to apply the statutory definition of 'estate' to the compound expression 'estate or interest in land'. The word 'right' in that definition does not in its context mean a public right; it means an individual right of a proprietary nature and I do not think that the word 'demand' in this context has any more extended meaning. In my opinion the ordinary meaning of the compound expression 'estate or interest in land' is an estate or interest of a proprietary nature in the land. This would include legal and equitable estates and interests, for example, a freehold or a leasehold estate, or incorporeal interests such as easements, profits à prendre, all such interests being held by persons in their individual capacity. It does not embrace interests in which the individual concerned has no greater claim than any other member of the public. All members of the public have a right to pass

51. (1977) 51 A.L.J.R. 672.
52. Ibid. at 679.

freely along and across public highways but none have in their capacity as members of the public any estate or interest in such land. Likewise, members of the public generally may be entitled pursuant to particular statutes to use specified areas of Crown Lands for the purpose of recreation. However statutes such as the *National Parks and Wildlife Act* 1970 (Tas.) were relied on to give rights to members of the public as such. All members of the public may have the right to go upon such land in the sense that they may freely walk thereon or in defined portions thereof and may resist attempts by the Crown or anyone else to eject them from such land. The fact that some of them are more disposed to go upon the land than others, derive more benefit therefrom and use the statutory right more often than others, does not elevate that which is a public right enjoyed by all members of the public equally into a private right capable of being described as an estate or interest in the land.''

[19.30]   Similarly, the mere use of land for a public purpose does not constitute any rights in the public to enforce that purpose and the Crown is free to change the use as it sees fit. In *Williams v. Attorney-General (N.S.W.)*[53] (1913) 16 C.L.R. 404, a challenge was brought against a decision by the government of New South Wales to convert to a park certain land that had from 1845 been used as the Governor's residence. As was put most simply by Gavan Duffy and Rich JJ.:[54]

"It is true that the land was reserved, and has long been used, as a residence and domain for the Governor of New South Wales; but the reservation was not intended to confer on the public of New South Wales any rights as against the sovereign. Its intention and its effect were to retain the land for the purpose of the king's government in the colony. It created no right which could be enforced in a court of law by any individual or set of individuals, or by the public of New South Wales; the sovereign still retained complete and undivided ownership and dominion, and he alone could complain of any interference with the land or with the method of dealing with it. The reservation gave to the public no more than it would have given had the land been reserved and used for a post office, a court of justice, or a custom house. Such purposes are commonly called public purposes, but the public has no right with respect to them which can be enforced in a court of law, apart from the proprietary right which the sovereign can enforce and defend.''

This principle was applied by Fox J. in *Kent v. Cavanagh*[55] in which objection was made to the erection of a communications tower on Black Mountain, Canberra. Part of the objection was that land on the mountain had been declared to be a public park under a relevant ordinance. A further declaration was made revoking that designation and establishing a new park which did not include the site for the proposed tower. Fox J.

53. (1913) 16 C.L.R. 404.
54. Ibid. at 467.
55. (1973) 1 A.C.T.R. 43.

held that subject to any statutory procedures, the Commonwealth could do as it liked on its own land. The procedures for the revocation of declarations had been complied with. Similarly in *Attorney-General; Ex rel. Carkeek v. West Torrens Corporation*[56] a local council resolved to open a road through a public park. The court held that a declaration by a council that land was to be held at a public park to be retained for reserve and recreation purposes did not create any trust for a public purpose. The statute under which the declaration was made did not impose any statutory restriction nor statutory obligation as to the use of the land in perpetuity. No irrevocable purpose had been stated. A declaration of a trust required a clear intention. No such intention existed.

2. Dedication of Public Land

[19.31] Commonly reference is made to land dedicated for particular public purposes. Such land may be removed from that capable of alienation or other dealing by the Crown. Such land may be given exemptions from various tax impositions. It seems that in Australia dedication for a public purpose involves a formal creation of a trust for that purpose. In *Randwick M.C. v. Rutledge*[57] the High Court denied a rating exemption for the Randwick racecourse on the basis that it was not dedicated for a public reserve. The court reached that conclusion even though the land was vested in trustees because the terms of the trust deed did not require the trustees to preserve the land as a public place.

The nature of public reserves and dedication for that purpose was considered by Windeyer J. in the *Randwick Case*:[58]

"The term 'public reserve'—and the word 'reserve' alone, when not controlled by a definition or a context indicative of a different sense—have come to be used in common parlance in Australia in an imprecise way to describe an unoccupied area of land preserved as an open space or park for public enjoyment, to which the public ordinarily have access as of right. This use of the word is not new. For example, in *Town Life in Australia* by Twopenny, published in 1883, the author said of Melbourne, 'there are several pretty reserves notably the Fitzroy, Carlton and University Gardens, and the Regent's Park which are well kept'; and of Sydney, 'Unfortunately Sydney has very few reserves, and those few she keeps in bad order, with the exception of the Botanical Gardens'.

The meaning of 'dedicated' in the definition of 'public reserve' with which we are concerned was discussed before us, but without reference to the main decisions. It is convenient to deal with the matter at this point because the word had come into fairly common use in New South Wales before its appearance in the *Crown Lands Act 1861* to which we were referred. At common law the only way in which land can properly be said to be dedicated to a public use is

56. (1981) 26 S.A.S.R. 472.
57. (1959) 33 A.L.J.R. 367.
58. Ibid. at 372-373.

when it is dedicated as a highway.[59] Although a private right to enjoy a park can be created as an easement appurtenant to an estate,[60] our law does not recognise a public ius spatiandi vel manendi apart from charitable trust or statute.[61] Nevertheless, in England a right in the inhabitants of a locality to use the village green for recreation and games could exist on a basis of ancient custom—a circumstance which may well have influenced the above-mentioned directions to the governors to provide reserves for the recreation and amusement of the inhabitants of towns and villages. It is possible that, since 'public roads and internal communications' headed every early list of public purposes for which land was to be reserved, the expressions 'dedicated and set apart' were thought to be applicable respectively to roads and other objects. The reservation of a road in a Crown grant amounted to dedication.[62] But it seems more probable that 'dedicate' came to be used in New South Wales without any concern for its limited common law sense. It seems to have been thought to indicate something more formal than mere reservation from sale, something binding the Crown and creating some right in members of the public or of a section of the public. Land reserved from sale did not pass from the control of the Crown. But lands granted for public charitable purposes were removed from the control of the Crown and were properly described as dedicated.

. . .

Attorney-General v. Eagar established that lands *impressed with a trust* could not be diverted by the Crown to purposes alien to the trust. Its authority that such lands were dedicated is undiminished. And in connection with the very lands there in question, the legislature later adopted the word 'dedicated' in the Church and School Lands Dedication Act 1880. But, in so far as the decision in Attorney-General v. Eagar appeared to place dedicated lands outside the authority of the legislature, it was mistaken. It was a later and even greater mistake to think that lands appropriated and taken into use by the Crown for a particular purpose (without the creation of any trust) became dedicated to that purpose and could not thereafter be used by the Crown for another purpose. All this was fully considered in Williams v. Attorney-General (the Government House Case).[63] It suffices to say here that there can be no dedication in any strict sense unless a public trust be created.''

3. Trusts for Public Purposes

[19.32] Land may however be set aside for a public purpose in such a way that the reservation does create a charitable trust. Such a

---

59. Ex parte Lewis (1888) 21 Q.B.D. 191 at 197; Attorney-General v. Williams (Government House Case) [1915] A.C. 573 at 579; and per Isaacs J., in New South Wales v. Commonwealth (Garden Island Case) (1926) 38 C.L.R. 14 at 91.
60. Re Ellenborough Park [1956] Ch. 131.
61. Attorney-General v. Antrobus [1905] 2 Ch. 188.
62. Rapley v. Martin (1832) 4 S.C.R. 173.
63. (1913) 16 C.L.R. 404 and on appeal [1915] A.C. 573.

reservation is more likely to occur where land is transferred by an individual to a public authority for a particular purpose. That purpose is likely to be set out in the documents by which arrangements are made for the transfer. Once a charitable trust exists, procedures such as a relator action by the Attorney-General are available to enforce the purpose.

In *Brisbane C.C. v. Attorney-General (Qld)*[64] the trustees of a society conveyed land to the Brisbane City Council on the following conditions:

> "(a) the area to be set apart permanently for showground, park and recreation purposes; (b) the show ring to be levelled off; (c) the show society to be granted the exclusive use of the ground without charge for a period of two weeks in each and every year, for the purposes of and in connection with the district annual show."

Some years later the Council contracted to sell the land for use as a shopping centre. In a relator action the Attorney-General sought a declaration that the land was subject to a valid and enforceable charitable trust. The Privy Council held that the conditions showed unequivocally an intention to create a trust for the purposes specified binding the land in the council's hands. Park and recreational purposes were clearly accepted charitable objects. Consequently, a valid and enforceable charitable trust was created.

64. [1978] 3 W.L.R. 299.

Index

[All references are to paragraph numbers]